The Works Of Mrs. Amelia Opie

You are holding a reproduction of an original work that is in the public domain in the United States of America, and possibly other countries. You may freely copy and distribute this work as no entity (individual or corporate) has a copyright on the body of the work. This book may contain prior copyright references, and library stamps (as most of these works were scanned from library copies). These have been scanned and retained as part of the historical artifact.

This book may have occasional imperfections such as missing or blurred pages, poor pictures, errant marks, etc. that were either part of the original artifact, or were introduced by the scanning process. We believe this work is culturally important, and despite the imperfections, have elected to bring it back into print as part of our continuing commitment to the preservation of printed works worldwide. We appreciate your understanding of the imperfections in the preservation process, and hope you enjoy this valuable book.

THE WORKS

OF

MRS. AMELIA OPIE;

COMPLETE

IN THREE VOLUMES.

VOLUME III.

PHILADELPHIA:
JAMES CRISSY, 4, MINOR STREET.
1843.

STEREOTYPED BY J. FAGAN.
PRINTED BY T. K. AND P. G. COLLINS, PHILADELPHIA.

CONTENTS OF THIRD VOLUME.

	PAGE
TEMPER	5
A WOMAN'S LOVE	175
A WIFE'S DUTY; being a continuation of a Woman's Love	209
THE TWO SONS	269
THE OPPOSITE NEIGHBOUR	300
LOVE, MYSTERY, AND SUPERSTITION	321
AFTER THE BALL; OR, THE TWO SIR WILLIAMS	363
FALSE OR TRUE; OR, THE JOURNEY TO LONDON	375
THE CONFESSIONS OF AN ODD-TEMPERED MAN	394
ILLUSTRATIONS OF LYING, IN ALL ITS BRANCHES:	
CHAP. I.—Introduction	414
CHAP. II.—On the Active and Passive Lies of Vanity—The Stage Coach—Unexpected Discoveries	415
CHAP. III.—On the Lies of Flattery—The Turban	427
CHAP. IV.—Lies of Fear—The Bank-Note	431
CHAP. V.—Lies falsely called Lies of Benevolence—A Tale of Potted Sprats—An Authoress and her Auditors	434
CHAP. VI.—Lies of Convenience—Projects Defeated	437
CHAP. VII.—Lies of Interest—The Screen	441
CHAP. VIII.—Lies of First-Rate Malignity—The Orphan	445
CHAP. IX.—Lies of Second-Rate Malignity—The Old Gentleman and the Young One	451
CHAP. X.—Lies of Benevolence—Mistaken Kindness—Father and Son	455
CHAP. XI.—Lies of Wantonness and Practical Lies	465
CHAP. XII.—Our own Experience of the Painful Results of Lying	467
CHAP. XIII.—Lying the most common of all Vices	470
CHAP. XIV.—Extracts from Lord Bacon, and others	471
CHAP. XV.—Observations on the Extracts from Hawkesworth and others	478
CHAP. XVI.—Religion the only Basis of Truth	480
CHAP. XVII—The same subject continued	491
Conclusion	493

MRS. OPIE'S WORKS.

TEMPER.

"Shut the door, Agatha," said Mr. Torrington to a beautiful girl of four years old; "the wind from the passage is intolerable."

But Agatha stirred not.

"Did you not hear what I said?" resumed her father; "shut the door, for I am cold."

Still, however, the child continued to build houses, and her father spoke in vain.

"I will shut the door myself," said her fatally indulgent mother;—"Agatha is not yet old enough to understand the virtue of obedience."

"But she is old enough to understand the inconveniences of disobedience, my dear Emma, if properly punished for disobeying."

"Surely it would be cruel to punish a child when she is incapable of knowing that what she does is worthy of punishment. When she is old enough to have reason, I will reason with her, and make her obedient and obliging on principle."

"It is lucky for society, Emma, that the keepers of lunatics do not act on your plan, and allow them to follow all their propensities till they are reasonable enough to feel the propriety of restraint."

"There is a great difference between mad people and children, Mr. Torrington."

"Undoubtedly, but not in the power of self-guidance and self-restriction. The man who has lost his reason, and the child who has not gained his, are equally objects for reproof and restraint, and must be taught good and proper habits by judicious and firm control, and occasionally by the operation of fear."

"Fear! Mr. Torrington, would you beat the child?"

"If you were a foolish mother, and by weak and pernicious indulgence were to *brutify* Agatha so much as to render her incapable of being governed in any other way. But in my opinion, if corporeal chastisement is ever necessary, it can only be where the parents by neglect and folly have injured the temper and destroyed the mind of their offspring."

"Could you ever have the heart to beat Agatha, Mr. Torrington?"

"If Agatha's good required it. If it were necessary that she should take medicine in order to cure her body, even you, Emma, would not hesitate, I conclude, to force the medicine down her throat."

"Certainly not."

"And is not the health of her mind of even greater importance? and should we hesitate to inflict salutary punishment in order to preserve *that* uninjured?"

At this moment, Agatha, unconscious, poor child! how important to her future welfare was this conversation between her parents, interrupted it by seizing a pair of sharp-pointed scissors, and carrying off the forbidden plaything to the furthest part of the room.

"Agatha, bring back the scissors this moment," cried Mr. Torrington; but Agatha kept them still.

"Give them to me this instant," he repeated, rising from his chair, and approaching to take them by force; when Agatha, unaccustomed to obey, as she was, when not in her father's presence, always used to command, instantly threw the scissors on the ground with violence.

"Take them up, and give them to me."

But Agatha only turned her back, and putting her hand under her chin threw out her raised elbow at her father with the gesture of sulky defiance.

Mr. Torrington now found that he was seriously called upon to practise as well as preach.

"Agatha," said he, firmly, but mildly, "obey me, and give me the scissors, or you shall go to bed this moment, and without your supper." But as the child continued obstinate and disobedient; in spite of her cries, blows, and kicks, Mr. Torrington took her up in his arms, and carried her into the nursery.

"Put Miss Torrington to bed directly," said he; "and on pain of instant dismissal, I forbid you to give her any thing to eat or drink."

He then returned to her mother, in the midst of the screams of the spoiled and irritated Agatha. He found Mrs. Torrington in tears.

"Why are you distressed thus, dearest Emma?" cried he, affectionately.

"I cannot bear to hear Agatha cry, Mr. Torrington."

"It does not give me pleasure," coolly replied he.

"Ah! Mr. Torrington, but you are not a mother."

"I know it, my love. I have had, it is true, many comical nervous fancies; but I never fancied myself a mother yet."

"This is a bad joke, Mr. Torrington."

"I grant it."

"And *I*, Mr. Torrington, am in no humour for joking; this is too serious a subject."

"Emma, I joked, to show you that *I*, at least, did not think this temporary affliction of our violent child, a cause for sorrow."

"No! Hark: how she screams! Indeed, Mr. Torrington, I must go to her."

"Indeed, Emma, you must not."

"Her agonies distract me; I cannot bear it, I tell you."

"You must bear it, Mrs. Torrington, or forfeit much of my respect."

"O, a mother's feelings——"

"——are natural, and therefore honourable feelings; but I expect a rational being to be superior to a mere brute mother."

"A brute mother, Mr. Torrington!"

"Yes; a brute mother. The cat that lies yonder, unable to bear the cries of its kitten, would, from mere natural instinct (the feelings of a mother, Emma, which I have not, you know,) fly at the animal, or human creature, that occasioned those cries; and the cat, wholly guided by instinct, could not do otherwise, though an operation were performing on its offspring that was requisite to save its life. But from you, Emma, who have reason to aid and regulate the impulses of mere instinct,—from *you* I expect better things than a selfish indulgence of your own tenderness at the expense of your child's future welfare; nay, even of its present safety. For had she been allowed to retain the scissors, she might have destroyed an eye or laid open an artery with them. If you must weep because she weeps, let it be for the alarming obstinacy and violence which she is now exhibiting; a violence which may, perhaps, be big with her future misery and ruin."

"I am a weak, a foolish woman, Mr. Torrington, and——"

"Not so, Emma. If you had been weak and foolish, though young, rich, and beautiful, and I only a younger brother, I would never have made you my wife. No; I saw in you a woman capable of being a rational companion, and the instructress as well as the mother of my children; and I do not recognise you, my dear Emma, in the puerile tenderness that shrinks appalled at the cries of an angry child.

"Let me put a case to you, Emma;—Suppose in one house a mother informed by the surgeons attending, that her beloved daughter must undergo a painful operation in order to save her life, or prevent the progress of a pernicious disease; suppose that mother unable from maternal tenderness to remain in the room while the operation is performing, and giving way to tears and hysterics in the adjoining apartment;—

"Suppose in another house a mother under similar circumstances, suppressing all selfish emotions, by thinking only of the beloved sufferer, and hastening to the scene of trial, to cheer by her presence, to soothe by her caresses, and to support in her arms, the object of her anxiety; while maternal tenderness checks the tear that maternal tenderness urges, and firmly, though feelingly, she goes through the painful task assigned her by affectionate duty. Now, in which of these two do you recognise the highest order of motherly love?"

"In the latter, undoubtedly."

"And such, my dear Emma, is the conduct of those wise parents who, in order to ensure the future good of their children, refuse them indulgences pernicious to their health, or inflict on them salutary punishment regardless of the pain they themselves suffer from giving pain to the resisting and angry child, and consoling and comforting themselves with knowing that, though the duty they are performing is even an agonizing one, the good of the beloved object requires it of them;—while the parents who suffer their children to tyrannize over them, and have their own way in every thing, because, forsooth, it gives them pain to deny and afflict them, are like the hysterical mother, who had rather indulge her own feelings in tears and exclamations, than punish and constrain herself in order to endeavour to be of service and of comfort to her child."

The cries of Agatha at this moment began to grow fainter and fainter, and at length ceased altogether; for she had cried herself to sleep. But now a new alarm took possession of Mrs. Torrington.

"Bless me!" she exclaimed, "perhaps she has screamed herself into convulsions! I must go up and see her, indeed, Mr. Torrington."

"No, Emma. I will spare you the trouble and go myself."

Accordingly he did so, and found Agatha in a calm and quiet slumber; though on her full and crimson cheek still glittered the tears of turbulent resentment.

Mrs. Torrington, whom love and reverence for her husband made submissive to his will, did not venture to follow him into Agatha's bed-room; but she stood in the hall anxiously awaiting his return.

"Away with these foolish fears," said Mr. Torrington, "the child is in a most comfortable sleep;—or, if you must fear, let it be, as I said before, for the health of her mind, not of her body; and avoid in future the conduct that may endanger it. Should the child with which you are about to bless me be a son, Emma, I shall expect you to assist me in forming him for a hero, or a legislator; and you must not disappoint the expectations so honourable to you, and so dear to me."

What is there that a wife, a woman so flattered and encouraged would not have promised, and would not, at the moment, have felt able to perform? Mrs. Torrington fondly pressed the kind hand that held hers; declared her consciousness of past weakness, and her hope of future strength, and retired to rest one of the happiest of human beings.

A very few weeks beheld an amendment in the behaviour and temper of Agatha, under the firm but gentle authority of her father, assisted by the now well-regulated indulgence of her mother. But, alas! in a few weeks more this husband so devotedly beloved, this father so admirably fitted to take on himself the awful responsibility of a father, was carried off, after a short illness, by consumption, the hereditary scourge of his family; and his almost distracted widow, overwhelmed by the suddenness as well as violence of the blow, gave birth to a dead infant, and was for some time incapable of attending in any way to the duties which she was lately so solicitous to perform.

But when time had ameliorated her grief, and Agatha regained her usual power over her affections, she was continually saying to herself that she would show her regard for her late husband by acting implicitly on his system for the education of Agatha. Still, at first she gave way to the childish whims of her daughter, from want, she said, of energy in her afflicted state to contradict her; and afterwards from want of power to distress, even momentarily, the beloved being who reminded her of the husband she had lost; and as that lamented husband was the only person who had ever possessed power to overcome her usual obstinacy of decision, and indolence of mind, and prevail on her to use her understanding uninfluenced by the suggestions of temper or prejudice, with him for ever vanished Mrs. Torrington's inducements to the exertions which he recommended, and Agatha became the tyrant of her mother and her mother's household, and the pity, the torment, and detestation of all the relations and friends who visited at the house.

But when Agatha approached the age of womanhood, and with her years the violence of her uncorrected temper increased, she became an object of fear even to Mrs. Torrington; for, having been long accustomed to tyrannize in trifling matters, she showed herself resolved to govern in matters of importance. Mrs. Torrington, however, loved power as well as Agatha, and a struggle for it immediately took place, which gave rise to a great deal of domestic discord, and had no tendency to improve the already impetuous temper of Agatha. Still she loved her mother, for her affections were as violent as her disposition; but her virtues, her beauty, and her talents were fatally obscured by the clouds thrown over them by the obliquities of temper.

There is nothing more likely to soberize the intoxications of self-love, than the reflection how soon even the most celebrated of men and women are forgotten; how soon the waters of oblivion close over the memory of the distinguished few, whose wit or whose beauty has delighted the circles which their reputation had attracted round them; and that even they, when they cease to be seen and heard, at the same time also cease to be remembered.

Mrs. Torrington (when Emma Bellenden) had shone brightest of the birthday beauties, and besides being nobly born, was rich both in personal property and estates; consequently, she was the little sun of every circle in which she moved. But when, at the age of eighteen, she gave her hand and her heart to Mr. Torrington, and retired with him to a remote residence in the country, where, like a virtuous and affectionate wife, she found her best pleasure in the enjoyment of her husband's society, and in attention to her husband's comforts; the circles which she had herself forgotten, forgot her in their turn; and some new beauty, some new heiress, filled the place which she had vacated, and soon banished all remembrance of the once celebrated Emma Bellenden.

The seclusion which love had taught, affliction and habit continued; and when Agatha became old enough to be introduced to general society, her mother found that, having for so many years dropped those acquaintances whose knowledge of the world would be of use to her daughter, she should re-appear in "those scenes so gay," as a stranger, or one long since forgotten, where she had once shone "the fairest of the fair," and should be forced to form new connexions, or to solicit a renewal of friendship with those whose self-love she had wounded by long and undeviating neglect. She knew, notwithstanding, that the effort must now be soon made, and Agatha be presented to that gay world which she seemed formed to adorn.

Previously, however, to their taking a journey to London, it was agreed upon that Agatha should be allowed to visit a relation a few miles distant from home, unaccompanied by her mother, who was confined to the house by attendance on a sick friend; and the beautiful heiress, in all the bloom of seventeen, made her appearance at a race-ball in the neighbourhood of her relation's abode.

"I conclude," said Mrs. Torrington to her daughter before she departed, "that my cousin will take care to prevent all possibility of your dancing with improper partners, and forming improper acquaintance."

"I flatter myself," replied Agatha, "that my own judgment will enable me to avoid such risks without the interference of any relation whatever."

"You forget that you are very young, Agatha, and new to the world; but I trust your pride will teach you the propriety of dancing with men of rank and consequence only, even though they be neither single nor young."

"I will not answer for obeying my pride, if the only rich and titled in the ball-room be the old, the ugly, and the married; for my taste certainly leads me to prefer the young and the well-looking at least."

"But it is my request, Agatha, that—"

"Hush, hush," cried Agatha, laughing and jumping into the carriage. "I will not allow you, dear mother, to fetter my first moments of liberty with any restraints." Then singing,

"My heart's my own, my will is free;
No mortal man shall dance with me,
Unless he is my choice,"

she kissed her hand to Mrs. Torrington, and drove to the house of her relation.

Agatha had not been long in the ball-room before her hand for the first two dances was solicited by the eldest son of a viscount, and she began the ball with a partner such as her mother would have most cordially approved. But as her partner was neither young nor handsome, Agatha resolved that, having done homage to pride and propriety in her first choice, she would either dance no more that evening, or dance with one more calculated to please than the right honourable partner whom she had just quitted.

At this minute her attention was directed to a very handsome young man, who, apparently uninterested in anything that was going forward, was leaning against the wall, and seemingly looking on in vacancy.

"Look, Miss Torrington, look! that is the handsome Danvers," said the young lady on whose arm Agatha was leaning; "there he is! in a reverie as usual! and though almost all the women in the room are dying to dance with him, the insensible creature looks at no one, and dances with no one; but after exhibiting his fine person for an hour, he will lounge home to bed."

"Perhaps," said Agatha, "the poor man is in love with an absent lady, and thence his indifference to those who are present. He is very handsome."

"Yes, and very agreeable too, I am told, when he pleases; but he is so proud and fastidious, (for he is not in love, they say,) that he does not think any lady in this part of the world worth the trouble of pleasing."

"Who is he?" asked Agatha; "and whence does he come?"

"What he is I know not; but he came hither from London, on a visit to Captain Bertie, who is quartered here, and who assures me that he is a man of family, though not of fortune."

"And so he never dances!" said Agatha, whom this handsome and indifferent man was beginning to interest, while her self-love piqued her to wish to conquer the indifference of which he seemed to make so provoking a parade. While these thoughts were passing in her mind, she and her companion were approaching the spot where Danvers stood; and as he chanced to glance his eye on Agatha, an obvious change in the expression of his countenance took place, and with evident interest and admiration he gazed on the beautiful girl before him; and when she moved to another part of the room, his eye followed her with undeviating attention.

Agatha, blushing and delighted, observed the effect which she had produced; nor was it unseen by her companion, who could not forbear, in an accent of suppressed pique, to rally her on having subdued at once a heart supposed to be impregnable. In a few minutes more Mr. Danvers was presented to Agatha by a lady of whom she had a slight knowledge, and led his ready and conscious partner to join the dance. In vain did her relation tell her she had engaged her to one baronet, and that another had also requested the honour of dancing with her, and that it was quite improper in her to dance with a man whom nobody knew. Agatha persisted in her resolution to dance with whomsoever she chose; and when Danvers came to claim her, she curtsied with a look of proud independence to her monitor, and joined the dancers.

To be brief; Danvers found opportunities to see Agatha often enough, in spite of the vigilance of her chaperone, to deepen the impression which his appearance, his manners, and still more the marked preference which he had given her over every other woman, had made on her heart; and when two gentlemen of rank and fortune asked Mrs. Torrington's leave to address her daughter, Agatha peremptorily rejected their addresses, and replied to her mother's letter of expostulation on the subject, in terms which wounded both the love and pride of Mrs. Torrington. Soon after her relation informed her that Danvers was endeavouring to gain the affections of Agatha, and that it was evident he would only too soon succeed. On hearing this, the alarmed mother resolved to summon Agatha home; but as she well knew that, being a stranger to the virtue of obedience, her daughter would refuse to obey the summons if the cause of it were told to her, Mrs. Torrington had recourse to the weakness and the vice of falsehood; the same weakness which led her to spoil Agatha in her *childhood*, naturally enough prompting her to make use of fraud in order to influence her in her *youth*; and she wrote to her, requesting her to return home, as she was very ill, and required her attendance.

The filial affection of Agatha immediately took alarm. She fancied that her mother had caught a fever of the friend whom she had been nursing. Without a moment's delay, therefore,—for even Danvers and the pleasures of a growing passion could not detain her from the sick bed of her mother,—she set off on her return home, and arrived there even before Mrs. Torrington could think her arrival possible. But when Agatha saw in the unimpaired bloom of her mother's cheek the evidence of uninjured health, and observed in her countenance at the same time the expression of grave resentment, she felt that she had been recalled on false pretences. Consequently she understood the motives for the summons, and with a sullen, haughty demeanour, she received without returning her mother's unendearing kiss, and, throwing herself into a chair, awaited in angry silence the lecture which she had no doubt was prepared for her.

Nor was she mistaken. But unfortunately the angry mother reproached her daughter for encouraging the attentions of a man whose fortune was contemptible, whose character was equivocal, and of whose connexions she had no satisfactory knowledge, in terms so violent and provoking, that they aroused all the rebellious feelings of the equally angry daughter; till at length, overcome by a variety of conflicting emotions, Mrs. Torrington gave up the fruitless contention; and yielding to the suggestions of maternal tenderness, alarmed for the future happiness and welfare of its object, she melted into tears of agony and affection, and told her daughter, that if she persisted in marrying Mr. Danvers, she would give her consent; but she knew that she could not long survive a union which would utterly destroy her peace of mind.

The proud rebellious heart, which anger and reproaches could not subdue, was overcome by gentleness and affection; and Agatha, throwing herself on her mother's neck, promised that she would endeavour to conquer a passion which was likely to be so inimical to her mother's peace. But the next day Mrs. Torrington, on a renewal of the subject, and on being more and more convinced, even by the confession of Agatha herself, that a union with her lover would be the most imprudent of actions, gave way immediately to a new burst of passion, and desired Agatha to remember, that by the will of her father she was left wholly dependent on *her*, and had only ten thousand pounds left her by her godmother which she could call her own. This ill-timed remark was of all others the most likely to awaken the pride and irritate the feelings of Agatha.

" Do you then threaten me, madam," cried Agatha indignantly, "after having had the meanness to impose on me by a tale of feigned illness!" then, with a look and gesture of defiance, she suddenly left the room, and retired to her own apartment, where she remained all day.

That evening, that fatal evening, she received a messenger from Danvers, to inform her that he was waiting to speak to her in a wood near the gate of the park; and urged by the dictates of ill-humour, and resentment against her mother, even more than by the suggestions of affection, she stole out unperceived to the place of rendezvous, whence her lover, who had a chaise waiting, had little difficulty in persuading her, in the then irritated state of her temper, to elope with him, and become his wife without the privity or approbation of Mrs. Torrington. In order to avoid pursuit, Danvers took care to have it reported in the neighbourhood that he had carried Miss Torrington to Scotland; but he preferred taking his victim to a village near London; and at the end of a month, Agatha was led to the altar by a man who knew that at the moment he pledged his faith to her, he had left a wife and family in India.

There were two circumstances, relative to the ceremony that united Agatha to Danvers, which it is proper for me to remark. The first is, that the only person present at it, besides those concerned in it, was the mistress of the house where they lodged, who, though far gone in a decline, which carried her off in two months afterwards, chose, as she had never seen a wedding, to accompany Agatha to church. And the second is, that the clergyman who married her was in a few weeks after their marriage killed on the spot by a fall from his horse.

Agatha for a few weeks thought herself happy; but she soon found that it was easier for her to violate her duty than to be easy under the consciousness of having done so; and with the entire approbation of Danvers she wrote in affectionate and even humble terms to Mrs. Torrington, to implore forgiveness. But the still irritated parent did not even vouchsafe an answer to her letter; and this silence soon became intolerable to Agatha; for, ere she had been a wife six months, she discovered that she had married a man of no tenderness, no affections, and who, now the novelty of her beauty was passed, and her fortune nearly expended in paying his debts, regarded her in no other light than as an encumbrance, and ran from the loud reproaches of her indignant spirit, and soon irritated temper, to the society of other women, to the tavern and the gaming-table. Nor was there any chance of his ever being reclaimed; for it was not in the nature of Agatha to soothe any one; and still less could she subdue her feelings so far as to endeavour to please a man who was now on the point of becoming the object of her contempt as well as her resentment; and Agatha, the repentant Agatha, was, as a wife, in every point of view completely miserable.

" Well, sir," said she one day to her tormentor, "if you will not give me your own company, let me seek that of your friends. Introduce me, as you promised you would do, to your relations." Danvers turned round, looked at her with a smile of great meaning and contempt, saying, "Never!" and left the room in disorder.

Agatha was motionless with amazement and fear of she knew not what; for why should she not be presented to his friends and relations? From this moment a feeling of forlornness took possession of her mind, which not even the consciousness that she was soon to enjoy the happiness of being a mother, could overcome,—and she again sat down to address Mrs. Torrington; who, though she had not written to her daughter, had so far relented as to send her trunks and trinkets, as soon as she knew where she was to be found. On this indulgence Agatha built hopes of future pardon, and she wrote in the fulness of her hopes and of her gratitude. Mrs. Torrington answered her letter; but she told her she would never forgive her; and, had not a tear evidently dropped upon the paper, and proved that she was more full of grief than indignation when she wrote, Agatha would have despaired perhaps of ever being pardoned. But in the first place her mother had deigned to write, and in the next place she had wept while she wrote.

"Courage!" said Agatha to herself; "I will write to her again when I am become a mother; and I think, I am *sure* that the image of her only daughter giving birth to her first child, unsoothed and unsupported by her presence, will soften her heart in my favour, and she will receive me and my poor babe into the safe asylum of her bosom;"—and then she shed tears of bitterness at the recollection that, though a wife, she was likely some time or other to need such an asylum.

At length Agatha gave birth to a daughter; and my heroine came into the world welcomed, fondly welcomed, by the caresses and tears of her mother, and received with sullen indifference by her vicious and cold-hearted father.

"Now then," thought Agatha, "I will write my intended letter;"—but in a few days she became so ill that her life was despaired of; and Emma was four months old before Agatha was able to announce her birth to Mrs. Torrington. Indeed she had scarcely courage to begin the task ; for she had to entreat from her mother's bounty, the means of living separate from her husband, if she would not receive her and her child into her own house; and Agatha hesitated to narrate the sad tale of her sorrows and her injuries.

Danvers was now never at home; but she observed that he went out more carefully dressed than usual, and commonly returned home sober, and at a decent hour. She also observed that he wrote notes frequently, and in a very neat hand, and on expensive paper. From these and other circumstances, she conjectured that the present object that drew him so frequently from home, and seemed to engross his thoughts when there, was a woman of character and respectability, who might perhaps encourage his addresses, not knowing that he was already married, and whose affections might become irrevocably and fatally engaged.

Soon after, as she was taking an evening walk in St. James' Park, with her child and its maid, feeling herself tired, she sat down on one of the chairs in the principal promenade,—when she saw her husband approach, in company with some ladies elegantly dressed, and apparently of great respectability. To one of these ladies, who leaned on the arm of an elderly gentleman, she observed that Danvers paid the most devoted attention, and that he addressed her in a low voice, while she replied to what he said, with evident confusion and delight. She had sufficient leisure to make these observations, as the party walked backwards and forwards, slowly and frequently ; and as she wore a thick veil, she could observe them without any fear of being known even by her husband, if his attention had not been wholly engrossed by his companion; while the nursery-maid, though she wondered why the husband and wife did not notice each other, was too much in awe of Agatha, even to say, " Look, madam! there is my master!"

What Agatha now beheld, confirmed all her suspicions. She saw in Danvers, that dangerous expression of countenance, and gentle insinuation of manner, which had won her inexperienced heart; and she left the Park, resolved to expostulate with him the next morning.

That night Danvers returned early, and in good-humour,—so much so, luckily for Agatha, that he threw a purse of thirty guineas into her lap, telling her that he had won the money at cards, and that she had a right to share the luck she had occasioned; "for," added he, laughing, "you know the proverb says, 'That if a man has bad luck in a wife, he has good luck at cards.'" The fulness of Agatha's torn heart, deprived her of the power of answering him, and she deferred her intended expostulation till the next day; when, in all the bitterness of a wounded spirit, she told Danvers what she had witnessed ; and disclosing to him her suspicions of his intentions towards the young lady whom she had seen, she declared that she would do all in her power to warn her of her danger.

"She is in no danger," replied Danvers, thinking the moment was now come for him to throw off the mask entirely, "as you are no obstacle to my marriage with her; for I am a single man now, and you never were my lawful wife. Know, madam, when I led you to the altar, my friends and relations could have informed your mother, if you had given her time to make the proper inquiries, that I was married six years ago in India, and that when

I married you, I had a wife living in that country."

Agatha heard him with speechless and overwhelming horror. Now then his reluctance that she should see or correspond with any of her relations and friends was explained, and his refusal to present her to his own; now then the whole hopeless wretchedness of her fate was disclosed to her. She saw that she was a mother, without being a wife; and that she had given birth to a child who had no legal inheritance, and though not the offspring of a mother's guilt, was undoubtedly the victim of a father's depravity! With the rapidity of lightning these overwhelming certainties darted across her mind, and with the force of it they stretched her in a moment senseless on the earth.

Slow and miserable was her recovery; and such was her frantic agony when she took her child in her arms, that though her manners, too often under the influence of her temper, had not conciliated the regard of the persons where she lodged, the mistress of the house, whom Danvers had sent to her assistance previously to his leaving home, when she found her senses returning, hung over her with the appearance of compassionate sympathy; and at length by her soothings moved the broken-hearted Agatha to tears, which in all probability saved her from immediate destruction.

In a few hours she was able to form some projects for the future. To remain even a night longer in the house with Danvers, was now, in her just conceptions of propriety, criminal;—but whither should she go? Would her mother consent to receive that child when proved to be only the mistress of Danvers, whom she had refused to receive when she appeared to be his lawful wife? She dared not anticipate the probable answer of Mrs. Torrington;—but to fly from Danvers and implore the protection of her mother was now her sole hope, her sole resource.

While she sat lost in mournful reverie, she heard Danvers return; and shutting himself into his own apartment with great force, he continued to walk about some time in violent agitation. At length he entered the room where she was, and looked at her in silence with a countenance of such savage and cruel defiance, that the original violence of her sorrow returned, and she was carried to bed in a state of insensibility.

Had Agatha suspected the cause of Danver's agitation, and the severity in his expression when he looked at her, she would have felt emotions of thankfulness, not of sorrow; for he had that morning received intelligence which defeated the expectations of his love, and showed him that his villany towards Agatha had been wholly unsuccessful. When he informed her that he had, at the time of his marriage with her, a wife living in India, he told her what he imagined to be true, (as he had received information of his wife's death only a few days preceding that conversation;) and she, to whom the practice of falsehood was unknown, implicitly believed the horrid truth which he asserted. But he had scarcely left the house when a letter was put into his hands, containing not only a detailed account of his wife's illness and death, but also the exact day, and even hour when she breathed her last; by which he found that she had been dead full three weeks before he led Agatha to the altar, and that consequently AGATHA TORRINGTON WAS HIS LAWFUL WIFE! He also met at the house of his agent a woman of colour just arrived from India, who was inquiring his address, and who, by the mother's advice, had brought over to England his only child, a beautiful boy of five years old; and from her he received ample confirmation of the intelligence which burthened him so unexpectedly with a wife whom he disliked, and made it difficult and dangerous perhaps to prosecute his endeavours to marry the woman whom he loved.

But as he grew calmer, he began to reflect that he had told Agatha she was not his lawful wife, and she believed him; therefore he hoped he should have no difficulty in keeping the real state of the case from her knowledge. But in order to make "assurance doubly sure," he resolved that the woman of colour before mentioned should be introduced to Agatha, in order to confirm his statement.

Nor was this woman averse to do so, when she heard his reasons for requiring this service from her. In early life, this unhappy being, when living at Calcutta in his father's family, had been the favourite mistress of Danvers; and she had ever remained so warmly attached to him, that when he married, her affliction, and her hatred of his wife, were so great, as to make it advisable for her to be sent up the country, lest, in a transport of jealous fury, she might gratify her hatred on her innocent and then beloved rival. But when she heard that this rival was in her turn forsaken, and was separated from her inconstant husband, she forgot her animosity; and hearing that Mrs. Danvers was in want of a nurse maid to attend on her child, she returned to Calcutta, where Mrs. Danvers resided, and became the attached and confidential servant of that lady, who, on her death-bed, consigned her son to her care, and charged her to see him safe into his father's arms.

This charge of her dying mistress the faithful creature punctually obeyed; and when, while inquiring for Danvers of his agent, he, as I have stated before, unexpectedly entered, the sight of him renewed in all its force the passion of her early youth; and as soon as he told her that he had a wife whom he hated, and whom he wished to get rid of, she was very ready to assist him, in the weak but natural hope that she might, for a time at least, be his again. Had she known that Danvers wanted to get rid of Agatha in order to obtain another woman, she would not have shown such a pernicious alacrity to oblige him; but she now readily promised to tell the falsehood which he dictated; and the next morning, while Agatha, buried in thought, was leaning on her hands and endeavouring to decide on some immediate plan of action, Danvers entered the room, leading in his little boy, and followed by the woman of colour.

At sight of the author of her misery, Agatha started, trembled, and rose from her seat, with a look so terrible and so wild, that the frightened Indian gazed on her with mingled awe and terror. Agatha, in compliance with the wishes of Danvers, had never worn powder; she usually, when at home, wore her hair, which was very thick and glossy, and had a natural wave amidst its other beauties, parted on the forehead, and hanging down on either side of her long and finely-formed throat. This flowing hair, which was commonly kept in the nicest order, was now neglected, and it fell disordered and dishevelled, while a long white bed-gown, loosely folded round her, completed the disorder of her dress, and added to the frantic appearance of her countenance and action.

"Who are these?" she demanded in a tone of desperation.

"This," said Danvers, "is the faithful servant of my late wife, who attended her in her last moments; and I have brought her hither, lest you should be inclined to disbelieve my assurance that you never were my lawful wife, in order to tell you the very day and hour on which she died, namely, two months after my marriage with you."

"It was wholly unnecessary, sir," said Agatha, turning still paler than before; "for I believed your own statement implicitly. But surely, sir, you are liable to a prosecution for bigamy?" added Agatha.

"Undoubtedly I am," replied Danvers; "but even if you had it in your power to adduce evidence of my two marriages,—which you have *not*, nor ever *can* have,—still, I know your pride and delicacy to be too great to allow you to proceed against me, especially as by so doing, you would neither establish your own marriage, nor legitimate your child."

"True,—most true," said Agatha, shuddering. "But what child is this?" said she, drawing near the little boy, who hid his face in his nurse's gown, as if alarmed at the approach of a stranger.

"It is my son," replied Danvers.

"Ay," returned Agatha, "your legitimate son. But what then is *this* innocent babe?" snatching to her heart the child sleeping on a sofa beside her.

Danvers, despite of his dauntless callousness of feeling, turned away in confusion.

"Poor boy!" continued Agatha, "why shouldest *thou* hide thy face, as if in shame? for THOU art not the child of shame. Nor art thou either, poor unconscious victim! Let me do myself justice," she exclaimed, pressing her child closely to her bosom; "it is for thy father, thou wilt have to blush, not for thy mother!" Then with an air of proud insulted dignity, she bade Danvers and the woman of colour, to be gone immediately;—and as if awed by her manner, and conscious of her superiority, they instantly and rapidly obeyed.

The rest of the day was spent by Agatha in forming plans for her future conduct; and after long and varied deliberation, she resolved to write to her mother again, but not till she could date her letter from a roof unpolluted by the presence of the man who had betrayed her, and inform her she had parted with him to behold him no more.

That night Danvers, to whom the dread of a discovery, in spite of the pains which he had taken to prevent it, occasioned considerable agitation, indulged more than usual in the excesses of the bottle, at the tavern where he dined, and was brought home and put to bed in an apoplexy of drunkenness. In the middle of the night, Agatha, who, unable to sleep, was pacing the floor of her chamber in morbid restlessness, thought she heard an alarming noise in Danvers' apartment, from which she was separated only by a dressing-room; and aware of the state in which he returned, she stole gently to his door, from an impulse, not of alarmed affection, but of principled humanity. She listened a few moments, and all was still again; and the stillness alarming her as much as the previous noise, she entered the chamber, and anxiously surveyed her flushed and insensible betrayer.

But a few moments convinced her that she had nothing to apprehend for his life; and she was gently returning, when she saw on the floor, papers that had evidently dropped from the pocket of the coat, which was thrown in a disordered manner on the chair, by the side of the bed. Involuntarily she stooped, in order to replace them, and her eye glanced on an open letter, sealed with black, addressed to George Danvers, Esq., Bruton Street, Berkely Square, London, *England*. An impulse not to be resisted, urged her to read this letter. It probably was the one he alluded to, containing the account of his wife's death! and setting the candle on a table, she opened it, and read the contents; which were such as immediately to throw her on her knees in a transport of thanksgiving. It was indeed the letter giving an account of Mrs. Danvers' last moments, and also of the very day and hour that she died; and Agatha, as Danvers had done before, saw that beyond the power of doubt she herself WAS THE LAWFUL WIFE of Danvers, and her child the offspring of a LEGITIMATE MARRIAGE. When the transports of her joy and gratitude had a little subsided, she folded the letter up and deposited it in her bosom, resolved to keep it as a defence against the evidently villanous intentions of Danvers; and with a lightened heart she returned to her own apartment.

The next morning she made a small bundle of the clothes most requisite for herself and child; and leaving a note for Danvers, informing him of the discovery which she had made, and of her intention to take every legal means to substantiate her marriage, bidding him at the same time farewell for ever, she walked with her child in her arms, to a stand of coaches, and having called one, desired the coachman to drive to a street which she named, at some distance from Danvers' lodgings, and then to stop wherever he saw "Lodgings to let" in the window.

Luckily for Agatha, she found two apartments to let on the ground floor, in a distressed but honest family; and having taken them for one week, she sat down to deliberate on her best mode of proceeding. To obtain a certificate of her marriage seemed a necessary step; but first she resolved to write a full detail to her mother, flattering herself that, as the conduct of Danvers was calculated to injure the fame of her daughter, Mrs. Torrington's pride might be roused to resent it, though her tenderness might remain unmoved.

Unfortunately for Agatha, Danvers was of the same opinion; and as soon as he found that Agatha was in possession of the letter, he took every possible means in his power to frustrate the success of her application to Mrs. Torrington, and to deprive her of every evidence that a marriage with him had taken place. Danvers knew, though Agatha did not, that her mother was at a retired watering-place, about a day's journey from London; and thither he immediately sent the woman of colour, and his little boy, whose deep mourning and excessive beauty were, he well knew, likely to attract the attention of all women, but more especially of *mothers.*

Nor was he mistaken in his expectations. Mrs. Torrington observed and admired the perhaps orphan child, who was constantly led along the walks which she most frequented; and at last she could not help stopping the servant to inquire the name of that beautiful child, and the cause of the deep mourning which he wore.

"He is in mourning for Mrs. Danvers, [at this name Mrs. Torrington started,] his poor mamma, who died a little while ago in India."

"But has he no father?" asked Mrs. Torrington.

"O dear! yes," replied the woman of colour, "A fine gentleman indeed, Mr. George Danvers, formerly of —— regiment, who lives in Bruton street, Berkely square, just now."

"Impossible! quite impossible!" answered Mrs. Torrington, tottering to a bench which was near her. "Surely that Mr. Danvers has a wife living!"

"A wife!" resumed the artful Indian with a look full of sarcastic meaning. "No! my master never had any wife, I am sure, but my poor dear mistress. That miss (Miss Torrington I believe her name is) who lives with him only goes by his name, and is only his miss."

It was too much for a mother to bear; and believing implicitly a tale which seemed so plausible, Mrs. Torrington fell from her seat in a state of insensibility, and it was many hours before she recovered her senses and recollection. But at the very moment she did so, a letter from Agatha was put into her hands, and torn unread into a thousand pieces; while the woman of colour remained a few days longer at the watering-place, in order to avoid any appearance of having come thither merely to effect a purpose,—and then returned to the delighted Danvers, who had no doubt of the success of his scheme in order to prevent the money and power of Mrs. Torrington from being exerted in her daughter's favour.

But his machination did not end here. In the clerk at the church where they were married, he had recognised an old friend and his assistant in the unprincipled seduction of a farmer's daughter; and who, though he had to his great surprise, when he last saw him, found him in a situation of trust and respectability, he was very sure was a being so completely unprincipled as not to scruple any action, however bad, for which his avarice was to receive a single gratification. Accordingly, he set off for the village where he had been united to Agatha; and while the church register was lying in the library of the rector, for the purpose of having extracts made from it, the clerk, bribed by Danvers, contrived to tear out the leaf which contained the evidence of his marriage; and as, owing to circumstances, no copy had yet been taken of the register, Danvers returned to his own apartments with the consciousness of successful guilt.

Agatha, meanwhile, watched the arrival of the post every day with vain and fruitless anxiety, till her feelings approached the very verge of insanity, and the nourishment which she had hitherto afforded her child began to be dried up; for dark and hopeless was the prospect before her. At length, she wrote again to her mother. And this letter Mrs. Torrington opened; but seeing that Agatha, presuming as she conceived on her superior understanding, was trying to impose on her, by making her believe that she was the deserted *wife* of Danvers, she read only the first sentence or two; then, in a letter of reproach and invective, she returned it to the expecting and half-distracted Agatha.

Agatha received her own letter back, and read her mother's with the calm firmness of desperation, and also with the indignant pride of conscious and outraged innocence. But where could she turn for assistance, advice, and redress? She was too proud to confide in inferiors, too proud also to apply, in that

Vol. III.——2

equivocal situation, which even exposed her to be called infamous by a *mother*, to the scorn or suspicions of her own relations and friends.

Yet something she must do; and her good sense taught her, as before, that she must try to obtain a certificate of her marriage. Accordingly she hired a coach, and drove, as Danvers had done, to the village where they were married. She was directed to the clerk's house; and little did Agatha suspect with what malignant joy this base agent of her unworthy husband saw her arrive at his door, and knew the errand on which she came. For during her childhood this man had been a hanger-on in her mother's kitchen; and his little girl, a most lovely child, the darling of his heart, had been often the playfellow of Agatha, and the slave of her tyrannical humours. One day this uncorrected tyrant, in a fit of passion, gave a blow to the poor child, who was forced into the misery of playing with her; and though the blow itself could have done her little injury,—in endeavouring to avoid it, she struck her head against a marble table so severely that she was taken up stunned and apparently dead; and while the terrified and therefore penitent Agatha was by her criminally weak parent soothed and comforted as tenderly as her little victim was by the parents who feared for her life, the father of the endangered child breathed curses on the head of the unamiable Agatha, and wished from the bottom of his soul to be revenged on her.

True—Agatha meant not to hurt so seriously the offending child, but who can say where may terminate the consequences of a blow aimed by the hand of passion! True—many presents were lavished on the child, when she recovered, both by Mrs. Torrington and her daughter;—but the darling of a father's heart had suffered pain, and had experienced danger; and the man hated the being that had inflicted them; for this darling did not live to womanhood, and her father always believed this blow was the occasion of her death.

Soon after he left the neighbourhood, and he never saw Agatha again till he beheld her at the altar. He now saw her once more, and he had had the *revenge* on her which he desired. But his vengeance was going to be more *amply* gratified;—he was going to see her writhe under the misery to which he had contributed.

Agatha was requested to alight, and the well-remembered face of the clerk met her view. Still she had no idea *where* she had seen him, and he had no inclination to inform her; while with suppressed agitation she begged to have a copy of the register of her marriage, mentioning the day and hour when it was solemnized. The clerk feigned astonishment, and looked at her as if he doubted her being in her senses. But Agatha persisted in her statement and her demand, and the clerk at last accompanied her to the church, having procured the keys of the vestry closet from the sexton; and the register was opened at the month which she mentioned. But in vain did she seek the record which she required;—it was not there! and the helpless, injured Agatha stood speechless with surprise! At length, however, indignation gave her words, and turning scornfully round to Cammell—

"You are a villain!" she exclaimed, "and the mean agent of a greater villain still. Let me see your rector himself; to his justice I shall appeal."

Cammell bowed; and said, "if the lady insisted on it, he would go to him."

"No," replied Agatha; "I will accompany you, nor shall you quit my sight till I have seen him."

The clerk again bowed, and saying the lady must be obeyed, led the way to the rector's house. At the door the servant said his master was dressing, but that the clerk might be admitted; and Agatha was, unwillingly, forced to submit to this separation.

Her suspicions of its consequences were not unfounded. The clerk described her as a maniac; a woman deprived of her senses by the marriage of a man who had seduced and abandoned her; that she was become mad, on the idea that she was his wife; and was in the habit of going to different churches demanding a copy of her marriage register. It is not to be wondered at, therefore, that the clergyman should, when he beheld Agatha, discover immediately in her looks the frenzy attributed to her;—and to her appeal for justice, and her accusation of her husband and Cammell, he replied with shrugs of the shoulders, shakes of the head, and "Really, ma'am, I can't say,—I cannot believe——" which drove the proud, irritable, and aggrieved Agatha into the real frenzy which the clerk had feigned. And when the clergyman wished her good morning, and attempted to leave the room, she, to his great consternation, suddenly seized his arm, and commanded him to stay. Then turning to Cammel, she started, mused a moment, and exclaimed,

"Where have I seen that dark and gloomy face before? It haunts my recollection like some miserable remembrance of pain endured long since!"

Here the clerk and the clergyman exchanged significant glances; and the clerk, prefacing his words with a look of pity, and "Poor, distracted creature!" assured him that he had never seen her before in his life.

"You are both in a league against me, I perceive," said she, "and where to turn, and what to do, I know not.—Sir," (turning round so quickly as to make the clergyman start,) "sir, who keeps the keys of the place where you deposit the register?"

"Myself."

"And you never trust them to others, except as I have myself witnessed this day?"

"Never."

"You never have it at your own house?"

"Yes; and, having found her coach, returned in an agony of unspeakable wretchedness to sight?"

"Never! And this you would swear in a court of justice?"

"I would."

"And there, sir, you *shall* swear it then," replied Agatha.

Then darting at them both a look of ineffable and fierce disdain, she walked majestically away; and, having found her coach, returned in an agony of unspeakable wretchedness to London; while those whom she left behind remained differently affected, though equally glad that she was gone. The clergyman was really afraid of her, on account of her imagined disorder, though at the same time he felt charmed by her beauty, and awed by the evident dignity of her manner—the natural result of conscious importance; while Cammell, though he rejoiced in his revenge, was every moment afraid that Agatha would recollect him and his name, and prove beyond a doubt that he had lied in declaring he had never seen her before.

Meanwhile Agatha, with despair in her heart, arrived at her lodgings, and was eagerly knocking at the door, having scarcely waited till the step was put down; while, so anxious was she to see her child, whom she had never left till now, that she forgot to ask the driver his fare. But he surlily reminded her of her neglect, and made a most exorbitant demand.

Agatha, however, complied with it immediately; and taking the purse which Danvers had given her, and which once contained thirty guineas, but was now reduced to much less than a fourth of the sum, she paid the man what he required. But he, his avarice being awakened by a compliance he so little expected, seized her arm, and told her she had not given him enough, and he must and would have more.

Against this evident imposition even the fast-clouding intellect of Agatha revolted, and she refused to comply; but alarmed at the violence of the coachman, and the crowd that began to gather, her hand dropped the purse, which scattered the guineas around as it fell.

The coachman immediately let go his hold; and Agatha feeling herself at liberty, and hearing her child cry, rushed into the then opening door, and was not conscious she had dropped her purse till the maid of the house brought it to her a few minutes afterwards, declaring that the coachman and the crowd had run away with all but one solitary guinea.—But she spoke to one who heard her not.

The mistress of the lodging-house had met Agatha on her return, holding her screaming child in her arms, who had been vainly for some time requiring the food which her fevered and agitated mother, even when she arrived, could no longer bestow on her. And while the poor woman, who had never been a mother herself, was lamenting her inability to offer either advice or assistance, Agatha sat in still, desponding silence, clasping the gradually sinking child to her heart, and ruminating sad and desperate resolutions.

At length she started up, and, wrapping her child in a large mantle, with outward composure but inward perturbation, told her landlady that she was obliged to leave the lodgings directly; and on begging to know what she was indebted to her, she heard with horror, that the sum exceeded, far exceeded, the guinea which, Agatha now comprehended, was all that remained of her once well-filled purse!

"Do not distress yourself thus, madam," said the kind-hearted woman, to whom her own sorrows had taught sympathy with those of others, "it is not much, and we can wait; and if you never pay us, it does not signify."

"I shall never be able to pay you if I do not pay you now," replied Agatha in a mournful and solemn tone; "but I believe my clothes are more than worth the money. I shall therefore leave them behind me; and if you do not hear from me in a month's time, look on them as your property."

The woman, alarmed, she scarcely knew why, by the manner of Agatha, earnestly entreated her to remain one night longer where she was, and offered to go in search of a wet nurse for the child. But Agatha, by a commanding look, imposed silence on her importunities; and, borrowing a shilling to pay her coach-hire, desired a coach to be called, and took a feeling, though distant, farewell of her anxious and kind hostess.

The coachman had driven Agatha, who knew little of the geography of London, as far as Windmill-street, on her way to Westminster-bridge, when she recollected that probably a shilling would not be sufficient to pay her fare thither. Accordingly she stopped the coach, and, desiring to be set down, got out, offered the shilling as payment, and was relieved to find that it was immediately accepted.

"I can ask my way thither," said Agatha to herself, "it is the only trouble I shall ever again give my fellow-creatures;" and she pressed her sleeping, because exhausted, babe still closer to her bosom; while the grave appeared her only place of refuge. For Agatha was married, yet had no husband; had a mother, yet was motherless; she was herself a parent, without the means of prolonging the existence of her child; she was spotless in virtue, yet was believed criminal even by the mother who bore her in her bosom; she had uttered her just complaints, and had been treated as a maniac; and discarded by the only being who could enable her to redress her wrongs, where on *earth* could she look for succour and for sustenance!

"I will seek the mercy and pardon of my God!" she exclaimed, and with a firm voice she desired to be shown the way to Westminster-bridge. But she was told it in vain; and in Cockspur-street she was again at a loss, and was debating of whom she should next inquire, when, just as a most severe summer shower began to fall, she was forced to stand up against the door of a shop in order to avoid a carriage. The pale face of Agatha was slightly shaded by so very costly a lace veil, depending from a small straw bonnet, and around her tall majestic figure was wrapt a laced muslin mantle of such curious texture, and her air and mien were so pure and so commanding, that it was impossible for her to be mistaken either for a servant, or for a depraved woman, or indeed for any thing but what she was—a gentlewoman. Yet this lady, as every thing about her proved her to be, was wandering alone in the streets of London, and carrying, like a menial, an infant in her arms.

"This is very strange," said a Mr. Orwell to himself, as Agatha stopped against his door; and his wife's countenance expressed equal surprise with that of her husband.

It was a bright evening in the first week of July, undimmed even by the shower then falling, for that glittered with the evening rays; and many of the inhabitants of Cockspur-street stood at their doors to enjoy the genial season. The door of Mr. Orwell's shop was very near that of his parlour, which also stood open, and he and his wife were drinking tea, and seeing the carriages and people pass; when Agatha, after throwing a wild unconscious look into the shop, stood up, as I before said, for safety. There was something in her look, her dress, her air, which irresistibly impelled Mr. Orwell to start from his seat and approach her; and an impulse equally strong led his wife to follow his example. Coach after coach continued to impede the progress of the passengers, and barrow after barrow; while the increasing rain made all who were not provided with umbrellas, seek shelter in some friendly doorway. But Agatha remained in the wet, unconscious that it rained; and, turning round, her wild, yet sunk eye, met that of Mr. Orwell.

"Pray, madam, come in," said he, in an accent of kindness, an accent made kinder than it was wont to be, by recently-experienced affliction; "it rains very hard, and you will be wet through, ma'am."

"Ay, pray do come in, and sit down till the rain is over," said his equally kind wife; and Agatha, though she scarcely knew why she did so, complied with their request, and entered the shop.

"Here is a chair, ma'am," said Mr. Orwell; and Agatha took it; but to sit was impossible. She hastily arose, and began, ill-suited as the narrow bounds of the place were for the purpose, to pace backwards and forwards, with the maniacal walk of overwhelming misery. Here a faint cry from the infant called her attention to it, and awakened still more forcibly that of the Orwells.

"I thought it was a child you were carrying, madam," said Mrs. Orwell. "May I, without offence, beg leave to look at it?"

"It is not worth looking at *now*," replied Agatha, unclosing the mantle; and Mrs. Orwell brushed away a tear, caused by a painful recollection, as she saw in its pale and sunken cheek, the evident approaches of death. Agatha saw her tear, and understood it.

"It will not suffer long!" said she; "neither shall I;" and she pronounced this in a tone of voice so deep, so solemn, and with a look so expressive of the resolution of despair, that Mr. Orwell, who was gazing on her when she spoke, guessed the misery, and suspected the desperate purpose of her soul.

"I will follow and not lose sight of her," said he, mentally; "but first I will endeavour to draw her into the relief of conversation."

Agatha had resumed her walk, and extended it into the parlour, where the tea yet smoking in the cups, and new bread, attracted her unconsciously, and she recollected that she had not eaten food for days. Mrs. Orwell observed the eager look she cast on the well-filled table, and with great humility,—for she saw that Agatha, as she afterwards expressed it, was "somebody,"—asked her to take a cup of warm tea, to counteract the cold, should her wet clothes have exposed her to it; and Agatha, her wonted pride yielding to her sense of fatigue and hunger, gave a ready assent; and in a moment more she was seated at the humble board of Mr. and Mrs. Orwell.

"Well; I am degraded for the last time!" said Agatha to herself; and she immediately began to ask her way to Westminster-bridge.

"To Westminster-bridge!" said Mr. Orwell, looking at her steadfastly; "It is past eight o'clock, and it will soon be dark; what can a young lady like you, burthened too with an infant, do at such a place at this late hour?"

"I am going to meet a friend there," said Agatha, sighing deeply.

"Indeed!" said Mrs. Orwell. "Well, Mr. Orwell, I'm sure, will see you safe so far, if you will allow him."

"No, madam," replied Agatha, haughtily, "I shall go *alone.*"

Mrs. Orwell was awed, and begged her pardon submissively, but Mr. Orwell coolly replied, "You shall go alone, or with me, as you please, madam, but not till you have had a hearty meal here, so pray condescend to sit down again;" while, presenting Agatha with some bread and butter, he opened a cupboard and offered her some cold meat, to tempt and gratify the ravenous appetite with which she devoured whatever was set before her.

"You are very kind," said Agatha, "and this is so welcome to me! I had not tasted food for hours—no, not for days."

"No! Then to be sure you are not a *nurse?*" observed Mrs. Orwell.

"I *was* a nurse," said Agatha; "but all is dry here now," putting her hand on her bosom.

Mr. Orwell left the room.

"No wonder;—if you starve yourself, you must starve your child."

Agatha started. "True—most true," she replied, "but if——" ("If I have no money to buy food," she meant to say.)

"If you were to eat and drink, the poor little thing might still live and do well," resumed Mrs. Orwell, who in her zeal in the cause of maternity, forgot her fear of Agatha; "and I wonder you can answer it to your conscience, not to do all you can for it. In the meantime, let us see what *I* can do."

Immediately, and while Agatha, now alive only to the idea of relieving her famished infant, sat gazing in wild but still expectation, Mrs. Orwell ordered some milk to be warmed, and in a very few minutes by artificial means, known to her who had been herself a mother, the exhausted infant sucked nourishment eagerly and copiously while she lay on Mrs. Orwell's lap;—and Agatha, encouraged by Mrs. Orwell to expect with certainty the restoration of her babe, uttered a wild hysteric scream of joy, and sank back, laughing and almost convulsed, into the arms of Mr. Orwell, who at that moment returned.

"My dear," said Mr. Orwell, while his wife was administering remedies to her interesting charge, "I trust we have not saved the child only!" And as he gazed on Agatha, tears in quick succession rolled down his cheek. "My dear," resumed he, "I see a likeness; don't you?"

"Yes," replied Mrs. Orwell, with a deep sigh; "especially now that her eyes are closed, and she looks so like death. Our poor child, when dying——" Here emotion broke off her speech.

"I wish she was not a lady," said the old man; "else for the child and grandchild we have just lost, it should seem that Providence had thus sent us this distracted stranger and her poor babe."

At length Agatha completely recovered her senses and her powers, and found her head resting on the compassionate bosom of Mr. Orwell, who if she had been a neighbour's child, would have pressed the poor forlorn one to his heart, and bidden her be comforted. But Mr. Orwell's feelings towards Agatha, were checked by the cold and haughty dignity of her mien, which not even affliction could subdue; and before she could herself proudly withdraw from his supporting arm, he had resigned her to the care of his wife.

Strange, mixed, and almost insupportable sensations returned with her senses to the heart of Agatha; and pride yet unsubdued,—for I believe the proud are rendered prouder still by adversity,—urged her to leave these kind but lowly strangers, who had stopped her on her way to the peace and independence of death.—"But *must* she die? Could she not live and her poor infant too?" And the moment she had once borne to ask herself the question, the reign of despair was beginning to cease, and that of hope to return.

"It still rains," said Mr. Orwell, "and is now nearly dark; your friend, madam, at Westminster-bridge cannot expect you now! Allow me to see you to your own house."

Agatha started, shuddered, and hid her face in her hands.

"Madam, I wait your commands," said Mr. Orwell, taking his hat down from the peg; "Shall I call a coach, and see you home?"

"I have no home!" exclaimed Agatha wildly. "Nor, when I leave this hospitable shelter, know I where to seek another, except—"

Here she remained choked by violent emotions; while Mr. Orwell, replacing his hat, eagerly locked the street door of his shop, ordered the shutters to be closed, and drawing a chair seated himself by the side of Agatha.

"My dear young lady," said he, "excuse my freedom; but my home is yours for this night at least; and were you not so much our superior, it should be yours as long as we lived, as I am sure guilt has had no share in your evident distress."

"Bless you! bless you for that!" said Agatha. "*You, you* do me justice; you a stranger, while *she*—"

"Allow me," said Mr. Orwell, "to tell you something of the man who thus presumes. Perhaps it is merely the suggestions of my own conceit; but I cannot help thinking you must have considered my language as superior to my situation in life."

Agatha only bowed; for she had not thought on the subject; and Mr. Orwell continued thus:—

"I have known better days, and having been heir to great wealth, received a suitable education. But unfortunate speculations ruined my father, and I was glad at last to settle in this little shop, where in the bosom of my family I became obscurely indeed but thoroughly happy; and I blessed the present goodness, without ever repining at the past severe dispensations of Providence. I had not, however, yet suffered my appointed share of affliction. I had an only *daughter;*—she married, had a child, and came to die in *our arms;*—she *did* do so; but still we were resigned; despair was never in our hearts nor its expressions on our lips; but we suffered, suffered deeply, and we still suffer——"

Here he hid his face, and wept; and Agatha, though at first felt inclined to resent being thus *preached* to, conscious of the obligations she owed him, sat and listened with evident attention and sympathy.

Mrs. Orwell, meanwhile, was still nursing the sleeping babe of Agatha, and weeping as she did so; while her husband went on.

"My dear young lady, you resemble our poor child, and——"

"Ay, you do indeed," cried Mrs. Orwell with a violent burst of sorrow; "and when you lay just now looking so like death, I could not help kissing your pale lips, and fancying you my poor Mary. Oh! that you were not, as I see you are, a lady, though now so sad and friendless; for then I could throw myself on your neck, and call you my lost daughter, my dear—dear Mary!"

Agatha's heart could not stand this appeal to its best feelings; every emotion of pride was annihilated; and bursting into a flood of tears, the first she had shed for many days, she threw herself on the neck of Mrs. Orwell, and exclaimed, "Do call me your child, your Mary, if it will relieve your poor heart!" And when composure was a little restored, Agatha, whose oppressed head and bosom had been greatly relieved by crying, blessed her in the most affectionate manner for having saved her child and her also from destruction.

"Well, but you will stay here till you can do something better?" said Mrs. Orwell.

"You shall have a room to yourself," said her husband; "and you shall pay me what you will, either little or much."

"I have not a shilling in the world!" cried Agatha.

"I am glad of it," replied Mrs. Orwell; "for then you may be pleased to stay with us."

"I fear not," observed Mr. Orwell; while Agatha gratefully and gracefully pressed his wife's hand to her quivering lip. But a sudden thought struck across her brain;—she jumped up, she ran into the shop, examined the contents of the shop windows; and returning with a countenance radiant with renewed hope and joy, she fell on her knees, and audibly returned thanks to God for having allowed her to be snatched from irremediable perdition.

Her new friends listened and beheld her with considerable alarm, and feared her frenzy had only taken a new turn. But they were relieved when Agatha, as soon as tears—tears of joy—would allow her to speak, told them she had discovered that they sold prints, patterns, water-coloured drawings, and paintings of flowers.

"To be sure we do," said Mrs. Orwell; "but what then, my dear young lady?"

"Why then you can employ *me*, and I shall be able to maintain myself and child by the exertion of those talents which to the rich heiress were only the source of most pernicious vanity."

"And you are a good artist then, are you?" said Mr. Orwell doubtingly; for he knew something of art, and of what lady artists too often are.

"You shall *see* what I can do," said Agatha; and she took from her pocket a miniature of her mother.

"Excellent!" said Orwell. "A copy, I presume?"

"No! an *original*; but that is not all; give me a pencil and paper, and let me sketch that dear group."

He gave them to her; and in a few minutes she designed with great skill and accuracy, Mrs. Orwell and her child upon her lap.

"Admirable!" said the delighted and convinced old man. "It is not so handsome as my old woman, to be sure; but it is a very pretty sketch. Why, madam, you may make my fortune and your own too. And what else can you do?"

"I can paint much better than those unnatural, stiff, ill-coloured groups of flowers for patterns are painted. In short, I am somewhat skilled in every branch of your trade, and you will save me from distraction and death by promising to employ me to the very utmost."

Words cannot express the joy of the benevolent and affectionate old couple, as Agatha spoke thus.

"Then you will *stay* with us now?" said Mrs. Orwell.

"Yes," said Mr. Orwell, "now you can do so without incurring pecuniary obligation; —for I see, young lady, that you have your full share of the pride of a gentlewoman, and have not yet been afflicted *long* enough to be humble. However, *who* you are, and *what* you are, you will tell us when *you choose*."

"All I *can* tell you, I will tell you *now*," returned Agatha. "I am a *deserted wife*, and a discarded daughter; but I am *innocent*; and now that I have a prospect of being able to earn a livelihood, I may one day live to triumph over my enemies. Perhaps some time or other I may tell you more;—but now I wish to suspend the operation of painful images on my mind. O ye kind, generous, Christian beings, who, though I was a stranger, took me in, and cherished me!—may you in your last moments be soothed by the reflection that you were the means of saving from destruction, from *self*-destruction, a wretched, injured, but *virtuous* fellow-creature!"

"Hush! hush! don't speak so loud," said Mrs. Orwell, smiling through her tears; "you'll wake the dear babe. Well, I'll put it to bed, for the bed is ready for you, my dear —*madam*, I mean." And Agatha, affectionately pressing Mrs. Orwell's hand, followed her to her apartment. It was a clean and quiet though not a spacious chamber, and Agatha, with a relieved and grateful heart, retired to the prospect of rest which it afforded her; and having again fed her evidently recovering infant, she soon sank into repose by its side.

In the morning, Agatha, wondering, humbled, sad, yet no longer despairing, awoke to mingled and overpowering sensations; amidst which, gratitude to her Maker for preservation from a sinful death, was the predominant feeling;—and happy would it have been for her, had not the sentiment of grateful adoration to God been nearly paralleled by one of vindictive resentment towards a fellow-creature, and that fellow-creature the mother who had given her being. But TEMPER, the bane of Agatha's existence, and the ruler of her conduct, towered in all its strength by the side of her religious emotions, and rendered vain the resources against the evils of her situation, to which a person uninfluenced by temper would gladly have had recourse. True it was that her husband had denied her to be his wife, and destroyed, as she could not doubt, one evidence of his marriage with her;—but did it follow that there was no other remaining, which legal means might not enable her to procure? True it was, that her mother had renounced her, and declared her belief that she was only the mistress of Danvers. But she had powerful though not near relations in London; and it was most likely that the tale she had to tell them, though they might at first disbelieve it, would at last find its way to their hearts, and through them, to her mother's, by the irresistible and omnipotent power of truth.

But Agatha derived a sad and sullen joy, a malignant consciousness of future revenge, from the idea that one time or other, when no one could know and no one disclose the fate of her lost daughter, the mother who had dared to suspect the virtue of that daughter, and to discard her in consequence of that suspicion, would regret her lost child, would wish she had been less hasty to condemn her, and feel in all its bitterness, the agony of a fault, for which it was no longer in her power to make any reparation. It was perhaps an angry feeling like this, that, adding force to the other source of misery, prompted her to the resolution of committing violence on her and her infant's life;—for there is little doubt that suicides have been often, very often, occasioned merely by the vindictive wish of planting an everlasting thorn in the breast of the parent, the lover, the mistress, the wife, or the husband, whose conduct has in the opinion of the weak sufferer, the slave of an ill-governed temper, excited the terrible cravings of a vicious resentment.—Sure is it, that Temper,—like the unseen, but busy subterranean fires in the bosom of a volcano, is always at work where it has once gained an existence, and is for ever threatening to explode, and scatter ruin and desolation around it. Parents, beware how you omit to check the first evidences of its empire in your children; and *tremble* lest the powerless hand which is only lifted in childish anger against you, should, if its impotent fury remains uncorrected, in future life be armed with more destructive fury against its own existence, or that of a fellow-creature!

"No," said Agatha to herself, "I will conceal my name and my wrongs in oblivion the most complete. Not even the good and generous beings to whom I owe my life and its continuance, shall be informed of them; but sustained by the proud consciousness of my own desert, I will be all-sufficient to myself and to my child; and the injured heiress of thousands shall derive more honourable pride from the exertions of her talents in honest industry, than she ever felt as the idol of an interested crowd."

And, unfortunately, the persevering obstinacy of Agatha, led her to adhere rigidly to the determination which Temper led her to form. Had she not done so,—had she opened her heart, and told the tale of her injuries to the benevolent Mr. Orwell,—it is possible that his representations might have induced such a line of conduct as would have been the means of restoring her to her mother, and might have enabled her to establish her marriage beyond dispute; for Mr. Orwell would have advised her to have immediate recourse to legal advice, and would gladly have afforded her the means of doing so.

But her resolution was taken, and she never allowed herself to suppose that from her resolves there could ever be any appeal.

At an early hour Agatha, who with the feeling of a real gentlewoman wished to conform to the hours of her hosts, took her seat at the breakfast-table, and with a quivering lip beheld her child received into the arms of Mrs. Orwell, while her husband took his seat and occupation at the board. Still, spite of the even parental kindness of these excellent people, Agatha felt that she was not in her place; and notwithstanding her efforts to be affable, she was at last only graciously condescending.

"You are not so like our poor Mary today," said Mrs. Orwell, attentively regarding her.

"No," said Mr. Orwell; "our Mary was not a lady, and therefore, had not the look or air of one; nor had she this lady's beauty."

"Our Mary was very pretty, my dear," interrupted Mrs. Orwell, "and looked so good and sweet-tempered!"

"She was certainly quite perfect in her parents' eyes," replied Mr. Orwell, the big drops swelling in his eyes;—"but she is gone—and it is a comfort we cannot be too grateful for, that we were allowed to administer to her wants during her last illness:—

' On some fond breast the parting soul relies,' " added he, willing perhaps to show off his little reading to Agatha. But he was interrupted by her starting from her chair, and pacing with distempered haste the narrow floor of the room.

"Excellent people!" said she at length, taking a hand of each, and pressing them affectionately;—"you feel as parents should feel;—and would I had been in reality your Mary! for then I should have breathed my last on a bosom which loved me.—But now——!"

Here her voice failed her, and she burst into tears. And as she viewed her softened eye, her languid air, poor Mrs. Orwell again recognised her lost Mary.

"But come," said Agatha with a more cheerful countenance, as soon as breakfast was over; "let us to business—I long to be earning money; procure me some flowers, and I will paint a group immediately." And in a very short time Mr. Orwell had procured the best flowers Covent-garden afforded; while Agatha was diligently employed in copying them.

As soon as the group was finished, it was exhibited by the delighted Mr. Orwell in the shop-window; and to his and Agatha's satisfaction, it was sold as soon as it was seen. It was bought by a gentleman of some rank and distinction in society, and he bespoke eleven more by the same artist, as he wanted them to decorate some particular room in a villa which he had lately purchased; promising, at the same time, to recommend Mr. Orwell's shop to all his friends.

"It was a kind Providence for me as well as you, madam," said Mr. Orwell, "that brought you to my house."

"I trust it will turn out so," said the gratified Agatha, who worked with such assiduity, that in a very short time the twelve paintings were completed, and declared admirable by the satisfied purchaser.

By this time Mrs. Orwell, who was become used to Agatha's "grand manner," as she called it, and who naturally enough was attached to her by a sense of the benefit she had conferred, was very desirous to learn whether she meant to continue with them, especially as she had contrived, by removing their own bed to the top of the house, to make a sitting-room for Agatha. But the latter, though her heart glowed with gratitude towards these excellent people as her preservers, could not prevail on herself to remain an inmate of their house, nor indeed of any other in London. She felt, in this respect wisely felt, that though Mr. Orwell had been a gentleman, and had had the education of one, (however his manners might have lost some of their habitual polish by collision with vulgar society,) Mrs. Orwell was only a tradesman's wife; and she knew that not only her pride but her taste would be offended by constant association with one so much her inferior; and whose affectionate familiarity she might, however reluctantly, be at times forced to repel. For it is not pride alone, but a sense of fitness, that makes persons prefer living with their equals to association with their inferiors.

It is the want of equal education that makes the great difference between man and man; and the bar that divides the vulgar man from the gentleman is not a paltry sense of superior birth, but a feeling of difference, a consciousness of different habits, ways of thinking, and manners—the result of opposite situations.

"No, no—I cannot, must not stay here," said Agatha to herself;—"besides, I long for the country, and some wild sequestered place where my infant may derive health and strength from the mountain breeze, and I may escape all chance of being known."

But in order to reach "this mountain breeze," it would be necessary for Agatha to undertake a long and expensive journey, and live at a most inconvenient and expensive distance from the metropolis. Her drawings and paintings for sale would in that case be some days on the road, and the carriage to London, consequently, considerably diminish the profits of her employers. She was therefore at last prevailed upon by Mr. Orwell to reside in a village in Sussex, sufficiently lonely, bleak, and desolate, to satisfy the gloomy and unsocial taste of Agatha; sufficiently near the sea to make it a healthy residence in her opinion for her child, and near enough to the metropolis for purposes of business; while Mr. Orwell pleased himself with the idea that he could occasionally step into a stage-coach, and in twelve hours' time be set down within a walk of the habitation of Agatha. Besides, his benevolence was gratified by being enabled from Agatha's choice of the abode he had recommended to be of pecuniary service, without her knowledge that he was so. He had hired rooms for her in the house of a dependent relation of his, and binding the woman to secresy, he had desired her to ask of Agatha only such a sum for the apartments, paying her himself the real rent which she had a right to demand.

Agatha, when she arrived at her new abode, resolved in solitude the most rigorous, to devote her days to unremitting industry, in order to maintain herself and child; endeavouring at the same time to impart to her little Emma those accomplishments and refinements which she had herself been taught, in order that she might be able to acquit herself with propriety and elegance, when (as Agatha had no doubt she would be,) she should be called upon to emerge from obscurity, and move in that sphere of life in which her birth had originally designed her to move. For Agatha was sure, she scarcely knew why perhaps, that her mother would not always remain inexorable; and though resolved never to hold communion herself with her tardily relenting parent, she looked forward with angry pleasure to the time when she would become an object of unavailing regret to her mother, and her daughter an object of pride and of t nderness. In the meanwhile, her natural activity, both of body and of mind, being rendered still more vigorous by an almost frenzied sense of injury and unkindness, she exerted her varied talents to the utmost, and had the satisfaction of knowing that she thereby increased, to a considerable degree, the profits of her affectionate benefactors; though they could not often prevail on themselves to sell a drawing, however good, that seemed taken from Agatha or her child; for "if we did not give, we at least saved their lives," said Mr. Orwell; "and every memorial of their persons is precious to us from that recollection."

But to return to Mrs. Torrington,—who, deceived by the arts of Danvers into a belief of her daughter's infamy, gave way to all the indignation which a proud and virtuous woman would feel on such a conviction; and while she returned to brood in solitude over her shame and her distress, to her sequestered seat in Cumberland, she was surprised there by a visit from her cousin, the honourable Mr. Castlemain, one of her earliest friends and admirers, but whose suit she had rejected in favour of Mr. Torrington.

Mr. Castlemain, faithful to his first attachment, had never married; and hearing of the distress in which Agatha's conduct had involved her mother, he hastened from the continent, where he had long resided, in order to express to her in person his sympathy in her sorrow, with a hope perhaps as yet scarcely defined to himself, that in her forlorn and childless state Mrs. Torrington might be induced to listen to his addresses, and secure to herself an attached and affectionate companion. Nor was he deceived in his expectations. Mrs. Torrington, grateful for his long and faithful affection, and eager to lose in new ties the remembrance of those which appeared dissolved for ever, consented to become his wife; and the birth of another daughter had in a degree reconciled her to the loss of Agatha, when, four years after her marriage with Mr. Castlemain, death deprived her not only of a husband whom she sincerely esteemed, but of the child to whom she looked for a renewal of all that happiness which Agatha's conduct had deprived her of. At first she almost sank under the blow; but as she recovered her powers of reflection, the idea that Agatha, though disgraced and distant, was yet alive, presented itself, and spoke peace to her wounded mind. "After all, she is my child!" said Mrs. Castlemain to herself, "and it was cruel to discard her for a first and only fault; for who knows what base arts were used to mislead her!" And from the moment she had allowed herself to think and feel thus, she became constantly solicitous to discover the residence of Agatha. But her solicitude was heightened almost to frenzy by the following circumstance.

There is probably no heart so callous, no human being so thoroughly depraved, as not to feel at some moment the agonizing pang of remorse and compassion towards the victim of its successful villany.— When Danvers recollected that he had put it out of the power of Agatha to obtain a copy of the certificate of her marriage at the church where the ceremony took place, and that owing to accident no copy of it had been previously transmitted according to the usual forms to any other register, he knew that he was perfectly secure from any legal prosecution in order to establish the fact of the marriage having taken place, and that his subsequent conduct, in order to make Mrs. Torrington discard her daughter entirely, had been a piece of villany as needless as it was detestable. Concluding also from Agatha's temper and disposition that her mother's rejection of her on the plea that she was only a mistress, though she endeavoured to make herself be received as a wife, would in all probability drive his unhappy victim to the frenzy of desperation, and involve his child also in all the misery incident to a deserted orphan,—he in a moment of remorse and self-condemnation wrote to Mrs. Torrington before he sailed for the West Indies, to assure her that he had really led Agatha to the altar, and that, as she never even suspected he had a wife living, she was consequently in intention as pure and virtuous as when she left her mother's house; adding, that as soon as she found she was not his lawful wife, she had fled from him for ever, carrying her child along with her; and he ended by conjuring Mrs. Torrington to give her innocent and injured daughter an asylum under her roof.

Though no representations from a man of such confessed profligacy as Danvers was, were worthy of credit, still Mrs. Castlemain did not for a moment hesitate to believe even his testimony to the innocence of Agatha, a belief at the same time precious though agonizing to her heart; and wild with remorse, regret, and anxiety, she left no means untried to find out the retreat of the sufferer, and induce her to return to the arms of her repentant mother. Danvers, meanwhile, satisfied that if Agatha lived she would be restored to the favour of her mother, or that his child at least would receive from her the protection of a parent, left England with a mind lightened of a considerable load, and felt himself less painfully haunted than he had lately been by the image of his victim. Of Mrs. Torrington's second marriage he had never heard, nor of her change of abode. The letter, however, as I have stated above, reached her in safety, and occasioned her repeated and long unavailing endeavours to discover the retreat of her daughter.

But no traces could be found of this long-lost daughter; and at last, despairing of any other means, Mrs. Castlemain caused a paragraph or advertisement, addressed to "Agatha," to be inserted in every paper, desiring that an answer should be directed to her lawyer in London. But as Agatha never saw a newspaper, this advertisement would have appeared in vain, had not Mr. Orwell seen it, who suspecting that the Agatha so addressed was the interesting object of his benevolence, sent the newspaper immediately down to her.

Agatha, in the mean time, had been endeavouring to make herself amends for the loss of other ties, by inspiring her child with an exclusive attachment to herself. "She is all to me, and I will be all to her!" was her constant exclamation; and when she fancied "Agatha," as she *now* called her, (since "Emma," the name of her mother, after whom she had christened her, was become odious to her,) was old enough to understand her, she used to delight in telling her the story of her cruel treatment; and she took a sad and savage pleasure in hearing her express hatred of her grandmother and her father, because they had been so cruel to her dear mamma;—while the lesson of deep resentment for a mother's wrongs was daily inculcated. But, though Agatha hated, or rather despised her husband, she was far from feeling sentiments of this nature in reality towards her mother; for her conscience told her she had violated her duty in marrying contrary to the laws of decorum and the express will of a parent; and though she could not remember without indignation that her mother had presumed to question the purity of her conduct, she felt that it was but justice to make allowance for those violent and resentful feelings, which after all were the result of her own disobedience.

Such was her frame of mind when she received a parcel from Mr. Orwell; and the address to " Agatha,"—an address so worded that she could not but immediately feel that she was the person addressed,—met her eager eye, and convulsed her whole frame with emotion.

"So then," cried she, "I am at last forgiven, regretted, and solicited to return to the home so long denied me:—Be it so; and when I am on my death-bed I too will forgive, and be contented to be forgiven—but not before."

Still, in spite of this angry resolution, she read the welcome address of parental affection over and over again; and several times she caught herself calling her daughter by the long prohibited name of Emma, the name of her mother; and as she did so the last time, she burst into tears, and folded the astonished child to her bosom with emotions of a various and contending nature. But the name so recalled to her memory and her tongue, was not again banished thence.

"I am Agatha, not Emma, mamma," said the little girl.

"You are both, my dear," replied her mother, making an effort to restrain her tears; "and henceforth I shall call you Emma."

Another and another week elapsed; the advertisement was repeated again and again, and the paper sent down to her every day; while the resolution of Agatha, never to let her mother hear of or from her but on her death-bed, grew weaker and weaker; and she began bitterly to repent of the pains which she had taken to make her child imbibe an aversion to her grandmother.

"Let me endeavour," said she to herself, "to eradicate this aversion while it is yet time." But she found the task a much more difficult one than she at first imagined.

Other persons had helped to deepen the feeling of dislike which she had originally inculcated. The surgeon of the village had several children, with whom Emma was occasionally permitted to associate, and sorry am I to add that they were frequently sufferers from the violence of her uncorrected temper. The consequence was, that her little playfellows, finding her grandmother was an object of terror and aversion to Emma, used to frighten her into submission by threatening to send her to her grandmamma. And Agatha found too late, that she had inspired her child with a sentiment of hatred unworthy of a Christian to feel or to inculcate.

Shuddering at this conviction, and at her own guilt in having cherished so vile a feeling in the heart of her child,—"How criminal I have been!" she exclaimed in the anguish of her soul; "but let me now make all the expiation I can."

"My dear child," cried Agatha, "you are to forgive your enemies, and to love everybody."

"Yes," replied Emma, "forgive and love everybody;—No, no,—forgive and love everybody but grandmamma."

Agatha was confounded at the tenaciousness of Emma's memory and feelings, and eagerly answered;—"No;—you must forgive and love grandmamma too; for she is a very good woman."

"No, no,—she is not a good woman; she is cruel to you, and uses you ill, and beats you!"

"Indeed she is good, and you must love her, Emma," replied the distressed Agatha; "for she will love you and me very dearly, and perhaps we shall live with grandmamma very soon."

Words would fail to express Agatha's consternation at the violent expression of rage and aversion which this information excited in her child; for she was not in the least aware that her mother had long been a bugbear to Emma, through the means of her play-fellows.—And with painful surprise she heard the child, stamping with terror and passion, declare that she never, never would go nigh so wicked, so very wicked a woman.

"I deserve this," said Agatha mournfully;—"I violated my duty both as a child and mother, when I tried to pollute that innocent heart with the angry and disturbed passions of mine." Then melting into tears of tenderness, she sighed over the injury which she had done Mrs. Castlemain, by steeling her child's heart against her; and the feelings of returning affection towards her were deepened by the consciousness.

The next week the advertisement was again repeated; and Agatha's heart was completely overcome. "Mother! dear mother!" she exclaimed, "you shall not long sigh for me in vain."

It so happened, that on the Sunday following the parable of the prodigal son was read at church. Agatha listened to it with emotions the most overwhelming; and when the preacher came to those words, "I will arise and go to my father,"—her feelings became uncontrollable; and throwing herself on her knees, she hid her face on the seat, and nearly sobbed aloud.

Her emotion had not escaped the observant eye of the amiable being who was officiating; and when the service was over, he followed her, resolved that he would no longer permit her to reject, as she had hitherto done, his advances to acquaintance, since he was now convinced that something weighed heavily on her mind; and he believed that conversation with him in his professional capacity, if not as a friend, might be the means of lightening her sorrows. But he soon found that Agatha was no longer averse to form the acquaintance which he sought. Her mind was wounded by the reproaches of conscience; and knowing the character of this truly pious man, she hoped that if she unbosomed herself to him, he might speak peace to her self-upbraiding spirit.

Accordingly she requested an interview with him, which he readily granted. She then detailed to him the eventful history of her short life, and of the feelings of regret, remorse, and repentant affection excited in her by her mother's advertisement.

"Let me advise you," cried Mr. Egerton, sighing as he spoke, "to lose no time in writing to your mother! Let her feel no longer the agony of 'hope deferred!'" And as he said this, overcome by some painful recollection, he brushed a tear from his eye. Agatha promised that she would write the next morning;—and cheerfully acceding to her request, that he would give her the benefit of his society as often as he could, he took his departure, leaving Agatha full of regret that she had allowed the feelings of disappointment and proud resentment to shut up her heart so long against the comforts of society and the consolations of religion.

But, alas! Agatha had neglected to profit by the past, and the present, and for her there was no future in store.

Whether the agitation which she had experienced in church was the cause of illness, or whether it was only the effect of an illness then impending, it is impossible to determine; but that night she was seized with all the symptoms of a low and dangerous fever, and was soon pronounced to be past any hopes of recovery.

In one of the intervals of delirium she sent for Mr. Egerton; and after having gone through with him the duties of religion, she earnestly entreated him to take her child under his care, till her mother, to whom she was about to write, should make known her will concerning her.

"I will do more," replied Mr. Egerton;—"I will myself deliver your daughter and your letter into your mother's hands."

"What! undertake so long a journey yourself?"

"Can I be better employed?—Remember that your mother will need consolation;—and who so likely to give it to her as the man who attended you in your last moments? for believe me," continued he, "I shall not leave you till all is over."

"May God reward you!" cried Agatha, grasping his hand fervently—"O that I had known you sooner!"—Then, making a violent effort, she scrawled, with a trembling hand, the following lines:

"I presumed to indulge the bitterness of resentment, and towards a mother too; and I am punished for it! for just as I was going to throw myself into your arms, and accept your protection for me and my poor child, I was seized with a mortal malady; and when you receive this, I shall be no more.—Take then my last blessing and farewell! Would I could have seen you before I died!—but I have a child,—named Emma, after you; love her;—she will be presented to you by the pious and generous being whose kindness has soothed to me the agonies of my last moments. If you and he think it right, let my claims and my Emma's, on my deluded husband, be prosecuted legally; and let him be told, if you bring forward my claims, that with my last breath, I forgave and prayed for him!

"A thousand sad and fond thoughts, my dearest mother, struggle for utterance, as I write; but —— I can no more —— I —— farewell —— I ——"

Here she fell back exhausted on her pillow; and in a few hours she expired.

Emma, in the meanwhile, had been kept as much as possible at the house of the surgeon, where she had been in the habit of visiting; but the affectionate child could with difficulty be restrained from going home, though forbidden to go thither; for Agatha, as soon as she found that her disorder was infectious, had courageously determined not to see her child again.

When Agatha had breathed her last, Mr. Egerton went in search of the poor, unconscious orphan, who eagerly ran up to him, and begged him to take her to her mamma.

"My dear child," replied Mr. Egerton, tears starting in his eyes, "your mamma has desired that I should take you home with me."

The child for a moment sullenly refused to go; but when he gravely added, "and can you have the cruelty to disobey your poor sick mamma?" Emma burst into tears, and suffered him to lead her to his house.

But it was some time before he had resolution to tell the quick-feeling child that she could see her mother no more! nor, when he did so, had he fortitude enough to retain any thing like self-command, when he witnessed her frantic agony at hearing it. Of death, indeed, she could have but a vague idea; but not seeing her mother, was a positive and intelligible evil; and hour succeeded to hour, and still the little sufferer was not consoled. But the next day the violence of her feelings had abated; and though she occasionally gave way to dreadful bursts of sorrow, the pains which Mr. Egerton's house-keeper took to amuse her were not thrown away upon her.

On the fourth day after Agatha died, the funeral took place; but Mr. Egerton did not allow Emma to attend it. He knew how little used to restraint she had been; and he dreaded, from a degree of curiosity and proneness to inquiry above her years, questions and conduct ill-assorted to the solemnity of the scene.

But he desired that Emma might be put into deep mourning. And on his return from the performance of the last melancholy duties to Agatha, with a heart full of sadness, and a cheek pale with emotion, he started and shuddered at witnessing the childish joy with which Emma ran forward to meet him, and showed him her new clothes and her fine black sash.

"Poor child!" said Mr. Egerton, shedding tears as he clasped her to his generous bosom, "one day thou wilt know how dearly they are purchased!"

A few days after, Mr. Egerton, having learnt from Mrs. Castlemain's agent in London her change of name and her present abode, set off with Emma for the house of her grandmother. But he was careful not to let her know whither they were going, as he was aware of the child's aversion to Mrs. Castlemain, and knew that it would be better to conquer it by degrees, than attempt to overcome it by violence. Mrs. Castlemain still lived in Cumberland, and her house was situated about three miles from Keswick; it was therefore some days before Mr. Egerton reached his journey's end, and beheld at the foot of a mountain the beautiful mansion of Mrs. Castlemain. But the journey had not appeared long to him. Emma, though not much more than six years old, had found the way to his heart, and had unlocked his long dormant affections. By turns he had been charmed by the quickness of her perceptions and had been terrified by the quickness of her sensibilities. He soon saw that she required a strict and unusually watchful eye to be kept over her; and long before they were arrived at their journey's end, he had convinced himself that Emma could have no guardian so watchful over her as he should be.

"Poor thing! how useful I could be to her!" he had said to himself;—and having once admitted the truth of that proposition, it was impossible for a man so conscientious as Mr. Egerton not to resolve to act accordingly; and his heart had fondly and for ever adopted the orphan Emma, when the postilion informed him that the house he saw before him was the house of Mrs. Castlemain, and by that means recalled to his recollection that he was going to present Emma to one who had real and natural claims on her, which might entirely annihilate those which he had resolved to put in force. "But if her grandmother should not be willing to receive her!" thought Mr. Egerton; and he was shocked to find how much he wished that Mrs. Castlemain might give them a cold reception.

While these ideas were passing in his mind, and while Emma, sitting on his lap, was leaning against his bosom, and playfully parting the unpowdered locks that hung over his forehead, among which sorrow, not time, had scattered the grey hairs of age, the chaise stopped at the door of the White Cottage, as it was called, and a lady, whose dress and manner bespoke her the mistress of the house, while her appearance proclaimed her worn with sorrow and anxiety, came to the green gate at which they stopped, and in a faint and languid tone demanded their business.

"Do I see Mrs. Castlemain?" said Mr. Egerton.

"Yes, sir," replied the lady; and struck with compassion at sight of her evident and habitual state of depression, he forgot the wish which he had just expressed, of keeping Emma to himself; and thought of nothing but the probable comfort which she would prove to her forlorn and miserable relation.

"I have some business with you, madam," answered Mr. Egerton; "and with your leave I will alight."

In a few moments Mr. Egerton, leading Emma by the hand, whose features were shaded from the view by her ringlets and the bonnet which she wore, followed the anxious and uneasy Mrs. Castlemain into the house, and prepared himself to give her the information which she was too anxious to demand.

But Mr. Egerton felt himself unable to speak before the child; he therefore requested that she might be allowed to play in the garden before the house; and Emma having eagerly accepted the permission given her, he found himself at last alone with the mother of Agatha.

"Is that your little girl, sir?" said Mrs. Castlemain, while with an anxious and inquiring look she gazed on Emma from the window, and saw her bound along the lawn with all the untamed vivacity of childhood.

"O, no!" answered Mr. Egerton, "she is not my child;—would to heaven she were; She——" Here he paused, for he had not yet courage to enter on the mournful task that awaited him.

"You were going to say something, sir," said Mrs. Castlemain, seating herself by him, and speaking in a faltering voice, as if her heart foreboded something unusual. "That sweet child, sir, by her dress seems to have lately sustained a great loss?"

"Yes, madam, the greatest of all losses," replied Mr. Egerton, making a great effort; "poor Emma has just lost——her mother!"

"Emma! did you say?" cried Mrs. Castlemain, catching hold of his arm, and gazing wildly in his face. "Who was her mother, sir?"

"You——you had a daughter, madam," replied Mr. Egerton.

"I *had* a daughter!" exclaimed Mrs. Castlemain, and fell back insensible in her chair.

Mr. Egerton immediately rang for assistance; and while the servants ran backwards and forwards with restoratives, Emma, who saw them pass to and fro, imagined that refreshments for them were preparing, and instantly returning to the house she re-entered the parlour just as Mrs. Castlemain had recovered her senses, and had learnt from Mr. Egerton that Agatha on her death-bed had bequeathed her orphan child to her care. Mr. Egerton was going to add, that Emma had conceived so great a terror and hatred of her grandmother, that it was advisable Mrs. Castlemain should not for the present be known to her as anything more than a friend of her mother's,—when he was prevented by her unexpected entrance.

As soon as Mrs. Castlemain saw her, a thousand fond and uncontrollable emotions urged her towards the unconscious orphan; while tears of tenderness trickling down her wan cheek, she stretched forth her arms to the astonished and affrighted child, and dropping on her knees entreated her to come to the arms of her grandmother.

At that name Emma, starting from Mrs. Castlemain's grasp as if from the touch of a serpent, uttered a loud and piercing shriek, and darting through the open doors flew over the lawn; while Mrs. Castlemain, shocked and surprised, sank almost fainting on the floor, and demanded of Mr. Egerton an explanation of this strange conduct.

"By some unfortunate means or other," replied he, "she has learned to associate with the name of her grandmother ideas of fear and dislike, which her poor mother has vainly endeavoured to remove."

"But then she did endeavour to remove them?" eagerly remarked Mrs. Castlemain.

"She did," said Mr. Egerton.

"Thank God!" returned the unhappy and repentant mother; (and Mr. Egerton immediately gave her Agatha's letter;)—then begging Mr. Egerton to go and find Emma, and endeavour to soothe her, she hastily left the room to read it in the solitude of her own apartment.

Mr. Egerton went immediately in search of Emma. He found her in a paroxysm of rage and terror. At sight of him she stamped with all the violence of passion, and protested that she would go away that moment. Mr. Egerton replied, that he had brought her there by her poor mother's express command; but that, if she would not stay where she was, he must take her away again; still he could not and would not go till he had eaten his dinner; he therefore expected that she should return into the house with him. But the violent child refused to comply; for she said the house belonged to her wicked grandmamma.

"So does the bank on which you are sitting, my dear," replied Mr. Egerton; and Emma started from it immediately. "The place on which you are standing is hers also; every thing you see is hers except the post-chaise," observed Mr. Egerton; "therefore while I dine I know not what can become of you, as you can't bear to remain on your grandmother's premises."

"I will sit in the post-chaise," said Emma, sobbing violently. And Mr. Egerton having ordered the postilion to put the horses into the stable, and to go into the house himself, he assisted Emma into the chaise, and then left her to herself, expecting that solitude and hunger would at length subdue her as yet untamed and pernicious anger and animosity.

It was near an hour before Mr. Egerton was sufficiently composed to venture into the parlour again, and during that time the cloth was laid for dinner, and he saw that Emma from the chaise window could see the preparations which were going on.

Mrs. Castlemain at length came down, and with a countenance so full of woe, that Mr. Egerton could not speak to her, when he beheld her, but was forced to turn to the window to hide his emotion.

"Where is my child, my all now?" said Mrs. Castlemain in a voice almost extinct with sorrow.

"I have left her to herself," replied Mr. Egerton; "for at present she is too headstrong for me to attempt to bring her hither."

"Shall I go to her? shall I humble myself before her?"

"By no means. On the first impression

which you now give her of yourself will depend her future conduct towards you; and if she finds you submissive, depend on it she is discerning enough to act accordingly."

"No matter," cried Mrs. Castlemain, "so that she does but love me."

"But for her sake as well as for yours, my dear madam, it is necessary that she should respect you too. At least allow me to advise you to-day, and we will see what to-morrow will produce."

"You shall direct, and I will obey you," replied Mrs. Castlemain; "for a mind so injured by distress as mine is, scarcely knows what is right; and indeed," added she, "I would have seen no one but you, after the sad intelligence which I have just received; but you have such claims on me! Besides, from you I can learn all the particulars of——" Here her voice failed her. Mr. Egerton was at no loss to fancy the remainder of the sentence.

Soon after, dinner was announced, and Mrs. Castlemain, as she seated herself at the table, asked Mr. Egerton if she must really not invite Emma to join them.

"Certainly not," he replied; "but let us open the windows, that she may see what is going forward."

Mrs. Castlemain, whom sorrow kept fasting, sat opposite the window; and as she could not eat, her whole attention was directed to Emma: she saw her continually looking out of the window of the chaise, as if she wished to be a sharer in what was going forward; and Mrs. Castlemain begged to be allowed to carry her some dinner. But Mr. Egerton requested that she would not be so perniciously indulgent. When dinner was ended, and a dessert of fine fruit brought on the table, Emma proclaimed by her gestures and her angry screams the violence of her rage and disappointment.

"I cannot bear this; I must go to her," said Mrs. Castlemain.

"Forgive me, but it is not yet time."

"But there is a mist rising from the lakes, Mr. Egerton, and she will catch cold."

"I had rather, madam, her health should be temporarily affected, than her temper ruined eternally,—which it must be, if she be allowed to see that by persisting in violence she can gain a point."

At these words, at this sentiment, Mrs. Castlemain sighed deeply, and became silent; for she had heard them before; she had heard them from that beloved husband whose precepts she had disregarded, whose rules for education she had neglected to act upon, and had by that means occasioned the ruin of her daughter!

Terrible are the wounds inflicted by self-reproach; and Mrs. Castlemain felt them severely.

When Mr. Egerton had finished his fruit, he went out to Emma. He found her quiet but sullen; and he took care to let her know, that, but for him, her grandmother Mrs. Castlemain would have brought her out some dinner; but that he told her he knew very well that she would take nothing from her hands. The child hung her conscious head on her bosom at these words, and, bursting into a loud fit of sobbing, replied, "But I am so hungry!"

"Indeed!" answered Mr. Egerton; "I am sorry to hear it; for hungry you must remain, unless you choose to eat some of your grandmother's excellent pudding and fruit."

"I am so hungry!" cried Emma again; and Mr. Egerton immediately letting down the step of the chaise, Emma allowed him to lead her in silence into the house; while with all the grimaces and distortions of sheepishness and sullenness she accepted a chair and plate at the table, and, turning her back on Mrs. Castlemain, eagerly ate the good things which were set before her.

When she had satisfied her hunger, she got up and begged Mr. Egerton to order the chaise, and take her away again.

"Not to night," said Mr. Egerton coolly; "for I have promised to stay and sleep here."

Emma heard him in sullen silence; but it was not long before she gladly consented to be undressed and put into a warm bed; where, with the happy forgetfulness of her age, she soon ceased to remember on whose bed she was, and fell into a deep and peaceful slumber.

"Thank God!" cried Mrs. Castlemain when she heard of it, gratefully pressing Mr. Egerton's hand as she spoke, "the child of my poor Agatha is reposing under my roof."

The rest of the evening was passed in anxious and interesting questions on the part of Mrs. Castlemain, and as interesting answers on the part of Mr. Egerton; who, though prejudiced greatly against Mrs. Castlemain by knowing Agatha, and the faults in her temper, a character which he attributed to a defective education, was so deeply impressed by her evident distress, so affected by the "venerable presence of misery," (as Sterne calls it,) that he retired to rest full of kindness and regard for his unhappy hostess, and resolved to do all that lay in his power to console her afflictions.

The next morning, when Emma awoke (and worn out with the fatigue and angry agitation of the day before she had slept much later than usual,) she found two servants watching by her bed-side, and ready to assist her to dress as soon as she was disposed to rise. It is difficult to say how soon a child loves to be made of importance; and certain it is, that Emma was fully capable of feeling the delight of being waited upon. She was also equally alive to the pleasures of a repast far more luxurious than she had ever seen; and the sight of a breakfast consisting of hot bread, honey, cream, preserved gooseberries, potted char, and fruit, immediately had power to suppress the emotions of terror and aversion which the sight of Mrs. Castlemain again occasioned her.

Mr. Egerton was also careful to let her receive every thing which she desired from the hand of Mrs. Castlemain; and the latter, having received the hint from Mr. Egerton, called the servants into the room; and after introducing Emma to them as her granddaughter and sole heiress, and their future mistress, desired them, as they valued her favour, to show her every possible attention.

Where one association is already powerful, it can be destroyed only by one as powerful, or still more so. The grandmother, hitherto an object of dread to Emma, and a being with whom she associated nothing but ideas of hatred and aversion, was now, because she had ministered to Emma's pleasure and ambition, become associated with agreeable images only in her mind; and with the versatility of childhood, she now no longer shrank from the offered kiss of Mrs. Castlemain, but gazed on her with a propitiatory smile as the dispenser of plenty and happiness.

Mrs. Castlemain beheld with delight the victory she had gained; and eager to insure its duration, she went in search of some old toys which had belonged to her daughter; and not waiting to indulge the painful recollections which the sight of them occasioned her, she soon returned laden with them into the parlour; where Emma, uttering a scream of joy, ran forward to meet her, and with eagerness received in her lap the precious case. The scream, the eager look of joyful impatience, the mottled and extended arms, reminded Mrs. Castlemain so powerfully of her lost daughter, that, with a heart oppressed almost to bursting, she rushed out of the room, and walked on the lawn to recover herself. But then she recollected how foolish she was to allow herself to be so painfully overcome by a resemblance which must endear Emma to her, and she resolved to re-enter the parlour, to contemplate the likeness from which she had before fled.

But the lapse of years, on her return, was entirely forgotten, and the illusion complete. Emma was seated on the carpet, encompassed by her mother's toys, and in the same room which had so often witnessed the childish sports of Agatha! and as she shook back her auburn and clustering ringlets from her face, and smilingly held up one of the playthings to Mrs. Castlemain on her entrance, she rushed forward to embrace Emma, exclaiming as she did so, " My dear, dear child!" Then, suddenly recollecting herself, she left the room, overcome by the mixed and painful feelings which overwhelmed her.

At this moment, as she slowly walked down the lawn before the house, she met Mr. Egerton, to whom she expressed the emotion which Emma occasioned her to experience from her strong likeness to her poor mother.

"The likeness strikes even me," replied Mr. Egerton, " who saw your daughter only when pale and faded by uneasiness of mind.—And I fear," added Mr. Egerton, " that the likeness in one respect extends still further; and that in the quickness of feeling and in the ungovernableness of her temper, she also resembles her mother."

" Perhaps she does," said Mrs. Castlemain; but so as she be but like her, I care not, however dear the complete resemblance may cost me!"

Mr. Egerton forgave the irrationality of this speech, for the sake of the feeling which it contained; but he felt it his duty to convince Mrs. Castlemain, that she was bound in conscience to endeavour to correct and eradicate those defects in Emma's temper and disposition which had had so fatal an effect on her mother's happiness. And he did so in a manner so kind and soothing, at the same time that he expressed his sentiments firmly and unequivocally, that Mrs. Castlemain confessed the impropriety of the sentiment which she had before indulged, and promised that it should be the study of her life to make Emma's temper as mild and tractable as her poor mother's had been otherwise.

" But, indeed," said Mrs. Castlemain, " I fear my own weakness, my own want of resolution. Sorrow and remorse have changed almost into imbecility and incapacity of resistance that proud tyrannical spirit to which I attribute all my woes;—and against the child of my injured Agatha, never, never can I use severe measures, even though they may be deemed necessary."

" I can enter into the feelings which produce that conviction," replied Mr. Egerton, " and have no doubt but that you will sometimes act upon them to Emma's disadvantage; therefore, you will want an assistant in the important office of educating your dear charge."

" I shall;—but where, O! where can I find the person with the proper requisites to undertake that office? If you, sir, would and can undertake it, believe me, my fondest hopes for Emma's welfare would at once be realized."

" To say the truth, madam," answered Mr. Egerton, " I have been wishing to offer you my services."

" Indeed!" cried Mrs. Castlemain eagerly; " then all my fears are at an end. Name your own terms, and I will instantly accede to them. I should think my whole income cheaply spent in securing to my Agatha's child those advantages which I was incapable of affording to her mother."

" Believe me, my dear madam, that the pecuniary reward which I shall ask for my trouble will be very little; my best and dearest reward will be your esteem and respect, and the affection of Emma. I *was* a solitary, insulated, unattached being; but I feel *now* that I have still affections, and that my heart is not entirely buried in the grave; and while I travelled from Sussex hither with your orphan grandchild, I learnt to love her so tenderly, that I thought I should never have the courage to separate from her again."

"I hope you never will," replied Mrs. Castlemain.

"I don't mean to do so at present.—In a fit of gloom, and disgust to the world, I solicited the curacy of the village near which your daughter resided; but I found not there the comfort which I sought. I had been used to society, and I saw myself in a desert;—true, there were poor around me, and I could minister to their wants; but they were as ignorant as they were indigent, and I felt the wretchedness which made me leave the world, increased by the fancied remedy which I had chosen. Therefore I was resolved to give up the situation and seek a less gloomy one, when I became acquainted with your lost Agatha, and learnt to know the value of that society which the sullen, proud reserve, springing from a consciousness of unmerited misfortune, was always careful to withhold from me.—But this is not to the point in question; you wish me to assist you in the education of Emma, and I wish to afford you such assistance. My terms then are these;—you shall give me the same sum (and no more) which I received as a curate; and as preaching does not agree with my health, I will give it up entirely, and content myself with performing the other duties of a parish priest, namely, visiting the sick and the afflicted, and bestowing on them the consolations of religion.—But I must have a house to myself."

"What! will you not live with me?"

"By no means; but as near you as you please. And should any one in the neighbourhood have another pupil to offer me, I will agree to receive another pupil, either boy or girl."

"Nothing can be more fortunate," eagerly replied Mrs. Castlemain; "Mr. Hargrave, a gentleman who lives about two miles off, is at this time greatly in want of a tutor in some way or other, for his nephew, Henry St. Aubyn, whom, from some caprice or other, he has taken from Westminster school; he has a very pretty little cottage on his estate, which is now to let; therefore, if you will not indulge me by living in my house—"

"Indulge you, my dear madam!—What! make you and me the theme of all the gossips in the town of Keswick! No;—we are neither of us old enough to set busy tongues at defiance; besides, as we are to educate Emma, we must not set her the example of a violation of decorum; for I deem an attention to decorum one of the first bulwarks to female chastity."

Mrs. Castlemain in a happier moment would not perhaps have been sorry to be told that she was still too young to escape scandal; but she was very sorry that she could not make her arrangements such as to enable her to enjoy the comfort of Mr. Egerton's conversation at all times. She however rejoiced at having succeeded so much to her own satisfaction in procuring a preceptor for the orphan Emma.

"But what sort of man is Mr. Hargrave?" asked Mr. Egerton.

"O! a humorist, and a domestic tyrant; a man who can't bear contradiction, and who likes to keep even those whom he pretends to love, in an abject state of dependence on his will."

"Was he ever at College for a short time?"

"Yes."

"At Cambridge?"

"I believe so."

"Is he rich?"

"Very rich."

"And is his name Henry?"

"It is."

"Then it must be the same Hargrave whom I knew at College. He is my senior by some years, but I occasionally associated with him during his short stay there."

"I flatter myself he is the Mr. Hargrave whom you know; for I hope there are not two such queer-tempered beings in the world."

"This Henry Hargrave had a very beautiful sister, who came to visit her brother, a very showy, dressing, dashing girl, and her name was Henrietta."

"That convinces me," replied Mrs. Castlemain, "that my neighbour and your College friend are the same person; for Henrietta Hargrave married Mr. St. Aubyn, a gentleman of an old and honourable family and large estates; and having ruined him by her extravagance, he died, it is said, broken-hearted; and she as well as her son is now dependent on the bounty of Mr. Hargrave, and at this moment she resides at Keswick, and Henry with his uncle."

"So," replied Mr. Egerton, "I am here then *en pays de connoissance;* and for your sake, Mrs. Castlemain, I rejoice in being so, for you can now receive proper testimonials to convince you that I am the man of education and honour, which I have professed myself to be; for, my dear madam, you must own that you have at present only my own word to prove that I am the reverend Lionel Egerton, and no sharper or swindler."

"Sir," replied Mrs. Castlemain, with great feeling, "it is enough for me that my poor child named you with gratitude and affection in her letter, and that you have been the protector of her orphan hither."

"But suppose I have robbed the real Egerton of the letter and the child?" replied Mr. Egerton, smiling.

"O! my dear sir, your looks and manner are sufficient proofs that——"

"Well, well,—I see you are determined to think well of me, and that it was not imprudent in you to receive me into your house without a certificate of my good intentions; however, I feel at this moment, so satisfied with myself, with you, and with my present prospects, that, as I am in a conversable humour, I will trouble you to tell me my way to Mr. Hargrave's; and I will call upon him, and beg him to assure you that your confidence is really not ill-placed."

Then, having received the necessary information, Mr. Egerton set off on his visit to the Vale House, as Mr. Hargrave's seat was called.

I will now give a short sketch of Mr. Egerton's history. But it is a history common to many men. Events in life are often not important in themselves, but rendered so by the effect which they produce in the person to whom they occur.

Mr. Egerton was the youngest son of a very numerous and respectable family, and brought up to the Church, in the prospect of being provided for by a noble relation. At College he soon distinguished himself by his knowledge of the classics, and his conversational powers; and he was so deservedly a favourite of the circle in which he moved, that, having become a fellow at the age of twenty-eight, he was contented to await at the University, a good College living, or one from his long-promised patron; when, unfortunately for his peace, he was introduced to the beautiful sister of a College friend, and became passionately and irrecoverably in love for the first time in his life. Nor was the young lady slow to return his passion;—but to marry was impossible.

Miss Ainslie was the daughter of an extravagant man of fashion, and her habits had been expensive in a degree far beyond what her fortune warranted. True, she was willing, in a transport of youthful enthusiasm, to share the poverty of the man of her heart, and to quit "the scenes so gay, where she was fairest of the fair." But Mr. Egerton knew that it was the nature of enthusiasm to subside, and that love, when exposed to the assaults of poverty and the teasing details of severe domestic economy, is only too apt to struggle against them in vain; and though sure that his passion was proof against all attacks whatever, he was unwilling to expose that of Miss Ainslie to the trial which he did not fear for his own. It was therefore settled, on mature deliberation, that the lovers should not marry till Mr. Egerton obtained a living; and in the meanwhile Mr. Egerton and Miss Ainslie's friends were both very active in their endeavours to obtain, from the noble relation mentioned before, the long-promised living. But year succeeded to year, application to application, and still Mr. Egerton's claims were overlooked or forgotten; and the sickly hue of "hope deferred" began to be visible on the once blooming cheek of Clara Ainslie. To her a union with Mr. Egerton was desirable, not only because he was a man whom her heart and her reason both approved, but she longed to seek shelter in the protection and quiet of a house of her own, from the profligate and dissipated company which frequented the house of her deluded father, and sometimes insulted her with addresses, to which her well-known poverty but too frequently exposed her. But her hopes of emancipation from her sufferings still continued fruitless; and she saw herself at the age of five-and-thirty the ghost of what she was, and vainly endeavoured, by the faint glimmerings of a distant hope of a union with her still devoted lover, to cheer her drooping spirits, and light up the languid radiance of her eye. But the frame, weak and delicate while warm with youth and the consciousness of happiness, shrank and faded before the constant and corroding power of restless wishes and certain distresses; while Egerton, only kept alive himself by a sure though distant prospect as he thought, of having his long-raised expectations gratified, hung over her drooping form with still increased affection and anxiety.

At length he heard in the fourteenth year of their courtship that the incumbent on a very considerable living in Lord D.'s gift was a very old man, and at the point of death; and he hastened to the house of a friend at about forty miles' distance, where Clara was then staying, in order to impart to her this welcome intelligence. He arrived, and found her in the last stage of a rapid decline. Her constitution had at length yielded to the constant demands made on it by her feelings;—and she had scarcely smiled on the welcome news which her lover brought, had scarcely received the kiss on her pale cheek, with which he hailed her his in prospect for ever—when, laying her head on his bosom, she murmured out, "We shall then at length be happy!" and expired.

On the day of her funeral, and while Egerton with the calmness of deep-rooted anguish was visiting the body for the last time and gazing on it in solitary woe, the letter announcing the death of the incumbent above mentioned followed him to the chamber of mourning; and he found that a living worth a thousand a year waited his immediate acceptance.

Oh! what agony did he not endure, while in a hollow and mournful tone he exclaimed, "It comes too late!"—and stooping down as he did so, rested his cheek on the cold brow of Clara.

"*It comes too late*, and I reject it;—I scorn the wealth of which she lives not to partake;

and now welcome poverty and solitude!" was his only answer to his patron; and with a sort of spiteful sorrow and savage grief, he gave up his fellowship, and sought for the trifling curacy above mentioned, resolved to court the difficulties and privations of a narrow income. But when time, the great soother, had calmed the first transports of his sorrow, he became dissatisfied with his situation;—not that he wished for means of living better, for on principle he had always practised the strictest denial, nor had he ever found his yearly savings insufficient to relieve the really deserving indigent around him; but he was conscious of having other treasures which he could not in solitude bestow—the treasures of his learning, his knowledge of mankind, and his experience. He saw himself amply possessed of the power of being useful, but completely shut out from the means of employing that power. If he talked, there were none to listen to or understand him; and though he felt convinced that his affections were for ever buried in the tomb of Clara, he sighed for a kindred mind, and wished for an intelligent companion, if it was only to listen to the tale of his sorrows. As soon as he saw Agatha he thought he had found this companion. He read an expression of fixed sorrow in her countenance that interested him; but he soon found that it was a sort of savage, proud, sullen sorrow, like what his own had originally been; and though he felt her endeared to him by this conviction, he also felt that this disposition was a bar to all hopes of intimacy; and he had lived in the same village with Agatha two years before he had exchanged two words with her. But when he saw her melted into tears at church at the pathetic parable of the prodigal son, he felt that the power of sullen grief was past, and he doubted not but that the moment was arrived when the voice of consolation would be welcome to her, and when her heart, as I before observed, would be lightened of half its load, could she but tell the tale of her sorrows to one who would listen to and pity them. Accordingly he did speak to her;—he heard her mournful tale; and while he hung over her death-bed, and received her last parting wishes, and promised to obey them,—with the consciousness of being useful, returned a degree of tranquillity to his mind; and the death of Agatha awakened him to new life and the prospect of new enjoyment. Besides, he read in her deep and guilty resentment,—in that sullen indignation which had caused her to put off the day of forgiveness till the pardon which she longed to pronounce and to implore was arrested on her lips by death,—a warning lesson and a salutary reproof to himself. Because a patron had neglected to fulfil his promises till, according to his long-treasured hopes, he could no longer profit by his bounty, in the sullenness of resentment,—a resentment which could injure and mortify himself alone,—he had fled from the society of men, to brood in retirement over the proud consciousness of injury. He had allowed the powers of his mind to droop, unstimulated by the influence of collision; and had suffered hours, precious hours, to be wasted in the languor of unavailing regret, which he might have employed to amuse, to instruct, and to enlighten his fellow-creatures.

"I have erred; but I will endeavour instantly to repair my error," he exclaimed, as he stood by the corpse of Agatha;—adding, as he imprinted a kiss on the cold unconscious hand beside him, "Thou shalt not have suffered and repented in vain. And I will repay, by endeavouring to benefit thy child, the gratitude I owe thee for the good I have derived from thy warning example."

He kept his resolution; and the child of Agatha became the pupil of his affection.

When Mr. Egerton returned from his visit to Mr. Hargrave, who happened to be in a good humour, and therefore received him graciously, he was pleased to find that when the postilion had come to the door with the chaise, according to the orders given the preceding day, Emma had burst into tears at sight of him, had protested that she would stay where she was, and had screamed as much at the idea of leaving her grandmother as she had before done at the idea of staying with her; nor could she be at all pacified till Mrs. Castlemain had paid and discharged the driver and his chaise.

"May all her hatreds through life be as evanescent as her hatred of you has been, my dear madam!" said Mr. Egerton; "for the being who hates easily and eternally, is a curse to himself and a pest to his fellow-creatures."

Mr. Egerton returned, accompanied by Henry St. Aubyn, the nephew of Mr. Hargrave, and now the pupil in prospect of Mr. Egerton, who ever and anon regarded him with such looks of interest and affection, as, considering the shortness of their acquaintance, were matter of surprise to Mrs. Castlemain.

Henry St. Aubyn was a tall, lank, unformed boy of fourteen; his figure all bone, and his face all eyes; for the rest of his features had not as yet grown sufficiently to bear any proportion to the large dark grey eyes, shaded with long and silken black eyelashes, which formed the striking feature in his sun-burnt yet blooming face. His hair, which once curled in luxuriant ringlets down his shoulders, was, to the great mortification of his mother's vanity, cropped close to his head, to gratify the arbitrary will of his uncle. But to prevent his hair from curling was impossible;— short, but full, his dark ringlets still clustered round his straight low forehead, and gave his head the resemblance of the bust of some young Greek. Still, though his appearance was certainly picturesque and interesting, he was not yet handsome enough to deserve the earnest gaze of affectionate and silent admiration which Mr. Egerton bestowed on him; but Mrs. Castlemain ceased to be surprised, when Mr. Egerton, sighing deeply as he turned away from a long examination of St. Aubyn's features, said to her, "That dear boy, madam, is, by his father, I find, second cousin to the Ainslies, and to *her* whom I have mentioned to you. And I am sure, quite sure, that in the cut of his dark-grey eye, and in countenance particularly when he smiles, he greatly resembles her. Judge then, madam, with what delight I shall undertake the task of instructing him."

Before Mrs. Castlemain could reply, Emma, who had just been fresh washed and dressed, came running into the room; and jumping on Mr. Egerton's lap, told him with a scream of joy that the post-chaise was gone, and that they were to stay where there were, and go away no more. "I am glad of it," cried Henry St. Aubyn; "for I hope you will stay and play with me, and love me."

Emma at first drew back from his offered hand; but after looking at him some time under her ringlets that hung over her eyes, she ventured to give her hand; and in a short time she very kindly took him to see her baby house.

The intimacy thus happily begun, was as happily matured by time. Mr. Egerton became the inhabitant of a small house at an equal distance between Mr. Hargrave's and Mrs. Castlemain's: but he taught Emma and St. Aubyn together at the house of the latter; while Emma, urged on by the example and praises of St. Aubyn, learnt eagerly and readily every thing which Mr. Egerton taught her, and was soon the pride and delight of her grandmother, her preceptor, and her companion.

But it was not in her studies only that Emma profited by the society of St. Aubyn; her heart and her temper were benefited by his example. It was at first a difficult task for Mrs. Castlemain by kindness, and Mr. Egerton by judicious severity, to break their pupil of those habits of violence and ill-humour which the unfavourable circumstances in which she had been placed had exposed her to acquire. But this task was rendered easy at length by the model of fine temper and obedience exhibited to her every day by St. Aubyn.

Henry St. Aubyn's most striking characteristic was filial piety. He was an only child, and his mind and feelings exhibited that precocity which is often observed in those children who have been the exclusive objects of attention and instruction. But he had also been in situations which never fail to bring forward permaturely the sensibility and the intellect. He had been nursed and educated in scenes of domestic distress;—the tears of his mother had mingled with her caresses of him, while she loudly lamented that extravagance, though she had not resolution to relinquish it, which would unavoidably destroy the future fortune of her son. He had also wept on his father's neck, while in unavailing agony the self-condemned parent had implored his forgiveness, for having weakly allowed his fond folly as a husband to get the better of his duty as a father, and suffer Mrs. St. Aubyn to pursue that ruinous line of conduct which had made them all beggars and dependants.

But luckily for Henry it was only as a husband that Mr. St. Aubyn was weak and criminally indulgent; as a father, he knew how to unite kindness with restraint, and tenderness with firmness, so judiciously, that the temper of his son was neither soured by cruel privations, nor injured still more by blind and excessive indulgence.

Henry St. Aubyn obeyed his father in infancy, because he knew that on disobedience awaited certain punishment; and thus the habit of obedience to proper restraint and proper commands was acquired without trouble. As he grew older, he found that he was thus constrained, because his ruler knew better what was good for him than he for himself, and he continued to obey from respect as well as from habit; and as his father possessed that command of temper himself, which he endeavoured to teach, St. Aubyn both from precept and example became mild without abjectness, and good-humoured without effort. Besides, he had the great advantage of being his father's constant companion; and being thus early the witness of his parent's sorrows, he learnt to feel and to reflect deeply at a time of life when children in general only know "the tear forgot as soon as shed," and the almost uninterrupted sunshine of the breast. He also felt himself the sole comfort of his father; and his young self-love flattered by the consciousness, he often preferred his own lonely fireside and the sad society of his unhappy parent, to the sports of childhood and the heartless mirth of his companions.

When his father was on his death-bed, he called St. Aubyn to him, who had then not long reached the age of thirteen; and telling him that he knew he was in virtue and understanding considerably above his years, he bequeathed his mother to his care and protection; desiring him whatever might be her errors, to behave to her with tenderness and forbearance, and to prove himself in every thing not only a fond and obedient son, but a guardian and a defender.

"The charge was needless," replied St. Aubyn melting into tears; "but, to give you all the satisfaction in my power, *hear me swear, that in all emergencies whatever, my mother's peace and comfort shall be my first care and my first motive of action.*"

Mr. St. Aubyn accepted the oath; called

him the best of children, prayed for his welfare; and the last words he pronounced, while with clasped hands he awaited his final struggle, were a prayer for Henry.

St. Aubyn's father had not been dead above nine months when he first saw Emma at Mrs. Castlemain's, and her mourning habit for her mother he beheld with a sympathetic interest.

"Poor child!" said he one day, as he looked at her black dress.

"Ay!" replied Mrs. Castlemain, "unhappy child!—it is very hard to lose a parent so young!"

"Say rather, happy child!" said St. Aubyn bursting into tears, "to lose a parent when she was too young to know the greatness of her loss!"

"Don't cry, master Henry," said Emma, putting up her pretty mouth to kiss him; "grandmamma is not angry with you." And St. Aubyn caught her to his bosom with mixed pity and affection.

When Mrs. Castlemain was again alone with Mr. Egerton, she said to him after some little hesitation, "but by what name, my dear sir, shall I call our Emma?"

"By what name, my dear madam? By her own name certainly,—that of her father—Danvers."

"No, sir, no!" replied Mrs. Castlemain with great agitation; "I cannot bear to be every moment reminded of that villain."

"But consider, madam, that by not calling your granddaughter and heiress by the name of her father, you would seem to admit her illegitimacy, and that she was not born in wedlock."

"No, sir, no; because I mean to call her Castlemain!"

"But, madam, her name is not Castlemain; and I am a decided enemy to all sorts of fraud. For whom, and what, madam, do you wish this dear child to be imposed on the world?"

"Sir, I scorn the idea of imposition as much as you."

"Then, to prove it, call her the child of Agatha Danvers; for then, and then only, will the real truth be told."

"No, sir; I will call her by the name of my late husband, who was my first cousin; for I mean, as soon as she is of age, to give her an estate left me by Mr. Castlemain, and shall solicit leave for her to bear the name and arms of Castlemain."

"But in the meanwhile, madam, for what do you wish her to be taken by strangers?—for your child by Mr. Castlemain?"

"I do not see, sir, that it is necessary for her own and her mother's story to be told to every one. Our intimate friends know it of course; and should any gentleman pay his addresses to Emma, he also will be told the truth."

"But suppose, madam, that, believing Emma to be the daughter of the honourable Mrs. Castlemain, a gentleman allows himself to become in love with Emma, under the sanction of a father's approbation; do you not think that gentleman will have reason to reproach you, when he finds he has been deceived by the change of name; and that your heiress is the fruit of a marriage, which, in all human probability, will never be proved to have taken place?"

"Sir," said Mrs. Castlemain angrily, "you are putting an extreme case, and fancying, I hope, an improbability that does not *exist*! Sir, my peace of mind depends on my not hearing the hateful name of Danvers; and in this respect, sir, I must beg, sir,—nay, sir, I must *insist* on having my own way!"

"Well, madam, then I must submit, though against my principles and my judgment; for never yet did I know any good the result of deception,—and God grant that from this no material mischief may ensue!"

Accordingly the orphan of Agatha was in future known by the name of Emma Castlemain.

But before I go on with the history of Emma, and her young companion, Henry St. Aubyn, I shall make my readers acquainted with two persons, who will be prominent characters in these pages, and on whose influence, directly and indirectly, will in a great measure depend the fate both of my hero and my heroine.

Mr. Hargrave was one of those fortunate men whom a series of unforeseen accidents, aided by quickness of talent and industry, elevate from a mean and obscure situation of life to one of opulence and gentility; and, as is often the case with persons who are the makers of their own fortune, he valued himself greatly on the extent of his possessions, and had a particular spite against family pride, and what he denominated "a poor, proud gentleman." Mr. Hargrave's understanding was good, but he fancied it better than it really was; or rather, perhaps, he did not so much overvalue his own ability, as undervalue that of those who surrounded him. He did not fancy, while measuring himself with others, that he was a giant; but he erroneously imagined them to be pigmies, while he piqued himself on his talent of overreaching and imposing upon his less acute companions. This propensity alone would have prevented him from being a desirable companion; as, though he was unconscious of it, his attempts were often discovered by the objects of them; and however politeness might prevent them from disclosing the discovery, they felt an indignant resentment at being supposed weak enough to be so deceived. But there was a still stronger reason why, though he might be an active citizen, an upright tradesman, and a generous relation, he could never be an amiable man, an agreeable companion, or a beloved friend. He was the slave of a bad and incorrigible temper; and this slave to himself became the tyrant of others. The spoiled child of a weak and ignorant mother, whose understanding he despised, and of an indolent and sottish father, whose helpless, yet contented indigence disgusted him,—he was thrown upon the world with all his irritable feelings uncorrected and unsubdued, except where interest and ambition made it necessary for him to assume the virtue which he had not.

At the age of thirty, love asserted its turn to reign over his yet unwounded heart; and the object of his affection had extreme youth, loveliness, and gentleness, to recommend her to his notice. Her fortune was small; but that he did not consider as any obstacle to his wishes, as he had wealth enough for both; and her birth and connexions were such as to flatter his pride. Nor was he long before he made known his passion and his views; and the lady seemed so fully to return his affection, and to share in the warm approbation of his suit which her parents expressed, that even a time for their union was fixed; while the prospect of happiness as perfect as this world can afford, seemed to soften the usual asperity of Mr. Hargrave's disposition, and he felt desirous of imparting to others the cheerfulness which he was conscious of himself. But his hopes and his benevolence were only too soon clouded, as it were for ever, by the most cruel and unmerited of disappointments. A better connexion, and perhaps a more amiable man, were offered to the mercenary parents of Mr. Hargrave's betrothed wife; and in a short time, by a number of little neglects and petty affronts, he was given to understand that both the lady and her family were become tired of him and his pretensions; and while by letters of earnest expostulation, he was daily requesting to be informed how he had deserved to forfeit the favour of the parents and the tenderness of the daughter, he received the overwhelming and heart-rending intelligence that the woman of his affections was married to another!

It would be needless for me to point out to my readers the natural effect of an injury and a disappointment like this, on a proud and irritable temper like that of Mr. Hargrave. Suffice that, having shortly realized by a successful speculation, a fortune sufficient even for his lofty ambition, he resolved to give up business and retire into the country, in order to brood in solitude over the recollection of promised joys to him for ever lost, and the wrongs which, though common to many, his resentment magnified into injuries never experienced before by any one but himself.

But the affair did not end here. The brother of his mistress, hearing that Mr. Hargrave in the bitterness of just resentment had used very opprobrious terms when speaking of her conduct, insisted that he should either retract what he had said, or give him the satisfaction of a gentleman. With this latter demand Mr. Hargrave eagerly complied, and his second fire stretched his adversary on the ground, apparently deprived of life. But though the surgeon in attendance declared that life was only suspended, his wound was so dangerous a one that Mr. Hargrave and the seconds thought proper to abscond. During a whole twelvemonth, the former was forced to be an exile from his country, and to experience the tormenting fear of being obliged never to return to it, or of standing a trial for his life.

At length, however, the cause of his distress was declared wholly out of danger, and Mr. Hargrave returned to England;—but both from principle and feeling he was become so decided an enemy to duelling, that he solemnly declared he would discard, pursue with implacable hatred, and disinherit a relation, however dear to him, who should either give or accept a challenge. He returned, too, so disgusted with the world, that he immediately went in search of an estate in some distant part of the country; and having on the death of his parents made his orphan sister the mistress of his house, he took her with him on his journey. It was while making the tour of the Lakes that chance introduced Mr. St. Aubyn to their acquaintance, who, captivated with the beauty of Miss Hargrave, formed that hasty and ill-advised union with her, which was the ruin of his fortune, and the bane of his peace of mind.

The marriage of his sister with Mr. St. Aubyn, though welcome to Mr. Hargrave in some points of view, as he got rid by it of a sister whose want of management hourly offended him, was very unpleasing to him in others. Mr. St. Aubyn, whose estates were deeply mortgaged, owing to the extravagance of his father, was a poor and proud gentleman, and Mr. Hargrave, as I have before observed, hated persons of that description; and the dignified refinement of Mr. St. Aubyn's manners, which as he could not imitate he therefore pretended to despise, was ill-suited to the coarse banter and unpolished demeanour of his brother-in-law. Nor could Mr. St. Aubyn always command his temper when the latter was determined to put him off his guard; and at such moments the just and haughty resentment of the man of family, used to show itself in a manner which the man of wealth never pardoned. And as Mr. Hargrave, like all angry persons, was apt to dwell on the provocation which he received, and to forget that which he gave, the proximity of the St. Aubyn estate to that which Mr. Hargrave purchased in the county of Cumberland soon made it a very undesirable residence for him; he therefore removed with his wife and infant son to a house which he still possessed near the west end of the metropolis. But he soon found reason to repent of his removal, as his wife's extravagance became such, that in a very short time he saw himself reduced to the alternative of going to a gaol, or of parting with his paternal estate; and as a purchaser for St. Aubyn (the name of his seat) offered at this critical moment, he with a sort of desperate resolution accepted the offer, and bade for ever farewell to the dear abode of his ancestors.

Soon after, he discovered that the real purchaser of a possession so valued by him was the purse-proud Mr. Hargrave; and the agony of his situation was considerably increased by the news. But he recollected that if Mr. Hargrave did not marry,—and he had solemnly resolved that he never would marry,—his son would in all probability be his heir, and St. Aubyn would revert to its original possessor! This thought was rapture to him; and in the happy state of mind which it occasioned, he even fancied that Mr. Hargrave made the purchase from the benevolent wish of preventing the estate from going out of the family; and as Mr. St. Aubyn was resolved to act upon this idea, and in Mr. Hargrave's supposed generosity to forget his unkindness, the latter soon after received a most affectionate letter from his brother-in-law, requesting him to forget all that had passed, and to receive them for a few weeks as his guests. Mr. Hargrave, flattered at being thus courted to a reconciliation, promised to forget and forgive every thing; and the St. Aubyns came to Vale-House on a visit. But in less than two years Mr. Hargrave, either in a fit of spleen against Mr. St. Aubyn, or from the love of accumulation, sold the highly-prized estate for a very large premium to another possessor; and Mr. St. Aubyn never recovered the blow.

"How I have mortified the pride of that poor gentleman!" said Mr. Hargrave to himself in one of his angry and malignant humours.

But he had it in his power to inflict still greater mortification on him. Debt succeeded to debt, embarrassment to embarrassment,—till so little of his once-comfortable fortune remained, that Mr. St. Aubyn on his death-bed saw himself obliged to recommend his wife and child to the protection and bounty of Mr. Hargrave! It was a moment of triumph for Mr. Hargrave; the representative of the ancient family of the St. Aubyns was thenceforth thrown by his high-born father on the pity and dependence of a man of yesterday. How humbled was now the pride of the man of family! But a better feeling succeeded to the throb of ungenerous exultation.

Mr. Hargrave gazed on the pale and careworn cheek, the imploring and sunk eye of Mr. St. Aubyn, with pity, not unmixed perhaps with remorse. "She shall not *ruin me*," said he with ungracious graciousness; "but I will maintain her handsomely; and if he behaves well, I will be a father to the child."

The eyes of the dying man beamed with momentary joy,—for he knew Henry would "behave well,"—and visions of future greatness, and even of the recovery of the family estate, danced momentarily before his closing eyes; while a blessing, a fervent blessing, faltered on his quivering lips, and wrung a tear from the usually dry lid of Mr. Hargrave.

Mr. St. Aubyn died; and he fulfilled his promise to the dying: he hired a small house for his sister in the town of Keswick, and allowed her a respectable income, but took Henry to reside with him, proposing to provide for and to educate him as if he were his own child.

But it was impossible for a man of Mr. Hargrave's temper and disposition to make conscious dependence easy to be borne. On the contrary, every day, every hour, every moment, reminded the St. Aubyns that they were eating the bread of dependence; and Mrs. St. Aubyn had at once to dread from her brother the sneer of contempt, the frown of reproof, and, what was still more painful to endure with composure, the coarse and noisy banter of sometimes well-deserved ridicule.

The circumstances in which Mrs. St. Aubyn had been placed in early life, were the most unfavourable in every point of view, to form a well-principled and respectable woman.— Praises of her beauty were the first sounds that met her ear; while, as she grew up, her weak and unprincipled mother, in order to obtain means to purchase ornaments for the child whose personal graces were her pride, used to set apart for that purpose, with her knowledge, small sums from the slender allowance given her by her husband for their daily meals; and by this means her daughter's young mind learnt a lesson of artifice and disingenuousness to which it could never rise superior. Nor was her father's sense of moral rectitude much greater than that of his wife, as a love of truth made no part of his precepts or his practice; and the ready lie with which his daughter usually endeavoured to hide the faults which she committed, was looked upon, both by him as well as Mrs. Hargrave, as a proof of talent and quickness above her years, and received with a wink of the eye at each other, and an ill-suppressed smile, which convinced the young delinquent, that the only crime in lying was that of being found out.

In addition to this sort of training, was a constant assurance from her mother that nothing was so necessary to a young woman as to look well, and that if she set off her person to advantage there was no doubt but that her beauty would make her fortune. But spite of her attention to her dress, and the splendour of her personal charms, Miss Hargrave's apparent folly and flippancy had so far counteracted the power of her beauty, that she had reached the age of twenty-five without having had one offer of marriage worth accepting; when, on the death of her parents, her brother invited her to reside with him, and Mr. St. Aubyn saw her with Mr. Hargrave, as I before mentioned, on his tour to the Lakes.

The vivacity and perhaps even the silliness of her expression, gave Miss Hargrave the appearance of extreme youth, an appearance which her manner strongly confirmed, and the bloom of her fine complexion, heightened by air and exercise, considerably increased. Mr. St. Aubyn gazed on her, the first moment that he beheld her, with admiration and delight. He saw in her youth, beauty, grace, every thing that his heart had ever sought in woman; and when he became acquainted with her, and accompanied her hanging on his arm, through the romantic scenes around him, he felt that she was become the arbiter of his fate, and that it was impossible for him to be happy without her. Indeed she appeared to Mr. St. Aubyn under peculiar advantages. The fear of her brother made her always silent and timid in his presence; therefore her lover heard not her usually insipid volubility, and her occasional he considered as general timidity. When they were alone, indeed, he found that she talked a great deal, but this he attributed to the sort of intoxicating relief which she felt at being removed from the alarming eye of her tyrant; and judging thence how great must be her sufferings from a residence with such a man, pity assisted to fan the flame of love, and he felt that it would be both a just and generous action to remove so fascinating a victim from the fetters that galled her.

Her want of fortune was indeed a serious obstacle to his wishes; as Mr. St. Aubyn, in order to pay off several heavy mortgages on his estates, had been living many years on a very inconsiderable part of his income, and it was necessary that he should continue so to do, in order to effect the honourable design which his integrity had dictated. But if Miss Hargrave loved him, he thought every obstacle would vanish; for she had been accustomed to live on a narrow income, and that which he had to offer her was certainly larger than the one on which she had been accustomed to live. Accordingly, rendered blind and confiding by the illusions of passion, Mr. St. Aubyn revealed his love to the object of it, and received from her an avowal of mutual regard. Immediately transported with joy, and the hopes of future happiness, he declared to her his situation, his well-principled plans of economy, and all that he required of his wife during the first years of marriage, in order to assist him in clearing his estates, and in rescuing from obloquy the memory of a much respected though improvident father.

Miss Hargrave listened to and approved his plan, promised every thing that he desired, and performed nothing. Still her infatuated husband admired and adored her; and even while they remained at their country-seat, he indulged her pride and her vanity by resuming much of the ancient state of his family in his mode of living. But when, in consequence of repeated differences with Mr. Hargrave, they removed to the vicinity of London, her extravagance knew no bounds, and her husband had not the heart to reprove or restrain her; for was she not called "the beautiful Mrs. St. Aubyn?" was she not the most admired woman in the drawing-room? and while her charms administered thus to the gratification of his vanity and his affection, Mr. St. Aubyn endeavoured to forget that the mortgages remained unpaid, and that debts were accumulating around him.

The result I have before detailed, and the consequences of that fatal uxoriousness, that want of proper energy, which led to the utter ruin of his fortune, and precipitated him into an early grave. But, let me speak it to his honour, he never, in his consciousness of the errors of the wife, forgot for a moment the respect which he, as a gentleman, thought due to her as a woman. Though too late convinced of her folly, her vanity, her extravagance, her disregard of truth,—he behaved to her before his servants and his son with as much politeness and deference as if her words were oracles. He took no mean revenge on her for her weakness, by wounding her self-love either in public or even in private; and though her foibles were such as to make her often an object of ridicule, he deplored but never scoffed at her weakness; whatever she ordered respecting her son, he never contradicted; if wrong, he told her it was so in private, and the order was repealed by herself, as if from her own conviction, and not his desire; and it was owing to this kind, generous, and manly conduct in her husband, that Henry St. Aubyn, in the midst of his convictions of his mother's follies, never lost sight for one moment of the respect due to her as his parent. His father had accustomed him to treat her with respect by his own example; and when crushed to the earth by the avowed contempt and ridicule of her brother, Mrs. St. Aubyn's tearful eyes could turn on her son with confiding and never-deceived affection, and her self-love was immediately soothed by his respectful attention to herself, and the firm, decided, but cool and gentle manner in which he defended and supported her under the attacks of his uncle;—while Mr. Hargrave feared, approved, oppressed, admired, and envied his nephew—love him he did not; it is not in nature for us to love those whom we feel to be our superiors in those qualities which entitle a person to the appellation of amiable. No one loved Mr. Hargrave, and every one loved St. Aubyn. How then could he possibly forgive his nephew an advantage which he had never possessed, and never could possess himself? But he could torment him occasionally, and that pleasure he often gave himself by speaking slightingly of his father; and once with ingenious malignity he tried to wound St. Aubyn to the utmost by leading Mrs. St. Aubyn to join him in disrespect to the memory of her husband. "After all, Harriet," said he, "St. Aubyn turned out a very bad match for you; with your beauty and power of pleasing, you might have done better; a rich London merchant would have been a more proper husband for you, than a poor and proud country gentleman; and I dare say you think so yourself; for then, you know, whatever you had spent, he could have supplied you by his increasing gains; and instead of now being dependent on a queer tempered fellow like myself, perhaps at this moment you might have been Lady Mayoress."

St. Aubyn turned pale at this ensnaring speech, and sat in fearful expectation for his mother's reply, who, trembling with agitation, rose from her seat, and pressing both her hands upon her bosom, as if to keep down the emotions that struggled there, indignantly exclaimed,

"What, sir, do you think I ever wish that I had been the wife of any other man than Mr. St. Aubyn? — No, sir; I know he was only too good for me; I know how faulty I am, and how indulgent he was. — No, Mr. Hargrave, believe me, with all my faults, I can never forget what I owed to the best of husbands; and I had rather have the proud consciousness of having been his wife, than be married to an emperor!" Here sobs interrupted her; and while Henry, with whom this energetic tribute to his father's worth effaced a score of her faults, ran to her, and laid her head on his bosom, Mr. Hargrave, struggling himself with a little rising in his throat, held out his hand affectionately to her, and said,

"Come, come, Harriet, don't be a fool, I only said what I did to try you.—So, I find you have a *heart*; and as St. Aubyn, but for his confounded pride, was a very fine fellow, if you did not feel concerning him as you do I should despise you;—but you have said what you ought; so shake hands, and be friends."

She gave him her hand, smiled, and forgot what had passed. But her son could not so soon forget this wanton trial of his mother, and the torture inflicted on himself; but with a look of reproach, which Mr. Hargrave felt, though he did not choose to notice it, he folded his arms in a sort of contemplative sadness, and left the room.

But to return to the inhabitants of the White Cottage.——I shall pass over the details of the succeeding eight years, contenting myself with saying, that during that time Emma's progress in acquirements had fully equalled the expectations of her preceptors, and that her improvement in temper, from the firm though gentle authority of Mr. Egerton, and the influence and example of St. Aubyn, had surpassed even their warmest hopes.

Indeed, in that difficult part of good temper which consists in forbearance and accommodation to the ill-humour of others, St. Aubyn was unrivalled; and Mr. Egerton was never tired of dwelling on his praises, and holding him up in this instance as an unfailing and admirable example.

"Excuse me, Mr. Egerton," said Mrs. Castlemain one day, piqued perhaps at the evident superiority which he attributed to St. Aubyn over Emma in this particular, "excuse me,—but I think you consider Temper as a quality of more importance than it really is."

"I am surprised at such an opinion from you, madam," replied Mr. Egerton gravely, "as I should have thought that you must have been aware, the chief part of your misfortunes and those of your daughter were occasioned by Temper."

Mrs. Castlemain looked down and sighed, conscience-stricken.

"So far from agreeing with you, madam," continued Mr. Egerton, "in what you have just advanced, I consider Temper as one of the most busy and universal agents in all human actions. Philosophers believe that the electric fluid, though invisible, is everywhere in the physical world; so I believe that Temper is equally at work, though sometimes unseen except in its effects, in the moral world. Perhaps nothing is rarer than a single motive; almost all our motives are compound; and if we examine our own hearts and actions with that accuracy and diffidence which become us as finite and responsible beings, we shall find that of our motives to bad actions Temper is very often a principal ingredient, and that it is not unfrequently one incitement to a good one. I am also convinced," added he, "that the crimes both of private individuals and of sovereigns are to be traced up to an uncorrected and uneducated temper as their source."

"You seem to have considered this subject very carefully, and in a manner wholly new to me," answered Mrs. Castlemain in an accent of uncomfortableness; "and you probably are right; but if you be, how many then are wrong!"

"Alas!" replied Mr. Egerton, "the many are indeed, in my humble opinion, wrong; for few persons are sufficiently aware how much the virtue, the dignity, and the happiness of life depend on a well-governed temper. You may remember that the Bourgeois Gentilhomme in Moliere finds, to his great surprise, that he has been speaking prose all his life without knowing it; and I have often observed, that parents and preceptors have in their gift the best and most compendious of all possessions, that of a good and well-governed temper, without at least the seeming consciousness that it is in their disposal; and that to watch over the temper of a child, ameliorate it by salutary or proper indulgence, or control it by salutary restraints, is far, far more necessary to its future welfare, than to reprove a fault in grammar, or to correct an exercise."

"Well, sir," said Mrs. Castlemain, "education and care may do much; but I suppose you will allow that some persons have tempers naturally good,—and there is no merit in that."

"No, madam," answered Mr. Egerton smiling; "but there is great convenience. I will allow, as the contrary does not admit of proof, that there are persons who seem to come into the world with good tempers, and that therefore they have no more merit in being good-humoured than in having fine eyes. But then what a world of trouble they themselves are spared! as they have no ill-humours to subdue; and how pleasant is an intercourse with them! because you are not afraid that their temper, like a tiger chained, should occasionally break loose and tear asunder the scarcely well-knit tie of affection, destroying the confidence and comfort of society. But many possess this sort of good temper, which may be called the physical part of it, without having an atom of the other sort, which may be called the moral part."

"I do not understand you, sir; you are too deep for me," observed Mrs. Castlemain.

"I will explain my meaning, madam, if you will permit me to talk a little longer.—I own that I am given to preach,—but preaching you know is my vocation,—therefore I hope you will excuse it. I mean by the moral part of good humour, that which shows itself in bearing with the ill-humour and provoking irritability of others; and this necessary and valuable power, I must say, is rarely, in my opinion, possessed by any one who has not a good understanding. Now St. Aubyn possesses both sorts of good temper, and—"

"Ah!" interrupted Mrs. Castlemain, "I thought how this long harangue would end; namely, in the introduction of your favourite's name, and of his praises; but they are not *new* to me; therefore, excuse my staying to hear more." So saying, she left the room with a toss of the head and a quick step; not conscious, perhaps, how much she herself was at that moment under the dominion of temper.

Mr. Egerton smiled, but not in derision. It was not for Mrs. Castlemain that he had harangued, but for the silent and attentive Emma, who was present, and in whose young and conscious heart every word that he had uttered had made a due and salutary impression.

"Sir," said Emma, coming to Mr. Egerton, and leaning on the back of his chair; "pray, sir, go on with what you were going to say about Henry; for I like to hear him praised for his temper, though I can't help thinking, sir, that grandmamma does not."

"Indeed!" said Mr. Egerton, suppressing a smile; "and what makes you think so?"

"O! her look and her manner, and I think I know why too; I think—"

"What dost thou think, my dear child?" said Mr. Egerton, taking her hand.

"I think, sir, that she looks upon such praise as a reproach to me; for you know, sir, I am not half so good-tempered as Henry St. Aubyn."

"O yes, much more than *half*, my dearest girl," replied Mr. Egerton; "but I believe you are right in your observation; and as Mrs. Castlemain is hurt at the praise of Henry, merely out of her affection for you, you ought to love her the better for being so."

"Certainly, sir," said Emma; "but you know her love to me need not make her unjust to others; and I am *sure* Henry deserves *all* you can say of him."

"True, very true. Well, then it is in your power to put a stop to Mrs. Castlemain's affectionate error, as you think it, by becoming as tractable, as mild, and as forbearing, as Henry himself."

"I will, sir, indeed I will," said Emma; and Mr. Egerton saying "I believe thee, dear child!" set out for his evening walk. But to resolve and to execute are, alas! very different things; and even that evening, as well as the next day, exhibited proofs of Emma's love of excellence being stronger than her power of imitating it.

That very evening Mrs. Castlemain invited Emma to walk with her to the town of Keswick; and when there, business led the former to the shop of a milliner. In the shop, unfortunately for Emma, was that weak, vain, inconsiderate woman, the mother of St. Aubyn; and on the counter, as unfortunately, lay a straw bonnet trimmed with pale-blue ribands. Emma's eyes were soon attracted to the bonnet; which the shopwoman perceiving, she instantly begged the young lady would put it on, assuring her it was the last new fashion, and amazingly becoming. To resist this entreaty was impossible. Emma's own bonnet, though nearly new, became immediately of no value in her eyes, especially as the milliner and Mrs. St. Aubyn declared, when Emma put on the new one, that there never was any thing so becoming, and that it seemed made on purpose for her.

Mrs. Castlemain was silent, her look grave and unapproving; but Emma had a quarterly allowance, and enough remaining of it to pay for the bonnet at least. Ay; but she did not want it, and she knew that Mr. Egerton and Mrs. Castlemain would both disapprove her incurring so unnecessary an expense. Yet the bonnet was so pretty and so becoming, and Mrs. St. Aubyn advised her so earnestly to buy it, that Emma had faintly articulated "Well, I think I must have it," when Mrs. Castlemain, who recollected that Mr. Egerton had said no opportunity of inculcating the practice of self-denial in Emma should be passed over, gravely observed,

"You must please *yourself*, Miss Castlemain, as I have made you in a measure independent of *me* in your expenses; but I must say, that if you are so extravagant as to purchase, for the indulgence of a whim, a hat which you do not want, I shall be very seriously displeased."

Emma's proud spirit revolted at this threat, uttered before so many witnesses; and saying within herself, "What signifies my independence if I am not allowed to use it?" she had half resolved to disobey her grandmother, when her resolution was completely confirmed by Mrs. St. Aubyn's indiscreetly and impertinently observing,

"Dear girl! it does not signify how much she spends! but do, dear madam, buy it for her! she looks so beautiful in it!—I assure you, Miss Castlemain, my son Henry says nothing becomes you so much as *pale-blue*."

This was *decisive*; and after a short struggle between duty and inclination, Emma threw down the money for the hat on the counter, and desired it might be put into the carriage, which now came to the door, as they were to walk only one way.

The drive home was gloomy and uncomfortable. Mrs. Castlemain was too greatly irritated to speak; and Emma, to the painful consciousness of having indulged a refractory temper, and displeased and disobeyed her grandmother, added that of having unnecessarily expended nearly the last farthing of her allowance, forgetting that it wanted some weeks to the quarter-day.

Mr. Egerton, who met them on their return, soon discovered that something unpleasant had happened, and he sighed as he observed that the ingenuous vivacity which had sparkled in Emma's eyes when she set out on her walk, from having formed a virtuous resolution, with the full intention of keeping it, was replaced by a sullen downcast look, indicative of self-upbraiding, and the consciousness of having failed in some necessary duty.

Mrs. Castlemain was silent, and spoke and answered in monosyllables; but as soon as Emma, tired and dejected, had retired to bed without her supper, she told her tale of grievances to Mr. Egerton, who, though much mortified at hearing of the weakness of his pupil, hoped that the inconveniences to which the want of money would expose her, would at once punish and amend the fault of which she had been guilty; and after volunteering a promise to Mrs. Castlemain that he would neither give nor lend Emma any money, however she might require it, and receiving a similar promise from her in return, he could not help hinting to Mrs. Castlemain that this was a fresh proof of the importance of a good and yielding temper; and he obliged her to own that, under similar circumstances, Henry St. Aubyn would not have gratified his own inclinations at the expense of a frown or a pang to his mother.

"But," added he, "depend on it, my dear madam, that our joint and incessant care will at length succeed in abating, if we cannot entirely remove this only fault in the object of our solicitude, and one entirely owing to the pernicious effect of early and erroneous habits."

The next day, to the joy of Emma, was a day of splendid sunshine; so much so, that there seemed no likelihood any rain would fall during the day; and as this was the case, she looked forward with all the delight of her age to a party of pleasure, in a beautiful vale about two miles distant from Mrs. Castlemain's house, which was to take place if the weather promised to be fine and settled. This party was to consist of Mr. Hargrave, Mrs. St. Aubyn, her son, some young ladies in the neighbourhood, and Mrs. Castlemain, Mr. Egerton, and Emma. It was in order to look well on this occasion that Emma was so eager to have the new hat, and when told that she might prepare for this promised expedition, as the weather would certainly be good, the pleasure she felt on putting on this dearly purchased ornament, almost deadened her regret for having disobeyed and displeased Mrs. Castlemain.

The place of their destination was Watenlath, or the valley on the top of rocks; a scene as beautiful and sequestered as the warmest fancy can conceive, and beyond the power of the most finished pencil to describe. It was agreed that Mr. Egerton, Mrs. Castlemain, and Emma, should walk thither, and meet the rest of the party there, they having resolved to go on horseback, as to them the vale was well known; but Mr. Egerton and Emma had never seen Watenlath, and its peculiar beauty could best be felt if approached on foot, and by means of one particular pathway.

The party were to dine in the valley, and a pony well-laden with provisions was to follow at a certain hour.

The party from the White Cottage were to go in the carriage as far as Keswick; and at length nine o'clock, the time for setting off, being arrived, Emma, dressed to the very utmost of her wishes, joined Mrs. Castlemain and Mr. Egerton, on the lawn.

"So — you have gotten a new bonnet, I see!" observed the latter; "but I don't think you look so well in it as you did in your old one. Not that the hat is not a pretty hat, and the colour of the riband becoming to you; but you don't look so happy as usual, and your countenance has not that open vivacity which I saw on it when you set off on your walk yesterday. Believe me, my dear girl," added Mr. Egerton, taking the hand of the conscious and blushing Emma, "the best ornament to a young woman is a mind at peace with itself, and a brow unruffled by a frown."

This remark, though well-meant, was perhaps ill-timed. It convinced her that Mrs. Castlemain had told tales; and the resentment of the preceding evening, which had nearly subsided, was again called forth.

Within a mile of Keswick, one of the wheels came off, and obliged them to alight; when on the road, which in places was exceedingly heavy and dirty, (and against which Emma's feet were fortified by a pair of thick shoes which fastened high on the instep, and were buckled on one side by a pair of small but substantial silver buckles, which had belonged to Mrs. Castlemain's grandfather,) the interest of the party was excited, and their course arrested, by the sight of a woman fainting by the side of a hedge, whom a child, seemingly of eight or nine years old, was vainly attempting to recover. But Mrs. Castlemain was more successful in her efforts; and when the poor creature, whose tattered garments bespoke her extreme poverty. recovered her senses, she said that she was a soldier's widow, and was travelling with her child to her parish, which was in Carlisle; but that, being worn down with sorrow, hunger, and fatigue, she had lain down, as she thought, to die on the road.

The woman's countenance bore a strong testimony to the truth of her narration;—and her auditors listened to it with the sincerest compassion. But to pity her distresses was not sufficient; they resolved to alleviate them; and having procured refreshments both for her and her child from a neighbouring cottage, they resolved to walk on briskly to Keswick, and hire a man and cart to convey her to Penrith, where she was to stay a night or two to recruit her exhausted strength. Longer time she said she could not spare, as she had a mother on her death-bed, whom she wished, if possible, to see once more. When she was quite recovered, and was seated comfortably at the cottage-door, awaiting the arrival of the cart, Mrs. Castlemain and Mr. Egerton took out their purses; and both not only relieved her present wants, but gave her money sufficient, as they hoped, to procure her a conveyance as far as Carlisle.

Now then the moment was arrived to fill the generous heart of Emma with sorrow, for the needless extravagance of the preceding evening, and Mrs. Castlemain was amply revenged. For the first time in her life since she had money to bestow, she had it not in her power to add her mite to the bounty of her friend and her relation; who, as soon as they had given the poor woman what they intended, walked forward to escape from her thanks, and hasten the intended conveyance for her; while Emma, sad, mortified, and irresolute, lingered behind, reading, as she fancied, in the sufferer's looks, an expression of wonder that she gave her nothing, and also of expectation and supplication.

"I have no money in my pocket," said Emma, mournfully; "but I will borrow some;" and having overtaken Mr. Egerton, who was behind Mrs. Castlemain, she begged him in a faltering voice, to lend her five shillings.

"I have no silver, my dear," cried he: "ask Mrs. Castlemain." But the latter angrily turned round and said she would not lend her money, as she did not deserve it; adding, "this is a proper punishment for your obstinate folly and extravagance in buying what you did not want last night."

This was only too true; and angry, sorry, abashed yet irritated, Emma ran back to the cottage, and soon, to her great satisfaction, lost sight of her monitors. Immediately she stooped down, took out her old-fashioned silver buckles, drew the twist out which confined her gloves over her dimpled elbows, endeavoured as well as she could to re-fasten her shoes by tyeing them; and then, as much impelled, I fear, by spite as by generosity, she entered the cottage, and telling the woman that she could not give her money, but that those buckles were silver, and would sell for some, she waited neither for an acceptance nor a denial of her gift; but, almost afraid to reflect on what she had done, she ran violently forward to overtake Mr. Egerton and Mrs. Castlemain; not liking, however, to show her tied shoes in the town of Keswick, she called out to tell them they would find her on the lake, and turned off to hasten to the boat in waiting to convey them to the spot whence they were to ascend the mountain; which having entered, she sat silently, sorrowfully, and even fearfully; for she dreaded the discovery of what she had done, and began to wish that she had had more self-government.

At length, Mrs. Castlemain and Mr. Egerton, with the expression of satisfied benevolence on their countenances, arrived at the boat, having procured the promised cart for the poor soldier's widow. But the joy of both of them was soon damped by observing the clouded countenance of Emma, who could with some difficulty contrive to hide her feet under the bench on which she was seated.

At length they landed near the foot of the Lodore waterfall, and began their laborious walk; when to Mr. Egerton's surprise, he not only found that Emma, so remarkable for the agility with which she used to climb mountains, could now with difficulty keep up with her companions, and evidently walked up with uncomfortable effort; but that ever and anon she was stooping down to adjust her shoes.

"This is very strange," thought he, turning round and offering her his assistance, (while Mrs. Castlemain, whom nothing impeded in her progress, was nearly out of sight;) but Emma in so pettish and peremptory a manner rejected his assistance, and turned her back while she stooped, that a suspicion of the truth darted across his mind; and when she again turned round, he saw that his suspicions were just. He said nothing, however, but contented himself with observing Emma, as first one string broke and then another, till at last they were too much broken to be used again; and poor Emma, almost crying with vexation, was forced to proceed with the straps of her shoes hanging loose, and threatening to throw her down every moment. To add to her distress, the road was wet and full of bogs; and at last both her shoes stuck completely fast in the mud, and unable to help herself, she was precipitated forward on her knees,—when a new calamity befell her; for before she could put her hand to her head to prevent it, the new hat was blown off by a sudden gust of wind, and the blue ribands disfigured with mud!

In spite of his love for Emma, his compassionate vexation at her distress, and his self-command,—when Mr. Egerton saw this last accident, and beheld the hat, the cause of all the mischief, on the ground, he could not refrain from a violent fit of laughter; which so irritated the poor prostrate Emma, that, as he stooped to raise her from the ground, she attempted to strike him.

Mr. Egerton, shocked, but instantly recovering himself, said with great calmness, " I shall address you, my dear, in the words of a celebrated Greek general on a similar provocation; I shall say to you, ' Strike, if you please; but hear me!' "

" No, no," exclaimed the sobbing and now subdued Emma; " hear me, hear me! I beg and entreat your pardon. O do, do, Mr. Egerton, forgive me! but I am sure I shall never forgive myself."

" I do forgive you, my dear, and will not say what I meant to say, and I scarcely regret what has passed; because I am sure that to a mind ingenuous and generous as yours is, it will afford an indelible lesson, and one for which you will be the better as long as you live; besides, I am well convinced that your own reproaches are more severe, and will be of more benefit, than any I should have the heart to address to you."

" You are too, too good," replied Emma, almost convulsed with sobs, and leaning her head against his arm.

" But recover yourself, my child," said Mr. Egerton, " and let us see what we can do for you, for you are in a terrible condition—shoes, stockings, petticoats, hat covered with mud!"

" Well, I must bear it patiently," said Emma meekly, " for I deserve it all."

" Good girl!" said Mr. Egerton affectionately; and Emma was able to look up once more. " But, my dear girl," added Mr. Egerton, " let me put you on your guard. You know Mr. Hargrave, and you know that to tease and to torment is one of the great delights of his life; and that I always hold him up as constantly as an example to deter, as I do his nephew as an example to invite. Then you will readily believe that he will make a number of provoking and teasing observations on your draggled appearance; but ' forewarned, forearmed ;' and as you owe some reparation for the pain your conduct has occasioned me, make it, by bearing with temper and calmness the sneers and sarcasms of Mr. Hargrave."

" I will try to obey you, sir," replied Emma; " but indeed I have lost all confidence in myself." Then leaning on the now welcome arm of Mr. Egerton, Emma slowly and with difficulty renewed her walk; but though dirty and fatigued from being scarcely able to lift her feet from the slippery and tenacious ground, her mind was considerably lightened, and she even began to observe the beauty of the richly-wooded rocks, and the flowery and velvet carpet, which, the further they advanced, still more and more kept spreading under their feet; while the sound of the cataract of Lodore, lately so distinctly heard, grew every moment fainter and fainter, and the lake of Keswick became diminished to the eye. Yet so gradual had been the ascent that they had scarcely perceived it, and now could only ascertain its length and height by the effect exhibited to the sight. They now began to approach the expected valley, and beheld with wonder that they were still, though on the top of mountains, surrounded by mountains and rocks, and were eagerly gazing around them, when some of the party whom they expected to join appeared in sight coming to meet them.

" Now, Emma, now your hour of trial begins; and I see by the sneer flickering on Mr. Hargrave's upper lip, and the expression of his fierce projecting eye, that I was right in my forebodings," said Mr. Egerton.

Mrs. Castlemain at this moment was expatiating to Mr. Hargrave on the great progress which Emma had made in the study of Latin, and even of Greek, as Mr. Egerton had readily acceded to her wish of learning those languages, because he wisely considered that it was the ostentatious display of learning in a woman, and not the learning itself, that was to be objected to; and telling Emma that all he required of her was a promise never to quote a Latin saying, or talk of Greek quantities, he tried to make her as good a classical scholar as he did St. Aubyn. And at this moment, as I before stated, this unlucky moment, Mrs. Castlemain was reporting her progress to the cynical Mr. Hargrave, who, as soon as he saw poor Emma with the straps of her shoes hanging down, a draggled frock, and dirty stockings, observed, as many men, ay and many women too, would have observed on a similar occasion—" Yes, madam, I don't doubt but that her progress has been considerable; for, see, she looks very like a learned lady indeed ! There 's a smart figure for you! Pray admire her!"

On hearing this, the eyes of all the company were turned on Emma; and Henry St. Aubyn kindly ran forward to inquire what had happened.

"Bless me! Where are your buckles, Emma!" asked Mrs. Castlemain, half suspecting the true state of the case; and Emma could not answer her.

"O!" said Mr. Hargrave, "I suppose she forgot to put them on; geniuses cannot attend to such trifles, you know!"

"You don't answer my question, Emma," resumed Mrs. Castlemain; "Was Mr. Hargrave's conjecture right?"

"No, madam," answered Emma, sobbing as she did so; while Mr. Egerton preserved a grave silence.

"Come, come, Mrs. Castlemain, don't distress the fair classic," exclaimed Mr. Hargrave; "but let us return to the valley, or we shall not see all its beauties before dinner;" and she, suspecting she had nothing to hear that would give her pleasure, consented to his proposal; while Emma, having begged her young companions to walk on without her, remained behind with Henry St. Aubyn, who declared he would not leave her; and Mr. Egerton, who was better pleased to gaze on the beauties of the surrounding scene alone, than surrounded by loquacious companions, walked slowly on before Emma and Henry, yet was not so far before them but that he heard their conversation.

"Now do tell me, dear Emma," said Henry, "why you have neither riband nor buckles in your shoes;—you who are generally so neat in your dress!"

"Why then, I must tell you," replied Emma, "that as I had no money to give, I gave my buckles to a poor distressed woman whom I saw on the road."

This explanation, so flattering to the generous pity of Emma, if not to her judgment, alarmed Mr. Egerton for the sincerity of his pupil; and he listened anxiously for what was to follow.

"Dear, generous girl!" cried Henry; "so this was the truth; and yet you bore my uncle's taunts in silence! But I will go and tell him."

"No, no, Henry," returned Emma, detaining him; "for, if you knew all, I doubt you would blame rather than praise me."

Here Mr. Egerton breathed freely again.

"Indeed! Well, what is this dreadful all?"

"Why, you must know, Henry, that I yesterday spent my last shilling most foolishly and unnecessarily; therefore, to the joy I believe of my mother and Mr. Egerton, I was punished by having no money to give the poor woman."

"Well, but you gave her your buckles, you know."

"True; but I tried to borrow some money first, and was refused; therefore as much out of spite as charity I gave her my buckles; and now what do you think of me?"

Here Mr. Egerton almost bounded forward with joy.

"Think of you!" replied Henry; "why, even more highly than before, for so nobly disclaiming the praise that was not due to you."

"You are right, quite right, my dear boy," said Mr. Egerton turning round; "ingenuousness like this is a much rarer quality that that of a disposition to relieve distress. I have overheard all that passed, and I own, Emma, I am again proud of my pupil. But be not elated by this well-earned praise; remember, you have still a terrible defect to conquer—a defect of temper; and that on the excellence or badness of temper chiefly depends not only one's own but the happiness of others. But come, let us forget everything now, except the beauties that surround us."

But Emma pointed sorrowfully to her shoes, and declared she must sit down on a piece of rock near them; while Mr. Egerton, producing a piece of strong cord from his pocket, (which from principle he had not produced before,) contrived, though rather awkwardly, to fasten Emma's straps over her feet, and enable her to walk with less effort.

While thus employed, neither of them was conscious of the disappearance of St. Aubyn; but when they looked up again he was out of sight.

"This is very strange!" said Mr. Egerton.

"This is very strange!" echoed Emma.

But the next moment a suspicion of the cause of St. Aubyn's absence came across the mind of both, though neither of them communicated it to the other.

Emma was now sufficiently rested to proceed as fast as her admiration would let her, while Mr. Egerton pointed out to her the picturesque beauties which met her eye as she advanced. They now found themselves on the banks of a clear and rapid river called the Lodore, whose waters fall into the cascade known by that name, which forms one of the great features on the shores of Keswick Lake. The green and velvet banks of this river were bounded on either side, and at no considerable distance, by bare, by wooded, and nearly perpendicular rocks, of which, as Gilpin observes, the particularity consists in their being nearly as much asunder at the bottom as at the top. It was then the hay season, and the unrivalled verdure of the scene was beautifully contrasted with the golden haycocks that were reared almost profusely around; while in places the dark green alder, and the mountain ash then decorated with its brightest berries, met across the stream, and united their well-assorted branches. At some distance a small lake was discoverable, on whose shores were scattered a few white cottages.

Near the lake, and on the point of entering a boat, Mr. Egerton and Emma now discovered their whole party, and amongst them Mrs. St. Aubyn, who was endeavouring, though evidently she was angrily repulsed by her brother, to assist him in getting ready his fishing-tackle, as the lake contained excellent trout.

On not seeing St. Aubyn with the companions with whom he had left him, Mr. Hargrave angrily desired to know what was become of his nephew, that he was not there to assist him with his fishing-tackle, which was entangled.

Mr. Egerton coldly replied, that he knew nothing of Mr. St. Aubyn;—but that he doubted not, when he returned, he would be able to account for his absence in a satisfactory manner.

"Oh, that I am sure he will," said Mrs. St. Aubyn; then seeing a frown gather on her tyrant brother's brow, she exclaimed, glad to turn the conversation, " Dear me, what a pity ! Why, the ribands on the beautiful hat of Miss Castlemain are covered with dirt ! Still, young ladies, pray look, is it not very becoming ? She would not have bought it if I had not persuaded her, and told her that I had heard it observed how becoming *blue* was to her."

"So, Mrs. St. Aubyn !" said Mr. Hargrave with a provoking sneer; "you are not content with being a coxcomb yourself, but you must endeavour to make one of a mere child !"

"Dear me, brother, you are so——," but her declaration of *what* he was, was stopped on her lips by a frown so terrible, that the poor woman almost trembled with apprehension; while Mr. Egerton was not sorry to find that Emma's obstinate extravagance was occasioned as much by the folly of another as by her own. But still St. Aubyn came not; and his uncle was so discontented at his absence, that nothing pleased him; nobody could steer a boat so well as Henry, he declared, as he was not there to steer it; for had he been there, his excellence would not have been allowed; and after rowing about the lake some little time, stopping occasionally to let Mr. Hargrave endeavour to angle, in order, if possible, to get him into good humour, the party returned to shore; and soon after, his cheek crimsoned with heat and exercise, and bearing a bundle under his arm, St. Aubyn appeared.

"I thought so," cried Emma, running forward with artless delight to meet him, and hanging affectionately on his arm, while he told her the bundle contained clean stockings, shoes, petticoat, and frock for her.

"So !" cried Mr. Hargrave, " it was well worth while, was it not ? for you to go and heat yourself into a fever in order to make a little girl clean, who, I dare say, does not care whether she be clean or dirty !"

"But I *do* care very much, sir," said Emma; "and I am sure I am so obliged to Henry——"

"It is more than I am," muttered his uncle; " but I am always to be last served."

"Nay, I am sure, brother," observed Mrs. St. Aubyn, " Henry is always ready to wait on you; and it was only his good nature that led him to ——, for I am sure Henry is the sweetest and most obliging temper !"

"That he is," exclaimed Mrs. Castlemain, giving Henry her hand; " and this is a proof of it." And so said all the young ladies, and Mr. Egerton too.

This praise of his now well-grown nephew, and for a quality which Mr. Hargrave was conscious that he did not himself possess, either in reality or reputation, was more than he could bear, as he had already begun to be so jealous of his nephew's virtues, and the general love which they excited, that he felt a sort of malevolent consolation in the knowledge of his complete dependence on him, and on his will.

"Come, let us have no more of your flattery, if you please," he angrily exclaimed ; " the boy is a good boy enough, but no such paragon as you represent him to be."

St. Aubyn, more gratified by the praise he had received than wounded by his uncle's ungraciousness, now attempted to turn the discourse by following Emma, who was going into an adjacent cottage to change her dress ; and producing a paper he said, " Here, dear Emma, here is some blue riband to supply the place of that dirty one ;—pray accept it as a present from me."—And while Emma with a sparkling eye and dimpled cheek received this new proof of Henry's kindness, Mr. Hargrave, who had overheard him, observed with a look of more than common malice,

" I am glad, Mr. St. Aubyn, to find you are *rich* enough to make *presents.*"

"This is a present," said Mr. Egerton eagerly, " which *I* must beg leave to make my young pupil,—and not Mr. St. Aubyn ; as I know that, if the riband be *my* gift, it will recall to her mind some events of this day, from the recollection of which I trust she will never cease to derive improvement."

"I dare not dispute this matter with you," replied Henry timidly, " as your right is so much beyond mine; but, dear sir," said he in a whisper, " do tell her that what I have done was meant as a reward for her *ingenuousness.*"

In a short time after, and before the beauty of the scene and the pleasant tone of spirits which it inspired had begun to pall upon the feelings, and to allow any sensation of hunger to prevail amongst the party, Mr. Hargrave proposed having dinner; and as he was generally conscious of being the richest individual in company, (an advantage of which he was very proud,) his proposals were usually uttered in the tone of commands.—Mrs. Castlemain, indeed, had some right to oppose his will; but she was on this occasion willing to accede to it, in hopes that he might eat himself into good humour; dinner therefore was served up as soon as ever Mr. Hargrave expressed his wishes on the subject.

But the angry particles of a bad temper, when once they have begun to effervesce, do not soon subside again. Mr. Hargrave was still dissatisfied; the meat-pie was too salt, the fruit-pie too sweet, the potted char wanted seasoning, and the home-brewed ale wanted strength. Every word from his poor dependent sister called forth from him an expression of insulting contempt; while his nephew, whom he could not even pretend to despise, was treated by him with sullen disregard.

"He is nothing but an old baby," whispered Emma to Mr. Egerton.

"True," replied Mr. Egerton; "but remember that all this disgusting conduct is the effect of *temper;* and be warned by his example!"

At this moment Mr. Hargrave asked Emma to help him to some tart which stood near her; and in her haste to comply with his request,— a haste perhaps occasioned by her consciousness of having just spoken of him in a degrading manner,—she unfortunately spilt some of the juice on the table-cloth, which happened to be his; and this trifling accident irritated him so much that he exclaimed,

"Pshaw! I might have known better than to have employed you to help me, as geniuses are above knowing how to do common things."

Henry blushed with indignation at this coarse speech, and Mr. Egerton looked ready to resent it; but Emma meekly replied,

"I am very sorry for my awkwardness, sir, as I wish to do every thing well. I am certainly a bad carver, but I will try to become a good one."

Mr. Egerton and Henry looked at each other with an expression of mutual satisfaction while she said this; and Mrs. Castlemain, looking proudly around her, exclaimed,

"You are a good girl, Emma, for you can return good for evil, and that is better than being a good scholar, as you certainly are."

"But is she a good workwoman? and can she make a pudding or a pie?" cried the implacable Mr. Hargrave.

"No, sir; but I can learn—"

"Can learn!—But will you? would you not think such things beneath you?"

"I am sure, sir," cried Henry eagerly, "Miss Castlemain has too much good sense to think it beneath her to be useful."

"I did not speak to you, you puppy," replied Mr. Hargrave; "What says Miss Castlemain herself?"

"That time will discover how justly Henry St. Aubyn answered for me." And Mr. Hargrave, pleased at the trimming which, as he boasted afterwards, he had given these uncommon folks, was tolerably good-humoured the rest of the day. Nor was this change lost upon the rest of the party; for it had an agreeable effect on their spirits. So paralyzing is the influence that one splenetic, sullen, and unamiable person in company has on that company!

Mr. Hargrave, now deigning to be agreeable, offered Mrs. Castlemain his arm, and even complimented her on *wearing well;* while Mr. Egerton offered his to the now loquacious and simpering Mrs. St. Aubyn, who, no longer awed by the dark and frowning brow of her brother, began to play off all the artillery of her airs and graces on the unconscious Mr. Egerton.

Little indeed did he think that even the vanity of Mrs. St. Aubyn could have imagined his affection for his amiable pupil Henry was at all increased by admiration of his mother;— yet such was this weak woman's belief;— and while with the common care and attention of a gentleman he handed her over broken pieces of rock, or little rivulets difficult to cross, which ever and anon obstructed their path, she fancied his supporting grasp was one of overflowing tenderness; and if he sighed, she sighed audibly in return.

"What a countenance that young man has!" cried Mr. Egerton, as Henry bounded past, and smiled on them as he went.

"He has indeed," simpered Mrs. St. Aubyn; adding, with affected and hesitating timidity, "Do you see any *likeness?* Some people say that———"

"A likeness! O yes, I do *indeed,* madam," replied Mr. Egerton in a faltering voice, "I do *indeed* see his likeness to one very dear to me;"— for he concluded she alluded to her husband's cousin, Clara Ainslie, whose image was always present to his mind, and whose name he thought Mrs. St. Aubyn from delicacy forbore to mention.

"Do *you* not see the likeness yourself, dear madam?" asked he, pressing her arm gently as he spoke.

"Why—yes," replied the lady, "I believe I do; but I must be a bad judge you know———"

"You are too modest," rejoined Mr. Egerton, again pressing her arm kindly, and hoping she would gently hint some praise of his regretted love; but Mrs. St. Aubyn only pressed his arm in return, and he felt the action to be an expression of her sympathy in his affliction and sorrows; which being recalled to his mind by this supposed allusion of Mrs. St. Aubyn's, he fell into a melancholy reverie, mistaken by his companion for a tender one, with her for its object. But at length, tired of his long and unnecessary silence, she ventured to express to him how happy she esteemed her son in having found in him such a friend and preceptor, nay even a *father,* as it were.

"A father!" cried Mr. Egerton enthusiastically, and suddenly starting from his reverie; "you say well, madam; I hope I shall one day or other prove a father to him!"

"Dear me!" said Mrs. St. Aubyn, affectedly disengaging her arm from Mr. Egerton's, for she thought this speech amounted to little less than an offer of his hand. But Mr. Egerton, wrapt in his own thoughts, heard not her exclamation, neither was he conscious of the delicate scruple which unlocked her arm from his, nor of the action itself;—and seeing Emma before him evidently waiting for his approach, he walked hastily forward; then taking her under his arm, he left Mrs. St. Aubyn to walk alone,—but at the same time to hope also; as she attributed his abrupt departure from her to the fear of having disclosed too much of his intentions on so short an acquaintance; and she earnestly wished she had let her arm remain where it was. But she had no opportunity of regaining the station which she had lost; for when the party, who all walked home, reached the town of Keswick, they separated and went to their respective homes; and as Mr. Egerton before he entered Mrs. Castlemain's carriage which met them at Keswick, bowed low to Mrs. St. Aubyn without looking her in the face, the tenderness which she had thrown into her last look was wholly thrown away; but she mused for hours after on her prospect of becoming the wife of Mr. Egerton, and had in fancy made him exchange his greyish unpowdered locks for an auburn Brutus.

Meanwhile Mr. Egerton, wholly unsuspicious of his power and of the dangerous hopes which his words and attentions had excited, was, together with Mrs. Castlemain, conversing with Emma on the errors which she had committed in the beginning of the day, and the virtues with which she had made amends for that error; while Emma, penitent yet pleased, and smiling through her tears, promised to turn the events of that day to profit the most unfailing.

The next day Henry, being obliged to go to Penrith on business for his uncle, did not attend at the usual hour for lessons; and Mr. Egerton, observing that Emma was very absent, desired to know the reason. On which she confessed that she thought herself pledged to learn those branches of housewifery which Mr. Hargrave had reproached her for not knowing.

"I have no objection," said Mr. Egerton, smiling, " to your close initiation into all the mysteries of the kitchen and the pantry, provided the motives for learning them be good ones; — but if your only motive be a wish to triumph over a splenetic old man, I object to it; for then it would be only *your* temper taking its revenge on *his*."

"I own," replied Emma, blushing, " that I *should* like to prove to him that the fair classic can be useful; but I do assure you that I had a painful feeling of *shame* during Mr. Hargrave's coarse speech, from the consciousness how little I knew of what I have often heard that all women should know; therefore for my own sake, I wish to learn all a woman's learning."

"And so you shall," replied Mr. Egerton, " as it is for your own gratification; for if you wished for it on any other account, you would be terribly disappointed. Men, and women too, scarcely, if ever, part with certain prejudices; and in spite of the evidence of their eyes, if they once find out that you have learning and talents, they will still taunt you with the reproach of being a slattern, and ignorant of every thing which it is necessary and becoming for women to learn. And yet, though in trifles like these prejudice is so difficult to be eradicated, we sit and wonder at the slow progress we make in eradicating prejudices of a more important and pernicious tendency."

"And is the world so full of prejudice then!" asked Emma, sorrowfully.

"More than you can imagine," replied Mr. Egerton; " but still in some respects mercy and justice have triumphed over it."

Here they were most unexpectedly and painfully interrupted; and Emma felt, in its full force, how true it is, that when once we have committed a fault, however trifling, it is impossible to calculate what may be the mischievous consequences of that single error.

Mrs. Castlemain ran into the room, an open letter in her hand, and exclaimed, " There, Miss Castlemain! see the effect of your preposterous generosities! There, read and tremble."

Emma did read, and did tremble; for the letter was an official letter from Penrith, stating that a poor woman had offered a pair of silver buckles for sale there, on the inside of which was engraved the name of Bellenden; and that, on being asked how she came by them, she had said that a young lady who had no money in her pocket had given her the buckles out of her shoes; and that this story had appeared so improbable, that the silversmith concluded she had either taken the buckles from the young lady's person by violence, or had stolen them in some other way; and had therefore carried the woman before a magistrate; who having on inquiry found out that Mrs. Castlemain of the White Cottage had hired the cart in which she came to Penrith, had committed her till further information could be procured from Mrs. Castlemain herself; and she was requested to send such information directly.

It would be impossible for me to describe the clamorous grief of Emma on this unexpected consequence of her foolish conduct; or her frantic eagerness to set off immediately to the relief of the poor woman, whom she had not only been the means of exposing to the disgrace of being committed as a felon, but who might probably be prevented by the delay from reaching Carlisle time enough to see her mother before she died. But Mrs. Castlemain and Mr. Egerton were just as eager to go as Emma herself was; and soon, as fast as four horses could carry them, they were on the road to Penrith. In the meanwhile the story of the poor woman's commitment and its cause was told to Henry St. Aubyn and his mother, who had accompanied him to Penrith that morning; and he, filled with pity for the prisoner, and grief for what Emma would feel on the occasion, ran immediately to the magistrate who was then sitting in court, to tell all he knew on the subject, and exculpate the poor woman. But unfortunately Mrs. St. Aubyn went with him; and while Henry was telling his story to the magistrates, she was relating the same at the door of the hall to the crowd that was collected; while, pleased to be listened to, and as she thought admired, she dwelt with raptures on the noble generosity of Emma; describing her as an angel not only in mind but person, till she worked up her audience to such a pitch of enthusiastic admiration of Emma, and of pity for the woman who had been so unjustly confined, that they huzzaed Mrs. St. Aubyn, and declared they would huzza Emma as soon as she arrived.

Mrs. St. Aubyn was so delighted at this homage paid to her eloquence, that she went on haranguing, flattering herself all the time that she should be exalted by it in the opinion of Mr. Egerton, and that he would feel the greatest gratitude towards her, as having been the means of his pupil's receiving so public a tribute to her virtue; and she was waving her white hand gracefully in the air, and expatiating on the duty and charm of charity to the poor, when the party from the White Cottage stopped at the hall, and beheld the delighted Mrs. St. Aubyn.

"I wonder what that fool is about!" said Mr. Egerton in no kind tone of voice; for he had taken alarm at seeing Mrs. St. Aubyn directing the attention of the crowd to the carriage; and his brow assumed a frown almost terrific, when, as soon as he lifted out the trembling Emma, the crowd greeted her with three loud huzzas; while the self-satisfied simper, nods, and glistening eyes of Mrs. St. Aubyn explained at once the cause and the effect.

"O that grinning idiot!" muttered Mr. Egerton, as he hurried the confused Mrs. Castlemain and the weeping Emma through the crowd; while the latter, seeing instead of the angelic beauty whom Mrs. St. Aubyn's description had led them to expect, a pale girl with blubbered eyes and discoloured cheeks, could not help muttering, "Well, I see no beauty in her, howsomever."

"But handsome is that handsome does," said one; and "That is the good young lady that gave her buckles to the poor woman out of her own shoes," was whispered on every side; while poor Emma wanted to stop and assure them that she did not deserve the good character they gave her.

"My dear girl," said Mr. Egerton, "you must bear in silence this new but severe punishment to an ingenuous mind like yours, that of being praised undeservedly."

Henry St. Aubyn had but just finished his story when the party arrived in the court, where Emma was again received as an object of curiosity and admiration; but she had not long to undergo the pain of interrogatories and praises. The poor woman was soon discharged, and she was made ample amends for the disgrace, delay, and terror she had undergone, by a promise from Mrs. Castlemain to send her in a light open chaise to the end of her journey.

Henry St. Aubyn undertook to procure this chaise, and see the soldier's widow comfortably settled in it; and as soon as the money necessary to defray expenses had been deposited by Mrs. Castlemain, they hastened from the court, the self-judged Emma being eager to hide her confusion in the carriage. Accordingly they passed so rapidly along to it, their speed being hastened by a renewal of the shouts, that Mrs. St. Aubyn, who was still waiting at the door, and had been too much elated with the attention she excited there to follow her friends into the court, had not even an opportunity of speaking to them, which for two reasons she earnestly desired; the first was, that she might show her intimacy with the lady who arrived in a carriage-and-four; and the second was, her wish to borrow money of one of the party to give the lower order of the crowd which she had collected round her, some of whom had seemed to hope her ladyship would give them something to drink her health, and had certainly lost a little of their respect for her when she declared she had (as was usually the case with her) no money in her pocket. "But," added she, mortified to observe the almost contemptuous expression of countenance which her avowal called forth, "I can borrow some of my friends when they come out."

But this was rendered impossible by the celerity with which they passed her and drove off. However, she knew she could procure some from her son, "the best of sons," who would soon appear.

Meanwhile, as it was market-day, the surrounding crowd was increased by several farmers whom curiosity had led to the spot, and whom the love of fun kept there when they heard all that had been communicated by the loquacious Mrs. St. Aubyn; who, while she went on to dwell on her son's great kindness in hastening to relieve the poor woman before the parties concerned arrived, applauded by clapping of hands, and sometimes cried "*Angcor*" in a manner so evidently intended to ridicule her, that she began to feel the impropriety of her situation, and resolved to go in search of St. Aubyn, who had been detained by an unexpected circumstance. While he was endeavouring in the sword-room to hire a chaise of a person present; an attorney, who was always on the watch for jobs of the sort, took the poor woman aside, and informed her that an action would lie against the silversmith for false imprisonment, which St. Aubyn overhearing, he eagerly interfered to prevent a proceeding which was, he thought, both unnecessary and unjust. Nor did the sufferer, worn down as she was with sickness as well as sorrow, feel any inclination to revenge herself, especially when the silversmith, in order to make her some compensation for the distress which his ideas of duty had occasioned her, came forward and offered to send her in his own chaise to Carlisle free of all expense; and begged that the money deposited by Mrs. Castlemain, should be given to her for other uses. To this proposal St. Aubyn gladly acceded, and the lawyer had the mortification of losing his job, and of seeing those whom he hoped to make enemies, part as friends. At length St. Aubyn appeared, and as soon as his mother saw him, she joyfully exclaimed, "There he is! there is my son!" On which one of the group archly cried, "Come then, let us huzza *the best of sons!*" and St. Aubyn, to his infinite confusion and surprise, was greeted by loud huzzas.

"What is the reason of this?" said he to his mother, and looking fiercely round on the mob.

"Oh, nothing, nothing," replied she, at that moment seeing to her great relief the horse and chaise come to the door, in which they were to return home; "only do lend me five shillings, that's all;" and with a deep sigh Henry obeyed her, and entered the chaise, into which she immediately followed, throwing the money amidst the crowd as she did so. This action immediately gave rise to such violent, repeated, and loud acclamations from the populace, that the horse took fright and ran with alarming violence through the town and along the road, till he overtook Mrs. Castlemain's carriage, which he passed, and soon after, by a sudden and unexpected shock, St. Aubyn and his mother were thrown out, and the gig nearly broken to pieces.

In an instant Mr. Egerton, followed by Mrs. Castlemain and Emma, who were scarcely able to support themselves from terror, hastened to the spot, and were greatly relieved by seeing St. Aubyn unhurt running to raise his terrified and nearly fainting mother.

"Lean on me, my dear madam," cried Mr. Egerton, seeing St. Aubyn too much alarmed to be of much use; and Mrs. St. Aubyn, who even then was sufficiently alive to certain impressions to be aware of the affectionate anxiety with which Mr. Egerton spoke, threw herself on his arm, and leaned against his shoulder with such prompt and energetic obedience, that his fears subsided, and he was well convinced that by the aid of Mrs. Castlemain's salts she would soon be herself again. Nor was he mistaken; after a little hysterical laughing and crying, Mrs. St. Aubyn resigned the support of Mr. Egerton, and, relinquishing the cold and trembling hand of her still terrified son, began to set her dress to rights, and to replace the *flaxen* ringlets, that had wandered from her forehead to her ear.

"But where's my bonnet?" she exclaimed. And when it was brought to her, covered with dirt and completely spoiled, "I am glad of this," said she, as she surveyed its discoloured beauties; "I have *now* a good excuse to get a new one; and I shall get one like yours, my dear," she added, addressing Emma; while St. Aubyn, deeply blushing, turned away.

"But what is to be done with this broken whiskey?" asked Mr. Egerton. "We can take Mrs. St. Aubyn in the carriage with us; and as the horse will soon be caught and brought back, Henry can ride it home. The chaise is then our only difficulty."

"I must get it taken back to Penrith," replied St. Aubyn, "and cause it to be mended as fast as possible, or my uncle will never forgive me."

"Bless me!" cried Mrs. St. Aubyn, "and must I go home without you, Henry? I am sure I dare not face my brother unsupported and alone. He will be so angry about his ugly old chaise."

"O we will go with you," said Mrs. Castlemain; "and perhaps our presence will be some restraint on him." And Henry and his mother being both relieved by this promise, the former went to a neighbouring farm-house in search of assistance to remove the broken carriage, and the latter took her seat in the chariot of Mrs. Castlemain.

An uncomfortable silence took place during the ride to Vale-House, rarely broken in upon even by the loquacious Mrs. St. Aubyn, as the dread of her brother's anger was the feeling continually uppermost, and the rest of the party had not as yet recovered the terror which they had experienced from the accident of the overturn. But at length, Mr. Egerton begged to know what had frightened the horse.

"O, the people's shouting."

"And why did they shout?"

"Why, the first time they shouted because they saw Henry, and were pleased with him on account of his kindness in going to try to exculpate the poor woman."

"But how came they to know that he had been so kind?"

"Because——because I told them."

"And how did they know him when they saw him?"

"Because I said it was he; and my son, the best of sons; so then they huzzaed him."

"But you have not yet explained why they shouted so as to frighten the horses?"

"O that was because I gave them five shillings."

"So then," replied Mr. Egerton, "they were resolved you should have your money's worth of huzzas. And now, madam, be so good as to tell me why we were greeted in the same noisy way; was that owing to you too?"

"It was," said Mrs. St. Aubyn, drawing up her head and smiling with satisfaction as she informed Mr. Egerton of the obligation which his pupil owed her; while she proceeded to tell him how lavish she had been in the praise of the abashed and humble Emma.

"And you said all this?" they all three asked at once; and Mrs. St. Aubyn, convinced they were filled with gratitude and delight, answered, "Yes, and a great deal more," with such a simple, confiding, and self-admiring expression on her distended mouth, that, even more amused by her folly than angry at its disagreeable consequences, Mr. Egerton gave way to a violent burst of laughter, in which he was joined by Emma and Mrs. Castlemain.

Mrs. St. Aubyn gazed on them with wonder. Instead of thanks, to be repaid with laughter!—but she was too good-humoured to resent it; and in a few moments she laughed as much as they did, though why she did not exactly know. They gave no explanation, and Mrs. St. Aubyn did not demand one; but conceiving the business of the shouting to be a better joke than she had fancied it, she felt satisfied that all was as it should be, and was convinced that Mr. Egerton's pride was gratified by what had happened, though he was too politic to acknowledge it.

But the white chimneys of the Vale-House now began to appear in sight; and Mr. Egerton, who wished Mr. Hargrave to remain ignorant if possible of their journey to Penrith and its disagreeable cause, proposed that they should dismiss the carriage, as it was drawn by four horses, and walk the rest of the way; a plan highly approved of by Mrs. St. Aubyn, as she hoped by that means to enter the house unobserved, and change her dirty and disordered dress before she was seen by Mr. Hargrave. Accordingly they alighted, and walked to the house, which they entered by a back door; but not unperceived by Mr. Hargrave, who, being in an adjoining parlour, called his trembling sister, who was therefore forced to appear before him, leaning for support on Mr. Egerton, he having engaged to explain the cause of her strange appearance, and of the absence of Henry.

"Heyday! whom have we here?" cried Mr. Hargrave. "I did not expect so much good company. And why this extraordinary humility of coming in at the back door? Well, where is Henry?—What! not a word? And you all look as glum as if you had just come from a funeral."

"We were very near being present at a death," replied Mr. Egerton gravely.

"A death! What do you mean? No accident to Henry, I hope?"

"No, thank God! no serious accident."

"Nor to me neither, as it happened," returned Mrs. St. Aubyn.

"As it happened!—Ah! and now I look again, your wig is on one side, old girl, and you have lost some of your bloom. And, why, 'sdeath! you have been in the *mire*, madam!"

"I have indeed, I have been *overturned*."

"Overturned!—No harm come to my horse and gig, I hope?"

Here Mrs. St. Aubyn, afraid to answer "Yes," thought it best to give way to a gentle hysteric; she had known such an expedient succeed with her husband, and she had a mind to try it on her brother. But scarcely had she begun to raise a few notes, when Mr. Hargrave rang the bell and ordered in a pail of water.

"Good heavens! what for?" cried Mrs. Castlemain.

"For my sister," he coolly replied; "to souse her,—that 's all."

And while Mr. Egerton turned round indignantly to reprove him for his brutality, he saw to his infinite surprise that Mrs. St. Aubyn was quite recovered.

"There!" said Mr. Hargrave exultingly, "now am I not a good physician?—I have known St. Aubyn on such occasions send for a surgeon, and wine, and brandy, and hartshorn, and the deuce knows what, and almost go into a responsive and sympathetic hysteric himself;—while madam kicked and squalled very much at her ease.—But I, you see, had no sooner—"

Here he paused; for real tears, the tears of wounded sensibility, now coursed each other down his poor sister's cheek, as she recollected the tenderness of her husband, and contrasted it with the coarseness of her brother;—while she indignantly exclaimed,

"It is cruel in you to remind me of that fond indulgence which I have lost for ever, and which the behaviour I now experience serves to endear to me every day more and more."

"Humph! well put, that," replied Mr. Hargrave; "and I like to see you cry for St. Aubyn, for he deserved it from you; though he was a confounded proud fellow, and I hate pride.—But come, now let us hear about the accident; are my horse and gig safe? I ask you."

"Your horse is, I hope;—but your gig—"

"Is broken to pieces, I suppose?"

"Not quite."

"Not quite!! 'sdeath! I had rather—but how did it happen?"

"The horse ran away," said Mr. Egerton, "and threw your nephew and sister out, and broke the chaise, which Mr. St. Aubyn has taken to be mended!"

"The horse ran away! That must have been the fault of the driver; for he is as gentle as a lamb, and not given to such freaks."

"Indeed it was no fault of Henry's," said Mrs. St. Aubyn; "but the people at Penrith *shouted* so loud that they frightened the horse."

"And what did they shout for, pray?"

"Why, for *us*."

"For you! What the deuce could they shout for at the sight of a fantastical old woman, and a tall gawky boy?"

"Well, they shouted for others besides us."

"So," thought Mr. Egerton, "all will out!"

"They shouted when they saw Miss Castlemain too."

"Amazing!" cried Mr. Hargrave; "Why, what ails the people of Penrith? — are they going mad? or are old women and pretty girls so rare at Penrith, that the sight of them turns their heads? — Do, Mrs. Castlemain, or Mr. Egerton, explain this business; for the fair classic looks sulky, and so does my sister."

Mr. Egerton immediately, as succinctly as possible, related what had passed; but could scarcely go on in his story uninterrupted by Mr. Hargrave, who was impatient to give a loud vent to the suppressed bursts of laughter which evidently shook his frame. When he had concluded, Mr. Hargrave put a restraint on his inclinations no longer; but gave way to so loud and hearty a laugh, that even the mortified Emma could not help joining in it. But her inclination to laughter soon ceased, when Mr. Hargrave recovering his speech exclaimed,

"This is glorious fun. It is a great consolation to poor ignoramuses like myself to see these uncommon folks getting themselves into such ridiculous scrapes! Oh! ho! ho! ho! I protest I don't think it would have entered into the head of any one, but a little Miss who learns Greek and Latin, to give away her buckles out of her shoes, in a fit of unnecessary generosity, and bear to go about like a slattern the whole day after! Oh! ho! ho! I shall burst my sides! I think I see you, Miss Emma, with your straps hanging down, and your draggled petticoats! But what did that signify? You had done something out of the common road, and that was enough for you, you know!"

Mr. Egerton, who felt deeply this coarse and unmerited attack on his pupil, was so angry he dared not trust himself to speak; but Mrs. Castlemain was beginning a—

"Let me tell you, Mr. Hargrave," when he interrupted her with,

"Stop, madam, I have not done yet.—Tell me, my pretty classic, were you not much elated when those fools at Penrith applauded you for what you had done? I dare say your little heart beat high with exultation and conceit, ha!"

Mr. Egerton was going to answer for her, dreading that Emma would make an angry reply, as he had marked the varying colour of her cheek, and the quick heaving of her bosom; —but she spoke before he was aware of it, and in a voice so gentle, that his alarm subsided.

"No, indeed, sir," she mildly replied; "for I did not add to the folly of giving away my buckles that of valuing myself on what I had done;—on the contrary, sir, my conscience told me that my fatal present was given more from ill-humour and spite than generosity; and the moments which you fancy I thought so flattering, were to me the most humiliating that I ever experienced."

"There, sir!" cried Mrs. Castlemain, in a tone of triumph.

"Heyday! what is all this? what new stage-effect have we here?"

"No stage-effect, nor attempt at it," said Mr. Egerton; "but a plain matter-of-fact, as I will condescend to convince you; though you hardly deserve that I should do so. But no, Emma shall tell her own story."—And thus encouraged, the blushing girl gave a circumstantial account of her extravagance and all its consequences, and blamed herself so unaffectedly, where Mr. Hargrave had fancied her valuing herself on her nobleness of feeling, that even he, though mortified to find he had not been able to mortify Emma, allowed she was a very good and well-disposed girl;—but he was afraid they would *educate* her into a pedant in petticoats.

It was now near Mr. H.'s dinner-time, and his guests rose to depart; but he would not allow it, and insisted so violently on their staying to partake of his family meal, that they at length consented, especially as they were anxious to await the return of Henry St. Aubyn, and be convinced that he had not at all suffered from his accident. Their compliance put Mr. Hargrave into great good-humour; still he could not entirely forget the destruction of his chaise; and he declared that Henry was a lad to be trusted alone anywhere; but that, if his ridiculous mother went with him, he was always led by her into some scrape or another.

"I am very certain," observed Mr. Egerton, "that Henry would not feel obliged to you for this compliment to him, at the expense of his mother."

"No, to be sure," answered Mr. Hargrave; "I know he is your pious Æneas;—or rather, I dare say you think pious Æneas was bloody Nero to Henry St. Aubyn.—— But, huzza! here he is! here is pious Æneas at last, and my chaise too, I declare! But I vow Henry shall pay for the mending!"

By this time the wine which Mr. Hargrave had drunk had made him more than usually kind. He therefore received Henry most graciously; declared he was an honest fellow, and he was very glad he had not broken his neck as well as the chaise. Then filling up a bumper, he desired him to drink it off to Madam Castlemain's health, and wish her another husband, and soon, (winking his eye as he spoke, at Mr. Egerton;)—then he chuckled his sister under the chin, by the title of old mother St. Aubyn; and telling Emma she was a beauty, and he should come a courting to her soon, he gave her so loud a kiss, that St. Aubyn started from his seat with a feeling of pain, which he would as yet have found it difficult to define even to himself.

When the company separated, an early day was fixed for their meeting again, at the house of Mrs. Castlemain; and Emma anticipated the arrival of that day, with more pleasure than she had ever before felt, when expecting to be in company with the dreaded Mr. Hargrave. But an attack of the gout deferred that gentleman's visit even some weeks longer.

At length, however, Mr. Hargrave's malady left him, and he was able to pay his long-promised visit to Mrs. Castlemain; and Mr. Egerton was not a little amused to observe that Emma was an interested partaker in the preparations making for Mr. Hargrave's reception.

"You take such pains to please this odd-tempered man," said he laughing, "that one might suppose you were in love with him!"

"Indeed," replied Emma with great simplicity, "I don't even like him; still I had rather please than displease him; for he is Henry's uncle, you know."

Mr. Egerton smiled again, but turned away as he did so, conscious that his smile had now assumed an arch expression, which he would not have liked to explain to her who called it forth.

At the appointed hour Mr. Hargrave, his sister, and Henry arrived, and the former in good humour. But when Emma helped him to some fruit-pie, and did it without spilling any of the juice, he observed that she took better care of Mrs. Castlemain's table-cloths than she did of other people's.

"Let me tell you, sir," said Mrs. Castlemain, "that you are very ungrateful to Emma, considering the pains which she has taken to please you. The custard which you are now eating and commending, was made by her; and you reward her by reverting to past grievances."

"He! what!" replied Mr. Hargrave; "Why, how should I know this? How should I suspect that the young genius had so condescended!—Here, give us your hand, my girl; and believe me, this pretty hand will look prettier covered with the remains of paste and pie-crust, than daubed with ink from writing Latin themes, or scribbling verses."

"Every thing in its season, Mr. Hargrave," replied Mrs. Castlemain, piqued at his ungraciousness; but she hoped that the present which Emma had in store for him would make him repent, and perhaps amend his harshness; and in a low voice she desired her to bring down her work.

Emma obeyed. Then timidly approaching Mr. Hargrave, she begged his acceptance of a silk handkerchief to replace one which he had mentioned having lost.

"He! what!—What have we here?" said he; "and whose work is this? and why is it given to me?"

"It is Emma's work; she both made and marked it; and now she begs you will reward her for her trouble by accepting and wearing it."

"Nay, madam," returned Mr. Hargrave, "I am not much obliged to her, I believe. Come hither, girl; and so you did all this to prove to me that I was an old fool, and to give me the lie, did you?"

(Here Henry with indignant emotion started from his seat.)

"No, sir," answered Emma, her eyes filling with tears as she spoke; "I did it merely to gain your good opinion and my own; as I agree with you in thinking that a woman should learn every thing that is useful."

Even Mr. Hargrave was not proof against this meek and modest reply; and catching her in his arms, he swore she was the best little girl in the world. "But," added he, as if afraid of being too amiable, "I shall never dare to use my handkerchief; but I shall lay it up in lavender, and show it as a wonder—Neat work by a learned young lady."

Mrs. Castlemain, Mr. Egerton, and Henry looked their indignation at this ungracious and sarcastic courtesy; but Emma, as if she did not feel the bitterness of it, replied, "Pray, sir, do not do that; for when it is worn out I should be very happy to make you another."

Mr. Hargrave looked at her a moment in silence; then said, taking her hand and kissing it respectfully, "You have conquered, young lady; and I will never call you learned again." While Emma, venturing to raise her eyes to those of Mr. Egerton and Henry, read in them such lively approbation of her forbearance as amply rewarded her for her efforts to obtain it, and flattered her much more than Mrs. St. Aubyn's repeated assurances, that to be sure she was the sweetest temper in the world.

In the evening Mr. Hargrave and Mrs. Castlemain played chess, and unfortunately the latter was the conqueror,—a circumstance which was particularly galling to the former, because he had an avowed contempt for the talents of women, and piqued himself on his skill as a chess-player; and secretly displeased as he had before been, and as Mr. Egerton suspected he would be, by Emma's triumph, his ill-temper became ungovernable; and on his poor dependent sister's coming near him, he vented some of his spleen on her by desiring her, with an oath, to get out of the way, and accompanying what he said with a push violent enough to send her almost on her face to the other end of the room.

Soon after, on Mrs. Castlemain's venturing to contradict him, he was so gross in his abuse of her that she replied in no very gentle manner. The consequence was, that they parted immediately, resolving never, on any terms, to meet again. Vain were Mrs. St. Aubyn's tears, and Mr. Egerton's remonstrances. Mr. Hargrave persisted in leaving the house, and Mrs. Castlemain in approving his departure; and meeting Henry at the gate, returning with Emma from a walk in an adjacent valley, he seized his arm, and exclaimed, "Come along, you puppy! and mark me, I do not choose you should be inveigled by any artful old woman, or her base-born brats; so come home, and never presume to enter these doors again."

"What has happened? for mercy's sake, tell me what has happened?" cried Henry; while Emma ran into the house; repeating his "Come away, I tell you!" Henry had only time to say, "Good night, my dear Emma, and I will try to see you to-morrow."

But that very night, Mrs. Castlemain told Emma, that as Mr. Hargrave and she, in consequence of a violent quarrel, had parted, never to meet again, it was not at all likely that Henry would be allowed to continue his visits; and Emma did not behave like a heroine on the occasion, for she retired in great distress to her apartment, and literally cried herself to sleep. The next morning Henry did not appear according to his promise, either at Mrs. Castlemain's or Mr. Egerton's; and Mr. Egerton, after endeavouring with some little success to calm the violence of Mrs. Castlemain's resentment, set out for Vale-House, with the benevolent intention of appeasing that of Mr. Hargrave. But his efforts were wholly unsuccessful, and he was forced to return with no prospect of a reconciliation between the parties, unless it should be in the power of time or accident to effect it; and, however deeply his want of success might affect the heart of Emma, it was not less sensibly felt by Mr. Egerton himself.

Emma could not be more desirous of pleasing Mr. Hargrave, because he was the uncle of St. Aubyn, than Mr. Egerton was. He allowed his paradoxes to pass uncontradicted, his asperities of temper to remain unresented, rather than offend the man on whose caprice the destiny of St. Aubyn depended; for his heart was bent on a union between Emma and Henry; and he well knew, that by displeasing Mr. Hargrave he should run the risk of weakening, if not of destroying the chance of this desired union's taking place. But all his forbearance was now rendered vain, and by a circumstance more likely to prove fatal to his views than a dispute between him and Mr. Hargrave could have been. The near relation of Emma had mortally offended the arbiter of Henry St. Aubyn's fate; and when Emma ran out to meet him, as soon as he appeared in sight, she discovered by his countenance, before he answered her interrogating eyes, that he had no pleasing intelligence to communicate. But to submit with patience to a positive evil, even though it be unavoidable, is a hard task for youth to learn; and to bear with fortitude the loss of her companion, her monitor, and her example, was a lesson which Mr. Egerton found it difficult to teach his usually docile scholar.

In a few days, however, Mrs. Castlemain observed that Emma had recovered her spirits; and she also observed, that though she herself rose very early, Emma rose still earlier, and immediately went out to take a walk. At first, this unusual circumstance excited no suspicion in the mind of Mrs. Castlemain, and she forgot to question Emma concerning it. But one morning, it occurred to her that these early walks must have a motive, and she determined to follow her. She did so, and found that she went to meet St. Aubyn. On seeing Mrs. Castlemain, Henry and Emma advanced towards her, afraid perhaps of being received with some degree of coldness, but not conscious that they deserved the severity of reproof. St. Aubyn, therefore, was shocked, and Emma irritated, at hearing himself accused by Mrs. Castlemain of having seduced her child into the commission of a disobedient, indelicate, and clandestine action, and secret, unbecoming intercourse.

"You astonish and distress me," cried St. Aubyn; while Emma was too indignant to speak. "You know I am forbidden to visit both at your house and Mr. Egerton's, (a command which I dare not disobey,) but I am not forbidden to associate either with you, Mr. Egerton, or Emma, if I happen to meet you; therefore, having been so fortunate as to meet Emma by chance one morning, I prevailed on her to indulge me with her company, and in hopes of enjoying the same pleasure again, though not by appointment, I have walked the same way every morning ever since; and——"

"She has been so complaisant as to do the same, I suppose!"

"She has," replied St. Aubyn, blushing; "nor did either of us imagine that in so doing we were guilty of an impropriety."

"Sweet innocents!" said Mrs. Castlemain, reddening with resentment; "but though you, Mr. St. Aubyn, may, and no doubt *do*, disapprove your uncle's unwarrantable conduct to me, and therefore do not at all feel disposed to enter into his quarrel, Miss Castlemain ought to have resented my injuries so far as to scorn to have meetings with the nephew of the man who has offended me; especially when she knows that her intercourse with you, if known to Mr. Hargrave, would be disapproved by him, and consequently forbidden. But if she does not know how to act with proper spirit, I must teach her; therefore, sir, while Mr. Hargrave and I are at variance, I positively forbid you to see or speak to Miss Castlemain; and I forbid her to see or speak to you." So saying, she turned hastily away, refusing to listen to St. Aubyn's remonstrances, and desiring Emma to follow her immediately.

Emma obeyed, but slowly and sullenly; and till she lost sight of St. Aubyn, she continued to kiss her hand to him, while the rapid tears that coursed each other down her cheek, sufficiently betrayed her sorrow at this cruel and in her opinion unnecessary prohibition.

"And you expect me to obey you, madam?" said Emma, in a tone more akin to defiance than submission.

"I do," hastily replied Mrs. Castlemain; "or you must take the consequences."

It happened unfortunately that Emma, who had been told by a tattling old servant who waited on her, some imperfect particulars of her mother's rash marriage, and Mrs. Castlemain's bitter and long resentment of it, had asked St. Aubyn if he could give her any information on the subject; and he, though he endeavoured to soften his account of Mrs. Castlemain's implacability as much as possible, had said enough to recall to Emma's mind the recollection of the dread and hatred which she used to feel towards her grandmother, and to account for her mother's having, as she concluded, inspired her with them.

It was at this moment, this unlucky moment, that Mrs. Castlemain, having kept Emma in sight, followed her at a distance; and seeing her walking with St. Aubyn, suddenly appeared before them with determined severity and resentment in her look; and while Emma listened to her words with a heart bursting with indignation, her mother's sorrows, her mother's wrongs alone were present to her view; and she forgot all Mrs. Castlemain's kindness to herself, and her own daily sense of that kindness, and she only saw in her indulgent and fostering parent the object of her early and just terror and aversion. No wonder then that her proud spirit rose at hearing a sort of threat from Mrs. Castlemain of future vengeance if she dared to disobey her; and that she listened with a rebellious heart to the lecture on propriety, which after breakfast (of which Emma refused to partake) Mrs. Castlemain thought it her duty to give her.

"I see no harm in what we have done," replied Emma; "and as an uncle is not one's father, nor a grandmother one's own mother, and therefore their right to command may very well be disputed, I should not at all scruple to meet Henry St. Aubyn again, and walk with him, in spite of your prohibition and Mr. Hargrave's."

Mr. Egerton who had entered the room just before Emma made this unbecoming reply, now came forward in great emotion; but she was too angry to be awed even by his presence.

"I see by your countenance, Mr. Egerton," said Mrs. Castlemain, "that you have heard what this ungrateful girl has been saying, and that you are shocked at it."

Mr. Egerton bowed in silence.

"I am glad you are here, sir," she continued, "that you may also hear what I am going to say; namely, that if in defiance of my express commands, and all the laws of propriety, Miss Castlemain persists in meeting Mr. St. Aubyn, I shall——"

"Renounce me for ever! I suppose," cried Emma rising, and pale with anger; "for I know you are not very forgiving in your nature. My poor, injured, discarded mother knew that to her cost!"

A thunderbolt could not have had a more overpowering effect on Mrs. Castlemain than this cruelly reproachful speech. She fell back in her chair; she spoke not—she stirred not—but lay with her eyes fixed in glaring unconsciousness.

Emma, on seeing this, gave a loud shriek, and sprang forward to her assistance; but Mr. Egerton, indignantly pushing her away with violence, exclaimed, "you have killed her! or you have driven her to frenzy!" and ringing the bell for the servants, he would not suffer Emma to share in his endeavours to restore her victim, as he called her, to life and reason; and Emma, screaming dreadfully, threw herself in frantic agony on the ground.

This roused Mrs. Castlemain from her stupor; she sobbed violently, and in a few moments tears came to her relief; while a "thank God!" that seemed to come from the bottom of her heart, burst from the self judged Emma.

In a short time Mrs. Castlemain was able to speak; and as she then begged to be left to recover herself alone, Mr. Egerton took Emma away with him, and led her into a room which she but rarely entered; namely, the dressing-room of Mrs. Castlemain. "Poor child of passion!" cried Mr. Egerton, seizing Emma's hand; "what an act of brutality have you been guilty of! Do you see that picture?" (pointing to a picture hanging over the chimney-piece, and drawing aside the curtain which concealed it as he spoke;) "know then that the life of that indulgent parent whose heart you have so cruelly wounded, is already tortured by incessant repentance and self-upbraiding; and that it was only yesterday, when unperceived I entered the adjoining apartment, that I overheard her, as she looked at that picture, speaking aloud in all the agonies of a broken and contrite spirit, and calling on her lost daughter to witness her sufferings and pardon her injustice! Cruel unnatural child! was it for you to inflict a still severer pang on a heart already lacerated and bleeding with remorse?"

Emma stayed to hear no more; but rushing out of the room, she almost flew into the apartment where she had left Mrs. Castlemain, and throwing herself on her knees before her, earnestly conjured her to pity and forgive her, though she declared that she never, never should forgive herself.

"Forgive thee! my child," replied Mrs. Castlemain in mournful and faltering accents; "ay, from the bottom of my soul do I forgive thee; for I have only too much need of forgiveness." Here she pressed Emma almost convulsively to her bosom; and as she again wished to be left alone, Emma returned to Mr. Egerton.

But, as she had foreseen, it was not easy for her to obtain her own pardon for the wound she had inflicted on the feelings of Mrs. Castlemain; during the whole of that day she was occasionally in paroxysms of frantic anguish, and the death-like figure of Mrs. Castlemain was present to her view; for what agony can exceed that of a young and virtuous heart that feels for the first time the horrors of remorse!

That evening, after Emma, exhausted by exertion, was retired to rest, Mr. Egerton told Mrs. Castlemain that he thought, as Emma was more than fifteen, she was old enough to be told her unhappy mother's story; "and at this moment," added he, "that her mind is melted and humbled by self-upbraiding, the warning moral which it inculcates will sink into it deeply, and she will also learn to understand and hold sacred your claims, your just claims, to her obedience and affection."

"I believe you are right," replied Mrs. Castlemain; "but as the narration would only call into additional force feelings and recollections which are already only too present to my mind, I shall order the carriage and go out for a long drive, that I may be out of the way of it. But here," said she, taking a letter out of a case deposited in her bosom, "here is my child's last letter to me; show it to her daughter, who in some respects I see too nearly resembles her, and as soon as I shall have driven from the door to-morrow, begin your melancholy task."

Mr. Egerton approved of Mrs. Castlemain's intended absence; and having on his return to his own cottage that night looked over some papers containing particulars necessary to be accurately explained, he was prepared the next morning to give Emma the desired and necessary information.

As soon as Mrs. Castlemain had left the house, Mr. Egerton told Emma that he wished to have some conversation with her on some circumstances very interesting to her feelings; and leading her into Mrs. Castlemain's dressing-room, he again undrew the curtain that concealed the picture of Agatha. "I am going," said he, "to relate the history of that dear unhappy woman."

"I am glad of it, very glad of it indeed," replied Emma bursting into tears; "but is it possible that that can be my mother's picture? I believe my grandmother showed it to me some years ago, and told me it was so; but I have never seen it since, and I had quite forgotten there was such a picture." Then going close to it, she regarded it some moments in silence, and, turning mournfully round, exclaimed, "O, sir, is it possible that my mother could ever have looked so young, so happy, so beautiful?"

"Yes, my dear," replied Mr. Egerton gravely, "till she became the slave of an imperious temper and ungovernable passions, and by an act of disobedience paved the way to her own misery and early death."

Emma blushed, looked down, and remained silent for a moment; but looking again at the picture, she suddenly observed, "Surely I have seen a face like that, for the features seem quite familiar to me!"

"You have," said Mr. Egerton with a significant look, which as Emma's eyes involuntarily turned towards a pier-glass opposite to her, she was at no difficulty to explain, and she blushed again; (but from emotions of a mixed nature, for pleasure was one of them,) as " the consciousness of self-approving beauty stole across her busy thought."

"Yes, Emma," cried Mr. Egerton, replying to the deepened and expressive glow of her cheek, and the involuntary complacency that dimpled the corners of her closed mouth; "that picture is as like you as if it had been painted from you; and you yourself have pronounced it beautiful. But be not elated by the conviction which it gives you; for,

What's female beauty, but an air divine
Thro' which the mind's all-gentle graces shine?

Therefore, how easy it is for temper and passion, by leaving their traces on the countenance, to injure if not to destroy loveliness even perfect as that is! Such as is that picture was your dear unhappy mother at the age of sixteen;—and such as is *this* picture was the same woman at the age of *twenty-four*; (giving Emma a large miniature of her mother as he spoke;) so great and so obvious were the ravages which the passions had made in her appearance."

Emma, surprised and affected, took the picture with a trembling hand, but had no sooner beheld it, than she exclaimed in a voice inarticulate from emotion, "this is indeed my mother!" and sunk back in her chair almost choked with the violence of her feelings.

When she recovered herself sufficiently to speak, she asked why this resemblance of her mother as she was accustomed to see her, had been so long concealed from her; and Mr. Egerton informed her that Agatha had desired him to let it remain unknown to her till she was old enough to hear the story of her mother's wrongs.—" When that time arrives, and not till *then*, show Emma," said she, " this picture which I have painted on purpose for her."

" I have obeyed your mother, my dear child," added Mr. Egerton, " in the one respect; it now only remains for me to obey her in the other."

" How many heartaches should we spare ourselves," said Mr. Egerton, as he prepared to narrate to Emma the history of her mother's sorrows, " if we were careful to check every unkind word or action towards those we love, as it is occasionally suggested to us by the infirmities of our temper, by this anticipating reflection;—' The time may soon arrive when the being whom I am now about to afflict, may be snatched from me for ever, to the cold recesses of the grave; secured from the assaults of my petulance, and deaf to the voice of my remorseful penitence!' O Emma! had Mrs. Castlemain fallen a victim last night to the strong emotion your cruel reproaches occasioned her, what to-day would not have been your bitter and unavailing agonies!"

Emma, conscience-stricken, did not attempt to answer him even by a promise of future self-control; and Mr. Egerton continued thus:

"' She is dead, and never knew how much I loved, and how truly I forgave her!' was the exclamation of Mrs. Castlemain, when I informed her that your mother was no more; and the tone in which she spoke conveyed to my mind such an impression of remorse and agony as no time can eradicate from my memory! and when you shall learn how much both of your mother's and of Mrs. Castlemain's miseries was the result of ill-humour, improperly indulged, I trust, my dear child, that you will not wonder at the incessant care with which I have endeavoured to teach you the virtue of self-command."

Mr. Egerton then proceeded to his long and melancholy detail, with which my readers are already acquainted;—but I wish to observe, that when Mr. Egerton said her mother was led to the altar, Emma eagerly interrupted him, and exclaimed with great emotion,

" Is it indeed true that my mother was really *married* to my father?"

" Certainly," replied Mr. Egerton, amazed at her agitated manner.

" Bless you! bless you! sir, for telling me so!" returned Emma, bursting into tears; " Oh what a load have you taken off my mind! I thought I had been told —— but now that agony is over, and I have not the misery of blushing for a mother's guilt!"

" But," replied Mr. Egerton, affectionately, " it is only too probable your mother's fame may never be cleared in the eyes of the world."

" It is cleared, sir, in the eyes of her daughter," replied Emma, " and other considerations are comparatively indifferent. I know her to be innocent, and I bless God that I know it; but pray go on: I think I can now bear to hear the detail of my father's depravity."

Mr. Egerton, satisfied with his pupil, pressed her hand kindly, and proceeded in his narration.

It is not in the power of words to describe the force or the variety of the emotions which agitated the heart of Emma while she listened to the tale of her mother's wrongs and sorrows; nor of the affectionate eagerness which she expressed to see the Orwells, the humble but admirable friends of her mother, to whom Mr. Egerton was in the habit of writing occasionally, and sending little presents in the name of Emma.

" I should like to go to London on *purpose* to see them," said Emma; and Mr. Egerton kept alive in her young heart a sense of gratitude so honourable and so just.

But he soon found that the praises of the Orwells, which Emma was for ever indulging in, sounded harshly on the ears of Mrs. Castlemain; for they recalled her own hasty renunciation of Agatha to her mind, and she felt that if *she* had done her duty by her, she would not have been forced to incur such vast obligations to the benevolence of obscure strangers.

" My dear child," said Mr. Egerton to Emma when they were alone together, " do not mention the Orwells again in the presence of your grandmother." And Emma, who immediately discerned the cause of his request, implicitly obeyed him.

It was now that Mr. Egerton thought the time was come for some inquiries to be made concerning the father of Emma, and for some steps to be taken in order to force him to acknowledge her as his legitimate daughter; and to the propriety of these measures, as a justice due to the memory of her child, Mrs. Castlemain reluctantly consented. Hitherto, the terror of being forced to resign her to a father's claims, when those claims were established, had kept them from bringing the affair forward; but selfish considerations could not now with propriety be acted upon any further; and Mr. Egerton employed an agent in London to inquire what was become of Danvers. And it was with no small degree of satisfaction they heard that, after many inquiries, the agent could only discover that Danvers had sailed nearly fifteen years back for the West Indies, and was supposed to have died there of the yellow fever, as no person of that name was known upon any of the islands.

" Then you are mine, exclusively mine *now*," said Mrs. Castlemain affectionately embracing Emma, " and all that is necessary to be done, is to procure a copy of the register of your mother's marriage, in order to clear her fame from the shadow of suspicion."

But though sure of still remaining under the protection which she loved, though *in hopes* of being proved the legitimate child of her mother, and lawful heiress of her grandmother, gaiety no longer lighted up the eye nor bloomed on the cheek of Emma; for Mr. Hargrave remained at variance with Mrs. Castlemain, and Henry St. Aubyn therefore was no longer a visitor at the Cottage. Mr. Egerton too missed his pupil as much as Emma her companion. Still at church they met; but for two successive Sundays Emma had vainly looked both for St. Aubyn and his mother, and she wondered at an absence so unusual. But she heard the reason of it only too soon from the gossip of the town of Keswick; and learnt with indescribable emotion, that St. Aubyn and his mother were gone on a tour of the Lakes with the honourable Mrs. Felton, a beautiful widow with a large jointure, to whom report said St. Aubyn was shortly to be united.

"This is a mere gossip, I am sure," said Mr. Egerton when the report of St. Aubyn's marriage reached him; "for I am certain Henry would have done me the honour to inform me of his marriage prospects, had any such existed."

And while Mr. Egerton said this, dear as he had always been to his affectionate pupil, she felt him at that moment dearer to her than ever;—but, as yet unacquainted with the nature of her own feelings towards St. Aubyn, she attributed her emotions to the indignation of injured friendship, which resented not being in the confidence of its object.

"No, no," continued he, "I can never believe that he would take a fancy to this fashionable belle and blue stocking."

"Pray, sir, what is a blue stocking?" said Emma.

"That is a question which I am not able to answer with perfect accuracy; especially as the term 'blue stocking' is one that has, like many others, varied from its original signification."

"I believe, I am *sure*," replied Emma, "that I am most interested in knowing what is its present meaning; still, I should like to hear all you can tell me on the subject."

"I have heard that it had its origin in the mistake of a foreigner, who, on being invited to a party of ladies and gentlemen that were in the habit of meeting for the purpose of conversation, asked whether he must come in full dress? and was told in answer, by no means; you may come in blue stockings;—meaning by that, that any undress was admissible."

"But what could be meant by blue stockings?"

"I conclude worsted or thread stockings of that colour, occasionally worn even by gentlemen in a morning. The foreigner, however, conceived that *bas bleus* were the livery of the party to which he was invited; and he went about describing them as wearing *bas bleus* at their meeting, and requiring their visiters to do the same. Hence arose the title of 'the blue stocking society,' given to the ladies and gentlemen in question; amongst whom were some of the first wits, scholars, moralists, poets, and painters of the day."

"I thought," said Emma, "that 'blue stocking' was a term applied to ladies only?"

"So it is now; but originally it must, from its origin, have been common to both sexes."

"Now, however, it is used to women only, is it not, sir? and is it not used as a term of reproach rather than of commendation?"

"I fear it is," replied Mr. Egerton, smiling at the eagerness with which Emma asked the latter part of the question, and which he accounted for by his having denominated Mrs. Felton a 'blue stocking;' "but whether justly or not, you shall judge for yourself. A 'blue stocking' is now, I believe, strictly speaking, nothing more than a woman who loves reading and literature, and who courts the society of literary men and women. Sometimes, perhaps, she is herself a writer, but not a professed one; and she occasionally makes her friends happy and flattered by the sight of manuscript verses and translations."

"Oh! then surely, sir," interrupted Emma smiling, "there are strong symptoms of blue stockingism about me!"

"Wait till I have finished, Emma. The 'blue stocking,' however, after all, only dips her foot in the waters of Helicon, without daring, like the bolder published authoress, to plunge in altogether. But giving the name of *bas bleus*, to the amateurs of literature of both sexes, I will point out the great advantage in society which *bas bleus* have over professed authors and authoresses. 'Blue stockings,' who write and read for pleasure, not profit, can afford to cull the richest flowers from the garden of their fancy in order to decorate their conversation. But not so the author or authoress;—they, as they write probably either to procure a necessary addition to their income, or even perhaps to obtain a subsistence for themselves and family, cannot afford to exhaust in society that produce of their imagination which is requisite for their works. The florist in Covent-garden market, whose flowers are in greatest profusion there, does not probably spare his own wife even a single sprig of geranium to adorn her bosom; and authors and authoresses, while 'blue stockings' are splendid and eloquent in their conversation, deny to theirs the brilliancy that might teach it to charm. I have often pitied authors, when I have seen them exhibited on these occasions in what are called conversationes, and expected to become what Dr. Johnson calls 'intellectual gladiators,' and have wondered at the wonder expressed, that men who could write so well should talk so ill; when the truth is probably, in the first place, that they do not choose to exhaust their minds in society; in the next, that the mind, which is often at full stretch in the study, requires relaxation in the drawing-room; and therefore they rather shun than court literary converse; while the love of display, which causes men and women of letters to delight so much in literary subjects, being gratified in authors on a wider and a prouder field, they have not in company the same motive to intellectual exertion."

"Then, my dear sir, you would not have professed authors and authoresses invited to blue stocking parties, because they are of no use when they get there?"

"Pardon me. I would have every attention possible paid to talents, at least in one point of view. Authors and authoresses are useful and ornamental too on such occasions; for every one feels a desire to see the being whose works have either interested or enlightened the world."

"Then I think," replied Emma, "that authors and authoresses are the costly heavy chairs in a drawing-room, which are there to be looked at only, and not used; while blue stockings of both sexes are the gilt cane chairs, which are set promiscuously about the apartment, for use as well as show, and formed of a lighter material."

"Bless me, child!" cried Mrs. Castlemain, who, lost in reverie, had only heard part of what had passed, "what are you saying about *bas bleus?* I hope you are not going to set up for one!"

"Dear grandmother," returned Emma, "I have a shrewd suspicion that I am one already; at least I shall henceforth take all *bas bleus* under my protection."

"What! Mrs. Felton and all, Emma?" archly asked Mr. Egerton.

"Yes, sir, certainly; for I think them very harmless and even commendable persons; for their greatest crime seems to be, preferring having full to having empty minds; literary conversation to gossip, scandal, and cards; nor do they do any thing which you and I and Mr. Egerton and St. Aubyn do not do every day."

"Perhaps not," replied Mrs. Castlemain; "still there is such a prejudice against blue stockings that I should be very sorry to hear you called by the name."

Emma was going to answer in a way that would not have pleased Mrs. Castlemain, and with more sarcasm on the prejudices of the world in general than would have become her age, her ignorance in many respects, or her relative situation to the speaker; but recollecting herself, and put on her guard perhaps by a look from Mr. Egerton, she replied, affectionately hanging over Mrs. Castlemain's chair as she spoke, "I shall endeavour, dear grandmother, to avoid deserving to be called any thing that you disapprove, and my highest wish will always be to please you."

Mrs. Castlemain kissed her affectionately as she said this, but suddenly rose up and left the room in tears, affected probably at the consciousness, that had the unhappy Agatha received from her the same judicious education and control which had been the safeguard of her more fortunate orphan, she might have been blessed with meeting from her the same respectful and affectionate deference to her will, and been at that moment free from those self-upbraidings that in solitude and secresy too often invaded her peace.

But to leave my heroine for a little while, and return to St. Aubyn. Part of the story was undoubtedly true. St. Aubyn and his mother were on a party of pleasure with the honourable Mrs. Felton and other friends.

This lady, whose charms in early youth had captivated the younger son of a nobleman, and induced him to raise her from the situation of governess to his sisters to the rank of his wife, was now, according to her own account, about seven-and-twenty. She had vivacity, grace, and accomplishments; and if not regularly handsome, there was an expression in her countenance, a something so attractive in her altogether, that women dreaded her for a rival quite as much as a more perfect beauty; and as the fine though full proportions of her form were set off by the most exquisite taste in dress, Mrs. Felton ranked in the calendar of fashionable belles. But presuming on her situation and talents, and not being a woman possessed of such delicacy of moral feeling as to shrink nearly as much from the imputation of guilt as from guilt itself, too proud to bear to be indebted to the candour of the world for believing her innocent spite of appearances, Mrs. Felton had been a flirting wife, and was now a flirting widow, dragging on a sort of sickly reputation, shunned by some few of her own sex from jealousy as much as from propriety, and extolled or abused by many of the other, according as their self-love was flattered by her fancied preference, or wounded by her neglect.

Mrs. Felton was now attended by a companion, on a visit to a lady and gentleman, friends of the St. Aubyns, who lived on a fine estate in the neighbourhood of Carlisle, meaning to go thence on a tour to all the Lakes, on which tour she had expected to have been joined by some of her London admirers. But having been disappointed in this expectation, she was anticipating a very dull expedition, when Mr. and Mrs. Selby, her host and hostess, thought it would be a good opportunity to claim an old promise made by Mrs. St. Aubyn, that she and her son would one day or other accompany them on a tour through the beauties of Westmoreland and Cumberland. Mrs. St. Aubyn's company would, they knew, be of no value to their fair guest, but as St. Aubyn was a handsome young man, of nearly four-and-twenty, was of a studious turn, and wrote pretty verses, they imagined that he would be a great acquisition to Mrs. Felton, whose aim was universal conquest, and whose pretensions to literature and taste were as decided and as universally acknowledged as her pretensions to fashion and to beauty.

To a woman of this description, it was, therefore, very certain that the expected arrival of a young, handsome and accomplished man, was an event of some importance; and on the day on which the St. Aubyns were expected, Mrs. Felton appeared dressed evidently for the purposes of conquest.

Mrs. St. Aubyn meanwhile had commenced her journey with feelings and anticipations of pleasure the most unalloyed. She wore a new and in her opinion most becoming riding-habit, and a straw bonnet exactly resembling that which in an evil hour she had recommended to Emma. True, in order to procure these decorations of her person, she had been obliged to increase an enormous old bill, and begin an enormous new one; enormous, I mean, according to the slenderness of her income; but that was a trifle in the estimation of Mrs. St. Aubyn, and the idea that for a whole month perhaps she should not meet the awful frown of her brother, excited in her such even girlish gaiety, as she sat by the side of her beloved son, who had hired for the occasion a low chaise, and a horse warranted steadiest of the steady, that she called a frequent and sometimes sympathizing smile to the now grave countenance of her companion, who, since he had been banished the dear society at the White Cottage, had felt a void at his heart, and a propensity to silence and abstraction, which were before unknown to him. But whatever were St. Aubyn's cares, the sweetness and benevolence of his nature always forbade him to make them a source of pain, or even uncomfortableness, to others; and nothing could be more foreign to his feelings than that selfishness which leads many persons to give way to the expression of their sorrows, even before those to whom the sight of their sufferings is an affliction difficult to endure. If St. Aubyn ever gave way to grief, it was in the solitude of his own chamber; for, as a social being, he thought he had no right to mix with his fellow-creatures without contributing his share of cheerful conversation, and endeavouring to do all in his power to fill the passing hour with innocent amusement.

After a pleasant and safe journey, though a few gentle screams from Mrs. St. Aubyn, on the road, seemed to imply that she had been in some danger, they arrived at their journey's end time enough for Mrs. St. Aubyn to dress for dinner. And when Mrs. Felton and herself entered the drawing-room, it would have been difficult to say which of the two ladies had taken the most pains at their toilet. The effect which the appearance of each had on the other, was, however, very different. Mrs. St. Aubyn certainly beheld Mrs. Felton's dress with unqualified admiration; but the latter could scarcely restrain a smile as she rapidly surveyed the long uncovered and meagre throat of the former, and the flowers which nodded on one side of the flaxen tresses which shaded the once polished brows of the faded but still self-admiring beauty. Yet Mrs. Felton was used to such exhibitions in town, but she did not expect them in the country; and she expected that Mrs. St. Aubyn's conversation would confirm the impression of her character which her dress had given.

St. Aubyn undoubtedly found more favour in Mrs. Felton's sight than his mother, on his introduction to her; and the look and smile with which she received his graceful bow, were calculated to convey to him how much she already appreciated him; but their force was lost on St. Aubyn, and he was only conscious that Mrs. Felton was a good-looking, and Miss Spenlove, her companion, an ill-looking woman.

But as he sat opposite to Mrs. Felton at dinner, he could not but discover that she had very fine eyes, though he was unconscious of what was visible to every one else, how often those eyes were turned expressively towards him, reminding one of the simile, "as on impassive ice the lightnings play." In vain too did the fair widow court every possible opportunity of carving, that she might show the beauty of her hands and arms, which were uncovered to the very extremity of fashion. St. Aubyn did not notice them; but, unconscious of her motive, he admired within himself that attentive politeness which made her willing to take so much trouble to help and please other people.

After dinner, Mrs. Felton introduced literary conversation, and brought in her taste and understanding in aid of her personal graces; but her evident wish to show off, counteracted her power of pleasing him in this instance, and St. Aubyn would have admired her more had she not talked so well. But the singularity of taste in the auditor for whom she talked was wholly unsuspected by Mrs. Felton, who, having displayed her own powers and gratified her own vanity sufficiently, thought it was incumbent on her at length to gratify the vanity of her intended captive; and before the evening ended she took care to insinuate to him that the fame of his literary talents had reached her, and she hoped that he would indulge her during their tour with a sight of some of his beautiful verses.

Nothing but St. Aubyn's surprise could exceed his confusion at being thus invested with the dignity of authorship, and told of the celebrity of his literary talents; for he was not conscious that his having written at all was known beyond the dear circle at Mrs. Castlemain's, and he gazed on Mrs. Felton with looks of wonder, confusion, and inquiry.

"Who can have so much misrepresented

me and my pretensions to you, madam?" said St. Aubyn, blushing deeply.

"Misrepresented!" exclaimed Mrs. Felton. "Fy, Mr. St. Aubyn! With that ingenuous countenance, how is it possible you can be so deceitful? However modest your pretensions may be, Mrs. Selby assures me she has seen very beautiful verses written by you on different occasions;—but I see, Mr. St. Aubyn, that you 'write verse by stealth, and blush to find it fame.'"

"However the verse on these occasions, madam," replied St. Aubyn, "may have been written, I am sure it must have been seen by stealth, as I never gave a copy of it to any one but my mother."

"But in the first place you own that you have written?"

"I do—a few schoolboy's verses."

"In the next place, you plead guilty to the charge of having given a copy to Mrs. St. Aubyn?"

"Certainly."

"And you know there is such a thing as *parental pride*; and Mrs. St. Aubyn, in the amiable pride of her heart, showed these stanzas so given to some of her friends; and these friends mentioned them with the praise they deserved to me.—Have I not clearly made out my case, Mr. St. Aubyn?—Verdict against the defendant, who is adjudged to pay a fine of so many stanzas into the Muses' court."

"A severe judgment," replied St. Aubyn, "when the poverty of the condemned is considered,—and I move for an arrest of judgment."

"What is the matter?" said Mrs. St. Aubyn, drawing her chair closer to her son's.

"The matter is, that Mr. St. Aubyn is called upon, as a punishment for his offences, to write some poetry, and he wishes his sentence to be revoked."

"My son refuse to write poetry! Well, that is droll indeed. Why, he writes such beautiful poetry!—Oh, I could show you, madam, such sweet things!"

"Admirable! just what I wished! These 'sweet things' are what I want to see; but Mr. St. Aubyn looks as if he would forbid you to show them."

"What! when he knows I wish to show them? No; Henry never denied me any thing yet, and I think he will hardly begin now."

St. Aubyn bowed to his mother with a look and smile of affection, and, seeing the display of his manuscripts was unavoidable, withdrew to another part of the room.

From Mrs. Felton's severity of criticism St. Aubyn had little to fear; for to him she was disposed to be particularly indulgent, as his person and manners were likely to make his poetry appear even faultless in the eyes of a female critic.

Henry St. Aubyn was above six feet in height; but the fine proportions of his form made it almost impossible for any one to deem him too tall; and now that all his features had acquired their due size, the beauty of his face, though not as perfect, was as striking as that of his figure. Still his beauty was chiefly the charm of countenance and expression, heightened by a rich and ever-mantling bloom, the result of health, temperance, and exercise. His manners, though he had seen little of the world, were the manners of a finished gentleman; for they had been modelled on his father's; and in those of his most intimate associate Mr. Egerton, he had a daily example of the politeness and graceful attention of the old court, as it is called, without any of its formality; and while his lofty and dignified carriage seemed to speak him born to command, the affectionate gentleness of his manner, and the mildness of his address, spoke him eager to oblige and willing to obey.

"What a highly gifted creature it is!" said Mrs. Felton, wiping a tear from her eye, as she read some lines by St. Aubyn, to the memory of his father.

"Henry! come hither, Henry," cried the delighted mother; "see, see! you have made Mrs. Felton shed tears!"

Henry obeyed the summons, and *saw* tears in the fine eyes of Mrs. Felton; but he either did not see, or would not see, the hand which she held out to him, and which he ought to have pressed or kissed according as his inclinations prompted.

"Here," said Mrs. Felton, "take away your odious verses; I wish I had not seen them!"

"Odious verses! and wish you had not seen them!" cried the literal Mrs. St. Aubyn —"well; that is funny!"

"But very true; for they will make me out of love with every thing else of the kind for ages to come. They are so beautiful, that I shall be as fastidious in future as I have hitherto been indulgent."

"There, Henry! do you hear?" asked Mrs. St. Aubyn.

"Yes, madam, and would I could *believe* what I hear!"

"You may, for I never flatter; not even myself."

"Nor do I; therefore I must think that your kindness rather than your judgment speaks."

"May be so," replied Mrs. Felton; "but I trust that the world will some day or other decide between you and me. Mr. St. Aubyn," added she, lowering her voice and looking archly at him, "these are pretty lines entitled 'To Emma, aged twelve years, on her birthday.' I wonder how you will write 'To Emma, aged *eighteen*.'"

"'To Emma, aged eighteen,' I shall probably not write at all," replied St. Aubyn blushing.

"Perhaps not," returned Mrs. Felton with quickness, and heaving a sigh as she spoke;

"and in that case she will be a more enviable object than if you *had* written."

"I do not exactly understand you," said Henry.

"No matter," was the answer; and the artillery of glances, sighs, and occasional pressures of the soft white hand on the sleeve of his coat, were again played off on the still insensible St. Aubyn, who when they retired for the night kept repeating to himself till he dropped asleep, "What could she mean? and why would she not explain herself?"

Had she not contrived to occupy his mind by this affected mystery, St. Aubyn would not have thought of Mrs. Felton at all. However, she had contrived to make him think of her, whether directly or indirectly, and that was a point gained; and had Mrs. Felton been sure she had done so, she would have been of the same opinion, and looked forward with some certainty to a time when she should occupy his attention and thoughts still more.

The next morning the whole party were to begin their tour through Cumberland and Westmoreland. It consisted of Mrs. Felton and her companion, the St. Aubyns, Mr. and Mrs. Selby, and Miss Travers, a young lady on a visit to the latter. At nine, the carriages drove to the door, consisting of Mrs. Felton's landaulet and the one-horse chaises of Mr. Selby and St. Aubyn.

As Mrs. Felton, it was known, preferred a chaise to her own carriage, it was resolved that Mrs. Selby, Miss Spenlove, and Miss Travers should go in the landaulet; accordingly, they took their seats and drove off from the door before Mrs. Felton, who had been writing letters, was equipped for her journey; and before she came down stairs, St. Aubyn had handed his mother into his chaise, and was preparing to follow the carriage. Nothing could exceed Mrs. Felton's astonishment and mortification at finding, when she reached the door, that, instead of requesting leave to drive her in his chaise, he was already contentedly seated by the side of his own mother, and preparing to drive off, as regardless of her as if he had never seen her. To such neglect and indifference, she had never been accustomed, and knew not how to endure it; and her countenance assumed so gloomy an expression, that even Mr. Selby, who was not the most penetrating of men, discovered the cause of her disquietude; and calling to St. Aubyn to stop, he in a low voice asked Mrs. Felton whether she would not oblige Mr. St. Aubyn, by taking his mother's place beside him, while he would condemn himself, for the sake of his young friend, to the pain of relinquishing her society. At this speech, which soothed her wounded self-love, her countenance brightened, and she allowed Mr. Selby to oblige St. Aubyn by making the proposal; but what could exceed her astonishment and angry mortification when St. Aubyn returned for answer, that he must beg leave to decline the honour intended him, as his mother was so fearful in an open carriage, that he knew she would be miserable if driven by any one but himself, as to his driving she had been accustomed!

Too much provoked to speak, Mrs. Felton seated herself beside Mr. Selby, and followed the other chaise in perturbed silence, debating in her own mind whether she should not show her sense of St. Aubyn's rudeness, in preferring his mother's comfort to her society, by treating him with disdain. But in the first place, he was the *only beau*, therefore she could not *afford* to affront him; and in the next place, she felt conscious, that by seeming to resent his indifference, she should only gratify his vanity, by proving that indifference gave her pain; therefore, before they had gone two miles, she had recovered her good-humour. Mr. Selby, who had waited in patient silence till the clouds of mortified vanity had dispersed, now led her into conversation, and took occasion, on her making some inquiries concerning St. Aubyn, to panegyrize his filial piety, amongst his other virtues, of which, he said, his refusal to have the honour and happiness of driving her was another instance; and Mrs. Felton, gratified to find she had been sacrificed to an habitual, and therefore irresistible duty, forgot all her displeasure, and made numberless inquiries concerning St. Aubyn's age and expectations in life.

"But who is that Emma," said she, "to whom he has written verses?"

"Oh! a little girl with whom he has been educated."

"But is she still a little girl?" And Mr. Selby, who had forgotten the insensible lapse of years, answered, "Yes; her age is only thirteen or fourteen."

"But who, and what is she?"

"The heiress of the honourable Mrs. Castlemain."

"But what did St. Aubyn mean, think you, by saying in answer to a remark of mine, on my mentioning his verses 'to Emma, aged twelve,' 'to Emma, aged eighteen, I should probably not write at all'?"

"That he should not dare to take the liberty of writing to her at that age."

"And why not?"

"Because he is poor, and utterly dependent on a capricious uncle; and she is a rich heiress."

"Oh! that is all that he meant, is it?" replied Mrs. Felton; "I suspected that he meant much more." And she immediately fell into a pleasant reverie, of which St. Aubyn was certainly the object.

It was the intention of the party to go to Cockermouth, and thence to Cromack Water and Buttermere, whence they were to make the complete tour of the lakes, ending it at Ulswater. When they stopped to bait the horses, and explore some of the fine scenery on the road from Carlisle to Cockermouth, Mrs. Felton eagerly approached Mrs. St. Aubyn, and offering her her arm as she did so, regretted having been so long deprived of her society, declaring at the same time, her resolution not to undergo a similar privation again. This speech, which Mrs. St. Aubyn received with smiles of unexpected satisfaction, was overheard by Mr. Selby with wonder and mortification; for he could not help thinking that his conversational powers were quite equal, if not superior, to Mrs. St. Aubyn's; and as he was a simple-minded, straight-forward man, as the phrase is, he had no suspicion that Mrs. Felton was saying what she did not think.

"I have a proposal to make to you, my dear madam," added Mrs. Felton, "which is, that you will do me the honour of going with me, when we resume our journey, in my landaulet, as you are apt, I find, to be alarmed in an open carriage."

"Dear me, you are vastly obliging! I am sure I should prefer going in the landaulet, and then my son may have the honour and happiness of driving you."

"Me! Oh, by no means; that would entirely defeat my purpose; which is, to procure myself more of your company. Therefore, if he pleases, Miss Spenlove shall be Mr. St. Aubyn's companion, and dear Mrs. Selby go with you and me, while Miss Travers takes my place in Mr. Selby's chaise."

From Mrs. Felton's decisions there was usually no appeal; and as his mother looked delighted at the marked and flattering attention of Mrs. Felton, and wished to accept her offer, St. Aubyn cheerfully acquiesced; though Miss Travers, who was a very pretty girl, and therefore perhaps not fixed upon by the fair widow to accompany St. Aubyn, would have been better pleased if the latter had not been so quiescent, but had insisted on driving her instead of Miss Spenlove.

Mr. Selby meanwhile said nothing,—but he thought the more,—and wondered within himself to hear Mrs. Felton professing such eagerness to enjoy the conversation of a woman who, but a few hours ago, she declared was as insipid as she was fantastical! "Well, it is very strange," thought Mr. Selby; for her refusal to be driven by St. Aubyn had completely succeeded in blinding the simple-minded Mr. Selby to her real motives of action; and he resolved to consult his wife on the subject, as she prided herself on her sagacity, and had persuaded him to think very highly of it also.

At length the horses were refreshed, the scenery sufficiently explored, and Mr. Selby handed Mrs. St. Aubyn and Mrs. Felton into the landaulet, and then his wife; who, as she seated herself, stooped down, and laying her finger on the side of her nose, (a habit which she had,) significantly and sarcastically said to her husband in a low tone of voice, "Oh ho, is it so?" a jingle she was fond of. And on this expressive but mysterious couplet, as it may be called, Mr. Selby mused for at least half an hour; but recollecting that it was deemed unmanly to be curious, the vice of curiosity being said to be exclusively that of the other sex, he resolved to wait patiently till bed-time for an explanation of what Mrs. Selby's penetration had discovered, and valued himself not a little on being a man, and consequently not at all curious. How often is one reminded of the fable of the Sculptor and the Lion!

During the drive, his sagacious wife was much amused at observing how completely "dear Mrs. Selby," as Mrs. Felton affectedly called her, was neglected for the new acquaintance, Mrs. St. Aubyn, and she was very eager to arrive at her journey's end, in order to indulge herself in another "Oh ho!" proof of her penetration.

"My dear madam," said Mrs. Felton with great tenderness of manner, "believe me, I consider you as a sort of cousin!"

"Dear me, do you! How so?" said the flattered Mrs. St. Aubyn.

"Oh, not without reason. Lady Mary St. Aubyn, your Mr. St. Aubyn's mother, was second cousin to my Mr. Felton; therefore, by marriage, you and I are certainly cousins."

"Dear me! to be sure we are," replied the delighted Mrs. St. Aubyn; "are we not, Mrs. Selby?"

"Oh ho!" replied Mrs. Selby, looking very arch, "and pray what relation then is Henry to you, Mrs. Felton?"

"I protest I—I never considered," said Mrs. Felton in some confusion.

"But why, my dear madam," continued Mrs. Selby, "is it necessary for you to discover a relationship to Mrs. St. Aubyn in order to account for your sudden affection for her——"

"No, certainly not," answered Mrs. Felton.

"O dear me!" said Mrs. St. Aubyn.

"There is," resumed Mrs. Selby, "a sympathy, a natural adhesion between some persons, stronger than any which are the result of blood. The ivy, dear ladies, clings much more closely to the oak than any of its own saplings do; and I am convinced that the cause of your growing attachment will make it much stronger than if relationship had really anything to do with it."

"You are very figurative in your language, Mrs. Selby," said Mrs. Felton, conscious that she saw through her designs.

"Oh! there is nothing like a simile to illustrate one's meaning. But which of you in this case is the ivy? *You*, Mrs. St. Aubyn, resemble it in one respect; that is, in being an evergreen; but sober green is not smart enough for your taste; no, you would rather be likened to the China rose, that blooms even in winter."

Not one word of this conversation was thoroughly understood by Mrs. St. Aubyn; however, she bowed and smiled, and said "Dear me!" as if she did understand it; though she was not at all sure that by comparing her to a blooming rose, Mrs. Selby did not mean a sarcasm on her rouge.

Luckily for the maintenance of Mrs. Felton's good-humour, the conversation was soon interrupted by their arrival at Cockermouth; for Mrs. Felton feared Mrs. Selby's sarcastic penetration, and she was not likely to be backward in the use of it on this occasion, as she in her heart disliked that lady; for whenever there was no other gentleman present, the fair widow, whose aim was universal conquest, and who always kept her fire-arms in order by constant exercise, used to flirt most unmercifully with the simple-minded Mr. Selby; and to use a vulgar but expressive phrase, the jealous wife was now paying off old scores, while Mrs. Felton was not backward to return the dislike which she felt conscious of exciting; and she spoke of and to her hostess by the name of "dear Mrs. Selby" on the same principle that we often throw perfumes about a room in order to hide an unpleasant smell.

At length, after the duties of the toilet were gone through, the company assembled to a late dinner, and St. Aubyn saw in the happy countenance of his mother an expression of satisfied and conscious importance which he had not for years beheld on it; and as he was certain that she derived it from Mrs. Felton's marked attentions to her, he felt grateful to that lady for the benevolence which dictated them.

"But is it benevolence?" thought St. Aubyn, for he sometimes had a suspicion that Mrs. Felton was laughing at his mother; as, spite of his filial piety, his uncle's just though coarse raillery had so often held her up in his presence to deserved ridicule, that he could not help fearing that this superabundant passion for her society which Mrs. Felton evinced, was founded on a wish to make her what is denominated a butt; for St. Aubyn had no suspicion that it was through his mother that the fair widow was aiming at him; and watchful, and suspicious, and pensive, he sat down to dinner as before, opposite to Mrs. Felton. But, with all his distrustful vigilance, he saw nothing in her manner to his mother but what demanded his grateful approbation.

Mrs. Felton evidently endeavoured to give her consequence, and she succeeded. She talked to her of her former residence near London, of the birth-day and the birth-day balls, of Lady Mary St. Aubyn, her husband's mother. And Mrs. St. Aubyn, who in her brother's presence had always the appearance of a frightened fool, thus encouraged, resumed the ease and gaiety natural to her; and her son, who had never seen her to such advantage before, and was now convinced he had undervalued his mother's talents, felt the liveliest gratitude to that benevolent woman, as he now believed she might really be, who had thus gratified his filial affection, and caught himself several times saying mentally, "She is certainly very beautiful!"

Never for an instant did a suspicion of Mrs. Felton's motives come across the mind of St. Aubyn. But Mr. Selby was now become more enlightened, for he had seen his wife alone; and having been informed by her of the plan of operations which was going forward, the corners of his good-humoured mouth were during dinner dimpled with more arch meaning than usual, and though he did not give utterance to any "Oh ho's," he looked even more of them than Mrs. Selby herself.

Not but that it required all his confidence in his wife's penetration, to be entirely convinced of the truth of what she asserted; for instead of directing her discourse to St. Aubyn, and paying him those pointed attentions which he had witnessed the first day they met, Mrs. Felton talked less to him than she did to any one else; and her seducing looks, her *agaceries* were so exclusively directed to himself, that he began to fear his wife would be jealous again.

But Mr. Selby was not aware that St. Aubyn, being opposite to Mrs. Felton, could see her every look and motion; and that the play of her countenance while speaking to him, and the graceful bend of her finely-formed head and neck while leaning towards him, with the occasional display of her fine hand and arm, could not escape St. Aubyn's notice, especially as now he was become unconsciously interested in her from her attention to his mother; and they were more likely to have their full effect on him, from not being *apparently* intended to captivate him; while ever and anon she addressed Mrs. St. Aubyn in a tone and manner so kind and so respectful, that Mrs. St. Aubyn's countenance was quite radiant with pleasure, and she forgot there was such a person in the world as her formidable brother.

During the course of the evening, Mrs. Felton was asked to sing; and having immediately complied with the request, she sung the following song:—

The soft blooms of summer are fair to the eye,
Where brightly the clear silver Medway glides by;
And rich are the colours which autumn adorn,
Its gold chequer'd leaves, and its billows of corn.

But dearer to me is the pale lonely rose,
Whose blossoms in winter's dark season unclose;
Which smiles in the rigour of winter's stern blast,
And smooths the rough present by signs of the past.

And thus when around us affliction's dark power
Eclipses the sunshine of life's glowing hour,
While drooping, deserted, in sorrow we bend,
O sweet is the presence of one faithful friend!

The crowds whom we smiled with when gladness
   was ours;
Are summer's bright blossoms, and autumn's gay
   stores;
But the friend on whose breast we in sorrow repose,
That friend is the winter's lone beautiful rose.

Mrs. Felton did not increase her power over St. Aubyn by singing; for though she sung with taste and science, she only recalled to his recollection a sweeter voice, and tones which he dearly loved; and for a few moments the White Cottage and its beloved inhabitant swam before his glistening eye. He soon, however, recovered himself; and suppressing a deep sigh, he hoped Mrs. Felton would be more generous than to excite their wishes by a proof of her musical talents, and then refuse to gratify still further the wish she had excited; and as he said this, there was so much softness in the expression of his eyes, the result of recent recollections, that Mrs. Felton flattered herself his evident emotion was caused by her, and that the look which accompanied his speech was also caused by the feeling of tenderness with which she had inspired him.

"You overrate my musical talents," said Mrs. Felton modestly; "but, such as they are, you and this good company may command them; and I hope Miss Spenlove will join me in a duet."

"Certainly, if you desire it," replied Miss Spenlove, "and I shall at least be an excellent foil to you."

"Ridiculous!" said Mrs. Felton; and she said right, as my readers will also say when it suits me to give a short history of Miss Spenlove. As soon as Miss Spenlove had given her consent to sing, Mrs. Felton fixed on a duet, which was received with more applause even than the song had been; and it was evident, even to the most untutored ear in the company, that, so far from being a foil to Mrs. Felton, Miss Spenlove's voice was of a richer and finer tone than her friend's, and her delivery of it proved her a performer of great excellence. She could not, however, be prevailed upon to sing any thing but a second to Mrs. Felton, and the latter was again requested to favour the company alone.

"But pray," said Mr. Selby, "who wrote the words you have just been singing?"

"Well, Mr. Selby," cried Miss Spenlove, "I am surprised you should ask. I thought you must suspect, if you did not *know*—that they are—"

"Hush! hush! you foolish woman," said Mrs. Felton, putting her hand before Miss Spenlove's mouth.

"No, I will speak," exclaimed she; "the words are this dear creature's!"

"Oh, fy!" cried Mrs. Felton, as well she might if she had valued truth; for, though Mrs. Felton wished them to pass for hers, as she had the reputation of never singing any words but her own, they were in reality the production of a friend, who did not value himself on them, and was contented to let them pass as productions by Mrs. Felton. It is to be supposed that when the company heard that the songs were Mrs. Felton's, they were so complaisant as to admire them.

"And who composed the music?" asked St. Aubyn.

"Oh! the music is—" replied Mrs. Felton.

"By the same person, I suspect, that wrote the words."

"You may say so," said Miss Spenlove. And indeed with equal truth so he might; for the tunes were both old tunes; but, as they were not much known, by a few judicious alterations by Miss Spenlove, and some pretty cadences and shakes well introduced by Mrs. Felton, they passed for the original composition of that lady, and were handed about in MS., in fashionable circles, as little *chef-d'œuvres* by the honourable Mrs. Felton.

"What a monopolizer of talent you are!" said St. Aubyn.

"A monopolizer!" exclaimed Mrs. Selby; "it is well you did not call my fair friend a regrater too."

"Dear me!" cried Mrs. St. Aubyn, "what is a regrater?"

"One," answered Mrs. Selby, quickly, "who buys up other persons' commodities, and retails them according to their own fashion and their own price."

"Well, well," said Mr. Selby, hastily, alarmed at his wife's coarseness, (for he well knew her suspicions,) "considering you are a woman, and therefore know nothing of business, the explanation, though not a correct one, is a tolerably good one, and I shall not take the trouble to amend it, but beg our friends to indulge us with some more singing."

Henry St. Aubyn had listened to Mrs. Selby's observation, and seen Mr. Selby's alarm, with ill-disguised astonishment. It seemed to him so unnecessary for a woman to write verses, or compose music, in order to be either charming or estimable, that he never suspected it possible for a gentlewoman to forfeit the indispensable requisites of truth and honesty, in order to obtain the reputation of being so gifted. He therefore unwillingly attributed Mrs. Selby's evidently intended sarcasm to the spite of an envious woman, while his admiration of Mrs. Felton was increased by the temper with which she bore the imputation, and consented to sing again.

"Might I be allowed to choose your song?" said Miss Spenlove fawningly.

"Certainly you shall," replied Mrs. Felton

with apparent kindness; "for no one will dispute the excellence of your judgment, and you certainly know which song I sing best."

St. Aubyn did not know it; but the rancour which Mrs. Selby had excited, Mrs. Felton vented thus on poor Miss Spenlove, who had once been a professional singer, and had taught music; but who having, on an accession of property, commenced woman of fashion, had not strength of mind enough to like to be reminded of her former situation. Miss Spenlove therefore blushed, from mixed feelings excited by this masked battery, which, "this dear creature," as she had just called her, had opened upon her; but returning good for evil, she requested her to sing the song she was famous for singing with such irresistible pathos; "though indeed," added she, "I wonder you can have the heart to sing it at all, as the unhappy writer was most fatally in love, and—"

"No more on that subject," replied Mrs. Felton, affecting to sigh very deeply, "for I wish to sing my best;" and she began the following stanzas, which she had adapted to an old Scotch melody;

Then be it so, and let us part,
Since love like mine has fail'd to move thee;
But do not think this constant heart
Can ever cease, ingrate, to love thee.
No—spite of all thy cold disdain,
I'll bless the hour when first I met thee,
And rather bear whole years of pain
Than e'en for one short hour forget thee,
    Forget thee! No.

Still Memory, now my only friend,
Shall with her soothing art endeavour
My present anguish to suspend,
By painting pleasures lost for ever.
She shall the happy hours renew,
When full of hope and smiles I met thee,
And little thought the day to view
When thou wouldst wish me to forget thee,
    Forget thee! No.

Yet, I have lived to view that day,
To mourn my past destructive blindness,
To see now turn'd with scorn away
Those eyes once fill'd with answering kindness.
But go—farewell! and be thou blest,
If thoughts of what I feel will let thee;
Yet, though thy image kills my rest,
'Twere greater anguish to forget thee.
    Forget thee! No.

"Brava! brava!" cried Mr. Selby, when Mrs. Felton had finished her song.

"I think," said St. Aubyn gravely, and conceiving by what Miss Spenlove had said, that the song had been addressed to her friend, "I think a man who could love as well as the poor man who wrote those lines must have loved, ought not to have loved in vain; but it seems he did; and he also complains of encouragement given and then withdrawn." St. Aubyn said this with a severity of manner which Mrs. Felton, spite of her aptitude to flatter herself, could not impute to apprehensive jealousy merely, but was obliged to see in it an implied censure of suspected coquetry; and she replied as composedly as she could, that men were very apt to flatter themselves, and to fancy encouragement given where none was intended.

"True, very true," observed Mrs. St. Aubyn, looking, or trying to look, wise; "I have often found it so to my cost. But, poor man! I should like to know what became of the gentleman who wrote that song; —I hope he did not drown or shoot himself for love!"

"I hope not too," said Mrs. Selby, "for that would have shown he was more in earnest than such a jilting mistress would have deserved; for you know, Mrs. St. Aubyn, our friend Hudibras says,

'If a man hang, or blow out his brains,
The deuce is in him if he feigns.'"

"Upon my word, madam, I have no friend of that name," replied Mrs. St. Aubyn, "at least not that I recollect; to be sure, when I lived in town, I had many foreigners on my visiting list, and this person might be one of them."

St. Aubyn blushed—Mrs. Selby bit her lip—while Mrs. Felton kindly said,

"I protest, my dear madam, I know no more of Mrs. Selby's friend Hudibras than you do; and indeed it is a book not usually liked by ladies, and you served Mrs. Selby quite right in affecting not to understand her allusion."

St. Aubyn, though grateful to Mrs. Felton for this attempt to veil Mrs. St. Aubyn's mistake, could not allow even his mother to be defended at the expense of truth; and therefore replied,

"I am sure, my dear madam, that my mother had not the intention which you obligingly impute to her; especially as, though she does not know the poem of Hudibras by name, she is familiar with many passages in it, for my poor father was fond of quoting Hudibras; and you must remember," added he, addressing his mother, "how much you used to admire one burlesque simile which he was often repeating—

'Now, like a lobster boil'd, the morn
From black to red began to turn—'"

"Dear me! yes to be sure I do; and that was by Hudibras, was it?"

St. Aubyn finding it was a hopeless case to attempt to set her right, sighed and was silent; but no one even *smiled* at Mrs. St. Aubyn's mistake. The filial piety of her son cast such a shield over her on all occasions, that when he was present it would have seemed sacrilegious to make her an object of ridicule; and even Mrs. Selby, who, because Mrs. Felton seemed to protect Mrs. St. Aubyn, felt inclined to attack her, was awed by respect for the son's feelings into forbearance towards the mother; and Mr. Selby took advantage of the temporary silence to change the conversation by observing,

"Your father, Henry, was a most amiable man, and I shall regret his early loss to the end of my existence. However, my dear boy," squeezing St. Aubyn's hand affectionately, "he survives still in you. Do you not think, Mrs. St. Aubyn, that your son is an improved likeness of his father?"

"My Mr. St. Aubyn was a very handsome man also," she replied; while her son's deep blushes at this implied compliment to his beauty called forth some good-natured raillery, and the evening terminated in mirth and good humour.

The next day Mrs. Felton persisted in going in the landaulet with Mrs. St. Aubyn and Mrs. Selby, though St. Aubyn requested the honour of driving her; but she was gratified at his having made the request; and when they arrived at Buttermere, she accepted his offered arm, and the assistance of his hand in passing miry paths and pieces of projecting rock; and sometimes while he sat down to sketch the most striking parts of the scenery, she leaned over him as he did so, and occasionally leaned her arm on his shoulder.

"Oh ho!" said Mrs. Selby to her husband as she observed this familiarity; and Mrs. St. Aubyn, as she delightedly gazed on them, asked Miss Spenlove in a whisper, if she did not think they would make a very handsome picture.

As the weather was fine, and Buttermere and Cromack Water were well worth visiting again and again, they did not quit the banks of the latter lake till twilight, and then took up their abode for the night in the neighbourhood, that they might return to the same scenes again the next day; Mr. Selby's servants having in the meanwhile joined them with fishing tackle, and a tent which they could pitch wherever they thought proper.

But late as was the dinner-hour, neither the ladies nor the gentlemen sat down to table without changing their dress; and had St. Aubyn continued to distrust Mrs. Felton's motives for behaving with such marked kindness to his mother, the appearance of the latter when she came down to dinner would for ever have lulled his suspicions to rest. Mrs. St. Aubyn appeared in a very elegant lace cap tied under her chin, the gift of Mrs. Felton; and as it was a style of head-dress more becoming her time of life than any cap she was in the habit of wearing, St. Aubyn saw that Mrs. Felton endeavoured to remove rather than promote his mother's follies; and his heart glowed towards her with a fervour that she had never excited in him before, and which all her beauty, all her coquetry, and all her seducing familiarity, would have failed to excite. She had really attacked St. Aubyn on his weak side, if I may call by such a name his attachment to a most foolish mother; and the fair widow was not at all blind to the advantage which she had gained.

As the day had been a day of fatigue, the party separated early. Nothing worth relating took place during the evening, except that Mr. and Mrs. Selby looked a number of ho ho's at each other, on observing several kind and corresponding glances exchanged between the grateful St. Aubyn and the fascinating Mrs. Felton.

The next and the two succeeding days were passed amidst the scenery of Buttermere and Cromack Water, or on the Lakes themselves; and the whole party walked from and to the inn. But as the lake which they meant to visit the next day was at some distance, the carriages were again necessary, and again St. Aubyn requested leave to drive Mrs. Felton, and was graciously permitted to do so, to the petitioner's great satisfaction, as he was become tired of both his companions, Miss Travers and Miss Spenlove. The former, though very pretty, was very insipid; and towards the latter, St. Aubyn, though not at all apt to dislike any one, was inclined to feel something rather resembling aversion.

Miss Spenlove, as I have before said, had once been a teacher of music, and had sung, for hire, in many respectable societies, contented with the honourable distinction of gaining an honest livelihood by virtuous industry; but having become mistress of eight or ten thousand pounds by the death of a distant relation, Miss Spenlove wished to set up for a woman of fashion. But to do this was a difficult task as a *noun substantive;* therefore Miss Spenlove resolved to become a noun *adjective;* and, by making herself useful to some leader of ton, get herself passed into the circles of high life, as an appendage to the aforesaid leader; like a *burr* sticking to a velvet petticoat.

At the time when Miss Spenlove's good fortune, as she called it, had led her to form this resolution, Mrs. Felton was a leader of the ton; and having known that lady when she was poor, and dependent on her talents for support, Miss Spenlove took the first opportunity of calling on her now her style of living was changed, and that she walked nowhere without a servant behind her. The pretence for calling on Mrs. Felton was, that she had composed a song hitherto unheard by any one, on purpose for Mrs. Felton's beautiful voice and manner of singing, and Miss Spenlove had little doubt but that under the auspices of the fair widow she should move in those circles after which her ambition panted; not that Miss Spenlove was romantic enough to suppose that Mrs. Felton would introduce her into fashionable circles from motives of kindness; no, she knew too much of the world and of human nature, and also of Mrs. Felton's nature, to suppose that. But she knew she could make it a traffic of mutual accommodation, and that she could purchase the services which it was not in her power to command.

After Miss Spenlove, who was immediately admitted, as Mrs. Felton had nothing better to do, had presented her song, which was most graciously received, she told Mrs. Felton that she knew her generous heart would rejoice to hear of her good fortune; that in consequence of it she had given up all professional pursuits, and had made a vow never to sing even gratuitously for any one again, "except," she added, "for *you*, my dear Mrs. Felton, whose musical talent is such as to entitle you to demand an exertion of the best efforts of others."

Mrs. Felton, whose heart was not at all given to rejoice at the good fortune of other people, received the first part of the intelligence very coldly, but heard the other with unfeigned delight, though she could not at first divine why this kind exception was made in her favour.

Miss Spenlove perceived the satisfaction her proposal had given, and went on to the complete furtherance of her project.

"My dear lady," said she, "I know you compose pretty melodies;—perhaps you have some by you to which you would like that I should put a bass. It would give me the greatest pleasure to be of use to you in that way; and perhaps you would sing over with me the song which I have brought."

Mrs. Felton complied; and without at all wounding her self-love, Miss Spenlove contrived to give her a most instructive lesson in singing; and she was too clever not to perceive immediately how useful to her a friend would be who could insure to her fame as a composer, by doing for her what she was too ignorant to do for herself; and reputation as a singer, by teaching her to sing in the first style of excellence, without her being at the expense of having a master.

The little melodies were produced; song succeeded to song, duet to duet; graces were noted down for the acquisition of Mrs. Felton, amateur, by the obliging fingers of Miss Spenlove, now amateur also; and, after some hours spent by Miss Spenlove thus in conferring obligation, she returned home, having at length received obligation in return; for Mrs. Felton begged, till her kind friend Miss Spenlove could meet with lodgings entirely to her mind, that she would make her house her home.— And that very night Miss Spenlove, who was elderly and ugly, removed to the house of the young and beautiful Mrs. Felton; being qualified to serve at once both for a foil and for a companion.

Nor, though the ladies had no great affection for each other, had their union during three years ever known interruption, so powerful is the tie called mutual convenience; and as Miss Spenlove paid Mrs. Felton very handsomely for her board, it was impossible for either lady to think herself more the obliger than the obliged.

But they knew each other too well to add to the tie of interest that of esteem and affection. Mrs. Felton, whose temper was not good, used to vent on her companion the ill-humour she was forced to restrain towards others; and as she knew Miss Spenlove wished it to be forgotten that she had ever been a musical professor, Mrs. Felton used to take a malicious pleasure in alarming her by distant allusions to this circumstance, which in time would have been wholly forgotten but by Miss Spenlove's almost pettish refusals to sing anywhere but at Mrs. Felton's, as the reason for her refusal was immediately suspected and whispered round the room, with sneers at her pride and affectation.

But Miss Spenlove took her revenge amply on Mrs. Felton behind her back for the mortification she endured sometimes in her presence; for she had a custom in seeming friendship, but with real malignity, to extol Mrs. Felton's personal charms and talents in so extravagant a manner to her rivals and acquaintance, as could not fail to provoke her hearers to deny her pretensions to such excelling attractions; for few persons can bear to admit the overwhelming superiority of any one, and on such occasions envy with propriety assumes the garb of justice, and may unoffendingly dispute the claims of the person so praised, to such extravagant eulogium. It was very evident therefore that Miss Spenlove set up Mrs. Felton in this manner as a ninepin, only for the pleasure of having her knocked down again;— after which she used with well-feigned concern to hint to Mrs. Felton what envious persons there were in the world! and how strenuously she had asserted her charming friend's rights to universal homage; well knowing, as she did so, that Mrs. Felton would be more hurt at the consciousness of being attacked, than gratified at being defended by such a person as Miss Spenlove.

But it was not by extravagant praise of Mrs. Felton that Miss Spenlove had disgusted St. Aubyn; it was only before women that she amused herself in this manner; to men she had a different way of proceeding;—as thus,

"Do you not think, Mr. St. Aubyn, my sweet friend is the most beautiful creature in the world?"

"She is beautiful certainly, madam, but—"

"Oh! I know very well what you would say,— that she looks differently at different times, and that when not a little rouged she is like all women of fashion, rather sallow."

"No indeed, madam," replied St. Aubyn, "I was not going to say any such thing, and I did not know till this moment that Mrs. Felton's colour was not at all times her own."

"Her own!" returned Miss Spenlove with a laugh as she meant it to be, but which was any thing *but* a laugh, " her own! yes, it is certainly her own, for she bought it with her own money."

"But what a sweet figure she is! though to be sure, at her time of life it is as well perhaps to grow fat."

"At her time of life, madam!"

"Yes, sir, after thirty it is always advantageous for a woman to get a little *em bon point*;" drawing herself up as she spoke with a proud consciousness of rotundity.

"After thirty! I did not suppose Mrs. Felton was above five-and-twenty, madam!" replied St. Aubyn.

"I do not wonder at that, sir; many persons have been so deceived; when dressed she certainly looks very young; for her great vivacity and cheerfulness give a youthful expression to her countenance. Not but that her temper is none of the *evenest*. She is *very* irritable at times;—however, I love her so much, dear creature! with all her faults, that I cannot help remaining with her, though, as I have an independent fortune, (bridling as she said this,) and could live handsomely *anywhere* for what I pay Mrs. Felton for my board, I need not stay with her if I did not like it."

"No, to be sure not," replied St. Aubyn, by way of saying something, and disgusted with this conversation; still, however, he felt less angry with Miss Spenlove, when he heard she was a woman of independent fortune, because till she said this he had looked upon her as a poor dependant on Mrs. Felton, who vented on her benefactress in this manner the hatred excited in her by a sense of obligation which she felt that she could never repay. Now the case was altered; however, disgust was still the predominant feeling in him towards Miss Spenlove; and though he was in a degree amused by the ingenious malice with which, while praising Mrs. Felton's beauty, she insinuated that her beauty was the result of art; that though she looked young, she was in reality old; that though she seemed cheerful and good-humoured, she was in truth the contrary; still he could scarcely refrain from putting a stop to this effusion of wormwood mixed up in syrup, by asking very seriously whether after this conversation he was to consider her as Mrs. Felton's friend or her enemy?

But as I am quite as much tired of this sickening though too natural conversation as St. Aubyn himself, I shall repeat no more of it, but go to pleasanter contemplations; namely, the very different subjects discussed by St. Aubyn and Mrs. Felton, when she became his travelling companion. They delighted to converse on literature, the arts, morals, and every thing connected with them, and it was with pain that they found themselves arrived at the end of their journey; where Mrs. St. Aubyn beheld with delight, but Mrs. Selby with pain, the mutual satisfaction which beamed in the countenances of Mrs. Felton and St. Aubyn, as they declared how pleasant their drive had been; and the expression of interest and pleasure with which St. Aubyn, apparently regardless of every one else, eagerly offered his arm to Mrs. Felton, when they began their walk to the lake.

Till this excursion took place, the first wish of Mrs. St. Aubyn's heart was, that her son should marry Miss Castlemain; but now her only ambition was to see him the husband of the honourable Mrs. Felton, while she in fancy beheld herself by this means reinstated in those gay and fashionable scenes which her own vicious folly had caused her to forego, but which she had never ceased most biterly to regret.

No such sanguine expectations for the aggrandizement of St. Aubyn entered into the more penetrating mind of her friend Mrs. Selby. She accurately read and justly appreciated the character of Mrs. Felton; and it was not only from dislike of that lady that she could not bear so precious a votary should do homage at the shrine of her vanity, but also from a conviction that Mrs. Felton in no one point of view was worthy to attach a being so excellent as St. Aubyn; the feeling of esteem for him being even more strong in the heart of Mrs. Selby than aversion to Mrs. Felton; whom she would never have admitted into her house, had she not been related to Mr. Selby's first wife, and had not he in early life been under obligations to Mrs. Felton's father.

To be brief; that evening St. Aubyn retired to rest more charmed than ever with the fascinating widow, especially when his mother, following him to his apartment, told him, almost with tears of joy, that Mrs. Felton had given her a most pressing invitation to visit her in London the ensuing spring, when London would be most full, and she could introduce her into such circles as she ought to be seen in.

"Kind Mrs. Felton!" exclaimed St. Aubyn, kissing his mother affectionately; "she is irresistibly charming; but of all her charms, the greatest she has for me is her affectionate attention to you!"

That night when St. Aubyn laid his head on his pillow he certainly did not recollect so vividly, nor think of so long as usual, a pair of dark-blue eyes peeping at him almost by stealth, between the crimson curtains of a certain pew in a certain church, from under the longest and thickest black eyelashes that ever were seen; while the blushing cheek beneath them was shaded by a large cottage bonnet tied with blue ribands.

Three weeks had already passed rapidly in exploring the beauties of the lakes, when the party arrived at Keswick or Derwentwater; and as that lake was well known to every one of the party, as neither Mrs. St. Aubyn's house nor purse would allow her to entertain her companions, and as Mr. Hargrave was absent from home, it was resolved that one day only should be spent in revisiting Borrowdale, Watenlath, and the other surrounding beauties; and that then, after visiting Bassenthaite and other scenes worthy of notice, they should proceed to Penrith, and devote all the time they could spare to the varied and extensive beauties of Ulswater and its environs. It was not without many tender and many painful recollections that St. Aubyn found himself once more in the vicinity of the White Cottage, and saw the church where, and where only, he had now for weeks beheld the dear companion of his youth and his studies; he therefore seized the first opportunity to steal from his party and mount a hill whence he could discern the chimneys of Mrs. Castlemain's dwelling. And when he returned he was absent and pensive during the remainder of the evening; but so marked had lately been his attentions to Mrs. Felton, that she, blinded by vanity, was sometimes inclined to attribute his abstraction to love for a present not an absent idol; and of the rest of the party some hoped and some feared the same thing.

Already before Mrs. St. Aubyn's sight swam white and silver favours and bridal finery, and she had nodded, and winked, and insinuated the same belief into pretty Miss Travers, who thought with a sigh that Mrs. Felton was a very lucky woman. But Mrs. Selby, who did not believe the dangerous widow was capable of being in love even with a St. Aubyn, and who believed her only aim was conquest, was alarmed lest the peace of a heart so valuable should be ruined by the wiles of a coquette. In this instance, however, Mrs. Selby was only right in part. Mrs. Felton had made no vow against marrying again; and if St. Aubyn had been already in possession of his uncle's immense fortune, she was so charmed with the beauty of his person and the graces of his manner, that she would willingly have resigned her liberty to him, and have been proud to exhibit her handsome husband in the circles of high life. But love in a cottage was not at all to Mrs. Felton's taste; and so Miss Spenlove assured Mr. Selby, when he hinted his suspicions of St. Aubyn's attachment to her, the first time they were alone together.

"Pho! nonsense!" said she, "I know her; she is only at her usual tricks. I endeavoured to put the young man on his guard, and tell him what she really is; but he is mighty conceited, and I saw by his look he did not believe me."

Mr. Selby, good man, listened, and was astonished; for he had been completely the dupe of Miss Spenlove's " sweet creatures," and " dear creatures," and supposed that she idolized her friend with even blind affection.

"My dear," said he to his wife at night, " would you believe it? I have discovered that Miss Spenlove's affection for Mrs. Felton is all put on."

"Oh ho! is it so?" replied Mrs. Selby; " what, have you only now found that out, Mr. Selby?"—who, poor man, sighed to think that he should never, if he lived even to the age of Methuselah, be as wise as his wife.

It was now an understood thing, that St. Aubyn was always to drive Mrs. Felton, and of course he handed her into the chaise as soon as it drove round. The preference he felt for her society he had no scruple in showing by his manner; and Mrs. Felton, though she had sometimes doubts herself on the subject, was charmed to discover, by the looks and conduct of the rest of the party, that most of them suspected St. Aubyn, though not yet her declared lover, was on the point of becoming so; and she felt authorized to add to the list of her captives, the name of Henry St. Aubyn.

Mrs. Felton had now in a great measure carried her point; still, she wished her conquest to be proved past doubt, by a regular declaration; and towards this she saw no symptoms of any progress; not that she meant to accept his offer, but most earnestly did she wish to have the honour of refusing it.

"I wish I could excite his jealousy," thought Mrs. Felton, " in order to bring him to the point; but that is impossible, as he can't be jealous of Selby, and there is no other beau." Fortune, however, as if eager to indulge so amiable a wish in this accomplished coquette, sent another beau, when she least expected it; and such a beau! no other than the man whom, of all others, she was the most desirous of charming, and to whom she would most willingly be made captive in return.

Mr. Wanford was, at the time I am speaking, one of the most admired and courted young men in the regions of fashion. Fortunately for him, when he first went to college, his fortune was so small, and his expectations so trifling, that he knew his only chance of distinction and success in life, was in having resolution enough to labour to deserve them; and Mr. Wanford had ambition; he had also talents and perseverance; and the same year that he took a very high mathematical degree, he was senior medallist also; while the ensuing year, having cultivated with great assiduity his poetical abilities, his poem on a given subject obtained the prize.

At this climax of his well-deserved celebrity, prosperities of another kind poured in upon him, but luckily too late to interfere with those virtuous habits of application in which poverty had fortified him. An uncle of his father died, and left him heir to a large independent fortune; and at the same time, his mother's brother, who had acquired an immense fortune in trade, had interest enough to obtain a peerage; and, having no children of his own, the patent was made out with remainder to the son of his sister—this fortunate Mr. Wanford.

It is not to be wondered at that such sudden prosperity should in some measure turn the head of the young and laurelled scholar; and that the expectance of title, and the possession of wealth, should not sit so gracefully on him as on those to whom such things have long been habitual. But to do him justice, he was quite as proud of his academical as of his other honours; and while he was abroad on his travels he published a volume of poems, consisting of some original pieces, and some elegant translations of Greek and other fragments.— This volume, coming as it did from the heir to a barony, and the possessor already of a very fine fortune, was received with much admiration by those ladies and gentlemen who unite literature with fashion. But the return of Mr. Wanford from abroad was anxiously expected not only by all who had read his works, and had heard of his reputation; he was considered as a prize worth trying for by illiterate mothers who had daughters to dispose of, and by widows of small jointures, who only knew that he was rich and lord Erdington's heir. To Mrs. Felton he was welcome, as scholar, poet, heir, and rich man; "and if I ever part with my liberty again," she had often said to herself, "it shall be to Mr. Wanford."

Being so highly gifted as I have described him, it was almost unnecessary for him to possess beauty of person or grace of manner; however, he was well made though not tall, and handsome rather than otherwise; and his manners, though at times rather haughty and important, were generally pleasing, and sometimes even insinuating. Of marrying he had at present not the most distant intention, and he had been so much the object of coquetry, that he was become no mean proficient in the art himself. Such was the man who was now making the tour of the Lakes, accompanied by his only sister, who resided with him, in a carriage of his own construction, which he drove himself, and of which the back part contained his man and his sister's waiting-maid.

Mr. Wanford had not returned to England long before the close of the season for parties in London; and it had so happened that though Mrs. Felton had been invited more than once to meet this gentleman, long the object of her secret wishes, he had either gone away before she had entered, or had come after she had left the house; while, in spite of her repeated invitations to him sent by friends of both parties, he never gratified her so far as to visit her either in a morning or an evening. She had therefore never seen him, nor he her; and when Miss Spenlove, who had seen Mr. Wanford arrive, and had heard his name from his servants, announced his arrival to Mrs. Felton at the inn at Patterdale, the joy she felt was so great as to make her jump off her seat, and exclaim, "The man here whom of all others I am most ambitious to see and know! What a fortunate event!"

"What a fortunate man! you might also have said," observed St. Aubyn, with perhaps a little feeling of mortification; while Mrs. St. Aubyn uttered a "Dear me!" in no cheerful tone, and Mrs. Selby drawled out a significant "Oh ho!"

But Mrs. Felton was too much engaged in her own speculations to attend to them.— Thought, that rapid traveller, had already gone through all the advantages accruing from meeting Mr. Wanford in such a spot; and could she but be introduced to him, could she but have such opportunities with him as she had with St. Aubyn, her success seemed sure, her marriage undoubted! But how could she contrive to make herself known to him? "Necessity has no law," says the proverb; and if nothing but a bold stroke can succeed, Mrs. Felton is too much a woman of the world to scruple it.

"My dear Mr. St. Aubyn," said Mrs. Felton, "will you do me an essential service?"

"Any thing in my power."

"It is absolutely necessary that I should be introduced to the gentleman (Mr. Wanford) who is just arrived, Lord Erdington's nephew and heir; would you then have the great goodness to tell him that Mrs. Felton wishes much to make his acquaintance, and begs the pleasure of seeing him? He knows me by *name* and reputation very well already."

"If then, madam," replied St. Aubyn gravely, "he knows you by name and reputation already, and learns, as no doubt he will do, or indeed as he shall do, (for I will take care of that,) that the honourable Mrs. Felton is at this inn, it will be his business surely to solicit the honour of knowing you."

"To be sure—certainly," said Mrs. St. Aubyn.

Mrs. Felton, who felt the delicacy of this reproof, blushed deeply both with a sense of shame and of resentment; though she fancied jealousy as much as regard for her dignity had dictated St. Aubyn's reply.

"My dear sir," she replied, forcing a laugh, "where a woman is conscious she confers full as much, or more honour than she receives by courting an acquaintance, there surely is no harm in her making the first advances."

"Not to a lady; but indeed I respect you, or any one of your sex, too much to endure the idea of flattering any man's vanity so far as to be the bearer of solicitations from a fair lady to a gentleman, requesting the pleasure of making his acquaintance."

"Mr. St. Aubyn," cried Mrs. Felton, too determined on her purpose to be withheld from it even by the risk of disgusting her friendly monitor, "it is necessary, as I said before, that I should know Mr. Wanford, as I have a message to deliver to him; and if you will not repeat to him what I said, I will go and introduce myself."

"Rather than you should do that, madam," said St. Aubyn, "I will, though reluctantly, obey you."

At this moment Miss Spenlove entered the room.

"So!" said she, "Mr. Wanford has a lady with him, I find!"

"A lady!" echoed St. Aubyn, immediately returning; while Mrs. Felton blushed from alarm, lest the lady should be such a one as to prevent the possibility of her introduction.

"Yes; but it is only his sister."

"His sister!" cried Mrs. Felton pettishly, but with her countenance brightening up; "why could you not say so before, Miss Spenlove? and then I should have felt no difficulty in this business; for Mr. St. Aubyn's delicacy will not be shocked by my requesting the honour of knowing Miss Wanford."

"Undoubtedly not," he answered, bowing profoundly, and left the room.

"Well, and may I ask who this great gentleman is?" asked Mrs. St. Aubyn in a tone of pique.

"He is a poet, a scholar, a fine gentleman, and the heir to a nobleman," replied Mrs. Felton.

"May be so; but I never heard of him before."

"It would not break his heart if he knew it," said Mrs. Felton contemptuously; "he is sufficiently known and admired where he wishes to be."

"Then if this be true, and you do not know him, it must be because, by you at least, he does not *wish* to be known and admired," sarcastically observed Mrs. Selby.

"Think what you please, ma'am," replied Mrs. Felton angrily.

"Dear me!" cried Mrs. St. Aubyn; "what a fuss there is about this man, who, I am sure, if that be he coming yonder, is not half as handsome as my son."

"Ridiculous! beneath my notice!" muttered Mrs. Felton, looking at Mrs. St. Aubyn with such a frown, that she almost fancied it was her brother whom she beheld.

Just then Mr. Wanford passed the window, at which stood Miss Travers, who had taken off her riding-hat from the heat of the weather, and let fall over her shoulders a profusion of fine light hair; while on her cheek not only the "sultry season glowed," but the bloom of healthy and happy eighteen!

Mr. Wanford gazed earnestly at her, and *almost* stopped as he gazed, but recovering himself passed on. Soon however he returned pretending to call his dog, though his eyes were riveted on the now blushing Miss Travers, who from native modesty turned away and went to a remote corner of the room; on which Mr. Wanford repassed the window and disappeared.

"Well, I declare," said Mrs. St. Aubyn, "my dear, you have made a conquest certainly of this Mr. Wanford."

"Ridiculous!" muttered Mrs. Felton.

"Not so ridiculous neither," cried Mrs. St. Aubyn; "for I am sure he had no eyes for any one else."

"That was very certain," observed Mrs. Selby; "and I think it was strange after your message to his sister, Mrs. Felton, that he should not look for you!"

"Perhaps," said Miss Spenlove, "he took Miss Travers for my dear friend."

"Impossible!" exclaimed Mrs. Selby. "Take that young thing for Mrs. Felton? Nonsense!"

"It is not the first time, madam," said Miss Spenlove looking grave, "that Mrs. Felton has been taken for a girl of eighteen."

At this moment St. Aubyn put his head into the room, saying, "Miss Wanford desires her compliments to you, madam, and she will wait on you presently." So saying, he disappeared, and the party soon after saw Miss Wanford walking along a path at a little distance, whither St. Aubyn had been in search of her.

However, instead of coming immediately into the house, she passed the window, after having asked of the waiters which way her brother went.

"Very odd that," said Mrs. Selby; "it seems as if she dares not make the acquaintance unsanctioned by her brother."

This remark gave Mrs. Felton as much pain as it was intended to give her; for the elegant widow knew very well, that though generally received in society, there were some squeamish and rigid persons who were not desirous of visiting her; and as Mr. Wanford had hitherto rejected all her advances to acquaintance, it was possible that his sister might be of the latter number. St. Aubyn, meanwhile, ever ready to oblige, was gone to gather some curious grass which he had discovered in a wet ditch behind the inn; a grass of which Mrs. Felton, who studied botany among other things, was desirous of obtaining specimens; and in this ditch he was standing mid-leg in water when Miss Wanford hastened to her brother, who was sitting on a bank and sketching a fine tree on the other side of the hedge under which St. Aubyn was.

"So, Frank!" cried Miss Wanford, as soon as she saw her brother; "who do you think is here, and has sent the handsomest young man I ever saw to solicit the pleasure of making my acquaintance? No other than Mrs. Felton!"

"What! *the* Mrs. Felton—"

"Yes, her own honourable self."

"Fairly hooked, by Jupiter! Now I must

know her whether I would or no," returned Wanford; while St. Aubyn coughed and hemmed very audibly to inform them they were overheard, though he stooped down as he did so, lest the young lady should recognise him and be shocked at finding he had heard her praises of his beauty. But regardless of St. Aubyn's honourable notice, they went on.

"I never could understand why you would not know Mrs. Felton, brother."

"Because, when I found she was so desirous of making my acquaintance, I suspected she had designs on me."

"Well said, my modest brother! and so I suppose you think, in soliciting my acquaintance, all she aims at is yours?"

"To be sure I do."

"And so do I. For, from what I have heard of Mrs. Felton, I do not believe she ever cares an atom for the females of a family, unless she can through them best obtain ascendency over the males."

Here Mr. St. Aubyn smiled to himself, and again hemmed audibly, though in vain.

"I see you know this sweet enslaver as well as I do, Bell. Well—as I must know her, I must; but if marriage be her end, I can tell her she cannot catch me in that snare; and if her only aim be to make a fool of me as she has done of other men, that I defy her to do. But, pray, have you met?"

"No; I sent word I would wait on her soon; but as I never mean to make an acquaintance till it is approved by you, I chose to consult you first, especially as Mrs. Felton is——"

"Generally received, Bell, and that is enough for me. I do not wish my sister to set up for being more wise and more virtuous than two-thirds of the world; besides, you know, Bell, you are very desirous to be invited to Mrs. Felton's parties. But come, since the fair widow will attack us, who's afraid? Besides, in her party I suspect is a lovely Hebe of a girl that I should like to be better acquainted with; and I shall have no little fun in playing off this inexperienced blushing beauty against this celebrated and dangerous coquette."

So saying they walked towards the inn, leaving St. Aubyn warned and enlightened sufficiently, if he had needed such warning; and not pleased with Wanford for his worldly and convenient morality; for, if it was to be more wise and virtuous than two-thirds of the world to avoid association with women of doubtful reputation, he proved in St. Aubyn's opinion, by not wishing his sister to be thus wise and virtuous, that his sense of propriety was not over-nice, and that he was not a very fit guardian for the honour and reputation of a young and pleasing woman.

"And this formidable coquette, whom they have thus freely discussed, is my amiable friend Mrs. Felton! and this woman whom I so much respected and admired, was really *mean* enough to want to solicit the acquaintance of a man who, it seems, has purposely hitherto rejected all her overtures to acquaintance! Sure is the saying, that where there is much vanity there is no pride, (virtuous pride I mean)!" And with a feeling of pity not unmixed with contempt for Mrs. Felton, he returned to the inn to change his shoes and stockings, before he joined his companions in a party on the lake.

But new arrangements had taken place during St. Aubyn's absence, in consequence of a violent thunder-storm, and it was agreed that in order to lose no time they should take a cold dinner while the bad weather lasted, and when it was over go on the lake, and remain on the water or its banks till the approach of night should force them to return to Penrith, their head-quarters.

Mr. and Miss Wanford, therefore, when they arrived at the inn, found the party preparing to sit down to dinner; but having been graciously met at the door by Mrs. Felton, and being pressed to sit down to their meal by her and Mr. and Mrs. Selby, they complied with the request, and soon felt themselves as much at ease as if they had been old acquaintances. When the dinner was completely served up, and the ladies seated, Mr. Wanford took the chair at the head of the table between Mrs. Selby and Mrs. Felton; on which Mrs. St. Aubyn hastily said, "You have taken my son's place, sir."

"Your son's place, madam!" replied Wanford coldly; "pray, where is he? I have not the honour of knowing him. Oh! I suppose that gentleman at the bottom of the table is your son."

"Dear me! if I ever heard the like! Why, Mr. Selby is as old as I am."

"Not happening to know how old that is, I hope you will excuse me, madam, and your son too when he makes his appearance, for I must keep my seat." And this he said with an air, as if he felt that the heir of Lord Erdington had some right to sit at the head of the table next to the honourable Mrs. Felton.

"Gracious goodness!" whispered Mrs. St. Aubyn to Mrs. Selby, "what airs the man gives himself! I can't abide him. And then for Mrs. Felton not to tell him it was my son's place!"

Wanford, who was only too fond of that mean order of fun denominated quizzing and banter, and to which those who reside in college are but too much addicted, soon discovered that Mrs. St. Aubyn was an excellent subject for this sort of diversion; and perceiving by her fanning herself violently, and other symptoms, that she was displeased, he very coolly exclaimed, leaning towards her as he did so, "Are we not friends?"

"No, sir," she replied, "nor even acquaintance."

"But I hope we shall be, dear madam," returned Wanford; "no endeavours on my part, I am sure, shall be wanting to bring about so desirable a circumstance. Shall we drink wine together?"

"No, sir, I never drink wine so soon; though stay—yes, I will take half a glass, for I remember my husband's mother, lady Mary St. Aubyn," (whom by the by she always talked of when she wished to impress any one with an idea of her consequence,) "yes, lady Mary used to say that it was rude to refuse to drink wine with any one."

"Lady Mary is a very sensible woman, and here's her good health."

"Good health, sir! Why did one ever hear the like! The poor soul has been dead these sixteen years."

"Indeed; I am very sorry for it."

"Sorry! Why, sir, you did not know her, I dare say."

"Not I, madam; I was only sorry on your account; as you seem so fond of her, you cannot help bringing her into company by head and shoulders."

"Indeed, sir, lady Mary was not a woman to be brought into any company against her will, and those whom she associated with might think themselves honoured; for, sir, lady Mary was none of your upstart yesterday quality; she was of the old and right sort, and a duke's daughter, sir."

"So much the better for her, madam," returned Wanford, who thought this was meant as a sarcasm on his want of family antiquity, and the bought peerage of his tradesman uncle. "So much the better for her. It is a fine thing to be a duke's daughter!" Then, with mock pathos, he added, "I wish I was a duke's daughter! but I fear it is impossible for me to be one now."

"Dear me!" whispered Mrs. St. Aubyn to Mrs. Selby, "did you ever hear the like! This your wit and your scholar indeeed! Why, he appears to me no better than a fool or a madman!" And while the rest of the party were laughing spite of themselves, at Wanford's nonsense, St. Aubyn entered the room. There was such an air of command about St. Aubyn's person and manner, that he always inspired strangers at first sight with a sort of involuntary deference; and Wanford, who felt himself irresistibly impelled to laugh at the mother, was as irresistibly impelled to respect the son. When St. Aubyn saw Wanford occupying his usual seat, and that the table seemed completely filled elsewhere, he exclaimed with a smile,

"The table's full."

On which Miss Spenlove said,

"Here is a place reserved."

offering him a vacant seat between herself and Miss Travers, which he instantly accepted. But Wanford, with more graciousness than usual, said—"I understand, sir, that I am occupying your usual place, and I earnestly wish to exchange it for that you have now taken."

"Impossible, sir! I know its value too well," he replied, smiling, "to bear to inflict on any one the pain of quitting it."

"And it is, sir, because I feel its value equally," answered Wanford, "that I am resolved not to expose a fellow-creature to the misery of regretting it."

"Well, sir, if I must be made happy at another's expense, I must;" and they exchanged seats. Mrs. Felton felt excessive mortification during this dialogue, which in words appeared so flattering to her vanity; for she saw that Wanford, whose eyes were oftener turned on Miss Travers than herself, was glad of an excuse to sit next that young lady; and in St. Aubyn's smile, and his extravagant compliments, so unlike his usual manner, she read that his heart was quite at ease, though she had carried her point, and the man she so much desired to know was sitting by her side. Nor was the pleasantness of her feelings increased by witnessing the entire devotion of Wanford to the pretty Miss Travers, or the good-humoured archness with which St. Aubyn rallied her on her evident discomposure and absence of mind when he addressed her.

"This man is too much at his ease to be jealous!" thought Mrs. Felton; and she thought right; therefore, as she did not like to lose one admirer before she had gained another, she renewed her attentions to Mrs. St. Aubyn. And though that lady was inclined to resent the epithets of "ridiculous! and absurd!" which she had addressed to her, and also her not keeping the place next her for her son, she was completely pacified by a "when you come to stay with me in town, Mrs. St. Aubyn."

After a hasty meal, as the thunder-storm soon passed away, leaving the scenery of Ulswater still more beautiful than it found it, they went on the lake, and as usual Mrs. Felton and her friend were requested to sing; while St. Aubyn, who, though no coxcomb, could not help looking on Miss Wanford with complacency, as she thought him "the handsomest young man she ever saw," hoped that she also would favour the company with a song, as her brother had hinted that it was in her power to do so. But that lady having declared that her brother had not spoken truth, Mrs. Felton and Miss Spenlove sung a duet; after which which Miss Wanford hoped that Mrs. Felton would sing the song of "Forget thee! No," of which she had heard so much; and Mrs. Felton, as usual, complied with graceful and unaffected alacrity.

"You know who wrote that song," said Miss Spenlove, significantly to Wanford, while Mrs. Felton sighed and hung down her head.

"Oh, yes," replied Wanford, carelessly; "poor Trevor! Ay—he was desperately in love when he wrote it! at least he thought so, and that is pretty much the same thing."

"Thought so! Why, I understood," cried Mrs. St. Aubyn, "that the poor gentleman was near hanging or shooting himself. Did not you say so, Mrs. Selby?"

"Me! Oh, dear no," replied Mrs. Selby, smiling at the inaccuracy of Mrs. St. Aubyn's memory.

"Then, sir, you know the author of this song," addressing Wanford, (for she did not believe it was addressed to Mrs. Felton,) "and did the gentleman recover his disappointment? and is he living, sir?"

"He was living, madam, in 1798, at Florence, when I parted with him."

"Poor man! Retired into a convent, I presume, disgusted with the world?" asked Mrs. Selby in an ironical tone.

"What an absurd idea!" cried Mrs. Felton. "Mr. Trevor was too wise a man, however disappointed, to seek a remedy in seclusion."

"True, madam," answered Wanford, archly smiling; "though your cruelty drove my friend to despair, I see you appreciated his wisdom justly. You are right — my friend sought a better remedy than seclusion or the cloister's vows for his misery."

"How, how is his health, sir?" asked Mrs. Felton.

"Never better; and in the smiles of one beautiful woman he sought consolation for the *frowns* of another."

"What, sir!" cried Miss Spenlove, "is Mr. Trevor married?" for Mrs. Felton was too confused to speak.

"He is, madam, to a most lovely and admirable woman, indeed; and I am sure Mrs. Felton's generosity and tenderness of heart are such as to make her rejoice to hear, that my friend's eternity of woe exists no longer anywhere than in his song."

"Certainly, sir, certainly," said the lady; while Mr. Selby, laughing heartily, exclaimed, "So much for the constancy and sincerity of a poet!"

"*Apropos*," said Wanford. "I should like to read those doleful verses. I will not ask *you* to *repeat* them, Mrs. Felton; but perhaps you can favour me with a sight of them."

"I cannot! but Mr. St. Aubyn can, for I wrote them out for him."

"Indeed, I am very sorry, and ashamed to own," replied St. Aubyn, blushing, "that I have *lost* them."

"Lost them!" said Mrs. Felton, pale with mortification; "it is a proof that my gift was not of much *value* in your opinion."

"You do me great injustice then; I valued it so much that I had it constantly about me."

"But not in a safe place, it seems."

"I thought it so; but I suspect that in stooping over the boat yesterday, it fell into the water."

"Oh ho!" said Mr. Selby, borrowing a phrase and a look from his wife, "then I suspect you wore it in your bosom, and it fell out from thence."

"No, indeed I did not, sir," hastily replied St. Aubyn, blushing with a sort of indignant feeling, and conscious *that* place was sacred to the hand-writing of only one being in creation; "no, indeed, sir, I wore it in my waistcoat pocket."

"Ay, ay," said his sapient mother, "he does not like to own that he did so, but I have seen a piece of folded paper in his bosom."

"Madam," replied St. Aubyn firmly but respectfully, "I know no motive sufficient to justify a falsehood. I wore the valuable verses which I have unfortunately lost nowhere but in my waistcoat pocket, and the paper to which you allude is still where you discovered it, and this is it." Then, with many blushes, St. Aubyn produced a folded paper from his bosom, and holding it towards Mrs. Felton, said, "You see, madam, this cannot be the paper in question, for that was embossed paper, and edged with green."

"It was sir," said Mrs. Felton in a tone of pique.

"Yes," observed Mrs. Selby, "Mrs. Felton wrote it with her best pen on her best paper, and in her best hand; and *yet* you lost it! O fie, Henry, to set so little value on a lady's favours!"

"But *all* ladies' favours he is not so negligent of, it seems," said Wanford.

"On that subject, sir," replied St. Aubyn, proudly, "I do not admit of any comments."

"I dare say," cried Mrs. Selby, in hopes of laughing off what might grow serious, "that treasured paper contains the white satin bandeau that I lost off my hair the other day.— Well, at my time of life, who could have thought it?"

"But, my dear," said Mr. Selby, "as at your time of life you are too wise to wear satin bandeaus, this is no stray charm of yours that has met with so sure a pound."

"No, but I remember now that Mrs. Felton lost *her* bandeau," archly observed Mrs. St. Aubyn.

"Oh ho!" cried Mrs. Selby.

"Yes, yes," nodded Mr. Selby, while St. Aubyn blushed so deeply, that every one *but* Mrs. Selby and Mrs. Felton herself, was convinced the guess was a just one. However, the former being anxious to drop a subject displeasing to St. Aubyn, and the latter being willing to let it be supposed her bandeau was so highly honoured, were silent, while nods and winks went round; and here the conversation dropped.

The day, on the whole, was one of mortification, and therefore of pain, to Mrs. Felton. In the first place, she had lowered herself in

St. Aubyn's esteem, by wishing to force herself on Wanford's notice; and she had pretty plainly shown Mrs. St. Aubyn that her temper was not so mild as self-command had hitherto made it appear. In the second place, it was evident that Wanford, as yet, admired Miss Travers more than he did her; and that St. Aubyn, who she fancied was all but her slave, was wholly from love towards her, for he was free from jealousy; besides, he had lost her precious hand-writing, and wore some one's else she believed in his bosom. And lastly, Mr. Trevor had forgotten her, and was happy with another woman!

But though a little disappointed, Mrs. Felton was not disheartened. She expected that Mr. Wanford, as the friend of Mr. Trevor, who had been in reality the victim of the most consummate coquetry, would feel prejudiced against her; and she made it her study to remove this prejudice as fast as possible, even though she gave up St. Aubyn wholly in order to effect it, and resigned his weak mother to the insignificance in their party from which her notice had raised her. But the difficulty was, how to obtain enough of Wanford's society to make him willing to acquit her towards his friend, by feeling her power to charm himself. She saw that it was a matter of indifference to him whether she noticed his sister or not; therefore she could not make any impression on his heart by gratifying his affections. Alone, she never saw him; for having dared to ask him to let her go with him in his very pretty and novel equipage (which was in truth the ugliest thing ever seen,) Wanford had coolly replied, he was very sorry, but that he was already engaged to drive Hebe, as he called Miss Travers, but hoped at some future time that he should be able to devote himself to the *maturer* charms of Minerva.

This was insupportable, especially as it had been overheard by St. Aubyn, who, with a smile too natural to be the result of pique, said, "You see, after all, you must take up with me; so you had better submit to your fate with a good grace, and let me hand you into my humble chaise, which, when you are in it, I consider as a triumphal car;" and Mrs. Felton, with assumed gaiety, complied.

I must mention here, that St. Aubyn wrote out from memory a copy of the song which he had lost, and gave it to Mrs. Felton in his *own hand-writing*.

Mrs. Felton would have been still more assured, that St. Aubyn's admiration of her was wholly unmixed with love, had she known of the dialogue that had taken place the preceding evening between him and his mother. Mrs. St. Aubyn had followed her son into his chamber, requesting a few minutes' conversation with him, when she exclaimed, "Oh! my dear Henry! it grieves me to the soul, to think how you are going on with Mrs. Felton!"

"What do you mean, my dear mother? I protest I do not understand you."

"Why, to see you so grave and so queer, and her so cold and so pettish, after you have been so loving together, and I thought and hoped all would soon be settled between you."

"Do I hear right, madam? For pity's sake, what can you mean? as I said before."

"Why, that you are going wrong together, I am sure, only owing to your not speaking *out*, as she expected you would do. Now pray come to an explanation with her; for I can't bear to see that pert jackanapes going to put your nose out of joint, as the saying is."

"I protest I cannot yet comprehend what your meaning is, and what I am to explain."

"Nay, dear child, this is all jealous spite and pride, I see very clearly; but do conquer it, do, my darling, to make me happy, and do what she expects and wishes, that is, pop the question to her."

"Pop the question, madam! I have no question to ask Mrs. Felton. To what question do you allude?"

"Now as if you did not know, Henry, what popping the question means! Why, asking her to *marry* you, to be sure."

"Marry me! ask Mrs. Felton to marry me! And is the state of your son's heart so little known to you, that you could suppose him capable of loving, and wishing to marry Mrs Felton?"

"Well, did one ever hear the like! I could have sworn, and so could other people, I'm sure, that you were in love with each other; and I was so, rejoiced to think that I should call the honourable Mrs. Felton daughter, and go and live with her and you in a fine house, and be as happy as the day was long!"

"My dearest mother, you greatly distress me! Is it possible that my attentions to Mrs. Felton, such as she had a right to command from any man, could lead you or any one to suppose I was seeking to gain her affections? Certain am I, however, that, great as is her vanity, she knows too much of the human heart to have been herself deceived; and therefore I have nothing to reproach myself with,—else I should be miserable!"

"Miserable!" replied Mrs. St. Aubyn in a whining tone, "miserable! I am sure you have made *me* so. There! to be thus disappointed, when I thought I had got a daughter-in-law, that was so fond of me, and had invited me to go and see her! Dear me! I shall not have half the pleasure in staying with her in London, now I find there is nothing serious between her and you."

"My dear madam, you will never be asked, depend upon it, to visit Mrs. Felton."

"No, child! Why, how can you be so provoking? Why, she repeated her invitation only yesterday; and I am sure, if she does not again, it will be all *your fault*."

"Believe me, she never meant you should be her guest. I have reason to think Mrs. Felton is not the amiable woman she seems to be, and that under that apparent kindness and good-nature she conceals a cold heart and a bad temper."

"Indeed! Well, and now I recollect, when you were not present to-day she called me 'ridiculous! absurd!' and looked as if she could have eaten me, just like my brother!"

"Very likely; and now you will see that the attentions she paid to you and me she will transfer to Mr. Wanford and his sister, and neglect us."

"No, child, no; I can't think she is so bad as that, neither."

"Well, we shall see. However, I thank her; for I am indebted to her for many pleasant hours, and for making me forget awhile the secret care that oppresses me; for surely, my dear mother, you cannot have forgotten that I undertook this journey not only to oblige you, but also to dissipate the uneasiness I felt at being forced to relinquish the beloved society at the White Cottage, and even that of Mr. Egerton, in compliance with my uncle's will!"

"Dear me! Why, what a fool I have been! Well, to be sure I see it all now; and so you have not forgotten Miss—"

"Hush! hush! dear mother! and let me try to rest. So, good night, good night! and do not be so cruel as to wish your son to be the husband of Mrs. Felton."

Mrs. St. Aubyn reluctantly departed, and St. Aubyn retired to bed, but not to sleep; for so nice was his sense of honour, that he was apprehensive lest his attentions to Mrs. Felton should have gone beyond what admiration alone warranted, and he began to consider how he ought to behave to her in future.

"As I have hitherto done, to be sure," said St. Aubyn mentally, after long deliberation. "If I change my manner now, it would prove that I am self-condemned, and that I think my behaviour hitherto has been improper, while of aught dishonourable my heart acquits me; but for my mother, who *knows* Emma Castlemain, to think that a Mrs. Felton could drive her from my thoughts! Emma, dear Emma!" and thinking on her he fell asleep.

The next day he accosted Mrs. Felton with the same attentive manner as usual; and as he saw her earnest desire to captivate Wanford, and now knew her to be a most determined coquette, he anticipated some diversion from observing her plan of operations, in the same manner as a person who has already witnessed a display and an explanation of optical delusions, is amused at observing their power to deceive those who are as yet unacquainted with their nature.

During the walks on the banks and rocks surrounding the lakes, Mrs. Felton, just before they returned to Penrith, contrived to begin a long enumeration to Wanford, whose arm she had as it were seized, of the very fine things a friend of hers had said of him; but just as the carriages were announced, she had come to the most interesting part of the eulogy, which was she declared too flattering for her to indulge his vanity with. The bait took; Wanford vowed she should not leave him till she had told him all, as she had excited his curiosity to an intolerable degree.

"No, no,—the carriage is here,—adieu! au revoir," cried Mrs. Felton.

"No adieu for me. You stir not from my side, or sight, till you have told me all," replied Wanford. "Therefore, Mr. St. Aubyn, will you do me the favour to take my place and drive Miss Travers, while I drive this lady?" And St. Aubyn, knowing that in making the exchange he should greatly oblige Mrs. Felton, smilingly agreed to the proposal.

During their ride to Penrith, Mrs. Felton, by feeding all the varied sources of vanity which were abundant in Mr. Wanford, won on him so far that he did not once regret the pretty Hebe whom he had forsaken; and he made himself so agreeable to the fair widow, that it was not till St. Aubyn, with a cheek glowing with exercise, and eyes sparkling with a number of arch meanings, met her at the supper table, that she secretly wished, with a sigh more tender than usual, that he, and not Wanford, had been heir to Lord Erdington. During supper, however, she had no eyes or ears but for Wanford; she took no notice of her dear Mrs. St. Aubyn; and to the great amusement of St. Aubyn, having prevailed on Wanford to repeat some of his poems and little pieces, she had tears for his elogies, smiles for his epigrams, and a loud laugh for his comical songs; in short, she acted over again the same scene with which she had endeavoured to charm him the second evening that they met.

During this time, Mrs. Selby's oh ho's, Miss Spenlove's meaning sneer, Miss Wanford's arch smile, and Mr. Selby's sly winks at his wife, were not unobserved by St. Aubyn, and added to his diversion; but he had no pleasure in observing the comic-pathetic of his mortified mother's expression, nor her evident resentment at seeing her son thrown into the back-ground entirely, and even his poetry forgotten,—that poetry which Mrs. Felton had declared was so fine that it would be a long time before she relished any other! At last maternal vanity got the better of all restraint, and she said to Mr. Wanford,

"My son can write poetry too, sir, and a very pretty poet he is, as that lady can testify. Come hither, Henry, and repeat to that gentleman some of your *beautiful* verses, as Mrs. Felton called them."

"Forgive me, dear madam, if I do not obey you," replied St. Aubyn, blushing, and leaving the room.

"Dear me! see what it is to be modest," added Mrs. St. Aubyn; "my son could no more repeat his own verses than he could fly; though, as I said before, he is so pretty a poet."

This remark excited a general smile at the implied contrast it contained between Wanford and St. Aubyn in respect to modesty; and he, in order to hide his confusion, said,

"A *pretty* poet, madam! your son a pretty poet! That is impossible!"

"Well, did one ever hear the like! to tell me my son *can't* be a pretty poet!"

"I repeat my words, madam, and I appeal to the whole company for the *truth* of what I say. 'Pretty' does not describe St. Aubyn! No—the appellation is unworthy of him. If he be a poet at all, he must be a *handsome* one; his height, his size, the size of his features, pretty indeed! Ask the ladies if they ever thought of calling him the *pretty St. Aubyn*. No, no—that appellation belongs exclusively to his mother," bowing low to her as he spoke.

"Well, good folks, you may laugh, and all this may be true," replied Mrs. St. Aubyn, a little pacified by the compliment to her beauty; "but Mrs. Felton knows my son writes finely, does he not madam? I ask you the question point blank; for I suspect that you do not like to answer me, lest you make your new friend envious and jealous."

"Madam!" replied Mrs. Felton contemptuously, "your suspicions proclaim the depth and nature of your understanding. Mr. St. Aubyn *is* a fine writer, a very fine writer; and so is Mr. Wanford, with this *additional* claim to admiration, a claim which must set him above the fear of competition with your son, that his talents have been stamped with the seal of public approbation, and that the university where he was educated, is proud of calling him her own."

"Not prouder, I'm sure, than I am of calling *Henry* my own, madam, for that matter," said Mrs. St. Aubyn; and Mr. Selby declaring it was past midnight, broke up the party.

The next day, when they all assembled at breakfast, Mrs. St. Aubyn made known the intention of herself and son to take their leave and return to their respective abodes; a resolution which, if she could, Mrs. Felton would have been glad to attribute to the pain St. Aubyn felt at seeing her growing partiality to Wanford; however, she flattered herself that the *rest* of the party would attribute this intended defection to a cause so flattering to her vanity. But Mrs. St. Aubyn, who now disliked her as much as she had formerly liked, was resolved neither she nor any one else should labour under an error which she thought so injurious to Henry, and into which he had hinted to her it was just possible they would fall. She therefore told the company, who expressed universally great regret at the idea of parting with them, that it was quite useless to pretend to alter their determination, for that the reason that could alone have induced her son to leave home so long existed no longer; as the unhappiness which he travelled to dissipate was removed by the removal of the cause.

"Unhappiness!" exclaimed Mrs. Selby.

"Yes; my brother had quarrelled with Mrs. Castlemain; therefore Henry was forbidden her house, and could no longer be with Miss Emma and Mr. Egerton, whom he loves better than the whole world, myself excepted." (Here Mrs. Felton changed colour, in spite of her self-command.) "To-day, however, my son has received a letter from my brother, telling him they are all reconciled, and Henry is so impatient to see his dear friends again, that to make him easy, I promised to set off directly; besides, as my brother is returned, I think it right to go home, lest he should be angry at my staying away so long."

This story was not only true, but had such an air of truth also, that Mrs. Felton was forced to believe in it implicitly, and felt that the rest of the company would believe it also,—therefore all idea of St. Aubyn's ever having had a serious thought of her, must vanish from every mind; and had any doubts remained, the countenance of St. Aubyn, who now entered, would have been sufficient to banish them. His heightened colour, and the joy that sparkled in his eyes, spoke such internal happiness, that his former gaiety appeared languid to his present animation; and there was not a woman in the room that did not feel inclined to envy "Miss Emma," if not Mr. Egerton.

"Hush! mum!" said Mrs. St. Aubyn, "pray don't tell my son *why* he is so happy, and so impatient to be gone."

"So, you are going to leave us, Henry?" cried Mrs. Selby, affectionately.

"Ay, cruel boy!" said Mr. Selby, "and you seem as if you were glad to leave us too."

St. Aubyn blushed, and, suspecting that his mother had been communicative, told him that he was sorry, very sorry, to leave so many kind friends and companions, but glad, very glad to return to others from whom he had long been separated.

"That's enough; we cannot expect more. And pray, Henry," asked Mrs. Selby, interrupting her husband, "how old is Miss Castlemain now?"

"I believe she is, that is to say, I think, yes, she is between sixteen and seventeen now."

"So old! I had no idea of it."

"And she is so tall and formed for her age," observed Mrs. St. Aubyn, "that she might pass for eighteen or twenty; then she is the most beautiful creature that ever was seen;—no art; all pure nature there; and then so learned and so sensible, and yet she never gives herself airs, and sneers at other people who may not know so much as herself!"

"Quite a prodigy!" said Mrs. Felton, with a laugh in which there was no mirth.

"My dear friend," said Mrs. Selby, "Miss Castlemain's merits have made you quite eloquent; but what says *Henry?* does he confirm your account?"

"Oh, yes! my mother has scarcely done her justice; the greatest charm of her character is ingenuousness, and, and——"

"Do not distress yourself," said Mrs. Selby kindly, "you are not on your oath, and you have said enough and looked enough to convince everybody that Miss Castlemain is the most charming of girls, and you the most *impartial* of judges. I *hate* her for being one of the magnets to draw you hence; and so I dare say do some others in the company, if they were as ingenuous as Miss Castlemain and I."

"But is she very intelligent, Henry?" asked Mr. Selby. "I met her a year ago in a large party at your uncle's; and though I thought her face and form perfection itself, I did not hear her say any thing extraordinary."

"No, my dear sir; no, I trust not.—Emma —Miss Castlemain, I mean, has all the modesty becoming her sex and age. She is, as Mr. Egerton once said of her, like the six-hour primrose, that closes its flowers in a bright and dazzling day, and only displays its beauties in shade. At home she talks; uttering with the simplicity of a child, observations that would do honour to a woman."

Here Henry paused and deeply blushed, shocked and astonished to find that he had had nerves enough to say so much; then saying he must go and see after his chaise, which was gone to have one of the wheels mended, he left the room.

Before the company could make any remark on what he had said of Miss Castlemain, Miss Spenlove, who had been absent a few minutes, returned, and told Mrs. Felton that a gentleman with whom she had entered into conversation knew her, and spoke in raptures of her beauty, and would like to renew his acquaintance with her.

"Oh! pray, show the gentleman in," cried Mr. Selby; and Miss Spenlove, who was eager to have him introduced, desired him to enter, before Mrs. Felton could ask a single question.—I have before said that Mrs. Felton, who was a native of a sea-port town, had not been born to the rank of life in which she then was, though education had fitted her to shine in it. Still, her family was respectable, and some of her connexions opulent, though not calculated for companions to the *honourable* Mrs. Felton; and one of these very relations, introduced by Miss Spenlove, now entered the room. He was a thick-set, short-necked, vulgar-looking man, very rich, very purse-proud, and the wit of his own family, a family that he thought the wisest and most virtuous in the world,—and had consequently a thorough contempt for every one not belonging to it; therefore, though he admitted Mrs. Felton, because she had once been a Stokes, might be both clever and handsome, yet, when he heard of her marrying a lord's son, he observed, 'A fool! she had better have married me, or cousin Simon, than a pert sprig of quality." And as Mrs. Felton was conscious that quality and the Stokes family would not agree well together, she had not seen any of her cousin Stokeses since her marriage. Judge then of her consternation, when, while in such company, she saw the door open, and cousin Peter Stokes enter the apartment!

"How do you do, cousin, how do you do?" cried Peter Stokes, advancing to the petrified Mrs. Felton; "I dare say you did not expect to see me;" attempting at the same time to salute her; but she drew back with a sort of horror, and offering him her hand, coldly said, "Bless me, is it you? how are you, sir?"

"Ha! what, I suppose it be n't the fashion to kiss! But I think the children of two own brothers, as you and I are, should not meet like strangers." Then, looking round, he said, "Your servant, gentleman; how do you do, ladies!" and leading Mrs. Felton to a chair, took a seat beside her. "Well, cousin Lucy," he cried, "you look monstrous glum. Ha! there is a pretty girl!" in a half whisper, looking at Miss Travers. "Ay, Lucy, I remember you just such another; but beauty's a blossom—the fairest rose at last is withered. However, I must say you wear well—though all 's not gold that glitters," grinning maliciously; "and as you are now set up for a fine lady," rubbing his cheek, "you may have more there than what's your own."

Never was woman more distressed than Mrs. Felton; to affront so near a relation was impossible, especially a man who was coarse and brutal enough to say the most offensive things if offended; yet she scarcely knew how to forbear resenting his vulgar rudeness.

"Well, cousin, though you are grown so sad and so silent, I'm glad to see you. Ah! poor thing! when you were only Lucy Stokes you used to be as merry as a grig; but honours change manners!"

"True," said Wanford, turning to Mrs. Selby, to whom this scene was highly gratifying:—

'—— new-made honour doth forget men's names;
And if his name be Dick, I'll call him Peter.'"

"What's that you are saying, sir, about Peter?" cried Stokes to the astonished Wanford; "Peter's a good name; I have a great respect for it; *my* name's Peter, sir."

"Sir, I have a great respect for the name too; and I shall have the more since I hear it is the Christian denomination of——Whom, sir—pray, whom have I the honour of addressing?"

"Why, as to the *honour*, sir, that's neither here nor there; though Peter Stokes, sir, is a name on '*Change* as well known and as honourable perhaps as any in the land. My pockets, sir, have no gold outside, but plenty *within!*"

"Not more, I dare say, than this gentleman has," said Mrs. Felton.

"No! who is he?" (whispering.)

"Mr. Wanford, Lord Erdington's heir."

"Heir! a fig for heirship! 'A bird in the hand is worth two in the bush.' But hark ye! as you are so fond of lords and their heirs, I'll inquire, if you please, into the truth of such reports of riches, and let you know the result, that you may not be swindled." This was said in a whisper, but so loud a one that Wanford and the rest of the party were forced to turn to the window to hide their laughter.

"Well, good folks, you are very merry there," said cousin Peter; "as to your names, I have only heard the name of one of you; and my own I was forced to tell myself, thanks to my cousin here, who did not choose to introduce us,—but may be that's the fashion; or perhaps she thinks Peter Stokes is not smart enough, nor grand enough for her to own him, now she has got *honourable* before her name."

"Indeed, sir, you wrong me."

"Sir, indeed! No sirring me, if you please."

"Well then, cousin, allow me to present you to——"

"*Present* me! There's an affected word! Why can't you say *introduce?*"

"Well then, let me *introduce* you to Mrs. Selby — Mr. Selby — Mrs. St. Aubyn — Miss Wanford—Miss Spenlove—Miss *Travers*."

"Ay, that's something like; I wish I was your cousin, young lady, and I would not be put off with a shake of the hand, as I was with cousin Lucy here. All's pure and wholesome on that round cheek, you pretty smiler; but come, tip us your dandy, will you not?" And poor Miss Travers, half-alarmed, complied.

"I admire your taste, sir," observed Wanford; "but allow me to ask, is there a *Mrs.* Peter Stokes?"

"No, sir; but perhaps there may be, one day or other; there's no hurry."

"No, sir, no, you are quite a young man yet."

"Why, yes; but not so young as I was, nor my cousin, here, neither, and she and I are much of a muchness with respect to age."

"You and Mrs. Felton, sir! Impossible!" cried Wanford.

"What, sir, do you doubt my word? I tell you, when I *die*, cousin Lucy may begin to quake in her shoes."

"Really, Mr. Stokes, really," faltered out Mrs. Felton, "you must be——"

"Ay, coz! what am I? Two-and-thirty next birth-day, and so are you?"

"Sir," replied Mrs. Felton almost ready to cry with vexation, "you must not be contradicted, I know; therefore I shall not dispute the point with you."

"Dear me!" whispered Mrs. St. Aubyn to Mrs. Selby, congratulating herself that the register of her parish was out of his reach, "did you ever hear such a rude, vulgar brute?"

"No whispering there, that an't manners, I'm sure, Mrs.——What did you say this lady's name was?"

"St. Aubyn—Mrs. St. Aubyn."

"Mrs. St. Aubyn! What, the widow of St. Aubyn, once member for Cockermouth?"

"The very same, sir, the very same," eagerly replied that lady.

"Well," said the incorrigible Peter Stokes, after looking long and earnestly in her face, "to see how things come about! Why, I dare say then you are Henny Hargrave that was?"

"To be sure I am; but what then, sir?"

"What then? Why, only that five-and-thirty years ago my uncle, Dick Stokes, was so in love with you!"

"Dear me! I am sure, sir, I never knew such a person as Dick Stokes in my life, and you must mean some one else."

"No such thing, I tell you; I know what I say; and his father, my grandfather, would not let him marry you because you had not the cash."

"It is all a mistake, sir, I tell you," cried Mrs. St. Aubyn, provoked at being made so old.

"No, no, madam, it is not; and where's the wonder that some thirty years ago you were young and beautiful? I say, sweetheart," to Miss Travers, "don't be vain of your youth and your beauty; for as the man says in the play,

'To this complexion you must come at last.'

"And a very good complexion it is to come to, sir," said Wanford; "'t is beauty truly blent,' as I see you are fond of quotations, 'whose red and white—' But to speak more to the purpose, sir; give me leave to hint, that if a Mrs. Peter Stokes be not already fixed upon, this young lady whom you admire, Hebe I call her, would perhaps be—"

"Mr. Wanford," said Mrs. Selby angrily, "you distress Miss Travers, and I must desire you to desist." While Mrs. Felton, at length recovering her vexation a little, asked him how his family did.

"My family!" he replied; "why not say *our* family, as your and my family are the same? And if your husband had not been honourable by nature, as well as by name, and done so handsomely by you, as to leave you a good 2000*l.* per annum, you would have been glad enough to have come to *my* family for support."

"Never, sir, never," cried Mrs. Felton, fire flashing from her eyes, "never; I would have begged my bread sooner."

"Well said, spirit, but I don't believe you; however, I am glad to find you so well to do in the world, with your fine landaulet which I saw in the yard; however, as I know nothing about coats-of-arms, I should not have known to whom it belonged but for that chatty lady yonder, Miss or Mrs. Spenlove; but she began talking to me, and she told me that it belonged to Mrs. Felton (the honourable Mrs. Felton,) with whom, she contrived to tell me, she was living, and on the present tour. Oh, thinks I to myself, if so be she is so proud of being the *friend* of this bit of quality, what will she think I ought to be when she hears I am her relation?"

"So then it is to Miss *Spenlove*, is it," said Mrs. Felton with a most malicious expression, "that I am indebted for this happiness!"

"Yes; she knew how fond you were of your own flesh and blood, and so she said she would *present* me."

"Miss Spenlove, you may depend on it I shall not *forget* the obligation."

Just then St. Aubyn entered, and Mrs. Felton introduced him.

"What! is this your son, madam?" cried Stokes, rising and bowing low to St. Aubyn.

"Yes, sir, it is."

"Then, madam, you have deserved well of your country. Why, he looks like a prince! The finest young fellow I ever set my eyes on!" in a half whisper to his cousin; "one would have thought she had him by my uncle; out of my own family, I never saw such a man!"

St. Aubyn now said his chaise was at the door; and having gracefully taken an appropriate leave of each of the company, and received from Mrs. Felton her card of address in town, he handed his mother down stairs; to whom, when she bade her adieu, her faithless friend had said, "Should you ever happen to come to town, Mrs. St. Aubyn, I hope you will not forget to give me *a call*."

"So much for your visit to London, my dear mother," said St. Aubyn as they drove on. "But come, be cheerful, we are hastening to real friends; to fond, affectionate, faithful friends; to beings who mean all that they say, and by whom it is an honour to be respected and beloved."

"My dear child," cried Mrs. St. Aubyn dolefully, "to be sure you forget we are going home to my brother."

As soon as they were gone, the carriages were ordered round; and Mrs. Selby, not out of kindness to Mr. Stokes, but malice to Mrs. Felton, asked the former if he would not do them the honour of joining their party, and accompanying them to and on Ulswater lake.

"I was thinking, madam," said he, "that considering it is so many years since we met, my cousin here might have had the kindness to invite me."

"Impossible! I could not take the liberty," replied Mrs. Felton. "I consider myself as Mr. and Mrs. Selby's guest, and cannot ask any one to join our party."

"Except," retorted Mrs. Selby laughing, "that one be a gentleman of certain agreeable qualities and rank in life;" for it was Mrs. Felton who invited Wanford.

"Well, madam, whether so be my qualities and rank in life," cried Stokes, "be agreeable or not, is neither here nor there—I am her own flesh and blood—but not that I should have accepted her offers, had they been ever so pressing. None of your going on your lakes for me."

"Excuse me, sir," said Wanford, "I thought you came on purpose to see the lakes."

"Well, and so I did; but going on the lakes and *seeing* them are two very different things, I take it."

"Certainly, sir," replied Wanford; "then I conclude you are afraid on the water."

"I afraid on the water! that's a good one —I that have crossed the Atlantic half-a-score times! I that have been for logwood to the bay of Honduras, I afraid of the water! No, indeed—but after being tossed about on waves as high as a house, this going along on smooth water is poor insipid work."

"True, sir, who after having ridden an elephant would cross a donkey!"

"Besides, angling in fresh water is poor milk and water fun."

"Certainly, sir, to one," replied Wanford, "whose pleasures, like yours, are all of the sublime kind; you I conclude never bob but for whales. May I ask how many you have ever caught?"

Stokes, having shrewdness enough to perceive that Wanford was laughing at him, replied, half in joke and half in earnest, "Caught whales! No, sir, no,—I never caught anything of the sort; but I'll tell you, sir, what you'll soon find you have caught to your cost."

"Bless me, sir, what have I caught?"

"Why, in me you have caught a *Tartar*," he replied in a voice of thunder, which turned the laugh against Wanford, and made Stokes very vain of his own wit.

The carriages were now announced, Stokes persisting in not accompanying them, even though, he said, nodding and winking at Miss Travers, they had with them a nice decoy duck.

Mrs. Felton coldly gave him her card of address in London, and said she should be glad to see him; that she breakfasted at ten or eleven commonly, and dined at seven.

"Thank ye, thank ye," said he; "and when you come into our parts, cousin, I hope you will come and smoke a pipe and drink a bottle of wine with me."

"A very extraordinary proposal to a lady, sir!" said Wanford.

"Not more so than her inviting me to a breakfast at ten, and a dinner at seven; for I am just as fit for one as she for the other."

"No, no, my honourable cousin, your habits and mine don't suit,—so we shall not come together often,—and luckily the world is wide enough for us both. But come, let us see you off." So saying, he handed Mrs. Felton down stairs; when finding she was to go with Wanford in his carriage, "what, is she going with you?" said he to Wanford. "I thought you would have preferred that pretty young thing. But every one to his taste, as the old gentlewoman said when she kissed her cow."

"Stay, sir, one moment's conference," cried Wanford. "Have you any ground for what you have just said? Is there any historical evidence for supposing that the sensible person whose saying you have just quoted, was an old gentlewoman, and not an old woman only, as she is usually called?"

"Whom do you mean?"

"I mean the cow-caresser, sir, whom you honoured by speaking after; perhaps amongst your own family archives you may possess her pedigree?"

"Why, no, sir," returned Stokes, with a malicious laugh; "I have not much to do with pedigrees; but if the *cow* in this case had a pedigree, I should not be surprised to find your name in it as one of her descendants, by the name of a *calf*." Then he laughed so loud at what he fancied wit, that Wanford, glad to escape from a contest in which he was not likely to come off unhurt, set his horses into a quick trot, putting his whip-hand to his ear, as he did so, and exclaiming, "A most extraordinary and overpowering person, 'pon honour!" while Stokes, after shaking the rest of the company heartily by the hand, and looking as if he wished to give Miss Travers a warmer farewell, allowed the other carriages to drive off, and then mounted his horse. But he overtook Wanford's vehicle on the road; and riding up to Mrs. Felton, to the great mortification of her pride, he desired her to see how independent he was,—for that he carried his linen and portmanteau before him.

"How shockingly vulgar, sir!" exclaimed she; "why, you look like a rider!"

"Ay, ay, and like a very good thing too; for if your ancestors and mine, cousin, had not been riders, you and I should not have been as genteel as we are now. But look, those powder-monkeys are, I see, grinning to hear a man with saddle-bags call their mistress cousin. So my service to you, I and my bags will shock you no longer." So off he galloped, much to the joy of Mrs. Felton, but the regret of her companion—to whom his oddity was a source of amusement.

The next morning, as the lake had been sufficiently explored, the party resolved to return to Mr. Selby's house, where after staying two days, Mr. and Miss Wanford continued their journey to Scotland; whither, had she been invited, Mrs. Felton would have accompanied them. But Wanford, now he had lost his rival St. Aubyn, from whom he was proud to have gained the fair widow, was tired of a conquest which he had made with so little trouble; and as he clearly perceived Mrs. Felton would accept his hand if he offered it, his vanity was sufficiently gratified, and he thought his honour required that he should leave the lady before she had lost her affections beyond the power of recall. Accordingly he and his sister pursued their original plan, and set off; while the mortified and disappointed Mrs. Felton returned to London soon after, out of humour with herself, Miss Spenlove, and all the world.

But while St. Aubyn and his mother are on their road home, I will relate how this happy reconciliation with Mr. Hargrave took place.

"I am come," said Mr. Egerton, one morning abruptly entering the room where Emma and Mrs. Castlemain were sitting, "I am come to tell you that Mr. Hargrave is dangerously ill with the gout in his stomach."

"O dear! if he should die!" exclaimed Emma, with nothing like alarm in her countenance.— Here she stopped, checked by a look of displeasure from Mrs. Castlemain, and one of sad surprise from Mr. Egerton.

"I doubt, Emma, you do not always think before you speak," said Mrs. Castlemain.

"At least," replied Emma with blushing ingenuousness, "I do not always speak well, and I must own that there is not to me any thing very terrible in the idea of Mr. Hargrave's death."

"Do you think him then so well prepared to die?" said Mr. Egerton gravely.

"But he shall not die if I can help it," exclaimed Mrs. Castlemain; "I have a prescription for the gout in the stomach, which I have known perform wonderful cures; and if you, Mr. Egerton, could but contrive means of getting it administered to Mr. Hargrave, without his knowing from whom it came——"

"I will attempt no such subterfuge, madam," replied Mr. Egerton; "but I will go to Mr. Hargrave myself immediately, and if he will consent to be saved by your means, well and good; but it is always the best, as well as most virtuous mode of proceeding, to tell the truth, regardless of consequences."

"I dare say you are right," said Mrs. Castlemain, rising to go in search of the prescription; while Emma, starting across the room, kissed her affectionately, exclaiming, "Kind, good grandmother! how I respect you! and after all his ill-usage too! But you forgave *me*, and that was more difficult still;" not being aware that the difficulty lies in preserving enmity towards those we fondly love.

Mr. Egerton found Mr. Hargrave so seriously alarmed for his life, that he was willing to try any medicine, and from any hand; and though he said with an oath, that Mrs. Castlemain was a very conceited, obstinate old woman, he was quite willing to take her medicine, adding, that to be nurses and Lady Bountifuls was all old women were good for; and Mr. Egerton left him fully resolved to profit by the cure which Mrs. Castlemain had sent.

In two days' time, whether the medicine was infallible, or the disorder transient, certain it is, that Mr. Hargrave was cured; and on the morning of the third day, he presented himself in person at the door of Mrs. Castlemain, who graciously received him, and his hearty thanks for her kind and salutary attention, which were accompanied by a salute, at once a pledge of reconciliation and gratitude, —while he swore, that no infernal chess-board should ever in future make any words between them.

"But where is Henry? is not he returned yet?" asked Mr. Egerton.

"No, he is still on his frolics."

"And on his *preferment* too, we hear," observed Mrs. Castlemain, while Emma turned to the window to hide her involuntary emotion.

"Pho! nonsense! all stuff!" cried Mr. Hargrave, "Henry is not such a goose as to marry any honourable madam, any fine lady whatever. Besides, I flatter myself that I must have a spoke in that wheel, and I promise you, I have no taste for any thing like quality-binding; and I value my banker's book more than all the red-books that were ever printed."

Emma listened with anxious attention to this speech, and thought she had never seen Mr. Hargrave so amiable; still he only spoke what he believed, not what he knew; and though consciously easier than before, she was delighted to think St. Aubyn was probably on his road home, and she eagerly anticipated his return to the Vale-House.

But a new event now took place, of more importance even than Mr. Hargrave's reconciliation with Mrs. Castlemain. Mr. Egerton, who, as I have before stated, was the younger son of one of the branches of a noble family, became, by the death of a distant relation, heir to a very large fortune, not less than 60,000*l.* in money, besides estates, which were capable of being raised to some thousands per annum. The news of this great accession of property, was received by him at first with a feeling of anguish, rather than of joy. It re-awakened the agony he had felt before, when good tidings reached him, for then he was mourning by the dead body of her who could alone, he thought, give value to riches, by sharing them with him; and as he read the letter, informing him of his acquisitions, he clasped his hands convulsively together, and exclaiming, "It comes too late," as he had formerly done, he threw the letter to his alarmed friends, and rushed into another apartment.

"No," said Emma to Mrs. Castlemain, "it does *not* come too late, and so his benevolent heart will own when he recovers his first feelings; he will then recollect the good which this money will enable him to do, and he will rejoice in it, I am sure he will." Emma was right, and in an hour's time Mr. Egerton returned to them composed and even cheerful. But neither Emma nor Mrs. Castlemain could speak to him: they each took and held his hand in silence, while the full and glad heart betrayed itself by the swelling and quivering lip.

"So, ladies, I am a rich old fellow at last," said he, brushing a tear from his eye.

"And I bless God that you are so," said Emma, "for your wealth will be the source of blessing to many."

"My dear sir," said Mrs. Castlemain, "your present residence will not be good enough for you now!"

"I am sure I shall have no other," replied Mr. Egerton, "I shall make no difference in my mode of life—*none*. I have long had a melancholy pleasure, and shall have to the end of my existence, in rejecting *all* but the bare necessaries of life, as she who would have joyfully shared my poverty cannot share—— Pshaw!" cried he abruptly, and hastily left the room; while Emma, whose young heart was rendered unusually susceptible by the anxieties of a dawning passion, wept over these affecting reminiscences of a virtuous, faithful, and unhappy love, and almost envied the lost, but still fondly regretted Clara Ainslie.

"Mr. St. Aubyn is like Miss Ainslie, in Mr. Egerton's opinion," observed Emma.

"*Mr. who*, my dear?" said Mrs. Castlemain.

"M—Mr. St. Aubyn."

"Bless me, child! why do you *Mr.* him? I never knew you do so before."

"Well," replied Emma, deeply blushing, "then Henry St. Aubyn is like Miss Ainslie; therefore it is no wonder that Mr. Egerton loves him so dearly; nor," thought Emma sighing, "if she was really like Henry, is it to be wondered at that he was fond of *her*."

It was some hours before Mr. Egerton could conquer his own heart, and meet his good fortune with the thankfulness of a Christian and the fortitude of a man; but at length he was quite himself again, and re-entered the drawing-room.

"Well, Emma," he exclaimed, "to whom shall my *first* present be given? whom does your heart suggest as the first object for my riches to be exerted on? Come, speak; I do not mean you should openly and boldly point out who are to be my heirs."

"No, sir," replied Emma, "for I hope your only heirs will be your own children."

"My children, Emma! I suppose you mean the heirs or children of my adoption?"

"No, sir; I mean that I hope you will marry and have children."

"Very disinterested that in you," replied Mr. Egerton forcing a smile; "but consider my grey hairs, child."

"What are they, sir?" she returned; "only a little snow on the top of a green mountain; you are a young man yet, and formed as you are for domestic life, I—"

"Say no more on that subject, if you love me," hastily returned Mr. Egerton, "the vibrations of that string thrill through me yet too painfully. No, Emma, no, talk to me only of feasible plans,—of the St. Aubyns probably by my means rescued from dependence on Mr. Hargrave!"

"Oh! my dear sir, do that, do that," eagerly exclaimed Emma, "and you will be good indeed!"

"Well, well, we shall see," replied Mr. Egerton, smiling at her eagerness; "but Henry, you know, is said to be on the eve of independence already."

"I have not yet answered your question, sir," said Emma (glad to get rid of that subject,) "relative to your first gifts on this accession of fortune."

"True, and to whom shall they be given?"

"To the Orwells, sir, if I may advise."

"Right; you guessed my meaning;" and Mrs. Castlemain, with a deep sigh, observed that they deserved every attention.

The next day, and before etiquette warranted, as breakfast was scarcely over, St. Aubyn appeared at Mrs. Castlemain's gate; for though he had been home two days, his uncle, on pretence of business, had not allowed him to leave the house. Immediately, in spite of her repeated declarations that she would fly to him as soon as she saw him and reproach him for not confiding in her, Emma ran up stairs to hide the perturbation which the sight of him occasioned her; and when she had resolution to enter the room where he was, and alone too, her manner was involuntarily cold, distant, and restrained.

"Dear Emma," said St. Aubyn, "what an age it is since I have seen you, and how glad I am to see you once more!" while Emma, walking awkwardly across the room, for the first time in her life smiled languidly, coldly gave him her hand, and seated herself at a distance from him.

"But how *well* you look!" cried St. Aubyn, following her and gazing with delight on her mantling cheek; "yet surely you are not well, —you seem out of spirits, and so so,—I can't tell how, but certainly not like *my* Emma;" and he kissed her hand as he spoke.

"Your Emma, Mr. St. Aubyn!" said Emma, putting up her pretty lip, and angrily withdrawing her hand.

"I desire you will not take such liberties with me; I dare say you dare not do so to Mrs. —Mrs. Felton."

"Mrs. Felton!" replied St. Aubyn, laughing.

"But perhaps you are on very familiar terms with that lady?" resumed Emma.

"Ay, to be sure I am, or was, dear Emma," he replied, again approaching her; but with a look of serious displeasure, she desired him to keep a respectful distance, for that she did not consider herself any longer as a child.

"Emma, dearest Emma, for pity's sake," exclaimed St. Aubyn, "tell me how I have offended you!"

"You have *not* offended me, but, but—"

St. Aubyn now saw tears in her eyes, "But what?"

"Only I think it very unkind that you should not let me know yourself that you were to marry Mrs. Felton, but leave me to hear it from strangers."

St. Aubyn, surprised but delighted beyond measure, again seized her struggling hand, and exclaimed,

"Is this then the reason of all this coldness and displeasure? Oh! if I dare interpret these signs as I wish," said he to himself, for he was too delicate to utter the sentiment, "I would not give one of those frowns or starting tears for all the smiles or distinction that Mrs. Felton could bestow.

"And *could* you for a moment, Emma, believe that I was in love with, or going to marry Mrs. Felton? O Emma! are you indeed so unacquainted with my heart?"

It was unnecessary for St. Aubyn to say any more. Emma felt that the report was entirely false; and with a heart suddenly lightened of a load, the weight of which she was not conscious of till it was removed, she smiled archly through her tears, gave him her hand freely, and saying, "So then I am disappointed of my wedding favour!" jumped up suddenly with her usual velocity, bounded along the lawn to meet Mr. Egerton, and told him with great eagerness, that Henry St. Aubyn was come, and not going to marry Mrs. Felton.

"I told you so," said Mr. Egerton, his countenance beaming with satisfaction, and observing with delight that the countenance of his pupil also had an expression of happiness on it which he had not seen for some time,—for certainly his fondest wish was a marriage between Emma and St. Aubyn. And weeks and months lasted the happiness that was thus restored to the bosom of Emma, by the presence of St. Aubyn. Every hour that he could spare from his exacting uncle he spent at the White Cottage, and every hour seemed to insure to him a dearer interest in the heart of all its inhabitants. Emma had not a sorrow, a care, or a hope, which she did not communicate to her friend as she called him, save one lurking anxiety which she did not like to own even to herself. St. Aubyn, in relating to her the events of his tour to the lakes, had owned that he thought Mrs. Felton very handsome, very clever, very accomplished, and very insinuating; and she was not without her suspicions at times, being naturally inclined to jealousy, that had not Mr. Wanford come in the way, St. Aubyn's affections might really have been captivated by this dangerous woman, and her *friend* have been lost to her for ever. This idea used sometimes to come across her mind, and fill her eyes with tears, while St. Aubyn was talking of Mrs. Felton, which he perceiving, used tenderly to inquire their cause.

"Oh! it is nothing, nothing," she was in the habit of replying; then, ashamed of her weakness, she endeavoured to change the discourse, and was very soon herself again. To St. Aubyn she now confided every circumstance of her poor mother's history; while he used to gratify her by declaring, that whenever he went to London, his first wish would be to see the benevolent Orwells, to whom *he* owed so much. In short, nothing of love was wanting between them but a declaration of it; and that, St. Aubyn, aware of the obstacles to their union, hesitated to make, lest, as honour forbade him to do so without having first obtained the consent and approbation of his uncle and Mrs. Castlemain, his suit should be at once rejected, and the present delightful intercourse be entirely forbidden. Of Mr. Egerton's intentions in his favour he knew nothing; and he knew his uncle too well, not to fear that, were it only from the suggestions of temper, he would oppose his wishes; he therefore reluctantly resolved to conceal his secret in his own breast, (if that can be said to be concealed, which every look, every tone, and every sentiment betrayed,) and to wait patiently, contented with the privileges of a friend, till Emma, no longer secluded from an admiring world, should be the object of other vows, and he must either speak, or lose her for ever.

It may be asked why St. Aubyn with his honourable feelings, and possessed as he was of health, industry, and talent, should so tamely submit to dependence on a tyrannical and coarse-minded relation? But, alas! his reasons for so doing were cogent and even unanswerable. He knew that were he to throw off the yoke of dependence, his uncle, in revenge, would cast off Mrs. St. Aubyn, and leave her to be wholly maintained by him; a duty which he would have delighted to take on himself, had his mother been like, I may venture to say, *most* women under similar circumstances; but St. Aubyn well knew that by no probable and even possible exertion of his could he ever *maintain* his thoughtless, wasteful, and extravagant parent. With a mother of other habits he was conscious that he could have lived on the income of a fellowship or clerkship, and on whatever trifle she could have added to their income by keeping a school, or the exertions of her needle; while with such a one he felt that he could have supported the difficulties of a narrow fortune with a light, contented heart, and have gladly braved the danger of being disinherited by his unamiable relation. But it was clear even to a mathematical demonstration, that should he venture to disoblige his uncle, and be turned adrift by him with the helpless Mrs. St. Aubyn, a jail for his mother, if not for himself, was the only prospect that awaited him, such were her inveterate habits of needless extravagance; and thus did this otherwise affectionate parent, by this pernicious vice, hang like a millstone round the neck of her noble-minded son, palsying all the energies of his free-born soul, and reducing to the slave of a tyrant's nod, a creature born with the best and proudest aspirings of a virtuous and highly-gifted being.

While St. Aubyn was thus continuing to bear the burthen of dependence from the best of motives, a little cheered indeed under the load by the consciousness that it was only as the heir of his uncle that he could pretend to the hand of Emma Castlemain, (for of Mr. Egerton's intentions in his favour Emma was at present forbidden to inform him,) Mr. Egerton was considering the best mode of putting those plans in execution, flattering himself that they would further an immediate union between Henry and Emma, as he well knew that only the half of his fortune ceded to them during his life, would be sufficient for the gratification of all their wishes. "But the race is not to the swift, nor the battle to the strong;" and the benevolent man, however good his intentions may be, must only be too often forced to content himself with the consciousness that he meant well, though chance or error may frustrate the accomplishment of his designs.

Mrs. St. Aubyn looked upon herself, it is true, as rather an extravagant woman,—but then she smoothed over the acknowledged fault thus; "To be sure I like to spend money,—but then I have been used to it, and I like to have things *genteel* about me; and I know my brother is rich enough to keep me a carriage if he would; and therefore I *must* have things a little smart, and I *will* have them too."

But like all of us in our turn, Mrs. St. Aubyn did not look to the consequences of her own actions. She was not aware that errors, like *sorrows*, "come not as single spies, but in battalions;" that the consequence of her determination to have "things genteel about her" was running in debt; that the consequence of running in debt was lying and mean evasions in order to put off the pressing demands of creditors; and she chose to forget that though she talked of making her *brother* provide for her elegant wants, she dared not make any one of them known to him, but that she drew from the filial piety of her noble-minded son even the money he wanted to enable him to support the appearance of a gentleman. Still Mrs. St. Aubyn called herself only a *little extravagant* or so; but she had soon to learn that an extravagant being, like an avaricious one, is never sure of remaining completely honest.

St. Aubyn and his mother both returned home with all their little stock of wealth expended on their tour, and two months must elapse before Mr. Hargrave, who never paid money before it was due, would pay them their quarterly allowance; and debts and duns awaited Mrs. St. Aubyn at home.

"I will pay you in two months' time positively," said she; and soon after her return, all but one creditor went away relying on her promise; but he telling her she had so often deceived him that he would have the money that evening, or half of it, or apply instantly for it to her brother the squire; poor Mrs. St. Aubyn saw herself reduced to the necessity of either borrowing what she wanted herself, or prevailing on Henry to borrow it, or of being exposed to the terrible and fierce resentment of her awful brother. But already had she asked her son for the money, and he, eager to oblige her, had asked it as a loan to himself of his uncle, who had *obligingly* told him he must wait for it till it was his due, and that he need not have been so extravagant as to spend his money in journeys and frolics. Still she thought St. Aubyn might be prevailed upon to borrow the money elsewhere; and as she was to dine at the Vale-House that day to meet Mr. Egerton and the families from the White Cottage, she hoped to have an opportunity of seeing her son apart, and of disclosing her distresses to him. To Mr. Egerton she dared not apply, because, though he was come to a large fortune and was very generous, she did not like to make a disclosure which might lead him to suppose her extravagant, as she had not yet given up the idea that he secretly loved her, and might one day or other make her his wife.

As it was a wet day, Mrs. Castlemain sent her carriage for her when it had taken them to Mr. Hargrave's,—therefore, Mrs. St. Aubyn had not the relief she expected, of unburthening her mind to her son when he came to fetch her in the chaise,—and full of agitation she took her seat at her brother's table.

Nor was the humour in which she saw Mr. Hargrave at all likely to calm her perturbation; for he was in one of his worst moods, a mood, indeed, in which his nephew was but too often accustomed to see him, but which he did not frequently exhibit before any one that was not a dependant.

"Where is St. Aubyn?" said Mr. Egerton, seeing that they were summoned to dinner without his having yet made his appearance.

"He is gone some miles off on business of mine," gruffly replied Mr. Hargrave, "and he can't be home for an hour yet."

"I am very sorry to hear it," cried Mr. Egerton.

"Yes, no doubt," returned the other, "I know I am nobody to Henry; and it is him and not me whom you came to see."

"Not so, Mr. Hargrave; but surely, if you invited me to come and partake of turbot and turtle-soup at your table, I should have a right to be disappointed if you gave me only the latter!"

"So, you make Henry the turbot, and me only the soup! But you are right there, for certainly I have more cayenne in me than he has."

Just then, Henry himself arrived, having ridden very fast; and was received by his uncle with—

"How dare you, sir, ride my horse as hard as you must have ridden him in order to get back so soon?"

"I have not ridden him harder than humanity warranted, sir," replied St. Aubyn.

"It is a lie," answered Mr. Hargrave.

"As you know, sir, that I never told you a falsehood in my life, and am incapable of doing it, I am satisfied that you are not in earnest in what you have now said," replied St. Aubyn mildly but manfully.

"Meaning to say then that I lie, I suppose?" retorted Mr. Hargrave.

"I hope my words will not bear so coarse an interpretation, sir."

"Come, come, let us eat our dinner," interrupted Mr. Egerton; and Mr. Hargrave, full of sulky irritation, took his seat.

St. Aubyn then produced some letters which he had written for his uncle; but they were all condemned as ill-worded and ill-written; and Mr. Hargrave added,

"But you never do any thing well for *me*; you think any thing good enough for me. If Mr. Egerton had employed you, the case would have been very different."

But neither that gentleman nor St. Aubyn chose to notice this splenetic remark, and the subject was dropped.

It was the time for Mr. Hargrave to receive his dividends on his East-India property; and though the contemplation of his riches had usually power to put him in good-humour, it had not done so to-day; as he was not fond of his expected guests; and he really disliked Mr. Egerton more than ever since his accession of fortune,—he, like most other rich people, not being able to endure a rival in wealth, and having great pleasure in undervaluing the fortunes and gains of others, while he not unfrequently boasted of his own.

"Alas!" thought Mrs. St. Aubyn, while

her brother at dinner talked of the pleasure of a well-filled purse, and seemed to wish to measure his with Mr. Egerton's; "I wish he would impart this blessing to some one whom I could name!" and her wishes were not a little increased, nor her alarm heightened, by the intelligence that some one wanted to speak with her, and by seeing that it was the dreaded creditor. With some difficulty she however got away from him, and returned to Mrs. Castlemain, who was busily reading the paper in the drawing-room, whither the ladies had already retired, while Emma was walking in a grove near the house.

"O that I dare borrow this money of Mrs. Castlemain!" thought Mrs. St. Aubyn; "the half, which would satisfy him, is only *five pounds*." But before she could make up her mind to do it, Mr. Egerton and Henry came in, and the latter sat down to copy a letter of business for the former, which he wanted to have written immediately. Consequently, Mrs. St. Aubyn could not speak to her son as soon as she had intended. Soon after Mr. Hargrave entered the room, and taking a handful of bank-notes out of his pocket, which he was going to deposite in the drawers of a book-case which stood at the end of the apartment, he told them over one by one with all the pride of riches, naming the amount of the precious hoard.

"It is right," said he, "to tell money, they say, even after one's own father;" then preparing his keys, he was going to lock up the sum, when he was called out to speak to a tenant, and he left the notes piled up upon the table at which St. Aubyn was writing. At this moment St. Aubyn's whole attention was riveted on his letter; Mr. Egerton's back was towards the company, while he was employed in making a new pen for Henry; and Mrs. Castlemain was completely absorbed in reading the newspaper; while on the top of the notes lay a five-pound note, the very sum which would extricate Mrs. St. Aubyn from her difficulties; and Mr. Hargrave had told the notes once, therefore it was very unlikely he should tell them again. The temptation was irresistible; and she flattered herself that she could own what she had done when her brother paid her allowance, and return five pounds; so it was taking what would soon be her *due*; till at last she drew near the table; and while she pretended to be admiring Henry's fine writing, she contrived by degrees to separate the five-pound note from the rest; and having done so, with a sort of desperate resolution she put it in her pocket and retreated to a glass door leading into the garden, meaning to join Emma who was walking there, and avoid the perturbation which her brother's return would unquestionably expose her to feel. But to effect this was impossible. Mrs. Castlemain followed, and, detaining her, insisted that she should read a long and interesting account in the newspaper of a mysterious murder; and Mrs. St. Aubyn, too ill at ease to find a ready excuse for refusing, submitted to her request and read the story, wholly unconscious of a single character before her, for Mr. Hargrave's loud voice was heard in the hall, and in another minute he entered the room.

"A plaguy puppy!" said he in no very placid frame of mind; "I thought I should never have gotten rid of him. But now for my notes. Hey-day!" exclaimed he, "how is this? why, I thought I left a five-pound note at top! Some one has been meddling with these things," darting a look of suspicion around.

"I am positive, sir, that no one has touched them," said St. Aubyn mildly, and looking up as he spoke; "for I do not recollect that any one has been near the table but myself."

"Well, I shall soon see that," said Mr. Hargrave, and began to re-tell the notes,—while Mrs. St. Aubyn wished herself in the centre of the earth.

"I was not mistaken," said Mr. Hargrave, scowling suspicion and accusation from under his bushy brows; "the sum was right before, and now there are five pounds wanting; besides, the note was a remarkable one, and could not but be missed. Ha!" cried Mr. Hargrave, "and now I remember, five pounds was the sum you wanted to borrow of me yesterday, Mr. St. Aubyn; and here, sir, before all these witnesses, I accuse you of having stolen my note!"

At this dreadful speech, uttered with almost maniacal vehemence of look and gesture, Mr. Egerton, Mrs. Castlemain, and even Mrs. St. Aubyn approached the scene of contention; while St. Aubyn rising with all the dignified indignation of conscious and outraged innocence, was about to deny the charge with firmness equal to his uncle's violence, when his eye glanced on his self-convicted and guilty mother, who more dead than alive, awaited the consequence of her too late repented guilt, and seemed to regard him with a look of supplication. In a moment the truth flashed on his mind; and aware that his denial of being guilty, and the proof which Mr. Hargrave would require of him, namely, submitting to be searched, would immediately fix the accusation on the *real* culprit, his courage failed him, his indignation was swallowed up in agony, and sitting down he leaned in silence on the table, and hid his face in his hands.

"What, sir! you will not speak then, you will not confess your guilt! But silence gives consent, they say, and—"

Here Mr. Hargrave was again called out of the room, and muttering a curse or two, he obeyed the summons.

"What is the matter?" said Emma, hastily entering.

"A mystery," replied Mrs. Castlemain:

"Mr. Hargrave misses a bank-note, and accuses his nephew of having taken it; and it is very certain no one was *near* the table but he."

"And what then, madam!" cried Emma, turning pale with anger. "If fifty Mr. Hargraves accused St. Aubyn of the theft, I would not believe him guilty. Nay, I would not believe, if I had even seen him take the note,—but I should have doubted the evidence of my senses."

"Mighty fine and romantic indeed!" cried Mrs. Castlemain; "and pray who do you think then *did* take the note, I, Mr. Egerton, or Mrs. St. Aubyn?"

"Me!" said Mrs. St. Aubyn almost convulsively; "Dear me!"

"I accuse no one," said Emma gravely, "but I only say, I *know* that St. Aubyn is innocent; and to the base charge, I would have him 'let his only answer be *his life!*'"

"Well said, my dear child," cried Mr. Egerton, "and well felt too;" while St. Aubyn, too miserable to be even capable of joy at being thus defended, could only reply to the "dear, dear St. Aubyn, be composed," which she addressed to him, by wringing her hand with the convulsive violence of agony. Mrs. St. Aubyn meanwhile, unable to stand, tottered to a chair, for again the alarming voice of her brother was approaching.

"I see, madam," said Mr. Egerton, "that the scene which must follow will be too much for your nerves; therefore, allow me to lead you into another apartment;" and Mrs. St. Aubyn, leaning on his arm, staggered out of the room. In a few moments, Mr. Egerton returned, just as Mr. Hargrave was again accusing his nephew, and demanding a confession of his guilt. Oh, then, what were not the struggles in St. Aubyn's mind! Scenes, long past, rapidly flitted across his recollection. He remembered his father's death-bed; and the promise he made, to make his mother's good his first rule of action, to screen her from every ill, to shelter from every sorrow; and now, one word from his lips would plunge her in irremediable disgrace.

"No," said St. Aubyn to himself, "I can better bear my own; and *Emma* will not believe me guilty."

During this struggle, Emma, amazed and alarmed at his hesitation, exclaimed,

"Mr. St. Aubyn, why do you hesitate? why are you silent? You surprise, you *terrify* me, Mr. St. Aubyn!"

This was a stroke indeed; and his resolution almost failed him.

"So, then, *she* too will believe me guilty!" But filial piety prevailed, and with a look of desperate resolution, St. Aubyn said, "Sir, I own, and I deny, nothing; but I beg you to dispose of me, and to proceed as you think proper."

"There, you see!" said Mrs. Castlemain; and Emma, though even *yet* she thought him innocent, bewildered and miserable turned aside and wept.

"I shall certainly not harbour a thief in my house, sir," said Mr. Hargrave; "therefore, you may decamp immediately;" and St. Aubyn, bowing, was about to leave the room, when Mr. Egerton, in a voice hoarse with emotion, seized his arm; "Mr. Hargrave," said he, "if you turn this young man out of your house, why then, as the old lord says in the play, 'I will receive him into mine.'"

"Yes; out of spite to me, I suppose?"

"No, sir; out of justice to him. Look up, look up boldly, thou noble-minded being, and tell this hasty-judging uncle of yours, that no guilt has ever stained either your heart or hand; and that you are now holily, though mistakingly, taking on yourself the guilt of another."

"Heyday! What is the meaning of all this!" cried Mr. Hargrave.

"Oh, sir! what are you saying? what are you going to do?" said St. Aubyn; "I see you know; I am satisfied; pray let me—"

"Peace!" cried Mr. Egerton; "you have done your duty, young man; now let me *do mine*. Mr. Hargrave, your nephew did *not* take the note,—but your sister did!"

"Very likely," replied he, "you persuaded her to take the fault on herself to screen her child;" vexed, Mr. Egerton imagined, to find that the virtue and high reputation of his nephew were not stained with the fault imputed to him, but were likely to shine out greater than ever.

"Indeed!" said Mr. Egerton, sarcastically; "Mrs. St. Aubyn's known virtue and Henry's known vices make this likely, do they? You know *better*, Mr. Hargrave; but here is the note which your penitent and miserable sister desired me to give you. However, sir, to put her guilt beyond dispute, know that I *saw* her take it. My back was towards the table, but my face fronted the pier-glass, and I happened to look in the glass just as Mrs. St. Aubyn took the note and put it in her pocket. At first I thought she did it on purpose to alarm you; but the moment I looked at her, I saw in her countenance and manner, all the perturbation of guilt, and was meditating how I should act, when your return brought the matter to a crisis, independent of me, and showed that excellent young man in—"

"There, there, you have said quite enough in his praise," interrupted Mr. Hargrave; while St. Aubyn left the room abruptly, in order to go and speak comfort to his mother. While he was gone, Mr. Egerton told Mr. Hargrave that he had informed Mrs. St. Aubyn that he had *seen the whole transaction*, and must, to save her son, disclose the truth; begging to know what the great distress was which could alone have led her to commit such an action, —and she had told him much to palliate, though not to excuse, her guilt; declaring her satisfaction at knowing her son's fame would be cleared, though terror of her brother prevented her from doing it, and he hoped Mr. Hargrave would be as merciful to her as he could.

Emma and Mrs. Castlemain, though greatly shocked at a delinquency which they could not conceive possible in a rank of life like Mrs. St. Aubyn's, earnestly joined the cry for mercy; but Mr. Hargrave vowed he would reduce her allowance one-half.

"That is," said Mr. Egerton, "you will increase the poverty which was the occasion of her error. Is that wise?"

"May be not; but it is my will."

"Well, then," said Mr. Egerton, "hear with indulgence the plan that I have to propose. Allow *me* to maintain Mrs. St. Aubyn in future, as the mother of my adopted son should be maintained; and let me also maintain Henry St. Aubyn, and send him to College as my future heir."

At first Mr. Hargrave, irritated to madness by this well-meant, but most injudicious and ill-timed proposal, a proposal which, however it might flatter the avarice of this man of wealth, was calculated to wound a passion more dear, namely, that of his pride, was speechless with unutterable rage.

"S'death, sir!" cried he, at length, "do you take me for a pauper, that you offer to maintain my nearest relations for me? Have your newly-gotten riches turned your head, Mr. Egerton; and you think nobody is rich and benevolent but yourself? Sir! how *dare* you insult me thus? But mark me, sir, if either my nephew or my sister condescend to be your pensioners—I *will*—Yes . . . . ." he, as if triumphing in some malignant recollection which gave him pleasure; "yes, that will do; and he dares not displease me."

"Mr. Hargrave, only hear me!" said Mr. Egerton.

"No, sir, I will hear nothing more on this subject; but I am not angry, sir, no, not at all; I owe you, on the contrary, a great obligation. Ha, ha, ha! so you wanted to take your pupil, did you, out of the clutches of his old crabbed uncle! I see it, I see it all;—and instead of doing so, you have fixed him there firmer than ever. Ha! ha! ha! O these wise folks, how often they overreach themselves!" Then laughing within himself, and looking as maliciously merry as Sir Joshua Reynolds' Puck, he left the room.

"What does he mean?" said Emma.

"I can't exactly tell," replied Mr. Egerton, pacing the room in considerable agitation, "but I fear I have done harm." St. Aubyn returned no more that evening, or rather not till the ladies from the White Cottage and Mr. Egerton were gone; nor did Mr. Egerton see him the next day, as he had a right to expect, but he received from St. Aubyn the following hasty note, written in a hand scarcely legible:

"My kind friend, and intended benefactor, accept my best thanks and blessings for your generous proposal! which I *never, never* can accept, nor *any bounty from your hands.* Still how fondly my heart clings, and will *ever* cling to you and the dear inhabitants of the Cottage!—But I dare add no more, except that I am your faithful, grateful, and affectionate, though miserable,
"HENRY ST. AUBYN.

"Ask me no questions, for mercy's sake ask me no questions!"

This letter, evidently written in a moment of excessive agitation, and a total absence of judgment, because it said both too much and too little, gave excessive pain to Mr. Egerton, and still greater to Emma. Mrs. Castlemain bore it more heroically; for, conscious how great an heiress Emma would be, she was not sorry to see that the growing attachment between her and St. Aubyn might be checked by circumstances arising out of the strange temper of his uncle; for though she never would have opposed a marriage between them, out of respect and gratitude to Mr. Egerton, whose wishes she was well acquainted with; still, as she was of noble descent herself, and nobly connected, she wished her heiress to marry the heir or son of some great family; for though St. Aubyn's was ancient and honourable, it was not noble. Therefore, while Mr. Egerton, alarmed more than he liked to own to himself, at the probable result of his avowed wishes, and quick-sighted too late to what was likely to be the event of the transactions of the preceding day, sat brooding in melancholy reverie over St. Aubyn's letter, Mrs. Castlemain preserved a degree of composure which was most painful to his feelings, and said "All things are for the best—and Providence orders every thing for our good," so often and so provokingly, that, pious and good as Mr. Egerton was, he could scarcely help wishing to contradict her; while Emma wandered along the paths in solitary sadness, where she had lately roved with St. Aubyn, and tried to remember only his declaration, "that to the dear inhabitants of the Cottage his heart would fondly cling for ever." But when she again saw St. Aubyn, every hope that she had cherished, every prospect that she had contemplated, seemed extinguished and closed from her view. He came alone indeed,—but his manner was cold and restrained, his countenance bore the marks of excessive depression; he never looked at, and rarely spoke to Emma,—though Mr. Egerton thought, and Emma too perhaps, that whenever she spoke he seemed to hang upon her accents with the silent attention of love, and to reply in tones softened by the influence of ardent, though restrained tenderness. Mr. Egerton at last, unable to endure in silence a change so afflicting and so marked, took him by the arm, and demanded to speak to him in private. But as soon as he entreated to be told the cause of what he saw, S.. Aubyn, with a vehemence, an agony not to be resisted, conjured him for mercy's sake to desist, and not to require explanations which he could not give, but to leave to him uninjured the only consolation that was left him under his misfortunes, the consciousness of fulfilling his duty, and of an unblemished integrity. "But one day, one day, Henry," replied Mr. Egerton affected by his evident distress, " you will explain every thing, I trust."

"One day!" he exclaimed, "one day! Ay, sir, I trust that day will come, or I doubt I should want fortitude to bear up under the tortures of a lacerated heart and a wounded spirit."

"Your unhappy mother," said Mr. Egerton.

"Do not name that subject to me," interrupted St. Aubyn, "I cannot bear it—but she *is* my mother, she was left too to my care by a dying and revered father, and I *will* do my duty by her, come what may.—Sir, dearest and best of friends, I should say, I shall see you all once more, and only once; for I am going to College at last; I have prevailed on my uncle to send me, and in a few days I set off."

"In a few days! well, it is better not to see you at all, than to see you thus."

"Oh, much better," replied St. Aubyn with quickness; " in this at least he is kind—and absence will be salutary."

They then returned to the ladies, and St. Aubyn soon after took his leave; but, as he withdrew, he cast a look of mournful tenderness on Emma, which, during the many long months of absence which succeeded, was the only comfort which her agitated bosom knew; for St. Aubyn returned not to the cottage, but set off for Cambridge without bidding his friends farewell.

Various conjectures and ever-changing surmises mingled with the painful feelings which this conduct in St. Aubyn occasioned both to Emma and Mr. Egerton, and unfortunately neither of them could have the relief of imparting their different sensations and ideas to the other. Delicacy and pride, the pride and delicacy becoming her sex, forbade Emma to complain of St. Aubyn's conduct, lest the secret of her heart should be by that means discovered; a secret only recently discovered to herself; for Emma was not aware that her silence on this occasion was a proof of that love which she wished properly to conceal; as but for a conscious feeling of disappointed tenderness, she would naturally, from the quick feelings of a neglected friend, have clamoured against the strange conduct of St. Aubyn, and his blind obedience to what she considered the will and caprice of his uncle. But this well-meant silence spoke volumes of conviction to the heart of Mr. Egerton, and he felt with an agony of self-reproach, that he had done all in his power to encourage in his docile pupil an attachment which was likely to end in nothing but miserable suspense and unavailing wishes.

Yet he had one consolation under his distress, and that was the consciousness that Emma in loving St. Aubyn was loving virtue; and while he respected the feelings of Emma too much to allude even in the remotest manner to the cause of her evident dejection, and even to endeavour to account for St. Aubyn's altered manner and conduct, he felt a firm conviction that those very changes were the result of some imperious necessity of which duty was the source, and he looked forward with certainty to the hour which should clear up the present mystery, and restore St. Aubyn to their society. But in the meanwhile he felt it to be his duty and that of Mrs. Castlemain to do all in their power to suspend in Emma's mind the images which preyed on it, and he therefore proposed excursions into different parts of England. But as soon as a certain number of weeks or months had elapsed, they returned home again, and occasionally saw St. Aubyn, who, with his uncle, paid his respects formally at the Cottage during the vacation; and these meetings, Mr. Egerton soon discovered, though painful in the extreme, were sufficient to keep alive in Emma's mind, not only the image of Henry St. Aubyn, but the dangerous conviction that he loved her, spite of his behaviour, as an involuntary look of tenderness, and a sigh half-suppressed, continually gave marks of feelings wholly contrary to the coldness which he assumed, and added fresh fuel to a flame which absence and the total annihilation of hope might have been able to extinguish. But at length St. Aubyn ceased his visits entirely, and Emma became more and more dejected.

"This will not do," said Mr. Egerton to Mrs. Castlemain, who mourned in secret over the faded cheek and abstracted air of Emma; "we had better resolve to leave this neighbourhood entirely;" and Mrs. Castlemain joyfully consented.

"But whither shall we go?" and Mrs. Castlemain answered, "To Roselands, to that seat which I have in the neighbourhood of the town of K——, in right of Mr. Castlemain."

"I did not expect," said Mr. Egerton to Mrs. Castlemain, " that you would propose going to Roselands, because I thought that place would be disagreeable to you, as it was there you lost Mr. Castlemain and your little girl."

"Some years ago," replied Mrs. Castlemain, " it would have been so; but I own to you that the presence of our dear Emma has so forcibly recalled to me the recollection of her mother, and of the ever-dear and regretted object of my first and fondest love, that all other recollections have faded before them; and though on my arrival at Roselands, mournful and tender remembrances will no doubt recur, still they will be bearable and evanescent feelings, and the most powerful possessors of my affections will again assert their influence unrivalled." Mr. Egerton felt that this must be a true statement, because what it asserted had its origin in natural feelings, and feelings which he could comprehend; and saying, "You must be the best judge of your own sensations," the subject was dropped, and the journey to Roselands agreed upon.

This removal was even more necessary than they imagined. True it was that even Mr. Hargrave at length gradually ceased, as well as his nephew, to visit at the White Cottage, because, in the first place, he had never forgiven the scene at his own house, in which Mr. Egerton had been so foremost an actor; and in the second, because he knew that without St. Aubyn his company had little charm for any one of the family; besides, he always disliked those who preferred his nephew's society to his, though such a preference was very natural and irresistible. It should seem therefore that all intercourse with St. Aubyn, or knowledge of where St. Aubyn was, would have been wholly at an end, especially as Mrs. St. Aubyn also, too conscious to be easy in her company, had not returned the visit which Mrs. Castlemain had kindly made her, and had declined the acquaintance—but the fact was otherwise.

However short were St. Aubyn's visits to his uncle, during his residence at College, he always contrived to steal out at night before the clock had struck eleven, and conceal himself in the neighbourhood of Mrs. Castlemain's abode, in order to catch a sight of Emma as she crossed the landing-place, on her way to her own apartment; and once, when Emma, unable to sleep, had arisen, and come in the dark to an open window, she saw, unseen herself, a tall figure of a man walking slowly away, who, by his height and manner, she was convinced was St. Aubyn; and having once seen him, she watched for him several successive nights, and saw him come again and again. Once too she had left a small ruler in a summer-house at the end of a wood, and when she went back for it the next day it was gone; and as its real value was too trifling to tempt a common thief, she suspected that St. Aubyn, having visited the spot, had, for her sake, purloined it as a remembrance; and her suspicions were confirmed a short time after, by the seeming reappearance of her ruler in the same place; but on examining it she found it was not her own, though it was one so like it as to have made it impossible for her to have distinguished the difference, had she not been conscious of having scratched with a pin on the ivory her own initials and those of St. Aubyn.

Often, very often, too, did she see the footsteps of a man on her most favourite walks, the walks which she had trodden with him, which her heart whispered were the footsteps of St. Aubyn.

These proofs of still-remaining and still-ardent, though concealed affection for *her*, kept alive in its utmost force, her deep-rooted love for *him*; and though her pride and her delicacy revolted at the idea that she loved a man who had never solicited her love, yet she could not but feel an internal conviction, that he would have made such a solicitation, had not an imperious necessity commanded him to forbear; while she lived over and over again in memory the happiness she had experienced only the evening before the sad exposure at Mr. Hargrave's, when on her falling from a piece of projecting rock, St. Aubyn, though she was not in the least hurt, was as much alarmed as if she had actually sustained an injury; and by the tenderness of his expressions, and the affectionate manner in which he supported her as they walked home, declared so plainly how fondly, how entirely, he was devoted to her, that she almost wished to meet such an accident every day, in order to be so questioned and so supported.

But all these consciousnesses and these recollections were food to a passion which she felt she ought to conquer, because it promised to be hopeless; and Emma forced herself to rejoice that she was going to leave scenes so destructive of her peace; for though she was sorry to be obliged to leave the school she had established in the neighbourhood, and some other useful and praise-worthy occupations, she felt that to go was right, and to stay as improper as it was dangerous.

K—— was a provincial town, near the northern coast of England; and, though partiality to the beautiful estate in Cumberland, which she inherited from her ancestors, had made her prefer her White Cottage to Roselands, still Mrs. Castlemain was not sorry to have a sufficient motive for incurring the expense and trouble of removing to the latter residence.

"Besides, I was once there for some months," said Mrs. Castlemain to Mr. Egerton, "and I thought the society at K—— very good, though it was that of a country-town."

"No wonder, my dear madam," said Mr. Egerton; "the society in country-towns is composed of men and women made up of the self-same passions, the same virtues, and the same vices, as those are who inhabit the country itself, or a metropolis."

"I begin to feel impatient to be at K——," exclaimed Emma, "and wish we were to set off this moment!" Not that Emma anticipated in reality much pleasure from her new residence, but that morbid restlessness which ever attends a mind ill at ease, made motion and change desirable to her; and as she drove away from the Cottage, she fancied she was driving away also from the associations there, which were wearing away her health and undermining her peace. This happy illusion was prolonged by the sight of the new mansion itself; for it had every charm of architecture, and of situation, to recommend it; and in the richly-decorated and spacious apartments, Emma found some pictures, by rare and excellent masters, which gave her a degree of pleasure to which she had hitherto been a stranger. But as the environs of the White Cottage, and even the town of Keswick itself, did not afford much society, and that variety of human character and liveliness of event so interesting to a young and inquiring mind, Emma looked forward with eagerness to the hour when she should become acquainted with the wider society of K——, and make her appearance at a K—— ball. Nor was it long before her wishes were gratified.

As soon as it was known, that Mrs. Castlemain, after an absence of many years, was returned to Roselands, many of those families, whom she had formerly visited, came to pay their compliments of welcome to her.

Contrary to her expectations, Mrs. Castlemain felt embarrassed while presenting Emma as Miss Castlemain to these acquaintance, especially when she saw in their countenances an expression of wonder and inquiry, who Miss Castlemain could be! However, as Mrs. Castlemain did not explain, they were forced for the *present* to remain in ignorance; I say for the present,—because, as a gossiping spirit of inquiry is proverbial in a country-town, it was not likely that any one of the parties should long remain ignorant on this subject, especially as amongst them was one lady who piqued herself on knowing the marriages and intermarriages of every noble or ancient family in the kingdom. Their curiosity indeed was soon gratified, as the ladies and gentlemen in question met that very evening at a rout, and naturally enough the first persons whose merits and demerits were discussed, were the inhabitants of Roselands.

"I think," observed a gentleman, "that Mrs. Castlemain looks excessively well."

"Indeed, poor woman!" returned a Mrs. Evans, a lady who affected great feeling, benevolence and sentiment, and who had not yet called on her; "I am surprised at that, considering her years, and what she has gone through! I have not yet been to Roselands, for I dread going. Poor dear Mr. Castlemain and I were such old friends, that the meeting between me and his widow, whom I have not seen since her loss, will be a very affecting one."

"Especially," observed another lady sarcastically, "as the afflicted widow is on the point of marriage with a third husband, if report says true."

"Impossible!" replied Mrs. Evans; "I can't believe my friend capable of a measure so derogatory; really if I thought she was, I would not go near the house."

"What, for fear such improprieties should be catching!" bluntly replied a gentleman to this lady of alarmed susceptibility, who, like Mrs. Castlemain, had buried her second husband. Mrs. Evans answered him only by a look of disdain.

"But pray," said she, "who may this third husband be?"

"Oh, that handsome, keen-looking, greyheaded man who lives with her."

"*Lives* with her!" exclaimed Mrs. Evans.

"Yes, madam," resumed Mr. Vincent, the gentleman who had before spoken; "may I beg leave to ask what are the improper ideas which your delicacy annexes to the term! But Mr. Egerton, whom I knew at College, is only on a *visit* to Mrs. Castlemain here, and does not live with her when in Cumberland; but he resides in a cottage near her, and is the preceptor of Miss Castlemain."

"Of Miss Castlemain!" exclaimed several ladies at once; "and pray who *is* Miss Castlemain?"

"Ay," said Mrs. Rivers, the lady skilled in pedigrees, "ay, who is she? I am sure *I know*, whatever *you* may do."

"And I too, I hope," replied Mr. Vincent.

"Nay, I can't guess," said one. "We all know that Mrs. Castlemain left Roselands, because she could not bear to remain in the place where she had lost a husband and an only child."

"No, that is a mistake; she had a daughter then living by her first husband."

"She had indeed," said Mr. Vincent, sighing.

"O dear, yes!" cried another; "a fine handsome girl, who ran away with a man named Danvers, a fellow whom nobody knew."

"No! there you must excuse me," observed Mrs. Rivers, conceitedly, and speaking very fast; "I know something on such subjects, and I can assure you the Danverses are a very old and respectable family. There's the Danverses of Shropshire, and the Danverses of Cheshire. The heiress of the Shropshire Danverses married Sir Henry Douglas, whose sister married Lord Clanross; and the Cheshire Danverses by marriage are related to the Duke of Montagu; and a daughter of that family married General Nugent, whose sister was drowned on her voyage to the Cape of Good Hope."

"But what is all this to Miss Castlemain?" said Mr. Vincent, as soon as Mrs. Rivers had talked herself out of breath.

"O dear!" resumed she, "I only meant to show that Mr. Danvers was not a man whom nobody knew; for that people of family themselves, and who therefore prize it in others, *know* that his family is both ancient and honourable."

"I am much more interested in what he was himself than what his family was," returned Mr. Vincent, "for the sake of the beautiful creature whom he married. I saw his wife, Agatha Torrington, when, in the pride of her youth, her beauty, and her expectations, she made her first appearance at a race-ball, and for the first time in my life I regretted that I was not a man of high birth and fortune."

"Bless me!" cried Mrs. Evans, "who should ever have suspected Mr. Vincent of being tender and sentimental?"

"Those few, madam," returned he, "who look beyond the surface, and therefore might fancy me both because I affect to be neither."

"Well, but Mr. Vincent," said Mrs. Rivers eagerly, "if you were so much charmed with Miss Torrington, you will be pleased to know that there is every reason to believe this Miss Castlemain her daughter."

"I suspected as much, madam," replied Mr. Vincent, "and am happy to find that Mrs. Castlemain received to her favour her daughter's unoffending orphan, though to her daughter herself she continued inexorable."

"How can you be so cruel and unjust," resumed Mrs. Evans, "as to blame my friend for her virtuous severity? How could she receive her daughter into favour when she knew her to be only Mr. Danvers's mistress, not his wife?"

"I am convinced, madam, that she could know no such thing, for I am sure Miss Torrington would never have been the mistress of any man."

"I fear it is only too true," said a lady who had not yet spoken, "that Miss Torrington was never married to Danvers; and on his marriage with another woman she lost her senses, and used to go about to different churches demanding a copy of her marriage register. I know this to be true, because I had it from a clergyman to whom she applied, and whom she accused, together with the clerk, of having destroyed the register, threatening at the same time to prosecute them."

To an assertion so positive as this Mr. Vincent had nothing to reply. At length, however, he said, that as to Danvers, he believed him to be capable of any villany; but that whether Miss Castlemain was born in wedlock or not, he knew, from a servant who then lived with him, (but who lived with Mrs. Castlemain when Mr. Egerton arrived with the little Emma,) that the day after their arrival she called her servants into the room, and introduced the child to them "as her daughter and heiress."

"*There!*" cried Mrs. Evans; "you hear that—' as her *daughter;*' and then she gave her the name of Castlemain; whereas, if the child had had a name of her own, she would have introduced her as her *grand-daughter*, Miss Danvers! Oh, it is as plain as possible; and I fear the other story is only too true, namely, that this Miss Castlemain was Miss Torrington's child, *not* by Danvers, but the man with whom she lived when she died, this very Mr. Egerton! O, my poor dear Mrs. Castlemain! it breaks my heart to think what you must have suffered from the errors of your daughter!"

"Surely, madam," said Mr. Vincent, "a lady of your exquisite benevolence, who feels so severely for the faults and griefs of her friends, should not be so ready to believe reports that militate against the fame and peace of others! What ground have you for the calumny which you have now uttered against that most respectable man, Mr. Egerton?"

"Oh, sir, I had it from undoubted authority."

"Name it."

"Excuse me, sir, I never give up names."

"No, you only make free with them. Mr. Egerton, to my certain knowledge, had never spoken to Mrs. Danvers more than once, till he saw her on her death-bed."

"Dear me! Egerton! Egerton!" exclaimed Mrs. Rivers; "I wonder whether he is a relation of the noble family of that name; or perhaps he is of the Durham Egertons. The heir of that family, by the by, married a Castlemain, so it is very likely——" Here, luckily, she was interrupted by a summons to the card-table; and Mrs. Evans and Mr. Vincent being called away for the same purpose into different apartments, they had no opportunity of resuming their angry altercation.

The next day Mrs. Evans was amongst the earliest of the visiters at Roselands; but her meeting with the lady of the house was not, as she apprehended, such as to affect the acuteness of her feelings. Mrs. Castlemain, who was usually cold and stately in her manners, did not at all relax in her usual stateliness at sight of Mrs. Evans; nor did the gathering tear in her eye declare that she either recollected "poor dear Mr. Castlemain" tenderly, or Mrs. Evans as his friend. The latter lady, therefore, who had taken out her pocket-handkerchief, and was beginning to sigh and look very pathetic, was obliged to resume her natural look, as reminiscences were not, she found, the order of the day, and she was soon able to answer Mrs. Castlemain's inquiries concerning her acquaintances at K——, with her usual assumed benevolence and real malignity.

"Pray, how are the Johnsons?" said Mrs. Castlemain.

"Oh, they live in a *great style*, and make a very fine appearance; and it is all very well if they can go on so; but there is such a family! Poor dear little things! my heart bleeds for them when I think what their fate may be!"

"Set your bleeding heart at rest then,"

observed another lady archly, "for their fate will be a very good one; as I know from authority that Mr. Johnson is worth at least 150,000*l.*"

"I don't believe it," hastily replied Mrs. Evans, reddening violently; "that is, I mean I wish I could believe it."

"Pray, madam," interrupted Mrs. Castlemain, "let me inquire after that sweet little girl, the daughter of an attorney at K——, who promised to be a perfect beauty."

"Oh, poor thing! she grew up to be both a wit and a beauty, and——"

"And what, madam? I hope no harm has happened," said Mr. Egerton, smiling, "to a young lady so proudly gifted?"

"Harm, sir! No, not harm in the common sense of the word, certainly,—for she is married very much above her sphere in life,—she is married to a young baronet of very large fortune, and who is also heir to a higher title, who fell desperately in love with her."

"She is is very much to be pitied, indeed," said Mr. Egerton, ironically;—"no wonder you called her 'poor thing!' So, she is young, beautiful, and clever, and is the wife of a rich young baronet, who married her from disinterested affection!"

"You may laugh, sir," replied Mrs. Evans, but "'all is not gold that glitters.' It is said that her husband is a very gay man."

"Well, madam," said Mr. Egerton, affecting not to understand her; "and if she be a gay woman, and loves to laugh, so much the better for her."

"Nay, sir, by gay I did not mean lively, I meant that he was a very, very libertine man, sir; and that she, poor thing! is pining herself very fast into a consumption! I am sure I did not believe this story till I could not help it, and I have felt a great deal for the anguish of her poor parents, who were so proud of their daughter's elevation!"

"For which, if this be the case, she has paid dear indeed," observed Mrs. Castlemain; "but I never approved of unequal marriages."

At this moment Mr. Vincent was announced, and received by Mrs. Castlemain with marked cordiality. When she presented him to Mr. Egerton, he too seemed glad to see him as an old College acquaintance; but Mr. Vincent was so struck with the strong likeness that Emma bore her mother, who had really captivated his young heart the first time he beheld her, that he could scarcely speak the welcomes which he felt; and Emma, blushing at his earnest yet melancholy gaze, turned to the window.

"I have been making inquiries of Mrs. Evans, sir," said Mrs. Castlemain, "concerning some old acquaintances of mine at K——, and I am sorry to find that beautiful girl, Mary Beverly, has been so unfortunate in her marriage, and is fretting herself into a consumption!"

"And you told this lie to Mrs. Castlemain, madam, did you?" said Mr. Vincent sternly, looking steadfastly at Mrs. Evans.

"Sir! sir! I told it because I do not believe it is a *fib*, for I scorn to repeat your vulgar word again."

"Yet you well know, madam, that I told you only two days ago, when you were repeating the same rancorous tale, which you and others believe true only because they wish it to be true, as they cannot forgive the sweet girl her good fortune; you know, I say, that I then told you, that from my own knowledge I could assert the whole story to be false.

"Madam," added Vincent turning to Mrs. Castlemain, "I must beg you to excuse my warmth, but I love the lady concerning whom you have kindly inquired; and as I have lately been staying at her house, I am qualified to assure you, that if being unhappily married is having a husband that adores her, and if growing fat be any proof of pining in consumption, then is this lady right in her assertions, and my poor friend in a miserable way indeed!"

"Well, sir," replied Mrs. Castlemain, "I have no doubt you are right, and——"

"I have great doubts still," angrily exclaimed Mrs. Evans; "for Mr. Vincent is so pleased with being this great lady's guest, that he is *bribed* to say what he has done."

"It is well for you that you are a *woman*, madam," replied Mr. Vincent, "or I should soon convince you that my honour is not to be questioned with impunity."

"We had better call another subject," coldly and proudly observed Mrs. Castlemain; and Mr. Vincent, again apologizing for his warmth, soon after took Mr. Egerton by the arm and led him to the end of the room, where with many apologies for the liberty he took, he begged leave to ask him whether that young lady was not, as report said, the daughter of Mrs. Danvers; on which Mr. Egerton gave him a short detail of Agatha's history, and, to his great joy, gave him another opportunity of contradicting the representations of Mrs. Evans.

In a short time Mrs. Evans was the only visiter remaining; when looking out of the window she exclaimed,

"Oh! that's the mayor's coach, here comes his lady, I protest."

"Who is mayor now?" said Mrs. Castlemain.

"Your old acquaintance, Mr. Nares the banker; he has married a second wife, and she is coming to pay her compliments to you; —but I wish just to say something concerning this charming but giddy creature."

"Giddy! Has then Mr. Nares married a young wife?"

"Yes, poor man! he has indeed! and I think it right to let you know that she has been a great deal talked of; there was a sad business about her and an officer, and almost half the town will not visit her; but *I* do, for I believe she was only *indiscreet*, not *guilty;* and therefore out of Christian charity and kindness I thought it right to take her by the hand, poor young creature, when no one else would; and now she is very well received. Still, lest some evil-disposed person should tell you this tale in order to prejudice you against her, I thought it right to be beforehand with them."

"Upon my word, madam," replied Mrs. Castlemain, drawing herself up even higher than usual, "I cannot see that it was at all necessary for you to give yourself this trouble; for I flatter myself there is nothing about me to encourage any one to tell me a gossiping tale of scandal, as I have long been convinced that no one is ever told by another any thing but what that other supposes the person so addressed is likely to relish."

The mortified Mrs. Evans was at first too much confounded to speak; at last she stammered out,

"That really there was so much ill-nature in the world, that——"

"Ay, madam, so there is indeed," observed Mr. Egerton; "but never is ill-nature so odious as when it tries to hide itself under the mask of pity and benevolence;—don't you agree with me, madam?"

"O yes! certainly, sir," she answered in a hurried manner; and at this moment Mrs. Nares was announced.

In spite of the well-principled aversion and the well-grounded distrust which the quicksighted family at Roselands were beginning to feel towards Mrs. Evans, they could not help being a little influenced by what she had said respecting the lady who now entered the room. But distance, suspicion, and reserve, vanished before the charms of her manners and her countenance, and Mr. Egerton did not wonder, if she added indiscretion to youth and beauty, that half the town of K—— were too strictly virtuous to visit her. But Mrs. Castlemain's stately carriage evidently disconcerted her. However, blushing as she did so, she gracefully requested her acceptance of tickets for a public ball, to which Mr. Nares was to be steward; and Mrs. Castlemain expressed her readiness to accept them. Mrs. Nares then sought relief from the awe impressed by Mrs. Castlemain, in a more familiar intercourse with her kind friend Mrs. Evans, who welcomed her with a sort of protecting air,—while the countenance and manner of Mrs. Nares to her, denoted such unsuspecting confidence in the reality of her friendship, that even Mrs. Castlemain, filled with pity and indignation at the treachery of Mrs. Evans, forgot that her new guest was said to be a woman of suspected character, and entered with alacrity into conversation with her. But in the meanwhile she had advanced greatly in the good opinion of Emma and Mr. Egerton, and rose in proportion as Mrs. Evans declined; for both ladies had brought a child with them. Mrs. Evans's was a girl about five years old, so spoiled and so humoursome, that it was very evident the mother had either not known or not practised her duty towards it. When desired to say or do any thing, its only answer was, "No, I won't;" while it ever and anon interrupted conversation with loud clamours of "Mamma, I will go home!" till Emma did not know which was most disagreeable, the mother or the child.

Mrs. Nares's little boy, on the contrary, though he was so beautiful that some mothers might have thought themselves excused for spoiling him on that account, was under such pr per restraint, and so well brought up, that he always spoke when spoken to, and never otherwise; and the whole appearance and manner of the child argued so forcibly in favour of the good sense and propriety of the mother, that all Mrs. Evans had said was soon forgotten; and *indiscretion*, a great and pernicious error in every woman, was judged wholly incompatible with the evident good qualities that Mrs. Nares as a parent possessed.

At length the ladies departed, and the family were left to comment on the variety of persons and characters, many of which I have not mentioned, who that day came under their review.

"Do you not remember," said Emma, "an interesting anecdote of the poor Dauphin, who, when those horrible *poissardes* besieged Versailles, was taught by his mother, who held him in her arms, to clasp his little hands, and say '*Graces pour maman!*'"

"To be sure we do."

"Well then, Mrs. Nares's little boy's manners seem to cry '*Graces pour maman!*' for I find it difficult to believe that so good a mother should be so bad a wife."

"And so do I, Emma," replied Mr. Egerton; "for I think it a very fair conclusion, that when a woman performs one duty well, she is not very negligent of others; for I believe the virtues, like the vices, are so fond of one another, that they are seldom or never found separate; and if a virtue or two be sometimes found crowded in amongst many vices, they are there only like sprigs of geranium set without roots in a garden, which before they have time to take root, are thrown down by the first shower or gust of wind, and are no more seen or heard of. But did you ever see so odious a child as that little girl?"

"Hush! hush! dear sir," cried Emma, laughing and blushing, "I cry '*Graces pour cet enfant*' for my sake; for *indeed* I saw in that disgusting child my own likeness when I first knew you, and I could hardly help saying, 'Pray, my dear, is not your name Emma?'"

"Indeed, Emma," cried Mrs. Castlemain,

in great emotion, "I cannot bear to hear you calumniate your mother so far as to compare yourself to that rude and spoiled child!"

"I calumniate my mother! God forbid!" cried Emma, "My poor mother! it was no wonder if she did spoil me, for I was her all, you know."

"I *do* know it, I know it but too well, Miss Castlemain;" while Emma, shocked at the inconsiderateness of her reply, was, like Mr. Egerton himself, unable for a few minutes to change the conversation or give a pleasanter turn to it. At length however she said,

"Yet fond of me as my mother was, she had strength of mind enough to correct me very severely when she thought such correction necessary for my good."

"Ay, indeed!" said Mr. Egerton, "as when, pray?"

"Oh! never but once, and then I shall remember what passed to the last day of my life. She had given me a piece of cake, and I some time after asked her for another; on which she replied, 'Have I not already given you some?' when I, thinking it better to tell a fib than lose my cake, replied, '*No*, indeed you did not.' In an instant her face became quite terrible with rage; and giving me a blow that almost felled me at her feet, 'You are a base and mean-spirited liar,' she exclaimed, 'and I am ashamed to own you for my child! Hence from my sight, nor dare to come into my presence again all day.' It was the first and last time I ever saw her angry with me; but her wise resentment did not end with the impulse of passion. She made me go to church the next day in my oldest and dirtiest coloured frock, telling me that any thing was good enough for a liar to wear; and that till I had the *spirit* of a gentlewoman's child, I should not wear the dress of one."

"Well! I think for a first fault my daughter need not have been so severe."

"Surely, dear grandmother, as it was a first fault, it was the more necessary to be so; for, though I did not know why, I considered lying to be so terrible an offence, from this unusual severity in my indulgent mother, that I was terrified from committing it again; and as I grew older, and found myself fondly caressed whenever I spoke the truth, fearless of consequences, the habit of ingenuousness which you have so often commended in me, was impressed on me too deeply, I trust, to be ever eradicated."

"Well, well, I am sure I am disposed to think your poor mother right,—but let us drop the subject, and tell me what you think of Mrs. Evans."

"Think of her!" cried Emma, "Why, do you remember, grandmother, that I used to say to you when you wanted me to take a pill wrapt up in currant-jelly,—'No, no; when you give me physic, give me physic; when sweetmeat, sweetmeat;' and so I used to make a wry-face, and swallowed the physic as physic."

"Well, and what is this to the purpose?"

"Why, Mrs. Evans appears to me physic wrapt up in sweetmeat; for under her jelly of pity and feeling is hidden the bitter herb malevolence and so forth. Now, this is as odious to me as your physic wrapt up in sweets; and I should like to say to her, 'Good Mrs. Evans, say at once, I rejoice in the distresses of my fellow-creatures, and that's the truth of it.' I fear I was wicked enough to wish that honest gentleman, who looked at me so comically kind, had knocked her down."

"So then, you did observe something particular in his expression when he looked at you?"

"Yes, my dear sir; and that he took you to the other end of the room. Well, sir, what was it for? Did he make proposals?"

"Proposals! What is she talking of?" cried Mrs. Castlemain. "To think of that child's talking of proposals, indeed!"

"And to think of a young lady who is going to a K—— ball, and will probably open it with the mayor himself, being called a child!"

"How the girl's tongue runs to-day, Mr. Egerton," said Mrs. Castlemain smiling.

"I am glad of it," replied Mr. Egerton, "for it shows a heart at ease." But Emma, knowing this was by no means the case, suddenly turned round and hastily retired to her own room.

Mr. Egerton soon discovered, however, that her heart was by no means as much at ease as he imagined. Going into her apartment one day, which she had only quitted meaning to return to it immediately, he saw some verses lying on the table, evidently wet from the pen; and, concluding that verses not meant to be seen could not have been left so exposed to view, he ventured to read them.

When Mrs. Castlemain came to Roselands, she found the garden had been so much neglected, that weeds grew along the parterre, and the spring flowers had planted themselves in the gravel-walks. This circumstance occasioned Emma to write the lines in question, which were as follows:—

IRREGULAR SONNET
ON A NEGLECTED BUT BLOOMING GARDEN.

Not on the weeded bed of yielding earth
Bloom the bright flowers that in my garden grow;
Midst rougher soil they force their beauteous birth,
And on thick turf or pebbly gravel blow.
Self-call'd they came, like friends in sorrow's hour,
Who wait not forms, but aid uncourted bring;
And like yon welcome, yet obtrusive flower,
O'er our rough path a rainbow splendour fling.
Sweet flowers! while wrapt in pensive thought I stray,
Where still unlooked-for in my path ye bloom,
Fond fancy whispers that some cheering ray
Of future joy may chase my present gloom;

May, like your buds, opposing powers o'ercome,
And light, with gladness light, my clouded home.

"I wish I had not read it," Mr. Egerton had just said to himself, when Emma returned and saw the sonnet in his hand, as he had purposely kept it that she might know he had read it, though he knew not what to say to her relative to it.

"So, I see you have read my lines," said Emma, blushing deeply as she spoke.

"Yes," replied Mr. Egerton, "and approve them too; my only objection to them is their solemnity,—but I hope your next will be of a gayer turn;" then, without looking at her, he left the room. While Emma, conscious how little likelihood there was that his hope would soon be gratified, vented her feelings in tears; and, afraid of being seen while under the influence of such painful sensations, set off for a walk in the gardens and the woods adjoining.

The assembly-day at length arrived; when Mrs. Castlemain and Mr. Egerton, for the first time for many saddened years, and Emma, for the first time in her life, prepared for a public ball. Not one of them, however, looked forward to the busy scene with any one feeling unalloyed by pain. Mrs. Castlemain recollected, as if it had been yesterday, the hour when she had parted with Agatha, that she might be present at her first ball, that *fatal ball*, which stamped with woe the future destiny of her life; and Mr. Egerton remembered that the last time he had been present at such an amusement, he had danced with the lost object of his constant affections; while Emma recollected, in the secret recesses of her heart, how often she had hoped, and how certainly expected, that her first partner at her first assembly would have been Henry St. Aubyn! But no one communicated to the other the feelings that were common to each, and they met with seeming cheerfulness in the drawing-room to await the arrival of the carriage.

Mrs. Castlemain, in order to do honour to her old acquaintance the mayor, and to show her respect to her K—— friends, made a point of appearing in a new and handsome dress, and in her family jewels. As her mind had now been for many years in a degree lightened of its overwhelming load, she had recovered her usual *embon-point*, and her complexion had lost but little of its original loveliness. At this time, therefore, she looked considerably younger than she was,—an illusion heightened by the judicious manner in which she dressed herself; for, conscious that after fifty, the less of the skin and form that is exhibited, the more is gained in personal appearance, as well as in propriety, Mrs. Castlemain concealed, either with lace or fine muslin, the whole of her figure; while round the only part of her once beautiful throat that met the view, she wore a black velvet collar, which at once hid the as yet only threatened wrinkles, and set off its still remaining whiteness. Her dress for this evening was black velvet, of which the only ornaments were point-lace and jewels; and on her still dark and glossy hair, she wore a simple though costly cap composed entirely of lace.

When she entered the drawing-room at Roselands, her smoothed and finely-grained complexion flushed with emotion, and a sort of anxious expectation, occasioned by the idea that she was going to introduce the child of Agatha at her first ball, Mr. Egerton was struck with wonder at her beauty, and the general magnificence of her appearance, and was gazing at her with respectful admiration, when Emma appeared, glowing with youth and expectation, simply habited in a white crape dress, ornamented, as well as her head, with pearls only. Both Mrs. Castlemain and Mr. Egerton looked at her with delight, though a tear glistened in the eye of both. Nor was Emma as unmoved as she seemed to be; but, substituting, like many other people, gaiety for cheerfulness, she held up her white and dimpled hands with wonder as she looked on her grandmother, and making a pirouette, exclaimed, "Well, I know who will be the handsomest woman in the room to-night!"

"That is very conceited in you, Emma," said Mrs. Castlemain smiling, and affecting to misunderstand her.

"What! is it conceited to be vain of one's own grandmamma?" replied Emma, caressing her as she spoke.

"I believe I may look well enough for an old woman," she answered; "and considering——," then overcome by many tender and many agonizing feelings, she burst into tears, and hastily retired.

"I suppose she is thinking of my poor mother," said Emma in a faltering voice; "but how well, how even beautiful she looks!"

"She does indeed," said Mr. Egerton; "and how judiciously she dresses herself!"

"Judiciously!" replied Emma.

"Yes; and were she, instead of being indifferent to her personal graces, at all inclined to the hope or wish of conquest, I should even have said, how *coquettishly* she is dressed! for I never saw any one who, at her time of life, better understands the art of clothing judiciously. I have often thought, that a beauty of fifty should imitate the example of a skilful general after the battle of the day is over, and a retreat is sounded. The general, previous to beginning another attack, takes an accurate survey of his remaining forces; and when he enters the field again, he puts in front and in full view the strongest part of them, but takes care to conceal from the sight that in which he is conscious of weakness. In like manner, a faded beauty should be careful to hide by dress whatever, according to the regular progress of decay, is the indication of age in the female figure, and to set off to the best advantage, whatever beauty time has touched with a more gentle hand."

"Really, dear sir," replied Emma, "it would be only kind in you to publish a magazine of instructions for elderly ladies in the art of dress, embellished with a vignette of my grandmother by way of illustrating your meaning."

Before Mr. Egerton could reply, Mrs. Castlemain returned, and soon after they set off for the ball.

"I hope," said Emma when they were seated in the coach, "that the greater part of the inhabitants of K—— resemble the pretty mayoress rather than Mrs. Evans."

"My dear child," replied Mr. Egerton, "very possibly the pretty mayoress herself may resemble Mrs. Evans, as most human beings resemble her also."

"What a libel on human nature!" exclaimed Mrs. Castlemain.

"If the truth be a libel on human nature, I am sorry for it; but I am sure that I speak only the truth."

"I hope not; but if it be so, why, my dear sir, do you wish to throw a gloom over the prospects of this young charge of ours, by representing human beings in so unamiable a point of view?"

"Do you wish me to deceive her?"

"I would rather that you should, than speak truths calculated to destroy those blissful illusions on which so much of the happiness of youth depends."

"But admitting, which I will never admit, that happiness can have a stable foundation on delusion, youth is but a small part of human existence; and I think it is the duty of a preceptor to prepare his pupil's mind in such a manner as to fit it for every stage of life. Illusion, we all know, must end in disappointment; and there is nothing that has such a tendency to sour the temper, and deprive the mind of energy, as disappointment. The young, who are not taught to believe all human character imperfect, are only too apt to set up idols to worship, and to fancy the acquaintance, the friend, the lover, or the mistress, devoid of blemish either of mind, heart, or temper; but time, circumstances, and rivalship, most probably unveil the real character, and the poor dupe learns not only to mourn past confidence betrayed, but to give up all hope of ever feeling confidence in future. But this would not be the case, if to the young was exhibited a picture of things as they are."

"Disappointment, I own," said Mrs. Castlemain, "would be avoided, but years of happiness or confidence would also be lost; and what then would they gain by the exchange?"

"Much, in my opinion, of the greatest importance to the improvement of the heart and character, and to the safety of the temper."

"Explain."

"I would wish to impress on the young mind this painful, degrading, but salutary truth, that 'envy, hatred, malice, and all uncharitableness,' are the most frequent, and the most general of all human passions. If they were not so, should we have been taught to pray publicly every week, to be delivered from them? I would impress on the young mind, that even those who are capable of honestly and deeply feeling the distresses and misfortunes of their friends, are often very much mortified at their success and elevation. That, generally speaking, the elevation of a friend or acquaintance above ourselves, either in fame, rank, or wealth, is a crime against our self-love, which we never thoroughly forgive; and that we seize with eager avidity on any dirty story, however improbable, which tends to lower the individual, so favoured and so envied, in the scale of happiness or reputation."

"A dreadful, but I trust an exaggerated picture!"

"You are a strong painter, Mr. Egerton, but you are one of the black masters!"

"I am particularly fond of those masters," replied he smiling; "and as I am convinced even their darkest tints and shadows are all to be found in nature, I think you flatter me by the comparison."

"But I am anxious to know how a young mind can be benefited by being taught to believe ill of all the world."

"That is not a fair statement;—but let me go on;—It would be benefited thus: A tendency to overrate the virtues, and to be blind to the weaknesses of others, has a most pernicious effect on our own character; our self-love forbids us to suppose that we ourselves are not as virtuous and as free from weakness as other people; therefore to those best and most necessary friends, self-examination and self-condemnation, we become wholly strangers; whereas, if we look upon certain mean but natural passions to be common to all, we cannot deceive ourselves so far as to believe that we are exempt from them. Consequently, we shall be on the watch for every rising tendency to them in our own breasts; and being conscious of a fault is one very important step to an amendment of it. I have sometimes, with disgust and contempt, heard hoary-headed sentimentalists, persons grown old in worldly experience, with whining candour and pretended generosity declare that it is most unjust and cruel to judge thus harshly; while, like the simple girl in the play, they exclaimed, on being told of the errors of others, the result of malice and envy,

'Can there be such, and know they peace of mind?'

Yet, before an hour was at an end they would

themselves utter something dictated by those very passions, the existence of which, as common agents on the actions and language of men, they had so strenuously denied."

"I feel the weight of what you say," replied Mrs. Castlemain; "still, I doubt not our poor Emma here would have been glad to have thought higher of human nature."

"But, my dear madam, it would have been more cruel to deceive her by a false representation of it. Suppose, Emma, (for I know you love a metaphor,) that you and I were approaching a large city, and I were to inform you, on hearing you admire the handsome churches, towers, and buildings, which we beheld before us, that the whole city was composed of such, and every part of it equally worthy of admiration; surely you would have great reason to reproach me with your subsequent disappointment, when you found, on your arrival, that these edifices were encompassed by mean, little, ill-built houses, and narrow streets, and dirty lanes?"

"Certainly, sir."

"But if, on the contrary, I told you that these fine buildings were so surrounded, but that the small houses, narrow streets, and dirty lanes, were necessary to carry on the common business of life, you would not only feel no disappointment on entering the city, but you would be contented to bear with its defects for the sake of its beauties. It is thus with human life and human character, Emma; we must all of us forgive each other's faults for the sake of each other's virtues; but we must not be guilty of the pernicious vice, not virtue as some call it, of blinding ourselves to the faults of others; in the first place, it has, as I have before observed, a tendency to blind us to our own; in the next, it only prepares for us the agonies of disappointment; for disappointment is always the offspring of error, by blind and ill-founded expectation. You see, ladies," added he, "that I cannot leave off the habit of preaching; and a pretty long sermon you have had!"

"I thank you for it, for more than one reason, sir," cried Emma; "for I thought I was only going to a ball; but you have convinced me I am going to a ball and *masquerade*, where many Mrs. Evanses will be walking about, affecting to be the thing they are not."

"Ay, Emma, till passion and circumstances, like the call to supper, or the morning light, cause the mask to be taken off, and the person to appear what it really is."

Here the coach stopped at the assembly house, and Mr. Egerton had not an opportunity of preaching any longer.

Though out of compliment to Mrs. Castlemain the steward would not have allowed the ball to begin till she arrived, had she come ever so late, still, as she knew the usual hour of beginning was nine o'clock, she was too well-bred not to accommodate herself to the custom of the place, and she entered the ball-room before many persons of less consequence had made their appearance.

Emma, having no rank, could not have begun the ball, because there were young ladies present who had claims to precedence, if she had not been a stranger; but according to the polite, and I may add benevolent, regulation of the K—— balls, a stranger lady was always provided with a partner if she wished to dance, and was uniformly allowed to begin.

The mayor himself, having given up dancing, presented his son to Emma, who accordingly was led by him to the top of the set.

The unfortunate mother of Emma was a remarkably fine dancer, and it was fortunate for her child that she was so, as otherwise her proficiency in dancing could not have been very great. But Agatha, knowing that grace of motion and activity of limb are only to be acquired by practice and habit in the earliest years of childhood, began to teach Emma to dance when she was only four years old; and when she died, Emma knew in that art all her poor mother could teach her;— therefore a lesson which she received once a week from a master who resided at Kendal, and gave lessons in the neighbourhood, was sufficient to keep in her memory all she already knew, and to teach her whatever she was still ignorant of. But notwithstanding she had reason to think herself a very good dancer, she trembled with diffidence and emotion at performing before so many spectators; while the natural bloom of her cheek was heightened by the mantling glow of modesty.

Mr. Egerton's eyes followed her down the dance with admiring and gratified affection; but Mrs. Castlemain, still unable to separate the idea of Agatha from that of Emma, was so agitated, that it was with difficulty she could command herself so far as to remain in the room.

The first two dances being over, Emma's partner, a young barrister of very agreeable manners and conversation, begged leave to introduce a partner to her for the next two dances. Accordingly, a vulgar-looking young man, who was, as Mr. William Nares had informed her, one of the first beaux in the town, was presented to her by the name of Popkison; while Mrs. Castlemain, leaving Emma to the care of a lady, was glad to join a party to the card-room, and endeavour to calm her mind by cards.

Though Emma had never been at a public ball before, she had been at private ones in the neighbourhood, and was therefore conversant with the usual rules on such occasions; but if not, her own good sense and love of justice would have taught her, that it was only fair that the person who had stood at the top during two dances should go to the bottom during the two next. She accordingly took her place at the bottom of the dance.

"Why, what's that for, Miss Castlemain?" said her new partner. "Why, to be sure you don't mean to stand here?"

"Indeed I do, sir: it is my proper place, as I began the two last dances."

"Well, but what does that signify? The misses here, I assure you, never mind that; but 'tis first come first served, and there is always such pushing and pushing! Come now, let us go up higher. I know some kind body or other will let us in. I see a good-tempered girl yonder, she will let us in above her."

"I cannot suppose, sir," said Emma, "that any young lady will be kind to me, a stranger, at the expense of other young ladies her acquaintances; nor has she any right to oblige one at the expense of many."

"Oh, that is her concern, so don't be so scrupulous, it is always done; and I assure you nobody here, that is *somebody*, ever stands at the bottom."

"I should rather think, sir," replied Emma, smiling, "that it is somebody who is *nobody*, that is thus presuming; as persons of real consequence are usually better bred than to assume rights which they have not;" and the young man finding that he could not gain his point, said within himself, "What a queer fish she is!" and was silent for a minute or two.

"Well, Miss Castlemain, how do you like these parts?" resumed he, after a pause.

"Very much, sir; the country around is pretty, and well-cultivated, though not grand. There is a gentleman's seat a few miles off that is a very desirable residence."

"Oh! I suppose you mean Mr. Wells's, or Squire Wells's, as we call him?"

"I do."

"Ay, ay, let you young ladies alone for finding out the rich bachelors. There, there he is! Now what say you to setting your cap at him? Shall I introduce you?"

"No, sir," coldly and proudly replied Emma, disgusted at his forwardness; "I am not in the habit of courting the acquaintance of any one." Then, in order to change the discourse, she inquired the name of a fine-looking woman who was standing near them.

"That! Oh, she is one of the has-beens. She has nursed me on her knee many is the time and oft."

"That lady! I should not have supposed she was thirty!"

"Thirty, and sixteen added to it, more likely. But what do you think of our mayoress? is not she a pretty creature?"

"Oh, very; and pleasing too."

"Yes; and *fond* of pleasing. But you know, if an old man will marry a young wife, he must take the consequences—ha!"

"Mr. Nares is a very young and well-looking man," said Emma, gravely.

"So he is for his years, fifty-six turned; but he is grey; so the joke here is, that he is the grey mayor, but not the better horse, for madam drives."

"Drives! a gig, or a curricle?"

"Poh, poh, you are a rogue; you know what I mean; that is, she has her own way."

At this moment Emma caught the eye of a lady whom she had seen at Roselands, and curtsied to her.

"What," said Popkinson, "do you know old Peg?"

"Not I, sir. Pray who is old Peg?"

"Why, you curtsied to her this moment."

"That, sir, was Miss Mortimer."

"I know that; but we call her old Peg, or Peggy. *Miss* Mortimer! yes, and a fine old Miss she is! I know the year she was born in."

"But why, pray, sir, do you call her old Peg? she seems a very well-bred, pleasing woman; and age, if she be aged, is not a crime in K——, is it?"

"No. But by way of fun and joke we call her so. To be sure she is a good-natured, inoffensive, excellent creature."

"You seem to be great jokers here, sir. And so the distinguishing reward for good-nature, inoffensive manners, and excellence, in the town of K——, in a woman, is the appellation of 'Old Peg!' I suppose, sir, you call a good-natured, inoffensive, excellent man, Old Harry?"

"Ha, ha, ha! very good indeed! A good joke, eh?"

"I am sure, sir, I did not mean it for one. Really, sir, you are very facetious persons here."

"Why, that's true. There is a set of us, to be sure, who do love fun and joking, and who make very free with our neighbours sometimes."

"I hope your neighbours return the compliment."

"Oh, they are welcome; 'Give and take' is my motto. Why, there's Dick Mullins, and Jem Hanway, and two or three more, when we get together we are very funny, sure enough; and we do give comical names to people. Jem Hanway is a most excellent mimic, and it is such fun to see him take off everybody!"

"I dare say; and how pleasant it would be for you to get unperceived behind a screen, and hear him take yourself off!"

"Why, that's true, to be sure, that one should not much like."

"Oh! you forget—'Give and take' is your motto; and if you like to see your friends served up for your amusement, it is only fair you should be served up in your turn for theirs."

"Yet if I thought he *did* mimic me, I would break every bone in his skin."

"Right; and all I wish is, that every one whom he does mimic would do the same."

Here Popkison left her for a moment to go

and whisper in a gentleman's ear who was dancing with a lady who had only one eye; and coming back with a face brimful of laughter, he said, "I beg your pardon for leaving you, but I could not help going to whisper Sam Vernon, who is dancing with that one-eyed beauty; I told him, as she is so rich, it would be wise in him to get on the blind side of her."

"And did you really whisper concerning the poor girl's personal defect to the gentleman with whom she was dancing? Suppose she had overheard you?"

"Oh, she would not have minded; for she knows she is called Miss Polypheme."

"And is she?"

"Yes; and once Dick Mullins, from use, forgot to call her by her own name, and called her Miss Polypheme to her face."

"How cruel!"

"Oh, but he did not mean it; and after all it was only a joke."

"*Only* a joke! If, sir, you and this Dick somebody are capable of being amused with jokes on the deformities of your fellow-creatures, you can never want for mirth certainly; but you obtain it at the expense of all the finer feelings of human nature."

Popkison, piqued at the animated contempt which beamed in Emma's expressive face as she spoke, and unable to answer her, looked up saucily in her face and said, "Pray, madam, are you bringing up to the church? for I never heard a young lady preach such fine sermons before."

"No, sir," replied Emma, laughing at this fair retort; and was going to say, "I conclude that you are already brought up to the bar, by your ready impudence;" but she wisely recollected that it would be unbecoming her to imitate the pertness and sarcasm which she condemned.

Emma was little aware what ample revenge for her just severity it would soon be in Popkison's power, unintentionally, to inflict.

"I think, Miss Castlemain," said he, "that I know some one from your part of the world. Does not Harry St. Aubyn live near you?"

"He does, sir," replied Emma, blushing and alarmed at hearing that name pronounced, and pronounced by such a person.

"I was at College with him; he is a fine-looking fellow, though rather a quiz, and a formal chap, for he would not drink, and used to study all day."

"Is that uncommon, sir? I thought young men went to College on purpose to study."

"Ha, ha, ha! What an antediluvian idea! Study is very well in its way, but to do nothing else is a horrid bore. Do you know one Alton?"

"No, sir."

"Why, he is a great friend of St. Aubyn's. Alton is a short, thick-made, fat little fellow, and so nervous, that if he is alarmed or agitated at all, he stutters most laughably; so some of us, who loved fun, used to like to tease him in order to set him a-stuttering; and you know there was no great harm in this—only a little sport or so."

"No, certainly,—only the fable of the Boys and the Frogs."

"Ay, so St. Aubyn used to say; and he never would let us make fun of Alton in his presence, and as he is a devilish strong-built fellow, and has a good large fist of his own, we thought it as well to let Alton alone; but we nicknamed St. Aubyn Don Quixote, and Alton his Sancho Panza."

"That was witty indeed; but no doubt the same laudable fear of consequences which led you to avoid laughing at Alton in St. Aubyn's presence, prevented you from calling him and his friend by their nick-names in his hearing?"

"Why, yes."

"And pray, sir, may I ask you in what you took your degree at College?"

"Degree! Why I did not stay long enough. Bless your heart! I thought it a horrible bore to be forced to get up willy-nilly to prayers at seven o'clock in the morning, or incur certain consequences; and really, as I never got up time enough to tie up my stockings before I went to chapel, I used to get the rheumatism in my knees."

"Poor man! The rheumatism!"

"Oh, poh! you need not look so compassionate; that's a joke."

"What, the rheumatism, sir?"

"No, that's no joke certainly; but I mean that I was laughing when I said I had it."

This was indeed a joke which Popkison had repeated several times as a clever thing, though our heroine was too stupid to understand it.

Just then the pretty mayoress passed, and Popkison stopping her said, "Here is Miss Castlemain knows your cousin Harry St. Aubyn."

"No doubt she does," replied Mrs. Nares. "It is many years since I saw Henry; but I well remember to have heard him talk of his little playfellow."

"I did not know that you were relations," said Emma in some confusion.

"Very distant," replied Mrs. Nares. "It is through the Ainslies I am related to Mr. St. Aubyn."

Here they had reached the top of the dance, and the conversation, to Emma's relief, was put a stop to.

Having danced down with only half the couples standing up who had begun, Popkison told Emma he supposed she would rest herself, and not join the second dance till it was near her turn to begin.

"No, sir," replied Emma, "let us do as we would be done by. If all dancers did as you recommend me to do, those who are at the bottom of a set would be served as you and I were just now, and would have scarcely couples enough to form a dance."

"Well, and what is that to us? I always take care of number one. Pray, madam, are you related to Don Quixote, alias St. Aubyn?"

"No, sir."

"But you were playfellows together, Mrs. Nares said; and, upon my soul, I believe you read out of the same primer, for I never heard two people talk so alike as you and he."

"Sir," replied Emma warmly, "I thank you; for you have now, in my opinion, paid me the highest compliment I could receive from any one."

"So so," cried Popkison, "the Don has gotten a Dulcinea, I see;" and would have gone on on this scent much longer had not the dance been a double one, and the set so small, that to talk while they went up it was impossible; and Emma, as soon as she had danced to the bottom, made her courtesy to her partner, and happy to be released from him, joined the lady to whose care Mrs. Castlemain had left her. For she was indeed completely tired of him, as his whole conversation consisted of such jokes as I have enumerated above, hints and sneers against every one whom he mentioned, and an account of the age of every man and woman in the room, and the age of the latter given with such spiteful accuracy as Emma could only have supposed possible in the worst species of female envy. But spite is of no sex, and it is not always born of rivalship; it is as often the result of a mean malevolent pleasure taken by the person who indulges in it, in traducing and lowering every one that happens to come within reach. Nor can I allow that gossiping is a fault more common to women than to men. Emptiness of mind, and want of proper and wholesome occupation are common to both sexes, and consequently their result a gossiping spirit and a traducing tongue; and though some faults like some diseases are for the most part confined to women; yet backbiting and slander, like the attacks of a fever, are common equally to both women and men.

Before Emma made Popkison her parting courtesy, she assumed a very arch look, which he in vain tried to understand, and said, "I could not for some time imagine how you could have opportunities of knowing the ages of all those persons whom you have named to me; but at last I have found it out;" and before the inquisitive beau could tease her, as he meant to do, into an explanation, she had entered into conversation with Mr. William Nares.

"I am going to quarrel with you, sir," said she to the latter, assuming a very angry look. "I did not expect that you would have paid me so bad a compliment as to introduce to me so improper a partner."

"Improper! Believe me, madam, he is one of the first young men in the town."

"Then so much the worse for K——, sir; for I am convinced, by his knowledge of every one's age, what his situation in life must be, and that he is the clerk of the parish."

Young Nares immediately understanding her sarcasm, and disliking Popkison, told it to his father, his father to another, that other to two or three more; and the mortified beau had at last the pain of finding, through the means of some good-natured friend, that he, who had no pleasure so great as that of turning others into ridicule, was now the object of ridicule himself; and he saw that he would be called the Parish Clerk for the rest of his life. In vain did he take his revenge, by calling Emma the young Parson. He was told the idea was not new, but borrowed from Emma's name for him; and though he related his happy repartee to her over and over again, no one believed it, till wearied and angered beyond measure, he quitted the ballroom, wishing Emma had been a man, that he might have had the satisfaction of caning her.

Emma having refused to dance again, and Mrs. Castlemain being tired of cards, she proposed they should return home, and Mr. Egerton and Emma cheerfully acceded to her desire.

"Well, ladies," said Mr. Egerton, as soon as they were seated in the coach, "how has your evening pleased you?"

"For my part," said Mrs. Castlemain, "I fear I must own that pain has preponderated over pleasure; and much of this was owing to you, Mr. Egerton. The picture of human nature which you had drawn previously to our reaching K——, in spite of myself was ever before my eyes, and made to me a sort of glass, distorting like a concave mirror, through which I viewed the actions and conduct of every one during the whole evening."

"Say rather that you viewed every one, not through a distorting medium, but with clearer optics than you did before."

"And what have I gained by that? Oh, what ill-nature there is in the world! Would I could get back my happy ignorance! for really I must say with the poet,—

'——where ignorance is bliss,
'Tis folly to be wise.' "

"A very pretty thing, my dear madam, for a poet to say, but a very bad rule to be acted upon in our passage through life, and for this best of all possible reasons, that it is not true. But what was this ill-nature? I suppose you heard of several marriages that were going to take place?"

"Yes."

"And I dare say, not one of them was allowed to have any prospect of happiness."

"Scarcely one, certainly," replied ⬛ Castlemain.

"Ay, I can imagine what was ⬛ I once lived in a country-town, and I always observed that a reputed marriage ⬛ sure to call forth all the malignity, not only of acquaintances, but friends. Madness, scrofula, bad-temper, libertinism, extravagance, and all the curses of life, were immediately imputed to one or other of the poor creatures that were looking forward, in the simplicity of their hearts, to conjugal felicity; and it is astonishing how long the town used to feast on this cheap dainty. Indeed, a projected marriage in a place like K——, is a treat, given at the expense of the lovers and their families, to the whole town, while ' envy, hatred, malice, and all uncharitableness,' like the harpies of old at the table of Phineus, cover the entertainment with their filth; though, unlike that of the harpies, their presence is not known to the entertained; but the good souls, while indulging their bad passions to the utmost, believe that they are only actuated by a sincere interest in the well-being of the poor victims of their busy tongues. The wise son of Sirach," added Mr. Egerton, "says, ' There be three things that my heart feareth, and for the fourth I was sore afraid;—the slander of a city,—the gathering together of an unruly multitude,—and a false accusation; all these are worse than death.' Now all these things, my dear madam, you probably have encountered this evening; for you have heard the slander of a city, and many a false accusation, no doubt; and what is a crowded assembly but the gathering together of an unruly multitude?"

"An unruly multitude, indeed!" cried Emma, laughing; "there was amongst the dancers, at least, such jostling and crowding and trying for precedence! and such a selfish disregard of other persons' pleasure exhibited, by many couples sitting down as soon as they had danced down the dance!"

"That is a most base practice indeed," said Mr. Egerton. "I declare that were I a marrying man, I should be afraid to marry a girl who made a practice of quitting the dance when she had taken her own pleasure, and, regardless whether others had theirs or not, did not join the dances again till it was near her turn to begin."

"But why judge a girl from this action? this one action too?"

"Because the general temper and disposition are often shown in one action, however trifling; and it is evident that she who is thus selfish in her amusements is selfish in little things; a terrible trait in a wife! The happiness of the married life depends on a power of making small sacrifices with readiness and cheerfulness. Few persons are ever called upon to make great sacrifices, or to confer great favours; but affection is kept alive, and happiness secured, by keeping up a constant warfare against little selfishnesses; and the woman who is benevolent, and habitually fond of obliging, will, regardless of herself, be benevolent and obliging even in a ball-room."

"But tell me, Emma, how have you been entertained?"

"Oh! much, very much, on the whole. I was pleased with my first partner, and I had agreeable conversation with two or three persons, and wholly unstained with scandal or calumny. My second partner, however, was a sad counterbalance to these advantages."

"Yes," replied Mr. Egerton; "but I was sorry to find that you took such ample revenge on him for his delinquency."

"How!" exclaimed Mrs. Castlemain; "pray what was the delinquency, and what the revenge?"

"Why, madam, it seems that as he amused her with a minute detail of the ages of every person in the room, Emma had the malice to tell Mr. William Nares that she concluded he was the parish clerk; and the Parish Clerk the poor man was not only called during the rest of the evening, but will be all the rest of his life, for a nick-name sticks to every one like a bur."

"Well, but, dear sir, where was the harm of this? Why was I wrong in throwing a poor little harmless bur at a man who himself throws darts and dirt at every one within his reach?"

"Such a man, I own, my dear Emma, deserves punishment, and I am only sorry that you were the inflicter of it. Your youth and your sex make you an improper person to go about reforming the world; and silent contempt would have been in my opinion the only weapon for you to use against him; for you must see that what you said was only too much in his own way."

"I feel that it was so," replied Emma ingenuously; "but I assure you the error carried the punishment along with it; for I overheard a very pleasing young man say, on being asked to dance with me by Mr. Nares, ' No, no; she is a wit, I find, and I am not fond of encountering that sort of person.' But fore-warned fore-armed, and I hope to profit, dear sir, by your lessons and my own experience."

And Mrs. Castlemain and Mr. Egerton, who forgot her fault in the ingenuous readiness with which she confessed it, forbore any further comments except those of commendation.

As it was now generally known that the family at Roselands wished to visit and be visited, invitation succeeded invitation, and in paying and receiving ⬛ several cheerful if not happy weeks passed away; for the society of K—— might be ⬛ on the whole good society, though tainted with the usual vices of a country place,—or should rather say, of human nature, called ⬛ frequently into action by the operation of circumstances, the result of closer collision, and the greater jarring of interests and self-love, from the narrowness of the field of action. But at length that morbid restlessness which ever attends disappointed affection again took possession of Emma; again her colour faded, her spirits flagged, and she ventured to hint that she was tired of Roselands.

"Then suppose we go to London," said Mrs. Castlemain, whose anxious and observant tenderness immediately took alarm. "We have," added she sighing, "business of some importance to transact there, and it is now the prime of the London season."

"The proposal delights me," replied Mr. Egerton.

"Then when shall we set off?" returned Emma.

"In a few days," was the reply, and Emma again vainly hoped to escape from her own heart. Three or four days before that fixed upon for their departure, they went to another public ball at K——. As Emma had complained of indisposition lately, she had promised her grandmother to decline dancing; therefore the family appeared at the ball merely to have an opportunity of taking leave of those friends and acquaintance to whose civility they had been principally indebted during their residence in the neighbourhood.

During the course of the evening Emma had an opportunity of entering into conversation with Sir Charles Maynard, the gentleman who had refused to dance with her because he fancied that she pretended to be a wit; and she had the satisfaction of finding that by the reserve of her conversation, and the modesty with which she gave her opinions, she succeeded so well in her endeavours to remove his prejudice, that he never left her to join the dance, but was her constant and assiduous attendant.

But her amusement was not derived entirely from Sir Charles Maynard. A young man made his appearance at the ball that evening, whose dress, manners, and countenance amused her excessively, though she had no conversation with him. His name was Varley; and the place of his residence, London; but he was come down to K—— on a visit to a relation. His mother, who was a widow, kept a lodging-house in Westminster, and a relation of hers had interest enough to procure the son, who was about one-and-twenty, a small place in the War-office, with the promise of future promotion. Meanwhile Varley, who was industrious and frugal, contrived in different ways to increase his little income; and to do him justice, had a great variety of talent—for he could paint watch-papers and transparencies, copy music to admiration, play on the tenor and flute very well for an amateur; he could dance admirably, and spout speeches, and enact scenes from plays with great excellence, so infected was he with a love for the theatre, that his conversation was amusingly interspersed with quotations from Shakspeare and other dramatic writers. But I must now speak of his higher pretensions and attainments; he had a great command of language, and wrote prose and verse with equal facility, and I might add of equal merit; for though he had some talents, as he had no strength of understanding, they were like a thick embroidery on a flimsy gauze, and were of more detriment than service; while, like many people, he mistook a taste for literature for a power of excelling in it.

But Varley was of a very different opinion, and while he kept his muse in breath by constant exercise in diurnal and monthly publications, he looked forward to the time when he should distance past and present competitors in the race for fame, and shine a planet in the sphere of literature and the beau monde. For it was Varley's ambition to blend the poet and the man of fashion, and to be at once a beau and a bel esprit. Nature had indeed made him a very pretty man; he was tall, slenderly but gracefully formed, had a regular set of small features, a pink and white complexion, light hair and light eye-brows; but the judicious application of some dark substance improved the latter, and sometimes his natural bloom looked as if it was heightened by art. It must be owned, therefore, that Varley, with these pretensions to be reckoned very pretty, might without any great stretch of vanity fancy himself very handsome; and as his dress made him a beau, and reading and natural capacity in his opinion, had made him a bel esprit, it is certain that as a beau and bel esprit, he had a right to present himself to the town of K——, and to hope to astonish the natives, to use his own phrase, when in the spring of 1802 he made his appearance at a K—— ball, dressed in all the extremity of the mode. Fashion, indeed was his idol, and he meant to be what he considered as fashionable in his attachments. He wished excessively to be in love, but as yet had found no object worthy of his heart and his muse; for as yet he was not introduced into that high life for which he panted. Therefore lady —— ——, the countess ——, and the honourable Miss ——, could only be gazed at by him through a glass from the pit at the Opera; and as yet, at least, these admired ladies had not apparently noticed his personal beauty, or the graceful lounge which distinguished him in fop's alley. In the meanwhile, he wished to become the lover of some beauty rather advanced in life, provided such beauty was of rank or fashion, and he was on the look-out for such an object when he came to the ball.

Varley had so much of the true cockney feeling about him, that he fancied it was impossible there could be anything so knowing or so tasty as himself in the room; and he walked up and down, concluding there was no one present fit for a Town-man to dance with, when he was requested by a gentleman whom he could not refuse, to dance one dance with a young lady who had sat still all the evening. Accordingly, with an air and a grace, he complied, saying,

"Since you will buckle fortune on my back."

When he had begun the dance, not being yet satisfied with the notice he excited, he took a pair of castanets out of his pocket, and by the novelty of the exhibition and the admirable though affected manner in which he danced with them, called the attention of the whole room to him and his terrified partner. When he had done, he looked round with an air of great self-satisfaction; and the young lady declining to dance any more, though Varley said,

"Oh, do not tear thyself away from me,"

he volunteered a few steps with the castanets at the end of the room, while Popkison went about proposing to go round with a hat for him, adding, "He is very poor, and I dare say the cash would be welcome." And to the ladies he observed, "Are you not fascinated by that rattlesnake?" and on these two new jokes Popkison valued himself highly.

By this time Varley found that he was become an object of attention to every one, and that delighted him; he also saw the eyes of our heroine, and those of the friend on whose arm she leaned, observing him with great attention; and concluding admiration was the cause, he began to look delightfully with all his might.

"Ha! Varley, are you there?" said a gentleman who then entered the room.

"Ay, my good lord, and your poor servant ever," he replied, bowing very low and affectedly. Then extending his hand to a young man, who now approached, he exclaimed, seeing that Emma and her friend were listening,

"I prithee, shepherd, if that love or gold
Can in this crowded place find entertainment,
Bring me where I may rest myself, and drink.
I am a youth with dancing much opprest,
And faint for succour."

"What! I suppose, in plain English, you want a seat, and some porter?" cried his friend bluntly; "the one you may fetch from the bar, and the other is behind you."

"I thank your courtesy,"

said Varley, with a sneer, and seated himself beside him, on the seat to which he pointed.

"Is all right in that poor young man's brain?" said Emma to Sir Charles.

"Yes, if a brain can be said to be quite right that is nearly turned by vanity."

Varley, still seeing Emma's fine eyes following him, asked, "Who is that pretty girl

'That falls to such perusal of my face
As she would draw me?'"

"That pretty girl, as you call her, is a great heiress."

"The devil she is!" cried Varley, immediately adjusting his neckcloth, and stretching out one leg in what he imagined a becoming posture; "but is her fortune in her own power yet?"

"No; for her grandmother, the honourable Mrs. Castlemain, is not dead, nor like to die, but as strong and as good-looking as ever."

"What! has she a grandmother, good-looking, rich, a widow, and an honourable into the bargain?"

"Yes."

"And is she here?"

"Yes."

"Show her to me."

"She is not in the room at present; but surely a young heiress is a better thing than an old one."

"That is as people think," replied Varley, conceitedly; "you country-folks have vulgar every-day notions; the girl, that young thing, is not despicable certainly, but let me see her grandmother."

"Well then, so you shall, for here she comes!" and Mrs. Castlemain entered the room, her cheek flushed with a very brilliant bloom, and looking, being attired in French grey satin, even younger than she did at the preceding ball.

Varley really was, to do him justice, as much struck with her beauty as he pretended to be; while turning away from Emma, and gazing on her grandmother, he theatrically exclaimed,

"So doth the greater glory dim the less;
A substitute shines brightly as a king,
Until a king be by."

"My dear grandmother," said Emma, running up to Mrs. Castlemain, "here is the most amusing person! I think him a little mad and——"

"Mad! child!" she replied, "I see nothing amusing in madness, that climax of human misery. But where is he?" And Emma pointed Varley out to her, who now rose in order to walk and show his fine person off, in hopes of charming as much as he was charmed—

"Oh! she doth hang upon the ear of night,
Like a rich jewel in an Ethiop's ear,"

he exclaimed, as, taking hold of his companion's arm, he lounged up and down the room after Emma and Mrs. Castlemain, looking at the latter languishingly through his half-closed eyes; while she, wholly unconscious of her own power, imagined those dying looks and those sighs were all aimed at Emma. Emma herself was of the same opinion; and though not remarkably vain, she also took to herself the "beautiful! charming creature!" which Varley occasionally uttered when behind them. And as the ladies when they turned round saw

9*

Varley using extravagant gesticulation, Mrs. Castlemain's opinion of his madness became a much more positive one than Emma's had been. Therefore, though she attributed his behaviour to admiration of Emma, she began to be seriously afraid of him. In early life, and when a young and beautiful heiress, Mrs. Castlemain had been excessively alarmed by a madman, who fell in love with her, and she was also in some danger from him. She therefore, naturally enough, feared for Emma, the risk she had incurred herself; and when Emma said, "But if he were really insane, he would not be here," she with great propriety replied, "The gentleman who persecuted me was at large, and went to balls, like other people; therefore, I really wish to go home directly; for you see the poor man never once takes his eyes off you, and his dress, his looks, and his manners are all proofs of a deranged mind." She then requested Mr. Egerton to call up the carriage directly. Mr. Egerton did so; and Emma began talking to Sir Charles Maynard, who said, that in order to mortify her pride of youthful beauty, he must inform her he had discovered the object of Varley's passion was not herself, but her grandmother, and that Mr. Egerton could tell her the same.

While Emma was enjoying this information, and laughing with Sir Charles, the carriage was announced; and Mrs. Castlemain desired Mr. Egerton to take Emma between him and Sir Charles; "for indeed," said she in a low voice, "I do not like the looks of that young man."

"That is very ungrateful in you, and very hard upon him," said Mr. Egerton smiling; "but pray, if we do as you bid us, who is to take care of you?"

"Me! I want no guard."

"There, madam, you are deceived. It is you who are the prize aimed at; you are the Hesperian fruit that requires a dragon to guard it."

"I cannot understand you, Mr. Egerton; and as the horses are waiting," replied Mrs. Castlemain angrily, "I must beg you will take Emma, as I desired, and let us be gone."

Mr. Egerton and Sir Charles immediately bowed and obeyed, while Mrs. Castlemain, thinking herself quite secure on the shady side of fifty, feared not the fate of Proserpine for herself. When Varley saw her going, he exclaimed to his companion—

"I now do penance for contemning love,
Whose high imperious thoughts have punish'd me.
Oh! gentle Tomkins, love's a mighty lord,
And hath so humbled me, as I confess
There is no woe to his correction,
Nor to his service no such joy on earth!
Now, no discourse, except it be of love;
Now can I break my fast, dine, sup, and sleep,
Upon the very naked name of love."

"A very lucky thing," observed the purse-proud Popkison, "for a man of no fortune." While Varley, exclaiming,

"I must be gone and live, or stay and die,"

ran out of the room to catch another look at his idol. Varley overtook Mrs. Castlemain just as she was left alone at the door, the gentlemen being gone to see Emma into the coach. This was an opportunity not to be lost. With a smile which he meant to be irresistible, Varley said, "Allow me the honour of conducting—" when Mrs. Castlemain, with a half scream, bounded forward, and did not stop till she found her hand in Mr. Egerton's.

When they drove off, and before Mrs. Castlemain was sufficiently composed to speak, Emma exclaimed, "Well, grandmother, whenever I mean to make conquests, I will not go into public with you; my youth has no chance against your beauty, I find; and the wretched Varley has received a mortal wound."

"I desire, Miss Castlemain, you will not presume to laugh at me," she angrily answered. "Besides, it is very inhuman to laugh at the vagaries of a madman. Would you believe it, he spoke to me! and I was so terrified!"

"Believe me, madam," said Mr. Egerton, "he is no madman; though I fear he may be one when he finds you cruel, for he is dreadfully in love."

"If this be true, sir," replied Mrs. Castlemain in her most angry manner, "I wonder you can presume to assert that he is not mad; for what boy in his senses would think of falling in love with an old woman like me?"

Neither Mr. Egerton nor Emma could help laughing at the modesty of this speech. "Pardon me, madam," said the former, "but there is something irresistibly comic to me in your manner of proving Varley's insanity, who, I dare say, would be ready to exclaim,

'O! madam, who'd ever be wise
If madness be loving of thee!'

There is so much modest simplicity, and 'bonhommie' as the French say, in that answer!"

"I am glad it amuses you, sir. But I must say the whole thing is to me very disagreeable. Poor crazy boy! I am sure my heart bleeds for him."

"That is only retributive justice then," resumed Mr. Egerton; "but I assure you I met him this morning in a bookseller's shop, and had some conversation with him on books; and he, being a collector of old editions like myself, I was much pleased with the meeting. He told me he possessed one very scarce book, but had it not with him here, else he would have shown it to me."

"What an escape!" cried Mrs. Castlemain, "for then he would have come to Roselands to bring the book! However, we are going away in a few days, so it is not worth fretting myself about such nonsense!" Then, as soon as they alighted, Mrs. Castlemain retired to her own room, in no little perturbation, and some indignation of mind; while Emma, though neither perturbed nor indignant, retired to bed any thing but calm and happy; for the pretty mayoress had told her that she had just heard from London, that St. Aubyn was seen there very gay and gallant, and escorting the beautiful Mrs. Felton everywhere; while report represented them as shortly to be married.

It had been with great difficulty that Emma had summoned resolution to say, "and where is Mr. St. Aubyn now? in London?"

"No, he is, I believe, returned into Cumberland;" and Emma felt relieved to hear she was not likely to meet St. Aubyn and his mistress in town.

The next morning, when Emma and Mr. Egerton set out for their usual walk, they met Varley very near Roselands, who had really walked that way in hopes of seeing Mrs. Castlemain, with whose person as well as rank and fortune he had persuaded himself that he was violently in love, and he had lain awake all night thinking over his chances of success. In the first place he had convinced himself that both Mrs. Castlemain and her daughter had married at fifteen, and that Emma was only seventeen; therefore, that Mrs. Castlemain was not fifty. In the second place, he knew that many women older, and probably as wise as she, had married young men for love; and he flattered himself that his personal graces and acquirements were such as to excuse such a tender weakness in any woman. In the third place, he had a great idea of the power of perseverance; and could he once get introduced into the family, he was sure that his powers of pleasing would establish him there. In the fourth place, Mrs. Castlemain had had two husbands already; and so far from that circumstance appearing to him likely to militate against the success of any third suitor, he looked upon it as a favourable omen of the success of his suit. But he well knew that he must appear to suffer long, and in secret, and that his best way to obtain hope was to personate *despair*. And *happier* than ever he was in his life, for he had found a lady of rank to be in love with, and to *boast* also of being in love with, feeling that it would tell well to be in love with the honourable Mrs. Castlemain, Varley set off for Roselands to *look* as *unhappy* as possible.

When Mr. Egerton saw him, he bowed, and that gentleman courteously entered into conversation with him, presenting him at the same time to Emma, who was much diverted with his dress. He wore a white hat lined with green, and a pair of striped pantaloons of pink linen, which gave a most offensive air of effeminacy to his appearance. But his conversation was, though affected, not unmanly, and sufficient to convince Emma that his love for her grandmother was no proof of madness, but a great one of worldly wisdom and presumptuous ambition; and she had *no mean* idea of his *courage*, to call it by the mildest term, when she heard him say, looking at Roselands,

"'How reverend is the face of that tall pile!'

The views from the *house* must be very *fine*, I should think." But as neither Emma nor Mr. Egerton took the hint, and asked him to return with them, he was forced to wish them good morning, and trust to chance for giving him a sight of the goddess of his idolatry.

"It will be better, I think," said Emma, "not to tell my grandmother we met Varley so near the house;" and Mr. Egerton coincided with her in opinion. But the well-meant caution was vain.

As soon as Varley lost sight of them, he proceeded to Roselands; and discovering a lane that led by the park-palings, he entered it, and found at the end of it a high gate that commanded a wood, in which were several walks; then climbing this gate, he got up a convenient hedge, and, putting his head between the branches of a tree, awaited there the chance of seeing Mrs. Castlemain.

That lady, being full of other thoughts, had forgotten Varley, and was, as usual, taking her morning walk in this her favourite wood; and Varley had not acted Hamadryad long, when she came in sight, and passed very near him. The second time she passed still nearer, and Varley ventured to sigh.—Mrs. Castlemain started, looked round, but saw nothing, and passed on. When she was approaching again, Varley, by moving, moved the branches through which he looked, and the motion attracted Mrs. Castlemain's notice, on which she looked steadily forward, and saw a *face* in the tree;—and whose could that face be? Instantly, the idea of Varley recurred to her; and turning round, regardless of her age and her dignity, she ran towards the house with all possible speed; —while Varley exclaimed in transport,

"Just so the fleet Camilla scour'd the plain,
Flew o'er the unbending corn, and skimm'd along the main!"

The Camilla in question, however, not being quite so young as formerly, did not find flying agree with her; and when she reached home, she began to doubt her own wisdom in having run so rapidly from what at last might be an imaginary danger. For was it certain that she *had* seen a man's face,—and if she had, was it certainly Varley's? However, she thought it better to ascertain the fact, by sending the gardener to search the lane; who soon returned, saying he had seen nothing; for Varley, being conscious that Mrs. Castlemain had acted Camilla merely in consequence of seeing a man's face in the hedge, without at the same time suspecting that man was his charming self, wisely conjectured that she would, in her alarm, be likely to send some one to search for the intruder, and ask what he wanted; therefore he thought it wise to make a precipitate retreat.

"I shall certainly not tell Mr. Egerton and Emma of my alarm," said Mrs. Castlemain to herself, "for they would only laugh." While Varley, on his return to K——, took care to look very pensive and lovelorn, and to let every one know that he had been wandering near Roselands all the morning, and had seen Mrs. Castlemain; adding, with a sigh, "What a fine creature she is! O Heavens!"

The next day, Mrs. Castlemain had a great struggle with herself, whether she should take her usual walk or not; but ashamed of her own want of courage, she determined to conquer her fears, and walk through the wood, and cross a field to visit a poor neighbour. Varley, meanwhile, had stationed himself in his old place, having resolved, if Mrs. Castlemain saw him and was alarmed, to discover himself, and beg her pardon for having alarmed her; by which means, he should have an opportunity of speaking to her, and also rendering her a service; for he had seen a furious bull in the field, and he did not know whether he had not better at once watch for Mrs. Castlemain, and accost her, in order to warn her against this identical bull.

Mrs. Castlemain, meanwhile, timidly but rapidly approached the spot where Varley stood, and again she saw a face; on which, as before, she turned about and fled. But Varley, according to his previous resolve, immediately jumped from the hedge and pursued the fleet Camilla, in order to assure her it was *only he!* little suspecting that that *only he* was the only person of whom the flying lady was afraid. The faster she ran the faster Varley pursued; till at length, unable to run any further, Mrs. Castlemain, nearly fainting, leaned against a tree, and Varley stood before her hat in hand, begging leave to assure her that it was he, and no evil-disposed person, whom she had beheld, and that he had followed her to assure her of her safety, and to warn her against a mad bull that was in the field.

Mrs. Castlemain only bowed and trembled, for she was conscious of being afraid of a mad something, but not of a mad bull; then, with faltering steps, she proceeded towards the house, Varley still following.

"Might I presume, madam," said he, "to take advantage of this opportunity to present a little petition?" taking a paper from his pocket, from which also at the same time dropped a German flute——

"Bless me!" cried Mrs. Castlemain, starting, for she thought it a pistol. But Varley, taking it up, said, "It is only a flute, which sometimes

'Discourses most eloquent music.'

But this paper, madam," he added, bowing and presenting it. And Mrs. Castlemain, having heard he was poor and a poet, concluded it was a proposal to print his poems by subscription; and hoping to get rid of him, she eagerly said, giving him a half-guinea which she had loose in her pocket,

"It is not necessary for me to read this paper,—but take this."

The astonished and mortified Varley, who was merely presenting her with a copy of verses which he had written on her and Emma, comparing them to a full-blown rose and a rosebud, surveyed the money with a look which Mrs. Castlemain mistook for one of fierce indignation; and fearing she had offended him by the smallness of her donation, she immediately took out her purse, and putting it in his hand, was ready to exclaim like the old lady in the play,

"Take all I have, but spare my life."

But she only said, "Take whatever you please,—you are quite welcome." Then, seeing the gardener approaching, she walked rapidly forward; and before Varley, who was lost in amazement at the offered purse which she left in his hand, could recover himself, she had entered a conservatory communicating with the house, and having locked the door, sat down to recover herself.

"I have it! I have it!" at last exclaimed Varley. "She thought I was asking her to subscribe for the relief of some distressed object; and having a hand

"Open as day to melting charity,"

she gave me her *purse* to dispose of. But what could frighten her so? What caused her emotion? Certainly my approach fluttered her, and flutter they say is a sign of love;

"Deep confusion, rosy terror,
Quite expressive paint her cheek!"

Oh! Varley, Varley! what a lucky dog art thou!" Then resolving to call the next day to return the purse and explain the mistake, he went home in the most happy of reveries.

Poor Mrs. Castlemain, meanwhile, had no such enviable sensations; and her companions discovered that something disturbed her, though what it was they were unable to conjecture. At about ten in the evening they heard the sound of a flute at a distance, which seemed to be drawing nearer and nearer, and as it did so they saw Mrs. Castlemain become much agitated.

"How finely the person, whoever he is, plays!" cried Emma; "let us open the window."

"Open the window!" exclaimed Mrs. Castlemain. "Not for the world! And I will have every door and window closed and barred directly."

"Dear grandmother! What danger can you apprehend?"

"No matter what; I will be obeyed, Miss Castlemain;" and immediately she ordered every window and door to be fastened.

"I suspect," said Emma to Mr. Egerton, "my grandmother thinks it is Varley come to serenade her!" And Emma was little conscious how truly she spoke.

The flute meanwhile drew nearer; and had Mrs. Castlemain been a catholic, she would have crossed herself; while her visible alarm astonished her companions.

"Surely, madam, if it be a blunderbuss approaching, it comes in the sweetest shape possible, and I should like to see who carries it."

"I beg, I *entreat*, you will not think of such a thing," replied Mrs. Castlemain, and though reluctant to obey, Mr. Egerton's respect insured his obedience.

The flute now came very near, and then the sound appeared to grow fainter and fainter, till at length it ceased. But when Mrs. Castlemain had retired for the night it was heard again; and Emma expressed an earnest wish that her grandmother had not forbidden her to peep at the musician.

"But I conclude that you recollect her prohibition, strange as it was, and will attend to it," replied Mr. Egerton.

"Certainly," returned Emma. "I am incapable of being so base as to do behind my grandmother's back what I should not dare to do in her presence." Then, listening to the flute as they went, which was now evidently under Mrs. Castlemain's window, who slept in the front of the house, they retired to their apartments wondering at that lady's emotion and commands, and suspecting that they were occasioned by some idle or well-grounded fear of her young admirer.

Varley, for it was he, having played

"How imperfect is expression,"

and other love ditties under Mrs. Castlemain's window, for he had contrived to find out which was her room, retired, resolved to come again early in the morning, though not to approach the house; but he meant to awake his Juliet by his melting strains, and perhaps draw her to the window. Accordingly he came; and as he foresaw, he soon saw a curtain gently drawn aside and closed again. But as it was partly of clear muslin, he was sure that he could be seen through it; and immediately ceasing to play, he began to assume despairing looks, and apostrophize with much action the house that contained his beloved; while, as he paced the banks of a fine piece of water opposite Mrs. Castlemain's window, he seemed as if he had a great mind to throw himself in, to the terror of that lady; who now being more than ever convinced that he was insane,

was on the point of sending a servant to watch him, when Varley, feeling hungry, and having had no breakfast, thought he had exhibited love enough for one morning, and went quickly back towards the town.

Mrs. Castlemain now began to think seriously of consulting Mr. Egerton, and telling him of her alarm; but still the dread of ridicule prevailed, and she remained silent.

"I will certainly not walk in the woods and lane again," said she to herself; accordingly she went on the other side of the house, and taking a book with her, sat down, when tired, in a sort of summer-house at the end of a walk, surrounded by what had been a ha-ha, but was now filled with water.

But what can escape the prying eye of love? Varley, having breakfasted, and till the time for his visit to the wood had arrived, had gone round the premises, and had seen Mrs. Castlemain go up and down the walk in question, and then seat herself in the summer-house.

"What an opportunity," thought he, "to return the purse, and have a conversation with her in that sweet spot! besides showing my grace and agility in jumping that watery barrier."

Mrs. Castlemain was reading at this moment the "Victim of Magical Delusion," and was pitying the poor man, who, like herself, was haunted by one particular person and face; when looking up she saw Varley, who had leaped over the water, standing before her; and instantly uttering a loud scream, she sprang forward, locked the door, and fell back almost insensible in her chair. The gardener was, however, luckily for her, and unluckily for poor Varley, very near at hand; and hearing his mistress scream, he came running, armed with his spade.

Varley, who stood trembling and abashed at sight of Mrs. Castlemain's situation, had added to the strangeness of his white and green hat, and his pink pantaloons, a branch of May, which he thought would give him a pastoral and picturesque appearance, and had therefore gathered as he came along, and put on one side of his hat. It was no wonder, therefore, that the gardener should take him for a sort of mad Tom, (every village having occasionally its mad Tom or its crazy Betty,) and lifting up his spade, he desired Varley to go away, and not to frighten his mistress.

"I must speak to her, I must indeed," cried Varley.

"Not you, indeed, poor crazy soul!"

"Crazy! I am not crazy.

'When the wind 's southerly I know a hawk from a hernshaw,'"

said Varley. "Nay, let me speak to her."

"There, there, go away! If you are not a little wrong in the head, more shame for you to go about such a figure, looking like a Miss

Molly, and drest up in flowers. But whosoever you be, as you came over the water, back over it you shall go again; so off with you, my lad; you shall be 'Charley over the water.'"

In vain did Varley entreat to be permitted to go out by some path. The man was resolute, and Varley was forced to attempt the jump; but not being on the vantage ground as he was before, he could not effect it, and he fell into the water, whence with great difficulty he contrived to scramble up on the other side. However, he did reach the land at last, but in such a condition that he was glad to hide himself all day in the adjoining wood, and not return to K——, till it was quite dark, lest the boys in the streets should hoot at him, as did the ploughmen who saw him run across the field, and pursued him with shouts and derision. The gardener, meanwhile, was quite vain of his exploit; and looking in at the summer-house window, assured his lady, who was only just recovering her senses, that the poor madman was gone, and she had nothing to fear.

"There!" thought Mrs. Castlemain; "even the servant sees the poor wretch is mad; and when we have left Roselands I will own all that has passed, and make Emma and Mr. Egerton ashamed of their obstinacy."

That evening poor Varley stayed quietly at home, excessively chagrined at his morning's expedition, and only consoled by the reflection that he had not his best coat on when he fell in the water.

The next morning he dressed himself in his best coat, waistcoat, and breeches, and a black hat; and, looking like other people, set out to put in execution a plan which he had now enabled himself to realize.

"Well, my alarms are now almost over," said Mrs. Castlemain mentally that morning when she arose. "In another day we leave K——, and it is only giving up one walk; and I will take a drive if I wish for air, and then I shall certainly be safe." When, therefore, Emma and Mr. Egerton set out, as usual, for one of their long rambles, Mrs. Castlemain, instead of going out, sat down to read in her library. The servants had just brought in the luncheon, and Mrs. Castlemain was preparing to lay down her book, having ordered the carriage round, when one of the men came in and told her that a gentleman had called to inquire for Mr. Egerton; but that hearing he was not at home, he had requested to see her.

"To see me!" exclaimed Mrs. Castlemain, turning very pale. "What sort of looking man is he, John?"

"Oh, he is a queer-looking gentleman, madam; but it is not the poor man, certainly, that frightened you so much." And Mrs. Castlemain had just desired he might be admitted, when, introduced by another servant, in walked the queer-looking gentleman in the shape of Varley himself; while John, not understanding his lady's nods and winks for him to stay in the room, retired, shutting the door after him.

At first Varley only bowed; while Mrs. Castlemain, rendered respectful through fear, courtesied as much as he bowed. At length he stammered out an apology for having unintentionally alarmed her so often, and she begged him to make no apology. He then approached her, while she retreated to a door behind her, and, presenting a book to her, begged she would do him the honour of giving it to Mr. Egerton, he having sent to London for it, in order to show it to that gentleman; and as it was a very scarce work, he did not like to leave it in any hands but hers. He then, with a deep sigh, and a look of such love that Mrs. Castlemain could not mistake the expression, begged leave to return her purse, as he had had no other petition to prefer to her than one in the success of which his heart was much interested; namely, that she would deign to peruse a little poetical effusion, presenting the paper as he spoke, which he was unable to restrain. And Mrs. Castlemain took it, begging he would sit down, she herself still keeping near the door, and exhibiting evident emotion, which the vain boy attributed to her consciousness of feelings of tenderness towards him which she was ashamed to indulge.

"What a fine piece of water is that in the park, madam!" said Varley; "and it looks so calm, so tranquillizing, that a man forced to endure 'the proud one's contumely,' or 'the pangs of despised love,' might easily be tempted to plunge into its silver bosom, and forget his woes for ever."

"*Begin* his woes for ever," replied Mrs. Castlemain, "if he thinks properly of the crime of suicide, sir; and I am sure I should never look at that water again with any pleasure, if a fellow-creature were to drown himself there." Then fancying Varley looked very wild, she got up, saying, "Perhaps you would like to take some refreshment, there it is, ready." Then opening the door, she made a precipitate retreat into the next room, while the delighted Varley seated himself at the table.

As soon as Mrs. Castlemain escaped from the dreaded presence of Varley, she called the two footmen, and desired them not to lose sight of that gentleman, (who was the very man, though differently dressed, who had alarmed her before,) till they had seen him safe out of the grounds, and into the town of K——, or in the custody of some of his acquaintance, for she had reason to believe he was mad; and they were to take particular care that he did not go near the piece of water. The servants promised to obey her punctually; and Mrs. Castlemain, finding the coach at the door, jumped in, desiring the man to drive very fast.

Varley, meanwhile, was regaling himself, much at his ease, on excellent cold pigeon-pie, flattering himself that Mrs. Castlemain was gone to read his verses. His pride too was gratified by the attendance of the two servants, who, seeing his very odd faces and gesticulations, when, laying down his knife and fork, he indulged in a tender reverie, and congratulated himself on his cleverness in having so well introduced himself at Roselands, kept looking at each other very significantly, as much as to say, "Ay, poor man! I see my mistress was right!"

But Varley continued eating till he was ashamed to eat any longer. Then, beginning to wonder at Mrs. Castlemain's long absence, which he vainly tried to flatter himself was owing to the sweet bashful reluctance she felt to re-enter the room after having perused his verses, he asked the servants if their lady was particularly engaged.

"My lady, sir! Why, she is gone out; that was she who drove away just now."

"Zounds!" cried Varley, starting up with mortified dismay; then, with a theatrical air, exclaiming,

'And must I leave thee, Paradise!'"

by which the servants thought he meant the pigeon-pie, he put on his hat and walked out of the house, not knowing exactly what to make of the behaviour of its mistress, but satisfied with the eclat, as he thought it, of being known to the honourable Mrs. Castlemain, of being in love with her, and of having dared to hint his passion to her in verse. Full of these thoughts, which made him sometimes jump, dance, and bound forward as he walked, he was not conscious that the two servants were behind him; and when he was, he certainly felt no small surprise. But having that happy vanity which was capable of converting every thing into a source of pride, he recollected that there were gates to open in the park, and that Mrs. Castlemain being a lady of the old school, she had, with old-fashioned politeness, ordered her servants to open the gates for him — and so they did — by that means confirming his suspicions. But nothing could exceed his astonishment, when, as he approached the beautiful piece of water above mentioned, and was dancing towards its brink to look at some swans, the two servants came up, one on either side of him, and told him he must walk along the path willingly, or they must make him.

"Make me! make me! A man like me be controlled by two impertinent footmen!" cried the indignant Varley.

"Why, look ye, sir," said John; "it is a good thing for you to have two anybodies to take care of you; and as to your calling names, if it was not in consideration of your infirmities, why, we'd soon cure you of that fun."

"My infirmities! rascals! I'll go and complain to your mistress of your insolence."

"Ay, do, and she will tell you that we only obeyed orders in not letting you go near the water."

"Obeyed orders!" exclaimed Varley;

'———Man, proud man,
Dress'd in a little brief authority———.'"

Then recollecting what he had said about drowning himself, and his gestures as if he meant to do it, he imputed this order to weak but alarmed tenderness, and, clasping his hands in an ecstasy, exclaimed—

"I see what Emma meant to say,
My Varley, live for me.'"

And he bounded along the path with such swiftness, that the servants, now more convinced than ever of his insanity, could hardly keep him in sight. But at this moment he met two gentlemen whom he knew, who each took him under the arm; and the servants seeing him thus, as they thought, in custody, and being now long out of the grounds of their mistress, returned to Roselands, satisfied that they had done all that was necessary.

When Mrs. Castlemain returned home, she questioned the servants relative to what had passed, and received from them an account completely corroborative of all her ideas relative to Varley.

"Well," said Mrs. Castlemain to herself, "shall I, or shall I not, tell all that has passed to Mr. Egerton and Emma, and triumph in my superior penetration? No, I dare not; for they will very likely still assert that this youth is not mad; and that I can't bear; for, if not mad, his pursuit of me is an insult not to be endured, and one which I have not deserved. Had I painted my face, and gone about half undressed, and without a cap, I might have been taken for a woman of intrigue, and a silly, vain boy might have dared to make love to me; but for a woman of my propriety of conduct and appearance to be the object of a pursuit like this! — No, no, 'tis impossible; I must, in self-defence, think the poor wretch insane. However, I will desire my servants not to mention what has passed to Mr. Egerton and Emma, and I will be equally silent myself." Accordingly, she only said when they returned, "Mr. Varley has been here, and left this book for you;" and, seeing an arch smile on the lip of him and Emma, she suddenly left the room to avoid further questions. The book was that evening returned, with a note of thanks to Varley from Mr. Egerton.

The next morning they set off for London, having given the town of K—— something to talk of for at least a week. One person reported that Mr. Egerton and Mrs. Castlemain were privately married; another, that they were going to town to be married; a third, that Mrs. Castlemain, having vainly tried to get Mr. Egerton for herself, because he was in love with Emma, and not willing his wealth should go out of her family, was going to sacrifice that beautiful young creature to that old fellow through avarice. Popkison said, he supposed the young Parson was going to get ordained. Mrs. Evans declared it made her heart ache to think that poor dear Mrs. Castlemain had so little regard for her reputation as to go about everywhere with that Mr. Egerton, especially as it was shrewdly suspected he had been the gallant of her daughter. But this she took care never to say in the hearing of Mr. Vincent.

"Now then," said Emma, "we are on the road to this boasted metropolis. But do you think, my dear sir, that I shall certainly admire the style of life and the society which I shall meet with there?"

"Not at first," replied Mr. Egerton. "You will feel, even though conscious of wealth, and of the importance which wealth gives, like a drop in the ocean, or like an atom in creation, when you find yourself in the immense crowd of London, an unknown individual. You will probably wonder at first that there should be so many persons in the world whom you neither know nor are known by; and it will be so impossible for you to believe this almost mortifying truth, that, as you drive along the busy streets, you will fancy at every turn that you meet some one whom you have seen before; but in time you will form so many acquaintances, that this illusion of your fancy, or your self-love, will become a reality. Admirers, if not friends, will soon surround the carriage of Mrs. Castlemain's heiress when it stops at a shop in Bond-street, and all the adulation which can attend on youth, wealth, and I will venture to add beauty, will in a very short time, my beloved girl, be yours! And——" Here Mr. Egerton paused; for Emma suddenly leaned her head on the table, and burst into a violent flood of tears; for she felt how contemptible, how valueless would be to her the admiration of the whole world, if unaccompanied by that of one being whom she might never behold again;

"——an atom to creation, yet of power
To hide the whole creation from her."

Mr. Egerton and Mrs. Castlemain both understood the cause of her tears, but delicately forbore to notice them; and at length Mr. Egerton continued thus: "But in the conversation of flattering men and flattering women you will not find that society of which I have so often boasted; and it will require a long residence in London to procure an entrance into it. It will soon be known that you must be an ornament to a ball-room, or any assembly which you will honour with your presence. But those whom good taste and a respect for talent lead to assemble at their houses persons of both sexes for the purposes of conversation, will not even suspect, perhaps, that a young and admired woman has similar tastes with themselves, and had rather listen in modest silence to the converse of the intellectual and the learned, an unobserved, though not uninterested auditor, than shine the gazed at meteor of a ball-room, or form the centre of an admiring crowd in a fashionable assembly. But we will endeavour to teach them this, and then, I trust, my dear Emma will feel how just is my partiality to London society."

"I wish it may be so," said Emma; "but at any rate we shall have gained something; we shall no longer be forced to listen to dirty gossip, to stories of vice and folly, which often have no foundation; and as no one in this great world of London can know the private concerns of his neighbour, because in London there are no neighbours—and as Mr. D. cannot speak ill of Lady S. because he can't be sure that he is not in company with some near relation of the lady's, I am convinced that my good feelings will be more often called forth than my bad ones, during my residence in the great city; and I shall scarcely sleep to-night for joy at thinking, that in two days more we shall be in London."

At this moment, as they turned up a hill, on which was a sort of seat made of turf, Mrs. Castlemain, looking out of the window, started back in great trepidation, declaring that there was the madman again, and more wild than ever, for he was using violent gesticulations, and even in the carriage she felt afraid of him.

"My dear madam, let me assure you," cried Mr. Egerton, "he is not mad, poor youth!"

"I don't like to be laughed at," said Mrs. Castlemain.

"Nor would I presume to laugh at you; but it is very certain that this ton-studying, affected, poetical boy has set you up as an idol to worship, and I doubt not but he is standing there on purpose to catch a last glimpse of you."

"Nonsense!" cried Mrs. Castlemain, throwing herself back in the carriage, drawing up the glass first; while Emma, laughing violently, was peeping at Varley through the front windows. The truth was, that he had taken this early walk, not only for the purpose, as Mr. Egerton suspected, of endeavouring to see Mrs. Castlemain, in order that he might write a sonnet on the occasion, and paint to his companions at K—— the elegant woe he had experienced; but in the hope that he should be favoured with an invitation from Mr. Egerton to call on the family in London. Finding, however, that the coach was not even in sight when he got to the top of the hill, he thought he might as well amuse away the pangs of tender expectation, by rehearsing a speech which he was going to make at a debating society in London, whither he was soon to return; and thence arose the vehemence of gesticulation which Mrs. Castlemain beheld. When the coach drew near, Varley took off his hat; and while it passed him, he made a most obsequious bow, but vainly tried to behold the object of his passion. Greatly also was he discomforted by receiving only a cold bow from Mr. Egerton, instead of the expected invitation, while his countenance and affectation had an immediate effect on the risible muscles even of Mr. Egerton, which were so rarely acted upon; an effect which was not at all counteracted by a "Let me tell you, this is *mighty disagreeable*," and "I am very glad we have left K——," from the incensed Mrs. Castlemain.

They little suspected, nor even did Varley himself, the mortification that awaited him on his return to K——; a mortification infinitely greater than that of not having received an invitation to call on Mr. Egerton in town, nor even a gracious smile and bow of adieu from the divine widow, in return for his elegant verses.

Popkison was riding along the road to Roselands, at the very time when the servants of Mrs. Castlemain were following Varley; and from a hill commanding the park, he saw Varley's approach to the water, and the singular conduct of the men in consequence of it. "This is very strange," thought Popkison; and soon after seeing Varley running along the footway to the town, while the men turned back towards Roselands, he clapped spurs to his horse; and being of a very inquisitive, as well as malevolent and gossiping spirit, he rode after the men, and began questioning them relative to what he had seen. Delighted to tell all they knew on the subject, and proud, not only of their valour in taking charge of a madman, but also of their spirited humanity in having dared to oppose him in order to save his life, they told him every thing he asked, calling Varley "the poor distracted creature!" thereby gratifying Popkison's most favourite propensities so much, that he sincerely regretted that an indispensable engagement to dine in the country that day, prevented him from going back to K—— to tell this story, and raise a laugh at Varley's expense. But this benevolent indulgence he was forced to put off till the evening of the ensuing day, when he knew he was to meet Varley at a rout; and he entered the room just as the poor young man was haranguing to a group of ladies and gentlemen, on the beauties of Roselands, and on the excellent pigeon-pie which Mrs. Castlemain's cook made; having before informed the company, in order to give them an idea how intimate he was already become with the family, that he had seen them that morning also.

"So!" said Popkison with a malevolent grin, "Mrs. Castlemain gave you cold pie, did she? I wonder she did not give you cold pudding to settle your love, or rather your brain."

"My brain, sir! Do you think that wants settling?"

"Not I; but no doubt Mrs. Castlemain does. So she sent her two servants home with you!"

"Home! No—only to open the gates for me."

"But would not *one* have done as well?"

"Yes; but it would not have been so *respectful*; and persons of ancient families are always remarkable for carrying good breeding and ceremony even to a fault."

"But where was the servants' good breeding, I wonder, when they *insisted* on your not walking by the water's side?"

"Amazing! How should you know that?" replied Varley, too much thrown off his guard to deny it.

"No matter how I know it,—is it not a fact?"

"Yes; but a fact of so delightful a nature, and originating from so charming a cause! Excuse me, but I cannot explain myself."

"What's all this nonsensical rhapsody, Varley?" replied Popkison, "I shall begin to think Mrs. Castlemain's idea was right." Then to the amusement of the company, but the shame and agony of poor Varley, he related all he had heard from the servants, and even mimicked Varley while eating and walking, as the servants themselves had mimicked him,—till the mortified and self-adoring Varley left the house in a rage. And not being able to bear the ridicule which he knew would continue to be his portion, he threw himself into a coach that very night, having told his friends he was summoned away on business; and having crossed the country to a friend's house, about fifty miles from London, on the Windsor road, he stayed there one night, and proceeded to town on top of a stage-coach, the day our travellers arrived at most elegant apartments provided for them in the best part of Piccadilly.

But to return to them; at length, on the third day of their journey, the distant dome of St. Paul's burst on their sight, and proclaimed their approach to the metropolis.

"Now then I shall soon see the good Orwells!" exclaimed Emma. "Oh! how glad I shall be to see *them*, how glad they will be to see *me*, the poor little babe whom——" Here a look from Mr. Egerton broke off her discourse; for the gloom that had during the whole day been evidently gathering on the brow of Mrs. Castlemain, now burst into a convulsive fit of sobbing, which both alarmed and affected her affectionate companions. Yes, they were approaching the metropolis, that place where her discarded daughter, with the lovely girl who sat beside her in her arms, was about to commit the crimes of self-murder and infanticide, in consequence of her unrelenting severity; and she was also about to behold, humbled and conscience-stricken to behold, the benevolent beings, the good Samaritans, who had poured oil and wine into the wounds which she had made, and had proved more truly parents to her child than she herself had been!

"But you are spared to me, and I trust I have done my duty to *you*," she at length articulated, catching Emma convulsively to her bosom.

"You have done your duty by us, and by the Orwells too, my dear madam," said Mr. Egerton in a soothing tone of voice, "and would have done so by your daughter, but for the representations of a villain."

"A villain!" echoed Emma, turning pale with painful emotion, for that villain she remembered was the man who gave her birth. "Alas!" thought Emma, whose mournful recollections 'and blighted prospects in love' had been, unknown to herself, dissipated for some hours by the consciousness of the favourable circumstances under which she was going to be introduced into fashionable life, and who was feeling the advantages attending on being young, handsome, accomplished, and an heiress,—"alas! how many, perhaps, are the drawbacks on the apparently most brilliant situation, could one but commune with the closely veiled heart! Who will suspect, while I am smiling amidst the glittering crowds of London, that I *know* my father to be a villain, and that I feel in the secret recess of my heart all the torments of a virtuous but hopeless passion?"

Mr. Egerton observed the reverie into which she had fallen, and, in order to put an end to it, directed her attention to the beauty of Highgate Hill and the surrounding country. And soon the everywhere increasing promises of an approaching London, the regularly built rows of houses stretching on every side, bearing the pompous names of Paradise-Row, Paragon-Place, Phœnix-Terrace, by awakening a new train of ideas in her mind, weakened the force of old and painful associations, and substituted in their stead a variety of new and pleasant ones.

At about three in the afternoon they arrived at their place of destination,—not without Emma's having, as Mr. Egerton predicted, several times fallen into the error of fancying she saw persons whom she knew; while Mrs. Castlemain beheld, in the brilliant scene of wealth and business and existence around her, nothing but that London where her daughter had suffered, and where she had nearly died the death of the despairing. Her feelings therefore in consequence of this remembrance were indeed insupportable; and as soon as she alighted, she retired into her own apartment, unable even to bear to witness the delight of Emma at the novelty and splendour of every thing which she beheld from the windows.

"How much more interesting, my dear Emma, would this scene, pleasant as it is, become to you," said Mr. Egerton, "if I could tell you the names of some of the gentlemen whom you see standing in groups near the windows, or lounging up and down the street! for among the throng are probably men of rank without name, and men of name without rank, generals and admirals, who have fought and bled for their country, and orators who have endeavoured to promote her interests in the senate. Perhaps at this moment some fashionable poet, whose works have delighted you, is passing under the window, or some distinguished pleader, whose eloquence, even in newspaper reports, has aroused your feelings in the cause of oppressed innocence."

"How tantalizing," cried Emma, "and how mortifying it is to think, that of so many well-known persons I know not one!"

At this moment a stage-coach passed; and seated on the top of it, though muffled up, as it were, Emma beheld and recognized Varley, who, with laudable economy, was contented to be an outside passenger to the great city, whither he was hastening to gain a livelihood by the exertion of his industry and talents. Immediately Emma, being thrown off her guard by the pleasure of seeing one face that she knew, exclaimed "It is Mr. Varley!" kissing her hand in even delighted recognition; while poor Varley, mortified at being known in such a situation, and too angry with Mrs. Castlemain to wish to be recognised by any of her family, turned away his head without noticing her salute, in hopes by so doing she would imagine she had mistaken some one for him.

"It certainly *was* Varley," said Mr. Egerton. "The foolish young man would not return the bow, because he is evidently ashamed of what he ought to be proud of, namely, the virtue of squaring his expenses to his circumstances."

"He is certainly following my grandmother," said Emma, laughing, "but I will not tell her of his arrival for fear of alarming her."

At this moment they heard a violent crash and loud screams, and throwing up the window, they saw that owing to a hole in the street the coach had been overturned, and poor Varley precipitated from his elevated station into the kennel. The first impulse of Emma was to run out herself, and inquire if any mischief had been done. But Mr. Egerton prevented her; nor did he go himself, as he saw that the only inside passenger was taken out unhurt; and he soon beheld Varley on his feet, evidently suffering no inconvenience but that of being covered with mud.

"But surely, sir," said Emma, "it would

be only kind in you to ask Mr. Varley to come in and take a glass of wine after his fright!"

"No, my dear girl," he replied. "I suspect, from Varley's manner, that it would be very unkind; for his self-love would be more wounded by the conviction that we had witnessed his distress, than by our desire to comfort him under it; and I dare say the foolish boy is more mortified at the possibility of our having seen him on the top of a coach, and thence precipitated into the dirt, than he would have been had we seen him reeling home from a tavern in a state of inebriety. Such are the false estimates of good and evil appearance, which we all in our turns make." They now saw a fat, vulgar, loosely and dirtily dressed woman run across the street, who going up to Varley with open arms, exclaimed with loud sobs and many tears, "Oh! my dear Billy! my dear Billy! are you sure you are not hurt, my Billy! my poor dear child!"

It was Varley's mother, who expecting his arrival, had gone out to meet him, and had seen the accident happen before she had reached near enough to ascertain the degree of damage that had ensued.

It was not in the nature of Emma or Mr. Egerton to experience any thing but respect and sympathy for the fears of a mother for the safety of a darling son, however ridiculously expressed; and at first even the populace respected her alarm. But knowing it to be groundless, and poor dear Billy wholly unhurt, they could not survey without excessive laughter, the endeavours of Mrs. Varley to clean her son; who, taking from her pocket a handkerchief begrimed with snuff, wiped the poor youth's face with it so elaborately, that it was streaked from one end to the other; and the sight produced such excessive mirth in the spectators, that Varley, suspecting the Roseland family were witnesses to his mortification, broke from his poor mother's grasp, and running down the street was out of sight in a twinkling; while he from that time cherished a spite against them, which he took the earliest opportunity of indulging.

It is curious to observe in the history of men, and even of kingdoms, how often the destiny and the most important event in the lives of both, are to be traced up to the most apparently trifling and insignificant of events.

While watching the motions of the discomfited beau, neither Emma nor Mr. Egerton was conscious of the effect which the appearance of the former had had on the gay crowd between them; but when Varley had disappeared, Emma blushed with confusion, at finding herself the object of universal attention, while many glasses were levelled at her, and some gentlemen absolutely stopped in order to gaze more at their ease at the new and beautiful face before them.

Emma instantly drew back, sorry to find her indiscretion had deprived her of the pleasure which she derived from watching the passers-by, as she saw several persons pass and repass evidently from the hope of seeing her again; for, whatever satisfaction her vanity might derive from this tribute to her charms, it was dearly purchased, she thought, by being forced to forego that of standing at the window. But after all this was a heartless enjoyment, and a mere gratification of the eyes and the curiosity. A dearer and a more respectable one awaited her the next day, as every feeling most near to her heart decided her to pay her first visit to the Orwells.

The next morning, when they assembled at the breakfast-table, Emma proposed going at eleven o'clock to call on the Orwells.

"You are in a great hurry, I think," said Mrs. Castlemain, starting, and in a tone of pique.

"Not in too great a hurry surely, madam," replied Mr. Egerton, "to see persons to whom we all owe so much!"

"Well, well," she returned with a deep sigh, "but you had better send them word that you are coming."

"They know it already; I never like what are called agreeable surprises; I think that by depriving persons of anticipations of pleasure, one robs them of more than half the pleasure itself; I therefore wrote to the Orwells last night to announce our visit to-day."

"I think you might have consulted me first," said Mrs. Castlemain, angrily; "but I suppose you will not insist on *my* going with you."

"Certainly not, though we shall regret your absence; but why, dear madam, should you not go?"

"Oh! because—because it will be for many reasons a painful visit to me."

"Then get it over."

"Besides, the Orwells don't wish to see me."

"Not to see you! Not to see their benefactress!"

"*Their* benefactress! Oh, Mr. Egerton!"

"Yes, madam, their benefactress. My dear lady, why will you always dwell on your past and repented errors, and forget the virtues by which you have made such honourable atonement? The Orwells owe you *much*, and I am sure that they will be cruelly disappointed if you do not accompany us."

"Do you think so?" said Mrs. Castlemain, in a gentler tone, soothed and encouraged by this speech; and on Emma's tenderly approaching her, and begging her to go with them, she consented, and as soon as the carriage came to the door, they got in and drove to the house of Mr. Orwell.

It was in a small street in Kensington, and was pleasantly situated on the side of a wide field, while the back-windows commanded the well-cultivated country adjoining. This house, furniture and all, was the gift of Mrs. Castlemain, who accompanied it by a deed of settlement of a handsome annuity on Mr. and Mrs. Orwell for their joint lives, sufficiently large for them to give up half the produce of their business to their nephew, and enjoy the blessing of comparatively country air; while, as they gazed with ever-new delight on the comforts that surrounded them in their new habitation, their grateful and conscious hearts whispered, "All these are the reward of an act of kindness to a suffering and friendless fellow-creature!"

The Orwells, as soon as the church-clock struck eleven, began to count the moments which must still intervene before they beheld their anxiously-expected guests; while Mrs. Orwell endeavoured to beguile the time by calling the maid again and again to rub the mahogany tables,—being never satisfied with their brightness, so eager was she to show Mrs. Castlemain the care she took of the furniture which she had bestowed. Mr. Orwell, unable to sit still, walked up and down before the door; and Mrs. Orwell had stroked down her bustling because clear-starched muslin apron, at least twenty times, as she heard the sound of an approaching carriage, before the expected party arrived.

"I wonder who the child is like, my dear," said she, joining her husband in his walk.

"The child! You forget, old woman, that the child is now a young lady."

"True, true; but I think I see her now as when—" Here affecting recollections made emotion break off her speech; and the old man, equally affected, spoke not, but pressed her arm, which was locked in his.

"I wonder whether she is like the drawings we have of her," resumed Mrs. Orwell; and in spite of her knowledge that Emma was now indeed a woman grown, her idea of her could not get beyond those drawings, and she clothed the image of Emma in the childish form which they exhibited.

The expected visitants, meanwhile, were not without their agitations. Mr. Egerton was much affected by the sight of Mrs. Castlemain's agitation; but in Emma's he participated, for it was the flutter of joyful sensibility. She was to see the preservers of her and her mother's life! and the tear that trembled in her eye, was one of grateful pleasure. At length they arrived at the little gate which opened into the small garden leading to the house in which Mrs. Orwell had intended to await her guests; but as soon as the coach was drawing up, overcome with trepidation, she hastened back into the parlour, and, scarcely knowing what she did, began to set the chairs and wipe down the table with her handkerchief. Meanwhile, Mr. Orwell stood bowing at the door. Mr. Egerton got out first, and seizing the old man's hand, pronounced, "God bless you, sir!" with such earnestness of feeling, that he took from Mr. Orwell the power of replying.

Mrs. Castlemain then, leaning on Mr. Egerton, tottered into the house; and Emma bounded out after her; while Mr. Orwell followed, raising his eyes in pious thankfulness for having been allowed to save the life of such a creature. Mrs. Orwell stood at the door of the parlour to courtesy if not to speak her welcome. But Mrs. Castlemain did not notice her; she rushed past her, and throwing herself on the sofa, hid her face with her hands.

"Shall I get the lady anything?" said Mrs. Orwell to Mr. Egerton.

"No; you had better take no notice of her," he replied in a low voice; and Mrs. Orwell turned from Mrs. Castlemain to look at Emma.

"Bless me!" cried she, "is it possible? Can that fine young lady be—"

"It is the child whom—" replied Emma; she could say no more, but gracefully throwing herself into the extended arms of Mrs. Orwell, she sobbed out her thanks on her shoulder; and Mr. Egerton, seizing Mrs. Orwell's hand, raised it to his lips as respectfully as he would have done that of an empress.

"But where is Mr. Orwell?" said Emma recovering herself; while the old man, wiping a tear from his eyes, came forward and affectionately saluted the wet and glowing cheek which Emma presented to him.

"This is a proud day for you both," said Mr. Egerton, as he and Emma seated themselves on the offered chairs.

"Yes," observed Emma, "it must give you great pleasure to see one who owes you so much."

"But I am the person the most obliged," cried Mrs. Castlemain uncovering her face, "and I—I cannot even articulate one thank."

"Madam," replied Mr. Orwell, "it is for us to thank you! Look round! all the comforts we enjoy are, you well know, the gift of your benevolence!"

"Say rather of my *gratitude*," she resumed, "for obligations which I can never sufficiently repay. Let me," she added, taking a hand of both Mr. and Mrs. Orwell, "let me clasp in mine the hands of the preservers of—" and as she pressed their trembling hands, she bowed her head on them with the humility of a contrite spirit.

"You have a very pleasant house here," said Mr. Egerton.

"Yes, indeed," replied both at once; "and I am sure," continued Mr. Orwell, "that coming to it has lengthened both our lives."

"God be praised!" cried Mrs. Castlemain, smiling through her tears, and bowing to the gratified Orwells. Soon after, as she followed the eyes of Emma towards some drawings which decorated the room, she saw enough to convince her those drawings were by Agatha; and she again hid her face in her handkerchief.

"But why is there no drawing *here?*" said Emma, pointing to a vacant space over the chimney-piece. "If you have not one large enough for that place, I will give you one of mine."

"I should rejoice to have it," said Mrs. Orwell, "but——"

"My dear," interrupted Mr. Orwell hastily, "*some other time*, not now, we will explain."

Mrs. Castlemain at this moment raised her head; and seeing by the nails in the wall that a drawing or picture had once hung in that place, suspected the truth, and desired to know whether a picture or drawing had not for some particular reason been removed.

"Yes, madam," replied Mr. Orwell, "one which we thought it might give you pain to see."

"No matter," rejoined Mrs. Castlemain with quickness, "I would rather you should inflict pain on me than not;"—and Mrs. Orwell brought in the drawing. It was a coloured drawing representing Mrs. Orwell with Emma pale and dying on her lap; while Agatha, on her knees beside her, was awaiting with clasped hands and a look of wild anguish the effect of the nutriment which Mrs. Orwell was going to convey into the infant's mouth.

"It is *very* like her," said Mr. Egerton with a quivering lip.

"It is like, indeed!" said Emma, gazing wistfully on the beloved face of her unhappy mother.

"It is not like my child as *I knew* her!" exclaimed Mrs. Castlemain wildly, and falling back on the sofa in an agony almost too great to bear.

"I would not be that poor lady for all the world!" thought Mrs. Orwell;—"my poor Mary died in my arms!—— Sir, sir," said Mrs. Orwell, affectionately pressing Mr. Egerton's arm, "were not you the gentleman who were with——"

"We will talk of those things another time, my dear madam," interrupted Mr. Egerton; then approaching Mrs. Castlemain, he asked her if she had not better return home; to which proposal she thankfully assented; and Mr. Egerton having put her into her carriage, and well knowing she would prefer solitude to company, desired the carriage to return for them as soon as it had set down Mrs. Castlemain.

"Now, my dear friends," said Mr. Egerton, "I will tell you all you wish to know." And Emma, as well as the Orwells, listened with eager interest to the description of Agatha's last illness and death, and the journey Mr. Egerton took with his orphan charge; while ever and anon the deeply interested old couple interrupted him with exclamations of "Dear child! poor little girl!" then turning to gaze with pleasure almost amounting to rapture on the lovely and expressive face of the being whom they had been the means of preserving.

Almost daily did Emma and Mr. Egerton visit the Orwells; and Mrs. Castlemain too very often forced herself to call on them; but she was never easy in their presence, and was also conscious that, however gratefully they felt towards her as their benefactress, a chill came over their feelings when they thought of her as the unforgiving mother of Agatha; and at such times she could not help recollecting, that in Agatha's narrative she had herself contrasted with her own mother's conduct the benevolence of these strangers. But to the pleasure which Emma and Mr. Egerton derived from being with these good old people there was no drawback, and many a day did Emma spend with them alone; for she thought that they had a right to some hours of that existence which they had preserved; and the joy that sparkled in their countenance whenever she appeared, gave her more heartfelt satisfaction than the homage paid her by admiring crowds. They were more at ease with Emma than they had ever been with her mother; for she united to the dignity of Agatha a degree of graciousness and playfulness of manner wholly unknown to her; and never once were the Orwells reminded by Emma's manners, though they had often been by Agatha's, that there was any difference between them in rank and situation.

But the pleasure which Emma derived from visiting the Orwells was not wholly the result of a feeling of duty fulfilled. They had informed her that a very handsome young man had called on them a few months preceding her arrival in town, and had told them that he came to see them, from the respect their conduct to Mrs. Danvers and her child had excited in him; and that having stayed with them an hour or two, during which time he had informed them that he knew Mrs. and Miss Castlemain and Mr. Egerton, he had taken his leave without letting them know his name or place of abode. But Emma was at no loss to discover who this visitant to the Orwells was; and the consciousness that St. Aubyn, actuated no doubt by the interest he still felt in her, had been at that house, had sat in that apartment, and had conversed with the owners of it, gave a degree of charm in her eyes to them and to their residence, which other feelings, though very powerful, could not alone have bestowed.

Emma often recollected that Mr. Orwell had once been opulent, and had probably been no stranger to the luxuries which opulence bestows; she therefore could not rest till she had seen his old age in possession of most of the enjoyments which his youth had known.

"I wonder whether he ever kept a close carriage?" thought Emma; and she contrived to find out that he had not, but that for many years he had had a one-horse chair, in which he used to drive his mother. This intelligence, and her wishes in consequence of it, were immediately made known to Mr. Egerton, who joyfully undertook to purchase a low-built open chaise, and a steady horse to draw it; while Mrs. Castlemain and Mr. Egerton disputed which of them should defray the expenses attendant on this new appendage to the establishment of the old couple. But at length Mr. Egerton carried his point; and till Emma came of age, and had an allowance of her own, it was agreed that Mr. Egerton should be at all the charges incident to this gift.

"Dear me! see what a pretty little carriage has stopped at our door!" said Mrs. Orwell to her husband, when Emma, who had come to spend the day with them, was standing by her side at the window.

"A pretty carriage, indeed!" replied he; "I wonder whose it can be; for see, the servant who is in it is getting out, and coming hither. It must be a mistake, unless he brings some message to you, Miss Castlemain."

"He has made no mistake," cried Emma; "and I have to request that you, my dear sir, will drive me a little way on the road, that I may see how the horse goes."

"I drive you, my dear!"

"Yes; you know you used to drive your mother, and I hope and trust that for many a day to come you will drive Mrs. Orwell in that chaise for my sake; for that chaise and horse are yours, if you will do us the honour of accepting them."

The delighted old couple, well aware that in accepting this gift they should impart more pleasure than they received, gratefully acceded to her request, and Mr. Orwell had the pride and satisfaction of driving Emma through the beautiful environs of Kensington.

But though Emma derived unmixed satisfaction from her visits to the Orwells, they frequently beheld her with mingled pleasure and pain; for Mrs. Orwell, like all women, quick-sighted to the feelings of her sex, soon discovered that some secret disquiet preyed on the mind of Emma, and she suspected her young favourite was in love.

"And if she *were*," said Mr. Orwell, petulantly, when Mrs. Orwell communicated her discovery to him,—" if she be in love, as she can't love in vain, that I am sure of, her cares, if she has any, can't proceed from that source."

"But perhaps she loves some one whom her grandmother does not approve! for you remember that very handsome young man's calling on us, to see us as the preservers of Miss Castlemain, and who knows but it may be her mother's sad story over again?"

"God forbid!" ejaculated Mr. Orwell; and he resolved to watch Emma as attentively as his wife had done; nor was he slow to discover in her symptoms which alarmed him for her future peace, though they *both* thought that Emma's spirits seemed to grow better from day to day.

Nor were they mistaken. Though Emma thought that she could love one alone, she was not insensible to the pleasure of being admired and addressed by sensible and respectable men, amongst whom Sir Charles Maynard had pleaded his suit, but pleaded in vain. And now, Mr. Egerton and Mrs. Castlemain having both renewed some of the acquaintance of their youth, she often associated at her grandmother's table with persons of acknowledged talents and great conversational powers; and she had also been introduced into those parties which she and Mr. Egerton used to discuss under the name of conversationes. These parties were held at a house where she would infallibly have met Mrs. Felton, had not that lady been at variance with the mistress of it; nor did they resume their acquaintance till Emma left London.

On these evenings they used to arrive at the lady's house at an early hour, and were introduced into a most elegant and tastefully decorated apartment, containing a party sufficiently large to admit of its being formed into many groups, but not large enough to preclude the possibility of walking about with ease and comfort. Amongst the company were usually men and women of the highest rank in the country, but waiving all the distinctions of their rank and situation, and only desirous of recommending themselves by their own talents, or their graceful and respectful attention to the exhibited talents of others; for many of both sexes who held a distinguished place in the literature, the arts, or the sciences of the day, were mingled in this fashionable throng, and joining in that greatest of all delights, rational conversation. Emma, though her polite hostess frequently endeavoured to call her forth, was always contented to listen; but it was in silence so animated and intelligent, that once, as she timidly declined giving a decisive opinion on a subject which she was hearing discussed, an elderly gentleman, turning to his neighbour, observed that that young lady need not speak in order to charm, for that she reminded him of the lines of the poet with one word altered—

" Alike her speaking and her silence move,
  Whose voice is music, and whose looks are love."

At the close of one of these evenings our heroine and her friends observed that the party had increased so much that the adjoining room was full of company, while they heard one voice, louder than the rest, speaking alone; and as the folding-doors which divided the rooms were at this moment thrown open, Mrs. Castlemain, with infinite amazement, beheld Varley, standing up in the middle of the room, speaking with great vociferation, and using gestures of the most violent description.

It was indeed Varley, exercising for the amusement of the company a talent, which, as I have before observed, he possessed in no mean degree, viz. that of spouting, or acting. He was not the mimic or copier of others; on the contrary, he gave his own conception of certain parts, both in comedy and tragedy, from which, with the occasional aid of paint and dress, he was in the habit of acting detached scenes, in a very amusing and interesting manner. It had long been the first object of Varley's ambition to get introduced into fashionable circles; and to do that he would willingly have consented to play Punch, or grin through a horse-collar, had such accomplishments been deemed necessary to procure such an introduction. At this acme of his ambition he luckily was introduced to a gentleman of some rank, who was a Pidcock or a Polito in his way, and was famous for assembling at his house those rarities, or monsters, or wild-beasts, denominated remarkable persons, or persons possessed of curious and amusing talents. Dwarfs, giants, ventriloquists, Turks, parrots, monkeys, mimics, often formed the rare and entertaining menagerie of this gentleman when he opened his house to fashionable society; and having been told by his hair-dresser that a young man of his acquaintance in the war-office had great talents for spouting, the delighted Varley received an invitation to dine with this gentleman, who, finding he really had the talents imputed to him, invited him to a party; and thence he gained admission to the still more tonish house of the lady where Mrs. Castlemain saw him.

It was the first time of Varley's appearing there, when his evil genius led the family from Roselands thither also.

Such is the power of prepossession, that even seeing Varley at this house had not power to remove Mrs. Castlemain's impressions concerning him, and she said to a gentleman near her—" How shocking it is that no one has humanity enough to interrupt that poor young man, and lead him home!" Then seeing Mr. Egerton, she exclaimed, "There, Mr. Egerton! here is your boasted London society, indeed! How dreadfully cruel and unprincipled it is for persons to amuse themselves with the ravings of a madman!"

"Indeed," said Mr. Egerton, "Mr. Varley is only showing off as a spouter, and is now acting Benedict. Approach, and you will be convinced of it." And as Emma, who was already listening to him, smilingly beckoned her, Mrs. Castlemain leaning on Mr. Egerton's arm timidly drew near. But as Varley's eye happened at this moment to turn towards Mrs. Castlemain, the consciousness that she had it in her power to tell a ridiculous story of her mistaking him for a madman, so completely overset him, that after fruitlessly endeavouring to recollect himself, and go on with his speech, he complained of illness occasioned by the intense heat of the room, and made a precipitate retreat before any one could stop him.

But when was excessive vanity unaccompanied by malignity? Varley, who was never happy except he was in all places the prominent person, was so provoked at the power which Mrs. Castlemain's appearance had on him, as it prevented his continuing to be that evening a centre of attraction, that he determined to be revenged; and whether she did or did not tell the story of his love, and its results, he was resolved to inflict mortification to the best of his power on her and Emma, in return for that which they had occasioned him that evening, and at K———. Accordingly, being at this time a writer in a fashionable newspaper, he inserted the following paragraph:—

"We hear from undoubted authority, that the Hon. Mrs. C———, grandmother to the beautiful Northern star that now glitters in our hemisphere, intends to obtain letters patent for this young lady to bear the arms and take the name of C———n, as she was not born in wedlock, and therefore could not otherwise be called by the ancient and noble name of C———n, though she will inherit some of the estates of that family; thus endeavouring to hide this terrible stain on the purity of the T———n family, by the spotless shield of that of C———n. This may be called *an escutcheon of pretence* indeed!"

This paragraph had all the power to wound the mother and daughter of Agatha which he expected it would have; for he had heard at K———, that Mrs. Castlemain's feelings were most painfully alive to any allusions to the illegitimacy of Emma, and he took a malignant pleasure in thus exercising the most dangerous of all powers, that of wounding anonymously. Deeply indeed was Mrs. Castlemain distressed to see the fame of Agatha publicly injured, and her child declared illegitimate, without the power of vindicating her in any convincing or satisfactory manner; for the only evidence which they could at present adduce, even to their friends and relations, was the declaration of Agatha, that she was the lawful wife of Danvers, because he had led her to the altar *after* the death of his first wife, as was proved by the letter to him which she had found and preserved;—while Danvers on the contrary asserted in his letter to Mrs. Castlemain, that his first wife was *alive* when he married Agatha. And as no register had yet been found to contradict by its *date* the truth of the assertion, there was only too much reason to believe that Emma's claims to legitimacy would always remain disputable.

"This paragraph must have been written by some secret enemy," said Mr. Egerton thoughtfully.

"But whom can we have offended?" demanded Emma. "I flattered myself that I had no enemy."

"No enemy!" replied Mr. Egerton. "Then, my dear child, you must have thought you had no merit. But whoever wrote the paragraph in question, it is very certain that it calls upon us imperiously to endeavour once more to procure a copy of the registry of your mother's marriage. And I must advertise again, in all the papers, a considerable reward to whoever will procure one."

"Advertise!" exclaimed Mrs. Castlemain, who had hitherto preserved a gloomy silence, "advertise, and we in London! I could not endure it, indeed I could not."

"Well, then, let us leave London." And Emma, disgusted and alarmed at this effusion of secret malice, consented joyfully to the proposal.

"But whither shall we go?" she added.

"What say you, ladies, to a trip to Paris?" replied Mr. Egerton; while Emma almost screamed for joy at the idea.

"I should like it excessively," said Mrs. Castlemain, "as being out of England during the time we are advertising would be a most desirable circumstance indeed."

"Then let us take the necessary steps immediately." And in a few days everything was ready for their departure.

Thus did the paltry spite of a vain, malignant boy, the result of a wound to his self-love, disarrange the plans and disturb the quiet of these respectable individuals; and thus did a paragraph in a newspaper, lead them to a scene pregnant with the fate of their future lives, and fraught with events of the most serious and important nature.

This paragraph, however, stimulated afresh Mr. Egerton's intention, to call on the minister of the parish where Agatha had been married; and at her earnest request, Mrs. Castlemain and Emma, as well as Mr. Orwell, accompanied him. They found, on inquiring for Mr. Jones, that he was still alive, and still minister of that parish; therefore they knew that they had met with the object of their search. He was also at home, and they were immediately conducted to him in that very room where the poor Agatha, nearly nineteen years since, had vainly opposed the representations of injured and helpless innocence to the successful machinations of a villain.

Mr. Egerton told the cause of their visit, and the subject of their inquiry, in as few words as possible; and Mr. Jones assured him, that he recollected the *poor lady's* calling on him, and her evident derangement, perfectly. But on Mr. Egerton's asking him, whether he had judged her to be insane from his own observation only, or from the previous suggestions of another, he owned, that he entered the room prepared to see a madwoman, because his clerk, Cammell, had assured him she was notoriously so, and told him the cause of her madness.

"Then, sir, that Cammell was a villain; for the poor lady was in her perfect senses, though driven perhaps into the temporary frenzy of passion by the consciousness of being the victim of treachery.—But where is this man, this Cammell?"

"Cammell! Cammell!" exclaimed Mrs. Castlemain, in an agitated manner, "What sort of man was he, sir? and how long had he been clerk of this parish?"

"For about nine years, I believe, madam; and he was a man marked with the small-pox, with small light eyes, and turned-up nose, and very red hair."

"And whence did he come, sir?"

"From somewhere in the North,—Cumberland, I believe."

"It is he! it is the same man!" cried Mrs. Castlemain, turning pale as death; "he left Cumberland about that time; and I was told, after he left my neighbourhood, and went to London, that he had often wished to be revenged on my poor child."

"Revenge! for what, madam?" asked Mr. Egerton.

"Ask me not now!" she replied in agony the most overwhelming. "The miseries of my child are on my head, and I feel sinking under the load."

"However," observed Mr. Egerton, "we have gained much by finding that Cammel had a motive to join Mr. Danvers in his scheme against his unhappy wife. But where is this man? Let him be confronted with us."

"That, sir, is impossible," replied Mr. Jones in some confusion; "for he absconded about two years ago with all his family, and it is supposed he went abroad, having been detected in some very dishonest practices; therefore I really should have thought it very likely, if I had not been conscious the registry had never been from under my eye, that the poor lady's accusation was just."

"I am sorry he is gone off," said Mr. Egerton; "though this evidence of the man's villany gives still greater credibility to the fact we wish to establish. And now, sir, you shall hear what happened to this injured lady, on the evening of the day on which *you* saw her, from the mouth of that benevolent being who succoured her in her distress; the good Samaritan who poured oil and wine into her wounds, while the priest passed by on the other side." So saying, he led Mrs. Castlemain into the room where they had left Emma and Mr. Orwell, and returned to Mr. Jones accompanied by the latter.

As soon as Mr. Orwell had told his tale, which clearly proved the sanity of Agatha,—as whatever might be called insanity in her vanished as soon as the power of the operating causes was removed,—Mr. Egerton desired to introduce to Mr. Jones the orphan of Agatha, whose claims to legitimacy it was now the first desire and purpose of Mrs. Castlemain and himself to prove. But before he did so, he gave him a short detail of Agatha's life, and the circumstances attending her death, in order to interest that gentleman as much as he could in the fate of her injured child, and induce him to do all in his power to aid their efforts to discover Cammell and bring him to justice.

"But allow me, sir," said Mr. Jones, "to make one remark;—I recollect perfectly, that the unhappy lady said to Cammell, who was certainly a most ill-looking man, ' Where have I ever seen you before?' and she added words importing the consciousness of having seen his ' dark and gloomy face,' as she called it, without being able to recollect where; on which Cammell, saying half aside, ' Poor distracted creature!' declared he had never seen her before in his whole life."

"Well, sir,—and what then?"

"Why, sir, as Cammell must have been the clerk at the time of the lady's marriage, if she really was married; and as, according to your own statement, he must have even officiated as father to the lady, it is very strange that she should not have remembered *where* she had seen him; and I confess that this appears to me a strong proof that at this church, at least, the marriage between her and Mr. Danvers never took place."

"There is some plausibility in what you say, certainly, sir," replied Mr. Egerton; "but you should make allowance for the perturbation of mind Mrs. Danvers was under while questioning Cammell, and also for that which she felt during the ceremony of her marriage; for she has declared to me, that she had not the slightest recollection of the clerk who gave her away, nor indeed was she sure that she even looked at him.—She added, that she had forgotten to ask how long this man, whose name she did not know, had been clerk of that parish; but she had a consciousness of having seen him before, when she conversed with him in this house; and, to use her own expression, that the recollection of him was ' associated in her mind with the idea of pain endured long since.' And how *correctly* she judged and felt on this subject, we have now her mother's testimony to prove. However, sir, that a marriage *did* take place, we have Mr. Danvers's own evidence in a letter to Mrs. Castlemain, at which time *he* says he had a wife *living*. But this we could prove false, could we obtain a copy of the marriage register, as we have a letter to him proving his wife to have died some time previously."

"Well, sir, well," returned Mr. Jones, this may be true as you say;" and Mr. Egerton, leaving the room, returned, leading in Emma.

As Mr. Egerton had conducted her, he gave her to understand that Mr. Jones was not very friendly to their cause, and was unwilling to give up the idea of her mother's insanity. Emma, therefore was not disposed to regard that gentleman with much complacence; and she assumed on her entrance so much haughtiness of manner and expression, that her resemblance to Agatha was rendered thereby even more striking than usual. To her cold and dignified courtesy Mr. Jones returned a low bow; when venturing to look up in her face he exclaimed,

"I protest I never saw such a likeness! It seems as if her mother really stood before me! Only that this young lady's complexion is more brilliant, and her cheeks and person are fuller."

"No wonder, sir," replied Emma, tears involuntarily filling her eyes, "for I have been the child of happiness and kindness; my poor mother was that of misery, and was the victim of the depravity of others."

"The very voice too, as I live!" returned Mr. Jones.

"Well, sir," said Mr. Egerton, "this is the injured orphan, in order to assert whose rights you see us prepared to bring the whole matter into a court of justice; and your evidence, though not as favourable as we could wish, we shall undoubtedly call for."

"Such as it is, sir, and such as I can conscientiously make it, you may command it, sir."

"It now only remains that we should examine the register," said Mr. Egerton; and the book was produced. After a long and a most minute examination, even Mr. Jones himself declared, that it did seem as if a leaf might have been torn out much about the time when Agatha stated her marriage to have taken place; though, as he was *positive* the book was under his sole care, he did not see how it could have happened. And having to their own satisfaction established *this* fact, the party returned to London. On their way thither Mrs. Castlemain, with many compunctious feelings, explained the cause of Cammell's inveteracy towards Agatha, and by that means made his compliance with the infamous proposal of Danvers the less to be wondered at.

On their return home a circumstance happened mortifying to the pride, though not painful to the affections, of Emma. A young nobleman, the eldest son of a peer, had been so charmed with Emma's beauty and other attractions, that he had solicited his father to make proposals in his name to Mrs. Castlemain; and the earl, imagining Emma to be Mrs. Castlemain's daughter, did what his son required.

Mrs. Castlemain, in her reply, referred the gentleman to Emma for his answer, declaring that she would never influence her in her determination on such subjects, though in the present instance she earnestly desired that Emma might approve of the proposal as highly as she did; but that she thought it proper to inform his lordship that Miss Castlemain was not her daughter, but her grand-daughter; her daughter's child by a marriage of which hitherto, and at present, there was no possibility of procuring proofs.

The answer to this letter she received on the day of her return from visiting Mr. Jones; and it added not a little to their wish of quitting England, as the earl politely, but coldly, declined for his son all further thoughts *at present* of a union with Miss Castlemain.

During the ride home Mrs. Castlemain remarked, that she thought it was not right for Mr. Egerton, who wished to conciliate, to call Mr. Orwell the good Samaritan, and insinuate that poor Mr. Jones was the priest.

"I agree with you," replied Mr. Egerton laughing; "and I can only say, that I was too much at that moment under the dominion of TEMPER, that domestic enemy against which I am so fond of guarding others; but I am not at all sure that good Mr. Jones had sense enough to make the application."

The next step they took was to prepare an advertisement for a copy of the registry of the marriage of Agatha Torrington and George Danvers, in case such a copy had been made, offering a very considerable reward.

A few days before their departure they went to the Haymarket Theatre, when just as the play was finishing, Emma heard a gentleman in the next place say, "What fine fellow now has Mrs. Felton caught in her chains? Who is that good-looking youth to whom she is talking?"

"It is a Mr. St. Aubyn," was the answer, "a North-country man, who has just entered into the dragoon guards." And Emma, following the direction of the speaker's eyes, as surprised and agitated she involuntarily turned round to look at him, beheld St. Aubyn, apparently gay and animated, listening with smiling attention to a tonish-looking woman, whose beauty she unconsciously exaggerated to herself. In a moment the stage, the audience, every thing disappeared from her view, but St. Aubyn and Mrs. Felton. Still, however, in the midst of her emotion she felt that seeing St. Aubyn as she *now* saw him, seemingly absorbed by another woman, would be of great service to her heart on reflection; it was the idea that he loved her, spite of his neglect, which made his image so dangerous to her; could she but once be convinced he loved her no longer, and loved another, she was *sure* that time and absence would in the end entirely annihilate his power over her. But *absence* was, she thought, the *surest* remedy; and not seeing him at all, a better cure than even seeing him paying attention to Mrs. Felton. She therefore gladly acceded to Mrs. Castlemain's proposal to return home as soon as the play was finished, as she felt oppressed by the heat of the house.

"But surely," said Mr. Egerton to Emma, "you will stay to see the entertainment! You came on *purpose*, and Mrs. Castlemain has no objection to returning alone."

"Not in the least," she replied; "do, my dear Emma, stay;—Mr. Egerton will take care of you, and I will send the carriage back."

"Indeed I had rather, *much* rather, go home," said Emma deeply blushing.

"Are you unwell? Are you oppressed by the heat of the house?" And Emma, too great a votary to truth to violate it on any occasion, professed herself neither ill nor *warm*, but declared that she had rather go home with Mrs. Castlemain.

"'Tis very strange!" said Mr. Egerton;—when at this moment the same gentleman who had spoken before observed,

"See! see! Look at St. Aubyn! How attentive he seems! Egad, I believe the fair widow has him." On hearing this, Mr. Egerton himself turned round, and seeing St. Aubyn, no longer thought Emma's wish to leave the house an unaccountable one. But he took no notice to her of what he saw and thought; only he could not help gently pressing the cold hand which trembled in his.

"I will see for the carriage directly," said he, "and do you remain in the box."

While he was gone, lounging on the back seat of the box next her, Emma saw Varley; and actuated not only by the wish to be civil to him, but also by the desire of turning her attention from St. Aubyn and Mrs. Felton, she courtesied very kindly to him, and, leaning forward to speak to him, lamented that she came into the room too late at Mrs. C.'s to be gratified like others with his admirable recitations. At this tribute to his vanity from a quarter so unexpected, and from one too whom mortified vanity had led him to injure to the best of his mean ability, Varley's conscience gave him some well-merited pangs; and scarcely could he with all his impudence reply to the benevolent and lovely girl who addressed him, little suspecting that he was the adder who had stung her and Mrs. Castlemain through the medium of a newspaper.

In a few moments Mr. Egerton returned, accompanied by Sir Charles Maynard, who assisted in seeing the ladies to their carriage, Varley crossing them on their way, in order to be noticed, in sight of some of his fellow clerks, by the beauty of the day.

"You are a lucky fellow, Varley," said one of his companions to him, just as Sir Charles returned into the lobby, "to have such a bow and smile from that angelic being."

"Do you think so?" cried Varley conceitedly, and pulling up his neckcloth, "she really is a fine creature, and I mean to patronize her."

"Presuming coxcomb!" said Sir Charles, loud enough for Varley to hear, and giving him a look of fierce disdain; while Varley, pretending not to notice it, slunk away into the crowd and disappeared.

A day or two after, however, Sir C———

M——d was stated in a certain newspaper to have been one of the unsuccessful suitors to a certain Northern heiress. Had Varley been contented to let his revenge stop here, it would have been better for him; but when the intended departure of Sir Charles and other men of fashion for France, was a few days after announced in some paper, he inserted another paragraph, which was as follows:—

"We hear that Sir C——— M——d, being disappointed in his matrimonial speculations, is glad to escape into a foreign land, from certain troublesome remembrancers, and is on the eve of his departure from England."

The consequence of this was, that Sir Charles was arrested at Dover by an alarmed creditor, whose bill he was fortunately able to discharge immediately,—vowing as he did so, that as soon as he returned, which would be in a few months, he would leave no method untried to discover the author of so foul a libel.

The proprietor of the paper in which Varley wrote, was himself abroad, when this paragraph concerning Sir Charles was inserted, else it would have been rejected as libellous and unsafe; but the person who officiated for him, knowing Varley was a favourite writer of his employer, concluded what he sent must be admitted and approved, and therefore he either did not know or did not regard the risk. But when the proprietor himself returned, he was so justly incensed at the paragraph in question, and apprehensive of its consequences, that he paid Varley whatever he was in arrears to him, and dismissed him from all future employment, having first drawn from him a confession of his motives for this calumnious insertion; severely reproaching him for having meanly dared to make the power of anonymous attack with which he was vested, the engine of venting his own petty spite, and the means of gratifying the malignity of his offended vanity.

The sum of money thus earned, Varley, afraid he should never again have so large a sum in his possession at once, resolved to spend in a trip to Paris; and there I shall again introduce him to the notice of my readers.

It was well for Emma that they could leave England so soon, as she had ceased to drive along the streets with any security and pleasure. She fancied every gentleman she met was St. Aubyn, and cast a timid inquiring glance round every company she entered, dreading to behold him accompanying her fascinating rival. But at length they set off for France; and when Emma landed at Calais, "thank Heaven!" she mentally ejaculated, "now the sea rolls between me and them!"

I am well convinced that no two persons can receive exactly the same impressions from any one object or scene, but that, however like the impressions might be in the aggregate, they would be different in detail; therefore there would be something of variety, and consequently of interest, in the account given by each passenger in the same boat of his voyage even from Dover to Calais. Still I shall not fatigue my readers with a relation of what my heroine and her companions saw, thought, or felt, during their passage to France, or on their landing on the Calais Pier. But no sooner were they arrived at their hotel, namely that kept by Grandsire, the one formerly the residence of the Duchess of Kingston, than Mrs. Castlemain became alarmingly ill, and Emma and Mr. Egerton endured an increased degree of anxiety on her account, from their very natural want of confidence in a foreign medical attendant; but luckily for them, Mr. Egerton learnt on the second day of her illness, that an English physician in the suite of an English nobleman had just landed.

Immediately, though a stranger to both gentlemen, he waited on them at their inn, to request the physician's attendance on the invalid, —a request instantly granted; and he had the satisfaction of hearing that three or four days of rest, with the aid of medicine, would remove every unfavourable symptom, and enable them, without any fear of a relapse, to proceed on their journey. Accordingly, after having passed a week at Calais, they set off in their own open barouche, drawn by four horses, with the footman and the lady's maid on the dicky.

The ladies, who had never been out of England, were surprised, as well they might, at seeing the horses fastened together and to the carriage by ropes; and as one never values health sufficiently till one is attacked by sickness, so our travellers, for the first time in their lives, felt the value and the elegance of an English equipage.

"Yet, as far as it can affect national happiness, of what consequence is it," said Mr. Egerton, "whether the harness and the other accoutrements be of leather or rope — if the French be as well contented with the one as the other?"

"No," replied Emma; "nor does it signify that the boasted view from the Calais ramparts commands in reality nothing but a miserable barren flat, and the uninteresting meanderings of the treeless road into Flanders, if all the inhabitants, as no doubt they do, like that good old gentleman in the steeple-crowned hat, can point it out to strangers with, 'Mais voyez donc! quelle vue superbe! Mais, mon Dieu! c'est magnifique!'"

Nothing either of event or of interest worth narrating, happened on the road till they approached Chantilly; when the increasing beauty of the country, the distant view of the palace and its celebrated stables, awakened their as yet dormant feelings into life.

"Alas!" said Mr. Egerton, "*I* saw that fine building in its splendour! However, I will see it in its *décadence*, were it only to impress on my mind the frail tenure of earthly greatness."

But as Chantilly has been frequently described by travellers, and is likely to call forth the same feelings in every one, I shall pass by in silence our travellers' visit to the palace and the environs, and content myself with giving the following lines, written no doubt in the days of its magnificence, which Mr. Egerton desired Emma to copy and preserve, as one of the instances in which the double meaning of a word is the same in both languages.

The following lines are written either on a wall or window of an inn at Chantilly:

"Beaux lieux, où de plaisirs Condé fixa la source,
A ne vous point quitter l'on feroit son bonheur,
Si vous n'étiez à notre bourse
Plus chers encore qu'à notre cœur."*

When they were about twenty miles from Paris, they were passed by a curricle and four driven by a gentleman, another gentleman sitting beside him. The one who drove looked earnestly at Emma as he passed, and turned back several times to repeat his gaze (evidently one of admiration) till they were out of sight; and when they had proceeded about two miles further, they saw the same equipage standing in the road, having evidently been just overturned, while the gentlemen belonging to it and the servants were employed in arranging whatever had been discomposed by the accident. The truth was, that the gentleman who drove had been so absorbed in admiration of Emma, that he had been unconscious of the horses' increasing speed till it was too late to stop them, and in trying to turn them short on one side, the vehicle had upset. The gentlemen, however, were both unhurt; and the poor youth, who had thus been put in peril of life by the power of beauty, was resolved to repay himself by another look at the beauty that had endangered him, and he still found something to do to the carriage, long after his companion had assured him that every thing was properly adjusted.

"I hope, gentlemen," said Mr. Egerton, in very good French, "that you have sustained no injury?" To which the gentleman who drove, with a bow and a blush, and a look at Emma, answered "No," in the same language.

"At least, not such an injury as the gentleman apprehends," observed his companion in English, (concluding Mr. Egerton was a Frenchman,) and laughing archly as he spoke. While Mr. Egerton, who found by this speech, which he perfectly understood, that the gentlemen were English, smiled involuntarily; but not choosing to expose Emma any longer to an intensity of admiring observation, which, though respectful, evidently distressed her, and displeased Mrs. Castlemain, he, with a bow, and an expression of pleasure at their safety, desired the postilions to proceed. But the curricle again overtook, and passed them, and its driver had another opportunity of looking at Emma, while he made a distant bow of recognition to the party.

At length, our travellers were approaching Paris; and if Chantilly had awakened strong emotion in their hearts, what must they have felt on entering that great city, that Paris, whose decrees had for years influenced three quarters of the globe, and whose inhabitants had, by turns, excited the pity, the horror, the detestation, and some few the admiration, of the world!

"I saw the church of St. Denys in its pride," said Mr. Egerton, as they entered that fauxbourg, "when the royal and the mighty dead slept undisturbed within its walls, and rapacious avarice had not thence removed the costly offerings of piety and superstition!"

"But is there nothing worth seeing there still?" asked Emma.

"No; I am told not," replied he. "However, some pious hands have conveyed to a place of safety many of the statues, the mausoleums, and perhaps the bones of those who here were 'quietly inurned,' and I expect to feel great interest and pleasure in beholding the former once more in, I trust, their last home; together with many other things of the same description, gathered from distant provinces, and all arranged under one point of view at Paris."

"Ay, but how much," observed Mrs. Castlemain, "must they not lose of their interest by being no longer seen in the spot where they were first placed?"

"True, madam, much of local and associated interest; still they have an interest appertaining to themselves, of which no change of situation can deprive them. Architectural beauty and propriety, and powers of sculpture, must exist, to charm and to instruct, whether in the church of St. Denys, or in the Petits Augustins at Paris; and I shall certainly not scorn the pleasure of looking at them where they now are, because I have once seen them to better advantage. On that principle, we might despise the gratification of seeing the Apollo of Belvidere, because Paris is not Florence, where he was originally situated, and, as I hear, in a better point of view. But to go from inanimate to animated beauty,—What did you think, ladies, of the young Jehu who passed us just now?"

"I think," said Mrs. Castlemain, "that he is almost the handsomest man I ever saw; I wonder who he is. — But what say you, Emma?"

"That he is certainly very handsome."

---

* "Fair scenes, where Condé fixed the source of pleasure,
One's happiness would consist in never leaving you,
If you were not to our purse
Still *dearer* than you are to our heart."

"Well, I dare say," replied Mr. Egerton, "we shall see him again; and in the meanwhile I shall fancy him somebody of great consequence."

They were now entering Paris, and Mr. Egerton was amused by the surprise which Emma expressed at seeing melons piled up against the walls, and lying one on the other in baskets in large heaps, like turnips in Covent-garden market.

"Well," exclaimed Emma; "What a superiority over England this circumstance proves them to possess! Melons, a luxury only served up in our country at the tables of the rich, are here, you see, a mere common fruit, like apples with us."

"Yes," replied Mr. Egerton, laughing; "and perhaps you may find out occasionally, that carpets and clean floors, which are every-day necessaries with us, are luxuries here."

They took up their abode at the Hotel des Etrangers, Rue de la Concorde, the best and widest street in Paris, and particularly interesting from its being so near, not only the finest objects in the city, but the scenes most pregnant with impressive associations. At one end of it, was the place where the perpetual guillotine stood; at the other, was the church of La Madelaine, where so many victims of revolutionary fury were buried; and the stones of that street, now so peaceable and so smiling, had lately reverberated from the heavy steps of a ferocious multitude, and, almost without a metaphor, had been dyed with rivers of blood.

The next day, for Mrs. Castlemain was too tired to venture out the evening of their arrival, was impatiently hailed by Emma; and as soon as she saw Mr. Egerton, "To the Louvre!" cried Emma; "I cannot rest till I have seen the Gallery." And Mr. Egerton, breaking from the mournful reverie into which he had fallen, led the way thither. It lay across the Place de la Concorde, and through the garden and palace of the Thuilleries. But while Emma and Mrs. Castlemain, struck with the uncommon beauty and grandeur of the surrounding objects, stopped on the above-mentioned place to gaze with delight around them, Mr. Egerton, with an exclamation of horror, darted down the passage which led into the gardens, and awaited them at the entrance.

"My dear sir, what impelled you to leave us in that abrupt manner?" cried Emma: "Why were you in such a hurry to quit the sweetest spot of the kind that my eyes ever beheld?"

"Because a friend, a venerable abbé whom I dearly loved, was butchered on that spot; because, Emma, the guillotine was erected in the midst of that smiling plain!"

"Is it possible?" exclaimed his auditors.

"I fear," added Emma, "that I shall never think it beautiful again." Yet the next moment she wished to go back again to see the very spot where the guillotine stood; but the Palace of the Thuilleries now caught her eye, and by calling forth other feelings urged her forward on her way.

Emma could not help stopping in the hall of the Palace, as certain recollections came across her mind; and going up to a soldier on guard there, she said in French, "And was it on those stairs that the poor Swiss were massacred?" The soldier, colouring deeply, replied, "Mais oui, mademoiselle:" while Mr. Egerton seizing Emma's arm, all the terrors of the revolutionary government recurring to his mind, hurried into the Place du Carrousel, saying, "For the future be more guarded. Why could you not have said killed, instead of massacred?"

"Because my pity got the better of every other consideration."

"But had your pity been so powerful in those days, when there was neither pity nor justice, that small mistake of yours might have sent us all three to the guillotine."

But all unpleasant remembrances of the past, or fears for the future, were absorbed in delight when they entered the saloon of the Louvre, and beheld in one room the scattered glories of the first painters whom the world ever saw. Yet great as was the pleasure which this first room afforded them, where the pictures were not only fine, but seen in a fine light, amongst which the St. Peter Martyr of Titian shone conspicuous, their sensations on entering the long gallery adjoining were of a still higher nature. There was a vastness, a magnificence in the idea of the whole space before them being crowded with chef d'œuvres of art, that filled and elevated the mind in a manner too vast for utterance; and choked with the emotions that overwhelmed them, they paused at the entrance as if too much overawed to proceed. But recovering themselves they slowly walked up the room, unable at first to fix on any one picture as an object of admiration; and they went to the top of the Gallery and back again without stopping before any one in particular. At length, however, Mr. Egerton was fixed by the St. Jerome of Dominico, Mrs. Castlemain was gazing on the Three Crosses by Rubens, and Emma was contemplating with admiring interest the Deluge by Poussin, when it was loudly rumoured that the First Consul was going in state to the Conservative Senate, and would very soon be on the Place du Carrousel.

"That I could but see him and the procession!" exclaimed Emma, eager to forsake a picture for a reality; and running up to Mr. Egerton, "Could we not see him from these windows?" she added, running to the window near her; when one of the guardians of the Gallery, hearing her name Buonaparte, and suspecting her wishes from the expression of her countenance, told her if she would follow him he would lead her to a window whence she could see the sight to the greatest advantage; and immediately Emma, followed by Mrs. Castlemain and Mr. Egerton, eagerly kept up with the rapid pace of her guide. He led them to the very extremity of the Gallery, which joined the Palace of the Thuilleries, and introduced them into an unfurnished apartment, full of lumber and of unframed pictures, where they found sitting in the window two French ladies and a gentleman engaged in earnest conversation. The women immediately, with French politeness, made room for the stranger ladies, and the gentleman also rose to offer his seat to Mr. Egerton; and when he turned round, our travellers, though with less delight pictured in their countenances than beamed on his at the meeting, recognised in him the driver of the curricle who had been so endangered by looking at Emma.

"Countryman and countrywomen of mine, I presume!" said the young man; "and indeed I earnestly hope so for the honour of England," he added, looking at Emma, while Mr. Egerton, smiling, replied in the affirmative, and hoped he had experienced no ill effects from his accident.

They were now, all, except the young stranger who insisted on Mr. Egerton's taking his seat, most commodiously placed for beholding the whole sight from the windows; but one of the ladies assuring them that it would be some time before the First Consul entered his carriage, she earnestly requested the gentleman, whom she called "mon cher Balfour," to go on with the subject of their dispute. "But, perhaps," said she to our travellers, "as it is connected with a story of a countryman of yours, it may be interesting to you to hear it; so suppose you tell the whole story over again, Balfour!" And Balfour declaring he was never tired of telling a story so much to the honour of any one as he thought it to be, smiling archly at the lady who spoke, said, with the English ladies' permission, he would relate what had occasioned a disagreement between him and the French ladies present.

"There are several English and Irish officers here; amongst the latter of whom is a man of brutal manners, who used very improper language to a young lieutenant, a great favourite with the ladies present."

"O mon Dieu, oui!" exclaimed one of them; "Il est fait à peindre;* c'est grand dommage qu'il soit poltron!"

"But is he so?"

"That is the point in dispute between us," returned his animated historian. "From you, ladies, and you, sir, he added, bowing to Mr.

Egerton, "I hope a milder verdict. But to proceed;—the young lieutenant replied with temper, yet with proper severity, and the consequence was a challenge from the other, which to the astonishment of his brother officers, he refused to accept; and he even declared, on their telling him that they expected him to fight, that duelling was against his principles, and fight he would not."

"How I honour him!" cried Mrs. Castlemain.

"But the consequence, sir?" eagerly demanded Emma.

"The officers, who had a sincere regard for him, earnestly entreated him to behave as officers on such occasions were expected to behave, telling him that they did not think his reasons sufficient as a military man for declining to fight.

"'But,' replied he, 'before I became a soldier, I was a man, a son, and a responsible being; and, as all these, I deem myself forbidden to fight a duel. As a man, and a member of society, I think it right to bear my testimony against a custom worthy only of savage nations; as a son, I think it my duty not to risk a life which is of the greatest consequence to a fond and widowed parent; and as a responsible being, I dare not, in express defiance of the will of my Creator, attack in cold blood the life of a fellow-creature.'"

"Well said!" cried Mr. Egerton.

"Ah!" cried one of the ladies, sarcastically looking at Mr. Egerton's coat, "apparemment Monsieur est prêtre!"†

But, without answering her, he begged to know of the stranger whether he was present at this conference.

"I was," he replied; "and perhaps, being hasty and rash in my judgments, I should not have judged more candidly than the officers, had the lieutenant been an every-day-looking man; but his look, his voice, his air, his manner are so full of truth and manliness, as at once to carry conviction to the heart that cowardice is unknown to him; and I could swear that, in his refusal to fight, principle, and principle alone, was his motive of action."

"Ah! le pauvre petit crédule!"‡ exclaimed one of the ladies affectedly.

"I believe we are as credulous as you, sir," said Emma with a smile that well repaid him for his candour, "but again I ask what was the result to this interesting being."

"Sorry am I to say," he replied, "that the officers of the lieutenant's own regiment, amongst whom was his colonel, who is, I believe, jealous of him, told him he must either fight, or they must abjure his society, and insist on his leaving their regiment when they returned to England. He still however persisted in his refusal, and met the threatened

---

* "He is so handsome, it is a great pity he should be a coward!"

† "Probably the gentleman is a clergyman."

‡ "Ah! poor credulous being!"

consequences with the manly firmness which might be expected from him."

" Poor young man!" said Emma.

" Poor! Rich rather," cried Mrs. Castlemain, " rich in the best of all fortitude, that of being able to act up to his principles, unawed by the fear of shame!"

" True, madam," said Mr. Egerton; " and believe me, I honour you, sir," addressing Balfour, " for daring to defend this young hero (hero in my sense of the word) against these fair accusers."

" But where is this gentleman, sir?" said Emma.

" I am told that he is gone into Poitou, madam."

" What led him thither?"

" Kindness and pity. An emigrant friend of his in London is so anxious concerning his father, — who is or was living in that part of France, and whom he has not heard of for some time, — that he got his address, and is gone in search of him."

" I am afraid," said Mrs. Castlemain to the ladies, " that you think our opinion on this subject very outré."

" O! pour cela non," one of them replied; "but I wish cet exquis St. Aubyn had not entertained the same."

" St. Aubyn!" exclaimed Mrs. Castlemain. " What St. Aubyn?" pronouncing the name in English, and addressing herself to Balfour.

" A Mr. Henry St. Aubyn," he replied, " who has but lately entered the army, to oblige his uncle, a Mr. Har—Har—"

" Hargrave, perhaps."

" The same."

" 'T is he! 't is he himself then!" exclaimed Mr. Egerton, " our own St. Aubyn!"— while Emma leaned forward and looked out of the window to hide her emotion — " Just what I should have expected from him! consistent! manly! pious!"

" Do you then know him, sir?" asked Balfour, glancing a look of suspicion towards Emma; when at this moment, luckily for her, " Le voilà! le voilà!" exclaimed both ladies at once; but before he could be distinguished, the First Consul was in his carriage, and the procession began.

But neither the different corps of Mamelucs, their sabres glittering in the sun, nor the eight bays harnessed to the Consul's carriage, nor the splendid consular guard bringing up the rear, could draw Emma's attention from the narration which she had just heard! St. Aubyn in France! St. Aubyn disgraced, though more deserving of honour than before! St. Aubyn gone on a mission of benevolence into a remote part of the country! St. Aubyn lost to her, probably for ever; though why, alas! she knew not;—but at least he was not with Mrs. Felton, and on that idea she could dwell, and dwell with pleasure. Mr. Egerton, meanwhile, was informing Balfour of his long intimacy with St. Aubyn, and lamenting that some circumstances which he did not think necessary to mention had interrupted their intercourse for the last two years; and Balfour immediately suspected that this circumstance was either unrequited love for Emma on the part of St. Aubyn, or parental disapprobation perhaps of a mutual attachment between the parties; and he felt his latter suspicions confirmed by his having observed the anxious look of inquiring affection which Mrs. Castlemain turned on Emma when St. Aubyn's name was mentioned, and her evident emotion.

Soon after, the sight being over, Emma rose, wishing to return to the Gallery; and as she did so, she gave the defender of St. Aubyn so kind and fascinating a smile, that he earnestly hoped St. Aubyn had never been her favoured lover; and he was eagerly anticipating a hope that Mr. Egerton, whose name and that of the ladies he had yet to learn, would express a wish of being better known to him, when he was summoned out of the Gallery to speak to a messenger from his father; and before he returned, Emma having complained of indisposition, and Mrs. Castlemain of fatigue, Mr. Egerton had called a fiacre, and they had returned to their hotel. Mr. Egerton however, more fortunate than he had been, had learnt his name and rank from a gentleman in the Gallery, and found that he was the Honourable George Frederic Balfour, only son of lord Clonawley, an Irish viscount then at Bareges for the recovery of his health;—he also learnt that the son had some thousands a year, independent of his father, left him by his grandfather. The whole of this information gave great satisfaction to Mrs. Castlemain, who saw Balfour's evident admiration of Emma, and wished for nothing more than to see her addressed by a man worthy to obtain her, in order to give her a chance of forgetting the ever admirable and still too dear St. Aubyn; while she rejoiced to find that her illness, by delaying their arrival at Paris, had prevented their meeting St. Aubyn there.

Perhaps Mr. Egerton ought to have wished as she did relative to this new acquaintance,— but he could not; the idea of seeing Emma the wife of any other man than his beloved pupil was agony to him; and though he was much prejudiced in favour of Balfour because he did justice to St. Aubyn, the prospect of his becoming the avowed admirer of Emma almost called forth, even in his subdued feelings, a sensation of aversion towards him, and he was inclined to retard an acquaintance which he clearly saw that he could not prevent. Accordingly, when, on finding that a lady to whom they had brought letters was gone to the valley of Montmorenci, a favourite spot some miles from Paris, Emma proposed that they should go thither in pursuit of her, he eagerly acceded to the proposal, and to Montmorenci they went, leaving Paris as yet unseen, in compliance with the wishes of the restless, because secretly unhappy, Emma.

In the castle of Montmorenci then resided two or three families, who had separate apartments, but met at dinner at a common table.

As soon as they arrived, they made themselves known to the lady for whom they had letters; but finding her an insipid, uninteresting woman, they would not have remained in the valley for the sake of her society, had not the ease and cheerfulness of the way of living there, and its vicinity to interesting objects, induced them to stay and take apartments for a fortnight; especially as Mrs. Castlemain fancied herself much better for the air.

The second day after their arrival, Emma was seated at dinner between two Miss Balfours, West Indians, who, with a little sister and a governess, were awaiting their father from Bareges and their brother from Paris. Emma immediately concluded that this brother was the young man whom she had seen at the Louvre; and she took occasion to say to Miss Balfour,

"I believe I saw your brother, Mr. Balfour, two days ago at the Louvre Gallery."

"Oh, very likely. Frederic is an extremely handsome young man, very tall, and rather thin."

"Yes; that describes him."

"Oh! dear Mary Ann," cried Miss Harriet Balfour, "I dare say Miss Castlemain is the young lady whom my brother mentions in his letter, in such raptures, and whom he is seeking all over Paris!"

"Very likely," said Miss Balfour turning to look at Emma with a critical stare, which ended in a look of disappointment; after which she said, "you have great reason I am sure to be proud, Miss Castlemain; for Frederic, who is, I assure you, very difficult to please, and is a great judge of beauty, thinks you the most beautiful creature he ever saw."

"Then I am tempted to believe," replied Emma blushing indignantly at this gross speech, "that it was not your brother whom I met; as I could not be very proud of the commendation of the gentleman I mean, since his extreme youth makes it impossible for his experience to give much value to his praise."

"Young! Why, Frederic is near four-and-twenty; and I assure you he knows every thing. Why, he is such a critic in dress, as well as in beauty, poetry, painting, and music, that neither Harriet nor I dare wear even a riband that he disapproves."

"But deciding on every thing, and knowing every thing, are very distinct things; and I suspect that if I were Mr. Balfour's sister I should choose ribands for myself."

"No, you would not," said Harriet; "for you would love Frederic so much that you would have a pleasure in doing every thing he bids you."

"That," cried Emma, taking her hand with kindness, "is the best proof of your brother's worth that has been given yet, and shows that he has merit beyond all the connoisseurship in the world."

"Poor Frederic!" exclaimed Miss Balfour, "there is he roaming about Paris to find a bird that is safe in his own nest at Montmorenci! I declare I must write and tell him you are here." But this Emma positively forbade; and that evening, weary of his fruitless search, Balfour arrived.

Unconscious that the beautiful girl he so much wished to see was observing him from the windows, Balfour, as soon as he saw his sisters, began to show off to them in his usual consequential way; and giving one his gloves to carry, another his hat and whip, and leaning on a third, he lounged into a room next to that where Emma was sitting with the door open, and threw himself on the sofa.

"I am dying with heat and thirst!" cried he. "Do, Harriet, come and fan me; and you, Mary Ann, fetch me the shaddock which I desired might be saved for me."

"I'll get it directly," she replied. "Fanny was feverish last night and wanted to have it, but I would not let her lest you should want it."

Emma, who overheard all that passed, expected Balfour would regret that the poor feverish child had not been gratified. But she was mistaken; he declared that he would not for the world have lost the luxury of eating it then. The shaddock was brought; and one sister having pulled off the young despot's boots, another his coat, and exchanged it for a loose chintz gown, and the third having rubbed his head dry, then sprinkled it with eau de Cologne, he cut the shaddock and was preparing to devour it, when one of his sisters, looking up in his face archly, said,

"Pray, brother, have you found the beauty you were in search of?"

"Pshaw! do not mention that subject, for I can't bear it.—No, I have not found her, though I have searched all Paris; and I suspect she was suddenly translated from the Louvre to her kindred skies, angel as she is, as soon as I was called away that morning!"

On hearing this, Emma, who had promised the sisters to come in and surprise Balfour, was rendered incapable, by delicacy, of fulfilling her promise, and she endeavoured to escape into another apartment; but they, being on the watch, ran after, and prevented her. Then, almost dragging her up to their brother, they presented her to him, as Miss Castlemain; while Balfour, blushing with delight, not unmixed with confusion, lost in a moment the important airs which he had assumed with his family, and like a timid youth stammered out something about surprise, pleasure, and soforth, setting down his untasted shaddock while he spoke.

"Do not let me disturb you," cried Emma; "pray eat your fruit."

"Impossible!" replied he, "unless you partake with me."

"I don't know that I should like it, as I never tasted shaddock."

"No!" cried the little feverish girl, "it is so good!"

Emma smiled, and ate a piece; while Balfour, seeing that she liked it, insisted on her eating the whole.

"In Jamaica," said the little Fanny, "every body has a whole shaddock, me and all."

"But as that is not the case here," replied Emma, touched by the poor child's diseased wish for the forbidden fruit, and willing to give the spoiled child (as she considered Balfour) a lesson, "I shall insist on sharing this fruit equally amongst us all; for participation makes pleasure sweeter."

"But my sisters," cried Balfour, "know what shaddock is."

"And they do not like it, I presume, as you were going to eat all this yourself!"

"Indeed we do," cried the girls, "but—"

"Then eat this to oblige me," said Emma. "But you, dear Fanny, whose lips look so parched and feverish, shall have the largest piece;" which Fanny ate with great eagerness, wishing that she was again in Jamaica, that she might have a whole shaddock to her own share.

All this time Balfour, who saw he was lessened in Emma's eyes by the circumstance of the fruit, was silent from mortification; and Emma became silent also. She was shocked at the little girl's greedy and selfish wish for solitary pleasure, and could not help attributing it to the bad example of her brother, whose habits, as she saw, being those of selfish gratification in trifles, had taught her to value unparticipated enjoyments. "No doubt," thought Emma, "Balfour has had a bad education!" and fancying, though mistakingly, that he had been chiefly brought up in the West Indies, she began to consider him as an unfortunate young man, spoiled by having been placed in unfavourable circumstances, especially as he had been for some years in possession of an independent fortune. While these things were passing in her mind, she was roused from her reverie, by little Fanny's whispering in her ear,—

"Brother must love you very much to offer you all his shaddock!"

"Nonsense!" cried Emma, blushing very deeply; and the sisters declaring Miss Castlemain looked warm, proposed taking a walk, —to which Balfour, forgetting his fatigue, gladly assented. Immediately the obsequious sisters ran to fetch his coat and shoes, and get his white hat.

"I think," said Emma, "you should have brought some of your slaves over, to wait on you."

"I have none; but my father would have brought over some of his," replied Balfour gravely, "had there been any chance of their being properly obedient in England;—but there, you know, as soon as they land, they are free."

"And would they were so all the world over!" cried Emma warmly, "or rather, would that the detestable traffic in slaves was everywhere put an end to!"

"We will talk together coolly on that subject one day," replied Balfour gently, contrary to his usual custom when any one expressed opinions differing from his own, "and I have no doubt but I shall make a convert of you."

"Never," exclaimed Emma indignantly, "but I hope to be more successful in my endeavours to convert you." And immediately, with all the sanguine expectations of a young and virtuous mind, Emma, presuming on the influence which she saw she was going to acquire over Balfour, beheld visions of freed negroes, and schemes of benevolent utility float before her fancy; which determined her, romantically eager as she was to do good, to encourage rather than repress his growing attachment.

Mr. Egerton, meanwhile, little thinking that the intimacy which he was willing Emma should go to Montmorenci to retard, had been hastened by that very plan, was at Paris on business; and Mrs. Castlemain, seeing at the end of a fortnight that Emma was pleased with her new companions, and that Balfour improved every day upon acquaintance, joyfully consented to the entreaties of the Balfours that they would stay another fortnight. And when Mr. Egerton returned, he saw with pain, that another fortnight spent together under the same roof would, in all probability, mature Balfour's passion into a serious attachment; and though it could not eradicate Emma's love for St. Aubyn, it would at least weaken his power, and very likely induce so strong a feeling of gratitude and esteem in her heart towards Balfour, as to make her willing to listen to his addresses with a view to accept them in future.

And he was right in his conjectures. Before the end of the month Balfour made proposals of marriage to Mrs. Castlemain for Emma, which she decidedly approved, provided his father approved them also; and Emma, though she positively refused to give a decided consent, on the plea of the shortness of their acquaintance, yet allowed Balfour to continue his addresses, and do all in his power to overcome her dislike to marry. But, in spite of the shortness of their acquaintance, his character was already known to her; and when she contrasted the disrespect with which he spoke of his weakly indulgent parent, with the filial piety of St. Aubyn,—and his violent despotic temper, with the mild forbearance of the latter,—her heart died within her, and she felt it would be equally impossible to forget St. Aubyn and marry Balfour. Still, however, new hopes and new views on the subject presented themselves occasionally to her mind; hopes and views too much, perhaps, the result of vanity and self-confidence. But Emma was only nineteen, and was, from motives dear to the heart of every delicately-feeling woman, anxious to get rid, if possible, of an attachment which she felt derogatory to her *delicacy* and her *pride.*

"Balfour," thought Emma, "has great faults; but then he is conscious of them, and he owns them to me with tears in his eyes, declaring, at the same time, that if I would but become his monitress, the result of the errors of his education will be removed!" And she also remembered that he looked so handsome and so humble when he said this, that Emma could not help wishing to lend her aid towards making so charming a being perfect; especially one whose self-importance, great as it was, was surrendered at the feet of her beauty. And then she reasoned thus: "St. Aubyn's character is perfect already, according to Mr. Egerton; to him, therefore, I could be of no use, and to him the defects of my character, were it possible we could ever be united, would be painfully apparent; whereas, by becoming the wife of Balfour, I should improve and exalt, perhaps, the character of a being capable of great actions, and be, besides, not only beloved by him, but looked up to by him as one of the first of women."

Emma forgot, at that moment, how often she had brought it as an argument for loving St. Aubyn, that his wife would have in him a friend to whom she could look up for instruction and improvement, while she learnt to correct the errors of her own judgment by the calm experience of his. But, unknown to herself, it was wounded pride and pique against St. Aubyn, two of the varieties of Temper, that urged her to marry a man she did not love; and Mr. Egerton, almost convinced that he must give up the darling wish of his heart, resolved, for Emma's sake, to study the character of Balfour, and endeavour to ameliorate it to the best of his powers. He found the young man more docile than he expected, and even willing to give up opinions, after having long and manfully defended them, on conviction of their fallacy. "This young man," said he to Emma, "has a heart, but it has never been taught to feel; he has a head, but it has never been taught to reason. However, I believe I shall like him in spite of his faults, and that his greatest defect in my eyes is not being——"

"What?" asked Emma, eagerly.

"Not being St. Aubyn;" and Emma understanding him, blushed, sighed, and turned away.

The month being now expired, they returned to Paris; while Balfour, having heard Emma express great admiration of filial piety, had the resolution to accompany his two elder sisters on the road towards Bareges, whence Lord Clonawley was proceeding by slow journeys to Paris. Accordingly Emma and Mrs. Castlemain, attended only by Mr. Egerton, prepared to explore all the scenes and beauties of that city. The day after they returned thither, the First Consul was to review the troops, and to have a grand levee afterwards. Accordingly our travellers procured tickets of admission to enable them, when the review was over, to get into one of the passage-rooms, in order to see the company pass to be presented.

The review being ended, they went from the ground-floor of the palace, whence they had beheld it, into an upper apartment, and were commodiously seated there, when an English gentleman entered into conversation with them, and said, that he was not come thither to see the review, or the company pass, they being sights familiar to him—but that he was curious to see an English officer go by, to whom the First Consul was going to present an elegant sword as a reward for his personal bravery.

"And shall we see him pass?" said Emma.

"Certainly, or I should not be here," he replied. "But in the mean while, suppose I tell you, ladies, the story of this young man's noble daring." On which Mrs. Castlemain begged him to begin the narration immediately, and he proceeded thus:

"It seems that during the troubles in La Vendée, many robbers by profession, calling themselves royalists, took possession of places of concealment in the woods and caverns there, and used to murder, or otherwise ill-treat the passengers; and as yet the government has not been able to hunt them all from their hiding-places. The young officer in question was travelling by himself one evening in this unhappy part of France, when he heard the cries of women; and spurring his horse up to the spot from whence the cries proceeded, he saw two women and their two servants in the power of some of the Vendéan banditti, one of whom was holding a pistol to the head of one of the ladies, while another ruffian was carrying the other off in his arms. Our young hero did not stop a moment to deliberate; with the butt-end of his whip he knocked down the ruffian who was standing over the lady, and, seizing his pistols, attacked the wretches who were plundering the carriage and the servants; the latter of whom, being thus reinforced, struggled with the plunderers, while their champion shot dead the man who was carrying off the lady, but who, leaving her, was coming forward to attack him. Then, though severely wounded, he, assisted by the servants, succeeded in mastering the banditti; and being reinforced by some peasants whom the noise called to the spot, they were all secured and carried to prison; while the rescued ladies overwhelmed our gallant countryman with their praises and their blessings.

"They were on their way to Paris; but as their preserver bled profusely, they insisted on going back with him to their chateau, and his weakness obliged him to comply with the proposal.

"The ladies are the widow and daughter of an early friend and favourite comrade of the First Consul, who, on hearing from the lady's letter to madame Buonaparte of the gallantry of their champion, insisted on their bringing him with them to Paris, that he might see and publicly thank one who had so materially served friends so dear to him. But these public thanks, and this elegant sword, are not the only good things, I find, which are likely to be the portion of our countryman; for the young lady has a large fortune and is very handsome, and it is supposed that herself and her wealth will both be bestowed on one who has so well deserved her."

"But his name, his name, sir?" demanded Emma.

"I have heard it, but I have forgotten it."

Then, while her companions thanked the gentleman for the interesting narration he had given them, Emma fell into a reverie.

At length the levée began, and a French gentleman said to their communicative companion, that he was sure, when the gallant Englishman drew near, the heart of the little girl opposite would beat violently, for it was she whom he saved from the ruffians; "and I have seen her have recourse to her salts several times to keep her from fainting." On hearing this they all followed the direction of the gentleman's eyes, and saw a pretty interesting girl with blonde hair, who was fanning herself with great violence, and seeming oppressed by the notice which she excited. But their attention was soon called to a more interesting object.

"Le voilà qui vient ce brave Anglois!" cried the Frenchman, the friend of their companion; when pale from recent loss of blood, his left arm in a sling, and dressed in full uniform, they beheld St. Aubyn.

"There!" said Mr. Egerton, and it was all he could say; while Emma, pale and trembling, caught hold of Mrs. Castlemain's hand, who, full of emotion herself, retained it in her grasp; while St. Aubyn, looking neither to the right nor to the left, went forward to the presence-chamber.

On the opposite side Mr. Egerton saw the French ladies who had accused St. Aubyn of being *tant soit peu poltron*; and having caught their eye, he made them a bow of very sarcastic meaning, which they perfectly understood, and by their gestures made him comprehend their penitence and their admiration.

Emma meanwhile spoke not a word; but Mr. Egerton and Mrs. Castlemain, while the French and English gentlemen were admiring the beauty and grandeur of St. Aubyn's face and person, assured them that they had once known him intimately, and that his mind and heart were not inferior to his personal graces.

In an hour some of the gentlemen who had been presented began to return, and amongst the rest St. Aubyn,—but not pale and languid as when he had passed them before; his cheek was flushed with pleasure, and his eyes were beaming with animation, while in his hand he held the promised sword of honour. Nor was he unattended. Those officers who had desired him to leave their regiment were crowding round him, offering him any apology that his offended pride might require; and Mr. Egerton, who approached them unseen, heard him answer, "I require no apology; you, according to the rules of military etiquette, did your duty, and I did mine; but there is one justice, sir," said he, addressing his Colonel, "which I shall require of you in due time."

While this was passing, Emma and Mrs. Castlemain heard a gentleman repeat the First Consul's address to St. Aubyn, which was such as could not fail to be gratifying to his pride.

Was all this likely to assist the endeavours of our heroine to drive him from her heart? Ah! no. And Emma felt in all its bitterness the cruelty of her situation. While he was thus congratulated, and pressed, and gazed upon, St. Aubyn's eyes met those of the young lady and her mother for whom he had fought and conquered; and with a look of delighted eagerness he made his way up to them, and, kissing a hand of each, pressed the young lady's hand to his bosom without speaking, while the poor girl's head sunk on her mother's shoulder.

"We shall meet in the evening, I trust, dear St. Aubyn," said the mother, who saw that St. Aubyn's presence overcame her daughter, whose nerves had been greatly injured by the fright which she had received; and St. Aubyn, taking the hint, withdrew; while Emma, who had witnessed the scene, felt the anguish of the preceding moments comparatively trifling.

In the door-way, in order to intercept St. Aubyn on his passage, stood Mr. Egerton. St. Aubyn, on seeing him, started and turned pale; but he held out his hand to him with affectionate pleasure, and while Mr. Egerton, speechless with strong emotion, could only press the hand he held, his eyes filled with involuntary tears.

"I did not expect," said he at length, "to see you here, my dear sir." Then looking round, as if he wished, yet dreaded, to see some one, his eyes rested on Mrs. Castlemain and Emma;—and all the animation of his countenance fled. Mrs. Castlemain kissed her hand to him with a look which powerfully expressed the affectionate interest which she took in all that had passed; Emma tried to smile also, but her lip quivered with emotion, and she knew that her bow was cold and devoid of grace; while St. Aubyn, instead of making his way up to them, bowed in a hurried manner in return, and taking Mr. Egerton's arm, left the room with him.

"We have heard all your adventures here, Henry," said Mr. Egerton, (who, alive only to the pleasure of seeing his beloved pupil, and witnessing his successes, could not feel any resentment towards him for his long estrangement from his society,) "and you are really quite a hero of romance;—but what is the justice you mean to require of your Colonel?"

"Why, you know my uncle——"

"Yes, only too well."

"And you know, perhaps, that he has always declared he would never forgive a relation of his who ever accepted a challenge?"

"Yes."

"Well then, when I on principle refused one since my arrival here, I wrote him word of it, telling him that, though I should have done just the same if he had not been in existence, it gave me great pleasure to reflect that my conduct in this instance was conformable to his opinions, and would procure for me his approbation."

"And what was his answer?"

"That he did not believe principle had any thing to do with my refusal to fight, and that he thought the officers quite right in wishing to get rid of such a chicken-hearted fellow."

"Shocking!" exclaimed Mr. Egerton; "here is another proof of the obliquities of Temper. But what will he say when you write him word of your chivalric exploits?"

"I shall *not* write to him on the subject; but I shall desire my Colonel to do it, and let him know that his 'chicken-hearted nephew' is no longer considered by the regiment as a disgrace to them; and this is the service I told him I should require."

At that moment St. Aubyn was told that he was wanted at the hotel of Madame de Coulanges (one of the ladies whom he had saved.)

"But we shall meet again, I hope?" said Mr. Egerton, impatiently.

"Not for some time, I doubt," replied St. Aubyn, confusedly, "for I expect a summons to England. My poor mother is very unwell, and unless to-morrow's post brings me a better account, I shall set off immediately;—so farewell! all happiness attend you and your friends till we meet again."

He then disappeared, and Mr. Egerton returned to the ladies.

Mr. Egerton's countenance bore evident marks of vexation and disappointment; and in reply to Mrs. Castlemain's "Well, what says St. Aubyn?" he almost pettishly repeated his conversation. But Emma, who had accurately observed the change in St. Aubyn's countenance when his eyes met hers, was so conscious that the sight of her occasioned him to experience very strong emotion, emotion which neither hatred nor indifference could cause, that her heart felt considerably lightened of its load, and though she thought it might be true that St. Aubyn was going to marry Mademoiselle de Coulanges, she fancied, she was sure, that he was not positively in love with her. Still she was unhappy, and could not help comparing Balfour and St. Aubyn so long and so often, that the former seemed to lose every moment the little ground which he had gained in her heart, and she began to dread his return to Paris.

That evening she at first refused to go to any public place, lest she should see St. Aubyn and Mademoiselle de Coulanges; but her delicacy being wounded at the idea that it was necessary for her to avoid St. Aubyn, she consented to the plan proposed, and neither at the Opera nor at Frescati did she behold him; while had admiration been her passion, the admiring gaze which greeted her whithersoeve. she went, and the name of la belle Angloise which on every side met her ear, would have gratified her feelings to the utmost, and healed perhaps the wounds of secret and ill-requited love. But admiration, though pleasing to Emma, was only dear to her from those she loved, and the greatest satisfaction she derived from it, was the look of pleasure and exultation which the notice she excited called forth in the expressive faces of Mrs. Castlemain and Mr. Egerton. That evening when they returned from Frescati, and Emma had left them, Mrs. Castlemain and Mr. Egerton began to discuss St. Aubyn's singular conduct, but still attributed it to some caprice of Mr. Hargrave, whose obliquities of temper they could not help recalling.

"It is very plain, by Mr. Hargrave's vulgar violence," said Mrs. Castlemain, "that he is a low-bred man, and was not born a gentleman." (Mr. Egerton on hearing this smiled significantly.)

"Why do you smile, Mr. Egerton?" added she.

"Because, madam, I am convinced that the conduct of the low and the high born, when under the dominion of temper, is commonly the same; that temper is the greatest of all levellers, the greatest of all equalizers; and that the peer and the peasant are, when under the influence of passion, equally removed from having any right to the name of gentleman."

"Indeed, Mr. Egerton," replied Mrs. Castlemain, "I cannot agree with you; consider the force of habit, that the language of a gentleman being habitually genteeler than that of the peasant, even his angry expressions must partake of this induced difference."

"But do you consider, my dear madam, that we are talking of a feeling powerful enough to overturn even the most powerful thing, itself excepted, namely, habit? It is a notorious fact, that even ladies delicately and carefully brought up, when in a state of derangement, use such language and such oaths as are only to be heard amongst the lowest of the sex; and what is passion but a temporary derangement, a maniac unrestrained by the usual decorums of life, and only to be kept in bounds, like other maniacs, by the operations of fear?"

"This is a mortifying and I hope an exaggerated picture, Mr. Egerton."

"No, madam, would it were! Still it is not temper, as exhibited in the shape of violent passion, that has the most pernicious influence on human conduct and happiness. It is temper under the shape of cool deliberate spite, and secret rancour, that is most to be guarded against.

'It is the taunting word whose meaning kills;' the speech intended to mortify one's self-love, or wound our tenderest affections; it is temper under this garb that is most hateful and most pernicious; when inflicting a series of petty injuries with a mild and smiling face, then is temper the most hideous and disgusting. The violence of passion, when over, often subsides into affectionate repentance, and is easily disarmed of its offensive power. But nothing ever disarms the other sort of temper. In domestic life it is to one's mind, what a horsehair shirt is to the body, and, like the spikes of Pascal's iron girdle, whenever one moves it lacerates and tears one to pieces."

The next morning, the same principle which forced her to the Opera and Frescati, led Emma to the Louvre Gallery, though at the risk of meeting St. Aubyn.

Mr. Egerton had gone to the Louvre Gallery very early that morning, in order to gaze on some of his favourite pictures alone and undisturbed. Not that he pretended to be a great connoisseur in painting, and fancied, because he had during a short residence in Flanders and Italy seen fine pictures, that he must understand them; his judgment taught him a more correct idea of his own powers, and he felt that a person by looking at Greek manuscripts might as well suppose himself capable of understanding Greek, as pretend to set up for a correct judge of painting from having gazed on pictures without some previous knowledge of the rules of art. But he had a correct eye and a poetical fancy, and on such paintings as interested his feelings he delighted to dwell,—while, by comparing the style of one master with another, he endeavoured to form an idea of the different merits of each. He was thus employed in that precious depository of the best works of the best masters,— and particularly precious to artists, because they can in the same room compare in a consecutive series the French school with the Flemish, and the Florentine with the Venetian,—when he saw a man pass him in a Highland dress.

"Another countryman arrived, I see!" said he to himself; "but why is he so clad?" Then supposing it might be some officer of one of the gallant Highland regiments, who had particularly distinguished themselves during the war, he followed him from a motive of respect and curiosity, and also probably from that warming of the heart which one feels when in a foreign land towards any native of our own beloved isles.

This sensation, however, was somewhat damped in Mr. Egerton, when he recognised in the stranger, on his turning round, no greater person than Varley. Still operated upon possibly by that feeling which makes one willing, when meeting countrymen abroad, to consider strangers as acquaintance, and mere acquaintance as friends, Mr. Egerton welcomed Varley most cordially to Paris; though, considering the personal vanity of the young man, he had his suspicions that Varley had assumed this very singular dress for an Englishman and a clerk in the War-office, from an idea of its being becoming and likely to attract notice to his really graceful form.

"Well, Mr. Varley, what brings you hither?" said Mr. Egerton.

"A truant disposition, good my lord," was the reply.

"Have you brought letters with you? have you any acquaintance here?"

"No," replied Varley, sighing, "I am

'Remote, unfriended, solitary, slow!'"

"Unfriended," returned Mr. Egerton, "you shall not be if I can serve you; and I will do all in my power to make your residence here agreeable to you."

"I rest much bounden to you," replied Varley, concluding that his charm of manner and conversation had interested Mr. Egerton in his favour. But he was mistaken.

Varley owed the benevolent wish which that gentleman felt to serve him, not only in trifles but essentials, to his having witnessed what Varley was ashamed of, namely, the laudable economy that had made him travel on the outside of the coach; and the anxious affection of his poor dowdy-looking mother. Even the dirty pocket-handkerchief which she had employed in a vain endeavour to wipe him clean, had had a pleasant effect on Mr. Egerton's feelings, as a proof of maternal tenderness; and when he recollected that Varley had some talent, and was, he had been informed, industrious, and a good and dutiful son, he could not help wishing to employ some of his large income in ameliorating the condition of these poor people, could he do so in such a manner as to stimulate, not check, the industry he so much approved. For never did the Christmas gift of a piece of money burn a child's pocket, as the phrase is, more certainly than did Mr. Egerton's purse burn his since his accession of wealth; and as he had no personal expense, he had so much money to give away, that it was quite a piece of good fortune for him to discover objects on whom to exercise his benevolence. His fixing on Varley, therefore, (for one of his protégés,) was more perhaps an act of necessity than of choice. He saw the young man's foibles, and was not a little disposed to resent his daring to cast a look of love on Mrs. Castlemain, little suspecting how far his conceit had led him; but he thought that a judicious friend might correct these follies, and convert him into a useful if not an ornamental member of society.

"Yes," said he mentally, "I will be that friend." Then, as the Gallery began to fill, he took Varley's arm, and, saying he wished to have some conversation with him, led him into a solitary part of the gardens of the Thuilleries. He then told Varley how much he had approved the manner in which he travelled,—a manner so contrary to the habits which he had attributed to him; he also expressed the interest which his affectionate mother had excited in him; and while Varley listened with amazement to hear that what he thought must have degraded had exalted him in Mr. Egerton's opinion, he added, that he wished to prove himself his friend, and must begin by telling him, that if he wished to be introduced into gentlemen's society, he must dress like a gentleman, and leave off every thing outré in his appearance, especially the dress he then wore, — begging to know what could induce him to assume it.

Varley, who did not want shrewdness, immediately saw that he could turn this circumstance, which originated in the motive Mr. Egerton had suspected, to good account; therefore, with downcast eyes, and affected reluctance, he answered,

"'My poverty, but not my will, consented,'

when my poor mother proposed to make up for me a plaid, which was a present to her from her native country, into the dress you see; — this, made at home to save expenses, and another by a smart London tailor, are all the wardrobe of one

'Who would buy more, but that his hand wants means.'"

Varley had formed a right judgment of the probable effect of this avowal on the man to whom it was addressed; and it deepened the interest which Mr. Egerton felt for the mother and the son.

"My dear sir," said Mr. Egerton with an air of great respect, and a blush of deep confusion, "I shall not believe that you pardon the great liberty I have taken in speaking to you with such freedom, if you will not confer on me the obligation that it is in your power to confer, namely, to accept this," sliding a purse into his hand; "for, having presumed to find fault with your dress, it is only just that I should furnish you with the means of procuring another;"—while Varley only bowed, and spoke his thanks in half-sentences, then put his handkerchief to his face to hide not his tearful, but his *dry* eyes.

"Mr. Varley," said Mr. Egerton, "you must dine with me. Can you come to-day? My ladies dine out, and I shall be happy to see you."

Varley, still more delighted at attention so unexpected, gratefully promised to wait on him; then telling Mr. Egerton he would go to his hotel immediately, and lay aside a dress so displeasing to his benefactor, he took his leave; and, as soon as he was out of sight, eagerly examined the contents of the purse which he had received. Its amount was as much beyond his expectations as it was his deserts; and while he felt some few stings of conscience for having written a certain spiteful paragraph, those feelings were soon forgotten in anxiety lest his delinquency should come to light, and cause him to forfeit the favour of that benevolent but credulous being, as he thought him, whose purse was thus generously opened to his suspected wants.

The real truth which Varley concealed from Mr. Egerton was, that he, in imitation of the celebrated Dr. Goldsmith, intended to walk through some part of France, hoping by the charm of his flute, and his dancing, to obtain food and lodging amongst the peasantry, and perhaps gain admittance into some chateaux on the road; and he thought his Highland dress would have not only a becoming but *pastoral effect*, and give him still more the air of a *héros de roman*. But the plea of poverty would, he was sure, do more with Mr. Egerton than that of picturesque effect, and certainly his scheme succeeded beyond his utmost expectations.

Mr. Egerton, out of respect to Mrs. Castlemain, would not invite Varley to dinner when she was at home; for, though he had no suspicion what good grounds she had for disliking that ridiculous boy, he felt that he had no right to ask him to a table where she presided, though with her conviction of his insanity her terror of him had vanished. Nor when he told her that he had invited a friend to dine with him, did he inform her who that friend was. But if, after some hours' conversation with Varley, he should appear to him deserving his notice, he resolved to endeavour to interest the excellent heart and benevolent nature of Mrs. Castlemain in his favour; and he had no doubt but that she would conquer her present dislike to Varley the forward coxcomb, in compassionate consideration for Varley the ingenious, industrious son of a poor, affectionate, and widowed mother.

At the appointed hour Mrs. Castlemain and Emma went out, and Varley arrived; and Mr. Egerton, under the unconscious influence of an eager desire to find an object for his benevolence to exercise itself upon, found Varley intelligent and interesting beyond his expectations, and was resolved in a day or two to arrange with the young man some scheme for serving him essentially.

During the course of the afternoon, Mr. Egerton, seeing a flute stick out of Varley's pocket, asked him to play to him; and he had not long complied before he was convinced that the flute he had heard in the park at Roselands was Varley's. He did not, however, think proper to notice this discovery,—to the great joy of his guest, who did not wish to have any allusions made to the transactions at Roselands.

"You are really a very fine performer on that instrument," said Mr. Egerton when he had ended; "can you play on any other?"

"Yes, sir, on the tenor and the violin."

"You must be quite an acquisition, then, to a private concert; and as I am going to join my companions to-night at a musical party, I will take you with me, if you have no better engagement."

And the gratified Varley had the satisfaction of hearing that he was about to be introduced into one of the best circles in Paris!

When they arrived, Mr. Egerton presented Varley as a young friend of his, who had great musical talents; while Mrs. Castlemain, seeing Varley before her, was ready to exclaim with the poor man in the story—"Vat! Monsieur Tonson come again!" and observing with surprise, not unmixed with resentment, that Varley was introduced by Mr. Egerton, she drew herself up, intending to receive both the introducer and the introduced with an air of haughty coldness. But Varley did not come within the reach of her disdain; for he soon took his place amongst the performers, and played the solo flute parts in a quintetto so well as to delight every one. Nor was he less successful on the tenor in a quartetto; and before the end of the evening, an English nobleman present was so charmed with his performance, that he invited him to a concert at his house the next week; and Varley thus saw an entrance into that sort of society which he most coveted, opened to him without any difficulty.

Emma, meanwhile, was lost in amazement at seeing Varley introduced by Mr. Egerton, who, purposely to enjoy her looks of wonder and curiosity, kept at a distance both from her and Mrs. Castlemain; nor till they returned home would he say anything on the subject. He then told Mrs. Castlemain his wish to serve Varley, and the interest he felt for him and his mother, and his hope that she would have the goodness to pardon the too open display of his admiration of her, which had, he believed offended her delicacy at the K—— ball; assuring her that he would answer for Varley's conduct and manners being in future all she could desire. To this speech Mrs. Castlemain, conscious that she had much more to pardon in Varley than his conduct at the K—— ball, did not vouchsafe an answer; but with an air of offended dignity she retired to her own apartment, leaving Emma to hear and approve Mr. Egerton's intended patronage of Varley, and to promise to assist him in removing her grandmother's prejudice against him.

As soon as Mrs. Castlemain reached her own apartment, dismissing her maid, she began to walk up and down it in violent agitation, debating with herself how she ought, consistent with her dignity, to proceed. She well knew that, if she were to tell Mr. Egerton how Varley had haunted and persecuted her at Roselands, he would resent his presumption so much as not to countenance him perhaps at all; but benevolence, and a sort of self-defence, *both* forbade her to make this confession. She felt that even to Mr. Egerton and Emma she could not bear to exhibit herself as an old Daphne flying before a youthful Apollo, and screaming and fainting at seeing a young man suddenly appearing before her, having jumped a ditch full of water in order to get at her. Then her mistake about the petition, and the verses on her beauty! Oh! it was impossible to disclose all this, because, though there was nothing derogatory to her in all this from Varley insane, it assumed the appearance of insult from Varley proved to be in his senses. What then could she do? and was it quite certain that Varley was as culpable as he appeared to be? Did not she, seeing through the prejudiced medium of conviction of his insanity, give a false colouring to actions in themselves excusable? When his face first alarmed her peeping through the branch of a tree, might he not be merely surveying the pretty walks in the wood? When he jumped down and ran after her, might he not be actuated really by the wish of informing her a mad bull was near? Might not his presuming to show her his verses, be excused by the very natural wish in a man like him, to obtain the patronage and notice of a woman of her rank in life? And might not the flute-playing in the park be justified by the same motive? while the jumping the ditch could be excused by the honest wish of returning her purse as soon as he had an opportunity. The call at Roselands was to Mr. Egerton, and the request to see her was satisfactorily accounted for by the value of the book which he was to leave. In short, Mrs. Castlemain's generous wish not to stand in the way of the welfare of an indigent, but en⁀owed young man, conquered even the suggestions of offended pride; and when she saw Mr. Egerton again, she assured him that *she* would throw no obstacles in the way of Varley's success with him. Accordingly, Varley was received at her table, and he, by his very judicious behaviour, a behaviour that spoke admiration, only kept in bounds by proper respect, soon made Mrs. Castlemain as much his friend as Mr. Egerton; and for his introduction to many pleasant parties, and the enjoyment of many pleasant evenings, Varley was indebted to our benevolent travellers.

It was on the very morning of Mr. Egerton's rencontre with Varley that another acquaintance was added to their list. I have before said that Emma had forced herself to go to the Louvre Gallery, though fearful of meeting there St. Aubyn and Mademoiselle de Coulanges; but neither he nor that young lady was to be seen, though there were Scotch, Irish, and English, in abundance. Amongst the English was a new comer, a widow of some rank, who, attended by a humble companion, and dressed à la Parisienne, was displaying her own lovely figure to great advantage, while admiring the plump person of Titian's mistress. This lady, catching a glimpse of Emma as, with her arms pensively folded in a long white veil, she walked along the Gallery, unconscious of the gaze of general admiration which followed her, was so struck with her beauty that she turned quite round to look at her, and with national pride exclaimed, "That must be *English* beauty!" And then, having eagerly inquired who she was, she smiled with great meaning, and unattended, followed Emma out of the saloon and down the stairs. Before she could overtake her, Emma had reached the Statue Gallery, and she did not come up with her till she had entered the "Hall of Illustrious Men," and was gazing on the statue of Phocion. As Emma turned away from it, she passed her hand affectionately over his chin, smiling, and shaking her head as she did so; when, looking up, she saw peeping from under a long black veil, the brilliant dark eyes of the above-mentioned lady, archly fixed upon her.

"What you said just now," cried the lady, "was very true."

"And what did I say, madam?" replied Emma, surprised at the familiarity of the speaker; "I do not remember that I spoke at all."

"No; but you shook your head, and according to our friend Bayes, that is the same thing, you know."

"And what did my shake say?"

"Oh! it meant, (for you looked at Phocion) 'Excellent, honest old fellow! these modern republicans are, alas, very little like you!'"

"I declare I will not stay near you a moment longer,—you are a conjuror, or something worse; for it is true that I thought nearly what you said."

"Not so, *ma belle*; we must not part so soon; by virtue of the art which you attribute to me, I also know that you are Miss Castlemain, commonly called here '*la belle Angloise*;' and out of pity to you, who have no devil to consult, I give you this (presenting her card) to tell you who I am."

On reading the card, Emma almost started as well as blushed, for it was, she found, Mrs. Felton who addressed her; but as she had now a new object of jealousy in Mademoiselle de Coulanges, she felt more kindly towards Mrs. Felton than she had done when she left England; and recovering herself, she said she should be happy to be better known to her.

Mrs. Felton, having made her a formal courtesy and received one in return, twisted her arm in Emma's, and exclaimed, "There, —now let us forget that we have not been acquainted these seven years." And Emma suffered herself to be led by Mrs. Felton back into the Gallery.

"So," cried Mrs. Felton, "it is full mall, I see! Come, my sweet old new friend, call up a look, and let us make

'Parisian nymphs with envy die,
Their shepherds with despair;'

for

'The Hotspur and the Douglas both conjoin'd
Are confident against the world in arms.'"

And saying this, she began to strut theatrically up the room.

"But let our arms be directed against the French, not the English world," replied Emma smiling; "for, or my eyes much deceive me, there are none but British in view."

"I believe you are very right," returned Mrs. Felton; "for so much do we abound here, that on a gentleman's asking who a man was at Frescati last night, he said on hearing the reply, 'Thank ye, sir. Now then I shall not return to England without having seen *one* Frenchman.' But, my dear, is not that Mrs. Castlemain approaching? Pray present me." And Emma did so. But that lady, to whom Mrs. Felton's character was known, and who thought her granddaughter might have made a more desirable acquaintance, assumed an air so proud and distant, that even the *woman of the world* felt awed by it.

But at this moment Mr. Egerton joined them; and when Emma presented him to Mrs. Felton, he made his bow with a look of so much satisfaction, and entered into conversation so courteously with the fair widow, that Mrs. Castlemain, conjecturing Mr. Egerton could not by his manner disapprove the acquaintance, and having implicit reliance on his judgment, relaxed in her repulsive hauteur, and condescended to be agreeable.

Mr. Egerton, though he certainly did not entirely approve of Mrs. Felton's character, was bribed into approbation of her present acquaintance with Emma, by seeing that the contagion of her vivacity had called back to her faded lip the smile so long a stranger to it; and if Mrs. Felton's varied talents, and the charm of her conversation could divert

Emma's mind from dwelling on depressing images, he thought it was the duty of both Mrs. Castlemain and himself to encourage the association, especially as Mr. Egerton believed no guilt, either of act or intention, stained the conduct of Mrs. Felton, and that his pupil's morals and reputation would neither of them be injured by her. With these feelings, he accosted Mrs. Felton, and his favourable intentions towards her were increased by her introduction.

Mrs. Felton possessed a great deal of what is called *manner*, a charm difficult to define, but certain to captivate. Mr. Egerton told Mrs. Felton, with an apology for alluding to the husband whom she had lost, that he had known Mr. Felton at College, and had so highly esteemed him, that he had cherished some spite against the irresistible charms which had made him give up being a fellow, in order to become a husband; and Mrs. Felton, in reply, said,—

"Is it possible that you, sir, can be the Mr. Egerton whom my husband knew and admired at College? I should have expected to have seen a much *older* man."

Thus, each offering a very innocent homage to the self-love of the other, (for it was not founded on falsehood, as Mrs. Felton was very handsome, and Mr. Egerton very young-looking, for his years,) they were disposed to regard each other with complacency;—for, whether Mr. Egerton's vanity was pleased or not by the implied compliment, his moral sense was satisfied, as he highly valued that sort of good-breeding, typical of benevolence, if not benevolence itself, which wishes to put every one in good humour, and call forth the good feelings only of those with whom we associate;—a habit of wishing and acting, which, when it does not militate against sincerity, in his opinion very nearly bordered on a virtue; while, on the contrary, he classed among the vicious those members of society, who, from coarseness of feeling, and a want of benevolence, (perhaps I should say of humanity,) are in the constant habit of wounding the self-love even of their best friends, by vulgar jokes on the defects of their persons, their dress, nay, sometimes on their professions, their trades, or their poverty.— And when not in good-humour, or when careless of pleasing, Mrs. Felton was as much given to speak daggers as any one;—but this he had as yet to find out.

But where was Miss Spenlove all this time? Miss Spenlove was Miss Spenlove no longer. A gouty, decrepit old Admiral, of seventy, who wanted a nurse, and had no objection to her 9 or 10,000*l.*, paid his addresses to her, and was immediately accepted,—to the great mortification and agony of Mrs. Felton; not that she envied Miss Spenlove her gouty husband, but, alas! this gentleman was the son of a *peer*, ay, and the son of a viscount too. Therefore, as Mrs. Felton's husband was only the son of a baron, Miss Spenlove, alias the honourable Mrs. Fitz-Walter, had precedence of the honourable Mrs. Felton; and it was amusing enough, to see the ill-concealed triumph of the one lady, and the mortified pride of the other. One day, the servant, at a small party, handed the tea first to Mrs. Fitz-Walter, when Mrs. Felton was sitting by her; on which, the former lady obligingly observed, "it shocks me, my dear creature, to take precedence of *you*,—but, you know, I *must* selon les règles;" and Mrs. Felton uttered a '*ridiculous!*' in a tone sufficiently expressive of her pique at the necessity her amiable friend was under. But Mrs. Felton was consoled for the pain she felt, at seeing a sort of dependant raised in rank above her, by the consciousness that she paid very dear for her elevation, as the old Admiral was said to use his gouty stick for more purposes than *one*, though its dimensions were larger than those allowed of by legal authority for the infliction of conjugal discipline; and no one could offend Mrs. Felton more, than by asserting that poor Mrs. Fitz-Walter was *not* the most wretched of women.

When they separated, Mrs. Castlemain assured Mrs. Felton that they should have the honour to call on her next day. Accordingly, they did so; and Emma would have felt quite at ease with her new and fascinating companion, but for the terror she experienced lest Mrs. Felton should talk to her of St. Aubyn. But of this there was no fear; for Mrs. Felton, who was in reality more in love with him than she had ever been with any man in her life, was extremely jealous of his attachment to Emma, and was as much averse to talking of him to her, as Emma could be to hear her do so; at least while such conversation could not assist in furthering the design nearest her heart.

I will here explain why St. Aubyn had renewed his acquaintance with Mrs. Felton, and had been seen escorting her to places of public amusement in London. Soon after Mrs. Felton's return to London, two pieces of intelligence reached her; the one was, that all hope of her ever marrying Wanford was rendered vain by his marriage with pretty Miss Travers; the other was, that Mr. Egerton, having become possessor of a large fortune, intended to adopt Henry St. Aubyn as his son, and settle on him immediately an independent property. This last information, which unhappily could not, as we have seen, be realized, made St. Aubyn appear as desirable a match in fortune, as he was before from merit; and Mrs. Felton began to repent her folly in giving up her chance of winning *him*, for the vain hope of captivating a man considerably his inferior in charms and agreeableness; and she immediately concerted a plan to

"Lure this tassel gentle back again!"

and a plausible one soon offered. St. Aubyn was much interested in the fate of a young man, who, having been brought up in affluence, was reduced to the extreme of poverty, and as this young man was in London trying to procure some employment, St. Aubyn mentioned him to Mrs. Felton, in the hope that she had interest, and might exert it in his favour. Mrs. Felton promised that she would so do; but she would never have remembered her promise again, had it not held forth a prospect of enabling her to please St. Aubyn, and induce him to renew his acquaintance with her when he visited London. For this purpose she wrote to him for the address of his protégé; and having received it, she not only was of great pecuniary relief to the poor youth and his distressed family, but she procured him by her exertions a place of increasing profit in a mercantile house.

When St. Aubyn, therefore, entered into the dragoon guards at the desire of his uncle, his first visit was indeed to the Orwells, but his second to Mrs. Felton; and more charmed with her than ever from her generosity to his friend, he allowed her to carry him about with her, a seeming captive in the chains of her attractions. But love and jealousy are quick-sighted, and though Mrs. Felton might deceive others, she did not deceive herself; she soon discovered that, whatever might be the cause of St. Aubyn's cessation of intercourse with the family at the White Cottage, his heart still sighed for the subject of his early muse; and that though to *Emma at eighteen* he had *not written at all*, to that Emma every faculty of his soul was devoted. But would it be so, if he was convinced she loved, and was likely to marry another? This query had occurred to her at Paris, and she resolved to proceed accordingly.

The new friends were now frequently in parties together; sometimes to Meudon, sometimes to Versailles; and not only were they at concerts and balls given by the English visiting at Paris, or residing there, but at some of the elegant fêtes given by a noble Russian family at a chateau about twelve miles from the metropolis. Mrs. Felton, meanwhile, gained so much on Mr. Egerton's good opinion, that she began to think, if she could not secure St. Aubyn, it would be no bad speculation to turn her artillery on *him*. And certain it is that, by way of preparation in case she was reduced to make such an attack, she continued on her guard in his presence, and did not give way to those airs and flippancies which, having been told that they became her, and were allowable in a woman of rank and fashion, the exuberance of her spirits sometimes prompted her to indulge in.

Mr. Egerton had seen her to great advantage in his opinion, namely, at her own table. It was one of his maxims, that it was easy for any woman to behave with graceful propriety at the table of another, where she has nothing to do; but the test of an habitual gentlewoman was seeing her at the head of her own;—and here it must be owned that Mrs. Felton always appeared in an attractive point of view.

They had met at a dinner given by Mrs. Felton two pleasant French families, and an English and an Irish family. But Emma's enjoyment of the conversation was damped by the terror she felt lest she should hear St. Aubyn named, and his late exploit expatiated upon. But though Emma was unfortunately ignorant of it, this was perhaps the only table in Paris, that day, where the circumstance was not likely to be alluded to; for the Irish gentleman present was the very officer whose challenge St. Aubyn refused, and the English one was the very lieutenant-colonel who sided with him in all he did. It was very certain therefore that Mrs. Felton would not name St. Aubyn, and she had given her French friends a hint to be as guarded.

The dinner itself was in the best style of French cookery; and Mrs. Felton's politeness had led her to learn all the difficult nomenclature of French dishes, and the meat of which they were composed, lest the appetite of her guests should be damped, as English appetites are so apt to be, by the terror of being betrayed into eating, in masquerade, something which in its ordinary dress is peculiarly repugnant.

This attention in their fair hostess was not thrown away on Mr. Egerton, who was an accurate observer of manners. "Well," said he as they returned home, "Mrs. Felton has gone through with honour to herself, in my opinion, one of the tests by which I try the understanding of a woman, and that is by her conduct at her own table."

"I never saw any one acquit herself better," replied Mrs. Castlemain, "and she is as well-bred as if she had been born to the rank of life in which good fortune has placed her."

"How attentive she was to her guests!" observed Emma.

"Yes," said Mr. Egerton, "and how well she preserved the medium between being troublesomely pressing, or painfully negligent in asking her guests to eat! In short, she never forgot that she was the mistress of the feast, and was not stuck up there to do nothing. I hate to see the master and mistress of a house sitting at the head of the table with their hands and arms crossed before them as useless as a carving-knife and fork before a fricassé, or serving only like their plateau to fill up a space."

"Yes, but, unhappily," observed Emma, "though just as useful, not so ornamental as that self same plateau, which is generally the prettiest thing in sight."

"I think," said Mrs. Castlemain, "that the master and mistress of a house should consider their guests as so many fire-works, and themselves as the *match* to be applied to them in order to make them explode for the general amusement."

"Ay, but there are some guests," observed Emma, "that, like phosphoric matches, blaze of themselves, requiring no external application; and I should like best to surround my table with them, as much the least troublesome as well as the most pleasant."

"And there are some guests," said Mr. Egerton, "who, if they are to be likened to fire-works at all, it must be to fire-works damaged by rain, and therefore incapable of going off let the match be applied ever so often. Some persons seem to think that they come to your table only to eat and drink, and not to contribute their share of conversation for the amusement of the company."

"Miss Castlemain," added he, "I hope you observed that Mrs. Felton condescended to know the name and quality of every dish. I have sometimes been amused, I confess, at the ludicrous distress of an unhappy John Bull eater, when he has been vainly exploring some made dish in his vicinity, and, often not daring to venture on the desperate step of eating 'a dish without a name,' has modestly inquired of the lady of the house what that tempting viand was; and then being informed that she knew nothing of the matter, I have seen the poor tantalized man apply to another dish, with equal doubt and equal curiosity, and receive the same answer to his question again; while, with all due deference, Miss Emma Castlemain, to your talents and latinity, I could not help thinking a woman could know nothing of more daily utility than what her table was composed of. For, after all, society is kept together, and our good feelings called forth, not by any *great* services that we can any of us do or receive, but by *little* services and attentions; attentions which show our friends when present, that we have thought of them when *absent*, and have felt interested in doing all in our power to gratify even their palates; for, such are the artificial wants that society creates, I never yet met with any one to whom dinner was positively a matter of no consequence. Therefore, Miss Castlemain, when you have a table of your own, I expect that you will never answer my question of what such a dish is, 'that indeed you don't know,' unless you mean by that to inform me you are rich enough to keep a housekeeper,— a fact that I should never have thought of doubting; and I do assure you that Mrs. Felton's conduct at table, to-day, was to me a much stronger proof of the soundness of her understanding, than if she had shown me a moral essay of her own writing, or descanted eloquently on a moral duty."

"Sir," replied Emma, "you may rely upon it, that the coroner, if called upon to sit on one of my visiters, shall never have to bring in his verdict, 'Died of eating an anonymous dish!' It should seem," added she, "that Mrs. Felton had modelled her conduct at her own table according to the wise son of Sirach's directions, who bids the master of a feast take diligent care for his guests, and so sit down. 'Then,' adds he, 'when thou hast done thy office, take thy place, and make thyself merry with them.'"

"This seems to imply," observed Mr. Egerton, "that the givers of the feasts should stand, and wait behind their guests, that probably being the custom of those days. But the advice to take diligent care for one's guests, that is, to be attentive in helping them, and providing for them, is a rule applicable to all ages of the world, and worthy of the illuminated pages from whence your quotation is taken."

"Your observation, Mr. Egerton," said Mrs. Castlemain, "on Mrs. Felton, reminds me of a story which poor lady Bellenden, my mother, used to tell. Lady Bellenden was, you must know, what is called a notable woman, and piqued herself on a knowledge of household duties. My father and mother were dining one day at the house of what are called here ' *les nouveaux riches*, or *new rich;*' persons who, though born only to a narrow income, and its usual paucity even of comforts, had been enabled by successful speculations in trade to keep a carriage, two men in livery, and a housekeeper; and the gentleman had been knighted for carrying up an address. The lady in this case was a very silly woman, and her weak head was nearly turned by the great change in her situation. The dinner was good and expensive, and consisted of many made dishes. As usual, some timid or some luxurious eater asked the lady occasionally what such a dish was. 'I am sure I don't know, you must ask my housekeeper,' was the reply with a smile, as if she had said a good thing. As this answer was amusing enough, another person, out of a malicious love of fun, and then another, asked the same question, and the same answer was given. At length, the master of the house ventured to ask what was coming at the bottom of the table, when the fish was removed. 'How can you be so ridiculous, Sir James,' replied the lady indignantly, 'as to ask me such a question? That is just like you! You know, since we have been rich enough to keep a housekeeper, I never trouble my head about those matters.' 'Suppose then, madam,' said a very sarcastic old gentleman, who was intimate in the family, and from whom they expected a legacy, 'suppose we have the housekeeper up; for she seems to have much more useful information than her lady.' The lady looked silly, but had not capacity enough to understand the full force of the speech, and profit by it; for she again made the same reply to the same question; and soon after, while she was talking to the person next her, a gentleman asked her if she would not like a piece of mince pie; and concluding it was the same tiresome question, she angrily answered, 'I am sure I don't know, you must ask my housekeeper.' This produced a general and most violent laugh; while the old gentleman observed, that as he did not approve of taking anybody's name in vain, he moved that the housekeeper so often named should be brought in to answer for herself."

"I thank ye, madam, for your story," said Mr. Egerton; "and in future, when I hear a lady say, 'I am sure I do not know what that dish is,' I shall translate her words into 'You troublesome person, ask my housekeeper.'"

"But silly as this lady was," observed Emma, "in her reply to her guests, she was still more offensive to me in that to her husband. There is nothing I dislike more than to hear a woman speak disrespectfully to the being whom she has sworn to honour."

"The same wise man from whom you have already quoted," replied Mr. Egerton, says, "'A woman that honoureth her husband shall be judged wise of all.' And Richardson, in his Clarissa, a book which many years hence I wish you to read, gives a fine monition to wives. When his hero Lovelace calls at a glover's shop, and desires to see the master of it, the wife replies that he is up stairs, and calls him down by the name of 'John!' on which Lovelace calls him also, and by the same familiar appellation of John. This gives great offence to the woman, and she reproaches him for taking such a liberty with her husband; to which he replies, 'Woman, learn to treat your husband with respect yourself, so shall you teach others to respect him.'"

"Admirably said," replied Mrs. Castlemain, "and the poor lady in my story might have profited by the hint. There is nothing so offensive, certainly, as the bickering of husbands and wives in company, especially in those conspicuous situations, the top and bottom of their own tables. I have sometimes seen *such* looks travel backwards and forwards!"

"Ay, so have I," returned Mr. Egerton; "looks sent like a shuttlecock backwards and forwards from the one to the other."

"But," observed Emma, "it was like a shuttlecock then, could such a thing be, with the quills not the feathers uppermost, and those of the porcupine kind."

"True," said Mr. Egerton; "and I am of opinion that conjugal quarrels, like conjugal endearments, should never take place before company; and that those parents who quarrel with each other, and correct their children, before even their intimate friends, are positive nuisances in society."

"This from you, Mr. Egerton!" replied Mrs. Castlemain laughing. "I thought you were so fond of having children corrected, that you would have no opportunity omitted; but, like King Arthur in Tom Thumb, you would bid the schoolmasters

'Whip all the little boys'

at any time."

"Not so, madam," answered Mr. Egerton smiling; "but if the alternative was, that they must be corrected in my presence, or not corrected at all, I should certainly say, whip away, and make no stranger of me. But let me quote in defence of that wise man King Arthur and myself, no less authority than that of the wise man in whose writings I am happy to see you, Emma, so conversant; 'He that loveth his son causeth him often to feel the rod, that he may have joy of him in the end.' Again, 'He that chastiseth his son shall have joy of him, and shall rejoice of him amongst his acquaintance.' 'A horse not broken becometh headstrong, and a child left to himself will be wilful.'"

"Ay, ay, all this is very wise, I know," said Mrs. Castlemain, and 'Spare the rod, and spoil the child,' is a well-known proverb; but there is also another proverb, Mr. Egerton, about bachelors' wives and so forth."

"True, madam, and a very sensible proverb it is; for it means that people are very apt, overlooking the difficulties of those tasks which they have not been called upon to perform, to arrogate to themselves a power of acting better and more wisely in a difficult situation than their neighbours and friends. But in this case the proverb does not apply to me; for I am fully aware of the difficulties of bringing up children properly; and though I am well convinced that the parents who have resolution to correct their offspring, love them more truly than those whose fine feelings, forsooth, forbid them to do it, I can make allowances for the obstacles thrown in the way of such corrections by a selfishness looking so very like the virtue of parental tenderness. But all I pretend to say is, that the conduct towards children which I admire, though rare perhaps, is very possible. Though not so fortunate as to be a parent myself, my mother was a parent; and I am well convinced, that whatever of good there is in my temper or disposition, I owe to her judicious corrections in the early stages of my childhood. I have also known many mothers, (for on mothers chiefly depends the conduct which forms the temper of the child,) whom I have surveyed with affection and veneration, while the firm and salutary frown of maternal severity could scarcely conceal the starting tear of maternal tenderness as they inflicted, magnanimously inflicted, punishment on present error, from the consciousness that it was the means of preventing more serious guilt in future. Some such mothers I have still the happiness of knowing; the grave has hidden others from my view, and circumstances separated me from many; but lovely and venerable is the recollection of them to my mind! And when all my conduct towards you, dear madam, has showed, during Emma's childhood, that I thought you capable, with a little exertion, of being all that these mothers were, I do not think I deserved to have a musty proverb thrown in my teeth as a sort of reproach, and I must say that it exhibited too much of pique and temper."

"Perhaps it did," replied Mrs. Castlemain, "and I sincerely ask your forgiveness."

"My forgiveness! O fy! the fault was too trifling to require such an apology. But I see by the light of yon lamp that you are looking very arch, Miss Castlemain. Pray why is this?"

"Nay, nothing; only that one has heard of a man's going to see that good-for-nothing person a house-breaker, executed in just punishment of his offences, and taking the opportunity himself of picking a pocket."

"Well, Emma, and now for the application."

"Why, sir, you reproached my poor grandmother with quoting a proverb against you, in spite and ill-temper, and in a manner at least as indicative of anger as hers was."

"True, child, true; and I beg pardon in my turn." Here the coach stopped at the door of the hotel.

When Emma had retired for the night, Mrs. Castlemain told Mr. Egerton that she wished to speak to him. "You said just now, sir, that some years hence you would wish Emma to read Clarissa, and I doubt not but your reasons for wishing her to defer reading it so long are very good ones. But, I must tell you, that Madame de Lamoignan reproached me the other day, because Emma at nineteen had not yet read that book,—a book which, she assured me, most French mothers think it right, as one of the first sources of moral instruction, to put into the hands of their daughters at seventeen. But I replied to her that I could see no necessity for this."

"No, madam, no more than to make a point of leading your pupil into a squalid and filthy cottage, the abode of dirt and poverty, in order to teach her the necessity of keeping her person clean. Can the death-bed of a Sinclair, and the horrible fate of Clarissa, be necessary to teach a young woman to hate vice, love virtue, and detest a villain? And as this otherwise admirable work contains very improper descriptions, and scenes of infamy with which it must sully a young woman's mind to be acquainted, I must think that putting this book in the hands of a girl, by way of improving her morals, is like giving a person a wound in order to bestow on them a plaister. Still, I consider the Clarissa of Richardson as a national boast; and so far from objecting to the formal manners of his Harlowe family, I think one might as well object to the dresses of Vandyke, and Lely and Kneller's portraits, because they are not according to the present fashion. The manners of the Harlowes are the manners of that time of day, and I cannot therefore wish to spare them an atom of their stateliness."

"I agree with all you have said," replied Mrs. Castlemain, "and am happy to find my opinions sanctioned by yours."

The next day Mrs. Felton was to accompany them to the Petits Augustins. It was agreed that they should meet in the Louvre Gallery, and walk thence to Mrs. Castlemain's hotel, whence they were to proceed in that lady's carriage. The walk from the Louvre lay, as I have before said, across the Place de la Concorde; and as the day was fine, the sunbeams beautifully illuminated the splendid objects which that scene exhibits. Our travellers, standing near the scaffolding then erected on the spot where the guillotine stood, and where once stood the equestrian statue of Louis Quinze, paused awhile to gaze upon the grand assemblage of objects. Behind them were the palace and gardens of the Thuilleries; on the right, the magnificent pile of building called Le Garde Meuble, divided by the widest street in Paris, the Rue de la Concorde, terminated by the numerous columns of La Madelaine. On the left were the river, and the Palais Bourbon, with the distant dome of the Invalides; and in front the Elysian Fields, with the grand vista leading to the hill beyond.

"Were all Paris like this spot," cried Mr. Egerton, "the world surely could not parallel it as a city."

"But it is not," replied Mrs. Felton; "and lovely as is this scene, I must forget the horrors transacted in it before I can relish its beauty as it deserves. Alas! this is a spot which the world cannot parallel for other reasons than its loveliness."

"True," said Mr. Egerton, the thought of his murdered friend painfully recurring to him. "And what a brief but eventful chronicle is the place in which we now are! In that palace lived and reigned Louis XVI. On the very spot on which we now stand, he was beheaded; in that church he lies buried; and all these striking memorials meet the eye as it were at once!"

"Ay," observed Emma, "in that church his remains, his unhonoured remains indeed, lie buried."

"Yes," replied Mrs. Felton, "amidst the bones of those humbler individuals who were crushed to death amongst the crowds assembled to witness the rejoicings which took place on his nuptials."

"True, madam," returned Mr. Egerton, "and I never feel more disgust at the operations of temper, (here he smiled significantly at Emma,) that universal agent in all human actions, and that soul of party spirit, than when they lead men to assume as it were the terrors of the Almighty, and presume to point the arrows of retributive justice. Often have I heard the circumstance of the poor king's being buried with the victims of his bridal-day, mentioned as an awful and signal instance of retribution; than which, nothing could be further from the truth, as no one can be properly said to suffer for a crime he never committed. Had the unhappy Louis ordered these persons so buried to be crushed to death, or had he by an act of sovereign power caused them to be put in a situation of which death was the unavoidable consequence, then might this circumstance be held up as a sign of retributive justice. But he was only an accessary to this dreadful fact, by having been, as a bridegroom, the cause of the festivity which called together those wretched people who perished in the gratification of their curiosity. This is one amongst many of those cruel deductions and observations which the virulence of party spirit makes, and partisans adopt as true without giving themselves the trouble of asking their own understandings whether it be really the truth or not; and this spirit caused Louis to be buried in that spot, as an expiatory offering to the manes of those unfortunate people!"

"As exhibiting an awful picture of human passions in uncontrolled action," said Mrs. Castlemain, "the history of the French revolution is an instructive volume to read, though every page be written in characters of blood."

"Alas!" replied Mr. Egerton, "in such characters must the history of *every* revolution be written; for private dislikes and personal resentments are commonly amongst the most powerful motives of the promoters of revolutions, and Temper reigns triumphant under the specious name of Public Spirit!"

"Conversations like these, and the sight of a scene like this," said Mrs. Felton, "are no bad preparation for what we are going to survey, — the tombs of those illustrious dead on whom the mean vengeance of Temper did indeed, under the mask of patriotism, vent itself with even Vandal barbarity."

At this moment Mrs. Castlemain's carriage appeared in sight, and the coachman came forward to meet them; while Emma slily whispering Mr. Egerton, said, "So, sir, you could not forbear mounting your hobby-horse just now. But I suspect, by Mrs. Felton's looking so grave when you began to talk about Temper, and your system concerning it, that your hobby gave her a kick or two. However, we shall find out if that was the case."

The Museum of Ancient Monuments which our travellers were now visiting, is in the Rue des Petits Augustins, and in the former monastery of that name. There are now deposited the tombs and monuments of the metropolis, as well as of other parts of France, which, saved from the destruction of Jacobin fury, are here historically and chronologically arranged.

With judicious accuracy, the chamber* containing the works of the twelfth century is decorated with the architectural ornaments peculiar to that age; and the same excellent plan is adopted in ornamenting the other chambers, containing in succession the monuments of the thirteenth, fourteenth, fifteenth, sixteenth, seventeenth, and eighteenth centuries; while the garden, dignified by the pompous name of the Elysium, contains forty statues, besides several tombs and urns raising their marble heads amidst pine trees, cypresses, and poplars. Here rest entombed the ashes of Abelard and Eloisa; here the illustrious remains of Descartes, Moliere, Lafontaine, and Boileau, and those of many other great men who are immortal in the pages of French history, and were judged worthy of having their names and actions recorded on monumental marble.

The interest which our travellers and Mrs. Felton expected to feel in these scenes, so calculated to call forth a variety of recollections and emotions, did not fall short of their expectations; and they gazed with gratified attention on the sculptured features of many a one whose valour, whose weaknesses, whose virtues, or whose genius, had been made known to them by the pages of history. The monument of cardinal Richelieu was already known to them by engravings; and there were others, amongst which was that erected by Le Brun to the memory of his mother, sculptured from a design of his own, of which they were happy to be enabled to perpetuate the recollection by similar means. When they entered the chamber of the sixteenth century, in which one of the most striking things is the monument of Diane de Poitiers, duchess of Valentinois, they saw a gentleman looking at this tomb with great attention, and contemplating the features of the once captivating beauty, whose kneeling figure was worthy of admiration; and when he turned round they recognised Varley, whom Emma immediately presented to Mrs. Felton, Mr. Egerton being too much engaged in consulting the book he held in his hand to do this kind office for his protégé. It was Lenoir's "Description Historique et Chronologique des Monumens de Sculpture réunis au Musée des Monumens Français."

"I am amused," said Mr. Egerton smiling, "with this sentimental gentleman's account of this tomb, that of Diane de Poitiers."

"Who was she?" asked Emma.

"The mistress of Henry the Second, who was the husband of Catherine de Medicis."

"A mistress! and of a married man too! And yet there is a splendid monument erected to her memory!" exclaimed Emma.

"There spoke the uncorrupted feeling of a virtuous heart," replied Mr. Egerton. "Yes, Emma, it is even so; but Diane de Poitiers, the lady of Anêt, whither she retired on the

* *Salle* is the French word.

death of Henry, and where she died at an advanced age, might have a tomb erected to her, as this was within her own chapel, without any offence to good morals. And I, as an Englishman, cannot object to it, when the remains of one of our celebrated actresses, a woman notoriously the unmarried mother of children by different men, after lying in state in the Jerusalem chamber, was interred in Westminster Abbey. But what strikes me, and *offends* me as contrary to decorum and good morals, is what this Frenchman *values* himself upon; and that is, that the 'emails or enamels, which he has introduced in the pedestal of her statue, suit it exactly, since, on one side is seen Francis the First, and on the other Henry the Second, at the feet of Diane, who is surrounded by love-ciphers, such as ornamented all the monuments erected by Henry's orders.' Thus does he show himself vain of perpetuating the remembrance of an adulterous intercourse, as if it were the bright spot on the life of the departed sinner, whom this breathing marble represents, instead of a stain on it, which it would be kinder to shroud in oblivion."

"But what does he say of this celebrated woman?" asked Mrs. Felton.

"Oh! he calls her 'illustre, aimable,' and soforth."

"And does he not regret that her talents and her graces were clouded over by her misconduct?" said Mrs. Castlemain.

"Oh, no."

"And does he say nothing of her age?" asked Mrs. Felton laughing.

"No; even when speaking of a dead beauty he is too gallant to talk of her age."

"Yet her age was one of the most remarkable parts of her history," returned Mrs. Felton; "for she was more than forty when Henry the Second, who was then eighteen, fell in love with her!"

"Astonishing!" cried Emma.

"Not at all so to me," observed Varley eagerly; "for, probably, as the poet says of Cleopatra,

'Age could not wither her, nor custom stale
Her infinite variety.'

For my part, *I* admire Henry's taste, and do not wonder that, like a modern poet, he should have been apt to exclaim,

'So lovely thou art still to me,
I had rather, my exquisite mother,
Repose in the sun-set of thee,
Than bask in the noon of another.' "

It would have been difficult to say whose cheeks were of the deeper crimson at this moment, Mrs. Castlemain's or Varley's. While Emma, who stood behind them with Mr. Egerton, could not help whispering to him, that for '*mother*,' she supposed Varley meant they should read '*grandmother*.' Mrs. Castlemain during this whisper, said hastily, "What nonsense! A boy of eighteen in love with a woman of forty! He indeed has youth for the excuse of *his* folly, but there can be none for the lady's."

"Nay," cried Mr. Egerton, "he had a still better,— economy; for, in choosing so sage and reverend a companion, he could make her serve both for privy counsellor and mistress *too;* and perhaps the lady, from a spirit of patriotism, consented to further this saving plan."

"Well," said Mrs. Castlemain pettishly, "I think this monument has detained us long enough; let us pass on to more."

"I cannot regret our detention," replied Mrs. Felton, "as it has drawn forth so many various comments;" and conscious that she was herself turned thirty, she looked with an eye of great complacency on the very pretty young man whose obliging taste led him, as it seemed, to value women, like wine, the more, rather than the less, for their age.

Emma was too *young* to feel thus gratefully, and her grandmother too *old* in her own sober judgment; but Varley soon observed that, whatever was the cause, this handsome Mrs. Felton paid great attention to what he said; and when he afterwards found that she was "an honourable, a fashionable, and a rich widow," he began to think that Mrs. Castlemain's place in his heart might perhaps be filled up even in a more stylish manner.

At length they reached the Elysium, where Varley, on having the tomb of Abelard and Eloisa pointed out to him, began to recite, with great propriety of action and sweetness of tone,

"If ever fate some wandering lovers bring,"

and so on to the line of

"Oh! may we never love as they have loved!"

"Thank you, Mr. Varley," said Mr. Egerton, "given with good emphasis and discretion."

"I beg pardon for my little effusion," replied Varley, "but at sight of that tomb enthusiasm conquered every other feeling.

"Surely," observed Mrs. Felton, "the sight of the tomb of those renowned and unfortunate lovers, Abelard and Eloisa, may well excite and excuse enthusiasm."

"Why so?" said Emma. "For, after all, those unfortunate lovers were guilty ones also. When Mr. Egerton first read aloud to me the poem whence Mr. Varley quoted those fine lines, I was charmed by the beauty of the verse, and interested for the sorrow that it expressed. But when I found that it was the sorrow of unlawful love, and not of a virtuous wife separated by force from a virtuous and beloved husband, that the writer too was a woman not ashamed of her error, but glorying in it, and preferring the title of mistress to that of wife, while the poet had only given more power and notoriety to her own profligate prose by clothing it in the most seducing poetical language, I lost the deep interest I originally felt for the eloquent nun, and can, I confess to you, gaze on this tomb with as much indifference nearly as on that of the mistress of Henry the Second."

"I am far from sharing in this indifference," said Mrs. Felton, "though on principle I ought; but the poem in question is so popular, that it is generally read long before one's ideas of right and wrong are precisely defined to our own judgments, and one's feelings are charmed without waiting for the leave of one's principles. But did Mr. Egerton, your grave preceptor," asked Mrs. Felton smiling, "really read that poem aloud to you?"

"Yes," interrupted Mr. Egerton, "all that I could read with propriety; for it is very certain that this poem, which, as you justly observe, is in general request with all ages, is one that a man who respects your sex could not read aloud to any woman."

"And were you, Miss Castlemain, contented with hearing it read?"

"Certainly; for surely what Mr. Egerton could not read *to* me, must be improper for me to read to *myself*."

"Her mind, I see," said Mrs. Felton, taking Mr. Egerton's arm, and leading him aside, "has all its original whiteness unsullied."

"It has been the endeavour of her most excellent parent and myself to keep it so," he replied, delighted, as Mrs. Felton foresaw he would be, at this tribute to his mode of educating Emma; "and I flatter myself that the correct judgment which in my opinion she displayed in her comments on Eloisa, she exhibits on all moral subjects; and that you will never see my pupil allowing a veil of sentiment to give a false loveliness to the face of female frailty."

"But are we not all too severe to one single error of that kind in our sex?"

"I think not; for, as the end of punishment is not to punish crime, but to deter from its commission, the individual delinquent must, I fear, be always on principle sacrificed for the good of the whole. Besides, I am much of Dr. Johnson's opinion. 'Chastity,' says that excellent moralist, 'is the great principle which a woman is taught. When she has given up that principle, she has given up every notion of female honour and virtue, which are all included in chastity.'"

"But where," said Mrs. Castlemain, "is the tomb of Turenne? I expected to have seen that."

"It has been removed from this place," replied Mrs. Felton, "and you will see it at the Invalides, where it stands by itself, harmonizing well, as the monument of a great hero, with the memorials of French valour which surround it. Striking is it also by its dignified simplicity, and worthy of the simple greatness of him whom it contains; for it is of undecorated black marble, and its only inscription is the name of 'Turenne' in gold letters."

"And that says enough," replied Mr. Egerton. "I always liked the character of Marshal Turenne, and when I read the account of his death, and of its effects on all ranks, as given by Madame de Sevigne in her inimitable letter on the subject, I learnt to love him, and to envy France her hero."

"O that the tomb of Madame de Sevigne were here!" cried Mrs. Castlemain. "Then indeed would my feelings be powerfully excited, and my judgment approve the utmost homage that they could pay!"

"True," said Mr. Egerton, "for she was an honour not only to her nation, but humanity. She was chaste in an age and at a court where to be unchaste was scarcely considered as a crime. Young, beautiful, and adored, she was faithful to a grossly unfaithful husband. The perfect wife became as perfect a mother, and at the early age of twenty-four she devoted herself exclusively to the children of her dear though unworthy husband; while in her maternal affection appeared a pure but decided passion as well as principle, as is exhibited by those admirable letters, which, though in some instances they are stained with passages not suited to the exemplary and matchless delicacy of Englishwomen, are models of wit, style, tenderness and friendship. I wish," continued Mr. Egerton, "that she had lived longer and happier; but it was no unfit end for this sweet and spotless lady to die the victim of maternal anxiety for the health of her daughter. And it is a comfort for me to think that she breathed her last at the house of that child for whom she had lived, and for whom she also died."

"Happy, enviable woman!" exclaimed Mrs. Castlemain with a faltering voice and a glistening eye; "for she died before her beloved daughter, and with the blessed consciousness of having fulfilled towards her every duty, and having displayed towards her the most unremitting tenderness and affection! Oh! how I envy her!"

Here Mr. Egerton, alarmed at her strong emotion, gently pressing her arm, recalled her to more self-command.

"I feel equal enthusiasm with you," said Mrs. Felton, "and wish much more strongly than you can do, that the monument of Madame de Sevigne was preserved in this interesting museum."

"Why so?" demanded Emma.

"Because I know the fate of that monument which was erected to her in the chapel of the castle of Grignan, her body being deposited in the vaults of the family.*

* See Miss Plumptree's Narrative of a Three Years' residence in France, and also an edition of Madame de Sevigne's Letters, published in 1801.

"During the reign of terror, the chateau with the church and family monuments were all laid in ruins; but when the destroyers came to the monument of this illustrious lady, on which was her effigy, a name so celebrated struck even them with a sacred awe, and the monument was left untouched."

"I thank you, I thank you heartily, madam, for this anecdote; it delights me to see such homage paid to the combination of exalted virtue with superior talent, even by barbarous ruffians like those."

"Ay, but the sequel, dear sir! So far, so good; but as avarice was of stronger influence over them, than enthusiastic reverence for virtue,—when they entered the vaults, and found that the body of this illustrious woman was incased in lead, they carried away the coffin, and left the body to the chance of what might befall it."

"Wretches!" cried Emma.

"Having been embalmed, it was found entire, and in a state of high preservation. It was dressed in a long robe of silk, fastened round the waist with a silver girdle. The girdle was carried away, as well as the coffin, and the body was in time deprived of its silken garment, by persons coming and taking a piece of it as a precious relic. The body remained amongst the ruins, and is probably now restored to its original dust,—while neglect and the injuries of the weather have laid this respected monument in ruins with the rest."

"O that the same pious hands which preserved these monuments had been busy at Grignan!" cried Emma.

"Would that the same *politic* hands had been busy there!" replied Mr. Egerton, "for I doubt their being actuated wholly by feelings properly called pious; and would that we possessed some of the silk that covered those sacred remains! For, however philosophy may laugh at such feelings, and learn to consider the unconscious body as unworthy the respect of rational beings, when the soul has departed from it, I believe it salutary to the affections, that of the mouldering relics of those we loved, or honoured, we should continue to think as if they were still conscious, and to consider them as too sacred to be polluted by mortal touch; and coeval with this world itself be those feelings that make our departed friends revive in our own creative sensations! What is it that throws a charm over all that we are now contemplating, but a reverence for, and a sympathy with, those very feelings? Taught by our own experience of similar emotions, fancy portrays the sorrowing affections which gratified themselves by erecting these memorials to those whom they loved; and whether the monument be one raised by private tenderness or national gratitude, it is by our power of entering into that enthusiasm, long since passed away and forgotten, which prompted the tributary erection, that we learn to feel so strongly while gazing on the cold unconscious marble, and to claim a sort of tender kindred with the dead who sleep beneath."

From the time of this visit to the Musée des Monumens, Varley became an invited guest of Mrs. Felton's, and he began to think that all the high-raised hopes of his vanity and ambition were likely to be gratified. I have before said that Varley danced admirably,—and he must indeed have been a good dancer to be admired as such in the circles of Paris; and as a man's dancing only tolerably well is a proof that he must be of a respectable class in society, as his friends were rich enough to send him to a dancing-school, it was natural that the very superior style in which Varley danced should lead the Parisian world to believe him a person to whom fortune had facilitated the means of having the first instruction; therefore he was soon named the Chevalier Varley. Indeed his excellence in this art was a matter of surprise to Emma, who knew that he was poor, and understood that he was born of obscure parents; she was also sure that whatever his father might have been, his mother was a vulgar woman. While these thoughts were occurring to her, which as they rose she communicated to Mrs. Castlemain, who was with her at a ball near Paris, to which Mrs. Felton had brought Varley, she resolved as delicately as she could to interrogate Varley on the subject. And while he was handing her some ice, she said, "There is no accomplishment, perhaps, Mr. Varley, in which it is more advantageous to a young man, who is a stranger anywhere, to excel, than dancing; as a proficiency in that art, such a proficiency as yours I mean, indicates *une éducation très soignée*; you must have had the first masters, to dance as you do."

"I had indeed a most admirable master; my poor father spared no pains for my improvement," replied Varley, sighing.

"So it seems; I know no one who does so much, so well. Your father must have been a great loss to you."

"He was indeed; for he never took a step but with a view to my future good; and had he lived, I should have certainly become rich by degrees."

"I am always sorry when the prospects of youth are thus suddenly blasted," said Emma kindly; "and I am very glad, Mr. Varley, that my admirable friend Mr. Egerton, is interested in your welfare, and has both the wish and the means of promoting it."

Little did Emma suspect the double meaning of Varley's words. The truth was, that his father was *a dancing-master*, and died before Varley was old enough to take his business.

Little also did she suspect that Varley, incapable of appreciating the generosity that he could not feel, was inclined to attribute Mr. Egerton's wish to serve him to a consciousness that Emma loved him; and that, finding she was bent on marrying him some day or other, he had resolved, by getting him forward in life, to make the match as little unequal as he could. But the end of his ill-deserved elevation was near at hand.

A Russian nobleman had invited all the French and British of rank and fashion, in and near Paris, to a dress ball at his chateau about twelve miles from the metropolis; and Emma had leave to bring any one she liked. Varley, though he had accomplishments, had neither rank nor fashion, and was therefore not invited; but he pined to be at this splendid fête, at which, though no one was to be admitted in a *mask*, every one was to wear a masquerade dress or a fancy dress.

"I wish, dear sir," said the kind-hearted Emma to Mr. Egerton, "you would go with us, and take Varley."

"I go, in a masquerade or a fancy dress, to a ball, child!"

"Why not? you would look so well as a Druid!"

"Fy, fy! consider my profession. But perhaps you think that a clergyman is not more bound to abide by certain restraints than another man; and that he may play high, attend cock-fights and boxing-matches, and go a-masquerading?"

"No, indeed I do not. On the contrary, I think that the man whose profession it is to teach self-denial to others, should first set an example of it himself, and should never be addicted to such amusements as must lead him occasionally to association with dissolute and bad people. But that would not be the case here, and a Druid is a very venerable character."

"My dear child, no man of my age and profession can assume any character without a total surrender of *his own*. I wish Varley to go to this fête, but I can't introduce him. However, you recollect that monsieur de Lamoignan and his son will go with you and Mrs. Castlemain as your protectors; therefore there can be no impropriety in Varley's being of the party."

Accordingly the delighted Varley was told that Mrs. Castlemain would, on such a day, send her carriage for him, and take him to this splendid fête, Mr. Egerton having informed him that he must go in a fancy dress.

"What say you, Mr. Varley," said he, "to going as a Highlander? What an opportunity would the Highland dress give you of showing off your Scotch steps, and playing Scotch tunes on your flute! and the dress ready provided."

Varley, conscious the dress was becoming, and that it would give him an opportunity of great display, acceded to the proposal. "But," said he, "I will go as the *Young Norval* and spout *Douglas*. Afterwards I can join the dance and play on the flute." And Varley could neither eat, drink, nor sleep, for thinking how his constellation of talents would charm and astonish every one at the ball.

But in the meanwhile Mr. Orwell, feeling great resentment against the unknown asperser of Agatha's fame, resolved to find out, if he could, the author of the paragraph. Accordingly, he seized an opportunity of forming an acquaintance with the proprietor of the newspaper in which it appeared, and did so, just as Sir Charles Maynard, being returned from his tour, had gone to the office, and insisted that the writer of the paragraph against him should be given up, or he would proceed against the editor. But, finding that the writer, whose name they told him was Varley, was dismissed for having written this libel, and that the proprietor was not in the least to blame, he contented himself with the insertion of another paragraph, apologizing for the false statement in the first; while the proprietor could not help inveighing bitterly against Varley by name, and did so before Mr. Orwell, who soon discovered that the Varley whom Emma mentioned as a protégé of Mr. Egerton's, was the same Varley that had written the slanderous paragraph; and, obtaining the original, in Varley's own hand, he sent it over to Paris, to let Mr. Egerton see that he was fostering in his bosom the serpent that had wounded Mrs. Castlemain and her family, and might wound them again.

The day, the long-desired and expected day of the Russian nobleman's fête was at length arrived; and Varley, dressed in his Highland habiliments, to which he had added a shield and spear, in order to represent the young and gallant Douglas, was admiring himself and practising attitudes and steps before a whole-length glass. Sometimes he laughed, to admire the effect of his white teeth; sometimes he added a shade of black to his eyebrows; sometimes he laid on a deeper tint of rouge; and then finished his interesting survey of his own person by making an entrechat, to the great diversion of his opposite neighbours, who supposed it was "un *fou Ecossais*," and stood at the window to watch him.

"The poor Emma Castlemain, how she will look and love to-night!" thought Varley; "but I shall make her horribly jealous of the divine and honourable Lucy Felton!" At this moment, while he was expecting the carriage that was to convey him to the scene of his triumph, instead of that anxiously-expected carriage, he received the following note from Mr. Egerton, enclosing the paragraph in the paper in *his own hand-writing.*—"Mr. Egerton is very much concerned at being forced to inform Mr. Varley that he does not consider the writer of anonymous libels as fit to be introduced to the house of a gentleman, or admitted to the society of one.—He therefore declines all further acquaintance with Mr. Varley."

I will not attempt to describe Varley's agonies at receiving this overthrow of all his splendid expectations, amongst which, the shame of detection, not the penitence of guilt, was predominant. The consequence was, that he the next morning put his plan in execution, and set off to walk through part of France in his Highland dress, with his flute in his pocket.

After a fortnight's absence, Balfour, unable to endure a longer absence from Emma, left his father two days' journey from Paris, and returned thither to see her for a day or two. He brought with him his father's unqualified approbation of his choice, and consent to his marriage, in a letter to Mrs. Castlemain, she having written to Lord Clonawley by his son, to explain who Emma was, and the particular circumstances of her situation. This letter, and what passed between him and Lord Clonawley, Balfour with great joy and animation communicated to Mrs. Castlemain alone. But when he entered the room where Emma was, and eagerly advanced to seize her hand and press it to his lips, she shrunk from his touch with such evident coldness, and seemed so little glad to see him again, that Balfour, stung to the soul at her behaviour, gave way to all the violence of his temper; which provoked such severe sarcasms from Emma, who could not help secretly drawing comparisons between him and St. Aubyn, that Balfour left the house in an agony of resentment and despair, and almost resolved in his own mind to give up for ever, the prosecution of a suit to which he met with so ungrateful a return.

As soon as he was gone, Emma severely reproached herself for her cruelty and ingratitude, and almost felt disposed to despise herself for behaving so unkindly towards a man who really loved her, and had with manly openness avowed his love, from the powerful and degrading influence, as she considered it to be, of one who, having gained her affections, had never offered her his own, but had left her for ever, as it appeared, in a manner at once offensive and incomprehensible. But Balfour did not return any more that evening; therefore he missed the opportunity of taking advantage of the whispers of her remorse. Nor did he come the next morning at his usual hour; for, being still too angry to see Emma with composure, he joined a party of young men to the Louvre Gallery, who flattered his vanity by begging him to tell them what pictures were most worth looking at; and while he was talking loud, and showing off with all the conceit of a connoisseur, Emma and Mrs. Felton, arm-in-arm, entered the Gallery. Balfour affected not to see Emma; but, being glad to display his real or supposed knowledge before her, he went on haranguing on the art of painting, and the beauty of particular pictures.

As they came up the stairs, at the bottom of which some gentlemen had left them who had accompanied them in a walk in the Thuilleries, Emma had been rallying Mrs. Felton on the provoking sarcastic severity with which she had treated their harmless beaux, asking her whether all women of ton resembled her.

"Oh! by no means," replied Mrs. Felton. "I assure you I am unique, no servile copy I, but a daring original."

"Daring indeed," said Emma, archly; "and who shall presume to follow such a leader?"

"No woman under the rank of an honourable, or without a certain reputation for talent, should attempt it, certainly," replied Mrs. Felton, piqued at Emma's meaning smile, and thrown off her guard so much as to give way to her natural love of mortifying the pride of others; "No, my dear child, no; as you are not a person of rank in society, what would only be thought whim and spirit in me would be called rudeness in you; not that I flatter myself so far as to suppose you are likely to copy me, far from it!"

"Indeed," cried Emma laughing, "I should not presume so far; and to prevent any foolish girls from attempting a task of so much danger, I think it would be a proper measure in the King to grant you a patent, running thus; 'We grant to the honourable Lucy Felton, the sole use and benefit of certain airs and graces of her own inventing, for such a term of years; when the said Lucy Felton having made her fortune and left off business, the said airs and graces shall become the property of any lady whose rank entitles her to become a purchaser, and who thinks them worth the trouble of acquiring.'"

"So," said Mrs. Felton colouring with resentment, and secretly resolved that she would not be long unrevenged; "you can be severe, I see, and I am not sure now that my caution was unnecessary.— But what have we here? Who is that gawky youth talking in that oracular tone of voice? Oh! I see now; it is a young man whom I saw at Frescati; Lord Clonawley's son." She did not add, though she had certainly not forgotten, that the said gawky youth had eternally offended her at Frescati, because, when pressed by a gentleman to be presented to Mrs. Felton, she had overheard him reply, "No, I like neither her face, her form, her dress, her expression, nor her manner;" a severity of criticism which few women, and certainly not a Mrs. Felton could be expected to pardon.

"Don't you think," said Mrs. Felton to Emma, "that youth is mighty disagreeable? —Yet, do you know, I hear a very pretty girl is in love with him, and is going to marry him!" Then, before the blushing Emma could reply, Mrs. Felton was standing near Balfour and listening to him with profound attention; while the vain youth went on with redoubled eloquence. Mrs. Felton then, with a half-courtesy to Balfour, begged leave to profit by his remarks, and asked him some questions relative to the names of certain pictures and their subjects; which Balfour, flattered by the appeal, gave most elaborately.

"But what were you saying to these gentlemen," said she, "concerning the ignorance of artists in general?"

"I was lamenting," replied he, "that modern artists take so little trouble to excel. A painter should be everything: He should be an anatomist, that he may be able to draw accurately; he should be a sculptor, that he may know how to put flesh properly on the parts when drawn; he should be a botanist, that he may know how to paint plants with such accuracy that every botanist might swear to the class of every separate flower; he should be an architect, that he may know how to exhibit buildings correctly."

"And," interrupted Mrs. Felton with great gravity, "he should be a tailor, that he may know how to fit coat, waistcoat, and breeches properly to the body." This speech occasioned a laugh, which disconcerted Balfour; "and," added she, "after all these *should-bes*, he should have the years of Methuselah, to enable him to complete so elaborate a course of study;" then, being tired of his harangue, and wishing to give him his coup de grace, she made him another drop, and, thanking him for the trouble he had taken, said that he was one instance amongst many, of the politeness of the French nation, which, for the convenience of English travellers, had provided them with a showman of their own country.

"A showman!" cried Balfour turning pale, "Do you take me for a showman, madam? The lady with you, by informing you better, might have spared me this insult."

"This lady does not know you, I believe, sir," she replied, "and how can you call my very natural mistake an insult? for who could suppose that a man would take so much trouble, unless he was employed and paid for it?"

"Miss Castlemain," cried Balfour, "surely, in consideration of the intimacy that subsists between us, you might have prevented me from experiencing the mortification of this moment!"

"Intimacy!" exclaimed Mrs. Felton. "Sir, she disclaimed all knowledge of you."

"How can you say so?" cried Emma. "You know, before I could answer, you accosted—"

"Ay, very true; so I did;—but pray Mr. Gaw—Gawky, forgive—"

"My name is not Gawky, madam," replied Balfour colouring.

"No! wrong again, I protest;—Why, my dear, I am sure you told me the gentleman's name was Gawky."

"Mrs. Felton," replied Emma indignantly, "I beg you will not attribute to me speeches which can become no woman 'under the rank of an *honourable*,' and of '*some reputation in the world for talent*;' but remember, that what is '*only whim* and *spirit*' in you, would be '*rudeness*' in me; and Mr. Balfour knows, that to raise a laugh at the expense of another is contrary both to my habits and my inclination."—There she stopped, and the grave rebuke,

"Severe in youthful beauty, added grace Invincible."

Mrs. Felton angrily bit her lip, and felt that Emma's retort had a little damped the triumphant revenge which she had taken on Balfour, for his speech concerning her at Frescati, and on Emma for her well-deserved sarcasms; while Emma held out her hand affectionately to Balfour. But he, too angry to accept it, and be just, indignantly left the room.

"So then, I suspect," cried Mrs. Felton, taking her arm, and making her walk up and down the Gallery, "I suspect you are the pretty girl who is going to marry that handsome savage; for handsome he is, and most uncommonly so; and when you have tamed him a little, he may be worth knowing. So no wonder you answered me so spitefully;—but is it really to be?"

"Possibly," replied Emma sighing deeply, "some time or other."

"But bless me! how dismal you look! Is that the effect of the sweet prospect of marrying the man of your heart? for I conclude he is the man of your heart; else, young, beautiful, and rich, as you are, I cannot see why you should marry him."

"Nor I neither," pettishly answered Emma.

"And really, to do him justice," coolly returned Mrs. Felton, "he has a great command of words, and is very handsome as I said before;—not," added she, thinking the time was come for her to strike the stroke she meditated, "not that I think him as handsome as another Englishman, who I am sorry to say is not now in Paris, a dear friend of mine, who has lately made a great noise here, and is quite the hero of the day. I conclude you know whom I mean." And so confused was Emma at this address, that nothing but her habitual reverence for truth could have prevented her replying, "No; I know not to whom you allude." But the rising falsehood was instantaneously checked, while in a faltering voice she said, "I conclude you mean Mr. St. Aubyn."

"To be sure I do," answered Mrs. Felton. "Oh! now I recollect, by the by, that St. Aubyn is or was an old friend of yours. Yes, yes, I recollect you are the little girl to whom he once addressed some pretty lines, entitled 'To Emma, aged twelve, on her birth-day.'"

"Did Mr. St. Aubyn show you those verses?" said Emma blushing.

"O, yes! and when I said 'I should like to see how you will write to Emma aged eighteen,' he made me an answer which, to use a French phrase, m'intrigua beaucoup."

"What was it?" demanded Emma in a voice faint from emotion.

"Why, he said, 'To Emma aged eighteen I shall probably not write at all.' But I believe," she added with affected carelessness, "I quite mistook his meaning, and he has not, I fancy, written to you at all since you was eighteen."

"No, ma'am, he has not," replied Emma almost in a tone of vexation.

"That's a pity, for he writes charmingly. Indeed, now I recollect, he has not seen much of you for the last two years. It is a pity he is not in Paris. If he were, I would ask him to meet you at my hotel one day. But he is gone to see a poor sick man, the father of an emigrant whom he knows in London, who on his way hither was taken ill, and is at a village twenty miles off; for St. Aubyn is, you know, a good creature. Poor fellow! he expects to be summoned to England to see his mother; but he has promised me to come back, unless she is in danger, in order to see me across the water. He came over with me; but when I went round by Flanders, he chose to come on to Paris, in a fit of jealousy forsooth, because I took some notice of a German baron who was of my party."

All this was said with an air so natural that it deceived Emma exactly as the speaker meant it should; however, struggling with her feelings, she replied, "But what will Mademoiselle de Coulanges say to Mr. St. Aubyn's attendance on you?"

"Oh! you have heard that idle report, have you?—But I assure you there is no truth in it, none. At least, I know from undoubted authority, that when the lady's friends hinted to him that if he offered he would certainly be accepted, he honestly confessed that his affections were fixed elsewhere.—Bless me! what is the matter with you?" cried Mrs. Felton at this moment; "I fear you are going to faint; let me lead you to a seat."

"Thank you," said Emma sitting down, "I feel a giddiness in my head."

"Well, thank heaven! the complaint is not in your heart." And Emma, roused to exertion by this speech, which she did not attribute to chance, regained her composure, and with a proud feeling of insulted delicacy looked her tormentor in the face.

"I beg your pardon," said Emma; "my illness interrupted you; you were saying something about mademoiselle de Coulanges and Mr. St. Aubyn, — then it is not to be a match?"

"A match! O dear, no!—how could you believe it?"

"Why not? She is very young, very pretty, and very rich."

"Ay, but a woman may be all these, and yet not be able to attach permanently such a man as St. Aubyn." And Emma felt that this truth as it *seemed* was aimed at *her*.

"Yet St. Aubyn can *love*," resumed Mrs. Felton; "I could show you some lines of his addressed to a friend of mine."

"A friend of yours," repeated Emma, scarce knowing what she said.

"Yes. By the by, I believe I have them about me." So saying, she took a pocketbook out of her *reticule*, and taking out some MS. verses, presented them to Emma, observing, "You know his hand."

"Perfectly," answered Emma, and opened the paper. The verses were those which St. Aubyn wrote out from memory for Mrs. Felton to show Wanford, when he had owned that he had lost the copy she gave him, and which were in reality written to her by a Mr. Trevor! But Emma, too guileless herself to suspect guile in another, saw it was really St. Aubyn's hand-writing, and implicitly believed that he had addressed them to Mrs. Felton. When therefore she read

"Then be it so, and let us part,
Since love like mine has fail'd to move thee,"

a mist came over her eyes; and unable to go on, she told Mrs. Felton she would, with her leave, keep them to read at her leisure.

"By all means," replied Mrs. Felton. "The poor soul was very dismal when he wrote them; but those hours of gloom are over, and I trust that happier days are in store for him. I have a miniature of St. Aubyn at home," she added, "which I will show you some day or other."

Emma now, affecting great gaiety, talked very fast, and laughed very loud, though she said nothing at all laughable; and seeing Mr. Egerton, she challenged him to walk three times round the Thuilleries gardens before dinner; while Mrs. Felton, thinking she had said all that was necessary to convince Emma that St. Aubyn was attached to herself, bade her farewell till the next day; convinced that, though Emma secretly preferred St. Aubyn to Balfour, pride would in all probability induce her to make an effort to overcome her passion, and thereby render certain a union which at present was only probable; "and then," thought Mrs. Felton, "St. Aubyn may perhaps be mine!"

It required all Mr. Egerton's speed to keep up in any degree with Emma during their walk. The restlessness of her mind imparted itself to her movements; and as she dreaded rest, since rest would bring leisure to think, it was not till Mr. Egerton pleaded excessive fatigue, that he could prevail on her to turn her steps towards the hotel. At dinner, Emma's total want of appetite alarmed her affectionate companions.

"Do, Emma, eat some of this dish," said Mrs. Castlemain; "I ordered it on purpose for you."

"You are very good," replied Emma, "but you know I am not dainty."

Vol. III.——13

"No, my dear girl; but your appetite has lately been so indifferent, that I wished to tempt it to the best of my power."

"You are ever kind and indulgent," said Emma, a tear filling her eye, "and I will try to eat."

"How unfortunate!" exclaimed Mrs. Castlemain. "I ordered most of these things for Emma and Mr. Balfour—and Emma can't eat, and Mr. Balfour did not come."

"Did you ask, did you expect him to dinner?" said Emma eagerly.

"Yes, to be sure I did; but just now he sent a note of excuse."

"I am sorry, very sorry for it," returned Emma. "Then I fear he is seriously offended with me, though without adequate cause.—Would he were here! For never since I have known him did I feel so affectionately, so warmly towards him, as I do at this moment."

"I am prodigiously glad to hear that," cried Mrs. Castlemain; while Mr. Egerton, who had been observing Emma in perturbed silence, sighed, but spoke not. At length Emma, complaining of a bad headache, said she would go and lie down awhile, and hastily retired to her apartment.

As soon as the servants were withdrawn, Mr. Egerton said, "This ought not to be, madam. It is evident to me that Emma has some terrible weight on her mind; and with your approbation I should like to tempt her to a disclosure of it, provided you yourself will not undertake the task."

"I had rather not," replied Mrs. Castlemain; "but I wish you by all means to do so." And as soon as Emma re-appeared, it was settled that Mr. Egerton should request a private conversation with her.

Emma meanwhile lay down, but not to *rest*. Busy memory recalled every hour of her past intercourse with St. Aubyn, since his acquaintance with Mrs. Felton; and she now recollected that he must (unconsciously to himself, she admitted,) have even then imbibed sentiments for that lady, which justified the jealous suspicions she herself always *felt* relative to her; which sentiments being now, as she evidently saw, returned, had ripened into sincere, ardent, and *successful* love,—for was it possible that a woman should have the picture of a man whom she did not expect to marry? Then her thoughts dwelt on poor Mademoiselle de Coulanges, who was also said to be attached to him. But could she have felt for St. Aubyn a real attachment in so short a time, unless he had given her reason to suppose he felt attachment towards *her*? No;—and when she considered his conduct towards herself and this young lady, she could not acquit him of being that most despicable character, a male coquette; for it was evident that Mrs. Felton was, and had ever been, the only real object of his affections. She then ventured to read the verses so falsely attributed to St. Aubyn; and having read them, she fell back on her pillow, in an agony of wounded pride and jealous love. But at length the soothing thought, that the extent of her weakness was known only to herself, and that St. Aubyn, if she married before him, would never suspect that her regard for him had exceeded the bounds of friendship, tranquillized her mind in a degree; and feeling more tenderly towards Balfour, in proportion as St. Aubyn decreased in her good opinion, she at length returned to the drawing-room tolerably composed. But her composure vanished, when on her entrance Mr. Egerton took her hand, and begging to have some conversation with her in her dressing-room, led her thither in silence.

"Emma," said Mr. Egerton, after a pause of great emotion, "I have hitherto forborne, from respect to the pride and delicacy of your sex, to endeavour to remove the veil which you have so properly drawn between the feelings of your heart and the curiosity of others. But both Mrs. Castlemain and myself are so alarmed and distressed, at witnessing the present agitated state of your mind, that we conjure you, by all our past and present affection for you, to confide in that affection, and let us know what are the secret sorrows that oppress you! My dear child," added he, "recollect that our peace of mind depends on you, and that we must be wretched while we see that you are so." Here emotion stopped him from proceeding; and Emma, every feeling of pride and reserve overcome by the claims of gratitude and affection, replied,

"Put to me, sir, any question that you please, and I will answer you."

"Well then," said Mr. Egerton, "are you not going to give your hand to one man, while your heart is wholly in possession of another?"

"Had you put that question to me, sir, yesterday," replied Emma, "I must, I fear, have answered *Yes*—but to-day I feel myself justified in answering *No*."

"Indeed! can a few hours have obliterated an image so long and so deeply impressed on your heart? Are you well assured that you are not under the influence of jealousy?" Emma paused for a moment, and then, without further comment, related to Mr. Egerton the progress of her attachment to St. Aubyn; her idea that it was mutual; her jealousy of Mrs. Felton after his return from his tour; her endeavours, on principle, to return the love of Balfour; the prospect she now had of succeeding in those endeavours; and finally, the whole of what had passed between her and Mrs. Felton relative to St. Aubyn.

"Amazing!" cried Mr. Egerton. "Is it possible that St. Aubyn can be in love with her, after having known you! Answer me, Emma; did his evident emotion when he saw you in the Palace appear to you a proof of indifference and aversion, or of still struggling but concealed love?"

"Of the latter. But I am now convinced that emotion proceeded from a remorseful consciousness that he had basely endeavoured to gain my affections, without any real intention of offering me his in return."

"Impossible!" warmly replied Mr. Egerton, "my life upon his honour!"

"At least you will own," answered Emma rather indignantly, "that his avoiding me, and attending Mrs. Felton, with those verses and the picture, are very suspicious circumstances; besides his having refused the hand of Mademoiselle de Coulanges, on the plea of a prior attachment."

"Nay, that proves nothing. You as well as Mrs. Felton may be the object of that attachment."

"Well, sir," resumed Emma proudly; "but suppose that I am the object of St. Aubyn's concealed affection, concealed through dire and invincible necessity, what would you have me do? Would you have me wait humbly and patiently till he thinks fit to come and say, 'Will you marry me, dear Ally, Ally Croker?' and would you then have me make him a courtesy, and say, 'Yes, if you please to accept me, kind sir!' No! forbid it every feeling of woman's pride and woman's delicacy!"

"But is it therefore necessary that you should marry a man you do not love?"

"There is no danger of that. It will very soon be in Balfour's power, I am convinced, to convert my present feelings towards him into positive tenderness. Besides, I have ever considered a woman who has so much meanness, and such a want of self-respect, as to pine in love for a man who has either never loved or has forsaken her, to be in the next degree of vice to a woman who has forfeited her honour; and I am well convinced that I shall be able to act up to this principle completely, as soon as, by a marriage with a man who adores me, the barrier of wedded duty will be raised between me and Mr. St. Aubyn."

"But suppose Balfour, from the obsequious lover, becomes the tyrant husband?"

"He will not do so; for he is conscious of his own infirmities of temper; and I am sure the influence over him which I possess, and which my not loving him as much as he loves me will allow me to increase, as I shall not be thrown off my guard by ungovernable tenderness, will enable me to keep his temper in subjection, especially as I am tolerably sure of my own now."

"Indeed," said Mr. Egerton doubtingly, "your temper is a *corrected* temper; and were you to be united to a man of such a disposition as is possessed by one that I could name, I have no doubt of your continuing to exercise proper self-command; but, when exposed to the contagion of a violent temper, I doubt the force of bad example will awaken dormant tendencies, and that you will too late repent the rashness which led you to marry a man in hopes of improving him. Yet one question more," he added, "have you disclosed to Mr. Balfour your attachment to St. Aubyn?"

"Not directly; but I have told him of our long intimacy and friendship, and of my sorrow at his sudden and apparently unmotived estrangement from me. But I will summon resolution to tell him more, and even to own that I had unsolicited bestowed my affections. For, though a delicate woman must feel agonies at owning so degrading a truth, an ingenuous woman feels still more from concealing it."

"I do not doubt it," replied Mr. Egerton; "still the task of disclosing such a truth is a difficult one, and one from which a common mind would shrink for ever. But I expect more from an uncommon mind like yours, and principles and practice usually so pure and upright. It is your duty to be as explicit with Balfour as you have been with me. Your future happiness depends on it; for on mutual ingenuousness must all connubial happiness be built."

"I agree with you," replied Emma, faintly, "and I will tell Balfour all directly; feeling at this moment, as I have often done before, great self-upbraiding at having so long delayed to tell the degrading tale."

"Not so, Emma. Loving a St. Aubyn is no degradation; and though he never in words solicited your love, I am witness that he did so every day by his attentions."

"Then how, sir, can you excuse or account for his present conduct?"

"That I cannot do; but I still believe that time will, and satisfactorily. However, I see that you will and must marry Balfour, provided his self-love, which is I think as strong as his love, strong as that may be, is proof against knowing that you *have loved*, if you do not *still* love, another. If, when he knows that, he still perseveres in his suit, I shall feel him raised considerably in my estimation, and shall with less fear commit to him the guardianship of your happiness."

"At every risk, however," replied Emma, "I will tell him the whole truth; and then, come what come may, I shall have done my duty, and shall not have to add to the sorrows I now experience, the aggravated misery of self-condemnation."

"Spoken like yourself, my dear child," replied Mr. Egerton; while with the lofty mien and open countenance of conscious integrity, Emma, on being told that Mr. Balfour was below, desired him to be shown into her dressing-room. He entered with an expression of joy on his countenance, which surprised Emma. It was occasioned by Mrs. Castlemain having, in the joy of her heart, informed him of Emma's affectionate feelings towards him, and her hope that their union was now not only probable, but certain. Soon after, Mr. Egerton retired; and Emma, putting an immediate stop to Balfour's expressions of penitence and love, begged that he would listen to her in uninterrupted silence.

I shall not detail what Balfour's feelings were during her confession, nor his expression of those feelings. Suffice that, when she had ended, Emma said, "And now, dear Balfour! I leave you to think over alone, uninfluenced by my presence, all that I have been saying; and if, after a night's calm deliberation, you still feel inclined to entrust your happiness in my hands, come to me to-morrow morning, and I pledge myself most solemnly to tender you this hand, as a pledge of grateful, faithful, and principled affection." So saying she ran out of the room, and Balfour saw her no more that night,—a night to Emma, as well as to himself, of anxious perturbation. The next morning by eight o'clock he was at the hotel, and Emma soon after joined him.

"I come," said Balfour, as soon as he saw her, "to claim this promised hand, as I am sure that my devoted affection will at length procure to me a full return, and to you with ardent and confiding love I willingly entrust my happiness."

"Take it! it is yours!" said Emma, blushing and sighing as she spoke; and Balfour, seeing Mrs. Castlemain enter the room, led Emma up to her, and begged her blessing on them.

"This is as I hoped," she cried, mixing tears with her blessings. And Mr. Egerton, on hearing what had passed, endeavoured to pronounce his congratulations as steadily as Mrs. Castlemain; but he could not do it; and it was a relief to him to hear that Balfour was forced to set off immediately to his father, who was taken very ill on the road.

Before he departed, he candidly told Emma that he did not approve her having much intercourse with Mrs. Felton. "And I think," said he, "you yourself cannot desire it now. For, if she is to be the wife of St. Aubyn, it will be impossible for you to talk with her on her prospects, without betraying the deep interest you once felt in him yourself; and if she be his mistress, she is an improper acquaintance for you."

"His mistress!" cried Emma; "such a suspicion never entered my mind."

"Very likely; but I dare say it may be a very just one, notwithstanding."

"At any rate," replied Emma, "I do not wish to see much of Mrs. Felton. Besides, I am not a little inclined to resent her rudeness to you."

This speech delighted Balfour, and he asked her how she would avoid Mrs. Felton.

"I will tell you how," said Emma. "Your sister Fanny is very unwell at Montmorenci, and has sent to request me to visit her. To-morrow morning I have promised to accompany two friends from K——, just arrived, to the Petits Augustins; but before the evening I will set off for Montmorenci, and stay there as long as my grandmother will spare me." And Balfour, satisfied with this arrangement, bade her adieu, to return to his father, with more tranquillity of mind than usual. Emma too, considering her fate as fixed, exerted herself to preserve the appearance of content, as one means towards procuring the reality, and she set off to the Petits Augustins, with a quiet heart and a calm countenance. A visit to the tombs was indeed congenial with her feelings; and what so likely to speak peace to each rebellious passion, and soberize the vanity of human wishes and expectations, as the contemplation of those mementos of mortality, and the lowly beds of kings and queens, of heroes and legislators, who having been the sport of their own passions and the passions of others, there, heedless of their enmity while living, sleep beside each other in the cold forgetfulness of the grave, reminding long suffering and patient affliction, that at last her miseries, like theirs, will find a resting place and an oblivion.

"When I look upon the tombs of the great," says Addison, "every emotion of envy dies in me; when I read the epitaphs of the beautiful, every inordinate desire goes out; when I meet with the grief of parents upon a tombstone, my heart melts with compassion; when I see the tomb of the parents themselves, I consider the vanity of grieving for those whom we must quickly follow."

Emma, in pensive silence, listened to the remarks of her companions, as they passed from the monuments of one age to those of another, till at last they entered the Elysium, and the tomb of Abelard and Eloisa was pointed out to them by their guide. As they approached, they saw a man evidently absorbed in a deep reverie, leaning his head on his hands against this interesting monument. The gentleman who accompanied Emma, on seeing him, said to her in a low voice,

"O'er the cold marble shall they join their heads,
And drink the falling tear each other sheds."

But this poor gentleman can only drink his own. What a pity that his love is not with him, to realize the fancy of the poet!"

Emma was about to reply, when, the gentleman raising his head, she could discern his profile sufficiently to see that she beheld St. Aubyn! and overpowered, bewildered, and surprised, she became heedless of her steps, and fell over a piece of marble that lay across the path.

St. Aubyn turning round, and seeing the accident, ran to her assistance as eagerly as her friends, and felt full as much emotion as she did when he recognised in the pale and trembling being whom he supported, and whom pain and emotion both made ready to faint, that Emma, whose probable marriage and attachment to another, having just been communicated to him by Mrs. Felton, had made him wander forth he scarcely knew whither, till, finding himself near the Petits Augustins, he had entered the garden, and almost unconsciously had drawn near the tomb of the unhappy lovers.

"I hope you are not much hurt," cried he in a tone of tenderness, with which Emma's ear and her heart also were but too well acquainted; while Emma, recovering herself a little, replied that the pain was only momentary, and that she was already better, withdrawing herself as she spoke from his supporting arm, and venturing to lift her eyes to his; but they shrunk immediately from the tender expression of his glance, and she felt relieved; when, sighing deeply, St. Aubyn bowing coldly round, wished them good morning, and suddenly disappeared.

"Is it possible," said Emma mentally, "that a man happy and successful in his love should be found almost in tears reclining against that monument? Is it possible, either, that the lover of Mrs. Felton could look at me with such an expression in his eyes?" And Emma certainly felt much happier than when she came to the Musée.

"Well," said her female companion, "I am afraid that uncommonly handsome young man is more hurt than you were, Miss Castlemain; for I never saw such a look of love as he gave you! Did you ever see him before?"

"O dear, yes," replied Emma in visible confusion; "it was Mr. St. Aubyn." And her companions, seeing her distress, forbore to press her further on the subject; while Emma, as they returned, forced herself to talk with unceasing volubility.

Mr. Egerton meanwhile had shut himself up in his own room, to reflect on the important decisions that had taken place on that and the preceding day; and in spite of his high reverence for Emma's principles, and his respect for the apparent motives that actuated her to accept Frederic Balfour, he was convinced that, unknown to herself, Temper was at the bottom of her decision. He was of opinion, that what is called pride, in a man and woman, both by themselves and others, is often nothing but temper in one of its various modifications, denominated *pique* or *wounded self-love*. And he felt assured that, had not Emma's pride and jealousy been roused by the communications of Mrs. Felton, she would have taken more time to deliberate, before she gave an irrevocable promise to bestow her hand on a man towards whom she well knew that she had not a sentiment resembling what she felt for St. Aubyn, and had long learnt to denominate love. Nor, indeed, did Mr. Egerton see in Balfour's attachment for her, the symptoms of a real affection. Her beauty had charmed him at first sight, and he found his taste justified by the admiration of all who beheld her; and as he was never accustomed to know an unsatisfied wish, he resolved to make himself the envy of others, by obtaining this valuable prize. But her coldness threw obstacles in his way; and obstacles to a temper such as his was, only induced him to persevere the more. His self-love indeed was very near getting the better of all other considerations, when he heard that Emma loved another; but it was counteracted by the wish he felt to triumph over St. Aubyn, who he believed loved Emma in spite of the representations of an artful woman, such as he considered Mrs. Felton to be, for he had become jealous of St. Aubyn's fame; who was now not only called the English hero, but "le bel Anglois," a title exclusively Balfour's till St. Aubyn reappeared at Paris.

"No, no," said he mentally, "he shall not triumph over me in every way, and I will marry the woman whom he loves, and have the felicity of forcing her to love me in return."

Accordingly he persevered, and Emma promised to be his. Meanwhile, though Mr. Egerton could not read Balfour's heart, he was so unhappy as to suspect that love alone was not the motive that overcame the influence of his pride, and induced him to forget so soon that Emma had loved, and probably still loved another.

He was still indulging these sad thoughts, when Emma and her companions returned. They found Mrs. Felton and Mrs. Castlemain, to whom the latter had communicated the news that Emma had accepted Balfour; and that lady could not help suspecting that her communications had been instrumental in influencing her determination.

Mrs. Felton expressed great surprise and sorrow, at the idea of Emma's departure for so many days, then begged to see her alone; when, taking a case from her pocket, she said she had brought St. Aubyn's picture to show her. Emma, provoked at her indelicate forwardness in displaying this picture, and also in her heart, a little distrustful of her truth, since the rencontre with St. Aubyn, was irritated into self-command, and, looking at the picture with great calmness, replied,

"It is like, that is to say, it is like what he now is, rather than what he was, for I never saw a man more altered; and I am sure he does not look like a happy and successful lover."

Mrs. Felton blushed at this observation; and hastily said, "Pray when did you see him?"

"Just now," she replied; and Mrs. Felton turned pale; while Emma, with great composure, added, "we found him reclining on the tomb of Abelard and Eloisa, and he evidently had been in tears."

"O, yes! O, yes!" in a hurried manner answered Mrs. Felton, "he is very uneasy about his mother, and thinks of setting off directly for England; that is all, I assure you, that afflicts him." And Emma with a sarcastic smile, which she meant Mrs. Felton to perceive, as she turned from her, in silence led the way back to the drawing-room.

The truth was, that Mrs. St. Aubyn was better, not worse. Still her son, unable to bear to be in Paris during the time of Emma's marriage, set off for England as soon as he left the Petits Augustins; and perhaps, like Emma herself, he was in his heart cheered and consoled by the meeting of that morning, and the emotion that he had witnessed.

As soon as Mrs. Felton and her friends from K—— had taken leave, Emma set off in Mrs. Castlemain's carriage for Montmorenci, and alone; for the only woman-servant that they had brought with them was wanted to attend on her grandmother, who had had at least the wisdom to teach both Agatha and Emma habits of independence, habits which rendered the poverty of the former more bearable than it would otherwise have been, and guarded the other against many inconveniences and difficulties to which those women are exposed who have been accustomed to depend entirely on servants for the duties of the toilette. Yes, Emma and Agatha, though heiresses, could really dress and undress themselves!

"I shall see you I hope during my visit, sir," said Emma to Mr. Egerton, as she got into the carriage, and proceeded on her journey,— little conscious what trials and what dangers awaited her at Montmorenci.

But to return to St. Aubyn. — It was lucky for him that he set off for England when he did, as by that means he avoided receiving a letter, desiring him, if he wished to see his mother alive, to return immediately; therefore, being already on the road when this letter reached Paris, he was spared the agony of travelling, an agony insupportable to an affectionate heart, in terror lest he should arrive too late. As it was, though he expected to find his mother ill, he did not expect to find her dying; and when he reached Keswick, he found that, so far from the account given in the letter, which never reached him, being the literal truth, Mrs. St. Aubyn was likely to live some weeks longer, though all hope of her recovery must prove to be vain.

After having shown Mrs. St. Aubyn in the degraded light of a detected criminal, I could not venture to obtrude her on the notice of my readers again, till I could exhibit her in that sad and fearful state in which one is disposed to pardon the most guilty their offences, because they can offend no more, and may soon be within the reach of that judgment, more terrible than any punishment which human justice can inflict.

When he arrived, the surgeon who attended Mrs. St. Aubyn, seeing him drive up, met him at the door, in order to prepare him for the change which had taken place in her during his absence. The wish of serving an interesting emigrant family, whom some peculiar circumstances of distress had thrown in St. Aubyn's way, as much as a desire of seeing France, had induced him to go abroad; an excursion in which his uncle, being by chance in a good humour when he requested his leave to undertake it, enabled him to indulge himself in a manner worthy of his expectations in life; while his poor mother taught herself even to rejoice in his absence, by the thought of the pretty things he would bring her from Paris. St. Aubyn, therefore, could not accuse himself, with justice, of having violated any duty by his foreign tour. Still, when he saw his certainly, though slowly, declining parent, his agony was so great as to make him bitterly reproach himself for having left her so long. In the first place, indeed, he had left her, to fulfil a military duty; but if he had not gone to France, he thought his attentive care and tenderness might have prevented her being guilty of the imprudence which brought on her complaint, as during his leave of absence he should have returned to the Vale-House, and been with her at the time when her love of youthful dress had made her go to a sort of fête champêtre on the lake, which was extended into the evening, too lightly clothed to bear the chill of the autumnal wind, especially as at that very moment she was oppressed with a severe cold.

When St. Aubyn saw her first on his return, she was sitting up in an easy chair, breathing with difficulty, and one meagre cheek pale as death itself, while the other was glowing with the bright red of fever. Her son, scarcely able to control his emotion, sprung towards her, and reclining her drooping head against his bosom, wept over her in silence.

"Ay, my dear Henry," she faintly articulated, "you little knew how ill I was, or I am sure you would have come sooner; but I am now getting well very fast; so don't distress yourself, for you know the sight of you will do me quite as much good as medicine.— Well, but I hope you have brought me some pretty gowns and trinkets from Paris. I have been quite reckoning upon them, I do assure you." And St. Aubyn, glad for an excuse to leave the room and give vent to his feelings, went in search of the expected presents. They consisted of fans, gold pins, brooches, &c., and two pieces of sarsnet for gowns.

The poor invalid was delighted with all she saw, and eagerly looked forward to the time when she should excite the envy and admiration of the town and country by wearing her Paris finery; while St. Aubyn, unable to bear this language of hope, which he well knew was the result of mortal disease, was again and again obliged to leave the room, in order to conceal the emotion which he felt. One of the pieces of sarsnet was dark, and his mother told him it was too old and grave for her; but the other, being what was called a French white, suited her taste exactly, as she pronounced it to be very becoming to the complexion.

That evening, while his mother by the aid of anodynes procured a little sleep, St. Aubyn visited Mr. Hargrave, who received him very graciously, nay, with a degree of involuntary respect; for the colonel had written to him a detail of his nephew's bravery, and the praises bestowed on him by the First Consul; and though his jealousy of his nephew was considerably increased by the means, his pride in him increased in proportion, and spite of himself he felt that he was in the presence of a superior.

St. Aubyn told him that he earnestly desired he would allow him to resign his commission, as, if he had not an insuperable objection to remain amongst men who had been so willing to disgrace and discard him, he could not bear to be under the necessity of leaving his mother, as his attentions and care, if they could not prolong her life, might at least smooth her way to death.

"Pshaw!" cried Mr. Hargrave, to whom the idea of his sister's death was as insupportable as to her son from different motives, "the old girl will recover again, never fear; however, resign and welcome if you choose. But harkye! don't come hither any more with that ugly long face, for your mother is in no more danger than I am, unless that ghostly visage of yours should frighten her into convulsions, by reminding her too powerfully of her latter end." And St. Aubyn, not feeling himself able to endure this sort of coarse banter, so uncongenial to his feelings, took an early farewell of his uncle and returned to Keswick, where he was resolved in future to pass every day and every night,—a determination very disagreeable to Mr. Hargrave; but as he was a little in awe of what other people might say, he did not venture to forbid St. Aubyn's performance of the duties of a son.

If Mr. Hargrave had been possessed of supernatural power, his sister would have borne about "a charmed life," and her existence would have been at least as long as his own. Not for any great affection that he bore her, but because with her life, he knew, all his power over St. Aubyn must end, as he, for her dear sake alone, had endured in patient silence the goadings of his tyranny, and even sacrificed on the altar of filial piety the best and deepest wishes of his pure and deeply feeling heart.

I will now explain the reasons of his mysterious conduct towards the family at the White Cottage. I have before said, that Mr. Hargrave in his heart never liked either Mrs. Castlemain or Mr. Egerton, for many cogent reasons. In the first place, they were of ancient families, and he was apt to hate any one who possessed an advantage which must be for ever unenjoyed by himself;—in the next place, he knew that they preferred his nephew to himself, another unpardonable fault; and finally, he had never forgiven what he considered as the triumph of that conceited girl, Emma Castlemain, over those splenetic effusions of his malignant disposition, of which, though he had not power to overcome them, he had sense enough to be conscious and ashamed. Still he knew not how, respected and respectable as Mrs. Castlemain was, to refuse what he saw would probably be proposed to him, namely, a union between his nephew and Emma, as he foresaw that every one of his acquaintance would blame him for such a refusal, and his detestable temper be more commented upon and abused than ever. But the guilt of his sister, and the disclosure which followed, put it in his power to prevent such an offer being made, and to cause his innocent nephew to appear at least as much in fault as himself in dropping the acquaintance of the family at the White Cottage. While his pride was irritated to madness by Mr. Egerton's proposal of emancipating St. Aubyn from his tyranny by maintaining both the son and the mother, the soothing consciousness came over his mind, that the reputation of his unhappy sister was now in his power, and by that means his noble-minded nephew also.

The day after that fatal business of the banknote, he called his nephew into his study, and told him that he saw very clearly his devoted attachment to Miss Castlemain; but as he never would consent to his union with her, he peremptorily forbade him to think of her more, or even to continue his acquaintance with any one of those three disagreeables, as he chose to call them; while St. Aubyn, who, had learnt from him the preceding evening Mr. Egerton's offer in his favour, and who thought he might at least accept from that gentleman's bounty the means of procuring a livelihood for himself, though he shrank from the idea of incurring a pecuniary obligation without the prospect of returning it, coolly assured his uncle, that he could not and would not resign those hopes and that society which alone gave a value to existence; but accepting Mr. Egerton's offer for his mother till by his aid he could, by labouring in a profession, be rich enough to maintain her herself, he should, though reluctantly, resign his claims to his uncle's favour and support, if they could be retained only at the expense of sacrificing his dearest affections and friendships.

"Then this is your decision, is it?" asked Mr. Hargrave with the smile of a demon.

"It is."

"Then hear me, sir," he replied. "I will this instant take the most dreadful and solemn oath that ever passed the lips of man, that if you persist in refusing to give up, gradually indeed, but finally, and without assigning any reason, all intercourse with those accursed people who have seduced your affections from me to fix them on themselves, I will proclaim to the whole town of Keswick and to its neighbourhood, that the mother who is the beloved object of your filial, nay, I might say, your paternal care, that mother bequeathed to you and your protecting love by your father on his death-bed, is an unprincipled wretch, and a detected thief. Her reputation, sir, shall be blasted wherever her person is known, till even the sentimentalists at the White Cottage shrink from her with aversion, and she pines away under the agonies of wounded vanity and pride, till she sinks into the shelter of the grave!"

St. Aubyn, on hearing this dreadful threat, which he well knew that Mr. Hargrave was capable of executing, sunk on a chair horror-struck, and almost heart-broken; and it was some minutes before he was composed enough even to think; and when he was, misery seemed to encompass him, till that filial piety, which in him was a principle as much as a feeling, held out to him consolation for the sorrows to which it doomed him; and convinced that in time, at least, every sacrifice to duty is rewarded, he faintly assured his uncle that his wishes should be obeyed, and he would gradually, but ultimately, break off all intercourse with the family at the White Cottage.

"But I must have your oath, sir!" cried Mr. Hargrave. And St. Aubyn, firmly grasping and devoutly kissing that book, whence his courage to devote himself was derived, took the oath required, and a few hours after wrote the letter which alarmed and distressed Mr. Egerton.

But spite of his oath, he felt that even the fear of betraying himself would make him do so involuntarily, if he continued to see or converse at all even with Mr. Egerton; and rigidly indeed did this most exemplary son fulfil the painful duty that his cruel relation imposed.

Now, however, the moment was come when the grave was in reality opening to shelter his mother from every evil that a tyrant could inflict, and free his noble victim from the chains that had galled him so long; but yet not, alas! time enough to restore to him those hopes which once he had delighted to indulge.

Mr. Hargrave, averse to believe the unwelcome truth, that the hour of St. Aubyn's deliverance approached, persisted to think his sister was in no danger; and, as he had never condescended to visit her, he could not be convinced of her situation by ocular demonstration.

But three days after St. Aubyn's return, and while he was watching in silent sorrow over that fading parent, who little suspected that she was the unworthy cause of his separation from the friends whom he loved best, he was informed that his uncle was in the next room, and desired to see him; and St. Aubyn, wondering at this unusual visit, waited on him in the adjoining apartment.

Mr. Hargrave met him with smiles unusually gracious; and after asking how the old girl was, more from habit than feeling, (for he did not wait to hear the answer,) he told St. Aubyn, that he came to speak to him on important business, and to put him in the way of making his fortune with very little trouble, and that of the most agreeable kind.

St. Aubyn, shocked at his levity at a moment so serious, only bowed his head as awaiting an explanation. It came too soon; for Mr. Hargrave called to propose to him a marriage with a young lady, the heiress of a very rich tradesman, who had seen him, and admired him prodigiously, and whose father was very desirous of the connexion. "For my part," added Mr. Hargrave, "it suits me exactly; for the girl's father is a man of yesterday like myself, and therefore can't be always throwing his rotten old ancestors in my face, like her majesty of Castlemain. So hark ye, my boy! I desire you will, as soon as your mother gets better, set off for town, and fall a courting with all your might."

"Never, never, sir," replied St. Aubyn. "To your will I resigned every hope of earthly happiness, except what arose from the consciousness of duty fulfilled; but never will I marry at the bidding of any created being, though utter ruin of every worldly prospect were the instant result of my determination."

"Do not provoke me, sir!" replied Mr. Hargrave, "remember, remember who is in my power."

"I do remember," solemnly replied St. Aubyn; "but at the same time I know that you dare not use that power against her."

"Dare not! It is false. If you refuse to obey me, before I return home, I will blast your mother's fame for ever!"

"No, sir, no," again resumed St. Aubyn, "I defy you to be so base and so brutal! Sir, I will not allow you to calumniate yourself thus. You are not the cruel and wicked man that you represent yourself to be. You have a heart capable of human feelings and human sympathies; and once more I *defy* you, at a moment like this, to utter aught against my dying mother, and your dying sister! Look there, sir!" he added, throwing open the door of his mother's chamber.

Mrs. St. Aubyn was sitting up in the bed, and looking at herself in a pocket-glass. On seeing her brother, an exclamation of joy escaped her, and she eagerly begged him to come in. At first he did not, for he could not obey her. With her face fallen away, even to the slender dimensions of sickly infancy, her teeth frightfully white from the transparency incident to disease, her eyes radiant from fever, and her cheeks glowing with the unwholesome bloom of consumption, while her oppressed breathing betrayed the nature and the danger of her illness,—Mr. Hargrave beheld that Henrietta, whose beauty had once been his pride, whose weakness had made her his dependant, and whose days he was conscious of having embittered by the terrible inflictions of his oppressive temper.

"Why do you not come to my bedside?" repeated Mrs. St. Aubyn, while Mr. Hargrave stood gazing on her in silence, the big tear swelling in his eye, and his voice choked by strong emotion. At length he drew near, and, grasping her meagre and burning hand, just articulated, "I did not think you had been so ill," and burst into tears.

"No; I thought you did not, or you would have come to see me," said Mrs. St. Aubyn, who always esteemed a visit from her rich brother as a great favour. "But I am getting well fast now,—only see what a fine colour I have got! all my own, too, I assure you—not rouge—you don't like rouge, you know. And Henry has brought me such beautiful gowns! and such pretty things! The first time I come to dine with you, brother, I shall put some of them on."

Mr. Hargrave, overcome by surprise and a variety of emotions, vainly endeavoured to answer her. At last, he grasped her hand convulsively, kissed that cheek, now becoming as wan as it was red before, then, without looking at St. Aubyn, left the room and the house.

"Well, did you ever see the like?" cried Mrs. St. Aubyn, as soon as he was gone. "But that is so like my brother! When I was very ill, he never came near me, as if he did not care a farthing for me; and now that I am so much better, he comes to see me, and cries as if I was dying!"

St. Aubyn could not answer her, but he felt certain in his own mind that his mother's reputation would remain *unhurt*.

The next day Mr. Hargrave sent a confidential servant to offer St. Aubyn any sum of money that he wanted, to defray the expenses of illness, and begging that he would send for a physician from London, if he thought any thing could save her. St. Aubyn was affected even to tears, at this proof of remorseful affection; but returned for answer, that the physician in the neighbourhood, on whose judgment he could rely, had assured him that all hope was over. The surgeon, meanwhile, who was brother to the rector of the parish, had thought it right to hint to Mrs. St. Aubyn, that she had better settle her affairs; and ventured to ask her, if he should request his brother to read prayers to her. On hearing this, her surprise and her anger were beyond description.

"What, sir, are you ignorant enough to think me dying," she exclaimed, "and cruel enough to tell me so? No, sir, I am not dying; and when I want you and your brother, I will send for you. Till then I desire you not to come near my house." This scene, when related to St. Aubyn, gave him increased pain; and he told the surgeon that those religious rites, which, when desired, were soothing and salutary to the conscious sufferer, would be only irritating and alarming to a being who persisted in the belief that her danger was over, and whose mind was therefore not in a state to profit by the visit he recommended.

Another month Mrs. St. Aubyn struggled with her disorder; but at the end of that period she sunk unconsciously into the sleep of death, breathing her last on the bosom of him whom, in the pride of her heart, she had proclaimed to be "the best of sons."

Though her death freed St. Aubyn from a thraldom that was become insupportable, he felt it with bitterness. He too felt as if he were alone in the world; as if he had lost the only being that really loved him, and whose interests were the same as his own. Besides, as we are all, I am convinced, more attached by the sense of the benefits we confer, than of those which we receive, St. Aubyn felt himself bound to his mother the more, from the consciousness of the sacrifices which he had made for her sake. He had not seen his uncle since his visit to desire him to marry; he now wrote to him to tell him all was over, and to say that he wished his mother to be buried by his father in the family vault at St. Aubyn, if he could gain leave to do so from its present possessor, that estate having passed again to a new owner.

Mr. Hargrave did not write an answer; but he sent his confidential servant again to say, that Mr. St. Aubyn was welcome to bury his mother how and where he pleased, and to draw on him for any sum that he desired. The servant at the same time informed him that his uncle was on the point of marriage with a young lady, who, with her mother, was then staying at the Vale-House; but that, out of compliment to his sister's memory, he meant to delay the ceremony a month.

It was indeed true that Mr. Hargrave, finding that St. Aubyn would now be no longer the slave of his will, resolved to marry, hoping to have a child of his own, in order to disinherit and punish his nephew.

But St. Aubyn felt more surprise than mortification at the news, and instantly prepared to fulfil the mournful task that awaited him; and having obtained leave from a Mr. Browne, the agent of the gentleman to whom St. Aubyn now belonged, and who was at that time abroad, to let his mother be interred in the family vault, he set off for that estate, which though only twelve miles off, he had not seen since the death of his father, to perform the last duties to the parent whom he had lost.

St. Aubyn was too conversant with the virtue of self-command to disturb the sacred solemnity by any bursts of grief, and in calm and silent melancholy he witnessed the last rites, and listened to the affecting service; but when it was over he desired to be shown into the vault, and suffered to remain there a short time alone. Then he gave vent to the long-smothered agony of his soul, and then he gratified his affectionate triumph also; then too he reaped the reward of his patient and self-denying virtue, for he threw himself on the coffin of his father; and as he did so his heart throbbed with the proud consciousness that he had punctually fulfilled the promise given to that dying father, and, to save the mother confided to his care, had not hesitated a moment to sacrifice himself. St. Aubyn had followed the dictates of a blind impulse, and had for the bravery that he displayed been honoured with the title of hero, and the praises of a hero. But his claims to that name were founded on a better right; he was a hero in domestic life; in the rugged field of self-denial he had fought the most difficult of all fights, he had warred against temper and his own conflicting interests and passions, he had struggled for, and had obtained the greatest of *all victories*, a conquest over *himself*.

When St. Aubyn had taken his last look at all that now remained of his parents, he asked permission to see once more the well-remembered house; and on entering it, he found that the servant who took care of it, had with officious civility provided refreshments for him and the surgeon who accompanied him. But St. Aubyn could not eat; and outstepping his guide, he passed with eager and breathless emotion from one room to another, till he entered an apartment decorated with family pictures, amongst which, the first that met his eye was a fine whole-length of his mother, with him, a child, on her lap. St. Aubyn looked at it, shuddered, and turned away; but recovering himself, he turned round again, and gazed on its companion, a whole-length picture of his father, the eyes of which, as they looked directly forward, seemed to meet the glistening eyes and affectionate glance of his son. St. Aubyn continued to gaze on this picture, and with a self-approving feeling that almost recompensed him for all his sorrows, "Thank God, I can bear to look him in the face!" he exclaimed aloud; then bursting into tears, he hurried through the other rooms, and hastened to the garden to visit the best-remembered walks.

"It was here," thought he, "that I bounded along with all the vivacity of childhood; and there, I remember, I used to sit while I learned my first lessons."

The sound of the village-clock had a peculiarity in it which he had not forgotten; and as it struck, it seemed to his ear like the voice of a long-separated friend. But at last the painful present proved superior to the pleasant associations and remembrances of past times; and not daring to trust himself in the manor-house again, he beckoned his companion, jumped into the morning coach, and bade, as he believed, an eternal adieu to the scenes of his childhood, and the last home of his beloved parents.

They were not above six miles on their return to Keswick, when the coachman was desired to stop, and a horseman rode up to the window. It was one of Mr. Hargrave's servants, who came to desire St. Aubyn to gallop with all possible expedition to the Vale-House, as his uncle, just as he had taken the pen in his hand to sign the marriage articles, was seized with a paralytic stroke, and his life was despaired of, though his senses were returned; that, when asked whether his nephew should be sent for, his countenance expressed pleasure, and with a nod of approbation, he tried to say "Yes—Henry;" and the servant came off immediately. St. Aubyn instantly mounted the servant's horse, and was out of sight in a moment.

He found his uncle quite sensible, but nearly speechless; and St. Aubyn, whose heart was rendered more than usually susceptible, sobbed audibly, as he leaned over the pillow of the invalid, who appeared evidently gratified by the emotion he expressed; and pressing his hand with that which was unstricken with disease, he said with difficulty, "Good—Henry—kind—" and he seemed uneasy whenever St. Aubyn left the bedside.

This chamber of death was not at all cheered by those quiet, yet touching attentions which sickness usually insures; and St. Aubyn could not help contrasting it with the sick chamber of his mother. He had found Mrs. St. Aubyn, whose manners had always been kind and unoffending, surrounded by all the little comforts which her sick state required. Her servant and her nurse were tender and attentive, her neighbours and friends assiduous and profuse in their offers of service; and all that could be done to save and assist her had been done even before he arrived. But no such anxiety, no such actively kind feelings had been called forth in Mr. Hargrave's family and acquaintance, by his sudden and mortal illness.

The violence and obliquities of his temper had alienated all hearts from him; and as it was soon ascertained that his recovery was impossible, his servants and dependants, no longer actuated either by fear or hope, administered to his wants with apathy and neglect; and like the beasts in the fable, trampled on the lion when dead, whom living they dreaded to encounter. While Mrs. Beaumont, the lady who was going to sacrifice her daughter to Mr. Hargrave, believing that he had made a will in favour of the latter, did not wish to have his life preserved, and therefore gave no orders to that purpose; and the servants, who loved St. Aubyn as much as they disliked their master, felt their indifference towards him increased by their resentment at his having resolved to marry, in order to injure the interest of his nephew.

But as soon as St. Aubyn arrived the scene changed; the first tears which he shed over the restless bed of the invalid, softened their hearts towards him also; and when he ordered the same physician to be sent for who had attended his mother, blaming at the same time their remissness in not having sent for him immediately, his orders were obeyed with the most exemplary alacrity, and all that attendance could do for the sufferer was instantly put in action.

Mr. Hargrave appeared evidently disturbed and angry when Mrs. Beaumont, the mother of his intended wife, came into the room; and when with officious civility she offered to shift his pillow, or give him any medicine, he waved her from him with a sort of horror, and would take nothing from any hand but that of his nephew. Here again was a triumph for St. Aubyn! His years of patient forbearance, and the fulfilment of painful duties, had won for him even the affection of this strange, wayward, and misanthropical relation; and at that awful moment when ourselves and others appear to us as they really are, St. Aubyn's virtues rose in full remembrance before Mr. Hargrave, and he coveted and enjoyed to receive from him those affectionate aids and attentions which forcibly spoke that all his unkindness was forgotten, and his cruelties forgiven.

The next day he grew evidently weaker and weaker, and seemed in great pain because he could not articulate what he wished to say; but towards evening he grasped St. Aubyn's hand repeatedly, and indistinctly uttered, "You—all—love—you—give—all—yours." —In a day or two after it was St. Aubyn's mournful task to close the eyes of his last surviving relation.

St. Aubyn, now accompanied by the medical attendants and the confidential servant, made a strict search for a will; for though what his uncle seemed struggling to say implied that there was no will, and he consequently would inherit every thing, yet he could not believe that, in his anger for his disobedience, Mr. Hargrave had not willed away his fortune from him. But he was mistaken. No will could be found. Therefore, after writing to the Cumberland and London bankers to inquire whether they had a will in their custody, and receiving an answer in the negative, St. Aubyn was convinced that his uncle meant him to be his sole heir, and he proceeded accordingly.

Poor St. Aubyn! How often, while reflecting on the immense possessions which now were his, did he recollect Mr. Egerton's expression, as he grieved by the cold corse of Clara Ainslie! "It comes too late!" said he in the bitterness of his heart, when he found that the long-expected living was his; and the same expression often hovered on the lip of St. Aubyn, for the same consciousness throbbed powerfully at his heart.

As Mrs. Beaumont had not offered to leave the house, and St. Aubyn, out of respect to his uncle's memory, wished to show her and her daughter every possible civility, he suffered them to continue his guests, and three days before the funeral was to take place he requested an interview with the ladies.

Mrs. Beaumont was a vulgar, unfeeling, tyrannical, avaricious, rapacious woman, and she had forced her mild and timid daughter to sacrifice herself for riches to an old and unamiable man; knowing too, as she did so, that her daughter was engaged to another whom she loved with the tenderest affection. Nothing could exceed Mrs. Beaumont's anger and disappointment when she heard that no will could be found; and she did not scruple to hint that wills had been known to be spirited away; for she knew that Mr. Hargrave's chief motive for marrying was pique against his nephew; and she flattered herself that, when every thing was fixed for his marriage with her niece, whom he met with during his last journey to London at the house of his broker, he would have made a will immediately in her favour. This idea had made her contented with the very paltry settlement of five hundred per annum, which this rich man offered her daughter, being much too wise not to make it his young wife's interest to behave well to him, that his will might remedy the scantiness of the settlement. But Mrs. Beaumont was apt to flatter herself, and her disappointments were of course frequent and violent.

When St. Aubyn waited on her, she was still so angry that he expected she would every minute declare that it was a scandalous shame his uncle should have presumed to die before he married her daughter; and she certainly did say she had never met with such usage before in her life. But seeing St. Aubyn looking at her daughter with admiring eyes, she changed her tone; and wisely considering that the nephew would make a much better son-in-law than the uncle, she took care to let St. Aubyn know that a marriage with Mr. Hargrave was much against Miss Beaumont's will; for, like all young women, she would have preferred a *young* man. Then followed a detail of all her daughter's qualifications to render the marriage state happy; and when it was ended, she had the pleasure of seeing St. Aubyn take her blushing and distressed child by the hand, and request a private conversation with her in another room, whither he conducted her. But while the delighted Mrs. Beaumont was saying to herself, "Ay; I am the woman to manage after all; let me alone; I am always sure of my market," St. Aubyn, with many apologies for the liberty he was taking, requested to know whether it was really against her will that the engagement with his uncle was entered into? And the poor girl with many tears assured him, that she would much rather have died than have been the wife of Mr. Hargrave.

"May I now venture to ask, if there was any man whom you preferred?" And her silence, her downcast eye, and blushing cheek evidently told that there was.

"Your silence answers my question sufficiently," replied St. Aubyn; "and I can only excuse to you my freedom in asking you the question, by telling you my reasons for it.—Had death delayed his summons to my poor uncle only a short time, you would have been enabled, by independence, to resist in future any attempt of your no doubt fond, but mistaken parent to force you into a hated, and, in my mind, unprincipled marriage; and marriages of such a nature are so abhorrent to my feelings, that I will always do all in my power to prevent them. Therefore, for my own sake, my dear Miss Beaumont, I beg you to accept from me a deed of settlement of two hundred a year on you for life." He could not go on; for the poor girl, overcome with his generosity, interrupted him with such clamorous expressions of feeling, that it was doubtful whether he must not have summoned her mother to her assistance. St. Aubyn had heard from his uncle's physician a very high character of this poor girl; and wishing to free her from the tyranny of her mother, of whom report spoke ill, he resolved to give her what he could not possibly miss from his income, in order to insure her the independence which she deserved. He felt also still more inclined to serve her, when he learnt that she was in love; and suspected that poverty might be the cause that that love was hopeless. As soon, therefore, as she recovered her composure, he asked her if her lover (politely saying that he concluded she was beloved in return) would have any objection to take orders; and the artless girl, thrown off her guard, replied, "Sir, Mr. Alton has been in orders some time."

"Alton!" cried St. Aubyn; "Alton! Was he of Trinity College, Cambridge?"

"He was, sir; and I have often heard him mention your kindness to him."

This information delighted St. Aubyn, for he found the lover of Miss Beaumont was that very Alton whom he used to defend against the vulgar, low-life banter of Popkison and his friends. St. Aubyn then informed her that he had long esteemed her lover, and that he now liked him still better for the choice that he had made; assuring her at the same time, that when the incumbent on a living in his gift was dead, (and he was at the point of death,) he would bestow the living on Mr. Alton.

"And now," added he, while Miss Beaumont could only weep her thanks, "do you wish that I should tell Mrs. Beaumont all that has passed?" And as she gladly acceded to this considerate offer, he led her back into the room where they had left her mother.

Mrs. Beaumont was quite amazed to behold her daughter in tears, and reproved her for her folly in spoiling her pretty eyes. But when St. Aubyn told her that he had taken the liberty to request Miss Beaumont's acceptance of two hundred pounds a-year for life, she thought it proper to squeeze a few tears into her eyes too, and to thank him for his generosity, which, in her heart, she could scarcely help suspecting was owing to a qualm of conscience for having suppressed a will. St. Aubyn, then, instead of hinting, as she hoped he would do, his wish to cultivate her acquaintance, in order to forward his intended suit to her daughter, began to plead the cause of Mr. Alton; which threw Mrs. Beaumont into a most violent passion, and she declared, she wondered at her daughter's want of spirit, for that with two hundred pounds a-year in her pocket, "who knew but that she might marry well!"

"But, madam, how do you know," replied St. Aubyn, "that I shall give your daughter this potent two hundred a-year, if she does not marry this identical Mr. Alton, my friend, to whom I destine a very fine living, now on the point of being vacated?"

"Oh! cried Mrs. Beaumont; "your friend! Mr. Alton is your friend, is he, sir? Oh! that alters the case entirely; and I shall be happy to call my daughter Mrs. Alton as soon as she chooses."

To be brief; St. Aubyn having made a short will, but according to the dictates of justice, affection, and benevolence, wisely considering that things of such importance should never be delayed a day, and having in that will settled the two hundred pounds a-year on the future Mrs. Alton, set off for France, buoyed up only too often by the idea that perhaps something had occurred to break off the engagement between Emma and Balfour, and thereby preparing for himself all the *bitterness of disappointment.*

But while he is on his way to Paris, let us return to our heroine. She had passed a quiet fortnight at Montmorenci, during which time she had been visited by Mrs. Castlemain, Mr. Egerton, and Mrs. Felton, who had, she observed, an air of great anxiety, and was very desirous of knowing how soon her marriage was to take place; when, just as she was preparing to return to Paris, Fanny Balfour, and her governess also, became alarmingly ill, and so did the other inhabitants of the chateau; and in three days' time it was known beyond dispute, that the disorder was that terrible scourge, the scarlet fever. Emma, who was busily employed in nursing Fanny, was excessively distressed on hearing what her complaint was, because she well knew the anxiety of mind that Mrs. Castlemain and Mr. Egerton would feel at knowing that she was exposed to such danger, especially as her grandmother had a decided horror and fear of infection, which her good sense could scarcely keep in any bounds. But hoping that neither they nor Balfour would learn the true state of the case, she wrote to them to say that Fanny Balfour was too unwell for her to think of her leaving her yet, and to wish that they would delay their next visit till she was better. In the meanwhile, she took upon herself the office of chief nurse both night and day.

It was several days before Fanny was declared entirely out of danger; and the disorder left her so weak, that she still required attentive nursing. But in the meanwhile the public papers had not been so discreet as Emma; and her affectionate friends and her impetuous lover had both read in the newspaper that an infectious fever had broken out in the chateau de Montmorenci! Mrs. Castlemain, though she had received a letter from Emma only the day before, expressing herself to be in perfect health, could scarcely retain her senses, at the idea of the danger she was in; and affection getting the better of all personal fear, she insisted on going to Montmorenci immediately. But Mr. Egerton fancying that in the present state of her feelings, she would be almost sure to catch the disorder, if she breathed the infectious air, insisted on being allowed to go alone to fetch back Emma to Paris; and to this proposal Mrs. Castlemain reluctantly agreed.

As soon as Emma saw what was published, she expected a summons to Paris, and was consequently on the watch for the arrival of her grandmother's carriage. Therefore, when she saw it approaching, she ran down stairs to prevent its coming near the door, and also to forbid whoever was in it to alight. Mr. Egerton, though charmed to see her so well, was quite agitated at beholding her, and conjured her to let him convey her immediately to Paris.

"I feel as I ought," replied Emma, "the kindness which dictates this request; but I am not the less resolved to refuse compliance with it."

"To refuse!"

"Yes. Would you have me so base and so selfish as to leave my young friend here at a time when she wants my assistance; and, in order to procure very problematical safety to myself, (for perhaps I should carry the seeds of the disorder away with me,) run the risk of spreading infection, and of infecting both you and my grandmother, and all the inhabitants of our hotel? No, my dear sir, thanks to you, far from me has ever been, and ever shall be, such sordid selfishness.—I am at my post, and never will I desert it;" while Mr. Egerton, though agonized at her probable danger, forbore to combat what his principles told him was just, and with a heavy heart returned again to Paris.

I will not attempt to describe the anxiety which he and Mrs. Castlemain experienced while the disorder lasted; and during six successive weeks it kept breaking out in different persons; consequently, Emma was obliged to remain where she was, lest she should, by removing, carry infection along with her.

During that period, Balfour had come over twice, and the first time he had with difficulty been prevented entering the house, and insisting on helping Emma to nurse his sister; but meeting him at the gates, she had at length succeeded in bringing him to reason, and had even prevailed on him to let three weeks pass before he came again.

His father, meanwhile, had come through Paris, and was gone to a lodging at Versailles, the air there being thought better for him than that of the metropolis; but he had been too ill to see any one on his way, and he still remained very much indisposed, though better, he believed, for the change of air.

When Emma had been at Montmorenci about a fortnight, an East Indian family took apartments in the castle; and in about three weeks after, an elderly mulatto woman, their servant whom illness had detained at Paris, joined them there when the fever was at its height.

At this time, so many both of servants and their masters and mistresses were ill of the disorder, that they had not nurses and attendants sufficient; and it was difficult to prevail on any new ones to come, so great was the panic occasioned by the disease. It is not to be supposed, therefore, that when the poor mulatto became in her turn attacked with this terrible disorder, she could receive proper attendance while persons of more consequence and more use than herself required it equally.

Dr. M——, a very skilful English physician, was regular in his attendance at the chateau, and Emma gave her friend nothing without his advice and approbation.

One morning, recollecting that she had forgotten to ask him a question of some importance, she lay wait for him on the landing-place which communicated with the mulatto's room, and as she stood there she overheard the following conversation in French:—

"Then you think this poor Indian is so bad that she must die?"

"I think," said Dr. M——, "poor creature, that she must die, because she cannot, I find, have attendance sufficient to save her. If you could get some good nurse who can be depended upon to sit up with her to-night, which is the crisis of the fever, and who can get medicine and wine down in large quantities, she might live; but I cannot sit up myself, as I must perform that duty by a patient at Paris;

therefore, I fear, the poor woman stands a bad chance for her life."

Emma now heard the voice of the mulatto, who, in the hoarse impeded utterance of disease, said in broken English,

"Ah! I must die, for nobody cares for and comes near poor Lola!"

Dr. M—— hearing this, kindly spoke words of encouragement to her; then turned away in some emotion, being conscious how fallacious were the hopes he gave.

Emma met him as he left the room, and drew from him a statement of the mulatto's case, like that she had overheard; but she found that though she had the fever worse than any one, the constant care of one night alone might give a favourable turn to the disorder. She then asked the question she wanted relative to Fanny Balfour; and finding that she was so well that she did not want her attendance, she went to bed, though it was noon, and soon fell into a sound and refreshing sleep.

It was evening before she awoke, and she found that Dr. M——, anxious about some of his patients, was come to visit them again. Emma immediately arose, hastily dressed herself in a long white bed-gown, and, fastening up her fine hair under a close morning cap, stole out of her room, and unseen took a seat by the bedside of the mulatto; being resolved to sit up herself with the poor neglected Lola.

Dr. M—— started with surprise when he saw Emma, who, with firmness not to be overcome, assured him, that as he believed attention might save the poor woman's life, and she was able and willing to afford that attention, she should consider herself as accessary to the death of a fellow-creature if she did not do all in her power to save her; "and," added she, "as I have already adjusted her pillow for her, and given her some drink, I conclude that I have incurred sufficient danger to make it a matter of no moment whether I remain here or not."

Dr. M——, rendered silent by respect for feelings so virtuous and benevolent, ceased to make any further objections; and having given Emma his directions in writing, she hung them up against the chimney piece along with her watch, that she might implicitly obey the instructions she received; and he took his leave, having promised to account for her absence to Fanny Balfour and her governess.

"Who are you?" said the mulatto, looking earnestly at Emma as she offered her a medicine at a stated time.

"I am your nurse," she replied, "and you must do as I bid you."

"You! Oh! what a pretty nurse!" Then, without much difficulty, she swallowed the medicine, though not before Emma, wisely concluding that she would be more likely to obey her if she knew she was a lady, and not a servant, told her she was a lady of fortune who liked mulattoes, and therefore came to nurse her. But during the greater part of the night, her delirium ran so high, that Emma could not without difficulty get down the necessary quantity of wine and physic. In the middle of the night, Emma finding sleep only too likely to overpower her, and that reading increased her drowsiness, was at first at a loss what expedient to fix upon in order to keep herself awake; at length she resolved to go in search of her brush, and rouse herself by brushing her hair. Like her poor mother's, her hair was of a rich auburn, thick, waving, and glossy; and whenever she let it loose over her shoulders, as Agatha often wore hers, her likeness to her mother became unusually striking.

She was busily employed in the above-mentioned office, when she heard the mulatto talking very loud; and fearful lest she should attempt to get out of bed, as she had once done before, she threw down her brush and ran to the bedside, where she saw the poor woman sitting up in the bed in the height of delirious agitation; but as soon as the mulatto looked on her, she gave a loud and fearful shriek, and hid her head under the bedclothes, ever and anon lifting up her head, and saying, "Go, go! Pray don't kill me! Go, go! take her away, take her away!"

The noise brought one of the nurses from the next chamber into the room; and Emma, while this woman stayed by the bed, twisted her hair under her cap again; and feeling chilly as morning began to dawn, she threw a red shawl round her, and, dismissing the nurse, resumed her station.

"Is she gone? is she gone?" whispered the mulatto, looking fearfully round; and Emma asked her whom she meant.

"Oh! I know! but I will not tell;—a terrible lady!" Then, examining Emma's face and dress minutely, she said, "No, it was all a dream; and I am easy."

By the time she expected to see Dr. M—— Emma had, with unwearied perseverance, forced the poor creature to take all the medicine and all the wine that he had ordered; and when he came, she had the inexpressible satisfaction of hearing him declare that the pulse was fallen from 140 to 130, and that she had, to the best of his belief, saved the mulatto's life.

"And now," said he, "go and do all you can to save your own more valuable life;—go and lie down, that if you persist, as I see you will do, in watching half another night, you may be prepared to encounter the fatigue." And Emma, with a light heart and self-approving conscience, obeyed him.

In another week or ten days, the fever seemed to have done its worst, and no fresh person was seized with its symptoms; while, whether she had had the disease in her infancy, or from whatever cause, Emma herself as yet remained in perfect health.

But to return to St. Aubyn.—As soon as he reached Paris, he set off for the hotel of Mrs. Castlemain, and, I believe, never recollected that Mrs. Felton was in being. His intimacy with that lady was owing to her having had art enough to draw from him the secret of his love, and cunning enough to indulge him in talking of it; by which means he preferred her society to that of any one; while she flattered herself that it was very common for the confidante of a passion to become the object of it. It was true, that he refused, in a fit of jealousy, to accompany her into Flanders, but not jealousy of *her*. The truth was, that he had heard Sir Charles Maynard had followed Emma from K——, and was her declared lover in London; and, when Mrs. Felton, finding Sir Charles a passenger in their boat, pressed him to join them on their Flemish tour, he owned to Mrs. Felton, that the society of a man who might one day or other succeed with Emma, was so insupportable, that he should proceed directly to Paris. As love for Mrs. Felton, therefore, had nothing to do with the motives that led him to associate with that lady, it is not to be wondered at that he should go to the Rue de la Concorde rather than to the Rue Vivienne. But on his way thither he met an English acquaintance, who was that odious being, a male gossip, and one of those idlers and loungers who will, if they meet you, insist on bestowing their tediousness upon you.

"Which way are you going, St. Aubyn?" cried this man.

"To the Rue de la Concorde."

"Oh! well, I don't care if I go that way, too."

Then, seizing St. Aubyn's arm, he began to tell him all the French and English gossip he had heard since he had been gone.

"So," said he, "I suppose you know the match between Balfour and Miss Castlemain is entirely off?"

"Off!" cried St. Aubyn, breathless with emotion.

"Oh! yes, quite. Egad, death was very near getting the lady, for she has been at Montmorenci all the time the bad fever has been raging there. However, she has escaped, and is coming soon to Paris, I believe."

St. Aubyn waited to hear no more; but rushing hastily from his astonished companion, he returned to his hotel, to write a letter to Emma, at Montmorenci. The letter, though almost incoherent from emotion, told her that every obstacle to his explanation of whatever had appeared ambiguous and capricious in his conduct towards his friends at the White Cottage was now removed, and there was not a secret of his heart, that, if allowed to see her, he would not reveal to one who always was, and ever would be, the sole unrivalled object of a passion ardent and eternal, even while it appeared entirely hopeless; but that now, as he understood, she was again *free*, he flattered himself that she would allow him to endeavour to win her affections from his now discarded rival. This letter he put in the post, directed to the Chateau de Montmorenci, and with a beating heart he went to the Hotel des Etrangers, and inquired for Mr. Egerton.

He found him and Mrs. Castlemain together, and amazed beyond expression at his appearance and his emotion; for he could not speak; but seizing Mrs. Castlemain's hands he pressed them to his lips and burst into tears.

"I conclude from your dress, what has happened," said Mrs. Castlemain kindly.

"No, not all," replied St. Aubyn. "I have lost both my mother and my uncle;" and Mrs. Castlemain thought in her heart he was a very fortunate person. He then begged to see Mr. Egerton alone, who immediately withdrew with him.

St. Aubyn then, as succinctly as possible, explained to him the reasons of his conduct; while Mr. Egerton interrupted him:

"I thought so,—I knew your reasons when explained would redound to your honour. But, O that ever Emma should have been so rash and inconsiderate!"

"Rash! what do you mean?" cried St. Aubyn turning very pale.

"That Emma is irrevocably engaged to Balfour!"

"And I was told," faltered out St. Aubyn, "that that affair was entirely at an end, or I certainly should not have written to her at Montmorenci!"

"And have you done so?"

"Yes, just before I came hither."

"Poor, lost Emma!" exclaimed Mr. Egerton wringing his hands; "how she will lament her hard fate! for I know but too well that her heart is still fondly yours!" Mr. Egerton, when he had uttered these words, earnestly wished he could have recalled them; but he could scarcely repent of them when he saw the joy they had given St. Aubyn, and heard him say, that he hoped Emma would feel the impropriety and dishonour of marrying Balfour, if in her heart she preferred him.

"There is one chance for you," said Mr. Egerton, after a pause; "I know that she will, on every principle of honour and justice, show your letter to Balfour, whom she will see to-morrow, and tell him whatever feelings that letter has revived in her bosom; and on his decision, in consequence, depends your fate."

St. Aubyn, then, too much agitated to pursue the subject further, tried to divert his attention by describing all that had passed since he saw him at the Palace. But he declined seeing Mrs. Castlemain again, as she was, Mr. Egerton said, very fond of Emma's marriage with Balfour, and would be greatly distressed at the struggle which she would foresee in Emma's mind between love and honour. St. Aubyn, therefore, returned to his own hotel, and endeavoured to fortify his mind against the dreaded morrow.

Emma, meanwhile, as she was preparing her mind to consider her union with Balfour as at no very distant period, (lord Clonawley having expressed a wish to see his son married and settled before his death, an event which his increasing infirmities made only too likely to occur,) received St. Aubyn's letter. With perturbation not to be described, she gazed on the well known characters, and, having perused the contents, sat for some moments in a state of seeming stupefaction. But uppermost of all her feelings seemed the joy of knowing she was so tenderly beloved; for every jealous thought vanished before the assurance of that word never pledged to a falsehood; and though St. Aubyn did not allege a single fact in his own justification, he was already, to the well-motived confidence of Emma, completely justified. But though the first moments were moments of pleasure, the succeeding ones were those of agony and despair.

At length she resolved, as Mr. Egerton had said she would do, to show Balfour the letter, and own to him all the feelings it had called forth.

After a night of restless anguish, she arose, and was told that Mr. Balfour awaited her in the parlour. As soon as she appeared, he ran to her, alarmed at her discoloured cheeks and swelled eyelids; and she answered him by putting St. Aubyn's letter into his hand.

"Well, madam," replied he, when he had read it, "what is this given to me for? Surely you cannot yet hesitate between Mr. St. Aubyn and me?"

"I wish you to decide," faintly returned Emma; "for I own to you, that this surety of his fidelity and entire innocence, has revived in their full force, my former feelings in his favour."

"Shame on you then!" replied Balfour, with fiercest indignation. "Where is your surety for this gentleman's innocence and fidelity? Does he even condescend to name a single proof of this vaunted innocence? But you, forsooth, merciful and credulous being, are no sooner informed that he is tired of his Mrs. Felton, (his convenient mistress,) and wishes to return to you, but you, condescending creature, are ready at his beck, to receive him again into favour, forgetful of the sacred claims of one who never loved any other woman than yourself, and whose honour and tenderness you have never had any reason to doubt."

What could Emma oppose to arguments so plausible as these? Not that she knew St. Aubyn's word was as sacred as the oaths of others; for he would be justified in answering that she only spoke from the partiality of a fond woman; and she could not but feel, that, all the circumstances considered, her ready acquiescence with the wishes of St. Aubyn, (which could only be the result of her discarding for ever the faithful lover before her, who told her he was convinced the pretence of her being free was only made as an excuse for his temerity in addressing her,) would be a degradation which pride and delicacy most powerfully forbade; and after a long, long struggle with her feelings, she told Balfour, whose deportment was more that of a maniac than of a rational being, that she hesitated no longer, but was willing to attend him to the altar as soon as they returned to England.

"When, then, shall we return to England?" said Balfour, his eyes sparkling with delight at this triumph over St. Aubyn.

"In four days' time, if my friends can get passports so soon, and are willing to go," replied Emma. And Balfour left her immediately, to expedite the means of their departure.

As soon as Balfour was gone, she wrote to Mr. Egerton, feeling that duty now forbade her to address St. Aubyn. She begged him to tell the latter that her engagement with Balfour had never been broken off, and that a very short time would make her his wife. More, every good feeling forbade her to say; except, that she wished the companion of her childhood and her youth as happy as he deserved to be, and greater welfare she could not wish him.

In another letter to Mr. Egerton, under the same cover, meant for his eye alone, she was more communicative. She told him all that had passed between her and Balfour, and her determination and wishes in consequence; but owning that she believed all St. Aubyn's declarations; and that, convinced too late that her first choice had been wise, and her second rash, she must request that in future the name of St. Aubyn should never be mentioned before her, nor the reasons of his conduct explained, as she was resolved to avoid every chance of having emotions excited which must militate against her duty to a fond and confiding husband. Mr. Egerton obeyed her wishes, and read the whole of her letter to St. Aubyn, (I mean that designed for his perusal,) except that part which mentioned that a very short time would make her the wife of Balfour. That overwhelming intelligence he had not the heart to communicate to him.

Mr. Egerton's sufferings were certainly next in degree to those of St. Aubyn; and even Mrs. Castlemain herself, who, by the death of Mr. Hargrave and Mrs. St. Aubyn, saw her sole objections to him as a husband for Emma entirely removed, felt the sincerest pity for his distress, and almost wished Emma had never met Balfour.

Soon after Emma had written her letter to Mr. Egerton, she retired to her room to dress;

but feeling her head considerably oppressed by the anxiety and watchfulness of the preceding night, she resolved to walk in the garden, in hopes that the air might revive her; and, throwing on a long, white wrapping-gown, she put her intention in execution. As the wind was high, and she walked rapidly backwards and forwards, the comb that fastened up her hair soon fell to the ground, loosened by the wind and the exercise, and her long tresses floated on her shoulders. At this moment she looked up at one of the windows, and saw at it the woman of colour; on which she was about to bow to her with a smile of congratulation on her being well enough to get up; when the smile was checked by a violent scream from Lola, who seemed, on seeing her, to shriek and fall back in the arms of her nurse. Emma immediately ran up stairs to inquire what had agitated her. She found the mulatto full of emotion, which increased still more on her entrance into the chamber, and she overheard her say, "But is that indeed the blessed angel who saved my life? Tell me, answer me," cried she, fixing her wild eyes on Emma—"Who are you? What's your name?"

"My name is Emma Castlemain," she replied.

"But your mother's name, your mother's name!"

"My mother's name was Agatha Torrington."

"'Tis she, 'tis she," cried the mulatto, clasping her hands and falling on her knees; "and I did not see your mother in a dream, but you awake. O blessed angel! you saved my life, while I did all I could to injure you, and your poor mother!"

Emma, at first, thought she was again uttering the rhapsodies of a disturbed brain; but, on reflection, she was convinced that she beheld the *woman of colour* who had been employed by her father to deceive both her mother and her grandmother; and, as she gazed on her with this consciousness, she almost shrank from the being whose success in deceiving Mrs. Castlemain had been productive of such pernicious consequences to her much injured parent. But when she recollected that the poor penitent, agitated, and ignorant wretch before her had only obeyed the will of her master, and that the crime, therefore, had been chiefly that of her father, she felt all her resentment vanish; and when Lola earnestly entreated her forgiveness, she granted it with as much solemn earnestness as it had been implored. But it was not from any compunction for the mischievous falsehoods she had uttered that Lola's conscience was haunted by the image of Agatha, and wounded by the certainty of the misery she had occasioned. Had the result of her obedience to her employer been what she expected, and that Danvers, on casting off Agatha, had resumed his connexion with her, or not taken another wife or mistress, she would never have thought of Agatha, or the probable result of her falsehoods, again. But Danvers, as soon as she had answered his purpose, paid her a small sum of money, and insisted on her returning to India by the next ship, as servant to a family to which he recommended her; and she also at the same time discovered, that Danvers was on the point of marriage with a lady, but one whose name and address she could not learn; else, it is most likely, she would have informed her, in revenge, that he had a wife living. But to India she was forced to return unrevenged, and haunted by feelings of painful and compunctious pity for the victim of Danvers's cruelty; who, as his first wife had been, was endeared to her by the conviction that she, like herself, had been deserted by him when his passion was extinguished. Vainly did she then wish that she had not obeyed Danvers, and endeavoured to learn whither Agatha had fled; and often very often had her dreams been haunted by the image of Agatha, as with wild eyes, pale cheek, dishevelled hair, and almost terrifying violence of mien and gesture, she had addressed Danvers on that fatal day, when, leading his little boy, she had followed him into his presence. It was no wonder, therefore, that in her delirium she should mistake Emma for Agatha, when with hair falling loosely on her neck she had approached her bedside; nor that on beholding Emma in the garden, dressed in every respect as Agatha was when she had seen her, she should experience emotion and surprise sufficient to occasion the scream which had led Emma to her apartment. Emma, indeed, had scarcely seen her since the night that she had watched by her bedside, as the mulatto had been in a state of mental derangement almost ever since her fever had left her; and it was therefore now for the first time that Lola had a perfect view of her "pretty nurse," and that "blessed angel," as she always called her, who had, she was told, been the preserver of her life.

"But where is the poor lady, your mother?" cried Lola.

"Dead!"

"Dead! Did she die from the sorrow I helped to occasion her?"

"No, she lived many years after; but on this very painful subject I must beg not to be questioned."

"And that poor lady, her mother, is she dead too?"

"No; she is now at Paris."

"Then perhaps I may see her, and ask her pardon also," said the mulatto with great eagerness.

"Perhaps you may," returned Emma, starting from a reverie; for it had occurred to her, that the singular coincidence that had thus made her acquainted with a being who had been one of the agents of Agatha's destiny, might lead her to some knowledge of her father's fate, and connexions, and perhaps clear away the stain upon the honour of her mother; for Emma had never believed in the report of his death. Still terror, lest she should hear her father was living, and too infamous for her not to shrink with horror from being acknowledged and claimed as his daughter, made her hesitate for a while to put the necessary questions; and before she had resolution to do it, the mulatto, overcome by the violent emotions which she had experienced, became again deranged, and was for some days too ill to be seen or spoken to.

In a short time the passports were obtained, and Mr. Egerton and Mrs. Castlemain left Paris in the carriage of the latter, Emma having preferred meeting them on the road, to joining them at Paris, owing perhaps to a fear of seeing St. Aubyn by chance. Accordingly, attended by Fanny Balfour, who had obtained leave to accompany her to England, while her governess joined her sisters at Versailles, Emma set off with Balfour in a landaulet and four, and Mrs. Castlemain had once more the happiness of pressing Emma to her bosom, endeared to her by a long separation, and by the danger which she had dared and surmounted.

The mulatto was so ill and so delirious when Emma left Montmorenci, that she could not bid her farewell; but she left a kind message for her, and a considerable present, as a proof of her entire forgiveness of her conduct towards her poor mother.

But now, in full view, and approaching nearer and nearer every day, was that trial, whose magnitude Emma was not conscious of before, and from which, now she was conscious of it, she shrank with agony and dismay, wondering, as she did so, that she could have been blind so long to the true state of her motives and her feelings, and have disdained to profit by the calmer reason of that admirable friend, who had vainly but conscientiously held up the mirror to her heart. She saw herself on the point of marriage with a man whose addresses, whatever were his charms and his talents, she was now conscious that she should never have admitted, had she not been influenced, however unconsciously to herself, by the suggestions of wounded self-love, wounded pride, irritated jealousy, and female pique; in short, by all those pernicious impulses to action, which, however called, are all to be resolved into one master feeling denominated Temper. But it was too late to retract, even though she felt her health impaired by the corrosion of her mind, especially as when, on her asking Balfour how he could think of persisting in his design of marrying her now she was become a sickly, pale, nervous being, he tenderly replied, because her sufferings endeared her the more to him, and that no one could prove to her so good and affectionate a nurse, as the husband who doted on her with the truest and best principled affection!

"Well then," replied Emma faintly smiling, "I will no longer hesitate to name a day for our union." And it was fixed for the day after this conversation took place. On which Balfour wrote to his father, informing him of the near approach of his happiness, he having sometime before caused articles to be drawn up preparatory to a regular marriage settlement; and Mr. Egerton wrote to St. Aubyn informing him, as he promised to do, that the day was really *fixed*, but sparing him the unnecessary pang of knowing that before he received the letter the ceremony would be over.

When Mr. Egerton and Mrs. Castlemain left Paris, St. Aubyn, knowing the cause of their return to England was the intended marriage, too wretched to remain stationary, mounted his horse, and rode towards the south of France, for no other purpose but to ride away from himself, if he could; and conscious occasionally of no pleasure but what resulted from the power his wealth gave him of relieving the distress which occasionally met his view on the road. He had, however, *one* source of enjoyment which he could impart to no one, but over which he brooded in solitude, like a miser over his treasure. And that was the assurance which had escaped Mr. Egerton, that Emma loved him! In vain did St. Aubyn say to himself, that if she loved him, she could not be happy with another man. Imperious love got the better of generosity; and when he dwelt on this idea, he felt that his misery diminished. But, as I before observed, this source of pleasure, honour and delicacy both, forbade him to impart to any one; therefore he avoided Mrs. Felton, with whom he formerly used to find relief in talking of his love, as he was happier alone than he could be in communicating to her his feelings, now he could divulge only half of them; and withstanding all that lady's almost frantic solicitations to an interview, he convinced her at length, that her hopes of succeeding Emma in his heart, were, at present at least, even more groundless than ever.

At length St. Aubyn, being impatient to hear some news from England, returned to Paris, and received Mr. Egerton's letter! Well indeed may the true lover be said,

"To hope, though hope were lost."

St. Aubyn, till he received that letter, had unconsciously flattered himself that something might happen to prevent the marriage; but now that the day was fixed, and that, though Mr. Egerton did not say so, by the time that he received that letter the ceremony might perhaps be over, he felt, from the anguish of his disappointment, the extent of the hope he had indulged, and he traversed Paris from one end to the other, too full of restless anguish to remain in his own apartment, experiencing the acutest of all misery, save that which springs from the agonies of remorse. So keen were his pangs that they seemed to change for a while his mild and compassionate nature, giving him feelings of petulance and hardness of heart, to him before unknown, and making creation itself appear "nothing but a pestilential congregation of vapours."

After long and almost unconscious wanderings, St. Aubyn found himself at midnight in the gardens of the Thuilleries; but as the sound of its trickling waters was painful to his feelings, he left the gardens, and turned his steps towards the Place de la Concorde. The night was stormy and starless; and at another time the quick emotions and busy fancy of St. Aubyn would have led him no unmoved wanderer over that scene of recent horrors and of guilt. The murdered great, the murdered good, would at another time have passed in rapid succession before his almost startled memory, and the oblivious dust would again have seemed reeking and red with the blood of the innocent and the unfortunate.

Absorbed either in misery or happiness must they be who can pass over the place where the guillotine stood, in the solemn silence of night, without a thrill of horror which probably no other spot in the creation can call forth. St. Aubyn was indeed absorbed in misery, and he forgot his youth, his talents, his possessions; and the wish to sink unnoticed into a quiet grave, was the only one that his sick soul delighted to indulge.

Being unable to retire to his hotel, as rest did not await him there, he turned his steps from the Place de la Concorde to the neighbouring Champs Elysées, and was just hailing the congenial gloom of its tall trees, when he heard a quick footstep behind him, whose solitary tread alone broke the deep stillness of night. St. Aubyn instinctively turned to face the danger, if any danger was nigh; and a feeble voice, in very imperfect French, exclaimed, "Charity, sir; for God's sake give me some relief." St. Aubyn, with all the savageness of grief, replied, that he had no money; and angrily bade the man begone. But he had scarcely indulged this sudden effusion of temper, so unlike his usual habits, before he bitterly repented of it, and was just going, in the words of Esdras, to exclaim, "Sufferer, what aileth thee, and why art thou so disquieted?" when the poor man faltered out in English, "O God, what will become of me, and all of us!"

"Ha! A countryman too!" cried St. Aubyn. "My poor fellow, tell me what you want, and what I can do for you;" and that love of life, which anguish had for a while suspended, returned immediately with the consciousness of being able to do good, and the inclination to put that ability in practice.

As soon as tears would allow the poor youth to speak, he told St. Aubyn that he, his mother, and sisters were starving, and his father in a high delirium; while for want of money, he could procure his unhappy parent neither food, medicine, nor advice.

"Well, well, I will remedy all these miseries," cried the revived St. Aubyn; and seeing some lights still glimmering in the Hemeau de Chantilly,* he led the way thither, desiring the young man to follow.

It was as he expected. The company who had assembled there had nearly all departed, and the owners of the house were very glad to dispose of what remained of their provision. The woman at the bar, seeing the greedy eye with which the youth regarded a dish of ham that stood by, desired him to take a piece, and St. Aubyn authorized him to eat all there was. He devoured the whole in an instant, in a manner so ravenous, as to call a tear into the eye of St. Aubyn, (who read in this a sad proof of the truth of his story,) and make the French woman exclaim, "Mon Dieu! que ce pauvre enfant a faim!"†

As soon as the poor youth had in a degree satisfied his hunger, and drunk two full goblets of the vin du pay, St. Aubyn desired to be furnished with a small basket, into which he put cold fowls and wine; then paying for all the different articles whatever the lady's conscience allowed her to ask, he desired the now-elated young man to take the basket on his arm, and to show him the way to his father's habitation. It was in the Rue Boulois, the very centre of Paris; and in a miserable garret, up three pair of stairs, St. Aubyn beheld a woman and three girls attempting, but with great difficulty, to confine down in his bed a man in all the violence of delirium.

"Joy, joy!" cried the youth as he entered; "I have brought you food, wine, and an angel!" Then, setting down and opening the basket, the hungry and eager group leaving the invalid, and too ravenous to wait, began to tear in pieces the relief that was set before them. The mother, however, had more self-command, and began to bless and thank St. Aubyn in the fulness of a grateful heart; while he put several questions to her relative to the state of her husband, and, writing a note to his servant, directed the son to carry it immediately to his hotel, and bring the man back with him.

St. Aubyn was now obliged to assist in confining the invalid, who was continually addressing some invisible object; "Ah, rascal!" he exclaimed; "so you pretended not to know me, did you? But I knew you, though you are grown so old, and so ugly, and are become a great man; and I will be revenged! I'll 'peach! So look to it! Here it is, here it is!" So saying, he took an old dirty pocket-book from under his pillow, and with a grin of

---

* A sort of Vauxhall in the Champs Elysées.
† "My God! how hungry the poor child is!"

maniacal defiance, hugged it, and hid it in his bosom.

This language, and this action, were repeated so often, that St. Aubyn at last asked what the pocket-book contained; but the wife assured him she did not know, and that it never was out of her husband's possession.

"What does he mean, think you, by 'peaching?" said he.

"I do not know," replied the woman; "I am sure I wish I had never seen his face; for I suspect he has done something that lies very heavy on his conscience."

"Woman," said St. Aubyn, sternly, "it is not for you to judge your husband. And whatever crime he may have committed, he is now a severe sufferer, and by you, at least, ought only to be considered as such."

Here the unhappy wretch began to rave again; and the eagerly-attentive St. Aubyn fancied he heard him utter names familiar to his ear. Again he spoke, again St. Aubyn listened; and at length was sure that he was not deceived; and breathless with agitated expectation, he hung upon the words of the unconscious speaker.

"Yes, yes," cried he, "I know you well, Miss Torrington! Agatha Torrington! Ha, ha, ha! I was revenged, but don't say I crazed you; I did not do it. And that fool Jones! But that rascal to refuse me money, and pretend not to know me! In black and white, you rascal, I have it, I have it, I have it!" Then, again was the book hugged and hidden; and St. Aubyn blessed the hour which led him to that spot; for, having heard every particular of Agatha's history, he had no doubt but he beheld that Cammell, who had been bribed by Danvers to destroy the registry of his marriage. But had he really destroyed it? St. Aubyn suspected not; and that the pocket-book contained it, Cammell having preserved it probably in order to extort money from Danvers wherever he should meet him. It seemed, then, that Danvers was *not* dead, and that Cammell met him, recently met him. Where then, and under what name, was the father of Emma to be found? And before St. Aubyn lost sight of Cammell, he was resolved to ascertain this fact; while sweet to his soul was the certainty that he should be able essentially to serve the woman he adored.

"Who are those people that he is talking of?" asked St. Aubyn.

"I am sure I don't know," said the woman, sulkily; "but for this last month he has done nothing but talk of some man who refused to give him money the other day, and against whom he has sworn to be revenged; while often he has started from his sleep, talking of one Agatha Torrington."

"Pray, what is your name?" said St. Aubyn. The woman hesitated, and answered, in some confusion, that their name was Williams.

"No, it is not," replied St. Aubyn, looking at her steadily. "Your name, I am convinced, is Cammell."

"Who speaks to me?" cried the invalid. "Who wants Cammell?" And the wife, assured that all further concealment was vain, dropped the food she was conveying to her mouth, and in a tone of terror exclaimed, "I see, sir, you know all about us; but pray, pray, sir, be merciful!"

"Did you," asked St. Aubyn, "ever hear your husband talk of having torn from a book the registry of a marriage?"

"Never, when in his senses; but very likely you will hear him talk of a marriage-register in one of his raving fits."

"Have you," said St. Aubyn, who saw the poor wretch sink back exhausted on his pillow, "have you any objection to my opening that pocket-book? for I have heard enough to induce me to set a guard on your husband, in order to bring him to justice for an act of a most wicked nature, by which he has greatly injured some of the dearest friends I have." The terrified woman, falling on her knees, begged he would do as he thought proper; and St. Aubyn, getting possession of the pocketbook, had the inexpressible delight to draw forth from it, doubled in many folds, and each fold ready to fall in pieces, the registry of the marriage of George Danvers and Agatha Torrington; with the date and every thing perfect. There would now, then, he believed, be no difficulty in publicly proving Agatha to be the lawful wife of Danvers, as Mr. Egerton had in his custody the letter from Jamaica to prove the day and hour when the first wife died; therefore the date of the marriage register would show, beyond dispute, the truth of what Agatha had always asserted, that when Danvers led her to the altar, his wife had been dead three weeks!

"Thus, then," thought St. Aubyn, "have I been the instrument to clear the fame of Mrs. Danvers from even a shadow of suspicion; and to prove that much-injured woman worthy to be the daughter of Mrs. Castlemain, and the mother of Emma!" For St. Aubyn felt, as every virtuous and unsophisticated Englishman must feel, that a stain on the chastity of its females, is a blot on the proudest escutcheon of the proudest family, which not even the splendour of royal descent and royal alliances can ever obliterate.

By this time the youth had returned with St. Aubyn's servant, whom he instantly despatched with a note describing Cammell's disorder to Dr. M——, he himself resolving not to leave the house till he had learnt where Emma's father was to be found.

In a short time Dr. M—— arrived; and having given his patient a composing medicine, he soon sunk into a profound sleep, from which Dr. M—— assured St. Aubyn that he would probably recover in a sane mind. But it was nine the next morning before Cammell awoke. However, when he did wake, St. Aubyn's tedious watchfulness was well repaid; for he appeared quite calm and sensible, though most alarmingly weak. He seemed excessively terrified at seeing a stranger, and turned pale as death on missing his pocket-book.

"Compose yourself," said St. Aubyn, mildly, "and look on me as your friend."

He then told him why he came, what discoveries he had made, and finally that the torn leaf was in his possession; while the poor abject wretch humbly begged for mercy at his hands.

"I am not able to grant it," said St. Aubyn; "but I think that as you were, in this affair, only the agent of a greater villain still, one whom I hope to make as penitent as yourself, I trust that you have nothing to fear; but you must make all the reparation in your power, by telling me where I can find Mr. Danvers."

"Mr. Danvers!" cried Cammell. "There never was such a person. To be sure, his christian names were George Danvers; but his surname was BALFOUR, and he has been many years LORD CLONAWLEY!"

At this dreadful intelligence, St. Aubyn was for a moment speechless with horror; but he at length exclaimed, "Perhaps it is not yet too late! Lord Clonawley the father of Emma, and of ———!" Then, learning from the astonished Cammell that Lord Clonawley was at Versailles, he told his servant not to lose sight of Cammell, but remain where he was till he saw him again. He then ran to his hotel, ordered a horse to be saddled, and set off full speed for Versailles.

"And who knows," said St. Aubyn to himself, "but that the present Lord Clonawley may not be the man in question?"

Lord Clonawley's mind was little prepared for the dreadful trial which awaited him. Though he had often inflicted misery he had never experienced it, except when he lost the mother of his daughters, a wife whom he had tenderly loved.

When St. Aubyn arrived at Versailles, he desired to be shown to Lord Clonawley's lodgings; while the hope he had indulged when he began his journey vanished entirely now the moment of explanation was at hand.

Having sent in to inquire for Lord Clonawley, the servant returned, saying his lord begged to see him instantly; for, on being told that a stranger in great agitation desired to see him, he feared something had happened to his son, and therefore resolved to admit him immediately.

"I beg pardon, my lord, for this intrusion," cried St. Aubyn on entering, "but may I beg to know where Mr. Balfour now is?"

"Sir!" replied Lord Clonawley, much relieved in mind on hearing this question, "my son is in England, and at this moment," parental affection lighting up his face as he spoke, "and at this moment, sir, he is one of the happiest of men;" (here St. Aubyn's heart misgave him;) "for, by a letter just received from him, he informs me that he was the next day to be united to the woman of his affections."

St. Aubyn, on hearing this overwhelming intelligence, reeled to a chair, and hid his face with his hands.

"What is the matter, sir?" exclaimed Lord Clonawley, little anticipating the wretchedness he was about to experience. "You seem distressed."

"I am indeed distressed," cried St. Aubyn, raising his head; "but wretched as I am, your fate is far more terrible than mine."

"This is strange, mysterious language, sir; and from a stranger too," replied Lord Clonawley, alarmed yet irritated.

"Answer me, my lord," returned St. Aubyn; "had you not a child, a daughter, by Agatha Torrington?"

"By what right, sir, do you ask that question?"

"Question me not, but answer me, my lord! Your fate hangs upon your answer; and I conjure you, by all your hopes of pardon for your crimes, to answer me truly."

And Lord Clonawley, awed and influenced, in spite of his haughtiness, by the air and words of St. Aubyn, replied,

"I had a daughter by Agatha Torrington, but not born in wedlock."

St. Aubyn's indignant eye momentarily reproved the despicable falsehood; but its fire was as instantly quenched in tears of anguish as he uttered, "Lord Clonawley, terrible is the retribution that has overtaken you! for your DAUGHTER, by Agatha Torrington, is, in all probability, at this moment, the wife of your SON!"

"Who are you," demanded the wretched man, terrified and averse to be convinced, "that dare to come hither to distract me with impossibilities? My son's wife is the daughter of Mrs. Castlemain."

"The granddaughter, my lord, bequeathed to her on her death-bed by the unfortunate Agatha. Mrs. Torrington's name became Castlemain on her second marriage; and as you had deprived your child of her rightful name, her grandmother gave her hers."

Lord Clonawley, on hearing this, could doubt no longer, but sat the tearless image of hopeless woe, not being so fortunate as to lose in happy forgetfulness the sense of suffering.

"But perhaps it is not too late," suddenly cried St. Aubyn, struggling against despondence.

"Perhaps not," answered Lord Clonawley reviving; "the marriage has once been delayed by the illness of—of the lady."

"Enough!" cried St. Aubyn. "At all events I set off for England as soon as ever I can get a passport. But let me first inform you, sir, that I have *here* (showing it as he spoke) the registry of your *marriage* with

Miss Torrington, and that CAMMELL is in my custody."

Lord Clonawley gazed at him with added horror and amazement, but spoke not; and St. Aubyn continued;—

" Therefore, before I go, I expect that you, in a letter to Mr. Balfour, which I shall deliver into his own hands, acknowledge Agatha Torrington to have been your lawful wife, and Emma to be your legitimate daughter."

Thus lord Clonawley at once beheld himself not only detected in all his guilt, but fully punished for it; and convinced that unconditional compliance was his only resource, he wrote the letter required, received St. Aubyn's address in London,—and in a moment after St. Aubyn set off for Paris.

It was lucky, perhaps, for his intellects, that his passport was expedited as it was, and that in a much less time than could have been expected, he was on his road towards England; having previously witnessed the last moments of Cammell, and received his dying confession.

When he reached Boulogne, he found a packet ready to sail; but just as he was going on board, the wind completely changed, and he was forced to return to his hotel. But motion being better for him than rest, and Calais at no great distance, he again took horses, and reached Calais in a few hours.

The wind, however, still continuing contrary, he resolved not to go to bed, as to rest was impossible, but to walk up and down the pier till a favourable breeze came up. It did so about day-break, and at length St. Aubyn hailed the fast-approaching shores of England.

But to return to lord Clonawley, who, after St. Aubyn was gone, feeling himself unable to remain sole depositary of his sad secret, summoned his daughters into his room, and went through the painful and mortifying task of owning to them his past guilt, and informing them of its terrible results. At present he had not the heart to tell them they were born of a marriage which he had contracted during the existence of his second wife, and that therefore Emma was his only legitimate daughter.

Three days after St. Aubyn was on the road to England, the mulatto, being restored to health and sanity, inquired why Emma had left Montmorenci so suddenly; and, on being informed that she was gone to England to be married, she fervently prayed that the blessed angel, as she always called her, might have a husband as good as she was. She then asked the name of her husband, and being informed that he was the honourable George Frederic Balfour, only son of lord Clonawley, she uttered a scream of horror, and jumping out of bed, insisted on setting off for England directly. The bystanders concluded she was again delirious, and did not alter their opinion when she added that she must go to prevent incest, as Balfour and Miss Castlemain were brother and sister. But the nurse, who had witnessed her recognition of Emma, was of a different opinion, and so were they all, when the mulatto becoming more calm, produced *proof* of the truth of what she asserted. However, they convinced her that it was too late to prevent the union; but as lord Clonawley was at Versailles, it was judged right by the mulatto's mistress, that she should go over and inform him of her discovery.

Accordingly, one day, while lord Clonawley, in all the horrors of remorse and despair, was pacing with feeble yet agitated steps his solitary apartment, the mulatto, in spite of the servants, forced open the door and tottered into his presence.

He knew her instantly; though time in the one, and time and vice in the other, had impaired in both that beauty of person, which in both had been the means of misery and guilt; and as lord Clonawley raised this self-condemned accomplice from the ground, addressing her by the kind appellation of " Is it you, my poor Lola?" he turned away his head, and gave way to a violent burst of anguish and remorse.

Lola was immediately convinced, by this kind greeting, so different from the one which she expected to receive, that lord Clonawley already knew what she came to inform him of; for nothing but misery and horrors great as these, were, she thought, likely to have so softened the destroyer of Agatha.

" I see, I see," said Lola, " that you know all I came to say; and that *blessed angel* is indeed the wife of her brother !"

" No; God forbid !" cried lord Clonawley, " there is yet a ray of hope,—and———"

" Indeed !" cried Lola; then falling on her knees in transport, she blessed God for having saved from destruction the dear preserver of her life!

" Whom do you mean," asked lord Clonawley impatiently, " by the blessed angel, and the preserver of your life? Do you mean my daughter, my poor injured Emma?"

" I do," replied Lola. Then, with all the eager animation of gratitude, and the eloquent exaggeration of her race, she detailed to lord Clonawley his daughter's beauty, and her active virtue; her generous nature, and her compassionate forgiveness; while the feeling of parental pride, which would, under other circumstances, have led the agitated parent to exclaim, " And this is MY child !" was checked in lord Clonawley by a consciousness too agonizing for expression. At the same time, as the slave of selfish passions can only be made to feel deeply through the certainty of incurred privations, his regret for his guilty conduct towards Agatha and her child, was rendered doubly acute by the idea, that if that child was capable of volunteering, and incurring a dangerous and a painful duty from the mere benevolent wish of saving the life of a distressed and *unknown fellow-creature*, what would she not have done for a sick, a helpless, and a long-suffering *parent!* And as he thought this, most painfully did he contrast his deserted and disowned daughter with his owned and cherished children. Bitterly did he remember how often Harriet and Mary Ann, though good and affectionate girls, had left him to the care of hired nurses, on pretence of being worn out by one night of watchfulness; and bitterly did he regret that the self-denying and benevolent being, who had so kindly watched by the bedside of an infected menial, was one whose tender offices he should have had a right to claim, had he not been deaf to every demand of affection, of justice, and of honour. And amply, injured and unfortunate Agatha, did thy child's virtues revenge thee on the vices of its unnatural father.

"Oh, Lola!" cried lord Clonawley, "think what I endure at the idea that this angel, as you call her, has probably been brought up to hate me, and will never deign to see or to forgive me!"

"You don't know her," cried Lola eagerly; "she forgave me, I tell you, and I doubt not but she will forgive you. Write to her, I say,—write to her." And lord Clonawley, in all the anguish of a contrite spirit, did write to Emma, and felt his mind relieved by the effort.

At this moment he received St. Aubyn's letter announcing his being landed at Dover; and both he and the mulatto felt a little comforted by the news.

But when lord Clonawley had despatched his letter, he resolved to follow it as soon as he could in person, not only because he was unable to bear the suspense he must undergo till he could hear from St. Aubyn again, but because he flattered himself, that if his letter produced any effect on Emma's heart, he might, by being ready on the spot, induce her to see him, and pronounce his pardon in person. He immediately, therefore, got all things in readiness for his journey, and was soon on his road to England.

But to return to St. Aubyn, who, on reaching Rochester, happened unfortunately, while waiting for horses, to take up a paper, by which he received a terrible confirmation that every hope of arriving in time was vain; for he read in that paper as follows:

"Yesterday was married by special license at St. George's, Hanover-square, the honourable G. F. Balfour, to Emma, grand-daughter of the honourable Mrs. Castlemain."

But he endeavoured to give himself courage to proceed, by the reflection that such paragraphs were often false, and only anticipations; and in a degree revived by this nearly frantic hope, he had courage to pursue his journey. When he reached London, he drove instantly to Balfour's lodgings; and almost too much agitated to be intelligible, he asked for Mr. Balfour.

"My master, sir," replied the servant with a look of great and complacent meaning, "is gone to church."

"To church!" said St. Aubyn.

"Yes, sir, to be married; he has been gone about twenty minutes to St. George's, Hanover-Square."

I will not attempt to describe St. Aubyn's feelings at hearing this, while agitated nature vented and relieved itself in a passionate flood of tears. He did not then come too late! and he passed from absolute despair to hope.

"Drive to St. George's church," cried St. Aubyn. But as the motion of the post-chaise was not rapid enough for him, he opened the door, jumped out, and in a few minutes was at the church-door.

"I *must* come in," he exclaimed to the man who opposed his entrance, "I come to Mr. Balfour from his father Lord Clonawley. And stop me at your peril!"

On hearing this, the man dared to oppose him no longer, and he walked up the middle isle. The minister who was officiating had just got to the words, "If any of you know cause or impediment, why these two persons are not to be joined together in holy matrimony, ye are now to declare it;" when St. Aubyn appeared in sight, loudly exclaiming, "I do"—and advanced to the altar.

At sight of him the same apprehension was felt by all who knew him; namely, that St. Aubyn, distracted by the loss of Emma, was come thither in a fit of frenzy; but this idea vanished, when the latter, premising that he came thither deputed by Lord Clonawley to forbid the marriage, presented his father's letter to Balfour, desiring him to read it immediately.

Then, while Balfour, pale and trembling, perused the unwelcome contents, St. Aubyn, as much agitated as himself, turned to Mrs. Castlemain.

"It has been my blessed lot, dear madam," said he, "to be the instrument to save those I most love from destruction! and in addition I am enabled to assure you that the fact of your daughter's marriage is established beyond a doubt; here is the registry of that marriage, (presenting it to her,) and here the dying confession of Cammell himself, and——" here his voice and strength began to fail—— "Lord Clonawley owns your beloved Emma to be his legitimate daughter, by——" Then, exhausted by several nights devoid of rest, and passed in misery and fatigue, he sunk into the arms of the person who stood near him, and was conveyed in a swoon into the vestry. Meanwhile his words had excited in his auditors, Balfour excepted, surprise the most unbounded and feelings the most varied. To Balfour, his father's letter had already told the same; but Balfour's feelings had, unlike those of Mr. Egerton, Mrs. Castlemain, and Emma, nothing of pleasure mixed with agony, except that of joy and thankfulness at being prevented the commission of a crime; he even sometimes doubted the fact of Emma's being his sister; which however his previous knowledge of her history, and now the testimony of Mr. Egerton, confirmed too strongly for him to doubt any longer; and unable to bear the various emotions that assailed him, he attempted to leave the church alone. But this Mr. Egerton would not suffer; and accompanying him to his hotel, he did not leave him till he was composed, and his sister Fanny was come to bear him company. Mrs. Castlemain and Emma, during this time, were anxiously awaiting the recovery of St. Aubyn; while Emma, though at a loss to guess how St. Aubyn had been the means of saving her from an incestuous marriage, felt happy at owing her preservation to him; and both ladies mingled, with pious thankfulness to heaven, blessings on their earthly friend and preserver.

It was therefore with almost overwhelming agony they found, on St. Aubyn's recovering from his fainting fit, that his eyes were wild, and his language incoherent; and that, not knowing any one about him, he raved of not getting to England in time; and was evidently so ill, that Mrs. Castlemain conveyed him to her own lodgings, and desired a physician to be sent for immediately. It was some days before St. Aubyn was conscious of his happiness in being nursed by Mr. Egerton and Mrs. Castlemain with even parental tenderness; while Emma, unseen, hovered near the bed that contained the being endeared to her heart by every tie that can bind one fellow-being to another.

At length St. Aubyn's danger was over, and he once more recognized the friends who, worn with anxiety, hung over his restless pillow. Emma's happiness amounted almost to agony; and she wondered what was become of those internal *intimations* of approaching *dissolution* which she had contemplated with such calm complacence, just before she fixed the day to be married to Balfour. The marriage day had been fixed as for the morrow, when Balfour wrote to his father; but Emma's health had yielded at length completely to uneasiness of mind; and on the morning fixed for the wedding, she was declared to be suffering under that painful disorder, a low and nervous fever.

When she recovered, however, she persisted in marrying Balfour; for she felt a conviction, perhaps *dear* to her mind, that she should not long survive the union, and she thought it her duty to let Balfour call her his before she died, as his persevering tenderness still desired to obtain this privilege. Weak, faded, and, in her own opinion, dying, she was therefore conveyed to church, and was about to pronounce the most sacred of all vows, when she was so happily prevented, and by a circumstance which in a few hours restored her love, and even her hope of life; and in a few days, that is, as soon as St. Aubyn was declared out of danger, her delighted friends saw colour restored to her cheek, and spirit to her eye.

As soon as St. Aubyn was sufficiently recovered to bear conversation, Mrs. Castlemain, who had hung over his sick bed with even a mother's tenderness, and bathed his unconscious face with many a tear of affectionate alarm, could no longer restrain her expressions of gratitude to him, for the signal services he had been enabled to render her, and those most dear to her; and she listened with painful interest to his explanation of the circumstances which led to it. When he had ended his narration, she exclaimed, "there is one way, Henry, and only one, in which I can ever hope to reward you; and it shall not be my fault, if all the happiness that is in my power to bestow, is not yours, whenever decorum warrants it." So saying, she left the room, and returned with Emma; then joining their hands, she said with great emotion,

"There, Henry, plead your own cause, and believe me that to witness your union with that object of my fondest care, will give me the highest happiness which an anxious parent can experience; for to whom can a parent confide the welfare of her child with such confidence of securing it, as to a man whose whole life has been an exemplary series of duties fulfilled?"

It cannot be supposed that Henry pleaded his cause in vain; and day after day glided by unheeded, while mutual and satisfactory explanations took place between the lovers. Still, as Emma had been so recently on the point of marriage with another, it was thought only proper that a year should elapse before she became the bride of St. Aubyn. When St. Aubyn was well enough to go out in the carriage, his first airing was to Kensington.

Emma had taken the earliest opportunity after her return to England, to call on the Orwells, and introduce Balfour to them as her future husband. Mr. Egerton, and she herself, had informed them by letter of her approaching marriage; but as it was not a subject on which either of them was fond of dilating, the good old couple had not heard enough of the intended bridegroom to satisfy either their affections or their curiosity; and they were particularly anxious to know whether Balfour was that handsome, benevolent-looking young man who had called on them and would not tell his name.

Accordingly they were delighted to see Mrs. Castlemain's carriage stop at their door, and Mr. Orwell eagerly ran out to receive his welcome visiters; while Mrs. Orwell, seeing from the window that the gentleman on whose arm Emma leaned was tall and blooming, readily believed what she wished, and concluded that Balfour was the identical unknown, who had so much charmed both her and her husband.

Hastening therefore to the door, she eagerly exclaimed, "Well! this is just what I——" but there she paused, for Balfour turned his face towards her, and with a look of disappointment she made him a cold courtesy; while Emma, conscious of what the old lady was about to say, and understanding the change in her countenance, hastily passed her, and, complaining of fatigue, leaned her head for a moment on the side of the sofa.

This visit to the Orwells was short, for Balfour was impatient to be gone; but it was long enough to convince Mrs. Orwell that Emma was not in love with the man whom she was going to marry, and with great bitterness did she inveigh against Mrs. Castlemain's cruelty in sacrificing her granddaughter for the sake of a title; while Mr. Orwell, though he angrily reproved his wife for what might be unjust suspicions, could not help entertaining similar ones himself, and he reluctantly owned that Emma looked alarmingly ill.

But now feelings of a very different nature awaited them. Emma had previously informed them, that she was coming to introduce to them her friend, Mr. St. Aubyn, to whom they all owed so much.

Impatiently, therefore, was this visit expected; and when in the pale, languid, but happy-looking invalid, whom Mrs. Castlemain and Emma fondly supported, and whose looks they affectionately watched, the Orwells recognised their unknown visiter, they exchanged looks of triumph and delight, and Mrs. Orwell could not help exclaiming, "Ay, this is just what I wished to see, and I am not disappointed *now*."

When their guests departed, after a long and satisfactory visit, Mr. Orwell, as he re-entered the house, exclaimed, rubbing his hands, as he always did when he was particularly gratified, "Well, old woman, I hope you are pleased *now*; and that our dear young lady is enough in love, and looks happy enough to satisfy even you?"

One morning, St. Aubyn received a letter, forwarded to him from Ibbetson's Hotel, the address which he had given to Lord Clonawley. It was from that unhappy man, and contained the unexpected intelligence that he was arrived at a hotel in Albemarle street, and begged to see St. Aubyn immediately; but adding, that having driven to his son's lodgings, as soon as he reached town, where Balfour's grateful anxiety made him remain till St. Aubyn was declared out of danger, he had had the happiness to find he was not married, and that that dreadful punishment for his offences was remitted. I shall observe here, that the already *improved* Lord Clonawley had made one of his daughters transmit this good news immediately to the *poor anxious Lola.*

St. Aubyn had only been abroad once since his illness. It was, therefore, on that account, and on many others, thought proper that Mr. Egerton only should go to him; and with a heart full of indescribable emotion, he prepared himself for an interview with the destroyer of Agatha, and the father of her deserted child.

It was late in the evening before Mr. Egerton returned; and never had either St. Aubyn, or Emma, or Mrs. Castlemain beheld him so deeply affected as he now was. For he had been endeavouring to awake a sinner to repentance; he had been listening to the painful narration of a life of profligacy. The profligate too, was the father of the child of his adoption and his love!

"However," thought Mr. Egerton, "his son, luckily for him, was never long enough with his father to be corrupted by his example; and the future Lord Clonawley will, I trust, be an honour, instead of a disgrace to his family!"

But even for Lord Clonawley, Mr. Egerton, who, like all good men, was indulgent to the faults of others, could make considerable excuses.

His father, a man of family, but of small fortune, married his mistress, a woman taken from the dregs of the people; but he kept his marriage a secret many years, and brought up his son, though born in wedlock, in the obscurity and humble education usually attendant on illegitimate children. The young man, therefore, instead of associating with his father's, lived with his mother's relations; instead of passing his time with gentlemen, was the companion of men whose manners were as vulgar as their morals were depraved. When he was eighteen, his father, having owned his marriage, gave him a private tutor, and at twenty sent him to College; but he had not one feeling or principle of a gentleman, on which to found the conduct of one, though his discernment, and his talents of imitation, soon taught him the necessity and the power of acquiring a gentleman's manners.

Shortly after his leaving the University, he was summoned to join his father in India, where he married, and remained a few years. Soon after, by the death of three persons, who were even in the prime of life, Mr. Balfour senior saw four lives only between him and the title of Clonawley, and there was only one life between Balfour and the succession at the time of his father's and mother's death, which was at the period of his rupture with Agatha. The fortune, therefore, which Agatha was heiress to, held out too remote a temptation to him to influence his conduct towards her, as a greater fortune would soon, in all likelihood, be in his grasp; and as he was most passionately in love with another woman, he was resolved to spare no villany to obtain possession of her. When he saw Agatha at the race-ball, he had dropped his surname, and was known by his christian name alone, in order to avoid a prosecution, with which he was threatened, for having seduced a farmer's daughter, in

Vol. III.——15　　　　　w

which guilt Cammell had assisted him; and while he was supposed on the continent, he was on a visit to one of his profligate friends, Captain Bertie, who was in his secret, and kept it most sacredly. The name of Danvers, he thought it advisable to retain, even when the idea of a prosecution was dropped; but after he had married his third wife, he owned his real name, telling her and her weak father, as they were sailing to Jamaica, where the latter had large plantations, that as he was next heir to a title, he concealed his name, that he might be sure his daughter did not marry him for the sake of his rank; and soon after he became Lord Clonawley. His son, meanwhile, was left in England, under the care of a tutor, of rigid morals, though not fitted to form the temper and correct the selfish habits which Balfour had contracted in childhood. Still, however, the outline was good, and only the filling-up defective; and Balfour certainly had none of his father's vices.

Mr. Egerton found from Lord Clonawley's discourse, that he had tenderly loved his third wife, whose sweetness of temper had won his affection; but that Agatha, instead of soothing, had always irritated him; and by the reproaches of her wounded pride, and her dictatorial, contemptuous manner, had changed all the passionate fondness which her person and her talents had first excited in him, into fear and aversion. Such were the bitter fruits to Agatha of an uncorrected temper.

Still, never without painful remorse, had Lord Clonawley remembered Agatha; and terror lest he should hear that some harm had happened to her and her child, in consequence of his desertion, had always prevented him from making any inquiries concerning them, in order to ascertain whether the mother of Agatha, in consequence of his letter, had received her and the little Emma to her favour and protection.

Bitterly now did Lord Clonawley lament the turpitude of his conduct towards her; and he listened to the narration of her despair, her poverty, her industry, her sufferings, and her death, with agonies that completely revenged her on her betrayer.

"But you tell me she forgave me," he repeated, "forgave and prayed for me!" And from that idea alone he derived consolation; but he had reparation to make to the living; and there again his punishment was severe; for he saw himself forced to punish the children whom he knew and loved, for the guilt he alone had perpetrated, by depriving them of their rank and name in society; and to own publicly, as his only lawful daughter, a child whom he never saw, and who had probably been brought up to detest him.

Mr. Egerton left him, however, calmed and composed, and Balfour with him, who, thinking he had better quit London, and not see Emma till he could behold her without emotion, determined to set off on a tour the next day. Balfour had been violent in his anger towards his erring parent, forgetting that Lord Clonawley had something to forgive his son.

Balfour, knowing how particular his father was with respect to family and connexions, was well convinced that, if he informed him Emma's claim to legitimate birth was equivocal, he would do all in his power to prevent the marriage. Actuated therefore by the impulse of that unyielding temper, which could not endure the slightest opposition, he suppressed Mrs. Castlemain's letter, explaining her relationship to Emma, and suffered Lord Clonawley to remain in the belief that she was Mrs. Castlemain's daughter. Nor, till Balfour confessed what he had done to Mr. Egerton, could the latter imagine why the discovery had not taken place as soon as Lord Clonawley received that letter. Thus the disingenuousness of Balfour, like all conduct of that nature, was very near being the cause of irreparable misery; and thus was Mrs. Castlemain convinced how judiciously Mr. Egerton thought and spoke, when he opposed Emma's being called Castlemain instead of Danvers; adding, "that he never knew any good the result of deception, and praying that from this deception no material mischief might ensue."

"Emma," said Mr. Egerton, "I have promised for you, that you will see your father."

"I am sorry for it, sir," replied Emma, proudly, "for never can I bear to behold the destroyer of my mother!"

"That mother," solemnly replied Mr. Egerton, "delayed to forgive her offending parent, till death made it impossible for her to see that parent, and pronounce the forgiveness which she then earnestly wished to bestow. Take warning by her mournful example, and remember that it is not for a child to take upon itself to punish even a guilty parent!" Here Emma, in great emotion, precipitately left the room; but, after a long struggle with herself, she returned, and going up to Mr. Egerton, assured him that whenever Lord Clonawley was willing to admit her, she would be willing to visit him; and the satisfaction which her lover and her friend expressed, amply repaid her for the conquest she had gained over her resentments.

Mr. Egerton immediately wrote to Lord Clonawley, desiring him to fix a day for seeing his daughter; but that very evening he was seized with a mortal malady. Agitation of mind brought on a return of bleeding at the lungs to which he had long been subject, and it was soon decided that all aid was vain. Just before this news reached Emma, she received Lord Clonawley's letter, which by some strange chance had not yet reached her.

Mr. Egerton, having sent an express for Balfour, who had left town two days preceding, came to inform Emma of her father's situation, and she instantly exclaimed,

"Oh! how glad I am that before I received his letter, and heard of his danger, I had consented to see him!"

"I come also to tell you," added Mr. Egerton, "that he cannot die in peace without beholding you, and asking your pardon in person for the wrongs he did you." And Emma, though pale and trembling with emotion, eagerly begged to be immediately conducted to him.

"No, my dear child," replied Mr. Egerton, "I will not conduct you to him, but I will follow soon. You shall go, supported and encouraged by the presence of that man, who was an example of filial piety himself, and who will have a pride and pleasure in seeing you fulfil the painful duty which filial piety now imposes on you."

"I have informed Lord Clonawley of St. Aubyn's claims and pretensions, which he warmly admits and approves; and he wishes to pronounce his dying blessing on your union."

This intelligence softened Emma's heart still more towards her dying parent; and with more emotion and less reluctance she set off for Albemarle-street, and was led by St. Aubyn to the presence of Lord Clonawley.

As soon as he beheld her, he exclaimed, "'T is she! my injured wife herself seems to stand before me!" Then, hiding his face in his hands, he sobbed audibly and convulsively.

From the generous and feeling nature of Emma, every trace of resentment vanished as she beheld the self-judged object before her, and no feeling but of pity remained. Lord Clonawley at length becoming able to bear to look at her, raised his eyes imploringly to hers, and extended towards her his damp and meagre hand.

"Will you, can you forgive me, my child?" he faintly exclaimed.

"From my very soul!" cried Emma, throwing herself beside him.

"Thanks! thanks!" he replied in a hurried manner, "her very voice too! and in the same sweet mournful tone as when I heard it last."

Emma now raised herself, and sat on the side of the bed, holding her father's hand in hers, while her sisters leaned over him on the other side, vainly trying to engage a little of his attention; but that attention was now so completely riveted on Emma, that he saw not St. Aubyn, whom he had wished so much to see, nor Mr. Egerton, who now entered the room, and for whom he had repeatedly inquired.

The delirium of death was indeed fast approaching; and mistaking Emma for her mother, lord Clonawley eagerly and repeatedly addressed her by the name of Agatha, and begged her to forgive her guilty husband all his trespasses against her.

"Pray for me, Agatha, pray for me, my beloved wife," he wildly cried; and Emma willing to indulge a delusion that might give him comfort, fell on her knees, and raising one hand to Heaven, while he grasped the other in his cold convulsive grasp,

"Merciful author of my existence," she exclaimed, "forgive this penitent sufferer as freely as I forgive him!"

The eyes of the dying man beamed with momentary brightness as she spoke; then, turning to the last on her, they soon after closed for ever.

Mr. Egerton immediately desired St. Aubyn to lead Emma away, while he remained with the poor orphans, in whose sullen grief he evidently beheld no heart-yearnings, but the contrary, towards their new-found sister, and therefore thought it best for the present to remove her from their sight.

Fanny, whose spirits were too weak to bear the scene that awaited Emma, had remained with Mrs. Castlemain, whom lord Clonawley had, luckily for her, not wished to see; and when Emma returned, the poor girl, who loved her tenderly, flew to her arms with every sentiment of tenderness towards her that Emma could desire; and they together wept, though with different feelings, the parent whom they had lost.

Lord Clonawley made a will the day before he died, in which he left only 2000*l.* each to his daughters, Mary Ann, Harriet, and Fanny; his estates of course coming to his son, who was, as my readers must be sensible of, the identical little boy, the only child by his first marriage, whom he had himself introduced to Agatha. To *Emma*, designated expressly by the name of Emma Balfour, his sole legitimate daughter by Agatha Torrington, his lawful wife, he gave the sum of 10,000*l.*

"Did you talk to my father *much* of me?" said Emma as soon as she recovered the violent emotion which she felt, on hearing the contents of the will.

"I did," he replied, "and spoke of you as I thought."

"I suspected as much," said Emma, bursting into tears, and hastening to her own room, where with a trembling hand she penned the following letter:

"My dear sisters,

"Our lost father, by willing to me so disproportionate a share of his fortune, relieved his conscience from a painful burthen. Now then let me relieve mine, and prove myself worthy of the reliance which, I evidently see, lord Clonawley placed on my justice and my affection. I insist on sharing equally with you the fortune he has bequeathed to me, and I conjure you to accept the offer as a proof of the affectionate regard of

"Your new-found sister,
"Emma Balfour."

For this offer, which Balfour allowed them to accept, his sisters employed him to express to Emma their grateful acknowledgments, promising to visit her at the White Cottage on their return from Ireland, whither they were going, with their brother, to follow the corpse of their father.

Mrs. Castlemain and Emma then set off for the White Cottage, and Mr. Egerton and St. Aubyn soon followed them to Cumberland.

On their road thither, as St. Aubyn was talking over his affairs, and telling Mr. Egerton what settlements he meant to make on Emma, the latter said,

"As I find, Henry, that you are now a much richer man than I am, I shall trouble you to pay me the little debt you owe me."

"A debt! my dear sir, I was not conscious that I ever owed you one."

"Very likely," replied the other, "nevertheless you do owe me a trifle."

"Name the sum, that I may repay it," cried St. Aubyn, taking out his purse.

"Pho! not a hundred purses could contain your debt to me; you owe me *only* the little sum of £80,000!" and while St. Aubyn, dumb with amazement, did not attempt to speak, Mr. Egerton proceeded to inform him, that hearing the St. Aubyn estate was again to be disposed of, he had purchased it for that money, meaning to restore it, either during his life, or at his death, to its original inheritor.

Next to the possession of Emma, there was nothing so near to the heart of St. Aubyn, as the recovery of his paternal estate; though he had never flattered himself with being able to effect it. His delight and his gratitude, therefore, were in proportion to this desire.

"Best of friends!" he exclaimed.

"Nonsense!" replied Mr. Egerton, "not the *best* of friends, but a *friend;* one who has not only the inclination but the power to prove his friendship by his actions. You had not money enough to buy St. Aubyn, and I had; and I am very sure that had you been me and I you, you would have done the same."

"Well," said St. Aubyn, "I have only to hope that you will always consider St. Aubyn as your own residence, and make Emma and me happy, by accepting apartments there."

"No," replied Mr. Egerton, "I will never be more than your guest, and my little cottage shall still be my *all* of mansion."

At length the time fixed on for the union of St. Aubyn and Emma, arrived; and Balfour, now lord Clonawley, accompanied his sisters, when they came to witness it; and having convinced himself that he mistook the instinctive regard of a brother for the impulse of passion, he felt no emotions but those of proper affection for the betrothed bride of St. Aubyn; and now he no longer looked upon him as a rival, his heart, which was really virtuous, and formed to love virtue, did ample justice to the merits of his new relation.

"Every wish of my heart is so completely filled," said St. Aubyn to Mr. Egerton, some months after his marriage, "that I wish, and so does Emma, to pass life between St. Aubyn and the Vale-House, and never, except for a few weeks at a time, encounter the busy scenes of the metropolis."

"I should approve your decision," replied Mr. Egerton, "if you had neither talents, virtues, nor energy enough to fit you for some public situation of life; but when I consider what you are, and the usefulness that you are capable of being, I must condemn, as inexcusable selfishness, those wishes which would lead you to bury yourself in retirement. I well know that the duties of a country gentleman are many, and that you can do much good by fulfilling those duties; but as the senate is the place where an upright and independent man can render the greatest service to his country at large, it is the wish of my heart, approved most warmly by my judgment, that you should divide your time between the metropolis and your estates, and exert in the House of Commons those powers of mind, and that rectitude of feeling and principle, which in a country life could only be exercised in duties comparatively of slender importance."

St. Aubyn, whose life had hitherto been spent in a surrender of his own wishes to those of others, was now naturally enough inclined to live, during his succeeding years, for his own good alone, and that of those whom he loved best.

But at length Mr. Egerton's reasoning, and Mrs. Castlemain's ambition, urged him to accept a seat in parliament; and Emma's first child was born in the metropolis.

Varley, meanwhile, returned from his wanderings, and had embarked for England in the same boat with Mrs. Felton, who remained in France long after our travellers, and left it just after she had heard of the discovery of Emma's birth from Mrs. Fitz-Walter; who had a pleasure in adding that St. Aubyn, to whom that discovery was owing, was supposed to be the betrothed lover of Emma. It was with great joy, therefore, that, when she recognized Varley, and asked why he had so suddenly displeased his friends, and left Paris, he told her he could not account for their behaviour, except in a way to call his modesty in question; insinuating, very adroitly, that Emma, the pure and precise Emma, had made him such advances as had alarmed the prudence of Mr. Egerton, and the jealousy of Balfour. And though Mrs. Felton did not in her heart believe the tale, she was delighted to act as if she did, and to give hints of the sort when she arrived in England, where Varley became a constant guest at her parties; and some confidential few he amused by mimicking Mrs. Castlemain's dignity, Mr. Egerton's long speeches, and Emma's girlish vivacity, which, to those who did not know them, appeared admirable likenesses. But it was at length suggested to Mrs. Felton, by a male friend, that the youth who thus made free with the reputation of his former acquaintance, Miss Castlemain, might be as free with his present one, Mrs. Felton; and hearing, from undoubted authority, that he had boasted of favours from her which he never received, and also called her, when speaking of her, his lovely Lucy, she indignantly forbade him her house; and as the lady, at whose house Emma first saw him in town, was now reconciled to her, and once more become her intimate friend, she also ceased to invite him to her conversation parties out of respect to Mrs. Felton. Thus Varley was restored to his original obscurity, and absence from those fashionable circles in which it was his first ambition to shine. But Mr. Egerton, just in his wrath, did not suffer the industrious and indigent mother to suffer for the faults of her son, and he sent her occasionally very handsome presents from an unknown hand.

But to return to St. Aubyn:

However averse he might originally have been to a residence of many months at a time in the metropolis, he could not help feeling his pride and tenderness amply gratified while there, by the flattering attention and admiration which his beautiful and accomplished wife excited; for it was such as could not have called forth one angry or unpleasant feeling in the most jealous of husbands, or most delicate of men, and was not only a tribute to the charms of her mind and person, but to the propriety of her conduct and her manners. Well and justly indeed, was it said of Emma, that though any one might have fallen in love with her before marriage, no one would have thought of doing so after it; the highest eulogium that can be passed on a young and beautiful woman.

While the delighted St. Aubyn seemed to follow his graceful wife, wherever she moved, with eyes of approving fondness, Mrs. Fitz-Walter had great satisfaction in observing to her dear friend, Mrs. Felton, with whom the St. Aubyns were on civil though distant terms,

"Was there ever such a doting husband as Mr. St. Aubyn? I am sure he is not conscious there is another woman in the world besides his wife! and, indeed, I do not think there is another woman in it worthy of such a man!" and Mrs. Felton, by exclaiming,

"Ridiculous! absurd!" her only answer on these occasions, sufficiently betrayed, that she felt all the mortification which her kind friend meant to inflict.

Mrs. Castlemain, though much distressed at a separation from Emma, had wisdom and self-denial enough to refuse to accompany her to London. For, as she felt the most certain conviction that Emma was worthy of implicit confidence, she thought it but right that she should mix in London society without any other guard than her husband, and her own prudence.

Mr. Egerton, too, now he had reaped the reward of his own paternal care of her, in seeing her the wife of St. Aubyn, felt that it was no longer necessary for him to forego his own tastes and pursuits. And having no surviving relations, or even friends, who required his society or assistance, he resolved to pass in studious retirement, and in benevolent exertions for the instruction and benefit of the poor in the neighbourhood of the White Cottage, those hours hitherto passed in superintending and accompanying his beloved pupil. But though he and Mrs. Castlemain had persisted to remain behind in the still shades of Cumberland, it was always with affectionate and almost painful impatience that they awaited the hour that should restore to them their best treasures. And when they beheld their carriages and servants winding down the opposite mountain, the tear of ill-restrained delight glistened in the eye of both.

"See," said Emma to Mr. Egerton, when she returned from the metropolis the second time after her residence there; "see, my dear sir, (giving her little boy into his arms,) I have brought you another pupil; and I trust that, by dint of my own watchful care, your precepts, and his father's example, he will be in temper and disposition all that he ought to be."

"You are too modest," replied Mr. Egerton as he kissed the babe, and returned it to its mother; "you omit to mention the probable usefulness of your own example, as well as watchfulness."

"Mine!" exclaimed Emma; "mine! Surely you must forget to what a violent, headstrong creature you are talking."

"Pardon me," returned he; "I do remember you were once what you describe; but I also remember how readily you undertook the difficult task of conquering your temper, and how admirably you succeeded in it. Sweetness of temper is often, as I have before observed, the result of a happy conformation and perfect health, and is no more a virtue in its possessor than beauty of person. But when a sense of duty leads the self-judged slave of an unhappy temper to conquer that irritability, then is good temper exalted into a virtue; and this virtue I have seen so often exhibited by you, that I shall, if I live to see your child old enough to understand my advice, have no scruple in holding up his mother, as well as his father, as a model to be imitated."

"The author of that interesting poem, The Triumphs of Temper," observed Mrs. Castlemain, "is of your opinion, Mr. Egerton, with regard to the importance of good temper, for he says;

' Virtue's an ingot of Peruvian gold;
Sense, the bright ore Potosi's mines unfold;
But Temper's image must their use create,
And give these precious metals sterling weight.' "

"I thank you, madam," replied Mr. Egerton, "for reminding me of my coincidence in opinion with the author of that poem; but I should wonder if any one, who thinks at all, were to deny the truth of this sentiment. There is no situation in life in which fine temper is not of use. In affliction it disposes the sufferer to dwell more on the blessings it still retains, than on those which it has lost, and thereby prepares the mind for the influence of pious resignation. In sickness it induces patience and quiet endurance, lest complaint should wound the feelings of affectionate attendants; while it disposes those affectionate attendants themselves to bear with the often provoking and ungrateful petulance of disease; for though religion and principle may in time clear away every obstacle to their desirable ends, the way to them is made easy and quick at once if Temper be the guide."

"But surely," said St. Aubyn, who entered the room at this moment, "it is not enough to consider what temper can enable us to do; one should reflect how many things without its assistance one cannot do. Without command of temper no one can be sure of always speaking truth; for many persons, of both sexes, utter, while under the dominion of passion, what they are glad to disown and to explain away when their passion is over."

"True," observed Emma laughing, "as for instance, in the Commons house of parliament, when one honourable member gets up and begs to know whether the honourable gentleman on the other side of the house meant really, by such and such words, what such and such words really mean; on which the honourable gentleman appealed to, assures the honourable appellant, that by such and such words he did not mean what such and such words really mean, (to translate these things into the language of truth,) on which the honourable appellant professes himself entirely satisfied that *black* is *not black* but *white*."

"Fy, Emma, fy!" replied St. Aubyn, laughing, "this is more severe than true; for, after all, these explanations are understood to be only modes of speech."

"So, so," cried Mr. Egerton, "I see you have acquired an esprit du corps, Henry, already, and do not like to have your respectable body attacked even by a joke."

"I have surely a right, sir," returned St. Aubyn, "to insist on Emma's extending her remark to the Lords, and owning that respectable body to be as liable as our own to these façons de parler, which she chooses to call falsehoods."

"Oh! by all means," answered Emma, "and I dare say similar scenes occur among them as frequently as amongst you; for no doubt there is nothing so like a commoner in a passion as a lord in one; and I beg leave to add to the list of what one cannot do without command of temper, that one cannot be always *well-bred* without such self-command; for both gentlemen and gentlewomen when angry, say and do what, for the time being, makes them neither the one nor the other."

"I am inclined to think also," resumed St. Aubyn, "that one cannot *love* perfectly without temper. We often hear that there is nothing so like *hatred* as *love;* and that lovers have a great delight in tormenting each other. Now, though I admit that love, and lovers as we see them every day, exemplify the truth of these observations, still I am convinced, that were the cultivation of good temper as universal as it ought to be, these fine definitions of love, and these descriptions of lovers, would be known no more. The truth is, that our habits of temper and feeling are formed in childhood, and long before the passion of love can be felt; consequently, however powerful love may be, temper being still more so, it gives its *own* obliquity to the *tender* passion as it is called. And when love resembles hate, and lovers take delight in tormenting each other, such horrors are to be explained thus; that, in the first instance, temper has more sway over the individual so erring than real affection; and in the second, that the lover who torments and tyrannizes over his mistress, or the mistress who torments and tyrannizes over her lover, would, if they could and dared, torment and tyrannize over the rest of their species; and that they take this liberty chiefly with one alone, because they believe that, as the tormented being loves them, they can give way to their temper with impunity."

"Well, Mr. St. Aubyn," replied Emma, "you are sure of my assent to this doctrine; for, as I can safely declare that you never yet thought proper to torture me in order to convince me of your love,—if I did not believe in its truth, I must doubt the sincerity of your affection, and that would be rather disagreeable."

"I agree entirely, and without such an inducement," said Mr. Egerton, "in all that Henry has advanced."

"But who can be always on their guard?" cried Mrs. Castlemain. "Occasional irritability of nerves, or secret anxiety, may sometimes overset the finest temper."

"True," replied St. Aubyn; "and after all, we must denominate as fine-tempered, not those who are never out of humour, for where are they to be found? but those who are most rarely thrown off their guard."

"I think," said Emma, "that Temper, like other great potentates, has her levées and her gala days. I know, sir, (addressing Mr. Egerton,) that you consider a revolution as a time when Temper is seated on her throne of state, with all her ugly ministers around her. And what think you, sir, of a contested election? That surely is one of her gala times; but then she wears ribands, and goes about with flags and music, and looks so pretty and so animated, and so like something very charming, that we forget what her real nature is."

"I am glad," returned Mr. Egerton, "to find that you are so conscious of the influence of Temper at elections, Mrs. St. Aubyn, as this knowledge will enable you, should your husband ever be opposed, to keep a guard over *your* temper; for those only are safe from falling who are conscious of their danger."

" And that danger lies more in trifles than great events," returned Emma. " I have often heard the trials of Serena blamed as being too trivial ; but I have considered the critics on this occasion, as no attentive observers of human nature and life; for it is very certain that trifles irritate the temper more than things of importance; and that great trials call for that higher order of exertion and virtue known by the name of fortitude and resignation. But the man or woman who can support loss of relations and fortune with dignified calmness, might very likely give way to impatience and angry fretfulness at the carelessness of a servant, a peevish contradiction from a relation, or a spiteful remark from a companion."

" True," replied Mr. Egerton ; " and I feel very happy in the consciousness that you are thus deeply impressed with the importance of a well-governed temper, as this impression will constantly influence you in the management of your children. To borrow the words of a great man,

' 'T is not in mortals to command success.'

But you 'll do more, my Emma, you 'll deserve it. Events over which we have no power often cloud the prospects of us all, and change our joy to sorrow. But parents, in giving their children good habits, bestow on them the best chance of virtuous prosperity; and good habits are gifts which it is chiefly in a mother's power to bestow, and what her offspring are capable of being benefited by, even in the earliest stages of childhood, since that is the time to begin the formation of the Temper; for, considering *happiness* as the goal in view, VIRTUE and TALENT are two Arabian coursers, which, however fleet and powerful, would never reach the desired and destined point unless managed and guided by the hand of TEMPER."

THE END OF TEMPER.

A WOMAN'S LOVE, AND A WIFE'S DUTY.

You command, and I obey: still, so conscious am I of the deceitfulness of the human heart, and especially of my own, that I am doubtful whether I am not following the dictates of self-love, when I seem to be actuated by friendship only; as you have repeatedly assured me, that the story of my life will not alone *amuse* and *interest* you, but also hold up to an injudicious and suffering friend of yours, a salutary example of the patient fulfilment of a *wife's duty.*

There is something very gratifying to one's self-love, in being held up as an example: but *remember*, I beg, that while to oblige you I draw the veil from past occurrences, and live over again the most trying scenes of my life, I think myself more a warning than an example; and that, if I exhibit in any degree, that difficult and sometimes painful task — the fulfilment of a wife's duty—I at the same time exhibit the rash and dangerous fervour of a *Woman's Love.*

I must begin my narrative, by a short account of my progenitors.

INTRODUCTION.

My grandfather and the grandfather of Seymour Pendarves were brothers, and the younger sons of a gentleman of ancient family and large possessions in the county of Cornwall; some of whose paternal ancestors were amongst the first settlers in America. Disappointments, of which I never heard the detail, and dislike of their paternal home, determined these young men to leave their native country, and embark for the new world, where the family had still some land remaining, and on the improvement of which they determined to spend a sum of money which had been left them by a relation. They carried out with them, besides money, *enterprise, industry, integrity*, and *talents*. After they had been settled in Long Island three years, they found themselves rich enough to marry ; and the beautiful daughters of an opulent American farmer became their wives.

My grandfather had only one child—a son; but his brother had a large family, of whom, however, one only survived — a son also. These two cousins were brought up together, and were as much attached to each other as if they had been brothers.

Never, as I have been told, was there a scene of greater domestic happiness, than my grandfather's house exhibited, till death deprived him of his beloved wife. He did not long survive her; and my uncle soon afterwards lost her equally-beloved sister, whose health had been destroyed, first by the fatigue of attendance on her sick children, and then by grief for their loss.

George Pendarves, the sad survivor of so many dear ones, now lost his spirits—lost that energy which had so much distinguished him before; and he soon sunk under the cessation of those habits of exertion and temperance, which he had once practised, and, after two or three years of protracted suffering, died. Thus the two youthful cousins found themselves both orphans before they had reached the age of twenty.

They had not inherited their parents' dislike of Europe. On the contrary, when their fathers imparted to them the learning and the elegant arts which they had acquired at the university, and in the society of England, they were impressed with respect and admiration for the sources whence such precious stores were derived, and resolved to enter themselves at an English college.

Accordingly, having put a confidential agent into their farms, they set sail for the land of their ancestors, and arrived at PENDARVES CASTLE, the seat of their eldest paternal uncle, who had come into possession of the estates on the death of his father.

At this time, my mother and Lady Helen Seymour, the daughter of Lord Seymour, were both on a visit there. The young Americans had now been some months expected, and their relations had long been amusing themselves with conjecturing what these SAVAGES (as they fancied them) would be like; while they anticipated much pleasure from beholding their surprise at manners, scenes, and accommodations, so different from their own. Nor was my mother, though she was their relation, and herself a Pendarves, less forward than her friend Lady Helen to hold up these strangers in a ridiculous view to her imagination, and to express an unbenevolent eagerness for the arrival of the *Yankees*.

At length, they came; and it was on the evening of a ball, given by Mr. Pendarves, to celebrate the birth-day of his wife. The dance was begun before they arrived; and their uncle was called out of the room to receive them. He went with a heart warmed with fraternal affection, and yearning towards the representatives of his regretted brothers: but the emotion became overpowering when he beheld them; for those well-remembered brothers seemed to stand before him in improved loftiness of stature, dignity of person, and beauty of feature. From their mothers, they had inherited that loveliness and symmetry, which so peculiarly distinguish American women; and in stature they towered even above their father's family.

The young men, at the same time, were considerably affected at sight of Mr. Pendarves, as he reminded them strongly of their parents. While these endearing recollections were uppermost in their minds, Mr. Pendarves at first wholly forgot how different his nephews were from the pictures his laughter-loving family had delighted to draw of them. But when he did recollect it, he enjoyed the idea of the surprise which their appearance would occasion.

Their dress, as well as their manners, bespoke them perfect gentlemen; but their hair was not yet spoiled by compliance with the fashion of England at that period; for it curled, uncontaminated by powder, in glossy clustering ringlets on their open brows.

Such were the young men who now followed Mr. Pendarves to the apartment in which his lady received her guests.

"Dear me! how surprising!" cried that lady, who was very pretty, very volatile, and very apt to think aloud. "Are these the Yankees? Why, I protest they look more like Christians than savages, and are like other people, except that they are much handsomer than other people."

This last part of her speech made some amends for the first part; but had she been of a contrary opinion, Mrs. Pendarves would have uttered it; and the glow of indignation on their cheek was succeeded by that of gratified vanity, for their hostess added to her compliment, by asking Mr. Pendarves if he was not quite proud of his nephews.

He replied in the affirmative, declaring himself impatient to show them to the assembled family. It was therefore with cheeks dyed with becoming blushes, and eyes sparkling with delight at the flattering welcome which they had received, that they followed their uncle to the ball-room, but at his desire were stopped within the folding-doors, whence they surveyed the gay groups before them. Mr. Pendarves made his way amongst the dancers, and accosting his guest, Lady Helen Seymour, and Julia Pendarves, his niece, told them they must leave the dance a little while, for he must present to them the *Yankees*, who were just arrived.

"I will come as soon as I have been down the dance," they both exclaimed. "But how unfortunate they should come to-night! for what can we do with them in a fine party like this? because," said Julia, "though they may do to laugh at in our own family circle, one should not like to see one's relations supply subjects for laughter to other people."

The dance was now beginning, and Mr. Pendarves, smiling sarcastically as he listened to his niece, allowed her to dance to the bottom of it, secretly resolving that she should now *ask* him for that introduction which she had thus delayed; and in the meanwhile he amused himself with watching for the first moment when Lady Helen and Julia should discover the two strangers, which he knew they could not fail to do, as the dance down which they were now going, fronted the folding-doors.

Mr. Pendarves did not watch long in vain; Lady Helen and her companion saw them at the same instant, and were so struck with their appearance, that they were out in the figure, and wondered to their partners, who those strangers could be.

"I cannot think," replied one of the gentlemen; "but they look like brothers, and are the finest and handsomest men I ever saw."

Julia whispered Lady Helen, "Is it possible these can be your Yankee cousins? If so, I am so ashamed."

"And so am I; and do look at my uncle, he is laughing at us."

"Oh, it must be they, I am so shocked!"

When they reached the bottom of the dance, they vainly looked towards Mr. Pendarves; he cruelly kept aloof. The strangers turned, however, eagerly round at hearing some one behind them address another by the name of Miss Pendarves.

Their glowing cheeks, their animated looks, were not lost on their equally conscious observers, and Mr. Pendarves now good-naturedly came forward to put a stop to this embarrassing dumb show, by presenting the cousins to each other, and then introducing them to Lady Helen.

You remember my mother, and you have seen a picture of Lady Helen; you will not wonder, therefore, that the sudden admiration which Lady Helen felt that evening for George Pendarves, and my mother for Charles, was as warmly returned. It even seemed that their attachment foreran that of their lovers, for the cousins went to college without disclosing their love. On their return, however, finding the dangerous objects whom they meant to avoid still at Pendarves, they ventured to make their proposals; and unsanctioned by parental authority, Lady Helen and my mother accepted the vows of their lovers, and pledged theirs in return.

I shall pass over the consequent misery which they underwent, and simply state that the two friends were at last so hurried away by their romantic affection, that they allowed the cousins to carry them to Gretna Green; and that after the ceremony they embarked from the nearest Scotch port for America.

At first Lady Helen was too happy in the new ties which she had formed, to feel much sorrow or much compunction when she remembered those which she had broken. But when she became a parent herself, and learnt the feelings of a mother, she thought with agonizing regret on the pains which she had inflicted on her own, and in the bitterness of awakened remorse, she supplicated to be forgiven. The answer to this letter was sealed with black, and was in the hand of her father! It was as follows:

"Your mother is dead, and it was your disobedience which killed her. Expect, therefore, no forgiveness from me.   SEYMOUR."

A fever of the brain was the consequence of this terrible stroke, and her life was despaired of. In the agonies therefore of anxious affection, George Pendarves wrote to Lord Seymour, retorting on him his own blow, for he told him that his letter had *killed Lady Helen*.

The wretched husband inflicted as much pain as he intended; for Lady Helen, however faulty, was Lord Seymour's *favourite* child—his only daughter; and the next letters from America were expected with trembling anxiety. The information, therefore, that Lady Helen was better, was *received* with gratitude, though it did not procure an offer of forgiveness.

My mother, though not quite such a culprit as Lady Helen, because she was one of many daughters, left an aged grandmother and an affectionate uncle with whom she lived; but the former pronounced her forgiveness before she breathed her last, and suffered the will to remain in force in which he had left her a handsome legacy. Nor was her uncle himself slow to pronounce her pardon. She therefore had no drawbacks on her felicity but the sight of Lady Helen's constant dejection, which was so great that my father thought it right to make an effort to procure her the comfort of Lord Seymour's pardon.

The troubles in America were now on the eve of breaking out, for it was the year 1772; and the joy of my birth was considerably damped to my affectionate parents by the increasing agitation of the country. But George Pendarves was too miserable and too indignant to write himself; he therefore gladly deputed my father to write for him. While they were impatiently awaiting the reply, they both busied themselves in politics, in order to escape from domestic uneasiness; and though undetermined which side to take, they were considerably inclined to espouse the cause of the mother country, when Lord Seymour's answer arrived, in which he offered Lady Helen and her husband his entire forgiveness, on condition that the latter took part against the rebels, as he called them, and accepted a commission in the English army, which would soon be joined by his son, Colonel Seymour.

It is impossible to say which at this trying moment was the governing motive of George Pendarves,—whether it was chiefly political conviction, or whether he was influenced insensibly by the wish of conciliating his father-in-law, in order to restore peace to the mind of the woman whom he adored; but certain it is that this letter hastened his decision, and that my father, who loved him as a brother, coincided with him in that decision, and resolved to share his destiny.

Accordingly, both the cousins *accepted* commissions in the British army; and when Colonel Seymour met his brother-in-law at head-quarters, he presented to him a letter from his father, containing a fervent blessing for Lady Helen and himself.

The husband and the brother soon after obtained permission to visit the one his wife, and the other his sister; and something resembling peace of mind, on one subject at least, returned to the patient Lady Helen, while with a mother's pride she put into the arms of her brother her only child, Seymour Pendarves, to whom, unpermitted, she had given the name of her family, and who was then seven years old. But now a *new* source of anxiety was opened upon her. Her husband was become a soldier, and she had to fear for his life; nor was she in a state to follow him to battle, as she would otherwise have done, because she had lately been confined with a dead child. My mother was in this respect more fortunate; for she was able to accompany her husband to the seat of war, and she persisted to do so, though both my father and his cousin earnestly wished her to stay with Lady Helen and myself, I being at that period only two years old.

But my mother had set up her husband as the only idol whom she was called upon to worship, and before that idol she bowed down in singleness of adoration; nor could the inconvenience to which her resolution exposed him at all shake her constancy. She was equally insensible also to the anxiety which her leaving Lady Helen at such a time occasioned, both to the husband and the brother of that amiable being.

The reply of, "It is my duty to accompany my husband as long as I can," silenced all objections from others, and all the whisperings of her own affectionate heart; and she tore herself away, though not without considerable pain, from the embrace of her friend, and committed me to her maternal care.

Dreadful was the moment of separation between Lady Helen and her husband: but the former bore it better than the latter; for, as her mind was impressed with the idea that she had deserved her afflictions, she believed that by patient submission to the divine will, she could alone show her sense of the error which she had committed. Yet, independently of the violence thus done to the enjoyment of affections, it was impossible for a feeling heart and a reflective mind to contemplate that awful moment without agony — that moment, when brother was about to arm against brother — when men speaking the same language, and hitherto considering themselves as subjects of the same king, were marching in dread array against each other, and breathing the vows of vengeance against those endeared to them perhaps by habits of social intercourse and the interchange of good offices. Such was the scene now exhibited at Lexington, in the April of 1775; for there the *first* blood was spilt in the American contest.

In that hour of deadly strife, my mother's trial was not equal to Lady Helen's; for she could linger around the fatal field, she could ask questions of stragglers from the army, and her daily suspense would end with every day; while other anxious wives around her, by sharing, soothed her uneasiness. But Lady Helen was in a sick chamber, surrounded by servants and by objects of interest which only served to heighten her distress; for, as she gazed upon her son and her charge, she knew not but that she was gazing at that moment upon fatherless orphans. There is certainly no comparison in strength between the uneasiness which can vent itself in *exertion*, and that which is obliged by circumstances to remain in *inaction*.

But not at the battle of Lexington was the heart of Lady Helen doomed to bleed. Her husband escaped unwounded, and once more he returned to her and to his children. The interview was indeed short, but it was a source of comfort to Lady Helen, which ended but with her life. His looks — his words of love during that meeting, were treasured up with even a miser's care; for, after their parting embrace — after that happy interview, they *never met more.*

George Pendarves fell in the next decisive battle, which was fought near his residence. By desire of his afflicted brother, the body was conveyed to his own house, which was near to that of the unconscious widow. The bearers mistook their orders, and conveyed it home. Lady Helen, who was at that moment teaching me my letters, after having set Seymour his lesson, broke off to listen to an unusual noise of feet in the hall; then gently opening the door, she leaned over the baluster to discover the cause. Young as I was, never can I forget the shriek she uttered, which told she had *discovered it!* while, wildly rushing down stairs, she threw herself upon the bloody corse. We, echoing her cry, followed her in helpless terror; but fear and horror were my only feelings. Poor Seymour, on the contrary, was old enough to take in the extent of the misery, and I yet hear his fond and fruitless exclamations of "Papa! dear papa!" and his vain, but still repeated supplication, that he would open his eyes and speak to him.

Lady Helen now neither screamed, nor spoke, nor wept; but she sat in the *silent desolation* of her soul on the couch by the body of Pendarves, with eyes as fixed and even as rayless as his. There was a something in this still grief which seemed to awe the by-standers into stillness also. No hand was lifted to remove *her* from the *body*, nor the *body* from *her*. The only sounds of life were the *sobs of Seymour;* for my cries had been checked by alarm and the groans of the compassionate witnesses, or the grief of the servants. But this state of feeling could not last long, and I remember that Seymour destroyed it; for, looking terrified by his mother's changed countenance, he threw his arms passionately around her, conjuring her not to look so terribly, but to take him on her lap, and speak to him. The attendants now came up to take her away; but she resisted all their efforts with the violence of frenzy, till she sank exhausted into their arms, and could resist no longer. The month that ensued was a blank in the existence of Lady Helen: that pressure on the brain from which she had suffered so much before returned, and delirium, ending in insensibility, ensued. When consciousness was restored, her feelings of humble piety and deep contrition returned with it, and kissing the rod which had chastised her, she resolved for our sakes to struggle with her grief, and enter again upon a life of usefulness.

My father meanwhile fought, and my mother followed his fortunes. Once he was brought wounded to his tent, and she was allowed to nurse him till he recovered. After that, she had to cross the country, and endure incredible hardships; but her husband lived, and hardships seemed nothing to her.

During this time—a period of two years—I have heard Seymour Pendarves say, that he dreaded his mother's receiving a letter from the army, because it made her so wretched. He used to call my father and mother uncle and aunt; and when, in seeing her affliction, he asked her whether uncle Pendarves was shot, or aunt Pendarves ill, she was accustomed to reply, "No—they are indeed sufferers, but have much to be thankful for; for *he lives,* they are *together,* and SHE IS HAPPY!"

In the October of 1777, the British army, commanded by General Burgoyne, under whom my father now served, and held a major's commission, were obliged to lay down their arms at Saratoga—yet not before my father had been severely wounded, and taken prisoner. This was a new trial to my mother's constancy; but her courage and her perseverance seemed to increase with the necessity for them; and had she wanted any other incitement to fortitude than her conjugal affection and her sense of duty, she would have found it in the splendid example of Lady Harriet Ackland, whose difficulties and dangers, in the performance of a wife's extremest duty, will ever form a brilliant page in the annals of English history.

Some of the dangers and many of the difficulties of Lady Harriet, had been endured by my mother, but had ended in her being allowed to share the prison of my father; when, on the surrender of General Burgoyne's army, the officers were allowed to return on their parole to England.

My father, therefore, was glad to hasten to that spot from choice, to which he might be ultimately driven by necessity; and my mother, who never liked America, was rejoiced to return to the dear land of her birth. Lady Helen, meanwhile, had undergone another sorrow; but one which, during its progress, had given a new interest to life. Her brother, Colonel Seymour, had been desperately wounded at the beginning of the year 1777, and had been conveyed in a litter to the house of his widowed sister.

Had the wounds of Lady Helen's heart ever been entirely closed, this circumstance would have opened them afresh. "So," she was heard to say, "would I have nursed and watched over my husband, and tried to restore him to life; but to go *at once*—no *warning*—no *preparation!* But God's will be done!" and then she used to resume her quiet seat by the bedside of her brother; whom, however, neither skill nor tenderness could restore. He died in her arms, blessing her with his last breath.

Colonel Seymour was only a younger brother; but having married an heiress, who died soon after, leaving no child, and bequeathing him in fee her large fortune, he was a rich man. This fortune, as soon as he was able to hold his pen, he bequeathed equally between his sister, Lady Helen, and her son, desiring also that his remains might be sent to England to be interred in the family vault of his wife.

I was five years old, when my father and mother returned to us, to prepare for their departure to England, and to prevail on Lady Helen to accompany them; and I have a perfect recollection of my feelings at that moment —or rather, I should say, of my first seeing them; for Seymour and I were both in bed when they arrived. I have heard since, that my father's resemblance to his brother awoke in Lady Helen remembrance even to agony, and that he was not much less affected. I also heard that my mother soon hastened to gaze upon her sleeping child, and to enjoy the luxury of being a parent, after having been so long engrossed by the duty of a wife; for, though she had been confined once during her perils, her confinement had not added to her family.

The next morning, I remember to have felt a joy—I could not tell why—at hearing that my father and mother were come, and that I was both pleased and pained when Seymour ran into the nursery, screaming out, "Oh, Ellen! my uncle and aunt are come, and I have seen them; but they are very ill-looking, poor souls! and my uncle is so lame!"

"Ill-looking, and my papa lame!" thought I. It was with difficulty the nurse could prevail on me to obey the summons; and I behaved so ill when I got to their bedside, that they were glad to send me away. It was impossible that I could know either of them, they were really so pale and haggard through fatigue and suffering; and I shrunk frightened and averse from their embraces.

True, the name of mother was associated in my mind with all that I best loved, for by that name I called Lady Helen. But why did I so? Because she had been to me the tenderest of guardians, and had fulfilled the duty which my real parent had been forced to resign. On returning to the nursery, I found Lady Helen, to whom I clung in an agony of tears, satisfied that *she* was my *own dear mamma*.

But when my father and mother were seated at the breakfast-table, and gave me some of the nice things set before them, I became less averse to their caresses, and before the day was over, I consented to have one papa and two mammas, while Seymour assured me he thought my papa, though *ill*, very handsome, and like his own poor papa.

At first, Lady Helen shrunk from the idea of returning to England; but she at length consented, from consideration of the superior advantages which her two young charges would receive from an English education, and as it was evidently in conformity to her brother's intention. Accordingly, in the beginning of the year 1779, we arrived at Liverpool, bringing with us the bodies of Colonel Seymour and George Pendarves.

Well was it for Lady Helen that we reached the inn at Liverpool at night, and that she had some hours of refreshing slumber, to prepare her for the surprise which awaited her the next day. While she and my parents were at breakfast the following morning, and Seymour and I were amusing ourselves with looking out at the window, we saw a very elegant carriage drive up to the door: our exclamations called Lady Helen to us.

"What are those pretty things painted on the sides, mamma?" asked Seymour.

"An earl's coronet, and supporters to the arms, my dear!" repeated Lady Helen in a faint voice, and suddenly retreating, as she saw there were gentlemen in the carriage, who looked up, on hearing the children's voices. It was her father's.

Nor had time, suffering, and sickness so altered her beautiful features as to render them irrecognizable by a father's heart. Catching the arm of Lord Mountgeorge, his son, who was with him, Lord Seymour exclaimed—

"O Frederic! surely I have beheld your sister!" and with trembling limbs he alighted, and reached the rooms bespoken for him.

He was on his way from London to the seat of a gentleman near Liverpool, from whose house he was to proceed to his own place in the North.

He now sent for the landlord, and begged to know if there were not some American strangers in the house; and on receiving from him a confirmation of his suspicions, he desired one of the waiters to tell Major Pendarves that a gentleman begged to see him.

On entering the room, Major Pendarves took in silence the hand which the agitated earl in silence tendered to him. The past and the present rushed over the minds of both; while Lord Mountgeorge, whose emotion was less violent, begged the major to prepare his sister to receive them.

In the meanwhile, Lord Seymour, with his heart full of his lost son, surveyed with respectful pity the faded cheek and altered form of the once-blooming Charles Pendarves.

"You did not look thus when we last met," said he; "but you have suffered in a noble cause, and you have only lost your *health*."

Here the lip of the bereaved parent quivered with agitation, and Lord Mountgeorge turned mournfully away.

My father then rejoined his party with evident agitation.

"What new sorrow awaits me?" cried Lady Helen; "for I see it is for me you are affected, not for yourself."

"No, my friend; these tears are tears of emotion, but of pleasure also."

"Pleasure!"

"Yes: Lord Seymour and your brother are in the next room, and eagerly long to see you."

The feelings which now strove for victory in Lady Helen's breast were too much for her weakened frame to support; and shuddering and panting, she caught hold of my mother to save herself from falling, while the scream of the terrified Seymour, as he beheld her nearly fainting on the sofa, was heard by the anxious expectants, who hastily entered the room.

Lady Helen, who had not lost her senses, instantly sunk on one knee before her agitated parent, and pushing her son toward him, desired him to plead for his unhappy mother.

"Helen!" cried Lord Seymour, in a voice broken by sobs, "you need no advocate but my own heart!" and Lady Helen was once more clasped to his bosom.

"And is this fine creature my grandson?" said he, gazing with delight on Seymour, while he kissed his open forehead; then seating himself by his daughter on the sofa, while Lord Mountgeorge sat by her on the other side, he drew the wondering boy to his knee.

My father now presented my mother and myself to Lord Seymour.

"I am disappointed," said he, civilly: "I hoped, Mrs. Pendarves, that this lovely girl was my grandchild also."

This was enough to conciliate my young heart; and I wondered to myself, I remember, why my Lady mamma should have seemed so sorry at seeing such a good-natured old gentleman; nor could I conceive why Lord Seymour, as he kept looking on Lady Helen, should shed so many tears.

"My poor Helen!" cried he, "your face tells a tale of sad suffering—and Augustus, too —both gone! But they fought bravely."

"Ay—but they *died!*" cried Lady Helen, clasping her hands convulsively.

"And they shall both have a magnificent monument erected to their memory, my child," cried Lord Seymour.

Lady Helen looked gratefully up in her father's face, as he said this.

Lord Seymour now wrote to his friend, to say that he and his son were prevented paying him the promised visit; and the next day we all set forward for the seat of Lord Seymour.

I forbear to describe poor Lady Helen's feelings when we reached Seymour Park, and what she endured, when she visited, at her own family vault, the remains of her beloved mother, after she had seen her husband and brother interred in that of the *latter*. But she had the consolation of knowing that Lord Seymour's resentment had made him unjust, as a mortal malady had long been preying on her existence.

Having only visited Seymour Park in order to witness the funeral solemnities, my father and mother soon took their leave, and, to my great agony, insisted that I should accompany them on their projected visit to Pendarves Castle, and also to my grandfather and grandmother; and I well recollect the violent sorrow which I experienced when I was torn from Seymour and Lady Helen. I was told, however, that I should certainly come back to them, and not soon leave them again; and that pacified me. Indeed, it was my father's intention to settle near Lady Helen Pendarves, who meant to fit up a cottage in her park for their residence.

When my father and his cousin first came over to England, they had found some property due to them in right of their father's will. This property was vested in the English funds, and there it had remained untouched, both principal and interest, for eight years. During this period, it had accumulated so much as to be sufficient for us to live upon, should the event of the war be such as to cause the confiscation of our American estates; and my mother had also to receive the legacy bequeathed by her grandmother. Their present enjoyment, therefore, was not clouded over (to my parents) by the fear of pecuniary distress; and after their first arrival at Pendarves Castle, (that scene so fraught with grief in its results to friends most dear to them,) they looked forward with joyful anticipations to the future.

They were speedily joined there by my mother's uncle and her parents. Thither, too, Lady Helen had at last resolution to venture also; and I was again united to my brother Seymour, as I always called him.

On leaving her carriage, Lady Helen desired to be shown to my mother's apartment, in order to recover herself before she saw the rest of the family; for she dreaded to encounter the thoughtless Mrs. Pendarves, who would say things that wounded the feelings in the most susceptible part.

On the third day, while she was administering a nervous medicine to her widowed guest, she could not help exclaiming,

"Poor dear! what will all the physic in the world do for you, cousin Helen? as the man says in the play—

'What can minister to a mind diseased?'

And—

'Give physic to the dogs.'"

Here my mother, with a pathetic look, motioned her to be silent—but in vain.

"Nay, my dear Julia!" said she, "I must speak: my dear cousin Helen will not know else how I have cried and lain awake all night with thinking of her miseries."

"She does not doubt your kind sympathy, dear aunt—she does not, indeed!"

"But she cannot be sure of it, Mrs. Charles, unless I tell her of it, and tell her

'I cannot. But remember, such folks were, And were most dear to all.'

Oh! he had

——'An eye like Mars!'

and that is quite appropriate, you know, as he died in battle. I mean your poor husband, poor George Pendarves! not your brother—I never saw him."

My mother looked aghast. Since the death of George Pendarves, no one had ever ventured to name him to Lady Helen;

"But fools rush in where angels dare not tread."

And Lady Helen hid her face in agonizing surprise on my mother's shoulder.

"Ah! one may see by your eyes that you have shed many tears. Why, they tell me you never knew what had happened till you saw the poor dear love lying dead and bleeding. There was a shock! Oh! how I pity you, dearest soul! I have often thought it was a mercy that you did not fall over the balusters, and break your neck!"

"It broke my heart!" screamed out Lady Helen, in the voice of frenzy, unable to support any longer the horrible picture thus coarsely brought before her; and in another moment the house resounded with her hysterical cries; while Mrs. Pendarves added, she could not but think Lady Helen was very bad still, as she could not bear to be pitied; though pity was said to be very soothing—and though she,

——"Like pity on one side, Her grief-subduing voice applied."

As my mother expected, Lady Helen now conceived a terror of Mrs. Pendarves, which nothing could conquer; and her health became

Vol. III.—16

so visibly worse, that she quitted the place the following week, accompanied by my father and mother, and my mother's uncle, to London, leaving Seymour and myself behind, to be spoiled by our too-indulgent relatives.

In a short time, my father and mother had settled their pecuniary concerns, and purchased furniture for their new habitation, of which they now hastened to take possession; and there we soon joined them.

I have detailed thus minutely the sentiments and sorrows of those with whom my earliest years were passed, as I believe that by them my character was in a great measure determined; and that I owe the merit which you attribute to me, and the crimes of which I am conscious, to having been the pupil of *Lady Helen*, and the daughter of *Julia* Pendarves.

The next three years passed quietly away; but my parents observed with pain that Lady Helen's visits to Seymour Park became more and more frequent, though Lord Seymour had married a young wife before his daughter's return, who was jealous to excess of Lady Helen's influence over her lord, and that she had evidently lost much of her enjoyment of their society. The truth was, that though Lady Helen did not envy the happiness of my parents, it was not always that she could bear to witness it; because it recalled painfully to her mind the period of her life when *she was equally* happy; and she had no longer that sympathy with my mother which is the foundation and the cement of friendly intercourse; so true is it, that *equality of prosperity*, like *equality of situation*, is necessary to give *stability* to friendship. My mother, though she felt this, was too delicate openly to repine.

My intercourse with her, and the benefit which I derived from her instructions, remained the same, for I was always allowed to accompany Lady Helen to Seymour Park.

But, alas! the tide of sympathy towards my poor mother, which had been checked in Lady Helen's bosom by happiness, now flowed again with increased fulness, when she was summoned to console her under a sorrow kindred with her own.

My father had been saved from the dangers of war, to perish at home by a *violent death*. He was thrown from his horse, struck his head against a stone, and died upon the spot.

Lady Helen having removed her to her own house, devoted her whole attention to the offices of a comforter. In proportion as my poor mother's sense of happiness had been keen, her sense of privation was overwhelming.

But, so curiously, so mercifully are we fashioned, that we are sometimes able to derive medicine for our suffering from its very excess.

My mother was, as you well know, a woman of *high aspirings*, and loved to be pre-eminent in all things. She was proud of her conjugal love; she was proud of the dangers which she had dared under its influence, and of the sufferings to which she rose superior, to prove the tender excess of that love; she was proud, also, of her good fortune, in having her husband's life so long preserved to her, and she gloried in his devoted and faithful affection. But now of this idolized husband she was bereaved in a moment, and without any alleviating circumstances.

Soothing, though painful, are the tears which we shed for those who fall in battle; and sweet, "like music in the dead of night," heard after distressing dreams, or while we are kept waking by mournful realities, falls the sound of a *nation's regret* on the ear of those who weep over a *departed hero*.

But my father died *ingloriously*, and YET my mother felt pride derived from that *very source*, for it made her, in her own estimation, *pre-eminent* in trial; for how hard was it, after having shared her husband's dangers, and the struggles of war, to see him perish at home, the victim of an ignoble accident!

"Had he died in the field of glory, I might have found," she cried, "some solace in his renown; and I was prepared to see him fall, when others fell around him. But to perish *thus!* oh! never was woman's trial so severe!"

And thus, while descanting on the pre-eminence of her misfortunes, she got rid of much of their severity.

You remember with what eloquence my mother used to describe what she had endured in America; you have also, I believe, heard her speak of the manner of my poor father's death: but you never heard what I have often listened to, with the pity which I could not utter, Lady Helen's assertion of her *own* trying sorrow, when my mother had harrowed up her feelings by the painful comparison.

"You may remember, that *you* were happy *many years;* but I" (here tears choked her voice) "remember, that while you were allowed to prove your love by soothing the sufferings of the being whom you adored, and had his smile to reward you, *I* was forced to prove mine only in the privacy of solitary and almost maddening recollections. Till recently, *you* have never known a *real affliction;* and I—oh! when have I *for years* experienced an enjoyment?"

This language used to *silence*, if it did not *convince* my mother.

But however they might dispute on the superiority of their trials, they loved each other the better for them, and were now scarcely ever separated.

Hence, Seymour and I were in a measure educated together, till it was judged fit that he should go to a public school. This painful trial was imposed on Lady Helen by her relations, and approved by her own judgment against the suggestions of her feelings; when I was eleven, and Seymour near fifteen years old; and when our mothers (as I was not long in discovering) had projected a union between us, and had promised each other to do all they could to ensure it.

Thus ends my *Introduction*.

Here begins, my dear friend,

THE HISTORY OF SEYMOUR AND HELEN PENDARVES.

Forgive me, if I introduce my narrative with a very vulgar but a most excellent proverb — which is, that "Little pitchers have wide ears;" or, that children hear many things which they ought not to hear, and which they were certainly not intended to hear. Now, to illustrate the truth of this proverb, and this explanation of it.

It certainly could not be the intention of two such sensible women that I should know I was designed for the wife of Seymour Pendarves; and yet they talked of their plans so openly before me, that I was perfectly mistress of their designs; and that precocity of mind which they had often remarked in me was increased so much by this consciousness, that while they fancied I was thinking on my doll or my baby-house, I was in reality meditating on my destined husband, till my heart was prepared to receive the passion of love at an age when it would have been better for me to have been ignorant of its existence. And this passion I was authorized to feel, and for a most engaging object! I leave you to judge how pleasant I found this permission — how much, young as I was, the idea of Seymour Pendarves now mixed itself with every thing I thought, and did, and said. Small was the chance, therefore, that even my highly honoured mother could ever succeed in changing the bent of those inclinations which she had herself given in the pliant hours of childhood and earliest youth.

It was some time before Lady Helen recovered her spirits, after the departure of her son. I also gave myself the air of being very dejected; but as with me it was the season of "the tear forgot as soon as shed," and of the preponderating influence of animal spirits, I bounded over the lawn as usual, after the first three days were gone by, and at length won Lady Helen from her reveries and her gloom; but I had the satisfaction of hearing the mothers say to each other,

"What sensibility! She really seemed to regret his absence with a sentimental dejection unusual at those years."

This idea, so flattering to my self-love, I took care to keep alive, by frequently inquiring how long it was to the Christmas vacation; and when that long-expected time arrived, and I found it settled that Lady Helen should meet her son at Lord Seymour's in London, and spend the holidays with him there, I gave way to the most violent lamentations, declaring that she should not go without me. Nor in this instance did I at all exaggerate my feelings of disappointment; for Seymour's absence made a sad void in my amusements, and I had looked forward to his return with the sincerest satisfaction. But my entreaties and my expostulations were equally vain.

Seymour, however, wrote to me twice at least from London. These letters I treasured up with the fondest care, and read them once every day; though I could not but think there was not quite love enough in them, and that I was too big to be called little Helen, and to be told by my correspondent that he blew me a kiss. I remember, also, that when I showed my mother my answers, which were those of a little old woman, and not of an artless girl, she used to say,

"I wonder where the child got those ideas."

When the holidays were over, Lady Helen returned, and brought me a beautiful writing-box, as a present from her son, with a guitar, as a present from herself. We immediately began our practice upon this instrument; and I made a rapid progress, from the hope of being able to charm Seymour when we next met.

But again Lady Helen went to meet her son in London; and it was not till two years after his first departure, that he revisited the North. Never shall I forget the flutter which I felt at the idea of his return; for I am very sure that I was more taken up, in spite of my sentimentality, with thinking what effect I was likely to have on him at our meeting, than with the idea of the pleasure which I should have in seeing him. Two years had made a great improvement in my person; but I was not tall for my age, and I was so thin, that I looked much younger than I really was. My glass, however, and the injudicious praises of flattering visiters, had told me I was handsome; and I really believe I expected to take Seymour's heart—of the actual possession of which I had some doubts—by a *coup de main*; for I had both heard and read of "love at first sight." Never before had I been so difficult to please in the shape of my frocks, which I in vain tried to persuade my wiser mother to alter into *gowns*—as vainly did I try to persuade her to let me have my hair dressed, and wear ear-rings: she coolly told me simplicity was the beauty of a *child's dress*; and I, swallowing as I could that mortifying appellation, was obliged to let my auburn ringlets fall in natural glossy curls into my neck, unfrizzed and untormented. But unable to keep my vexation to myself, to the great amusement of my mother, I said, rather petulantly, as I was leaving the room one day, "Well, I must do as you please, mamma; but I am sure Mr. Seymour Pendarves, who is used to London young ladies, will think me a great fright."

"Mr. *who*, my dear?—whose opinion is of so much consequence to you?"

"Seymour Pendarves," replied I blushing, and leaving out the Mr.

"Oh! Master Pendarves! Really, my dear, I can't think it matters much, what such a mere boy as that thinks; and it is enough for you that you are a good child, and obey your mamma."

At length, Seymour arrived, and the delighted Lady Helen brought her idol to our house; while I gazed with wonder as well as pleasure and embarrassment, on the change which two years had made in my youthful companion. He, though only seventeen, had assumed the dress of manhood: his throat was tied up with a large cravat — his hair was powdered, and worn in a club behind, according to the then fashion—his hat was set on one side, and he was dressed in a grass-green coat. Nothing so smart had ever met my sight before; and what with his fine teeth, his dimpled cheek, and his sparkling eyes, I thought I had never even *read* of any one so beautiful: and this lovely youth was intended to be my husband. But had he himself any such intentions? That I could not say; and I was both mortified and displeased at the way in which he first addressed me, even though I drew up my long neck as high as possible, to look as tall and womanly as I could. He flew up to me, calling me—

"Dear *little* Helen! how are you? I am so glad to see you again!"

And then, in spite of my dignity, he clasped me round the neck, gave me a kiss which might have been heard in the next room, and left the mark of his metal sleeve-buttons on my throat. My mother saw my confusion, and, as she did not approve such familiar and boisterous ways, coolly said, "My daughter is not used to such rough salutations, my dear Seymour; and I did not expect such a remnant of the great romping boy from you."

Alas! all remnant of youthful unrestraint and of the boy now vanished; natural feeling, which the sight of his early companion and playfellow had called forth, disappeared, and the manners of the young men of the world *then* and *for ever* replaced them. But what provoked me was, though he seemed to consider himself as a *man*, he never even for a moment treated me as a *woman*. I was his "little Helen," and his "chicken," and his "tiny pet;" and then, dreadful degradation! he used to chuck me under the chin: nay, once he asked me, pulling up his neck-cloth, and looking in the glass, whether the neighbourhood was improved, and whether there were any *fine women* in it, who visited our mothers.

I had a mind to answer, "What does it signify to you whether there are or not?" but as I dared not so reply, it was a relief to me when my mother came in, and put a stop to his inquiries.

But never, indeed, have I since felt more jealousy than I experienced during Seymour's residence at home, in various ways. Soon after his return, I went with one of my cousins from Pendarves Castle, then on a visit to us, to a public walk in a neighbouring town, which was then much frequented, and Seymour accompanied us: I, conscious that my straw hat and purple ribands became me, and that my young friend, who was remarkably plain, served only as a foil to my charms.

"Now, then," thought I, "his hour is come." While glorying in this imagined security, I was hurled down into the depths of despair; for we scarcely reached the Mall, when we met some fine showy-looking women, whom I thought *old*, as they seemed past five-and-twenty. Seymour, to my great consternation, inquired who these *lovely creatures* were, declaring they were the handsomest women he had seen since he had left London.

"My cousin can introduce you," said Harriet Pendarves.

"I! not I, indeed!"

"Why not, dear Helen!" cried Seymour.

"Because — because I have only lately known them."

"Oh! that is quite enough," he hastily returned; but I still refused.

However, the ladies returned, accompanied by a young man of Seymour's acqaintance; and in a few minutes we beheld him laughing and talking with the party. My feelings at that moment still live in my memory as vividly as ever. I was thunder-struck. "What! Seymour Pendarves, the friend of my childhood, to leave me for women whom he never saw before; and call them handsomer than any thing he had seen since he left London! It was in vain that two youths of my acquaintance—one of them a young lord—joined my deserted side: I was silent, absent, and unhappy; for Seymour remained with his new acquaintance.

It never occurred to me to talk and laugh with my beaux, for I was a stranger to coquetry, and the natural feelings of my heart were allowed to display themselves: still, an untaught delicacy made me try to hide the cause of my oddness from my companions; and a headache, which was not feigned, was my excuse.

The ladies, however, at length left the walk, and Seymour was forced to return to us. He immediately launched forth into rapturous praises of their charms and elegant manners, while I listened in angry silence, as I had expected him to apologize for leaving me; and nothing, I perceived, was further from his thoughts.

"But what is the matter?" cried he. "Are you not well, Helen, that you do not speak?"

"Not quite."

"Helen has a headache," said my cousin.

"Poor child!" cried Seymour kindly; "then let us go home directly; it grows late, and I believe you do not sit up to supper yet, Helen, except on great occasions."

Here was an affront. I angrily replied, "Indeed, Mr. Seymour Pendarves, you seem to know very little about me, and to *care* very little about me now."

"*Mr.*, and a tossed-up chin, and a flushed face! Why, really, Helen, I find I did *not* know much about you: I took you for a sweet-tempered girl; but I have often thought you captious and pettish of late, and I never could imagine why; but let me tell you, Miss Helen Pendarves, that if you lose your good-temper, you will lose your greatest charm — *any woman's greatest charm.*"

This reproach I could not bear from him; for I knew, if I was become pettish and captious, affection for him was the cause; and I burst into tears. But struggling with my feelings, I sobbed out, "And I suppose, sir, you think I *have* no *other* charm than my good-temper."

"*I*, Helen! No such thing: I think quite the contrary; and I do assure you, the ladies I have just left, they——"

"O yes!" cried I, "they, I suppose, have every charm possible."

"They have great charms, certainly, both of face and person; still, they are only *fine women*; but *you*, Helen, are quite a *little beauty* — only you are as yet but a *child*, you know."

Away went my ill-humours, and even my jealousy; for I was sure, though the boy of seventeen thought it more manly to talk to women grown, I knew as he advanced in life, and I too, he would be of a different opinion; and I also knew a few years would fade the ladies whom he so much admired, while the same number of years would leave me still young, and *still a beauty*. Yes, he thought me a beauty, and he had told me so; and I repeated his words to myself so often, that in a reverie I once spoke them aloud, and my mother asked, "Child, what are you saying about Helen and beauty?"

"Helen was a great beauty, mamma—was she not!" said I, blushing at my own duplicity; but the subterfuge weighed heavily on my mind, nor could I rest till I told the whole truth to my mother, who, in consideration of my ingenuousness, merely observed to me, that when, from the exaggeration to which even boys were much given, Seymour called me a beauty, he only meant I was a pretty girl: but *I* thought *differently*.

Seymour now remained at home full six months, with a private tutor, as he was too old to go back to school, and Lady Helen thought him too young for Oxford. During that time, my mother, from (as I suspected) some private information, began to form an unfavourable opinion of his steadiness of conduct; and the anxieties of a mother for his future well-being clouded the still beautiful countenance of Lady Helen.

Once, as I was apparently engaged in reading, I overheard Lady Helen say to my mother, "Do you not discern any symptoms yet of a growing attachment on his side? he may be on his guard before me."

"None whatever: he seems to consider her still only as a beautiful child; and she is certainly not at all more womanly in her appearance this last year."

"I am sorry for it," was the answer; "for there is no guard so good for the morals of a young man, as a virtuous attachment."

"Yes," said my mother; "and I had hoped, that by being so much with Helen, he would have loved her, as it were, by anticipation."

I never could find out whether they *meant* me to hear this conversation or not; but the assurance which it conveyed, that Seymour did not love me yet, was not lost upon me; and it was possible that all this was said for that purpose. The consequence was, that I put the strictest guard over my words and manners, lest Seymour should discover the attachment which I had with much confidence indulged; and the attachment itself, I resolved to resist, with all the energy possible: for surely, thought I, if I am too young to inspire love, I ought to be too young to feel it; and I am too proud to love where I am not beloved. And I kept the former part of my resolution, for my attachment remained unsuspected; nor did its strength hold out entirely uninjured against the conviction of the utter indifference of its object. However, an affectionate grasp of my hand, and a respectful salute of my cheek, replaced the boisterous familiarity of his greeting, when we first met.

"Surely," said I to myself, "his feelings towards me have undergone a change;" and while hope was thus restored to my bosom, I felt that my former feelings would, on the slightest encouragement, return with undiminished force.

I have since learnt — though not till long after the period in question—that Lady Helen had thought proper to have a conversation with her son on the subject nearest her heart; namely, a marriage between him and me, in the course of a few years.

He listened to her, I found, with great surprise, but great complacency; only exclaiming, "But she is such a child at present, dear mother!"

"But she will not always be a child," replied Lady Helen; "and though I believe she is quite indifferent to you *now*, I am much mistaken if that 'child,' as you call her, did not at your first arrival feel something resembling love and jealousy too."

"Is it possible!" exclaimed Seymour, "and I not to be conscious of it! *Dear* little Helen!" And then he recollected the scene in the walk, and my petulance, silence, and tears, for which he now accounted in a manner flattering to his vanity; and it was so new—so *piquant*, to be loved by a child, that he was charmed with the idea of his conquest. But then Lady Helen had told him he had lost this affection; and as none can bear to renounce the power which they have once possessed, he was resolved to pay me those attentions by the want of which I had been alienated. He was too conscious, however, to be able to act upon his resolves; and he had learnt to consider me in so new a light, that he felt embarrassed when he should have been assiduous; and though I saw a change in his manner during the last four days, it was far from being a favourable one. It was only on the last of the four days that he seemed to have shaken off the trammels which hung about him. That day, as I was drawing at the window, and he was reading aloud by his mother, I saw him lay down his book, and whisper in her ear.

"Helen," said she, "what do you think Seymour says? He says, that he has now found that you are no longer a child."

"Indeed!" replied I, blushing, but in a tone of pique: "and since when? That is a discovery which I have long made."

"And since when have you *yourself* made it, dear Helen?" said he, with that saucy smile of his which you have often said was irresistible.

"These four years, at least," I answered, trying to avoid his eyes.

"Do not fib, Helen," was his impertinent reply.

"You make Helen blush, my dear son."

"So much the better; she never looks so beautiful as when she blushes, and I dare say some little time hence, we shall have some English Priam exclaiming of this modern Helen—

'No wonder, Britons, that such heavenly charms
For ten long years have set the world in arms!'

While *I* shall sit and sing—

'Ah, Chloris! could I now but sit
As unconcern'd as when
Thy infant beauty could beget
Nor happiness nor pain!'"

I was now so pleased, so confounded—yet so happy, that I knew not where to look or how to behave; but remembering that the "best part of valour is discretion," I fled from the danger I could not face, and had just presence of mind enough to run away.

"What is the matter with Helen?" cried Seymour, when I was gone. "Is she angry?"

"No," replied Lady Helen, more skilled in the nature of woman's feelings; "she is only conscious of being too well pleased — that's all;" and from that time — had not Seymour left us the next day—the chances are that we should soon have become lovers.

I, meanwhile, had gone into my own chamber, where I found my mother. I threw myself into her arms, without saying a word, and hid my blushes and my tears in her bosom. My mother, untold, knew those tears were not tears of sorrow, and soon drew from me a part of the truth; for I told her Seymour had been so full of his compliments that I came away.

During the course of that day, Seymour was continually exclaiming, "How provoking it is, that I should be forced to go away just now!"

"Ah!" cried I, pertly enough, and insincerely too, "what will poor Miss Salter do?" This was the name of one of the ladies with whom he had fancied himself charmed.

"Miss Salter!

'I think not of Miss Salter——
My fancy has no image now but—'"

Here my mother rather pettishly interrupted him.

"I think, for Miss Salter's sake, young man, it is well you are going, as you certainly took great pains to make her think you admired her; and I must say, I am no friend to coquetry, be it in man or woman."

"Nor I," said Lady Helen; "and I trust the next time my son makes love, he will do it with his whole heart, and not mistake the illusions of fancy for the dictates of attachment."

"I trust so too, my dear mother," he replied, "and that the object will be one whom you approve."

The next morning he set off, and every thing at first seemed a blank to me. He wrote frequently during the first weeks of his residence at Oxford, but my mother discouraged my answering his letters, and he soon grew remiss in his correspondence even with Lady Helen, who found that his allowance, though handsome, was insufficient for his wants, and suspected that the life must be dissipated which required such an exorbitant expenditure. My mother knew that it was so; why she imparted what she heard to her friend, I cannot tell, because it made Lady Helen unhappy, and she wrote to her son in the language of expostulation. I was vexed to find that my mother gave such implicit credence to the stories of Seymour's errors, as the accounts might be exaggerated; and when I had once admitted that he was the victim of misrepresentation, pity for Seymour added force to my attachment.

It seemed a very long time to me till the next vacation came; but Seymour passed it in London, at his grandfather's; my mother was glad, but I was disappointed. Nor did he come down into the country till half of the long vacation was expired; and after he had spent a week with Lady Helen, my mother took me to pay a visit to a relation of her's. In vain Lady Helen remonstrated, and Seymour entreated; she replied she had put off her journey in the expectation of seeing him in June, and she could no longer delay her visit. He sighed, looked conscious and confused, and forbore to urge her again.

My mother was certainly right in thus resolving; for she knew, though I did not, that Lady Helen had communicated to him her views and wishes with regard to me; and she left home with a firmness and decision of manner which promised ill for the success of her hopes.

When we came back, Seymour was returned to Oxford. The following Christmas, Lady Helen, whose health seemed evidently declining, went to London for the advice of physicians, and Seymour attended her home; but he only stayed a week, as he was under an engagement, he said, to accompany some friends abroad. He departed, however, with evident dejection and reluctance, and seemed while with us to enjoy the quiet of our domestic scenes; but as his actions were not regulated by a steady principle of *right*, and under the restraint of moral and religious obligation, no sooner was he removed from our purifying influence, than he became again the follower of pleasure, while as he was driven backward and forward upon the ocean of the world, my image, which his poor mother thought would save him from temptation, appeared to him only as a beacon at a distance to remind him of that shore of safety which the waves forbad him, however much he wished it, to approach. During the next term, and in spite of his dissipation, Seymour obtained a prize for writing the best prose essay; and he sent it to his mother just after some very unfavourable accounts of the society which he frequented in London, had reached her, and had been only too strongly confirmed by my mother's secret informant. These reports had not been communicated to me, but I happened to be present when Lady Helen received two copies of the essay, accompanied by a letter, in which he begged that his dearest friend Helen, would not only accept, but do him the favour to criticise the little production which he had sent, as he knew no one whose praise he should so highly value, or to whose censures he should pay greater attention. Methinks I still see the delight yet gleaming mournfully through tears, which beamed from Lady Helen's countenance when she received the essay and read the letter. Alas! that renewed and increased brightness was but too like the flame of an expiring taper.

"My dear Julia!" cried she to my mother, in a voice almost inarticulate with emotion, "what a foolish thing is a fond mother's heart! Now it is all fear, and now all hope; now it is broken, and now healed again. This boy, this dear, naughty good boy! it was but yesterday I cried for his weakness, and now I cry for his strength."

"No one, I believe, ever doubted your son's talents," said my mother coldly, and I thought crossly.

"True," replied Lady Helen meekly; "and this prize, I own, is not proof of amended conduct."

"I know not," cried I eagerly, "what fault poor Seymour has committed; but of this I am sure, that if he was so very idle as ill-natured people say he is, he could not have found time to write for a prize, and still less have been able to gain it."

"Thank you, my dearest girl, for being my poor boy's advocate; for what you say is very just: and Seymour shall know how kindly you took his part."

"I must beg he may not know," said my mother, angrily.

"Indeed!" answered Lady Helen mournfully. "But I cannot now blame your change of feeling on this subject, for I myself should hesitate to give my daughter to a youth such as Seymour is said to be."

I now turned round, and looked at Lady Helen with so alarmed and inquiring a countenance, that she could not withstand the appeal. She took my hand, and said—

"Yes, Helen, your mother and I had pledged our words to each other, to do all in our power to promote a union between my son and you, and to cherish every symptom in you of a mutual attachment; but now, owing to some too well-founded reports, I fear, of his faulty conduct, she wishes to retract her promise; and here, as one of my last acts and deeds, (for I feel that I shall not be with you long,) I solemnly give her back that promise in your presence! declaring to you, my beloved child, that unless your mother thinks Seymour deserving of you, I cannot wish you to be his wife; and that it will be my parting injunction to you, Helen, never, never to marry an immoral man."

Lady Helen had scarcely said this, while I listened with downcast eyes, when my mother threw herself into her arms, sobbing out convulsively, "My own dear generous friend! for your sake I will try to think well of your son, and to believe he will reform—only don't talk of dying; I can't bear *that!*"

"But I wish to prepare you for it."

"Prepare, Helen! prepare. Do you think anything can make me endure the idea of losing you? Oh! it will be losing all I ever loved a second time!"

Lady Helen shook her head, but did not speak; for she knew that her friend must soon undergo this dreaded trial—and *she*, too, felt that for *some* blows there is no such thing as *preparation*.

The night that followed was the first of real agonizing sorrow which I had ever known. I had heard that Seymour was believed, even by his own mother, to be unworthy of me, and that mine was decidedly averse to that union which she had originally made the first desire of my heart; I had also heard from Lady Helen's own lips a solemn assurance that she was dying.

At my time of life, however, the spirits are never long depressed, especially by an uncertain and remote sorrow; but as a captive butterfly, when the pressure on its wings is removed, flutters them again in air, with all their glittering dyes and buoyancy uninjured, so do the spirits of youth quickly resume their brilliancy and their elasticity.

When I rose the next morning, I was *sure* that Lady Helen would *recover*; I was sure that Seymour would *reform*, even if the reports concerning him were *not* exaggerated; and I was also sure that some time or other I should be his wife.

But, alas! Lady Helen had not spoken from momentary dejection, and still less from the ungenerous wish to excite interest and alarm in the hearts that tenderly loved her: she spoke from her deep conviction—a conviction only too well founded.

In less than two months, she was attacked by fever and inflammation of the brain, such as had before seized her on the death of her husband. She had, however, lucid intervals; and though my mother and myself felt our hearts wrung by her delirious ravings—during which she called upon her son's name in the most affecting language—still we suffered more, when, on recovering her senses, she asked for this darling son, and we were obliged to reply that he was not yet arrived.

And where—oh! where was he, at a moment like that? We knew not.

As soon as Lady Helen's attack was judged to be a dangerous one, my mother wrote to him at Oxford, desiring him to set off immediately, or he might come too late; and as Oxford was only a ten hours' journey from home, he might have been with us the next morning, had he been at college. It was also term time; but yet he came *not*, though on such an occasion, leave of absence was easily to be obtained. My mother was too angry to be as wretched as I was at this distressing circumstance—for indignation often swallows up every other feeling, and once she hinted to me that he must have received the letter, and that mere idle neglect kept him away; but the poor invalid, who, unsuspected by us, overheard our conversation, exclaimed—

"No, Julia; whatever are his other faults, my poor boy loves me—tenderly loves me; and even from a sick-bed he would hasten to his dying mother. Oh no! he has never received your letter—he is not in college."

"Then where is he? In college he ought to be."

"True, Julia; but he is young and thoughtless, and we ought to remember that we were so *once ourselves*. We ought not to have run away from our parents—yet we *did* so, Julia."

"We did, indeed," cried my mother, abashed and silenced.

"Yes," continued Lady Helen; "and therefore I have always endeavoured to be mild in my judgment of other people—especially of the young."

"Helen," cried my mother, "forgive me, thou blessed spirit! I will be merciful to him, even though it makes me unjust to——"

"No, your first duty is to your daughter: but listen to me, Julia! Be *sure* to convince Seymour, when I am no more, that I did not impute his absence to want of love, but merely to *accident*. Be *sure* you do; for he will feel only too much, when he comes and finds that he has no longer a mother!"

The afflicting image thus presented to my mind, of what would be Seymour's misery if he indeed arrived too late, was more than I could bear, and I was forced to leave the room. Soon afterwards, Lady Helen's senses wandered again; but when I returned, she was sensible, though exhausted; and as I entered, she hastily put back the curtain, and said—

"Oh! I hoped it was my dear, dear boy!" Her breath now grew fainter, and she exclaimed, "Oh! where, where is he? must I die without seeing him once more, and giving him my blessing? Helen! Julia! be sure to speak very kindly to him, and tell him that I blessed him! But thy will, O Lord! be done!"

Still, as long as consciousness remained, her eyes were anxiously turned towards the door, as if looking for that beloved object whom she was never more to see, we thought, in this world. At that moment, however, my watchful ear heard a quick step on the stairs, and an exclamation of agony, not mistaken by me.

"*He* is *here!* I am *sure* he is here!" cried I, bending over her pillow; and in another moment Seymour was on his knees at the bedside. Never shall I forget his look of speechless woe, when he found her last agony approaching: but it seemed as if *affection* struggled successfully with death for a few short moments. She could not speak, but her eyes were eloquent; and as she laid her hand upon the head of her child, those eyes were raised to heaven in earnest supplication: they then turned on him, while she reclined her head on my mother's bosom, and her right hand was clasped in mine. I cannot go on: the scene is still too present to my view.

* * * * *

Deep as was my affliction, it sunk into nothingness, compared with that of the bereaved and self-reproving son. It was really a *relief* to me to see his sense of anguish suspended by his insensibility.

When he recovered, there was something so full of woe, and yet of a woe so stern, in the look with which my mother ordered me away, that I had not the heart to resist it. It was near an hour before she came to me; and never before had I seen her so overpowered with affliction. She called upon Lady Helen by the tenderest names; talked of her patient gentleness—of the sweetness of that temper which she had so often tried—and reproached herself for having thus tried it. But she spoke not of Seymour; and deep as my regret was for the dead, it was equalled by my anxiety for the living. I therefore ventured to say, "But how is poor Seymour?"

"Unfeeling girl!" cried my mother; "you can think only of him when his angel mother lies dead!"

"*She* would have *thanked* me for my anxiety," I replied, rendered courageous by distress. "I shall go and inquire after him."

"Hold, Helen! he is extremely wretched; so much so, that I could not bear to listen to his self-upbraidings, nor to witness his caresses of that hand which replied no longer to his grasp; and then his wild entreaties, that she would speak to him once more, and say that she forgave him!"

"And could you have the cruelty to leave him alone in such a state?" cried I. "Do you think his mother would so have left *your* child?"

My mother started—"You are right!" said she: "I will return, and do my duty by him."

"Oh! let me go with you!"

"No, Helen; I must do my duty by you too—and the poor youth at this moment is only too dangerous."

She was right, and I submitted; but I had gained my point, and she was gone back to the poor afflicted one. Before she went, however, she insisted on my going to bed; where, wearied with three nights of watching, I fell into a heavy slumber. But, oh! that wretchedness on waking, which attends the recollection of a recent affliction! and I was giving way to all the misery I felt, when, soon after eight in the morning, my mother came into my room.

She told me she had not been in bed all night, for that she dared not leave Seymour.

"How kind it was in you, my dearest mother!"

"No, it was only right," she answered, in great agitation: "he was a bitter and penitent sufferer; and if my departed friend is conscious of what is passing here, I trust that she was satisfied with me, for I tried to do a mother's part by him. And now, my dear child, we must both return home: this, you know, is no place for you, Helen."

"And must I go without taking leave of poor Seymour?"

"What leave is there to take?"

I had nothing to reply, and we came away.

As my mother knew that Seymour's sleep was likely to be long, she did not return to the house of death for some hours; but when she did, I earnestly conjured her to let me accompany her. I pleaded, however, and wept in vain : in vain did I urge, that Seymour would think me unkind in forsaking him wholly at such a time as this was.

My mother said she feared that Seymour would only be too ready to attribute his not seeing me to her commands, rather than my own inclinations; and, disappointed and wretched, I threw myself on the bed in an agony of grief, and never rose from it, feeding my distress by every means in my power. I must own, however, that temper and contrivance had some share in this self-abandonment, or sensibility, which I thought would at once punish my mother for her obstinacy, (as I called it,) and induce her to give up her resolution. How often is grief, like love, made up of materials which we dream not of —and how often has temper much to do with it! But my seeming unmixed sorrow had no effect on my excellent parent, whose decisions, where I was concerned, were the result of firm principle. Her first observation was—

"This excessive misery, Helen, accompanied, as I see it is, with a degree of sullenness, is not likely to make me change my purpose, but rather to confirm me in it the more; because it proves to me the great extent of the danger to which my compliance would expose you, when you can thus, in spirit at least, be rebellious; and this at a time, too, when I want every comfort possible."

These words subdued every particle of resentment in me: I threw myself on her neck, and assured her she should never have so to reproach me again; nor did I even venture to inquire for Seymour—but she was generous enough to speak of him unasked. She told me he woke, after a long sleep, more composed than she expected; "though, on his first waking, he started me excessively," she said, "by asking for his mother, and wondering to see me instead of her. My tears seemed to force back his recollection; and in a faint voice, and with a look of wretchedness, he added, 'Ah! I remember now;' and hiding his face in the pillow, he wept aloud.

"And I—I was but a sad consoler, for I wept in silence by him. When he was calm again, I wished him to rise; and before I left him, in the fulness and tenderness of my heart, poor child! I stooped down, and kissed his burning forehead. But I soon repented; for he exclaimed, "Oh! that was so like *her!* But she never—no, never more——" and again he lay almost convulsed with his feelings.

"When this fresh paroxysm was over, I left him."

"But I am sure," said I, "that he will be soothed by that kind kiss in remembrance, though it affected him painfully at the time."

"Perhaps so: but his grief, violent though it be, will soon go off, and be after a time forgotten. Lady Helen was his mother, and he loved her; but she had not been the chosen playfellow of his childhood—the friend of his youth—the companion of his riper years—the sharer of every joy—the soother of every sorrow—and the being endeared to him by daily she had ceased I was too uneasy to close my eyes.

When I rose the next day, and was walking in the garden before breakfast, I found my mother's windows still shut, and it was very late before she came down stairs. I had previously felt disposed to indulge my own dejection; but as soon as I saw her, all thought of myself vanished. For never did I see the expression of hopeless grief stronger than in her speaking face. As she did not talk, I vainly tried to converse of indifferent things. She smiled; but every smile was succeeded by a sigh; and once she exclaimed,

"No! they cannot come to *me*, but I shall go to *them*."

"Dearest mother," cried I, rising and looking up in her face, "you forget *me*. Surely you do not wish to leave me?"

"Do not ask me," she cried, clasping me fondly to her bosom; "I fear I am ungrateful for my remaining blessing."

From that time she struggled with her grief, and became, as you know, in *company*, at least, the agreeable companion; for about that time it was, I think, that your amiable husband succeeded to the living, and you came to enliven and adorn the rectory. However, as your friend, for whose inspection this is written, does not know any of the subsequent events, I shall proceed with the detail of my story.

During the ensuing six weeks we had only one letter from Seymour, but that was a pleasant one: for he told us that he had been studying very hard, and had gotten another prize, and he sent us his composition, adding in a very touching manner, that as the eye which he most wished to please by his production was for ever closed, his proudest desire now was to have it approved by those whom he and she best loved.

My mother was gratified by this compliment as well as myself; for she augured favourably of his amendment from this close application, and she owned to me in the fulness of her heart, that she had informed him, his obtaining my hand depended entirely on *himself*. I have said that my mother appeared quite recovered in company; but such was the constant recurrence of one anxious subject to her mind in private, that every thing unconnected with it soon became uninteresting to her; this was the renewal of virtuous friendship in another world; and she read and tried to procure every thing in the shape of a Sermon or Essay that had ever been written on the subject. One sermon, and it was a most eloquent one, bearing the title, "The renewal of Virtuous Friendship in another World,"* delighted her so much, that it was never out of her reach; and though she found it difficult to de-

---
* See a volume of Sermons written by the Rev. P. Houghton.

duce from the Scriptures any certain grounds for this consoling doctrine, still she delighted to indulge in it; and as she could never rest till she had tried to convert others to her own opinions, especially where those opinions were likely to increase individual happiness, those only with whom she was not intimate could avoid hearing her descant on this subject, with all that plausible and ingenious fluency which usually attends reasoning from analogy and imagination. While her mind was thus employed, it ceased to prey on its own peace; and though her system sometimes failed to satisfy her, she still found a soothing conviction in the thought, that should we not be permitted "to know and love our friends in heaven," we should be sure not to be *conscious* of the want of those who had been the dearest to us when on earth, but should find all the "ways of God" vindicated "to man."

It was now, while my mother was too constantly thinking of the regretted dead, and I of the still tenderly-remembered living, that a new acquaintance was introduced to us, who had power to withdraw our thoughts from these interesting speculations, and fix them for some time at least upon himself.

Methinks, my dear friend, I see you smile at this distance, and remark to your husband, "Now we shall see what she says of the impression which Count Ferdinand De Walden first made on her, for I never could understand how she could ever prefer another man to him."

You forget how very early in life my affections were turned towards Pendarves, and how soon I learnt to look on constancy in love as a sort of virtue; you also forget the "fascinating graces," and the "irresistible archness," to use your own expression, of Seymour's smile. But this is perhaps an ill-timed digression. Where was I? Oh! at the introduction of a new acquaintance.

My parents had made an acquaintance in America with the Count De Walden, the elder, whom curiosity and the love of travelling had led thither. On the breaking out of the war, he returned to his native country, Switzerland, by way of England; where he was so much pleased with the manners of the people and constitution of the government, that he resolved his nephew and heir, Ferdinand De Walden, who was like himself a protestant, should come over and enter himself at one of the universities. When the time for his admission arrived, the count remembered with renewed interest his acquaintance with my parents and their cousins; and that they now resided in England. Nor was it difficult for him to obtain particulars of their present residence and situation.

His uncle heard with pain that my mother, Seymour, and myself, were the only survivors of that happy family which he had so much loved in the new world. To my mother, however, he was still anxious to introduce his nephew; and he hoped that in Seymour he would find a durable friend at college; but in this expectation he could not be gratified, as he had resolved that Ferdinand should go to the mathematical university, and Seymour was of Oxford. This impossibility my mother, they thought a fortunate circumstance for Ferdinand.

When De Walden came, and showed, among other letters, one of recommendation to Mr. Seymour Pendarves, she coldly observed, " That letter need not be delivered yet;" and certainly, the appearance of Ferdinand De Walden did not promise much congeniality of disposition and pursuit with Seymour; for the latter, from the light gaiety of his manner and countenance, seemed as if he never thought at all; and the former, from the grave pensiveness and reserve of his, appeared at first sight as if he did nothing but think. The open eye of Seymour invited confidence, the penetrating one of De Walden repelled it; and as the one, when first seen, was sure to inspire admiration if not love, the other was as sure to excite alarm, if not a feeling resembling aversion. For myself, I must own that when De Walden was presented to me by my mother, I experienced towards him a little of the first, though none of the second sensation; for I had been accustomed to look on Seymour as my model for personal beauty and captivation; and the young Swiss, therefore, had not a chance of charming me at first sight. I had not seen my mother so animated for years as she was on the arrival of her foreign guest; for she had greatly esteemed his uncle, and Ferdinand strongly resembled him. With him of course were associated the ever-remembered hours of youth and friendship, wedded love and happiness; and De Walden shone with a radiance not his own. But my mother, much to my annoyance, was not conscious of this: she insisted that his brilliancy was all self-derived; that if she had never known *his uncle*, she should still have admired *him*. By this admiration, I am ashamed to confess, I was piqued and mortified, because I fancied it interfered with the rights of Seymour; and I suspected that, if he should repay the regard of the mother by loving the daughter, I could not without disobedience remain constant to my first attachment.

As De Walden was not to go to college till October, he had leave to stay with us till that time, since it was rather an unusual thing for a fine young man, unless he was a relation, to be the guest of a widow lady and her daughter for so long a period. I was therefore certain that my mother must have some particular point to carry, and that point was, I believed, the alienation of my heart from Seymour Pendarves. These suspicions certainly made me regard Ferdinand the two first days of his arrival with prejudiced eyes, not unmixed with fear of his keenness of penetration. But, in spite of myself, my fear of him vanished, and much of my prejudice with it, when I found that this grave sententious personage, who talked theology with my mother, and tried, poor man! to explain to us some new German philosophy, could laugh as heartily as if he never read and never thought, and had a sense of the ridiculous, which he found sometimes dangerous and troublesome to his good-breeding.

This welcome discovery happened to me at breakfast, while he was reading to us aloud some amusing extracts from a kind of periodical paper, published in France by the Baron De Grimm, one of which was so ludicrous, that he laid down the book to laugh at his ease, while I exclaimed, " Is it possible ?"

" Is what possible, my dear ?" said my mother.

" That Mr. De Walden," I repeated rather uncivilly, " can laugh so very heartily."

"*N'est-il pas permis en Angleterre, Mademoiselle ?*"* was his answer.

"Oh, yes!" said I, blushing, and looking very foolish, "only—"

"Oh! Je comprends: apparemment c'est Mademoiselle qui ne veut pas qu'on rit devant elle. Hélas, belle Helène! il faut rire tant qu'on le peut, quand on a le bonheur de jouir souvent de votre aimable société; car il me semble qu'en ce cas là, on pourroit bien avoir raison de pleurer bientôt, et peut-être pour la vie."†

Here was *gallantry* too, and returning good for evil; though I was rude, he was polite. I was humbled and ashamed, while, he with increasing archness said, "*Mais qu'est-ce que vous voulez dire avec votre*—' Is it possible ?'‡ What! you think me a disciple of Crassus, and fancy me never laugh till I see an ass eat a thistle ?" he added in his foreign English.

" Shall I tell you what I take you for now ?" replied I, venturing to look up in his face, which, for the first time, animated as it now was by pleasantry and the consciousness of appearing to advantage, struck me with the conviction of its excessive physiognomical beauty; and I ceased to wonder at my mother's regard for him, not because he was possessed of great personal attractions, but because beauty of physiognomy cannot exist without corresponding beauty of mind, if not of heart.

" Well, he replied, " and what do you take me for ?" speaking with that accent which in him I have often thought an additional charm.

* Is it not permitted in England?

† Oh! I comprehend: you do not like any should laugh in your presence. Alas! beautiful Helen, one must laugh while one can, when one has the happiness of being in your society; for one runs the risk of crying very soon, and perhaps for life.

‡ But what did your mean with your ' Is it possible ?'

VOL. III.——17   z

"A kind-hearted man and a good Christian; for you returned good for evil, and repaid impertinence by making it the foundation of a compliment. Still, I must presume again, and tell you that I believe your laughs are like *jours de fête;* they do not come *every* day."

"Pour les jours de fête, non; ils ne me sont point venus tous les jours que depuis mon arrivée ici; mais à présent, Mademoiselle, tous les jours sont pour moi des jours de fête, et ma sainte est Sainte Helène."*

I was not yet old enough to know how to receive compliments like these without embarrassment; and to hide my awkwardness I exclaimed, "Why, what can have become of them? I have lost them; they are quite gone."

"*Qu'avez-vous perdu, Mademoiselle? Permettez-moi de le chercher. Dites donc.*"†

"My fear and awe of you."

"Fear and awe of me! *Oh! qu'ils s'en aillent tout de bon. Ce ne sont pas les sentiments que je voudrais vous inspirer pour moi.*"‡ As he said this, there was an expression in his dark eyes which made me turn mine away; and addressing my mother, I told her that our guest reminded me of a little French paper toy which I had seen, called *deux têtes sous un bonnet;* that at first view, it was a monk with a cowl on, but that when the cowl was thrown off, there was a gay and smiling young man. So it was with Mr. De Walden: when he first came, he seemed a grave philosopher, and now he is an absolute lover of fun, and a laugher of the first order.

"De grace, Mademoiselle, dites-moi lequel des deux caractères vous plait le plus; mais, ne me dites pas, je vous le demande en grâce, que je vous offense le moins dans mon rôle de philosophe; Hélas! auprès de vous qui pourroit rester philosophe?"§

"I wish you," said I, "to resemble Democritus, who united the two characters of laugher and philosopher; and you, if you please, shall be the latter with my mother; you shall talk wisely and gravely with her, but laugh and talk nonsense now and then with me."

"Vous convenez donc de la justice de ma proposition, qu' auprès de vous on ne peut être philosophe?"‖

I shook my head and held up my hand at him, not knowing exactly how to answer: he seized it, and pressed it fervently to his lips. My mother, I saw, enjoyed this dialogue; but my own heart reproached me for having allowed myself to be amused and flattered into a sort of infidelity to Seymour, by a man too who would be, I foresaw, warmly encouraged by my mother.

By this conversation, which has never been effaced from my memory, you will suspect that my flippancy and the evident pleasure with which I kept it up, were proofs that nothing but a prior attachment could have preserved my affections from the power of De Walden, when he once displayed to me all the variety of his talents, and the graces of his mind. Even as it was, they would have had a more certain effect, but for the injudicious eagerness with which my mother tried to force a conviction of them upon me; for then my alarmed feelings took the part of Seymour, and I was piqued into underrating her idol, because she seemed to *overrate* him. How very rarely is it that one can obtain or give an opinion uninfluenced by temper, prejudice, or interest!

"Is he not very handsome?" she used to say.

"Yes, but I have seen a handsomer man."

"Oh, you mean Seymour; he is handsomer certainly, but then he is not near so tall."

"No, but he is better made."

"That *I* never remarked; and I hope you will only impart the result of your observation to *me:* others might think it indelicate. What a fine countenance he has!"

"Yes, *sometimes,* but not always; and I prefer one that is always so: I like *perpetual* rather than *occasional* sun-shine. — It is disagreeable to have to watch the sun peeping out from behind clouds."

"Helen, Helen!" replied my mother, "weak, foolish girl! to like what no one can on earth obtain—perpetual sun-shine in the moral world! And after all, when one considers what this life is, its *long pains* and its *short pleasures,* the *riches of one* day succeeded by the *poverty of* the *next,* the ties which are *firmly knit* only to be *severed* in *a moment,* and our *capacity* and *cause* for *enjoyment* never equal to our *capability* and *cause* of suffering; my child, what a *poor, thoughtless, frivolous* being must that be, whose *lip* can always *smile,* and whose *eye* can always *sparkle,* whom fears for *himself* can never *depress,* nor fears for *time* or for *eternity,* or anxiety for the welfare or the peace of others, can alarm into *self-government!*"

You know that when my mother was roused into any mental emotion, she did not talk, she harangued, she spoke as if she read out of a book; it was, as you perceive, the case now.

"My dear mother," replied I, "such a being as you describe would be as odious to me as he could be to you; and his vivacity either of manner or countenance must be the result of want of feelings, affections, or intellect. To

---

* For holidays, no: they never came to me every day, till I came hither; but now, all days are holidays to me, and my saint is Saint Helen.

† But what are you seeking? let me look for it. Tell me.

‡ Oh, let them go away entirely! These are not the sentiments with which I wish to inspire you.

§ In pity tell me, which of these two characters pleases you the most; but pray do not tell me that I offend you less as a philosopher, for who that is near you can long remain a philosopher?

‖ You agree then to the justice of my proposition, that near you no one can remain a philosopher?

such perpetual sun-shine, I, like you, should object. But then the *clouds* must not be occasioned by the absence of good-humour, or by the presence of sulkiness and ill-humour, or by hypochondriacal tendencies."

"You do not suppose, Helen," she cried, with quickness, "that De Walden is grave only because he is cross, and thoughtful only because he is hypochondriacal?"

"Were we talking of individuals, mamma?"

"If not, you know we were thinking of them, Helen; and I feel only too sensible that the pique with which you answer when I praise Ferdinand, springs from your still powerful attachment to Seymour."

I could not deny it: but my conscience reproached me for having, from a feeling of jealousy on poor Seymour's account, not only seemed to insinuate an ill-opinion of Ferdinand, which I did not entertain, but for having also given unnecessary pain to my mother. Oh, my dear friend! how often since I lost her have I reproached myself with these little offences! and what I suffered for the more painful trials which I inflicted on her, no words can describe, no regret can atone. Sad state of human blindness, and human infirmity, when one seems conscious of the duties which one owes to a parent, only after one is utterly deprived of the means to atone for the neglect of them!

By what I have said of my jealousy of my mother's admiration of Ferdinand, you will see how much I had forgiven Seymour's imputed ill-conduct, and how little I adhered to my resolution of forgetting him. His letter and his new prize had much contributed to this. The latter was a proof that he had been leading a regular and studious life; and the former declared that my mother and myself were dearer to him than *any one else* in existence, and that our approbation was what he most coveted.—Alas! when one loves, one easily believes what the beloved object asserts.

Still, however, spite of my constancy, De Walden, by his varied talents, his rational pursuits, his instructive conversation, and his active benevolence, gained on my esteem every day. He was constantly occupied himself, and his example stimulated us to equal industry.—Weeks, therefore, fled as if they were days; and I felt raised in my own estimation, by seeing myself the constant object of interest to such a man, and also by feeling myself able to appreciate him.

If Seymour had not been able to write elegant prose, and gain prizes, my constancy would have been in great danger. But as it was, there was intellectuality on both sides; and I had only to weigh talent against strength of mind and extensive information, throwing a great many pleasant make-weights beside into the scale with the first.

My feelings towards Seymour were now called into fresh vigour by a letter from him, informing my mother that instead of having a monument made on purpose for his beloved parent, which would not have been ready for a considerable time, he had purchased one which had been nearly finished for a gentleman who died before it was completed, and who had intended it for his wife, and which the sculptor had been desired by the heir-at-law not to trouble himself to complete.

This monument Pendarves said had met all his ideas of simple and classical beauty, and it would soon be ready for the inscription. This, he added, he had also enclosed for the approbation of my mother and "his cousin Helen," as he called me; considering the former as the representative of his mother, and *me* as the only woman after her whom he wished to consult on any of his plans.

We were excessively affected at the receipt of this letter; and De Walden, who was present, appeared distressed at the sight of our emotion. "What do you think of the inscription, my dear!" asked my mother.

"Ask Mr. De Walden what he thinks of it," I replied.

It was as follows:

HERE LIETH ALL THAT WAS MORTAL
OF
THE LADY HELEN PENDARVES.
READER,
PITY ONLY HER SURVIVORS.

On the reverse side were to be the following words:—

THIS MONUMENT
IS ERECTED TO HER MEMORY
AS A TOKEN OF LOVE AND GRATITUDE,
BY HER ONLY CHILD,
WHOSE PROUDEST BOAST IT WILL ALWAYS BE,
THAT HE WAS
THE SON OF SUCH A WOMAN.

As I expected, he exclaimed in its praise; and as he was a great *theorizer*, he added much that delighted me, and much that consequently made my mother uncomfortable.

"It is," cried he, "simple and comprehensive. Oh! I must know him: simple virtues, simple manners, and simple heart. Pompous writers not much real feeling — not *true*. I must know Pendarves; a good son makes a good friend, good every thing. When shall I see him?"

My mother looked grave, and I saw that the observant eye of De Walden remarked our contrary emotions with surprise, if not with uneasiness.

"Then, I may tell Pendarves that you like the inscription; may I, Helen!" said my mother.

"Oh yes, that it is every thing I could wish;" and she retired to write.

When she returned, it was evident that she had been weeping violently; and De Walden, without saying a word, took her hand and pressed it respectfully to his lips.

This action, though it was at once feeling and affectionate, displeased me; for it seemed to my oblique manner of viewing such things, an injury to Pendarves, and in no very pleasant disposition of mind I left the room. Nor can I doubt but that my absence gave my mother an opportunity of telling De Walden all the circumstances of our situation with Seymour; for on my rejoining them I found my mother looking agitated, though also much pleased, and De Walden dejected, abstracted, and silent. Need I add that I had long since had the pain of discovering that he had conceived an attachment for me?

You may easily believe that this letter from Seymour, and my mother's assurance that he would certainly come to see the monument put up, did not tend to further the suit which I foresaw in process of time would be urged to me by De Walden. But the monument was sent down and erected, and yet Pendarves did not arrive. Consequently we thought he would not come at all; still, as precaution is wisdom, my mother with much earnestness conjured me to pledge my solemn word to her, that if he came I would not converse with him alone, should he be ever so desirous of an interview, and that I would avoid him when he called at our house. This was a trial of my filial duty for which I was not prepared, but my mother was so bent on carrying her point, and she so solemnly expressed her conviction that his conduct when in London was not amended, that I gave at last the promise which she requested.

"Now then," said I to myself, "I hope poor Seymour will *not* come down."

Lady Helen's monument was placed next that of her husband, on which, by desire of Lord Seymour, an account of the two families and of the manner of his death, had been engraved in an ostentatious manner. Consequently it had not been necessary for Seymour to give any additional details. My mother likewise had found herself at liberty, when she hung up a beautiful tablet to the memory of her husband, to confine herself to the simplicity which she loved, and these last furnished a curious contrast to the pompous copiousness of the first.

Still it was not to enjoy the superiority of my mother's and Seymour's taste, that I now so often visited the church, and resumed the custom which I had adopted in America, of strewing the graves I honoured with flowers. Oh no! it was because the *mother of Seymour Pendarves* the *dearest friend of my youth* slept beneath that spotless marble; and I not only gratified my own feelings, but was sure my tribute would be gratifying to those of Pendarves.

Of *his* father I had *no* recollection, and of *my own* not sufficient to make such a tribute, had I paid it to him, more than an act of coldly remembered duty; but my whole heart was interested when I performed it in honour of Lady Helen; and the chill and colourless marble looked warm and glowing, from the profusion of blooming flowers which I loved to scatter on it.

One morning, after offering, as usual, my tribute on this precious monument, and while kneeling beside it, a deep sigh startled me, and I beheld Seymour Pendarves, who had entered at another door, standing in pleased contemplation of me; but the view which I allowed myself of him was short indeed; my promise to my mother forcibly recurred to my mind, and the shriek of surprise and even of alarm which I uttered on beholding him so unexpectedly, was succeeded by my flying with the speed of phrensy to the door behind me, before Seymour, thunderstruck, mortified, and overcome by my seeming terror on observing him, could recover himself sufficiently to prevent or overtake me.

Alas! by the beating of my heart, and the trembling of my whole frame, I knew too well that on hiding myself from him depended my only chance of keeping my promise. I therefore took refuge in a cottage, the owner of which was well known to me, instead of hastening home along the park, where he must with ease have overtaken me. Accordingly, I followed a sharp turning which led through a little lane to the cottage, and making my way through the first room into the back one, I threw myself on a bed, trembling and breathless.

"What is the matter, my dear young lady!" cried the cottager.

"Ask no questions, but shut the door," was my answer.

She obeyed me, and I listened for several minutes for the sound of rapid footsteps, but in vain. I felt mortified at finding that Seymour did not trouble himself to pursue me; still I dared not go home, lest I should meet him on my road. I was therefore obliged to tell the cottager that I had a particular reason for wishing to avoid seeing Mr. Pendarves, and I would thank her to watch, if she could do it unsuspected, for his quitting the church, and inform me which way he went.

"Yes, yes," replied the woman, shaking her head, "he shall not see you if I can help it; for though to be sure I hear he is very good to the poor, folks say he is but a wild one, and they do say—"

Here, with an agonizing heart, and a gesture of indignant impatience, I bade her begone and do as I desired. When she had disappeared, I clasped my hands together convulsively. I sobbed aloud in the anguish of a wounded spirit; "And can it be," I cried, "that he whose sweet and pensive countenance so full of mournful tenderness I have just gazed upon for a moment, and shall never be able to forget again; can he be a man whose notoriously profligate habits make him the theme of abuse to a person like this?" No; there is not one pang in the catalogue of human suffering so acute as that which the heart feels from the consciousness of the decided depravity of a being tenderly beloved.

The woman on her return told me, "Mr. Pendarves was certainly seeking me; that he had, on leaving the church, looked round, and then ran several yards at full speed down the park, after which he stopped and she thought it probable that he would soon be past the front window, but she would look out and see." She did so, and having told me in a whisper, adding that "through a hole in the little muslin curtain I could see him without being seen," I was weak enough to take advantage of the opportunity. He walked dejectedly and with folded arms; the glow on his cheek, which the sight of me had deepened, was now succeeded by a deadly paleness; and I felt a bitterness which not even my sense of his errors could assuage, that he was wretched, and that I had made him so. My spy watched him into his own house, and only then I ventured to return to mine. I must say that I look back on this morning, spite of the sufferings which I endured, with much self-satisfaction, as I had completely acted up to the dictates of filial duty under the strongest temptation of disobeying them, as my mother was gone with De Walden to spend the day from home; and had I not conscientiously avoided Seymour, I might even without any positive infringement of duty, havé exposed myself to the risk of seeing him undisturbed by her presence. Happily, however, my principles were too firm to allow me to be satisfied with this subterfuge, and, as I before said, I recall this day with satisfaction.

Every hour I expected that Seymour would call, but he did not come: however, I saw his servant ride up to the gate, deliver a note, and wait for an answer. I gave it verbally to my own maid. It was, that Mrs. Pendarves was gone out for the whole day. Shall I confess that I *hoped* Seymour would, on hearing this, make an attempt to see me, though I was resolved to refuse him attendance; and I was *mortified* that he did not? Just before I expected my mother and De Walden would return, I saw Seymour's servant come to the door again, and deliver another note, as it seemed; but when it was brought into the room, I found it was a letter to me! I was at once relieved, agitated, miserable and delighted; yet my hand trembled so much I thought I should never be able to open the letter. The following were its contents:—

"When this letter reaches you, Miss Pendarves, I shall be at a distance from that scene which to me can now never again be a home, but which is endeared to me by such tender recollections, that not even by the miserable ones which now must succeed to them can they be ever effaced.

"Oh, my beloved mother! could you have believed that your son could be refused admittance within the doors of your dearest friend, and forbidden even to speak to the play-fellow and companion of his childhood, and the once appointed sharer of his heart and his fortunes? Could you have thought that the friend who adored you would have gone from home purposely to avoid him, and to avoid his just reproaches; because, without any *new* offence on his part, she had not only *resolved* never to allow him to address her daughter, but had pledged that daughter's hand, as he is informed, to another? And yet her parting words were, 'Your marriage with Helen depends wholly on yourself!' These words I never have forgotten; they regulated my conduct, they gave strength to my resolutions; I came hither full of hope, and I go hence overwhelmed with despair. For my claims, claims which I have *never resigned*, have been disregarded, and Helen will be the wife of a stranger, the acquaintance of yesterday!

"Nay more, at sight of me, Helen herself, the conscious Helen, fled as from a pestilence! And at what a moment too, when I had surprised her in an office the most flattering to your memory, and the most precious to my heart!

"Cruel Helen! what have you done? and what have *I* done to be so treated? Surely it was from your mother herself that I should first have heard of your intended marriage. But no: I refused to believe it till your flight and your countenance of terror on seeing me confirmed the horrible truth.

"But though you might not be able to tell it me yourself, why did Mrs. Pendarves avoid me? why; when I wrote to tell her I was coming for a single day, did she not make a point of seeing me either at her own house or at mine? But I will not detain you much longer from your attention to the happy stranger.

"Oh, Helen! had you continued to encourage my hopes, I might have been a happiness to myself and an ornament to society. But now—yes, now, it will be well if I am not a disgrace to it. But why do I continue to write? Shall I tell you, Helen? It is because I feel that I am addressing you for the *last time;* for the wife of the Count De Walden must not, I know, receive letters from
"SEYMOUR PENDARVES."

Though I now think, and you will probably think so too, that this letter was written full as much from the head as from the heart, you will not wonder that it bent me to the earth in agony; and that when my mother entered the hall on her return, she heard my voice uttering the tones of loud lamentation, and found me in the arms of the terrified servants. Never have I since suffered myself to be so weakly overpowered. I try to excuse such weakness by the state of my health at the time. Indisposition, and a tendency to a severe feverish cold, had prevented me from accompanying my mother and De Walden. Nor did the sudden surprise of seeing Pendarves steady my nerves, or decrease my fever; but these circumstances prepared the way for the letter to affect me as it did, and to excuse in some measure the state in which my mother beheld me.

An open letter near me, in the hand-writing of Pendarves, accounted for all that she saw. I was become more composed, though I did not speak, and she then eagerly inquired, but she soon desisted, to express her surprise at the charge of having gone out purposely to avoid him; for no such letter had ever reached her: in consequence of some accident it did not arrive till the next day. She declared she could not sleep till she had written to Seymour to exonerate herself from so heavy a charge. I wished to say, " and to assure him, I hope, that I am not engaged to De Walden, that, on the contrary, he is not even a declared lover:" but I *dared* not say this; and my mother read on—but she read hastily, and wished, I saw, to conceal from me the painful emotions which the letter occasioned her. She therefore insisted on my forgetting these ill-founded reproaches, as she called them; she then left me, to write to Seymour.

The next morning Seymour's servant came to say, he was going to rejoin his master, and wished to know if we had any commands for him. To him, therefore, was consigned the exculpatory letter. But of this I had no knowledge at the time; for when my mother and the servant entered the room next day, they found me in all the restlessness of fast-increasing illness, and my mother, before night, was assured by the medical attendants, that I was suffering under a very formidable attack of the scarlet fever.

For three days and nights my life was despaired of; and as, according to the merciful dispensations of Providence, "good always springs from evil," my mother learnt to know, from the danger of her only child, that life was not so valueless to her, as she was sometimes disposed to think it. But hope succeeding to fear, on the fourth morning from my seizure I was pronounced out of danger. Yet a cloud, and that a dark one, still hung over my mother's prospects; for I had named Seymour in my delirium, in such terms as convinced her that he was ever uppermost in my mind, and that my illness had been the consequence of misery endured on his account.

De Walden, during this time, was in a state of painful anxiety. Scarcely could he be prevailed upon to keep out of the infected chamber; his nights were never once passed in bed, till I was declared to be in safety; and on my recovery, I had to experience the mortifying necessity of owing gratitude where I believed that I could never make an adequate return of affection.

Well, I recovered, though I remained for many weeks thin, languid, and afflicted with the disagreeable local complaints which often attend on the subsiding of a fever like mine, particularly inflammations of the eyelid, and I could not bear for some time to have my eyes uncovered. During this period of suffering, De Walden devoted his whole time to amusing me. He read to me while I reclined upon the sofa, and I forgot my complaints while listening to his intelligent comments on what he read. It was therefore with considerable concern that I saw him depart for Cambridge, in October; but my concern was joy to his. Never did I see any one more agitated on such an occasion, and scarcely could the presence of my mother restrain the declaration of love which hovered on his lips, and which I dreaded to hear! but he did restrain it; for he had promised her that he would do so, on her assurance that the time was not come for its being favourably received.

At Christmas he returned to us, and the surprise which he showed at sight of me, convinced us of the great change which had taken place in my appearance, in consequence, as is sometimes the case at my age, (for I was not yet seventeen,) of a severe fever. I was become taller by several inches; that is, I had become from five feet five, full five feet eight, and from my upright carriage, as I have heard you remark, I look considerably taller. But I am quite sure, that had the attachment of De Walden been founded on my personal appearance, it would, during his stay with us, have completely vanished; for my eyes were inflamed, my *embonpoint* had not increased, and my colour was not only gone, but my complexion looked thick as well as pale. I perceived, however, no diminution in the ardent devotion which his manner expressed, and I sighed while I thought, that had Seymour Pendarves seen me, he perhaps would not have remained so constant.

What an argument was this belief for me to try to conquer my attachment! But certain it is, that the example of Lady Helen and my mother influenced me even unconsciously to myself, and that I considered eternal constancy as praiseworthy, and not blameable. Love had led my mother and my admirable friend and monitress to leave their parents and country, and they had wept the loss of husbands thus exclusively beloved, in sacred singleness of attachment. It was in vain, therefore, that my mother told me love was to be conquered, and that she insinuated it was even indelicate to pine after an object who was perhaps unworthy, and certainly negligent, if not faithless. Her example, as I before said, had raised the passion in my estimation; the object of my love was one on whom my eyes had first opened, one who was associated with my earliest and happiest recollections, one too, who, she must remember, had at an early age saved my life at the hazard of his own, (a story I shall tell by-and-by); and I could not but think she wished me to forget Seymour, chiefly because she preferred Ferdinand. I believe I have forgotten to mention, that Seymour Pendarves went abroad as soon as he left our village, and that he did not receive my mother's explanatory letter till several months after it was written.

In January, De Walden returned to college, and I was still so unwell, that my mother wished me to change the air; and as business required her to undertake a journey, we set off, in February, on a tour.

I have never, I believe, during my whole narrative, mentioned some of my relations more than once, and this has been from a wish of not encumbering it with unnecessary characters. The uncle with whom my mother had lived previously to her marriage, who occasionally spent months at our house, and whom we visited in return, died suddenly, at a very advanced age, during my illness. It was this event which called my mother, as one of the executors, as well as residuary legatee, from her home.

The weather was cold, dry, February weather, and the brightness of the road, from the effect of frost and sun, was so painful to my eyes, that my mother resolved to travel all night, and repose in the day, after our second stage from London; and we set off for Oxford at one in the morning. From the ruggedness of the road, however, and the care which our coachman always took of our horses, we had full leisure to dwell on the possibility of our being robbed; when about three in the morning, two horsemen rode past the carriage, and one of them looked into the window next my mother, which she had just let down: but he rode on, and we were grasping each other's hand, in terrified silence, when he came back again, and desired the postilions to stop. Our footman, who was on the box, was disposed to resist this command; when a faint voice, the voice of the other gentleman, who now rode slowly up, conjured them to stop for mercy's sake, for they were not highwaymen: the first now came up to the window, and begged to be heard.

He and his friend, he said, were Oxford students, who had been to London, without leave; and if they were missing another morning at chapel, they were liable to a punishment which they wished to avoid; but they should certainly have reached Oxford in excellent time, had not his companion been taken extremely ill; and unless we would take him in, he must stop at the next house, at whatever risk.

You may suppose that my mother did not hesitate: she instantly desired the footman to assist the gentleman into the coach, and mount his horse — a plan which was thankfully acceded to. His companion instantly galloped off at full speed for Oxford.

The invalid, unable to speak, sunk back exhausted in one corner, and seemed most thankful, though he spoke almost inaudibly, for the use of my mother's smelling-bottle.

The weather had now experienced such a change, that the frost was gone; though the night was so dark, that the stranger could not distinguish our faces, nor we his. Indeed, he appeared to be insensible of external objects, and heedless of sounds, for he did not always answer my mother's kind inquiries.

I, meanwhile, was as silent as the invalid, and sat back in the coach, to indulge in the feelings which agitated me at the idea, that before long I should be in the very place which probably contained Pendarves, but without the remotest chance of seeing him. At length, we heard a village-clock strike four, and day began to dawn: my mother let down the glass, to feel, for a while, the refreshing breeze of morning. As she did this, desiring me to keep my thick veil wrapped close round my face, for fear of cold, the invalid said he would put his head out of the window, for he thought that the air would revive him. My mother drew back to make room for him; when, as the rays of the red and yellow dawn fell on his wan face, she recognized in this object of her kindness, Seymour Pendarves himself.

He, too, as her veil was thrown back, knew her at the same moment; and faintly ejaculating—

"Is it possible?" he turned his eyes eagerly toward me, then seized both her hands, and resting them on her knees, buried his face in them, and burst into tears; while, with the hand next me, he grasped mine, which was involuntarily extended towards him.

A painful silence ensued — the result of most uncomfortable feelings, which, on the side of Pendarves, were accompanied by the most distressing consciousness; for we had as it were detected him in a breach of college rules; and, but for us, his irregularity of conduct might, perhaps, have exposed him to the disgrace of expulsion; so much for that amendment on which *alone* depended his union with me. That was an event, however, which, though we knew it not, he had ceased to make probable; for the report of my engagement to De Walden was still current, wherever we were known; and if he had not known that Mr. Pendarves, the head of the family, knew nothing of this intended marriage, Seymour would have been convinced it was a fact *himself*.

My mother's tears now fell silently down her cheek, and in spite of herself she pressed her forehead on the head of Seymour, as it still rested on her knees. Certain it is, that she loved him with much of a mother's tenderness — loved him also because he resembled his father and mine—and loved him still more because he was all that remained to her of her ever-regretted friend. The opposition to our union, therefore, was the strongest proof possible of the strength of her principles, and of her affection for me; for, though she thus loved, she rejected him, because she was sure that he was not likely to make her daughter happy.

My mother was the first to break silence. In a voice of great feeling, she said, "Seymour! unhappy young man! why do I see you *here*, infringing college rules? and why do I see you thus? Have you been ill long? have you had no advice?" It was now quite day; and, as he raised his head, the wild wanness of his look was terrible to us both, and it was with difficulty that I could prevent myself from sobbing audibly, while I anxiously expected his answer.

"Spare me! spare me!" cried he mournfully, "a painful confession of follies."

"Did not business carry you to London, Seymour?"

"No—nor kept me there. It was the search of pleasure; and I have scarcely been in bed for three nights. Yet no; let me do myself some little justice: I was unhappy, and I *am* unhappy. By denying me all hope of Helen, you made me desperate, and I fled to riotous living, to get away from myself; therefore, do not reproach me; I am quite punished enough by seeing before me the intended wife of the Count de Walden—curses on the name! Tell me," cried he wildly, seeing that my mother hesitated to speak, "am I not right? Is not my Helen, as I once thought her, betrothed to De Walden?"

"Oh, no—no!" cried I, eagerly, and I caught my mother's eye rather sternly fixed upon me; but I regarded it not, for I felt at the very bottom of my heart the sudden change from misery to joy which Seymour's face now exhibited. He could not speak—his heart was too full; but leaning back, overcome both with physical and moral exhaustion, he nearly fainted away. He was soon, however, roused to new energy by the indignation with which he listened to what my mother felt herself called upon to say. I shall not enter into a detail of her observations; suffice, that she candidly told him her objections to his being allowed to address me remained in full force, as did her ardent wish that I should marry De Walden, who had offered himself as my lover, and who (she was certain) would as surely make me happy in marriage, as he would make me *miserable*.

When she had ended, he thanked her for her candour, but coldly reminded her that he had always said he would never take a refusal from any lips but mine—and he retained his resolution.

"And now," said he, "the opportunity is arrived. Helen! such as I am—not worthy of you, I own, except as far as tender and constant love can make me so—I offer myself to your acceptance. Speak—Yes or No,—and speak as your heart dictates!"

I remained silent for a minute; then faltered out, sighing deeply as I spoke, "I have no will—can have no will—but my mother's."

"Enough!" replied he, in a tone and with a look which seemed to me to be the climax of despair. "Hark!" cried he, "the Oxford clocks are striking six—why do I linger here? for here I am sure I have no longer any business!"

He let down the glass, and desired the postilions to stop, while the footman rode up to the door. This little exertion seemed too much for him, and he sunk back quite exhausted, while my mother tried to take one of his hands.

"Pshaw!" cried he, throwing her hand from him—"give me love or give me hate; no half-measures for me; nor hope, when you and your daughter have given me my deathblow, that I will accept of *emollients*. I thank you, madam, as I would a *stranger*, for your *courtesy* in admitting me here, and I wish you both good morning."

Again his strength failed him, and he was forced to wipe the dews of weakness from his forehead.

"Go, I must—even if I die in the effort!" he then exclaimed.

I could not bear this; and while my mother herself, greatly affected, held me back, I tried to catch him by the arm; and, in a voice which evinced the deep feeling of my soul, I exclaimed, "Stay, dear Seymour! you are not fit to go—you are not, indeed!" But I spoke in vain: he mounted his horse, assisted by the servant, while I broke from my mother, and stretched out my clasped hands to him in fruitless supplication; then giving me a look of such mixed expression, that I could not exactly say whether it most pained or gratified me, he was out of sight in a moment, while I looked after him till I could see him no longer; and even then I still looked, in hopes of seeing him again. I did see him again, just as we had entered Oxford, and were passing Magdalen; he *stood at the gate;* he had, therefore, *seen* my long, earnest gaze, as if in search of him; and though I felt confused, I also felt comforted by it. In another moment we were near him, and his eyes met mine with an expression mournful, tender, and I thought, grateful, too, for the interest which I took in him. He kissed his hand to me, and then disappeared within the gates.

"Helen!" said my mother, "I meant to have stopped here, to refresh the horses and ourselves; but after what I have seen this morning, I shall proceed immediately."

She left the footman, however, behind, to bring us word the next day how Mr. Pendarves was. Oh! how I loved her for this kind attention! But then she was a rare instance of the union of strong feelings with unbending principle.

Methinks I hear you say, "I hope you were now convinced that Seymour's attachment as well as Ferdinand's, was founded on too good a basis to be shaken by your altered looks."

No, indeed, I was not; for so conscious was I that my looks were altered, I *never once* lifted up my veil before Pendarves. I dare say, both he and my mother imputed this to the wish of hiding my emotion, whereas it was in fact only to hide my inflamed eyes, and my *ugliness*. But what a degrading confession for a heroine to make! to plead guilty of having bad eyes and a plain face! It is as bad as Amelia's broken nose. But *n'importe:* my eyes, like her nose, will get well again; and, like her, I shall come out a complete beauty, when no one could expect it.

We awaited with great impatience the return of the servant, from whom we learnt that Mr. Pendarves had been seized with an alarming fit on leaving the chapel, and was pronounced to be in an inflammatory fever.

"O my dear mother!" cried I, wildly, "he has no one to nurse him now that loves him!"

"But he *shall* have," she replied; and in another hour we were on our road to Oxford. My mother insisted on being admitted to the bedside of the unconscious sufferer, who in his delirium was ever blaming the cruelty of *her* who was now watching and weeping beside his pillow. Long was his illness, and severe his suffering: but he struggled through; and the first object whom he beheld on recovering his recollection, was my mother leaning over him with the anxiety of a real parent. Never could poor Seymour recall this moment of his life without tears of grateful tenderness.

He was too much disappointed, however, to find that her resolution not to allow him to address me remained in full force; for the circumstances on which it was founded were added to, rather than diminished. Nor could his assertion, that his dissipation was owing to the despair into which she had plunged him, at all excuse him in her eyes, for she could not admit that any sorrow could be an excuse for error.

This, indeed, far from its being a motive to move her heart in his favour, closed it the more against him; as it proved she thought that from his weakness of character he never could deserve to be intrusted with the happiness of her child.

Bitter, therefore, was his mortification, when, on expressing the hopes to which her kindness had given birth, she assured him that her sentiments remained unaltered.

"Then, madam," cried he, "why were you so cruel as to save my life?"

"Young man," she gravely replied, "was it not my duty to try to save your life, that you might try to amend it? Were you prepared to meet that terrible tribunal from which even the most perfect shrink back appalled?"

On his complete recovery, my mother and I proceeded to the house of my uncle, now become our property; and thence we returned home. The following vacation Seymour finally left college, and again went abroad.

He wrote a farewell letter to my mother, as eloquent as gratitude and even filial affection could make it: she wept over it and exclaimed,

"Oh, that the generous-hearted creature who wrote this should not be all I wish him! He is like a beautiful but unsupported edifice, fair to behold, but dangerous to lean against!"

There was one part of the letter, however, which my mother did not understand: I fancied that I did, though I did not own it. He assured her, that in spite of everything he carried more hope away in his heart than he had ever yet known: hope, and even a *precious conviction* which he *had never known before*, and which he was sure his cousin Helen would wish him to possess, as it would be to him the *strongest shield* against *temptation*.

"My dear," said my mother, after long consideration, "how stupid I have been not to understand this sooner! He certainly means that he is become very religious: and that this hope, this sweet conviction, are faith and another world. Dear Seymour, I am so glad! for though I do not choose you should marry a Methodist, and one extreme is to me as unpleasant as another, still I believe Methodists to be a very happy people; and I hope Seymour, for his own sake, will not change again."

I smiled, but said nothing; for I put a very different interpretation on his words. As it appeared to me, his *hope* and *conviction* were that he possessed *my love*, and that my compliance with my mother's will was wholly against my own; for I recollected the tone in which I had replied to his question concerning my engagement to De Walden, "Oh, no! no!" and also my scream of agony in spite of his alarming weakness when he persevered in leaving us, and the anxiety with which I looked at him at the gates of Magdalen. Yes, when we exchanged that look, I felt that our hearts understood each other, and I was sure that the shield to which Seymour alluded was his conviction of my love.

But alas! he was absent—De Walden was present. He came to us at the beginning of the long vacation, and was to remain with us till he returned to college.

My mother now urged me to admit the addresses of De Walden, showing me at the same time a letter from his uncle, in which he expressed his earnest desire that his nephew should be a successful suitor, and offering to make a splendid addition to his fortune whenever he should become my husband. In short, could the prospect of rank and fortune, could manly beauty, superior sense, unspotted virtues, and uncommon acquirements, have made me unfaithful to my first attachment, unfaithful I should soon have become; but though the attentions of De Walden could not annihilate, they certainly weakened it. No wonder that they should do so, when I was so little sure of the stability of Seymour's affection, that I was fearful it would be weakened by any change in my external appearance, and as I had often heard him say, he did not admire tall women, I own I was weak enough to be uneasy at the growth consequent upon my fever; and 'I was glad, when we met in the coach, not only that my veil concealed my altered looks, but that, as I was seated, he could not discover my almost may-pole height.

De Walden, on the contrary, admired tall women; and declared that I had now reached the exact height which gave majesty to the female figure without diminishing its grace; and as I really thought myself too tall, his praise (for flattery it was not) was particularly welcome to me. Whatever was the cause, whether I liked De Walden so well, that I liked Seymour so much less as to cease to be fretted by his absence, I cannot tell; but certain it is that I recovered my bloom, and that from the increase of my *embonpoint*, my mother feared I should become too fat for a girl of seventeen: my spirits too recovered all their former gaiety, so that October, the time for the departure of De Walden, arrived before I was conscious that he had been with us half his accustomed time.

My mother now naturally enough augured well for the success of his suit; and I owned that I was no longer averse to listen to his love, but that I would on no account engage myself to him till I was *quite sure* I had conquered my attachment to Pendarves.

This was certainly conceding a great deal, and De Walden left us full of hope for the first time; while I, who felt much of my affection for him vanish when I no longer listened to the deep persuasive tones of his voice, should have repented having gone so far, had I not seen happiness beaming in my beloved mother's face.

At Christmas De Walden came to us again, and I then found that in such cases it is impossible (to use an expressive phrase) "*to say A without saying B;*" I had gone so far that I was expected to go further; and but for the secret misgivings of my own heart, and the firm dictates of my own judgment, De Walden would have returned to college in January my betrothed husband. But, though we had not received any tidings from Pendarves, and my mother felt assured of his inconstancy, I persevered firmly in my resolution not to *engage* myself till I *had seen him again*, and could be assured, by seeing him with indifference, that my heart had really changed its master.

You will wonder, perhaps, how a man of Ferdinand's delicacy could wish to accept a heart which had been so long wedded to another, and that other a living object. But my mother had convinced herself, and had no difficulty in convincing him, that I was deceived in the strength of my former attachment; that she had originally, though unconsciously, directed my thoughts to him; that, like a romantic girl, I had thought it pretty to be in love, and that my fancied passion had been irritated by obstacles; but that, when once *his* wife, I should find that *he alone* had ever been the real possessor of my affections.

It is curious to observe how easily even the most sensible persons can forget, and believe, according to their wishes. My mother had absolutely forgotten the proofs of my strong attachment to Seymour, which she had once so much deplored. She forgot my illness, which if not caused was increased by his letter of reproach; she forgot the tell-tale misery which I had exhibited on the road to Oxford, and she did not read in the firmness with which I still persisted to see Seymour again, a secret suspicion of still lingering love.

But the crisis of our fates was fast approaching: I received an invitation to spend the months of May and June in London, with a friend who had once resided near us, and who had gone to reside in the metropolis.

I felt a great desire to accept this invitation; and my mother kindly permitted me to go, but declined going herself, saying that it was time *I* should learn to live without *her*, and *she* without *me*. Accordingly, for the first time we were separated. But this separation was soon soothed to me by the charms of the life which I was leading. I was a new face: I was only seventeen, and I was *said* to be the heiress of considerable property. This, you know, was an exaggeration; my fortune was handsome, but not very large: however, I was followed and courted, but none of my admirers were in my opinion at all equal to Seymour or De Walden: they gratified my vanity, but they failed to touch my heart.

One day at an exhibition, I met a newly-married lady, who when single had been staying in the neighbourhood of my mother's uncle during our last visit, and was much admired both by my mother and myself. This meeting gave us great pleasure, and she hoped I would come and see her at her lodgings. I promised that I would.

"But there is nothing like the time present: will you go home with me now, and spend a quiet day? You must come again when my husband is at home and I have a party; but he dines out to-day, and I shall be alone till evening."

"But I am not dressed."

"Oh! I can send for your things and your maid; and such an opportunity as this of telling you all about my love and my marriage may never occur again."

I was as eager to hear as she was to tell; my friend consented to part with me, and I accompanied her home.

In the afternoon while we were expecting two or three ladies of her acquaintance, and were preparing to walk with them in the park, my friend received a little note from her husband.

"That is so like Ridley," said she. "However, this is an improvement; for he often goes out and invites half-a-dozen people to dinner without giving me any notice: but now he has only invited one man to supper, and has sent to let me know they are coming. His name I see is the same as yours, Seymour Pendarves: is he a cousin of yours?"

"What!" cried I, almost gasping for breath, "Seymour Pendarves in England, and coming hither!"

"Yes; but what is the matter, or why are you so agitated?"

"If you please I will go home, I had rather go home."

Mrs. Ridley looked at me with wonder and concern, but she was too delicate to ask me for the confidence which she saw I was not disposed to give. She therefore mildly replied that if I must leave her, she would order her servant to attend me.

A few moments had restored my self-possession: and I thought that as the time was now arrived when I could, by seeing Pendarves, enable myself to judge of the real state of my heart, I should be wrong to run away from the opportunity.

"But pray tell me," said I, "when you expect Mr. Ridley and his friends?"

"Oh not till it is dark, not till near supper-time."

Immediately (I am ashamed of my girlish folly) I had a strong desire to discover whether Seymour would recognise my person, altered as it was in height and in size; and I also wished to get over the first flutter of seeing him without its being perceived by him. In consequence I told Mrs. Ridley that Seymour was my cousin, but that he had not seen me *standing* since I was grown so very tall; and I had a great wish to ascertain whether he would know me. "Therefore," said I, "do not order candles till we have sat a little while."

Mrs. Ridley smiled, fully persuaded that, though I might speak the truth, I did not speak *all* the truth. I was at liberty in the mean time, during our walk in the park, to indulge in reverie, and to try to strengthen my agitated nerves against the approaching interview. But concerning what was I now anxious?— Not so much to ascertain whether I loved *him*, but whether he loved *me*. Alas! this anxiety was a certain proof that he was still the possessor of my heart, and that of course I ought not to be and could not be the wife of De Walden.

Just as we stopped at the door, on our return from our walk, Mr. Ridley was knocking at it, accompanied by Seymour. I felt myself excessively agitated, while I pulled my hat and veil over my face: to avoid a shower, we had crowded into a hackney-coach. Luckily I had not to get out first; but judge how I trembled when I found Seymour's hand presented to assist me. My foot slipped, and if he had not caught me in his arms, I should have fallen. Mrs. Ridley, however, good-naturedly observed, that she had been nearly falling herself, the step was so bad, and her friend *Miss Pen* was also very short-sighted. I now walked up stairs, tottering as I went.

"Fanny," whispered Mr. Ridley to his wife, "who is she?" She told him I was a Miss Pen, and she would tell him more by and by.

"Pray, Fanny, when do you mean to have candles?" said Mr. Ridley.

"Not yet; not till we go to take off our bonnets. I like this light, it is so pleasant to the eyes."

"Yes, and so cheap too," replied her husband. "But I wonder you should like this sort of light, Fanny, for you are far removed yet from that period of life when *le petit jour* is so favourable to beauty: you are still young enough to bear the searching light of broad-eyed day, and so I trust are all the ladies present; though I must own a *veil* is always a suspicious circumstance," he added, coming up to me.

"Yes, yes," said his wife, "I always suspect a veil is worn to conceal something."

"But it may be worn in mercy," he added; "and perhaps it is so here, if I may judge of what is hidden by what is shown: if I may form an opinion indeed from that hand and arm, on which youth and beauty are so legibly written, I—"

Here, confused and almost provoked, I drew on my gloves; and Mrs. Ridley, who loved fun, whispered her husband,

"Do not go on; she is quite ugly, scarred with the confluent small-pox, blear-eyed, and hideous: you will be surprised when you see her face."

She then begged to speak to me; and as I walked across the room in which we sat to join her in the next, I saw Ridley whisper Pendarves.

"May be so," he replied: "but her figure and form are almost the finest I ever saw."

"And yet I am so very tall," said I to myself with a joy that vibrated through my frame.

The conversation now became general; and on a lady's being mentioned who had married a second husband before the first had been dead quite a year, Pendarves, to my consternation, began a violent philippic against women, declaring that scarcely one of us was capable of a persevering attachment; that the best and dearest of husbands might be forgotten in six months; and that those men only could expect to be happy who laid their plans for happiness independently of woman's love."

It is strange, but true, that the indignation which this speech excited in me enabled me to conquer at once the agitation which had hitherto kept me silent. Coming hastily forward, I exclaimed, while he rose respectfully,

"Is it for you, Mr. Seymour Pendarves, to hold such language as this? Have you forgotten Lady Helen, your own blessed mother, and her friend and yours?"

So saying, while he stood confounded, self-judged, and full of wonder, for the voice and manner were mine, but the height and figure were no longer so,—I left the room; and a violent burst of tears relieved my oppressed heart.

Mrs. Ridley then rang for a candle and considerately left me to myself.

Oh! the flutter of that moment when I re-entered the drawing-room, which I found brilliantly lighted up! Seymour, who had I found now doubted, and now believed, the evidence of his ears in opposition to that of his sight, was standing at the window; but he turned hastily round at my entrance, and our eyes instantly met.

"Helen!" exclaimed he, springing forward to meet me, while my hand was extended toward him; and I believe my countenance was equally encouraging. That yielded hand was pressed by turns to his lips and his heart; but still we neither of us spoke, and Seymour suddenly disappeared.

Mr. Ridley, who was that *melancholy* thing to other people a *professed joker*, to my great relief (as it enabled me to recover myself,) now came up to me bowing respectfully, and begged me to veil my face again; for he saw that my excessive ugliness had been too much for his poor friend, and he hoped for his sake, as well as that of the rest of mankind, I would conceal myself from sight.

I told him, when his friend came back I would consider of his proposition, and if he approved it I would veil directly.

Before Seymour returned, I asked Mr. Ridley whether he suspected who his presuming monitor was.

"Pray, madam," he archly replied, "say that word again. What are you to Mr. Pendarves?"

"I said 'Monitor.'"

"Oh—*monitor!* I thought you were *something* to him, but did not exactly *know what*. No wonder he was so alarmed at sight of you, for monitors, I believe, have a right to chastise their pupils; and I begin now to fear he will not come back. Do you use the ferule or the rod, Miss Pendarves?"

"You have not yet answered my question, sir!"

"Oh! I forgot. 'Heavens!' cried he, as you closed the door, 'is it possible! Could that be my cousin, Helen Pendarves? Yes, it could be no other; and yet'——Is that like him, madam?"

"Oh! very!"

"'Well,' I, in the simplicity of my heart, replied, 'your cousin she may be; but my wife told me her name was Pen.'"

"'Oh yes, it must be Helen—it was her own sweet voice and manner!'"

"'She is given to scolding, then—is she?' said I."

"'Oh!' said he, 'she is!' But I will spare your blushes, madam; though I must own that I could not believe you *were* the lady in question, because my wife told me you were hideous to behold, and *he* said you were a beauty: besides, when he last saw you, he added, you were thin and short; but then he eagerly observed, that a year and a half made a great difference sometimes, and you had not met during that period. But here comes the gentleman to answer your questions himself. What I further said did not at all please him."

"No! what was it, sir?"

"That, if you were indeed Miss Helen Pendarves, you were a great nuisance, for that you had won and broken at least a dozen hearts; but that it was a comfort to know you would soon be removed from the power of doing further mischief, as you were going to be married to a Swiss gentleman, and would soon leave the kingdom."

"And you told him this?" cried I, turning very faint.

"Yes, I did; and he had just turned away from me, when you made your appearance."

Seymour now entered the room; and I was, from this conversation, at no loss to account for the gloom which overspread his countenance, while he hoped Miss Pendarves was well.

"My dear Fanny," said Mr. Ridley, who must have his joke, "I hope you will make proper apologies to this gentleman and me, for having exposed us to such a horrible surprise as the sight of that lady's face has given us. Pray, was this ungenerous plan of concealment Miss Pendarves's or yours?"

"Her's, entirely."

"But what was her motive?"

"She wished to see whether her cousin would know her through her veil."

"Oh! she was acting Clara in the Duenna; you know she plays Don Ferdinand some such trick."

"True; but Ferdinand and Clara were *lovers*, not cousins."

"Cannot cousins be lovers, Fanny?"

Here the entrance of the servant with supper, interrupted the conversation, and Seymour and I sat down to it with what appetite we could.

"It is astonishing," said Mr. Ridley, "what use and habit can effect; I have already conquered my horror at sight of your friend's face; and I see Mr. Pendarves has not only done the same, but I suspect he is meditating a drawing of it, to send to the Royal Society, as a *lusus naturæ*."

In spite of himself, Seymour smiled at this speech, and replied, while I looked very foolish, that he was gazing at me with wonder, as he could not conceive how I had gained so many inches in height since he saw me.

"I grew several inches after my fever," I replied.

"Fever! When—where—what fever, Helen? I never heard you were ill."

"Oh yes, I was—and my life was despaired of."

"You in danger, Helen, and I never knew it!"

"It was really very unkind," said Ridley, "to keep such a delightful piece of intelligence from you."

"But *when* was it, dear Helen?"

"When I saw you on the road to Oxford, I was only just recovered."

"Only just recovered! You did not look ill; but I remember you had your veil down, so I really did not see your face."

"So, so; wearing her veil down is a common thing with her—is it? I am glad she is so considerate."

These jokes, however, had their use; for they tended to keep under the indulgence of feelings which required to be restrained in both of us, in the presence of others.

"But, when was you first seized, Helen? and what brought on your fever?" said Seymour, as if urged by some secret consciousness.

You will not wonder that I blushed, and even stammered, as I answered, "I was not quite well when I saw you in the church—and —and——"

"And what?"

"I was seized that night, and when my mother returned, she found me very ill indeed!"

"That night!" Here he started from his seat.

"Ah Fanny!" cried Mr. Ridley, "you *would* buy them! I always objected to them."

"Buy what, my dear Ridley?"

"These chairs; I always said they were such uneasy ones, no one could sit on them long — you see Mr. Pendarves can't endure them."

I was very glad when Seymour sat down again; when he did, he leaned his elbows on the table, and gazed in my face as if he would have read the very bottom of my soul. But hope seemed to have supplanted despair. Mr. Ridley now suddenly rose, and holding his hand to his side, cried, "Oh!" in such a comic, yet pathetic manner, that though his wife really believed he was in pain, she could not help laughing; then, seizing a candle, he went *oh-ing* and limping out of the room, leaning on her arm, and declaring he believed he must go to bed, if we would excuse him.

There was no mistaking his motive, and Seymour was not slow to profit by the opportunity thus good-naturedly offered him.

"Helen!" he exclaimed, seating himself by me, and seizing my hand, "is what I heard true—am I the most wretched of men—is this hand promised to De Walden?"

"No—not yet promised."

"Then you mean to give it to him?"

"Certainly not *now*."

"Why that emphasis on *now?*"

"Because I am sure I do not love him sufficiently."

"And since when have you found this out?"

I did not answer; but my tell-tale silence emboldened him to put his own interpretation on what I had said; and now, for the first time, unrestrained by any unwelcome witness, he passionately pleaded the interests of his own love, and drew from me an open confession of mine. Nor was there long a secret of my heart which was withheld from him; and while he rejoiced over the certainty that his rival's hopes were destroyed by this interview, I rejoiced in hearing that the conviction he had received of my affection for him, had preserved him from temptations to which he would probably otherwise have yielded.

"But they are returning," cried he; "tell me where you are, and promise to see me tomorrow, my own precious Helen! Never, never was I so happy before."

"Nor I," I could have added; but I believe my eyes spoke for me, and I promised to see him the next day at eleven. He had just time to resume his chair when Mr. and Mrs. Ridley returned.

"I have been very unwell," said Ridley, "and am so still; but I would come back, as she would not leave me, because I was sure, what with the uneasy chairs, and Miss Pen's ugly face, you would be so fretted, Mr. Pendarves, that you would never come hither again."

"'But then, my dear,' said Fanny, 'you forget they are relations, and must love each other.'

"'That I deny,' said I, 'if they are not both loveable.'

"'And then, says she, 'they have not met for so long a time, and have so much to say.'

"'I don't believe that,' says I: 'if so, they would have taken care to meet sooner'——but pray what has happened to you both since we went away? Well, I declare, such roses on cheeks, and diamonds in eyes! and, I protest, Miss Pen has learnt to look straight-forward, and is all dimples and smiles! and this, too, when, for aught you both knew, I might be dying!"

Seymour and I were now too happy not to be disposed to laugh at any absurdity which Ridley uttered; and never before or since did I pass so merry an evening. Seymour was as gay and delightful as nature intended him to be: you will own that the word "*fascinating*" seemed made on purpose to express him; and I, as he has since told me, appeared to him to exceed in personal appearance that evening (animated as I was with the consciousness of loving and being beloved) all the promises of my early youth; nor could he help saying—

"Really, Helen, I cannot but look at you!"

"That is very evident," observed Ridley.

"Yes, but I mean that I look at her because —because——"

"You cannot help it, and it requires no apology. I have a tendency to the same weakness myself."

"But I mean you are so surprisingly altered—so grown—so——"

"Say no more, my dear sir," cried Ridley, interrupting him, "for it must mortify the young lady to see how much she has outgrown your knowledge and your liking! and she is such a disgrace to your family, that it is a pity there is no chance for her changing *her name*, poor thing! those blear eyes must prevent that. I see very clearly, indeed, she is likely to die *Helen Pendarves*."

This observation, much to Ridley's sorrow, evidently clouded over the brows of us both; for we both thought of my mother, and I of poor De Walden. But the cloud soon passed away; for we were together, we were assured of each other's love, and *we were happy*.—Nor did we hear the watchman call "past one o'clock," without as much surprise as pain. However, Pendarves walked home with me, and that walk was not less interesting than the evening had been.

But, alas! my mother's image awaited me on my pillow. I could not help mourning over the blighted hopes of De Walden, nor could I drive from my startled fancy the suspicion that I had committed a breach of duty in receiving and returning vows unsanctioned by her permission, or satisfy my conscience that I had done right in allowing him to call on me the next day. But I quieted myself by resolving that I would instantly write to my mother, tell her what had passed, and see Seymour only that once, till she gave me her permission to see him more frequently.

He came at eleven, and I told him what I meant to do. He fully approved, but declared he would not consent to meet evil more than half way, and give up seeing me. On the contrary, he was resolved to see me every day till she came; and as Mr. Pendarves our uncle was just come to his house in town, he meant to tell him how we were situated, and he was very sure that he would approve our meeting as much as possible. On leaving me he proceeded to lay his case before our uncle, while I sat down to write to my mother. It was a long letter bathed with my tears; for was I not now pleading almost for life and death? If I loved Pendarves when my affection was not fed by his professions of mutual love, how must that flame be now increased in fervour, when I had heard him plead his cause two days successively, and had enjoyed with him hours of the tenderest uninterrupted intercourse! Wisely had my mother acted in forbidding us to meet, as she wished to annihilate our partiality; for absence and distance are the best preventives, if not the certain cures of love.

My letter, which was full of passion, regrets, apologies and pity for De Walden, was scarcely finished, when I was told that a gentleman who was going immediately into Warwickshire, and would pass close by my mother's door, would take charge of it. I foolishly confided it to his care; I say "foolishly," because the post was a surer conveyance. However, I could not foresee that this gentleman would fall ill on the road; that he would not deliver my packet till ten days after it was written; and that I was therefore allowed to spend many hours with Pendarves unprohibited; for my uncle approved our meeting, and desired our union, declaring that he had always thought my mother severe in her judgment of his nephew, and that while considering the fancied interests of her own child, she had disregarded his.

"Besides," added he, "I am the head of the family, and I command you to meet as often, and to love as much, as ever you choose."

Alas! I obeyed him only too well, though my judgment was not blinded to the certainty that he had no rights which could invalidate those of my mother; and though I rejoiced at not receiving her command to cease to receive Pendarves, I was beginning to feel uneasy at her silence, when a letter from her reached me, saying, she was on her road to London, where she would arrive that night, and should take up her abode with our friend Mr. Nelson.

Never before had I been parted from my mother, and till I met Pendarves I had longed for her every day during my stay in London; but now, self-reproved and ashamed, I felt that a yet dearer object had acquired possession of my thoughts and wishes, and the once devoted child dreaded, rather than desired, to be re-united to one of the best of mothers.

She came; and we met again, as we had parted, with tears; but the nature of those tears was altered, and neither of us would have liked to analyze the difference.

Long and painful was the conversation we had together that night, before we attempted to sleep. I found my mother fully convinced that there was a necessity for my not marrying De Walden, a necessity of which he was now himself convinced; for she had gone round by Cambridge, in order to see him: but she was not equally convinced that there was a necessity for my marrying Pendarves, as all her objections to that marriage remained in the fullest force.

The next morning she opened her heart on the subject to Mrs. Nelson, who was Seymour's warm advocate, and assured her, that if she made proper inquiries, she would find that the character of Pendarves was universally spoken of as unexceptionable; and that whatever might have been the errors of *the youth*, they were forgotten by other people in the merits of *the man.*

"Ay, but a mother's heart can't forget them," she exclaimed, "when her child's happiness is at stake!" and she begged to have no private conversation with Seymour till the next day. In consequence, she saw him only in a party at my uncle's, where she was struck with the great improvement both of his face and person, for both now wore the appearance of health; and the countenance which, when she last surveyed it, bore the stamp of sickness and sorrow, now beamed with all the vivacity of youth and hope.

The party was a mixed one of cards and dancing; and as she gazed on Pendarves when he stood talking to me, he recalled forcibly to her mind the image of my father, as she first beheld him in a similar scene, four-and-twenty years before.

The next day Seymour obtained the desired interview with my mother. She brought forward his former errors in array against him, his debts, his dissipations, and his love of play; and though she expressed her readiness to believe him reformed, still, as he ingenuously admitted that his improvement was chiefly owing to my influence over him, she could not deem it sufficiently well-founded to obviate her objections; and he was still pleading, and she objecting, when Mr. Pendarves insisted on entering. Mrs. Nelson and I accompanied him.

"I tell you what, niece," said he, "you do not use this young man well: you bring up a parcel of old tales, and dwell upon the naughtiness of them, as if he was the only young man who ever erred. I know all his sins; he has made me his confessor. In the affair to which you allude he was much more to be pitied than censured, and yielded at seventeen to temptations which might have overcome seven-and-thirty. Since then he has distinguished himself at college: he has paid all his old debts, and incurred no new ones; he has steered clear of the quicksands of foreign travel, shielded (as he says) by the hopes of one day possessing Helen, and by the idea that he was the object of her love; and what would you have more? Besides, Helen tells me he once saved her life."

"I did so," cried Seymour, eagerly seizing her hands, "I did so, and you promised to be for ever grateful!"

"How was it, my dear nephew?"

"*I* will tell you, sir," cried I, gathering hope from my mother's agitation. "It was at the Isle of Wight, soon after we came to England: he and I were playing on the shore, and I, not knowing the tide was coming in, paddled across a run of water to what I called a pretty little island, and there amused myself with picking up sea-weed, when the sea flowed in, and he saw that I must perish; no one was near us. Luckily, he spied a boat on the dry land, which, with all his boyish strength, he pushed off to my assistance, and jumped into it. In one minute more it floated towards me, just as my cries had reached the ears of my mother, who was reading on the rock, and who now saw my situation."

"Helen! Helen!" cried my mother, "I can't bear it—the scene was too horrible to recall." But I persevered.

"Seymour seized my hand just as I was sinking, and dragged me into the boat; but in another moment the waves came swelling round us, and, without oar or help, I and my preserver were both tossed to and fro upon the ocean."

"Helen!" cried Seymour, with great feeling, and clasping me fondly to his heart, "I could almost wish we then had died, for then we should have died together!"

"Go on," said my uncle, "I hope you will live together yet!"

"I have not much more to tell, except that my mother's screams had now procured assistance, and a boat was sent out to follow our uncertain course. When we were overtaken, they found Seymour holding me on his lap, and crying over me in agony unutterable, for he thought that I was dead, and he had come too late. Who can paint my mother's transports, when she received me safe and living in her arms?"

"And how she embraced me, Helen," cried Seymour, "and called me her noble boy—the preserver of her child! (for she saw all I had done;) and how she owned she should ever love me as her own child—and vowed her gratitude should end but with her life!"

"It never *will* end but with my life!" cried my mother, throwing herself on Seymour's neck. "But is your having saved my child's life an argument for my authorizing you to risk the happiness of that life?"

"Julia, Julia, I am *ashamed* of you!" cried my uncle. "Was there ever a better or more devoted wife than yourself? Yet, what did you do at Helen's age? You ran away from your parents, out of an ungovernable passion for a handsome young man."

"But is my error an excuse or justification of his?"

"No; but you are a proof that error can be atoned for and never repeated, as you have been a model for wives and mothers. But beware, Mrs. Pendarves, of carrying things too far; beware, lest you tempt Helen and Seymour to copy your example, rather than conform to your precepts."

"Ha!" cried my mother, clasping her hands in agony.

"Now, then," said Seymour, with every symptom of deep emotion, "the moment is come when I am authorized to obey the commands of the beloved dead, and fulfil the last injunctions of my mother."

A pause which no one seemed inclined to break, followed this unexpected observation; and Seymour, taking a letter from his bosom, kissed it, and presented it to my mother.

"'Tis Helen's hand," cried she.

"And her seal, too, you observe," said Seymour: "the *envelope*, you perceive, is addressed to me, and I have therefore broken it; the other is entire."

My mother read the *envelope* to herself, and these were its contents:—

"My conscience reproaches me, my beloved son, with having too lightly surrendered your rights, and probably your wishes, in giving my friend back her promise to promote your union with her daughter, as I know Julia's ability to act up to her strict sense of a mother's duty, even at the expense of her own happiness, and risk of her child's safety. But I have given up that promise, which might have pleaded for you, my poor child! when I was no more, and ensured to you opportunities of securing Helen's affections, which may now, perhaps, be for ever denied to you. However, I may be mistaken; therefore, if Helen's affections should ever be *yours* — *avowedly* yours, and her mother still withhold her consent, give her the enclosed letter, and probably the voice of the dead may have more power over her than that of the living.

"For your sake I have thus written, with a trembling hand, and with a dying pulse; but value it as a last proof of that affection which can end only with my life.

"HELEN PENDARVES."

The letter to my mother was as follows:—

"I speak to you from the grave, my dearest Julia! and in behalf of that child on whom my soul doted while on earth. But this letter will not be given you till he is *assured* he possesses the heart of your daughter; and when, if your consent is denied to their union, nothing but an act of disobedience can make them happy in each other. Are you prepared, Julia, to expose them to such a risk, and thus tempt the child you love to the crime of disobedience? that crime which, though it dwelt but lightly on your mind, weighed upon mine through the whole of my existence, as it helped to plunge my mother in an untimely tomb. Perhaps you flatter yourself that Helen's education has fortified her against indulging her passion at the expense of her duty. But remember, that your precepts are forcibly counteracted by your example.

"Anxious, however, as I am that Helen should not err, I am still more anxious that my son should not lead her into error, as I feel that he is doubly armed against her filial piety, by the example of her mother and his own.

"And must my crime be thus perpetuated by those whom I hold most dear? must the misery of my life be renewed, perhaps, in that of her whom I have loved as my own child? and must my son be the cause of wretchedness to the dearest of my friends, through the medium of her daughter?

"Forbid it Heaven! I conjure you, my beloved Julia! by our past love—by *tanta fede, e si, dolce memorie, e si lungo costume,* listen to this my warning, my supplicating voice; and let your consent give dignity and happiness to the union of our children.

"HELEN PENDARVES."

My mother, after having read this letter, covered her face with her hands, and rushed out of the room. It was in a state of anxious suspense that we awaited her return. When she appeared, her eyes were swelled, but her countenance was calm, her look resigned, and her deportment, as usual, dignified. Her assumed composure, however, failed again, when her eyes met those of Pendarves.

"My son!" cried she, opening her arms to him, into which Seymour threw himself, as much affected as she was; then, beckoning me to her, she put my hand in his, and prayed God to bless our union.

Little of this part of my life remains to be told. My mother had given her consent, and in two months from that period we were MARRIED.

Here ends my narrative of a WOMAN'S LOVE. When next I treat of it, it will be as united to a WIFE'S DUTY.

A WIFE'S DUTY,

BEING A CONTINUATION OF A "WOMAN'S LOVE."

PART THE SECOND.

I am only too painfully aware, my dear friend, that in my history of a "Woman's Love," I have related none but very common occurrences and situations, and entered into minute, nay perhaps uninteresting details. Still, however common an event may be, it is susceptible of variety in description, because endlessly various is the manner in which the same event affects different persons. Perhaps no occurrence ever affected two human beings exactly in the same manner; but as the rays of light call forth different hues and gradations of colour, according to the peculiar surfaces on which they fall, so common circumstances vary in their results and their effects, according to the different natures and minds of those to whom they occur.

My trials have been, and will no doubt continue to be, the trials of thousands of my sex; but the manner in which I acted under them, and their effect on my feelings and my character, must be peculiar to myself. And on these alone, I can presume to found any expectation of affording to you, while you read, the variety which keeps attention alive, and the interest which repays it.

In the same week which made me a bride, Ferdinand de Walden left England, unable to remain near the spot which had witnessed the birth of his dearest hopes, and would now witness the destruction of them.

I could have soothed in a degree the "pangs of despitefulness," by assuring him that I was convinced nothing but a prior attachment could have prevented my heart from returning his love. I could have told him, that I seemed to myself to have *two hearts:* the one glowing with passionate tenderness for the object of its first feelings, the other conscious of a deep-rooted and well-founded esteem for him. But it was my duty to conceal this truth from him, as such an avowal would have strengthened my hold on his remembrance, and it was now become his duty to *forget.*

My mother, not very long after my marriage, wounded my feelings in a manner which I could not soon recover. I was speaking of De Walden with that warmth of regard which I really felt for him, and lamenting that I should probably now see him no more, when, with a look of agony for which I was not prepared, she begged me never to mention the name of De Walden to her again; for that her only chance of being able to reconcile herself to the marriage which I *had made,* was her learning to forget the one which she had *so ardently desired.*

Eagerly indeed did I pledge my word to her, that I would in future *never name De Walden.*

The first twelve months of my wedded life were halcyon days; and the first months of marriage are not often such,—perhaps they never are, except where the wedded couple are so young that they are not trammelled in habits which are likely to interfere with a spirit of accommodation; nor even then, probably, unless the temper is good and yielding on both sides. It usually takes some time for the husband and wife to know each other's humours and habits, and to find out what surrender of their own they can make with the least reluctance for their mutual good. But we had youth, and (I speak it not as a boast) we had good temper also. Seymour, you know, was proverbially good-natured; and I, though an only child, had not had my naturally happy temper ruined by injudicious indulgence.

You know that Seymour and I went to Paris, and thence to Marseilles, not very long after we married, and returned in six months, to complete the alterations which we had ordered to be made to our house, under the superintendence of my mother.

We found our alterations really deserving the name of improvements, and Seymour enthusiastically exclaimed, "O Helen! never, never will we leave this enchanting place. Here let us live, my beloved, and be the world to each other!"

My heart readily assented to this delightful proposition, but even then my judgment revolted at it.

I felt, I *knew* that Pendarves *loved* and was *formed for* society. I was sure, that by beginning our wedded life with total seclusion, we should only prepare the way for utter distaste to it; and, concealing my own inclinations, I told him I must stipulate for three months of London every spring. My husband started with surprise and mortification at this *un-romantic* reply to his sentimental proposal, nor could he at all accede to it: but he complained of *my passion* for London to my mother, while the country with *me* for his companion was quite sufficient for *his* happiness.

"*These are early times yet,*" replied my mother coldly; and Seymour was not satisfied with the mother or the daughter.

"Seymour," said I one day, "since you have

declared against keeping any more terms, and will therefore not read much law till you become a justice of the peace, pray, tell me how you mean to employ yourself?"

"Why, in *the first place*," said he, "I shall read or write. But my *first* employment shall be to teach you Spanish. I cannot endure to think that De Walden taught you Italian, Helen."

"But you taught me to love, you know, therefore you ought to forgive it."

"No, I cannot rest till I also have helped to complete your education."

"Well, but I cannot be learning Spanish all day."

"No; so perhaps I shall set about writing a great work."

"The very thing that I was going to propose, though not exactly a great work. What think you of a life of poor Chatterton, with critical remarks on his poems?"

"Excellent! I will do it."

And now having given him a pursuit, I ventured to indulge some reasonable hopes that home and the country might prove to him as delightful as he fancied that they would be; and what with studying Spanish, with building a green-house, with occasional writing, with study, with getting together materials for this life, and writing the preface, time fled on very rapid pinions; and after we had been married two years, and May arrived a second time, Seymour triumphantly exclaimed, "There, Helen! I believe that you distrusted my love for the country; but have I once expressed or felt a wish to go to London?"

"The Ides of March are come, but not gone," I replied; "and surely if I wish to go, you will not deny me."

"No, Helen, certainly not," said he in a tone of mortification; "if I am no longer all-sufficient for your happiness."

Alas! in the ingenuousness of my nature, I gave way when he said this to the tenderness of my heart, and assured him that my happiness depended wholly on the enjoyment of his society; and I fear it is too true that men soon learn to slight what they are sure of possessing. Had I been an artful woman, and could I have condescended to make him doubtful of the extent of my love, by a few woman's subterfuges; could I have feigned a desire to return to the world, instead of owning, as I did, that all my enjoyment was comprised in home and him; I do think that I might have been for a much longer period the happiest of wives; but then I should have been, in my own eyes, despicable as a woman; and I was always tenacious of my own esteem.

May was *come*, but not GONE—when I found my husband was continually reading to me, after having read to *himself*, the accounts in the papers of the gaieties of London.

"What a tempting account this is, Helen, of the Exhibition at Somerset-House! I should like to see it. Seeing pictures is an elegant rational amusement. And here are soon to be a ball and supper at Ranelagh. A fine place Ranelagh for such an entertainment."

Here he read a list of routs and cotillion balls at different places; but one day he read with infinite mortification, that our uncle, Mr. Pendarves, had given a ball on the return of his son-in-law to parliament.

"How abominable," cried Seymour, "for my uncle to give a ball, and not invite us to go up to it!"

"You forget," replied I, "that, knowing our passion for the country, and that we had abjured the world, he did not like to ask us, because he knew he should be refused."

"I am not so sure he would have been refused, Helen; or, as to having abjured the world—no, no, we are not such fools as to do that—are we, my dearest girl?"

"We are bound by no vows, certainly; and as soon as retirement is become irksome to you, we can go to London."

"Did I say that retirement was grown irksome? O fy! such an idea never entered my thoughts: besides, as this fine ball is over, what should we go to London for?"

"There may be *other* fine balls, and fine parties, you know."

"True: but really, Helen, I begin to believe you wish to go to London."

"If you do, I do *certainly*."

"I? Not I, indeed! Ah, Helen! I suspect you are not ingenuous with me; and you do wish to go."

I only smiled; but I soon found that the book did not get forward—that the newspapers were anxiously expected — and that my Spanish master sometimes forgot his task, in the indulgence of reverie; and I debated within myself whether it would not be for our interest and our domestic comfort to propose to go to London, in order to conceal from him as long *as I could*, that I was not sufficient for his happiness, and that he would live and die *a man of the world*. I was the more ready to do this, because I wished that my mother should not see my empire was on the decline. Why did I so wish? I hoped it was because I was desirous to spare her any anxiety for my peace; but I fear it also was because I did not like that she should have cause to suspect her choice for me was likely to have proved a better one than my own. (I believe I have observed before how strong my conviction is, that there is scarcely such a thing in nature as a *single motive* of action.)

I therefore, in the presence of my mother, hinted a wish to go to London for six weeks. She started, and looked suspiciously at Pendarves; while he, with an odd mixture of surprise, joy, and mortification in his countenance, exclaimed—

"Do I hear right, Helen? Are you, after

all you have declared, desirous of going to London?"

"I am: 'Variety is charming,' says the proverb; and here, you know, it is *toujours perdrix*."

"Well, there, madam," said Pendarves, turning to my mother, "you will now, I hope, believe what I assured you of some time ago, that Helen had a passion for London."

"*C'est selon,*" replied my mother, "to use a French phrase in answer to Helen's;" and darting, as she spoke, a penetrating glance at me.

"I assure you," replied I, "that my wish to go to London originates with *myself*, as I believe that this journey to the metropolis is the *wisest* as well as the most *agreeable* thing I could desire."

My mother sighed, and a "Well, my child, I have no reason to doubt your word," broke languidly from her lips, while she suddenly rose and left the room.

"And are you *really* in earnest, Helen?" said Pendarves.

"Never more so; and unless my proposal is very distasteful to you, I beg you will write directly, and engage lodgings."

"Distasteful! Oh no! quite the contrary. I shall be *proud* to exhibit my lovely wife in London, where no doubt she will be as much admired as she was abroad. Do you think," he affectionately added, "that I have forgotten the exquisite pleasure I experienced at seeing you the object of general attraction wherever you moved?"

This was said and felt kindly; still it did not inspire me with that confidence which it seemed likely to inspire; for *I*, though I was conscious of my husband's personal beauty, had no vanity to gratify in exhibiting him to the London world. I had no wish to be the most *envied* of women—it was sufficient for me to know that I was the *happiest*; and I thought that if Pendarves loved as truly as I did, the consciousness of his happiness would have been sufficient for him. Still I am well aware how wrong it is to judge the love of others, according to our own capability of loving. As well and as justly might we confine beauty, or the power of pleasing, to one cast of features or complexion. All persons love after a manner of their own; and woe must befall the man or woman who expects to be loved according to their own way and their own degree of loving, without any consideration for the different character and different feelings of the beloved object.

"How absurd I am!" said I to myself, after I had shed some weak tears in the solitude of my chamber, because Pendarves did not love me, I found, as I loved him. "How absurd! True, *he* delights in the idea of exhibiting *me*, and *I* have no wish to exhibit *him*. After all, he loves more *generously* than I do, and my selfishness is nothing to be proud of."

Thus I reasoned with myself, and tried to fortify my mind to bear the cares and the dangers which I had on principle provoked.

"One word, Helen," said my mother, when she was alone with me after what had passed relative to my projected journey, "are you sure, my dear child, that in urging your husband to go to London, you have acted wisely?"

"As sure as the consciousness of my bounded vision of futurity can allow me to be. I thought it better to *forestall* my husband's wishes, than to wait for the *expression* of them."

"If not *better*, it was less *mortifying*," replied my quick-sighted parent; and we said no more on the subject.

In three days' time we had lodgings procured for us near Hanover Square; and on the fourth day from that on which I made known my wishes, we set off for London. But how different were the feelings of my husband and myself on the occasion! He was all joy and pleased expectation, unmixed with any painful regret or any anxious fears. But I left for some time a tenderly beloved mother, and the scene of tranquil and certain enjoyment. I was going, I knew, to encounter probably the influence of rivals, both men and women, in my husband's attentions, and the dangerous power of long and early associations. And how did I know, but that into a renewal of intimacy with his former associates I was not bringing my husband? But I had done what I thought right; and if I had presumptuously acted on the dictates of human wisdom alone, I prayed, fervently prayed, that the divine wisdom would take pity on my weakness, and avert the courted and impending evil.

I was many miles on my journey, before I could drive from my mind the recollection of my mother's countenance when we parted. It did not alone express sorrow to part with me—it indicated anxiety, foreboding of evil to happen before we met again; and it required all my husband's enlivening gaiety and fascinating powers to revive my drooping spirits. His gaiety, I must own, however, depressed rather than enlivened me at first; for I was mortified to see with what delight he anticipated our return to the great world: but, as I had no ill-tempered feelings to oppose to the influence of his buoyant hilarity and his winning charm of manner, they at length subdued my depression, and imparted to me their own pleasant cheerfulness.

"Dear, dear London!" cried Pendarves, as our horses' hoofs first rattled on its pavement; "dear London! how I love thee! for here I was first convinced how fondly Helen loved me!" So saying, he pressed me to *his* heart, and a feeling of revived confidence stole over *mine*.

We found my uncle and Mrs. Pendarves still in London; but I did not feel as rejoiced on the occasion as they and my husband did.

The latter was glad because he had in them proper protectors for his wife, whenever he was obliged to leave me, and the former, because they had really an affection for us. But I knew so much of Mrs. Pendarves, by the description I had heard of her from Lady Helen and my mother, and what I had observed myself, that I dreaded being exposed to her home truths and her indiscreet communications.

It was not long before we found ourselves completely in the vortex of a London life. And as for the most part my husband's engagements and mine were the same, I lost the gloomy forebodings with which I left home, and even lost my fears of Mrs. Pendarves.

One day, Pendarves told me he was going to dine with an old friend of his—Maurice Witred; but as I was not going out, he hoped to be back to drink tea with me; but I expected him in vain, and he did not return till bed-time.

He told me he was sorry to have disappointed me; but his friend had prevailed upon him to go to the play. This excuse was so sufficient, and his wish to accompany Mr. Witred so natural, that I should have had no misgiving whatever, had I not observed a certain degree of constraint in his manner, and a consciousness as if he had not told me all. However, I was satisfied with the alleged cause of his absence, and I slept as soundly as usual. But the next morning came Mrs. Pendarves, saying she was glad to find me alone. She told me she had met my husband, and she had given him such a set-to! (to use her own elegant phrase.)

"And wherefore?"

"Oh! for going to the play with Maurice Witred and his lady."

"Lady! I did not know he was married."

"He is *not* married; and it was very wrong, and had an ill-appearance, for a young married man to be seen in public, though it *was* in a private box, with a profligate man and his mistress. I thought he would not tell you; but I was resolved you should know it, that you might scold him with the 'grave rebuke of a severe *youthful beauty* and a grace.'"

I did not reply, even to assure her that I was better pleased that she should scold my husband than that I should do it myself, for I knew she was incorrigible, and her communication had thrown me into a painful reverie; for I found that Pendarves had begun to practise disingenuousness and concealment with me, and in the most dangerous way — for he had concealed only half the truth, by which means persons make a sort of compromise with their integrity, and lay a *salvo* to their consciences; for they fancy they are not *lying*, though they are certainly *deceiving*—whereas, if they tell a *downright lie*, they at least KNOW they are sinning, and may be led by conscious shame into amendment. But there is no hope for those who thus delude themselves; and as *ce n'est que le premier pas qui coute*, I felt that I had lost some of my confidence in my husband's sincerity. Alas, when perfect confidence between man and wife is *once destroyed*, there is an end to *perfect happiness!* But I tried to shake off my abstraction; and I listened as well as I could to my talkative companion, whose passion was to give advice, that troublesome though common propensity in weak people; and like such persons, she was always boasting of the advice she had given, that which she would give, or of the *dressings* and *set-tos* which she had bestowed, or meant to bestow. At length, however, much to my relief, she went away, and not long after Pendarves returned.

"So," said he, "I find Mrs. Pendarves has been with you; and I suppose (blushing as he spoke) that she has been telling tales of me!"

"And of herself," I replied, smiling as unconcernedly as I could; "for she owns to the presumption of having given you a *set-to*, as she calls it."

"Yes; but I suppose she told you the cause?"

"No doubt."

"And do you think it deserved so severe a lecture?"

"I think it was not right in a respectable married man to seem to give his countenance to such a connexion as the one in question; and I suspect that you are of the same opinion."

"I am; but why do you think so?"

"From conceit; because I believe that fear of my censure made you conceal from me what you had done."

"True — most true; and my repugnance to tell you all proved to me still more how wrong that all was."

"My *dearest* Seymour!" I replied, "believe me, that no *all* which you can communicate to me can ever distress me so much as my consciousness of your want of ingenuousness and of your telling only half the truth can do. I saw by your manner something was wrong, and I shall ever bless the weak indiscretion of Mrs. Pendarves, because it led to this salutary explanation; and I trust that the next time you go with Mr. Witred and his *lady* to the play, you will mention *both*."

"But I shall *never* go with them again," eagerly replied my husband, "as you, Helen, think it improper."

"But I may be too rigid in my ideas; and I beg you to be ruled by your own judgment rather than mine. All I ask is, to be told the *whole truth*."

Pleasant to my feelings then, and dear to my recollection since, is the look of tenderness and approbation which Pendarves gave me as I spoke these words; and when he left me, peace and confidence seemed restored to my mind.

The next evening was the fashionable night

for Ranelagh, and my husband and I, who dined out, were to accompany a large party to that scene of gay resort.

Ranelagh was the place for tall women to appear to advantage in. Little women, however beautiful, were likely to be unnoticed in that circling crowd; but, even unattended with beauty, height and a good carriage of the person were sure to be noticed there. The pride which Pendarves took in my appearance was never so fully gratified as at Ranelagh; for while I leaned upon him, I used to feel my arm pressed gently to his side as he heard or saw the admiration which my lofty stature (to speak modestly) excited. This evening, as I was quite a *new face* in the splendid round, I was even followed as well as gazed at; and I was not sorry when our carriage was announced, though I was flattered on my own account, and pleased on my husband's; for I was eager to escape from some particularly impertinent starers, especially as I found that Pendarves was disposed to resent the freedom with which some men of high rank thought themselves privileged to follow and look at me. Before we separated, some of the party proposed that we should meet again at Ranelagh on the next night but one, and while I hesitated my husband exclaimed, " No mock modesty, Helen; no declining an opportunity, which you must enjoy, of being admired. So, pray tell our friends you gladly accede to their proposal."

" I gladly accede to your proposal," cried I laughing, but blushing with conscious vanity at the same time.

" What an obedient wife!" cried one of the ladies: "public homage has not spoiled her *yet*, I see."

" Nor can it," replied I, " while I possess my husband's homage, which I value *far more*."

" *While* you possess it! Then, if his homage should fail you, you might perhaps be pleased with the other?"

" I humbly hope *not*: but if exposed to that bitter trial, I dare not assert that I should not yield to it as scores of other women do every day; for I must say, in defence of my sex, that good husbands, generally speaking, make good wives; and that most women originally value the attentions of their husbands more than those of other men. On your sex, therefore, O false and fickle man! be visited the crimes of ours!"

This grave discourse provoked some laughter from my audience, from which I was glad to escape to our carriage, which had waited for us while we alighted.

" So, Helen," said my husband as we went home, " it is your opinion,

> That when weak women go astray,
> Their lords are more in fault than they."

" It is."

" And you said what you did as a gentle hint and a kind warning to *me* how I behaved myself?"

" Not so," said I eagerly : " I humbly trust that even your example would not make me swerve from my duty; and my observation was a general one. Still, my favourite and constant prayer is, ' Let me not be led into temptation;' and believe me, Pendarves, that she who is able to admit that she may possibly err, is less liable to do so than the woman who seems to believe she is incapable of it."

" Helen," said my husband, " I never for one moment associated together the idea of you and *frailty*: therefore, dear girl, I will carry you to Ranelagh again and again; for I *do love* to see you admired; and I feel proud while I think and *know* that even princes would woo your smiles in vain."

He kept his word, and we never missed a full night at Ranelagh. But one evening completely destroyed the unmixed pleasure which I had hitherto enjoyed there.

We had not been round the room more than twice when we were joined by Lord Charles Belmour, a former associate of my husband's, who, after a little while, begged to have some private conversation with him; and taking his arm, Pendarves consigned me to the care of the gentleman with us, on whose other arm hung a lady to whom he was busily making love: consequently, his attention was wholly directed to her, and I had nothing to divert mine from the conversation which occasionally met my ear between my husband and his noble friend, who walked close behind us.

Sometimes this conversation was held in a low voice, and then I ceased to listen to it; but when they spoke as usual, I thought I was justified in attending to them.

" Look there!" said Lord Charles, as we were passing a box in which sat two ladies splendidly dressed, accompanied by two gentlemen, " look, Pendarves, there is an old friend of yours!"

" Ha!" said my husband, lowering his voice, " I protest it is she! I did not know she was in England. Who are those men with her?"

" What, are you *jealous?*"

" Nonsense! Who are they!"

" The man in brown is husband to the lady in blue; and for the sake of associating with a titled lady, which your friend is, you know, he allows his wife, who is not pretty enough to be in danger, to go about with her and her *cher ami* — the young man in green. You know she was always a favourite with *young* men."

" True, and young indeed must the man be who is taken in by her fascinations."

" But she is wonderfully handsome still."

" I hardly looked at her."

" We are passing her again. *Now*, then, look at her *if you dare*."

" Dare!"

"Yes: for her eyes are very like the basilisk's."

"I will risk it."

I too now looked towards the box we were approaching; at the end of which stood a young man in green, hanging over a woman, who though no longer young, and wholly indebted to art for her bloom, appeared to my now jealous eyes the handsomest woman I had ever beheld. I also observed that she saw and recognised my husband; for she suddenly started and looked disordered, while an expression of anger stole over her face. A sudden stop in the crowd to allow the PRINCE and his party to pass, who were just entering, forced us to be stationary a few minutes before her box. Oh! how my heart beat during this survey! But one thing gratified me: I was sure, as I did not see her bow her head or curtsy, that Pendarves did not notice her. And yet Lord Charles had, uncontradicted, called her his *old friend!*

Who, then, and *what* was she? would he tell me? Perhaps he would when he got home; if he did not, I felt that I should be uneasy.

We soon moved on again, and I heard Lord Charles say,

"Cruel Pendarves! not even to look at or touch your hat to her! Surely that would not have committed you in any way."

"It would have been acknowledging her for an acquaintance, which I do not wish now to do, especially *in my wife's presence*," I conclude he said, for he spoke too low for me to hear; but I judge so from the answer of Lord Charles.

"Oh! then, if your wife was *not* present, you would not be so cruel?"

"I did not say so."

"No; but you implied it."

"I deny that also."

Then coming up to me, my husband again offered me his arm, and Lord Charles left us. I soon after saw this beautiful woman walking in the circle, and heard her named by the gentleman next me as Lady Bell Singleton — a dashing widow more famed for her beauty and her fascinations than her morals. But Pendarves said nothing; and though she looked very earnestly at him, and examined me from head to foot as I passed, I saw that he never turned his eyes on her, and seemed resolved not to see her.

I had therefore every reason to be pleased with my husband's conduct; but I felt great distrust of Lord Charles. I thought he was a man, from what I had overheard, whom I could never like as a companion for Pendarves; and I disliked him the more, because, if I had given him the slightest encouragement, he would have been my devoted and public admirer, and would have been delighted to make his attachment to me and our intimacy the theme of conversation. I also saw that my cold reserve had changed his partiality into dislike; and I could readily believe that he would be glad in revenge to wean my husband from me. Still, I could not wish that I had treated him otherwise than I did; for I could not have done it without compromising my sense of right, as *half measures* in such cases are of no avail; and if a married woman does not at once show that pointed and particular admiration is offensive to her, the man who offers it has a right to think his devoirs may *in time* be acceptable.

Here I may as well give you the character of this friend of my husband.

Lord Charles Belmour was the son of the Duke of ———; and never was any man more proud of the pre-eminence bestowed by rank and birth; but to do him justice, he began life with a wish to possess more honourable distinctions; and had he been placed in better circumstances, the world might have heard of him as a man of science, of learning, and of talents. But he had every thing to deaden his wish of studious fame, and nothing to encourage it. Besides, he was too indolent to toil for that renown which he was ambitious to enjoy; and instead of reading hard at college, he was soon led away into the most unbounded dissipation, while he saw honours daily bestowed on others which he had once earnestly wished to deserve and gain himself. But he quickly drove all weak repinings from him, proudly resolving in future to scorn and undervalue those laurels which could now never be his.

He therefore chose to declare it was beneath a nobleman, or even a gentleman, to gain a prize, or take a high degree; and this assertion, in which he did not himself believe, was quoted by many an idle dunce, glad so to excuse the ignorance which disgraced him.

But, spite of this pernicious opinion, Lord Charles never sought the society of those *who acted* upon it; and Pendarves, who had *distinguished* himself at Oxford, was his favourite companion there.

When Lord Charles entered the world, he gave himself up to all its vanities and irregularities. But he was conscious of great powers, and also conscious that he had suffered them to run to waste. Still, if he could not employ them in a way to excite admiration, he knew he could do so in a way to excite fear; and after all, *power* was *power*, and to *possess* it was the *first wish* of his heart.

Accordingly, though conscious he had himself the follies which he lashed, he had no mercy on those of his acquaintances; for, as he himself observed, "it is easier to laugh at the follies of others than amend one's own;" and though courted as an *amusing* companion, he was often shunned as a *dangerous* one.

Women, also, who defied him either as a suitor or an enemy, have rued the day when they ventured to dispute his power; but as I at length discovered, there was *one* way to dis-

arm him; and that was to own his ability to do harm, and try to conciliate him as an *active* and *efficient* friend.

In that case his generous and kind feelings conquered his less amiable ones, and his friendship was as sincere and valuable as his enmity was pernicious.

But with no uncommon inconsistency, while he declared that he thought a nobleman would disgrace himself if he sung well, or sung at all, or entered the lists in any way with persons à *talens*, he condescended to indulge before those whom he respected in the lowest of all talents, though certainly one of the most *amusing*, that of mimickry—a gift which usually appertains to other talents, as a border of shining gold to the fag end of a piece of India muslin, looking more showy indeed than the material to which it adheres; but how inferior in value and in price!

But to resume my narrative. My husband did *not* mention Lady Bell to me. The next time I went to Ranelagh with *mixed feelings*—for I dreaded to see this lady again, and to observe that Pendarves had chosen at length to own her for an acquaintance; for, had he been sure of never renewing his acquaintance, why should he *not* have *named her to me?*

It was also with contending feelings that I found myself obliged to have Mrs. Pendarves as my companion; for though I *wished* to be informed on the subject of my anxiety, I dreaded it at the same time: and I was sure that she would tell me *all she knew.*

A nephew of Mrs. Pendarves was our escort to Ranelagh; and my husband, who dined with Lord Charles Belmour, (much to my secret sorrow,) was to join us there.

My eyes looked everywhere in search of Lady Bell Singleton, and at length I discovered her. My companion did the same; and with a sort of scream of surprise, she said, "Oh, dear! if there is not Lady Bell Singleton! I thought she was abroad! Do you know, my dear, when she returned to England?"

"How should I know, madam? The very existence of the lady was a stranger to me till the other evening."

"Indeed! Why do not you really know that is the lady on whose account your mother forbade your marriage with Pendarves?"

"No madam, my mother was too discreet to explain her reasons."

"Well, my dear, you need not look so uneasy—it was all off long before he married you—though she is a very dangerous woman where she gets a hold, and looks

'So sure of her beholder's heart,
Neglecting for to take them.'"

I scarcely heard what she said, for a sick faint feeling came over me at the consciousness that I was now in the presence of a woman for whom Pendarves had undoubtedly felt some sort of regard; but it was jealousy for the past, not for the present, that overcame me, though my husband's total silence with regard to this lady was, I could not but think, an alarming circumstance. And "it was on her account your mother forbade your marriage with Pendarves," still vibrated painfully in my ears, when Lord Charles and he appeared. With a smile by no means as unconstrained as usual I met him, and accepted his proffered arm. Lord Charles walked with us for a round or two—then left us, whispering as he did so, "Remember! *do* notice her, she expects it, and I think she has a right to it."

Pendarves muttered, "Well, if it must be so," and his companion disappeared.

Soon after we saw him with Lady Bell Singleton leaning on his arm; and I felt convinced he had made the acquaintance since we were last at Ranelagh, as he never noticed her till that night. We were now meeting them for the second time, and passing close to them, when I saw Lady Bell pointedly try to catch my husband's eye: and no longer avoiding it, he took off his hat, and civilly, though distantly, returned the cordial but silent salutation which she gave him.

"This," thought I, "is in consequence of Lord Charles's interference, and explains what Pendarves meant by 'Well, if I must, I must.'"

How I wished that he would break his close silence on this subject, and be ingenuous! But I felt it was a delicate subject for him to treat—and I resolved to break the ice myself.

"That was a very beautiful woman to whom you bowed just now," said I, glad to find that Mrs. Pendarves was looking another way.

"She *has* been beautiful indeed!" was his answer.

Then looking at me, surprised I doubt not at the tremour of my voice, he was equally surprised at my excessive paleness, and with some little sarcasm in his tone, he said,

"My dear Helen, is my only bowing to a fine woman capable of making your cheek pale, and your voice trembling?"

"No," said I, "not so—you wrong me indeed; nor did I know that my cheek was pale." I said no more, shrinking from the seeming indelicacy of forcing a confidence which he was disposed to withhold.

"Helen," said he, looking up in my face, "I see our aunt Pendarves has been at her old work, and telling tales of me. I protest I shall insist on my uncle's sending her *muzzled* into your company."

"The best way of muzzling her would be to anticipate all her communications yourself. It would be such an effectual silence to a woman like our little aunt, to be able to say, 'I know that already!'"

"That's artfully put, Helen! But, really, there are some things which I have respected you too much to name to you. A *general* knowledge of my past faults and follies you have long had; but from no unworthy motive I have shrunk from talking to you of any *particular* one; and I feel pained and shocked, my beloved wife, to know that you are aware of that lady's having once been very near, if not very dear, to me in the days of my early youth."

"Enough," said I, "enough! Forget that I know any thing which you wished me *not* to know, and assure yourself that I will forget also."

"You are a wise and good girl," he replied, kindly pressing the arm that reposed in his; "but my little aunt is capable of making much mischief between married persons, where the mind of the wife is weak, and her temper suspicious."

But how irritated I was against Lord Charles that evening! He forced conversation with Pendarves whenever we passed him, and gave Lady Bell an opportunity of fixing her dark eyes on him in a manner which having once seen, I took care never to see again. I am sure it offended him as much as it did me; for though Lady Bell was not absolutely excluded society, she was by no means a woman to be forced on the notice of any man who had a virtuous wife leaning on his arm; and in returning her bow, Pendarves had done all that civility required of him: but I am convinced that Lord Charles wished to give me pain; and he was also in hopes that I should resent the appearance of any acquaintance remaining between the quondam lovers, and thereby occasion a coolness between my husband and myself.

This was the longest and the only painful evening I had ever passed at Ranelagh; and from that moment I took such a dislike to it, that I was very glad when the great heat of the weather made my usual companions at such places substitute Vauxhall for Ranelagh. But at Vauxhall the same lovely and unwelcome vision crossed my path; and I once overheard a gentleman say, looking back at my husband, who had stopt to speak to some ladies, "What a lucky fellow that Pendarves is! The two finest women in the garden—ay, or in London, are his wife, and his quondam mistress." The compliment to myself was deprived of its power to please me, by these wounding words, my husband's "quondam mistress." And was then that disgraceful connexion so well known? The thought was an overwhelming one, and I began to resent my husband's having bowed to this woman in my presence. But perhaps he was entreated to do so in order to shield her reputation? If so, could he do otherwise? And as I was always glad to find an excuse for Pendarves, I satisfied myself thus, and my recent displeasure was forgotten.

When we had extended the six weeks which we meant to pass in London to two months, I expressed a wish of returning into the country; and Seymour complied with so little reluctance, that I prepared to return home with a much lighter heart than I had expected ever to feel again. But Mrs. Pendarves had a parting gift for me in her own way—a piece of intelligence which clouded over the unexpected brilliancy of my home-prospects.

"Well, my dear niece," said she, "I am glad you are going, though I am sorry to part with you; for I do not like Seymour's friend, Lord Charles Belmour. He seems to me, my dear, to have, in the words of the poet—

'That low cunning which from fools supplies,
And aptly, too, the means of being wise.'

And I have thought no good of him ever since I saw him come out of Lady Bell Singleton's house with your husband."

"What!" cried I, catching hold of a chair, for my strength seemed suddenly to fail me, "does my husband visit Lady Bell?"

"Yes, that once I am sure he did; but then I do not doubt that Lord Charles took him there: for I am told his great pleasure is to alienate his married friends from their wives."

Alas! from what a pinnacle of happiness and confidence did this foolish woman cast me down in one moment! Reply I could not; and she went on to give me one piece of advice—and that was, never, if I could help it, to admit Lord Charles within my doors, and to discourage his intimacy with my husband as much as I could.

By this time, I had a little recovered this overwhelming blow, and I resolved, in *self-defence*, and in defence of my husband's character, to tell her I must believe she was mistaken in thinking she saw Pendarves come out of Lady Bell's house; but whether that were true or false, I must request her to keep such communications to herself in future, as a wife was the *last* person whom any one should presume to inform of the errors of her husband. But company came in; and soon after my uncle drove up to the house in his travelling carriage, and in a few minutes more they were both on the road to Cornwall. If Seymour, when he came in, had found me alone with Mrs. Pendarves, he would have attributed the strange abstraction of my manner to some information which she had given me; but he now imputed it to the headache of which I with justice complained; and when my visiters went away, he tenderly urged me to go to my chamber, and lie down.

This was fortunate, as I should have disliked excessively to tell him what his aunt had seen, and to let him observe how uneasy the communication had made me; for I was aware that a wife whose jealousy is so very apt to take alarm, is as troublesome to a husband as one whose nerves are so weak that she goes into a fit at the slightest noise, and starts at the mere shutting of a door. Still, my husband's ignorance of the cause of my indisposition was a great trial to me, for it forced me to have, for the *first time*, a secret from him. And *he*, too, it seemed, was keeping a secret from *me*; for, spite of my entreaties that he would always tell me himself what it might grieve me to hear from others, he had called on Lady Bell Singleton, without telling me that he had done so!

Alas! I did indeed lie down, and I did indeed darken my room; but it was to hide my agitation and my tears: nor till Pendarves went out to dinner, which with some difficulty I prevailed on him to do, did I suffer the light to penetrate into my apartments, or my swollen eye-lids to be seen of any one. But then I rose—then, too, I rallied my spirits; for, in the first place, I was cheered by my husband's affectionate unwillingness to leave me, and in the next, I had nearly convinced myself that Mrs. Pendarves had not seen him when she fancied she did.

By this resolute endeavour to look only on the *bright side*, I was enabled, when my husband returned—which he did very early—to receive him with unforced smiles and cheerfulness.

The next day we set off immediately after breakfast, on our journey home; and I met my mother with a countenance so happy, that the look of anxious inquiry with which she beheld me was immediately exchanged for one of tearful joy.

"Thank God! my dearest child," she fervently exclaimed, "that I see you again, and see you *thus!*"

Why had she looked so anxious, and so inquiringly? and *why* was she thus so evidently surprised, as well as rejoiced?

No doubt, thought I, she is in correspondence with our gossiping aunt, and she has told my mother all she told me: no doubt, also, *she* has all along been that secret source whence was derived my mother's fear of uniting me to Pendarves. But then, was not her information derived from her husband—and was it not always only too authentic?

As these thoughts passed my mind, it was well for me that my mother was talking to Seymour, and did not observe me.

Two months had greatly embellished the appearance of our abode; and it looked so green and gay, and was so fragrant from the summer flowers, that Pendarves, always alive to present objects and present impressions, exclaimed, as we followed my mother through the grounds, "Dearest Helen! why should we ever leave this paradise of sweets? Here let us live and die!"

"Agreed," said I; and my mother looked at us with delighted eyes, but eyes that beamed through tears.

Calm and tranquil were the months that followed—though my husband's brow was always clouded when letters arrived bearing the London post-mark; and when I asked who his correspondent was, he answered, "Lord Charles;" but never communicated to me the contents of these letters.

In walking, riding, receiving and paying visits, passed the time till September, when my husband had an invitation to spend a few days in Norfolk, on a shooting excursion; and when he returned, he found me confined to my sofa with indisposition. Never had woman a tenderer nurse than he proved himself during the three succeeding months; at the end of that time I was quite recovered; and as he had business in London, he declared his intention of going thither for some days, as he could not bear, he said, to leave me some few months later, and when a time was approaching so dear to his wishes and expectations.

To London, therefore, he went, and left me to combat and indulge, alternately, the fears of a jealous and the confidence of a tender wife.

His letters became a *study* to me. I tried to find out, by his expressions, in what state of mind he wrote. Sometimes I fancied them hurried, and expressive of a mind not at ease with itself; then, in another passage, I read the unembarrassed eloquence of faithful and confiding love.

During his absence, my mother found me a bad companion: I was for ever falling into reverie, and a less penetrating eye than hers would have discovered that my symptoms were those of mental uneasiness.

At length he returned, and he gazed on my faded cheek and evidently anxious countenance with such tender concern, that my care-worn brow instantly resumed its wonted cheerfulness; and when my mother came to welcome him, she was surprised at the alteration in my looks.

"Foolish child!" said she, in a faltering voice, when Pendarves left the room, "foolish child! to depend thus for happiness — nay, health and life itself, perhaps, on one of frail and human mould! I see how it is with you: you were ill and anxious yesterday, but *he* is come, and you need no other physician."

"Did you see much of Lord Charles?" said I the next day, looking earnestly for my needle while I spoke, as I was conscious that my countenance was not tranquil.

"No—yes—on the whole I did. But why do you ask? I believe he is no favourite of yours."

"Certainly not."

"But I hope, Helen, you are not so *very* a wife as to wish me to give up an old friend merely because he does not please *you?*"

"No; I am not so unreasonable, even though I could give substantial reasons for my dislike."

"And pray what are these reasons? Oh! that reminds me of a joke Lord Charles has against you, Helen. He tells me he is sure you thought that he fell in love with you, when, on being first presented to you, he expressed his admiration in his usual frank way, which *means nothing;* for he says your prudery took alarm, and you drew up your beautiful neck to its utmost height, and have My lorded and Your lordshipped him ever since into the most awful distance."

"'True; but for a manner that *means nothing,* I never saw a manner more offensive to a modest wife. However, I am very glad he has been so clear-sighted as to my motives; for I wish him to know that *I* do not love such marked homage from him, or any other *friend of yours,* even in a joke."

"You are piqued, Helen."

"I am."

"Perhaps you wish me to call Lord Charles out? But, indeed, were I to call out all the men who look at you with admiring eyes, I should soon sleep with *my* fathers, or send numbers to sleep with *theirs.* No, no, excuse me, Helen; I will not quarrel with Lord Charles; for even if the fire ever was kindled, your snow has now completely extinguished it; and I do assure you, he is a very good fellow, though odd, and not always pleasant."

"Is he paying his court to that Lady Bell?" said I, speaking her name with difficulty, and preceding it with an impertinent *that.*

"I really — I — cannot say positively. But *that Lady Bell,* as you emphatically call her, has quarrelled with that fine young man whom you saw at Ranelagh, and perhaps it is on his account."

I said no more, for I saw his colour heighten, and that his manner was hurried; and I tried to believe that the quarrel was wholly on Lord Charles Belmour's account.

I now, however, took myself seriously to task, for was I not violating a wife's duty, in trying to find errors in the conduct of my husband? and was I not, by so doing, endangering my own peace of mind, my health, and consequently, in my situation, my life? Was I not also depressing those spirits, and weakening those powers of exertion, which ought to make home agreeable and alluring to the dear object of my weak solicitude?

The result of this severe self-examination was, that I resolutely determined to turn away from every anxious and jealous suggestion—to believe, as long as I could, that my husband was as deserving of my love and confidence when absent as he was when present, and to make a vigorous effort to stop myself on my way to being a fretful, jealous, and miserable wife.

Nor did I break my resolution, as you well know, my dear friend; for, if I had, you would never have even fancied that I deserved to be exhibited as an example of a wife's duty. But if I had not begun to *school* myself when I did, all would have been over with me.

I cannot help observing here, that this painful jealousy, which I endured so early in my married life, was owing to my having, in despite of my mother's wise prohibition, united myself to a man, of the steadiness of whose principles I had had too much reason to doubt; and I could not help saying to myself sometimes, "If I had married De Walden, I should have had none of these misgivings."

As the hour of my confinement drew nearer and nearer, Seymour's tender attention increased; and at length, after severe suffering, I became a mother; but scarcely had I been allowed to gaze upon my child—scarcely had I heard its first faint cry, (that sound which thrills so powerfully through the heart,) when its voice was stopped by death, and it closed its eyes for ever.

I am afraid I should have borne this affliction very ill, had I not been obliged to exert myself to quiet the fears of my husband and my mother for my life, as they thought that the shock might be fatal.

I had also to console them, for they were both grieved and disappointed. But their feelings were transitory: mine were still in full force when they believed they were forgotten; for, besides the sorrow I felt for the loss of that being whose helpless cry still vibrated in my ears, I felt that I had lost in it a strong cement to the tie which bound my husband to me: nor, till I found myself again likely to become a mother, was I really consoled.

A circumstance happened which induced me to conceal my situation; and this was an invitation which my mother received from the Count De Walden, to accompany his sister and her husband back to Switzerland, when they left England, which they were then visiting, and to stay some months with him and Ferdinand De Walden.

This invitation I well knew she would refuse, if she knew that accepting it would prevent her being with me during my period of suffering; and I allowed her to depart for Switzerland, with the expectation of being returned time enough to attend on me.

I own that this was a great trial to my selfishness, as I knew I should miss her greatly; but I thought the excursion would be so pleasing a one to her, that I felt it my duty to make the sacrifice. I suffered my husband to remain in ignorance also, lest he should betray me to her: and I had judged rightly; for when I owned the truth to him, it was with great difficulty I could prevail on him not to write, and say I had deceived her.

Alas! I had but too much reason to regret even this deception, which might be called a virtuous one.

It so happened that I had no married friend, or near relation, who could come to be with me at that time; and as Pendarves wished me to have a female companion, I was induced to accept the eagerly proffered services of a young lady, the eldest daughter of a numerous family, who had conceived a great attachment to, my husband and me, and was very solicitous to be with me during my confinement.

This girl had such a warm and open manner, that I fancied her one of the most artless of human beings; I was so weak as to consider the gross flattery which she lavished on me and on Pendarves, as the honest overflowings of an affectionate heart.

I was, I own, a little startled when she used to kiss my husband's picture as it lay on my table, when she became my guest, and when I saw her come behind him, and cut off a lock of his hair. But as she afterwards begged for a piece of mine, that she might unite them in a locket, I considered this little circumstance as nothing but a flight of girlish romance.

What Pendarves thought of it, I know not; but he blushed excessively when he saw that I observed it, and tried to take the hair from her; on which a sort of romping ensued, that I thought vulgar, I own; but it called forth no feeling.

Perhaps had she been handsome, I should not have been so easy; but she was, in my eyes, plain, and could scarcely, I thought, be called a fine girl. Besides, I had heard Seymour say she was dowdy and awkward. But few men are proof against the flatteries and attentions of any woman who is not old and ugly; and I soon found, though without any jealous fear, that Charlotte Jermyn had power to amuse my husband, and that her enthusiastic admiration of every thing which she liked was a source of never-failing entertainment to him.

He now was sufficiently intimate with her, he thought, to venture to hint the necessity of a reform in her dress; and she wore better clothes, became clean, if not neat, and in time she even learnt to look rather tidy; while Pendarves was flattered to see the effect of his admonitions, and used to reward her by challenging her to a long walk.

At length, after I had been confined to my sofa some weeks, I had the happiness of giving birth to a daughter; and my young nurse was most kind and assiduous in her attendance upon me; indeed, so much so, that she often shortened my husband's visits, on the kind plea that I was not yet strong enough to bear long ones from one so dear; and I, though reluctantly, dismissed him.

But I soon observed, that her own visits became very short; that she used still to kiss me, and call me "dearest creature!" and tell me how beautiful I looked in my night-cap; but now, when I asked for her I was told that she was gone out with Pendarves. And once, as he was standing by my bedside, she was not contented with saying he had been with me long enough, but she linked her arm in his, and dragged him away, in a manner at once hoidenish and familiar.

I also saw, that though she loaded my sweet baby with caresses when he was present, and tried to take her from him, she scarcely noticed it when he was absent.

Still I felt no distrust, because I had confidence in my husband's honour and affection. But I now saw that the countenances of my nurse and of my own maid, when I inquired for Miss Jermyn, used to assume an angry expression; and once my maid muttered, that she supposed she was with her master, for he could not stir but she was after him.

This I did not seem to hear; but it made me thoughtful.

When I had been confined three weeks, I was able to leave my chamber for my dressing-room, which overlooked the garden; and one day, as I ventured to the window for the first time, I saw Charlotte Jermyn walking with my husband, and ever and anon hanging on his arm, almost leaning her head against him occasionally, and looking up in his face (he the while reading a book) with an expression of fondness which alarmed and disgusted me. I then saw her snatch the book from him; and as he tried to regain it, a great romping match ensued, and lasted till they ran out of my sight, and left me pale, motionless, and miserable. For I found that I had been exposing my husband to the allurements of a coquettish romp; and though I acquitted both him and her of aught that was wrong, I still felt that no prudent wife would place the man she loved in such a situation.

Many, many a wife, it is well known, has had to rue the hour when, at a period like this, she has introduced into her family a young and seemingly-attached friend.

What was to be done? I saw that the servants were aware of what was passing, and they would not judge with the candour that I did. I therefore convinced myself, that regard for my husband's reputation, and not jealousy, determined me to get down stairs, and out again as fast as possible, in order that I might make some excuse for sending my dangerous attendant away, or at least be a guard over her conduct.

But to my great surprise and joy, my beloved mother arrived most unexpectedly that morning; for I had insisted on her not returning sooner on my account, as I was so well. However, she did come; and I received her with rapture, for more reasons than one; for now I had an excuse for sending Miss Jermyn away directly, as I wanted the best room for my mother.

Accordingly, I told her that in two days' time my mother would take up her abode with us for a few weeks; and that, as Miss Jermyn had long been desirous of her return, I hoped she would hold herself in readiness to set off for home on the next day but one, as my mother always slept in the room which *she* occupied.

"O dearest Mrs. Seymour! do not send me away from you!" cried the strange girl, clasping and wringing her hands," or I shall die with grief—for I shall think you do not love me, and I shall never survive it!"

The time for my belief in such rhodomontade was now happily past, and I coolly replied, that " in no other but the best and most convenient room in the house could I allow my mother to sleep; therefore, she *must* go."

" Why so, Mrs. Seymour? I can sleep anywhere. There is a press bed in the little room; and I care not where I sleep, so I am but permitted to stay."

Here she attempted to throw her arms fondly round me, while she repeated, " Do—there's a sweet woman! *do* let me stay !"

" Impossible!" I replied, disengaging myself, with a look of aversion, from her embrace. On which she started up, and exclaimed—

" I am sure some one has been telling you stories of me, and you are set against me."

" There is no one in this house, Miss Jermyn, who would presume to say any thing to me against any guest of mine."

" And, pray, does Mr. Pendarves know I am to be sent away at a moment's warning?"

" He does not yet know that you are going away at *two days' notice*, to make room for my mother, and that I may enjoy her society, after a long absence, uninterrupted."

" Oh! if that be all, I will promise never to interrupt your *tête-à-têtes*."

" They will not be *tête-à-têtes*; my husband will be of our party."

" And, pray," answered she, with great sullenness, " how am I to go home? I am sure Mr. Pendarves will not approve of me going home in the stage without a protector."

" Nor would his wife: and I will settle the mode of conveyance with him."

" Oh! if I must go, I will see if I cannot settle that myself."

At this moment, my mother entered the room, and with her my husband; and Miss, to hide her disordered countenance, abruptly disappeared.

" What is the matter with Miss Jermyn?" said Seymour: and I told him; but in a voice that was not as assured as I wished it to be.

" So soon!" cried he, starting. " Is it not too sudden? Will it not look as if she was sent away in a hurry?"

" Sent away in a hurry!" exclaimed my mother, looking earnestly in his face. " Why should any one suspect that?"

" O dear! no one ought, certainly; but after her having staid so long — however, I think she has been here long enough, and the sooner she goes the better."

" Then, as you think thus, and her mother has long wished for her, her departure shall remain fixed for the day after to-morrow, and——" Here I was interrupted by Seymour's being called out of the room. He did not return for some minutes: when he did, he seemed disturbed.

During his absence, the nurse brought me my child; and both my mother and myself were too agreeably engaged with her to talk of Charlotte Jermyn. But Seymour's evident abstraction and uneasy countenance drew my mother's attention to him; and after a moment's thought she said, " That seems a very strange, presuming girl, Seymour; and I really think with you it is time she were gone."

" Oh yes — certainly; and she is very willing to go."

" So much the better," replied my mother; while I suppressed, for fear of alarming her suspicions, the " How do you know that?" which was on my lips; for, if her feelings were so changed, he must have changed them; and she it was who had desired him to be called out of the room.

Seymour's horses now came to the door; but before he left us, I begged to know how he meant Miss Jermyn should travel.

" She came," said I, " in the coach which passes our gate; but then her mother's maid came with her, and I cannot spare a servant to attend her."

" I can drive her home in my curricle: if we set off at five in the morning, we can perform the journey with ease before dark."

Pendarves said this in a hurried, conscious manner, which did not escape the quick eye of my mother; and while I hesitated how I could best word my decided objection to this plan, which would, I knew, excite disagreeable observations among the servants, that ever-watchful friend replied, " Hear my plan — it is far better than yours. The mornings are yet cold and dark at five: lend me your horses for my chariot: and as I want to visit a friend of De Walden's, who lives half-way to Mr. Jermyn's, with whom I have business, I will take this opportunity of going. My maid shall accompany us; and while I stay at Mr. Dumont's, she shall see Miss Jermyn safe to her father's."

" Well, if Miss Jermyn likes this plan."

" She would prefer going with you, no doubt," said I, smiling; " but as this plan will be a convenience to my mother, we need not consult her wishes."

" Oh no — very true, very true," said he, in a fluttered tone (but not owning that he had promised to drive her) : " and when I return from my ride, I shall expect to find you have arranged everything with her."

He then ran down stairs, and galloped off, as if to avoid speaking to Charlotte; for I saw her from the window run along the path to the road, to catch his eye if she could, and give him a signal to stop and speak to her.

Soon after she joined us; and I thought I saw a triumphant meaning on her countenance, which increased to a look of almost avowed exultation; when, on my saying, "Now, let us tell you how we have arranged matters for your journey," she eagerly interrupted me, and exclaimed, "Oh! I have arranged that with Mr. Pendarves, and he is to drive me in his curricle."

I did not answer her, for her look disconcerted me; but my mother did, coldly saying, "Mr. Pendarves did mean to do so, but for my convenience he has altered his plan."

She then went on to inform her what the new plan was; and the mortified, indignant girl burst into tears, and left the room.

"That is a very self-willed, pernicious young person, I suspect," observed my mother; "but I flatter myself that her journey with me will do her some good—at least, if it does not, it shall not be my fault."

Then, being too wise and too delicate to say more, she changed the subject; nor was any allusion made to Miss Jermyn till Seymour returned on foot; for he left his horses at the stables; and as he saw us in the drawing-room, which was on the ground floor, he came in at the window, being impatient, he said, to welcome me *down stairs*.

But he had probably another reason for that mode of entrance; he feared, I suspect, that Charlotte Jermyn would want to speak to him, and he was not disposed to listen to her reproaches, for having given up his design of driving her home.

My suspicions were confirmed by my seeing her walking along the path which commanded the approach to the house; and this path Seymour had avoided by going to the stables, but she did not long remain there, for on looking towards the house, she saw my husband standing at the window with me, with one arm round my waist, while with his disengaged hand, he was stroking the cheek of the child which I held to my bosom, and was rocking to rest.

Happy as I was at this moment, I could not help throwing a hasty glance towards this strange girl, who now rapidly drew near, and as she passed the window, curtsied to us with a countenance in which every unamiable feeling seemed to be uppermost.

She then threw open the half-door with violence—threw it to with the same force—then ran to her own chamber, and closed the door of that with such energy, that it could be heard all over the house. Nor did we see her again till dinner, when, although she had taken uncommon pains with her dress, her eyes were swelled with crying, and her whole appearance so indicative of gentle sorrow, that Seymour's voice softened even into tenderness when he addressed her, and mine was consequently as strikingly cold and severe. Meanwhile, my mother was a silent, but an observant spectator, and both Pendarves and Miss Jermyn seemed oppressed by the penetrating glance of her eye.

In the evening, Seymour proposed reading to us aloud; and as I wished to sit up late, for reasons you may easily guess, I was glad of so good an excuse as staying to hear an interesting book. But I had reason to repent having allowed feeling to prevail over prudence, for when my mother came to me the next day, she found I had caught cold, and together with the fatigue of sitting up too late, was in no condition to go down that day *at all*. Nor could my mother bear to leave me; consequently, I had the mortification of finding that in trying to avoid a slight evil, I had fallen into a greater. But my mother, who had, I doubt not, heard from her maid what the servants had observed, requested Miss Jermyn would be so kind as to sit with us, and teach her two sorts of work which she excelled in; and she could not, without great incivility, refuse compliance. However, at the hour when she was accustomed to walk with Seymour, she started up, declaring she could stay no longer, because it was her last day there, and she was sure Mr. Pendarves would walk with her. We could not object to this on any proper ground, and she was putting her knitting and her netting into her work-bag, when we heard a carriage drive to the door, and a servant came up to inform me that Lord Charles Belmour was below, and his master desired him to say he meant to dine with us.

Little did I think that Lord Charles would ever be a welcome guest to me; but at this moment he was so, for I saw that Charlotte Jermyn looked disappointed. My joy, however vanished when I recollected that it was by no means desirable Lord Charles should witness this indiscreet girl's evident attachment to Pendarves; and just before she went to her own apartment, my mother said, to my great relief, "You must then dine with us to-day, Miss Jermyn; for you are too young and too old at the same time to be the only female at a table where Lord Charles Belmour is."

"Well, if I *must* I must," was her reply, and she left us.

But while I was rejoicing that circumstances would force her to dine with us, I heard her rapidly ascending the stairs; and throwing open the door hastily, she told us with a look of delight, that she was going to walk; for Lord Charles had brought his sister, Lady Harriet, with him, whom he was conveying home from school for the holidays, and Mr. Pendarves had told her she must do the honours to the young lady, as *I* was not able to attend her. "And *so*," she added, "I must also dine below, for he *told* me so." And without waiting for our opinion or reply, she again disappeared; and we soon after saw her laughing with Lord Charles on the lawn, as if she had known him for years.

"How he will *show her off*," said my mother, "to-day! That young man has more ingenious malignity about him than any one I ever saw. When I was nursing Seymour at Oxford, he came to see him, and in order to make the poor invalid laugh, he used to make masters, deans, and fellow-commoners pass in rapid succession before us, like the distorted figures in a magic lantern."

This view of what was likely to happen was a relief to my mind, for I had not expected that Lord Charles would try to draw her forth for his own amusement; I had feared he would be contented to amuse himself with observing her admiration of Pendarves.

When they returned from their walk, I was vexed to observe that Lady Harriet held her brother's arm, not my husband's; and I also saw that Charlotte leaned on him and looked up in his face in the same improper manner as she did when they were alone. I was very glad that Lord Charles and his sister walked before them.

Pendarves now came up-stairs to beg, as I was not able to dine below, or see Lord Charles otherwise, that I would go to the window and kiss my hand to him in token of welcome; for that he was afraid to stay, because he believed he was a disagreeable guest, and that I kept up-stairs merely because he was come. He also begged that I would, after dinner, admit Lady Harriet for a few minutes.

I promised compliance with both these requests, and went to the window directly.

Lord Charles answered my really cordial salutation with a most lowly bow, and a countenance meant to express every thing that was respectful and courteous, and drew from my mother, to whom he also bowed, the observation of, " Graceful coxcomb! Now do I fancy him saying within himself, 'There, I have made that haughty old woman believe that I respect her and her loftiness, to her heart's content.'"

Pendarves could not help smiling at this right reading, as it probably was, of his satirical friend's thoughts; but he assured her that admiration the most unbounded was, as well as respect, felt by his friend towards her; and that he considered a woman of her age as in the prime of her charms.

"Nonsense!" cried my mother; and my husband, laughing, returned to Lord Charles.

Charlotte Jermyn did not come to us before she went down to dinner, as she had Lady Harriet with her, but when they left the room, I desired to see them in mine, and for the first time I thought her pretty, for her cheeks glowed with a very brilliant and becoming colour, which added to the fire of her eyes; and her dress was neat and lady-like. She had the countenance, too, of one who had been much commended, and felt certain that the commendations were sincere.

"I am glad she is going to-morrow," said I, mentally, and I sighed at the same time. Lady Harriet was a good foil to her, except in *manners*—for there, there could be no comparison; and by the side of Lady Harriet, Miss Jermyn was pretty.

As soon as they had had coffee, the brother and sister drove off, but not before Lord Charles had fixed to return that day fortnight to dinner, on condition of my dining below.

When they were gone, my mother went down to make tea; and after that meal was ended, she asked if there was any objection to Seymour's going on in my dressing-room with the book which he began the night before, and in his reading till it was time for me to go to rest.

He complied instantly, and read till I was tired.

My mother then proposed that he should read me to sleep: to this also he agreed; and while I lay with the curtains closed round, my mother, he, and Charlotte sat round the fire; and it was eleven before I ceased to hear, and Pendarves retired to his own chamber.

My mother then went away, desiring Charlotte to be ready at six, as she should breakfast with her at that hour. But, as I afterwards found, she reached our house on foot before six, and just as Pendarves came down stairs.

By these apparently undesigned circumstances, my mother prevented any scene that might have called forth unpleasant observations in the family; but she could not prevent a most sorrowful parting on the side of the young lady. She wept, she soothed, she leaned against Seymour's shoulder, when he put his lips to her cheek; and he was nearly obliged to carry her to the carriage, for she declared she would not go till she had taken leave of me; but my mother was as positive that I should not be disturbed, and Pendarves gently forced her to the door.

What passed between my mother and her when they were on the journey, and alone— for the maid always preferred travelling outside—I do not know; but I suspect that she animadverted on her conduct and want of self-control in a manner more judicious than pleasant.

During these vexatious occurrences I must own that it was a sort of comfort to me that my aunt Pendarves had such inflamed eyes that she could not write; for otherwise the chances were that she might hear some exaggerated accounts of our visitor's conduct, and might think it necessary to address one of us on the subject, and give us *good advice.*

Well: this pernicious girl was gone, and my mind at ease again. Still I feared that she had done me a serious injury: not that I believed she had alienated my husband's heart from *me,* or from propriety; but she had been the first person to accustom him to find amusement at home *independent of me* and of the exertion of my talents. He was an indolent man, and she had amused him, and beguiled away his hours, without obliging him to any *exertion of mind*. Besides, she was not only a new companion but a new conquest. He was certainly flattered by it, and evidently interested. I was led to draw these conclusions by observing the gapish state into which Pendarves fell the day of her departure. He seemed to miss an accustomed dram. He gave me indeed, on my requesting it, a lesson in Spanish, which I had long neglected; but he seemed to do it as if it was a trouble, and he was too absent to make the lesson of much use. I however forbore to remark what I could not but painfully feel, and I fancied that my best plan would be to contrive some new objects of interest at home, if I could; but on second thoughts I resolved to propose that he should visit a sick friend of his at Malvern hills, for a few days, as I believed it not to be for my interest he should stay to contrast his *present* with his *late* home; but that he should go away to return from *an invalid* and the *cold* hills of *Malvern*, to me and his own comfortable dwelling.

I no sooner named my plan to him than he eagerly caught at it, declaring that he had wished to go, but feared that I should think the wish unkind. Accordingly, he only staid to see my mother comfortably settled as my guest, and then set off for Malvern. Nor did he return till three or four days before he expected Lord Charles. By that time I had recovered my bloom and my strength, and our infant had acquired *a fortnight's growth*,—an interesting event in the life of a young parent: and I assure you it was thought such by Pendarves; and while he complimented me on my restored comeliness, and held his little Helen in his arms, I felt that he had no thought or wish beyond those whom he clasped and looked upon.

I could now join him again in his walks, and in his rides or drives.

My mother threw a great charm over our evenings by her descriptions of the country which she had so lately seen, and of the scientific men with whom she had associated. But Seymour and I both fancied that she was rather reserved and embarrassed when she talked of Count De Walden. Nor could I help being desirous of finding out the reason. One day I told her how sorry I was to think that she had shortened her agreeable visit entirely on my account; but, as if thrown off her guard, she eagerly replied, "Oh, no! I was very glad of an excuse for coming away;" and this was followed by such manifest confusion of countenance and manner, that I suspected the reason, and at last I prevailed on her to confess it.

The truth was that Count De Walden, who had admired her in America, when she was a wife, as much as an honourable man can admire the wife of another, could not live in the same house with a woman still lovely, and even more than ever intellectual and agreeable, without feeling for her a very sincere affection; and as their ages were suitable, he made her proposals of marriage of the most advantageous and generous nature. But my mother could not love again: and though at her time of life, and that of her lover, she thought that mutual esteem and the wish to secure a companion for declining years was a sufficient excuse for a second marriage; still, she had an unconquerable aversion to form any connexion, and more especially one which would remove her to such a distance from me. When she told me how strongly she had been solicited, and that the advantages which she should ultimately secure to *me* by this union were held up to her in so seducing a light, as nearly once to overset her resolution, I was so overcome by the thought of the escape which I had had, that I threw my arms round her, and bursting into an agony of tears exclaimed, "What could ever have made me amends for losing you? The very idea of it kills me."

My mother was excessively affected when I said this; but I soon saw that her tears were not tears of tenderness alone; and looking at me with an expression of sadness on her countenance, she said, "Two years ago, my poor child, you would have better borne the idea of such a separation; and had I been a jealous person, I should have been hurt to see how completely a husband can supersede even a mother. But I was pleased to see this, because I saw in it a proof that you were a happy wife: but perhaps you have now an idea, though still a happy wife I trust, of the great *value of a parent*, and can appreciate more justly *that love* which nothing can ever alienate, or ever render less."

What could I answer her, and how?

I did not attempt to speak, but I continued to hold her in my arms, and at last I could utter, "No, no, I never, never can bear to part with you."

That day Lord Charles Belmour came, according to his promise, and just as I had convinced myself that it was my duty to overcome my dislike to him, and to endeavour to convert him from an enemy into a friend. Accordingly, I went down to dinner, prepared to receive him even with smiles; but recollecting, when I saw him, his impudent assertion, that his admiration of me had *meant nothing*, and that I was an alarmed prude, my usual coldness came over me, while the deepest blushes dyed my cheeks.

However, I extended my hand to him, which he kissed and pressed; and, as he relinquished it, he turned up his eyes, and muttered, "Angelic woman!" in a manner so equivocal, that, consistent as it seemed with "his joke against me," I could not help giving way to evident laughter.

Lord Charles was too quick of apprehension to be affronted at my mirth; on the contrary, he felt assured and flattered by it. He had expressed his admiration only in *derision* and *impertinence*, and as he saw that I *understood* him, he felt that we were much nearer being friends than we had ever been before; and when our eyes met, a look almost amounting to one of kindness passed between us. Lord Charles now became particularly animated; but some allusion which he had made to Lady Bell Singleton, while addressing my husband, made me distrustful again, and I relapsed into my usual manner; and he was *My lord*, and *Your lordship*, during the rest of the dinner. Nor could I be insensible to the look of menace which I subsequently beheld in his countenance. It was not long before the storm burst on my devoted head.

"My dear madam," said he, in his most affected manner, "you are a prodigiously kind and obliging helpmate, to provide your *cara sposa* with so charming a *locum tenens* when you are confined to your apartments. I found my friend here with the prettiest young creature for a companion! and then so loving she was!"

"Loving!" said I, involuntarily.

"Oh, yes. Allow me to give you an idea of her." Immediately, to the great annoyance of my husband, with all his powers of mimicry, he exhibited the manner and look of Charlotte Jermyn, when looking up in Seymour's face and leaning against his arm, as I had myself seen her do.

"Is not that like her?"

"Very," replied I, forcing a laugh.

"Now, shall I mimic your husband, and show you how *he* looked in return! Shall I paint the bashful but delighted consciousness which his look expressed—the stolen glance, the——"

"Hush, hush!" cried Pendarves, anger struggling with confusion. "This is fancy-painting, and I like nothing but portraits."

During this time, I observed a struggle in my mother's breast, and I sat in terror lest she should say something severe to the noble mimic, and make matters worse.

But after this evident struggle, which I alone observed, she leaned her arms on the table, and fixed her powerful eyes steadfastly on Lord Charles, looking at him as if she would have dived into the inmost recesses of his heart. It was in vain that she endeavoured to escape their searching glance; even his assurance felt abashed, and his malignant spirit *awed*, till his audacious and ill-intentioned banter was looked into silence, and he asked for another bumper of claret to drink my health. I was before overpowered with gratitude to the judicious yet quiet interference of this admirable parent, and the recollection of our morning's conversation were still present to me. No wonder, therefore, that my spirits were easily affected, and that I felt my eyes fill with tears.

At this moment I luckily heard my child cry; and faltering out, "Hark! that was my child's voice," I hastened to the door; but unfortunately the pocket-hole of my muslin gown caught in the arm of my mother's chair, and Lord Charles insisted on extricating me.

I could now no longer prevent the tears from flowing down my cheeks; which being perceived by him, he said, in a sort of under tone, "Amiable sensibility! There I see a mother's feelings!" On which my mother, provoked beyond endurance, said, in a low voice, but I overheard it, "My lord, my daughter has a WIFE'S FEELINGS ALSO."

I was now disengaged happily, and I ran out of the room.

When I arrived in the nursery, I found I was not wanted. I therefore retired to my own apartment, where I gave way to a violent burst of tears. I had scarcely recovered myself, and had bathed my eyes again and again in rose-water, when my husband entered the room.

He had witnessed my emotion, and he could not be easy without coming to inquire after me, on pretence that the child's cry had alarmed him.

This affectionate attention was not lost upon me, and I went down stairs with him with restored spirits and perfect composure.

My mother, who had walked to her own house, was only just entering the door as we appeared; therefore, Lord Charles had been left alone; and whether he thought this an affront to his dignity or not, I cannot tell; but we did not find him in a more amiable mood than when we left him.

After looking at me very earnestly, while sipping his coffee, he came close up to me, and said, resuming his most affected tone, "Pray, what eye-water do you use!"

"Rose-water, only," was my reply.

"Very bad, 'pon honour; I must send you some of mine, as you are a person of exquisite sensibility, and I fancy it is likely to be tried. Upon my word, it took me a week to compose it; and as I occasionally read novels, and the *Tête-à-tête Magazine*, (which is, you know, exceedingly *affecting*,) I use it continually in order to preserve the lustre of my eyes; and you see that in spite of my acute feelings they retain all their pristine brilliancy."

As he said this, neither Pendarves nor myself, though provoked at his noticing my swelled eyes, could retain our gravity; for the eyes, which he thus opened to their utmost extent, were of that description known by the name of boiled gooseberries, and were really dead eyes, except when the rays of satirical intelligence forced themselves through them; for the sake of exciting a laugh, he had now dismissed from them every trace of meaning, and consequently every tint of colour.

His purpose effected, he resumed his sarcastic expression; and turning from me with a look full of sarcastic meaning, he said,

"Ah! *comme de coutume*—after tragedy comes farce."

My mother now asked him whether he had ever seen her house and garden; and on his answering in the negative, she challenged him to take a walk with her.

"I never," replied he, bowing very low, "refused the challenge of a fine woman in my life; and till my horses come round, I am at your service, madam." Then, hiding his real chagrin under a thousand impertinent grimaces, he followed my mother.

"I would give something to hear their conversation," said Pendarves, thoughtfully.

"And so would I: no doubt it will be monitory on her part."

"Monitory! What for!"

"If you do not know, I am sure I shall not tell you."

And with an expression of conscious embarrassment on his countenance, my husband asked me to walk with him round the shrubbery.

My mother and Lord Charles did not return till the carriage was driving up. We examined their countenances with a very scrutinizing eye; but on my mother's all we could distinguish was her usual expression of placid and dignified intelligence; that of Lord Charles exhibited its usual *catfish* and alarming look.

What had passed, therefore, we could not guess; but we saw very clearly, that we should not be justified in joking on the subject of their *tête-à-tête*; and simply saying that it was beyond the time fixed for his departure, Lord Charles now respectfully kissed my hand, and told Pendarves he hoped he should soon see him in London. He then left the room without taking the smallest notice of my mother, and was driving off before my husband could ask him a reason of conduct so strange.

"Pray, madam," said Pendarves, when he returned into the room, "did Lord Charles take leave of you?"

"*He did not.*"

"Then I solemnly declare that before we ever meet again he shall give me a sufficient reason for his impertinence, or apologize to you; for there lives not the being who shall dare, while I live, to affront you with impunity!"

"My dear, dear son," cried my mother, "look not so like, so *very* like——"

Here her voice failed her, and she leaned on Seymour's shoulder, while he affectionately embraced her. Dear to my heart were any tokens of love which passed between my mother and my husband.

Seymour's strong likeness to my father, in moments of great excitement, always affected her thus, and endeared him to her.

When my mother recovered herself, she desired Pendarves would remain quiet, and not trouble himself to revenge her quarrels.

"Indeed," said she, "I am much flattered, and not affronted, by the rudeness of Lord Charles, as it proves that what I said to him gave him the pain which I intended. The wound, therefore, will rankle for some time, and produce a good effect. Nor should I be surprised if he were to send me a letter of apology in a day or two; for, if I read him aright, he has understanding enough to value the good opinion of a respectable woman, and would rather be on amiable terms with me than not."

"I hope you are right," replied Pendarves, "for I do not wish to quarrel with him; yet I will never own as my friend the man who fails in respect to you."

"I thank you, my dear son," said my mother, with great feeling, and the evening passed in the most delightful and intimate communion: nor, I really believe, were Charlotte Jermyn or Lord Charles again remembered; so true is it, that when the tide of family affection runs smooth and unbroken, it bears the bark of happiness securely on its bosom.

Shortly after Lord Charles's visit, I was so unwell, that I was forbidden to nurse my child any longer, and I had to endure the painful trial of weaning and surrendering her to the bosom of another. But most evils in this life, even to our mortal vision, are attended with a counterbalancing good.

At this time, it was the height of the gay season in London, and I saw that my husband began to grow tired of home, and sigh for the busy scenes of the metropolis, whither, had I been still a nurse, I could not have accompanied him; but now, however unwilling I might be to leave my infant, I felt that it must not interfere with the duty which I owed its father; for my mother had often said, and my own observation confirmed the truth of the saying, that alienation between husband and wife has often originated in the woman's losing sight of the duty and attention she owes the father of the children, in exclusive fondness and attention to the children themselves—and she often warned me against falling into this error.

She therefore highly approved my intention to leave my babe under her care, and accompany Pendarves to London, where she well knew he was exposed to temptations and to dangers against which my presence might probably secure him.

"Yes, my child," said she, as if thinking aloud—for I am sure she did not intend to grieve me—"yes, go with your husband while you can, and have as few separate pleasures and divided hours as possible; for they lead to *divided hearts*. But if you have a large family, you will not be able to leave home. Go, therefore, while you can, and while I am with you, and turn me to account while I am still here to serve you. That time, I know, will be short enough."

It is not in the power of language to convey an adequate idea of the agony with which I listened to these words. Never before had my mother so pointedly alluded to her conviction that her health was decaying; and if the idea of separation from her by a happy marriage was so painful to my feelings, what must be the idea of that terrible and eternal separation?

Pendarves came in the midst of my distress, and almost fiercely demanded who had been so cruelly afflicting me — fearing, no doubt, that I had heard something concerning him, and naturally enough conceiving that no great grief could reach me, except through that, or from him.

My mother gently replied, "She has been afflicting herself, foolish child! I said, unwillingly, I allow, what might have prepared her for an unavoidable evil; but she chooses to fancy, poor thing! that I am not mortal; yet, see *here*, Seymour!" As she said this, she turned up her long, loose sleeves, and showed him her once-firm arm fallen away comparatively to nothing!

I never saw my husband much more affected: he seized that faded arm, and pressed it repeatedly to his lips, turned away, and burst into tears; then, folding us both in one embrace, he faltered out, "My poor Helen! well indeed might I find you thus!" But my mother solemnly promised that she would never so afflict me again.

In the midst of this scene, a letter was brought to my mother: it was from Lord Charles, and was so like the man, that I shall transcribe it.

"Madam — I doubt not but you were amazed, and probably offended at my quitting the house of your son-in-law without taking my leave of you, as you are not a woman likely to think my silence at the moment of parting from you was to be attributed to the tender passion which I had conceived for your beauty and accomplishments. But, madam, if my silence was not attributable to love, so neither was it caused by hate; and I beg leave, hat in hand, and on bended knee, to explain whence my conduct proceeded. In the first place, madam, you had given me a blow — a *stunning* blow; and after a man has been *stunned*, he does not soon recover himself sufficiently to know what he is about, and how he ought to behave. In the next place, I endeavoured to remember how the great Earl of Essex behaved when Queen Elizabeth gave him a blow, or, in other words, a box on the ear — for *blow* I need not tell a lady of your erudition is the *genus*, and box on the ear the *species*. Now, that noble earl did not return the blow, (which, I own, I was very much inclined to do,) but he departed in silence from her presence, I believe: and so did *I*, in imitation of *him*, from *yours*. Methinks I hear you exclaim, 'The little lord is mad — I gave him no blow!' Not with your hand, I own, but with your tongue, that 'unruly member,' as St. James so justly calls it: you gave me a tingling blow on the cheek of my mind, which it still feels, and for which, perhaps, it may be the better. It is this consideration, and the belief that your motives were kind, though your treatment was rough, and that you only meant, like the bear in the fable, to guard me from a slight evil, though you broke my head in doing it; it is this belief, I say, that now throws me thus a suppliant at your feet, and makes me beg of you to excuse all my rudeness, and all my faults, whether caused by imitation of lord Essex, or my own sinful propensities, and to raise me up to receive, not the kiss of peace — for to that I dare not aspire — but to grasp and carry to my heart the white hand tendered to me in token of forgiveness.

"I am, madam, with the liveliest esteem and the deepest respect, your obliged, though stricken servant,
"CHARLES FIREBRAND."

"Ridiculous person!" said my mother, when she had finished the letter, giving it to me at the same time.

When I had read it, I asked her to tell us what she had said to him. "And why," said Pendarves, "does he sign himself Charles Firebrand?"

"Oh! thereby hangs a tale," said my mother blushing, "which I, I assure you, shall not tell: therefore, ask me no questions. If ever Lord Charles and I meet again, the white hand shall be tendered to him: nay, perhaps I shall answer his letter."

And so she did, but we never saw what she wrote; however, I am convinced that she had CALLED him a firebrand, and reproved him for his evident desire of making mischief between my husband and me. Nor can I doubt that the justice of her reproofs made them more stinging to the heart of the offender; and that he felt at the time a degree of unspeakable and unutterable resentment, on which his cooler judgment made him feel it impolitic to act; for he had, as my mother said, too much good sense not to value her acquaintance.

I must now return to Charlotte Jermyn. I forgot to say that she wrote a very fawning letter of thanks to me after her return home, thanking me for my kindness to her, and hoping that I would send for her again whenever she could be of any service to me. I have reason to think that she also wrote more than once to my husband: but he never communicated what she wrote to me; and I had the mortification to find how vainly I had tried to give him those habits of openness and ingenuousness which can *alone* render the nearest and tenderest ties productive of confidence and happiness.

Now, after a silence of four months, she

again wrote to me, to inform me that she was married to a young ensign in a marching regiment quartered near her father's house; but as it was against her father's consent, she had been forced to go to Gretna Green—and that her father, Mr. Jermyn, continued inexorable.

This letter I communicated to my husband, who was, I found, already acquainted with the circumstance, though he did not tell me by what means he knew it. He also told me that her father had since assured her of his forgiveness; but told her, at the same time, that he could bestow on her nothing else, as he had ten children, and a small income; and that the young couple had nothing to live upon except the pay of an ensign of foot.

"I am sure *I* can do nothing for her," Pendarves added, "for my own wants—or, rather, my expenses—are beyond my means."

"And were they not," answered I, "I do not feel that Charlotte Jermyn—or, rather, Mrs. Saunders—has *any claims* on you."

"Still, I would not let her starve, if I could *help* it; but I *cannot*."

I did not like to ask whether she had applied to him to lend her money; but I suspected that she had, and that he had refused; for soon after I saw him receive a letter, which he read with an angry and a flushed countenance, and thrust into the fire, muttering as he did so—

"Confounded fool—insolent!"

I felt, however, that her visit to me, and the terms which we had been upon, made it indispensable for me to give her a wedding gift, and I sent her money instead of a present, in consideration of her poverty, desiring her to buy what she wanted most in remembrance of me. My letter and its contents, much to the annoyance of us both, she answered in person, bringing her husband with her; and they came with so evident an intention of staying all night, spite of the coldness of their reception, that we were forced to offer them a bed.

The next day, however, even their assurance was not proof against the repelling power of our cold civility; and they departed, neither of us prejudiced in favour of the husband, and leaving me disgusted by the wife's forward behaviour to Pendarves.

I now, according to my mother's advice, proposed to Pendarves a visit to London; but, to my great surprise, he seemed to have no relish for the scheme, and telling me we would talk further about it, he dropped the subject.

Most gladly should I have welcomed this unwillingness to go to London, if I could have attributed it to a preference for home and for the country; but I had no reason to do this, and I feared it proceeded only from inability to meet the expenses of a London establishment, even for a few weeks; and of this I was soon convinced.

I told you, a few pages back, that I was so cruel as to rejoice in my aunt's being rendered unable to write, by a violent inflammation in the eyes; but as that did not deprive her of locomotion, most unexpectedly one day, Mr. and Mrs. Pendarves drove up to my mother's door, and soon after she accompanied them to our house. I was dressing when they arrived, and I saw myself change even to alarming paleness when my mother came up to announce them. I also saw that she was as much disconcerted as I was.

"Oh! if my dear uncle had but come *alone*," said she, "the visit would have been delightful." But here we were interrupted by Pendarves, who came in with, "So, Helen, I suppose you know who is come. Oh! that one could but transfer the disease from the eyes to the tongue, and bandage that up instead of the former! What shall we do? for, probably, as she can't use her eyes, she makes her tongue work double tide."

"Suppose," replied I, "we bribe our surgeon to assure her that entire silence is the only cure for inflamed eyes."

"The best thing we can do," observed my mother, "is to bear with fortitude this unavoidable evil; and also to try to remember her virtues more than her faults."

When I went down, I found my mother admiring her beaver-hat and feathers.

"Yes," she replied, "I think my beaver very pretty. What is it the mad poet says about 'my beaver?' Oh! I have it—

'When glory, like a plume of feathers, stood
Perch'd on my beaver in the briny flood.'"

"Do you, then, bathe in the sea with your beaver on?" said my mother.

"Well, there 's a question for a sensible woman!" cried my aunt, not seeing the sarcasm; then, turning to me, she welcomed me with a cordial kiss: but I was struck by the great coldness with which she greeted Seymour.

My uncle, however, received us both with the kindest manner possible.

But I forgave all her oddness, when she saw my child—for praise of her child always finds its way to a mother's heart; and she was in raptures with its beauty. She pitied me, too, for being forced to give her up to a nurse: but she added, "I hope she is not, to use the words of the bard, a

'Stern, rugged nurse, with rigid lore,
Our patience many a year to bore.'"

Then, renewing her caresses and her praises, she banished from my remembrance for a while all but her affectionate heart.

At dinner, however, she restored to me my fears of her, and my dislike to her visit; for she called my husband Mr. Seymour Pendarves at every word, though my mother she called Julia, and me Helen — wishing, as I saw, to point out to every one that *he* was not in her good graces. But why? Alas! I doubted not but I should hear too soon; and, feeling myself a coward, I carefully avoided being alone with her that evening.

What she had to tell I knew not, and whether it regarded Charlotte Jermyn or Lady Bell; but I summoned up resolution to ask Pendarves whether he had ever visited Lady Bell Singleton in company with Lord Charles; and without hesitation, though with great confusion, he owned that he had.

"What! more than once?"

"Yes."

"Why did you not tell me of it?"

"Because I thought, after what you had heard, it might make you uneasy."

"Should you ever do," I replied, forcing a smile, "what, in our relative situation, it would make me uneasy to be informed of?"

"Not if your uneasiness would be at all well-founded."

"But concealment implies consciousness of something indiscreet, if not wrong; and had you told me yourself of your visits to Lady Bell, I could have set Mrs. Pendarves and her insinuations at defiance."

"And can you not now?"

"Perhaps so; but no thanks to your ingenuousness. However, I must own," said I, smiling affectionately, "that no one answers questions more readily."

I had judged rightly in preparing myself for my encounter with Mrs. Pendarves, as she took the first opportunity of telling me how much she pitied me; for she had heard of the affair with the young lady who came to nurse me in my lying-in, which was of a piece with the renewal of intercourse with Lady Bell Singleton. "But I assure you," she added, "his uncle means to tell him a piece of his mind; and if he does not, *I will*."

On hearing this, I thought proper to laugh as well as I could, which perfectly astonished my aunt, as I knew it would do, and she demanded a reason of my ill-timed mirth. I told her that I laughed at her mountain's having brought forth a mouse; for that the *affair* with the young lady ended in her marrying a young ensign, soon after she left us, for *love*, and that I had given her a wedding-present; and that I knew from Seymour himself that he visited Lady Bell Singleton: I therefore begged she would keep her pity, and my uncle his advice, for those who required them.

My mother entered the room at this moment, and I had great pleasure in repeating to her what had passed; for I was glad to impress her with the idea that my husband confided in me. I saw that I had succeeded.

"Mrs. Pendarves," said she, gravely, "I am sorry to find you are one of those who act the part of an enemy, while fancying you are performing that of a friend. What good could you do my daughter, by telling her of her husband's errors, had the charge been a true one? Answer me that. Sure, where 'ignorance is bliss, 'tis folly to be wise.'"

"But she could not be ignorant long—she must know it some time or other; and it was better she should hear it from a sympathizing and affectionate friend like me. However, I did not mean to be officious and troublesome, and I am glad Mr. Seymour Pendarves is better than I supposed he was."

"Madam," replied my mother, "Seymour, like other persons, is better—much better than a gossiping world is willing to allow any one to be. And it is hard, indeed, that a man's own relations should implicitly believe and propagate what they hear against him."

"Take *my advice*, my dear little aunt, and always inquire before you condemn; which advice is your due, in return for the large store of that commodity which you are so willing to bestow on other people."

My aunt was silent a moment, as if considering whether in what was said there was most of compliment or most of reproof. Be that as it might, she was too politic not to choose to believe there was much of compliment implied in the mention made of her willingness to bestow advice. She therefore looked pleased, declared her pleasure at finding all was well, and that she found even the best authority was not always to be depended upon. At dinner that day—to show, I conclude, that Seymour was restored to her favour—she asked him to pay her a visit at their house in town; but on my saying that I expected she would include me in the invitation, as I wished to go to London, she turned round with great quickness, and exclaimed, "What! and leave your sweet babe?"

The censure which this abrupt question conveyed, gave a sort of shock to my feelings, and I could not answer her; but my mother instantly replied, "My daughter's health requires a little change of scene, and surely she can venture to entrust her infant to *my* care."

"Oh yes; but how can she *bear* to leave it?"

"The trial will be great, I own," said I; "but I am not yet so *very* a mother as to forget I am a *wife*; and as I must either leave my child or give up accompanying my husband, of the two evils I prefer the first."

"Oh! true, true—I never thought of that," was her sage reply: "and you are right, my dear, quite right, as husbands are, to go to take care of yours; and I advise you to keep a sharp look out—for there are hawks abroad."

"Hawks!" said my uncle, smiling—"turtle doves, more likely; and they are the more dangerous bird of the two."

This observation gave Pendarves time to recover the confusion his aunt's speech had occasioned him, and he told me he was much amused to see that I had positively arranged a journey to London for him and for myself, without his having ever expressed an intention of going at all.

"But I knew you wished to go, and I thought it was your kind reluctance to ask me to leave my child which alone prevented your expressing your wishes."

"Indeed, Helen, you are right: *I* never *should* have thought of asking you to leave your child; and I own I am flattered to find I am still dearer to you than she is: therefore, if my uncle and aunt will be troubled with us, I shall be very happy to visit London as their guest."

"Is it possible," cried I, "you can think of going anywhere but to a lodging!"

"Is it possible," cried Mrs. Pendarves, "that you can prefer a lodging to being the guest of your uncle and aunt!"

"To being the guest even of a father and mother; for when one has much to see in a little time, there is nothing like the liberty and convenience of a lodging."

"Well, well, Helen," said Pendarves, rather impatiently, "that may be; but *this year*, if you please, we will go to Stratford Place."

I said no more, and it was settled that we should follow my uncle and aunt to town, and take up our residence with them. But the next day my mother, who thought the plan as foolish and disagreeable as I did, desired me to find out, if I could, why my husband consented to be the guest of a woman whose society was so offensive to him: "And *if*," said she, "it is because he cannot afford to take lodgings, you may tell him, that I have both means and inclination to answer all the necessary demands, and moreover I have a legacy of 2000*l.* untouched, which I have always meant to give you, Helen, on the birth of your first child; and that also is at your service."

I shall pass over my feelings on this occasion, and my expression of them. Suffice that my husband owned his "*poverty*, and *not his will, consented*" to his acceptance of our relation's offer; and that he thankfully received my mother's bounty. The legacy, however, he resolved to secure to me, as my own property, and so tied up that he could not touch it. We found, however, that we must spend part of our time with my uncle and aunt; but at the end of ten days we removed to lodgings near them.

I was soon sensible of the difference between the present time in London and the past. I found that Pendarves, though his manner was as kind as ever, used to accept in succession, engagements in which I had no share; and if it had not been for the society of Mr. and Mrs. Ridley, and my uncle and aunt, I should have been much alone; and have pined after my child and mother even more than I did. Still ardently indeed did I long to return home; and had I not believed I was at the post of duty, I should have urged my husband to let me go home without him.

Lord Charles was frequently with us, and, had I chosen it, would have been my escort everywhere; but I still distrusted him; and I suspect that it was in revenge he so often procured Pendarves dinner invitations, from which he rarely returned till day-light; and once he was evidently in such low spirits, that I was sure he had been at play, and had lost everything.

We had now been several weeks in London, and I grew very uneasy at my prolonged separation from my child, and at my mother's evidently declining health — besides having reasons to think that my husband would have enjoyed London more without me; for Lord Charles took care to tell me often, that had *I* not been with him Pendarves would have done this, and would have gone thither; always adding, "So you see what a tame domestic animal you have made of him, and what a tractable obedient husband he is." There is perhaps nothing more insidious and pernicious, than to tell a proud man that he is governed by a wife, or a mistress, provided he has great conscious weakness of character; and Lord Charles knew that was the case with Pendarves. And I am very sure that he accepted many invitations which he would otherwise have declined, because his insidious friend reproached him with being *afraid of me.*

Ranelagh was still the fashion, and my husband had still a pride in showing me in its circles; but even there I was sensible of a change. He now was not unwilling to resign the care of me to other men, while he went to pay his compliments to dashing women of fashion, and give them the arm once exclusively mine. Still, these occasional neglects were too trifling to excite my fears or my jealousy, and I expected, when we returned to our country home, that it would be with unclouded prospects. But while I dreamt of perpetual sun-shine, the storm was gathering which was to cloud my hours in sorrow.

I had vainly expected a letter from my mother for two days, — and she usually wrote every day, — a circumstance which had depressed my spirits in a very unusual manner; and I was consequently little prepared to bear with fortitude the abrupt entrance of my husband in a state of great agitation: but pale and trembling I awaited the painful communication which I saw he was about to make.

"Helen!" cried he, "if you will not, or cannot assist me, I am liable to be arrested every moment."

"Arrested! What for?" cried I, relieved beyond measure at hearing it was a distress which *money* could remove.

"Ay, Helen, dearest creature! There is the pang — for a debt so weakly contracted!"

"Oh! a gaming debt to Lord Charles, I suppose?"

"No, no, would it were! — though I own that that way also I have been very culpable."

"Keep me no longer in suspense, I conjure you."

"Why, you know what a rash marriage that silly girl, Charlotte Jermyn, made."

"Go on."

"Well—her husband was forced to sell his commission to pay his debts; but that was not sufficient; and to save him from a jail, I had the folly to be bound for him in no less a sum than several hundreds."

"But who asked you?—Are they in London?"

"They were."

"And you saw them?"

"Yes."

"Why did you not tell me they were here?"

"Because they were persons with whom I did not choose my wife to associate."

"Were they fit associates for you then?" was on my tongue, but I suppressed it; for mistaken indeed is the wife who thinks reproach can ever do aught but alienate the object of it.

"But do you often visit them? and what made them presume to apply to you?"

"Necessity. She wrote to me again and again, and she way-laid me too—what could I do? I was never proof against a woman's tears, and I was bound for him."

"Well, and what then?"

"Why, the rascal is gone off, and left his wife without a farthing, to maintain herself as she can."

"Is she in London?" cried I, turning very faint.

"No, at Dover; but, as soon as it is known that he is off, I expect to be arrested for the money; and for me to raise it is impossible; but you, Helen—"

"Yes, yes—I understand you," I replied, speaking with great difficulty: "the legacy—I will drive instantly to the banker's—and take it *all*, if you wish."

Here my voice, and even my eye-sight totally failed me, and almost my intellects; but I neither fell nor *fainted*.—Miserable suspicions and *certain* anxiety came over me, and in one *moment* life seemed converted into a dreary void. My situation alarmed Pendarves almost to frenzy. He rang for the servants, sent for the nearest surgeon, without my being able to oppose anything he ordered—for I could not speak;—and I was carried to my room, and even bled, before I had the power of uttering a word.

"The lady has undergone a violent shock," said the surgeon; and the conscience-stricken Seymour ran out of the room in agony too mighty for expression.

I was now forced to swallow some strong nervous medicine; and at length, feeling myself able to speak again, I ejaculated, "Thank God!" and fell into a passion of tears, which considerably relieved me.

My kind but officious maid had, meanwhile, sent for Mrs. Pendarves, who eagerly demanded the original cause of my seizure.

"Dearest Helen, do you tell your aunt," said Seymour, "how it was."

"I had been fretting for two days," I replied, "on account of my mother's silence; and while I was talking to Seymour, this violent hysterical seizure came over me. Indeed, I had experienced all the morning, my love, *previous to your coming in*, a most unusual depression." This statement, though true, was, I own, deceptive; but I could not tell all the truth without exposing my husband. Oh! how fondly did his eyes thank me! My aunt was satisfied; she insisted on sitting by my bedside while I slept;—for an anodyne was given me,—and I consented to receive her offered kindness. Nay, I must own that, in the conscious desolation of my heart at that moment, I felt strangely soothed by expressions of kindness, and was covetous of those endearments from her, which before I had wished to avoid.—But my hand now returned and courted the affectionate pressure of hers; and I seemed to cling to her as a friend who, if she knew all, would have sorrowed over me like a mother; and while sleep was consciously stealing over me, I was pleased to know that she was watching beside my pillow.

I had forbidden Pendarves to come near me, because the sight of his distress prevented my recovery, and perfect quiet was enjoined.

But, when I was asleep, he would not be kept from my bedside; and he betrayed so much deep feeling, and exhibited so much affection for me, that when I woke, and desired to rise and dress, as I was quite recovered, my aunt was lavish in his praise, and declared she was now convinced he was the best of husbands.

Pendarves would fain have staid at home with me that day; but I insisted on his going out, as I thought it would be better for us both; and I told him, with truth, that I preferred his aunt's company to his. Our next meeting alone was truly painful; for we could neither of us advert to my excessive emotion. He could not explain away its cause, nor could I name it: but he, though silent, was affectionate and attentive, and I tried to force my too-busy fancy to dwell only on what I knew and saw, and not to fly off to sources of disquiet, which, spite of appearances, might really not exist.

The next morning, as soon as breakfast was over, we drove to the banker's, resumed the whole of the deposit, and I insisted that Pendarves should accept it all. This he was very unwilling to do—but I was firm, and my mind was tranquillized by his consenting at last to my desire. Yet I *think* I was not foolish enough to suppose I could buy his constancy.

One thing which I said to him I instantly repented. I asked him whether Mrs. Saunders was likely to remove to London. He said, he did not know: "But if she does, what then? O Helen! can you suppose I will ever see her *now?*" he added.

"And why *not?*" thought I, when he quitted me—"If it was ever proper to see her, why not now? And why should I seem to be accusing him, by appearing solicitous to know whether he would see her or not?"

Alas! his reply only served to make me more wretched; but, fortunately I may say, my mother's continued silence made a sort of diversion to my thoughts, and substituted tender for bitter anxiety.

That very day the demand was made on my husband by the creditor of Saunders, and while he was gone out with this man on business, in bustled my kind but mischievous aunt.

"How are you to-day," said she, "my poor child? but I see how you are—sitting like patience on a monument, smiling with grief!"

"With grief! dear aunt?"

"Yes: for do you think I do not know all? Oh, the wicked man!"

"Whom, madam, do you call wicked?"

"Your husband, child: has he not been keeping up an acquaintance with that girl who married? and has he not been bound for her husband? and is not the man run away, and he liable to be arrested for the debt? and where he can get the money to pay it I can't guess —I am sure *my* Mr. Pendarves will not pay it. Nay, *I* know 'tis all, all true—my maid, I find, met him walking in the park with her, and the creditor is *my maid's brother*."

Here she paused, exhausted with her own vehemence; and I replied, "I am sorry, madam, that you listen to tales told you by your servant: I am also sorry that a transaction, which, though rash, was kind, is known to more persons than my husband and me. I know, as well as you, that Pendarves visited at Mrs. Saunders's lodgings, and he was very likely seen in the park with her. To the money transaction I am also privy, and I assure you my Mr. Pendarves need not apply to yours on this or, I trust, on any occasion; for the creditor has been here, and he is paid by this time."

"Then he must have borrowed the money, for I *know* he has lost a great deal lately."

"Mrs. Pendarves," said I, rising with great agitation, "I will not allow you to speak thus of the husband whom I love and honour. I tell you, that he has paid the creditor with his *own* money; and if you persist in a conversation so offensive to me, I will quit the room."

"How! this *to me?* Do you consider who I am—and our relationship?"

"You are the wife of my great-uncle, madam, *no more;* and were you even *my mother*, I would not sit and listen tamely to aspersions of my husband, and I must desire that our conversation on this subject may end here."

I believe there is nothing more formidable while it lasts, than the violence of those who are habitually mild—because surprise throws the persons who are attacked off their guard; and it also magnifies to them the degree of violence used.

The poor little woman was not only awed into silence, but affected unto tears; and I was really obliged to soothe her into calmness, declaring that I was sure she meant well, and that I had never doubted the goodness of her heart.

The next day brought the long-expected letter from my mother; and its contents made all that I had yet endured light, in comparison; for they alarmed me for the life of my child! She was, however, declared out of danger for the present, when my mother wrote.

It is almost needless to add, that as soon as horses could be procured, Pendarves and I were on the road home.

I must pass rapidly over this part of my narrative. Suffice, that she vacillated between life and death for three months: that then she was better, and my husband left me to join Lord Charles at Tunbridge Wells, whither he had been ordered for his health; that he had not been gone a fortnight, when her worst symptoms returned, and my mother wrote to him as follows:—

"Come instantly, if you wish to see your child alive, and preserve the senses of your wife! When all is over, your presence alone can, I believe, save her from distraction.
"J. P."

He instantly set off for home, and arrived at a moment when I could be alive to the joy of seeing him; for my child had just been pronounced *better!* But *what* a betterness! For six weeks longer, watched by us all day and all night with never-failing love, it lingered on and on, endeared to us every day the more, in proportion as it became more helpless, and we more void of hope, till I was doomed to see its last faint breath expire, and——no more on this subject—

* * * * *

I believe my mother was right; I believe that dearly as I loved her, her presence *alone* would not have kept my grief within the bounds of reason: but the presence of him whose grief was on a par with mine, of him whom love and duty bade me equally exert myself to console, had indeed a salutary effect on me; and it at length became a source of comfort to reflect, that the object of our united regrets was mercifully removed from a state of severe suffering, and probably from evils to come. But my progress towards recovered tranquillity bore no proportion to Seymour's; for, when I was capable of reflection, I felt that in losing my child I lost one of my strongest holds on the affections of my husband. Consequently, the clearer my mind grew after the clouds of grief dispersed, the more vividly was I sensible of my loss.

I also became conscious that the habitual

dejection of my spirits, which was pleasing to Seymour's feelings while his continued in unison with mine, would become distasteful, and make his home disagreeable, as soon as he was recovering his usual cheerfulness. Still, I could not shake it off—and by my mother's advice I urged him to renew his visit to Lord Charles, who was still an invalid.

To Tunbridge Wells he therefore again went, leaving me to indulge unrestrained that pernicious grief which even his presence had not controlled, and also to impair both my health and my person in a degree which it might be difficult ever to restore.

When Pendarves returned, which he did at the end of six weeks, during which time he had written in raptures of the new acquaintances which he had formed at the Wells, he was filled with pain and mortification at sight of my pale cheek, meagre form, and neglected dress.

What a contrast was I to the women whom he had left! And even his affectionate disposition and fine temper were not proof, after the first ebullitions of tenderness had subsided, against my dowdy wretched appearance, and my dejection of manner.

"Helen," said he, "I cannot stand this—I must go away again, if you persist to forget all that is due to the living in regard for the dead. I have not been accustomed lately to pale cheeks, meagre forms, and dismal faces. I love home, and I love you; but neither my home nor you are now recognisable."

I was *wounded*, but reproved and amended. I felt the justice of what he said, and resolved to do my duty.

Soon after, he told me he was going away again; and on my mother's gently reproaching him for leaving me so much, he replied that he could not bear to witness my altered looks, and to listen to my mournful voice.

When Pendarves was gone, I resolved to renew my long-neglected pursuits. I played on the guitar; I resumed my drawing, and sometimes I tried to sing; but that exertion I found at present beyond my powers.

After three weeks had elapsed, Seymour wrote me word that he was about to return from the Wells, with some new friends of his, who were coming to the large mansion within four miles of us, which had been so long uninhabited, called Oswald Lodge. He said he should arrive there very late on the Saturday night; but that after attending church on the Sunday, to hear a new curate preach, whom they were to bring with them, he should return home.

I was mortified, I own, to think that he could stop, after so long an absence, within four miles of home; but I felt that I had lately made so few efforts for his sake, that I had no right to expect he would pay me an attention like this. But to repine or look back was equally vain and weak; and I resolved to act, in order to make amends for what I could not but consider an indolent indulgence of my own selfishness, however disguised to me under the name of sensibility, at the expense of my husband's happiness. And as six months had now elapsed since the death of my child, I resolved to throw off my mourning, and make the house and myself look as cheerful as they were wont to do.

I also resolved to meet him at the church, which was common to the parish whence he would come, and ours also, and not to sit, as I had lately done, in a pew whence I could steal in and out unseen; but walk up the aisle, and sit in my own seat, where I could see and be seen of others.

My mother, meanwhile, observed in joyful silence all my proceedings; and when she saw me stop at the door in the carriage on the Sunday morning, dressed in white, with a muslin bonnet, and pelisse lined with full pink, and a countenance which was in a measure at least cheerful, she embraced me with the warmest affection, and said she hoped she should now see her own child again.

Spite, however, of my well-motived exertions, my nerves were a little fluttered when I recollected that I was going to encounter the scrutinizing observation of Seymour's new friends, who, if arrived, would no doubt, from the situation of the pew, see me during the long length of my progress towards mine, which was opposite. They were arrived before me, for I saw white and coloured feathers nodding at a distance; but I remembered it was not in the temple of the Most High that fear of man ought to be felt, and I followed my mother up the aisle with my accustomed composure.

Oh! how I longed to see whether my husband was with the party! but I forbore to seek the creature till the dues to the Creator were paid. I then looked towards the pew, but soon withdrew my eyes again, for I saw my husband listening with an animated countenance to what a gentleman was saying to him, who was gazing on me with an expression of great admiration. I therefore only exchanged a glance of affectionate welcome with Pendarves, and tried to remember him and his companions no more.

When service was ended, Seymour eagerly left his seat, and coming into mine, proposed to introduce me to his friends: "For now," said he in a low voice, "I again see the wife I am proud of." I smiled assent, and a formal introduction took place.

The party consisted of Mr. and Mrs. Oswald, who after a long residence abroad were come to live on their estate, and resume those habits of extravagance the effects of which they had gone abroad to recover; of a Lord Martindale, the gentleman I had before observed; and of one or two persons—a sort of hangers-on in the family—who ministered, in some way or other, to the entertainment of the host and hostess.

Mr. and Mrs. Oswald now politely urged my mother and myself to favour them with our company at dinner, my husband having promised to return to them by five o'clock; but we declined it, and Seymour attended us home. Seymour expressed more by his looks than his words, the pleasure my change of dress and countenance had occasioned him; for he was too delicate to expatiate on what must recall to my mind only too forcibly the cause of the difference which he had deplored; but when he rejoiced over my recovered bloom, and *embonpoint*, I reminded him that my bloom was caused by my lining, and my seeming plumpness by my pelisse. This was only too true. Still I was, he saw, disposed to be all he wished me: and when we reached our house, and he beheld baskets of flowers in all the rooms, as usual; when he beheld the light of day allowed to penetrate into every apartment, except where the sun was too powerful; when he saw my guitar had been moved from its obscurity, and that my portfolio seemed full of drawings;—he folded my still thin form with fondness to his heart, and declared that he now felt himself quite a happy man again. Nor would he leave me, to dine at Oswald Lodge; and he sent an excuse, but promised to call there on the morrow, and take me with him. The next day he summoned me to get ready to fulfil his promise, and I obeyed him, but with reluctance; for I felt already sure that I should not like these new friends.

In Lord Martindale, I already saw an audacious man of the world; and those spendthrift Oswalds—those beings who seemed to think they came into life merely to amuse it away—did not seem at all suited to my taste or principles, and were certain to be dangerous to a man of Seymour's tendency to expense.

On our way thither, I asked if Lord Martindale was married; and with a cheek which glowed with emotion, he replied, "Married! Oh, yes! Did I not mention Lady Martindale to you? How strange!" But I did not think it so, when I heard him descant on her various attractions and talents with an eloquence which was by no means pleasing to me.

"Indeed," said I, sighing as I spoke, "I feel it a great compliment that you preferred staying with your faded wife to dining with this brilliant beauty."

"Brilliant beauty! Dear girl! in beauty, *she* is not to be compared to you! She is certainly ten years older, and never was a beauty in her life. She has very fine eyes, fine teeth, fine hair, and a little round, perfectly-formed person: *au reste*, she is sallow, and, when not animated, plain; in her expression, her endless variety, her gracefulness, and her vivacity, lies her great charm. Altogether, *c'est une petite personne des plus piquantes;* and with even more than the usual attraction of her countrywomen."

"Is she French, then?"

"Yes; she was well-born, but poor; and her great powers of fascination led Lord Martindale, who was living abroad, to marry her in spite of his embarrassed fortune. They came over in the same ship with the Oswalds, and thence the intimacy."

By this time we had reached Oswald Lodge, and were ushered through a hall redolent with sweets to the morning-room, where we found Mrs. Oswald, splendidly attired, stringing coral beads, and the gentlemen reading the papers. If there ever was a complete contrast in nature, it was my appearance and that of Mrs. Oswald. Figure to yourself the greeting between a woman of my great height, excessive meagreness, and long neck, and one not exceeding five feet, with legs making up in thickness for what they wanted in length, with a short neck buried in fat, and the rest of her form of suitable dimensions, while the dropsical appearance of her person did not however impede a short and quick waddling walk. Figure to yourself also a fair, fat, flat face, full of good-humour, and betokening a heart a stranger to care; and then call to mind my different style of features, complexion, and expression, particularly at that melancholy period of my life.

"What a fine caricature we should make!" thought I; and it required all my dislike to employ the talent for caricature which I possessed, to prevent my drawing her and myself when I went home. But I was ashamed of the satirical manner in which I regarded her, when she welcomed me with such genuine kindness: and ill befall the being whom welcome and courtesy cannot disarm of even habitual sarcasm! Mr. Oswald was as courteous and kind as his wife, and Lord Martindale *looked* even more soft meanings than he *uttered* —adding, "When I saw *you* yesterday, Mrs. Pendarves, I did not expect to see Mr. Pendarves return to us to dinner. Nay, if he had I never could have *forgiven* him."

"My lord," cried Oswald, "*I* did not expect him for *another* reason, though I admit the full force of yours. He knew Lady Martindale was too unwell to dine below, for I told him so myself; and my 'fair, fat, and forty' here was not likely to draw him from 'metal more attractive—'" bowing to me.

"So then," said I to myself, "his staying with me, for which I expressed my thanks, was no compliment after all; and, disingenuous as usual, he did not tell me Lady Martindale would not be visible!" I am ashamed to own how this little incident disconcerted me. I had been flattered by Seymour's staying at home, but *now* there was nothing in it. Oh! the weakness of a woman that loves!

Seymour, who knew that I should be mortified, and he *lowered* in my eyes by this discovery, was more embarrassed and awkward than I ever knew him, in paying his respects and making his inquiries concerning the health of Lady Martindale, and had just expressed his delight at hearing she was recovered, when the lady herself appeared; she paid her compliments to me in a very easy and graceful manner, and expressed herself much pleased to see the lady of whom her lord had raved ever since he saw her; and I suspect her broken English gave what she said much of its charm. At least I wished to think so *then*. I found Seymour had painted her as she was, as to externals; whether he had been as accurate a delineator of her mind and general manners, I was yet to learn.

That she could dance, I had soon the means of discovering; for she had a little French dog with her, which had been taught to dance to a tune; and while Mrs. Oswald played a slow waltz, and then a jig, Lady Martindale, on pretence of showing off the little dog, showed herself off to the greatest possible advantage.—Whether she glided smoothly along in the graceful abandonment of the waltz measure, or whether she sprung lightly on the "gay fantastic toe," her fine arms floated gracefully on the air, and her beautiful feet moved with equal and as becoming skill. When she had ended, she was repaid with universal bravos and clapping of hands.

Nothing could exceed the grace with which she curtsied; and snatching the dog under her arm, she went round the circle, extending her beautiful hand to each of us, saying "*De grâce! donnez des gâteaux à ma Fanchon;*"* and the plate of macaroons that stood near us was immediately emptied before the little animal, who growled and ate to the great delight of his mistress, who knelt in attitude *fait à peindre* beside him.

I cannot express to you what I felt when I saw Seymour's eyes riveted on this woman of display. He watched her every movement, and seemed indeed to feel she possessed *la grâce plus belle encore que la beauté.*†—But who and what was she? A Frenchwoman, well-born, though poor.

Was it the quick-sightedness of jealousy, I wonder, or was it that women read women better than men do, where their love or their vanity is concerned, which made me suspect that she had been not only a *femme de talens*, but a *femme à talens*, and that Lord Martindale had married a woman who had been in public life? However, what did that matter to me! Whatever she was, she possessed fascinations which I had not; she had a power of amusing and interesting which I had never possessed; and I feared that to him who could admire *her*, I must soon cease to be an object of *love*, though I might continue to be one of *esteem*. But did I wish to please as she had been pleasing? Did I wish to be able to exhibit my person in attitudes so alluring? Would it have been consistent with the modest dignity of an English gentlewoman? Nay, would my husband have liked to see me so exhibit in company? Notwithstanding, to charm, amuse, and fix his roving eye, and enliven our domestic scenes, I could not help wishing that *I* could do all *she* did. But I *could* not do it, and I *feared* her. We were eagerly asked to stay to dinner, but we refused; however, another day was fixed for our waiting on them, so the evil was only delayed.

And *what* were we doing? and *wherefore?* We were entering into dinner visits, and with a reduced income, with persons who lived in all the luxuries of life, and of whom we knew nothing but that ten years before they had been forced to run away from their creditors, and that the chances were they would be forced to do so again. The *wherefore* was still *less* satisfactory to me. We did it that my husband might amuse away his hours; and, as I had reason to fear, forget in this stimulating sort of company and diversions the anxieties and the unhappy feelings which were in future likely to cling to him at home. For I was sure he was involved in debts which he could not pay, and those who are so involved are always forced to substitute constant amusement for happiness. If they do not, they fly to intoxication; but agreeable company and gay pursuits are the better intoxication, I own, of the two.

And was it come to this? Was my husband for ever unfitted for the enjoyment of domestic comfort; and was I reduced to the cruel alternative of seeing him abstracted and unhappy, or of parting with him to the abode of the Syren? while I was sometimes forced to accompany him thither, and witness his evident devotion to *her*, his forgetfulness of *me?* Alas! such seemed to be my situation at that moment: but I was resolved to talk with him seriously on the state of his affairs, and to make any retrenchments, and offer any sacrifices, to remove from his mind the burthen which oppressed it. But, for some time, like most persons so distressed, he was decidedly averse to talk on the subject, and liked better to drive care away by pleasant society, than to meet the evil though it was in order to remove it. In the mean while I went to Oswald Lodge occasionally, and occasionally invited its owners and their guests to our home, till the party there grew too large for our rooms to receive them : and then I had an excuse for not accompanying my husband often, in not having carriage-horses, as I had prevailed on Pendarves to drop that unnecessary expense. This produced urgent invitations to sleep there; but that I never would do; I would not consent to be with these people, on so intimate a footing, especially as I had not my mother's countenance or presence to sanction it; she

---

* Pray, give cakes to my Fanchon.
† Grace more beautiful still than beauty.

having resolutely declined visiting them at all, as she disliked the manners and appearance, as well as the mode of life, of the whole party. But she confirmed me in my resolution never to seem to *undervalue*, though I did not *commend*, Lady Martindale, as she well knew my disapprobation would be imputed to envy and jealousy even by Pendarves, and she advised me to endure patiently what I could not prevent. Not that she for a moment suspected that my husband was seriously alienated from me, and was acting a dishonourable part towards Lord Martindale; but she could not be blind to Seymour's long absences at Oswald Lodge, and his now passing nights there, as well as days. But his pleasures were, for a little while at least, put a stop to; for he received at length so many dunning letters, that he was forced to unburthen his mind to me, and ask my aid, if possible, to relieve his distresses. He positively, however, forbade me to apply to my mother, and I was equally unwilling to let her know the errors of my still beloved husband.

Yet what could I do for him? I could dismiss one, if not two servants, and he could sell another horse; but then money was wanted to pay debts. There was, therefore, no alternative, but for me to prevail on my trustees to give up some of my marriage-settlement; and as I knew that my mother's fortune must come to me and my children, if I had any, I was very willing to relieve my husband from his embarrassments, by raising for him the necessary supplies. Nor did I find my trustees very unwilling to grant my request, and once more I believed my husband free from debt. I also hoped that my mother knew nothing of either the distress, or the means of relief. But, alas! one of the trustees concluded our uncle knew of these transactions, and was probably desirous to know why he had, though a very rich man, allowed *me* to diminish my marriage settlement, in order to pay debts which *he* could have paid without the smallest inconvenience, as he had only two daughters, who were both well married.

Accordingly, he mentioned the subject to my astonished and indignant uncle, who, with his usual indiscretion, revealed it to his wife. The consequence was inevitable: she immediately wrote a letter of lamentation to my mother, detailing the whole affair, adverting to the other transaction concerning Saunders's debts, pointing out the great probability there was that what every one said was true—namely, that my husband had prevailed on Saunders to marry Charlotte Jermyn, and therefore was bound in justice to assist him, and concluding with a broad hint concerning his evident attachment to a Lady Martindale.

What a letter for a fond mother to receive! But to the money transactions alone did she vouchsafe any credit; and relative to these she demanded from me the most open confession, saying, "The rest of the letter I treat with the contempt it deserves." I had no difficulty in telling her every thing which related to the last transaction; but my voice faltered and my eye was downcast, when I described the other, because I had never been entirely able to conquer some painful suspicions of my own, and her quick eyes and penetrating mind soon discovered, though she was too delicate to notice it, that in my own heart I was not sure that all my aunt suspected was unjust. But if I shrunk from the searching glance of her eyes, how was I affected when she fixed them on me with looks of approving tenderness, and told me, with evidently suppressed feeling, that I had done well and greatly in concealing my husband's extravagant follies even from her!

That day's post brought a letter of a more pleasant nature from my uncle to me. He informed me, that though he utterly disapproved my giving to an erring husband what was intended as a provision for my innocent children, he could not bear that I should suffer by my erroneous but generous conception of a wife's duty, and had therefore replaced the sum which I had so rashly advanced, desiring me on any future emergency to apply to him.

Kind and excellent old man! How pleasant were the tears which I shed over this letter! but still, how much more welcome to my soul were those which it wrung from the full heart of Pendarves!

But amidst the various feelings which made my cheek pale, my brow thoughtful and sad, my form meagre, and which deprived me of every thing but the mere outline of former beauty, was the consciousness that my mother's heart was estranged from my husband. He had even exceeded all her fears and expectations; and her manner to him was full of that cold civility, which, when it replaces ardent affection, is of all things the most terrible to endure from one whom you love and venerate. He felt it to his heart's core, and alas! he resented it by flying oftener from his home and the wife whom he thus rendered wretched.

At this period, my mother was surprised by a most unexpected guest, and, situated as I was, an unwelcome visiter to both—for it was Ferdinand De Walden.

Business had brought him to England; and as time had, he believed, mellowed his attachment to me into friendship, he had no objection to visit my mother, and renew his acquaintance with me. But though she prepared him to see me much altered—as I had not, she said, recovered the loss of my child—he was so overcome when he saw me, that he was forced to leave the room; and the sight of that faded face and form—nay, I may say, the utter loss of my beauty—endeared me yet more to the heart of De Walden.

Had I been an artful—had I been a coquettish woman, this was the time to show it, for

I might have easily roused the jealousy of my husband, and perhaps have terrified him back to his allegiance. But I should have felt debased if I had excited one feeling of jealousy in a husband's heart; and my manner was so cold to De Walden, that he complained of it to my mother.

Mr. Oswald called on De Walden, as soon as he heard of his arrival, for he had known him abroad, and a day was fixed for our meeting him at Oswald Lodge: nay, my mother, to mark her great respect for her guest, would have joined the party, had she not sprained her ancle severely the day before.

It was now some weeks since I had dined there; therefore I had not seen the great increase of intimacy which was visible between Seymour and Lady Martindale, and which I dreaded should be observed by Lord Martindale himself: but he did not seem to mind it, and looked at me with such an expression of countenance, lavishing on me at the same time such disgusting flatteries, that the dark eye of De Walden flashed fire as he regarded him, and he beheld my absorbed and inattentive husband with a look in which scorn contended with agony. But if Seymour was completely absorbed in looking at and listening to the Syren who bewitched him, *she* was not equally absorbed in *him :* but I saw that when he was not looking at her, she was earnestly examining De Walden, and that his eye dwelt on her with a very marked and scornful meaning.

Lady Martindale was solicited, at the dinner-table, to promise some new guests who were there to exhibit to them the scene with the dog; but, on pretence of having hurt her foot, she refused. This led to a conversation on dancing, of which art, to my great surprise, De Walden declared himself a great admirer in the early part of his life. "When I was very young," said he, in French, "I saw such dancing as I shall never forget. It was that of a young creature on the Paris stage, who was then called Annette Beauvais, and she quite bewitched my young heart, both on and off the stage; for I once saw her in a private party—but then I was quite a boy. She was at that time the mistress of a *fermier général :* since then, she has figured, as I have heard, in many different capacities, and I should not be surprised to hear of her as a peeress, or a princess, so great and versatile were her powers."

This discussion, so little *àpropos*—for what did any one present care for Annette Beauvais?—convinced me De Walden had a meaning beyond what appeared; and casting my eyes on Lord Martindale and his lady, I saw they were both covered with confusion; but the former recovering himself first, said, "Annette Beauvais! My dear Eugéne, is not that the name of the girl who was reckoned so like you?"

"*Mais oui—sans doute*—I was much sorry —for I was take for her very oft—*et cependant elle est plus grande que moi.*"*

"She may look taller on the stage, my lady," said De Walden, again speaking in French, that she might not lose a word; "but I would wager any money, that off the stage, no one would know Annette from you, or you from her."

"*À la bonne heure,*" said she in a tone of pique, and avoiding the searching glance of his eye; then on her making a signal to Mrs. Oswald, she rose, and we left the dining-room.

With the impression which I had just received on my mind, of Lady Martindale's former profession—or, rather, *character*—I could not help replying to the attentions which she now lavished on me with distant politeness; and I saw clearly that she observed my change of manner, and, resenting it in her heart, resolved to take ample vengeance; for, as I stood with my arms folded in a long mantle which I wore, lost in reverie, it happened that I did not answer Lady Martindale when she first spoke, and when I did, it was in a cold and absent manner, and as if I addressed an inferior; on which the artful woman, who sat in a recess by the side of my husband, threw herself back, exclaiming, "*Mais voyez donc comme elle me traite! Ah! comment ai-je mérité cette dureté, de sa part?*"† She accompanied these words with a few touching tears.

On seeing and hearing this, for the first time in his life since we married, Seymour felt irritated against me; and coming up to me, he said, in a voice nearly extinct with passion, "Mrs. Pendarves, I insist on your opologising to that lady for the rudeness of which you have been guilty." For one moment my spirit revolted at the word "insist," and my feelings were overset by the "Mrs. Pendarves;" but it was only for a moment.

I felt that I *had* been rude; and I also felt that I should not have acted as I did, spite of my suspicions, if I had not been jealous of Seymour's adoration for her.

Accordingly, drawing so near to her that no one could hear what passed, I told her at the command of my husband, I assured her I did not mean to wound or offend her, and that I was sorry I had done so.

"Ah! 'tis your husband spoke den, not your own heart—dat's wat I want."

"The feelings of my heart," said I, "are not at the command even of my husband; but my words are, and I have obeyed him—but I am really sorry when I have given pain to any one." Then, with a low curtsy, I left them, and retired to a further part of the room.

During this time I saw that Seymour looked still angry, and was not satisfied with my

* Yet she is taller than I.
† Only see how she treats me! How have I deserved such hard treatment from her!

apology, or the manner in which I delivered it; and I repented I had not been more gracious. But now I was requested to sing a Venetian air to the Spanish guitar, to which I had written English words; and I complied, glad to do something to escape from my own painful reflections, and also from the earnest manner in which De Walden examined my countenance, and watched what had just passed. But in order no doubt to mortify my vanity by calling off the attention from me to herself, the moment I began, Lady Martindale set her little dog down who was lying in her lap, and began to make him dance to the tune; but as she did not get up herself and dance as usual with him, the poor beast did not know what to make of it, but set up a most violent barking. I had had resolution to go on both singing and playing during the grimaces of the dog and its mistress, even though my own husband, instead of resenting the affront to me, had seemed to enjoy it; but when the dog spoke I was silent; on which De Walden seized the little animal in his arms in spite of Lady Martindale's resistance, and put it out of the room. Then stooping down he whispered something in her ear which silenced her at once. During this scene I trembled in every limb; for I feared that Seymour might be mad enough to resent De Walden's conduct. I was therefore relieved when Lord Martindale came up to him, as if he meant to resent the violence offered to his lady's dog; but on his approaching De Walden, he said, with great good-humour—"That was right, Count De Walden; and if you had not done it, *I* should. Only think that a beast like that should presume to interrupt a seraph!"

"Ah! if but he it was alone that presumed in this room, it would be well; but we often make example of one who is guilty the least."

Lord Martindale did not choose to ask an explanation of these words, but turning to me, requested me to resume my guitar and my song. But I had not yet recovered my emotion, nor perhaps would it have been consistent with my self-respect to comply.

Certainly De Walden thought not; for he said in a low voice, "*Ma chère amie, de grâce ne chantez pas!*"* and I was firm in my refusal.

Perhaps it was well that I was not allowed to go on with my song, as the words were only too expressive of my own feelings, for they were as follows:—

SONG.

How bright this summer's sun appear'd!
 How blue to me this summer's sky!
While all I saw and all I heard
 Could charm my ear, could bless my eye!

The lonely bower, the splendid crowd,
 Alike a joy for me possess'd;

* My dear friend, pray do not sing.

My heart a charm on all bestow'd,
 For that confiding heart was *bless'd*.

But thou art changed!—and now no more
 The sun is bright, or blue the sky;
Now in the throng, or in the bower,
 I only mark thy *alter'd eye*.

And though 'midst crowds I still appear,
 And seem to list the minstrel's strain,
I heed it not—I only hear
 My *own deep sigh* that mourns in vain.

My carriage was announced soon afterwards, and I saw by the manner of both, that Lady Martindale was trying to persuade my husband to stay all night, but as De Walden came with us, propriety, if not inclination, forbade him to comply, and he sullenly enough followed De Walden and me to the carriage. When there, that considerate friend refused to enter it,—declaring as it was moonlight, he preferred walking home.

What a relief was this to my mind! for I dreaded some unpleasant altercation, especially if De Walden expressed the belief which he evidently entertained, that Lady Martindale and Annette Beauvais were the same person.

When he entered the carriage, my husband threw himself into one corner of it, and remained silent. I expected this; still I did not know how to bear it; for I could not help contrasting the past with the present. Is there—no, there is not—so agonizing a feeling in the catalogue of human suffering, as the first conviction that the heart of the being whom we most tenderly love, is estranged from us? In vain could I pretend to doubt this overwhelming fact. Seymour had resented *for* another woman, and to *me!* He had even joined in, and *enjoyed*, the mean revenge that woman took, though that revenge was a public affront to *me!* And now in sullen silence, and in still rankling resentment, he was sitting as far from me as he could possibly sit, and the attachment of years seemed in one hour destroyed !

All this I felt, and thought during the first mile of our drive home; but so closely does hope ever tread on the heels of despair, that one word from Pendarves banished the worst part of my misery; for in an angry tone he at length observed, "So, madam, your champion would not go with us; I think it is a pity you did not walk with him—I think you ought to have done no less, after his public gallantry in your service."

"Ha!" thought I immediately, "this is pique, this is jealousy, and perhaps he loves me still!" What a revulsion of feeling I now experienced! and never in his fondest moments did I value an expression of tenderness from him more than I did this weak and churlish observation; for he was not silent and sullen on account of Lady Martindale's fancied injuries, but from resentment of De Walden's interference. In one moment therefore the face of nature itself seemed changed to me; and I eagerly replied, "I was certainly much obliged to De Walden—I needed a champion, and who so proper to be it as himself, the only old friend I had in the room, yourself excepted, and the only person in it probably who now (here my voice faltered) has a real regard and affection for me?"

"Helen!" cried Pendarves, starting up, "you cannot mean what you say! You do not, *cannot* believe that De Walden loves you better than *I* do."

"If I had not believed it, I should not have said it."

"But how could you believe it? Has he dared to talk to you of love?"

"Do you think he could forget himself so far as to do such a thing? or if he did, do you think I could forget myself so far as to listen to him? Surely, sir, you forget of whom and to whom you are speaking."

"Forgive me—I spoke from pique. And so, Helen, you think I do not love you?"

"Not as you did, certainly: but I excuse you. I know grief has changed me; and it had been better for me to have died, if it had so pleased God, when my poor child died."

"Helen, dearest! do not talk thus, I cannot bear it!" he exclaimed, clasping me to his heart; and though I then wept even more abundantly than before, I wept on his bosom, and all my sorrows were for a while forgotten.

The next morning, Pendarves told me he should certainly breakfast with me; but he must leave me soon, to partake of a late breakfast at Oswald Lodge, as he had promised to go with the party to call on a family, with whom they were to arrange some private theatricals.

"And are *you* to engage in them?"

"Oh! to be sure: it will not be the first time of my acting."

"And will Lady Martindale act?"

"Yes, but not with us. We shall act in English: she will favour us with a monodrame, a ballet of action, and perhaps read a French play, which she reads to perfection."

"Not better than she dances, I dare say; for dancing, I suspect, was once *one* of her professions."

"What nonsense is this, Helen? and who has dared to give such an erroneous and false impression of this admirable woman?"

"Surely you must have perceived that De Walden meant to insinuate that she and Annette Beauvais are the same person?"

"Then he is a vile calumniator."

"Not so—he is only a *mistaken* man."

"But it seems you think he *cannot* be mistaken: he is an *oracle*."

"My love," replied I, "we had better not talk of De Walden."

"You are right, Helen—quite right, for I am conscious of great irritation when I think of him; for I feel — I cannot but feel, how much more worthy of you he is than I am; and yet, foolish girl! you gave him up for me. O Helen! when I saw him, impatient of affront to you, step forward with that flashing eye, that commanding air, to seize the offending brute, though I could have stabbed him, I could also have embraced him; and I said within myself, "And to this man Helen preferred *me!* How she must repent her folly *now!*"

"She never has repented—she never *can* repent it," said I, throwing myself upon his neck. "You know I took you with all your faults open to my view."

"Yes; but you fancied love and you would reform them."

"I did — and I think that we may do so still; but you must not let me fancy you do not love me, Seymour: if you do, I shall pine and mope, and become the object of your aversion."

"Impossible! do you think I can ever dislike you?"

"Is thy servant a dog, that he should do this thing?" said I, returning to his embrace.

"I will hear no more of such horrible surmises: I have now outstaid my time."

Then, mounting his horse, he was out of sight in a moment.

Soon after, my mother appeared, and, to my surprise, unaccompanied by De Walden.

"Where is our friend?" was my first salutation.

"On the road to London."

"London! And why?"

"He had his reasons for going; and, as usual, they do honour both to his head and heart."

"May I not know them?"

"I would not tell them to all women under your circumstances; but I can trust you. He finds that he has not conquered his attachment; and that he cannot behold the affecting change in your appearance, and reflect on the cause, without feeling what his principles disapprove. Besides, he is afraid of getting involved in a quarrel with Pendarves, as, I suppose, you guess who this Lady Martindale is."

"I do. Well, I am glad De Walden is gone, for I know Pendarves will rejoice."

I then related to her my conversation with my husband, and did it with so much cheerfulness, and such an evident revival of hope, that I imparted some of the feelings which I experienced; and my mother's heart was visibly softened towards Seymour, while she uttered, "Poor fellow! he does indeed justly judge himself: you did prefer the brilliant to the diamond! But where is he?"

"Gone out with the party at the Lodge, on particular business, and will not return till night."

On hearing this, my mother's countenance fell; and kissing my cheek, she shook her head mournfully, and changed the conversation.

Pendarves came home that evening in great spirits. Every thing was arranged for the theatricals, and the play fixed upon. It was to be the Belle's Stratagem, and he was to play Doricourt—a part he had often played before. The part of Letitia Hardy was given to a young lady who was famous as an actress on private theatres; and every part was filled but that of Lady Frances Touchwood.

"O Helen!" cried he, "how happy should I be, if you would give over all your dismals, lay aside your scruples, and make me your slave for life, by undertaking this mild and modest part."

"You bribe high!" I replied, turning pale at the apprehension of any thing so contrary to my habits, and my sense of right: "but you know my aversion to things of the sort."

"I do: but I also know your high sense of a wife's duty; and that you cannot but own a wife ought to obey her husband's will, when not contrary to the will of God."

"You seem to have *high*, though *just* ideas of a wife's duty," said I, smiling: "now, perhaps, you will favour me with your opinion of a *husband's* duty."

"Willingly. It is to wean a beloved wife, if possible, from gloomy thoughts; to keep amusing company himself, and make her join it; in short, when he has engaged in private theatricals, it is his *duty* to get his wife to engage in them also; and if you think such things dangerous to good morals, you are the more bound to engage in them, in order to watch over *mine*."

I suspected he was right, and that the general duty should, in this instance, give way to the particular one; but I shrunk with aversion from the long and intimate association with these disagreeable, if not disreputable people, to which it would oblige me; and after expressing this dislike, I begged time to consider of his request.

The next day I went to consult my mother, who at first would not hear the plan named, and declared that her child should not so far degrade herself as to allow her person to be profaned by such familiarities as acting must induce and she must suffer. But when I told her Mr. Oswald was to act Sir George Touchwood—a quiet, elderly, married man—she was more reconciled to it on that score, but she disliked it as much as I did on other grounds. However, having convinced myself, I at length convinced her that my duty to make myself as dear and as agreeable to my husband as I could, and not leave him thus exposed to the every day increasing fascinations of another woman.

"But can you, my child," said she, "have fortitude enough to bear for days together the sight of his attentions to your rival? Will it not make you pettish, grave, and unamiable, and cloud your eyes in tears, which will incense and not affect, because they will seem a reproach?"

"It will be a difficult task, and a severe trial, I own, but I humbly hope to be supported under it; and though the risk is great, the ultimate success is worth the venture."

"Helen," said my mother, "till now I thought *my* trials as a wife great, and my duties severe; but I am convinced that they were easy to bear, and easy to perform, compared to what a fond wife feels, who is forced to mask misery with smiles—to substitute undeserved kindness for just reproach—and to submit even her own superior judgment, and her own sense of right and wrong, to the will of her husband."

"But, dear mother! I shall be repaid and rewarded at last."

"Repaid, rewarded, Helen! how? Who, or what, is to repay you? As well can *assignats* repay bullion, as the love of a being who has grossly erred can reward that of one to whom error is unknown."

"But he has *not grossly* erred; and if he had, I *love* him," cried I, deeply wounded and appalled at the truth of what she said.

"Ah, *there it is*," she replied; "and thus does love level all in their turns; the weak with the strong, the sensible with the foolish. One thing more, Helen, before you go—You shall have your mother's countenance and presence to support you under your new trials: I will condescend to invite myself to attend *rehearsals*, and *I* will be at the *representation*."

I received this offer with gratitude, and then returned to tell my husband that I would perform the part of Lady Frances Touchwood.

He was delighted with my compliance; and on making me read the part aloud directly, he declared that I should perform to admiration.

"I should have played Letitia Hardy better," said I.

"You! how conceited!"

"I got that part by heart once, and I have often acted it quite through for my own amusement, when I was quite alone. But I prefer playing Lady Frances now, for the days of my vanity are pretty well over."

"No, no, child, they are only now beginning, according to this; and little did I think I had married a great actress!"

Pendarves then departed in high spirits to his friends, and I sat down to *study my part*. But bitter were the tears I shed over it. And was I, so lately the mourner over a dying and dead child, was I about to engage in dissipations like these?—But humbly hoping my motive sanctified my deed, I shook off overwhelming recollections, and resolved to persevere in my new task.

For some days, and till all was ready for rehearsals, Pendarves rehearsed his part to me, and I to him; but at length he found it pleasanter to have Lady Martindale hear him, he said, for her broken English was so *amusing*.

I could not oppose to *this excellent reason* my being a better judge of his performance, but I was forced to submit in silence. Now, however, I was soon called to rehearsals, and my mother was allowed to accompany me.

My first performance was wretched, and I thought Seymour looked ashamed of me; but my mother said she should have been mortified if I had done better the *first time*. The next I gained credit; but on the third day I found the party in great distress. The Letitia Hardy had been sent for to a dying father, and there was no one to undertake her part. You may easily guess that Seymour immediately told tales of me, and I undertook that prominent character: but I did not shrink from it, for my husband was to act with me; and Letitia Hardy was not more eager to charm Doricourt than I to charm my husband.

You know there is a minuet to be danced, and a song to be sung; and as Le Piq and Madame Rossi were the first dancers when I was young, I had taken lessons of both in London, and was said to dance a minuet well. Pendarves was equally celebrated in that dance; and as we rehearsed our minuet often at home, each declared the other perfect; nor was the little song less warmly applauded, which I substituted for the original, and adapted to a Scotch air. It applied to my own situation and feelings, as well as to those of the heroine, and was as follows:

SONG.

If now before this splendid throng
　With timid voice, but daring aim,
I strive to wake my pensive song
　And urge the minstrel's tuneful claim,
One wish alone the anxious task can move,
The wish to charm the ear of HIM I LOVE.

If in the dance with eager feet
　I seek a grace before unknown,
And dare the critic eye to meet,
　Nor heed though scornful numbers frown,
This wish to fear superior bids me prove,
The wish to charm the eye of HIM I LOVE.

And if, my woman's fears resign'd,
　I thus my loved retirement leave,
My humble vest with roses bind,
　And jewels in my tresses weave:
One wish alone could such vast efforts move,
The wish to *fix the heart* of HIM I LOVE.

The rehearsals, meanwhile, were pleasanter than I expected. My husband was *forced* to be a great deal with me, as he had to *rehearse* so much with me; and Lady Martindale chose to practise her ballet in her own apartment, in sight of a long glass. Therefore I had not to bear, as I expected, my husband's complete neglect; and I could smile at the meanness which led her to come in while I was rehearsing, and lament, as she looked on, loud enough for Seymour and me to hear, that the *charmante* Henrietta Goodwin was summoned away, and could not perform the heroine, because she did it *à ravir*. I saw Pendarves change colour often when she said this, and she said it daily; but as he thought I much excelled Miss Goodwin, he attributed it to female envy, and perhaps to *jealousy* of me as *his wife*.

At length the first day of our theatricals took place, and a company far more select, and less numerous than I expected, was assembled. My mother had insisted on defraying my expenses, and both my dresses were elegant. You must forgive my vanity when I say, that, with rouge replacing my natural bloom, and clad in a most becoming manner, I looked as young, and as well, as when I married;—while to my grateful joy, my husband seemed to admire me more than any one. Indeed, he pronounced my whole performance beyond praise, and I know not what any one else said. I made one alteration, however, in the text, on the night of representation, which called down thunders of applause. The author makes Letitia Hardy say, "that if her husband was unfaithful, she would elope with the first pretty fellow that asked her, *while her feelings preyed on her life*." I could not make my lips utter such words as these; I therefore said, "I *would not* elope like some women, &c., but would patiently endure my sufferings, *though* my feelings preyed on my life."

Seymour was so *surprised*, so confounded, and so affected, that he seized my hand and pressed it to his heart and lips before he could reply: and my mother told me afterwards, that she could scarcely control her emotions at a change so worthy of me, and so welltimed. The *next* representation was deferred for a week; and, whatever was the reason, Lady Martindale deferred any exhibition of herself to that future opportunity.

But the comfort and the joy of all to me was, that during this intermediate week I recovered my husband; and with him some of my good looks; while that odious lord would very fain have bestowed on me equal attention to what Seymour had bestowed on his wife, and of a less equivocal nature.

Lord Charles Belmour at this period paid us an unexpected visit, having entirely recovered from his late indisposition. I certainly was not glad to see him, though I believed he regarded me with more kindness than formerly, and he was evidently solicitous, by the most respectful attentions, to conciliate the regard of my beloved mother.

Out of compliment to Lord Charles, Seymour dined at home two days; but on the third, he insisted on taking his friend to call at Oswald Lodge, whose hospitable master had called on him, as soon as he heard of his arrival, and was anxious to have the honour of his acquaintance. Lord Charles thought the honour would all be on Mr. Oswald's side, and probably the pleasure also; but he was at length prevailed on to return the call, and to my great joy he returned, wondering at Seymour's infatuation in living so much with such a vulgar set; declaring, that even the Lady Martindale had more the air of a French *petite maîtresse* than of anything akin to quality. He said this in my mother's presence and mine, and he could not have made, I own, better court to either.

"My daughter and I always thought so, and I am glad to have our judgment confirmed by your lordship," answered my mother. "But my son thinks differently."

"I do, indeed," said Pendarves blushing; "and when Lord Charles sees her to advantage,—which he did not to-day,—he will not, I am sure, wonder at my admiration."

"Well, we shall see," said he: "but I trust I shall not change my mind, if the future exhibitions of her exquisite ladyship be like that of to-day. You were not there, ladies; therefore, for your amusement, allow me to open my show-box, and give you portraits of the inhabitants of Oswald Lodge."

He then stood up, and Mr. and Mrs. Oswald lived before us—air, voice, attitude, all perfectly given. Then came Lord Martindale, and at these pictures Pendarves laughed heartily; but when Lord Charles exhibited the dog and the lady, by turns, dancing, and sometimes barking for the one, and throwing himself into attitudes and smiling for the other, my husband looked much disconcerted, and said it was a gross caricature. But we did not think so; and though neither my mother nor myself approved such exhibitions, and on principle discouraged them, still, on this occasion, I must own, they were very gratifying to me. But the feeling was an unworthy one, and it was soon punished, for Seymour said, with a look of reproach, "You have mortified me, Helen: I had given you credit for more generosity; I did not think you would thus enjoy a laugh at *any* one's expense—especially that of one whose graces and talents you have yourself acknowledged."

I felt humbled and ashamed at the just reproof, though I thought he should not thus have reproved me, and I was silent; but my mother haughtily replied, "I am glad to hear you own you are mortified to find your wife has *some* leaven of human frailty, as I am now for the first time convinced that you appreciate her justly."

"I have many faults," he replied; "but that of not valuing Helen as she deserves was never one of them; and oh! how deeply do I feel, and bitterly lament, that I am not more worthy of her and you!"

My mother instantly held out her hand to him, while Lord Charles exclaimed, "What a graceful and candid avowal! No wonder the offender is so soon forgiven! But believe me, dear madam, there is no hope of amendment from persons who are so ready to own their faults; for they consider that candour makes amends for all their errors, and throws such a charm over them, that they have no motive to improve, especially if they are young and handsome, like my friend here; for really, he looked so pretty, and modest, and pathetic, that I wondered you only gave him your hand to kiss."

"Be quiet, Lord Charles; you are not a kind commentator."

"But I am a just one. Oh! believe me, there is more hope of an ugly dog like me, who can't look affecting, than of such a man as Seymour. I *cannot* make error look engaging if I would, and therefore must reform in good earnest when I wish to please."

That night, Seymour, who sat up with Lord Charles, did not come to bed till some hours after me. I was awake when he entered the room, and could not help asking him what had kept them up so late, anticipating his answer only too well.

"We sat up playing piquet," said he, in a cheerful voice; "and I am a great winner, Helen. If Lord Charles stays some days, and plays as he did to-night, I am a made man: only think of my winning a hundred pounds since you left us."

"But if Lord Charles should *not* always play as he did to-night, and you should *lose* a hundred pounds, what is to become of you then?"

"Psha, Helen! you are always so wise and cautious; there, there, go to sleep, and do not alarm yourself concerning what may never happen."

But I could not go to sleep, though I said no more; and I saw that our guest would probably upset those resolutions to which Pendarves had for some time adhered. True, he had not been tempted to break them; but had his desire for play been strong, he could have sought means to indulge it. He had not done so,—and therefore I thought him cured; though, as most persons have recourse to gaming merely to produce excitement, and the stimulus of alternate hope and fear, I could not but see that Oswald Lodge and Lady Martindale amply supplied to my husband the place of play; and so that he was interested and amused, it mattered not whence that feeling was derived. And this was he who had declared himself the votary of domestic habits, home amusements, and literary pursuits! But now he was most unexpectedly and unnecessarily assailed; for he had not gone to temptation, but it was come to him—and my resolution was taken.

The next morning, while we were at breakfast, a chaise stopped at our door. It was sent from Oswald Lodge, to convey my husband thither immediately, as a note from Lady Martindale informed him that she could not make arrangements for the next evening's exhibition without his advice and assistance; for nobody, she added, had any taste but himself.

This note Lord Charles playfully snatched from him, and would read aloud, much to Seymour's annoyance; as, though the language was elegant, there was not a word spelt right, and every rule of grammar was violated.

"The education of this well-born lady was much neglected, I see," said Lord Charles: "would she could spell as well as she can flatter!"

He then read the concluding compliment aloud.

"*C'est un peu fort*," he observed, returning the note, which Seymour angrily observed he ought not to have allowed him to read.

"Well; but you obey the summons, I suppose?"

"Certainly."

"And when may we hope to see you again?"

"As soon as I can get away."

"That may not be till bed-time."

"Impossible! Have I not promised to give you your revenge this evening?"

"Yes; but when a lady's in the case——"

"Nonsense! I shall return to dinner."

"And not before? How mortifying it is to me to see that you are not afraid of leaving me so many hours at liberty, to pay court to your wife—with whom, you know, I am desperately in love."

"If my wife were not what she is, I should be so; and my confidence, I assure you, is not in *you*, but in *her*."

"Besides, we shall not be alone, my lord, for I am going to challenge you," said I, "to call on my mother."

"Agreed! And now I am flattered. Your lady, you see, thinks me a more formidable person than you do. Suppose, my dear lady, that we go off together, only to punish him for his weak confidence?"

"We will consider of it," said I, laughing, "and in the meanwhile we will visit my mother."

My husband then drove off, and I prepared for my walk. When I returned, I found Lord Charles walking up and down the room, and with a thoughtful, disturbed countenance.

"Mrs. Pendarves," cried he, "I have no patience with that infatuated husband of yours! Here am I come on purpose to see him, and for a short time only, and yet, at the call of this equivocal French peeress, he leaves me— and has the indecorum, too, to go away, and leave me with his beautiful wife! Tell me, do you not believe in love-powders and philters? for surely some must have been administered to him."

"Not necessarily: my ill health, the consequence of sorrow, and that sorrow itself, made poor Seymour's home uncomfortable to him. He did not like to see me suffer; therefore, he acquired a habit of seeking amusement elsewhere; and the flatteries and invitations of these gay and agreeable people have at last obtained a complete ascendency over him."

"That I see; and such people, too! And to think of what the foolish man leaves! Mrs. Pendarves, I think that if I had had such a wife as his, I could not have left my home as he does."

"Lord Charles," replied I, "this is language which I will not listen to; but I laugh at your self-deception. The habits of all men of the world are similar, and alike powerful, and *your* wife would be left as I am: but I assure you that I am convinced my husband loves me tenderly notwithstanding; and I am trying, by conforming to his habits, to make myself as agreeable to him as others are."

Lord Charles seemed about to break into violent exclamations of some kind or other; but I stopped him, and begged to lead the way to my mother's. He bowed respectfully, and followed me; then, taking his arm, I tried to begin the conversation I meditated: and luckily, he made my task easy by saying, "I conclude Pendarves told you how completely he beat me at cards last night. But he has promised to give me my revenge to-night. The truth is, I have not played piquet these two years; but before I leave you I expect to recover my knowledge, and to turn my visit to account; for I have been very unsuccessful at Brookes's lately."

I now stopped, and said, "Hear me, Lord Charles! I believe that you can be a kind and honourable man, and that you are really disposed to be a friend to me."

"To be sure—to be sure I am."

"I feel, I own, your power to be my foe in many essential points, but I am equally sure that you can be my friend if you choose; and I request you, if you value my peace of mind, not to tempt my husband to renew that habit and fondness for play, which he had lost, which he cannot afford to indulge, and which, I assure you, has impoverished and distressed us."

"You amaze me! Impoverished!"

"Yes; we have been forced to part with our horses and dismiss servants. Surely, therefore, it would not be the part of a friend to lure Pendarves to the risk of losing a hundred pounds a night. My lord, I throw myself on your generosity, and say no more."

"You have said enough; and the admirable wife's prudence shall make amends for the rashness of her husband. Besides, I am so flattered by your confidence in me! At last to find you considering me as a friend, confiding in me as a friend, and asking assistance from me as a friend! I protest I am more flattered by your friendship than I should be by the love of twenty other women.—Take my revenge! No, indeed. He shall keep his hundred pounds; 'I will none of it.'"

"Hold; not so: play with him this evening; but whether you win or lose, declare you will play no more. I would rather you should win back the money, and even more; for it may be dangerous to Seymour to feel himself enriched by play, and he may go on, though not with you: but after this evening forbear."

"Excellent! excellent! O that ever I should come hither! I shall be a lost man: for I shall fancy it so charming a thing to have a wife to take care of me, that I shall marry, and find too late there is only one Helen Pendarves!—But tell me, do you wish me to go away to-day, to-morrow, or when—in order to put you out of your pain?"

"By no means: I rely implicitly on your promise; and I owe it to you to assure you, Lord Charles, that your company is most welcome to me, and that I shall not forget your kindness."

I now offered him my hand, which he was going to kiss; but suddenly dropping it, he said, "No—no; take it away.—You must not be too good to me: I am not a man to be trusted with much flattery and kindness; for, ugly as I am, the women have so spoiled me, that I may fancy even you are kind to me '*pour l'amour de mes beaux yeux*,'"* opening his gooseberry eyes as wide as he could, and in a manner so irresistibly comic, that I gave way to that laughter which he delighted to excite. I therefore entered my mother's parlour looking more animated than usual, and she looked most graciously on my companion as the cause: but she seemed displeased when she found Pendarves was gone to Oswald Lodge, and had left me to entertain his noble guest.

I now took my departure, having some poor cottagers to visit. When I came back, I saw by the thoughtful brow and flushed cheek of both, that their conversation had been of a very interesting nature; and I also saw that there was an air of confiding intimacy between them, which I never expected to see between two persons so little accordant in habits and sentiments.

But every human being has a capacity for good as well as evil, and the great difference in us all, results chiefly, I believe, from the favourable or unfavourable circumstances in which we are placed. Lord Charles had been so circumstanced, that his capacity for evil alone had been cultivated; and till he knew my mother and myself, he had never met in women any other description of companions than those whom he courted, conquered, and despised,—and those whose rigid morals and disagreeable manners threw him haughtily at a distance, and made him hate virtue for their sakes. But now, trusted, noticed, liked by women of a different kind, his good feelings were awakened; and while *with us*, he really

* For the love of my fine eyes.

was the amiable being which he might, differently situated, have always been.

"I love to be with you," said he to us: "your influence is so beneficial over me, and you wrap me in such a pleasing illusion! for while I am with you, I fancy myself as good as you are; but when I go away, I shall be just as bad again.—Well; have you nothing to say in reply? How disappointed I am! for I thought you would in mercy have exclaimed, 'Then stay here for ever!' Would I could."

And indeed, when he did go, I missed him. But to return to the place whence I digressed. Pendarves came home time enough to take a ride with Lord Charles, but he took care to let him see that he expected more attention from him. That evening he challenged my husband to piquet; and having won back nearly the whole of what he had lost, positively declined playing any more: and, much to Seymour's vexation, he would not play again while he staid. The second night's performances at Oswald Lodge now took place; but though Lord Charles staid to be present at them, he could not help expressing his astonishment to me, when alone, that a modest, respectable gentlewoman like myself should ever have joined in them, and that my husband should have permitted it.

"It is very well for these fiddling, frolicking, fun-hunting Oswalds," said he, "to fill their house with persons and things of this sort, and rant and roar, and kick and jump, and make fools and tumblers of themselves, and such of their guests as like it: but never did I expect to see the dignified and retiring Helen Pendarves exhibiting her person on a stage, and levelling herself to a Lady Martindale. As your friend, your adoring friend, I tell you, that such an exhibition degrades you."

"It would do so were it my *choice*, but it is my *necessity*; and the fulfilment of a painful duty *exalts* rather than degrades."

"Duty!"

"Yes; my husband required me to act, and I obeyed."

"I understand you. Oh! what a rash, ill-judging being he is! But I beg your pardon, and will say no more. Yet I must add, *you* are *justified*; but alas! what can justify *him?*"

This conversation did not give me any additional courage to undertake and execute my task; especially as I had now reputation as an actress to lose, and other circumstances increased my timidity.—Lady Martindale had purposely reserved all her powers for this evening, and, as she herself said, she was very glad to have her performance witnessed by such a judge as Lord Charles Belmour—a man whose opinion, she knew, was looked up to in all circles as decisive, with regard to beauty, grace, and talents. No wonder, therefore, that to throw her spells round him was become the object of her ambition. Hitherto he had avoided her, and she seemed conscious that he did not admire her. Her only hope was, I believe, therefore, to charm him at once by a *coup de théâtre;* and while she convinced Pendarves that for *him* alone she would exert her various powers, her fascinating graces were in reality aimed at Lord Charles: so I thought and suspected,—and though jealousy *blinds*, it also very often *enlightens*. She was to begin the entertainments by acting a French proverb with a French gentleman, an *émigré*, who was staying at the house; and having no doubt of her transcendant powers, I felt very reluctant to enter into competition with her. Yet, was not the prize for which I strove my husband's admiration? But then was I not degrading myself from the dignity of a wife and a private gentlewoman, by putting myself into a competition like this? The question was difficult to answer, and while I was thus ruminating, the curtain drew up.

I shall not describe her performance; suffice, that the exhibition was perfect. The dialogue was epigrammatic, and the scenes too short to let the attention flag. Every word, every gesture, every look told; and the curtain dropped amidst the loudest applauses.

I could only see from the side-scene; but I saw enough to make me feel my own inferiority, and I went on for Letitia Hardy in a tremour of spirits of which I was quite ashamed; nor could the kindest of the audience applaud me, except from pity and the wish to encourage me; while I saw that Lord Charles could not even do that, and sat silent, and I thought uneasy. However, I recovered myself in the masquerade-scene, though my voice when I sang still trembled with emotion; and now I was overwhelmed with plaudits, and even Lord Charles seemed pleased; for, as I was masked, I could examine the audience.

Still the play went off languidly, after the lively petite piece, and I saw I had mortified my husband's vanity, which my first performance had gratified.

Much impatience was expressed for the next entertainment, which was Rousseau's Pygmalion. Pygmalion, by the French Marquis; the Statue, by Lady Martindale. This was received with delight; and I saw that the beautiful statue, whose exquisite proportions were any thing but concealed by the dress she wore, absorbed completely the attention of Pendarves; and when she left the stage, apparently exhausted, how different were the look and manner with which he led her to her dressing-room, to those with which he had so handed me!

"Why, why," said I to myself, "did I *attempt* a comparison, in which I was sure to fail?" But if I had erred, I had meant well, and my mother had approved my conduct, and that must console me under my want of success; for, instead of winning Seymour back, I now saw that, feeling my rival's superiority over me, he would be more her slave than ever.

The whole concluded with a ballet of action, a monodrame, by Lady Martindale, to which I was too uncomfortable to attend; but what I saw I thought admirable. She pretended to be overcome with fatigue when it was ended, and fell into my husband's arms, who in his alarm, called me to her assistance. I went; but her lip retained its glowing hue, and I saw in her illness nothing but a *new attitude*, and that the statue was now *recumbent*. Having been long enough contemplated in this posture, she opened her eyes, fixed them with a dying look on Pendarves, and then desired him to lead her to her apartment; whence she returned, attired in a splendid mantle, which seemed in modesty thrown over her statue dress, but which coquettishly displayed occasionally the form it seemed intended to hide.

I never saw Lord Charles so disconcerted as he was during the whole of the time. He could not bear to praise the heroine of the evening, yet he felt that praise was her due. Nor could he bear either to find fault with or to praise *me*. In this dilemma, he seemed to think it was best to be silent; and drawing himself up, he entrenched himself in the consciousness that he was *Lord Charles Belmour*. But while Lady Martindale leaned on Seymour on one side, and I on the other, as we were awaiting the summons to supper, surrounded by our flatterers, one glance at my dejected countenance brought back his kinder feelings, and turning to my mother, who held his arm, he said, "Shall I tell your fair daughter how enchanted I was with the masquerade scene?"

"I assure you," said Seymour, "Helen did not do herself justice to-night; she did not act as well as she *can act*."

"I should have been very sorry, so much do I esteem her, to have seen her act *better*," was his cold reply. "Would you have your wife, Pendarves, perform as well as a professional person, and as if she had been brought up on the stage?"

"I would wish my wife to do well whatever she undertakes," replied Seymour.

"And so she does, and so she *did*; but if you do not love her the better (as I *am sure you do*) for the graceful *timidity* which she displayed, I am sure I could not esteem you."

Lady Martindale, who watched his every look, now bit her lip, and Seymour did not look pleased. My mother owned afterwards, that what with pinching Lord Charles's arm, to see how Lord and Lady Martindale both were confused by the *first* part of his speech, and squeezing it affectionately with delight at the last, she is very sure Lord Charles carried her marks with him to London. I, too, could scarcely keep the grateful tears from flowing down my cheeks, which his well-timed kindness brought into my eyes; but I saw that my expression was not lost upon him.

Seymour led Lady Martindale to the head

of the supper-table, and Lord Charles, on account of his rank, was forced to sit next her.

"Painful pre-eminence!" he whispered to my mother, who, as I was one of the queens of the night, insisted on my taking her place on the other side. Lord Martindale seated himself next me, and Seymour took the seat vacant by Lady Martindale. As Lord Charles scarcely noticed her, except as far as civility commanded, Lady Martindale soon turned her back on him, and Seymour and she seemed to forget any one else was present.

Lord Charles endeavoured, by the most unremitting attentions, to conceal from me what must, he knew, distress me. But he could not do it: I heard every whisper of their softened voices, and I dare say my uneasy countenance was a complete and whimsical contrast to that of Lord Martindale, who seemed perfectly easy under circumstances which would have distressed most men, and talked and laughed with every one in his turn.

The lord and lady of the feast, who were never tired of exhibitions, now began their usual demands on the talents of their guests, and were importunate in soliciting several of them to sing—a custom which I usually think "more honoured in the breach than the observance;" but on this occasion it was welcome to me, especially as I knew that it must for a time interrupt Seymour's attention to Lady Martindale. But as the hypochondriac, when he reads a book on diseases, always finds his own symptoms in every case before him, so I, in the then existing state of my feelings, always brought home every thing I heard or read to my own heart; and two of the songs which were sung that night accorded so well with my own state of mind, that I felt the tears come into my eyes as I listened; and during the following one Pendarves sighed so audibly, that I imagined *he* felt great sympathy with the sentiments; and that idea increased my sufferings:—

SONG.

Oh that I could recall the day
　When all my hours to thee were given—
And, as I gazed my soul away,
　Thou wert my treasure, world, and heaven!

Then time on noiseless pinions flew,
　And life like one bright morning beam'd;
Then love around us roses threw,
　Which ever fresh and fragrant seem'd.
And are these moments gone for ever?
And can they ne'er return? No—NEVER.

For, oh! that cruel traitor, Time,
　Although he might unheeded move,
Bore off our Youth's luxuriant prime,
　And also stole the bloom of LOVE.

Yet still the thought of raptures past
　Shall gild life's dull remaining store,
As sinking suns a splendour cast
　On scenes their presence lights no more.

But are those raptures gone for ever?
And will they ne'er return? No—NEVER.

The other song was only in unison with my feelings in the last lines of the last verse. Still, while my morbid fancy made me consider them as the expression of my own sentiments, I listened with such a tell-tale countenance, that my delicacy was wounded; for I saw that my emotion was visible to those who sat opposite to me.

The song was as follows:

FAIREST, SWEETEST, DEAREST.
A Song.

Say, by what name can I impart
　My sense, dear girl, of what thou art?
　Nay, though to frown thou darest,
I'll say thou art of girls the pride,
And though that modest lip may chide,
　Mary! I'll call thee "FAIREST."

Yet no—that word can but express
The soft and winning loveliness
　In which the sight thou meetest:
But not thy heart, thy temper too,
So good, so sweet,—Ha! that will do!
　Mary! I'll call thee "SWEETEST."

But "fairest—sweetest," vain would be,
To speak the love I feel for thee:
　Why smilest thou as thou hearest?
"Because," she cried, "one little name
Is all I wish from thee to claim—
　That precious name is 'DEAREST.'"

You will not, I conclude, imagine that I remember these songs only from having heard them that night, especially as they have very little merit; but the truth is, I was so pleased with them, because I fancied them applicable to my own feelings, that I requested them of the gentlemen who sung, and they were given to me.

Lord Charles meanwhile listened to the singing with great impatience, as he had enough of the entertainment, and still more of the company, which was very numerous, and by no means as select as it had been before. Indeed, at one table were many persons in whom the observant eye of Lord Charles discovered associates whose evident vulgarity made him feel himself out of his place. However, he could not presume to break up the party; and as our indefatigable host and hostess still kept forcing the talents of their guests into their service, song succeeded to song, and duet to duet. From one of the latter, however, sung by a lady and gentleman, I at length derived a soothing feeling, and in one moment, an observation of Seymour's, with, as I fancied, a correspondent and *intended* expression of countenance, removed a load from my heart, and my clouded brow became, consciously to myself, unclouded again.

The words of this healing duet were as follows:—

DUET.

Say, why art thou pensive, beloved of my heart?
Indeed I am happy wherever thou art:

21 *

My eyes, I confess, towards others may rove,
But never, believe me, with wishes of love.
And trust me, however my glances may roam,
Of them, and my heart, THOU ALONE ART THE
HOME.

ANSWER.

Perhaps I am wrong, thus dejected to be:
But my faithful eyes never wander from thee:
On beauty and youth I unconsciously gaze;
No thought, no emotion, in me they can raise;
And ah! if thine eyes get the habit to roam,
How can I be certain they'll EVER COME HOME!

"Oh! trust thy own charms! See the bee as he flies,
And visits each blossom of exquisite dyes;
There culls of their sweetness some store for his cell:
But short are his visits, and prompt his farewell:
For still he remembers, howe'er he may roam,
That hoard of delight which AWAITS HIM AT HOME.

"Then trust me, however thy Henry may roam,
I feel my best pleasures await me at HOME."

I'll try to believe, howsoever thou roam,
Thy heart's dearest pleasures await thee at home.

"That is a charming duet," cried Seymour, when it was ended; then leaning behind Lady Martindale and Lord Charles, and calling to me, he said, with a look from which my conscious eye shrunk, "Oh! Helen, I admire the sentiment of that duet. I think, my love, we will get it: we should sing it *con amore*—should we not?" I could not look at him as I replied, "*I* could, I am *sure*."

"Silly girl!" he added, in a low and kind tone; "and so, I am *sure*, could I."

I then ventured to raise my eyes to his; and his expression was such, that I felt quite a different creature, and was able to enjoy the rest of the evening.

But why do I enter into these minute and unimportant details? Let me efface them — but no; perhaps they may chance to meet the eyes of some whose hearts have felt the anxieties and the vicissitudes of mine, and to them they may be interesting.

Lord Martindale was now requested to favour the company with a song, and with great good-nature he instantly complied; while Lord Charles whispered across to my mother,— "What a disgrace that fellow is to the peerage!"

"By his vices I *grant* you," replied my mother, "but not by his obliging compliance."

Lord Charles shrugged up his shoulders, and was about to reply, when—Silence was vociferated rather angrily by the lady of the house, who had not been blind to the airs which, as she said, Lord Charles had given himself the whole evening. Lord Martindale, as may be supposed, was greatly applauded, on the same principle as that mentioned by the poet with regard to noble authors:

"For if a Lord once own the happy lines,
How the wit brightens! how the taste refines!"

And the noisy expressions of admiration which rewarded a very mediocre performance did not increase the good-humour of our noble guest, against whom I saw an attack preparing at the bottom of the table. At length, a very pretty girl, who had sung with considerable skill, tried to engage the attention of Lord Charles; and finding "Sir" was not sufficient, she added, "Mr. Belmour, sir!" But some one whispered, "He is a lord;" on which she said, "Dear me! Well, then, my lord, Lord Belmour;" and Lord Charles turned toward the pretty speaker, while a half-muttered "Vulgar animal!" was audible to my mother and myself, and formed a ludicrous contrast to the affectedly respectful attention and bent head with which he had to observe. But when he found that the young lady was requesting him to *sing*, and that she declared she had a claim on him, his expression of mingled *hauteur*, astonishment, and indignation, was highly comic, and we, who knew him, were eagerly expecting his answer, when we heard him say, having bowed and smirked his hand affectedly to his heart at the same time, "With the greatest pleasure in life;—which wine, claret or champagne?"

"Dear me," cried the young lady, "I did not ask you to drink, but to sing, my lord."

"Oh! Champagne; very good. — Carry a glass to that young lady;" but she indignantly rejected it, and repeated her request.

"I beg pardon," replied the impracticable Lord Charles. "I thought you said champagne; then take claret to the young lady," who in vain exerted her voice. He remained quite deaf, holding his ear like a deaf person, much to the amusement of the company, and the confusion of the fair suppliant, who had been encouraged by the admiring glances which Lord Charles had till now bestowed on her, to think that any request from her would have been attended to.

Thus far Lord Charles's endangered dignity had come off with flying colours, as it was no great affront to be requested to sing by a pretty girl, even though she had told him that he had a *singing face*, and *looked like a singer;* for the turn which he had given to her application got the laugh on his side, and he was very sure that she would not so presume again. But he was not to be let off so easily; for Mr. Oswald, who, being almost "as drunk as a lord," felt himself quite as great as one, now came behind Lord Charles, and giving him a sounding blow across the back, exclaimed with an oath, "Come, now, *Belmour*, there is a good fellow, do sing, for I have heard you are a comical dog when you like."

If a look could have annihilated, that instant would have the little fat man have disappeared from off the face of the earth. The glance of Lord Charles was powerless even to *wound* Mr. Oswald;—and he was equally unmoved when, scorning even to answer his importunate host, our friend suddenly addressed my mother, saying, "I think, Mrs. Pendarves, you desired me to call your carriage?"

"You are mistaken, my lord," replied my mother, with a reproving look which he well understood; and his tormentor was going to assail him again, when Seymour, to relieve Lord Charles, drew him into conversation; and I had just advised his still-irritated guest to remember that he was intoxicated, when our attention was attracted to a conversation between Mrs. Oswald and another lady, of which Lord Charles was the subject; and it was evident that Mrs. Oswald spoke of him in no friendly tone.

"Yes, my lord," said she, "you may look; we were certainly talking of your lordship."

"You do me much honour, madam."

"That is as it may be, my lord; but I was trying to do you justice, for my friend said it was *pride* that prevented your singing; but *I* said (and here she raised her voice to a shriller and more ludicrous pitch than usual) yes, I said, says I, "That is *impossible*, my dear; it cannot be *pride;* for if a real *peer* of the realm," says I, "the *real thing*, condescends to sing and amuse the company, surely Lord Charles Belmour need not be above it, who is only a *commonly called*, you know."

Instantly, to my consternation, and afterwards to his own, Lord Charles, thrown off his guard by this sarcasm, *echoed* her last words, and gave her tone and manner so exactly, that the effect upon the company was irresistible, and a general laugh ensued;— which, to do him justice, shocked more than it gratified the self-condemned mimic, who could only for a moment be provoked to violate the rules of good-breeding: and he was completely subdued, when Mrs. Oswald, with a degree of forbearance and good-humour which exalted her in my esteem, observed, "Well, my lord, you have condescended to exert your talent for mimicry, though you would not sing; and though it was at my expense, I am grateful to you, as you have contributed to amuse my company."

"Admirably replied!" exclaimed my mother.

"Excellent, excellent, bravo!" cried Pendarves;—while Lord Charles, admonished, penitent, and ashamed, was not slow to redeem himself from the sort of disgrace which he had incurred. Rising gracefully, and bowing his head on his clasped hands, he solicited her pardon for the liberty which her evident good-nature had emboldened him to take, declaring at the same time, that if she forgave him, it was long before he should forgive himself.

Mrs. Oswald, who was really as kind-hearted as she seemed, readily granted the pardon which he asked, and he respectfully pressed her offered hand to his lips. He did more; for while the carriages were called, he suddenly disappeared, and in a moment we could have fancied ourselves at the door of Drurylane or Covent-Garden; for the offered services of link-boys, the cries of "Coach, coach," and "Here your honour," with all the different sounds, were heard in the hall; and while the guests listened delighted to this new and unexpected entertainment, the Oswalds were, I saw, evidently gratified at finding that it proceeded from the talent of Lord Charles. O the unnecessary humiliation to which pride exposes itself! Had he civilly, though firmly refused the young lady's and Mr. Oswald's request to sing, and not discovered in the evening his haughty contempt for the company and his host, or insulted his hostess, he needed not to have condescended to an expiatory exhibition, from which under other circumstances his pride would have properly revolted.

Thus ended this to me disagreeable evening, which extended far into the morning. The drive home was pleasant; for Lord Charles having reconciled himself to himself by his ample *amende honorable*, and by the generous candour with which he received our reproofs, thought he was privileged to indulge his less amiable feelings by turning some of the company into ridicule, and exhibiting them to the very life before us. I must own that I again felt an ungenerous pleasure in some part of the entertainment, namely his mimicry of Lady Martindale, which I vainly endeavoured to subdue, and I was glad that, as Pendarves rode on the box, he did not witness my degradation. I must add, that both my mother and myself were gratified to observe that Lord Charles forbore to mimic our kind but vulgar host and hostess; and my mother took care to let him know indirectly that his delicacy was not lost upon her.

Another performance was fixed for that day week; the original Letitia Hardy, however, was expected, and most gladly did I offer to resign my part to her. Still, I was mortified to see with how little concern Pendarves heard me offer my resignation, and saw it accepted. Alas! not even Lord Charles's and my mother's joy at my being removed from a situation which they thought unworthy of me, could reconcile me to his indifference on the subject.

The next day Lord Charles was to leave us; but I saw that his departure was more welcome to my husband than to my mother and myself. In the morning he had requested Pendarves to walk with him round the grounds, and they returned, I observed, with disturbed countenances.

Lord Charles then called, and sat some time with my mother. What passed between them I do not know; but their parting was even affectionate, and his with me was distinguished from all our other partings by a degree of emotion for which I could not account.

"How I shall miss you!" said I, softened by his dejection.

"Thank you! I can better bear to leave you now:" and springing into his carriage he drove off, and I felt forlorn; for I felt that I had lost a friend: and I also felt that I wanted one who, like him, had some check over my husband.

What more shall I say of this painful period of my life? for which however, painful as it was, I would gladly have exchanged that which soon followed; one day was a transcript of the other. Pendarves, ever good-natured and kind while he was at home, seemed to think that he was thereby justified in leaving me continually; but, as I was not of that opinion, to use a French phrase, *je dépérissois à vue d'œil;* and though I affected to be cheerful, my mother saw that my feelings were undermining my existence. But not even to her would I complain of my husband, and she respected my silence too much to wish me to break it. However, *she* was with me,—she, I felt, never would forsake me, or love me less; and while I had her, I was far from being completely miserable. Alas! what was she not to me? friend, counsellor, comforter!

But the decree was gone forth, and even her I was doomed to resign!

Not long after Lord Charles had quitted us, I perceived a visible alteration in my mother's appearance. I saw that she ate a little, that she was very soon fatigued, and that her fine spirits were gone. I had no doubt but that she fretted for my anxieties. I therefore laboured the more to convince her that I was not as uneasy as she thought me.

But how vainly did I try to veil my heart from her penetrating glance! If there be such a thing as the art of divination, it is possessed by the eagle eye of interested affection, and that *was hers.*

My mother saw all my secret struggles; she pitied, she resented their cause; and I have sometimes feared that she *sunk* under them.

One morning, Pendarves on his return from Oswald Lodge came in with a very animated countenance, and told us that a new description of amusement was introduced there, namely, *archery*, and he must beg me to go with him the next day, and learn to be an archer: "Lady Martindale," cried he, "already shoots like Diana herself."

"The only resemblance, I should think," said my mother, "which she has to Diana. But what do you say to this proposal, Helen? *I* must take leave to say that, as *your mother*, you can never go to Oswald Lodge again with my consent on *any* terms: and to engage in this new competition, oh! never, never!"

"And why not, madam? There is nothing indelicate in such an exhibition; and I own my pride in Helen, as a husband, made me wish to see her fine form exhibited in the graceful action of shooting at a target. Besides, as I really wish if possible to associate her in all my amusements, I was delighted to think this new pursuit would have led her to join me in my visits to the Lodge, and I am really desirous to know on what grounds you object to her obliging me."

"On account of the company there. Mr. and Mrs. Oswald are weak, vain people, fond of courting persons of quality; and so as they can but be intimate with a Lord and Lady, they care not of what description they are. This Lord Martindale is, I find, a man not much noticed by his equals; and as to Lady Martindale, the woman who could so expose her person in the dress of the Statue is not a fit companion for my daughter, nor your wife."

"You are severe, madam; but what says Helen?"

"That my mother does not make sufficient allowances for the difference of manners and ideas between a French and an English woman; and that dress which shocks us in the former does not necessarily prove incorrectness of conduct."

"Incorrectness of conduct! and can your mother possibly suppose I would introduce my wife to a woman whom I knew to be incorrect in her conduct?"

"No, Seymour, no: I do you more justice. But it is my duty to inform you that it is suspected this person is Lord Martindale's mistress only, not his wife."

"*Not* his wife!" interrupted Seymour.

"No, so I am informed. As to him, you know his character is so infamous that one can wonder at nothing he does; and *he* has been suspected of being a spy for the French convention, as well as the lady."

"Madam," said Seymour, "I thought you had been above listening to tales like these, and I cannot think myself justified in acting upon them. On the contrary, by taking my wife to the Lodge, I think it right to show my disregard of them, especially as by staying away, and by her distant manner when there, Helen has already injured the character of Lady Martindale, and made even my attentions to her the source of calumny. This the afflicted lady told me with tears and lamentations, and Helen's renewed visits can alone repair the injury her absence has done."

"So, then, *this* is the real reason of your wishing to make Helen a sharer in your amusements, and to exhibit her fine form to advantage!" exclaimed my mother, indignantly. "But, Mr. Pendarves, if your constant visits are injurious to the fame of this afflicted lady, you know your remedy—*discontinue* them; for never, with my consent, shall my virtuous daughter lend her assistance to shield any one from the infamy which they deserve."

"Deserve, madam!" cried Seymour, as indignant as she was: "*repeat* that, and, spite of the love and reverence I bear you, I shall exert a husband's lawful authority, and see who dares dispute it."

"*Not I*," she replied, folding her arms submissively on her breast, "and still less that poor trembling girl. No, Pendarves, my only resource now is supplication and entreaty: and I conjure you, by the dear name of your beloved mother, and by the memory of past fond and endearing circumstances, and *hours*, to grant the prayer of a *dying woman*, and not to force your wife to this abode of revelry and riot. I feel my days are already numbered; and when I am taken from you, *bitter* will be your recollections, if you refuse, my son, and soothing if you grant my prayer. I *know* you, Seymour, and I know that you cannot do any great cruelty without great remorse."

It was some moments before Pendarves could speak; at length he said "Your request *alone* would have been sufficient, without your calling up such agonizing ideas. Helen, my best love, tell your mother you shall *never* go to Oswald Lodge again." He then put his handkerchief to his eyes, and rushed out of the room.

"The foolish boy's heart is in the right place still," said my mother, giving way to tears, but smiling at the same time.

But I, alas! could neither smile nor speak. She had called herself a dying woman; and through the rest of the day I could do nothing but look at and watch her, and go out of the room to weep; and my night was past in wretchedness and prayer.

The next day I found my husband cold and sullen in manner; and I suspected that, having engaged to bring me to Oswald Lodge, he was mortified and ashamed to go thither without me, and would, I doubted not, make some excuse for my staying away which was not strictly true.

No one could feel more strongly or more virtuously than Pendarves: but good feelings, unless they are under the guard of strict principles, are subject to run away instantly when summoned by the voice of pleasure and of error: and before he set off for the archery ground, he told me he sincerely repented his promise to my mother.

I did not reply, but shook my head mournfully.

"Psha!" said he, "that ever a fine woman like you, Helen, should wish to appear in her husband's eyes little better than a constant *memento mori!* Helen, an arrow cannot fly as far in a wet as in a dry day; and a laughing eye hits where a tearful one fails. You see I already steal my metaphors from my new study. But good-bye, sweet Helen! and when I return let me find you a little less dismal."

This was not the way to make me so; nor were his daily visits at this seducing house, which began in the morning, and lasted till he came home to dress for dinner: he then returned thither to stay till evening. At last he chose to dress there, and he did not return till night; nor, perhaps, would he have done that, had there not been some house-breaking in our neighbourhood, and he was afraid of leaving the house so ill-defended. I think that pique and resentment had some share in making him thus increase in the length as well as constancy of his visits: for I saw but too clearly that he continued offended with my poor mother; and I doubted not but that he had owned she was the cause of my refusal to visit at the house, and that Lady Martindale had added force to this bitter feeling.

But he soon lost all resentment against my beloved parent.—Not very long after his painful conversation with her, I was summoned to her, as she was too ill to rise, and had sent for medical advice.

"Go for my husband instantly," cried I.

"My mistress forbade me go for him," replied her faithful Juan, (one of my father's manumised slaves,) "and I cannot go."

"Then she does not think very ill of *herself?*" said I.

"No, but I think very bad indeed."

And when I saw her, my fears were as strongly excited.

"I am going, I am going *fast*, my child," said she: "but I do not wish to have Pendarves sent for yet: I wish to have you a little while without any divided feelings, and *all my own* once more; when *he* comes, the wife will seduce away the child."

"How can you think so!" said I, giving way to an agony of grief; "and how can you be so barbarous as to tell me you are dying!"

"My poor child! I wished long ago to prepare you, but you would not be prepared. For your sake I still wished to live. You would have *better* spared me years ago, Helen! But this is cruel; and I will try to behave better."

As soon as her physician arrived, and had felt her pulse, I saw by his countenance that he was considerably alarmed; and the first feeling of my heart was to send for my husband, for him on whom I had been accustomed to rely in the hour of affliction. But I *dared* not, after what had passed; and I tried to rally all the powers of my mind to meet the impending evil, while I raised my thoughts to Him who listens to the cry of the orphan.

The physician had promised to come again in the evening. He did so; and then I learnt that there was *indeed* no hope; and I also learnt, by the agony of that moment, that I had in reality hoped till then; and, more like an automaton than aught alive, I sat by the now fast-exhausting sufferer.

Pendarves returned at night, and heard with anguish uncontrollable, not only that my mother was dying, but had forbidden that he should be sent for; and he arrived at the house in a state little short of distraction, nor could he be kept from the chamber of death.

His countenance, as he stood at the foot of the bed, told all the agony of his mind. They tell me so, for I saw him not; I could only see that object whom I was soon to behold no more!

My mother knew him; read, no doubt, all his wild wan look expressed; and smiling kindly, held out her hand to him. He was instantly on his knees by her bedside; and she seemed, from the look she gave him, to feel all the maternal love for him revive which she had experienced through life.

Your husband, my dear friend, now came to perform his interesting duty, and we left her alone with him.

Oh! what a night succeeded! but Pendarves felt more than I. My faculties were benumbed: I had made such unnatural efforts for some time past to appear cheerful, while my heart was breaking, that I was too much exhausted to be able to endure this new demand on my fortitude and strength; therefore already was that merciful stupor coming over me, which saved, I firmly believe, both my life and my reason.

My mother frequently, during that night, joined my hand in that of Pendarves, grasped them thus united, while her eyes were raised to heaven in prayer, but spoke not. At length, however, just as the last moment was approaching, she faltered out—"Seymour, be kind, be very kind to my poor child; she has only you now."

He replied by clasping me to his breast; and in one moment more, all was over!

You know what followed; you know that for many weeks I was blessedly unconscious of every thing, and that I lay between death and life under the dominion of fever. My first return of consciousness and of speech showed itself thus:—I heard voices below, and recognised them, no doubt, as female voices; for I drew back the curtain, and asked my mother's faithful Alice whose voice I heard. But the joy my speaking gave the poor creature was instantly damped, for I added—"But I conclude it is my mother's voice, and I dare say she will be here presently."

Alice, bursting into tears, replied—"Your blessed mother never can come now."

"Oh, but by and by will do:" and I closed my eyes again.

Alice now ran down to call my husband, and tell him what had passed. The voices I heard were those of Mrs. Oswald and Lady Martindale, who had called every day to inquire for me; and Pendarves had been this day prevailed upon to go down to them. But he bitterly repented his complaisance when he found I had heard them talking; though he rejoiced in my restored hearing, which had seemed quite gone. He hastily, therefore, dismissed his visiters, and resumed his station by my bedside. I knew him, and spoke to him; but damped all his satisfaction by asking for my mother, and wondering where she was. He could not answer me, and was doubtful what he ought to reply when he recovered himself.

At this moment the physician entered; and hearing what had passed, declared that the sooner he could make me understand what had happened, and shed tears (for I had shed none yet,) the sooner I should recover; and he advised his beginning to do it directly.

Accordingly, when I again asked for her he said—"Do you not see my black coat, Helen! and do you not remember our loss?"

"Oh, yes; but I thought our mourning for the dear child was over."

"You see!" said Pendarves mournfully.

The physician replied—"Till her memory is restored, though her life is spared, a cure is far distant; but persevere."

In a fortnight I was able to take air; but I still wondered where my mother was, though I soon forgot her again.

But one day Pendarves asked me if I would go and visit the grave of my child, which I had not visited for some time. I thankfully complied, and he dragged me in a garden-chair to the church-door.

It was not without considerable emotion that he supported me to that marble slab which now covered my mother as well as my child, and I caught some of his trembling agitation.

"Look there, my poor Helen!" said he.

I did look, and read the name of my child.

"Look lower yet."

I did so, and the words "Julia Pendarves," with the sad *et cetera*, met my view, and seemed to restore my shattered comprehension.

In a moment the whole agonizing truth rushed upon my mind; and throwing myself on the cold stone, I called upon my departed parent, and wept till I was deluged in tears, and had sobbed myself into the stillness of exhaustion.

"Thank God! thou art restored, my beloved, and all will yet, I trust, be well," said my husband, as he bore me away.

From that time my memory returned, and with it so acute a feeling of what I had lost, that I fear I was ungrateful enough to regret my imbecility.

I now insisted on hearing details of all that had occurred since my illness; and I found that my uncle and aunt had come down to attend the funeral of my mother, and that Lord Charles had attended uninvited, to pay her that tribute of respect—nor had he returned to London, till my life was declared out of danger. How deeply I felt this attention! I also heard that the ladies at the Lodge pestered my husband with letters, to prevail on him to spare his sensibility the pain of following my lost parent to the grave: but that, however he shrunk from the task, he had treated their request with the utmost disregard, saying, that if he had no other motive, the certainty that he was doing what *I* should have wished, was sufficient.

When I was quite restored to strength, both of mind and body, Pendarves gave me the key of my mother's papers, which he had carefully sealed up. My mother left no will, as she wished me to inherit every thing; but in a little paper directed to Pendarves, she desired that an income might be settled on Juan and Alice, which would make them comfortable and independent for life; that her friends, the De Waldens, might have some memorial of her given to them; and that Lord Charles might have her travelling writing-desk.

Oh! what overwhelming feelings I endured while looking over papers, containing a sketch of her life—her reflections and prayers, when I married Pendarves—a character of Lady Helen, of her husband, and of my father—and many fragments, all indicative of a mother's love and a mother's anxiety. But tender sorrow was suspended by curiosity, when I found one letter from Ferdinand de Walden! It was evidently written in answer to one from her, in which she had described me as suffering deeply, but, on principle, trying to appear cheerful, and for her sake dutifully trying to conceal from her the agony of my heart. What *else* she had said, was very evident from the part of the letter which I transcribe—translating it from the French:—

"Yes! you only, I believe, do me justice. I should have been a more devoted husband than Pendarves, having my affections built, I trust, on a firmer foundation than this—*viz.* a purifying faith, and its result, pure habits. Still, I know not how to excuse his conduct towards such an angel! for, oh! that faded cheek, and that shrunk form—that dejection of spirits from a mother's sorrows which seem to have alienated *him*, would have endeared her to me still more fondly——"

I had resolution enough, my dear friend, to pause here, and *read no more;* nay, distrusting my own strength, I had the courage to commit the dangerous letter to the flames—and that was, indeed, an exertion of duty.

I shall pass lightly and rapidly over the next few months. My husband gradually resumed his intercourse at the Lodge, while I, to conceal as much as possible his neglect, paid and received visits; and Mrs. Ridley and my aunt were by turns my guests, for I had now lost my dread of the latter. She had nothing to tell but what I knew already, except that she believed my husband more criminal than I did or could think him, and that I positively forbade her ever to *name* him to me again. I also visited you, and did all I could to fly from a feeling of conscious desolation which was ever present to me since I lost my mother. In all other afflictions, I had her to rely upon—I had her to soothe and to comfort me; but who had I to console me for the loss of her? on whose never to be abated tenderness could I rely? Other ties, if destroyed, may be formed again; but we can have parents only *once*—and I had lost my mother, my sole surviving parent, at a moment when I wanted her most. Still, I roused myself from my lethargy of grief, and "sorrowed" *not* like "one without hope." But the misery of disappointed and wounded affections preyed on me while tenderer woes slumbered, and my health continued to fade, my youth to decay.

My kind aunt and Mrs. Ridley were both just come on a visit to me, when Pendarves signified his intention of accompanying his friends on a tour to the Lakes. He said his health had suffered much from his anxiety during my illness, and he thought the journey would do him good.

"Then take your wife a journey," cried my aunt bluntly: "she wants it more than you do."

"She will not accompany my friends," replied he; "and my *word* is pledged to go with them."

"Is a pledge given to friends more sacred than duty to a wife, Mr. Seymour Pendarves?"

"Is it a husband's duty never to stir without his wife, madam?"

"My dear aunt, you forget," said I, "how unfit I am to travel: quiet and home suit me best."

"It is well they do," said my aunt, and Seymour left the room.

I will pass over the time that intervened before Seymour's departure: suffice that I tried to attribute his still frequent absences from home to his dislike of his aunt's society; and in the meanwhile I masked an aching heart in smiles, that no one might have the authority of my dejected spirits to found an accusation of my husband upon.

At length the day of Seymour's departure arrived, and we had an affectionate and on my side a tearful parting: but I recovered myself soon; and though I deeply felt the unkindness of his leaving me after my recent affliction, I declared it the wisest thing he could do, and that I hoped he would find me fat and cheerful on his return. But I saw that I did not make converts of my *auditors;* and that Lord Charles Belmour, who called to inquire after my health, absolutely *started* when he found that Seymour was gone away on a journey. I could not bear this, but left the room; for I could not—would not, either by look or word, blame my husband; and I could not bear to observe that he was blamed by others.

At the end of three weeks, my uncle came down to fetch his wife; and I heard, with a satisfaction which I could not conceal, that my uncle hoped he should be able to prove that Lady Martindale, as she was called, was a spy of the Convention, and that he could get her sent out of the country on the Alien Bill — for that she was undoubtedly the mistress, not the wife, of Lord Martindale. I also learned that Lord Charles had been indefatigable in using his exertions and his interest to effect this purpose, in hopes, as my aunt said, of opening my husband's eyes; and she thought, when he saw that his uncle and his friend were thus active and watchful to save him from perdition, that he could not refuse to be convinced and saved.

Alas! we none of us as yet knew Pendarves. We did not know that in proportion to conscious strength of mind is the capacity of conviction, and that no one is so jealous of interference, and so averse to being proved in the wrong, as those who are most prone to err and most conscious of weakness. My uncle and aunt went away in high spirits, at the idea of the good which was going to accrue to me from their exertions; and left me much cheered in my prospects, little thinking of the blow which these exertions were ensuring to me.

My husband wrote to me on his journey about twice a-week; but as he rarely did so till the post was just going out, or the horses were waiting, I was convinced either that he had lost all remains of tenderness for me, or that, conscious of acting ill, he could not bear to write.

When he had been gone two months, I was expecting his arrival in London every day, and with no small anxiety; for my uncle had written me word, that as soon as Annette Beauvais (for that *was* her real name) arrived in town, she would be seized by the officers employed by Government, and be shipped off directly for Altona, whither Lord Martindale, who was reckoned a dangerous disloyal subject, would be advised to accompany her.

But while I was pleasing myself with the idea that Pendarves, when convinced of the real character of those with whom he associated so intimately, would return to me, thankful for the discovery, and that in the detected courtesan and spy he would forget the fascinating companion, a very different end was preparing for the well-intentioned plans of our friend and relation.

Pendarves, not choosing to fail in respect to his uncle, and resolved to consider himself as on good terms with him, called at his house in Stratford Place; but unfortunately found only Mrs. Pendarves. The consequence you may easily foresee. She reproached him with his cruel neglect of his wife, and then triumphed in the approaching discomfiture of that wicked woman who had lured him from her; informing him with great exultation, that his uncle had procured her arrestation; that she would be taken up directly, and sent abroad; and that his angel-wife was expecting his return to her with eager and affectionate love.

"And was my wife privy to this injustice and this outrage?" asked Pendarves, with a faltering voice and a flashing eye.

"To be sure she was."

"Then she may expect me, madam, but I will never return!" Having said this, he rushed from the house, and hurried back to the lodgings. He found Lady Martindale, as she still persisted in calling herself, in fits, and Lord Martindale threatening, but in vain. The warrant was executed, and the lady forced to set off, her lord having a hint given him, which made his retreat advisable also.

"You shall not go *alone*, my friends," said Pendarves as soon as he saw that their banishment was certain; "and as my family have presumed to *procure* your exile, they shall find that they have exiled me too."

So saying, he left the house, gained a passport as an American, which you know he was, as well as myself, by birth, and soon overtaking them, he travelled with them, and embarked with them for Altona.

He wrote to me from the port whence they embarked, and such a letter! I thought I should never have held up my head after it. He reproached me for joining the mean cabal against an injured and innocent woman, and declared that as I and his uncle had caused her exile, he felt it his duty to soothe and to *share* it.

In a postscript, he told me he had drawn for all the money that was in his banker's hands, before he set out on his journey; that he wished me to let our house, and remove into my mother's, which was still empty; that he trusted I would not let him want in a foreign land, for in *some* respects he knew I could be generous; but he feared the income of *his* fortune *must* be appropriated to the payment of his debts, which were so many, he feared he could not return, even if he wished it, except at the danger of losing his personal liberty. He trusted, therefore, that I would join my uncle in settling his affairs; and if he wanted money to support him, he knew I would spare him some out of the fortune which came to me on the death of my mother, the income of which I, and I alone, could receive.

In the midst of the wretchedness inflicted by this letter—for it was my nature to cling to hope, I eagerly caught at the high idea of my conjugal virtues which this cruel letter implied; and I trusted that, when intimate association had completely unmasked this syren and her paramour, he would prize me the more from contrast, and hasten home to receive my eagerly bestowed forgiveness. But the order to let the house was so indicative of a separation *meant* to be long, if not eternal, that again and again I went from hope to despair. But there was one sorrow converted into rejoicing. Till now I had grieved that my mother was no more, but *now* I rejoiced to think that this last terrible blow she was spared her; that she did not live to witness the grief of her worse than widowed daughter, nor to see the degradation of the beloved son of her idolized Lady Helen. Degradation did I say? Yes: but I still persisted to excuse my husband, and would not own, even to *myself*, that he was without excuse for his conduct. I thought it was *generous* in him not to forsake his friends in their distress, nor would I allow any one to *hint* at the probability that his female companion was his mistress.

I also resolved to justify his reliance on my exertions and my generosity. I wrote to my uncle. I made myself acquainted with all his embarrassments, I dismissed every servant but Alice and Juan, and I set apart two-thirds of my own income also for the payment of the debts.

My uncle would fain have interfered, and advanced me the money; but I had a pride and a pleasure in making sacrifices for my husband's sake, and I wished Mr. Pendarves to leave him money in his will, as a resource for him when he should return to England, and I should be no more; for I fancied that I was far gone in a rapid decline. But I mistook nervous symptoms, the result of a distressed mind, for consumptive ones; and to my great surprise, when I had arranged my husband's affairs, and had, while so employed, been forced to visit London once or twice, and associate with the friends who loved and honoured me, my pain of the side decreased, my pulse became slower, my appetite returned, and I recovered something of my former appearance. But it was now the end of the winter of 1793, and the reign of terror had long been begun in France, while we heard from every quarter that the English there were in the utmost danger on account of the unpopularity of the English Government; that all were leaving France who could get away; and Pendarves was gone to Paris! But then he was an American. Still, I could not divest myself of fears for his life; and the horrible idea of his pining in a foreign land, in a prison and in poverty, (for though he had written to say he was arrived in Paris, he had not drawn for money, nor given his address,) haunted me continually. To be brief; you know how the idea of my husband's danger took entire possession of my imagination, till I conceived it to be my duty to set off for Paris.

You remember, that you and your husband both dissuaded me from the rash and hazardous undertaking; and that I replied, "I have now but one object of interest in the world, the husband of my love! True, a romantic generosity, and what he calls just resentment, have led him for the present to forsake his country and *me;* but that is no reason why I should forsake *him*, and who knows, but that the result of my self-devotion may restore him to me more attached than ever?" You know that you listened, admired, and almost encouraged me, and that you have always considered this determination as the crown of my conjugal glory, and held it up as a bright example of a wife's duty. But, my dear friend, my own sobered judgment and the lessons of experience, together with reproof from lips that never can deceive, and a judgment that can rarely err, have convinced me that I rather *violated* than *performed* a wife's duty when I set off on this romantic expedition to France.

No: if ever I deserved the character of a good wife, it was from the passive fortitude and the patient spirit with which I bore up against neglect, wounded affections, and slighted tenderness. It was the sense of duty which led me to throw a veil over my husband's faults, which held him up when his own errors had cast him down, and which led me still, in strict compliance with my marriage vows, to obey and honour him by all a wife's attentions, even when I feared that he deserved not my esteem.

But to go on with my narrative. My uncle and aunt came down to reason me out of my folly, as they called it; and my uncle thought he held a very persuasive argument, for he told me he felt it *indelicate* for me to intrude myself and my fondness on a husband who had showed he did not value it, and had chosen to escape from me.

"But I did not *mean* to intrude upon him," I replied; "I mean to be concealed in Paris, and with Alice and Juan to attend me; I fear nothing for myself; nor need you fear for me."

"What!" cried my aunt, "be in Paris, and not let the vile man know you are there? *I* should discover myself, if it were only for the sake of reproaching him; for *I* should treat him very differently, I assure you. *I* should show him,

"Earth has a rage with love to hatred turn'd,
And love has fury by a woman spurn'd."

"But you are not *Helen*, my dear," said my uncle, meekly sighing, as he always did over her misquotations; and still he argued, and I resisted, when I obtained an unexpected assistant in our kind physician.

"My dear sir," said he, "if your niece remains here in compliance with your wishes, I well know that her mind and her feelings will prey upon her life, and ultimately destroy it, if they do not unsettle her reason. But if she is allowed to be active, and to indulge at whatever risk her devoted affection to her husband, depend on it she will be well and comparatively happy; nor do I see that she runs any great risk. She is an American; her two servants are the same, and are most devotedly attached to her; and I give my opinion, both as a physician and a friend, that she had better go."

Oh, how I loved the good old man for what he said! and my uncle and aunt were now contented to yield the point; but my uncle insisted on defraying all my expenses.

"They will be trifling," said I; "for I

shall not choose to travel as a lady, but to dress as plainly, travel as cheaply, and attract as little attention as I can."

This he approved; but, in case I should want money to purchase services either for myself or my husband, he insisted on my sewing into my stays ten bank-notes of a hundred pounds each; and I accepted them in case of emergencies, as I thought I had no right to refuse what might be of service to my husband.

"Would I were not an old man!" said my uncle; "then you should not *go alone*, Helen." But I convinced him that any English friend would only be a detriment to me.

Lord Charles Belmour, on hearing of my design, left London, and the career of dissipation in which he was more than ever engaged, to argue with me, to expostulate with me, to *entreat* that I would not go, and risk my precious life, which no man living was worthy to have sacrificed for him, and then burst into tears of genuine feeling when he bade me adieu, wishing that " Heaven had made *him* such a woman;" and, while envying the husband of a virtuous wife, went back to a new mistress, and renewed his course of error.

At length, the day of my departure arrived; and, plainly attired, I set off for the port of Great Yarmouth, attended by my two faithful servants.

Juan and Alice were both slaves on part of our American property; but they were born on the estate of a French proprietor; therefore French was their native tongue, which was a fortunate circumstance. As soon as my father was their master, he made them free, and they became man and wife. They had lived with my mother ever since. She, as I before said, had desired they should be made independent for life. It is no wonder, therefore, the faithful creatures were devoted to the daughter of their benefactress, and I had the most cheering confidence in the tried sagacity as well as integrity of both. Their colour, you know, was what is called mulatto, and their appearance was less distinguished by ugliness than is usually the case with such persons.

I thought it necessary to give this little history of two beings whom I learnt to love even in my childhood, and who, in the season of my affliction, added to that love, the feeling of interminable gratitude.

Well, behold us landed at Altona, and designated in our passports, as Mrs. Helen Pendarves, and Juan and Alice Duval, Americans. After a tedious journey in the carts of the country, and sometimes in its horrible waggons, behold me also arrived in the metropolis of blood, passports examined and approved, and all my greatest difficulties at an end. So relieved was my mind, when every thing was arranged, and I had hitherto gotten on so well, that my affectionate companions observed with delighted wonder that my cheek glowed and my eyes sparkled once more; but cautious Juan advised me to hide my face as much as possible, for there were no such faces in Paris, he believed. When, however, I found myself in Paris, when I knew that the being I loved best was there, and yet I dared not seek him, sorrow destroyed my recovered bloom again, and tears dimmed my eyes. Yet still I felt a strange overpowering satisfaction in knowing that I was *near* him; and when we had found out his abode, I thought that I could perhaps contrive to see him, myself unseen. But I found a letter addressed to me, *poste restante*, which not only dimmed the brightness of my prospects, but damped much of my enthusiastic ardour in the task which I had undertaken, and even abated some of my tenderness for Pendarves: for I could no longer shut my eyes to the nature of his attachment to Annette Beauvais.

My uncle told me in his letter that Lord Martindale was returned to London, but could not stay there, and was on his way to America; that he had met him in a shop; that, on hearing his name, Lord Martindale had the effrontery to introduce himself, and thanked him for having enabled him so easily to get rid of a mistress of whom he was tired.

"Indeed," said he, "I am much obliged to the family of Pendarves; for the uncle forces my mistress to go back to her native place, and the nephew takes her off my hands, and under his own protection."

"And I have the honour to assure you, sir," said he, "that if you visit Paris, and the Rue Rivoli, *numero* 22, you will there find your nephew, romantically happy with a most fascinating *chere amie* who had once the honour of bearing my name."

"I turned from him," adds my uncle, "with disgust, as you, I hope, will turn from your unworthy husband, and come back, my dearest niece, to your affectionate and anxious uncle."

For one moment I felt inclined to obey his wishes — my husband really living with an abandoned woman, as her avowed protector! wife, country, reputation, sacrificed for her sake!

Horrible and disgusting it was indeed! But I soon recollected, that if it was really a duty in me to come to Paris for his sake at all, it was equally a duty now, for his criminality could not destroy his claims on my duty; nor could his breach of duty excuse the neglect of mine. In short, whether love or conscience influenced me, I know not, but I resolved to stay where I was. And so he was in the Rue Rivoli! I was glad to know where he was, but I did not as before wish to see him, and even gaze on him unseen. No: I felt him degraded, and I thought that I should now turn away if I met him.

We took a pleasant and retired lodging on the Italian Boulevards; but I soon found that in this situation we were not likely to learn any tidings of Pendarves; and by the time we had been ten days at Paris, Juan and I resolved, having first *felt our way*, to put a plan which we had formed into execution.

It was absolutely necessary that we should have opportunities of knowing what was going forward in public affairs, in order to learn the degree of safety or of danger in which Pendarves was; and if Madame Beauvais had really been a spy in London for the Convention, she must be connected with the governing persons in Paris.

Accordingly, we hired a small house which had stood empty some time, in a street through which most of the members of the National Convention were likely to pass in their way to and fro. The street-door opened into a front parlour, and that into a second parlour; of this, with a kitchen and two chambers, consisted the whole of the house. Humble as it was, I assure you it was on the plan of one which Robespierre occupied in the zenith of his power.

The windows of the front parlour Juan converted into a sort of shop-window; and as he and his wife were both good bakers, they filled it with a variety of cakes, which they called *gâteaux républicains;* and it was not long before, to our great joy, they obtained an excellent sale for their commodity. This emboldened us to launch out still more; and in hopes that our shop might become a sort of resting and lounging-place to the men in power as they passed, Juan put a coat of paint on the outside of the house, converted the parlour into a complete shop, and at length put a notice over the door in large tri-colour letters, importing that at such hours every day plum and plain pudding *à l'Américaine* was to be had *hot*, as well as *gâteaux républicains.*

If this *affiche* succeeded, there was a *chance* of Juan's hearing something relative to the objects of our anxiety from the members of the Convention, while I myself, hidden behind the glass-door of the back-parlour, might also overhear some, *to me*, important conversation. At any rate, it was worth the trial; and experience proved that the scheme was not so visionary as it at first appeared.

It was not without considerable emotion that I saw our shop opened, and business prospering. Never, surely, was there a more curious and singular situation than mine. Think of me, the daughter of an American loyalist, living an unprotected woman in the metropolis of republican France, and helping to make puddings and cakes for the members of the National Convention!

Though I have never paused in my narrative to mention politics, still you cannot suppose that I was ignorant of what was passing on the great theatre of the Continent, nor that the names of the chief actors in it were unknown to me. On the contrary, I often beguiled my lonely hours with reading the accounts of the proceedings at Paris; had mourned not only over the fate of the royal family, but had deplored the death of those highly-gifted men, and that great though mistaken woman (Madame Roland,) in whom I fancied that I perceived some of the republican virtue to which others only pretended; and though far from being a republican myself, I could not but respect those who, having adopted a principle, however erroneous, acted upon it consistently. But with Brissôt and his party ended all my interest in the public men of France, though their names were familiar to me, and aversion and dread were the only feelings which they excited.

Therefore, when, on the first of February, 1794, we opened a shop for puddings and cakes, and I, through the curtain of a glass-door, saw it thronged with customers, some of whom I concluded were regicides and murderers, my heart died within me. I felt as if I stood in the den of wild beasts, and I wished myself again in safe and happy England.

Juan was frequently asked a number of questions by his customers; such as who he was, and whence he came, and how long he had been there; and his answer was, that he was born in America, and born a slave, and so was his little wife, but a good master made him free.

"Bravo! and *Vive la liberté!* and you are like us; we were slaves, now we are free," always shouted the deluded people to whom he thus talked.

Juan used to go on to say that he had heard his master was in France, and poor, and so they left America, and came to work for him (applauses again;) but that he found he was dead. "And so," said he, "as I liked Paris, we resolved to stay here, and make nice things for the republicans in Europe."

This tale had its effect; Juan was hailed as the *bon citoyen* Duval, and promised custom and protection.

"Oh! dear Miss Helen," cried Juan, (as he usually called me,) "what bloody dogs some of them look! No doubt some of them were members of parliament. They govern a nation indeed, who were such fools as to be so easily taken in by my story! Psha! I should make a better parliament-man myself."

At length we saw some of the distinguished men.

Juan heard one of the party call two of the others Hebert and Danton; and he made an excuse to come in and tell me which was which. I looked at them, and was mortified to find that Danton was so pleasant-looking.

When they went away, which they did not do till they had eaten largely, and commended what they ate, a wild, singular-looking man entered the shop, in all the dirty and negligent attire of a *sans culotte*, and desired a plum-pludding *à l'Américaine* to be set before him; declaring that had it been *à l'Anglaise* he could not have eaten it, as it would have tasted of the slavery of that wretched grovelling country, England. When the pudding was served, he talked more than he ate, and made minute inquiries into the history of Alice and Juan; but when he heard who and what they were, he ran to them, and insisted on giving each the fraternal embrace—"for I," said he, "am Anacharsis Cloots! the orator of the human race; and dear to my heart is the injured being who was born in servitude. Blessed be the memory of the master who broke your chains!"

He then resumed his questions, and, to my great alarm, desired to know if they lived alone in the house. Juan, off his guard, replied,

"No; we have a lodger."
"Indeed! let me see him."
"Him! 'tis a woman."
"Better and better still! Let me see *her*, then. Is she young and handsome?"
"Hélas! la pauvre femme! elle ne voit personne, elle est malade à la mort."*
"Eh bien, que je la voye! Je la guérirai moi."†
"Tu! citoyen? Oh non! elle ne se guérira, jamais."‡
"Mais oui, te dis-je. Où est-elle? Je veux absolument faire sa connaissance."§
"C'est impossible. Elle est au lit."‖
"Qu'est-ce que cela fait?"¶
"Comment, les femmes chez nous ne reçoivent jamais les visites quand elles sont au lit."**
"Mais, quelle bêtise! au moins dis-moi son nom qui elle est, et tout cela."††

And Juan told him that I was the relation of his benefactor; that I was in reduced circumstances, having had a bad husband; and that he and his wife had taken me to live with them, and never would desert me.

"*O les braves gens!*" exclaimed he.—But what an agony I endured all this time! Afraid that this mad-headed enthusiast would really insist on paying me a visit, I ran up stairs, put on my green spectacles, which Juan insisted on my buying, (for he really thought me a perfect beauty, and that all who looked must love); then tied up my face in a handkerchief, pulled over it a slouch cap, and lay down on the bed, drawing the curtains round. But Alice came up to tell me the strange man was gone. He declared, however, that the next time he came, he would see *la pauvre malade*.

But fortunately we never saw him again, except when he stopped in company with others, and was too much taken up in laying down the law for the benefit of the human race, to remember an individual.

You will not be surprised when I tell you, that slight as was my knowledge of the persons of Hebert and Anacharsis Cloots, and little as I had heard of their voices, still, the circumstance of having seen their faces and heard them speak, made all the difference between rejoicing at their deserved fate and regretting it. They were guillotined during the course of the next month; and I shuddered when I heard they were no more, catching myself saying, "Poor men!" very frequently during the rest of the day.

I could give you some interesting details of many events that now happened in affecting succession; but they have been painted by abler hands than mine: I shall only say further, concerning our shop-visiters, that more than once the great Dictator himself took shelter there from a shower of rain, and ate a *gâteau républicain*. When he first came, Juan, who had seen him often before, sent Alice to tell me who he was; and I cannot describe the sensation of horror with which he inspired me: for nature there had made the outside equally ugly with the inside. He asked many questions of Juan, relative to who he was, and whence and why he came : and I saw his quick and restless eye looking suspiciously round, as if he feared an unseen dagger on every side: and so watchful and observant was his glance, that I retreated from the curtain lest he should see me. I was also terrified to perceive that my poor Juan was not so much at his ease with *him*, and did not tell his story with so steady a voice as usual. But perhaps, like Louis the Fourteenth, Robespierre was flattered with the consciousness of inspiring awe. Juan was, however, a little relieved by the entrance of Danton, who spoke to him as an old acquaintance; on which Robespierre turned to Danton, and said, "Then *you know* these people?"

"Yes—and their puddings, too. Do I not, citizen?" he good-naturedly replied; and soon after, Robespierre and he departed together.

Certain it is, that I breathed more freely after they were gone.

Not long after this, Danton and Camille des Moulins came together; and though they spoke very low, Juan heard them talk of *la citoyenne Beauvais*, and then they talked of *son bel Américain Anglois*,* (so it was clear they knew who my husband really was,) and they whispered and laughed. We then heard the name of Colonel Newton, an Englishman by birth, who had served in foreign armies all his life,

---

* Alas! poor woman! she is sick to death.
† Well, let me see her: I will cure her.
‡ You, citizen? Oh, no! she will never be cured.
§ Yes, I tell you. Where is she? I will absolutely make her acquaintance.
‖ Impossible. She is in bed.
¶ What does that signify?
** Our ladies never receive visits in bed.
†† What nonsense! But tell me her name, and all that.

---

* Her handsome American Englishman.

and had the melancholy distinction of being the only British subject who was put to death by the guillotine.* But Juan heard him mentioned by these men, and soon after we knew he was arrested; for Juan was in the habit of frequenting the Palais Royal and its gardens in an evening, and other places of public resort, and there he was sure to hear the news of the day. At first, he only heard that an Englishman was arrested; and his emotion was such, that if any one had looked at him it must have been perceived: but no one noticed him; and presently some one named Colonel Newton as the conspirator who had been denounced and imprisoned.

Was Pendarves acquainted with this unfortunate man? We could not tell; but certain it was, that the awful lips which mentioned the one had named the other.

In another month, Danton and Camille des Moulins were themselves no more! and fell with many others who were obnoxious to the tyrant; and again I wished that I had not seen or heard them.

As I never went out till it was quite dark, the great seclusion in which I lived injured my health. Since the death of Hebert, indeed, I was not so cautious, as I could wear a hat; but while he lived, he had decreed that every head-dress was *aristocrat*, except the peasants' cap.

Juan went, therefore, to find a lodging for me for a week or two, near or in the Champs Elysées, and in so retired a spot, that, with my green spectacles, and otherwise a little disguised, my guardian declared he allowed me to walk even in a morning.

Alice accompanied me, and Juan promised to come and tell us every evening what was going forward.—During my abode in this pretty place, Juan arrived one evening a good deal agitated, and I found that he had seen Pendarves.

"Did he see you?"

"Oh no! he saw no one but——"

"His companion, I suppose. Was Madame Beauvais with him?"

"She was, and her little dog; and the beast would not come at her call: and then she was uneasy, and so *he* took up the nasty animal, and carried it in his arm. I could have wrung its neck."

"It is a nice clean animal," replied I, trying to speak cheerfully. "But how did he look, Juan?"

"Well, madam—too well!" said the faithful creature, turning away in agony to think he *could* look well under his circumstances.

"You see he is not yet arrested," said I: "and for that I am thankful."

One night — the night before we were to return to our house — Juan disappointed us, and did not come at all. You, who have

* See Miss Williams's Letters.

always lived in dear and quiet Britain, cannot form to yourself an idea of the agitation into which this little circumstance threw us. We could not fancy he was ill: that was too common-place and too natural a circumstance to occur to the heated imaginations of women accustomed, as we were, to tales of terror and blood; and we thought no less than that he had been suspected, denounced, arrested, and would be *jugé à mort*. What a night of misery was ours! Early in the morning, however, Alice set off for Paris, conjuring me on her knees not to come with her, as Juan thought it unsafe for me to walk in the street unprotected; and promising to come back directly, if anything alarming had happened. I therefore allowed her to depart without me; but though her not returning was a proof that all was right, according to our agreement, I was half distracted when hour succeeded to hour, and she did not return; till, at last, unable to bear my suspense any longer, I set off for Paris, and reached the Place de la Revolution, (as it was then called,) just as an immense crowd was thronging from all parts and around me, to a spot already filled with an incalculable number of persons. In one instant, I recollected that what I beheld in the midst must be the guillotine, and I tried to turn back, but it was impossible. I was hurried forward with the exulting multitude; and just as the horrible snap of the murderous engine met my now tingling ears, I heard from the shouts of the mob that the victim was the Princess Elizabeth! Self-preservation instinctively prompted me to catch hold of the person next me, to save myself from falling, which would have been instant death — and the aid I sought was yielded to me; and while a noise of thunder was in my ears, and my eyes were utterly blinded with horror and agonizing emotion, a kind but unknown voice said in French, "Poor child! I see you are indeed a stranger here. We natives are used to these sights now:" and he sighed, as if use had not however entirely blunted his feelings.

"But why did you come to see such a sight?"

"Oh! I knew nothing of it, and was going home."

"Poor thing! Well; but shall I see you home—if you can walk?"

I now looked up, and saw that my kind friend was only a lowly citizen, and wore a Jacobin cap; and I was still shrinking from allowing of his further attendance, though I trembled in every limb, and felt sick unto death; when, as the crowd dispersed, I saw Juan and Alice coming towards me: in another moment I was in her arms, where I nearly fainted away.

"This is unfortunate," said the *citoyen*: "her illness may be observed upon, as it was a Bourbon who died, and she may be fancied no friend to the republic. What is best to be done?"

While he said this, I recovered, and begged to go home directly; but I could not walk without the aid of my Jacobin friend, who insisted on seeing me safe home, and we thought it the best way to consent.

On our way, the *citoyen* exclaimed, "*O mon Dieu! le voilà lui-même!*"* and we saw the dreaded Robespierre hastily approaching us. He desired to know what was the matter with that woman; and neither Juan nor Alice had recollection enough to reply; but our friend did instantly, taking off his cap as he spoke: "The poor woman, *citoyen*, was nearly crushed in the crowd, and but for me would have been trodden to death. Only see how she trembles still! She has not been able to speak a word yet."

"Oh! that is the case, is it?" said he, surveying me with a most scrutinizing glance. "It is well for her I find her in such good company, Benoit."

He then departed, and we recovered our recollection.

He was no sooner gone, than, to my great surprise, I saw Juan seize our companion's hand, while he exclaimed, "You! are you Benoit?"

"To be sure; what then?"

"Why then, you God for ever bless that's all! For many poor wretch bless you; and now, but for you, what might have become of *her?*"

"How!" cried Alice; "is this the kind jailor of the Luxemburg? Oh dear! how glad I am to see you!"

It was indeed Benoit; who, at a period when to be cruel seemed the only means to be safe, lightened the fetters which he could not remove, and soothed to the best of his power the horrors of a prison and of death.

A feeling which he could not help, but certainly not one of joyful anticipation, led him to witness the death of the royal victim; and my evident horror instantly interested and attached him to my side. This good man attended us home, and we had great pleasure in setting before him all our little stores: but *he could not eat then,* he said; and as he spoke, he sighed deeply. However, he assured us he would come and eat with us some other day: then desiring us to take heed and not go to see sights again, he ran off, saying he had been absent too long.

What a mercy it was that Benoit was with us when we met the tyrant! We also rejoiced that he did not see or did not recognise Juan and Alice: but after this unfortunate rencontre we did not feel ourselves as safe as we did before, and dreaded every day to see him enter the shop.

I now desired to know the reason of Juan's

* Oh! there he is himself.

not coming to us, and I found that his too great care had exposed me to even a far *worse* agony than that from which he wished to preserve me. The truth was, he heard that poor Madame Elizabeth was to be executed the next day: fearing, therefore, that he should be betrayed into saying so, and wishing me not to know of it till all was over, as he knew how interested I was in her fate, he resolved to stay away, not supposing we should be alarmed; and he and Alice could not return to me sooner, as the way led over the very spot which they wished to avoid. Besides, Alice had told me her *not* returning was a good sign. Well! this agony was past; but I had seen and met the suspicious eye of the tyrant, and it haunted me wherever I went. For my own life, indeed, I had no fear; and imprisonment, I thought, was all I had to dread, though poor Juan insisted on it that the wretch saw, spite of my dowdy appearance, that I was a handsome woman; and he thanked Heaven at the close of every day, that no Robespierre had visited us. Another evening Juan returned in much agitation from his walk, but I saw it was of an opposite nature to that which he experienced at sight of Pendarves: and on inquiry I found that he had, as he said, met that *good* young man, Count De Walden.

"Indeed!" exclaimed I; "and did he see you? and does he know I am in Paris?"

"No, he did not see me; and without your leave I dared not tell that you were here: so I thought it best not to speak to him."

I felt excessively disappointed; but after some moments of reflection I recollected that it would be *cruel* and *selfish* to force myself, in a situation so interesting and so anxious, on one who on principle had so recently left the place in which I was; and I told Juan he had done quite right.

"However," said I, "it is a comfort to me to know that I have a protector near."

"Ay; but not for long!"

"No! but what could bring a man like him to this den of wickedness and horrors? Some good purpose, no doubt."

"I suspect so: for I saw him in close conversation with Barrère and others, and I overheard him say, 'But can you give me no hope? I want excessively to return home: still, while there is a chance of Colonel Newton's being saved, I will stay.' Barrère, I believe, said all hope was over; for the Count cast up his eyes mournfully to heaven, and retired."

Till I heard this, I was inclined to suspect that my uncle had written to say I was here, and that he came on my account.

I shall now relate the motive of his journey: the object of it was connected with the fate of my husband.

A man of the name of Beauvais was executed with Danton and other supposed conspirators in the preceding April. This man was the father of Annette Beauvais; and she would have been denounced and executed with her father, had not one of Robespierre's tools become exceedingly enamoured of her, and for his sake she was spared. But Colonel Newton having been known to be rather intimate with Beauvais, and having also dared, like a free-born Englishman and a man of independent feelings, to reproach the tyrant with his cruelty, he was accused, imprisoned, and condemned to death. It was on *his account* that De Walden came to Paris. By some means or other, Newton informed him of his situation; and as he had known him in Switzerland, and greatly esteemed him, he hastened to try whether by solicitation, interest, or money, he could procure his acquittal or escape: but he tried in vain. As vain also were the efforts made,—to do her justice,—by Madame Beauvais herself. The wretch to whom she applied was made jealous of Newton by her earnest entreaties for his life; and his doom was consequently rendered only more certain. He also tauntingly bade her to take care of her own life and that of her American Englishman, assuring her she would not find it an easy matter to do that long. Nor did he threaten in vain; for, though she admitted his addresses and received his splendid presents, she still persisted in living with the infatuated Pendarves, who believed her constancy equal to her pretended love. The consequence was, that an accusation was brought against my husband for getting to Paris on false pretences, and as being a dangerous person: for, though he was born in America, his father was a loyalist, not a republican, and had fought, they found, against the republican arms; and his mother was that offensive thing a woman of quality and a nobleman's daughter. There were other charges equally *strong;* and even in the presence of his vile companion, Pendarves was arrested, and condemned for the present to be confined *au secret* in the Luxemburg.

He bore his fate with calmness; for he expected that she who had caused his imprisonment would be eager to share and to enliven it: but that was beyond the heroism of a *mistress*. She was not willing to prefer to fine apartments and liberty, love and a prison with him; but while he, agonized at her desertion, —for she bade him a cold and final farewell, —was borne away into confinement, she was led away smiling and in triumph by her now avowed protector!

All these circumstances I did not know at first—I only knew the result; which was imparted to me by the trembling Juan, who had seen Pendarves led away, had seen her farewell, and had vainly tried to make himself observed by him, that he might know he had a friend at hand.

"A friend!" cried I, with a flushed cheek, but with a trembling frame: "he shall know that he has the *best* of friends, a *wife*, near him!" and instantly, taking no precaution to conceal my person in any way, for I thought not of myself, I hastened rapidly along, Juan with difficulty keeping pace with me, till I reached the Luxemburg.

"Whom do you want?" said a churlish man on duty.

"Seymour Pendarves."

"You can't see him: he is *au secret*."

"Oh! but I must! Do let me speak to the *Citoyen* Benoit, and ask him to let me enter."

"You are very earnest; and perhaps he will let you."

"Who shall I say wants to be admitted to this Pendarves?"

"His wife."

"His wife! Well," added he, respectfully, "wives should not be kept from their husbands when they seek them in their distress."

He then went in search of Benoit, who appeared with his keys of office.

"*Citoyen*," said he, "here is a wife wants to see her husband."

"I fear she is an aristocrat, then," replied Benoit, smiling and approaching us.

"Ha!" cried he, "is it you? What is become of your spectacles? And do you want to see your *husband*, poor thing? Who is he?"

I told him. He shook his head, saying to himself—"Who could have supposed he had a wife, and such a one too!"

"*Citoyenne*," said he, "you cannot see your husband to-night, nor shall he know you are here; but to-morrow, at nine in the morning, I will admit you. Yes, and *for your sake*, I will show him all the indulgence I can. So it was for this, was it, you came to Paris? I thought there was a mystery. Good girl! good girl!"

So saying, he walked hastily away, and we returned to our home, at once *disappointed* and *cheered*.

Oh how I longed for the light of morning! Oh! how I longed to exhibit the superiority of the wife over the mistress! With what pleasure I anticipated the joy, mixed with shame and sorrow, no doubt, but still triumphant over every other feeling, with which Pendarves would behold and receive me! How he would value this proof of tenderness and duty! while I should fondly assure him that all was forgotten and all forgiven! So did I paint the scene to which I was hastening. Such were the hopes which flushed my cheek and irradiated my countenance.

At length the appointed hour drew near; and I had just reached the gates of the Luxemburg, had just desired to be shown to Benoit, when I looked up and beheld De Walden!

"You here!" cried he, turning pale as death, "O Helen! dear rash friend! why are you in Paris? Speak."

Here he paused, trembling with emotion. I was little less affected; but, making a great effort, I faltered out, "My *husband* is prisoner here, and I am going to him."

De Walden clasped his hands together, and was silent; but his look declared the agony of his mind.

Benoit now came to conduct me in; and De Walden, taking Juan's arm, led him apart.

"Have you told him I am here?" said I, turning very faint, alarmed, now the moment was come which I had so delightedly anticipated.

"No: I have told him nothing."

He now put the key into a door at the bottom of a long, narrow, dark passage, and it turned on its heavy and grating hinges.

"Some one desires to see you," said Benoit, *gruffly*, to hide his kind emotion; and I stood before my long-estranged husband. But where was the look of gladness? where the tone of *welcome*, though it might be mingled with that of less pleasant sensations? He started, turned pale, pressed forward to meet me; but then exclaiming in a faltering voice, "Is it you, Helen? Rash girl! why do I see you here?" he sunk upon his miserable bed, and hid his face from me. I stood motionless, pale, and silent as a statue. Was this the scene which I had painted to myself? True, I should have been shocked, if he had approached me with extended arms, and as if he felt that I had nothing to forget: yet I did expect that his eye would lighten up with joyful surprise, and his quivering lip betray the tenderness which he *would* but *dared not* express. However, for the first time in my life, indignation, and a sense of injury, were stronger than my fond woman's feeling; and I seated myself in silence, on the only chair in the room, with my proud heart swelling as if it would burst its bounds and give me ease for ever.

"Helen!" said he at length, in a subdued and dejected tone, "your presence here distracts me. This scene, this city, are no places for you; and oh! how unworthy am I of this exertion of love! What! must a wretch like me expose to danger such an exalted creature as this is?"

These flattering words, though uttered from the head more than from the heart, were a sort of balm to my wounded feelings; but I coldly replied, That in coming to Paris, in order to be on the spot if any danger happened to him, I had only done what I considered as the duty of a wife; and that now my earnest wish was to be allowed to spend part, if not the whole, of every day with him in prison, as his friend and soother.

"Impossible! impossible!" he exclaimed, becoming much agitated.

"Why so? Benoit is disposed to be my friend."

"No matter; but tell me who is with you in this nest of villains?"

I told him, and he thanked God audibly. I then entreated to know something concerning his arrest, its cause, and what the consequences were likely to be.

"Spare me!" cried he, "spare me! It is most painful to a man to blush with shame in the presence of his wife. Helen! kind, good Helen! I know you meant to soothe and serve me; but you have *humbled* me to the dust, and my spirit sinks before you! Go and leave me to perish. In my very *best* days I was wholly unworthy of you; but *now*—"

He was right; and my *parading* kindness, my *intruding* virtue were offensive. I *had* humbled him: I had *obliged him too much*: I had *towered over him in the superiority of my character*; and instead of *attaching*, I had *alienated* him. This was human nature—I saw it, I owned it now, but I was not prepared for it, and it overwhelmed me with despair. Still, it softened my heart in his favour; for, if I had to forgive *his errors, he* had to forgive my officious exhibition of *romantic duty*. I now at his request told him all my plans, and every thing that had passed since I came, not omitting to tell him that I had seen *De Walden*. Nor was I sorry to remark, that at his name he started and changed colour.

"He here! Then you are sure of a protector," said he, "and I feel easier. But, Helen! you are too young, too lovely to expose yourself to the gaze of the men in power. I protest that you are at this moment as beautiful as ever, Helen!"

"It is from the temporary embellishment of strong emotion only," replied I, pleased by this compliment from him. I then turned the discourse to the opportunity our shop gave us of hearing conversations; and I also promised to bring him some of our commodities. He tried to smile, but could not, and I saw that my presence evidently distressed instead of soothing him. Benoit now came to say I must stay no longer, and disappeared again; while, a prey to most miserable feelings, I rose to depart.

"I shall come again to-morrow," said I; "shall I not?"

"If you insist upon it, you shall; but, you had better leave me, Helen, to perish, and forget me!"

"Forget you! Cruel Seymour," cried I, bursting into an agony of tears.

He now approached me, and, sinking on one knee, took my hand and kissed it: then held it to his heart. A number of feelings now contended in my bosom, but affection was predominant; and as he knelt before me, I threw my arms round his neck, mingling my tears with his, "*Mais vite donc, citoyenne—dépêches tu?*"* said Benoit, just unclosing the door, and speaking outside it. Pendarves rose and led me to him; and, scarcely knowing whether pain or satisfaction predominated, I reached

* Quick, make haste, female citizen!

the gate, Benoit kindly assuring me I might command his services to the utmost.

I found De Walden still talking with Juan. They both seemed to regard me with very scrutinizing as well as sympathizing looks; and I still trembled so much that I was glad to accept the support of De Walden's arm. He attended me home; but we neither of us spoke during the walk. When I reached the door, I said, "Come to me to breakfast to-morrow; for to-day I am wholly unfitted for company." He sighed, bowed, and departed; but not without assuring me that he would inquire concerning the causes of my husband's arrest, and try to get him set at liberty.

"Well," cried Juan, "I have one comfort more than I had; Count De Walden has declared that while you remain in Paris *he* will." And I also felt comforted by this assurance.

I now retired to my own room, and, throwing myself on the bed, entered upon that severe task, self-examination; and I learnt to doubt whether my expedition to France were as truly and singly the result of pure and genuine tenderness, and a sense of duty, as I had supposed it was. For what had I done? I had certainly shone in the eyes of many at the expense of my husband. I had, as he said, "humbled him in his own eyes," and I had chosen to run risks for his sake, which he could not approve, and after all might not be the better for. In such reflections as these I passed that long and miserable day; ay, and in some worse still; for I felt that Pendarves no longer loved me—that he esteemed, he respected, he admired me; but that his tenderness was gone, and gone, too, probably, for ever!

I had, however, one pleasant idea to dwell upon. Deputies, if not an ambassador, were now expected from America, and De Walden had told Juan he should claim their protection for us.

The next morning De Walden came; but his brow was clouded, his manner embarrassed, and the tone of his voice mournful.

"Have you made the inquiries which you promised?"

"I have; and they have not been answered satisfactorily. My dear friend, there are subjects which nothing but the emergencies of the case could justify me to discuss with you. Will you therefore pardon me if I say——"

"Say any thing: at a moment like this it is my duty not to shrink from the truth. I guess what you mean."

He then told me the cause of my husband's arrest, which I have already mentioned; adding that the ostensible causes were so trifling, that they could probably be easily gotten over; but that the true cause, *jealousy*, was, he feared, not likely to be removed.

"But she left him," cried I, "left him as if for ever, and accompanied her new lover in triumph!"

"Yes: but I fear that he will not get quit of her so soon."

My only answer to this unwelcome truth was a deep sigh; and for some minutes I was unable to speak, while De Walden anxiously walked up and down the room.

"Perhaps you would go and see Pendarves?"

"No: excuse me: an interview between me and him must be painful, and could not be beneficial. The letter I had from him to inform me of a certain mournful event was cold; and though I answered it kindly,—for I thought of you when I wrote,—I was convinced that the less we met again the better."

"Then what can you do?"

"I know not—I could not save my *friend*, you know."

"If money can do it, I possess the means."

"And so do I; but Robespierre is inaccessible to bribes, and so I have found his creatures. I fear that I must seek Madame Beauvais herself."

"But she probably hates you?"

"True: but she does not hate Pendarves; and if I convince her that her only chance of liberating him is by seeming to have ceased to love him, the business may be done."

"And must he owe his liberty, and perhaps his life, to her? But be it so, if he can be preserved no other way—in that case I would even be a suitor to her myself."

"That I could not bear. But oh! dear, inconsiderate friend, why did you come hither?"

"Because I thought it my duty."

"And do you still think so?"

I was silent.

"Answer me, candid and generous Helen: do you not *now* see that it was more your duty to stay in your own safe country, protected by respectable friends, than to come hither courting danger, and the worst of dangers, to a virtuous wife? Believe me, the passive virtue of painful but quiet *endurance* of injury was the virtue for you to practise. This quixotic daring *looked* like duty; but *was not duty*, Helen, and could only end in disappointment: for tell me, have you not found that you have thus suffered and thus dared for an ingrate?"

My *silence* answered the question.

"Enough!" resumed De Walden; "and I feel that I have been cruel; but mine has been the reproof of friendship, *wrung* from me by the indignant agony of knowing that even *I* cannot perhaps protect you from the insults which I dread. Oh! *why* did they *let* you come hither? I am *sure* your mind was not itself when you thought of it."

"You are right. The idea had taken hold of my imagination, then unnaturally raised, and come I would. But my physician approved my coming; for he thought it safer for me, and thought, if I was not indulged, that my reason, if not my life, might suffer."

This statement completely overset De Walden's self-command; he blamed himself for what he had said—accused himself of cruelty —extolled the patient sweetness with which I had heard him, and had condescended to justify myself. Then, striking his forehead, he exclaimed,

"And I, alas! am *powerless* to save a being like this!—But save her, THOU," he added, lifting his clasped hands to heaven.

The hour of my appointment at the prison now arrived again, and De Walden accompanied me thither. I did not see Benoit; but I was admitted directly, and my conductor, opening the door, said, "A female citizen desires to see you."

"Indeed!" said Pendarves in a tone of joy; but he started, and looked disappointed, when he saw *me*.

"Is it you, Helen!" said he.

"Did you expect it was any one else?"

"Not much," he replied, evidently disconcerted; "not much. It is only a primitive old-fashioned wife like yourself, who would follow an unworthy husband to a prison."

"And to a *scaffold*, if necessary," cried I with energy.

"Helen!" said Pendarves in a deep but caustic tone, "spare me! spare me! This excess of goodness——"

I smiled; but I believe my smile was as *bitter* as his *accents*.

What meetings were these between persons circumstanced as we once were and were *now*! But it could not be otherwise, and all I *now* suffered I had brought upon myself. In order to change the tone of our feelings, I told him De Walden had breakfasted with me, and then asked him if he would not like to see Juan.

He said "Yes," but carelessly, and then added, "So, De Walden has been with you?" and fell into a mournful reverie till our uncomfortable interview was over.

I promised to send him by Juan all he wanted and desired, of linen, clothes, and food; for Benoit had assured me he would allow him to receive any thing for the sake of *his good wife*. He thanked me, shook my hand kindly, and saw me depart, as I thought, with pleasure.

I found De Walden waiting for me with Juan. The latter by my desire asked for Benoit, and begged to know of him at what hour that day or evening he might be admitted to his master. Accordingly, he went, carrying with him the articles I mentioned. He was gone some time; and anxious indeed was I for his return.

"I have *seen* her," said he.

"Seen whom?"

"That vile woman."

"Was she with him?" cried I, turning very faint.

"No, no: let the good Benoit alone for that. She desired to see the citoyen Pendarves, *her husband;* on which Benoit scornfully answered, "one wife is enough for *any* man; I allow him to see *one* of his every day, *but no more;* so go away, and do not return again."

"What!" exclaimed the creature, in great agitation, "is she, is Helen Pendarves in Paris."

"Yes; *she*, the *true* she,—the good wife is here; and *she* alone will Benoit admit to his prisoner. *Va-t-en le dis-je!*"

"And the creature went away," added Juan, "for I saw and heard it all, giving him such a look!"

I could not help being pleased with this account; but I sent him immediately to tell De Walden what had passed, that he might lose no time in seeking La Beauvais, to prevent her going to the prison, and thereby increasing the danger of Pendarves. — When Juan returned, I asked for a minute detail of all that passed between my husband and him.

"Oh! he is very wretched!" he replied; "but he told me nothing concerning himself; he only walked up and down the narrow room, asking me nothing but about you, and why they let you come, and if De Walden came on purpose to guard you. In short, we talked of nothing else; and then he did so wish you back safe in your own country!"

This account gave me sincere pleasure, and made me believe that Seymour's heart was not so much alienated from me as I expected; and a weight seemed suddenly taken from my mind. The next day I went again at noon, and I found La Beauvais in high dispute with Benoit. As soon as he saw me, saw that I recognised her, and that my countenance assumed the hue of death, he caught my hand, saying, "*Vite! vite! entre donc:* BELLE *et* BONNE! *et toi, va-t-en tout de suite!*"*

La Beauvais, provoked and disappointed, seized my arm. "Madame Pendarves," she cried, "the *same interest* brings us hither: use your influence over this barbarian to procure me admittance."

"The *same* interest!" I replied, turning round, throwing her hand from my arm, and looking at her with all the scorn and abhorrence which I felt: "*Madame, je ne vous connois pas.*"†

"*It is well*," she said. "Depend on it, I shall refresh your memory; and soon, too. I will be *revenged*, though my heart bleeds for it."

She then hastened away; and I, feeling the rash folly I had committed, and fearing I had irreparably injured my husband's cause, was forced to let the kind jailor conduct me to his own apartment, in order that I might recover myself before I went to Pendarves. I found him more cheerful, and also more affectionate

* "Quick! quick! enter: fair and good! but you, go away directly!"
† Madam, I do not know you.

in his manner towards me. He had been reading a letter which he hastily put into his pocket; yet not so soon but that my quick eye discovered in the address the hand of La Beauvais. It was the renewal of intercourse, then, that had made him cheerful! But why then was he more affectionate to me? I have since resolved that question to my satisfaction.

No one likes to give up any power once possessed. Pendarves had flattered himself La Beauvais fondly loved him; and his bitter grief at her apparent desertion of him, arose from wounded pride, and the fear of having lost his power over her, more than from pining affection. But she had *written* to him; she was trying to gain admittance to his prison; his wounded vanity therefore was at rest on one point, and the sight of me was grateful because it ministered to it in another.

But I did not, could not reason then; I only felt; and what with jealousy, and what with my fears for his life, *now*, I thought, endangered *by me*, I was ill and evidently wretched the whole time I staid. But Seymour's manner to me was most soothing, and even tender. At that moment I could better have borne indifference from him; for I was conscious that I had weakly given way to the feelings of an injured jealous woman, and had thereby probably given the seal to his fate!

Glad was I when the jailor summoned me; for I was anxious to tell De Walden the folly which I had committed; and I saw that Seymour was hurt at the cold and hurried manner in which I bade him farewell.

When I saw De Walden, he told me that he had called in vain on La Beauvais hitherto; but would try again and again. On hearing what had passed between us, he became alarmed, but declared that he could not have forgiven me, if I had spoken or acted otherwise. That day, some of the tyrant's creatures were in our shop, and one of them desired to see the other shop-woman, declaring Alice was not pretty enough to wait on them; and that they were resolved the next time they came, to see *la belle Angloise*—But every other fear was soon swallowed up in one.

Juan heard that night in the Thuilleries gardens, that the *Englishman*, Pendarves, would be brought before the tribunal *the day after the next*, and there was no doubt of his being executed with several others, *directly!!!*

The moment, the dreaded moment was now at hand, and how was it to be averted? De Walden heard this intelligence also, and came to me immediately. But all hope seemed vain, because he was to be condemned to satisfy private wishes, and not because any public wrong could be proved against him, and he left me in utter despair. But he also left me to reflect; and the result was a determination to act resolutely and immediately, and to risk the event. Suffice, that I called my faithful servants into my room, reminded them of that fidelity and obedience to me which they had vowed to my poor mother on her death-bed, and told them the hour for them to prove their attachment and fulfil their vow was now arrived. This solemn adjuration was answered by as solemn assurances to obey me in whatever I required of them. I *first* required that they should keep *all* I was now going to say, and all they or I were *going* to do, profoundly secret from *De Walden*. I saw Juan recoil at this; but I was firm, and he *swore* himself to secresy. I then unfolded to them my scheme, and had to encounter tears, entreaties urged on bended knee, that I would give up my rash design, and consider myself. But they might as well have talked to the winds. "I feel," said I, "by the suddenness of this proceeding, that my treatment of La Beauvais has done this, and it is my duty, at all risks to myself, to save my husband from the death to which I have hurried him." The faithful creatures were silenced, but not convinced. Still, finding they could not prevent my purpose, and that I declared I would cry, *Vive le Roi*, that I might die with my husband, they prepared in mournful obedience to consult with me on the best means of accomplishing my wishes.

My plan was this: I resolved to ask permission to take a last farewell of Pendarves at night, after I had seen him in the morning, and then change clothes with him, and remain in his stead.

"And as Benoit was ill in bed this evening, when you went," said I, "there is no likelihood that he will be well to-morrow; so my plan cannot injure him. Therefore, let us be prepared to execute what I have designed, directly."

"Well, my comfort is," said Juan, "that my master will never consent to risk your life in order to save his own."

"Not willingly; but I shall *force* him to do it."

"Well! we shall see."

You may remember how I used to regret my great height, because Pendarves did not admire tall women; but now how I valued it, as it made it more easy for Pendarves to pass for me, and therefore might aid my efforts to save his life!

We agreed that Alice and Juan should be in waiting with a covered peasant's cart, at the end of the Luxemburg gardens; that then he should drive him and her to our lodging in the Champs Eysées, which we had again hired, where he was to pass for me, and still hide his face as if in great affliction. The house was kept by a deaf, stupid old woman, who was not likely to suspect any thing. And at daybreak, Pendarves, in a peasant's dress, with Alice by his side, dressed like a peasant also, with her hood over her face, was to drive on day and night when he had passed the barrier, which we hoped it would be easy to do, till some place of safe retreat offered itself on the read. And I knew that on this road was the *château* of a gentleman whom we had known and had done kindnesses to in England, who had contrived like some others to take no part in politics, and had retained his house and his land.

All was procured and ready as I desired; and having written down my scheme for my husband, conjuring him to grant my request, I went to the prison in the morning with a beating heart, lest Benoit should be well enough to be at his post. But he was not only unwell, he was dismissed from his office. The *bon Benoit*, as he was called, was too good for his situation.*

Seymour beheld with wonder, and no small alarm, my cheek, now flush, now pale, my tremulous voice, and my abstracted manner; and I once more saw in him that affectionate interest and anxiety so dear to my heart.

"You are ill, my beloved," said he at length.

"Beloved!" How the word thrilled through my heart! I never expected to hear it again from his lips; and the sound overcame me. "I shall be better soon," cried I, bursting into tears.

The surly jailor (Oh! how unlike Benoit!) who had taken his place, now summoned me away, and I slided my letter into my husband's hands. "Read it," said I, "and know that your doom is fixed *for to-morrow*, therefore I conjure you by our past loves to grant the request which the letter contains, and if you think I have deserved kindness from you, comply with my wishes."

Seymour, who had heard nothing of his approaching fate, took the letter, and listened to me with a bewildered air; and I hastened from the prison. I had easily obtained permission to return to the prison at night.

"It will be the *last time*. You will never come again," said the brutal jailor; "your husband will never come back when he goes to the tribunal to-morrow, so come and welcome!"

I spent the intervening time in writing a letter to De Walden, inclosing one to my uncle, which I begged him to forward; and I arranged every thing as if death awaited me. Nay, how could I be assured that it did *not?* But I kept all my fears to myself, and talked of hope alone, to my poor servants, who wandered about, the pictures of grief.

When De Walden called that day, I would not see him, but lay down on purpose to avoid him; for I dreaded to meet his penetrating glance.

As it was now the middle of July, days were shortening, and by eight o'clock twilight was gathering fast. My appointment was for half-past seven, and by a bribe I obtained leave from Benoit's unworthy successor to stay till half-past eight.

---
* An historical fact.

Then summoning all my fortitude, I entered the cell of my husband. I shall pass over the first moments of our meeting; but I shall never forget them, and I am soothed and comforted when I recollect all that escaped from that affectionate and generous, though misguided being. Suffice, that all his arguments were in vain to persuade me, that he was not worthy to be saved, at even the smallest risk to a life so precious as mine.

"My life precious!" cried I; "a being without any near and dear ties! with neither parent, child, nor husband, I may now say," cried I thrown off my guard by the consciousness of a desolate heart.

"I have deserved this reproach," said Seymour; "you have indeed no husband, therefore, *why* should not I die? as, were I gone, Helen, I feel, *I know* that *you* would be no longer *desolate!*"

I understood his meaning, but did not notice it. Bitter was now the anguish which I felt; nay, so violent was my distress, and so earnest my entreaties that he would escape, as the idea that he refused me in consequence of *what I had just said*, would, if he perished, drive me, I was convinced, to complete distraction, that he at last consented to my request.

"But, take notice," said he, "that I do it with this assurance, that *if* my escape puts you in peril, I will return and suffer for, or with you; and then you shall again find that you have a husband, Helen, and our union shall be renewed in death, and cemented in our blood—I say no more. You command, and it is my duty to obey."

He then took off the *robe de chambre* which he wore in prison; and I dressed him in the loose gown I had made up for the occasion, and long enough to hide his feet; and even when he had my bonnet on, I had the satisfaction of seeing that he did not look much taller than I did. I now wrapped his robe tight round me, put all my hair under his night-cap, and with my handkerchief at my eyes awaited the jailor's summons; while Pendarves dropped the veil, and covered his face with his handkerchief as if in grief. But the anxious heavings of my bosom and the mournful ones of his were only too real. Every thing favoured us; the wind was high, and by blowing the door to, blew out the lamp which the jailor held: therefore the only light was from a dim lamp in the passage. At the door stood the trembling Juan.

"There, take care of her: for she totters as if she was drunk," said the jailor: "I warrant you she will never come again."

In five minutes more Seymour was in the cart, and very shortly after he reached our cottage in safety, and was, *as me*, lying in my bed in the Champs Eysées. I, meanwhile, went to bed, and made no answer, but by groans, to the "good night" and brutal consolations of the jailor, when he came to lock me up, without the smallest suspicion who I was. But when I heard myself actually locked up *for the night*, I threw myself on my knees in a transport of devout gratitude.

The next morning I rose after short and troubled rest, seating myself with my back to the door, that I might remain undiscovered as long as I could, in order to give my husband more time to get away. But I could no longer retard the awful moment; for my jailor came to summon me before the tribunal.

"I am quite ready!" said I, turning slowly round. I leave you to imagine his surprise, his indignation, his execrations, and his abuse. I forgave him, for the poor wretch feared for his place, if not for his life.

"Yes: you shall go before the tribunal," said he, seizing me with savage fury. "But no, I must first send after your rascally husband."

He then locked me in; and I saw no more of him for two hours, when I heard a great noise in the passage, down which my cell when open looked, and presently the door was unlocked by the jailor himself, who exclaimed with a malignant smile, "Your husband is taken, and brought back! Look out, and you will see him!"

I *did* look out, I did see him, unseen by him at first, and I saw him walking up the passage with La Beauvais weeping on his arm, and one of hers thrown across his shoulder.

An involuntary exclamation escaped me; and I retreated back into the cell. I have since heard that Henriot and his guards, De Walden, and Juan, were in the passage; but I only saw my husband and La Beauvais; and leaning against the wall I hid my face in my hands, oppressed with a thousand contending and bewildering sensations.

"There!" said the vindictive jailor, ushering in Pendarves, as if he felt how painful a *tête-à-tête* between us now would be; "there, citizen! I shall shut you up with your wife, till I know what is to be done with her. But perhaps you would like the other *citoyenne* better?"

"Peace!" cried Pendarves, "and leave us *alone!*"

"Helen!" said my husband.

"Mr. Pendarves!"

"I see how it is, Helen; nor can I blame you: appearances were against me. But I must and will assure you, that that person's appearing at such a time, and with her behaviour, were as unexpected as they were unwelcome."

Still I spoke not: no, not even to inquire *why* I had the misery of seeing him return; and ere I had broken this painful but only too natural silence, and had only just resumed my woman's gown, the door was again thrown open, and an officer of the National Convention came to say, that I was allowed to return to my own house for the present, till further proceedings were resolved upon.

"Take notice, sir," said Pendarves, "that this lady's only fault has been too great a regard for an unworthy husband; and that what you may deem a crime, the rest of Europe will call a virtue."

The officer smiled; and wishing my husband good night, I followed where he led.

At the gate I found De Walden, who accompanied me home, having first been assured by the officer that I should be under *surveillance.*

"And is it thus, rash Helen, you use your best friends, and risk an existence so valuable?" cried De Walden.

"Spare me, spare me your reproaches," said I: "I am sufficiently *humbled* already."

"Not *humbled* — those only are humbled who could injure such a creature. Helen, I was in the passage at the prison, and I saw all that passed.

"Now then, while this recollection is fresh on your mind, let me ask you if you think yourself justified in staying here where you are now exposed to insult and to danger, for the sake of one who at a moment which would have bound another man more tenderly than ever, could so meet and so offend your eyes?"

I was still silent.

"Now then hear my proposal. I have the greatest reason to believe that I can secure an escape both for you, Alice, and myself, through the *barrière* this very night on the road to Switzerland. There, my dear friend, I offer you a home and a parent! My mother will be your mother, my uncle your uncle; and well do I know, that could my revered Mrs. Pendarves look down on what is passing here, she would be happier to see you under the protection of my family than under any other protection on earth!"

"No, my dear friend, no; your just resentment and your wishes deceive you. My mother valued her child's fame and her child's virtue equal with her safety."

"Your fame could not suffer. I would not live even near you, Helen; I am as jealous of your fame as any mother could be; besides that *principle* would make me shun you. No, Helen; I would see you safe *in Switzerland*, and then sail for America."

"Generous man! But you shall not quit your country for my sake: besides I will *not* quit my husband in the hour of his danger. No, whatever be the fate of Pendarves, I stay to witness and perhaps to *share* it. The die is cast; so say no more."

By this time we had reached my home. Alice came to meet me.

"O my poor dear master!" said she: "but it was all his own seeking. We had passed the barrier; but he *would* go back. He declared he could not, *would* not escape till he knew you were safe: when just as I was got into the house in the Champs Elysées, and he was holding the reins in his hands, the officers seized him; and he said, "I am he whom you seek — I am quite willing to accompany you."

"This in some measure redeems his character with me," cried De Walden; and *I* did not feel it the less because I *said nothing;* but at length I said, "Generous Seymour! He never *told me* this. He did not make a merit of it with me."

Juan now came in, lamenting with great grief his poor master's return. "O that vile woman!" cried he; " It was at her instigation that he was to have been tried and condemned to-day; and then she repented, and came to the prison to watch for his being led out, when she saw him brought back, and then she had the audacity to hang upon him, weeping and making such a fuss! while he, poor soul, tried to shake her off, *assuring* her he forgave her, but *never wished to see her more!*"

"Did he *act* and talk thus?" cried I.

"He did indeed."

"A..d he came back from anxiety *for me!* O my dear friend, how glad am I that I had refused your proposal before I heard this!"— Sweet indeed was it to my heart to have the conduct of Pendarves thus cleared up.

That evening we learnt that Pendarves was to go before the tribunal the next day; and I was preparing to try to gain admittance to him, and to see him as he came out, when an order for my own arrest came, and an officer and his assistants *to lead me to a prison.* Juan instantly went in search of De Walden; but I was led away before his return.

On the road we met the tyrant: "*Ah, ah, ma belle!*" cried he, "where are your green spectacles?"

I haughtily demanded my liberty; but he said I was a dangerous person—and to prison I was borne. To such a prison too! My husband's cell was a palace to mine; but I immediately concluded that they wished to make my confinement so horrible that I should be glad to leave it on any conditions.

Two days after, and while I had been, I found, forbidden to see any one, I received a letter informing me that my decree of arrest should instantly be *cassé,* my husband set at liberty and sent with a safe-conduct out of the frontiers, if I would promise to smile on a man who adored me, and who had power to do whatever he promised, and would perform it before he claimed one approving glance from my fine eyes.

I have kept this letter as a specimen of Jacobin love-making. It was not signed by any name, except that of my *dévoué serviteur;** and I never knew from whom it came.

It told me an answer would be called for *in person* the day after the next; and anxiously did I await this interview — await in horrors unspeakable. There was however one com-

* Devoted servant.

fort which I derived from this letter; *till* it was answered, I felt assured that my husband was safe. Dreadful was the morrow: more dreadful still the day after it; for hourly now did I expect the visit of the wretch. But that day and the next passed, and I saw no one but my taciturn and brutal jailor, and heard nothing but the closing of the prison doors.

The next day too I expected him still in vain; but that night I marked an unusual emotion, and, as I thought, a look of alarm in my jailor; and my wretched scanty meals were not given me till a considerable time after the usual hour. The night too I and the other prisoners, I found, were locked up two hours before the customary time.

All that night I heard noises in the street of the most frightful description; and as my cell was near the front gates of the prison, I could even distinguish what the sounds were; and I heard the terrible tocsin sound to arms: I heard the report of fire-arms, I heard the shouts of the people, I heard the cry of *Liberty*, I heard '*Down with the tyrant!*' and all these mingled with execrations, shrieks, and, as I fancied, groans; while I sank upon my knees, and committed myself in humble resignation to the awful fate which might then be involving him I loved, and which might soon also reach me, and drag me from the dungeon to the scaffold!

At this moment of horrible suspense and alarm, and soon after the day had risen on this theatre of blood, my door was thrown open, not by my brutal jailor, but by DE WALDEN and JUAN! My jailor, one of the tools of despotism, had fled; the TWENTY-EIGHTH OF JULY had freed the country from the fetters of THE TYRANT: he was *then* at that moment on his way to the guillotine with his colleagues; and I, Pendarves, and hundreds else, were SAVED and FREE!

Oh! what had not my poor servants and De Walden endured during the four days of my imprisonment! Painful as that was, they feared worse evils might ensue; while Pendarves, confined with the utmost strictness, was not allowed to see even Juan!

But where was Pendarves? and why did I not see *him*, if he was indeed at liberty? De Walden looked down and replied, "He is at liberty, *I know;* but we have heard and seen nothing of him."

By this time we had reached my home, where I was received with tears of joy by my agitated attendants. But alas! my joy was changed into mortification and bitterness: and when my happy friends called on me to rejoice with them, I replied, in the agony of my heart, "I *am* thankful, but I shall never *rejoice* again!" and for some minutes I laid my head on the table, and never spoke but by the deepest sighs.

"I understand you," replied De Walden;

"and if I can bring you any welcome intelligence, depend on it that I will."

He then hastily departed; and worn out with anxiety, want of sleep, and sorrow, I retired to my bed, and fortunately sunk into a deep and quiet slumber.

When I went down to breakfast the next day, I found De Walden waiting for me. His cheek was pale, and his look dejected; but he smiled when I entered the room, and told me he brought me tidings of my husband.

"Indeed!" cried I with eagerness.

"Yes; I have seen him. He is at a lodging on the Italian Boulevards—and *alone*."

"Alone! And—and does he not mean to see me; to call and—"

"How *could* he? Have you forgotten how you *last* parted,—you resenting deeply his then only *seeming* delinquency; and *he* wounded by, yet *resigned* to, your evident resentment."

"True, true: yet still—"

"No: I have had a long conversation with Pendarves,—for after his late behaviour, and being convinced that he was *alone*, I had no objection to call on him,—and he received me as I wished. He even was as open on every subject as I could desire; and I found him, though still persecuted by the letters of La Beauvais, resolved never to renew any correspondence with her."

"If so, and if *sure* of himself, *why* not write to me, if he does not like to visit me? I am sure I have not proved myself *unforgiving*."

"Shall I tell you why? A feeling that does him honour; a consciousness that, fallen as he is from the high estate he once held in your esteem and that of others, he cannot presume to *require* of you, though you are his wife, a re-instatement in your love and your society; and he very properly feels that the first advance should come from you: for though, as I told him, the relaxed principles of the world allow husbands a latitude which they deny to wives; still, in the eyes of God, and in those of nicely-feeling men, the fault is in both sexes equal; and an offender like Pendarves is no longer entitled, as he was before, to the tenderness of a virtuous wife. Nay, Pendarves, penitent and self-judged, agrees with me in this opinion, and is thereby raised in my estimation."

"What! does Pendarves feel and think thus?"

"Yes; therefore I will myself entreat for him entire forgiveness; but not *directly*, and as if a husband who has so grossly erred were as dear to you as one *without* error."

Here De Walden's voice failed him; but he soon after added, in a low voice, "And I trust that to have aided in bringing about your re-union will support me under the feelings which the sight of it may occasion me."

"But does Pendarves think I shall be always inexorable?"

"He cannot think so, from your oft-experienced kindness."

"Then why prolong his anxiety? Why not offer to return with him to England directly?"

"Because I think there would be an indelicacy in offering so soon to re-unite yourself to him. I would have you, though a wife, ' be wooed, and not unsought be won;' but I should not dare to give you this advice, were I not convinced that this is the feeling of Pendarves. Besides, I *also* feel that he would be less *oppressed* by your superior virtue, if he found it leavened by a little female pride and resentment."

"Well, well, I will consider the matter," said I.

The next day, and the day after, De Walden called and saw Pendarves. "He is very unhappy," said he; "though he might be the envy of all the first men in Paris. The most beautiful woman in it, who lives in the first style, is fallen in love with him; but he refuses all invitations to her house, does not answer her *billets-doux*, and rejects all her advances."

"He does not *love* her, I suppose?" I replied, masking my satisfaction in a scornful smile.

"No, Helen. He says, and I believe him, that he never really loved any one but *you ;* and for a La Beauvais, who persecutes him with visits as well as letters, he has a kind of aversion. Believe me, that at this moment he has all my pity, and much of my esteem; and *could* I envy the man who, having called you his, is conscious of the guilt of having left you, I trust I should soon have an opportunity of envying Pendarves."

Oh! the waywardness of the human heart! or was it only the waywardness of mine! Now that I found my husband was anxious to return to me, I felt less anxious for the reunion; and having gained my point, I began to consider with more severity the faults which I was called upon to overlook; and though I had reclaimed my wanderer, I began to consider whether the reward was equal to the pains bestowed. And also I felt a little mortified to find De Walden so willing to effect our union, and so active in his endeavours to further it. These obliquities of feeling were, however, only temporary; and I had actually written to Pendarves, by the *advice* of De Walden, assuring him all was so much forgiven and forgotten that I was prepared to quit Paris with him, and go with him the world over —when the most dreadful intelligence reached me!—Even at this hour I cannot *recall* that moment without agony. I must lay down my pen—

* * * * * *

Pendarves continued to resist the repeated importunities of La Beauvais to visit her; but at length she sent a friend to tell him she believed she was dying, and trusted he would not refuse to bid her farewell.—Pendarves could not, dared not refuse to answer this appeal to his feelings, and he repaired to her hotel; in which, though he knew it not, she was maintained by one of the new members of the Convention, whom she had inveigled to marry her according to the laws of the republic. When he arrived, he found her scarcely indisposed; and reproaching her severely with her treachery, he told her that all her artifices were vain; that his *heart* had always been his wife's, though circumstances had enabled her to lure him from me; that now I had shone upon him in the moments of new danger more brightly than ever, and was dearer than ever; and that he conjured her to forget a guilty man, who, though never likely perhaps to be happy again with the woman he adored, yet still preferred his present solitary but guiltless situation to all the intoxicating hours which he had passed with *her*.

La Beauvais, who really loved him, was overcome with the solemn renunciation, and fell back in a sort of hysterical affection on the couch; and while he held her hand, and was bathing her temples with essences, her husband rushed in, and exclaiming, "Villain, defend yourself!" he gave a pistol into the hand of Pendarves; then firing himself, the ball took effect: and while De Walden was waiting his return at his lodgings to give him my letter of recall and of forgiving love, he was carried thither a bleeding and a dying man! But he was conscious; and while Juan, who called by accident, remained with him, De Walden came to break the dread event to me, and bear me to the couch of the sufferer.

He was holding my letter to his heart.

"It has healed every wound there," said he, "except those by conscience made; and it shall lie there till all is over."

Silent—stunned, I threw myself beside him, and joined my cold cheek to his.

"O Helen! and is it *thus* we meet? Is *this* our re-union?"

"Live! do *but* live!" cried I, in a burst of salutary tears, "and you shall find how *dearly* I love you still; and we shall be so happy—happier than ever!"

He shook his head mournfully, and said he did not deserve to live, and to be so happy; and he humbly bowed to that chastising hand which, when he had escaped punishment for *real* errors, made him fall the victim of an imaginary one.

The surgeons now came to examine the wound a second time, and confirmed their previous sentence, that the wound was mortal; on which he desired to be left alone with me, and I was able to suppress my feelings, that I might soothe his, during this overwhelming interview.

These moments are some of the dearest and most sacred in the stores of memory—but I shall not detail them: suffice, that I was able, in default of better aid, to cheer the death-bed of the beloved sufferer, and breathe over him, from the lips of agonizing tenderness, the faltering but fervent prayer.

That duty done, my fortitude was exhausted. I saw before me, not the erring husband—the being who had blighted my youth by anxiety, and wounded all the dearest feelings of my soul; but the playfellow of my childhood—the idolized object of my youthful heart, and the husband of my virgin affections! And I was going to lose him! and he lay pale and bleeding before me! and his last, fond, lingering look of unutterable love was now about to close on me for ever!

"She has forgiven me!" he faltered out; "and oh! mayest Thou forgive my trespasses against *thee!* Helen! it is sweet and consoling, my only love, to die here!" said he, laying his cheek upon my bosom — and he spoke no more!

* * * * *

Alas! I could not have the sad consolation, when I recovered my recollection, to carry his body to England, to repose by those dear ones already in the grave;—but I do not regret it now. Since then, the hands of piety have planted the rough soil in which he was laid; flowers bloom around his grave; and when, five years ago, I visited Paris, with my own hands I strewed his simple tomb with flowers, that spring from the now hallowed soil around.

Object of my earliest and my fondest love! never—no, never have I forgotten thee! nor can I ever forget!—But, like one of the shades of Ossian, thou comest over my soul, brightly arrayed in the beams of thy loveliness; but all around thee is dark with mists and storms!

To conclude. I have only to add, that after two years of seclusion, and I may say of sorrow, and one of that dryness and desolation of the heart, when it seems as if it could love no more, that painful feeling vanished, and I became the willing bride of De Walden; that my beloved uncle lived to see me the happy mother of two children; and that my aunt gossips, advises, and quotes, as well and as constantly as usual; that, on the death of his uncle and his mother, my husband and I came to reside entirely in England; that Lord Charles Belmour, with a broken constitution and a shattered fortune, was glad at last to marry for a nurse and a dower, and took to wife a first-cousin, who had loved him for years—a woman who had sense enough to overlook his faults in his good qualities, and temper enough to bear with the former; and he grows every day more happy, more amiable, and more in love with marriage.

For myself, I own with humble thankfulness the vastness of the blessings I enjoy; and though I cannot repent that I married the husband of my own choice, I confess I have never been so truly happy as with the husband of my mother's: for, though I feel that it is often delightful to forgive a husband's errors, she, and she alone, is truly to be envied, whose husband has no errors to forgive.

END OF A WOMAN'S LOVE, AND A WIFE'S DUTY.

THE TWO SONS.

In a populous village, on the borders of Westmoreland, lived an exciseman of the name of Douglas. He was descended from an old Scotch family, which had gradually become poorer and poorer, from generation to generation, till its representatives sunk into utter obscurity; and the father of him of whom I am writing thought himself very fortunate in procuring the place of exciseman, and in being allowed to resign it when he grew old to his son. This son sunk himself still lower in society, by marrying beneath him: and every spark of ambition seemed extinguished in his bosom, till he became the father of two boys, and then he suddenly recollected that he heard his father say, the name of Douglas was a good name; he therefore resolved to give his sons an education. But our exciseman inherited the indolence and wasteful habits of his progenitors, and the advantages bestowed by a village-schoolmaster were all he was able to give his children. Still, such as they were, the younger son made himself master of all the learning offered to him; while the other son, though three years his senior, was as ignorant when he left school as he was when he entered it.

It is natural to conclude therefore, that the parents would have been prouder and fonder of Ronald Douglas than of his elder brother; but it was not so; on the contrary, the petted and spoiled child was the dull, idle, unamiable boy; and he who was the pride of his master, and the favourite of the village, was treated at home with even brutal severity; while, if his warm heart was not chilled into apathy, his manners were rendered cold and reserved, and his temper apparently sullen.

The elder boy, John, was strikingly handsome; and so had Ronald been, but the smallpox injured the excessive beauty of his skin, and with his fine complexion vanished most of his mother's love. John, therefore, remained without a competitor in her good opinion and admiration. To her, the fair florid cheek, the bright unmeaning eyes, of John, were the perfection of loveliness, while she and her husband both mistook his pertness for wit, and thought his not being able to learn was to be attributed to his excessive quickness and cleverness. To their undiscriminating eye, Ronald's expressive countenance possessed no beauty; and his look of mild intelligence said nothing to their hearts, while they persisted to believe that he got forward in the school merely by dint of plodding, and that his excellence was as much a proof of stupidity as John's ignorance was of talent. This is a very common mistake; and often do parents attribute to superior quickness in their children, that incapacity to learn by which they are nevertheless secretly annoyed.

Poor Ronald was so often told that he was ugly, stupid, and disagreeable, that he at last believed it: the consequence was, that at fifteen, his spirits were depressed, his abilities checked, his hopes gone, and a sort of early blight seemed to have come over his heart. As he was now old enough to work for his living, he was soon informed by his father that he must choose a trade. He would have liked to have been a schoolmaster, for he loved books, and loved children; but he found that he was expected to choose a mechanical employment, and he was bound to a carpenter. His brother, meanwhile, did nothing: his foolish parents thought he was so handsome, that he might make his fortune by marrying; and they meant to try to raise money enough to buy him a commission in the army, for " how handsome John would look in a red coat!" They did not hit upon this sensible plan till they had tried another in vain. An old friend of theirs, an apothecary, took John out of kindness into his shop, with a very small premium; but being wholly unaccustomed to obey, he soon told his master he would not do any dirty work; and on his being reproved for disobedience and impertinence, he, without leave, returned home, where he met with sympathy and indulgence, instead of proper chastisement and reproof; and his parents resolved not to expose so fine a gentleman, and a youth of such a *proper spirit*, to such degradation in future.

At eighteen, John Douglas was the tyrant of the parents who doted on him, and the slave of his own uncontrollable temper and ungovernable passions.

It was soon certain that no money could ever be raised to buy a commission, as John ran in debt, and his father was not only forced to maintain him, but to pay money to save him from disgrace. "Sweet are the uses of adversity," and safer is it for a child to be thwarted and reproved, than to be petted and never contradicted; therefore, while John Douglas became more despicable every day, the virtues of Ronald Douglas every day increased.

The neighbours loved and pitied him; and if there was a kind action to be done, Ronald was asked to do it. His master said he worked hard and well at his business, and would be the best carpenter in the place; and while temperance, industry, and exercise, gave health to his cheek, and size to his manly limbs, he as much out-towered his brother in stature, as he excelled him in character.—This was an injury which John and his mother highly resented; and a sort of vindictive dislike of Ronald, whose superiority he felt, took possession of the heart of John Douglas, which already showed itself on his countenance, and impressed on it those traces of malignity which made his face, if once seen,—especially when under the influence of such feelings,—never to be forgotten.

Ronald Douglas was so formed for the tenderest feelings of filial love, that nothing could supply, to his disappointed heart, the want of parental affection. He therefore acquired habits of lonely musing and reverie, in which a sort of ideal world supplied the place of real objects; and life as it *might* be, was contrasted by him with life as it *was*. He was not, however, insensible to the kindness which he experienced out of his own family; and the heart shut up at home opened abroad.

A house in the village, which had been long uninhabited, had at length found a tenant; and before the new inhabitant took possession, he wished a vault or drain belonging to it to be wholly removed. Accordingly, four men were hired to go down the dark steps which led to it; and foolishly enough, they all went down together. But they had not been down five minutes, when they answered not to the signals which were made to them, and great apprehensions were entertained for their lives, as the vault had not been entered for years, and the vapours in it must consequently be of a most deadly nature.—Alarm now spread through the village and the wives and children of the poor men came clamouring and lamenting round. For who would have courage and benevolence enough to risk his own life in order to preserve theirs? No one could even be expected to do it; and all hope for the unhappy victims was at an end, when Ronald Douglas was walking near the spot, and seeing the crowd, came to ask what was the matter. They informed him; and his heart was melted to the most painful compassion, by the tears and agonies of the mourners.

"How long have they been down?" said he.

"A very short time; and they might be recovered probably. But who," added the person to whom he spoke, "will go down and risk his life for the chance of preserving theirs?"

"I will,"* cried Ronald: and whether it was from the impulse of benevolence, or that life had fewer charms for him than for the rest, he insisted on being allowed to descend, and on having the requisite precautions procured directly.

"But, dear Ronald," cried one, "we dare not let you do this without your father's and mother's leave."

"Their leave!" cried Ronald starting, and the hectic of a moment passing over his cheeks, while he replied in a bitter tone, "Oh! they would not deny it to me; and if you hesitate any longer, I will go *without* what I ask."—As he said this he descended two or three steps into the vault; and finding him resolved, they gave him what he required. This was a rope, one end of which was to be held by those above, a jug of vinegar, and a light in a lantern. Armed with these, he courageously descended to the bottom of the gloomy abyss, but was so suffocated by the vapours from it, that he scarcely had power to throw a little vinegar about it, when he fell nearly fainting to the ground. But his noble and generous spirit gathered new strength from the difficulty; and having applied the vinegar to his nostrils, he recovered, and threw a great part of the contents of the jug into the darkness before him. As he expected, the pestiferous damp dispersed, and he was able to distinguish the four men lying at the foot of the steps, and part of their bodies in the putrid stream. He instantly re-ascended the steps for a grappling-hook; and returning he tied a rope to the man nearest him, and called to those above to drag the rope up. They did so, while he assisted the senseless body in its unconscious progress, and preserved it from being dashed against the sides of the vault. It reached the top in safety; and Ronald, encouraged by his success, descended for another, and he too was drawn up without much difficulty. But the third was further in the stream; and as Ronald was forced to stoop lower over it than before, he felt himself turn sick and faint; and when he and his charge reached the air, he fainted away: but he soon

* This generous action, under circumstances similar to what I have described, was really performed in a village in France by a girl only twenty years old, whose name was Catherine Vassent; and she received in person, at the Academy in Paris, the yearly prize adjudged to virtue. She also received great honours in her own village. I have seen a French drama on this subject.

recovered, and insisted on going down again. He did so, and saved another from destruction. Again he descended; but the fourth was deeply sunk in the water, and it was with the greatest difficulty he succeeded in dragging him to the steps. However he persevered, and he too was once more restored to the eyes of his anxious relatives; but not to life. The others soon showed signs of returning consciousness, but he was gone for ever: and Ronald felt his joy incomplete, because he had not been able to preserve them all.

A scene now ensued that I would fain paint, but cannot; the wives and children hanging with suspended breath over the bodies, whose heaving bosoms began to give assurance of struggling existence: the widow and the orphans mourning over him whose eyes could never unclose again; and another group surrounding Ronald, blessing him, and calling him by the most tender and gratifying appellations! But he was one who was inclined "to do good by stealth," and "blushed to find it fame." Accordingly, he suddenly broke from them all, and springing over a hedge, escaped along a by-path to the back of his father's garden, and entering it unseen, by a gap in the hedge, threw himself under a favourite tree, hid his face in his hands, and burst into tears,—the result of mingled and contending emotions. He had saved the lives of three of his fellow-creatures, and these three were also his neighbours and acquaintance. They were husbands too, and they were fathers; and he was rich in the consciousness of not having lived in vain, and in being endeared and respected throughout his native place.

But oh! bitter was the drawback to his joy; for instead of being able to hasten to his parents to tell his tale of virtuous triumph to them, and cause their hearts to participate in the joy of his, he knew that they would receive the story with coldness and indifference, and would probably damp all his generous exultation by saying, 'What a busy fool you were for running such a risk!' Yet still he felt a sensation of happiness predominating over the rest of his feelings; and as he raised his eyes in heart-felt gratitude to heaven, he felt the repinings of his spirit gradually but entirely subside.

When the poor men were able to speak, and to ask how they were preserved, those around missed the generous Ronald, and told with tearful incoherence the tale of his benevolent daring.

"Where is he! Where is the noble boy!" cried many voices at once; and the rescued men were eager to see and bless him.

"We will go to his house; we will carry him round the village," said some sailors just paid off from the ship in a neighbouring port.

"Ay, and we will make him a civic crown," said Ronald's master, glad to display his learning in his beloved pupil's honour. Then running to his garden he pulled a branch of laurel; which, being tied together at the ends, the delighted old man carried in his hand as the procession marched, shouting and huzzaing through the road that led to the house of Ronald.

As they went, the pallid but animated look of the men, whom their wives and children supported, the civic garland, the procession— in short the whole scene together, attracted the attention of two sentimental travellers who were walking along to enjoy the pleasant weather, with their servants and carriage following at a distance; and they stopped to inquire the reason of what they saw.

Those to whom they spoke were as willing to tell as the travellers to hear; and they congratulated each other on their good fortune in coming through the village at such a moment.

"How I should like to see this noble boy!" said the lady.

"How I should like to serve him!" cried the gentleman.

On hearing this, the good schoolmaster begged they would join in the party, and go to the house with them; and then, as they walked along, he told them the history of poor Ronald in all its painful details.

The husband and wife now fell back from the rest, and held a conversation together, in a low voice.

I shall pause in my narrative to give some account of these travellers.

The husband, Mr. Fullarton, left his native land and Edinburgh, the city of his birth, to go as a writer to India. He went reluctantly, for he was in love; but, as he had no fortune independent of his father, and that father would give him nothing during his life, he was forced to accept the offered place, and try to earn the power of marrying the girl of his heart. To industry like his, stimulated by the tenderest of affections, fortune could not long remain a stranger;—and Grace Douglas was summoned to India sooner than even her sanguine expectations led her to hope. She was accompanied thither by her sister, who, some time after, had pledged her own vows to an English gentleman, of the name of Hatfield. But a different lot awaited her; for while Mr. and Mrs. Fullarton were the happiest of the happy, Mr. and Mrs. Hatfield were the most ill-assorted couple in Calcutta; and the only comfort of the latter was derived from the society of her brother and sister.

But they, happy as they were, had drawbacks to their felicity. They had an only child, who died at the age of six years, just as they were going to send him to England for education;—and as years rolled on without giving another child to their wishes, they had at length made up their minds to the disappointment.

Mrs. Fullarton now received a letter from Scotland, and from the aunt who had brought her up. This lady told her she was dying of an incurable complaint, but one that might not destroy her for months.—She therefore wrote to say, that should they have any intention of revisiting Britain, she hoped they would not delay putting it in execution, as she earnestly wished to embrace her niece, if possible, once more before she died.

"Poor dear woman!" cried Mr. Fullarton, as he read the letter.

"We had no intention of going, as you know, Grace; but, for her sake, we will set off directly. It is due to her, is it not, Grace?"

The delighted and grateful wife could only weep her thanks, and everything was put in train directly for their sailing.

"But what will become of me, if you never return?" said poor Mrs. Hatfield. "Your father, Mr. Fullarton, is supposed to be declining fast; and as you are now the only son, should he die, your return must be out of the question; as his estates will be yours. And how can I exist without the comfort and protection of your presence?"

"We will *certainly* come back at *all* events, on your account," he replied. "We have no children, and one place is the same to us as another: therefore, why not live in India, as the climate suits us? and if our living near you is a comfort to you, how can you think we will not return?"

"Kindest of men!" faltered out the grateful invalid, while her unhappy sisters folded her in an affectionate embrace, and sighed to think how unlike their husbands were. Soon after, the Fullartons embarked for Britain.

But, agreed as they were on most subjects, these good people differed on *one*. They were both not a little given to romance and enthusiasm, and were great admirers of heroism and self-devotion.—But Mr. Fullarton earnestly wished for the abrogation of that Hindoo law, which obliged a Hindoo wife to burn herself on the body of her husband. Mrs. Fullarton, on the contrary, reprobated as cruel the wish to prevent a widow from thus sacrificing herself, declaring, with tears in her eyes, that for her part *she* could not consider the law as inflicting any *hardship* on a woman, but that it was a mercy, not a cruelty. Mr. Fullarton probably was not convinced by what his wife said; but he always dropped the subject after she had thus spoken, and used to be troubled with a sort of hoarseness and choking cough, when she ceased to speak.

Such were the persons who, having closed the eyes both of his father and her aunt, were now on their way from Scotland to London, previous to re-embarking for India, when they came through the village of L——, and time enough to witness a scene so truly in unison with their high-wrought imaginations and benevolent hearts.

But to return. Our travellers were roused from their earnest conversation, by the shouts of the sailors and others, who declared that they were arrived at Ronald's door. Ronald, as I before stated, was lying under a tree in the garden, and his father and mother were taking their afternoon's sleep in their chairs. The noise which these unexpected visitants made roused them from their slumber, and the father, starting up, ran to the door and opened it.

"We want your son," cried they: "We want to carry the brave lad in triumph round the village, to do him *honour*."

"Honour to my son! Oh, I will call him directly!"

On which, he went to call John, asking him how he deserved such respect. He could not tell; but he eagerly followed his father down stairs, and with his exulting mother went to the door, bowing and smiling with ineffable conceit.

"Not you, you poor fair-weather sailor!" cried one of the tars, "it is your brother we want."

"You have *two* sons, Mr. Douglas," said Mr. Fullarton with emphasis: "We want that fine fellow, Ronald: where is *he*?"

"Dear me! I am sure I do not know," said his mother.

"Nor I," said John, pale with spite.

"I think I saw him jump the hedges, and enter the garden," cried one.

"Then we will have him out," cried another; and into the garden they all went, Mr. and Mrs. Fullarton eagerly following.

Ronald started up at the noise they made, and stood in silent wonder at their appearance; but, as soon as the reason of it was explained to him, he suddenly turned round, and attempted to run away. But he was instantly seized, and Mr. Fullarton gently assured him, that he ought not to deny his friends and neighbours the pleasure of expressing their gratitude and love for him, in any way they chose.

Ronald bowed respectfully, but remained silent; while Mrs. Fullarton was whispering her husband, "What a fine creature! I declare, he is like my poor brother, who died at sixteen. I dare say he is of our blood, for his name is Douglas, you know."

Mr. Fullarton now introduced himself and his wife to Ronald, and Mrs. Fullarton exclaimed—

"Noble boy! blessed is the mother who bore you! Mrs. Douglas, you must be proud of your son."

"If you will tell me why, madam, for I cannot think what you are all about, so crazy like, I take it."

Mr. Fullarton then told the wondering but not elated parents the whole story, corroborated by their neighbours, and the poor men themselves, who with their wives and children were surrounding Ronald, and blessing him with quivering lips.—This was more than he could endure; his breast heaved, his limbs trembled, and he wanted, nay, longed, to throw himself on the neck of his parents; but, alas! he could not do it, and invited by the glistening eye and kind look of Mr. Fullarton, who stood by him, he threw himself on his shoulder, and wept aloud.

"Ronald, for shame! what a liberty you are taking with the gentleman!" cried his mother.

"Ronald, what are you about?" said his father; "the boy's head is turned — he quite forgets himself."

"No," replied Mr. Fullarton, sternly, as Ronald withdrew from his embrace—"no; he only remembers too well, poor boy! and knows that the heart of a stranger yearned towards him more than that of his parents. But from this moment my heart adopts him."

"And so does mine!" cried Mrs. Fullarton, grasping his hand; "and I will be a mother to him."

"And I a father!" while the good old schoolmaster threw up his cap in the air, and exclaimed, "Ronald will be a gentleman, and need not neglect his Latin!"

"But come, we will not lose our frolic for all that—so, have at you, young man!" said two of the sailors, seizing Ronald as they spoke; while Norton, the schoolmaster, now presented him with the civic wreath, repeating, as he did so, some lines from Horace.

Ronald was too much overwhelmed by all he saw and felt, to be able to reply or to resist; and when they had led him to the door, they soon hoisted him on their shoulders, and led the procession. The poor men wished to join in it, though they still felt weak from their danger; but as Mr. Fullarton's carriage now drove up, that gentleman insisted on their entering it, and they, the most interesting persons in the show next to their preserver, brought up the rear. Mr. and Mrs. Fullarton, with Ronald's parents, stood at the gate looking at it till it was out of sight; and even the latter did not seem to hear unmoved those unbought shouts in honour of their son; but the former listened with glistening eyes, and with an exquisite feeling of gratified benevolence, which they felt grateful to Ronald for having so unexpectedly procured them.

But where was John Douglas, while these honours were conferred on his younger brother? Did he walk in the procession, and join in the general enthusiasm with a brother's heart? No; he shut himself up in his own room, till the procession was out of sight; and he held his ears, muttering curses as he did so, that the acclamations might not agonize his envious and ungenerous mind.

When he ceased to hear and to see what he disliked, he came down stairs, and was not agreeably surprised to find Mr. and Mrs. Fullarton sitting with his father and mother.

"Well, then, Mrs. Douglas, you say you have no objection to letting me adopt your son, and providing for him in life as I choose?"

"Not if you think him worth your troubling yourself, sir," said Mrs. Douglas. She dared not, in the presence of John, say any thing but what was uncivil of his brother. "But I must say, we have found him sulky and dull, and only good enough to be a working carpenter."

"I did not speak to you, Mrs. Douglas," said Mr. Fullarton. "What say you, sir? Will you part with your son, or not?"

"Why you see, sir, he is bound to a carpenter."

"Well, but, for a certain consideration, no doubt, he will give up his indentures."

"But who is to pay that, sir?"

"I, to be sure."

"Well, really," cried the incorrigible mother, "to think that any one should take such a fancy to Ronald! Had it been to John, indeed, I should not have wondered. Smooth down your hair, my darling! you do not look well to-day; the gentle-folks do not see you to advantage."

"Mother, hold your tongue—you are an old fool!" was the dutiful answer.

"Pray, Mrs. Douglas," said Mr. Fullarton, "did your darling John ever save the lives of three of his fellow-creatures, at the risk of his own?"

"La! no, he was never so silly; for suppose he had been suffocated, you know. Why, if John had done it, and been — O dear! the thought turns me all over, like——"

"There is no fear, I fancy, of his ever trying your sensibility thus; but may I ask in what way your son John has claims on any one's preference over Ronald?"

"Look at him," replied the fond mother.

"But what can he do? Is he clever in any trade or profession?"

"Oh, no! he was always too quick to learn."

"Peace, you silly woman!" said Mr. Douglas; "the truth is, John has good parts, but is very idle, and at present I am forced to maintain him; but he is a fine-looking, genteel lad."

"Ay, that he is—and he is a lad to make a gentleman of, *indeed!*"

"What a sarcasm on gentlemen!" said Mr. Fullarton. "So, then, a lad that calls his mother an old fool—that cannot learn — and who, at the age of twenty, chooses to be a burden to his poor father and mother, rather than work for his living, is exactly fitted for a gentleman, is he? But I beg pardon — I am taking great liberties here."

"Do not mind what my foolish wife says," replied Mr. Douglas, who had sense enough to feel the justice of this reproof; "but tell me all your goodness intends for Ronald."

"We are on our return to India, and we wish to take Ronald with us."

"To India!" screamed out Mrs. Douglas.

"Oh! then I do not care that John is not the favourite, for it would have killed me to have him go to the Indies."

"Hold your tongue, mother; if I like, I will go in spite of you."

"Yes," continued Mr. Fullarton, "I have had a writership offered me for a young friend, and I mean to give it to Ronald, if he likes to accept it."

"Likes to accept it!" cried the father; "I should like to see him dare to refuse it!"

"He shall refuse it, if he wishes to do so, sir; for I will not punish the virtue I meant to reward; but I believe from what I see of poor Ronald's home, that he will be glad to accept it. In that admirable woman, I assure you, sir, he will find a mother, and in me a father; and, if I read him aright, I doubt not but, when he has made a fortune, which he will do very soon, that he will remember you as his parents, and nobly, too."

"Mother," exclaimed John Douglas, with a face crimson with passion, and almost inarticulate with ungovernable feelings—"mother, if you let Ronald go to India, and be put so over my head, I will *kill* myself!" Then, with a malignant scowl at the strangers, he left the room, banging the door to with a violence that shook the house: on which his mother fell into an hysterical cry, and declared Ronald should not go, to kill her poor darling John.

This roused the now indignant spirit of her husband; and no longer awed by the presence of that child whom they had petted into a tyrant, before whose frown they trembled, the old man declared that he should scarcely lament if John was dead, for that then he would be safe from evils to come, and that he was the torment and terror of his life; adding, that no consideration for John should induce him to refuse to let Ronald go. In the midst of the conversation, the procession returned, and Ronald eagerly escaped from the oppressive kindness of his friends into his own house, and, followed by the delighted Norton, entered the parlour with a countenance full of emotion, and a cheek glowing with modest triumph.

"Is that the countenance of a dull and sullen boy?" said Mrs. Fullarton, smiling, and holding out her hand to Ronald.

"He dull and sullen!" said Norton, coming forward, but bowing very low: "he was the pride of my school, and the joy of my heart."

"And I trust that he will be the joy of ours," said Mr. Fullarton.

"Ronald, will you go with us to India, and make your fortune?"

"I will go anywhere with you," replied Ronald, eagerly. It was the first time that his new friends had heard his voice; and its deep but sweet tone added to the favourable impression which he had made on them.

"But will my father and mother consent? and can I break my indentures?"

"I think you were very ready to leave us, Ronald," said his father, consistently with his usual injustice: "the indentures can be broken."

"That they can, for his master is my brother, and loves him as I do," said old Norton, "and will never stand in the way of Ronald's promotion. To be sure, I shall miss him, and can never hope to see him again: but it is for his good, I trust." Here he turned to the window to hide his emotion.

"Then I may look on these matters as settled, Mr. Douglas: you consent to Ronald's acceptance of the writership, and to his going with us to India. But he must come up to London in three or four days, as he has to procure his outfit; and by that time he will have arranged all his affairs here, and taken leave of all his friends."

"Agreed, sir," said Mr. Douglas: "he is yours; do with him what you please, and God bless you for your goodness!"

"Now then, my love," said Mr. Fullarton, "we must go a stage on our way to London. We shall soon meet again, Ronald: till then, God bless you!" and Ronald, unable to speak, could only grasp the kind hands tendered to him.

The Fullartons did not quit the village without leaving marks of their bounty amongst all those who had done honour to their *protégé*; nor were the poor men whom he had saved forgotten. To old Norton, Mr. Fullarton promised the last new edition of Horace; and he declared he should not sleep that night for joy.

Ronald, still unable to believe that his good fortune was not a dream, looked after the carriage till he could see it no longer, and then returned to meet very different persons and looks from those which the departing carriage contained. He found his mother wondering what business any one had to come and make mischief by meddling and making in her family; and seeing him, she exclaimed, "Ah! here you come: you were never anything but a plague to me since you had the small-pox, and grew so ugly; and now you are going over sea, and that vexes John."

"Is John sorry to part with me?" said Ronald, joyfully.

"Sorry?" cried his father: "no, he is only sorry for your good-fortune."

John now entered the room, with the look of a fiend, saying, "There is something for the *new gentleman!*" and the maid-servant brought in a paper parcel directed to Ronald, which a waiter at the only inn in the village had brought. On opening it, it was found to contain a complete suit of black clothes, and linen to wear with them; and was accompanied by the following note from Mr. Fullarton:—

"My dear Ronald—My wife and I cannot bear that you should wear, longer than you can help, those coarse habiliments which, though proper for your former situation, are not so for that which you are about to occupy. I have therefore sent you a suit of clothes which I have not yet worn, and which, as we are of the same height and size, you will, I trust, be able to wear; and I charge you to go to church next Sunday in them.

"Your affectionate friend,
"W. FULLARTON."

Ronald told as much of the contents of the note as he thought proper, then retired to fit on the present of his benefactor. But seeing the storm on his brother's brow, he would not wear the clothes that evening; but he walked to Norton's house in his usual dress, and spent the evening with him.

Norton's brother gave up Ronald's indentures immediately, and was very unwilling to receive any recompense. Half the sum offered was all he would accept; and Ronald resolved that he should be no loser by it.

Ronald did not return home till bed-time: he found his mother sitting up for John, who was gone to sup with a rider from London, with whom he often associated, and from whom he learnt no good. This strange woman reproached Ronald for going out and leaving his parents during one of the three last evenings he was ever to spend at home. However unjust this reproach was, the good heart of Ronald was pleased at it; and he hailed it as a sign of affection—not seeing that it was nothing more than the ebullition of ill-humour, which had nothing else to vent itself upon.

"My dear mother!" said Ronald, "depend on it, I will not quit you again till I go."

"There is reason in roasting of eggs, child," replied Mrs. Douglas; "and I am sure I do not want you to be tied to my apron-strings."

They now heard John's voice at the door, in his loudest and surliest tone; and the weak, terrified parents, suspecting that intoxication had probably rendered John more fierce than usual, entreated Ronald to go to bed before she let his brother in, and to lock his door. Ronald instantly obeyed her in both particulars, and it was well he did, for John did try to enter his chamber; and as he could not, vented his ill-humour on the outside in oaths and execrations.

The next day was Sunday; and Ronald, dressed in his new apparel, descended to the breakfast-table. Spite of her folly, and her envious partiality to John, Mrs. Douglas could not see Ronald, with his really fine person, set off by the dress of a gentleman, without feeling both pride and pleasure at the sight—and, oh, unexpected favour! she desired him to come and kiss her, for he looked charmingly in his new dress.

"My child!" said his father, his voice faltering with a much deeper feeling, "God grant you long health to wear them, and many others! and I trust you will live to be somebody."

"I hope—I trust, sir," replied Ronald, "that under no circumstances shall I ever disgrace you."

"Disgrace! no; I expect you will prove an honour to us."

This was the happiest moment which his parents had ever given poor Ronald—a kiss from his mother, and flattering speeches from his father! and he went to church with a heart glowing with gratitude to Heaven. There was not an eye there which on his entrance did not welcome Ronald. The poor men whom he had saved were at church; and the clergyman, at their desire, returned thanks for their signal deliverance; while Ronald's feelings at that moment were such as any one living might have envied.

As soon as the service concluded, Ronald left the pew, wishing to escape without speaking to any one; especially as the clergyman, in his sermon and in his text, made an obvious allusion to Ronald's heroic, or rather *Christian* action. But he was not allowed so to evade notice; and he was asked by the rector to dine with him; an honour, he, however, refused, because it would be the last Sunday he might ever spend with his parents.

"I honour your motives, young man—they are worthy of you," replied the gentleman; "and I do not urge you further. Farewell, then! I trust, by the blessing of God, that I shall live to see you return to us, full of honours; for according to an old saying, 'A good beginning makes a good ending.'"

John Douglas had been so excessively intoxicated the night before, that he did not rise till late the next day; and as he was not present to prevent the natural flow of his parents' feelings towards Ronald, the morning and the dinner hours were unusually pleasant to him. His heart, therefore, yearned towards his father and mother with feelings which he had scarcely ever experienced before; and while he thought that he was about to leave them and home, perhaps for ever, his spirits sunk, till, in the delusive softness of the moment, he fancied that his home was worthy of regret, and he "sighed as he thought of the morrow."

While these ideas crossed his mind, and as he remembered how age would have changed his parents before he saw them again, he drew his chair close to his mother's, leaned affectionately on the arm of it, and would have taken her hand as it rested on her knee, but she pettishly drew back her hand and her chair, exclaiming,—

"There, child! do sit further off, or you will set your chair on my gown."

Ronald drew back as he was bidden to do, chilled and disappointed. Soon after, John made his appearance, when his mother pressed him to sit by her, asked him what he would like to have, and bestowed on the thankless elder-born what would have bound the younger to her for ever.

John replied, by telling her to hold her palaver, and not plague him; and on her saying, "Take this easy chair, love," he accepted the offer; but then, declaring the room was so hot he could not bear it, he ran to the window and opened the casement.

"I cannot bear the air at my back, John," said his father.

"Then change your seat."

"But your mother has a bad cold; you must not keep the window open long—it is a north wind."

"*Must* not!" he replied with a sort of defiance; then, lolling out of the window, he began to sing.

"It is Sunday, John," said his mother— "you forget that."

"So did you, I fancy—for you did not go to church; therefore hold *your* tongue."

"It is plain *you* never go to church," said his father, "for you seem not to have learnt the commandment, to 'honour your father and your mother.'"

"Did they ever *teach* me to honour them?"

"We have tried, John, to make you love us, however; yet I believe poor Ronald, to whom we have never been very kind, loves us better than you do."

"The more fool he —— but what have we here? Carpenter Ronald turned gentleman, I declare, and dressed out in his master's cast-off clothes! Turn about, Ronald, and let us look at you."

Ronald meekly obeyed; nor did he deign to notice the insulting word of "master," or the "cast-off clothes."

But his mother, who had felt great respect for Ronald's dress, if not for him, had the rashness to reply—

"Nay, John, the gentleman is not Ronald's master, he is to be his friend—not his servant; and as to the clothes, they are *quite new*, and the gentleman never put them on in his life."

"It is a lie—I know they are not new."

"A lie!" cried his mother, in a tearful voice; "I am sure I do not lie!"

"Yes, you do; and I wonder Ronald is not ashamed to wear any one's old clothes."

"Old or new," returned Mrs. Douglas, rising as she spoke with more spirit than was usual to her, and approaching to shut the window, "Ronald may be proud to wear them, for he earned them by his good deeds, and that is more than other persons can say for themselves."

The poor woman had scarcely ended her ill-advised speech, when John gave her a blow which made her stagger, adding, "And if you dare affront me again, or presume to shut the window till I choose, I will turn you out of the room." He then seized her by the arm with a violence which made her scream.

Ronald, who had borne his own insults with meekness, could not so endure the injuries of his mother; but, seizing his brutal brother with one hand in his nervous grasp, he opened the door with the other, and threw him into the passage.

"My noble boy!" sobbed out his self-accused father, "*you* have done what *I* should have done; but it is too late now."

His mother said nothing at first: she only listened to the angry threats of John, as he walked up and down.

At length, she said, "I will not have John turned out of the room by any one — he shall come in."

"Ay, go to your petted brute," said Mr. Douglas, "and make much of him: your weak indulgence, poor lad! has made him what he is."

"With a little of your assistance, my dear," said she, unbarring the door.

"John, my darling! I am not angry with you. I forgive you, dear! Do come in—pray do!"

"No, that I will not," he replied in a voice of thunder: "I will go away, and never come back—at least, never till Ronald is gone."

"Well, dear, well: Ronald goes to-morrow, you know."

"O heavens!" exclaimed Ronald, cut to the quick by the tone of joy rather than of sorrow, in which his mother said this; and rushing out of the room, passing his brother, who shrunk back terrified at his approach, he ran and threw himself under the tree where he had lain when his benefactors first approached him —that tree which was always his refuge when unhappy within doors, and was now dear to him from association and recollection. But it was long before he could succeed in pacifying his wounded spirit. It was, therefore, long ere he ventured to return to the house: when he did so, he found John was gone out, and his mother was in earnest conversation with his father.

"I tell you what, Ronald," said she, "I will not suffer you to take on yourself to correct your brother: the poor lad did not hurt me, nor mean to hurt me much, I am sure."

"Not much!" replied Ronald.

"No—there was no harm in what he did."

"No *harm*, mother? Is not the curse of the Almighty on the child who lifts his arm against his parent?"

"How shocking you talk, Ronald! But pray, was not that man Cain cursed who lifted his arm against his brother Abel? I wonder who was like Cain just now! Answer me that." But his heart was too full.

"You see what you get by taking your mother's part," said Mr. Douglas; "but don't mind what she says. I tell you that I am convinced the blessing of the Almighty will go with you wherever you go. O Ronald! I am justly punished for all my harshness to you: now that I feel your worth, I am going to lose you for ever!"

Ronald would fain have offered to stay, if he wished it; but he was conscious that these parental feelings were called forth by circumstances only, and might vanish again: he was, besides, pledged to accept the proffered kindness of his new friends. While this was passing, his mother angrily left the room, and went in search of her darling; but he was still absent, and till he came home, all quiet conversation between Ronald and his father was destroyed by her restlessness. He came home, however, to supper; but, though sullen, was not savage, to the surprise and comfort of Ronald. He did not, indeed, speak to him or to any one; but his silence after Ronald's spirited action in defence of his mother was a sign of abated hostility. When he was gone to bed, and Ronald rose to retire also, wishing his parents Good night, even Mrs. Douglas heard and was affected by his faltering voice, and could not help observing, " Dear me, Ronald! well, who knows if we shall ever wish each other good night again? There is something very awful, as I think, in that. Well, poor child! I am sure I wish you well, and hope you will forget and forgive whenever I was cross; for you did provoke me sometimes — that is the truth of it. But come, Ronald dear! kiss, and be friends."

He affectionately met her offered kiss; then turned to wring and press the trembling hand of his father.

"Ronald, my dear, ill-treated boy!" said he, "all I ask of you is to think as *little* ill of us as you can, and write to us when it suits you." Ronald's only answer was his tears; and he gladly hurried to his chamber.

The next morning he rose very early, visited all the scenes of his first and dearest recollections, and called on all his neighbours and friends, except the poor men whose lives he had saved: the clamorous expressions of their regret, good wishes, and gratitude, his delicacy and his nerves equally shrunk from encountering.

"But I will see my dear old master," said Ronald to himself, " in all his glory once more." Accordingly, he approached his school-room; but the bee-like hum of many voices was not heard, and all was still and silent. " How strange!" thought he; "and so long after the hour of meeting, too?" However, he knocked, and Norton's voice replied in a mournful tone, " Come in." He did so, and found the poor old man alone, sitting leaning his head on his arm, which rested on his knee, as if lost in mournful reflection. At sight of Ronald, he started up, and his countenance became cheerful, but it soon clouded over again.

" Why are you not keeping school to-day, my dear friend ?"

" Why, because you are going away. Not that your going away is a holiday, child; oh, no! with me it is one of sorrow and humiliation of spirit: but I could not have done my duty by the children when I thought of you, and that I had seen you for the last time."

" Come, come; you must not talk or think thus," replied Ronald in a faltering tone; " I have need of all my spirits, as I am going away."

" No, Ronald; they suffer most at parting who stay behind; and it will be so sad to look for you, and look in vain! But it is all for your good, and so I do not repine — at least I try to do so as little as I can help."

It is not to be supposed, when Ronald had taken leave of this attached old friend, that he returned home more fitted than before to bear parting with his parents with firmness. On the contrary, as he forgot their past unkindness in their present affectionate behaviour, he left them with a degree of tender regret and violent sorrow which their conduct to him had little deserved; and when the coach stopped, he could scarcely distinguish his way to it, so great was the disorder of his feelings. Just as he was going to get into the coach, John, who was not yet up, though it was twelve o'clock, and he knew his brother was to go at that time, opened his window, and cried out, " Good bye, Ronald, and be sure to write *often* to us."

Ronald's heart bounded with pleasure at this unexpected mark of kindness, while he kissed his hand in return, and nodded the adieu which he could not utter.

As the coach passed through the village, numbers came out to take their last look of Ronald; and amongst them, as he feared, the men whom he had preserved; nor would they allow the coach to go on till they had poured forth all their hearts were full of. Their children had culled the best flowers of their gardens as a parting gift to Ronald; and the fathers themselves had subscribed to buy him a keep-sake. By the advice of Norton, the money was laid out on a prayer-book with silver clasps, and this with blessings and with tears, and grasping of his extended hands, they now gave to the equally agitated Ronald, and then reluctantly allowed the coach to drive on; while he threw himself back in one corner, and hid his face in his handkerchief. When he had recovered himself, he opened the book, and read in the blank leaf written by Norton himself—

" The gift of Robert Jones, William Alsop, and Richard Merrick, in token of their affectionate gratitude to Ronald Douglas, who risked his own life to preserve theirs.—God prosper all your undertakings, and restore you with health and wealth to your native land !"

"Amen," said Ronald, and kissing the book, put it into his bosom.

There was only one passenger in the coach besides Ronald; and he had not beheld this parting scene unmoved.

"Those flowers will soon die," said he. "What a pity! as they are the tribute of grateful children to their fathers' preserver!"

"Sir!" cried Ronald.

"Yes, I know it is so; I know you cannot be other than Ronald Douglas, the adopted son of my friend Fullarton. I am proud, young man, to make your acquaintance."

To have such a companion was indeed a pleasant circumstance to Ronald, whose heart was sad, spite of his brilliant prospects; and who now catching the *last glimpse* of his native place, and the village spire, from a hill which they had just ascended, looked till he saw them no more; then tried, in order to escape from himself, to enter into conversation with this friend of his friends; and rapidly passed the time with our travellers till they reached London.

If Mr. and Mrs. Fullarton had been struck with Ronald's appearance, when they beheld him in the dress of a working mechanic, they could not but be still more pleased with it when they saw him in the apparel of a gentleman; and they congratulated each other on their fortunate visit to the village of L——. Again and again also did Mrs. Fullarton advert to the surprising likeness between Ronald and the brother whom she had lost, never failing to add, "I should not at all wonder, my dear, if this dear boy were really a distant relation of mine."

"Yes, and the *father* and *John* also, Grace," her husband used to reply, smiling at her enthusiasm. "Remember, if you own one of the family, you must own all."

"And for Ronald's sake, as I told you before, I do not care if I do own them all. If one gathers the rose, one must take the thorns along with it."

The summons to go to Portsmouth now arrived, and in a short time Ronald and his benefactors bade a long farewell to their native land.

There is a time when the most rational enthusiasm looks back appalled in some measure on the actions to which it has been impelled; and even the benevolent Fullartons began to consider with some sort of misgiving, their generous interference in Ronald's favour, and the responsibility which they had entailed on themselves.

They had been almost eye-witnesses of Ronald's heroic actions; they had witnessed the love and respect which his friends and neighbours felt towards him; and they had heard that he bore the unkindness of his parents, with dutiful forbearance. They had also discovered that he was a good scholar, and loved reading. But how would he appear in the circles of Calcutta?

"And yet," said they to each other, "what should we fear? Of his excellence of heart, we have seen undoubted proofs; it is not likely, therefore, that he should ever disgrace our protection, by his immorality and manners: the mere external polish of the man may be acquired; meanwhile, his countenance and his person are themselves letters of recommendation, and we may tell the story of his noble daring, without mentioning the obscurity from which we took him."

In the meanwhile, they were anxious to observe what effect Ronald would produce on the company on board ship.

This was a subject on which Ronald was equally anxious. For the first time he found himself in the company of persons who would expect from him manners and accomplishments befitting the situation in life which he now occupied; and Ronald trembled lest he should disgrace his benefactors by his ignorance and his awkwardness.

But this salutary fear made him silent, retiring, and cautious in what he said or did, till the pleasing certainty stole over him that all he said and did would be kindly received; for his quick eye soon discovered that his kind friends had told of his exploit; and his understanding taught him, that an action which they thought it an honour to him to relate, would be likely to throw a veil over his defects, and interest his auditors in his favour. Nor was it long before he was able to bring into use the little accomplishments which he possessed. He could sing, and play the flute; and though, being conscious of his own want of skill, he refused to join in the merry dance in an evening, he could play reels and waltzes for others; and before the ship reached Calcutta, Ronald was the most distinguished favourite on board: therefore, all his patrons' fears and misgivings were scattered to the winds; and Mr. Fullarton's hope that Ronald Douglas would do nothing to disgrace him, was lost in the pleasing certainty that Ronald Douglas would do honour to his adoption.

But for some weeks before the ship reached its destination, Mr. Fullarton thought he saw an alteration in his wife's manner, whenever he talked of his intended plans for Ronald. She seemed particularly restrained and reserved, whenever he conversed of him as his future heir. Mr. Fullarton was too tender a husband not to be anxious at witnessing any change in a wife so beloved, and his earnest solicitations at length drew from her a reason for her conduct: it was a reason which filled his affectionate heart with joy; and he soon convinced her, that if Ronald were the worthy being whom they believed him to be, he would rejoice in the circumstance which rejoiced his benefactors.

The truth was, that Mrs. Fullarton was

again likely to become a mother, after having for many years desired this blessing in vain; therefore Ronald's expectations of being their heir would be, if the child lived, entirely frustrated.

"Well, now we shall be able to try whether Ronald loves us for *ourselves*, or not," said Mr. Fullarton. But one glance at Ronald's expressive face, when Mr. Fullarton informed him of his wife's expectations, carried the most pleasing convictions to his heart; his eyes sparkled with unaffected delight, and seizing his benefactor's hand, he exclaimed,

"O my dear sir! this alone was wanting to your happiness; but now I trust it will be as perfect as I wish it."

"Then you do not think of *yourself*, Ronald," said Mr. Fullarton; "for we promised to consider you as our child, you know."

"And will still, I trust, in the only way in which I ever expected or desired to be considered."

"Then, pray, what meaning did you annex to our words, when we told you we should adopt you as our son?"

"I thought you engaged to treat me with the kindness of parents: that kindness, I mean, which parents *usually* show to their children," he added, deeply sighing. "But I never thought that you meant to provide for me as a son; and having given me the means of making my own fortune, I expected nothing more."

"Well, Ronald, then the only drawback to the pleasure which my wife's situation gives us is removed. Still, as *I* knew what my words meant, though you did not, I shall not think that in giving you the writership I have done all my duty by you."

"You must do no more, sir; I should hate to receive favours which I cannot repay. Money I cannot pay me back; but if you love me, I can love you again, and even probably love you more than you love me."

"Well, well; I respect your pride: and now let us go tell my wife all you think and feel on this occasion."

Mrs. Fullarton was as well satisfied with Ronald's assurance as her husband had been, and had great pleasure in communicating what had passed to her beloved sister. Mrs. Fullarton, though a sensible woman, was not an accomplished one: as she had been bred up at home, and in retirement, and her opportunities of improvement had been few. Besides, the man she adored had loved her without accomplishments; therefore she had no motive for endeavouring to acquire them. But her eldest and her youngest sister had been taken from the paternal roof by a lady of quality, their mother's first cousin, and had received from the masters which she provided them, and from the company which she assembled at her house, all the advantages and polish which education can bestow.

Emma Douglas, in an evil hour, had left the roof of this adopted mother, and had accompanied her sister Grace to India; where, as I have before stated, she became the unhappy and ill-treated wife of a Mr. Hatfield; who, though he had long ceased to love her, would not allow her to leave him, even for her health's sake, because he knew that her attractions alone drew company to his house, and that her presence alone made that house respectable.

Whatever her complaints had been, and whether or not a return to England might have removed them, they had now all settled in a complete paralysis of the lower limbs; but since that crisis took place, her mind seemed to recover all its brilliancy; and conversational powers of a very superior nature drew around the sofa, to which she was now confined, all those residents in Calcutta who had taste enough to relish her society, and talent enough to add to its charms. Mrs. Fullarton was well aware that it would be highly to Ronald's advantage to be a favourite with this accomplished woman, as she well knew, that to a young man who has mind enough to appreciate a woman of superior acquirements, constant intercourse with her is the greatest possible advantage. Accordingly, Mrs. Fullarton lost no opportunity of interesting Mrs. Hatfield in Ronald's favour, and he became very soon one of her most welcome and constant visiters. The consequence was, that he acquired too great a relish for the intellectual enjoyment which her house afforded him, to feel inclined to partake of the less-refined pleasure to which he was tempted elsewhere; and Mrs. Fullarton had the satisfaction of seeing, that the society of her captivating sister not only polished the manners and called forth the mental powers of her *protégé*, but preserved his morals from contamination, and threw a shield over his endangered youth.

I have before said, that Mrs. Fullarton delighted to think that Ronald might possibly be related to her, as his name was Douglas; "as all the *Douglases were related, no doubt.*" But she did not content herself with only thinking this; she also *said* it; and as her words were not accurately repeated, it was soon reported that Mr. Ronald Douglas was Mrs. Fullarton's cousin; and some declared that he was her nephew: while, much to Ronald's vexation, whose love of truth revolted against any deception, however flattering to himself, Mrs. Fullarton used to delight in aiding this belief, by calling him in sport, as she said, "Cousin Ronald."

In vain did he reply, "You do me too much honour, madam." No one heard or noticed this answer; and Ronald was, spite of himself, elevated to the dignity of Mrs. Fullarton's near relation. Nor would his benefactors listen to his expostulations on the subject.

"If you were going to be married, indeed,"

said Mr. Fullarton, "the case would be different, as on such occasions no truth must be withheld or can be by honourable persons; and you must tell all you know concerning yourself."

"What, *all?*" cried Mrs. Fullarton.

"Yes, all," replied Ronald; "and my own lowly *calling;* not forgetting," he added, laughing, "the ragged apron I wore when you first saw me. But this communication ought, I think, to be made before I am going to *woo;* for the love might be given to Mrs. Fullarton's cousin, which would have been refused to Ronald Douglas the exciseman's son and the carpenter's apprentice."

"Ronald, you provoke me," cried Mrs. Fullarton, resolutely resisting the appeal of her judgment from her feelings. "However, the girl that would not love you, even if she knew you to be the son of a shoe-black, could not be worthy of you."

"There is a declaration for you, from one of the blood of the Douglases! After that, Ronald, I am sure you ought to be satisfied," said Mr. Fullarton. Ronald shook his head; and if not satisfied, he was silenced. But the subject was soon renewed on the following occasion.

A Mr. and Mrs. Manvers, residents in Calcutta, determined to give a ball and supper to the governor-general; but as they wished the party to be more select than numerous, and were desirous of filling without crowding their rooms, they resolved to confine their invitations to masters of families and their relations only; as, had they invited all the residents in the family, no private house could have held the company; — because it often happens at Calcutta, as well as in other settlements, that gentlemen and ladies invite young persons of both sexes, when they arrive in port, to take up their residence at first under their roof. Accordingly, the invitations of Mrs. Manvers were to Mr. and Mrs. such an one, and their relations; that to the Fullartons was consequently to them and their relation, *Mr. Douglas.*

"What a fortunate mistake this is for Ronald, my dear!" cried Mrs. Fullarton; "I am told, this ball will be the finest thing ever given in Calcutta; — but if he were not supposed to be our relation, he could not go to it, for he would not have been invited."

Mr. Fullarton smiled significantly, and replied, "True: but as he is not our relation, I do not believe Ronald will go. Here he is, give him the card."

Mrs. Fullarton did so.

"Will you answer this card for me?" said Ronald, "or shall I answer it myself?"

"As you please: you go, of course?"

"No—how can I? None but the relations are, I know, invited; therefore I have no more right to go than the young lady and gentleman who are residing under your roof, as well as myself."

"But you are expressly invited."

"Yes, from an error I am."

"But it is an error so established now as a truth, that there can be no harm in taking advantage of it."

"Pardon me, I cannot go anywhere on a false pretence: I should know I had no right to be of the party, and that thought would poison all my enjoyment."

"There!" cried Mr. Fullarton, "I *told* you what Ronald would feel."

"And do I not feel right, sir?"

"You do, you do; and so Grace will tell you herself, when her principles have conquered her feelings a little."

"You are a disagreeable, scrupulous person, Ronald," said Mrs. Fullarton: "but I cannot help honouring you: and I see I must submit, as well as I can, to your provoking decision; so write what you please."

Ronald was going to obey; but suddenly recollecting herself, Mrs. Fullarton said she would write the answer: then, taking her husband's arm, she led him into another apartment. The result of the conference was, a resolution to inform Mr. and Mrs. Manvers of what had passed, of Ronald's honourable resistance to their entreaties that he would accept the invitation, and so on.

"There, my dear Fullarton!" said his warm-hearted wife; "if these people have moral taste enough to appreciate Ronald's conduct, they will keep the secret, and *insist* on his coming."

"Yes, Grace, yes, *if,*" replied Mr. Fullarton, who knew the world, and the people of the world, better than she did.

"Is the answer written?" said Ronald, when they returned.

"Yes, and sent too;—and it is *all* your primeval and puritanical scrupulosity could have *desired* it to be," replied Mrs. Fullarton, laughing.

But the day passed without Mrs. Fullarton's receiving, as she expected, an answer full of admiration of Ronald's conduct, and desiring him to come at all events. No answer came, and poor Mrs. Fullarton could only say—

"Well! how differently, my dear husband, should you and I have felt and acted!" She was right.

On receiving the note, Mr. and Mrs. Manvers only said, "Well, this is *lucky:* there is one less; and I am so afraid my rooms should be too full. — What could people mean, by saying Mr. Douglas was related to the Fullartons?"

It was a consolation to Mrs. Fullarton, under this disappointment, to be able to vent her feelings to her sister, as she knew that Mrs. Hatfield sympathized with them all; but even she rather displeased Mrs. Fullarton, by saying,—

"After all, I dare say, Ronald does not care much about balls."

"Do you mean then to undervalue the merit of what he did?"

"Certainly not: on the contrary, I am sure that to refuse the invitation gave him the sincerest pain; because he knew that it would hurt your feelings, as he is well aware that you have an affectionate pleasure in knowing that he is supposed to be your relation."

"Then would it not have been almost a virtue in Ronald to have gone to the ball, and said nothing on the subject?"

"No; at most, it would only have been an amiable weakness. But Ronald showed in what he did a degree of moral heroism, which is, of all others, the most difficult to practise. Ay, my dear sister, a heroism more difficult, I really believe, than to perform the action which recommended him to your favour."

"Indeed!"

"Yes; for his impulse then was of the highest nature, the daring was of the most generous kind, and the *success* would be the acme of virtuous delight."

"And you think Ronald felt this, and anticipated the *gratitude* and the *applause* which followed?"

"No; but, however unconsciously, he must have been governed by motives of this kind: therefore, great as was his self-devotion, it did not necessarily follow, that Ronald must be capable of that heroism which he displayed yesterday."

"Heroism!"

"Yes, I call it so; for there is nothing which requires so much *mental courage*, and so much firm principle, as to be able to tell the strict truth without being led from it by temptation to *lies of vanity*, of *interest*, of *pride*, or of *complaisance*."

"And why so?"

"Because no *fame*, no *honour*, awaits the person who so dares, as there is scarcely an individual in society who values a spontaneous truth, or indeed *any* truth. To tell a *little fib*, a *white lie*, is thought even meritorious on some occasions: while a strict adherence to truth, on small as well as great points, exposes the person who so adheres, to be *ridiculed*, if not *despised*, by people in general.—Therefore, he who can act up to his own sense of right, in defiance of ridicule and example, and also unstimulated by aught but the whisper of conscience, is capable of what I must call the most difficult of MORAL HEROISM."

"My dear Emma, how you charm me!" cried Mrs. Fullarton: "Ronald would enjoy such a tribute of praise from you—more than fifty balls. Here he is; and now, for curiosity's sake, I will ask him whether he really wished to go to this ball."

"Indeed I did," replied Ronald; "most earnestly did I wish it, as such things are quite new to me; and I love dancing, now I can dance without appearing very awkward."

"Then I am mistaken," said Mrs. Hatfield; "I thought you did not care for a ball for its own sake, Ronald; for I forgot that I was once young myself, and that my preference for my intellectual pleasures is probably the result of necessity, not of choice. Well, sister, this adds another leaf to our hero's laurel."

Six months after their arrival in India, Mrs. Fullarton gave birth to a daughter; and as the child lived and flourished, Ronald had the satisfaction of seeing his friends as happy as their virtues deserved.

Ronald was soon enabled by the assistance of Mr. Fullarton, who thoroughly understood business, to make two or three successful speculations; and there was no one in Calcutta who was judged more likely to make a fortune than Ronald Douglas. Whatever had been his causes for complaint against his parents, Ronald was too good a son to mention them even to the Fullartons, otherwise than with affection and interest; and ill-befall the child who can dare with unhallowed hand to point out to reprobation and notice the errors and infirmities of a parent!

His first letters to England were accompanied by presents which he knew only too well would be more welcome than the letters themselves; but it was Mrs. Fullarton who provided them, as he could not yet make presents. As soon, however, as he had realized a sum of money, he showed his sense of his friend the carpenter's kindness, by sending him what he thought an equivalent; and when he had remitted money for the use of his parents, he also remembered his old master Norton.

Precious to Ronald's heart were the letters which he received from England in return for his presents: those from the good Norton were certainly affectionate, but so he expected they would be. His anticipations of letters from his own family had not been so highly raised. It was therefore a most welcome surprise to him to find not only gratitude but affection in his mother's as well as in his father's letter, though he could not but smile more in sadness than in mirth at one characteristic and consistent trait in that of the former; for after telling him she could not decide whether the shawl cravat he sent his father or that to John was the prettiest, she added, "but I let John *wear both*; so sometimes he goes out in one and sometimes in the other; but don't tell your father so when you write, for he *does not know it*, as he is so careful of his!" But dearer,—perhaps, because wholly unexpected, written also with seeming affection, and with apologies for past unkindness,—was a letter from his brother: and Ronald in a transport of joy flew to his benefactors, exclaiming, "Only think John too has written to me, and written kindly!"

His friends tried to rejoice with him; but they could not do so with sincerity, though they would not damp his affectionate joy by telling him that they believed John only wrote to him in order to give himself a chance of profiting by his prosperity. But Ronald's nature was not formed for distrust: believing that absence had softened his brother's heart in his favour, as his home came over his recollection in brighter and dearer hues than he had ever beheld it before; nor could he help exclaiming, "Well, this is indeed one of the happiest days of my life!" Alas! It is painful to reflect how often we owe the enjoyment of our happiest days to *imagination* and *illusion*.

I shall pass rapidly over the next year of the life of my hero, during which he acquired a considerable fortune, and received frequent and kind letters from his brother John, who became his sole correspondent at last; as his mother, he told him, was threatened with blindness, and his father had sprained his right hand. This was a severe mortification to Ronald.

The little Grace Fullarton, the darling of her parents, and the happy pet of her aunt and Ronald, grew in the meanwhile in beauty and intellect. It has been observed that children born in India have a peculiar precocity and quickness of talent, and this child more than confirmed this observation; nay, so great was the readiness with which she learnt the Latin grammar, under Ronald's instructions, and music, drawing, French, and Italian from her aunt, that her fond parents hoped there would be no necessity to send her to England for education: but at eight years old her health became evidently affected by the climate, and they were forced to send her to the care of her eldest aunt, Miss Douglas, who resided in London. Mr. Fullarton had generosity enough to insist on his wife accompanying his child to England. But she refused to go, assuring him that, dear as Grace was, he was still dearer; nor while he, faithful to his promise, remained to watch over and cheer the hours of her slowly declining sister, would she forsake the post of duty either, but would submit patiently to a separation from her daughter. Accordingly, under the best possible care, and at the most favourable season, Grace Fullarton sailed for England, and arrived in safety at the house of her aunt. This lady had been left by the noble relation with whom she lived, a handsome fortune, and she now resided by herself in the neighbourhood of Hanover Square. It was not the intention of Miss Douglas to send her niece to boarding-school, especially when she found her education so well begun, but she chose that she should have masters at home. However, when Grace was thirteen, Mrs. Fullarton was prevailed upon to let her daughter follow the fashion of other persons' daughters, and to send her, at an enormous expense, to an establishment where the education of young ladies was what is called *finished*, and the last polish given to their manners.

Miss Douglas obeyed these orders, though it was most reluctantly, and Grace was sent to the lady who had been recommended to her sister. Nor did her aversion to this plan diminish when she found that her niece imbibed in this new situation very high ideas of her own consequence as the heiress of Mr. Fullarton, whose estates were known to be very great, as well as his personal property; and this empty pride it had been her aunt's study to discourage as much as possible. But now, all that her prudence had done, the governess and Grace's companions had entirely counteracted; and she feared that the simplicity and modesty of her niece's character and manner, which used to remind her of her sister Mrs. Hatfield, would be entirely destroyed by the pernicious flattery lavished on the heiress, who was enabled by her munificent parents to indulge her natural generosity by giving presents to her governess and her friends.

Fortunately, however, in one respect, as Miss Douglas thought, a circumstance took place, which, by diminishing her niece's expectations, also diminished her consequence, and furnished her with a pretext for taking Grace from this focus of pride and expense, when she had been there a twelvemonth.

Mr. Fullarton was only a younger son; but he succeeded to his estates in Scotland by the death of his father, as his eldest brother had died abroad, and died, as was supposed, without an heir; but it was now ascertained, beyond the power of doubt, that his brother had married the woman with whom he lived; and therefore, according to the law of Scotland, the son was entitled to his father's estates. Some circumstances, not worth detailing, had hitherto prevented the claims of the widow and the child from being brought forward; but now the most able lawyers declared those claims were indisputable, and the young heiress was divested of some of her adventitious splendours. With them, much to her surprise, and even to her great distress, she lost a considerable portion of the attention and the flatteries of her governess and her companions, as they fancied her pretensions to be a great heiress were wholly gone; and two only out of the twenty who had sworn to her eternal friendship, declared that she was as dear to them as ever. Therefore, when her aunt came to remove her from this now painful situation, her young heart was almost breaking with this first proof of the hollowness of professions; and it was some time before Miss Douglas could convince her, that the salutary lesson, which she had thus painfully acquired, was of more worth than the estates which she had lost.

"Oh! it is not the loss of wealth," replied the weeping girl, "which affects me; it is the discovery that I was loved merely on account of my father's consequence, and not on account of——"

"Of your own merit, my dear; I will finish the sentence for you. Well, then, you must be more circumspect in forming your future friendships, and choose those only for your friends, whose qualities are such as to convince you they are capable of loving you for yourself alone."

"Oh, how angry and how surprised too, my own dear Ronald Douglas will be, when he hears of the insincerity of the girls concerning whom I have written to him in such raptures!"

"You do not doubt the sincerity of Ronald's friendship, then?"

"Doubt of that! No. If all the rest of the world be false, I am sure Ronald would ever remain the soul of honour and of truth."

"There I believe you are right, my dear girl; and happy is the woman who has a real friend of the other sex."

Ronald, meanwhile, was becoming very rich, very popular, but very anxious. His wealth and his popularity made him thought one of the best matches in Calcutta; and he certainly could have always had his choice of *the market*. But it was evident to him that his friends the Fullartons did not wish him to marry; and as his own heart was wholly unmoved by the variety of objects which were presented to his view, he resolved at present to remain a bachelor, unless, during the visit which he was about to make to England, he should see a woman whom he could love, and the disinterestedness of whose attachment he could not doubt. Indeed, the poor declining Emma Hatfield threw a sort of shield over his affections, which defended them from others; for where could he meet with a woman who united the charms of face, of mind, of heart, and of manners, to the degree that she did? and, till he did meet a being who resembled her, he firmly believed that he could never love.

Yes—Ronald had resolved to visit England, though his heart bled at the thoughts of leaving his beloved friend. But then he was willing to spare himself the misery of seeing her die, and he also felt that a nearer duty called him to his native country; for he had not heard from his home, or even from England, for more than two years; and he feared that something had happened to his father and mother, if not to John. He now, too, recollected only too often, what he had forgotten while John wrote, and wrote so kindly to him, namely, that old Norton had said in his letter, that he feared his brother was doing *very ungainly*, and was a great trial to his father.

At this time, too, his health gave way, and he was ordered to try the air of England; therefore he could not remain where he was.

Accordingly, after a parting of the most affecting nature with Mrs. Hatfield, uncheered by the hope of seeing her again, and one of a more cheerful nature with the Fullartons, as they were pleased to think he would see their daughter, and that she would see him, and also that when he returned he would be accompanied by her, he set off for England.

Ronald carried with him a letter to young Fullarton from his uncle, worthy of the generous and affectionate heart of the writer.

"There is always good coming out of evil, my dear Grace," said Mr. Fullarton. "We have lamented that Hatfield would not let us take Emma to England, and therefore obliged us to stay here. But now, this loss of the estates would have obliged me to return, as my personal property would not have been sufficient for us to live as we have been accustomed to live, and give Grace a handsome marriage portion. Now, however, when we are able and willing to quit India finally, my fortune will still be equal to my most ambitious wishes."

At length, Ronald Douglas landed in England, after sixteen years of absence, and found himself once more in the streets of the metropolis. But as he arrived in the summer, and the air of the metropolis was hot and oppressive, he determined to hire a villa a few miles off, while he was forced to remain near London to transact business.

His first visit was to the daughter of his benefactors, to that engaging child whom he had loved from the hour of her birth, and whose quick talents and sweet temper had endeared her still more to his heart.

Grace, meanwhile, was counting the hours till Ronald arrived in England. For, dearly as she had loved him when she was a child, her affection for him had increased with her esteem, and she was now old enough to appreciate his character.

Nor was Miss Douglas slow to join in her niece's enthusiastic admiration of Ronald; on the contrary, she encouraged her partiality to the utmost of her power, and was as openly impatient for Ronald's appearance, as Grace herself could be.

At last, after rather a faint and unpromising knock at the door,—for Ronald felt some flutter at the idea of being reunited to the darling child of his affections, the servant announced Mr. Ronald Douglas; and Grace was bounding into the ante-room to meet him with open arms, when a feeling of unexpected timidity came over her, and she stopped at the door.

It seemed as if Ronald on his side had intended meeting her in a different manner; for his rapid step paused when he saw her, and he started back with evident emotion, while the kiss which he had designed for her cheek was respectfully imprinted on her hand.

"Is it possible? Can this tall, fine young woman be my own little Grace?" cried Ronald, after the first flutter of meeting had been recovered on both sides.

"Yes," replied Miss Douglas; "and you will find your own little Grace still,—only that she has become a lady of great experience, and out of *twenty professed friends*, she has found only *two* sincere and faithful."

This led to a discussion of poor Grace's little injuries; while she assured the sympathizing Ronald that she had quite recovered the blow, and forgiven the offenders, being of opinion that the young woman who is almost *seventeen* should not resent the wrongs of the girl of *fourteen*.

"*Seventeen!* Are you no more, Miss Fullarton?" said Ronald, gravely.

"I will only be seven again if you call me Miss Fullarton," replied Grace, her eyes filling with tears.

"Well, *Grace* then, *dear* Grace," he answered, taking her hand.

Ronald passed the whole of that day with the aunt and the niece. The next day they went with him to hire a villa near town which had been recommended to him; and for one whole week in succession, whatever was his business, Ronald dined or spent his evenings with Miss Douglas and Grace.

"This will not do," said he to himself at last. "I must set off for Westmoreland: I must not neglect my duty thus; nor indeed, if I am wise, shall I expose myself any longer to the danger of being with this fascinating girl. My benefactor's heiress! I take her back to India! I go in the same ship with her! Never, never."

After a hurried farewell, Ronald set off for his native village, having commissioned Miss Douglas to hire servants for him, and give orders for his house to be gotten ready against his return.

Ronald travelled rapidly till he came to an inn which he well remembered, that was only a few miles distant from his native place. To this inn he had previously sent his riding-horse. He then mounted, and while the sun was still high in the heavens, he set off unattended, for the village of L——. As soon as he caught the first glimpse of the well-known spire with its golden fane glittering in the sunbeams, while the village lay green yet dark in the still vale below, he stopped in his rapid career to take breath, to think, and to *feel*.

"In ten minutes more I shall be there," said Ronald to himself, "and I shall know the fate of my parents. My dear old master, too! will *he* be alive to welcome me? And the poor men whom I saved! Oh! how glad they will be to see me! I hope they are living."

Slowly did he make his horse go, as he thus thought and felt, while the recollections of days that were gone came mournfully over his soul. At length, feeling his spirits becoming painfully depressed, he put spurs to his horse, and soon found himself in the village.

The first well-remembered object was the school-room, the door of which was broken off its hinges, and told a melancholy tale of utter disuse.

"My poor old friend!" thought Ronald, "I doubt you are no more!"

The next object was an old friend with a new face, for it was the house of the other Norton, the carpenter; with smart sash-windows replacing the ancient casements, and the whole place wearing an air of neatness and comfort, the result of increased opulence. Ronald felt a sort of sob of pleasure in his throat as he saw this, for he trusted that *he* had contributed to this change; but on he went, for he was eager to arrive at the door of his own home. He did reach it, or rather what was once that home; for the modest tenement which he had left on that spot, was now converted into a handsome red brick mansion, and bespoke such wealth in its possessor as could not yet belong to the parents of Ronald. A high wall now enclosed the well-remembered garden; and his heart beat even to agony as the fear came over his mind that his *tree*—that dear willow-tree under which he used to conceal his early sorrows—that tree under which he lay when the beaming countenance of his benefactors first met his eye, had been cut down during this season of alteration, and that his wish to lie under it once more, and there lift his soul in humble gratitude to heaven, could never, never be gratified.

"But perhaps it is *not* down!" and he stood on his saddle trying to look over the wall. It was all in vain; some Lombardy poplars still towered above him, and interrupted his view.

"Psha!" cried Ronald, pettishly, "I always hated Lombardy poplars!" and he turned his horse away.

"So then, THEY are not there," cried Ronald, sighing deeply; "then where are they? In their graves, perhaps. Shall I seek them there? Shall I go to the church-yard? No, no, I dare not;" and while considering what he should do, he continued to ride slowly through the village.

But Ronald was not quite well when he began his journey; and as the agitation of his mind had not tended to make him better, he was now conscious of great exhaustion; and feeling rather faint, he beckoned to a little girl who had a milk-pail on her arm, and was entering a cottage-door. While she drew near, Ronald took off his hat to wipe the damps of fatigue from his brow, and as he stopped to speak to the girl, and, getting off his horse, requested a draught of her new milk, he was unconscious that he was surveyed with the most scrutinizing attention by a middle-aged woman at the cottage-door. But the moment he spoke, the woman bounded forward, exclaiming—

"Oh! 'tis Ronald—I am sure 'tis Ronald!"

"Ronald!" cried the girl, and she ran away

to tell every one she saw, that Ronald was come; while her delighted mother—the wife of one of the men whom he had saved—wiped down her best chair, and then shouted out to her husband in the field, that Ronald Douglas was come.

It seemed as if the grateful people had taught the name of Ronald to lisping infancy, and taught it also to bless it; for a little curly-pated girl looked up in his face, and said, "Is ou Ronald? den me *tiss* ou!" and in a moment she was on his knee, and fondling him as if she knew him.

The cottage was now thronged; and the men whom he had saved, with their wives, children, and neighbours, all came to welcome and shake hands with this tenderly-remembered friend. Ronald's heart was too full to speak; but joy made the others garrulous, especially the woman who had first seen and recognised him.

"I wonder you knew me, Sarah," said he.

"Know you! do you think I could ever forget you? But when you spoke, oh! then I was sure it was you: that kind voice, and yet so mournful too."

Ronald sighed deeply, and then said—

"Where are my poor father and mother?"

At first, no one spoke; but seeing his evident agony, one of the men hastened to reply, "We cannot tell you: they left this place two years ago, with your brother John, and we have neither heard nor seen any thing of them since."

"Thank God! then you do not *know* they are no more?"

At this moment, James Norton entered the cottage, and welcomed Ronald with a faltering voice and quivering lip.

"Where is your brother?"

"Alive and *sensible*—but speechless, and has lost the use of his limbs."

"Will he know me?"

"Oh yes, and be so glad to see you!"

"That is another comfort. But tell me, do you know any thing of my parents?"

"They are alive, I believe."

"But where are they?"

"I can't tell; a relation of ours lives near the house to which John took them, and she told us that John carried a woman home whom he called his wife; but that your father found out she was infamous, and he reproached John for bringing his mother such a companion; on which the unnatural son turned both him and your mother out of doors, and nothing has been heard of them since."

"Horrible!" cried Ronald. "But I shall go to John directly, and demand to know where they are."

"You must find him first: for he is gone no one knows where; and there are sad stories about him."

"Indeed! but however, my poor parents cannot be in want, wherever they are."

Another dead silence, which was broken only by tidings of the most afflicting nature.

The money which Ronald remitted for the benefit of his parents, did not minister to their comfort long, for it only induced John to launch into greater extravagance; and again and again his father had to exhaust his finances entirely to save him from a gaol. But as Ronald continued to write and to send remittances, though they did not rise, they did not sink in the world. Still, they had not the heart to write to him; for they could not bear to complain of his brother, and yet they hardly knew how to write, without betraying the melancholy truth. They therefore gladly allowed John to write for them. But at length they ceased to receive either letters or money from Ronald.

When James Norton got to this part of his narrative, Ronald eagerly interrupted him; declaring that he wrote letters and sent money to them *twice every year*.

"Then John intercepted both."

"Letters he might, but surely not remittances."

"Why not? Your father's name is John Douglas, as well as your brother's, and no doubt he was up to any thing. For my part," said Norton, "I always suspected there was some foul play; for I was sure that you would not neglect your parents."

"And did they think I neglected them?"

"They could not think otherwise; but then, poor things! they blamed themselves, not *you*, and said you had already done more for them than they deserved from you."

"Did they say so? I will find them, if I travel over England on foot, to do it. But, go on."

He did so; and Ronald learnt, that owing to John's villany, his father lost at last his place of exciseman; for it was discovered that John was connected with a gang of smugglers, and that he had assisted them to make the garden a deposit for their goods; that in consequence of some secret information, officers had examined the premises, and found a large cargo of contraband commodities. It was in vain that the poor old man declared his entire innocence: his place was taken from him, his reputation destroyed; and hating to look in the face of his old neighbours and associates, he gladly consented to accompany his unworthy son to the obscurity of the metropolis.

Indeed, though neither Ronald nor his neighbours knew it, he had no other alternative, for John had money, whatever might be the means by which he gained it; and till Mr. Douglas could receive a letter from Ronald, to whom he at last wrote, taking the precaution to carry the letter to the India House himself, and pay the necessary postage, he was forced to submit to be maintained by John.

These last particulars Ronald did not learn till afterwards: all he knew was, that his parents were turned out of doors by his brother, and were probably without any means of procuring a livelihood.

"Well, then, I know my duty," said Ronald, "and I will perform it. It is most likely that John will go to the post-office, as usual, for letters, when the next fleet comes in, and I will take care to have him watched, and then kept in custody till I have seen and interrogated him. But let me try to turn to pleasanter things."

Ronald now gratified the three cottagers, by showing them the prayer-book which they had given him: then he took out of his pocket-book a paper containing the flowers which their children gave him, as he passed through the village.

"Which of you gave them to me?" said Ronald.

"It was I"—"and I"—"and I," eagerly exclaimed two fine young women and a young man near him: "but we will give you some better now—throw away that trumpery." And away they ran, to cull for him the best of their gardens.

Ronald smiled mournfully, to think how little his feelings were understood, and carefully put the dried flowers back into their case: for to *him* they were certainly not trumpery. He, however, complaisantly waited for the promised flowers, then taking James Norton's arm, accompanied him to his house.

"Who lives in our house?" said Ronald, as he passed the well-known gate.

"A stranger—one Mr. Benson: a good kind of man, and well to do in the world."

"So his alterations seem to show; but I wish he had not done so much to the garden, for I am so disappointed: I did so wish to lie under my favourite tree once more; but I conclude it is down."

"No, no," replied Norton, with great emphasis. "No: we knew how much you loved that tree, and we thought you would be sorry if it should be destroyed; and so we made it our business, the three cottagers, my brother, and myself, to go to Mr. Benson about it."

"What do you mean?"

"Why, we went, and told him the story of you, the men, and the tree. My *brother* was chief spokesman; and we said we did so wish that he would let that tree stand for your sake, and because you loved it, and would like to see it again."

"Thank you! God bless you!" cried Ronald. "Well, and did he spare it?"

"Oh yes—and seemed so pleased! He said he would call it the good Ronald's tree, and teach his children to respect it for the good young man's sake."

"I will go and thank him to-morrow."

"Well," said he to himself, "at least there are many sweet and precious drops mingled in the bitter cup that awaited me here."

They had now reached Norton's house, part of which had been appropriated to the use of the elder Norton, ever since the poor old man had had a stroke of the palsy. Ronald's heart died within him, as the meeting with the poor paralytic approached; for he dreaded to see the conscious helplessness—the frequent tears—the involuntary sobs—the fruitless endeavours to articulate, which are so affecting in patients of this description.

"I should like to see whether my poor brother will know your voice," said James Norton: "I will go in and watch his countenance, while you stand behind him, and speak to my wife."

"As you please," answered Ronald, and followed where he led.

The good old man was sitting up in an easy chair, neatly dressed in a cloth wrapping gown, and everything about him bore the marks of cleanliness and comfort. The door of his room opened into a pretty garden, and the fragrance of the flowers gave freshness and sweetness to the apartment.

"I am glad to see you so well, Mrs. Norton," said Ronald.

The invalid started, looked round with eager anxiety, but saw nothing, and burst into tears. His brother motioned to him to speak again.

"What a pleasant room this is! and how glad I am to find my good old friend so comfortably situated!"

Ronald could say no more, for that good old friend was now certain Ronald was near, and he tried, though vainly, to rise from his seat to look for him, while his emotions were painful to behold. Ronald now rushed forward, and stood before him.

The next moment he supported the delighted but agitated old man, exhausted, against his bosom. When he recovered, he made signs to Ronald to kneel down. He did so. He then lifted up his eyes in prayer, and put his hand on his head, as if giving him his blessing.

"Thank you, thank you, my dear friend!" said he, rising: "your blessing is a gift that I truly value."

As he said this, the old man's eyes lighted up with a peculiar meaning, and a smile played about his features. He then took a key out of his pocket, and gave it to his sister-in-law.

"I understand," said she; and going to a small cabinet, she took out of it the Horace which Mrs. Fullarton had sent him.

He then gave it to Ronald, and made signs that he should put it in his pocket, showing him first what was written on the blank leaf.

"If I die before Ronald Douglas returns, give him this, to keep in remembrance of his loving friend, Robert Norton."

"How I shall value it!" cried Ronald, pressing it to his lips, and the delighted invalid wept out his joy.

Hitherto, such was the simplicity of Ronald's dress and manners, that every one had been able to forget, in the joy of seeing him, that he was now raised above them, and that he was become a *gentleman.*

But by this time Ronald's groom arrived on another horse, and was soon followed by his master's chariot, drawn by post-horses, while the servants desired to know where Mr. Douglas lived.

"Not here now," was the answer; and the servants did not know what to do, when Ronald came out, and directed them to an inn.

"So, then, those servants and that carriage are Mr. Ronald's," said one to the other.

At last, the arrival of *Mr. Douglas* reached the ears of the rector. The clergyman who possessed the living when Ronald went away, had resigned it for a better; but the present incumbent was well acquainted with his story, and he civilly sent to offer Mr. Douglas a bed at the rectory; but he preferred sleeping at James Norton's, especially as the invalid was delighted to think that *Ronald Douglas* was to sleep under his roof.

Before the good man went to rest, Ronald unpacked his portmanteau, and took out of it a cap made of shawl, which he had brought for his father, who usually replaced his wig with a cap at home. But as Norton did the same, and his father was not there, he gave it to the former. Ronald was gratified and affected to see the satisfaction which lighted up the old man's usually rayless eye, as he looked in the glass, and fitted it on his head. Nor would he allow the cap to be put out of his sight when he went to bed, but had it placed where his eyes could behold it on waking.

Perhaps it was the first object he beheld on waking — perhaps it was also the last he ever gazed on: and that kind and grateful recollections of his beloved pupil were uppermost even in his closing sigh. For, certain it is, that when his brother went to call him in the morning, he found him seemingly asleep, so placid and pleasing was his countenance; but on a nearer approach, he found that his sleep was that of DEATH.

Ronald could not help imputing this sudden dissolution to the agitation occasioned by seeing him. Still, though shocked and distressed, he was comforted; for a life of helplessness and privation had terminated in feelings of pleasure; and his last consciousness had undoubtedly been one of satisfied affection.

This event detained him a few days in the village, as he wished to pay the good old man the last tribute of respect, and also by so doing to gratify his survivors. But heavily moved these days to Ronald Douglas; for, after the first pleasing emotions of seeing his native place and of being cordially welcomed to it had subsided, he felt the want of companions such as he was now accustomed to, and he for ever relinquished the wish he had once indulged in of settling in his native village.

"No, kind and grateful beings!" thought he,

"I will be your friend and your benefactor, but not your neighbour and your associate; and so fades away for ever, one of the dreams of my youth!"

Ronald received a visit the day after his arrival from the Mr. Benson who occupied his father's house, and was courteously invited by him to go and visit the old tree. This offer he thankfully accepted, and Mr. Benson had delicacy enough to let him visit it alone.

When Ronald returned to the house, the voice was faltering with which he thanked Mr. Benson for having preserved the tree, and for the opportunity of revisiting it which he had now afforded him.

"Come every day and visit it," cried the good man; "and all I ask of you is to engrave on its bark the revered and beloved name of Ronald Douglas."

To beguile the time which intervened before the funeral took place, Ronald wrote a long account of his reception at L——, and of his disappointments, his sorrows, and his gratifications. But to whom was he to address it? His heart said, to Grace Fullarton; but his judgment, to her aunt; and the latter carried the day. Still, though he thought he had effaced every word which would have betrayed that it was of Grace he thought while he wrote, he still left in the letter the words *sweet young friend;* and Miss Douglas laughed at the discovery this expression made.

"Only think, my dear Grace," said she, while reading the letter, "Mr. Douglas calls me his *sweet young friend!* Did you think he had been such a flatterer?"

"He a flatterer! No, indeed; it is a mistake; he did not mean you, dear aunt."

"Then whom *did* he mean, Grace? He was writing to me."

"Yes, but——"

"But he was thinking of you, I suppose, is your modest inference."

"I hope he was, for I am sure I do not wish him to have any *other* sweet young friend."

The day was a welcome one to Ronald which conveyed the remains of his respected friend to the grave, because it set him at liberty to return to dearer society, and also to take measures for tracing, if possible, his unfortunate parents.

He had a pleasure in making the good schoolmaster's funeral as handsome as was consistent with propriety; and the brother was thankful indeed to Ronald, for having done all in his power to honour the kind and harmless being whom he had loved as a relation, and of whom he had been proud as the *scholar of the family.*

"This last kindness of yours," said he as he wrung Ronald's hand at parting, "I feel, somehow more, I think, than any other: and God bless you, and, if possible, make you happy with your parents!"

"Amen," cried Ronald, as he sprung into

his carriage, and drove along the village.—Again, but not in like manner as when he first left his home, did the cottagers come out to bid him farewell.

He had left with them such large tokens of his bounty, and his carriage, his *own carriage*, was so handsome, and so completely bespoke the gentleman, that respect was now mingled with their love, and they feared to treat him with their former familiarity. But Ronald's hand was as kindly tendered to them as before, the parting tribute of flowers was as gratefully received. Still, they felt he was no longer their equal only, and their blessings were given not to "Ronald," but to "*Mr. Douglas*," not to their *friend*, but to their *benefactor*.

"Alas!" cried Ronald, "they will never welcome me as heartily on my second as they did on my first visit;" and he regretted for a moment that they would *never call him Ronald again*.

Ronald was so impatient to get to London, that he only stopped on the road one night, and he drove to the house of Miss Douglas as soon as he reached the metropolis; but heard to his great surprise, that she and her niece were gone to a country-house near Southgate.

"Near Southgate! Was it possible they were gone to *his* house, then?"

His house was on the borders of Enfield Chase, he having preferred that side of London as being more convenient for transacting his city business.

When Ronald arrived at his own house, he eagerly inquired for Miss Douglas and Miss Fullarton, but found that they were in a house of their own, which they had hired since his departure, and which was only half a mile distant.

"So near me!" said Ronald mentally, sighing as he spoke.

Ronald was affectionately welcomed by both aunt and niece; and he was provoked with himself when he found that he could not be as unembarrassed as they were.

"You cannot think, Mr. Douglas," said the aunt, "what difficulty I have had in keeping my niece at home; she wanted to set off for L——, merely to thank and to see the nicely-feeling men who petitioned the new comer to save your tree. As for the tree itself, of that she wants to have a drawing: can you give her one?"

"Dear, enthusiastic girl!" cried Ronald, "would I could! I wish you had come to L——; I could not have been more surprised than I am to find you at Southgate."

"Really you will think we *haunt* you; but I must own that we came hither on purpose to be near you."

"Indeed!"

"Yes."

"Pray, aunt, speak for yourself," cried Grace, deeply blushing, "and do not say *me*. I assure you, Mr. Douglas, I had no share in hiring this house; it was all my aunt's doing."

Ronald felt hurt at her denying so eagerly any participation in her aunt's desire of being near him, and turning round was going to answer her in a tone of pique; but when he saw her blushes, her conscious downcast eye, and the extreme confusion of her countenance and manner, a hope, a suspicion, a consciousness, which he had never dared to entertain before, took possession of his mind; and tenderly taking her hand as he bent over her averted face, he said in a low, impressive tone, " But I hope, though you did not hire the house you were pleased when it was hired?"

"To be sure she was," cried her aunt. " I read her wishes; and know that in coming hither I obliged her full as much as I did myself."

"O fy, dear aunt!" said Grace; but she said no more, and her eyes fell beneath the glance of Ronald: but he soon put a check upon his looks and feelings, and with a deep sigh changed the conversation.

"You are looking better than when you left us," said Miss Douglas.

"Indeed! it is surprising to me that any one knew me, for I think I am grown a very ugly old fellow."

"You must say this in hopes of being contradicted; for I should have known you anywhere, spite of climate and indisposition: not that I mean to say, that a man of four-and-thirty can look like a youth of sixteen."

"*Am* I four-and-thirty?" said Ronald, starting—" true, so I am, I declare. Yes, Miss Fullarton, yes, I was *seventeen* the day you were born. Well do I remember that day, and I hope and trust I shall never *forget* it."

Grace was now called out of the room, and Miss Douglas said, " I hope you will be able to take Grace out to India in a year from this time; for as I must part with her, I wish the pang was over, as the longer she stays with me, the more cruel will the separation be."

"*I—I* take her out to India!—Oh! no, excuse me, I have no such intention."

"No! Why my sister expects you to do so, whether Grace be married or single."

"Married, ma'am! Is Miss Fullarton going to be married?"

"No, sir, not that I know of."

"Well, I can only say, that married or single, she will not go with *me* to India."

"And why not?"

"Why not? Though I *am four-and-thirty*, madam, I am not a *stock* or a stone: and to go in the same ship with a creature whom it is not safe for me to approach on shore! O Miss Douglas! how *can* you wish me to face such danger, and meet with such destruction?"

Grace now returned, and Miss Douglas was kind enough to drop the subject.

The next day and the day after, Ronald did

not call on the ladies, as he was resolved to struggle with what he thought a dishonourable passion in him, since its object was the heiress of his benefactors; but on the third day he went to them in the evening. Miss Douglas received him kindly, but openly reproached him with his long absence; but Grace looked dejected, and uttered not one reproach; and there was something in the softened, saddened tone of her voice, which went to his heart, and made him scarcely know what he said. Miss Douglas restored him to himself, however, by asking him if he had heard aught of his parents or his brother. He had not; but he said that he had taken every possible step to discover the latter, and that, he hoped, would lead to a discovery of the former.

"You will, I hope, dine with us to-morrow?" said Miss Douglas.

But Ronald was engaged: he was going to dine and spend the night at the house of a gentleman who lived in Surrey.

Accordingly, Ronald set off for Surrey; and spite of his hopeless attachment, and of his anxiety concerning his parents, he could not help being attracted by the variety of the external objects which he saw on the road, especially as these objects told a striking tale of the opulence of London and its environs. Nay, Ronald wondered where London would end and country begin: nor was it till he had driven round Clapham Common, and entered a green lane, where there was a grassy bank, shady trees, and no houses, that he felt he was beginning to breathe the air of the country.

The postilion now took advantage of a gentle rising, which could scarcely be called a hill, to walk his horses, and Ronald was on the point of giving way to a disposition to sleep, when his attention was arrested by the sight of two persons sitting on the bank, one of whom, a fine old man with an erect person, but silver hair, got up as the carriage approached, and, stepping from the bank, held out his hat, and asked charity for his poor blind wife and for himself!

To the voice of distress Ronald was never deaf, and there was something in the tone of this which thrilled to his very soul. He let down the glass, he gazed on the old man, who was now close to the carriage-door; then hastily bidding the postilion stop, he opened the door, sprung upon the neck of the beggar— and "Oh, my father, my dear father!" burst from his quivering lips.

The poor old man, overcome with surprise, stood motionless and speechless; but the ear of his mother, made more quick by the loss of sight, instantly recognised the voice of her child, and she screamed out, "T is Ronald, I am sure it is Ronald. Oh, guide me to him!"

Ronald now released his agitated father from his arms, and clasped to his bosom his sightless parent. But oh, with what agony did he gaze on their threadbare apparel, and the misery which their appearance, as well as their calling, displayed! "But come," cried he, recollecting himself, "get into the carriage; I have found you now, and never will I part with you again."

"Where are you putting me?" cried the poor woman. "Do not take me from Ronald."

"No, you are going with him, my dear mother."

"Indeed! Oh, anywhere with you, Ronald! We have now no friend besides, and we thought *you* too had forgotten us."

The postilion, who was a wondering spectator of this scene, now desired to know whither he was to drive.

"Back to where you took me up;" and he drove on.

"Where is that, my child?" asked Mr. Douglas.

"To my house."

"*Your* house! Oh, do not let us appear in this mean garb before your servants. If you are not ashamed of *us, we* should be ashamed to disgrace *you.*"

"Oh, no, Ronald, dear! pray do not take me anywhere in this trim; I should die with shame; I cannot be seen and known *thus* as your mother, Ronald."

"You shall be seen and honoured too, as my mother," replied Ronald; "but if it would give you any pain to be seen in this dress, let us go to *your* home, and you shall wait there till I have provided you with clothes."

"O, Ronald! we have *no* home now, none whatever: we were forced to leave our lodging, miserable as it was, this morning, and we have been walking about for hours; and but for meeting you—" Here he paused, and Ronald wept in company with his unhappy parents.

"Well, then," said he at length, "we will stop at the first decent lodging we see near Westminster bridge;" and it was not long before "Lodgings to let on a ground-floor" met their sight, and seemed far more than sufficiently good for the accommodation of the indigent couple.

Ronald got out, and told the mistress of the house that he had met, by accident, two near and dear relations, who had been cruelly deprived of their little property, and they must remain here till he could take them to his house.

The landlady promised them the kindest attendance; and Ronald did not leave them till he had partaken with them a comfortable dinner, and seen them lodged in as comfortable a bed.

"I now go," said he, "to order every thing necessary for your comfort; and when your wardrobe is ready, you shall remove to my house."

The poor old people were still too overcome

Vol. III.—25

with surprise and joy, to feel as if they were otherwise than in a dream; but they had heard, they had embraced, and the old man had *seen* Ronald; and blessing him repeatedly, and praying for blessings on him, the exhausted couple fell asleep, and forgot not only their sorrows but their prospects of happiness.

Ronald, when he quitted them, drove to the nearest livery stable in London, left his carriage there, and paid off his postilion, as he did not like to give him an opportunity of describing to his servants the scene which he had witnessed. He then procured fresh horses, and drove to Southgate.

" I have found them! I have found my poor father and mother," cried Ronald, as he entered the room; and his auditors sympathized with his emotion.

He then told them that his parents refused to come home to him till they were properly dressed; and Miss Douglas instantly consented to drive with him to warehouses for ready-made clothes and linen.

Grace insisted on accompanying them; and Ronald felt a secret pleasure, the extent of which was not known even to *himself*, in seeing the object of his fond idolatry busied in choosing apparel for his *poor blind mother.*

When the purchases were made, Ronald mounted his horse, which he had desired should follow them; and while the ladies returned to Southgate, he galloped to the lodgings where he had left his parents.

Their friendly landlady told him they were awake, and she had just sent them up some tea. Ronald, therefore, knowing he should not disturb them, went to their apartment, and, on opening the door, asked if he might come in.

" 'Tis Ronald's voice!" cried his mother. " Come in? Ay, to be sure ;—only too glad to see—No, no! I cannot see you, but I hear you, and that is more than I deserve."

His father did not speak; but grasped his hand and welcomed him with such a look of grateful affection!

" We have had such a sweet, refreshing sleep, my child!" said his mother. " I dreamt I had seen an angel, and that he spoke so kindly to me; and that angel must have been *you*, Ronald."

" You want more tea; shall I order some?" He did so; and when it was brought, he insisted on holding it himself to his mother's lips. But pushing away his hand, she cried out, in a sort of hysterical agony,

" No, no; I cannot bear such goodness. The tea will choke me if you give it to me;" and he had too much delicacy not to desist directly.

Ronald now assured them that some of their apparel would be ready during the course of the next day, and would be sent to them.

" In the evening, therefore," he added, " I shall come and conduct you to my house."

Blessed that night were the slumbers of the pious son, as well as of the grateful parents.

When Ronald went the next evening to take them to his home, he was painfully affected to see the childish delight which his mother expressed at *feeling* herself dressed in a manner far beyond what she ever was before, and her regret at not being able to see her finery. She was as much delighted at finding herself in her son's *own carriage*; and when she reached the house she insisted on being led round the drawing-room, that she might feel the furniture, while exclamations of pleasure and affection towards Ronald were continually bursting from her lips. But he was far more affected by his father's expressive silence, and the looks of deep feeling with which he ever and anon regarded him.

" My son!" said he at length, " did I not tell you that the blessing of the Almighty would go with you wherever you went? He has blessed *you*, and has enabled you to bless *others.*"

The next day the aunt and the niece called on Mr. and Mrs. Douglas, but they felt a sort of repugnance towards the parents who had so embittered the youth of their favourite. Afflictions, however, had given so touching an expression to the countenance of the father, whose fine person and dignified manner were themselves prepossessing, that when they saw him they lost most of their dislike to him, especially as they observed the looks of love with which he beheld his son. The mother too was made an object of interest by her blindness, and her utter helplessness under it; and when Grace found that she could not even knit well enough to amuse herself, she determined to procure the means, and undertake to teach her two or three works which she had seen taught in a blind asylum.

Ronald meanwhile was resolved to make the residence of his parents under his roof an excuse for not going so frequently to Southgate as he was expected to do; since every fresh interview strengthened his attachment, and consequently added to his hopeless unhappiness. Sometimes too, he suspected that Grace was only too much disposed to return his affections, and that was an additional reason for him to refrain from going to the house. But vainly did he form the resolution to avoid her.

When he returned from London, he used to find her benevolently employed in teaching his poor blind mother the works I have before mentioned. When he returned from a visit at a distance, he found his parents established guests in the house of Miss Douglas; and however determined he might be to *avoid them;* they seemed equally determined *not to be avoided.*

Miss Douglas all this time was fully sensible of what was passing in the heart of Ronald and her niece, though she seemed not to notice it; but once she complimented Grace on the benevolence which led her to take such pains to teach that stupid old woman what she really could never learn.

"My motive is not benevolence," replied Grace; "I will not take to myself credit which I do not deserve."

"Then what is your motive?"

"She is HIS MOTHER."

Miss Douglas smiled, but chose to make no further remarks.

Though Grace was not introduced into *the world*, she had not escaped the notice of *men* of the world; and her youth, her beauty, and her expectations, made her the object of matrimonial speculations to more than one gentleman in the neighbourhood of Southgate. Nor was it long before Miss Douglas received proposals of marriage for her niece from three gentlemen; one of whom was a young nobleman of considerable personal recommendations. The two first were satisfied with being told in a letter from Miss Douglas, that her niece positively declined receiving their addresses; but the young peer declared that he would take a refusal from the lips of Miss Fullarton only, and Grace was resolved not to grant him the interview which he required: but he still persisted in *request*, and she to *deny*; till wearied with his importunities, Miss Douglas determined to consult Ronald on the subject, and request him to prevail on her niece to put a stop to this persecution by granting the desired meeting. But she did not seem likely to gain any assistance from him; for he was no sooner informed that Grace had lovers, and that one was a young nobleman, in every respect worthy of her, than all self-possession forsook him, and he scarcely knew any thing that she said.

"And—and Miss Fullarton wishes to see this young nobleman, does she?" said he, in great perturbation.

"See him! No, I told you the exact contrary: she wishes to *avoid* seeing him."

"Does she *refuse* him, then?" he eagerly demanded.

"To be sure she does."

"But why?"

"Because she does not *love* him."

"Does she then love another?"

"I suspect so."

"And one likely to be approved by—"

"Oh, yes! by her parents you mean?"

Ronald could not speak, he only bowed his head in acquiescence.

"Yes, if my suspicions are just, Grace is disposed to love, or does love, the man my brother and sister would most approve. But you should judge for yourself, Mr. Douglas. Here is a letter from my sister, which I will leave with you, while I go in search of Grace."

Ronald took the letter, trembling in every limb, and with such a mist before his eyes that he could not read it for some minutes after Miss Douglas left him. At length, however, he *did* read it; but he read no more than the first paragraph. It was sufficient, for the letter began as follows:

"My Dear Sister,—This letter will be given you by our own dear Ronald. It was painful indeed to us to part with him; but we console ourselves by looking steadily forward to the moment of his return, when he will come accompanied by our darling girl. O Mary! what happy parents should we think ourselves, as you have long known, if Grace should return to us as the wife of Ronald! for we had rather see her married to him, than to the first peer of England. Do then, dear sister, let them be as much together as possible, and I doubt not but that all will be as we wish it."

Surprise, joy, gratitude, now nearly overpowered the susceptible heart of Ronald Douglas; and he threw himself on the sofa, unable almost even to think coherently, till he recollected that Miss Douglas might be mistaken, and that Grace might not love him. But now he had permission to woo, and to address her: and while this cheering thought was uppermost in his mind, the door opened, and the soft voice of Grace, "I thought my aunt had been here."

Ronald instantly started from his recumbent posture, and seizing the hand of the astonished girl, for his countenance proclaimed the now unrestrained tenderness of his heart, he breathed in her willing ear the tale of his authorized attachment; but, too delicate to presume on what her aunt had told him, he gave her mother's letter into her trembling hands, and quitted her.

When he returned, he found Grace in tears —but they were tears of joy—and holding out her hand to him, she said,

"I am sorry you showed me this letter."

"Why so?"

"Lest you should suspect I love you merely from a sense of duty."

Ronald could not desire a more explicit avowal, and he left her the happiest of men.

Letters were now expected every day from India; and as soon as they were arrived, Ronald intended to write for permission to become immediately the husband of Grace, though Miss Douglas thought that the letter which she had shown him made it unnecessary to wait till an answer from Mr. Fullarton arrived: and in the very next letter, Mr. and Mrs. Fullarton both desired, that if an attachment had taken place between Ronald and their daughter, they should marry immediately, and come out to them as soon as they could. Any further delay, therefore, was out of the question.

The young nobleman, being now assured by Miss Douglas that her niece was on the point of marriage, desisted from his suit, and preparations for the nuptials were immediately begun.

Ronald had now the satisfaction of succeeding, in what he had before vainly attempted, namely, to prevail on his mother to let her eyes be examined by an oculist; and he had the still greater satisfaction of finding that there was no doubt her sight might be restored by the operation of couching.

"May Heaven bless you, sir," said the poor woman to the oculist, " if you restore my sight! for then I shall see RONALD again, and that is enough."

The operation *was* performed, and successfully, while the delighted old woman uttered a cry of pleasure as she beheld the light of day again, and saying,

"Thank God! I shall see Ronald now," fainted away, overcome with contending emotions.

" Who is Ronald?" said the oculist.

" She means me," he replied, turning away much affected.

At length the bandage was allowed to be removed, as the eyes had recovered their powers, and she was suffered to gaze on her son;—while she hung upon his neck in a transport of grateful affection, and wondered at the mercies of God to so great a sinner. But Ronald had soon rivals in her looks and her attention, in his house and his furniture; and she was never tired of saying,—How pretty this is! and how beautiful that! and it required all his high-principled forbearance to make him patiently endure the troublesome and empty pleasure which these things afforded her.

"You absolutely fatigue both my ear and my spirits," said her husband one day, " by constantly saying ' Ronald, Ronald!' I wish you would call him ' My son,' or ' My dear son,' as I do."

" No, Mr. Douglas, *no*," was her reply.— "Nothing shall ever make me call him always ' My son,' as if he was our ONLY son."

" *I* own no other."

" But *I do*, however unworthy he may be. I cannot forget, though you may, that he was once most dear."

Her husband sighed, brushed a tear from his eyes, and said no more.

The day for the marriage was now fixed, and Mr. and Mrs. Douglas had a new source for joy in the " *beautiful*" and " *kind-hearted*" young lady who was to be the wife of Ronald.

One evening that they and their son were at the house of Miss Douglas, the latter went home at about nine o'clock to fetch a new publication which the ladies wished to see.

There is nowhere a road more infested by robbers than that round Southgate and Enfield Chase; and at nine in the evening, in the early winter months, the chances of being attacked are very certain. But Ronald had escaped so often that he had lost all fear, and he went on foot unarmed and unattended from the house of Miss Douglas to his own, though that part of the Chase which he had to cross was particularly unsafe and lonesome. But he did not now cross it with impunity. Two footpads started out upon him, one of whom held a pistol to his breast. Ronald's involuntary movement was to resist; with a powerful arm, he struck the pistol from the ruffian's hand, and with a blow levelled him to the earth. He then wrenched the murderous weapon from the hand of the other, and threw him to the ground. His gardener, who was coming home from work, now approached, followed by his man, and hastened to his assistance; his first assailant now rose, and seeing this reinforcement, ran precipitately away; but the man whom Ronald kept down in his athletic grasp, was unable to fly, and he was dragged struggling into the house.

"Lead him, for better security," said Ronald, " into an upper apartment; and as it is now too late to commit him, we must guard him there all night."

The men obeyed; and the footmen having seen that the windows were securely fastened with shutters hung with bells, which the slightest attempt to escape would instantly set ringing, assisted to fasten the hands of the wretched man behind him, and returned to their master, who was pacing the room below in great agitation, shrinking from the painful task of having to appear against a fellow-creature.

"I must do it, however," said Ronald to himself; " but I can recommend him to mercy." Then taking a candle in his hand, he went to the room where the prisoner was confined; and desiring to be left alone with him, he prepared to indulge the kindness of his heart, by interrogating him with a view to soothe and to serve him.

The man was sitting with his back to the door when Ronald entered and set the candle on the table before him, but he now turned round; while Ronald commanded the servants to withdraw, and the light fell full upon his fine but bloated face. One glance of that never-to-be-forgotten countenance was enough. Ronald instantly recognised it; and uttering an exclamation of agony, he leaned against the wall and hid his face with his hands. His wretched brother, for it was indeed John Douglas, did not recognise him, and looked at him with an expression of ferocious wonder.

" What the devil is this for?" said he. " If you cannot bear the sight of me, let me go."

" Do you not know me, John?" said Ronald, turning round and advancing towards him, shuddering as he recollected him. The conscious culprit laid his head on the table, and groaned aloud.

A pause of agonizing silence ensued. It was broken by the criminal, who said in a surly tone,

"Well, I conclude I am safe now, however; for your own sake you will not appear against me."

"Nor for yours either, John, nor for that of our poor father and mother."

"Dotards! Where are they?"

"They live with me."

"With you? That is more than they deserve, I am sure."

"Why do you speak so harshly of them? they do not deserve that from *you*, John."

"'Tis false! Their wicked indulgence made me what I am. They did not indulge *you*, Ronald, and see the difference! Curses on them!"

"Horrible!" cried Ronald. "Well, if they have injured you, John, you have amply revenged yourself; for you have made them suffer severely. Poor souls! they add one to the many proofs which are daily exhibited, that even in *this* world no duty is ever violated with impunity. They did indeed spoil you, and the evil has already been visited on their own heads. God grant that it may end here!"

"To punish them, I wish it may *increase*."

"Do not talk thus, John! You shut my heart against you."

"But not against your own *interest* shall I shut it, let me talk ever so horrible; and I tell you, you will not *hang your brother*, Ronald."

"Certainly not; and I will do still more: I will give him the means of becoming a respectable member of society."

"Indeed! but how?"

Ronald now told him, if he would quit England directly, he would allow him a comfortable income in a foreign land, where he might remain till it was safe for him to come to his own country. He then showed him that he might escape by the chimney, which was old-fashioned, and consequently wide, and he might then go along the top of the house and drop down. He also promised him bank-notes to a considerable amount. He then went to order wine and refreshments, and left the unhappy man to ponder on what he had said.

The servants were so used to their master's goodness, that they were scarcely surprised at their master's kindness shown to a robber and a ruffian; and there was something in the tone and look with which Ronald urged his guilty brother to eat when he returned, that for a moment softened even his callous heart, and brought a stranger tear into his eyes.

"But let me unbind your arms," said Ronald.

As he approached to do this, he observed such a malignant look in the full eye of his brother, as shocked his inmost soul, and bade him be on his guard. He therefore summoned all his self-possession, and looking him steadily in the face, he set his hands at liberty, then slowly retreated from him.

"You are a devilish strong fellow, Ronald; but that you always were; I remember your throwing me out of the room when you were quite a lad, because I struck my mother; and just now I felt how powerful you were. Yet in a deadly struggle I am not sure you would be victorious."

"In such a struggle I trust we shall never engage."

At this moment a carriage stopped at the gate.

"It is my father and mother," cried Ronald, double-locking the door lest the servants should tell them what had happened, and the former should try to enter.

The precaution was wise: for both his terrified parents came to the apartment, and his mother earnestly entreated that he would not sit alone with that *wicked wretch*, lest he should murder him.

An oath, a terrible oath, now burst from the unhappy man's lips.

"Let them come in: let them see the fruits of their folly," he cried.

While Ronald assured them he was in no danger, and having promised, that if they would but go down, he would come to them directly, they reluctantly obeyed; but as long as he continued to hear his unconscious mother's querulous and anxious tones, John Douglas muttered "*curses not loud but deep.*"

"Poor woman!" said Ronald in a faltering tone, "I could have changed her feelings in one moment; and the wicked wretch, as she called you, would have been converted into her '*dear, dear son!*'"

"Nay, she must *hate* me, and so must my father: for you know, I conclude, all my misdeeds——"

"I do; but it takes so much to make a mother's heart hate the child she has once so tenderly loved!"

"Then you think they do *not* hate me?"

"Oh, no! and one sign of penitence and regret from you would at any time make your peace."

"Really! Well, then, I do not feel, as that is the case, to hate them so bad as I did before; but when one believes one is hated, you know, it makes one hate in self-defence."

"True, very true."

"And it is easy to love when one is sure of being beloved. You have no merit, Ronald, in being what you are; for every one always loved you, except these unnatural old fools: if they had not spoiled me, I might have been like *you*, and *you* like me."

"True again; for we are all made what we are by circumstances."

"You admit it," cried John, with his face brightening even into complacency.

"Yes; and therefore you are to me an object more of *pity* than *blame*."

"Do you think so? do you say so? God bless you, Ronald! that is the kindest thing you *have* said yet."

"But tell me, John, have you considered my proposal? and will you go abroad, and lead a regular life?"

"I cannot promise; habit is so all-powerful. And so this is your house, and you have servants, and carriages, and honour, and esteem. And I, your elder brother, what have I, Ronald?" and again oaths and execrations burst from his lips.

"You may be any thing yet that you choose to be," replied Ronald.

"But I must be a dependant on a *younger brother's bounty*," he replied with the expression of a fiend.

"The obligation is no obligation; I serve myself in serving you: if you allow me to reclaim you, the obligation will be all on *my side*."

"Fine talking! as if you would not plume yourself on your generosity to an unworthy brother, while my accursed parents were for ever crying out, "Only think of *Ronald's kindness to his wicked brother John!*""

"They should never *know* of it; it would be easy to blind them to the truth."

"Indeed! Well, I will think of what you have said."

"But I must go, as I dread my father's coming to listen at the door, and he might recognise your voice."

"Let him," said his *impracticable* son.

"But now, God bless you! I will keep the key of this room in mine, and will rise very late, that you may have all the time possible to make your escape. Once more, God bless you!"

Ronald now forcibly took his brother's hand, which responded not to his pressure, and hastened from the apartment.

"What could you stay so long with that vile wretch for?" said his mother.

"I wished to make him penitent," he replied.

"And is he?" demanded his father.

"I hope he is."

Another ringing was now heard at the gate, and Miss Douglas and Grace Fullarton rushed in. They had heard what had prevented Ronald's return, and could not rest without assuring themselves in person that he was not at all hurt.

Ronald thanked them cordially for this mark of affectionate anxiety; but the quick eye of love discovered that his cheek was pale, his eye restless, and his manner hurried.

"You are not well; you are agitated," said the anxious girl, looking up in his face. "There is something more the matter than what appears," she added in a low voice.

"Hush! be composed, my best love," replied Ronald : "say no more, you shall know all to-morrow."

The ladies now returned home, and Ronald and his parents retired to their apartments: but Ronald could not sleep. He was continually on the watch to hear John begin his operations: at last, just as the clock struck one, he heard a noise in his apartment, and stole gently to the door of it. He now evidently heard the sound of climbing, and as if John made at first as many steps backwards as forwards: but at length he heard him no longer ; and opening a window at the back of the house, he distinctly heard, and thought he saw, some one drop down from a projecting parapet: and relieved from one overwhelming anxiety, he returned to his chamber, and near morning fell asleep.

It was near mid-day before Ronald rang for his servant, that he might make pursuit after the fugitive appear utterly unavailing.

When this man entered the room, he gave him the key of the robber's apartment, and desired him to let him have breakfast before the constables came for him.

"They have been here some time," replied the man; "but I did not like to disturb you, sir."

"Well, well; let them wait, and do as I bid you."

The man obeyed, but soon returned with a countenance of terror, to tell his master that the robber had escaped.

"Escaped! how could he escape?"

"By the chimney, no doubt, as there is dirt fallen on the hearth; but we can send after him."

"No, no, that were fruitless trouble indeed; for no doubt he has been gone many hours—so let him go, and dismiss the constables."

Bitter were the lamentations of Mr. and Mrs. Douglas, particularly of the latter, for the evasion of the wicked man; and what they said grated so harshly on poor Ronald's feelings, that he could not remain with them, but set off for Miss Douglas's.

But it was with pain and reluctance that he now took his way to that house which contained to him the dearest being on earth; for he was going to make a disclosure to her of circumstances which might perhaps separate them for ever. However, honour required that he should make it, and he bowed in humble resignation to the trying necessity.

"I am glad you are come, my dear friend," said Miss Douglas, as he entered; "for one of the *two* real friends out of Grace's supposed twenty friends, *cannot* attend her as bridemaid till two days after the time fixed: therefore, you must consent to defer your happiness *two* days longer, and I was now hastening to tell you so."

It was some minutes before Ronald could reply, while Grace gazed with silent anxious tenderness on his perturbed countenance. At length he uttered, in a mournful accent, "My happiness must be deferred for *months* not *days* —and perhaps *for ever*."

"What can you mean?" cried Miss Douglas, while Grace hung upon him, as if to say that nothing should have power to separate them.

He then explained; and declared, that if the sad, disgraceful circumstance that his brother was a *robber*, and connected with robbers, did not damp, as he believed it would not, the affection of Grace for him, still, he could not, as an honourable man, lead her to the altar while her parents were ignorant of the disgrace which now attached to him; that he should therefore write to India by the next ships, and await the answer of Mr. and Mrs. Fullarton.

"And is this all?" cried Grace. "Oh, how my mind is relieved!" while Ronald gratefully pressed her to his heart.

"All!" said Miss Douglas—"and enough, too, I think, to make you and Mr. Douglas anxious and uneasy."

"And wherefore? for I well know what the answer from India will be."

"I am not so sure; for, much as I esteem Mr. Douglas, and much as my brother and sister adore him, these are painful circumstances, and parents may well hesitate to give their only child to a man, however amiable, who is so connected."

"Not honourable—not just people, like my father and mother," cried Grace, her whole countenance kindling with indignation as she spoke.

"Indeed, dearest girl, you are wrong; even the honourable and the just must pay respect to the world they live in; and think, if my unhappy brother does not forsake his evil courses, he may one day expiate his crimes on the scaffold, and I be a disgraced and dishonoured man."

"Then let the just and honourable leave this world, which is so unfit for them to live in. What! shall a virtuous brother be the victim of a vicious brother's crimes? No, Ronald; your disgrace, as you call it, which after all may never happen, will only endear you the more fondly to me and to the good. And, oh! how *paltry* is this world, which you hold up in terror to my view, to one who looks above it. Your brother's crimes and punishment cannot lower you an atom in the esteem of your bountiful Creator."

"But beings of this world, my dear niece, must act and feel like and with the world; and you see that Mr. Douglas is so well convinced of this necessity, that he will not, as an honourable man, unauthorized by your parents, involve you in his possible disgrace."

"Disgrace! as if disgrace could attach to Ronald Douglas! I tell you, stain, dishonour, cannot *adhere* to him; but it would drop off from him innoxious and unfelt, as the viper dropped from the hand of the apostle. Aunt! I do not know you; you make one mad with your cold-hearted, worldly notions."

"Be composed, my generous, noble girl!" cried Ronald; "I expected no less from you."

This language was balm to the wounded spirit of Ronald, and Miss Douglas smoothed her ruffled brow, as she was not called upon to consent that the marriage should take place till an answer arrived from Calcutta, though Grace protested she was willing to go to the altar at the appointed time. But this, Ronald's high sense of honour opposed, and Grace acquiesced in its decision. The only difficulty now was, how to satisfy the wondering curiosity of Mr. and Mrs. Douglas, when they found the marriage was delayed; but it was imputed to Grace's scruples, as her father and mother were ignorant of her intentions, and no suspicion was entertained concerning the real cause. But a month had now passed away since John had escaped, and yet Ronald received no tidings of him. His hopes of his conversion and amendment, therefore, wholly vanished, and anxiety for the future sadly overclouded his enjoyment of the present.

At this anxious period, however, a most unexpected, and, but for one drawback, a most welcome occurrence took place.

Miss Fullarton received a letter dated from the Isle of Wight, to say that her father and mother were landed there, and that when she received that letter, they would be on their road to London. But the seal was black, and Ronald's joy was damped by the certainty that the welcome return of his benefactors was purchased by the death of his beloved friend, Mrs. Hatfield. Still, she was removed from a life of suffering, and he tried to remember that his regrets were selfish.

That very day, and just after the delivery of this letter, Mr. and Mrs. Fullarton arrived, and arrived to occasion and partake of those mingled feelings of joy and sorrow which those they loved were experiencing, and at sight of them experienced still more.

With what delight did they gaze upon their daughter! But her general resemblance to her regretted aunt, which to them appeared at that moment stronger than it was, threw a tender shade over their pleasures, while it endeared her still more to their hearts.

"I hoped to find you were become my son, Ronald," said Mrs. Fullarton; "but that is not at all a bridegroom's face. However, I am not sorry to think I shall be present at the ceremony, either. Are you, my dear Fullarton?"

"No, certainly not; for I shall have a pride and a pleasure in giving my child to a man whom I shall be proud to call son-in-law."

Ronald could not bear this, but ran out of the room, while Grace tried to look unconcerned, and Miss Douglas was very busy in looking for something which she said she had dropped.

"What can be the matter with Ronald?" said Mrs. Fullarton, struck by the oddness of his manner.

"He has only just heard of my poor sister's

death," observed Miss Douglas. Grace was silent; and soon after she joined Ronald in the garden.

That day was passed by the Fullartons, in giving details of poor Mrs. Hatfield's last illness—of the resolution taken by Mr. and Mrs. Fullarton to quit India for ever, now their only tie to it was removed—and in hearing Ronald's account of finding his parents.

"No, no," said Ronald to Grace Fullarton, "I will not embitter our moments of meeting, by telling a tale so horrible. But to-morrow I will know my doom."

To-morrow came, and Ronald repaired to the house of Miss Douglas.

No sooner did he enter on his story, and come to that part which disclosed the robber to be his brother, than Mr. and Mrs. Fullarton started, changed colour, and looked at each other in evident consternation. How Ronald's heart died within him at this sight! and he turned a mournful glance on Grace, who had herself observed this unpromising circumstance, and stood with her arms folded in her long shawl, looking all the proud indignant defiance which she felt.

When Ronald had finished his narration, and before he could add that he had delayed his marriage, and wherefore, Mrs. Fullarton, instead of taking any notice of what he had said, beckoned her husband out of the room, and left Ronald and Grace full of the most anxious suspense. However, they soon returned; and Ronald having mentioned the delay of the marriage, and his reasons for it, in faltering accents demanded to know his doom, and whether after what he had just told them they would still bestow their daughter on him.

"Why not?" was Mr. and Mrs. Fullarton's reply, at the same moment. And Grace exclaiming, "There! I told you so," threw herself on her mother's neck, and vented the fulness of her heart in tears.

"Yes, why not? I say again," said Mr. Fullarton. "Are you not the same Ronald we have always loved? And ought not your present conduct to endear you to us still more? Does your brother's guilt alter you? And as to the disgraceful punishment you fear, that may never happen; and even if it does, who is John Douglas? Nobody need know he is your brother."

"O sir!" cried Ronald, "how happy you make me! and I little expected to hear this; for the looks which you exchanged with Mrs. Fullarton, and your going out of the room, made us very uneasy."

"Ah! what did that mean?" said Grace, raising her head from her mother's shoulder.

"I will explain to Ronald," said Mr. Fullarton; and Ronald accompanied him into the garden.

The circumstance was this: Mr. Fullarton's gentleman came down the preceding night in the coach to Southgate, and one of the passengers observed, soon after they got in, that a wedding was going to take place in the neighbourhood of the Chase; for that Mr. Douglas, who lived in a fine house there, was going to be married to Miss Fullarton, a great heiress.

"Indeed!" exclaimed a bold-looking, showy-dressed woman, who was in the coach, her countenance assuming an expression of a most devilish nature, which the light of the lamps, as they passed Shoreditch church, made distinctly visible. "Indeed! many things fall out between the cup and the lip."

"Very true," replied another. "But though a young lord wanted to have her, she preferred Mr. Douglas; so I think he is sure of her now."

"Life is uncertain; and Mr. Ronald Douglas is not married yet," said the woman.

"How do you know his name is Ronald?" asked the man who before spoke.

"What is that to you?" was the surly answer; and she said no more during the journey.

When the coach stopped, which was within a mile of Southgate, she was met by some men who seemed of very suspicious appearance; and during the rest of the drive, the passengers, after expressing their suspicions of the woman and her companions, frightened the servants by accounts of the frequent robberies committed in the neighbourhood, and of a desperate gang who were believed to inhabit it. As soon as he came home, the terrified man, who was the husband of Mrs. Fullarton's own maid, related the conversation to his wife, lamenting that his young mistress and her intended lover should have taken up their abode in such a dangerous neighbourhood.

"But my dear sir," said Ronald, "what is there in this stage-coach conversation to alarm you and Mrs. Fullarton?"

"What! why every thing, since I have heard this account of your brother; and to say the truth, as women are more quicksighted where their affections are concerned than we are, my wife took alarm before she was fully acquainted with John's delinquency."

"Took alarm? What do you mean?"

"My dear Ronald, I must prefer truth to delicacy, and be explicit. In all seriousness, then, I assure you, that we do not think *your life safe*. Yes, you may look incredulous; but it is even so. Only recollect, that if you were dead, John would be your heir after your father's death, and he cannot be sure that you have made a will."

"I have *not* made a will; but why should you think he could be so very wicked as to assail my life?"

"Because he turned his fond parents out of doors to *perish*, for aught he knew, in the streets; because he joined a gang of robbers, and has raised his arm against *the life of a fel-*

low-creature. Is *such* a man, do you think, likely to be withheld by any principle from *conspiring,* at least, against the life of a brother whose death may bring him wealth and independence? Besides, is he not known to be under the guidance of a bad woman? and we all know, which is at least a compliment to the *powers* of the other sex, that no man can be completely wicked without the aid of a wicked woman."

"And do you think the woman in the coach was John's mistress?"

"I do; and I wish to send after her. Remember, you have not heard from your brother, spite of your generous offer. Remember, too, that he must hate you the more for having conquered him in bodily contention, and for your prosperity, and your great superiority in virtue and character — a superiority rarely forgiven, even by better men than he."

"But I was kind to him, and spoke kindly."

"What then? He would say, and say truly, that you let him go for your own sake, not his."

"True: but do tell me what I can do in this perplexity: and if my life be really unsafe from John or his accomplices——yet a dread of detection surely would—"

"They can have no such dread; for they cannot conceive of such a high sense of honour as yours. They cannot think that you would disclose a brother's guilt, though at the risk of losing your own happiness, and impart a disgraceful truth to me, which you might have entirely concealed; therefore, they would hasten to perpetrate their crime with very rational expectations of *impunity.*"

Ronald said no more; he shuddered and turned faint, at the too great probability of the *truth* of this statement; but he entreated Mr. Fullarton not to insist on his sending to inquire concerning the woman in the coach; for he was secretly afraid that it might lead to the discovery and detection of his brother and his accomplices. He listened more complacently, however, to Mr. Fullarton's proposal, that he should marry immediately, and set off for Westmoreland from the altar, and then join him and Mrs. Fullarton in Edinburgh, where they meant to pass the winter; and, in the meanwhile, though ashamed of being influenced by fears which he thought unmanly, Ronald promised to avoid being alone on the road after dark.

But unfortunately, Grace was so much indisposed, and she was also so resolved to wait till both her bridesmaids could attend her to the altar, that the marriage was of necessity still delayed to the day originally appointed; and, spite of his promises and his intentions, Ronald could not help visiting her every day; and would linger near her longer than Mr. and Mrs. Fullarton approved; but, as he always left them at twilight, he thought he fully kept to the agreement which he had made.

At length, the day before the intended wedding-day arrived, and Ronald went to Southgate to an early dinner.

But to return to his unworthy brother. Some months after the events which I am now describing, it was known, by the confession of one of John Douglas's accomplices, who was under sentence of death, that as soon as he left Ronald's house, he repaired to his mistress and his associates, instead of going abroad; and while he talked of his brother's offers, and of his wealth, his house, and all the comforts which surrounded him, the abandoned wretches at once exclaimed, " And *you* are heir to to all this, when a worn-out old man *dies.*"

"I am — unless my brother has a wife and children."

"That we will inquire into."

They did inquire; and found he was on the point of marriage.

"*Now,* then, or *never,*" said the woman; and John was prevailed on by his female companion to approve a plan for way-laying and murdering his brother.

But he wished to be excused sharing in the bloody scene. This indulgence was, however, refused him; as they could not, in the first place, trust him or his infamous associate; and, in the second, they justly thought that he who was to profit so largely by the *success* of the scheme, should share in the *danger* of it; John was therefore obliged to consent.

They now set spies to watch in the neighbourhood of Ronald's house, and to learn all particulars relative to his marriage; nor was it difficult for them to gain all the information they wanted. And they knew beyond a doubt the day and the hour fixed for the union; and one of the gang saw Ronald mount his horse dressed in a light-coloured great-coat, and a white hat —objects easily distinguished in a dark night— and proceed to the house of Miss Douglas to pay his last visit to his future bride. Ronald's horse was at the door some time before he could prevail on himself to shorten his stay; and though the hour was early, night was already come; nor could the moon be seen through the thick clouds and occasional misty rain which obscured her brilliancy.

"Have you no servant with you?" said Mr. Fullarton, who attended him to the door.

"Certainly not," replied Ronald; "but I am well-armed. Really, my good friend, you are enough to make me a coward. I am mounted on a swift and powerful horse, and I shall be home in five minutes. Why should I want a servant?"

"Well, I will say no more, as I know your obstinacy, Ronald; it is the only fault I can see in you; but obstinate *you are.* Good night, my dear son, as I may almost call you now; God bless you and *protect* you!"

Ronald was now out of sight of Mr. Fullarton's house in a moment; and all idea of danger had vanished from his mind, when suddenly he heard a shrill whistle, which was immediately answered by another; and his heart died within him while he recognised in the sound the signal of impending danger, and thought that perhaps a brother's hand might, at that very instant, be armed against his life.

His horse now suddenly recoiled, and flung himself on his haunches. No wonder; for a rope was held across the road by two of the lurking assassins, in order to throw the horse with his rider to the earth; but the noble animal instantly recovered himself, and clearing it at a bound, continued his rapid course.

This was an unexpected discomfiture; and the gang, rendered desperate, now advanced from their concealment, one of them firing a horse-pistol, just as Ronald was in sight of his own house, which shot the hat from his head.

The ruffians now approached at the instant when one of them, by another shot, had terrified the horse so much that he began to rear, and Ronald thought it best to dismount, and defend himself on foot. As he did so, he looked earnestly at the men who were seizing the horse's bridle and assailing him; and having assured himself that they were *strangers* to him, he fearlessly drew a pistol from his belt, and while his horse struck one ruffian with his forefoot to the ground, he fired and wounded another in the right arm, who, dropping his weapon, fled from the conflict. One ruffian alone remained to be contended with, and he had hitherto stood *aloof* from the scene of action; but he now eagerly drew near; and before Ronald could approach him with words of *expostulation* and *peace,* he fired at him with an agitated and trembling arm, and the ball whizzed harmlessly past him. On seeing this, the villain suddenly closed upon his intended prey, and dread and deadly was the struggle which ensued. In vain did Ronald try, in vain did he *wish* to bid his antagonist *forbear;* he found that he was engaged in the very strife of death, and that he must either *conquer* or *die*.

By this time, the sound of the fire-arms reached the ears of Ronald's servants, and of one more *watchful* and more *anxious* ear.

As Ronald's father had discovered that the Fullartons entertained fears for the life of his son, he was always uneasy, and on the watch every evening till Ronald returned.

He therefore had heard, what no one *else* could hear, the *single,* but *shrill agonized* cry which Ronald uttered for help, when his footing became slippery from the blood which had flowed from the ruffian whom he wounded, and he felt that he could not long sustain a struggle with his fierce competitor, who evidently aimed at his life with the vindictive fury.of despair. At length, he could no longer keep his feet; paralyzed by agony of mind, as well as fatigue of body, he fell beneath the weight of the triumphant assailant, just as his father, having snatched a loaded pistol from his apartment, flew to his assistance, with even the quickness of youth.

At this moment the moon burst through the cloud above them, and the old man beheld the *knife* of the ruffian aimed at the *bosom* of *Ronald!* But he *fired* at him, and his aim was mortal; for instantly uttering a trembling but *fervent* prayer for *mercy* to the God he had offended, the unhappy man fell a bleeding corpse across his intended victim.

"I have saved him! I have saved my child!" cried the exulting parent clasping the grateful but wretched Ronald in his arms.

"My God! my merciful God! accept my thanks."

Ronald heard and *shuddered;* but he was thankful that the broken accepts of the dying man which had carried an agonizing conviction to *his* soul, had fallen unnoticed on the ear of his father.

The servants now came with flambeaux; and Mr. Fullarton, who had heard the shots fired and had taken alarm, arrived, accompanied by his servants.

While Ronald and his antagonist had been engaged in mortal strife, the villain who had been momentarily stunned by the blow from the horse, had also disappeared, being disabled from renewing the contest; no vestige therefore remained of what had taken place save the *body* of *Ronald's assailant.*

"Take him away!" cried Ronald in a voice of agony, as the servants began to raise him: "let him be recovered if possible! but take him where we may never behold him!"

"Recovered! Oh, he is quite dead!" said the man who held him.

"There is a crape on his face," observed another of the by-standers, pulling it aside as he spoke.

"Let it remain on," cried Ronald with phrensied vehemence: but the crape was removed, and by an involuntary impulse the old man stooped to gaze on the features of his victim, which now glared horribly in their paleness beneath the light of their torches. He looked, and he recognized those features once so *beautiful,* and once so *dear!*

He spoke not one word, neither did he breathe one groan; but he turned round, and gave Ronald such a look of complicated meanings! then cast an imploring glance to heaven, and with a deep convulsive sigh fell back a lifeless corpse in the arms of his son.

"He is only in a swoon," cried Ronald; "send for assistance directly. I am sure he will soon recover;"—while feeling conquered not only the evidence of his judgment, but blinded him to the mercy of the Almighty arm which had thus suddenly destroyed that life which would otherwise have been passed in ceaseless wretchedness.

Aid was procured; but every aid was vain. And his *father* and his *brother*, the one the victim of the other's unconscious hand, both lay like "the *clod of the valley*" under the roof of Ronald. And oh! how did it increase his grief that he could not, dared not, lay them beside each other! Nor could he inter them together—but while the one would be followed with all the honour and attendance which he could bestow upon him, the other must, he knew, be consigned like a nameless vagabond to the grave, nor even might the coffin tell who rested in it. To the eye of reason indeed this was indeed no hardship; but to the heart of feeling it was a circumstance to add bitterness to the cup of sorrow.

The poor unconscious widow, meanwhile, who had gone to bed early with severe indisposition, slept soundly through the awful scene, and it was morning before she awoke, and missed her husband from her side: another glance convinced her that his pillow had not been pressed, nor were his clothes in the room. Instantly her bell rang through the house, and Ronald with a face full of mournful tidings obeyed its summons.

"Where is your father?"

Ronald only answered by his tears, and they left him little more to tell, or her to hear.

"But let me rise; I will see him," cried she, when her first burst of grief was abated; and Ronald led her where his father lay. But he could not bear to witness her lamentation; still less could he endure what she uttered when Mr. Fullarton told her that her husband had killed a robber with his own hand who was about to kill Ronald, and that in the effort and the alarm he had probably burst one of the vessels of the heart.

"Poor soul!" cried she: "I dare say if he had known it he would have been glad to die for Ronald; for he loved him so fondly now, so that he seemed quite to forget he had another son."

"*Forget!* Oh, no!" thought Ronald; "he *remembered that* only *too keenly:*" and rushing from the room he dared not then draw near his poor mother again.

But her feelings, never of the strongest nature, were now blunted by increasing years; and though Ronald remained dejected and unconsoled, though soothed by the sympathies of friendship and the tenderer sympathies of love, his mother soon recovered the usual tone of her spirits, and could not help exclaiming,

"How odd it does seem to me, that Ronald should be more inconsolable for the loss of his father, than I am who was his wife! But then, to be sure, he saved Ronald's life, and that gave him his death, poor soul!"

Alas! she little knew the dreadful consciousness that still and long haunted the memory of Ronald.

But the sorrows of the virtuous yield surely, though gradually, to the influence of time; and those pangs only are lasting and memorable which are inflicted by a self-reproving conscience.

The heart of the pious man clings closely, eagerly, and thankfully to every thought that offers comfort to his soul; and Ronald turned from the most agonizing of his recollections, to dwell on the faltering but ardent prayer which escaped from the lips of his dying brother; he also remembered that the wretched man had reluctantly entered into the strife of death, and that he had not assailed him till he was urged by the fury of despair. Nor did he fail to derive comfort from the thought, that his father had rejoiced greatly in having saved the life of one son, and had been mercifully snatched from the misery of mourning over the fate of the other, who had fallen beneath his own unconscious arm.

Ronald at length received the reward of his virtues and a balm for his sorrows in the possession of the object of his love; and as the nephew of Mr. Fullarton died young and unmarried, soon after the marriage, that gentleman resumed the possession of his paternal inheritance.

Ronald, at his mother's desire, bought her a comfortable house in his native village, where, to the day of her death, she always lived *in hopes* of hearing from her *elder son.*

On his marriage, he took his bride to L——, and she had the satisfaction of seeing those who loved Ronald, and of hearing his praises from their lips. They then proceeded to Scotland; and Ronald having purchased an estate near that of Mr. Fullarton, that gentleman and his amiable wife received the reward of their benevolence, by witnessing the *happiness* of their ADOPTED SON, and seeing him make the *happiness* of their DAUGHTER.

END OF THE TWO SONS.

THE OPPOSITE NEIGHBOUR,

A STORY FOUNDED ON A WELL-AUTHENTICATED FACT.

Though no one can deny that various are the evils which it has pleased our Creator to mingle with the blessings of existence; still, if we were to take from the catalogue of miseries those which are merely the result of our own diseased imaginations, and the distorted or *mistaken* view which we take of circumstances or persons—I am well convinced that the list of evils would be astonishingly diminished; and that many who consider themselves devoted to care and anxiety, would find that they are in reality possessed of every means for the quiet enjoyment of happiness.

To illustrate what I have observed, I beg leave to lay before my readers the history of two victims to imaginary distresses.

Mr. Evelyn was the eldest son of a rich father, and brought up to all the idleness, and all the comforts incident to the possession of wealth. But, fortunately for him, some counteracting circumstances in his early life made him eagerly change hours of idleness into hours of study; and value money, more for the power which it gave him of befriending others, than of gratifying himself.

He was born in the country; and he lived there, under the care of a private tutor, till he went to college;—and as the study of the mathematics, of languages, and of the belles lettres, had been not only the employment, but the favourite entertainment of his youth, he carried with him to the university the *mauvaise honte* and retiring manners of a recluse; and, by going to Cambridge, he only exchanged one place of study for another. But on his return home during the first long vacation, he was presented to a young and handsome heiress, who had long been designed for his wife by his parents and her own;—and this young lady took care to let him know that she would never marry a mere *bookworm;* but that the man whom she honoured with her hand must dress well, dance well, and have both the air and manner of a man of the world.

Evelyn, conscious that he was not likely to attain these accomplishments, and *certain* that he did not think them worth the trouble of attainment, would gladly have declined the honour of the hand designed him; but his father and mother had declared their hearts would break, if anything prevented the union of Miss Fanshaw and himself; and he was too good a son to refuse some sort of compliance with the conditions on which that spirited young lady was willing to gratify the wishes of her parents. Accordingly, Evelyn took pains to learn the newest steps, and to walk, move, and behave as much like a man of fashion as he could: *polite* he was by nature, for his disposition was benevolent; and when his hair was cut by the most fashionable hair-dresser, and his coat made by the most celebrated tailor, Miss Fanshaw condescended to declare, that he was not so ugly as she *once* thought him, and that in *time*, perhaps, she might become his wife.

Evelyn could have replied, " Just as you please; it is a matter of indifference to me:" especially as the liking which he was naturally disposed to feel towards her as his betrothed mistress, and as an uncommonly fine woman, was *checked* by his more than suspecting that she was trying to captivate a man of high rank, and that, if she succeeded in her attempt, she would break off her engagement with him.

But she failed to effect her object; and on her return from her second visit to the metropolis a disengaged woman, Evelyn was received at her father's house as her declared and accepted lover; but it was easy to be seen that the union would be one of *estates*, rather than of hearts. Evelyn, indeed, tried hard to love his intended bride;—but as she was always letting him see that she thought his face ordinary, and his manner awkward, he was so sure he could not be an object of love himself, that he was rendered averse to feel that passion for another; and his most favourite prospect was, that of being allowed to resume his retirement and his studies, after the bustle of marrying, of being presented, and of giving and receiving visits, was entirely over.

But while Evelyn was thus resigning himself to the necessity imposed on him, of marrying a woman who felt for him little more than indifference, there was one being in the world who hung on his looks with secret but adoring love;—who listened to his accents with eager and attentive ear, and thought that the wife of Evelyn must be the most enviable of mortals!

This hopeless, but faithful adorer, was the orphan cousin of Miss Fanshaw, who had been received into Mr. Fanshaw's house on the death of her own parents, and had been brought up as a sort of slave to the wants and humours of the petted heiress, who was six years her senior.

Another rich relation had taken the elder sister, and the brother was sent out as a cadet to India.

At the time this story begins, Rosabel Vere had just heard that her sister had formed a very advantageous marriage, and that it was likely she would be invited to supply her place in the family of the lady with whom she had lived.

"Thank Heaven!" poor Rosabel exclaimed, when she heard of this probability: "then I shall be able to avoid seeing him daily, as I now do, and may in time, perhaps, learn to forget him."

But she sighed while she spoke, and thought that till Evelyn was her cousin's husband, there was no harm in listening to him with such deep and absorbing interest.

Many circumstances had conspired to make this timid, delicate girl feel towards Evelyn a degree of preference, which certainly amounted to love. In the first place, he had saved her life during a violent storm at sea, when the boat in which they were was upset;—and when, in the conscious forlornness of her situation, she had said within her heart, "No one will think of saving me, and *I* must *perish!*"

While she said this, her pale lip had involuntarily murmured, "Oh, help me, Thou, who art the orphan's father!"

Low as was the tone in which this prayer was uttered, it reached the ear, and touched the heart of Evelyn; who, seeing his intended bride and the other ladies sure of assistance in the moment of coming peril, seized the poor helpless orphan in his arms—and from that moment became in her eyes a sort of image of the Being whom she had invoked.

In the next place, this great service was followed up by a series of little kindnesses —of kindnesses, opposed to unkindnesses from her cousin. Whenever Matilda capriciously abused and scolded her, Evelyn defended her; when she scornfully refused to answer her questions, Evelyn gave her the information which she wanted; when she ventured to inquire on subjects of literature, and to request explanations of passages in books, which she did not understand, Matilda would sneeringly tell her such subjects were above the comprehension of a dull girl of fifteen. But Evelyn took the trouble to answer all her inquiries, and never desisted till he had made her comprehend what her cousin declared was entirely beyond her capacity.

It is no wonder, therefore, that the ill-treated orphan looked up to Evelyn as the best and most engaging of his sex; and in all probability he would have learned to consider her with feelings inconsistent with his engagement to Miss Fanshaw, had not the period of his danger been rapidly coming to a conclusion. Rosabel had earnestly entreated to be allowed to go to the house of her relation, before the wedding took place; but Matilda insisted on her officiating as one of the bridemaids, and she was forced to stay.

"I think it very ungrateful in Rosabel," said Miss Fanshaw to Evelyn, "that she is eager to leave me. I did expect she would have wished to live with me after I married, and that I should have some difficulty in getting rid of her importunities——Why do you smile?"

"Because I never saw any one less likely to be *importunate;* but did you not ask her to live with us?"

"No; I thought you would not like it."

"I not like it! If you wish it, I am sure I ——but no," added he, with a sort of suppressed sigh, "it is better as it is. It is better she should go to her aunt's."

"Indeed! Well, I am surprised: I thought you would have liked to retain so docile and apt a pupil near you, Evelyn; especially one who listens to you as if you were an oracle, and grudges any one even the indulgence of *sighing* with weariness while you are prosing. You will miss Rosabel as a *listener*, I am sure."

"It is well," thought Evelyn, "if I do not miss her as something dearer.

"But there is one thing," said he, with some embarrassment, "that I wish to mention to you. I understand that Miss Vere is not *quite* dependent, as she has fifteen hundred pounds; but it would be an action worthy of your generous spirit, Matilda, to make that sum up to two thousand pounds—or more, if you wish it."

"Dear me! the girl will be maintained, you know."

"Yes; but suppose that she should wish to leave her aunt: in that case, her own fortune would not be sufficient to maintain her; and you would not like your first-cousin, and the descendant of one of the oldest families in England, to go out as a governess."

"No, certainly not; but could she live on a hundred a-year?"

"No doubt; and that sum would prevent her being forced to retain any situation which she does not like, or submit to the still worse necessity of marrying for a maintenance."

"Do you think she is likely to have many suitors, poor as she is?"

"Indeed I do: there are many rich men who would be glad to purchase so beautiful a creature for their wife."

"Beautiful!"

"Yes; she is more like a Greek bust than any thing living that I ever saw. She would never be noticed in a crowd—her cheek is too pale, and her features too small and regular, to be observed there: but the more her face is examined, the more wondrously handsome it seems. Then that modest, gentle expression, that——"

"Say no more, Mr. Evelyn," said the jealous, haughty Matilda: "*I* too am now convinced it is better that Miss Vere should *go to her aunt's.*"

Then quitting the room, she threw the door to with great violence, leaving Evelyn confounded and distressed, but echoing her last words from the bottom of his heart: "Yes, it is better that Miss Vere should go to her aunt's."

And hither Rosabel again solicited to be allowed to go before the wedding-day. But whether Matilda suspected the secret of her heart, and wished to punish her presumption, can be known only to the Searcher of all hearts: certain it is, that she insisted on her staying, and forced her to adorn her for the ceremony. Rosabel's was the only pale cheek and trembling frame amidst the numerous assemblage at the altar: and when the binding vows were pronounced, and Evelyn saluted his bride, Rosabel fainted away.

What others thought on the occasion I know not: Evelyn, however, who believed himself wholly incapable of winning the heart of any woman, even if he had endeavoured to do so, had no suspicion of the real cause of her illness; but while he assisted to recover her, he could not help thinking with a sigh, that there was something very endearing and interesting in such delicate health and helplessness—forgetting that the endearing quality lay probably more in the feminine beauty than the delicate health.

The bride and bridegroom set off from the church-door on a tour of some months; and Rosabel, after staying a few weeks with the father and mother of Matilda, took up her permanent abode with her aunt.

But I should say, that before they set off, Mr. Evelyn in the name of his wife, presented her with a bank note for five hundred pounds. Rosabel's pride and other feelings revolted against accepting the gift; but when Evelyn assured her that he should consider her acceptance as a personal obligation, she burst into tears, took the note, and suddenly left the room.

I shall enter into no details of the next ten years; suffice that during that time, Mrs. Evelyn became the mother of two daughters and a son: that Mr. Evelyn's parents died when they had been married nine years; that Rosabel continued to live with her aunt, and continued single; that she had endeavoured to return the long and tender attachment of a very amiable young man, but had tried in vain, and that he had gone to the West Indies in despair; that she had refused very advantageous offers of marriage, both from the rich and the titled; but that, though her heart acquitted her of loving Mr. Evelyn with any feeling but what the most rigid of her sex would have approved, that heart still rejected every other image, and remained cold to the addresses of the young and the distinguished.

At the end of ten years, Mrs. Evelyn's health suddenly declined; and as her mother was wholly taken up with nursing her dying husband, and she required constant attendance, she declared that unless her cousin Rosabel would come and nurse her, she must undoubtedly die. Accordingly, Mr. Evelyn himself wrote to request Miss Vere to obey his poor wife's summons. Rosabel complied directly; for she had no opposing duty to fulfil, as her aunt was just dead, having doubled her little fortune, and giving the orphan Rosabel an income fully sufficient to her humble wants.

Rosabel had not seen her cousin or Mr. Evelyn, since they married; and ten years had only matured in *her* the beauty of which they had robbed Mrs. Evelyn. Evelyn was become an old-looking man of three-and-thirty; and his wife, whose pretensions to be reckoned handsome were founded chiefly on a very high colour, bright eyes, and a full, finely-rounded person, was now rendered dim-eyed, pale, and thin, by the ravages of disease, and formed a striking contrast to the blooming, beautiful young woman of five-and-twenty, who now stood at the side of her sick couch, and kindly inquired how she found herself. But though the person was changed, the mind and temper remained the same.

"Good heavens! child!" cried Matilda, in a peevish tone of voice, "is it you? Why, you are painted, I protest; and you are absolutely grown as fat and coarse as a milkmaid! Well, poor Evelyn will be so shocked when he sees no traces left of his delicate classical beauty.—I hate the sight of such vulgar health: and yet I own, I envy it," she added, with a deep sigh. Then starting up, she said, "Tell me, Rosabel, am I not grown meagre and hideous-looking?"

"You are altered, certainly."

"Altered! You are cruel enough to tell me so, are you? There, child, you had better go away again, if that is what you came to say: I sent for you to comfort me."

"And so I will, if you will let me: for I mean to nurse you into health again, and then you know your beauty will all return."

"Meaning to say, that at present it is all gone, I suppose?" said the incorrigible Mrs. Evelyn.—Rosabel did not reply; and the entrance of a servant, who brought her something to eat which did not please her, gave her a new object to tease and to abuse.

Mr. Evelyn now came in to welcome Rosabel, who met him with the composure which became their relative situation, and with a dignity and gracefulness of manner which she had not when they parted.

Mrs. Evelyn's quick and jealous eye soon saw that his lingered long, and with evident pleasure, on the face and form of Rosabel; and she observed, in a hoarse and uncomfortable voice, "Ay, I do not wonder you stare at Rosabel, Mr. Evelyn. I declare I should not have known her, she is grown so fat, and red, and coarse. I see you wonder what is become of her Grecian beauty, that you used to talk about."

Evelyn was going to answer, "I see it still matured into new charms:" but as he gazed on the faded form of his wife, pity, and the dread of giving her pain, suppressed the just eulogy, and he contented himself with saying, "Miss Vere is certainly much taller and fatter than she was."

But the speech which soothed the apprehensive feelings of Mrs. Evelyn gave pain to those of Rosabel: for, if he had indeed admired her when she was pale and thin, she could not but be sorry that she had outgrown his admiration. "And surely," thought she, "if he had not shared his wife's opinion, that I am altered for the worse, he would have kindly contradicted her. But why should I wish him to admire me? It is very wrong." And when Rosabel retired at night, she took herself severely to task for having felt so reprehensible a feeling.

But she soon found that self-blame was by no means the only blame she was to be tormented with; for illness, and the consciousness of her altered person, and of the loss of that beauty of which she had been so proud, added every day some new bitterness to the temper of Mrs. Evelyn, which was never amiable, even when every wish of her heart seemed gratified; and though Rosabel waited on her caprices all day, and frequently sat up with her all night, she never gained from her an approving smile or a kind word. Rosabel's only comfort, therefore, was derived from the children, with whom she passed every hour that she could steal from their mother; and she soon endeared herself to them by kind words and affectionate caresses, such as they had never experienced before,—for even to her children, there was nothing caressing or affectionate in Matilda; and she also gained their respect, by instructing them in works and little employments which their governess was unable to teach them. With the boy she would sometimes whip a top, and she would help to make his kite; in short, her habitual love of children, and her wish of making them love her, by rendering herself useful to them, were here amply gratified whenever opportunities offered; and Rosabel, though unconsciously, had another motive for thus engaging the affections of the children—they were the children of Evelyn, and the two elder were very *like him*. In the third, she saw a likeness of herself; and one day Evelyn said, "I flatter myself, Miss Vere, that Fanny is a little like you." As he said this, he seated the child on his knees, and affectionately kissed her; and from that hour, spite of her laudable efforts and continual self-upbraidings, Rosabel could never see Mr. Evelyn caress that child, without emotion and confusion: "And yet," said she to herself, "I am sure he is not thinking of me!"

But while Rosabel was thus recommending herself to her cousin's *children*, she was every day losing ground in the affection of her *cousin*; and her motives, seen through the distorted medium of jealousy, were cruelly misconstrued. The children themselves assisted to alienate their mother's heart from her, even by what ought to have endeared her the more; for they were always saying, "Look, mamma! what a pretty thing cousin Rosabel has made for us!" "See, mamma, what a clever thing cousin Rosabel has taught us to make!"—till the unhappy Matilda used to exclaim, "There! go away, and take your trumpery along with you! I am sick of hearing of your cousin Rosabel and her clever doings!" while in her heart she accused Rosabel of paying court to her children, in order to please their father, and induce him to marry her when she was dead.

With increased vigilance, therefore, did she watch the behaviour of her cousin and her husband. Often, unable to bear to see them together, she used to send Rosabel away when Evelyn visited her; and if his eye followed her as she left the apartment, she used to reproach him with making the girl vain, by showing how much he admired her: and when Evelyn took care never to let his eye glance towards her in his wife's presence, she was still *more* unhappy, for she was sure that he would not have put such a restraint on himself had he not been conscious of having some improper feeling to hide. Rosabel gave her great offence by wearing her fine long hair twisted round her head and parted *à la Madonna*; for she told her she wore it in that manner because Mr. Evelyn had said she was like a Greek bust; and she insisted on her wearing a cap, as she hated such affected beauty-like airs. Accordingly, Rosabel wore a cap; but as it was that sort of close cap called a *dormeuse*, she reproached her bitterly for her delicate coquetry, declaring that she wore it to show how pretty she looked in her night-cap.

In short, what with tormenting her in the day, keeping her up all night, calling her up on some unnecessary pretence when she was in her first deep sleep, Mrs. Evelyn certainly deprived poor Rosabel of the look of robust health which she had when she first came to her; and she was not slow to remark to Mr. Evelyn how ill his beauty looked; "She looks very pale," he replied, "and worn out, I suspect, with watching; but hers is a beauty independent of complexion; it is the beauty of outline, you know."

"Yes," she replied with violent agitation, "I know it; and *I* had never any *outline* to boast—*mine* was all dependent on *filling up*; and see here! (turning up her sleeve and extending her shrunk arm,) see here! it is all gone; flesh, bloom, beauty, all vanished! Well, then, it is time that I vanish too!"

"My dear Matilda!" said Mr. Evelyn, "suppose what you say is true, do you think I love you for your outward charms alone; and that with them must vanish my affection?"

"What! then you own they are quite gone?" screamed the wretched woman, and vain were all Mr. Evelyn's efforts to pacify her; while Rosabel, who entered the apartment, was commanded by her to carry herself and her treacherous beauty elsewhere directly.

Evelyn had already observed the change in Rosabel's appearance; and in order to save her as much as possible from the necessity of such constant attendance and painful obedience to her tyrant, he secretly wrote to his sister, Mrs. Lewellyn, who had more power over his wife than any one, conjuring her to come to them for as long a time as she could be spared, in order to lighten a little the painful fatigue of that excellent and really suffering girl, her young friend, Miss Vere.

Mrs. Lewellyn, who had dearly loved the mother of Rosabel, and felt interested for her, did not hesitate to obey the summons; as she was very certain that her brother would not have written so urgently, had not his wife, whom Mrs. Lewellyn thoroughly understood, been inflicting torments on Rosabel and him, which even his patience and her gentleness made insupportable; and her kind husband allowed her to hasten to the relief of the sufferers.

Mrs. Evelyn's disorder now assumed all the various changes which mark decline; amidst which, that hope of life which is evidently born of certainly impending death, is the most affecting to the by-standers.

"How well you look to-day!" cried Rosabel, one morning: "quite like yourself again! Surely you must feel better!"

"Better! I feel quite well. Bring me the glass! Let me look at myself!"

Rosabel obeyed, and as the poor invalid gazed on her bright eye and flushed cheek, the tell-tale effects of her disorder, she delightedly exclaimed, "Hide your diminished head, Rosabel! Matilda is herself again!" Then seeing that Rosabel wore a very pretty morning-cap with pink ribands, she desired her complying cousin would let her wear it; and she adjusted it on the head of the invalid; while the fine long hair of Rosabel, as she was so employed, streamed in graceful luxuriance to the ground on which she knelt.

"How becoming it is! How well I look in it! I wish Evelyn would come in now!" said Mrs. Evelyn; and he at this moment asked admittance.

"Come in," cried Matilda, eagerly. He did so; and started with surprise and admiration, not at sight of his poor fevered wife in her becoming cap, but at the striking appearance of her companion.

"There!" exclaimed the irritable Matilda, "there! he does not even *see me!*" on which she tore the cap off her head, threw it on the ground, and gave way to such violent gestures, that Evelyn, alarmed for the consequences, held down her arms, and conjured her, for her own sake as well as his, not to give way to such fantastical and ill-grounded anger; but she continued to scream out, "Send the mischievous girl out of the room! I hate the sight of her!" But Rosabel was too terrified to understand what she said. At this moment Mrs. Lewellyn entered the apartment, who had arrived unheard by any one; and, alarmed at the noise in the sick-room, had immediately hastened thither. Her presence instantly stilled the angry sobs of the nearly exhausted invalid; and as she saw that the agitation proceeded from some improperly indulged ebullition of temper, she did not hesitate to comment in her usual manner on the scene before her.

"Mrs. Evelyn, I am rejoiced to see you are so well: to judge by the loudness of your voice, your lungs were never stronger than now. Private theatricals, I declare! the part of the fair Ophelia by Miss Vere; and you, I conclude, and your wife, brother, are the sympathizing king and queen. Have you many such exhibitions as these? If so, I shall be happy to take a part."

"I am no actor, dear Hannah," said Evelyn, smiling, "when I tell you I am glad to see you. Matilda has been a little agitated, and—"

"A *little* agitated! what then must her *great* agitations be! But now I am come I hope to keep you in better order; for you all three look as if the agitation had been pretty general. Heyday! what have we here? Pray, ladies, have you been at a game of romps? Why is this cap on the ground? did it escape in play from those dishevelled tresses?"

Rosabel now hastily picked up the cap, and retired to bind up her hair: while Matilda, afraid of the observant eye and sarcastic remarks of her sister-in-law, conquered her weak emotion, and thought proper to express herself glad to see her.

The fever had now subsided for a while: the sunk cheek regained its paleness, the brightened eye became dim; and while Mrs. Lewellyn replaced the discarded cap of sickness on the faint dishevelled hair of the invalid, who now lay back in exhausted helplessness on her couch, tears filled her eyes as she beheld the ravages which disease had made in her once healthy sister. Matilda saw her emotion, and saw it now without irritation; while, overcome with complicated feelings, she wept upon her shoulder; then worn out with fatigue and illness, she fell back in deep though uneasy slumber.

"What was the cause of the strange scene

I witnessed, when I arrived?" said Mrs. Lewellyn to her brother when she saw him alone.

"Upon my word, I do not exactly know myself; but poor Matilda seemed angry that I did not look at her when I first entered. I believe she had put on Miss Vere's cap; and I unfortunately looked first at the strange appearance of Miss Vere, with her long hair streaming on the ground."

"Well, and what then?"

"Why, then," replied Evelyn, looking very foolish, "I suspect poor Matilda was silly enough to be jealous."

"Jealous!" cried Mrs. Lewellyn, laughing violently.

"Yes, you may well laugh to think of my wife's being jealous of such a quiet personage as I am."

"Indeed, that is an absurdity Matilda in her senses would not have been guilty of. But it is no laughing matter, for in her state such another freak might destroy her; and I shall propose to take the place of Rosabel, as head nurse."

The next day, therefore, she told Mrs. Evelyn that, as Rosabel was evidently worn out with attendance and nursing, she would insist on taking her place during greatest part of the day and night.

"No, no," cried Matilda, eagerly; "for then you know Rosabel would be with my husband or the children."

"And why not?"

"Why not? Oh! because they are so fond of her."

"And what then?"

"Oh! why, I cannot bear they should love her; I fear they love her better than they do me."

"Nonsense! the children may love better for a little while the person that plays with them. But how can you suppose *my brother* so lost to himself?"

"Oh! but he always admired her Grecian beauty."

"But can you suppose that while his wife is lying on a sick-bed, he can be looking at or admiring beauty of any description? Fy upon you, Matilda!"

"I do not mind what you say; and Rosabel *shall not* be all day with my husband!"

"I must laugh indeed, Matilda, at the idea of my grave moral brother's being grown such a terrible Lothario."

Rosabel now entered, with her hair dressed, without a cap, as her cap of the day before had been nearly destroyed; and her appearance irritated the invalid, who passionately exclaimed, "There! look at her! look what pains she has taken to look pretty! Get out of my sight! Go!"

Rosabel, bursting into tears, was instantly obeying, when Matilda called her back: "No, no, you shall not go; stay where you are; I will not trust you from me."

On which Mrs. Lewellyn rose, and taking Rosabel's hand, said, "My dear girl, you shall go or stay, just as you please; I will not sit tamely by, and see my beloved Mrs. Vere's daughter treated like a slave by *any* one."

"Then I will go," said Rosabel, and quitted the apartment.

"How cruel — how unkind!" cried Mrs. Evelyn, "to take that girl's part against me, and contradict me, when I am a poor dying woman!"

"If you are *really* a dying woman, it is the more necessary that I *should* interfere, to prevent your indulging such wrong and culpable feelings towards an unoffending individual. I appeal to your own excellent sense, Matilda, are the angry feelings which you are cultivating towards your cousin proper ones to be indulged in a dying woman?"

"I cannot help feeling as I do."

"But, if you are withheld by no religious considerations from the indulgence of your evil passions, let *policy* withhold you. You are afraid, I see, that the contrast between Rosabel's personal appearance and yours should weaken Evelyn's attachment; but have you not much more to fear from the contrast between your tempers and conduct—between her patient forbearance and endearing gentleness, and your vindictive, tyrannical violence. Depend on it, that Evelyn, though blind I am sure to the beauty of Rosabel's face, will not be so to the qualities which you oblige her to display; and you are making your own danger."

"Do you really think so?"

"I do, indeed."

"Well, then, I will put a guard upon myself."

And for a few days this well-meant hint had the effect which Mrs. Lewellyn hoped for; but habitual violence and injustice, increased by disease, could not long be restrained, even by fancied self-interest, and jealousy and dislike of the patient attentive Rosabel again gained ascendency over the mind of the dying woman; while Evelyn beheld with silent admiration the gentle sweetness and affectionate submission with which she endured the trials inflicted on her.

Matilda had discovered the secret of Rosabel's heart, though hidden long even from herself. She had detected the deep affection which she felt for Evelyn; which had revived on her again becoming the inmate of his house, and witnessing his merits, both as a husband and a father; nor could she be insensible to the kindness and consideration which marked his conduct to herself. Still, she struggled against these feelings — criminal feelings, as she properly termed them. "But in a short time now," she cried, "all will be over, and I shall go and live far from him! and then, too, it will be no crime to love him!"

But in the meanwhile she vainly tried to suppress the tell-tale blush when he appeared, and the tremour of her frame when he addressed her; and these had been observed by the watchful eye of Mrs. Evelyn, who, though death now approached with rapid stride, retained all her painful irritability of feeling. One day, while Rosabel was alone with her, and was kindly adjusting her pillow, they heard Mr. Evelyn speaking, as he opened the door, to some one on the landing-place; and Rosabel, as usual, felt a betraying blush on her cheek, when she knew he was near at hand.

"Insidious girl! I see your secret passion, and I know your aspiring hopes!" said the invalid, with a look of cruel expression; "but I will disappoint you! I will tell him all, and forbid him with my dying breath to——"

Here she paused from the violence of her emotion, and Evelyn entered the room; while Rosabel, terrified for herself, and alarmed for Matilda, knelt by the bedside, watching with painful anxiety the countenance and words of the sufferer.

"Evelyn!" said she, in a nearly inarticulate voice, and grasping the arm of the trembling Rosabel, "I am dying—I know I am; and you see this girl, Rosabel Vere! Then, mark me, if you marry again, and give a mother-in-law to my girls, I charge you, Evelyn, with my last breath—yes, I desire, I insist, that——"

Here a short but violent convulsion came on, and in a few moments she lay a corpse before them!

Mr. Evelyn's sorrow on the loss of the mother of his children was consistent with his affectionate and justly feeling nature. As a wife, he had loved her more from duty and habit, than from taste and preference; and like most wives, who, carrying their point by violence rather than persuasion, are obeyed because contest is troublesome and compliance is unimportant, Mrs. Evelyn was rather *missed* by her husband than *regretted;* and, as Dr. Johnson said of a friend of his who had lost his wife, he was "*afflicted,* but *relieved.*"

As soon as the funeral was over, Rosabel resolved to leave Stavely (Mr. Evelyn's seat) and seek a lodging in a city near the house of her elder sister. One day, when she had just informed the children that she was going to leave them, Evelyn entered the room while they were hanging about her, and declaring that they would never part with her.

"What is the matter?" cried he: "my dears, I am afraid you are troublesome to Miss Vere?"

"O papa! she is so naughty—she says she is going away; and she will go, and we cannot persuade her to stay after—after *next Monday*, papa!"

"I am very sorry to hear it: but perhaps we can persuade her not to leave us so soon," said Evelyn, who felt almost as sorry as his children; "and I will go and speak to my sister on the subject."

Accordingly, he went in search of her, and found her with an open letter in her hand, over which it was evident she had been shedding tears.

"See!" said she, "here is my truant husband forced to go to Barbadoes, to look after his estates there, and he will not allow me to go, because he is afraid of the climate for me! How provoking!—But he talks of being gone only six months."

"Well, then, that six months you will, I trust, pass with me? I shall in that case feel that good comes out of evil."

"Yes, I will stay, if you wish it: but I do not like to part with Lewellyn, for all that; but he thinks it right to go, as our son and daughters have large families and small incomes: but still, I shall scold him when he comes to take leave of me. But what have you to say, brother? I see you have something to disclose."

"Why, yes; Miss Vere has been telling the children that after Monday she must leave us; but surely, as she has a home to seek, there could be no impropriety in her staying here as long as you do, and the poor children cannot bear to part with her."

"I see no impropriety in it, certainly; but young ladies have such refined notions of punctilio, that perhaps Rosabel may: however, I will tell her my mind."

But though Rosabel's sense of propriety did not disapprove her continued residence under Evelyn's roof, her sense of her own weakness did, and regard for her own peace of mind. Still, whether a hope unowned even by herself, operated to bend her resolution; or whether it was that she felt that she could not give a sufficient reason for refusing to stay, certain it is that stay she did.

"Poor Matilda!" said Mrs. Lewellyn one day to her brother, after Mrs. Evelyn had been dead two or three months, "what a strange, jealous dislike she seemed to have conceived against poor Rosabel!"

"Yes," replied Evelyn, "but not *always.* Sometimes she did her justice; and, strange and incomprehensible as it may appear, in her *last* moments she did indeed make her the most ample amends."

"Is it possible?"

"It is quite true, I assure you."

Here he paused.

"Well, go on: why do you hesitate? What did they say?"

"Why," and he blushed exceedingly as he spoke, "it really may seem incredible, but with her dying breath, she *insisted* that, if I married again, I should marry Miss Vere."

"Amazing! and did any one hear this beside you?"

"Yes, Miss Vere herself."

"Well, if any one but you had said this, brother, I could not have believed it; but, I heartily, as a Christian, rejoice that poor Matilda died in a better frame of mind than she had lately lived; and never did she show her good sense, or her love for her children more."

"What, dear Hannah! at my time of life, and with my inability to inspire love,—for you know Matilda never loved me,—did it show her good sense to wish me to marry a beautiful young woman? Absurd!"

"As to your time of life, brother, I will thank you not to talk of that; for I am some years your senior, and I do not *yet* begin to talk of '*my time of life*'—nor need you at three-and-thirty: and as to your inability to inspire love, *that* I doubt. Though certainly no *beauty*, you are a fine manly-looking man; and I am much deceived if Rosabel is not of my opinion. Here she comes! I shall ask her what she thinks."

"Not for the world: and I beg you to forget this ridiculous conversation." But that was impossible: and Mrs. Lewellyn, who still thought her brother's wishes, unconscious as yet to himself, had deceived him, had a great mind to ask Rosabel what Matilda said while she was dying. But she was afraid; for if Evelyn had mistaken what his wife said, and were to be undeceived, she thought that an event which she now believed this mistake would render certain, might be at least retarded; and she heartily wished it to take place. She therefore did not mention the subject to Rosabel, and took care to *assist* as much as she could, unobserved, the progress of her brother's evident attachment for the amiable orphan. "How surprised he will be," said she to herself, "when he finds by what he feels for Rosabel, that he never loved Matilda!"

During the six months which ensued, Evelyn, Mrs. Lewellyn, the children, Rosabel, and the governess, formed one happy and united family. Evelyn read aloud every evening, while the ladies either worked or drew. Time flew unheeded, because every moment of it was filled with pleasing or useful occupations; and when Mr. Lewellyn came to take away his wife, Mrs. Lewellyn was the only one who was conscious that the six months were really gone, and who was glad that they were so.

Rosabel had, in the meanwhile, received a letter from her aunt, Mrs. Evelyn's mother, who was now a widow, entreating her to consider her house as her future home; declaring, that she should always consider her as her daughter, and feel grateful to her for her kind assiduities to her poor child during her last illness. As she was now forced to leave Stavely, and as Evelyn was forced to let her go, a residence with Mrs. Fanshaw was the most welcome; and as she would be within a day's journey, and the children could often, Evelyn said, visit her and their grandmother:—he even urged her taking Matilda with her directly—Fanny, he said, he could not yet part with.

"Matilda is most like her poor mother," said Mrs. Lewellyn.

"Yes, so she is," replied Evelyn; "certainly so she is."

"I do not know whom Fanny resembles," observed his sister; "and yet she reminds me very strongly of *some one*."

Evelyn knew who this *some one* was, but he did not tell his sister.

To be brief. The day of parting came, and Rosabel tore herself, but not without difficulty, from the embraces of the children;—while Evelyn took leave of her with a degree of coldness, which, to a more experienced person, would have betrayed the intensity of his sorrow and regret.—But it misled her completely, and she could not help saying within herself, "How strange it is, that as the children love me so *much*, he should not love me a *little more!*"

When she had gone, Evelyn made a discovery of which he little dreamt; namely, that he was *alone!* that he had experienced a loss which his books and his studies could not console him for; and that he could sit for an hour or two with a book in his hand, and never get beyond the *first page!*—He also discovered, that, in his heart, he loved the little Fanny better than her sister, and he began to suspect why he did so; and one day, when he was gazing at her, as she sat upon his knee, he exclaimed, "Beautiful creature!"

"O fy, papa!" said the little girl: "cousin Rosabel used to tell nurse it was very wrong to tell children they were beautiful."

"But I was not thinking of you, Fanny!"

"No, papa! of whom then? of cousin Rosabel, I suppose, for do you know I am reckoned very like her; and what do you think, papa, (whispering,) my governess says? She thinks cousin Rosabel would make us such a nice mamma!"

"Nonsense! my dear—your governess does not know what she is talking about."

"O, but she does though; for cousin Rosabel says she is a very sensible woman."

Evelyn said no more; but kissing the little girl with more than usual tenderness, he sent her away, and retired to his library, but not to study, though he began to quote poetry, and repeated, as he walked up and down the apartment,—

"In vain would books their formal succour lend;
Nor wit nor wisdom can relieve their friend.
Wit can't relieve the pang I now endure,
And wisdom shows the ill without the cure."

"Yet, according to my sister, the cure may be within my reach.—Well! the best thing I can do is to go and consult her, when the year's mourning is expired; and in the meanwhile we will often go over to see my daughter, and her grandmother."

He did so; and when the twelvemonth was just past, he paid a visit to Mrs. Lewellyn.

That lady received his communications with undissembled pleasure; but with her usual sarcasm she observed, "Really, Edward, I find you loved Matilda much more than I ever suspected you did, as her wishes are *still* the guides of your conduct;—for if I understand you right, it is *merely* in compliance with her dying will, that you are going to propose to Miss Vere."

"No, no: not *merely* because Matilda wished it; far from it; I think her very, very charming, and—"

"In short you are in *love* with her, brother!"

"What! at my time of life?"

"There! talking of your time of life again! Nonsense! At some time or other of every one's life, it is said, love must be felt, and your time is only now come. So away with you! tell your tender tale, and Cupid speed you!"

Evelyn was by no means pleased to be treated and considered as a love-sick boy, but he could not help himself;—he knew his sister would have her sarcasm, and he set off for Mrs. Fanshaw's.

When he arrived, he found that lady alone; and having desired they might not be interrupted, he, with great effort, made known to the mother of Matilda, that he was desirous of marrying again; but that the mother-in-law that he wished to give his children, was one whom she, with her last breath and last action, pointed out to his choice; and he was happy to say that *her* choice was *his*.

"Then you must mean Rosabel Vere," cried Mrs. Fanshaw;—"and Matilda showed her usual good sense and judgment, even in her last moments, poor dear girl! Yes: and your marrying thus, Mr. Evelyn, will only be a *fresh* proof of your tender devotion to her will.—Yes, I see, I see how it is—dear good man! You were always the best of husbands, as well as she the *best of wives*, and *but to oblige her* you would never have married again.—Yes: I understand you."

Here her increasing sobs made her inarticulate, and Evelyn was glad of it; for *he* was not sure that he wished to marry Rosabel Vere, *merely* to please his late wife. However, he did not contradict the old lady, who, when her emotion was over, insisted on being the bearer of his proposals to Rosabel: and unfortunately his timidity made him consent.

The old lady was not slow to profit by this commission, and went in search of Rosabel; but when she saw her, instead of speaking, she threw her arms round her neck and burst into tears.

"What is the matter?" exclaimed the terrified Rosabel, returning her embrace. "Oh! has anything happened to the children, or to Mr. Evelyn?"

"Mr. Evelyn is *here*," sobbed out Mrs. Fanshaw; "and he is come to tell me he means to make proposals of marriage to you, my dear!"

Rosabel's arms were instantly unlocked from the old lady's neck, and she sunk nearly fainting on the sofa, overcome with a sense of happiness which she had never expected to know; for in proportion as Evelyn became sensible of what he thought his weakness, the more cold his manner became; and poor Rosabel, apt to torment herself, sometimes fancied she was become an object of dislike to him. But this overpowering happiness was not destined to last long; for Mrs. Fanshaw, seeing her pale and agitated, exclaimed, "Dear me, Rosabel! how terrified you look! To be sure, you will not refuse Mr. Evelyn! I am quite *set* on the match; for he tells me, he only acts in obedience to my poor dear daughter's dying wishes and commands, that he should give you as a mother to his children; and you know, my dear, that her wishes were always his laws, and so they *continue* to be,—though she is dead and gone! And no wonder, for she was such a woman!—so handsome, and such a COMPANION! Mr. Evelyn, poor dear! knows very well *he* could never meet such an one again."

Rosabel was now nearly fainting from *contrary* feelings; but recovering herself she said, "Surely, madam, you mistook Mr. Evelyn! he never could say what is untrue:—my cousin did not recommend me to him as a wife, I *assure* you she did not."

"Nay, Miss Vere, he *must* know—ay, and be very sure of what he says—or he would never, spite of your pretty face, have thought of marrying *you*. You are a very good girl; but Matilda! Oh! she was such a creature! and such a *companion!*"

Here she again paused to weep, and gave Rosabel time to consider whether she should or should not endeavour to convince the old lady, and next Evelyn himself, that, so far from her cousin's having wished her to marry her husband, she was sure she meant to forbid it: but love prevented it; for though pride said, and loudly too, "Reject the hand that is not offered to you by the heart, and from exclusive affection for yourself," apprehensive and deeply-rooted tenderness whispered, that on any terms it was for her happiness to make him hers; and Rosabel resolved to be silent. Matilda Evelyn now came into the room, and her grandmother instantly told her what her papa was come for. The intelligence was received by her with a scream of delight; and running to Rosabel, she kissed and embraced her, and said the dearest wish of her heart was now gratified.

"Ay, but I have not said Yes yet," said Rosabel.

"Oh! but you will, you *must*, for *my* sake you must."

"Well, for *your* sake I will," cried Rosabel, clasping her to her heart; but Matilda escaped from her to go in search of her father, whom she no sooner saw, than she sprang to him, and, overwhelming him with caresses, thanked him for having made her so happy! And on his asking her, she told him it was by intending to make Miss Vere her mamma; "for she has *promised* me," added the unconscious tormentor, " that she will say *Yes* to your proposal, for *my* sake."

Evelyn *started*, and felt his joy that Rosabel would be his, entirely damped by hearing that his children were the inducement. And thus were these two passionate lovers deceived into doubting the strength of each other's affection, while pride, false delicacy, and pernicious reserve of character, annihilated that ingenuousness and openness of conduct which alone is safe, and alone is truly respectable. It was after this impossible that the meeting of Evelyn and Rosabel could be otherwise than *cold*, though they met alone.

When Evelyn expressed his hopes that his little girl had not deceived him, but that she would consent to be his, Rosabel faltered out an affirmative, and Evelyn then said, he expected no less from her regard for the dead; and she well knew what was Matilda's dying wish. Rosabel only shook her head in reply to this, and burst into tears.

"Yes, dearest Miss Vere, you will, I am sure, make the kindest of mothers to my children," said Evelyn.

"How can I do otherwise," replied Rosabel, sighing deeply, "when I recollect *whose* children they are?"

The words were spoken, and the sigh was heaved, for Evelyn alone; but he believed they were both caused by the remembrance of Matilda; and there were moments when he thought it would be ungenerous in him to continue to urge a suit which consideration for the wishes and interests of *others* only led her to approve. But love conquered generosity, and Evelyn persisted.

Mrs. Fanshaw's establishment was now increased by the arrival of a widowed sister to take up her abode with her: therefore she could not miss the society of Rosabel as she would otherwise have done, and her warmest approbation was given to the marriage; but it was on condition that for six months to come the engagement should be kept secret, and that not till then the marriage should take place; for she was tenacious of all proper respect to the memory of her daughter, secretly resolving that she would take care to let every one know Mr. Evelyn's chief motive for marrying Miss Vere was compliance with his first wife's wishes.

Evelyn and Rosabel were both desirous of gratifying the old lady's feelings, by concealing their engagement till the time she mentioned: but the former, after a long struggle with himself, resolved to make this six months a test of Rosabel's attachment: and he told her it was his particular request that she should spend three of those months in London, and three at a watering-place; that his niece, Mrs. Lewellyn's eldest daughter, was going to London with her husband and family, and thence to a bathing-place; and he wished her to accompany them, and see the world, which she had not yet done, and young men of the world, before she had irrevocably doomed herself to live in the country with a man advancing in life. Rosabel, though very reluctantly, promised to oblige him. But while Evelyn was, when he left her presence, agonized at the risk to which he had thus exposed himself of losing her for ever, and while he fancied she was too ready to comply with his request, Rosabel, as soon as the door closed on him, shed tears of bitterness on her side.

"There!" cried she; "it is evident he already repents of his engagement, and hopes I may see some one whom I may like better than him!" And she was confirmed in this painful belief by the receipt of a letter from Evelyn, in which he conjured her, during this six months, to consider herself as a free and disengaged woman; and assuring her, that should she see during that time any man whom she preferred to him, he would give her up to that happy and more favoured mortal.

It took poor Evelyn many an hour of painful struggles to write this letter; and when he had written it, he had scarcely resolution enough to send it: but Rosabel saw in it, not a proof of generous magnanimity, but of cold indifference, and a decided wish to get rid of her if he could.

"And why should I not indulge him," cried she, "and give him back the vows of which he repents?" But love said No; and hope whispered that in time, perhaps, she might teach him to love her.

Rosabel went to London with the niece of Evelyn, and thence to a watering-place; and, spite of her repulsive coldness and abstracted manner, her beauty gained her admirers, and she had two avowed lovers—but they were refused; and though, when his niece informed Evelyn of Rosabel's conquests, he wrote word that he was ready to waive his claims, in favour of any man whom Rosabel preferred to himself, he followed his letter so *immediately*, and looked so wretched when he did come, that any one but the prepossessed Rosabel would have seen that his happiness depended on her keeping her engagement.

But Rosabel, instead of seeing in his visit a proof of anxious love, was only conscious how rarely he visited her; and saw in the self-restraint and the fear of influencing her by his presence, which made him keep away, nothing but a proof that he was going to marry her from fancied duty rather than strong inclination: "And perhaps he *sees* my love for him, and has had *pity* on me!" she used to exclaim, at another moment. "Well, I will take *care*, however, that he shall not long fancy that."

At last, after many misgivings on both sides, Evelyn and Rosabel were irrevocably united; and each would have been the happiest of the happy, but for the fantastical misery which they derived from the errors of imagination. In these errors, circumstances tended to confirm them; and I need not tell my readers, that a groundwork was laid, before they were married, for a very substantial superstructure of misery to be erected upon.

"*I* am *older*, both in habits and in look, than I am in years," thought Evelyn, "and my wife is much *younger* in *both:* therefore, I will sacrifice my habits to hers, to make her feel less the disadvantages of the union; and I will fill my house with company, and take her to places of amusement."

"I see," said Rosabel to herself, "that he has no enjoyment of my society: he cannot bear to be alone with me, and live quietly at home. How different it was in Matilda's time! But then, as Mrs. Fanshaw says, *she* was such a *companion!* And so am I, perhaps, if he would try to draw me out: but I know that my love makes me appear to such disadvantage before him, I can't converse at all at my ease. How I wish he loved me a great deal more, and I him a *little less!*"

But the greatest obstacle to the removal of these bars to their happiness, was one mistaken principle of action, which Rosabel had been taught to think a right one.

One or two of her earliest friends were women whose mothers had put into their hands a very erroneous book, in my opinion, but one formerly in much vogue, in which a reverend and sensible father inculcates in his married daughters the *duty, safety*, and *glory* of *dissimulation*, bidding them to consider it as a *virtue*, never to let their husbands know the extent of *their love* for them; and this doctrine was taught to the young and naturally close-tempered Rosabel. No wonder, then, that being painfully conscious of a deeply-rooted and even a reprehensible attachment, as its object was first an engaged, and then a married man, she should improve on her instructors, and guard her secret love with anxious care, even from the suspicions of Evelyn, after she became his wife.

The first winter after they married, Rosabel was presented at court, where the pleasure Evelyn experienced from seeing her admired, was damped by his overhearing one gentleman say to another, who had asked who that beautiful creature was—

"That! It is Evelyn's second wife — the Staffordshire Evelyn, who married Matilda Fanshaw."

"Evelyn's wife! What! that old fellow— is he married to that young thing? He is a bold and lucky man: but I conclude he is rich, and women now are so mercenary! He looked old enough, when I last saw him, to be her father."

How poor Evelyn longed to turn round, and say that his wife was actually six-and-twenty! But he dared not; and he went home saying to himself, "Yes, I dare say every one thinks Rosabel has thrown herself away for money; and perhaps she thinks so herself!"

Two uneasy years passed away; but Evelyn, though he feared Rosabel did not love him, had never hitherto suspected that she loved another. But now that species of misery was added to his other sufferings. Some thoughtless person told him that Rosabel and a young man in the neighbourhood where she lived with her aunt, had been tenderly attached to each other; that want of fortune alone prevented their marrying; and that the lover entered the army, and went to the West Indies.

This was the very young man whose affection Rosabel could not return, on account of her hopeless attachment to Evelyn: but he believed the story; and concluding that her coldness towards *him* was the result of her love for *another*, he became completely miserable. What increased his annoyance was, that his books, which in the time of his first wife were always the solace of every care, had now no power to soothe him : for read he *could* not. The passion of love was to him what drinking a quantity of wine is to a water-drinker — intoxicating and maddening, not exhilarating ; or like a large and unexpected fortune to a man long poor, and habitually self-denying — he feels more burthened than served by his riches, and his anxiety is greater than his enjoyment.

Evelyn, however, would have been happy, had not circumstances prevented his seeing that he had really all the means of being so: but this he could not see; and as he could not lose his uncomfortableness in reading, he flew to society; and he even became a member of a book-club in the neighbourhood of his country-seat, where gentlemen met to read, and discuss political tracts, literary subjects, or play whist, and whence Evelyn never now returned till a late hour of the night. He always desired Rosabel not to sit up for him, and she obeyed; but if the night was dark, she could never sleep till he returned in safety, as he went on horseback, and the road was not only bad, but she fancied that his horse was not a safe one. And often, very often, used she to open the window, and watch for the sound of his horse's feet: nor till she heard it approaching the house, would she retire to bed again. But when Evelyn in the morning hoped he had not disturbed her rest, she used coldly to answer, "No;" and he often said, mentally,

"If I did not return all night she would not be uneasy, but would sleep on, I dare say."

One evening, he was gazing fondly on Fanny, who resembled his wife, and he observed how much the likeness increased.

"I see it myself," said Rosabel.

"But she will always have one advantage over you, Mrs. Evelyn," he replied, "for her countenance is the picture of happiness."

"And is not mine? I used to have a very happy countenance, Mr. Evelyn."

"*Used* to have! You mean to insinuate, I suppose, that you had a happy countenance before you married *me*. I thank you, madam. Heaven knows we are both much altered in countenance since we married." So saying, he left the room, and pulled to the door with great violence.

"What is the matter with papa?" cried Fanny; "he is grown so cross lately; he never used to be so when mamma was alive."

"No, my dear, never. But then he loved your mother," she could have added, "and me he does *not* love." The truth was, that unhappy and jealous love had made him pettish and suspicious. To Matilda, whom he had never loved, he was never unkind; but to Rosabel, whom he adored, as he believed, with unrequited passion, he was now often what Fanny called "cross."

Not long after this, he received a letter from his sister, in which she desired him to tell Rosabel that her old lover, Captain Denbigh, was dangerously ill from a wound received in a duel, and was coming to England.

"Now, then," thought Evelyn, "I shall be able to try the state of her heart;" and he read aloud to her what his sister wrote, meaning to fix his eyes on her as he did so. But he did not find this an easy task, till Rosabel's excessive emotion made him gaze on her with the eye of indignant reproof.

"So, madam," cried he, "this gentleman was your lover, I find: I heard this from another quarter, and he loved you very tenderly, I am told."

"Poor fellow! he did, *indeed, very, very* tenderly," Rosabel falteringly replied, who had now learnt to feel the bitterness of unrequited passion.

"Yes; and I believe it was a long as well as an ardent attachment."

"Oh, very long!" and her tears redoubled.

"I think it a great pity, Mrs. Evelyn, that you did not marry Captain Denbigh;" and he rushed out of the room in an agony of jealousy.

"Alas!" exclaimed Rosabel, in the bitterness of her soul, "he is at least no *hypocrite!* No doubt, he speaks the truth here."

Not many days after, the papers announced the arrival of such a ship in port, with the gallant Captain Denbigh on board, who was declared in great danger from a wound received in a duel; but it was thought that his native air, a skilful surgeon, and *good nursing*, might restore him.

"It is a great pity," said Evelyn, as he showed Rosabel this paragraph, "that *you* cannot be his nurse. But you know, Mrs. Evelyn, I *cannot* break our fetters if I would; else the *gallant* Captain Denbigh should not be lost for want of a good nurse."

He said no more, for Rosabel fainted; and he imputed her illness not to his unkind speech, but her affection for Denbigh.

His determination was now taken. He resolved to leave his home, his country, and his wife; for every feeling of delicacy in him revolted from his continuing to live with a woman whose heart was evidently another's. Life was insupportable, and madness he felt must ensue, if he remained with her any longer. He therefore made preparations for his journey, and had even obtained his passport, before he informed his wife of his intentions, while Mrs. Lewellyn was on a visit to them. Rosabel turned pale, and instantly quitted the room; and while Mrs. Lewellyn, who saw some secret uneasiness was preying on both the husband and wife, was trying to laugh and argue Evelyn out of his strange fancy of going abroad without his wife, she was sent for to Rosabel, who earnestly conjured her to prevail on her brother to let her go with him, declaring that she should be wretched to stay behind.

Mrs. Lewellyn obeyed her, but she pleaded in vain.

"Why did not Rosabel come herself? But she was *afraid*, I suppose, of gaining her point. She was quite *safe*, however. I would rather *die*, than take her with me!"

"Brother!" cried Mrs. Lewellyn, after a long pause, during which she had examined his agitated countenance—agitated in spite of great effort, "Brother! I see you are playing the fool—I see you are trifling with your own happiness and that of Rosabel. Go abroad! and go alone! I foresee your folly will be its own punishment. Go, and come back *wiser!*"

Evelyn did not reply; but the next morning, when his wife and sister waited breakfast for him, they found he was gone, but had left a letter for them :—

"I hate *leave-taking!* therefore you will find me gone without, though I may be absent at least six months. I wish you, Mrs. Evelyn, to go to London at the end of that time, and reside there for the sake of masters for the children, if I do not return. In the meanwhile, I leave you uncontrolled mistress, to draw on my banker for what you please, and to go whither you please; for I KNOW that I leave my children and their interests in the hands of the safest and tenderest of mothers.

GOD BLESS YOU!

"I must leave off, ere certain recollections and feelings come over me, and unman me.

E. E."

"The man is *mad!*" cried Mrs. Lewellyn, affected by the evident agony of Rosabel. "To use a vulgar phrase, my dear, he is quarrelling with his bread and butter. What nonsense has he in his head, Rosabel? Can you tell?"

"No: all I know is, that he does not *love* me!"

"What! Why you are as great a fool as he, my dear. But I see there is some misapprehension, which time and a little proper *chastisement* may remove."

During the ensuing six months, Evelyn wrote three or four times, saying, first he was at Paris, then at Brussels, then at Geneva. At the end of that time, Mrs. Evelyn removed with the children to their town-house; and Mrs. Lewellyn in a letter to her brother, said that she was very angry with Rosabel for her prudish obstinacy; that poor Captain Denbigh was in London, and, fancying himself dying, wished to see her once more; but that she refused to indulge him, because she felt it improper, and because she fancied her husband would disapprove it. "I therefore beg," she added "that you will desire her not to be so unnecessarily hard-hearted."

Evelyn, as soon as he received this letter, in a sort of petulant bravado sat down to answer it, desiring Mrs. Evelyn would do whatever she wished to do, without considering him, and that she had his leave to visit Captain Denbigh. But as soon as this letter was gone to the post, he repented of the permission which he had given; and, impelled by jealousy and other uneasy feelings, he set off for England, and never rested till he reached London. Still, when he got there, he could not prevail on himself to enter his own house, or re-unite himself to a woman whom he fancied pining in love for another man. But a wild fantastic project took possession of his imagination, which, difficult and preposterous as it was, he immediately put in execution.

He concealed his return from every one but his bankers, and them he desired to sell stock for him to a very large amount indeed; and when the stock was sold, he called and took away the money, saying that he was probably going abroad for some time. But instead of doing so, he dyed his complexion of a dark colour, and by means of a black wig, false mustachios, and green spectacles, he disguised himself so effectually, that no one could have known him except by his voice. He then bought into the funds again in the name of Sanford, which name he now assumed, and hired a first-floor of a lodging-house, immediately opposite his own house, and which overlooked every thing that passed in its front rooms.

Here, then, he took up his abode: but to do him justice, it was not merely to be a spy on the actions of his wife, and from jealousy of her seeing Captain Denbigh. No; it was that he might indulge a painful but absorbing feeling—that he might be near the being whom he so fatally idolized; might gaze on her unseen; might perhaps find opportunities of hearing her voice, of finding out whether she regretted him. In short, it was the morbid resource of diseased but tender and impassioned feeling; and while his silence filled the heart of the equally fond and deceived Rosabel with agonizing anxiety, the object of her solicitude was *comparatively* easy; for he had converted himself into her OPPOSITE NEIGHBOUR.

I shall not attempt to describe the complicated feelings with which Evelyn gazed on the house which contained his wife and children; nor the effort it was to him not to indulge the wish which he felt to clasp them to his heart: and he was forced to make himself recollect that Rosabel, as he feared, still loved another, before he could resolve to persevere in the line of conduct which he had marked out for himself. "No, no: while I believe she loves this Denbigh, I cannot, I will not live with her again."

Evelyn now almost lived at the window, watching to see Rosabel or the children.

The room on a level with his chamber was his wife's dressing-room; and there she used to sit in the morning. There he now fancied he saw her sometimes behind the muslin curtains, and his heart used to beat with mixed pain and pleasure. Every night he watched for a light in that room; and he used to sit in the dark till that light was extinguished, and then, and not till then, he went to bed himself. In the morning his first care was to watch to see those windows thrown open; for then he knew Rosabel was gone down to breakfast; and he used to eat his by his front drawing-room window, where he sat watching to see Rosabel and the children come into their front-room when they had finished their breakfast. And there he often did see them; but Rosabel never came to the window. He every day saw the children walk out with their governess, and sometimes Rosabel went out in the carriage. Once he saw her stand on the step of the door a few minutes, and he was shocked to see how pale and thin she looked: but as she had a basket of hot-house fruit in her hand, he was sure she was going to visit the wounded Denbigh; and he pitied her no longer.

Evelyn could not help observing that Rosabel saw no company. Many ladies and gentlemen called at the house, but were not admitted. But one person, his agent and solicitor, Mr. Belfield, was admitted every day: but then *he* was a man of business, and his constant visits were accounted for. But why was Rosabel denied to every one else? He could not flatter himself that it was because she was uneasy concerning his absence and his silence. Still, spite of his jealousy of Captain Denbigh, he felt less uneasy than he did.

When he had passed some months in this monotonous but to him soothing manner, he saw that Rosabel came regularly to the window, and stood there at a certain hour every day for a considerable time. At length he found out that she was watching for the arrival of the general post; and when the postman knocked he used to see her run to the door, and as he believed down the stairs. He then used to see her return, and then he beheld her no more till he saw her in her dressing-room; of which she used to let down the curtains hastily, and where he fancied that she used to sit alone, to recover her disappointment. For no doubt she was expecting daily to hear from *him!* Oh, if this anxiety to hear from him had no other motive but *affection!* But he could not *believe* it, especially as every two or three days the coach conveyed her, as he suspected, to the sick couch of Captain Denbigh.

A new visiter was now admitted to Rosabel, one whom he never saw before, and Evelyn soon found that this gentleman lived *next door to him.* He also learnt from the neighbouring tradesmen, that his name was Monro; that he was the son of the steward of Rosabel's grandfather; that from him he had inherited large property, which his own fortunate speculations had increased; and that Rosabel had a great respect for him, for his father's sake.

"I must know this man," thought Evelyn; "and through him I shall receive daily intelligence of what is going on."

Fortune favoured him: for one day as he returned from his banker's, he saw Mr. Monro taking shelter from a very heavy rain under a gateway. Evelyn had a large umbrella as well as a thick great-coat; but Monro had neither. This was an opportunity of making his acquaintance, which was not to be passed by.—Evelyn stopped, insisted on his taking his umbrella, *forced* it into his hand, declared his great-coat was sufficient for him, told him his name, and where he lived, and rapidly left him. But Monro soon overtook him, vainly trying to make him take back the umbrella; and they walked home together.

The next day Monro, who had seen Evelyn ride out with a groom behind him, and saw that his horses were of the highest price, left his card at his door. Evelyn returned the call the next day; and by his pleasing manners, and the willing attention with which he listened to the lively and incessant gossip of his new acquaintance, he gained so much on him, that they met almost every day, and sometimes dined together.

Evelyn found that his friend was one of those happy persons who are vain of every thing that belongs to them, and was more especially vain of his large possessions; but he was a good-natured egotist, and was not disposed to wound, as many egotists are, the harmless self-love of others.

Evelyn very soon took care to lead the conversation to something which must make Monro talk of Mrs. Evelyn. Monro was not backward to tell him that he had known her from her birth; and at last he informed him, that her husband, a *very odd man*, whom he had never seen, was abroad; and that she was excessively uneasy because no one had heard of him for *a great many months;* and, what was very extraordinary, he had been in England; had gone to his bankers'; had received a great sum of money; and had told them he was going abroad instantly, perhaps for life.

"*For life!* No, surely not!" observed Evelyn, thrown off his guard.

"Ay, you may well doubt the fact," replied Monro, "as you see what a lovely wife and charming children he leaves behind him. For my part, I think he is mad; Belfield, his agent, says that he is only *liberty*-mad, and that he has no doubt he has gone to give money to the Spanish Patriots, if not to fight for them."

Spite of his indignant astonishment, and the state of his feelings, Evelyn could not help laughing at hearing himself represented as such a fighting Quixote.— Love, he thought, had made him quite enough of a madman and a fool; but liberty he did indeed defy to drive him to such extremities. "But pray," said he, "what does Mrs. Evelyn think of this extraordinary supposition?"

"She does not believe it; but Belfield— who, by the by, is, I suspect, desperately in love with her, tells her he has good ground for what he suspects."

"Indeed!" cried Evelyn, starting; and suspicions, by no means favourable to Belfield, took possession of his mind.

"This Belfield," said he, "what sort of a man is he? If Mrs. Evelyn were a widow, surely, *he* could have no pretensions to her?"

"Why not? He is a monstrously handsome man, a great favourite with women, very shrewd, very insinuating, very rich, and is lately come into parliament."

"Well; but we will hope poor Mr. Evelyn is *not* dead, nor likely to be."

"*Poor* Mr. Evelyn! I am sure I cannot pity him, a shatter-brained fellow, to go away and leave his beautiful wife in this manner without a protector, to all the dangers to which youth and beauty are exposed; and no one on earth but his own fantastical self knows the reason why. He is a pretty fellow for a husband and a father, indeed!"

"You are severe, sir, on poor Evelyn. You cannot tell but that he might have very cogent reasons."

"Well, may be so; but I only beg you will never call him poor Evelyn again, as if you pitied him." And Evelyn was very glad to drop the conversation.

The next day, as he was walking with Monro, they met the Miss Evelyns with their governess, and Monro stopped to speak to them, while Evelyn stood gazing on them unseen, and trembling in every limb while he heard the sound of their voices. At first, he was so bewildered that he heard nothing else; however, at length he heard, "My mamma very unhappy," "Captain Denbigh dying slowly," "Captain Denbigh grieved to leave mamma so wretched," "miserable to see her affliction," and so on. All this *mutual grief*, poor Evelyn, who did not hear the intermediate sentences, attributed to the agony of their being parted for ever by the sure but slow hand of death. He did not hear that the governess and Matilda both said, not *hearing of* or *from her husband* was the cause of Rosabel's misery; and that Denbigh said his great grief when he died, would be to leave her so unhappy. He therefore returned home with every doubt restored, and doubly confirmed, which had been gradually yielding to the influence of time and absence. But how had he overrated the strictness of her principles! Was the woman who could thus allow even a dying man to declare his passion for her, and own that it was agony to her to part from him, was such a woman calculated to train up his daughters in the path of propriety? Certainly no. But a glance at her pale cheeks, and pure innocent countenance the next day, made him think that by such a creature no one could be led into any material error.

As summer approached, Evelyn had a new enjoyment, which no one but a man in love would have delighted in.—Rosabel, who loved flowers, had mignonette in every window of her house; and as the street was not wide, Evelyn could inhale the perfumes from her windows; and to his love-sick fancy, as he sat without candles, inhaling this fragrance, with his windows open, and with his eyes fixed on her window-blinds, through which he fancied he saw her pass and repass,—it seemed as if he was holding some intercourse with her; and these hours in the day were to him the most soothing and most welcome. But it now occurred to him that he might have the still greater enjoyment of ministering to her gratification. Accordingly, he contrived a sort of shelter or awning for plants; and, having obtained permission from his landlord to substitute large balconies to his windows in the room of small ones, he filled them with the most fragrant plants that the most curious garden could produce. This rare sight attracted the attention and charmed the eyes both of Rosabel and the children; and as the former was botanist enough to know that the flowers she saw were uncommonly sweet, she removed her mignonette from her drawing-room windows, in hopes of smelling the delicious perfume opposite. Nor was she mistaken; for when the wind was in one quarter, and the evening moist, she could inhale all its mingled fragrance; and she used to stand in her balcony after it was dark, to enjoy the delicious gales from the balcony of her OPPOSITE NEIGHBOUR, who, himself unseen, could enjoy her pleasure. Once he distinctly heard her soft voice exclaim, "What exquisite, what singularly exquisite fragrance it is!"

But Monro exclaimed very differently when he saw the balconies put up, and the flowers come home! "What amazing extravagance! Why, Sanford! what can you mean by it? You tell me that you cannot afford to keep a valet, and yet you throw away money in *this* manner! and after all, a few boxes of mignonette would answer all the purpose."

"*Perhaps not*," replied Evelyn, sighing: "these flowers give me *exquisite satisfaction.*"

But another species of enjoyment awaited him. He had hitherto vainly listened for the sound of Rosabel's harp and voice; but he was consoled by the idea that her spirits were not good enough to allow her to sing or play. But one evening he saw that a lady was her guest, who would not, he knew, be restrained by any feelings of delicacy from endeavouring, by repeated importunity, to procure the gratification of hearing her; nor was he mistaken. He at length heard a few faint, preluding chords struck on the harp, and then the voice of Rosabel sung a *ballad*, his *favourite* ballad! But her voice was weak and faltering, till at length it entirely failed; she paused in the middle of a line, and he fancied he heard the sob of distress. Certainly, the sound of music was heard no longer; and on looking up he saw Rosabel, with her handkerchief at her eyes, standing at her dressing-room window, the curtain of which she in another moment as usual let down; and he had no doubt that she had retired to vent in solitude the mournful feelings which that ballad had called forth.

"Can this be, or am I deceiving myself?" thought Evelyn. "If I am not, Rosabel at length loves me; and we may yet be happy! But no: it is impossible!"

However, that night he went to bed happier than usual.

Evelyn now found out that his daughters sometimes came over to call on his neighbour, in order to see his collection of prints, and other curiosities. He therefore set about purchasing all manner of rare and curious things himself, and expensive Indian toys, that he might, some time or other, have an excuse for asking them to his house; and in the meanwhile, when he heard they were coming to see Monro, he sent over some of his purchases to add to their amusement. At length, he ventured to call in, when he knew they were there; but he was forced to quit the room suddenly; for he overheard both his daughters speaking of him in such affectionate terms, and grieving for his supposed death in so touching a manner, that, had he staid, he felt he must have discovered himself to them. Some days after, having in the meanwhile often seen and conversed with his daughters, he tied up his thumb as if it was gouty, and he could not write, and dictated a note to Rosabel, in which he begged she would allow the Miss Evelyns to accept the Chinese bonzes, which they had so much admired. Rosabel, overcome by their importunity, allowed them, though reluctantly, to accept the presents.—Still she did not choose to invite him to her house, as he was a stranger, and she in a state of deep affliction; but she came purposely to the window one day, when Evelyn was at his, and thanked him by her gesture and her expression for his kindness to her daughters. Evelyn stood like one entranced as she did so; for he was shocked and alarmed again at the recent change in her appearance, and her look was evidently that of deep, habitual dejection. Could *he*, could his absence, his silence, his supposed death, occasion it? If he could but be sure of that, he should indeed be satisfied! But it was more likely she was mourning for her *first love*.

However, he was not only beginning to be tired of his present mode of life, but to consider it as unworthy of him. True, he did not neglect the offices of Christian love :— he sought out the abode of the destitute, he enabled the industrious, but indigent, man to acquire the humble independence which he desired, he visited the prisoner, and he caused "the widow's heart to leap for joy;" for such were his *habits;* and even love, that *selfish* and *monopolizing* passion, could not render Evelyn forgetful of his fellow-creatures. But then he was neglecting his duties as a father, a magistrate, and a proprietor of large estates. He was also acting a part which, when it came to be known, must attach ridicule to his name, and perhaps affix to it the suspicion of *insanity*. And after these serious reflections, Evelyn was resolved to pave the way for his return, by writing to his sister, when a circumstance happened which determined him to let matters remain as they were a little longer.

Belfield, who had long and secretly been enamoured of Mrs. Evelyn, whose virtue was, he knew, beyond the reach of his profligate arts, had resolved to take advantage of Evelyn's strange silence, and probable death, in order to make her his; not doubting, if he kept other men away, by giving out that she was engaged to him, he should, with his importunities, soon gain her affections. But then it was necessary that he should convince her friends, and *her*, that Evelyn was dead. When she was once his, his vanity led him to believe she would follow him through the world, and leave England with him, should her husband return.

For instead of being a rich man, as Monro thought him, he was a distressed man; nay, he had contrived so completely to embarrass Evelyn's affairs, that he knew, he must, ere long, quit England for safety;—and he was desirous that Mrs. Evelyn should be the companion of his exile. With this view, though he promised Evelyn's brother and sister, that he would advertise for tidings of Evelyn, he never did. He went down to Liverpool, on pretence of having heard intelligence of Evelyn, and returned with a list of the crew and passengers in a frigate, which had sailed to South America on such a day, and sunk on the voyage. On the list, was the name of Edward Evelyn. He also brought with him a boy, who had floated on shore, and was the only person saved. This boy he tutored to describe Evelyn's person, and what he said when he found that all hope was vain : and such was the apparent simplicity of this artful youth, that even Mrs. Lewellyn was deceived, and believed, as well as the broken-hearted Rosabel, that her brother, in his mad enthusiasm and fantastical unhappiness, had embarked on this expedition, carrying his 40,000*l*. along with him.

Evelyn's first intelligence of this successful fraud, was from seeing the children and the servants in deep mourning; and, alarmed at the sight, he flew to Monro to know the occasion of it.

"Why, that mad fellow, Evelyn, is dead!" was the astounding reply.

"Indeed! Well—I could not have believed it! Nay, I *cannot* believe it."

"Why not? I tell you he is dead, and devoured, too—the *sharks* have him."

He then related to the wondering Evelyn the whole story of his own expedition, his shipwreck, his despair, and his *last dying speech!*

"Oh! this is too pathetic," cried he—"it really makes me laugh! And so Belfield has a *witness* of all this?"

"Yes, and they doubt the fact no longer. The poor widow is, I hear, overwhelmed with affliction; but then I *also* hear that she is to be Mrs. *Belfield*."

"What!" cried Evelyn, seizing hold of the arm of the sofa, to steady his trembling frame.

"Yes. Why, Evelyn has been gone near eighteen months, and has been dead eight; so, when the year is up, I do not see why she should not marry again—do you?"

"Yes, I see a few objections to it: but this must be a false report. However, *nous verrons.*"

Evelyn felt *this* was not the moment to discover himself, as he had now to detect and punish a villain. Time went on, and Belfield was, Evelyn saw, admitted every day. Nor was it long before Monro told him, that the servants assured *his* servant, preparations for a wedding were making; though it was to be a private one. Evelyn felt confounded by this astonishing information. Still, he derived consolation from it. He knew that as soon as he appeared, Belfield must vanish; and he trusted that he kept too strict a watch on what passed in his house, not to detect preparation for a marriage. Therefore, he set Belfield at defiance, and could allow his thoughts to dwell on the cheering consciousness, that if Rosabel had quickly forgotten *him*, she had also forgotten the dying Denbigh, and therefore could love him no longer.

He was now surprised one morning by seeing Belfield leave Mrs. Evelyn's house with a very disturbed countenance, and marks of high irritation and anger in his manner. But Monro was absent, and he could not learn the reason. The next day Belfield called, but was evidently refused admittance; and so he was the following day. That day Monro returned, and soon after Evelyn saw one of his own servants go over to him, and he returned with him to the house.

"What can this mean?" thought Evelyn; and while he stood at the window watching for Monro, the latter looked up, saw him, and came to him instantly.

"Here is a pretty piece of work!" cried Monro. "That rascal Belfield is foiled, however: he spoke too soon; and having addressed Mrs. Evelyn rather familiarly, and declared his passion, he received the most firm and disdainful repulse; on which he had the impudence to tell her, that if she did not marry him, her reputation was gone; for that he had told his friends he was to marry her, and every one knew that *he* was the *only* man admitted every day to her presence, and at all hours; and that, though *she* knew he came on business alone, the world believed he came for other reasons."

"Impudent scoundrel!" cried Evelyn, breathless with indignation. "But to these insults," thought he, "it is I who have exposed her?"

"This behaviour did not recommend him the more to the fair widow. She ordered her servant to show him the door, and desired him to make up his accounts directly, that she might put her affairs in the hands of another agent. But he refused; and he vows she *shall* see him, and hear him plead his cause again.

"In this dilemma, she sent for me, as her oldest friend at hand, to meet this man, when he comes to-morrow morning, and to be there, in readiness to receive and threaten him; and I can tell him I shall not spare him."

"No, be sure you do not — there is a good creature!" cried Evelyn, squeezing his hand. "But do you not now suspect that this man trumped up the story of Mr. Evelyn's shipwreck?"

"No, no, that is sure — at least, I hope so; for that fellow was certainly unworthy of her. What a sweet creature she is! and what a fortunate man he would be who should gain her! Beauty, virtue, *family*, and a large jointure—hey, Sanford! Was it not very, very flattering, and very *kind* in her, to send for *me* to protect her? I consider it as a proud day in my life — hey, Sanford! Should not you be proud to be the chosen protector of such a woman?"

"To be sure," replied Evelyn, sighing deeply, and turning away from him.

"Well, good-bye, Sanford! I will let you know what passes to-morrow; and if I go *out* with Belfield, perhaps you will be *my second*. I have the best pistols and the best arm of any man in England. Will you oblige me?"

"O sir! remember that such a ruffian as this is not worthy to meet an honourable man."

"That is true; and a little gentle caning will be sufficient. He can only take the law of me."

But no Belfield appeared the next day: his affairs came suddenly and unexpectedly to a crisis, and he was forced to fly his country.

His complete detection, though it involved the affairs in difficulties, was in secret a great relief to Rosabel's mind; for she suspected now that the story of her husband's death was false, and the whole a fabrication of Belfield's. But she owned this to no one, lest she should be contradicted, and feel that hope damped which alone gave energy to her drooping mind.

Evelyn was now resolved he would not long delay to make his existence known; but he still was anxious to know whence the report of a *private wedding* originated: perhaps she was going to marry Denbigh, who might wish in death to call her his—if indeed he was dying, for Monro had heard he was *better*.

He therefore interrogated Monro on this subject, who learnt at last, that the wedding was only that of the governess and a young man to whom she had long been attached, and they were to be married the next day.

"Indeed!" cried Evelyn; "and who is to replace her in the family?"

"A sister of Mrs. Evelyn's, who is there already — a very clever woman — a widow, who, with herself and masters, Mrs. Evelyn thinks, will be able to do all a governess is wanted for."

"Is she like her sister?" said Evelyn.

"No; but she is a very fine woman—some years older than Mrs. Evelyn."

"Now, then, the time is come for my return," said Evelyn to himself: "yet still my mind misgives me concerning Denbigh. Were I sure that I was regretted, and he no longer loved, I should look forward to a life of content, if not of happiness. Perhaps I have wronged her. She has not visited him now for months, and *never* since she heard of my death — at least, not that I know of." And he went to bed that night, happier than he had yet been since he left Rosabel. But the night was hot, and he feverish, and he rose at dawn, to throw open his window, and catch, if possible, a refreshing breeze; when, as he approached the window, he beheld a sight that riveted him with horror and agony to the spot, and made the fever of his body forgotten in the phrensy of his mind: for he beheld Rosabel supporting a young man's head on her arm, who reclined on a couch at the open window; while ever and anon *she* wiped the damps from his forehead and pale cheek, imprinting as she did so a kiss on the former.

Evelyn saw, and fell staggering against the wall. This then, no doubt, was Denbigh! and they were privately married; and she had ceased to visit him only because he was in the house! Yes, yes: it must be he! else why that kiss of love? Never had she bestowed such a voluntary caress on him! And while he execrated his own mad folly, which had thus made him the means of his own disgrace, he suffered torments beyond the power of language to describe. But what was he to do?

He never could receive Rosabel again as *his wife*. Therefore, after hours of almost distracting thought, he resolved to let the story of his death remain uncontradicted, as the discovery that he yet lived might endanger her life, if not unsettle her reason.

"I have brought all this on myself," said he; "and it is right that I alone should be the victim. Besides, I feel I shall not long survive this dreadful stroke."

He was, however, resolved to convince himself indisputably of the *fact*, before he took any new steps; and that instantly, for delay and suspense were death to him. Accordingly, as soon as he rose, he sent a note to Monro, to tell him that he wished he would prevail on the Miss Evelyns to come over to see his curiosities that *morning*, according to their promise, as he might leave London the next day; and to his great joy their mother allowed them to come; but their aunt accompanied them, as she thought Matilda, a tall, full-grown girl of fourteen, was too old to visit a bachelor, unless she was with her.

With a beating heart, and an aching head, Evelyn received his guests; and his evident indisposition elicited many kind inquiries and obliging *prescriptions* from Mrs. Edwin. But he wanted to get rid of her; and, telling Monro to show her a very fine book of prints, he took his daughters into another room to show them things of a different nature. The inquiry, however, which he longed to make, died on his parched and trembling tongue. At length he gained courage to say, as he showed Matilda a pearl necklace of great value, which he purchased abroad for Rosabel, "See here, Miss Evelyn! When your mamma appears as a bride again, she should have such a necklace as this!"

"My mamma will *never* be a bride again, I am sure."

"No! Are you sure she is not a bride *now?*"

"Oh dear, no; impossible! We had seen for some time she was not so low as usual; and at last she told us she was convinced papa was alive, and Belfield had invented the story of his death; and we were so glad!"

"Can this be? Well, then," he added, shaking with emotion as he spoke, "I am certainly delirious; for I thought I saw your mother, this morning at daybreak, supporting a young man in her arms at the window!"

"Hush, hush!" cried little Fanny; "you must not tell what you saw!"

"O yes, I may now, you know: but did you *really* see uncle? How very odd!"

"Uncle, uncle, did you say?" screamed out the agitated Evelyn.

"Yes: our uncle who was supposed dead."

Here Evelyn ran out of the room to vent his full heart in tears and thanksgiving! but soon returning, he told her to go on with her story.

"Well, sir, he got out of the prison at Goa, came to Europe, fought a duel at Cork, where he landed, and left his antagonist mortally wounded as he thought. So he fled to London, and to mamma, who was forced to conceal his being with her; for the parents of the young man had vowed, if their son died, they would hang him if possible. But to-day we heard the gentleman was out of danger; but uncle was wounded so badly that he cannot stir from his couch."

"What a comfort," said he in a faint voice, "your uncle's arrival must have been to Mrs. Evelyn!"

"Yes: if any thing could comfort poor mamma for papa's absence, and supposed death. My uncle's first letter came on the day twelvemonth that papa left us; and though she was glad to hear he was alive, she said she could not rejoice that day. But she shut herself up all the day, and would not see any one."

Evelyn heard, wondered, but was self-condemned.

"She is not your own mother, I think?"

"Oh, no: but we love her quite as well as we did our own mamma."

"As well!" cried Fanny: "Oh, better, better! Our mamma was very good and sensible, I dare say; but she was not kind, and this is *so* kind!"

"And to all equally?"

"Why, no. We are rather jealous of *Edward*, because mamma thinks he is so like *papa*, and so handsome, and she does *so* love him, and look at him!"

"Was your papa handsome?"

"Mamma thinks him so; and his picture is almost the only comfort she has."

"See, Matilda! see! what a fine piece of spar this is," said Fanny; and Evelyn was glad, while their attention was occupied, to escape again to his chamber. When he returned, he could not prevail on himself to converse with his children again. Their unconscious prattle wounded while it delighted him; for he saw his injustice, and sorrowed over it

27*

with unavailing regret. He therefore went into the room where he had left Monro and Mrs. Edwin; being resolved to have, if he could get rid of Monro, some conversation with the latter relative to her sister, and the disappearance of her husband.

"The young ladies are looking at the fossils now," said he to Monro: "there are some fine specimens which perhaps you never saw:" and Monro left them together.

"I am sorry, sir, to see you so exhausted," said Mrs. Edwin: "I doubt we are amusing ourselves at your expense? I dare say you wish us gone?"

"By no means, madam, if you are entertained."

"Can I be otherwise?"

"Perhaps you could prevail on Mrs. Evelyn to favour me with a call, if she is fond of prints and fossils?"

"My sister! Oh, no, sir. Poor dear creature! she is fond of nothing now but the memory of Mr. Evelyn and his children."

"Not even of Captain Denbigh?" was a question Evelyn wished to ask, but dared not.

"Pray, madam, was the reason ever known, why Mr. Evelyn returned to England *incog.*, and went abroad again without seeing his wife and family?"

"*Never,* sir.—Oh, sir! it is a most *mysterious* and distressing circumstance altogether, if you knew all."

"I wish that I did know all; for Mrs. Evelyn interests me much. Her story resembles that of one very dear to me, and if—that is, madam, if it be not impertinent, and you would condescend——"

"Certainly, sir; but shut the door first." And Mrs. Edwin, who loved to talk, and like every one else was fond of telling a very interesting story, was as eager to narrate as Evelyn to listen.

"What made Mr. Evelyn unhappy, no one exactly knows; but unhappy he was during the whole two years of his marriage, till he could endure to live no longer at home, and he went abroad. Poor Rosabel thought it was because he had taken an aversion to *her.*"

"*Aversion* to her! Impossible!"

"Yes, sir: she was always sure he married her, merely because he fancied his first wife desired him to do so, and that his children loved her. And Rosabel has always thought that she was justly punished for not having owned to him that she knew her cousin was going to forbid his marrying her, when death stopped what she was about to utter."

"Amazing! And why did not Rosa—Mrs. Evelyn I mean—tell Mr. Evelyn *the truth?*"

"Because she loved him, sir, and had long loved him." Mrs. Edwin then went on to describe all Rosabel's secret passion, and secret sorrows, to the amazed but gratified and agitated auditor. "Judge then, sir," said she, "how wretched and mortified Rosabel was to be assured by Mrs. Fanshaw that Mr. Evelyn told her, he only married Miss Vere because *his wife bade him!* No wonder that Rosabel concealed her feelings by coldness and reserve, and Mrs. Lewellyn says that proud and delicate coldness did the mischief."

"No doubt, madam."

"Mrs. Lewellyn says that her brother was the humblest of men, and thought no woman could love him for himself; therefore, she is well convinced he fancied Rosabel did not marry him for love: and afterward, Rosabel thinks, he believed she loved Captain Denbigh; whereas, it was her secret love to Mr. Evelyn which had prevented her returning Denbigh's passion."

Here Evelyn started from his seat in excessive emotion; but re-seating himself, motioned to her to go on. She did so, and blamed the dissimulation on principle which Rosabel practised in order to conceal her love, which she fancied unrequited. She even related her watching for the sound of the horse's feet, when Evelyn was out late; and gave, in short, a minute detail of her sister's devoted love to the man who for a whole year had not given her any tidings of his existence, and who, if he had not really perished, was acting a most cruel part towards a woman who adored him, and affectionate children. "'And all for *what?*' as Mrs. Lewellyn says. Not but that she very properly blames my sister. Had she allowed her husband to read her heart—and wives should have no secrets from their husbands—she would have given herself the best chance of securing the attachment and esteem, and in time the *love,* of any husband, had he *not* loved her already. And, as it happened, Evelyn was exactly the sort of man whom the consciousness of being tenderly beloved would have rendered as passionately in love in return, if he had not been so *already;* and Mrs. Lewellyn says, never was man more in love than her brother. However, sir, out of evil comes good; for, if her husband ever *does* return, (and *she,* poor thing, will not believe he is dead,) Rosabel says that, being made wise by past experience, her heart shall be—but you are *ill,* sir! I am sure you are!"

Evelyn was, indeed, too much overcome with joy, thankfulness, and other emotions, to contain himself any longer, and he sobbed in convulsive agony.

When he was a little recovered, Monro led him to his room, and his sympathizing visiters departed.

When Evelyn was alone, and could reflect on what he had heard, he could hardly believe but that it was all a dream. What! *he* the first and *only* love of Rosabel's heart! for that was the recollection uppermost.

"Then I will return to her *directly,*" said he; "and, oh! how much happier shall we be, than we have ever yet been! Therefore, however culpable, I *cannot* regret my folly.

"Away, hated disguise!" said he, trying to wash off the dye on his face, and throwing his wig and false mustachios indignantly from him. But, alas! the sudden transition of feeling which he had undergone, and his ceaseless anxiety during many months, had operated so powerfully and fatally on his health, that before morning Evelyn was raving in all the delirium of fever; and in two days his life was declared, by the medical attendants whom Monro kindly called in, to be in the utmost danger. The latter was very uneasy, because he could not tell where his relations lived, as he said he was not related to the Sanfords whom *he* knew. Rosabel, Mrs. Edwin, and the children were meanwhile most kindly interested in the recovery of the *lonely being*, as they called him, who had been so kind to Matilda and Fanny, and who seemed to have no one belonging to him; and Rosabel sent him home-made jellies, and whatever she thought could be of service to him.

"Command my services," said she to the physician, who was also her own, "and any thing in my power I will do for this poor man." Long was the struggle, and doubtful the recovery.

"It is very strange," said Monro: "I always understood he had neither wife nor family; and yet the poor soul, in his delirium, is always talking of his wife and children."

"Poor things!" cried Rosabel, deeply sighing, "if he dies, how much they will be to be pitied: *they, too, may expect and look for him they love in vain!*"

At length, the life now so precious to its possessor was mercifully spared, and Evelyn was declared out of danger. When he came to himself, he eagerly inquired of Monro, if he had named any one in his delirium. "No one," was the reply; "but you raved about your dear wife and children."

"Nonsense!" said Evelyn, blushing.

"But who could have thought," cried Monro, "that a fever should have so improved the complexion! You look like other people now, only rather pale; and as to your eyes, I never saw finer in my life. What should you want green spectacles for?"

"How are Mrs. Edwin and that family?" said Evelyn.

"Quite well, and they have been so anxious concerning you! That angel, Mrs. Evelyn, has sent you jellies and nice things every day."

"She! Mrs. Evelyn?"

"Yes—what is the matter?"

"How kind!" cried he bursting into tears. Soon after he desired Mrs. Evelyn's "nice things" to be brought him; and he would have eaten ravenously, if Monro would have permitted him, of all that was set before him.

A knock at the door was now heard, and Monro told him it was Mrs. Evelyn herself, come to inquire how he was.

Instantly, Evelyn, who was up and dressed, prevailed on him and the nurse to lead him to the banister, that he might hear what she said. They did so, though Monro said it was very absurd. But Evelyn heard Rosabel's sweet voice asking after the health of "Mr. Sanford," in the kindest accents, and *he* felt that it was *not* absurd: nor did he fail to watch for her calling again, that he might have again the same gratification.

In a very few days, he insisted on being removed down stairs, and he had a French bed put up on the first floor for him to repose on whenever his strength was exhausted.

He now resolved no longer to defer restoring Rosabel, and consequently himself, to peace and happiness; and he told the physician that in case he should die—and his life was perhaps not worth many months' purchase—he wished to impart something which was on his mind, in confidence, to Mrs. Evelyn: he therefore conjured him to prevail upon her to grant him a private interview. The physician, seeing him much agitated, promised compliance; and Rosabel, who always fancied every thing that she could not account for had a reference to Evelyn, was not very reluctant to indulge the request, especially as it was that of a man who fancied himself dying.

"Poor man! perhaps he wishes to tell me where to find his wife—from whom some adverse circumstances may have separated him!" and she sent word to Evelyn that she would call on him when he chose. The hour being appointed, Rosabel was ushered into Evelyn's apartments, who lay on the French bed, with the room so darkened, and the curtains so drawn around him, that Rosabel could not distinguish his features.

"Mrs. Evelyn!" said he, in a low, broken voice, when she approached him, "I dare not speak the request I have to urge; but if you will deign to peruse the letter which you will find lying on the table in the next room, you will see what I require."

Rosabel, relieved by hearing this, as she saw he *spoke with difficulty*, eagerly went in search of the letter; but a mist came over her eyes, and she became painfully agitated when she saw that it began, "Dearest, ever most beloved, and most injured of women!" What followed, she did not stay to read, but she passed rapidly on to the end; and when she saw, "Come, then, if you can indeed forgive him, to the arms of your penitent and adoring husband,   EDWARD EVELYN."

Rosabel uttered a faint scream, and rushing into the inner room, she threw herself on the neck of Evelyn, who was coming forward to receive her, and she nearly fainted on his bosom.

I shall pass over the scene that followed, of explanation, forgiveness and happiness; but I must say, that so difficult is it for any one to break through the restraints imposed by habitual reserve, especially if it be founded on a principle, however mistaken it may be, that till Evelyn told Rosabel he was aware of her long and secret attachment for him, she had not had resolution to confess all she had felt and suffered. But now an unreserved and mutual communication of thoughts, fears, and jealousies took place, and Evelyn exclaimed—

"*Now*, then, Rosabel! the foundation of our happiness is laid on a sure basis, and never can it be shaken again by our *own* faults!"

Monro called during the conference; and heard with wonder, almost amounting to indignation, that Mr. Sanford was engaged, and could not see any one, because Mrs. Evelyn was with him.

"How!" thought he: "Mrs. Evelyn visit a stranger, and alone! I wonder whether she would so honour me, if I were ill!"

"But my children!" said Evelyn; "how I long to embrace them!"

"Let me go for them!"

"No, not so, my best love! and I really do not like they should know, at present, at least, that their grave father has been playing the fool thus."

"O dear Evelyn! no more concealments—I have done with them for ever."

"But surely, Rosabel, you do not wish your husband to appear to disadvantage, if it can be helped?"

"No, certainly."

It was then resolved upon by Evelyn, that he should write a letter which Mrs. Evelyn was to go home and say she had just received from her husband himself, telling her he was on his road home, and desiring him to meet her alone at Barnet the next day. The next morning early he set off for Barnet, leaving a note for Monro, thanking him for all his kindness, and leaving him, as memorials of him, his collection of fossils and spars.

Accordingly, Rosabel tore herself away from Evelyn, but not before the length of their conference had excited great wonder. When she returned home, she soon summoned the family around her, read an affectionate letter from her husband, which Mr. Sanford, she said, (who was, she found, the confidential agent of Evelyn,) had been desired to give her, when he had prepared her for hearing he was alive. Great was the children's joy at hearing they should soon see their papa again, and the little boy was immediately sent for from Harrow.

"O mamma!" cried Matilda, "how glad you must be to think you were so kind to a stranger when he was ill, as you now find he was papa's friend!"

"I am *indeed* thankful for it," cried Rosabel, with no unpleasing tears trickling down her cheeks. "But come, pull off your mourning directly, girls! and tell the servants to pull off theirs." And she left the room singing—

And shall I see his face again?
And shall I hear him speak?
There's a downright madness in the thought!
Indeed, I'm like to greet!

"Come, Aunt Edwin," (as they called her,) said Fanny, "and put on a gay dress. But how thoughtful you look, and as if you were only half pleased that papa is alive, and coming home!"

"I am *quite* pleased, my dear," replied Mrs. Edwin; "but I am *perplexed*, and have my own private opinions and suspicions. However, to-morrow will satisfy them."

That evening, Monro called on Mrs. Evelyn, and saw with astonishment the changes that had taken place, and heard with equal astonishment of the resurrection of Mr. Evelyn. Nor was it long before he went to communicate to Evelyn what had happened, who now resumed his glasses and his black wig and mustachios.

"Well," cried he, "this is a day of wonders! There is the reserved, prudent Mrs. Evelyn, coming to visit a stranger, and shut up with him for hours! There is Mr. Evelyn come to life, and coming home to-morrow! and there is his wife, as white and as gay as a bride, with a face full of smiles! and there are the children in white also, and the servants in their gay liveries! In short, I neither know the house again, nor its inhabitants; and this all on account of the return of a cross, ill-looking, crack-brained fellow, who wants a strait-waistcoat."

"I see you are jealous and disappointed, Monro, because your chance of the fair widow is now quite over."

"Yes, poor thing! and for *her* sake I am sorry; for, *really*, not to be at all conceited, I dare say I am better looking than this Evelyn."

"I do not *doubt* it," replied Evelyn, smiling.

"But if I may be so bold, may I ask, what could your business be with Mrs. Evelyn?"

"You may *not* be so bold," replied Evelyn, laughing: "but I am tired, and must now bid you good-night."

The next morning, the astonished Monro heard he was gone, and received his letter and his present.

"There is something very mysterious about this fellow," said Monro: "I am afraid he is some sort of a spy—I am glad he is gone."

Early the next day, Mrs. Evelyn set off in her chariot, with four horses, to fetch her husband; and before the dinner-hour, Evelyn found himself in the embrace of his affectionate children, and once more restored to his home and his family!

Mrs. Edwin looked at him very earnestly before she gave him her hand; then, with a meaning smile, she advanced to receive his offered salute, saying, "I am satisfied—I see, or rather *hear*, that we have *met before*."

"How much papa speaks like poor Mr. Sanford!" observed both the girls.

"Who is poor Mr. Sanford?" said Evelyn; and he was amused to hear himself described as a poor, frightful-looking man, who had been very kind to them, and was *very ill.*

In the evening, Rosabel begged Monro would come over; and she took care that the children should be out of the way when he was presented to Evelyn.

When he first saw him, he started back with a look of astonishment and suspicion; but exclaiming, "No, it *cannot* be!" he gave him his hand, and welcomed him home again. But the moment Evelyn spoke, to doubt any longer seemed impossible; and Evelyn, with great feeling, told him he relied upon his oft-experienced kindness, and his judgment, not to disclose the secret which he now discovered. And Monro promised all he asked, while Evelyn took occasion to explain to him some of his reasons for the strange part which he had acted, and for which he had so wisely rebuked him.

But Colonel Vere and Mrs. Lewellyn, the former of whom he had never seen till now, mixed even a painful degree of reproof with their welcome, when they saw the self-judged Evelyn. Nor did Rosabel herself escape.

"I was for years," said Colonel Vere, "a prisoner, and in chains, and in the dungeons of the Inquisition, at Goa, and the iron ate into my flesh; but I vow to you, Mr. Evelyn, I had rather be so bound again, than endure those fetters which you and Rosabel have fastened round yourselves, to eat away your peace of mind — the fetters of a morbid sensibility and diseased imagination."

END OF THE OPPOSITE NEIGHBOUR.

LOVE, MYSTERY, AND SUPERSTITION.

——"My grief lies all within;
And these external manners of lament
Are merely shadows to the unseen grief
That swells with silence in the tortured soul:
There lies the substance."
Richard II.

INTRODUCTION.

By desire of the same gentleman who employed me to edit the narrative which I published two years ago, as a Tale of Trials, I now publish the following Tale—found, as he says, among the same hoard of family manuscripts.

When he looked over this manuscript, after I had fitted it for publication, he expressed his surprise and disapprobation that I had not, as Editor, exclaimed, as the story went on, against the superstitions and the mistaken zeal manifest in the events related; but as I thought that the events were in *perfect keeping* with the sentiments of the unknown writer, and of the heroes and heroines of the piece, I did not like to injure the unity of a *Catholic story* by the comments of a *Protestant Editor.*

"But are you not afraid," said he, " of being supposed to approve what you do not pointedly reprobate?"

I could not help smiling, as I replied, that I had no such fears, as *my* Protestantism, I trusted, was beyond the reach of suspicion. I did not wonder, however, that such a fear occurred to him, as he had only *recently* abjured the Catholic faith; and it was this circumstance, no doubt, which made him displeased with my forbearance.

"One thing I must observe," said I. "There are some observations made by two of the principal characters, which seem to me inconsistent with their religious belief; how does this happen?"—and I pointed to the passages as I spoke.

"They are interpolations of mine," he replied; " as they point out the moral which I wish to be deduced from the story."

I will not give the argument which ensued; suffice, that we entered into a compromise, that if he would allow me to print those passages in italics, I would, to oblige him, give up my original intention of calling the tale "Love and Mystery," and would name it—

LOVE, MYSTERY, AND SUPERSTITION.

PART THE FIRST.

"Who calls so loud, at this late, peaceful hour!"

In the winter of the year 1693, a family in the north of England was alarmed at midnight by a violent knocking at the gates of the mansion. But the noise was heard by the young lady of the house only — the Lady Barbara Delmayne; who, easily awakened from the light slumbers of youth, and terrified at the unusual sound, hastened to call the servant that slept near her, and then, opening her window, asked who was there.

"It is I my ownself, my lady! it is O'Carrol; and, for the love of the Holy Virgin, I conjure you to let me in; for I hold a dead woman in my arms, whom I want to bring to life—and I am quite dead myself."

Lady Barbara, who immediately recognised the voice, waited to hear no more; but scarcely allowing herself time to throw an additional clothing over that which she had already seized, she ran down stairs, and with her own delicate hands endeavoured to unbar the massy gates. She tried, however, in vain; but the summons of the bell was quickly obeyed by the rest of the family — O'Carrol and his burthen were admitted.

"Alas! I fear she is indeed dead!" exclaimed Lady Barbara, taking one of the passive hands that hung powerless over O'Carrol's shoulder; while her eyes rested on a face beautiful and pale as any statue in her father's gallery.

"Quick! quick! a fire!" cried the kind-hearted young man, following Lady Barbara into the kitchen, where, to their great surprise, they found a blazing fire already; and, on a table beside it, ale and spirits, and a jug of hot water.

"Here are wicked doings, indeed!" cried Mrs. Mendham, the housekeeper, (who in the absence of Lord and Lady Delmayne, was particularly tenacious of her authority.) "Come out, ye vipers! from where you have hidden yourselves;" and she dragged one of the housemaids and the under butler from their hiding-place; but Lady Barbara insisted that all discussion of their guilt should be deferred till the next day, and that she should come and assist in restoring, if possible, a fellow-creature to life.

"And how do we know," said the prudent Mrs. Mendham, "who it is that O'Carrol has picked up?"

"Faith, old jontlewoman, I only know she is a distressed creature, whom I found in the deep snow, in a violent storm, near the ruined shrine of the Holy Virgin, about a mile off, where she was praying, I'll engage."

"It does not matter who or what she is," cried Lady Barbara—"she is in distress."

"And a Catholic, too," said the priest; "and the victim of her piety."

"And a bonnie creature, too," cried Donald, a Scotch servant, who had lived many years in the family; "and I hope that——" But as he bent over her, he started back in a kind of agony, and ran out of the kitchen.

Lady Barbara, meanwhile, was desiring the maid to bring her a complete change of linen for the stranger, and the housekeeper to assist her in putting it on.

"Mighty fine!" muttered Mrs. Mendham, who had grown old in power, and scarcely knew how to obey the child whom she had seen in her cradle; "mighty fine!" but, without further objection, began reluctantly to undress the unfortunate pilgrim. She was soon converted into a willing assistant; for, on loosening the pilgrim's cloak, and the collar of the inner garment, she perceived a broad, black riband round the sufferer's throat, and following it with her hand down the folds of the gown, she found hanging to the end of it a miniature picture, set round with very large diamonds.

"What fine jewels!" cried Mrs. Mendham. "Poor dear lamb! she must be somebody!"

"What a beautiful face!" said Lady Barbara, looking only at the picture: "but take it away—we must not lose time," she added, handing it to Donald, who was now returned to the room.

In a few moments after the warm linen had been put on, and the friction resumed, the housekeeper declared that she felt the sweet lady's heart beat.—O'Carrol, hearing this, loudly gave thanks, for then he should have saved a fellow-creature; while Donald, giving him a hug that almost throttled him, laid the picture down, and hastily left the room, declaring that he had the toothache. Not a hand was now lifted from the limbs of the sufferer, for life seemed to return with every touch; not an eye was removed from her countenance, as every one expected to behold the heavy eyelids unclose, and returning consciousness beam from the first startled glance.

Lady Barbara hung with suspended breath over the object of her solicitude, watching every languid movement, and listening to every struggling sigh. At length, the anxiously-expected moment arrived; and dark, but as yet rayless eyes, opened upon the anxious spectators.

"Thank God!" ejaculated Lady Barbara, while the tears of grateful emotion glittered on her glowing cheek: "but," added she, mournfully, "alas! she is not yet conscious!"

Those dark and rayless eyes now assumed a different appearance; for they lighted up with sudden recollection, and throwing inquiring glances around, they at length fixed with wonder on Lady Barbara; then raising herself on her elbow, she exclaimed, "*Dove sono?—Rinaldo, Rosalie, dove siete?*"*

"How fortunate it was," thought Lady Barbara, "that my cousin Aubrey taught me Italian!" Then, in imperfect words, she informed the stranger she was amongst friends, though those whom she mentioned were not present.

"*Je parle François: Je le parle toujours,*" was the agitated and eager answer—"*et même l'Anglois quelquefois. Mais où suis-je, et où sont-ils?*"†

Lady Barbara now again assured her she was in safety, adding, that those whom she wanted to see should be sent for immediately.

"I wish, I wish to go home directly," she exclaimed in broken English: "they will be so wretched."

She then tried to rise, but her strength failed her, and she fell back, nearly fainting, on the mattress. At this moment, the door of the hall was heard to open, and O'Carrol appeared, followed by a neighbouring surgeon.

"Is it possible," eagerly asked Lady Barbara, "that this lady can undertake to go home to-night with safety?"

"No," said he, feeling her pulse: "it would be at the hazard of her life: the cold is intense, the night dark, and the snow so untracked, that even were she well, it would be tempting death to undertake it."

"Death!" said the stranger mournfully;—"oh! that were happiness! But I must live, must suffer, must—Well, God's will be done! I must stay where I am. But who are you, sweet creature?"

"I am called Lady Barbara Delmayne; and you are in the castle of my father, who, with my mother, is unfortunately absent; and this is Father Vincent, our chaplain."

The lady bent her head reverently to the priest, who gave her his blessing, and bade her be comforted: he then reminded her of her providential escape.

"Providential indeed!—But where is he who was made the instrument of my preservation?"

O'Carrol was now fetched forward by Donald, whose face was nearly enveloped in a large black handkerchief. The lady beckoned O'Carrol to approach her.

"You have saved my life; and, wretched as it is, I thank you. There are those who will thank you also, and reward you too."

"I ask no reward, lady; I only did my duty. I saw you perishing, and I tried to save you—that's all: and you are saved, and that's reward sufficient."

"An approving conscience is indeed its own reward," said the lady sighing, "and may it ever be yours, kind young man! But when will morning dawn? for I do so wish to go home!"

"We will send you home when you are able to go; and in the meanwhile, as soon as it is day, we will despatch a messenger to your friends. Do they live far off?"

"About four miles, I believe, at the village of Greenval."

"Oh! I know it well," cried Donald in a low voice; "and I will go myself."

Lady Barbara now asked, for whose house he was to inquire.

"For the house of Mr. Dupont," said the lady in a faltering tone; "and beg him to send for me as soon as possible."

Donald bowed very low, promised implicit obedience, and withdrew.

"I am sorry you are in such a hurry to leave us," said Lady Barbara; "but I have no right to interfere."

"Your ladyship must interfere to persuade this lady to try to sleep," said the surgeon.

"To sleep!" exclaimed the lady. "Oh, no! I have a terror of sleep."

She was at length, however, persuaded to take an anodyne draught, and, after much importunity, to go to bed. While she was undressing, she for the first time missed her picture, and inquired for it with trembling anxiety.

"I have it here," said Mrs. Mendham, taking it from her pocket, "and a precious thing it is. If those are real diamonds, they might make a duchess proud."

"But not happy," said the stranger, pressing the picture to her lips. "This inanimate ivory is what I value."

"So should I," observed Lady Barbara, "if I loved any one resembling that face."

"It is—yes, it is like *you*," said the stranger with surprise, and gazing on Lady Barbara: "how singular!" But not choosing to satisfy the curiosity which she saw depicted on the countenance of her young hostess, she fastened the riband round her neck herself, and hid the picture in her bosom.

Mrs. Mendham now brought the night-clothes, which the stranger insisted on being allowed to put on without help: but as the former had conceived some suspicions which she was eager to remove or confirm, she persisted so resolutely, that the latter was forced to accept her assistance; and as she gave it, she started back with an expression of horror in her face, and, crossing herself, stood gazing on the conscious lady with a look of strange scrutiny. Mrs. Mendham soon after abruptly quitted the chamber. The stranger was now removed to her pillow, and was comfortably settled when the house-keeper returned. Approaching the lady, she desired to know whether she would not wish to see Father Vincent before she settled for the night.

---

* Where am I? Rinaldo, Rosalie, where are you?

† I speak French: I always speak it; and even English sometimes. But where am I, and where are they?

"No," she meekly replied; "I have nothing to say to him."

"What means *this* interference?" cried Lady Barbara angrily.

"I am sure 'twas well meant," said Mrs. Mendham; "for few of us would like to die without confession and the rites of the church, my lady, and if—"

Lady Barbara was about to interrupt her with great indignation, when a tapping at the door was heard, and Father Vincent himself now entered the apartment.

"Whence this intrusion, father?" exclaimed Lady Barbara; but before he could reply, the lady, with a significant smile, desired him to approach.

"Shall I bid every one withdraw?" said he in a solemn tone.

"No, not one—I have nothing for your private ear. My mind is at present burthened by nothing but the fulness of gratitude to Heaven and to my preservers."

"But if you should have a relapse?"

"If I have, I trust there will be time allowed me to summon you and your holy aid, father. And if not, be satisfied to learn that before I set off on my pilgrimage, I had performed all my religious duties; and when you *remember*, father," she added, casting a meaning glance at him, "the severe duty in the performance of which I nearly lost my life, and *other circumstances* of which I believe you to be aware, you cannot suppose I do not feel comforted by the blest assurance that 'there is joy in heaven over the sinner that repenteth.'"

The priest looked confused, crossed himself, and departed; and while the latter in a petulant tone demanded of Lady Barbara what was next to be done, "Again, I beg, I entreat that you will retire to rest, and your lady, also," said the stranger. But Lady Barbara was fixed to stay: she however desired the other bed to be made ready for her, and insisted that Mrs. Mendham should go back to her own apartment.

Lady Barbara now seated herself in a chair, and prepared to watch by her interesting charge.

At fifteen and a half—and Lady Barbara was no more—the *importance* of such an office was very grateful; and what a fine incident she thought it would be to tell her cousin Aubrey! But as the stranger declared she could not sleep, her gentle nurse thought there could be no harm in a little conversation, with a view of eliciting some particulars of the lady's story; and she proceeded to give her a short detail of her own family and connexions.

"My father and mother," said she, "are gone to London to pay their respects at Whitehall; but it is for the first time, as the earl was a friend to the exiled family, and the oaths have not sat very easily on his mind. But William Tyrconnel, a distant relation, who is heir to my father's title, and Aubrey, his brother, are great favourites with the new sovereign, and have at last prevailed on my father to go to court. Tyrconnel is very clever, has travelled a great deal, and thought and read more. You must know that it is intended he should marry me, and therefore he has great influence here; but he and I intend no such thing. His brother Aubrey is far more lively than *he* is. Oh, so lively! and though he has not travelled much, he is quite master of Italian, and has taught me to read it at least. But he *speaks* it so well! Oh! I wish he was here for your sake."

"Not for my sake only."

"Oh no! not entirely; because I like my cousin Aubrey excessively."

"And does he not like you, sweet girl?"

"Oh dear, yes! I hope so. Nay, I am sure so."

"But then your parents' wishes are for your union with the elder brother?"

"Yes; but Tyrconnel is not in love with me."

"And Aubrey is?"

"Why, yes; I think he is: but there is a long time before us yet. I am not sixteen, and I assure you I have no wish to be married before I am *seventeen*. My elder sister, indeed, married at sixteen, but I think seventeen quite early enough."

"So do I," said the stranger, sighing; "and *then* it is necessary that a parent's blessing should accompany a child to the altar. No vows, I believe, are blessed of God our Father in heaven that are not first blessed by his representatives on earth." Here she paused in some agitation. Lady Barbara now felt her curiosity strongly raised, but it was as quickly suppressed by respect and delicacy; and when her companion stretched forth her hand to her, smiling through her tears, and looked at her as if expecting her to speak, she only said,

"I never will marry without my parents' consent; and I *think* they will let me marry the younger brother, as the elder will not have me. Aubrey has an independent fortune left him by an aunt. Oh, I wish you could see him! He will be here in a day or two, and so will my father and mother; and if you would but stay here till then! Is it impossible?"

"Quite, I am sure; even if I wished to stay, Rinaldo—that is, Mr. Dupont I mean—would never consent."

"Is Mr. Dupont's name Rinaldo?"

"It—that is, I call him sometimes, which is very foolish; he is called Bertram Dupont, a Swiss name; of a Swiss family."

"And he is your husband?"

"My husband!" exclaimed the lady. "Alas! he is my brother!"

"But pray who is the Rosalie you talked of?"

"I! did I talk of Rosalie? When?"

"When you first recovered."

"Ah! very likely; I awoke as from a dream.

"Rosalie is the name of a sweet girl that lives with Mr. Dupont and me, and is under our care."

"How I should like to know her!"

"Would you could!"

"But, as you are not Mr. Dupont's wife, your name is not Dupont."

"My name, the only name I wish to be called by, is Madeleine."

"Madeleine! How romantic!—what pretty names! Rosalie, Madeleine, Rinaldo!"

"No, no—not Rinaldo, I beseech you!"

"Well, then, he shall be plain Monsieur Bertram Dupont. But I am well read in Tasso, and Rinaldo is a favourite hero of mine; and I am sure, when well, you are, or must have been, quite handsome enough for Armida."

"An Armida! What a comparison!"

"I could only mean in beauty," hastily added Lady Barbara, distressed at the agonized expression which the stranger's countenance assumed.

"Alas!" exclaimed the lady, seizing her hand, "was not Armida a seducer?"

"Yes; but then the fault was mutual, and Armida loved Rinaldo quite as tenderly as he loved her."

"True, most true; but then had she not tempted, Rinaldo had not fallen. Let us, sweet girl, if we must talk of such things, talk of Tancredi and Clorinda, where love was united to purity and piety."

"It is not necessary to talk of either; and indeed," added Lady Barbara, "I had much rather talk of a more interesting subject, *yourself*."

"Of me!"

"Yes: but your voice grows faint, and your eyelids seem heavy."

"You are right. It is an exertion to me to speak loud. Come nearer me, dear child."

Lady Barbara obeyed, and, sitting on the side of the bed, leaned over her pillow. Never was there a more complete contrast than that exhibited by Lady Barbara and her charge. The latter was pale and thin almost to emaciation; her eyes were dark, and shaded with still darker eye-lashes; while her black and glossy hair, parted à la *Madonna* on the forehead, was twisted round her small and graceful head; and her countenance told a tale of deep sorrow, sorrow borne with resignation, but felt bitterly, and to be felt *for ever*. She seemed also to be faded by affliction, not by years.

The happy being who leaned affectionately over her, looked, on the contrary, all the happiness which she felt. Hope and gladness sparkled in her bright blue eyes, and her face glowed with the tints of health; while glossy ringlets burst from their confinement over her flushed and dimpled cheek, and her night-gown marked out the finely-fashioned form and limbs beneath it.

"Sweet, lovely girl!" cried the stranger, as she gazed on her, "may no cloud dim the brightness of the lustre! May no self-confidence betray thee! May thy course on earth be long and pure, and mayest thou resign thy breath innocent as thou art at present! And thou hast a mother. Happy woman! and she may kiss thee, and clasp thee to her heart, and shed over thee the delightful tears of maternal fondness. Happy, happy woman! how I envy her!"

Here she groaned aloud. The kind girl for a moment or two could not speak: at length, she timidly said, "Oh that I were worthy to know the *cause* of this mysterious grief! and oh that I could alleviate it!"

"*Both* are impossible," replied the lady, in a solemn tone of voice: "but it were better for us to talk no more. I feel as if I could sleep now." Then offering her faded lip to the full and crimson one of the youthful being beside her, she turned to rest.

Lady Barbara, left to silence and her own reflections, struggled some minutes against the approaches of sleep, but in vain; when seeing the lady was in a calm slumber, she gently stole to her own bed, and soon forgot her curiosity, and *even Aubrey Tyrconnel*.

The sun had been risen a full hour before she awoke to a recollection of where she was, and the transactions of the preceding evening. The fire still burnt on the hearth, and Lady Barbara, having heaped fresh fagots on it, turned on tiptoe to the bed of the stranger: but she forgot that no tiptoe motion could preserve the sleep of one whose slumbers were invaded by the crackling of green wood; and the noise soon awoke the lady so completely, that she was immediately conscious where she was, and held out her emaciated hand. To Lady Barbara's inquiries after her health, she replied, that she had passed the most comfortable, because the most *unconscious* night she had known for years; but that she felt great pain in her limbs, and wished, if the day was not far advanced, to remain in bed a little longer. Lady Barbara declared it was wise to remain there, however late it might be: then, ringing for servants, she insisted on it that breakfast would be the next best thing for her guest.

The housekeeper now entered the room with Lady Barbara's own woman; and while her lady was dressing, she approached the stranger, and told her that the gentleman whom she sent for would arrive very soon.

"Soon! Is it possible?" cried she, starting up with a countenance where pleasure and pain seemed struggling for mastery.

"Yes, very possible: for it seems a messenger set off for Greenval before day-break, and it is now near nine o'clock."

"As this is the case," said the stranger,

"I will endeavour to get up before Dupont comes."

"No, no," cried Lady Barbara, "I will not allow it indeed; and hither comes the surgeon himself to forbid such an act of suicide."

"Not absolute suicide, my Lady," he replied, after feeling her pulse: "there is no fever at present, and the night I find has been a good one. Let us now try to revive the patient by a little breakfast."

Soon the hand became trembling that conveyed the coffee to her lip, and vainly did she attempt to eat the offered viands; while Lady Barbara could not behold her suddenly increased emotion, and the universal shaking of her frame, without secretly wondering what had occasioned it. Father Vincent now knocked at the door, to say that the gentleman was arrived.

"I was sure of that, for I heard his voice at a distance," exclaimed the stranger in great agitation.—"Pray show him hither directly."

Lady Barbara, who was kneeling by the bed-side, now rose, and motioned to every one to leave the room. She was preparing to follow them, when the lady begged her to give her the cordial; which she had only just swallowed as the stranger hastily entered the apartment.

"What a Rinaldo!" involuntarily, though in a low tone of voice, ejaculated Lady Barbara; but what she said or what she did was alike unheeded by these two mysterious beings. The lips of the lady uttered no sound, although they moved; but her eyes swimming in tears were fixed on her brother, who with difficulty supported his trembling frame. He too was silent, and in his wild but steadfast glance sternness seemed strangely struggling with tenderness; till on observing Lady Barbara, with a look expressive of awe mingled with astonishment, he exclaimed, "What do I see? Lovely vision, what art thou?"

"It is Lady Barbara Delmayne," said the lady, with a meaning smile, which the stranger immediately returned. Lady Barbara believing that her presence was a check on their mutual feelings, was now hastening to the door, when Dupont in a deep and plaintive tone exclaimed, "Stay, young lady, stay! I have nothing to say to my sister which you may not hear; and I am impatient to thank you for your hospitality."

"No thanks are due to me, sir; give them all to O'Carrol, who snatched her from destruction and brought her hither."

"Bless him!" cried he, clasping his hands convulsively together, and fixing his eyes on his sister; then turning them away with a shuddering emotion, he buried his face in his cloak.

"Yes, Dupont," said she, "my escape from death was miraculous: I was found senseless, and—"

"Name it not," he wildly exclaimed: "it is over, and thou art here!"

"But I am not *alone*, Madeleine; Rosalie is with me. Shall she come in?"

"Oh, yes! do let me see her," cried a sweet voice; and in another moment a beautiful girl, after bowing timidly to Lady Barbara, was by the pillow of Madeleine. The lip of Madeleine, however, courted not the pressure of hers, nor did her arms open to receive her embrace; but such was the violence of her internal struggle, that she fainted away.

Rosalie screamed with terror; and Lady Barbara, ringing hastily for assistance, seemed in the meanwhile by looks to entreat aid from the hands of Dupont.

"O, sir! do help me to raise her," cried Lady Barbara.

"Let Rosalie," was his reply. But Madeleine now slowly recovered; and finding that it was on Rosalie's bosom that her head reposed, she folded her arms round her for one moment, then coldly desired her to withdraw, and conquer her emotions.

"I hope, sir," said Dupont, addressing the surgeon, who now entered, "that you think this lady able to bear a journey of a few miles?"

"Oh no — impossible, impossible!" cried Lady Barbara.

The surgeon, however, thought differently, and only stipulated that she should be well wrapped up, and be conveyed in the easiest manner.

"Come, Rosalie," cried Dupont; "and while our dear Madeleine *gets ready*, let us go thank the preserver of her life."

Lady Barbara was now attracted different ways: she did not like to leave Madeleine, yet she wished to witness their interview with O'Carrol, and also to see the beautiful Rosalie's manner on the occasion; for though Rosalie was near two years her junior, as she had been told, she perceived that she had a power of self-command even beyond her years. But the struggle in her mind was soon ended by Madeleine herself, who desired her to go after her friends, and hear what Dupont said to her preserver. Oh, how swiftly did Lady Barbara bound along the oaken stairs, cross the marble hall, and reach the parlour, where Dupont and Rosalie were awaiting O'Carrol! The former was traversing the floor, with long but rapid strides. At sight of her he stopped, and eagerly said, "She is not worse? No relapse, I hope?"

"Oh no! and she is dressing herself as fast as weakness will allow."

Dupont then bowed, sighed, and resumed his restless motion; while Lady Barbara gazed upon him with a variety of mingled sensations.

He was tall, almost to a fault; and sorrow or sickness had evidently worn him greatly; while the large proportions of his muscular figure were increased by a long mantle of black serge, worn like an Italian *ferriola*, and falling in graceful drapery from the shoulder. His features were large and regular; and his eyes!—Lady Barbara thought she had never seen such eyes before—so dark, so wild, so mournful, so stern, and yet at times so sweet and so expressive. His lips had once, she thought, been full and red; but strong emotion, or perpetual care, had given him a habit of contracting them, till the under one was rarely visible; and the same causes had prematurely printed, on the smooth front of manhood, the lines of old age. And then his voice! She had never heard so fine a voice — so full, and deep, and plaintive. To be sure, he is not the *Rinaldo* in the book: still, though not my hero, he looks as grand, and holds his head as loftily as any prince in Christendom. But who and what is he? *He* a private Swiss gentleman—and *she* a private Swiss lady! It cannot be; for lofty birth, and high pretensions, mark their port and countenance: certainly there is abundant mystery about them.

Then that sweet, though cold being, Rosalie! She *fancied* she was like them both. Oh! never was a romantic girl, not quite sixteen, so curious, and so bewildered, yet so *pleased*, as Lady Barbara Delmayne. This was *indeed* an adventure; and how Aubrey would enjoy it!

While all these thoughts were shooting with the rapidity of lightning through her head, Rosalie was not without her thoughts and her wishes. She had linked her arm in that of her lovely hostess, and was saying to herself, "Oh that I might stay a while in this fine castle, and with this beautiful young lady!" and Lady Barbara felt that she pressed her arm gently to her side. She replied to the pressure by clasping the hand next to her, and was about to express her hopes that this casual meeting would be followed by many others, when O'Carrol, introduced by Donald, entered the parlour.

"This is O'Carrol," said Lady Barbara to Dupont, who instantly grasped his hand with the convulsive pressure of strong emotion, while his right arm was lifted up, as if in the attitude of blessing him. "I thank thee!" burst in broken accents from his quivering lip.

Rosalie, meanwhile, had pressed O'Carrol's hand to her lips. "She can *feel* acutely, then," thought Lady Barbara; "and *he* too:" and while she gazed on those evident marks of strong, deep, though subdued feeling, an unconscious tear stood on her crimson cheek. Dupont now turned round, and his eye rested on that lovely face glittering with the tears of unaffected feeling.

Instantly, those speaking eyes lighted up with the most marked expression of pleasure and approbation; and taking her hand, in a manner at once affectionate yet respectful, he imprinted a kiss upon her fair and polished forehead, saying as he did so, "Daughter of a noble house! be thou ever as now thou art, its pride and its ornament!"

Lady Barbara could only answer by bending her head in silent and grateful reverence. "Strange, mysterious being!" thought she; "I, though an earl's daughter, feel myself flattered by a kiss and a complimentary wish from an odd-looking stranger—a private, obscure person whom nobody knows."

Lady Barbara at this moment almost started to observe how sternly Rosalie was gazing on her; and she was going to speak to her, when perceiving Donald, and remembering she had not seen him since his expedition to Greenval, she called him to her, and said, "You were always a kind-hearted creature, Donald; and I thank you for going to Greenval as you did, and in such pain, too, at an hour when no one could have required it of you. I assure you, you shall be rewarded."

Donald with great effort ejaculated, "God bless you, Lady Barbara! God bless my lord and lady!" then ran out of the room. He soon returned, however, equipped for a journey, and wrapped up in a large horseman's coat.

"But how is this?" cried Lady Barbara. "Whither are you going, Donald?"

"With your permission, madam," said Dupont, "he is going to ride back the horse on which he accompanied me hither."

"Oh! by all means!" courteously replied Lady Barbara: "but if you must go, may we not hope to see you here again?"

"That must depend on circumstances," was the evasive reply.

"But this young lady—may she not remain with me! or, if not, can we not fix a day for her return?"

But Dupont coldly replied, "Not now, not now: besides, you forget, young lady, that you are not the mistress of the house."

"Oh! if that be all the objection," she eagerly exclaimed, "I am sure my mother will wait on you to request this pleasure herself. Indeed, I cannot bear to think we shall not meet again."

Rosalie, at these words, turned suddenly around with a look of satisfaction; but when she saw that Dupont was raising Lady Barbara's hand to his lips, it seemed as if the sight was strangely displeasing to her, for she started back, and resumed her coldest manner and her sternest expression.

"Donald!" cried Dupont at this moment, "is every thing ready?"

"Yes, sir."

"Then we only wait for my sister—is she coming?"

"Yes, sir; the lady is now leaving her room, and here, I believe, she comes:" for the door of the saloon at the top of the high marble stair-case now opened, and Madeleine appeared, supported by the priest and the housekeeper.

"Now, then, my good man," said Dupont to Donald, "be so good as to go and see that my chaise is come round to the gate."

Donald bowed, but hesitated one moment before he obeyed. He looked at Lady Barbara, and seemed as if he wished to speak, but could not; then, without further word or look, he ran out of the apartment.

"I fear you were too hospitable to poor Donald," said Lady Barbara, "and gave him drink too potent for his head this morning, for he is not like himself. I hope your horse is a safe one, sir."

"Believe me," cried Dupont, "Donald is in no kind of danger."

Lady Barbara now turned to receive the last thanks and farewell of Madeleine. It was the first time she had seen her standing; and as she gazed upon her tall and graceful person, and on her fine though faded face, which were both set off by her black hood and cape, and the long pilgrim's cloak which hung loosely round her, she felt the expression of her affectionate feelings checked by a sensation of reverence and awe; and instead of meeting her with a kiss, she only pressed her offered hand.

"Come, Madeleine," said Dupont, in a hurried voice, "come, I hate long adieus;" and she advanced to embrace Lady Barbara.

"Oh! *do* promise that you will come hither again, or let me visit you!" cried Lady Barbara.

"It is my earnest wish," answered Madeleine, "to do both:" but Rosalie was silent.

Dupont now, turning to the priest and O'Carrol, begged that one of them would bear the lady to the carriage.

"Had you not better carry her yourself?" asked Lady Barbara, in a tone of surprise.

"No," was his laconic reply.

By this time, the great gates of the castle were thrown open, and O'Carroll advanced to assist Madeleine, who in tearful silence printed a fervent kiss on the lips of Lady Barbara.

"We shall meet again, sweet girl! I trust," said she in a faltering voice. "I leave you my blessing and my thanks."

O'Carrol then lifted her in his arms, and she was soon placed in the carriage.

Rosalie had now resumed her cold manner, and almost started back, as if with aversion, when Lady Barbara advanced to salute her. She then, at the desire of Dupont, took his arm down the last flight of steps, and seated herself in the chaise; while Dupont, accompanied by O'Carrol, returned into the hall, to take leave of his young hostess.

It was unwillingly that Lady Barbara had remained in the hall, and had not attended her guests to the bottom of the steps; but a sense of her dignity, as the "daughter of a noble house," restrained her eager feet.

When Dupont returned into the hall, he took a crucifix from his bosom, and turning to O'Carrol, said, "I am told that you are too rich, young man, to need a pecuniary recompense; but receive this, wear it for my sake, O'Carrol, and remember that it was given in reward of a humane and benevolent action: may it remind thee, and strengthen thee to persevere in the practice of Christian duty! Now, I have only to bid you farewell, kind and lovely being! I know you will often think of us; and I beseech you, do so with Christian charity. I shall always think of you with affectionate gratitude. Farewell! farewell to you all, and peace be with this house!"

While he said this, the priest, O'Carrol, the housekeeper, and several of the domestics, had ranged themselves on either side of their young lady, and fronted the majestic stranger, who, letting fall his mantle as he reached the gate, turned once more round, and raising his arms to heaven, gracefully waved them over their heads, as if bestowing his benediction, while they bowed themselves reverently before him; then, folding his mantle round him, he hastened down the steps, and in another minute the carriage was heard driving from the door.

Lady Barbara turned away with a full heart; and then slowly walking up the marble stairs, she locked herself into the saloon, and threw herself on a couch; but starting up again, she ran to a window in front of the house, which commanded the park, and followed with her eyes the course of the travellers.

"Well, at least I shall hear of them when Donald returns," she exclaimed; and remembering that she had not yet seen the crucifix which Dupont had given to O'Carrol, she summoned him into the saloon. He came, accompanied by the priest and Mrs. Mendham.

"It is very handsome," said O'Carrol.

"I have rarely seen one so handsome," observed the priest.

"And to give it away was handsomer still," cried the housekeeper. "I must say, whatever *else* she may be, the lady is very generous."

So saying, she produced a double louis-d'or, which Madeleine had given her.

"Whatever else she may be!" echoed Lady Barbara. "Remember the stranger's parting injunction, that we should judge them with Christian charity; and let me hear no more such insinuations as these."

Lady Barbara, seeing that the priest was going to speak rather angrily, asked him whether he did not think the stranger had the appearance of being an ecclesiastic.

"I have no doubt of it," he replied; "I have seen a print or picture like him somewhere, though where I know not."

"I wish *I* had a print of him," said Lady Barbara, "for he has the most striking face and he is the most graceful man I ever saw."

As soon as she was alone, Lady Barbara laid down the book which she had taken up, for she found that she could not read, and she sat for an hour or two leaning on her elbow, patting the floor with the point of her foot, and indulging in strange but interesting fancies and recollections; but she was sometimes inclined to think it was only a dream, all the occurrences of the night and of the day seemed so improbable and so romantic. However, she had perhaps, in spite of mysterious appearances, made a valuable acquaintance; and then she could not help wondering what Aubrey Tyrconnel would think of the young Rosalie. To be sure, she would be more to the taste of William Tyrconnel, as he liked dark eyes, and Aubrey could not bear them. Still he *must* think her very handsome—indeed she would not forgive him if he did not. As to William, he would probably fall in love with her. But then his father, Lord Bellamore, would never approve his marrying her, unless she was really *somebody*. But then could any one doubt who looked at all the three, but that they were *all somebody*, and *somebody* of consequence? At last she worked up her imagination to conceive that Dupont was actually a cardinal in disguise; that Madeleine was his sister, and Rosalie some other sister's daughter; and on those thoughts alone, however improbable they might be, her mind could find repose.

But how was she to get through this day? how beguile the time till Donald's return? At the utmost, indeed, he could not be gone *more* than four hours, and she would read concerning Rinaldo and Armida till then. But when four, six, eight hours had passed away, and even night, dark night, was come, and no Donald appeared, her alarm superseded her curiosity, for she feared that he had met with some accident; and it was a great comfort to her mind that O'Carrol, who had been passing the day in the servants' hall, volunteered to accompany the footman in search of him.

Upon reaching the house pointed out to them as the residence of Mr. Dupont, they knocked loudly at the door, but no one came; and the sounds seemed to echo through the empty apartments. However, a woman from an adjoining cottage advanced towards them; from her they learnt that Mr. Dupont, on the arrival of a messenger that morning, paid and dismissed his two servants, gave the key of the house to her care, with a letter to the landlord; and then taking Miss Rosalie and his trunks, he drove away in his queer-looking chaise, followed by the strange man on his honour's own horse: " and I have neither heard nor seen any thing of them since," she added: upon which, without further delay, O'Carrol mounted his horse and galloped back to the castle.

Lady Barbara listened to this story with the most painful interest. Why had they so suddenly left their habitation; and, as it should seem, in consequence of what Donald had said? Yet surely *he* at least meant to return, and not leave thus abruptly a family to which he seemed so much attached.

"But my lady," said the governess, "we do not believe they *were* strangers to *Donald:* his behaviour was very queer when he first saw the lady."

"I must own," she replied, "that I was struck with the oddity of Donald's manner then, and when on horseback. Gracious powers! who can these mysterious persons be? But no doubt Donald knew them when he was abroad. However, it is very certain that the *lady* did not know she was going back to Greenval."

"I think *I* understand all this but *too well*, and why poor Donald was asked to ride the horse *home;* which," cried the housekeeper, " no doubt he promised to do, *expecting to return*, but he will never return again; no, never!"

Here she burst into tears.

"And why not return again?"

"Because that vile man, that Italian,—for Italian he is, I am sure, will make away with him, now he is in his power, for fear he should tell who he is; as I dare say he has committed murder, and been forced to fly his country, spite of his crucifixes and his fine fly-about arms and blessings."

Lady Barbara started and shuddered; the priest crossed himself, and owned there was too much reason in what Mrs. Mendham said; for he did not like his countenance, and it was very strange that he should want to employ another person's servant, and one too who was in a nobleman's service.

"But," said O'Carrol, who was, like Lady Barbara, very averse to think ill of Dupont, "if Donald went away expecting to return when the service for which he was employed was performed, he has no doubt taken no change of clothes with him; and we shall find all his accustomed wardrobe in his room. — Then let us search that first, before we judge others in this unchristian manner."

"Spoken like yourself, O'Carrol," said Lady Barbara: " let the search be made directly."

It was made; and O'Carrol and the others returned to say, that upon examining his room, they found, that though Donald's liveries were on the bed, his own two suits of plain clothes and his Highland dress were gone. Upon the liveries was pinned a paper with these words: " God bless and preserve you all!"

"It is evident," said Lady Barbara, " that wherever he is, his life is in no danger; for he has, with his own free will, left our service, and gone into that of the strangers. — Why he has done so, is a different question, and one I cannot pretend to answer.— I am hurt and disappointed by Donald's conduct; but I should be ashamed to let the acquaintance and events of a few hours, however interesting, engross my thoughts any longer. Come then, good father! I challenge you to a game at chess, and let us talk no more of what we can neither help nor explain."

Lady Barbara "talked this well," though she spoke in a tone of pique: but she overrated her own powers; she could not forget beings so interesting, and circumstances so strange. She was therefore check-mated perpetually; and she was very glad when her supper was eaten, and the hour of bed-time arrived. It was late the next day before Lady Barbara awoke to hear the welcome tidings, that the earl and countess, with Mr. Tyrconnel and his brother, were within a few hours' journey of the castle.

Never had Lady Barbara felt any hours perhaps so long as these were; but she at length beheld the carriage enter the gate, and ran on bounding step to meet her parents. She reached the saloon at one door, just as her mother and the earl entered it at another, followed by Tyrconnel;—but when she saw them, her power of utterance failed her; and wholly unlike her usual self, she turned away and burst into tears.

"My darling child! my sweet girl! my dear little cousin! what has happened! what is the matter!" cried her parents and Tyrconnel at once.

Lady Barbara would have found it very difficult to explain with precision the causes of her emotion. Perhaps there is no feeling so painful, as that which we experience when, for the first time in our lives, we find that the attachment on which we relied had in reality no permanent existence.

Though Donald was only a servant, Lady Barbara had recollected him from her childhood; and she had believed him one of the firmest adherents of her father's house, and one, too, who felt the most devoted attachment to herself—yet he had left their service under most mysterious circumstances. This was one cause of her tears; the other, was the flutter of spirits occasioned by the strange occurrences of the eventful hours so recently passed; and a third,—though Lady Barbara would not have liked to own it,—was her disappointment in not seeing her cousin Aubrey: she had been told he was coming, and she saw him *not*!

This last cause, however, speedily vanished; for he entered the saloon, followed by the priest, who was earnestly conversing with him. The earl now received from the priest and the housekeeper, that information which Lady Barbara was as yet unable to give. Aubrey, meanwhile, stood aloof, looking at Lady Barbara, but not approaching her. This coldness made her tears flow faster.

"Nay, now, sweet cousin, the matter grows too serious," cried Tyrconnel; "this great grief appals me. Poor little dear! what is the matter?" and as he said this, he gently rested her head on his shoulder. "Your first tears I attributed to joy at seeing me, but these seem to flow in agony."

"Nonsense!" said Lady Barbara, "I am not at all unhappy."

"No! then be so good as to give me one of your smiles again. Why, child, gloom on thy merry face is like a frosty night in the dog-days—so impossible, one can hardly believe it though one sees its white legacy on the ground.—Aubrey, I begin to believe you have told Barbara she looks prettiest in tears, and some nonsense about blue flowers peeping through dew."

"I? Not I, indeed!" replied Aubrey; "and if I had, I have not influence enough with her ladyship, I dare say, to make her do anything to please me."

"Why, Aubrey! what ails you, man? You are as little yourself as her *ladyship*."

"Her *ladyship!*" echoed the wondering girl: but she had now courage to look up rather saucily in Aubrey's face; for, with that quickness which belongs particularly to women, where their affections are concerned, she now was certain that Aubrey spoke in pique; but she said no more. Her mother and Tyrconnel were both listening to the narrative of the priest.

"A fine-looking man, did you say, father!" asked the earl.

"He was a tall raw-boned man, with large dark eyes. I saw nothing fine about him; but Lady Barbara, as I was telling Mr. Aubrey, my lord, thinks him charming, and the most handsome, striking, and graceful person she ever saw."

"Indeed!"

"Yes, *indeed*, dear sir, when giving his blessing."

"His blessing! Was he a *priest*, then?"

"A priest?" cried Aubrey, coming nearer.

"Yes; we fancy so."

"And how old did he seem?" asked Lady Delmayne.

"Between thirty and forty."

"Nay, father," said Lady Barbara, "he must be full forty."

"Forty!" cried Aubrey, seating himself eagerly on a stool at Lady Barbara's feet, and looking up in her face with an expression which she understood; while Tyrconnel whispered her, "Aubrey unbidden has placed himself on the stool of repentance, for he is not jealous of a youth of forty."

"How absurd!" cried Lady Barbara, on whose face smiles had superseded tears.

"Absurd, indeed!" echoed Aubrey, and in another moment she felt the hand which she had suffered to hang down by her side, grasped in his trembling fingers and pressed to his lips, when no one but his brother could see it.

Lady Barbara could now enter upon her story, and had the satisfaction of hearing her conduct entirely approved; but the subject was not allowed to be dropped; and during the whole day Lady Barbara had to answer some new questions or other from each of the party.

"And so," cried William Tyrconnel, "this little Rosalie is very handsome—is she?"

"Little! Dear no! though only thirteen, she is taller than I am."

"And still she may be more like a pink than a holly-hock in stature. And her eyes are dark?"

"Yes: I am sure you would fall in love with her, Tyrconnel?"

"And why not *Aubrey?*"

"Because—because Aubrey likes blue eyes better than black."

"And is there no *other* 'because' that you could give us?" said Tyrconnel, archly smiling.

Lady Barbara blushed, and Aubrey whispered in her ear, "I *could* give another."

The next day, and every day for a week afterwards, the mysterious visiters were talked of, and the probability of hearing from them discussed: when, as no news of them was received, they were forgotten, except by Lady Barbara; who, in the midst of much nearer interests and dearer ties, used frequently to say to herself, "I wonder who they were, and whether or not I shall ever see them again!"

PART THE SECOND.

"To you and to your honour I bequeath her."

Six years had elapsed since the events above narrated had occurred, and Lady Barbara was become the wife of Aubrey, when William Tyrconnel, his elder brother, was travelling in an unfrequented part of the Isle of Wight.

He had been visiting Carisbrook Castle, and with no inconsiderable share of mournful curiosity; for, though a firm friend to William III., he could not survey without much interest, the scene of the imprisonment of Charles I., and the window whence he had vainly, alas! attempted to escape.

Lord Bellamore, the father of Tyrconnel, had recently purchased a seat near Portsmouth, whence his son, though it was now near the end of November, had set off on his journey. In truth, he was dissatisfied with his home. His father had wished him to marry Lady Barbara; he saw therefore his second son carry off the prize, with some feeling of disappointment; but there were other women as beautiful, as rich, and as much to be coveted for wives. Tyrconnel replied, and all he asked was, to be allowed to choose for himself. But this his father did not seem willing to grant, and he often filled his house with young ladies, in hopes that at last Tyrconnel's heart would be the victim of some one amongst them.

But against these schemes that independent heart rebelled; nor could he admire the delicacy of the parents or the daughters who were thus willing to bring themselves in array before him. Accordingly, when a party of beauties and heiresses were expected at Lord Bellamore's seat, he declared his intention of setting off for the Isle of Wight, not to return till he had visited its wildest and most sequestered retreats.

On hearing this, Lord and Lady Bellamore expostulated with him upon the folly of making such a tour in such a season, and in a country notorious for the badness of its roads in winter.

"But consider, dear sir," replied Tyrconnel, "that every commonplace tourist would visit the island in summer; it accords, therefore, with an eccentric being like myself to go thither when no one else would: besides, as I shall travel on horseback, the state of the roads does not signify much to me; and as you, dear madam, have often been so obliging as to fear for the safety of my lungs, you should rejoice, that in an English winter I shall breathe so mild and balmy an air."

"One question, William, and I have done," said his father, well knowing that his son had too much decision of character to give up a design which had evidently been much considered. "One question, and I charge you to answer it sincerely: have you no particular views in your intended tour?"

"Yes, my lord, I have; the views round Cowes in particular."

"You trifle with me, and you know I hate puns. I mean, is there an *Island Queen* to whom you are going to pay court?"

"Would there were, if she would allow me to share her dominion! But as I see you are serious in asking this question, I as seriously answer *No*, on *my honour*. I shall certainly pay a visit to my friend Clarges, who lives near Carisbrook Castle; but when I have seen him I shall have seen the only person whom I know in the island."

"Enough, I am satisfied; and shall only add, that we shall impatiently expect your return."

Tyrconnel smiled to himself when he recollected this conversation, to think that his father, by expressing his fear of there being a favourite lady of his in the Isle of Wight, had excited in him a wish to find one; and his imagination thus awakened, he delighted, as his bark glided across the ocean river, to picture to himself at the door of a myrtle-covered cottage, some beautiful recluse who should turn out to be a high-born beauty reduced to poverty; but who, unlike the high-born beauties of his acquaintance, should fly with unaffected modesty from his pursuit, and blush with endearing timidity at witnessing the effect of her charms.

"What an idiot I am!" thought he, when his arrival on shore woke him from his reverie; "what an idiot I am to fancy delights not likely to be realized!" But he sighed as he said this; and it is certain that he looked eagerly, for two days at least, at the door of every cottage which looked smarter than another.

After spending two or three days (as he had intended) in the neighbourhood of Carisbrook, he set off for the wild country below Cliff.

The hand of art had not then, as now, improved the luxuriance of the scenery; but nature had covered the hills with trees of the finest growth; and as the rocks and the shore had charms for the lover of wild and rugged scenery, Tyrconnel, though he had admired the charms of other countries, was too much an Englishman not to be eager to do justice to those of his own.

He was attended only by a servant on horseback, and even that attendant he had been obliged to leave behind him on account of the lameness of his horse: still, however, he persisted to continue his route that evening, desiring his servant to follow as he could the next day. But he regretted his decision, when, having missed the direct road to the place of his destination, he found himself, at eight o'clock in the evening of a November night, travelling in a mountainous country, without guide or companion, and sheltered only by a thin surtout, from one of the heaviest rains which he had ever experienced.

As the soil was of clay, it soon became almost impossible for his horse to keep his feet; Tyrconnel was therefore forced to dismount, and lead him by the bridle. But whither could he direct his steps? No twinkling light declared his vicinity to any house; and when he looked around, he could only be sure that on one side of him rose a mountain; on the other side there was, he suspected, a precipice; and he knew that the sea was at the foot of it. His only safety, therefore, lay in ascending carefully, the height above, and a sort of path, which he could with difficulty trace, seemed to afford him the means. Still his difficulties were great, as he was forced to drag after him his unwilling horse, who once was nearly precipitated down the steep and slippery path.

Tyrconnel, who was almost blinded by the rain, as his hat was turned up in front, according to the fashion of the times, was often forced to stop in order to take breath; and at these moments he could not help sighing, to think how his fond parents would be agonized were they conscious of his danger, and how gladly they would have welcomed fear for the heart of their son, in exchange for his more painful apprehensions.

"But am I really in peril?" exclaimed Tyrconnel, starting at his own suggestion. "Well, then, it is fit that I make one great effort to get out of it." Then breathing a silent prayer, he exerted his utmost strength, and found himself at last on the place which he had struggled to reach; but he fell as soon as he had reached it, and his horse fell beside him. However, he trusted that they were now both removed from danger, and his heart glowed with fervent gratitude; but it also glowed with joy, when, on proceeding a few paces further, he beheld, at no great distance, an extensive building, and at one end of it a light. Instantly remounting his now recovered steed, he soon reached what appeared to be the gate of a ruin.

Still, however hopeless of hospitality, he had resolved to knock loudly for admission, when a strain of sweet solemn music broke upon his delighted senses, from the illuminated corner of the building. It was the evening-service to the Virgin, accompanied by the chords of the harp; while ever and anon one female voice, clear yet touching in its tones, was heard above the other, and sometimes unaccompanied, while every pulse in his heart responded to the sound.

"This is indeed an adventure," thought Tyrconnel, while with suspended breath he continued to listen to the strains. But at length he gained courage to knock violently at the door, and the music suddenly ceased; a casement was cautiously opened, and a deep voice demanded who was there.

"A benighted traveller," replied Tyrconnel, "who only asks shelter, for a short time, for himself and his horse, and afterward, a guide, if possible, to the next town or inn."

The casement was then closed again; and in another instant, a man unbarred the gate, held up a dark lantern to the face of Tyrconnel, and, uttering some incoherent exclamation, admitted Tyrconnel and his horse into the porch, which led into a large Gothic hall, where a few faintly-burning fagots lay expiring on the capacious hearth, and hastily withdrew.

"A strange reception," thought Tyrconnel, "at once hospitable and inhospitable." But the idea had scarcely crossed his mind, when another person appeared, in whom Tyrconnel concluded that he beheld the owner of the mansion; for with great courtesy he bade him welcome to whatever comfort his roof afforded. As he said this, he heaped some wood upon the embers on the hearth, and Tyrconnel speedily disencumbered himself of his wet hat with its dripping feathers. On turning round towards the gate, meaning to speak to the servant, he found his host attentively regarding him; and if, as Tyrconnel fancied, that look of earnest inquiry was one of approval also, he was very sure that it was met by him with one of admiration; for never had he seen a countenance of more touching expression. But he was not allowed to remain long in quiet contemplation of it; for his host insisted on his taking off his wet garments, telling him with a smile which did not seem a frequent visiter of his faded lip, that he must submit, for that evening, to wear a garment resembling his, for he was sure that his own dress would not be dry till morning.

"Do you then mean to give me shelter for the whole night?" said Tyrconnel, shaking back, as he spoke, his auburn hair, which now fell, almost deprived of curl, upon his manly shoulders, and disclosed to full view, a face lighted up with an expression of grateful pleasure.

"To be sure I do," replied the other; "and a bed is already ordered for you. Why do you look surprised? Is my appearance so very unpromising, that you expected me to turn you out again into the pitiless storm? Were *such* my nature and my custom, (said he,) believe me, sir, for your sake I should forego them."

As he spoke these words, he grasped Tyrconnel's hand, with evident emotion.

"This is very strange," thought Tyrconnel, courteously returning the pressure, and bowing as he did so, in silent gratitude; for, though conscious that his figure was good, and his face handsome, he was surprised to find that he had made so favourable an impression under such circumstances.

"But I am not giving you a proof of my hospitality," observed the stranger, "while I let you remain in your coat;" and leaving the room a few moments, he returned with a wrapping-gown of black serge.

Tyrconnel, who hoped he should at length be introduced to the singer, was involuntarily solicitous concerning his appearance, and took pains to restore his hair to its wonted curling beauty; while he held his ruff to the fire, to make it again fit for use.

"Psha!" cried he the next moment, ashamed of his vanity: "and after all, the singer may be the wife of my host, or the wife of some one else, and ugly and disagreeable besides. What an idiot I am!"

He now followed his conductor into an apartment where supper awaited their coming. But neither wine, nor ale, nor viands of a very tempting nature, could at first make Tyrconnel amends, when he found no one in the apartment, and saw the table prepared for two persons *only*; for his imagination, which had for some time previously dwelt on the fancied recluse at the door of the myrtle-covered cottage, had now allowed itself to fancy a recluse as beautiful in the unknown singer of the ruined castle. But great as was his disappointment, it did not take away his appetite, though whenever he heard the tread of woman's feet over his head, he flattered himself there was going to be an addition to the party. But his host did not even mention that he had a lady residing with him, and Tyrconnel was too conscious of his own thoughts and wishes to make any inquiries. At length he ventured to say,

"I cannot but admire, sir, the generous confidence so indicative of a noble mind, which has allowed you thus to shelter a stranger travelling without a servant, and who might have thrown himself upon your hospitality with evil intentions."

"Your countenance," he replied, "is one that inspires confidence, and your air and manner bespeak the gentleman. Nay," he added with a smile of much meaning, "I should not be surprised to find that you are nobly born."

"Indeed!" cried Tyrconnel, blushing with pleased surprise: "If your penetration, sir, is so great, I shall be afraid to stay, lest you discover what I may wish to conceal."

"Heaven forbid," returned the other gravely, "that you should ever have a thought or feeling, while you are under this roof, which ought to be concealed!—Young man, *I believe* you are worthy of confidence, and to-morrow you shall have a proof of mine. To-night, however, I wish you to retire early to rest: you have undergone much fatigue. Permit me to show you the way to your chamber: but I must warn you, that this castle is old and full of strange noises. However, you may sleep too soundly to be disturbed by them; yet, should you hear aught unusual, do not be alarmed, but turn and sleep again."

"And will you not ask who I am, and what I am?" said Tyrconnel smiling.

"What would you think *I* am, were I to tell you that I know your name already?"

"Impossible!" cried Tyrconnel, surveying his host in his turn with a scrutinizing look. "No, no, I never saw you before, for, if I had, I could not have forgotten you."

"You never did see me, nor I you; and you shall, if you please, tell me your name and *quality*."

"Quality! What! then you are sure I am a man of rank? You are right: my name is Tyrconnel, and I am the son of Lord Bellamore."

"Are you Aubrey or William Tyrconnel?" eagerly asked his host.

"William, the *elder* son," replied Tyrconnel in an accent of surprise. "How strange it is that you should ask that question!"

"You may think so: but come, I am impatient till you are in a warm bed. To-morrow I will be more communicative."

They now reached the apartment designed for Tyrconnel; and the stranger, with a cordial pressure of his hand, wished him good night, and left him to his repose.

But though Tyrconnel slept, it was not with unconscious sleep. His dreams were full of the dangers he had passed: he still trod on the slippery edge of the precipice, still dragged after him a resisting horse, still heard the appalling roar of the ocean; and when he started from his unquiet slumbers, it was to hear, on awakening, the very sound which haunted his dreams. The wind, too, howled along the ruinous corridors of the building; mournful noises caught his attention, and struggled, though for some time vainly, with the power of sleep over his senses. But again he was locked in deep, though restless slumbers, when a sudden blast rocked his apartment, displaced his sword from his bed-side, and woke him completely — woke him not soon to rest again; for between every gust, deep groans as of one in agony burst on his ear, and he started from his bed in order to convince himself that what he heard was not the creation of fancy.

Immediate conviction attended his leaving the bed. The sounds were real, and came from a room at no great distance from his own. But what occasioned them? Perhaps the wind had shaken down part of a wall or chimney, and had buried some one in its fall. He could not, therefore, hesitate a moment to offer his aid; and gently, though rapidly, he drew near the apartment whence the noise proceeded, and distinctly heard, mixed with the groans, the following words — "Oh! mercy, mercy, thou offended God!" This was followed by groans as of a spirit in agony. He could no longer forbear to knock. "Who is there?" replied a stern voice; and immediately the door was opened by his host, who, having thrown his cloak over his apparently naked body, demanded, in an angry tone, and with a fierce look, why he did not remain in his bed.

"I could not," he replied, "for I heard the groans of some one in distress, and I came in hopes to assist the sufferer."

"Assist the sufferer! Kind, but deluded youth!" exclaimed his host with a laugh inconceivably horrid. "Tyrconnel, I told you, whatever noises you heard, to turn again and sleep. You have not regarded my request; but I honour the motives which prevented you. Now, return to your chamber; and forget, when we meet again, that we have met now and thus."

Tyrconnel, shocked, yet awed in spite of himself into instant obedience, returned as he was bidden to his apartment, but not to sleep; for had he not almost beheld a penitent sinner in the act of inflicting punishment on himself for some conscious crime? and if so, what was that crime, and who was the criminal?

He was now sure that the noise he heard mixed with the groans, was that of the knotted rope upon the uncovered flesh. But perhaps this mysterious man was a monk of the order of Flagellants; still, his cry for mercy to an offended God seemed to proclaim him suffering under the stings of conscience. Yet, if so, could his countenance ever look so placid as it had done the preceding evening? No, it was impossible. "But how weak it is in me to wear away the hours in these idle conjectures?" Then, laying his head once more on his pillow, in a short time he fell into slumber, deep, quiet, and refreshing.

The morning sun, darting its beams through his window, first awakened him as he thought, and awakened him time enough to hear some one leaving his apartment.

"Who is there?" cried Tyrconnel.

"I came to bring your honour's clothes," replied a voice which he thought was not unknown to him. "The family is ready for breakfast, if you are."

"Ready for breakfast!" cried Tyrconnel: but the man was gone, and on looking at his watch he was surprised to find that it was near ten o'clock. He made, therefore, a hasty toilet, even though he expected to meet "*the family*," one of whom was no doubt the singer herself: but he had no reason to be displeased with his appearance. Rest had restored the wonted bloom to his cheek, and his hair, which parted on his forehead, had recovered its waving beauty. Tyrconnel, except when obliged to appear at court, and in the circles of the metropolis, claimed the privilege of a young and handsome man of quality, to dress as he liked; and consequently never wore, but on such occasions, that encumbering wig which replaced the simple and picturesque style of wearing the hair adopted in the days of the first Charles, and which a traveller on horseback in the Isle of Wight would have found a very troublesome appendage.

When his host met him on the stairs, on his way (as he assured him) to call him to breakfast, his manner was so kind that it entirely removed Tyrconnel's embarrassment, and he was able to shake off every unpleasant impression and recollection.

"I must now introduce you to the ladies of my family," cried he, as he opened the door of the apartment in which he had supped the preceding evening.

"Ladies!" thought Tyrconnel: "I recollect to have heard a low and faltering female voice singing with the others; but I had forgotten it again, and only remembered *one*;" and Tyrconnel was now in the presence of her to whom *that one voice* belonged.

She was standing by the side of a couch on which reclined a female in a morning habit, whose pale cheek assumed a faint flush as if of pleasure on his entrance, while her dim eye lighted up with the brightness of former days.

"This, Mr. Tyrconnel," said his host, "is my sister Madeleine." He started at the name, while Madeleine, extending her hand, bade him welcome to their retreat.

"Oh! all is now explained to me," exclaimed Tyrconnel, "in one moment. I now know that I am so happy as to behold the visiters of my sister Lady Barbara."

"Your sister!" said Madeleine.

"Yes, she is now my younger brother's

wife; and you, sir, are no doubt Mr. Dupont, and this young lady is Mademoiselle Rosalie." As he spoke, a deep involuntary blush overspread his cheek; for he not only remembered Lady Barbara's prophecy, but he knew not what to call the fair creature before him. Rosalie *alone* seemed too familiar: the Lady Rosalie would have implied suspicion of their being persons of rank in disguise; and yet *Mademoiselle*, the appellation of a *French* girl, though the only one he could use, seemed the one least befitting her appearance, as she resembled more a statue which had been changed by some modern Pygmalion into a woman, but retained all the stillness and all the coldness of its original material—for *scarcely* could that beautiful head be said to move in return to Tyrconnel's bow, and certainly that faultless lip did not vouchsafe a smile of welcome. Whence did this insensibility proceed? Was it from bashfulness? In that case it might wear off — at least Tyrconnel hoped it would; and in the meantime he turned to meet the kinder glance of the faded but still beautiful Madeleine. Her dress was of black silk, her veil black also, and parted on her fair forehead was the dark hair which Lady Barbara had described to him, while the marked eyebrow and the long eye-lashes formed the strongest possible contrast to the transparent skin of the cheek beneath them.

That clear, pale cheek, told a tale of approaching dissolution, and the rapid heaving of the dress which was folded over her bosom declared that her fluttering heart had nearly beaten its last.

Tyrconnel, when he approached her, meant to speak of Lady Barbara, and of her enforced visit to the castle of Delmayne: but his power of utterance failed him; for he felt that he beheld a being on the brink of the grave — one to whom he had learnt to consider with mysterious interest, and spite of himself his countenance betrayed what was passing in his mind.

Madeleine, raising her expressive eyes, answered to his look, while Dupont stood with folded arms beside them.

"Yes, you see before you a poor dying creature; but one whose heart, while there is yet a spark of life left it, will glow with gratitude to your warm-hearted and lovely sister: and you are welcome hither for her sake."

"Welcome indeed," cried Dupont, in a hoarse tone of voice.

Rosalie at this moment changed her posture, and seemed about to speak; but, though her lip moved, she said nothing; and Tyrconnel, who was now earnestly gazing on her, felt himself mortified and disappointed.

A new recollection now suddenly came over Tyrconnel, and he ventured to say, "Where is Donald? for I suspect he it was who last night obtained me so courteous a reception."

"True," said Dupont gravely: "but Donald dares not appear before you, till I have assured you, that in leaving Lord Delmayne's family, he believed himself to be fulfilling a *superior duty*—and I am of his opinion."

"I am satisfied," replied Tyrconnel, "and I heartily wish to see him; for he was always a favourite of mine, and poor Barbara wept for his desertion."

"You may come in, Donald," said Rosalie, with a smile which almost made the youthful traveller start with pleasure; and Donald entered the room with a smile on his face, but a tear in his eye—for he was sincerely attached to the family of Delmayne. He hoped the Lady Barbara was well, and her bonnie laird.

Tyrconnel said she was well, and the happy mother of two children, the image of herself.

"Ay, indeed!" replied Donald: "then they must be bonnie bairns; for my lady hersel is a bonnie lassie, and I should like to see her blue een again."

"And Lady Barbara is now a wife and a mother!" said Madeleine. "Sweet girl! may she be happy in every relation of life! And she has married the man of her heart, too — for I soon discovered that she was in love with Aubrey Tyrconnel, and that he loved her."

"Pray, is your brother like you?" asked Rosalie with some eagerness.

"Very like."

"Oh!" was the answer of Rosalie—and Tyrconnel wished he could be sure what that "oh" meant, and whether it was complimentary or otherwise; but perhaps it meant nothing.

It was mid-day before the breakfast was over, for Tyrconnel purposely prolonged the meal, because he knew that he must offer to go away at its conclusion, as he had no excuse for staying; and at last he reluctantly desired to have his horse saddled.

"Surely, you are not going to leave us?" exclaimed the poor invalid.

"You cannot be so unkind," said Dupont, laying his hand on his arm, while Rosalie looked up and looked down again, and began to tear a piece of paper which she held in her hand.

"If you wish me to stay," said Tyrconnel.

"*Wish* you to stay!" echoed Dupont; "oh! indeed I do, and so I am sure does Madeleine."

"Yes, Tyrconnel; and if neither parent, nor friend, nor mistress, is counting the moments of your absence, you will oblige a poor dying woman by giving her a few hours of your company. I would have said days, if we had any thing to offer, capable of repaying you for the sacrifice."

"It would be no sacrifice," replied Tyrconnel, affectionately grasping her moist yet burning hand. "Command me as you please; my parents are prepared for my spending at least a month in the island; my friends do not want me, and I have no mistress; believe me, I came hither with a heart as free as air."

"And you will stay with us a day or two at least?" said Dupont, eagerly.

"Yes, *days*, if you desire it. After which, I shall probably directly return to my father's residence near Portsmouth, where I expect Barbara and the rest of my family."

"Will Lady Barbara be so *near* us?"

"Yes." A look of great meaning passed between Dupont and Madeleine.

"Have your brother and Lady Barbara a house of their own?" was Dupont's next question.

"They have: they live in London, as Aubrey is studying the law."

"It was a benevolent and merciful Providence that sent you hither;" and Dupont, as he said this, grasped Tyrconnel's hand, and quitted the room.

Rosalie, who had listened to this conversation with her usual statue-like stillness, now raised her eyes to Tyrconnel's with a look of evident pleasure; but they were instantly withdrawn again; and blushing at her own boldness, with a sort of bounding step she followed Dupont.

Madeleine, now beckoning Tyrconnel to sit down beside her, assured him that, by promising to stay a few days with them, he had made her last moments comparatively happy.

"Your last moments, dear lady! Do not say so. Surely, you do not expect that I should witness your———"

"I will fill up the sentence———I *do* wish you to be here when I breathe my last; that time is nearer than those beloved beings suppose; and for both their sakes, I am desirous that a man of feeling and honour like yourself should be present, to soothe and assist one whose agonies, I know, will be great indeed. Rosalie, too———But my brother will himself tell you of the service which we mean to request of you."

"If it be in my power to serve you, or any one belonging to you, command me; but do not talk of dying."

"It is a prospect too pleasant for me not to indulge in the anticipation of it. If you knew," said she, "what an hour of comfort that of death will be to a long-suffering heart like mine, you would be pleased to hear me talk of it as near."

"The interest and the mystery connected with these strangers, increase in exact proportion," thought Tyrconnel; "but I expect this day will end the latter. Yet if it does not, there is a something of dignity, nay, even of sacredness about them, which forbids the indulgence of idle curiosity."

At this moment, Dupont came in to invite Tyrconnel to take a walk with him.

"Donald tells me," said he, "that you draw from nature, and I can show you some very fine views. Rosalie also has a taste for drawing, and perhaps you will to-morrow have the kindness to give her a lesson?"

"Certainly; but why not to-day?"

"Because to-day I wish to have some serious conversation with you."

And Tyrconnel, on hearing such a reason given for the delay, was no longer averse to it.

Rosalie now returned with a book in her hand; and Madeleine telling Dupont that Rosalie was going to read her to sleep, he begged Tyrconnel to follow; and they quitted the apartment together.

As they began their ramble, Tyrconnel found that when he fancied he had attained the top of the mountain, he had only reached a terrace, half way up its uneven side, on which the house stood.

The mansion itself seemed originally, from its castellated towers and its still remaining fossé, now nearly overgrown with grass and weeds, to have deserved the appellation of a castle; but one wing only had survived the ravages of time, and was now converted into a comfortable habitation.

After they had proceeded a little way in silence, Dupont, turning to his companion and laying his hand on his shoulder, exclaimed, "Look round, young man, and see that not a trace remains of the winter's storm of yesterday, except what seems to add new beauty to the scene;—the storm of the passions alone, that storm, far more terrible in its course than the whirlwind of winter, leaves traces behind it of its awful visitation, although the visitation be past: *fearful* and *indelible* traces, which no earthly power can hope to remove. Tyrconnel, I have urged your stay, though at the certain risk of wounding the feelings of your susceptible heart. But *you* have, I trust, a long life of happiness before you, and can afford to let the afflicted draw upon you for a few agitated moments. Besides, before we part for ever, (and we shall so part, I trust, at no very distant day) you shall hear a story which may serve as a salutary warning to yourself, and to your children after you."

"Why not tell it *now*, sir?" eagerly asked Tyrconnel.

"Now! Impossible! A vow of the most solemn nature has sealed my lips: and it is only when I am beyond all question on my death-bed, that this warning tale can be revealed."

"Your death-bed, sir!"

"Yes; and I am happy to assure you, that I have within me the seeds of a mortal malady, and that when SHE goes *I* shall not long survive her."

Here he seemed for some minutes labouring with strong emotion.

"Let me now," he rejoined, "describe to you our route after we quitted the castle of Delmayne. We left the North road as soon as we could, and stopped for sleep and refreshment as little as possible, till we reached Southampton.

"As it had occurred to Donald, that the Isle of Wight was a most desirable residence for those who wished for retirement, and for a mild and genial air, and as he was well known there, his mother being a native of Newport, he knew he should have no difficulty in gaining leave from the governor for us to reside on the Island.

"From Southampton we sailed hither, nor was it long before one of our rambles led us to this deserted building. On inquiry we learnt that it belonged to a nobleman who had quitted his country on the murder of his king; and who chose to remain abroad. At a very low rent we were at last allowed to take possession: the result of our labours you have seen; and I have derived much comfort from my share of the occupation. Already, you see, the myrtle flourishes around us; and I trust that when the stone closes over Madeleine and myself, this abode, which sheltered the sorrowful, may one day be the dwelling of the cheerful and the happy."

"But, sir," said Tyrconnel, "if you and your sister realize these sad forebodings, surely, surely, Mademoiselle Rosalie will not remain here alone?"

"I trust *not*," replied Dupont, turning with a brightening glance towards Tyrconnel, "and *this* is the subject on which I am longing to speak to you. When Madeleine and I are no more, Rosalie, dear friendless girl, will have no protector but her God!"

"Say not so," cried Tyrconnel, grasping his arm; "she *shall* have a *protector*. I have a *brother* and a *father*."

"*Can* you promise for them that they will befriend the poor orphan, and secure for her a safe and honourable home?"

"For my brother, I am sure I *can* promise; and remember, Aubrey's wife was Barbara Delmayne."

"You have almost healed a broken heart," murmured out Dupont. Then raising his eyes and arms to heaven, he exclaimed, "Thou hast done this! I see the hand of mercy here! Blessed be thy name, and now let me depart in peace."

It was some minutes before Dupont recovered from the devout abstraction into which he had fallen, and Tyrconnel was too much awed by his manner, to break the silence himself. At length, with a placid smile, he said,

"How did this happen, Mr. Tyrconnel? How was it that I came to the end I had in view, before I had even begun my approach to it? I meant gradually to unfold to you my wishes concerning Rosalie, and to solicit your intercession with Lady Barbara: but somehow or other, we went a quicker way to work, and my heart is lightened of such a load! Lady Barbara will be delighted, I doubt not, to ratify your promise; for I never saw a face so expressive of benevolence and sweetness of temper as hers. When I came to Delmayne, I thought that the guardian angel of poor Madeleine, in a shape most dear to her, was made manifest to human eyes, and was watching beside her pillow."

"What! my rosy, bright-eyed sister, taken for an angel, and that by such a man as you, sir! O dear! I never dare tell her this; for I am sure her little head would be quite turned, and she would prove a very woman to my brother."

"Perhaps, mine," said he, "may be a *tête exalté*, and at that moment my feelings were particularly susceptible. Expecting only to see my faded, suffering sister, I beheld the image of youthful beauty hovering over her bed-side. A bright winter's sun shone through curtains of a golden hue, and its beams diffused an unearthly radiance round her, while her blue eyes were uplifted with an expression of the most benevolent pity. Tyrconnel, she *has* been to me a *guardian angel*; for, whenever anxiety concerning Rosalie has come across my mind, I have pourtrayed that face upon the gloom of night, and I have said to myself, 'Yes, to thee, sweet being, will I try, one day or other, to consign my poor orphan;' and then I used to invoke a blessing on her, and fall into a quiet sleep."

"Dear sir," said the gratified Tyrconnel, "I always loved Barbara dearly, but now I shall love her twice as much as ever."

"Let me add," said Dupont, "that Rosalie will be richly independent in fortune, and will want nothing *but* protection. It is not improbable that, a few years hence, she may wish to take the veil; but in my will, I have positively forbidden her, on pain of forfeiting her fortune, ever to enter a convent till she has mixed with the world some years, and given herself a chance for being a happy wife. No sir, no," he added, in a hurried manner, "Rosalie, while a young woman, shall not enter even the gates of a convent."

"I trust she will *never* enter one — such beauty as hers."

"Beauty! Ay, she is beautiful. But had you seen Madeleine in her pride, oh! Mr. Tyrconnel, that beauty indeed, but now!—"

Here he rapidly paced the turf on which they had been seated; then returning with a countenance still bearing the marks of violent agitation, "We will now," he said, "cross the mountain, and explore some of the scenes in the valley beyond."

Tyrconnel consented; and as his host talked of Switzerland, of Italy, of painting, and of music, the walk did not appear long to him: though he certainly sometimes felt a strong desire to return to Madeleine and to Rosalie.

When they were within a mile of the house, Dupont observed that they should scarcely get home by dinner-time.

"Indeed, sir," said Tyrconnel, "I am very

sorry to hear it, as I wished to do something to my dress."

"What can you want to do to your dress? You will see no one you know but Madeleine and Rosalie."

"*But* Madeleine and Rosalie!" thought Tyrconnel, with a conscious smile and an unconscious sigh.

"Quick! quick! there is no time to be lost," cried Tyrconnel, as he led his way to his room, followed by his servant, who had now arrived with his portmanteau, and who was surprised to see how difficult his young master was in the choice of a dress; but his surprise was at an end, when, as they descended the stairs, he saw Rosalie cross the hall. Tyrconnel now desired him to return to Ryde, and remain there till further orders.

Rosalie had no great variety of wardrobe; but she had folded her long hair round her head, and had fastened it on the top with more care than usual, and she had put on a gown of pink Lyons silk, which she had tried to shape after the fashion of Lady Barbara's. This gala dress was, however, thrown away on Tyrconnel: all he saw was, that her countenance was more animated than before, and that she was the most perfectly beautiful of women.

They found Madeleine still lying on the couch where they had left her; but her face wore a look of comfort added to that of resignation, which Tyrconnel had not before observed.

"Surely," said Madeleine, "I have now a hope of seeing Lady Barbara once more?"

"She will only be too happy to come," replied Tyrconnel; "and with your leave I will write to her directly, to tell her what an unexpected though clouded pleasure awaits her here: but then I fear she will not let Aubrey rest till he sets off."

"We must run the risk of that," replied Madeleine faintly, and wiping the damps of weakness from her brow; "for," added she in a low voice to Tyrconnel, "my time on earth is growing very short."

"Do not say so," cried he.

"Well, well, I will say no more;" then elevating her voice to its usual tone, she said, 'Once an enthusiast, always an enthusiast,' is a remark which I have heard, only that the objects of enthusiasm change; therefore, I expect to find Lady Barbara as enthusiastic as when I saw her at Delmayne, but perhaps for new objects."

"No, Barbara's heart is constant to its first loves. Aubrey and Tasso are still her two prime passions; but she has, I own, added to them two or three others."

"What are they?"

"Two lovely children, working chairs in tenth-stitch for her drawing-room, and making up baby-linen. All these in their turn are passionately pursued, and the dear enthusiast is alternately laughed at, praised, pitied, scolded, and fondled by us all; but loved also, loved to the greatest degree."

"Happy creature!" cried Madeleine.

"Happy indeed!" cried Rosalie mournfully.

"Shall you not be delighted, Rosalie, to see her again?" asked Dupont.

Rosalie, to Tyrconnel's great mortification, remained silent.

"Rosalie, why do you not answer your guardian?" said Madeleine.

"I hope to be glad," said Rosalie at last with a faltering voice; "but delighted is so *very* strong an expression."

"But is it possible you do not *love* Lady Barbara," said Dupont, "after the kindness she showed your best friend?"

"My best friend, and you, sir, seem to love Lady Barbara so much, that though I believe I *do* love her, my love is quite unnecessary."

Tyrconnel was hurt at this unamiable speech, and it was evident that Rosalie was jealous; but his attention was drawn from this disagreeable consciousness by his observing the look of extraordinary meaning which passed between Dupont and Madeleine. Dupont soon afterward suddenly quitting the room—

"Rosalie," said Madeleine in a voice of emotion, "you have distressed your guardian; he hoped that you had kinder feelings toward our young friend."

"Mistake me not," replied Rosalie, seizing her hand and kissing it while she strongly struggled to take it from her. "I do love Lady Barbara; but I should love her better, if you and my guardian did not seem to love her so much—seem, indeed, to love her better than poor Rosalie."

"Oh, this cup is a bitter one," cried Madeleine, raising one emaciated hand to Heaven, while she suffered the other to remain in that of Rosalie.

"Recollect, dear friend," she continued, "that I have seen you both embrace Lady Barbara; but when, in all these melancholy years, when have you ever caressed or fondled poor Rosalie? Till we went to Delmayne, and till I saw how differently you behaved to Lady Barbara, I did not feel this coldness; but I have ever since been so wretched at times! for I have feared——"

"What have you feared?"

"That there was something in my manner or nature to excite aversion rather than love; and I have wished — often and often I have wished—to *die*."

Here, she paused from excessive emotion: but the pause was unheeded by the unhappy being whom she addressed; for Tyrconnel, on looking at Madeleine, saw that she was lying insensible on the couch. He was trying to afford his assistance when Dupont entered the room; but without stirring from the spot where he stood, he only desired Rosalie to lend her aid. Tyrconnel could hardly help reproaching him with want of feeling; but he was disarmed by the excessive misery which his appearance displayed, as his hands were closely squeezed together as if from the agony of mental struggle. At length he sprung forward, exclaiming, "She is not dead! are you sure she is not dead?" and then hastening to the window he threw it open to its utmost extent. As the feeble invalid gradually returned to life and consciousness, joy seemed to agitate Dupont not less than grief had done. "Strange, inconsistent being!" thought Tyrconnel, "to stand aloof, and prove your fondness only by your agony!"

"Poor Rosalie! I can perfectly understand and excuse all you have said; for so, I see, they have both acted towards you."

Madeleine now raised her head from Tyrconnel's shoulder; and, opening her eyes, beheld Dupont tenderly gazing on her. Instantly she closed them again, and her head fell back on the shoulder not of Tyrconnel, but of Dupont. But there it was not suffered to remain: he started away from the evidently unwelcome burthen, and rushed out of the apartment.

Madeleine sighed deeply, took the crucifix from the fold of her robe, pressed it with lifted eyes to her lips, then begged Tyrconnel to replace her on the couch, desiring that Rhoda would watch beside her, and that Rosalie should take a walk with Tyrconnel.

"But you do not send me from you in anger, I hope?" said Rosalie.

"*In anger!* No, dear girl," said Madeleine; "but do leave me to Rhoda's care."

"Dear girl," cried Rosalie, kneeling beside the couch, and pressing a now passive hand to her quivering lips, "I go now almost happy! You never spoke to me so affectionately before."

"But how have I looked at you, Rosalie?" said Madeleine, with unwonted energy; "have my looks never loved you, dear ungrateful girl?"

"Oh, yes, yes; and I was almost contented till we knew Lady Barbara. But come, Mr. Tyrconnel, she waves me from her;—and I will *go*, now I am *sure she* loves me at least a *little.*"

"A *little!*" murmured Madeleine; and Rosalie, accepting Tyrconnel's arm, accompanied him to the terrace.

They walked some time in silence; for Tyrconnel's heart, like Rosalie's, was too full to allow him to speak, after the agitating scene which he had just witnessed. But as soon as he could compose his perturbed mind, he felt that it would be only kind in him to convince the distrustful heart of Rosalie, that however cold the manner of both her guardians might be to her, she alone was the object on whom their affections rested. The difficulty was how to begin the conversation, if Rosalie did not begin it herself.

It was not long, however, before Rosalie said, "I am afraid, Mr. Tyrconnel, you think me very ungrateful for not loving Lady Barbara as much as my guardians do;—but indeed—"

"But, indeed," cried Tyrconnel, pressing as he spoke the arm that was linked in his, "sweet Rosalie, I cannot blame you, even when I think you unjust; for I am sure your guardians love you better than anything in the world."

"Do you think so?" replied Rosalie, looking up in his face and smiling through her tears. "So poor Mary Anne thought, who lived with us when I first remembered anything: Mary Anne was such a comfort *to me!* and when she died, I thought I should never have been happy."

"But did you love Mary Anne better than your guardians?"

"Oh, no; but when they repulsed my caresses, and seemed to look upon me almost with horror, I used to fly to Mary Anne, who soothed me to sleep, and then all was well again."

"Happy Mary Anne!" said Tyrconnel, tenderly.

"Happy! She was not happy: she had been crossed in love.—Poor Mary Anne! I often wish that I could go and cry on her grave as I used to do. But she lies buried at Greenval; and I fear all the flowers are dead which I planted round her grave."

"If they are," said Tyrconnel, "I will plant new ones when I go next to Delmayne, and I will give orders to have them attended to."

"And *will* you do this?" cried Rosalie, clasping her hands together, and her countenance glowing with pleasure. "Oh! Mr. Tyrconnel, how *good* you are! They may talk of Lady Barbara: but indeed *I* think *you* the kindest person that I ever saw, and I dare say you will take care that the grave is *weeded* too?"

"I will weed it *myself,*" said Tyrconnel, who would have promised anything at that moment.

"*Will* you? Oh, how I shall love you!" she was going to add, but a feeling of innate delicacy restrained her, and she only said "*like* you."

Tyrconnel saw this, and, with a feeling of delicacy akin to her own, forbore to notice it; and though his looks were so expressive as to make Rosalie cast down her eyes in confusion, he only said, "I thank you for your good opinion of me;"— but then he repaid himself for his forbearance, by imprinting an impassioned kiss on the hand which he had taken.

"But surely," he observed after a pause, during which Rosalie had resumed her statue-like appearance, "surely your guardians never in reality seemed to feel horror at your caresses?"

"Oh, yes! indeed they did; and when I asked them who I was, they only told me I must remain contented with knowing that I had been under their joint care from the time of my birth, and that while I lived I should never want a friend. Upon such occasions, if I ventured to throw my arms around their neck, press their hands to my heart, and bless them for their kindness to a poor orphan, they invariably started from me with a sort of aversion, told me such importunate caresses were unbecoming, and dismissed me. But when I found that they could show their regard for another by caresses, though I was to be kept at a distance, I felt a sense of injury, and a feeling of resentment, which made me resolve, in the hall at Delmayne, to restrain every evidence of those strong affections which in me, and me alone, seemed not to be valued, and to be colder and more unperturbed even than I had lately been. Do not think me vain," she added, blushing as she spoke; "but as I cast my eyes on a statue in the hall of the castle, I fancied that I was like it in features, and I resolved to be also like it in character from that unhappy moment.—'They shall no longer be disgusted at my warmth of expression,' said I to myself; and I kept my word, till at last I fancied that my heart was as still as my face, and that I had ceased to love any one. Tell me, Mr. Tyrconnel, did I not freeze you when you first saw me?"

"Not *absolutely*, but I own that I thought I never saw anything alive so like a statue."

Dupont now appeared in sight, and they hastened to meet him. He looked dejected, and Rosalie felt her heart reproach her as the cause. Struggling therefore with her tears, she begged his forgiveness, and assured him that she would never, if possible, occasion him uneasiness again.

"I forgive you," replied Dupont solemnly and mournfully, "and I hope you will keep your word;—for, believe me, some time or other, if you do not, dear mistaken girl, you will bitterly repent it."

Rosalie, overcome by the epithet "*dear*," would, in the agitation of her feelings, have caught his hand; but he shook his head reprovingly, and waved her from him.

"You *see*," said she in a low voice to Tyrconnel.

"I see, and I *wonder*," he replied, looking at her with eyes that said, "*I* could not act thus towards you."

Rosalie sighed, but probably more from pleasure than pain, as she felt the kindness of his glance; and the rest of their walk passed in silence.

On returning to the house, they found Father Prevost, who officiated as their priest; and as he told them it was time to repair to the chapel, he, Donald, and Dupont bore the couch, with Madeleine stretched upon it, to the chapel. When there, Madeleine was laid upon her face on the floor, and Tyrconnel involuntarily started forward, in order to place a pillow under her bosom; but Rosalie mournfully assured him it was her custom so to lie, and he reluctantly drew back, while Rosalie seated herself at the organ.

The service now began, and Tyrconnel's devotion was disturbed by the attention which he could not help giving to that of Dupont and Madeleine. They were both prostrate before the altar, and the groans of agony seemed to mingle with the breathings of adoration. But he forgot even to attend to them when the exquisite voice of Rosalie joined in the service.

The offices of devotion ended now only too soon for Tyrconnel; and as he led Rosalie back to the parlour, he felt that he was indeed gone an age in love, and that whether as a statue, or as an affectionate accomplished woman, she was, and must be, most fondly dear to every feeling of his heart.

A letter from Lady Barbara was now given to Tyrconnel, which his servant had brought.

"Good news," cried he; "Barbara is already at my father's, and may be here any day, tide serving, in a few hours."

"The sooner the better," said Madeleine.

A servant now came in to say that Mr. Fenton, Madeleine's medical attendant, was come, and she was left alone with him.

Eagerly was his leaving her watched for by Dupont and Rosalie: but what he told them was far from encouraging, for the fainting fits of the poor invalid evidently grew more frequent; and that very afternoon, ere they had left the dinner-table, Dupont, laying his hand on Tyrconnel's, exclaimed, "Look there, she faints!" but never offered to go himself to her assistance, though he rang for her servants.

"How very strange!" again thought Tyrconnel; but he dared not inquire a reason for conduct so unusual.

That evening a servant brought a second letter from Lady Barbara in reply to one written by her brother.

"My dearest William,—Never was delight greater than mine! And so you have found the mysterious strangers, and are actually living with them? and they wish to see me and Aubrey? and they call me sweet and angelic? (But you are only laughing at me, I know.) Well, but, dear William, how trying it is that we can't come directly, as I wish, and you wish! and the cause too is so trying! My sweet little Aubrey is indisposed; but I hope he will be well again in two or three days, and then we will hasten over to you and your fascinating friends. But, alas! you say that the amiable Madeleine is very, very ill, and I must come, she says, directly, if I wish to see her alive. No, no; she must not, shall not, die. Rosalie and I will *nurse* her into *health*. I can't bear to think that I must lose her,

when I have just found her again. But I am called; depend on seeing us as soon as the child is well, if we sail at midnight.
"B. T."

"P. S. Ah, cunning William! Not a word of *Rosalie's* looks! it was very unkind in you not to tell me whether Rosalie turns out tall or not; and whether she is a beauty still, and whether you are in love with her or not; but I shall come and judge for myself, and find *you out*, that's *certain*. I can tell you, your silence looks very suspicious."

"Rosalie," said Dupont one morning, as she entered the room, "it is my hope that Tyrconnel and myself shall be able to prevail on Mr. Aubrey and his lady to become your guardians, and allow you to live with them, when our beloved Madeleine is taken from us."

"And do you mean," exclaimed Rosalie, bursting into a passion of tears, "to send me away from you?"

"It will be so much for your good, Rosalie, so much more cheerful for you to go about with Lady Barbara, that I certainly do."

"And do you think that I will obey you? Do you think I know so little what gratitude is, that I will leave you to live with strangers, and visit and amuse myself while you are here in solitude and sorrow? No, never, never. How could you be so cruel as to think of such a thing?

"There, Mr. Tyrconnel!" added the sobbing girl. "There now, tell me after this if you *dare*, that my guardian loves me!"

"Do you doubt it, Rosalie?" cried Dupont reproachfully.

"I shall, if you send me away from you. But mark me, sir," she added, wiping away her tears, and assuming all her dignity and self-possession, though evidently it was with great effort; "do what you will, say what you will, I never will forsake you. I do not say to you, that 'where thou diest, I will die, and there will I be buried;' but I *do say*, that evil be by my portion, and my days few upon earth, if aught but death part thee and me!"

Here her firmness again forsaking her, she hurried out of the room.

"Calm your disordered spirits, dear girl," said Tyrconnel, who followed her; "your guardian declares he will not urge you to live with Lady Barbara during his life."

"And I conclude that you think I am right, Mr. Tyrconnel?"

"To be sure I do; you have spoken and acted worthy of yourself."

"Oh! how happy you make me! Your praise has raised me in my own opinion. I sometimes flatter myself that you will in time like me almost as well as Lady Barbara."

"Almost as well! Believe me, I shall in time love you *better* than Lady Barbara; better than I ever loved, or can love, any other woman."

"*Better* than Lady Barbara! Oh! that is more than I asked for, or expected. I am sure now I shall love Lady Barbara dearly myself."

The breakfast meal passed in silence: Rosalie was too happy to talk, for Madeleine seemed better, and Dupont allowed her to stay, and Tyrconnel had been so kind! But Tyrconnel was silent, because he was perplexed. After what he had said to her that morning, he felt bound to disclose his attachment to Dupont and Madeleine, before he renewed the subject to Rosalie. Soon after breakfast, Dupont invited Tyrconnel to walk.

Madeleine now beckoning Rosalie to the side of her couch, said, "Let me make you amends, my dear girl, for the pain which was inflicted on you to-day, by assuring you that your determination has been a comfort to my mind, and that I always disapproved of your guardian's plan of sending you away, when I believe he will want your presence most. I bless you Rosalie, for what you have done, and I doubt not but your feeling and recollections will reward you when two broken and contrite hearts are quiet in the grave."

Rosalie, gratified yet affected by this address, would have thrown herself on the neck of Madeleine, but she *dared* not; and only murmuring out a blessing on her, she hurried from the apartment.

When she had vented her full heart in prayer, and regained her usual self-possession, she hastened to join Dupont and Tyrconnel on the terrace; and as she knew Tyrconnel was much interested in the study of botany, she offered to conduct them where they would find a variety of mosses and some curious lichens. They consented to follow her route, and set off with her to a romantic dell at no great distance. As Madeleine felt herself unusually well that morning, and the servants were particularly busy in preparing for the reception of Lady Barbara, she had forbidden any one to stay with her, and had taken up a book, when a sound reached her ear, which she knew from experience to be of *alarming import*.

Though our recluses during their six years' residence in the castle had avoided society, the indigent and the helpless were well known within their gates; and when Madeleine could walk, her smile of pious love and her words of holy peace had often whispered hope to the wretched, and led the trembling soul to reliance on its God.

Amongst the superior class of poor in the neighbourhood, was a young woman who had seen better days, and who had found beauty a most pernicious gift, especially as to beauty she united excessive ambition, an imperious spirit, and ill-regulated feelings. What her conduct and fate had been, no one exactly knew; but one day after a long absence, she returned to her mother's cottage in misery and madness. Whatever had been her woes and her wrongs (and in the wildness of her ravings she talked most touchingly of both,) they had left her just reason enough to know that the humble door which in the days of her pride she had disdained, would open to receive her in her state of degradation, and that the mother whom she had neglected in her hour of sunshine, would forgive and shelter her in the night of her despair. She therefore wandered as far as Portsmouth, though alone and unprotected, only by her evident insanity, from insult. She therefore reached the port in safety, and embarked in the packet-boat to Cowes, retaining on her person the few ornaments, the wreck of former splendour, in which the impulse of phrensy had led her to deck herself.

On reaching the shore, she ran along the road that led from Cowes to Newport with a speed which nothing but phrensy could have induced.

When the poor Anna saw the well-remembered field, and beheld at a distance the chimney-top of her mother's cottage, she stopped in her wild career; but it was only to tear the garments from her person which the thorns and briars as she passed had begun to destroy; while the glittering baubles which had so lately fed her pride were strewed upon the unthankful ground, and shone there as uselessly bright as the poor maniac's sparkling eyes in the midst of her phrensy.

In a few minutes the violence of the paroxysm abated, but not its unconsciousness; but by the mechanical power of habit the steps of the maniac were directed to the garden gate which led to her mother's door. That mother whose heart had been nearly broken by the neglect of her child, had at that moment forgotten all her sorrows in sleep, when she was half awakened by a sound resembling the voice to which she had so often listened with pride and pleasure in happier days, and which now she fancied her dreams were recalling to her. The song too was one which Anna used to warble, little thinking, poor girl, that the fate which it described would be her own; and the stanza of it which she now sung, was as follows:

O say, on a pillow of down can you rest,
While I on the earth or on straw must recline?
Oh! say, can you wrap the warm fur o'er your breast,
When bare to the winds and the tempests is mine?

No pillow have I, even that you deny one:
No garment have I—nor a penny to buy one.
He hears not! nor pities my frantic distress,
Yet sure he remembers mad wandering Bess.

As the tones came nearer, and were more and more distinctly caught by the still half-slumbering parent, she fancied that her child was dead, and that it was her spirit which she thus heard; and for a few moments the sorrows of her heart were soothed; for it was less bitter to believe she was no more, than that she was alive and undutiful; and she was lifting up her heart in thankfulness to her God, when the increased loudness of the voice banished the lingering remains of sleep, and a scream which vibrated to every pulse of her heart, convinced her that the being whom she heard was yet alive, and was her long-lost daughter: she therefore sprung from the bed, and beheld from her window the wretched but still dear being beneath. In another moment the door was unbarred, and she clasped the now laughing maniac to her heart.

"Oh, my child, my child!" said she, "welcome, welcome, though I see thee thus."

To be brief,—by the kindness of friends, but chiefly by the bounty of Madeleine and Dupont, Anna was sent to a place of confinement, and recovered her senses completely for a time, though it was with difficulty her mother had been prevailed upon to part with her, and she returned home apparently quite cured. But she was subject to relapses, which the fond but weak parent concealed as long as she could, lest she should be sent from her again, though sometimes she was very mischievous in her paroxysms, and had once endangered the life of a young woman who had, as she fancied, stolen her lover from her. It was a curious fact, that while she was well she never sang; but as soon as her phrensy was returning she used to resume her singing; and the sound of her voice which could be heard at a great distance, was the signal for those who feared her to get out of her way.

This was the sound which now burst on the ear of Madeleine, and, rapidly drawing nigh, struck terror to her heart; and she feared for Rosalie, whose life the maniac had once threatened as her supposed rival, till recollecting that she was well guarded, she began to fear for *herself*, and tried to pull the string of the bell which was usually within her reach; but this day it had been forgotten, and Madeleine found that she had no means of making herself heard by the servants, except by an exertion of voice to which she was wholly unequal. At this moment of alarming conviction she heard a noise behind her, and she beheld the unhappy maniac, who, probably knowing that she might be refused admittance at the front door, had climbed over a hedge behind the house, and at this moment stood at the window. She then threw open the casement, and in another moment was in the room, and at the couch of the trembling invalid.

"Tell me," she cried with great fierceness of manner, "where Rosalie is?"

"She is gone out," replied Madeleine gently.

"Is she gone to *him?*"

"She is with her guardian, and a friend of his."

"O yes! *that* friend is I know who—but I

shall find them. See," said she, "how beautiful I am! I have dressed my hair like hers, to be like her;" and Madeleine saw that the poor thing had fastened her long hair round her head with skewers, to look like Rosalie's. This method in her madness, which proved how full her brain was of the subject of Rosalie, overcame her so much that she fell back on her couch, catching hold of the maniac at the same time, and exerting her small remaining strength to draw her down beside her.

"What do you mean by holding me down?" screamed out Anna in an angry voice, and lifting up her arms as if to strike her, while her eyes glared with terrible expression.

Madeleine let go her hold, and her hand fell nerveless beside her; for she thought her last hour was come, and oh! how unlike that last hour which she had loved to anticipate! But who can calculate on the caprice of phrensy! Madeleine's eyes were closed, to shut out the terrible object before her; but she soon found that her life was in no danger, for in soft and mournful accents she heard her say,

"She is dead! quite dead! cold and pale! and she was very kind and good. There, there, I owe her much." She then laid Madeleine's limbs straight upon the couch, wrapt her cloak tight round them, pulled her black veil over her face, knelt beside her, and chaunted over her a kind of hymn for the dead, ending with these four lines. But it was all sung in a voice so subdued, that it frustrated poor Madeleine's hope the servants would overhear her, and come into the room:

" He gave me gems, and he gave me gold,
    And proud was I to wear them;
But the love he gave, Oh! it soon grew cold,
    And then I could not bear them."

She was soon, however, freed from her alarming guest; for after she had finished her song she rose up, murmured out "God rest her soul!" and made her exit the same way she came.

Not long after her departure Madeleine beheld Rosalie *alone*, pursuing with rapid step the same way that the maniac had taken; and she recollected with terror that she had seen something like a knife glitter in Anna's girdle. In an instant, present weakness, impending death, all was forgotten; and borrowing strength from despair, she sprung from her couch, and, rushing to the hall-door, flew out of it toward the path of danger, when she heard a scream which seemed to her startled ears to resemble the voice of Rosalie. It *was* the voice of Rosalie, who had left the gentlemen behind her in order to gather for Tyrconnel a plant which he had never seen; when, just as she was stooping, she felt herself seized by a powerful arm, and beheld the fierce eye of the maniac glaring upon her.

"I have caught you," cried she in a hoarse and hollow voice; "and now for vengeance! but we will die together."

She then tried to drag Rosalie towards a bush, under which she thought she saw something glitter like a knife; but Rosalie resisted her so powerfully, that she could not effect her purpose.

"Well then," said she, "we will roll down this precipice." The former now uttered those screams which were heard by Madeleine, and which fortunately were also heard by persons more able to assist her; for just as Rosalie's strength was failing, Dupont seized the maniac by the throat, and threw her from him with a violence which shook her to the earth, while Rosalie nearly fainted on his bosom.

At this moment Tyrconnel, who had been a considerable distance behind, came up just as the maniac, who had concealed herself, snatching up the hatchet which she had hidden, stole unheeded behind Dupont, and was about to inflict probably a mortal blow on his uncovered head; when Tyrconnel turned round just time enough to seize her uplifted arm, and snatch the weapon from her hand. The wretched woman, thus baffled again in her murderous intentions, ran with phrensied speed along the path to the shore, where she was seized by some sailors who were preparing their boat for sea, and was soon afterward sent again into confinement.

By this time the danger and the rescue of Rosalie were known to the servants and others whom her scream had summoned to her aid, and who had passed Madeleine on their way to the spot. But as soon as the danger was over, they remembered where they had left the invalid, and hastened back to her assistance: and now, with feelings of alarm not easy to be described, Dupont and Tyrconnel beheld Madeleine coming forward to meet them, supported by Donald and Rhoda.

"Is she saved?" exclaimed Madeleine wildly.

"She is."

"Who saved her?"

"I did," replied Dupont; "and Tyrconnel saved me."

Madeleine now looked at Tyrconnel with such an expression of love and gratitude! but seeing that Rosalie still seemed insensible, she screamed out, "But she is dead *now!*"

She was instantly answered by Rosalie, who threw herself into Madeleine's arms; but she had not power to hold her; and after pressing her cold cheek to Rosalie's, and calling her by every tender name her native language could furnish, her strength failed, and she fell back on her supporters, who bore her to the house. Rosalie, bewildered though not insensible, would have sunk on the ground again but for the supporting arm of Tyrconnel. At length she opened her eyes, and gazing wildly round her, exclaimed, 'Surely, I have been in a dream! Methought I had found a—a—and——"

"Rosalie," cried Dupont, "recollect yourself: there is no one present but your guardians and Tyrconnel."

Rosalie looked up earnestly in his face. "Oh! I feel very strangely," said she, putting her hand to her head:

"I fear madness is catching, for I have fancied strange things."

"But you see and recognise us now, dear girl?"

"Oh, yes! I do, I do," answered Rosalie, bending her head submissively, and crossing her hands devoutly on her bosom: "Oh, yes! I am convinced, entirely convinced now, and my senses are quite clear, quite." So saying she rose with the assistance of Tyrconnel, and begged him to lead her to the house.

"Do you now, dearest Rosalie, doubt the love of your guardians?" said Tyrconnel.

"No, Mr. Tyrconnel," she replied: "they have too, too well convinced me of it."

"Oh! do not fear that this exertion will shorten the life of the invalid. It has convinced me how strong she still is."

"Indeed!" replied Rosalie in a tone of the deepest dejection; and as soon as she had seen Madeleine on her couch, she retired to her chamber. But nothing could prevail on Madeleine to follow her example: she persisted in remaining below stairs: she consented, however, to allow the priest to read to her while she tried to rest; and as Dupont also retired, either to his chamber or the chapel, they now separated, and Tyrconnel was left to his own thoughts. But he was at present no pleasing companion to himself,—for in the lover he found that he could not wholly forget the son; and he knew that his attachment would entirely blast all the bright plans of his parents. Again, he was not sure that Rosalie loved him; and when a doubt of her affection came over his mind, he lost all consideration of the disappointment of Lord and Lady Bellamore, and was full of anxious reverie concerning the probable event of his love.

He had just resolved to speak first to Madeleine on the subject, when the priest came to tell him that she wished to see him. Tyrconnel found her alone; and when he besought her to approve his addressing Rosalie as a lover, that he might be enabled to give her the best of all protection, that of a husband,

"Joy does not *kill*, Tyrconnel," said she in a voice almost extinct from emotion, "or I should expire this moment. From the first hour I saw you, it was the dearest wish of my heart to see Rosalie your wife: but then I felt the improbability that such an event could take place; for how could I ever suppose that your noble parents would allow you to marry an obscure though not portionless girl; and over whose birth must hang, for some time at least, an impenetrable mystery?

"But that mystery, I am told, will one day or other be cleared up."

"But if not cleared up to the satisfaction of your parents, then I shall with my dying breath declare against your union with Rosalie."

"Yet, after all," cried Tyrconnel, rising from his seat, "this is but idle talk, for Rosalie herself may be averse to the union."

"Is Rosalie then ignorant of your love?"

"I have made no direct declaration, and she does not seem to understand indirect avowals."

At this moment they heard a carriage driving up to the gate.

"'Tis she her ain sel," cried Donald, hastily entering the room; "and she nodded her head tul poor Donald. O her twa bonnie blue een! there's na the like o' them in the known world!"

"What are you talking of?" cried Tyrconnel: "whose eyes have turned your head thus?"

"Whose but my ain young lady's?—She's come! my lady! the Lady Barbara, and Maister Aubrey!"

"Come! Then where are they? Who has let them in?"

"Oh! gude faith, I forgot that; the sight of her made me daft, and I forgot to open the gate."

But Tyrconnel got to the gate first, and opened it to admit the welcome visiters.

"Are we in time to see her alive?" asked Lady Barbara eagerly as she sprang into his arms.

"Oh yes, but we have had a day of terrible agitation."

"But shall I see her to-day?" said Lady Barbara.

"I dare say you will;" and Madeleine desired to see them directly.

"I come, I come to nurse you, and make you *well*," Lady Barbara would have said; but when she came near the poor sufferer—when she felt herself pressed to that quick-beating heart, her tongue refused to utter such a word of mockery, and she hid her tears on the shoulder of Madeleine.

"What a pleasure it is to me to see you again before I close my eyes on earthly objects!" said she, still gazing with joyful animation on her young friend.

After a short interview, however, she requested to be left alone, and the exhausted sufferer fell into a calm and refreshing slumber.

But the sight of her had had a very different effect on Lady Barbara; for it told her a tale of approaching death, and she dreaded to behold the grief which she could not alleviate.

"But where is my fancied rival?" said Aubrey, to turn his wife's thoughts from the painful sight which she had left.

"I dare say he is in the chapel."

Tyrconnel was right: on opening the door

of the chapel, he found Dupont prostrate on the steps of the altar, and he did not venture to disturb him: but the noise which the door made caused him to turn round, and he beheld Tyrconnel first, and then the head of Lady Barbara peeping in. He knew her instantly; but, instead of hastening to meet her, he let fall his mantle, which was before folded round him, and stretched forth his arms to her — in silence indeed, but with a countenance radiant with pleasure and benignity. Lady Barbara hastened to him as silent as himself, for emotion choked her utterance; and when he had embraced her, he lifted up his arms as if in prayer for a few moments, while she involuntarily bent one knee before him, and crossed her hands on her bosom. He then laid one of his hands on her head, while the other was elevated; and as he did this, Tyrconnel and Aubrey both beheld him as Lady Barbara and O'Carrol had done in the castle-hall at Delmayne; and they did not wonder at the description which had been given of his dignity of air and gracefulness of motion.

When his devout abstraction was ended, he courteously raised Lady Barbara from her knees, and desired her to present her husband to him. She did so; and as he grasped the hand of Aubrey, he surveyed his countenance with an inquiring eye; then observed to Tyrconnel, that they were so truly brothers in appearance, he doubted not but that they were the same in mind and in tastes.

"But tell me, Mr. Tyrconnel, where is Rosalie?"

"Ay, where is she? I long to see her."

As they said this, they were leaving the chapel, and Lady Barbara found an opportunity of whispering to her husband—

"Tyrconnel may say and think as he pleases, but I believe our host is nothing less than a cardinal."

Rhoda, who had overheard her master's question to Tyrconnel, now came forward and told him Miss Rosalie was in bed.

"In bed!"

"Yes, sir; she has been there ever since she came in."

"Do, Rhoda, go into her room gently, and, if she is awake, tell her who are come — the poor thing has undergone a great deal to-day, and I only wonder we are any of us at all recovered."

This led to a demand for an explanation; and it was scarcely ended, when Rhoda came to say that her young lady hoped Lady Barbara would take the trouble to come to her bedside.

"She must be ill, or I am sure she would have risen to receive you," said Dupont, with a countenance from which every trace of recent pleasure was banished; and Lady Barbara followed Rhoda.

When she reached Rosalie's bedside, she was shocked to see such marks of evident dejection in her countenance, and every vestige of colour gone from her cheek; nor was her distress lessened when Rosalie, having murmured out "Thank God! Oh! I am so glad you are come!" threw herself on her neck, and wept for some minutes in silence.

It were tedious to relate the conversation that followed, which consisted chiefly of inquiries concerning Rosalie's health after the fright of the morning, and mournful presages concerning the approaching fate of Madeleine. But when Rosalie declared her aversion to rise and join the party, as her spirits were too much depressed to allow her to mix in company, Lady Barbara began to fear some painful secret lurked within her heart, and could hardly be restrained by politeness and decorum from expressing her suspicions.

Rhoda now entered the room, to tell Rosabel that Madeleine sent her word, if she was not well enough to come down stairs, she would come to *her*; for that anxiety for her health would not allow her to stay where she was.

"If that be the case, pray assure her that I will dress and come down directly. Do, dear Lady Barbara, go down while I rise, and tell my guardians I am not really ill."

"I can tell them that with a safe conscience, believe me," replied Lady Barbara, shaking her head: "at least, I am sure your illness is not of the body." And with a slow step, a very unusual thing with her, Lady Barbara went down the stairs. She found Tyrconnel waiting at the foot of them.

"Tell me," said he eagerly, "how is Rosalie? And how did she receive you?"

"With the greatest kindness and cordiality. But she is ill—very."

"And not coming down stairs?"

"Yes, she is dressing. But her malady is of the mind: such a face of dejection I never saw before in one so young. O William! if I could think you were the cause of this!"

"But you *cannot* think so; for you know me to be a man of honour."

"But let a man be ever so much a man of honour, a beautiful girl may fall in love with him."

"She may be *likely* to do so; but if a man be really a man of honour, as soon as he sees that his presence is dangerous, he will fly the spot before it is too late. No, no, my dear sister, if you are inclined to pity, pity *me!* I see already that Aubrey does, and has read my heart."

"Is it indeed so? Then, poor Lord and Lady Bellamore! But perhaps Rosalie does not, cannot return your love, and *that* makes her unhappy! Yet, dear me! it would seem so *unnatural* for her not to love you!"

"But *you* did not love me, Barbara—you preferred Aubrey."

"Ay, but remember you did not love me, and Aubrey did."

"True. But come, there is an hour to dinner, and before you dress, I wish to show you and Aubrey some views."

Aubrey, who had been closeted with Dupont, now joined them; and the brothers and sister had an undisturbed conversation till they went to dress; but it was of no satisfactory nature.

Aubrey and Lady Barbara were quite willing to receive Rosalie as their ward and companion; but if she rejected the addresses of Tyrconnel, or if she accepted them, and was herself rejected by the parents as the wife of their son, how could Rosalie live where she and Tyrconnel were exposed to meet daily? And the way in which Tyrconnel obviated this difficulty gave great pain to his affectionate brother and sister; for, "In that case," said Tyrconnel, "I should go abroad, and never return till Rosalie was married or in a convent."

They were interrupted by the approach of Rosalie herself, who told her fair guest it was near dinner-time, and she came to assist her at her toilet. Tyrconnel now presented his brother to Rosalie, who was himself struck with the air of deep dejection which obscured the most perfect face that he had ever seen. But the form of Rosalie was not yet impaired by secret grief; and, as he surveyed her tall, majestic figure, and heard the touching tones of her voice, he did not wonder that his brother's heart, all the romantic circumstances also of their meeting considered, became the victim of her charms.

As they walked towards the house, Aubrey kindly told Rosalie that he had heard since he came of a most unexpected good fortune which was likely to befall himself and Lady Barbara; and on her asking what it was, he said it was the prospect of having her to reside with them when she was deprived of her present guardians.

"Unless," said Lady Barbara archly, "you are previously claimed by a better guardian—an amiable husband."

"*That* I shall *never* be," replied Rosalie, her face covered with the deepest blushes. "No man, I am sure, will ever solicit my hand in marriage; and if he did, he would solicit in vain."

A silence, a painful silence, followed this unexpected and unwelcome speech, which was soon broken, however, by Aubrey, who, casting a sidelong glance at his brother, was terrified at his excessive paleness, and exclaimed—

"My dear brother! Tyrconnel, you are ill! I am *sure* you are ill!"

"Ill!" exclaimed Rosalie, turning pale as death itself, while she seized Tyrconnel's arm, and looked anxiously in his face.

The husband and wife exchanged looks; and Tyrconnel, pressing her hand to his lips, assured her he was well, quite well again.

"What does all this mean?" whispered Lady Barbara to Aubrey.

"Mean!" replied he. "Why, that Tyrconnel has not offered as soon as he ought to have done."

And Lady Barbara thought he might be right.

"I am afraid you will find me a very awkward waiting-maid," said Rosalie to Lady Barbara, while with trembling fingers she officiated at her toilet.

"I do, indeed, my dear," replied she, laughing; "for you were intended to have women to wait on you, and never to wait on any one. I have no doubt I shall see you a lady of quality before I die, spite of your recent declaration against marriage. Believe me, your heart is more tender than you fancy it."

"Lady Barbara," cried Rosalie, "I told you I should not *marry:* I did not say that I could not *love*."

"What, my dear! would you love and not marry! Impossible! As soon as *I* was in love, I wished to *marry*—and so will you."

"Nay, Lady Barbara, think of the difference of our situations: you, highly born—you, blessed with noble parents, the pride and ornament of an illustrious house; and I, the poor, obscure, unknown Rosalie! No, believe me, if I loved to distraction, I would never be the wife of any man of family."

"Well, well, we shall see when the time comes," replied Lady Barbara, with an arch smile; and, taking Rosalie's arm, they proceeded together into Madeleine's apartment.

Rosalie, who had not seen her for some hours, was sensible that an evident change had taken place, and was not surprised to hear that the dinner, at her desire, was to be served in the front room.

"Would you could have come yesterday!" said Dupont, with more than usual despondency of manner. "Yesterday, we were all more like ourselves: our Rosalie was cheerful yesterday," he added, darting a penetrating look at her, which evidently distressed her; and so general a gloom seemed to pervade the party, that the summons to dinner was a relief to them all.

But nothing could long entirely depress the elastic spirits of Lady Barbara; and even Dupont and Rosalie were for a while enlivened by her sallies. The good priest seemed quite captivated with her vivacity, and Donald forgot he was waiting at table while gazing on Lady Barbara's bonnie blue een. Her countenance, however, was clouded, when Mr. Fenton, who had visited the invalid while they were at dinner, called Dupont out of the room, and informed him that he was convinced the forebodings of his patient were just; and that though she might outlive the night, she would never be able to come down again.

This information so completely overset the wretched man, that he was unable to remain with the company, and the priest felt it his duty to retire with him; while Rosalie went to take her station by the couch of the beloved sufferer, till the bell called them to vespers. When that summons came, for the first time Madeleine owned herself unable to obey it, but declared her resolution not to be carried up stairs till her usual hour; adding, with a melancholy smile, " I have my reasons for it :" and Mr. Fenton promised to stay with her till her friends returned.

Dupont and the priest were already there, when the guests and Rosalie entered the chapel; but words cannot paint the agony of Dupont's countenance, when he learnt that Madeleine could not attend the evening-service; and when the priest began, he threw himself on the very spot where he had been accustomed to see her throw herself; and there he lay enveloped in his cloak, heaving such sighs as spoke a spirit tried almost beyond its power. Ill, indeed, could Rosalie exert her voice, while witnessing the misery of one guardian, and anticipating the death of the other. At length, her devotional conquered her other feelings; and, with the exception of the broken-hearted Dupont, the tones of her voice breathed peace over the disturbed spirits of her hearers.

Mr. Fenton meanwhile took leave of Madeleine, recommending her to be carried to her own room without further delay, as the night-air was chilly, and she had to cross the hall.

" I shall soon be more chilly than the night-air," said Madeleine; " and a few minutes more or less here can do me no harm. Rosalie, my love!" cried she, while the epithet, never heard but once before, thrilled through the affectionate heart of the dejected girl, " Rosalie, hold up the candles, that I may gaze on every object in this room, where I have known so many different feelings, for the last time. Now," said she, " seat yourself at your harp, where I have been used to see you sit, and sing me the evening hymn to the Virgin."

She obeyed; and Madeleine joined in it with a voice so sweet, and tones and manner so overpoweringly affecting, that Rosalie's voice failed her before she came to the close, and Lady Barbara sobbed aloud.

" Enough," she cried : " now let me be removed to my chamber. I have sung my last hymn on earth."

That night, though Madeleine was unconscious of it, Rosalie watched, wept, and prayed by her bedside. That night, too, the wakeful ear of Tyrconnel heard those well-remembered groans from the self-tormented penitent, and wondered what new sin had called for such an expiation.

At length, the time of rising came, and the matin bell summoned the family to chapel. With what different looks did those who composed the congregation meet there! Aubrey and his wife, though their faces wore the expression of sympathetic sorrow, were still radiant in their complexions and features. But Dupont, Rosalie, and Tyrconnel bore in their dim eyes and pallid cheeks, the traces of the sleepless night of woe.

" I once thought," said Lady Barbara to Tyrconnel, as they left the chapel, " of bringing my little girl with me; but I am glad I did not, for I would not for the world put her out of love with good and pious persons; and really the countenance of poor Madeleine, Dupont, and Rosalie—and even of you, William, would frighten her into horrors; and *good* and *terrible* would ever after be associated in her mind."

Towards evening, Mr. Fenton called again, and positively, at Madeleine's earnest command, assured her that life was ebbing apace.

" Then I am actually on my death-bed, and in my *hour* of death ?" she said, with a countenance lighted up with joy.

" You are :" and her transparent hands were silently lifted, as if in praise and blessing.

" Enough ! God bless you, sir ! You may now leave me, and send Father Prevost hither. I thank you cordially for all your kindness."

The priest now came in, and administered extreme unction to the dying Madeleine. The sacramental rite followed, of which the brothers, Lady Barbara, Rosalie, and Dupont, at her earnest request, were summoned to partake.

" And now, where is Rosalie ?" cried Madeleine : " my beloved ! where art thou ?"

" Here," she replied ; hastening to meet the now offered embrace.

" Leave us," said Madeleine : " I would be alone with Rosalie."

They had been together near an hour, when Rosalie, pale and agitated, ran down stairs, and begged Tyrconnel to find Dupont, and send him to Madeleine, who earnestly requested to see him. He did so, and Rosalie returned to the chamber of death.

Tyrconnel found him in his own apartment, and was obliged to support him to that of Madeleine, and even to her bedside. They found Rosalie lying beside her, supporting the head of Madeleine on her arm ; while the dying sufferer was gazing on her with unutterable fondness.

" Leave me now, dearest," said Madeleine, pressing her lips to hers, and clasping her to her bosom. She then bid Tyrconnel lead her to Lady Barbara; while as the weeping girl withdrew, she followed her with her eyes till the door closed and she could see her no more.

" There !" said Madeleine with a deep sigh, " that *pleasure* and that *pang* are over, and now !—"

It was not long before the anxious fears of Rosalie, who had herself been forbidden to come again till she was sent for, led Tyrconnel, whose presence had not been forbidden, and who had always been desired by Madeleine to be with Dupont at the moment of her death, to go to the door of the room and listen to what was passing.

And he was very soon impelled to enter the room, for he heard the increasing loudness of the expiring breath; and he heard Dupont exclaim in the bitterness of his agony. Tyrconnel at this moment stood at the foot of the bed.

"I am dying, beloved of my soul," cried Madeleine, struggling as it were to repel the quick approach of death, and eager to indulge for one short moment that faithful tenderness, so long repressed and subdued: as she said this, she stretched out her arms to the agitated Dupont, who, clasping her with phrensied agony to his breast, wildly conjured her, as he kissed her damp brow, to live a little longer, and wait till *his* appointed hour was come.

"It will not be," she faintly replied.

Then, while she gasped for utterance, the priest gave the cross into her closing hand: she pressed it to her breast, fixed her last, long, expiring glance on that beloved being who now tenderly supported her; and as he pressed his cold and tearful cheek to hers, she smiled and expired.

For one moment all was as still as was the corpse before them; for Dupont was *stunned* by the blow, though it had been so long expected, and he stood gazing on his lost Madeleine as if he expected to see her move, and hear her speak again;—while reverence for such deep grief as his, forbade Tyrconnel and the priest to speak or move. But at length the unhappy man awoke to the full extent of his suffering;—and throwing himself beside the body, he called her by every endearing name, amongst which, however rapidly he spoke, and in Italian too, Tyrconnel could clearly distinguish the name of Angela, *amante, mia vita*, and all the words that denote the tenderest ties which bind the heart of man. It seemed as if that imperious love, which had for years been confined within oppressive bonds, and tyrannized over and trampled upon, now rioted in its recovered liberty, and gave way to that violence, which might be fettered, but could not be annihilated.

At last, when he had raved himself into insensibility, Tyrconnel and the priest removed him into his own room, and the latter promised to summon him whenever he thought his presence would be of service. He then proceeded to fulfil the painful task of imparting to Rosalie the death of Madeleine.

"Am I sent for?" said she eagerly; "I saw you remove my guardian from the room; I thought the scene would be too much for him. I shall go to her now."

"No, dearest Rosalie, you must go with my sister to your chamber," replied Tyrconnel, the tears trickling down his manly cheek.

"What do you mean?" cried Rosalie, catching his arm; "shall I see her no more?—Is—is—"

"Yes—all is over, and we can now only pray for her soul."

Lady Barbara did not leave the mourner that night, but partook of her sleepless bed and restless pillow.

Tyrconnel's night was a sleepless one; for Dupont's frantic grief, which was often succeeded by quiet and calm dejection, admitted of the soothings of friendship, and caused him therefore to pass most of the hours till daybreak in the mourner's chamber.

With what new and mournful feelings did the sleepers now hear the bell which summoned them to matins! with what painful emotions did the mourners hear that sound which, they at once remembered, she, whom they most loved, could hear no more! and with what overpowering wretchedness did they behold the beams of that sun, which diffused a general cheerfulness upon the face of nature, and called everything around them into new life, save her, more dear than even life itself! O the painful contrast between the still, cold, dark paleness of the dead, and the warm, revivifying sun, and the bright blue sky above them!

Lady Barbara and her husband arose indeed to renewed gratitude alone to the Giver of good: for they arose to a consciousness of their own still unimpaired enjoyments. But they could not forget that mourning was in the house: and Lady Barbara, bursting into tears, exclaimed, when she heard the matin bell, "The poor Madeleine hears it not!"

"She hears better music, I trust, my beloved," replied her husband. And Lady Barbara said she wondered she could be so foolish as to weep for her.

When they entered the chapel, they found Rosalie had taken her seat as usual at the organ, and Dupont was stretched along the selfsame spot as the night before; while Rosalie's voice only faltered occasionally, as some recollection, probably, came over her mind and agitated her feelings.

When the service was ended, Dupont moved not from his recumbent posture, and took no notice of any one. But Rosalie accepted the offered arm of Tyrconnel; and with a pensive but placid countenance gave and received the usual greetings, and accompanying her guests to the house, officiated at the breakfast-table; but when the meal was over, she retired again.

"It is very certain," said Lady Barbara the next day, "that Rosalie's countenance is not so dejected, not so full of woe, as it was before this event happened."

"Certainly not," replied Aubrey; "at least, if it be, bitter, hopeless dejection; but this has an air of placid sweetness, that only belongs to the occasion; and Rosalie, while sorrowing for the poor Madeleine, cannot sorrow like one without hope."

"True!" replied Tyrconnel, "and I myself have observed the change with great pleasure; and I also know exactly when the change took place.—I observed it after she came from her long conference with the deceased, as soon as ever she had recovered her first emotions, and was composed enough to converse; and I suspect this change in her was the result of the conversation. What it was that so affected her the day you came, I cannot guess; but that was the first time I had ever observed it in her. But I will go in search of her: I expect to find her in the chamber of death."

"Now Tyrconnel is gone, we must talk of our departure," said Lady Barbara. "When can it with propriety take place? for remember, I have left my dear children two days."

"But we cannot go before the funeral, Barbara."

"What necessity can there be for our attendance? Besides, I have no mourning; I can do no good here, and I am wanted at home."

"Is it doing no good, to show respect to that person when dead whom you loved while living? Is it doing no good, to show countenance and kindness to a poor orphan girl when she is in affliction, Barbara?"

"Yes, yes, it is: I own it, I own it. Still, I think a superior duty is owing to my own children."

"So I should think, if they were in danger, or in distress; but as they are all well and happy, and under the best possible care, not even excepting your own, I think your superior duty is to stay here."

"And do you not think a mother's duty paramount to all others, a wife's excepted?"

"Yes: but when a mother prefers going to her children to staying where she is wanted, because it is far more delightful to her to go than to stay, then I think her maternal tenderness looks very like selfishness disguised under the form of maternal duty."

"Well, Aubrey, well, rather than seem selfish in your eyes, I am sure I'll stay a month if you wish."

"Nay, Barbara, that would be still more selfish; for then you would really from *selfish* motives sacrifice your children."

"I am incapable now-a-days of arguing with you, Aubrey, since you became a barrister; therefore I shall only say, I am your wife, and I feel it my duty to obey your will."

"Is it not your pleasure too, Barbara? I have always flattered myself it was—are you *changed*, my love?"

"I! Oh no! but you are, or you would not have thought me selfish."

"I *did not* think so; and I was sure you only seemed so, because you had not allowed yourself to consider the point in question properly and on both sides. I was always certain that, if you do so consider it, you would give it up as quietly and good-humouredly (with an emphasis) as you have done *now*."

Lady Barbara, as he said this, looked at him with a suspicious and inquiring glance. Then, shaking her head, and holding up her hand at him in a threatening manner, she exclaimed, "Aubrey, you are a sarcastic person!" and went in search of Rosalie.

Lady Barbara found Tyrconnel with her standing by the dead body of her whom they loved: but she hesitated to enter the room; for what is soothing to strong feelings of affection is painful where the affections are not deeply engaged. And Tyrconnel, observing her reluctant step, whispered Rosalie, that they had better go to *her;* and they led the agitated Lady Barbara to Rosalie's apartment.

"I am afraid," said she, wiping her eyes, "you think me a great fool."

"Oh, no! I can understand your feelings!"

"It is more than I can; for how strange it is that *I* cannot bear to look on that which *you*, who loved her so much more, can like to contemplate!"

"There are many ways of accounting for that. In the first place, nothing can increase the grief already at its height; and it loves whatever suits and feeds it. In the next place, it is sweet to me to be with her as long as I can; and next to seeing her alive, it is pleasing to me to gaze on her when dead. I shall soon not see her at all, you know. But pray let us change the subject."

"Willingly; and I must venture to observe the change in your countenance: your expression is quite altered, not from woe to joy, but from one sort of sorrow to another."

"I can believe it; for so are my feelings changed. The woe you mean was a bitter, blighting distress; but my last conversation with the dear lost Madeleine removed the cause of it; and *now* I only feel a tender softening kind of melancholy occasioned by her loss."

"I do not understand this distinction, Rosalie. Your first woe was an acute wearing pain like the tooth-ache. Your present resembles a slight gentle headache, and is by the by rather agreeable than otherwise, when one may rest one's head on the shoulder one loves."

"I should think, Lady Barbara, that even *sorrow* when soothed by those one most loves would be sweet also."

"Try the experiment. I dare say Tyrconnel will be very glad to soothe your sorrow."

"How can *you* joke, Lady Barbara, and at such a time?"

"Indeed, it was wrong, and I sincerely beg your pardon. I am afraid I want to meet with a severe affliction, to prevent my growing hardhearted; for a life of continued blessings is a most fearful state, and very bad for the soul, I believe; and I never lost *any* thing I loved, except a very fine long-eared setter. There

Vol. III.——30

are some losses which I cannot *bear* to contemplate. I leave you to guess what I mean — the very idea—" Here she paused, and wiped the tears from her April face.

"Do you know," said she, "that I have often wondered at the fuss that is made in a Greek play about a wife who prevailed on the gods to let her die instead of her husband? *Alcestis* her name was. But I never could see so much in it. I am sure it appears to me a very easy and natural thing. I had much rather die for Aubrey, than endure the misery of losing him. Do you not think you should feel the same towards your husband, if you loved him?"

"I would never," said Rosalie solemnly, "marry any man, for whom I should not be willing to die."

So much for the enthusiasm of two-and-twenty and nineteen.

When dinner was announced that day, to their great surprise, Dupont himself took his seat at table, and with a countenance which spoke forcibly of recent sorrow, but of sorrow subdued into calmness by the consolations of religion. As Madeleine had not for many weeks partaken of that meal with him, he did not miss her at it, and that added to his composure. He ate a little himself, but was attentive to his guests, particularly to Lady Barbara, who had not at all lost her power to charm his imagination, and whom, to her confusion, he often gazed upon till tears came in his eyes; for he recalled the first moment in which he saw her, and when he was then fearing an event might happen, which had since taken place.

"How like Lady Barbara is," said Dupont starting from a reverie, "to one of Guido's angels!"

"She is a better thing to me, dear sir," said Aubrey affectionately: "she is a real angel, not a pictured one; and she is my own little wife: but I do wish you may not turn her head with your flattery: praise from most men to a sensible woman is no better than a temporary and trifling allowance, which is never to be depended on; but praise from you is a large fortune at once, which may make the person who receives it proud and independent."

"And what are you yourself now doing, Aubrey? have not *you* praised me enough to make me proud? Independent I never can be, never *wish* to be, of you and your affection."

"Tyrconnel," said Dupont with great feeling, "if I live long enough to *know* that you and that dear girl will one day be united, I shall almost think the miseries of my own existence repaid."

So saying he left the room.

"What does this mean?" cried Lady Barbara, turning to the blushing Rosalie: "have you changed your opinion since yesterday, and learnt to think that marriage may as *well* attend on love; and that love is a bad thing without it?"

"I never *did* think otherwise," replied Rosalie: "I only said, that I might love, though I could not marry."

"*Could* not marry! that is to say, *will not* marry: dearest Rosalie, do not conjure up such a distracting thought! why will you give up all hope thus?"

"I do *not* give up hope—I cannot *bear* to give it up—I am not ashamed to repeat to these kind friends what I owned to my departed guardian, and to my living one,—that I love you, Tyrconnel; and that I believe I can never love any other man: but then I must also assure you and in their presence, that without the consent of your parents I never will be *yours*. You best know what prospect there is of obtaining it; and alas! when I consider what a splendid marriage has been made by the *younger* son, can *I* believe Lord and Lady Bellamore will allow me to be the bride of the elder!"

"Very true," said Aubrey: "I did marry wonderfully well for a younger brother; and little *splendid* here, this small diamond, but of the first water, which I wear in my bosom, was thought a fit match even for my elder brother. But remember that, in the first place, a man who will be the representative of two rich and noble houses does not want so much money as his younger brother; and in the second place, a nobleman——

"Alas!" cried Aubrey, "though sure of the indulgence of my audience I cannot go on; for I cannot speak against my conscience—without a *yes* at least—and I own my fears of ultimate disappointment for you, my dear brother, are equal to my hopes of your success."

The next day the brothers challenged Lady Barbara to take a long walk with them; and as they went along they told her that in their rambles that morning before breakfast, they had seen in a cottage the prettiest children they had ever beheld.

"Do *you* say so, Aubrey?" asked Lady Barbara reproachfully.

"Yes: I do."

"What! prettier than your *own* children?"

"Prettier than they were when I last saw them."

"Ay: but that is three days ago, and one had not been well. *William* has not seen *my* children a long time; therefore *his* praise does not *mortify* me."

"And why should mine, my love? If your children were *ugly*, I should not think them so; nor should I love them the less, if I did: for are they not equally *yours* and mine, Barbara?"

"Yes: but still one likes to have pretty children."

"But *you*, it seems, want yours to be the *prettiest* children; and though I reverence maternal tenderness, I do not admire maternal vanity."

"But must they not always go together, Aubrey? Can you separate the weed from the flower?"

"But I can discourage the one, and cherish the other."

"Well, as you please; only do not, if you love me, think any children prettier than your own. But where are these wonders? am I to see them?"

They now entered the cottage; and Tyrconnel, with a countenance of affectionate pleasure, held out to the delighted Lady Barbara her own rosy girl, while the nurse made her appearance with the other child. "Oh! my dear considerate brother, how did you contrive this delightful surprise?"

"Why, you must know, Barbara, that when I found from Aubrey how reluctant you were to stay, though benevolence conquered selfishness, I resolved that my gain should not be your loss; and having despatched a note to my mother, I prepared Rosalie's friends at this cottage to accommodate your children for a few days."

"A few days, William! If you wish it," cried the enthusiastic Lady Barbara, "I will now stay months."

"But what would our *parents* say to that, Barbara?"

"And what would the *law* say to *me?*" said her husband.

"True, I see I am wrong; but my dear husband and brother," cried she, folding each child by turns to her bosom, "how difficult it is when one is *very* happy to consider other people!"

"But not difficult to consider one's parents?"

"No: to be sure not; but when one's *near* view is so delightful, it is very excusable, for a few moments at least, to forget a more distant one, however dear."

As they left the cottage, to which Lady Barbara made an excuse for returning at least half a dozen times, she said with great earnestness, "Do you think Rosalie will consider it a breach of decorum and feeling to come with me to the cottage before the funeral is over? for I do so *long* to show her my children!"

To shorten my narrative as much as possible, I shall only say that Madeleine was interred in the chapel, under the stones where she had been accustomed to prostrate herself; that the interment was attended by a numerous congregation, who had lost in the deceased the kindest of benefactors.

Sweetly soothing was this tribute to the souls of the survivors; and when Dupont rejoined his guests in the evening, his countenance was placid, and his conversation cheerful.

After breakfast the next morning, Tyrconnel entered the room where his brother and sister were sitting, with a disturbed countenance, and with an open letter in his hand.

"See here," said he, "what one of my father's servants has just brought me!"

Aubrey read the letter, and observed that it was what he expected: "Your servant," said he, "gave such a description of Rosalie's beauty to the lady's maid at Forest Lodge, that I foresaw what would happen."

"And pray, what has happened?" asked Lady Barbara.

"My father and mother, and your father and mother, with Lady Honoria Mandeville and others, are now at Cowes, on a tour round the island, if the snow does not fall; and you and Aubrey and I are expected to join them there immediately."

"What! and leave my children and Rosalie! No, no; you may go, but I shall stay here."

"Thank you; but if I go, you must go, or our parents would be offended; and Tyrconnel must go, I fear, at all events."

"I fear so, too. I must not run any risk of offending them, as on their favour now so much depends; besides, they have been such kind and tender parents, that till now I always found my best pleasure in my duty; but then, to leave Rosalie!"

To shorten my story:— when Tyrconnel communicated the contents of his father's letter to Dupont, the latter told him he was very glad that he had received a summons, for that he meant to propose that he should quit the castle immediately, and go to Lord Bellamore to acquaint him with his attachment, and the peculiar situation of the object of it; for that he could not think he himself was acting an honourable part, while allowing any man to address a ward of his, unknown to his parents. "Well do I know," continued he, "that your father will disapprove your passion, and forbid your marriage; but tell him not to bid you utterly despair, till he knows every thing concerning the birth and connexions of Rosalie. If, when acquainted with them, he objects to her as your wife, I have *now* to tell you, my dear young friend, that that objection must be final."

I shall not describe the parting hour — that hour, more trying to those who *remain* than to those who *go;* as a path, a view, a chair, the merest trifle, are to the former, melancholy memorials of departed pleasures; while, for the latter, new scenes, new objects, and even motion itself, possesses a power to lull the mind in temporary forgetfulness.

PART THE THIRD.

"——Most dangerous
Is that temptation which does goad us on
To sin in loving virtue."
SHAKSPEARE.

AFTER Tyrconnel had been gone more than a week, Dupont received the following letter from him:—

"It is only nine days since I left you, my dear friend, yet it seems to me nine months; and it will really be nine months, I believe, before we get round the island, if we travel as slowly as we have hitherto done.

"Oh! how time drags with me now! Did you ever see me weary while I was with you? Never. But how can I bear to enter on what must, however reluctantly, be told?

"I soon found that Lady Honoria Mandeville, and another beauty, were, like two greyhounds in one string, to be let slip against my poor heart, and that I was expected to gallant them about. But I was so undutiful as always to carry off our own dear Barbara under my arm, and leave the single woman to Aubrey. How could I do otherwise? I had been told that Lady Honoria was my intended bride, and that our parents had talked matters over. Could I then, as a man of honour, pay the young lady any attention, since that attention was liable to misconstruction? No, no, I *could* not. Besides, one thought of Rosalie was enough to render all pretenders to my love odious to me; especially as I was sure that William Tyrconnel, the son of a mere private gentleman, would not have obtained one of the kind glances cast on the Honourable William Tyrconnel, son of Lord Bellamore, and heir to Lord Delmayne. Oh, these titles! would I were indeed plain William Tyrconnel! Then, perhaps—yet no; she is worthy of coronets, and I am glad I can place them on her brow. But can I do so? Hear and judge.

"You may suppose that Lady Honoria was not pleased, nor at all amused, by my disagreeable silence; at the end of a week, therefore, she made an excuse for returning to London, and I then perceived that I should have a *scene* with my father. But of this I was desirous: my secret lay heavy on my mind; for never till now had I a thought or a wish concealed.

"I dreaded, however, to have the explanation *tête-à-tête* with my father. I therefore contrived to lead to it, when my mother, brother, and Barbara were present. Suffice, that after I had told my tale, after Barbara and Aubrey had pleaded better for me than I did for myself, (blessings on their generous natures!) all I could obtain was a promise not to forbid me entirely to hope, till the mystery hanging over Rosalie's birth be cleared up; and *then*, if no disgrace attends her birth, in favour of her accomplishments and virtues he will waive all other considerations, and for the sake of his son's happiness receive her as his daughter; but this only on *one* condition—that we do not *meet* till the time for solving the mystery arrives.

"I *cannot* go on. O sir! I know you will enter into my feelings, and will not suppose that selfish consideration for myself can make me fail in love and duty towards you. But surely, surely, your vow may be more generously interpreted. Surely, if, as you say, your health is wasting daily, and you are every day, therefore, expecting the approach of death, you are, as it were, on your deathbed; and it would be no infringement of your vow to disclose the secret; do it, then, while you can reasonably hope to witness the happy results. But forgive me! your own conscience is your best guide; and I respectfully await its decree.

"I write to Rosalie, but it is for the last time—*all* intercourse is forbidden—absolutely *all*. God bless you! My heart is too full to allow me to say more.

"WILLIAM TYRCONNEL."

*The Answer.**

"Your father, dear Tyrconnel, has, in my opinion, acted a wise and virtuous part; and has refused, as I myself should have done, to admit into his family a young woman of mysterious birth and unknown connexions; but he has, with a degree of justice which I honour, consented to receive her, if her birth be not stained with disgrace.

"That, time will soon reveal: and, in the meantime, his prohibition of intercourse between you is another proof of his wisdom; for, if you are *not* ultimately to be united to Rosalie, further intercourse would be cruel to you both, as it would only increase your mutual attachment; and if that attachment cannot stand the test of absence, your union ought never to take place.

"I have a pleasure in telling you, that Mr. Fenton confirms all my ideas of my own malady, and that the organs of life become more diseased every day; but be assured, that only when I am *literally* on my bed of death, will I make the promised disclosure. When I am *really* there, I shall despatch an express to you.

"Rosalie looks pale, but she bears up for my sake *wonderfully;* and so, I hope, do you, for the sake of *your parents.*

"Believe me, both in life and in death,
"Your faithful and affectionate
"BERTRAM DUPONT."

Three weeks had worn heavily away, and bad roads, heavy carriages, and occasional in-

* The letter to Rosalie, and her answer, do not appear.

dispositions, made long excursions impossible; when at length Tyrconnel one morning received, by express from the castle, a letter written in a hand scarcely legible. It contained only a few words.

"My prayers are heard—I am dying—and before you have left the island—come you! come *all*, at the earnest request of an expiring man!

"RINALDO, CONTE M. G."

Tyrconnel went instantly to his father's bedside, and obtained his promise, and that of his mother, that they would follow him, (as they hoped,) with the rest of the party, as soon as their six horses could be harnessed.

The brothers set off immediately. They found Dupont quite composed, and with an evident expression of satisfaction in his countenance; while his whole soul seemed in his eyes as he gazed on Rosalie, who sat on the bed beside him, wiping the damps of death from his brow, and giving and receiving the most affectionate caresses, scarcely turning from her interesting charge to welcome her long-absent lover.

"Here are the papers which I mentioned to you," said Dupont; "and they are so long, that *I* have wished, *earnestly* wished, your parents would arrive, as it would be a trial to me, indeed, to die uncertain of the fate of this most precious child. Yet, if it must be so, I shall not dare to murmur; for I have merited nothing but chastisements, and every mercy shown me surprises as much as it encourages me."

Tyrconnel received the packet with a trembling hand, and though he longed to open it, he *dared* not do it: besides, he wished to *hope* as long as he could, and those papers *might* bid him despair.

It was more than an hour before Tyrconnel, who was anxiously on the *watch*, hailed the arrival of the party; but at length they came, and Aubrey went down to receive them.

"Surely," said the dying man, "Rosalie ought to go down to welcome them."

"What! and leave you? I cannot—*indeed* I cannot."

"You can return again in a short time; and really my mind is so relieved, now I know they are here, that I believe death much more distant than I expected." And as Mr. Fenton, who now entered, declared that the pulse was rather stronger than when he felt it last, Rosalie allowed Tyrconnel to lead her down stairs. But it was as much against his inclination as against hers; for, as yet, Tyrconnel knew her by no other name than Rosalie; and as *Rosalie only* he could not present her to persons who to high rank and the pride of lofty birth, united formality of manners and rigid ideas of decorum. But there was no alternative; and Tyrconnel tried to repress in his beloved charge that reluctance which he was only too conscious of himself. In Rosalie, however, it was reluctance *only*, unmixed with any feeling of bashful trepidation; for how could that being who had just left the chamber of death, and the contemplation of the dying, feel awed at appearing before any one of mortal mould? "Dust and ashes as we are, or soon must be, is it for us," she might have said, "to plume ourselves upon the distinctions of worldly grandeur, and look down on our fellow-creatures, when the time perhaps is near that shall make one act of recollected virtue, and a single aspiration of present faith, however gently breathed, of more value than all the splendours of a coronet?" But it was not to such reflections, however just, that Rosalie was indebted for her present courage. It was *sacred sorrow* which lifted her above the admission of any other feeling, and even made her insensible to the wish of pleasing the parents of Tyrconnel.

When she entered the room, Tyrconnel was relieved at once from his embarrassment by Lady Barbara, who joyfully exclaimed, "Oh! here is my dear friend Rosalie."

The Countess of Delmayne and the Lady Bellamore, and their lords, immediately rose; and with a manner which they meant to be very gracious, and with the consciousness of condescension, the ladies advanced a step or two to meet the pale and tearful girl. But the long and fine-turned neck of Rosalie bent itself more courteously than humbly to their salutation; and her step was so firm, her manner so self-possessed, that they who came intending only to bestow protection were struck with involuntary respect.

Aubrey had set a chair for her near his mother, and every one seemed expecting her to speak. Rosalie, too, felt that she was called upon to do so; and in words nearly inaudible she thanked the visiters for their truly kind compliance with the wishes of a dying stranger: but as the recollection that *he* was *dying* recurred to her, she earnestly conjured them to excuse her, if she returned *instantly* to his room.

The expiring sufferer looked eagerly in the face of Tyrconnel, as he led Rosalie to the bedside, to read there, if he could, what impression she had made on his guests; for he had urged her going to them, in hopes that her beauty and her sorrow would make her an interest in their hearts. But he had seen little of the world, and knew not how much the habits and restraints of civilized society fetter not only the expression of the feelings, but the feelings themselves.

Deluded man! Rosalie's appearance had produced an unfavourable effect on the mother of Lady Barbara, who had never quite forgotten Tyrconnel's indifference to her daughter. Still, however, as she was a generous, goodhearted woman, she felt a wish to promise protection to a poor, friendless orphan: and pro-

tection implies *power*; and the love of power is not only a universal passion, but one that it is *gratifying to indulge*. And Lady Delmayne pleased herself with the example she should set Lady Bellamore, and with the anticipation of soothing the terrors of the trembling and embarrassed Rosalie. But lo! Rosalie was neither trembling nor embarrassed. Lady Delmayne, therefore, was mortified and disappointed.

Aubrey's observing eye discovered this, and he dared not ask what the family thought of Rosalie.

Not so Lady Barbara. With her usual warmth of heart, she exclaimed, "Well, is she not very beautiful?"

"We saw her to great disadvantage," said Lady Bellamore.

"Her face we did," said her lord; "but her figure is the finest that I ever saw, and her air dignified."

"Dignified!" cried Lady Delmayne: "*proud*, I think. Surely, no duchess could have carried her head more high."

"True," said Aubrey, coldly; "for Rosalie has great dignity of mind, and that usually gives dignity of manner and self-possession. Were she the child of a peasant, her manner would be the same. What you call pride, I call proper self-respect."

"But do you not think, Aubrey, that the consciousness of high birth gives a sort of grace and air to the person, however diminutive, which no one could mistake?"

"My dear madam," replied Aubrey. "do you think that if a stranger were not told who this laughing-eyed, bustling little person beside me was, he would instantly discover that she was an earl's daughter?"

"He would know at least that she was of rank; for you have often said yourself, sir, that it was impossible for Lady Barbara Delmayne to move ungracefully; and what can this be owing to but to that consciousness of her own consequence, which alone can give that ease to the manner, in which grace consists?"

"What a piece of pride and conceit, then, have I been loving so tenderly and so long without knowing it!"

"You are always laughing at Barbara about her littleness, Aubrey; but she is not so very short, though she is certainly not a May-pole."

"My dear lady, she knows she is '*as high as my heart*;' and knowing that, I know she is contented. Are you not, Barbara?"

"I was—but am so no longer."

"No!"

"No," replied she, seeing the storm gathering on her mother's brow, and wishing to avert it by a joke: "No, not since I have gained the high appellation of angel; and you know the poor Count says I *look* and *am* an angel—his *guardian angel*."

"Does the Count say so?" said Lady Delmayne, frowning no longer.

"Oh yes!"

Tyrconnel's entrance interrupted her. He came with the manuscript in his hand.

"Begin, dear brother, begin," cried Lady Barbara.

But finding he was too much agitated to command his voice sufficiently, he resigned the task of reading it to Aubrey; and he read as follows:

Confessions of Rinaldo, Conte Manfredi di Guastalla.

Little did you suspect that the son of one of the first families in Italy, a family which has given ambassadors, statesmen, and heroes to its country, was hidden under the unhonoured name of Bertram Dupont, and was wearing away existence in a foreign land, in solitude and in penance. Little could you imagine, that he who avoided the eye of curiosity, and whom real and imagined fears forced into concealment, was once the object of public veneration, and courted and applauded by the learned, the virtuous, the good, and the pious. Yet, so it was; till self-confidence hurled me down from my pinnacle of earthly exaltation, to prove a warning example to others, that he who trusts in his own strength shall fall; and that those who fancy themselves superior to temptation shall be cast down in the midst of their imagined security, to change the vauntings of a confident spirit for the agonies of a contrite one.

I was the second son of the Duke Manfredi, by his second wife, in right of whom I bore the name and enjoyed the fortune of the family of Guastalla: but at an early age I discovered a distaste for the things of this world, and a passion for retirement and theological studies, which seemed to prove me called by a voice from heaven to devote myself to the service of the church.

My father opposed my calling, but my brothers encouraged it. On them and their motives, however, I wish not to dwell: suffice it, that I persisted in my religious vocation, and that my *first degrees in sanctity* were taken by a violation of the *duty of obedience to my father*.

He menaced, he entreated, in vain; and at the age of sixteen, I began my novitiate in a convent of Benedictines at Rome.

With what delight did my ears drink in the praises bestowed on my early and distinguished piety! How was my pride gratified, when I found my acts of extraordinary self-denial and penance, the theme of admiration, and that I was held up as a model to the other novices in the convent! Infatuated being! not to feel that the heart which was elated by human praise for homage to its God, was actuated by an earthly ambition, not by the irresistible impulses of heavenly zeal!

But I thought myself the holiest of the holy, and I took my vows at the age of seventeen. Yes, the youthful Count Manfredi Guastalla laid down his worldly honours, to be known no more but as the Father Francesco. Still the ambition of my soul prompted me, in spite of my renunciation of my titles, to illustrate the name of Father Francesco by eloquence and learning; and in idea the sacred tiara already glittered on my brow. With this view, though I redoubled my austerities, I at the same time also redoubled my attention to my studies; and my fame as a preacher, when once I had been permitted to ascend the chair, spread from Rome through every town in the Pontificate; till, by the time that I was one-and-twenty, crowds collected wherever I was, to see me pass along, and kiss the hem of my garment; and the proudest beauties of Italy humbled themselves in the overwhelming consciousness of sin before the holy eloquence of the youthful Benedictine. But did not he who thus admonished others, require admonition himself?—Was he who called sinners to repentance, free himself from the consciousness of sin? Alas! undetected, the damning sin of pride clave unto my secret soul, and terrible was the humiliation preparing for me.

By this time, I was known personally as a theologian, a saint, and an orator, to some of the first men of the age; to Cardinal de Retz, and other distinguished men who visited Rome; and I was invited to go to Paris, to preach before the Grand Monarque: nor would my vanity have denied itself this gratification, had I not been suddenly stopped in my career by a power whose influence I despised, and against which, puffed up with self-righteousness, I had never thought of arming myself, by humble reliance on my God.

The Marquis di Romano, a distant relation of our family, who had married the heiress of the house of Visconti, died, leaving only two daughters to inherit his and his wife's possession.

The younger of these daughters, Seraphina Celesi, became attached, at the age of fifteen, to a Scotch nobleman, the young Earl of Monrose, who was travelling in Italy with a tutor and his servant, our faithful Donald. But her poor widowed mother, who could not bear that her child should marry a foreigner, though a catholic, violently opposed the union; she opposed it in vain, and at last she was brought to consent, that at the end of two years the marriage should take place, if Monrose returned at that time to Italy as much in love as when he left it.

The elder of these daughters, Rosmunda Celesi, who was two years my junior, believed herself, alas! incapable of any earthly love; and glowing with enthusiasm, resolved to resign the pride of rank, of wealth, and of beauty, and devote herself to a cloister.

The Marchioness opposed this *heavenly* union, as much as she had done the terrestrial one: but filial duty had no power against the impulses of a heated imagination. She was resolved, as I had been, to live and die in the odour of sanctity; and when she heard of my exalted sacrifice of the world and all its allurements, she declared that it was her ambition to prove herself worthy of the consanguinity which she bore me; and that she trusted I should one day be proud of my cloistered kinswoman.

Alas! I fear that I was proud of her already; proud of having made so distinguished a convert, and of having snatched from the snares of the world a being so beautiful, and a soul so precious. Emboldened by her conscious call, she addressed a letter to me, though we had never met, in which she solicited my advice and encouragement in the path which she had chosen, and I gave them with pride.

My letter, perhaps, nay *certainly*, put the seal to her fate, and her unhappy mother continued to plead in vain.

"Only wait a few years, my beloved child! you are too young yet to form any opinion on subjects of such importance; and remember, that if you become a nun, you leave me desolate and alone."

Such was the language of the Marchioness; but the poor victim of her own rashness thought it, as I did, the pleading of worldly selfishness, and prepared to enter upon her novitiate. But the time of her probation was delayed by an accident which happened to her mother, who by a fall from a carriage appeared to have been killed upon the spot: she recovered, however, to existence, though never to reason and perception. Still, her daughter resolved to leave her to the care of others, impelled (she fancied) by a higher duty, and began her novitiate in a convent of Benedictines at Ferrara.

In the meanwhile I was advancing in reputation, and was the delighted idol of kneeling crowds: and engravings of me, taken from the picture which you will find in the box I shall give you, were spread over the Continent. Scarcely, perhaps, will you believe, that I ever resembled that picture, which exhibits a man glowing with the bloom of youth, and in unblighted pride. The print, however, which is colourless, resembles me still; and little did Father Vincent think, when he looked on the mysterious stranger with so suspicious an eye at Delmayne, that a portrait of me was hanging up in his apartment, as the holy Father Francesco. This print was given, by one of our mutual relatives, to Rosmunda, who sent me in return, with a letter full of humble veneration, a miniature of herself, painted by a pensioner, in her nun's dress, soon after she had taken the vows, and when the austerities of her religious duties had begun to injure the roses on her cheek. But, though I knew it not, in spite of its languid eye and faded bloom, that face, when I first beheld it, even in painting, called forth in me emotions never known before. I fancied them the result of admiration for that zeal, which could resolve to bury such beauty in a convent: but though my proud heart disdained to believe that aught of human passion mingled with my adoration, certain it is, that I have often turned from the image of the Virgin, to gaze on Sister Angela (as Rosmunda was now called); and that, having done so, I have penned letters to her, glowing with all the fervour of earthly and forbidden ardour. — She, poor innocent, believed as I did; and we were far gone in a correspondence, which, though it treated wholly of religion, was written with the pen of passion, when we both of us fell ill—I, from the fatigues and austerities of my religious profession, which threatened me with consumption; and she, from her too rigorous observance of fasts and penances. We were both ordered by our physician to the baths of Baia, near which our mutual relative, the young Marquis di Romano, had lately purchased a villa. Our noble relatives were excessively devoted to holy books and holy beings; and the idea of having two such youthful saints near them was most gratifying to their enthusiastic minds. Nor was it long before they formed to themselves the delightful prospect of prevailing on us to take up our abode under their roof. And what should prevent it? No danger could accrue to two such sanctified beings from a familiar intercourse; and there was no doubt but that their whole family would be edified and hallowed by our presence.

Alas! our own betraying wishes agreed but too well with theirs; and I veiled my real motives from my view, by believing that I wished to converse on doctrinal points with my correspondent face to face, because I had reason, as I fancied, to apprehend that she was a little tinctured with Jansenism, as she had been deeply impressed with the high reputation and talents of Sister Angelica, of Port-Royal, where heresy was suspected to flourish, under the countenance of the celebrated Arnauds.

To be brief: We consented to stay at the villa of the Marquis, and still more eagerly consented to meet there. — O day of fate! a day big with inconceivable misery, when I first gazed upon that form of breathing loveliness, and viewed that face, where the woman's impassioned tenderness, and the saint's holy zeal, shed indescribable fascination over the features of a Grecian Venus! Never shall I forget my emotion, when she bent her knee with modest reverence before me, and, crossing her beautiful hands on her bosom, besought my blessing.

Those hands, so often lifted with confidence to call down blessings upon others, now trembled, as if palsied by conscious forebodings, while raised to heaven for *her ;* and the voice faltered which uttered the now inarticulate prayer.

When she rose, with a glistening eye and blushing cheek, and gazed upon me with a look of flattering regard and reverence, the tender impulse which made me wish to clasp her to my heart, ought to have convinced me, that though I proudly thought myself a teacher and an example, my breast was about to glow with a consuming fire, and one which other love than that of Heaven had kindled. But I was self-confiding; and I thought that for *me*, the gifted one, to fall from grace, was impossible, and I hurried blindly on to my destruction. Alas! I hurried not on alone.

We had *met*, and we were left daily together; for we feared not for ourselves, and who should presume to fear for us? When not alone, we witnessed the wedded happiness of the Marquis and his Paulina; and we judged by their parental transports, as they beheld the gambols of their children, how sweet it was to be a parent. Once, too, the inconsiderate Marquis said, as he held one of his babes up in his arms, to be kissed by Angela—

"See, my dear cousin, what a cherub this girl is! And such a blessing might have been yours, had you not been called upon to resign all worldly ties, and even the lawful indulgence of the purest affections, for the still higher joys of the self-devoted vestal."

"Ay, and you, too, holy father," cried his innocent wife, "you, too, gave up a great deal to gain the height at which you now stand. What a *beautiful* couple would you and sister Angela have been! Your children would have been little angels!"

It is strange, though true, that till this moment the veil had never been removed from the eyes of either of us; but it now *fell*, never to be replaced!

I felt a mist come over my sight, and should have fallen to the ground, had not a scream from the Marchioness restored me to myself; for Angela, conscious like myself, too late, of the sacrifice we had made through the delusions of a heated fancy, had sunk nearly insensible at her feet. However, my support she determinedly avoided, while to the arm of the Marquis she clung with conscious preference. But she had not an equal power over her eyes; for when she unclosed them again they involuntarily sought mine; and that look, given and returned, discovered by a single glance the heart of the one to the other.

Terrible was the night I passed. She, I conclude, had slept as little; and we appeared the next day with such altered looks, that our kind-hearted relations, who had rejoiced in our renovated bloom during our stay at Baia, now grieved to think they should restore us to our cells with the same pallid cheeks we wore at our arrival. Restore us to our cells! As well might they have hoped to restore the Neapolitan to his dwelling which had been covered with a burning tide of lava.

We had indeed recovered our health during our fatal visit, for we were happy in the *unconscious* gratification of the dearest feelings of our nature. We loved, and we were *near each other:* no pang of remorse clouded over our pleasure; and when we retired at night, we knew that we should meet and converse the next day, and nearly all the day with each other. But now, what was to be done? I felt that we must separate—at least I thought this in my cooler moments; but sometimes, as I was sure my passion was returned, I had serious thoughts of conjuring Angela to fly with me from the unnatural fetters in which the frantic dreams of our youth had bound us, and vow at another altar to pass our lives together. Next moment, shocked at my own delinquency, I shrunk not from the less criminal resolve, as I considered it, of self-destruction; for how could I bear to live, and live without Angela?

Weak, deluded being! *Now* was the time to prove the *reality* of that holy vocation, in whose imagined security I had so presumptuously gloried, proudly supposing myself raised above the frailties and temptations of human nature, because I had never been exposed to their assault. Now was the time to show my faith, by conquering my weakness: hitherto, I had claimed the honours of a triumph, before I had fought, or even beheld, a battle.

What was passing in the mind and heart of Angela was, as I afterwards found, a transcript of mine; but, more capable of self-command than I was, she continued to avoid me, and for two days, under pretence of indisposition, she kept her chamber. This conduct, instead of exciting my respect and my emulation, piqued my pride; for I began to fear I had deceived myself in thinking that she loved me, and that her avoidance of me proceeded from a desire to repress the daring hope which my looks had displayed. Not from principle, therefore, but from pique, I resolved to avoid her. I did so; and I had soon the cruel satisfaction of seeing that she was wounded by my averted eyes, and that her resolution of avoiding my presence was fast failing her. But where, you will say, was the penetration of the Marquis and Marchioness? Did they not guess the cause of your altered conduct? No; there are some persons, and such were they, who, when they have once conceived an opinion, never can be led to change it. They had believed, that for a monk, though he was only a monk of one-and-twenty, to feel the power of beauty and the force of passion was impossible; and that a nun, though only a girl of nineteen, could not be susceptible of any love but that of her Saviour. Therefore, they interfered not to save us from each other and from ourselves; and we were too faithless to our best interests to implore with sincerity of heart the aid of a higher being.

At this critical moment, Angela's sister, who had just been united to the man of her heart, came to pass the first days of her marriage at the baths of Baia; as she longed to make the sister whom she loved the witness of her felicity. Little did she think that the nun whom she had seen absorbed in her religious exercises had now learned to hold the cloister in abhorrence.

They came; and we, whose bosoms burned with as warm a flame, were doomed to witness the happy love which we were forbidden to know.

At length, my resolution was taken—I would return to my cell; I would resume my labours; the dreams of ambition should replace those of love, and by fasting and penance I would drive Angela from my thoughts. Yet, I was resolved to grant my passion one indulgence—I would own it to its object; I would wring from her a confession of a mutual attachment, and then resign her for ever. And I did not long watch in vain for an opportunity.

One day, as the shades of twilight stole over the lonely gardens filled with a thousand odours, and gently tinged with the beams of the setting sun, the two pair of married lovers left us alone together. Conscious of the weakness of her own heart, and suspecting that of mine, Angela rose, and would have followed them; but I forcibly detained her, and, grasping her trembling arm, pointed to the objects of our united envy, and exclaimed, "See, Angela! see those happy husbands! and think what torments I endure, who love as tenderly as they do, and never must hope to be as happy! Speak, thou whose beauty has undone me! Say, have you no pity for a wretch whom you have made? Tell me, Angela, do I suffer alone?"

As I spoke with passionate violence, but in a voice subdued even to woman's gentleness, I pressed her to my heart; and as her head fell upon my shoulder, she murmured out, "Yes, you *must* go; but know that my sufferings and my love are as great as yours!"

"Then why should we part?" cried I.

The scene, the hour, the sight of the wedded happiness before us, and my impassioned tenderness, laid the voice of conscience to rest; nor was it long before she bore to hear me talk of the means of our elopement. To attempt it would have been dangerous in the extreme, had we not each possessed, as if it had been granted us on purpose to lead us into temptation, a large sum in money, and Angela a considerable one in jewels. The Marchioness had breathed her last just before Angela came to Baia; and her share of the money, which she had just received, together with the jewels, which came to her as the eldest sister, were at that moment in her apartment. I too had recently received a considerable legacy from a relation.

It was dark before our companions, lost in pleasing converse, returned to the bower, and it was well for us that it was so; for though they believed our conversation had only been of spiritual things, our disordered countenances, where reigned by turns tenderness, alarm, and contentment, must have excited wonder, if not suspicion in their minds, could they have beheld them.

My plan was this: I was to purchase of one of the servants of the Marquis a complete suit of his oldest clothes; disguised in which I was to hire a mule, and proceed to Naples, where I should purchase the dress of a male and female peasant. In these, we were to contrive to escape to Bastia in a boat, which I was to hire; and there the first priest whom we met was at the *nearest altar to join our hands.*

Angela, as I *thought*, agreed to this proposal; and I bade her farewell, full of love and joy.

But that night was a terrible trial to her feelings, for her sister followed her into her room, and throwing herself on her neck, bewailed with an agony of tears the evident unhappiness which her countenance betrayed.

"You know how earnestly I opposed your religious profession," said she; "but when I thought it was for your happiness, and when I saw you happy, I was reconciled to it. But now that some secret sorrow is evidently undermining your health, I fear you find too late you have deceived yourself, and repent the sacrifice which you then made."

This affectionate appeal was more than the conscious Angela could bear; while with a beating heart she assured her beloved sister, that though she was dejected then, she should not be so long. Angela's heart, however, died within her, when she remembered that ere three days were past she should never perhaps see this darling being more! The thought was madness; and as I was absent, and this beloved sister present, her resolution to sacrifice every thing to love and me died away; and I waited for her at the appointed place in vain.

Oh! how desperate were my feelings, while I resumed the garb which I thought I had resigned for ever, and, hastening to the villa, walked with indignant mien to the balcony, where I saw Angela sitting alone. Terrified at my frantic gestures, she joined me in the garden; and when I swore never to survive another disappointment, she solemnly promised to follow me that night to the shore. Unseen we reached it, and embarked on board the vessel.

When we reached Bastia, we had no difficulty in finding a priest and an altar, and Angela became my wife; nor did any remembrance of our broken vows come over us, to cloud the first brightness of our joys, our *virtuous* joys, as we presumptuously called them. But thinking Bastia too near Baia, we embarked on board a vessel bound for the port of Marseilles: even there, I did not think we were safe from the pursuit which I fancied would be made for us; and with the terrors of the inquisition before me, I resolved to remove into Switzerland; nor did I allow the soles of our feet to rest till we reached Geneva, where we assumed the habit of the country, and called ourselves by the name of Muller. There we remained six months, but not as happy as we had been during the first weeks of our union, for now would be heard the voice of a reproaching conscience.—Angela, or Madeleine, as she had named herself, sighed to hear of tidings of that tender relative whose heart she was certain of having wounded, not only by her desertion but disgrace; and I remembered the father whose grey hairs I might perhaps have brought with sorrow to the grave, for I, who was once his pride, was now become his dishonour. But of these dear relations we had no means of hearing, except at the greatest risk to ourselves; and we found that short was the existence even of wedded happiness, when obtained by the surrender of the most sacred of duties.

At this time I had amused myself with improving by study of some knowledge of simples and of physic, which I had acquired in the convent; and I had performed one or two cures amongst the poor around me.

One night, the person whom I had last attended came to inform me, that an English servant, who was waiting for his master, an English nobleman expected at Geneva, was taken ill at his house, and he wished me to visit him. I did so; and with a mixed feeling of alarm and pleasure, I found in the invalid the faithful Donald, who was the foster-brother of Lord Monrose, and was attached to him with most devoted affection. For a moment, the terror of detection prompted me to leave him to his fate, as he was delirious, and could not as yet recognize me; but humanity conquered selfishness, and I staid. I took care, however, to be alone while I watched the effect of my medicines; and it was well that I did so; for, when he recovered his senses, he with surprise and joy vociferated my name, adding, "Oh! how glad my lord and my lady will be to see you! But where is the Lady Angela?" He was not yet well enough to listen to the explanation which he asked for: his delirium returned, and for two days and nights Madeleine and I watched beside the bed of this faithful creature. He was scarcely convalescent when intelligence came that his lord and lady had arrived, and Madeleine and I retreated precipitately to our own house, there to wait the result of Donald's communication respecting us. When he came, he came not alone, and Madeleine was pressed with forgiving tenderness to the bosom of her sister. Not such was the reception which I received from the high-principled Caledonian. He rebuked me as the seducer of innocence, and my conscious heart shrunk from the awful severity of offended virtue. But never can I forget the vehemence with which Madeleine repelled this charge against me. "He my seducer, my lord! Rather say I was his; for I have long been convinced that I loved him even before I saw him."

Even he shuddered at the thought of our being discovered. However, not believing us safe on that side of the German Ocean, he advised our flying instantly to Aberdeen, near which port his estate was situated, and hiring a cottage in the neighbourhood, that his nearly heart-broken wife might sometimes see her unhappy sister. He gave us also bills of exchange on his agent at Paris for our cumbrous specie, and thus facilitated to us the means of travelling.

He told us, that when our flight could no longer be concealed, and the circumstances were known at our respective convents, the consternation was great in proportion to our great reputation for sanctity; and in the same degree that we had been considered an honour to our order, was the disgrace which we had brought upon it. This disgrace, however, it was impossible to avoid; and the superiors resolved to give out to the world, that I had died, after my return from Baia, of a rapid decline, and that Angela had sunk a victim to her rigid fasts and penances. They also solemnized our funeral obsequies with due solemnity.

"Would to God," said Monrose, "that we could have been deceived like the rest of the world! Would to God that we could have believed you had died holy and virtuous! But we could not long flatter ourselves, as we at first did, that you were gone on some holy pilgrimage, or mission, and had perished in it; for the boatmen who rowed you to Bastia talked of the great reward which they had received for rowing two young peasants (and on the very night on which you were missing,) who looked more like a king and a queen than what their dress bespoke them to be."

"But if," cried I after a long pause, "we are supposed *dead*, what danger have we to apprehend from the pursuit of the Inquisition?"

"Every danger, if you remain *where its power can reach you*. Have they not to *punish* sinners, if they cannot *reclaim* them? Believe me, you will be most secure in England or Scotland; and I conjure you to set off directly. But even there, you must be on your guard while living on the coast; for Madeleine might easily be ensnared and seized, if you were traced to Aberdeen, and carried off unknown to the government, to a vessel stationed for the purpose."

"True, true," I exclaimed in an agony of apprehension, of apprehension the extent of which I would not reveal; for I feared that not by *violence*, but by *persuasion*, my beloved wife might be taken from me, and that she might be prevailed upon, by secret agents from Ferrara, to leave me, and return a voluntary victim to her cloister. Impelled by this horrible apprehension, I would have fled with her, had it been possible, to the end of the earth. No longer therefore did I hesitate; and, after a mournful farewell between the sisters, we proceeded to Bologne, and thence embarked for Aberdeen. Never, never did we behold the angelic face of Seraphina again! But we have seen one like it, as you yourselves will say, if you examine the picture which Madeleine always wore in her bosom; for Seraphina was a tall Lady Barbara; and when I told you that I thought she was Madeleine's guardian angel made visible to my sight, her likeness to Seraphina favoured the illusion. Seraphina was totally different to Italian women; for her hair and eyes were light, and this singularity she inherited from her grandmother, who was a noble Scotchwoman.

But to proceed with my narrative. Scarcely were we sailed, when a violent storm arose: and for several hours, nothing but different modifications of despair were visible or audible around us. But oh! the horror of that moment to us! to us, who with yet unrepented crimes upon our heads were about to be hurled, as we feared, into the presence of a just and omnipotent Judge! Never can I forget the moment when, holding the fainting Madeleine in my arms, I was about to vow unto that power whom I had offended, that if he would but spare our forfeited lives, we would break those ties which we had sinned in forming.—But at that moment the storm abated, and we landed at Aberdeen in safety.

Great, however, as were our joy and thankfulness, they could not equal the agony which we had endured, nor enable us quickly to forget it. Mine "was continually before me," and it had far exceeded that of Madeleine—nor dared I disclose it to her; for I knew that she would shudder to think of the vow which had so nearly escaped my lips, and which I could not recall without horror.

But soon a new train of delightful hopes took possession of my heart, and banished the gloom which the recollections of the storm had occasioned.

Madeleine was likely to become a mother; and to increase our comfort, we received letters from Lord and Lady Monrose.

I now, in order to legitimate my child as much as possible, procured a license, and we were married according to the rites of the *Protestant Church*. Our comfort, however, was not of long duration.

Alas! one night a ship was heard to fire signals of distress; and on hastening to the shore, I saw a vessel seemingly on the point of perishing in the storm!

With what eagerness did I join in the means taken to succour the distressed people! With what alacrity did I, at some risk to myself, enter the boat sent out to their assistance!—and we succeeded in saving some of the passengers. The crew, most of them, alas! were swallowed up with the vessel before our eyes.

But judge of my dismay, when I tell you that in one of them I recognised a monk, an officer of the Inquisition, whom I knew to be my most determined enemy; and who was of the same convent as myself!

And what could have brought him to Aberdeen? I could not but suppose that we were the inducement: but if not, still, if he discovered Madeleine, and demanded to see her, I could not prevent it; and I feared that his awakening eloquence might lend force to those compunctious visitings in her heart, which were too often difficult to be suppressed in mine. What was to be done? At present I saw that he was too full of his recent danger to be alive to external objects, and had, consequently, not yet seen me.

We were now approaching the shore; and while the rest waded to land, I was left alone in the boat with him. — Easy then would it have been for me to push him into the waves, when he had one leg over the side, and to hold him under them till he had ceased to breathe; for, busy as the rest of the people were in dragging the boat to land, and assisting the half-drowned crew, I could have committed this crime unseen and unsuspected. But I prayed to be delivered from the temptation, and I was enabled to resist it. I instantly quitted the spot, and reached my home unperceived by this alarming man. But I felt that there was no time to be lost, and we left Aberdeen.

When I reached the wide world of London, I felt once more secure; and there I should have spent the rest of my days, had I not found that the air disagreed with Madeleine: we therefore again bent our faces to the north, but kept far from its shores.

But now I had to endure anxiety of another kind: for three long days and three long nights, I was doomed almost to witness the agonies of the being on whom my soul doted, to expect that every moment was to her the moment of death, and to anticipate the still more awful moment of judgment to come. All that I thought, all that I felt and feared, I cannot reveal; but then for the first time was my *soul* awakened to deep and true repentance, and to the necessity of *expiation;* and I solemnly vowed, prostrate on the earth, that if she might be spared for contrition and amendment, I would break our unhallowed ties, and still further punish myself by never revealing to any one, except when I was on my death-bed, that I had a right to the dear name of *father*. Having taken this heart-rending oath, I became more composed, and waited the event with something like resignation.

The event was a merciful one: Madeleine lived through her agonies, and the delighted nurse gave a living infant into my arms, which eagerly opened to receive and embrace it; but the next moment, remembering my oath, I imprinted a long kiss on its unconscious brow, and gave it back into the nurse's arms—never, except in life's last hour, to be received into them again. This child was baptized by the name of Rosalie; and the register of her birth and baptism accompanies the certificate of both our marriages. I need not add, I think, that this child was our dear Rosalie.

Here Tyrconnel, in great agitation, interrupted his brother, and said, "Surely sufficient has now been read of the manuscript, to enable its hearers to form a judgment on the points on which my whole happiness depends?" Still they were silent.

"Go on," said Lord Bellamore, "with Count Manfredi di Guastalla's narrative."

Drowning men catch at a straw, says the proverb; and Tyrconnel caught a gleam of hope from his father's having given the father of Rosalie his title; and Aubrey continued:—

I shall pass over my first interview with Madeleine, the joy with which she showed me her child, and her wonder that I refused to nurse it; and proceed to that awful moment when I had to disclose to the woman whom I adored, and who loved me with all a virtuous woman's ardour, that *we must part*, and that I wished her with her child to reside near her sister, while I retired into some monastery in France, and spent the rest of my life in rigid penance.

"And this painful proof of love," she cried, but with a calmness that astonished me, "was wrung from you, my beloved, in a moment of agony. Believe me, I, in one of perfect self-possession, will give you one more painful, more convincing still: I will propose to you a penance to-morrow, more hard to undergo than any your *monastic* discipline can teach you."

The next day, to my surprise, Madeleine met me at breakfast, where I, with a beating heart, awaited what she had to propose to me.

"Rinaldo," said she at length, summoning all her fortitude, "have not absence and entire cessation of intercourse been always held up as most calculated to calm the agonies of hopeless passion?"

"Granted."

"And can any tortures inflicted on the body, equal the tortures hourly inflicted on the heart?"

"None."

"Well, then, if you leave me and enter the walls of a cloister, separation, however painful at first, will in time calm the yearnings of your affections towards me, and you will become resigned, and perhaps cheerful. Yours, then, will be no *expiation*, for you will endure no *constant struggle*. Mark me, then! *Do not let us separate!* Let us live together, not as brother and as sister only — for brothers and sisters may clasp each other's hand, may assist each other's steps, and by many little offices of kindness prove their mutual regard; but let us, my beloved, live wholly as the coldest and most distant strangers would live together. Let no fond epithet be used by either of us; and after this day let us glide along the path of life like ghosts, to each other *visible*, but *intangible, for ever!* You have sworn never to caress or own your child, except in the hour of death. I will make the *same* vow, and oh! to fulfil it will rend a mother's heart, far more than a father's. Still, when she is old enough to feel and to return caresses, from that moment most interesting to the parental heart, I will solemnly swear, in expiation of my offences, never to caress her, nor call her child, till I am *on my deathbed.* Rinaldo, the fulfilment of my *first* vow depends on *you.* Can you consent to live with me on those terms? or must we cease not only to love, if that be possible, but also to live together?"

I hesitated to decide; for terrible appeared the probation and the penance. At last, after a few hours of conflict and earnest prayer— for I was no longer confident in my own strength—I ventured to tell her that I approved of all she had proposed. And then we both of us, after humbling ourselves before the throne of mercy, besought its blessing on our task, and took the trying vow.

"Trying, indeed!" said Aubrey.

"And cruel and unnatural!" cried Lady Barbara. "What! deprive themselves of the indulgence of a parent's feelings—those purest and sweetest of feelings! They were great sinners, and they had a right to punish themselves, but not to punish their innocent child!"

"I wonder," said Aubrey, "they lived so long under such trials; not that they sunk under them so soon."

"Do go on, Aubrey," cried Tyrconnel, rather pettishly: and he obeyed.

Yes, Tyrconnel, yes, we took that painful oath; and, by the aid of heaven, we never can be said to have infringed it.

Once, when I was taken up apparently dead from a fall, poor Madeleine, as she wept over me, tried to revive me by the tenderest endearments; but on recovering my senses, she shrunk from my reproaching look and hurried from me with horror and self-abasement. In expiation of this involuntary offence it was that she resolved to go on that fortunate pilgrimage to the shrine of the Blessed Virgin, which led her to the hospitable kindness of Lady Barbara Delmayne.

But she previously inflicted on herself severe self-punishment of another kind: and the *marks* of this being perceived by the house-keeper, as she informed me, gave rise to her singular manner towards her, and to the uncalled-for visit of Father Vincent to her chamber.

But let me confess to you, what Madeleine herself owned in our last conversation, how utterly we *deceived ourselves*, in resolving to remain together on such hard conditions, and by the belief that we should thus perform the severest of penances. The truth was, that to us the GREATEST OF ALL TRIALS, and of *all penances*, was the idea of SEPARATION; and any trial was welcome, save that of ceasing to see and to hear each other. This I am convinced was the truth, so deceitful above every thing is the human heart! And well do I remember, that when assured I should not be forced to leave her, I became comparatively tranquil, nay comparatively *happy.* But, though happier than I *deserved* or *meant* to be, He who reads the heart knows that in this instance we *both* were *innocent* of *intentional* deceit; therefore, I do not regret the mitigated suffering which this self-deception occasioned.

But to return to the point whence I have digressed.

These vows which we have described will account for my strange coldness towards the dear sufferer, which I saw astonished and even displeased Lady Barbara.—I dare say she remembers the tone in which, when I told O'Carrol and Donald to carry Madeleine to the carriage, she exclaimed,

"Had you not better carry her yourself?"

And she must also remember how surprised she looked at my not approaching Madeleine when I first saw her after her escape from death.

("Oh yes! I shall never forget how strange I thought it!")

You too, Tyrconnel, reproached me with your looks, for not assisting her when she fainted. But one of the greatest pangs which we either of us felt was caused by our discovering the effects of our painful reserve upon our darling child.

But this was not of long continuance; for, deprived of recollection and self-command by her danger, both Madeleine and I called her by the name of our dear child, our beloved daughter: and Rosalie understood the deep yearnings of our hearts. She saw, and *sickened* at the sight; for, if she was our child, she feared she must also be the child of shame; and thence arose that bitter dejection for which we alone knew how to account. On her deathbed, Madeleine re-assured Rosalie upon this subject, and a change in her was instantly visible.

I have little to add, save that unalarmed we remained near fourteen years at Greenval; where, as I meant to educate Rosalie for the world and for retirement also, I made her mistress of Italian and French, and provided her other accomplishments. But though, owing to the extreme loneliness of our abode, we had no more fears of being found out, we there received information of an event which Madeleine, I believe, never recovered.

We had not been above two years at Greenval, when Madeleine grew uneasy concerning her sister; I therefore hired a peasant in the neighbourhood to go to the Castle of Monrose, and he returned with the sad intelligence that both the Earl and Countess were no more.

It was months before Madeleine held up her head after this terrible blow. She was always repeating, "No letter! no farewell! no notice from either of them!" At length, I convinced her that, while hiding ourselves so completely from our foes, we had hidden ourselves as completely from our friends.

I come now to the memorable night when Madeleine went on her pilgrimage. It was without my knowledge. I was asleep, unconscious of her danger, when a loud knock at the gate before day-break, roused and alarmed me. It was Donald. From him I learnt that a print of me was hanging up in the chamber of Father Vincent, *the priest*, an *officious prying man*, and a great *zealot*; and that should he suspect that I and Father Francesco were the same person, he would not rest till he found out the truth; which he would certainly do, by application to a brother of his, who was also brother to one of the Benedictines at Rome; and I could not in the end fail of being discovered. We therefore resolved that I should remove that very night, to avoid all risk of having my face scrutinized by the priest; and Donald advised us, as I told you before, to settle in the Isle of Wight.

The faithful creature, I found, was resolved to follow our fortunes, having on her deathbed promised his beloved mistress, if he could ever discover her sister, that he would never desert her.

I also found that Seraphina bequeathed her whole property, at her lord's desire, to Madeleine; that Monrose, feeling his death near, not knowing where to find us, as we had so suddenly left Aberdeen, had gone in person to his agent's in London, and there deposited the fortune left to Madeleine—taking Donald with him; and the agent, or his heirs, or executors, were to keep that money in trust, and never let any part of it be touched, except Donald Cameron brought an order for such a payment, or sent a person accredited to receive it by the said Donald Cameron.

Not long afterwards Lord Monrose breathed his last at his house in London, having left a considerable bequest to the niece of his Seraphina; and Donald, having long vainly sought us, entered into the service of Lord Delmayne.

You know the rest. I came and bore away Madeleine and Rosalie, escorted by Donald, to this retreat; and as I wished to restore the chapel to its former beauty, I sent Donald to claim some part of Madeleine's legacy, which in eighteen years had accumulated to a large amount.

But though obliged to give up the pleasure of seeing Lady Barbara, her image pursued me everywhere. "If she resembles the lost Seraphina so strongly in countenance," we used to say to each other, "surely she must resemble her also in mind; and that benevolent smile, and those courteous manners, must be the result of genuine kindness of nature." We therefore resolved to bequeath our Rosalie to her pity and protection.

Yes, dearest Lady Barbara! in the cheerless night of our desponding souls, anxious for the fate of our only treasure, your image beamed brightly upon us like the light from some building at a distance, which cheers the weary traveller on his journey.

More than protection, however we might wish it, we did not dare to hope—nor dare I now. And yet, listen ye happy parents of noble youths! listen, ye who are high in rank and rich in worldly prosperity, to the representation of one in birth *at least* your *equal*, and once as richly gifted with every thing that can call forth the glow of pride in man!

He is now on his bed of death! There he has learnt the emptiness of all worldly grandeur, and of all distinctions save those of virtue and piety!

Rosalie is pious; Rosalie is pure. But then I own she is the child of parents who committed great sin before they could be the authors of her being; and I should not wonder, if dread of the world's scorn on such an alliance deter you from approving it. But why must the world know that Rosalie, Countess Manfredi di Guastalla, is the child of *Sister Angela and of Father Francesco?*

No: if it be your will, the *stone* which covers my mouldering remains and those of the partner of my error, may also hide our sorrow, our shame, our names, and our penitence.

When this sad narrative shall be known to you, I probably shall be on the point of appearing before my final Judge!

Short and few have been my hours of happiness on earth: but you, Lord Bellamore, may, if you choose it, bestow on my expiring moments, a happiness denied me throughout a painful life. Give my daughter to your son, and let me go my way rejoicing!

RINALDO, COUNT MANFREDI DI GUASTALLA.

When Aubrey had finished the MS. a short expressive silence ensued. It was broken by Lord Delmayne, who observed, that certainly no one need know who Rosalie's parents were; and that if they took her abroad with them, and Lord and Lady Bellamore followed them with Tyrconnel, he might return to England, bringing with him a rich and noble Italian bride; and what more need transpire?

"But we should know more ourselves," said Lord Bellamore.

"Yes," said Lady Delmayne, "and we should also know that she was the child of wicked people."

"Nay, now, Lady Delmayne, you are very severe," said Lord Bellamore.

"And very unjust, too," cried her lord, whose heart had been softened toward the dying man, by the love and admiration which he had testified toward Lady Barbara. "And really I must say—"

"Remember, oh! remember," cried Lady Barbara, starting up with a look of terror, "that while you are deliberating, poor Manfredi is dying, and may die, perhaps, without ever having known one moment's real happiness. Think of that, you *happy, happy* people!"

"Dear father, must he die unblest?" cried Aubrey.

Tyrconnel did not speak; but he threw himself on his father's neck, and wept.

"My lord and father, hear us," cried Lady Barbara, falling at Lord Bellamore's feet, while Aubrey clasped his arm round his kneeling wife, and sunk beside her. Lady Delmayne spoke not. Her lord, too, was silent; for, though his heart was with the pleaders, he felt that Lord Bellamore ought to be left to the influence of his children alone.

"Hark!" cried Lady Barbara, "there is a noise in the room above; perhaps he is dying!" and Tyrconnel looked up imploringly in the face of Lord Bellamore.

"What says your mother, Tyrconnel?"

Tyrconnel clasped her knees in silence.

"Say! That she wishes her son happy, to be sure," she replied: and while Tyrconnel folded her in his arms, Lord Bellamore, in a fluttering voice, added, "Then the Countess Rosalie shall be Tyrconnel's wife!"

"Blessed hearing!" cried Lady Barbara, flying through the door; and in an instant she was at the bedside of the dying Manfredi.

"Angelic being!" cried he, "I see you bring me joy!"

"Yes," cried she, grasping his chill cold hand: "HE CONSENTS."

At this moment, Lord Bellamore, leaning on his son, and followed by the whole group, entered the room. Manfredi, with eager eyes, gazed on what was passing. Lord Bellamore, too full at heart to speak, then took the hand of Rosalie, and placed it silently in that of Tyrconnel. The action spoke for him; but recovering his firmness, he laid a hand on the head of each, as they kneeled before him, and faltered out, "My children! God bless you together!"

"Enough!" murmured out Manfredi: "I thank you, and I die happy!"

Rosalie now sprung forward to catch his last parting look. It was hers, and his lips moved as if he blessed her. The next moment, the movement was gone. He pressed his crucifix to his heart, and he lay in the STILLNESS and SILENCE OF DEATH.

END OF LOVE, MYSTERY, AND SUPERSTITION.

AFTER THE BALL;

OR, THE TWO SIR WILLIAMS.

THE family of Sir John Wallington, a Yorkshire baronet, consisting of Lady Wallington, a son, two daughters, and a niece (the daughter of an elder brother), were preparing one evening for a public ball in their neighbourhood, with great but varied expectations of pleasure.

The anticipations of Lady Wallington would have been the most enviable, had not the prospect of seeing the admiration which her daughters would excite, been sullied by the hope of witnessing the mortification of those mothers whose daughters were contesting the palm of beauty with her own; while Miss Wallington and her sister Laura were too conscious of their personal charms, and too desirous of having the best partners in the room, to experience any feelings dear to the heart of benevolence.

Their brother, perhaps, was actuated by a more amiable selfishness; for he expected to meet his old college friend, Sir William Dormer, who had lately succeeded to an estate in the neighbourhood, and was a desirable match for one of his sisters. He also hoped to meet there another friend, Sir William Maberley, who, though not possessed of so large a property, might, he thought, suit the other sister.

He therefore anticipated valuable additions to his domestic circle, and his head was full of family aggrandizement. Besides, Major Wallington had also views for himself; Sir William Dormer had a sister, who lived with him, and who had inherited an immense fortune from her grandfather; and she was to make her first appearance that evening, previously to presiding at a ball which her brother and herself were to give the ensuing week, and to which they had already invited those who had paid their respects at Park Place.

But neither the sister nor the brother was as yet personally known to any one in the county, except Major Wallington. He therefore thought, and on good grounds, that an immediate introduction to his own family would be a desirable thing to these young strangers. His cousin Caroline had also *her* anticipations; but they were of a more humble nature. She felt, that in the presence of Anna and Laura she was not likely to be noticed; still, however, she was eager to see the two young men who might be, as she was told, her future relations; and she was even more desirous to see Miss Dormer, as she had heard much of her amiable qualities, and fancied she might find in her a companion better suited to her retiring nature than the showy and flattered Miss Wallingtons.

The coach was now ordered round; and the Major had taken his mother's hand to lead her down stairs, when he received letters by express from his commanding officer, which compelled his immediate departure. He promised, however, to return as soon as he could; and telling him they must introduce themselves to his friend Maberley, for whom he should order a bed, and who would, he trusted, attend them home, he bade them farewell.

When the ladies reached the ball-room, they found, that though Miss Dormer was there, neither of the Baronets had arrived.

However, respectable partners offered immediately for the three young ladies, and they joined the set; but Miss Wallington, who had always been used to begin the dance in that room, could hardly see with complacence, Miss Dormer, as the daughter of the elder Baronet, taking the lead.

This ball in other respects had nothing in it to distinguish it from former balls; but the Miss Wallingtons found it different from what their high-raised expectations had anticipated. In the first place, neither their brother nor his two friends were there; in the next, Miss Dormer did not desire to be introduced to them; and a feeling of pique made them for once not willing to put themselves forward, and request to be presented to her. Thirdly, they saw, that though not presented, Caroline had already formed an acquaintance with the heiress, and that it was evident she was pre-possessed in their cousin's favour, as she made her a distinguishing curtsy on leaving the room. They were, however, made some amends by the sudden appearance of their brother, though evidently dressed for a journey, just as their carriage was ordered, bringing with him his friend the Baronet, whom he was introducing as his friend Sir William — when he was suddenly called away, and could only add, "I am very sorry that I am forced to leave you, Sir William; but I am sure my mother and sisters will be proud to do all they can to entertain you, and they expect you to accompany them home."

The Baronet bowed — Lady Wallington smiled and curtsied, as did her daughters, and the former saying that her carriage was at the door, Sir William, after placing them in it, took his station, in spite of all entreaties, on the coach-box, leaving the ladies at liberty to comment on his person and manner, and to wonder whether Sir William Dormer was as handsome as this, their new guest, Sir William Maberley.

When they reached Old Hall, Lady Wallington's first inquiry was for Sir John; but he was just gone to bed.

"Then he can't be asleep," murmured Lady Wallington; and she hastened to his bedside, to tell him Sir William Maberley was below, and he must rise to do the honours of Old Hall to him.

"And pray, what for?"

"Why, because he is James's friend—and —and for your daughters' sake, as it may be a good thing for them, you know."

"But a very bad thing for me to get up with the gout in my great-toe; therefore, for my own sake, I shall stay where I am; and I will not get up for all the Sir Williams, and all the daughters in the world."

"Selfish and self-willed as usual," muttered Lady Wallington, as she left the chamber, throwing the door to rather loudly, considering her husband's gout; and when she entered the dining-room, where a handsome supper had been prepared, she assured Sir William, that, but for a very bad fit of the gout, Sir John would have risen to welcome him to Old Hall, and that he desired her to assure her guest, he was *au désespoir* not to be able to enjoy his society.

The young Baronet, who was by no means a man of words, and from a sort of *mauvaise honte*, only too common to Englishmen, was never quite at ease with strangers, only bowed in return; and the party sat down to supper.

It was now increased by the presence of a lady whom Miss Wallington had graciously gone to summon, and now as graciously supported on her arm into the room; for youth and beauty appeared, she well knew, to great advantage, while lending their aid to infirmity.

This lady, on being introduced to Sir William by the name of Mrs. Norman, took care to call his attention to this trifling piece of benevolence, by observing,

"My sweet young friend's angelic attention makes me not feel my lameness;" while the sweet young friend seated her by herself, and, patting her on the shoulder, insisted on her making a good supper, as she had been so foolish as to sit up on purpose to hear all about the ball.

"Well, but you have told me nothing yet."

"No, nor can I, till I have supped. Sir William, be so good as to help me to a leg of that chicken."

He obeyed. In the meanwhile the lame lady was questioning Miss Wallington, and whether she and her sister had made *any new conquests*.

"Nonsense!" cried both the young ladies at once; but Mrs. Norman, who knew such questions were usually welcome, had not tact enough to feel that they might be ill-timed in the presence of a stranger; and she still went on with,

"Well! and was the handsome young baronet, Sir William Dormer, there?"

"No; he was not," petulantly returned Miss Wallington, while the handsome young baronet who *was* present, looked up with a strong expression of astonishment; but he said nothing, and Miss Wallington feared that he was shocked at the petulance with which she had replied.

"Well, my Lady, and how did you like the ball?" resumed the *impracticable* Mrs. Norman. "But no doubt you liked it, and, as usual, felt yourself favoured of mothers?"

Lady Wallington smiled complacently, and said, "Yes, I felt that I was a fortunate mother; but there were others as much so. The Miss Selvyns looked lovely to-night, only they were *comme de coutume*, over-dressed. Their mother, though she has long been a private gentleman's wife, can't forget she was once on the stage; and she loads them and herself with such trumpery finery!"

"Ay, she does indeed; but you are too candid: the Selvyns can't look lovely."

"Oh! mamma quite patronizes their beauty, you know, Mrs. Norman; and I am sure it needs patronage. To-night these lovely creatures looked as red as red cabbage, and red cabbage dipped in oil too."

"Oh, you clever creature! that was so like you!"

Miss Wallington, gratified by this praise of her wit, and fancying it would add to the piquancy of her beauty, went on with her observations.

"Yes, mamma is so over-candid. There was Mrs. O'Connor sprawling about her large limbs in a quadrille, and mamma looking on and asking me if I did not think the handsome widow improved in her dancing!"

"Well, indeed, *I* thought she was," said Caroline Wallington, with a timid manner and a blushing cheek.

"Ay, and so did I," said Miss Laura.

"There, Anne; it is three to one against you," observed Lady Wallington.

"No matter: I may be out-voted, but not convinced. All I can own is, that Mrs. O'Connor's foot has now a *plan to pursue*, since she took lessons in town; and before it was '*a mighty maze*, and *quite without a plan;*' and as this foot kicked in all directions, she ought in common humanity to have cried out to those nearest her, ' Gare toes, gare toes!'"

This lively sally, which she thought witty, drew forth smiles from Lady Wallington and her complaisant friend. But Miss Laura said, "You are always so severe, Anne!" and Caroline looked very grave, while she observed, "How handsome Mrs. O'Connor is, *even now!*"

"She would not thank you for that compliment, with the '*even now*' tacked to it; but you think everybody handsome, Caroline. I really do believe—don't blush—that you think *yourself* so."

"No, indeed, cousin Anne, that I do not," replied the poor girl, covered with the most becoming blushes; "and I am sure you do not think I ever did; and you only say it to—"

"To what?" cried Anne, rising and hiding her anger at the unuttered word under a smile, while she threw her beautiful arms gracefully round her agitated cousin, and kissed her cheek with seeming affection, "What did I do it for, dear Cary?"

Caroline had not courage now to say, "To tease me:" and while Sir William gazed on the exquisite form and graceful attitude of Miss Wallington, and saw her caressing manner towards her cousin, he forgot (as she thought he would) the unkind raillery which had produced it.

Miss Wallington returned to her seat, agreeably conscious that the Baronet's eyes followed her with admiration.

"Well," now observed the curious Mrs. Norman; "well, and so Sir William Dormer, to the disappointment of all the young ladies, was not there, after all."

"Not to my disappointment, I assure you," cried Miss Wallington, scornfully; "for I have been told he is very proud, reserved, and conceited, and not very good-looking."

"Dear me, Anne," cried her sister, "how changeable you are! It was only to-day that you said you would give any thing to know if he would be at the ball, and whether he liked fair or brown women."

"Nonsense! No such thing," replied Anne, blushing with anger at hearing her real sentiments thus exposed before Sir William Maberley; but Laura provokingly went on to say, "Yes, it is *true*, sister; and you know what you said about Miss Dormer's ball, and about opening it with her brother."

Miss Wallington's reply was now prevented by Sir William's rising suddenly, and saying that it grew late, and he must go. But it was in vain that he made the attempt; Anne, with an air and a manner which she had often found irresistible, playfully set her back against the door, and looked up in his face with a fascinating smile; and while Sir William muttered a few unintelligible words, he suffered himself to be persuaded back to his seat: but it was evident that he was not at ease, and that though he resumed his chair, he did not resume his composure.

"It is very strange," said Caroline, "that not one of us has yet mentioned the great novelty of the evening, the young heiress, Miss Dormer."

"The less that is said of her the better, perhaps," observed Anne, "though it is wrong to judge of any one at first sight. I own, I was terribly disappointed in her."

"Indeed!" replied Caroline: "I am sure she quite equalled my expectations, high raised as they were."

"High raised! And pray, child," said Lady Wallington, "what could you know of Miss Dormer?"

"Oh! I know an intimate friend, a schoolfellow of hers; and she described her as all that was amiable, and indeed she looks so. Why, is it possible, cousin Anne, that you do not think her face and countenance beautiful?"

"Beautiful! she is deformed."

"Her face is not; and the defect in her shape I should never have found out, if it had not been pointed out to me."

"No!—Why, her wretched style of dress called one's attention to it; it was so showy, and so unbecoming!"

"I must own it was too rich and splendid to suit my taste," said Caroline.

"Or your pocket either, my dear," said Lady Wallington: "and Miss Dormer could have no *eye*, no taste, to adopt it."

"I dare say, dear aunt," replied Caroline, "Miss Dormer did not choose her own dress: I suspect that sweet-looking old lady with her chose it for her."

"And why?"

"Because she seemed so pleased with her appearance, and surveyed her and it with so much delight; and then she *stroked it down* with such complacence just before Miss Dormer began to dance; and looking so affectionately and so like a mother at her, I really could not help envying Miss Dormer a friend so *like a parent*; and I am told she lives with her, and *is* quite a mother to her. How delightful!"

Here the eyes of the warm-hearted girl filled with tears of affectionate regret; for she had not very long been an orphan. But less tender tears succeeded, when Lady Wallington with no very soothing tone exclaimed, "Caroline,

you surprise me! I had flattered myself that you had found an affectionate mother in me, and sisters in your cousins; and that *you*, of *all* persons in the world, were not likely to envy Miss Dormer, or Miss *any* one. Really, Caroline, I did not think you had been so ungrateful!"

"Ungrateful! I! ungrateful!" cried the agitated girl, casting an appealing look at Lady Wallington. Then, unable to restrain her tears, she left the room.

"I assure you, Sir William," said Lady Wallington, in the gentlest accents, "that girl, when her father, a most extravagant man, died, was received into our family, to be maintained by us, and has ever been considered and treated as a daughter."

"*That* she has," cried Mrs. Norman: "you may say so indeed."

"Nay, I claim no merit for what I did; it was only our duty. But I am very sorry that I have hurt the child's feelings. I think, Laura, or Anne, you had better go to your cousin."

"Poor dear girl! I will go, mamma," cried Laura, who had the acuteness to see, by Sir William's downcast eye and continued silence, though addressed by his hostess, that the scene and the confidence reposed displeased him.

"Kind, good creature!" exclaimed Mrs. Norman. "Well, Lady Wallington, I have always said you are the happiest of mothers!"

When Caroline returned, the traces of recent tears were still visible on her cheek; and they almost began to flow again, on her aunt's kindly taking her hand, and, saying she was a foolish child to be so soon overset, told her she must, as a proof of forgiveness, eat the pastry which she offered her. Caroline obeyed her; looking up in her face as she prepared to do so, with so sweet and touching an expression of patient resignation, that Sir William, who caught the look, wondered he had not observed her sooner, and began to find out, that though Anne and Laura were strikingly handsome, they had not the beauty of countenance which distinguished Caroline.— Besides, he *pitied* her, and he remembered too, that she had eulogized and defended Miss Dormer.

"By the by, Caroline," said Miss Wallington, "you must explain to me, how it happened that you were the only one of our party whom the proud heiress deigned to notice. For my part, I thought it *her* place to desire to be introduced to *me*, as I saw that she felt herself my superior.—I *dare say* she only took her right precedence; but, as she was a stranger, and I, you know, usually begin the dance, I thought she might have *offered* me the place, though I should not have accepted it."

"You had no *right* to accept it, Anne," cried Laura, who was never sorry to mortify her domineering sister. "If Miss Dormer had waived her right at all, as the daughter of the elder baronet, it would have been in favour of Caroline, the child of papa's eldest brother, who ought always to stand above you."

"O dear!" replied the provoked Miss Wallington, "I always forget that Caroline has precedence of me; and I suppose from this time forward, as she and Miss Dormer seem to be already tender friends, I must make up my mind to see her *pressed* into the place of honour at balls."

"Miss Caroline knows *her* place better than to accept it, I am sure," observed Mrs. Norman, tossing up her head; "nor can I think, but that when Miss Dormer knows you, my sweet young friend, she will be eager to do you every honour in her power. But, perhaps, as she is very young, she might be *awed* by your dignified manner, and a little feeling of jealousy might prevent her seeking to know you; and—"

"Miss Dormer jealous, madam!" cried Caroline eagerly: "Oh! that is quite *impossible.*"

"Why, really the heiress and her smiles have turned thy head, Cary," said Anne, trying to conceal her spleen. "But come, explain how you were introduced."

"Oh! her waist-riband came unpinned in the dance; and,—and as that sweet-looking old lady was not near her, I offered to pin it for her."

"Well, for a modest, timid girl, that was tolerably forward, Cary."

"Dear! do you think so?"

"It was very *kind,*" said Sir William, breaking for the first time a long silence. "And what did Miss Dormer say to you?"

"She thanked me, and in such a tone of voice, and with such a smile, that I ventured, as I stood near her, to tell her I knew a friend of hers; and so we talked together the rest of the evening, whenever we had an opportunity."

"Quite a romantic friendship begun at first sight!" cried Miss Wallington: "I see, Laura, you and I have no chance now of pleasing either the brother or the sister; it is *place prise*, and Cary carries all before her."

"Nay, dear Miss Wallington," said Mrs. Norman, "how can you talk so? I would lay any wager that Sir William Dormer will begin the ball at his own house with you."

"What! in defiance of Caroline's *rights,* on which Laura has been so eloquent?" sarcastically answered Miss Wallington. "Cary," she continued, "I wish you would, as a friend, advise Miss Dormer not to dance quadrilles, for her's really is not a figure to exhibit. I own, by padding, her crookedness is as much hidden as possible, and it might be possibly unnoticed in a country dance, but in a quadrille it must be obvious to all the world."

"I conclude you are joking," said Caroline, blushing. "I could never presume to wound any one's feelings by such advice; and after all, where there is so much to admire as there is in Miss Dormer, it would surely be most unkind in the by-standers to remark only her sole defect."

"Unkind! Was that aimed at me, madam?"

"Oh dear! No; it was a *general* observation."

"Pray," said Mrs. Norman, seeing the cloud gathering on the brow of the haughty Anne, "do tell me who this Miss Dormer is like? Can you, Miss Caroline, describe your idol? or did her effulgence blind you too much?"

"Really, madam, I cannot say whom she is like."

"She is like you," said Sir William, smiling with great complacency on Caroline: "I never saw two countenances more alike."

"Like her!" exclaimed Mrs. Norman: "why, I thought some one said she was handsome."

"So she *is,* madam, in my eyes," returned Sir William coldly. Caroline blushed with surprise and pleasure, while the sisters bit their lips.

Lady Wallington at length, after hemming to get rid of an involuntary *hoarseness*, remarked, "You know Miss Dormer, then?"

"Perfectly, madam."

"Perhaps you will be at her ball?"

"Certainly," he replied, smiling; "for—and—and"——Here some strange embarrassment broke off his speech; and looking at his watch, he suddenly rose, declared it was very late, and hastily bowing, prepared to depart.

"Oh no, indeed! you must not leave us yet," cried Lady Wallington: "perhaps you are musical, Sir William! Anne and Laura, perhaps Sir William would like to hear a duet?" Sir William declared he should be delighted; and Caroline sat down to accompany her cousins, who sung a duet.

The sisters sung admirably; and Caroline, in Sir Willim's opinion, accompanied admirably; but her cousins found fault with her, and the poor girl humbly asked their pardon.

Anne now challenged Sir William to dance a reel of three, and he accepted the challenge; while Caroline continued at the instrument. The reel over, the graceful sisters, preparing for a waltz, desired Caroline to play slowly and as well as she could. She did so; and Sir William surveyed with admiration their fine figures and graceful motions; but Caroline, whose whole soul was in the bewitching air, and whose countenance, as she gazed on her cousins, expressed the generous pleasure with which she beheld their excellence, did *more* than share his admiration with the dancers, till, much to their surprise and hers, he moved to the side of the instrument, and cried, "Bravo! bravo!" to her expressive playing.

This was the signal for the sisters to leave off waltzing: they hoped, however, that Sir William would offer to waltz with them, and give them an opportunity to show their sense of propriety by assuring him that they only *waltzed with each other:* but he was hanging over Caroline's chair, and begging her to indulge him with that waltz again. She obeyed, but with a tremulous hand and a bewildered mind; for she was confused by such gratifying and unusual approbation, and observed her severely-judging relations with sarcastic smiles watching her execution, till at last she was forced to declare her inability to go on—begging her cousins, who were so much more able, would take her place. Anne did so, and played what she called a voluntary, in a masterly style. "There, Sir William!" cried Caroline, "that *is* playing!"

"And so was yours, in a different style."

He then complimented Anne on her perfect command of the instrument. She then played an *adagio* and a slow waltz; but Sir William did not praise the latter, nor encore it as he had done Caroline's.

Caroline now entreated her cousin Laura to sing her favourite song. "I will," she replied, "if you will accompany me, and promise *not to blunder.*"

"I will try," she meekly replied; and Laura sung as follows:—

SONG.

"Whene'er the moon, in silver pride,
   Illumes the soft-reflecting tide,
   And spreads reviving lustre wide,
Oh! then I think on thee, Henry.

For so upon my darken'd view
   Thy love reviving splendours threw;
   While life thou badest to shine anew,
And smile once more on me, Henry.

But ah! when o'er the rolling wave
   I see destructive tempests rave,
   While nought can struggling sailors save—
Then, *then* I think on thee, Henry.

For now thy heart is mine no more,
   To me life's cheering light is o'er;
   Despair's dark billows round me roar,
And thou *hast* shipwreck'd *me*, Henry."

The third verse was to a quick movement with a rapid bass, which Caroline executed so well, that Sir William could not help applauding her; and when the song was over, Caroline said with great *naïveté*, "Well! I could never have supposed that while Laura was singing, any one could have heard my accompaniment!"

Her cousins were as much surprised as she was; and when Sir William next declared he must go, they did not press him to stay, though Lady Wallington said, "We expected you would sleep here, and a bed is prepared."

"A bed! is it possible? I have but a very little way to go, and I ought to have gone away long since, as my carriage has been here some time."

Then, not allowing Lady Wallington time to ring, he darted out of the room, and they heard him drive off.

"I could lay any wager, Sir William Maberley is in love with Miss Dormer," cried Laura, as soon as he was gone.

"O heavens! if he is, how he must hate me!" said Anne.

"And like Caroline!" cried Laura.

"Yes; and if so, no wonder he thought Caroline by implication handsome. Upon my word, it would mortify *me* to be thought so by a man evidently so devoid of taste."

"Well said, Conceit!" cried Laura: "but you are always so satirical, Anne, and always cut up people so unmercifully."

"With a little of your assistance, my candid sister: if I use the knife, you hold the body."

"Be quiet, girls!" cried Lady Wallington: "you know I can't bear to hear your constant bickerings with each other."

"Well mamma, I did not begin—Laura attacked me first."

"I know it."

"And what did I say, mamma? Nothing very severe; and I am sure it is all true."

"Perhaps so; but——"

"*Perhaps* so! I like your saying that, Lady Wallington; for who is so severe as yourself? I am sure, if your daughters are so, they learnt it from *you.*"

"Very dutiful, indeed, Miss Wallington! But it is my own fault: my indulgence, and the tenderness of my nature, my exquisite maternal feelings, which led me never to deny you any thing, have brought on me this ungrateful return."

"Ungrateful! No, madam, we are not ungrateful!" exclaimed both the sisters at once, united now in a common cause.

"You talk of your exquisite maternal feelings, indeed!" cried one. "Your *selfish* ones you mean," cried the other, "which would not let you be at the trouble of correcting us. Had you done your duty by us, we should have been grateful. If I am violent in temper, who *made* me so?"

"If Anne and I quarrel more than sisters should, it is owing to your partiality for her when she was a child, which made me dislike her; and which your apparent love for me since I grew up and have been thought as handsome as Anne, has never banished from my memory."

"As handsome as *I* am!" cried Anne, fire flashing from her eyes: "you vain——"

Here she was interrupted by a violent scream from Lady Wallington, which ended in a fit; and this "happiest of mothers" was carried to bed in strong hysterics, brought on by the unkindness of her spoiled children.

Mrs. Norman, the *toad-eater* of the family, meanwhile, *now at least* was sincere, and gave way to a *natural* feeling, when she muttered to herself, though loud enough for Caroline to hear, before she followed her screaming friend and the now penitent daughters to Lady Wallington's apartment, "What vile tempers they all have! I am sure no one would live with them who could live anywhere else. Do you not agree with me, Miss Caroline?" shrugging up her shoulders, and looking up in Caroline's face, with all the contempt which she felt for her tyrannical relation.

But she met with no answering glance from the high-principled Caroline; who, elevating her head with the pride of virtuous feeling, replied to her, "I believe you forget, madam, that you are speaking to me of my relations, and that I am the object of their bounty."

So saying, she hastened to her aunt's apartment; and it was Caroline who performed a daughter's duty by her, and watched by her bedside. Lady Wallington woke, after an hour's forgetfulness, and asked, "Who is there? is it Anne or Laura?"

"No: it is *I*, dear aunt," replied Caroline.

"You!"

"Yes; my cousins were so tired, they were forced to go to bed."

"And were not *you* tired?"

"Oh dear! not in the least."

"And *you* did not make me *ill*!"

"Indeed, dear aunt, my cousins were very sorry to go, but they were quite overpowered. They, however, desired me to call them, if you were ill again."

"Indeed! Well, that was much for *them*: but it is all my own fault; and you, Caroline—you, whom —— You are a kind, affectionate creature, Caroline, and I will not forget it."

Here she heaved a deep sigh, and was silent, if not asleep again.

Caroline spoke the truth when she said she was not tired; for the occurrences of the former part of the evening had exhilarated her so much, that she was not conscious of fatigue. In the first place, she had become acquainted with Miss Dormer, and had evidently been regarded by her with partiality. In the next place, the handsomest and most agreeable-looking man whom she had ever seen had thought her like Miss Dormer, whom *she* believed *beautiful*, and *he* thought *handsome*. She, the plain Caroline, as she had always been taught to consider herself; she, who had always been told it was a wonderful thing if she had good partners and many of them, because she had so few personal pretensions, had that evening evidently *more* than divided with her cousins the attentions of this very pleasing man; and a feeling of self-complacency, which she had never experienced before, gratified her artless and innocent bosom. "*I* like Miss Dormer! impossible!" she said to herself: then going on tiptoe to the glass, she endeavoured to contemplate her features by the light of the lamp in the chimney; but she could only see them imperfectly, and she returned disappointed to her chair.

However, the same thoughts again recurred; while again the wish returned to gaze upon those features which now, for the first time, had gained importance in her eyes. She therefore made another effort, and took the lamp to the glass, instead of carrying, as she had before done, the glass to the lamp; but in so doing, she struck the lamp against the drawers, and awoke her aunt, who exclaimed, "What noise is that?" Luckily, however, for Caroline, who would not lie, and who would have blushed to own the truth, she fell asleep again, without waiting for an answer.

Caroline now returned the lamp to its place, without another attempt to profit by its light; for her rightly-feeling mind was shocked to think she had, in order to indulge a trumpery vanity, disturbed the rest of one whose slumbers she was pretending to guard; and she now sighed, while she thought how soon that mind which she had once fancied could not be upset, was capable of being misled, if the same incense was applied to her self-love. "I see that I should have been like my cousins, if I had had the same temptations:" and while her heart glowed with pious thankfulness for exemption from their dangers, she felt the most generous indulgence for their errors, and the sentiment of self-blame for having ever judged them severely.

It was not till six o'clock that Lady Wallington woke; when, assuring Caroline that she was quite recovered, she insisted on her retiring to bed, and calling her own maid to her.

The breakfast that morning at Old Hall was much later even than usual. Caroline, on entering the room, was surprised to see her uncle there, but not surprised to behold him looking, as usual, the stern dictator; especially as the gout, she knew, was no sweetener of the temper. The sight of her, however, smoothed his perturbed brow. "What! Cary up already?" cried he: "this is a comfort I did not expect, as thou hast been up all night, child! Come hither, my girl—come, and tie this handkerchief round my foot: those clumsy-fingered girls can't do it at all. I protest, there is no one in the house good for any thing but thy little self."

Caroline obeyed. "So, ladies," he then added, "I find you take advantage of my absence to quarrel with your silly fond mother, and throw her into those horrible squalling fits of hers. But, mark me! I will have no one abusive in this house but myself; and if you do not obey me, you shall rue it. And I find, too, that instead of staying with her, to show your penitence, you went to bed, and let that sweet unoffending girl sit up."

"Dear me, papa," cried Laura, "it was only an hysteric: there was no need to sit up, only Caroline chose to do it."

"Caroline always chooses to do right. Come hither, and give me a kiss, dear."

"What an owl the child looks to-day!"

observed Anne, spitefully, being piqued at her father's commendation of Caroline.

"She only looks like one who has had no *sleep*, Miss Pert! And why had she not? Because she was performing the duty you neglected. Though not the *handsomest*, Caroline is the *best* girl in the world."

Here the two sisters forced a violent "Ha! ha! ha!" as if in derision, while Caroline was secretly thankful that she had already restored her mind to its *wonted* state of humility on the score of her *own beauty*; else her cousins' remark and her uncle's comment would have mortified her exceedingly. She was also prepared for the further mortifications of which her cousins' laughter was, she knew, the forerunner.

"Pray what does that confounded cackle mean? for laugh it was not: explain," said Sir John, in a loud tone.

"Why, papa, there is a gentleman in the world, who, by *implication*, at least, thinks Cary *handsome*—no less a man than our guest of last night."

"Does he? Then he is a sensible man, and I honour him; for 'handsome is that handsome does:' and if he could only see Cary nurse me in a fit of the gout—see how lightly she trips along the floor, and how gently her beautiful little fingers tie on my shoes, I should not wonder if he thought her *beautiful*; and if he has a tendency to gout, Cary's fortune would be made directly. What say you, girl—could you like Sir William?"

This unexpected question made all the blood fly from her heart to her cheeks, for she had ventured to whisper to herself that perhaps she could have liked Sir William, if it had been possible that he could have liked her; and Mrs. Norman, enjoying her confusion, said, "Poor Miss Cary! what a pity it is Sir William seems enamoured of Miss Dormer!"

Here a sharp twinge of the gout caused Sir John to exclaim violently, and taking Caroline's arm, he hobbled to his study and his couch.

It was now only two days to Sir William and Miss Dormer's ball, and the sisters were busily employed in making preparations. They had bespoken dresses from London, which were the objects of daily admiration. Caroline was forced to content herself with an old dress; and she virtuously endeavoured to hush the murmurs of her vanity, by the conviction that a dress like that of her cousins', especially as her other was still as good as new, would have been highly unbecoming her dependent situation.

Still, in spite of her self-discipline, she could not help being most unphilosophically delighted, when, on Miss Wallington's asking Caroline whether she did not mean to wear some new trimming, her aunt replied, "There is no necessity for it, as I have by to-day's post ordered her a dress exactly like your own—except that, as she is not so tall or large as you are, she is to have a flounce less, and the branches of flowers are to be smaller."

The sisters were at first silent from mortification, and Caroline from pleasurable emotion; while Mrs. Norman exclaimed, "What attention and generosity!"

"Say, rather, 'What justice!'" said Lady Wallington: "I only have remembered as I ought that good girl's attention to me."

"My dear aunt," cried Caroline, seizing her hand, and finding her power to speak return, "how you overrate my little services! which, after all, are only your due. But I never wore a dress with such pleasure as I shall wear this: I wish it was come. How I long to see it! I hope Miss Dormer will admire it, because I shall have such pleasure in saying it was my aunt's present for the occasion!"

"I think, madam, you might have consulted my sister and *me*, before you ordered Caroline a dress exactly like *ours*. You know we always dress alike; but we make a point of Caroline's dressing differently."

"Then the more shame for you, as she is your first-cousin, and moreover the child of the elder brother."

"There is no reason for you to throw that in my teeth always."

"Dear me, Anne," cried Laura, "how can you be disconcerted at Caroline's being dressed like us? Dresses look so different on tall women to what they do on little creatures like her, that I dare say no one will see her dress is like ours; especially as it is to have a flounce less."

"True! But no: as Cary is coming out in a *new* character—that of a *beauty*—the chances are that she and her dress alone will be remarked, and we and ours utterly overlooked."

Here they attempted to laugh; while their mother, whose affection had been somewhat alienated by their undutiful behaviour, enjoyed their mortification, and, telling Caroline she knew she had too much greatness of mind to be annoyed by their raillery, desired her to go with her into her apartment, and read one of Crabbe's Tales to her.

When Caroline appeared at dinner that day, every one observed that she looked thoughtful, and was frequently on the point of saying something; and when her aunt and cousins remarked, that they thought it strange Sir William Maberley had not called, they saw that Caroline's countenance had a peculiar expression.

"Come, Cary, out with what you wish to say; for I have watched you for some time, and I am sure you have something to communicate, but want resolution," said Sir John.

"Yes; really I wish to say something; but I am afraid you will laugh at me, and—"

"Laugh at you, Cary? Who shall dare to laugh at you in *my presence*, ha!"

Here he gave his daughters one of his fiercest looks, and Caroline ventured to ask, "Pray, dear aunt, are you *quite sure* who the gentleman was that supped with us last night?"

"What fancy has she got in her head now?" muttered Anne.

"Silence!" vociferated Sir John. "*Answer*, Lady Wallington; I hope you did not bring home a *sharper* with you?"

"No: certainly not, for your son introduced him to us."

"Yes: but what did he call him? Did you hear him *distinctly* say, Sir William Maberley? I certainly heard him say only Sir William; for he just then turned away."

"Well Cary, and what then?"

"Why, sir, I have my suspicions that—that—"

"Oh! I see it all now," said Anne, with one of her most provoking laughs: "Cary thinks—nay hopes perhaps, that our guest was really Sir William Dormer, and not Sir William Maberley; and *if so*, she thinks *we* have no chance of being Lady Dormer, and she certainly has—"

"No, indeed," replied Caroline, "I am not so conceited; but I have some reason for my suspicions."

"I *hope* not, my dear," said Lady Wallington gravely; "for, if so, I should be ashamed to look Sir William Dormer in the face."

"And so should I, I am *sure*, mamma."

"I also, and all of us but Caroline. But quick, your *reasons*, Cary?"

"When I first began to have my suspicions, I asked the butler whither Sir William ordered his postilion to drive; and he said that he called out Home! Now Sir William Maberley lives in another county, and he certainly told us he had his own carriage and horses."

"I declare there is some probability in what Cary says. But go on."

"What made you first suspect?"

"The *gloom*, and the *very* odd look which I remembered to have seen on his countenance, when you were so—when you were criticising Miss Dormer, and the pleasure which his looks expressed when I defended her."

"Well, but if he was *her lover*, he would have looked the same."

"Yes; but remember that he got up and tried to go away when you talked of Sir William Dormer; and I saw every now and then, that though he looked confused, the corners of his mouth showed that he could hardly help laughing."

"I cannot say I watched the man's countenance," said Anne.

"Or the corners of his mouth either," cried Laura.

"But would any man who was not a fool sit there so long, when he found out our mistake, without explaining who he was?"

"I conceive," replied Caroline, firmly, "that a modest man would not have had nerve enough to do it; after what Anne said about his person, and his being proud and conceited, and so on; and after what passed about his sister, a generous man would have felt it still more difficult."

"So, so, child! you are far gone, indeed. She gives her hero credit for modesty and generosity already; and that after having been only one evening in his company."

"Ah! this comes of *gratitude*—this is because he thought you like your beauty."

"I told you you would *laugh* at me," said Caroline, blushing.

"Nay," exclaimed Sir John, "if this be as Caroline thinks it is, the laugh is on her side. And so you brought a gentleman home with you," cried Sir John, "to ridicule his sister, and affront HIM? S'death! women! I shall one day have to answer with my life for your impertinence!"

"Dear papa! there is no evidence of this after all, except Cary's suspicions; and is she the infallible in your eyes? But I suppose she is now to be the *oracle* as well as the *beauty* of the family."

"To me she has long been the *blessing* of it," he grumbled out; "and that is better than being either an oracle or a beauty."

"I declare," said Lady Wallington, "Cary has alarmed me: and I shall not be easy till Mr. Nowell comes. He can tell us whether Sir William Dormer arrived yesterday or not. What reason did our guest give for not being earlier at the ball?"

"He said he had been forced to attend a christening dinner on his way."

"And pray, most oracular cousin," cried Anne, "did Miss Dormer mention her brother to you?"

"Yes; she said she did not expect him that evening."

"There! And yet Cary has frightened us all by her ridiculous suspicions!"

"Why, really Cary, I begin to think Anne is right: as Miss Dormer did not expect her brother, it is most likely he did not come."

Lady Wallington now rose from table, and the ladies left Sir John to his nap, in his elbow-chair.

At tea-time, Mr. Nowell arrived, and was eagerly questioned concerning Sir William Dormer, and whether he was at Park Place or not.

"Dormer!" replied he. "Let me recollect, what did Lord John Rory write me word about Dormer? No: it was not Lord John, it was the Marquis. Oh, I have it: he said Dormer was going to dine with him the next day, at the Star and Garter at Richmond. So you see he can't be here, because he dined at Richmond yesterday."

"I am satisfied:" "And so am I:" "And so am I," said the three ladies, in great joy.

"What is all this?" asked Mr. Nowell affectedly; "I seem to have imparted great satisfaction."

"Oh, nothing: only Caroline was sure Sir William Dormer was come to Park Place, and we were sure to the contrary. What sort of looking man is Sir William? Is he tall?"

"About my height," replied Nowell, drawing up his head to the utmost.

"Is he stout or thin?"

"About my size," throwing back his shoulders as he spoke.

"Is he fair or dark?"

"Much such a complexion and hair as mine."

"Eyes dark or light?"

Here Mr. Nowell, instead of replying, fixed his own, stretching them to the utmost bounds, on his fair interrogator; and after a pause, during which the ladies could scarcely restrain their laughter, he exclaimed, "Look and judge for yourselves!"

"Do you mean to insinuate," said Anne, "that *you* are really Sir William Dormer himself in disguise?"

"No: but we are so alike that we have been spoken to for each other. Lord John calls us the two Amphitryons."

"Then I am sure, mamma," cried Laura, "we have never *yet* seen Sir William Dormer."

Caroline was silent; for so difficult is it for the most candid minds to part with a strongly conceived opinion, that she even thought she saw in the coxcomb before her, an ugly likeness of the handsome baronet.

Those who love to indulge in bantering are very glad of variety of object for it; and Anne ceased to laugh at her little cousin, in order to play off Mr. Nowell and Mrs. Norman, which she did in her own judgment so successfully, that she was good-humoured to her sister, kind to Caroline, and tolerably dutiful to her mother, though her father was not present; and their ambiguous guest was entirely forgotten.

Mr. Nowell was at all times a fit object for her ridicule; for he was in every way a consummate coxcomb; and at that moment he was dressed, though he was a gentleman of birth and fortune, in the extreme of dandyism; —that is, the breast of his coat and waistcoat were padded till they bestowed on him a protruding chest, while his waist was tightened in till it became small to an apparently wasp-like degree; and his pantaloons were plaited and gathered in at top till they assumed a petticoat fullness, giving an unnatural appearance of roundness to his person, and making him, like many other young men of the present day, look like a woman on the stage attired in boy's clothes; while the collar of his shirt was in almost loving contact with his nostrils, and his wristbands had formed an equally intimate connexion with his knuckles.

But, happy am I to say, that a less effeminate description of dress seems likely soon to prevail; a dress more worthy of the manly youth of Britain.

The next day was passed by the sisters some miles off at the house of a school friend; and by Sir John, Lady Wallington, and Caroline, at a little cottage near the sea, inhabited by his favourite physician.

When the family returned home, they found Sir William Maberley's call card, who had called during their absence; and while it filled the rest of the party with exultation, Caroline vainly tried to be equally glad; but when she reached her own apartment, she involuntarily said to herself, "So then it was Sir William Maberley after all! and he is certainly in love with Miss Dormer!"

The next day that dawned was the day of Miss Dormer's ball; but hour followed hour, and no dress arrived for Caroline: she summoned all the fortitude of eighteen upon the occasion: at last she observed, she had better prepare her other gown, thankfully accepting a trimming of Laura's to add to the necessary decoration.

By the latest coach the long-expected box appeared; and the dress, endeared still more by the dread of its not arriving, was received in uninjured beauty. When the ladies, ready dressed for the ball, were waiting for their carriage, they saw, to their great surprise, Sir John himself enter the room in his very best attire, save that one of his shoes was a gouty one, and declaring that he was resolved to witness the conquests he anticipated: for little Cary really looked so charmingly, that he foresaw she would be the cause of great trouble to him.

"And do not your own daughters look charmingly, too, Sir John?" said Lady Wallington, whose maternal pride now took the alarm.

"Yes; but that they *always* do, and look as if they knew it, too: but Caroline never looked so well before, nor was ever so well dressed before, I fancy: and her consciousness of it only just serves to deepen the colour of her cheeks to a most becoming hue."

The sisters tossed up their heads at this just description, while Caroline looked still prettier from the blush which it called forth on her dimpled cheek, and with sparkling eyes jumped into the carriage after her cousins.

For a mile before the carriage reached Park Place, the company approached the house through an avenue in which every tree was filled with pale green lamps, whose light increased by contrast the brilliancy that met their eyes on every side when they entered the hall, the dome of which was *studded* with white lamps, while magnificent cut-glass lustres were suspended from every ceiling in the suite of rooms on the first floor, and displayed to advantage the beauty of the pictures.

Miss Dormer received Lady Wallington and her daughters coldly, but politely; she looked more graciously on Sir John. But when she saw Caroline, she took her hand with a smile of animated welcome. Nothing could exceed the simplicity of Miss Dormer's dress that evening: and now, as Caroline said to herself, no eye, surely, but that of a very envious woman, could discover any fault in her shape.

The ladies looked round to try if they could see Sir William Maberley, but in vain; and as no gentleman came forward to receive them, they concluded Sir William Dormer was not present.

Miss Dormer now proposed to adjourn to the dancing-room, and, on the doors being thrown open, led the way into a long gallery brilliantly lighted and ornamented with fine statues. At the end of this gallery were a number of gentlemen, two of whom advanced from the group: in one of these the Wallingtons recognised Sir William Maberley; the other was, they concluded, the master of the house.

As the two gentlemen advanced to meet her, she said, "Give me leave, my dear brother, to present you to Sir John and Lady Wallington, and the Miss Wallingtons; and this is my friend Miss Caroline Wallington," taking at the same time the hand of the *supposed* Sir William Maberley!

Caroline was now full of pity, and even of mortification, on witnessing the consternation of her aunt and cousins, and the wonder, mixed with painful suspicion, with which Sir John observed the evident discomposure of his family.

"What does all this mean?" said he. "Answer me, Lady Wallington: is this the gentleman whom you mistook the other night for Sir William Maberley?"

"*I* am the *real* Simon Pure," said the other gentleman: "and I did myself the honour, though personally unknown, to call yesterday at Old Hall, to thank you for the civilities intended for me."

"Hark ye! Sir William Dormer," said Sir John, taking him on one side, "I trust you are too sensible a man to be affected by the impertinence of women, or to think the worse of me, because I have a foolish wife and prating daughters. I understand that all my family, little Cary excepted, said many things which they now wish recalled; but for my sake, and for Caroline's sake, who is a little angel, and I dare say behaved like one, pray forgive the rest of the family."

Sir William, who was a singular mixture of *mauvaise-honte* and dignity, felt embarrassed during this address; but at the end of it he cordially gave his hand to Sir John, and said, "Not only for your sake, and that of Miss Caroline, but for theirs, will I banish from my mind every recollection of what passed at Old Hall; though, for my own sake, I wish to remember it, as mortifications to our vanity are always salutary. What was said of one dearer to me than myself, she, also, I trust, will profit by. And now, Miss Caroline, let me reward your candour and kindness, by presenting you to that *sweet old lady*, my aunt, who promises, that when she chooses a dress for her niece again, it shall be such as your better taste approves."

While he said this, he led the delighted Caroline to Mrs. Fitzroy, who gave her such a reception as proved that her nephew had spoken most highly of her.

Miss Dormer now gave the signal for the music to begin. The sets were formed; and Sir William Maberley led Miss Dormer to the top of one of the dances, while Sir William conducted Caroline to the head of the other set.

To Anne and Laura, and, indeed, to Lady Wallington, the evening was now completely spoiled. Lady Wallington had great pride in her daughters; pride in their beauty and external graces, upon which she depended for their advantageous establishment in life. She had looked forward to the ball of that evening, with great expectation: but her views were now frustrated; and had she been a wise woman, she would have blamed herself for not having tried to give her daughters virtues as well as accomplishments, when she saw that Caroline, with inferiority of face, person, and acquirements, by the simple exertion of candour, and a kind, indulgent spirit, had contrived to make *friends* where they had made *enemies*, and was enjoying that ball-room, which was to them and to her a scene only of regret, envy, and resentment.

They had the pleasure of being engaged for every dance; but they were not dancing with the first men in the room, and Caroline was; nor could they hear without excessive mortification, how even BEAUTIFUL Caroline looked; and what marked attention she received from Sir William and Miss Dormer; for there is, perhaps, no feeling more trying to the self-love of both sexes, than that of being forced to own a SUPERIOR or EQUAL in one whom all your life you have considered as your *inferior*.

In the course of the evening Sir William Dormer owned to Caroline, that he had chosen, knowing his sister's strength of mind, to impart to her what Miss Wallington and Caroline had said concerning her dress, and her dancing quadrilles; and had expressed his wish, that she would be more simple in the one and discontinue the other.

"You see," he added, "that she has complied with my request; she did it with the greatest good humour; and though we have danced quadrilles this evening, she has declined doing so, and her dress is as simple as *you* would have advised. Let me add, however, that Augusta was more gratified by your defence, than she was wounded by the severity of the rest of the family. But see, hither, she and Mrs. Fitzroy are coming to speak to you, and I hope that you will receive what they have to say with a wish to oblige them."

As soon as Caroline heard what they had to communicate, she flew on the wings of hope and joy to seek her uncle and aunt; to whom her cousins were expressing their wish to return home.

"What! so soon?" cried Caroline, her look of joy suddenly changing.

"So soon! Why it is three o'clock, and we are both tired."

"Tired!"

"Don't echo my words, if you please,—it is very vulgar. Yes, tired; for I never passed a more disagreeable evening."

"Dis——" Caroline checked herself, and almost begged her cousin's pardon: then turning to Sir John and Lady Wallington, the former of whom observed her look of animated pleasure with kind satisfaction, she told them that Mrs. Fitzroy and Miss Dormer had asked her to spend a week with him, if they would allow it; and before Lady Wallington could reply, those ladies came in person to urge their suit.

"Ladies," said Sir John, "it is I, and I alone, who am the person to consult; for Caroline is my head nurse:—however, as the gout is nearly gone, I shall willingly spare her whenever you choose to summon her."

"Could she not stay to-night?"

"Why, yes," he answered, "I have no objection, and then the dear little girl may dance as long as she likes."

"Oh! my kind, good uncle," said Caroline, "I never can thank you enough!"

Caroline's joy, however, was not wholly on account of being able to rejoin the dance; she was glad to escape the sarcasms and ill-humour which her cousins, she knew, would vent on her defenceless head, and also perhaps on the master and mistress of the feast.

But to spend a *week* with such mild and blessed spirits as Mrs. Fitzroy and Miss Dormer! Mrs. Fitzroy, who had known, she found, her own dear mother! Never since that regretted parent died had Caroline felt so happy; and it was so kind in her uncle to spare her, before he had gotten his own shoe on again!

How worthy of love is that being who is fond of encouraging sources for thankfulness! and how salutary is the influence of such a one! Such a temper, like the Claude Lorraine glass, sheds a glowing tint over scenes which are already pleasing, and creates them where the prospect is gloomy and cheerless.

Caroline stayed a week at Park Place, and then obtained leave to stay another, and then another. At the end of the third, when Sir William Dormer and his sister conducted her to Old Hall, the former came to urge a still dearer and more important request to Sir John; namely, that he would part with his little nurse for life, and allow her to be the mistress of Park Place.

Sir John was luckily, at this moment, quite free from gout; therefore it was no trial to his selfishness to grant the request; besides, if it had been, it was so good a thing to part with a portionless niece to such a man, that even the gout would have remonstrated in vain. With a glow of affectionate pleasure, he said, "Take her, Sir William, she is yours; and I, who know her worth, for I have tried it, can assure you that I give you a *treasure*."

It is not to be supposed that the sisters could see, without great pain, their despised cousin Cary made the choice of a man of splendid fortune and high connexion; nor, that they could ever help regretting the supper " after the ball;" because they felt assured that, but for that unfortunate conversation, Sir William Dormer might have chosen one of themselves; for it was a little salvo to their vanity, to believe that it was by the incense offered that evening unconsciously to his fraternal vanity, that Caroline had obtained the preference; and when they were in a very spiteful mood, they worked up each other to suspect that *Caroline*, though *they* did not, *knew* him all the time to be Sir William Dormer.

Whether the mortifying results of that memorable evening made them more careful in future how they *pulled to pieces* and *cut up* (to use two expressive though common metaphors) their companions and friends, on their return home from routs or assemblies, I cannot determine; but certain it is, that Caroline continued to be as candid and averse from detraction, as she had then proved herself; and Sir William Dormer often declared, that his little wife never looked so lovely in his eyes, as when, on such occasions, she dwelt delighted on the looks or graces of the ladies whom she had met, and kindly threw their defects into shade,—proving herself, I must own from frequent experience, an exception to a general rule; as, what is more common than for a party to assemble round the table of refreshment, to talk over, criticise, and ridicule the company, and prove DETRACTION the greatest of pleasures " AFTER THE BALL?"

END OF AFTER THE BALL; OR, THE TWO SIR WILLIAMS.

FALSE OR TRUE;

OR, THE JOURNEY TO LONDON.

"Well then, Ellen, all is settled," said Sir George Mortimer to his niece and ward; "and you are resolved to go to London by the mail, from W——, next Monday?"

"Yes, dear uncle, it is the quickest conveyance; and as I am only to stay a month, I shall like to lose as little time as I can in travelling."

"Oh! certainly; to lose twelve hours of such delight as awaits you, Ellen, would be shocking indeed!"

"Oh! but it is not only *that*, it will be less trouble, and less expense, you know; and I shall want all my money for London; and as my aunt lets her maid go with me, and Mr. Betson, the attorney, will take care of me, I do not see why I should not go by the mail."

"Nor I neither, my dear; but, Ellen, I suppose you have written to desire your cousin, Charles Mandeville, to meet you at the inn?"

"No, indeed, I have not," Ellen replied, deeply blushing, "for I wish to surprise him; besides, I should not like to take the poor youth out of his bed so early in a cold May."

"A great hardship, indeed, to force a healthy young man of one-and-twenty out of his bed, in a spring morning, at five or six o'clock."

"Oh! but if I should give him cold! you know he often has a bad cough."

"Poor delicate creature! I am glad you have so much consideration for him."

"Nay, I am sure Charles is not *delicate*; he looks very manly, and has a fine healthy colour."

"Then why should he not get up to meet you?"

"Oh! but I wish to surprise him. I tell you, he will be so surprised, and so delighted!"

"No doubt; well, well, silly girl! have your own way." And Ellen, having sent for places in the W—— mail, ran to talk to her aunt and cousins on the only subject uppermost in her young and confiding heart;—namely, the joy of a first visit to the metropolis, and of the delight which her unexpected presence there would occasion her dear, dear Charles: for Ellen, though she had a fine understanding, had a heart even too fond and too confiding, and she was only eighteen. Charles Mandeville, who, at the age of five-and-twenty, was to come into possession of a handsome fortune, had finished his classical studies under the tuition of a country clergyman, in the village where Sir George Mortimer resided, and thence had had an intimate and frequent intercourse with Sir George's family, which had ended in a tender attachment between him and his cousin, Ellen Mortimer, whose mother was his father's sister. Not that anything like an engagement existed between them; that Sir George had positively forbidden.—He had represented to them, that they were as yet too young to know their own minds; and that, as Mr. Mandeville could not marry till he was of age, it would be better to prove the strength and reality of their attachment by absence, and by mixing with the world. The young lovers would have talked of eternal constancy, and declared their hearts were unalterably fixed on each other, if he would have allowed them to do so; but he forbade it, assuring them that their rhapsodies would not carry conviction to his mind, as he had known many a passion, which the retirement of a village had created, vanish away in the varied intercourse and pleasures of busy life. And very soon was absence, the great test of affection, to prove that of Charles Mandeville, for his guardian wrote to tell him it was time for him to enter himself at Lincoln's-inn. As Mandeville's father had been a strict dissenter, he had forbidden his son to be educated at College; therefore, instead of going to Cambridge, he received the private tuition which I have mentioned, and was then to commence his legal studies, as intellectual pursuit of some sort was wisely deemed necessary for him during the years that were yet to come of his long minority. But a young man, who knows that at five-and-twenty he shall have a large fortune, is not likely, from principle and the love of employment, to study very hard. The known expectations, the handsome person, prompt attentions, musical powers, and pleasing manners of Charles Mandeville, soon gave him entrance into some gay and fashionable circles in the metropolis; and at the end of six months after he left the village of R——, his letters to Ellen were neither so frequent nor so long as they had been, but they contained some tender words, such as "dearest, beloved girl," and so on; and Ellen tried to be satisfied; for how was it possible that Charles should have changed so soon, if at all; since her heart was unchanged, though she had had temptations to falsehood thrown in her way.

Sir Henry Claremont, a young baronet, came to reside on a beautiful estate, belonging to a friend of his, who was forced to live abroad on account of his health. This estate joined the Park-gate of Sir George Mortimer. Sir Henry, on losing a mother, whom he almost adored, felt himself unable to remain in his own house, where everything reminded him of his loss; he therefore hired the seat in question of its owner. But he declined visiting his neighbours, and had gained the title of the recluse, when he saw Ellen at church, soon after she finally left school, and from that moment he was a recluse no longer; for as soon as Sir George found that the young baronet sought, rather than avoided him, he invited him to his house; and a great deal of visiting intercourse took place, till, on the obvious intimacy and attachment which ensued between Ellen and Charles, Sir Henry gradually ceased his visits, and his love of solitude and home returned. But when Charles went to London, and when, on inquiry, Sir Henry found that no engagement existed between him and his cousin, he again became sociable, and at length, after a "series of quiet attentions, not so pointed as to alarm, or so vague as to be misunderstood," he ventured to ask leave to address Miss Mortimer. But Ellen was firm in her refusal of his addresses; and Sir George could not help saying,—

"Well, Ellen, I only hope that Charles may prove himself worthy of the sacrifice you are making for his sake."

"Sacrifice, my dear uncle!"

"Yes;— for is not Sir Henry Claremont everything a father would desire in a husband for his daughter, or his daughter for herself? Is he not handsome, young, good, pious, studious? Before his rich neighbours knew him, did not his poor ones bless him, Ellen?"

"Oh, yes, he is very good, and charming, I dare say; and if I did not love Charles, I— but I *do* love Charles, so I cannot have Sir Henry."

Sir George shook his head, sighed, and told Sir Henry he had nothing at present to hope. Sir Henry sighed also, but he contrived to remember the "at present" qualified the refusal from the lips of Sir George, and he resolved to hope on; in the meanwhile Ellen could not express a wish which was not immediately fulfilled; presents so delicately offered that they could not be refused, and attentions so well timed that they could not be dispensed with, proved the continuation of his love; a love which, though silent in words, spoke in every glance of his intelligent eye, and seemed resolved to burn unchanged even in the midst of despair. There were times when Ellen herself thought it was a pity she could not reward such love as that of Sir Henry; but this was only when she had for a few days vainly expected a letter from Charles. If the expected letter, when it came, contained its usual quantity of tender epithets, and one regret at being separated from her, then she forgot Sir Henry's incessant assiduity: she heard with calm approbation only of his benevolent exertions, and had no wish so near her heart as to see Charles again; no regret but that she did not receive the long-promised invitation to London from her mother's old friend, Mrs. Ainslie. At length this precious invitation arrived, and Ellen was requested to set off immediately, as at the end of the month her friend would be obliged to travel to the north. It was the suddenness of the summons which tempted Ellen to surprise Charles, as she hoped, agreeably; and Sir George, who suspected that Charles's attachment had not resisted the destroying power of absence as well as hers had done, was willing that he should be taken by surprise, as he thought that, if Ellen could see her favourite's heart off its guard, she might find out that he had ceased to love her, and might thence derive power to conquer her own attachment.

The parting hour with her relations, was, on Ellen's side, one of tears quickly succeeded by smiles when she found herself really seated in the mail, and really on her journey to London; that journey, at the end of which she was to see, though not, alas! immediately, the face which haunted her dreams, and gave interest to her waking hours; and to hear that voice whose parting accents still rung mournfully and melodiously in her ears. To Ellen, the novelty of the present scene, and the expectation of the future, gave a feeling of intoxication, which made her almost troublesomely-loquacious to her companion, Mr. Betson, for she could only converse concerning London, and ask incessant questions relative to the place of her destination. As they passed Sir Henry Claremont's park-gate, Ellen saw him leaning on it as if watching to catch a last look of her. She eagerly returned his bow of adieu, and kissed her hand kindly to him, but was soon again engrossed in questioning her companion. As it grew dark, Mr. Betson's answers were shorter and shorter; and, when night came on, his replies dwindled down into a plain "Yes," and "No." At last Ellen with dismay saw him, with a hearty yawn, put on his night-cap, and settle himself down in the corner.

"Dear me, sir!" she exclaimed, "to be sure you are not going to sleep?"

"Why not, Miss Mortimer? I am not a young man, and I really advise you to sleep yourself, for you will want all your spirits for the journey, and for London, when you get there."

Ellen was disappointed, but she saw that sleep was so much dearer to Mr. Betson as a companion than she was, that she submitted in silence to the preference; or rather she talked, as talk she must, to her aunt's maid, now, for the time being her own; and in projecting alterations which she was to execute in her old things, or in thinking over what new things she was to purchase, she beguiled part of the long night, which still separated her from London and her love, but at dawn she had talked herself into weariness, and sleep was not far behind. When she awoke, the approach to London, through Piccadilly, was in sight, and Ellen was in an ecstasy of admiration! Oh, the incessant questions with which she now assailed Mr. Betson. But the question nearest her heart was, "Pray, sir, where is Albany? Because this is Piccadilly, you say, and Albany, I know, is near it." But Mr. Betson had never heard of Albany, which Charles mentioned as a most fashionable residence: *ergo*, Mr. Betson was a vulgar man, and knew nothing of *ton* and life.

Ellen now began to regret that she had not written to request Charles to meet her, or rather to let him know she was to be seen at seven o'clock in the morning at the Golden Cross, Charing Cross. No doubt he would have been there, and then she would have seen him so much sooner. This consideration had led her into a deep *reverie*, when the mail turned into the inn-yard at one of the entrances, and she found Mr. Ainslie's carriage waiting for her.

It is easy to imagine that Ellen's ideas of London were considerably lowered as she turned her back on the west end of the town; and after going down the comparatively gloomy Strand, in which the current of human life had not yet begun its course, saw the carriage turn into the spacious but dark area of Serjeant's Inn; and Charles lived in Albany, and that was near *Piccadilly!* But the warm, affectionate greeting of her mother's friends, the cheerful fire, the refreshing breakfast, and the evidences of kind hearts, of taste and opulence, which surrounded her, suspended for a while even the remembrance of Charles and regret that he was so far off; and Ellen was so cheered, so alive, that she could not be prevailed upon by her kind hostess to go to bed for a few hours.

"Oh, no — it is impossible! I should not sleep if I did;" then blushing deeply, she said that she must write a note.

"You will find whatever you want for that purpose in your own chamber."

"No—not unless you go with me thither," she replied, blushing still more, "for I want you to write what I shall dictate."

Mrs. Ainslie accordingly accompanied Ellen to her room, and there she learnt what she wished her to write, as follows:

"If Mr. Mandeville will take the trouble to call at Mr. Ainslie's, No. —, Serjeant's Inn, some time to-day, he will learn some intelligence respecting his cousin Ellen Mortimer."

"But why," said Mrs. Ainslie, "not tell him at once that you are here."

The treasured fancy of her heart, however, was indulged, and Mrs. Ainslie did as she desired her, then sent her own servant to Albany with the note.

Mrs. Ainslie, in consequence of having been told in confidence by Sir George that he suspected Charles's heart of having played truant to Ellen, allowed the expression "some time to-day" to remain, and did not insist on changing it for a *particular hour*, as she thought that Charles's coming early or late, according to the suggestions of his own heart, would prove the state of that heart beyond a doubt to her eyes, though not, perhaps, to Ellen's; therefore, with some anxious expectation, though not equal to that of her young guest, Mrs. Ainslie awaited the arrival of Charles. But hour succeeded to hour, and yet he did not come;— while Ellen's cheek was now pale, now flushed, as disappointment or hope preponderated; yet it was in reality all disappointment, for if he had been interested in hearing aught concerning her, he would have come directly.

"Surely," said Ellen at last, no longer able to conceal her vexation—"Surely, Charles is not in town?"

"You shall question my servant yourself," said Mrs. Ainslie, and she rang for him, though she already knew what he would reply, which was, that he saw Mr. Mandeville's servant, who told him he would give the note into his master's hand immediately. Yet it was three o'clock, and he was not at Serjeant's Inn.

"Well," said Mrs. Ainslie, "I conclude, Ellen, you will not stay at home any longer in hopes of this truant's arrival. My carriage is coming round, and I must take you to see something, as you are neither tired nor sleepy."

No,—Ellen was neither, but she was something *much worse*—she was sick at heart. The bright prospect that love and hope had pictured was blighted, and she wished already, earnestly wished, that she had never come to London. But the next moment she excused Charles's delay thus:—

"He could not suppose he was to see me, and perhaps he thought it a *hoax*. Yes—yes—I dare say he believed it a take-in. Oh! why was I so *foolish* as not to write to him myself. I am *sure* he would have come then."

This internal colloquy served to tranquillize her mind so completely, that she ventured at length to repeat it audibly to Mrs. Ainslie, but that lady coldly replied,

"This is a fresh argument, Ellen, for you to consent to go out, and I hope you will no longer refuse."

However, she did refuse; for it was far more delightful to her to stay within, expecting and looking for Charles Mandeville, even though he did not come, than to see all the wonders of London. Mrs. Ainslie, however, took her accustomed drive in the park, with a feeling of kind vexation at her fond obstinacy, painfully subdued by pity for the apparent strength of an attachment, which was probably ill-requited. But she would not have left her, had she not wished to ascertain the truth of what she suspected; namely, that Charles Mandeville, feeling no particular eagerness or anxiety to know the intelligence concerning Ellen, had gone to Bond street, and St. James's street, or to some of his other daily haunts, and was probably, as usual, finishing his morning in the drive; and *there* Mrs. Ainslie saw him. For a moment she resolved to send her servant to say a lady wished to speak to him, then introduce herself, tell him who she was, and invite him to dinner; but she thought it was more for Ellen's good to let events take the direction which Ellen had given them by her note, and she left the park almost as soon as her end in going was answered, and returned home without speaking to Mandeville.

"Well," said Ellen, mournfully, as soon as she saw her, "he has not been here yet!"

"No, certainly not, for I met him several times in the park on horseback."

"Then you have seen him; and if I had gone with you I should have seen him too," said Ellen, the long-imprisoned tears trickling down her face, "but, oh! how unkind it is in him not to call; but surely, you told him."

"I only knew him personally, my dear girl, and he does not know me when he sees me; nor could I be sure that you would not be displeased with me for depriving you of your chance for surprising him agreeably."

Spite of herself, Mrs. Ainslie's voice drawled almost *sarcastically* when she uttered "agreeably," and Ellen, bursting again into tears, hurried to her own apartment.

I will not attempt to describe the misery which Ellen's confiding, fond, and inexperienced heart underwent when she reached it; but I fear many of my readers, young and old, can imagine what it was, from their own painful experience.

Whether Mrs. Ainslie's heart was experienced in the same way, I know not, but certain it is, that she allowed Ellen to indulge her feelings till the indulgence was probably become burdensome, before she knocked at her door. Oh! how tenacious, how clinging, even to a hair for life, is hope, in a young, impassioned heart! Ellen thought that, perhaps, Charles Mandeville was now really come, and she eagerly opened the door to receive the welcome tidings.

"Alas! No—he is not come," said Mrs. Ainslie, answering the asking eye.—Ellen blushed, and turned away with her handkerchief to her face.

"Come, come, my dear child! this must not be," said her kind hostess; "I want my Ellen Mortimer's daughter to be seen to advantage; and spite of what poets and novelists say, swelled eyelids and a red nose, however they may prove sensibility, are no improvers of beauty, and I expect some smart young men to dinner."

Ellen did not reply; she recollected but that for her own obstinacy Charles might have been one of the smart young men. However,

she felt ashamed of seeming to feel so much for one who appeared by his present conduct to feel so little for her, that she dried up her tears, washed her eyes with rose-water, called herself an idiot, conversed with Mrs. Ainslie on indifferent subjects, dressed herself as becomingly as she could, for perhaps Charles might call in the evening, and went down to dinner looking very pretty, and, to those who had not seen her before, unaffectedly animated: but Mrs. Ainslie saw that her spirits were forced; she also observed, with considerable pain, that every knock at the door made her start and change colour, and that she took little interest in aught that was going forward. Poor thing! thought she as she looked on her sweet and modest loveliness, and is thy fair morn so soon overcast? Is a blight to come so soon over thy beauties? Not if I can teach her to distinguish the *false* from the *true*. However, he might think the note a hoax.

At length the long weary day ended, and even before the company departed, Ellen, on pretence of fatigue, obtained leave to retire to bed, where, from the journey of the preceding night, she was able to sleep spite of her sorrows. Welcome, however, was the sight of the next morning, for *surely* Charles would call that day; and if he did not, it would be evident that he thought the note was an imposition, and then she resolved to write to him herself.

The truth, the mortifying truth was, that Mandeville, though surprised at receiving such a note, resolved to ride to Serjeant's Inn during the course of the day, but in the busy idleness of his London life he utterly forgot to do so, as Ellen no longer reigned the mistress of every thought; and consequently the desire of hearing "intelligence" of her was not, as it once would have been, one of the dearest wishes of his heart. But when he rose the next day, and saw the note lying on his table, he was rather ashamed of his negligence, and resolved to go to Serjeant's Inn as soon as he returned from breakfasting at the rooms of a fashionable friend of his in Albany, especially as Mr. Ainslie was, he knew, a man high at the bar, and his wife gave good parties for *that end of the town*. Still it was odd that an anonymous note should come from such a quarter; "intelligence concerning his cousin Ellen Mortimer." What could it be?—Surely Ellen was not false! Surely she was not going to be married! The idea was far from being a pleasant one; but he glanced his eye over his really handsome face, now embellished by the flush of apprehension, and muttering to himself "no, no, that cannot be;" he thoughtfully descended the stairs, and went to his apartment.

Ellen, meanwhile, unlike the Ellen of her uncle's house, took her seat at Mrs. Ainslie's breakfast-table, with a look of anxiety and uncomfortableness on her usually bright and

THE JOURNEY TO LONDON.

happy countenance, which gives age even to the countenance of youth; and Mr. Ainslie thought her some years older than she appeared the day before, ere the cloud of disappointed hope had passed over her brow, and the anxieties of love had begun to tread on the heel of its enjoyments. Mrs. Ainslie too was hurt and mortified; she had expected to give uninterrupted pleasure to Ellen by the invitation to London, but she found that she had been the means of misery to her. However, if Mandeville had ceased to love, the sooner and the more completely she was convinced of his falsehood the better it would be for her future peace; and the remedy, though very painful, would, she trusted, make the cure complete.

Ellen ate scarcely any thing, but Mr. and Mrs. Ainslie were too delicate to notice her want of appetite as they knew its cause; when the usual hour of breakfast for fashionable young men was, according to Mrs. Ainslie, passed, she began to recover a degree of hope that Charles would soon appear, and with it some of her vivacity and all her beauty; for the flush of anxious expectation deepened into even feverish brilliancy the colour on her cheek, and gave lustre and added expression to her ever bright and tender blue eye.

The boy has no heart! thought Mr. Ainslie, as he gazed on her, or he would have come post to receive intelligence of a creature like that. Oh, she would be better without him. So thought his amiable wife; and the next thing to be done was to convince Ellen, if possible, of the same obvious truth. But on what was Ellen's love of him founded? If, thought Mrs. Ainslie, her love be not founded on the supposed superior qualities of mind or heart of the man she loves, I believe any woman's love may be conquered, and I trust Ellen is like other women; then, if *gratified* self-love be the foundation of her attachment, *wounded* self-love may be the means of bringing it to the ground again, and I will see what can be done.

This day Ellen was not doomed to expect in vain; but after a tremendous knock from his groom, which made Ellen start from her seat, Mr. Mandeville was announced; he asked for Mrs. Ainslie, and was instantly admitted to that lady; she had asked Ellen whether she wished to receive Charles alone, but as she replied no, though very faintly, Mrs. Ainslie was glad of the slightest excuse to stay and witness the manner and conduct of Charles on the *surprise* which awaited him.

When he entered, Ellen stood in the next room by the open folding-door, where he could not see her; after the usual salutations, Mandeville said,

"I take the liberty of calling on you, madam, in consequence of receiving this note."

"You did right, sir, for I wrote it; but the intelligence to which it alludes you must receive from a lady in the next room."

He turned, and beheld Ellen pale and *agitated*; for at sight of her no glow of delight sparkled in his eyes, mantled on his cheek, or gave tenderness to his tone; he blushed, indeed, but it was evidently from embarrassed, not agreeable surprise; and his salutation of "Why Ellen! Is it possible? you here!" was spoken in the same drawling, affected tone with which he had addressed Mrs. Ainslie.

"Yes," faltered out the poor girl as she withdrew her hand from his unimpassioned grasp; "yes, I thought you would be surprised to see me."

"Surprised indeed!" but still the word *glad* did not escape him.

He is honest, however, thought Mrs. Ainslie; but as she saw her young friend's excessive emotion, and also saw if she had an opportunity she would give way to the mortification and apprehension which she could not but feel, and treat her unworthy admirer with a scene which might gratify his vanity without touching his heart, she resolved not to quit the room; therefore she seated herself at her table, and began to work. Mandeville's countenance she thought cleared up when she did so; but not Ellen's, who, unwilling to think that she and Mandeville were not still lovers, wondered excessively that Mrs. Ainslie did not leave them alone.

"And when did you come?"

"Yesterday."

"And how did you come?"

"By the mail."

"The mail! how could Sir George suffer it?"

"Oh! but I wished it."

"What a vulgar taste! The mail! How could you wish it, Ellen?"

"Oh! because, because"—here poor Ellen recollected that she wished it because she was anxious to *lose no time*, as her stay was to be short; therefore the contrast of her expectations then and *now* overcame her, and she turned aside to weep. Charles was more nettled than affected by this sensibility, and was about to say a kind word in a peevish tone; when Mrs. Ainslie interfered, and coldly said, almost mimicking, in spite of herself, the manner in which he pronounced "the mail,"—"I see no vulgarity, but much good sense, in my young friend's choosing to come up by the mail, Mr. Mandeville."

"Indeed, madam?"

"Yes, posting is very expensive."

"But could not Sir George have afforded to treat his niece with a post-chaise?"

"No; he has a large family, and cannot afford to spend ten or twelve pounds unnecessarily."

"Why could she not pay for herself then?"

"Because Ellen is not of age, and her allowance is small, therefore she wisely resolved to come by the odious, vulgar mail, attended by her aunt's maid and a gentleman of her acquaintance."

"A gentleman! what gentleman?" said he, changing colour.

"Oh! you need not be jealous," replied Mrs. Ainslie, maliciously, and Mandeville blushed still deeper; "it was not a *certain* gentleman, but a Mr., Mr. ——."

"Betson," said Ellen, who had now recovered herself, and was cheered by Charles's blush and manner, when he heard that a *gentleman* accompanied her.

"What, old Betson the attorney! what a beau! really Sir George is a strange guardian for a young lady of your fortune, Miss Mortimer, and a baronet's niece."

"On the contrary," said Mrs. Ainslie, "he is the wisest guardian possible; the income of £10,000 will not go far if its possessor must always travel post or not at all; and habits of economy are necessary even for persons of £10,000 per annum. Sir George has known the misery of a narrow income; and, though a baronet, was, you know, a penniless subaltern, and then a captain in the army for many years, dragging a wife and eight children about with him from one station to another, as he could, *on* coaches or *in* coaches; and, when comparative wealth came, it was too late for him to assume the fantastical airs, and fine gentleman disguests and shrinkings of those who have not, like him, been made superior to the unnecessary indulgences of life by a painful acquaintance with its realities. His girls were baronet's daughters then; yet, if it was *necessary*, they went with their nurse on a baggage-wagon; and now, if necessary, Sir George and Lady Mortimer would let them go in a *mail*, ay, and with Mr. Betson too."

Mandeville was surprised to hear such sentiments from a woman much as he, knew, reckoned rather proud, not easy of access, and was herself allied to nobility; and as he associated the idea of vulgarity with that of attention to economy, he would have thought Mrs. Ainslie *vulgar* if he could so have thought of a woman of her station in society; however, he judged it best to say no more concerning mail travelling, but bowing, as if convinced, he next asked Ellen how long she meant to stay?

"Only a month."

"Dear me; how unfortunate! for I have so many engagements for this month!"

"But when a lady's in the case,
All other things you know give place,"

cried Mrs. Ainslie, fixing her penetrating eyes on his countenance.

"Yes," said he, avoiding her glance as much as possible. "*all* other *things*, but not all other ladies; and my engagements are with ladies. I have to sing at Lady D——'s one night; at Lady C——'s another; then quadrille balls without end."

"I did not know, my dear," said Mrs. Ainslie, coldly, "that Mr. Mandeville was a singing and dancing gentleman."

"Oh yes; he does both exquisitely."

"But does he never think proper to sing and dance with you? Pray, Mr. Mandeville, would not Miss Mortimer, that is, your cousin Ellen's being in London for a short time be a sufficient excuse for your singing one duet and dancing one quadrille less in an evening where she is not, in order to enable you to dance and sing where she is?"

"Certainly, certainly," he replied in a hurried manner; "certainly, at some places; but I really did wish to have gone about with Ellen and shown her London."

"And can you not?"

"Never mind whether he can or not," said Ellen rather indignantly; "since, since"—here she paused, covered with blushes, for she was conscious of this feeling; "as he is not, I see, anxious to stay at *home* with me, I do not much care whether he goes abroad with me or not."

Mandeville now saw that Ellen resented his manner and conduct, and not being willing to break with her entirely, he soothingly replied; "*Nay*, my dear Ellen, do not make my misfortune, in being forced to relinquish your society, greater than it already is, by seeming to consider it as my fault. But why lose the time present? Ellen, let us now go somewhere. Ellen, do not frown on me! Dearest Ellen, forgive me!"

Mrs. Ainslie now thought, as Charles's manner was become humble, and his looks and tones tender, that she ought to quit the room. But she had scarcely reached the landing-place when another knock at the door announced the arrival of visiters, and she reseated herself, much, as she again fancied, to the relief of Mandeville and disappointment of the still believing Ellen; she now saw Mandeville speaking in a low voice to her, and what he said was received with a blush and an inquiring eye directed to her.

"What does that look say, Miss Mortimer?" cried she, smiling.

"That Ellen wishes to take a walk with me, and see some sights, if you have no objection."

"Certainly not: my footman shall attend you; I only require that you should return time enough for your cousin to go out with me in my carriage." Mandeville promised to be obedient to her wishes, and Ellen went to equip herself for her walk.

It was with mixed feelings in which pain predominated, that Ellen took out her bonnet which was made on purpose to wear in London; for it was exactly like one which Charles used to admire, and say that she looked remarkably pretty in; therefore when the original hat was worn out, the fond and flattered girl bought another to replace it, and had a tender pleasure in anticipating the satisfaction her lover would feel in seeing this proof of her attention to his taste. But now she felt a degree of delicate reluctance to wear this tell-tale hat before him; but she had no other, and with embarrassing consciousness she entered the drawing-room, in which she found Mrs. Ainslie and Charles alone.

"Dear me, Ellen," cried he, as soon as he saw her, "have you no other bonnet than that to put on?—that old-fashioned, odd-looking thing."

"I thought you used to admire it," said Ellen, almost in tears.

"Yes, so I did, when it was new and in the country; but here it would be so quizzed."

It is new, she was going to say; but she stopt, unable to make the now mortifying avowal; and, turning to Mrs. Ainslie, she timidly said, "What can I do? I see Charles will be ashamed of me in this bonnet."

"I own," said Mrs. Ainslie, "the bonnet is not fashionable, though becoming; and as I wish you to look like other people in your dress, Ellen, I will lend you my last new one till we can buy another."

"Will you, indeed? oh, that will be so kind!" said Ellen, following Mrs. Ainslie to her chamber.

When she reappeared, Charles eagerly exclaimed, "What a beautiful bonnet, and how becoming! really, Ellen, I think you will not disgrace me now."

Heartless, vain creature, thought Mrs. Ainslie; but surely, surely, Ellen cannot long bear this.

As soon as they were in the street, Charles said, "A very fine woman, that Mrs. Ainslie, still, but terribly severe; I would as soon encounter a wild-cat as a woman of that sort."

"She is very kind to me, Charles."

"Yes, and will be, till you displease her; but then beware of a *coup de patte*—did you not see how she scratched me?"

"Scratched you, Charles!"

"Metaphorically, I mean; but whither shall we go, Ellen? we are now at the Temple-gate, let us go and look at the gardens."

"And at the Temple too, if you please, Charles; for my dear father lived there many years, you know; and when there he fell in love with mamma. I should like to see his chambers! Shall we ask which were Mr. Mortimer's chambers where he fell in love with mamma? Nay, do not laugh at me, Charles, I am not quite so silly as you imagine; but I know papa lived in Paper-buildings."

"And so do many others."

"Indeed! but I should like to look even at the walls."

"Sentimental girl!—Well, you shall be indulged." And till Ellen had seen the buildings on both sides, the gardens had no power to attract her attention. But even then, pretty as they are, Ellen could not admit that they were equal in beauty to her uncle's; and one thought of the view she had of the lake in Sir Henry Claremont's ground annihilated all the beauty of the Temple river to her. "That river is the Thames, Ellen," he replied peevishly, not pleased at the mention of Sir Henry, for the jealousies of self-love are as powerful and strong as those of love; and after having taken a turn or two round the garden,—the footman was not allowed to follow,—the gate was unlocked again, and they went forward on their way to the *upper regions*, as Charles called the other end of the town. As they walked through some of the courts they met young barristers returning home, and Charles found by the evident admiration which Ellen excited that he had reason to be proud of his fair companion, and saying to himself, "she will do, I may venture to show her in Bond-street," he took her thither, after having first pointed out to her all the principal streets on that side of Oxford-road, and the best squares. However, I must own, my heroine was as yet more alive to the pleasure of being with Mandeville again, hanging on his arm, than to the charms of what she saw; even his conversation, egotistical and frivolous as it was, pleased her, because it was his; though she listened with ever renewed, and ever disappointed expectation, in hopes of hearing him speak the language of the *heart*, and of still faithful affection.

When they returned to Serjeant's Inn, Mrs. Ainslie asked Ellen how she liked her walk. "Oh! very much," she replied, but her observant friend saw that, though her eyes might have been satisfied, her heart was not. "You, I trust, Mr. Mandeville, have been pleased and proud too; for I dare say, as every new face is stared at in town, a new, young, and pretty one also, must have created a great sensation."

"It did, I assure you; and Ellen carried away gazers' hearts like burs sticking to her."

"Oh! fy, Charles; how can you say so!" replied Ellen, blushing and pleased.

"Well then," said Mrs. Ainslie, "suppose you go with us into the drive, and help Ellen to give back these hearts, as you there may probably see and know their respective owners." Mandeville said he was very sorry, but he could not go to the Park with them, as he had an appointment at White's at half-past four, but he would thank her to set him down in St. James's-street.

"You will dine with us, I hope?"

"Yes, with pleasure, if you dine late."

"At seven o'clock precisely."

"Then I will have the honour to wait on you."

Ellen now grew very thoughtful; and her internal world, poor girl! hid the external one from her view. Charles became his own rival, and by dint of thinking of him and his conversation, she almost forgot that he was present. She had been with him alone in a crowd, the next thing to being alone in a room; but no language resembling that of love, or even affectionate interest, had escaped him. He had talked incessantly, but entirely of himself and his fine acquaintance, and his singing, and the admiration it excited. Then he knew this lady, the most beautiful creature in the world; and that lady, the most fascinating and accomplished; and another, whom to see was to adore; but when Ellen, pale, spiritless, and jealous beyond expression, could scarcely ask the name of these charmers, she heard, with an odd mixture of pleasure and pain, that these irresistible creatures were married women or widows of a certain age; and though her jealousy suffered less, her morals suffered a great deal. "Oh!" thought she, "even one short walk in our village alone with Charles, was worth all our noisy, bustling, long walk to-day; and this is my eagerly expected pleasure in London! Sir Henry Claremont would hardly believe what I could tell him!"

"Ellen is in a *reverie*," said Charles to Mrs. Ainslie.

"Yes, thinking of the absent, I suspect," she replied.

That piqued him, and he tried to make her talk, but even the tone of his voice was altered; and while Ellen heard him she was so engaged in comparing his past with his present voice, his past with his present manner, that she scarcely heard what he said; and while she almost unconsciously fixed her meaning, and nearly tearful eyes on his face, he dared not encounter, because he could not respond to their appealing expression; therefore he was very glad when they reached St. James's-street. His adieus were soon spoken, and he disappeared without one of those lingering looks that speak the reluctance with which a beloved object is quitted, and a wish to see that object still, while it is at all visible. Alas! Ellen's eyes pursued *him* thus, and saw him till he could be seen no more.

"Your cousin is a very handsome young man!" said Mrs. Ainslie.

"Yes, very."

"How long was he at R—?"

"Two years."

"Indeed!" replied Mrs. Ainslie gravely, alarmed by the length of the intimacy.—"However," thought she, "as Mandeville's head has been turned, and his heart hardened by admiration here, why should not Ellen's be operated upon by the same process? I will watch her now that men are staring at her, and glasses raised at her as we pass."

But Ellen saw them not,—she saw only the Charles Mandeville with whom she used to associate at R—, till Mrs. Ainslie at length gained her attention by pointing at a succession of distinguished and well-known characters who were lounging in Piccadilly, or going on horseback into the Park. The eager look of curiosity with which Ellen received what her friend said, accompanied sometimes with an almost audible "which is he?" attracted even more eager observation than it evinced, and Ellen, no longer insensible of the admiring attention which answered her curious glance, became quite alive to the passing scene, and her own pre-eminence in it; till, after several turns in the drive, she fancied she saw Charles on horseback by the side of a very fine woman. After that, her eyes were incessantly wandering in search of him; and when he indeed passed, apparently without seeing her, her only hope, her only interest was to try and be more successful when he passed again.

"But how strange it was," said Mrs. Ainslie, "that Mr. Mandeville should not be on the look-out for you, Ellen?"

"Oh! no, you forget that he is with a lady——."

"But that lady is old and faded, and *fardée*. The man ought to have better taste than to prefer her to you."

True, but she was a woman of fashion, and Mandeville was flattered by being seen with her. Again Ellen tried to catch his attention, but in vain; and as Mrs. Ainslie saw that all her pleasure in the scene was over, she desired the coachman to get out of the Park as fast as he could, and drive to a French milliner's in Conduit-street. Had they gone down the drive again, Mandeville meant to have *seen* her.

After the mortified and even mournful Ellen had tried on two or three bonnets, with a degree of indifference painful to behold in so young a person, as it was unnatural at her age and only too indicative of an oppressed heart, she bought one, which Mrs. Ainslie admired; and having engaged a very fashionable hair-dresser, to cut and dress Ellen's hair, Mrs. Ainslie, as there was yet time, drove to the gallery of a fashionable painter. There her attention was riveted by an unfinished whole-length portrait of a gentleman, and she eagerly called Ellen to admire it. "What a countenance! what eyes! what a meek benignant expression about the mouth!—I never saw such a face!—I have seen handsomer, perhaps, but one so captivating, never! Is it not charming, Ellen?" As she said this, she looked at her, and saw her covered with blushes.

"I know the original," said Ellen, smiling. "It is Sir Henry Claremont."

"Indeed! Oh! Ellen! Ellen! that your Sir Henry Claremont?"

"He is not mine."

"Yes, yes, he is; the fine flower in one's garden is our's, Ellen, though we may not choose to pluck it and wear it. Silly girl, ungrateful, mistaken girl!—Is Sir Henry to sit again soon?" said Mrs. Ainslie to the attendant.

"No, madam, he will never sit again. The

picture is paid for, but it was begun for Lady Claremont, his mother; and Sir Henry, as she is dead, cannot bear to have it finished."

"I would give something," said Mrs. Ainslie, passing her arm through Ellen's, "to see that picture finished one day. What an attached, affectionate husband would such a son make! Ay, and I dare say he is a faithful lover!" Ellen did not reply, but she involuntarily turned her eyes on the picture. The pensive penetrating eye seemed to fix even reproachfully upon her; and what and whom had she preferred to him! Ellen sighed, and turned suddenly away. "Good bye, most captivating being!" said Mrs. Ainslie to the picture, "I will come and see you again very soon, and would that I knew the original!"

"He is handsomer than his picture," said the attendant, "and as good as he is handsome, madam. My brother is one of his servants, and my sister is married to one of his tenants, and they say he is an angel upon earth."

"Come away, Ellen,—come away! if your heart can stand this, mine can't, I assure you!"

Ellen smiled, spite of herself, with pride and pleasure too, for this admirable creature loved her, even though she loved another. Again she was absent and taciturn, while Mrs. Ainslie, wishing her to be left to her own reflections, made no effort to engage her in conversation.

Never had Ellen been so absorbed in the business of the toilet as she was to-day. Mrs. Ainslie kindly superintended and patiently answered all Ellen's inquiries, as to what was fashionable, rather than as to what was becoming: for she had discovered that fashion was every thing with Mandeville. At length not satisfied with her appearance, for her aim was to recall a strayed heart, and love makes every one humble, Ellen, attired entirely to the satisfaction of Mrs. Ainslie and to the loud admiration of Mr. Ainslie, seated herself on a sofa, that held *only two*, and with a beating heart awaited the arrival of Charles, for she could not help hoping, spite of all that had passed, that he would come early; but he came late, and was evidently not solicitous to sit next Ellen at table. Mrs. Ainslie, however, conscious that Ellen would be evidently disconcerted if he did not sit by her, desired Ellen to go next him, as he, of course, sat by the lady whom he had handed down stairs; and she tried to be happy. But Charles did not, as he used to do at R—, turn his back for her sake on the lady, whoever she was, that sat on the other side of him, and she felt glad when the ladies retired, that she might go to her own room, and relieve her full heart by weeping.

When Ellen returned to the drawing-room, she found a large party of newly-arrived guests assembled, and as the gentlemen left the table soon, it was not long before the necessary arrangements for music, which was to be the first entertainment of the evening, took place, and Charles was told by Mrs. Ainslie, that his musical powers would be put in requisition, till his quadrille dancing was equally wanted.

"I am glad," whispered Charles to Ellen, "that this music begins so early, as I must go away to other parties soon."

"Indeed!" said Ellen, forcing a smile, "you are quite a fashionable man, I see!"

"I flatter myself I am," he replied, with a self-sufficient look; and, as he turned away to promise Mrs. Ainslie that he would sing after the piano-forte lesson was over, he did not hear the deep sigh of poor Ellen.

Charles sung a duet with a young lady whom he had met at other places, and he sung so pleasantly that he was pressed to sing a song. He consented, on condition that Ellen would accompany him. She would fain have refused from mere timidity, but the wish to oblige him, and enable him to shine, conquered her repugnance, and she sat down to the instrument; but Charles was anything but encouraging to her.

"I declare," he said, "you don't play near so well as you did at R——."

Sometimes she played too loud, then too soft, sometimes too slow, sometimes too fast; however, she was at last piqued into indifference to his censure, and Mandeville's ill-humour vanished in the gratifying "bravos" and "charming," which attended his own success, and showed no consciousness in the hearers of Ellen's failures. At length the song ended, and Ellen gladly rose; but, while every one else murmured and applauded Charles, the lip which his petulance had paled, uttered no word of praise, and the mortified and indignant girl retired to her seat in silence.

In a few minutes, Charles was entreated to sing again, and he asked Ellen to accompany him again.

"No — I will not," was her cold and firm reply.

"Why not, Ellen?"

"Because I know I cannot please you, therefore I will not give fruitless pain to myself."

In vain he urged her — Ellen was resolute; and Charles, on a lady's saying that she had heard Mr. Mandeville sing sweetly without music, ceased to importune her, and sung unaccompanied. When he had ended his song, which was loudly applauded, preparations were made for dancing quadrilles, and Ellen hoped that Charles would come eagerly forward to request her to dance with him; but he staid so long in the next room, that when he did approach her for that purpose, she was already engaged; and, to her still greater mortification, he neither looked nor expressed regret, nor did he engage her for the next dances. As Ellen was not in the same set with Charles, she could not have the satisfaction of seeing him dance, though she had the mortification of observing that he had selected for his partner, the finest and most fashionable-looking girl in the room. The quadrille was succeeded by a Spanish dance, in both of which, Charles's dancing was thought equal to his singing. At the end of the last dance, when he had quitted his partner, Charles approached Ellen, and she hoped he was going to ask her to dance with him; but he told her he was very sorry, but really he could stay no longer.

"Oh! very well," said Ellen, trying to speak and look cheerfully.

Mrs. Ainslie now joined them, saying, "I suppose you are come to lead this dear girl to the dance now, Mr. Mandeville."

"Upon my word I should have been most happy, but unfortunately"—

"She is engaged, I suppose."

"No, but I am; that is, I must go, though most reluctantly. My presence is imperiously demanded at two parties this evening, near Grosvenor-square, and I fear I shall be waited for, as I have to sing one or two trios at one place, and to dance a new quadrille at another."

"But it is very early for any party in Grosvenor-square, and surely the delight of dancing with Ellen is temptation enough even to excuse your being vainly expected for a few minutes. The heart has its claims as well as other things, Mr. Mandeville."

"Oh, yes; oh, dear, yes," said Mandeville, looking very silly, "but—"

"I beg," cried Ellen, proudly, "that you will let my cousin please himself; I resign all right to keep him here."

"Nay, but Ellen, you are unjust; I am sure I wish to stay. Well, (looking at his watch) there is time for one *quadrille*. Will you do me the honour?" offering his arm.

Ellen looked at Mrs. Ainslie, who made her a sign to accept it, and he led her to the set. But he gave himself the air of dancing with languid indifference, and sometimes only walked through the figure.

"You did not dance thus with your last partner," said Ellen, indignantly.

"No—but I am sparing myself now for my next party; besides, what a fine dancer, and what a fine fashionable girl that partner was! but not so pretty as you, Ellen," he added, seeing her change colour, and look as if she had a mind to sit down.

These words, uttered in a faltering tone, assisted Ellen to recover herself, and she resolved that he should not, if she could help it, again perceive the mortification which he inflicted.

When the quadrille was over, Charles declared he was unable to stay a moment longer, and for the next dance of the set he must resign her to some one else.

"By all means," said Ellen, coldly, while her heart beat almost audibly with internal emotion, and a feeling almost approaching to misery.

At this moment, and just as Charles was hastening away, meaning to take French leave, as it is called, that he might not be detained again, Mr. Ainslie came up, and said that Lady Jane F—— and her daughters were just arrived; and as they were very desirous of hearing Mr. Mandeville sing, and were excellent judges of music, he hoped he would do them the favour of singing before the dancing was resumed.

Ellen listened with almost breathless anxiety for his answer, and felt sick at heart when he replied,

"Certainly, sir, I was going, but I will stay and sing to your noble guests."

He was then presented to her and her daughters.

Mrs. Ainslie said in a whisper to Ellen, "I thought Mr. Mandeville said that he could not stay a moment longer!"

"He even told me so, but—"

"I see — I understand," she replied; "he can stay for *vanity*, but not for *affection*."

"Alas! that is only too true," thought Ellen; and she seated herself where Charles could not see her, lest he should ask her to accompany him. But he did not; a ballad without music was requested, and Charles complied.

Lady Jane and her fair daughters were delighted; Charles was applauded to the skies; another song was requested, was granted, equally extolled, and a third earnestly solicited; but now Mandeville's vanity made him desire to show off in something more difficult, and he looked round for Ellen, that she might accompany him; but at this moment her good genius, in the shape of Mrs. Ainslie, stepped forward to her rescue; for that lady declared that she could not allow any further trespass on Mr. Mandeville's time and indulgence, for she knew he was eager to take flight to the upper regions, where he was anxiously expected; therefore he could not afford to give more time to the lower ones, and must instantly set off for the neighbourhood of Grosvenor-square.

"I really am willing to stay," stammered out Mandeville, provoked, yet ashamed; for he felt that though Mrs. Ainslie's words were flattering, her tone was *sarcastic*; but she interrupted him with,

"Not a word; the more willing you are to indulge us, the more incumbent it is on us not to abuse that good-nature; and I am sure Lady Jane is too generous to desire a pleasure purchased by disappointment to others."

"Certainly I would on no account detain Mr. Mandeville, but I hope to have the pleasure of seeing and hearing him in Grosvenor-place."

Charles bowed, blushed, murmured out, "You do me great honour—happy to wait on you,"—and, having once met the sarcastic look of Mrs. Ainslie, was glad to escape out of the room, without daring to raise his conscious eyes to Ellen, who now, spite of herself, came forward in hopes of receiving a kind farewell, for Ellen knew they should not meet the next day, as Charles was to dine in the country, and was not to return till late. But he was gone in a moment, without one adieu, either looked or spoken! However, he was no longer there to excite or disappoint her expectations in any way, and Ellen felt relieved, though saddened; but the attentions of a very agreeable partner, who talked to her of Sir Henry Claremont and his virtues, and delicately hinted that he had obtained an invitation to the party that evening, merely to be presented to her, as Sir Henry wished him to have the honour of knowing Miss Mortimer, diverted her thoughts from the unworthy engrosser of them, and the rest of the evening passed away pleasantly to her; but, when she retired to bed, she repeated to herself Mrs. Ainslie's forcible words: "Yes, yes; he can stay for vanity, but not for affection."

The next day, when Ellen rose, she said to herself, "Well, I cannot hope to see him to-day!" and was surprised at finding that a degree of repose stole over her feelings at the idea; for as it was no longer a pleasure *only* to expect him, but anxiety, and the dread of mortification, now mingled with that pleasure, she was conscious that her harassed mind was soothed by the certainty that for some hours, at least, she should be able to feel entirely alive to the enjoyments of the passing day, should really observe the objects and sights presented to her eyes, and be able to profit by the opportunities afforded her of seeing London.

"Good girl," said Mrs. Ainslie, when she returned to dine and dress for the theatre, "I am quite satisfied with you to-day, Ellen; and I really believe you will turn out to be the sensible girl I always thought you."

Ellen, as Charles was not present, was wholly absorbed in the illusion of the scene at Covent-garden, and as much charmed as Mrs. Ainslie wished her to be with all she saw and heard; till, just before the farce began, a gentleman who had joined their party said to Mrs. Ainslie,

"I expected to see Mandeville here, for he told me he should come hither, if he returned in any tolerable time from the country, and did not go to Lady D.'s."

"Depend on it, if he does return, he will go to Lady D.'s," replied Mrs. Ainslie, in a tone which Ellen well understood.

However, this conversation had awakened in her a faint hope of seeing him; and instead of attending any longer to what was passing on the stage, she was looking round every time her own box-door opened, or looking into the boxes opposite, or near her, to discover the object which even yet was, as usual, dearer to her than any other in creation; but not as usual did her judgment go along with her partiality; she felt that her heart and her head were now at variance; and that Charles Mandeville of London was very inferior to the Charles Mandeville of R——. But vainly did Ellen look for Charles; he came not, and the curtain dropt.

"I conclude Mandeville did not return from the country in time," said his friend.

"On the contrary, I conclude that he did, and is now singing and dining at Lady D.'s," replied Mrs. Ainslie; while pensive, and disappointed, and silent, Ellen walked to the carriage.

Mrs. Ainslie followed her into her room that night, and, seeing her melancholy countenance, kindly took her hand, and told her that she knew very well what was passing in her mind; and that she hoped she would see the necessity, which pride and delicacy equally imposed on her, to cease to feel so tenderly towards a man, who evidently had no longer any tender attachment for her.

"But is it possible that he can so soon, and for ever, have ceased to love me?" cried Ellen, melting into tears; "why, if you had heard how he reproached my uncle for his cruelty, in not allowing us to engage ourselves to each other.—Surely, surely, he does not know his own heart; and he loves me still, spite of appearances!"

"Ellen, dear child of my dearest friend, listen to me, with calmness," said Mrs. Ainslie: "believe me, that real and faithful love is a restless feeling, that cannot be satisfied without proving its existence by constant attentions to the object of that love. The true lover prefers the society of the woman he loves to every other engagement; and to him, no amusement is welcome which is unshared by her, unless she is far distant, and that he wishes to beguile part of the tediousness of absence by it.—There, Ellen, I have given you a little sketch of what a true lover is; and I leave you to compare your lover with it, and see if it resembles him. I beg leave to add, that I advise you also you also to compare Sir Henry Claremont's assiduity with your cousin's, and with the sketch."

"Oh! but Sir Henry has never been exposed to the temptations of a London life since he knew me."

"True, therefore the condition on which you accept Sir Henry's addresses, and I trust you will one day accept them, shall be, that he goes and lives six months in London to try his constancy, because you shall tell him, to speak *elegantly*, my dear, ' that a burnt child dreads the fire.' "

"No, no; I shall never love or accept any man now," cried Ellen, her tears redoubling.

"Not *now*."

"Oh! but I mean—"

"I *know* what you mean; but do not believe, my sweet girl, that I laugh at you, or that I do not enter deeply into your present feelings; I only think that they ought not to last, as the object is unworthy of *them;* I should not say so, if Sir Henry Claremont were the object, and by some strange inconsistency of conduct were to behave to you as Mandeville does, for then I should be tempted to say, ay, you may well weep, for you have lost a treasure. What I wish on this occasion is, that you should feel your own worth, justly appreciate the value of your own tenderness, and learn to despise the heartless boy who can thus prefer town pleasures, and women of fashion, to you and your invaluable love. There is a speech for you, Ellen! I did not think I had been so eloquent; but, the Arabian song says, ' who can live with the rose without imbibing some of its sweetness;' so the wife of Ainslie must catch some of his eloquence; and thus, having ingeniously contrived to compliment both myself and my husband at once, I will bid you good night, and join my prayers to yours, Ellen, for your being assisted through your present trial, and that you may live long and happy!"

But poor Ellen was not yet willing to resign for ever the illusions of love, so long dear to her heart; however, she slept at last: and, on waking, the image of Mandeville was sometimes replaced by that of Sir Henry Claremont: that of the latter was soon rendered more vivid to her mind's eye, by the entrance of her maid with a large hamper, and a flail basket. The former contained the finest pines and melons that she had ever seen, and the latter the most beautiful and rare hothouse flowers; but they were accompanied by no letter or note, and the direction was in a hand unknown. Ellen, however, could not doubt that they came from Sir Henry, whose hot-houses and pinery were the admiration of his neighbourhood.

"See!" said she, with a sparkling eye and a glowing cheek, when Mrs. Ainslie entered her apartment.

"And whence came they, Ellen?"

"From R——, I believe."

"And who sends them?"

"There is no letter, so I only suspect the donor, and he is Sir Henry, I dare say."

"So dare I. Well, this is a lover, if, as the man says in the play, *Le vrai amphitryon est celui où l'on dine, le vrai amant est celui qui donne des ananas et des fleurs.* Oh! sweet Sir Henry! I dare say he divined that I was going to have a bag-wig and feathered party to dinner to-day, and wished to be very elegant at as little expense as possible, and therefore, to bribe me to espouse his interest, he sent these gifts; for I suppose, Ellen, you do not mean to keep all the fruit to yourself, and wear all the flowers, appearing one day as Pomona and Flora the next."

"Oh, no; you are welcome to them all: but—one of the flowers I mean to wear in my bosom, and another in my hair."

"Bravely resolved, and if by any at present unforeseen chance Mandeville should come, as I own I have not *invited* him, I beg you will tell him that you wear them for the sake of Sir Henry Claremont."

The only part of this last sentence to which Ellen attended was the assurance Mrs. Ainslie gave that she had not invited Mandeville, for till then she had hoped he was to be one of the invited guests. However, she could not help owning to herself that it was not necessary *as things were* for Mrs. Ainslie to invite Mandeville every day, as it was evident that all his engagements were formed, and would be pursued, without any reference to her.

The end of the morning, as usual, was spent in sight-seeing; and on their return home they drove to the same painter's as before, for Mrs. Ainslie to indulge herself in looking at Sir Henry Claremont's picture, the dear man to whom she owed the elegant additions to her dessert and her flower-vases; and she saw by Ellen's countenance, when she now beheld the picture, that the original had gained ground in her favour.

The dinner went off well, but the evening would have been passed by Ellen in a state of vain expectation of *him who came not,* had not an acquaintance of Mandeville joined the party, who informed Ellen that Charles had found the day he passed in the country so agreeable, that he had been induced to stay longer, and that he had left him there singing, dancing, and acting to the delight of every one. Ellen changed colour, sighed, was glad her cousin was so well amused, when, after a great struggle with herself, she conversed, laughed, and seemed as cheerful as usual; but she could not help saying, when she retired to rest,—"This was a voluntary absence of a whole day—this was an engagement formed since my arrival! Why! why did I come to London? Yet, no—thankless girl! if I had not come, I might have been deceived still!"

The next day Mandeville called, and wanted to walk out with Ellen alone as he had done before, but Mrs. Ainslie would not allow it; she said that her young friend was to be with her *so short a time* that she could not bear to give her up *a whole morning,* he must therefore accompany them if they walked. Mandeville, though he felt the reproof, coolly said, her going would increase his pleasure and his pride; and he should be the envy of every one whom he met.

"*Plus galant, que tendre!*" murmured Mrs. Ainslie between her teeth, and Mandeville had feeling enough to blush. "But I think," added she, "we had better go in the carriage, and order it two hours sooner than usual."

Accordingly they did so; and Charles, equally attentive to both ladies, endeavoured to be most agreeable; but it was only by showing himself attached to Ellen that he could really succeed in pleasing either lady. He, however, obtained an invitation to dinner, which, with many blushes and regrets, he declared his inability to accept, as he was engaged to dine and go to the play with some friends whom he had met in the country; and the next day he was going, he said, to —— races, and thence on a tour to Windsor and Reading. But he was very sorry, indeed, to lose so much of his cousin Ellen's society, but it was her own fault — why not let him know she was coming?

"Yesterday, however," said Mrs. Ainslie, "you knew she was here, and *yet* you staid a day longer in the country than you intended."

"True; my host and hostess were so pressing and so charming."

"We think Ellen charming."

"So do I, I am sure," he replied; "and I hear she makes quite a sensation wherever she goes."

"She does; but I patronize the suit of only one of her adorers."

"May I ask his name?"

"No—he is not here, but mourning her absence at R——."

"Indeed!" said Mandeville, blushing, for he knew of Sir Henry's addresses.

"Yes, and if you had dined with us you would have seen some of his votive gifts, 'flowers to the fair,' adorning her hair to-day."

"If I had, I should have stolen or trodden them under foot."

"No — that you should not," said Ellen, hastily; "I prize them too much to have allowed it."

"This looks serious," replied Mandeville with a mixed expression of conceit and mortification on his countenance: but the former prevailed; and, wishing them good morning, he left them at Albany, assuring them he would call as soon as ever he returned.

"Ellen, forgive me," said Mrs. Ainslie; "but, surely it is *bad taste* to love this man."

Ellen blushed, looked down, and was *silent;* and Charles Mandeville was to be absent from London a week while she was there, preferring races to her company. Alas! what then were the protestations of man's love worth? to think that he loved her still, spite of appearances, was now impossible; and she resolved to try to repay indifference with indifference. A week's absence was a good preparation for the execution of this wise resolve; but Mrs. Ainslie thought there was still a better way of weakening Charles's power over her.

"Love," says the eloquent author of Ada Reis, "though strong in itself, receives great accession of strength from perceiving the admiration paid by others to its object;" and Mrs. Ainslie hoped, that if she could contrive to let her see Mandeville eclipsed in those very things which gave him such importance in her eyes; if she could hear his singing excelled, his pretensions to high fashion and fashionable acquaintance proved less real than they now appeared to her, and could be made to seem at all degraded or ridiculous in her sight, her end would be accomplished. But to effect this was difficult; as though Ellen already thought Charles grown conceited and affected, especially concerning his singing, he still appeared to her the height of elegance, and "the desired of all beholders."

The ensuing week passed more rapidly than Ellen expected or wished, as she found herself obliged to quit London at the end of the next week, since Mrs. Ainslie was forced to hasten into the North, on account of the increased illness of her sister. At the end of the week Mandeville called, and told Ellen that he had procured his friend Lady D.'s Opera Box for Mrs. Ainslie and herself, for the next Tuesday; this was delightful news to Ellen, who had not yet been at the Opera.

"We are really much obliged by this attention," said Mrs. Ainslie. "I conclude you will dine with us on Tuesday, and use one of the tickets yourself?"

"Impossible! I dine with some friends of mine at the —— Coffee-house that day; a dinner I am to give in consequence of my election into the Alfred, which will, I expect, take place the day before, as though success is difficult I am told that I am sure of getting in; but I shall certainly come to the Opera during the course of the evening. I have promised Lady B. to look in on her in her box, and I shall also make a point of coming to yours."

"You are only too good," replied Mrs. Ainslie, with a sarcastic smile; "but, seriously, I am glad to have so well situated a box as Lady D.'s is for Ellen to see the Opera, and Tuesday is the only night that she will be able to go thither."

"The only night?"

"Yes; she will leave me, and I London, on the following Friday."

"I am quite concerned to hear it; my dear Ellen, may I speak a few words to you alone?"

Ellen, fluttered, curious, anxious, paused for a minute, and then led the way into the next room.

"Ellen," said Mandeville, "I know you like to oblige me, and I have a favour to ask of you; I am invited to Lady Charlotte D.'s musical party on Monday, and I want to sing that song which I have altered so as to make it suit my voice, and which you accompany so well; but I dare not trust anybody but you to accompany me, I therefore told Lady Charlotte that I had a cousin in London whom I wished to bring with me to her party, if she would allow me, and she said yes, but she hoped you would excuse her calling on you; I said I was sure you would not stand on ceremony, therefore here is her card, and here an invitation."

Ellen at first was speechless at the utter selfishness of this project, and the indelicate coolness with which Mandeville seemed to make a convenience of her at the expense of herself, respect and proper pride, and desired to take her with him to a London assembly as his accompanier. When she recovered herself, she coldly and proudly said, that though always ready to oblige him, she must consult Mrs. Ainslie before she could reply to such a proposal; then, before Charles could prevent an appeal to which he instantly foresaw the certain answer, she threw open the folding door, and, with faltering voice, disclosed to Mrs. Ainslie what Mandeville required of her.

"Amazing!" exclaimed Mrs. Ainslie, after a pause, during which she fixed her fine eyes on Charles with an expression of indignant contempt: " I have seen selfishness before, but never, I think, to so unblushing an amount as now."

"Selfishness, madam! surely there is nothing selfish in wishing to procure my cousin Ellen a pleasant evening's entertainment; and you, I know, do not visit Lady Charlotte D."

"Nor shall Miss Mortimer, sir, if I can help it. No guest of mine shall go to the house of a lady who does not choose to trouble herself to pay the customary due of respect by calling on her, or at least by leaving a card at the house where she is; and I wonder, Mr. Mandeville, that you could bear so to compromise the dignity of your cousin. Then to want to drag the dear girl about with you merely for the purpose of your own vanity, but never to desire it at the prompting of affection!"

"How do you know, madam, that what I now desire is not from the prompting of affection?"

"Because it is inconsistent with your former conduct since Miss Mortimer's arrival in this town; however, let Ellen judge for herself. If she wishes to go to Lady Charlotte's, I can send her thither with a friend of mine; what say you, Ellen?"

"That I see the affair in the same light as yourself, and have not the slightest wish to go to Lady Charlotte D.'s. I must also add that I am hurt beyond measure to see that my cousin Charles has never wished for my company at any party before, and that now he wishes for me merely to make me the means of gratifying his vanity."

"You are too severe, and unjust, and ungrateful, Miss Mortimer."

"Indeed! would that I were so," replied Ellen, bursting into tears; " would you could make me think myself so; for then I should be spared the bitterest of all pangs to me—the pain of blaming you."

Mrs. Ainslie did not like the tenderness of this last part of Ellen's reply; but, on the whole, she was satisfied with the just view which she took of Mandeville's motives, and had little doubt of Ellen's being cured in time; as selfishness, in the beloved object, is of all qualities the most likely to break the tie that holds the heart in bondage. Ellen's tears, if they did not otherwise affect Charles, induced him to express his regret for having wounded her feelings, especially when it had been his sole intention to gratify them : but he hoped, he said, that she would excuse the unceremonious invitation to the party, for the sake of the Opera Box.

"Artfully put, Mr. Mandeville. Yes, yes, we will try to remember nothing but the obligation you have conferred on us. Will you dine with us on Sunday? we dine out to-day."

"I go out of town on Sunday to dinner; but on Monday I should be happy to have the honour to wait on you."

"So be it;" and Mandeville bowed and departed.

He was no sooner gone than Ellen threw herself on Mrs. Ainslie's neck and gave way to an agony of grief, which drew sympathizing tears from her affectionate friend.

"Oh! trying, but blessed visit to London, Ellen," said Mrs. Ainslie; " it has brought you to know the false from the true : but come, now your full heart has relieved itself, tell me, if you can, for what qualities you loved Charles Mandeville?"

"He is my cousin you know."

"Yes, that is a reason why you should love him, certainly; but not why you should be in love with him."

"And then—"

"Well, and then?"

"I thought he loved me."

"That is, was in love with you."

"Yes."

"Well, now for the reasons?"

"And then, you know, he is very handsome."

"Yes, but not so handsome as Sir Henry Claremont, in my eyes."

"And then he sang and danced well, and seemed very good-natured."

"And I suppose you read together, and conversed together?"

"We read novels together, but our conversation was chiefly about, about—"

"What!"

"Love, and each other."

"Ay, I suppose so: an admirable compendium of the substance and sense of a boy's and girl's attachment; but I conclude you never thought Charles a man of reading and reflection, or of active virtues, like Sir Henry Claremont?"

"I never thought *about* it," said Ellen, blushing.

"Then now, my dear, it is time that you should think about it, and seriously too; compare Mandeville with his rival, and let me soon hear that the poor Baronet is sent by you to undergo his six months' probation in London."

Ellen smiled, and looked as if the idea was not so impossible to be realized as she thought it, when Mrs. Ainslie last mentioned the subject; and by the time the carriage came round she had dried up her tears, and anticipated the drive, though Charles was not to be with them, with considerable pleasure. They called to take up a friend of Mrs. Ainslie in their way to the Park, and as the lady wished to see pictures, they went to the painter's gallery, nothing loth, and saw Sir Henry's picture again.

"What a countenance! what a fine man!" said their companion; and Ellen saw, not without pleasure, that a group of ladies and gentlemen were admiring this picture, and that two or three declared they had the happiness and the honour of knowing the admired original.

"Oh! what a happy woman you might be if you chose," said Mrs. Ainslie in a whisper; "and I think you might spare the poor man the six months' probation, as he is seven-and-twenty, and men know their own minds though boys do not."

As Charles had engaged to dine at Mrs. Ainslie's on the Monday, that lady had enabled herself to put in execution part of her scheme for curing Ellen of her love. Mrs. Ainslie was acquainted with a young man of good family and independent fortune, whose first passion and first pursuit in life unfortunately was music; as his health was delicate, he was ordered to Italy, and, during a residence in that country of some years' duration, his very fine voice was improved to the utmost, as was his general skill in music; and he returned to England the best possible amateur performer. He had within the last year become intimately acquainted with a singing-master and his sister, born of Italian parents in England; and with these young persons, who sang admirably, he passed so much of his time, that it was supposed the pleasing manners and vocal powers of Olivia Pedruglio would win so much on his affections that he would make her his wife. In the meanwhile, not the slightest stain attached to the lady's character from the intimacy; and when Mr. De Mornay was invited out to dinner, it was customary to invite Mr. Pedruglio and his sister also. But it was no easy matter to prevail on Mr. De Mornay to pay visits; he preferred receiving friends in an evening at his house, where music of various kinds was the usual amusement; but, as he greatly respected and admired Mrs. Ainslie, he promised to wait on her, and so did the Pedruglios, as soon as she told him that she had a very *particular* reason for wishing him and his friends to dine with her on the Monday. When Charles Mandeville arrived, Mrs. Ainslie took him on one side, and said, "I am going to tell you what will delight you; Mr. De Mornay, that first of gentleman singers, and his Italian friends, the Pedruglios, dine here to-day, and they will sing in the evening." Charles bowed, and said he was enchanted; but the discerning Mrs. Ainslie saw very clearly that he was excessively mortified, and had rather bear himself sing than the finest singers in the world. However, though mortified, he was not entirely dismayed, and was frequently lost in thought during dinner, saying to himself, "what can I sing? for Ellen is so cross or timid that I know she will refuse to accompany me; really I think I will sing without music, for every one likes ballads." When two or three persons were assembled in the evening besides the dinner-party, Mr. De Mornay, as soon as he was requested to do so, took his seat at the piano-forte with the prompt compliance of a gentleman, and the skill of a professor. The first song he sang convinced Mandeville that he could not presume to compete with a singer like that, and Ellen's eyes swam in tears, whilst the most touching *voice* she had ever heard, sung a sweet *cantabile* air, the words of which (for she knew enough of Italian to understand them) applied in many respects to her own disappointed hopes.

"Is it not exquisite?" said Charles, wishing to be contradicted.

"Oh! I could listen to him all night!" cried the enthusiastic girl.

"Indeed! an hour or two would content me," said the mortified Mandeville.

The friends next sang a trio; in short, duet succeeded to duet, song to song, from each of the three, when Mrs. Ainslie in a whisper desired De Mornay to ask Mr. Mandeville to sing. But he, alarmed at the evident superiority of the man who asked him, and mortified at the praises bestowed on him and his friends, refused with awkward bashfulness, not modesty, not real timidity, but its counterpart, which is self-love, afraid of not shining, fearful of not excelling; and it was not till after repeated pressing that he could be prevailed on to sing. Then what should he sing was the difficulty.

"Would Ellen accompany him?"

"No; she knew she could not satisfy him."

"How unkind!"

"Not at all; you would scold me, and I should not know a note that I played; and indeed you sing best without music; besides, you will then come into no competition with these great performers."

"So then, you think me very inferior to them?"

"Who is *not*?" said Ellen.

"There, even Ellen is gone over to them. Heigho! I wish I had not come, or had gone away after dinner," thought Charles.

However, he sang, but oh! the obvious difference between the singing of a frightened, husky, ill-assured amateur, and that which the company had lately heard. The friends kindly encouraged him, but, spite of his vanity, Charles felt that he had completely failed, and Ellen was quite surprised to think that Charles could sing so ill; she, however, good-naturedly assured the audience that her cousin was terrified out of his accustomed powers. Miss Pedruglio now asked Charles if he would take a part in an Italian quartetto. He said he believed he could, as he had once sung it before; but, as he could not sing by note, he made such blunders that the performance could not go on, and the friends were earnestly conjured by a gentleman whose love of music conquered his politeness, *not to lose time*, but to sing themselves together in their usual way.

Unfortunately, two ladies of consequence came in at this moment, who had heard Charles sing; and knowing nothing of music, declared that they were vulgar enough to dote on a ballad, and they hoped Mr. Mandeville would indulge them. Again, therefore, Charles sang, and hoped to recover his lost fame; but in vain, his voice was hoarse, and even his newly-come admirers said they saw he was very hoarse, and had a bad cold, and it was very kind in him to sing at all.

"Pray, sir, can you sing ballads?" said one of these ladies to De Mornay; "but I suppose English singing is beneath you."

"By no means, I will sing an English song directly."

"But not unaccompanied?"

"Oh! yes."

Then turning from the instrument, he sang a simple, touching melody in a plain unornamented style, which went directly to the heart. The words he sang, were as follows:—

I had a hope which now is o'er,
  It was the hope to live for thee!
But since I'm doom'd to hope no more
  I only bid thee pity me.

Yet had I been the favour'd one
  Allowed to live for love and thee,
I might, perhaps, have been undone,
  This world had then been *all* to me.

But now I bid its scenes farewell,
  A better world my aim shall be!
And I may hope one day to dwell
  In that eternal world with thee!

There, dearest, I again may love,
  And thou with smiles my love may'st see,
For 'twill be shared with saints above,
  And worthy them, and worthy thee.

Even Charles's passionate admirers were enchanted, and he had the mortification of hearing the same praises bestowed on De Mornay, which they had before lavished on him; and even Ellen, who had given sympathizing tears to the first two verses, and hung entranced and enamoured on the recollection of De Mornay's tones, was so *absorbed* in admiration that she forgot to feel for Charles's discomfiture. Not very long after, Mr. Ainslie saw Mandeville hastening out of the folding-doors.

"I hope you are not going yet?" said he.

"Oh! yes, I am; I was charmed into staying too long," he replied. "I have an engagement in St. James's-Square; I ought to have been there an hour ago."

"What is that?" said Mrs. Ainslie, on whose arm Ellen leaned.

"Oh! only that Mandeville is gone to *St. James's-Square*."

"Indeed! these grand *squares* are sure to take him from our humble *circle* in Serjeant's Inn."

"Is Charles gone?" said Ellen, "and without my seeing him go? what could I be thinking of?"

"Of Mr. De Mornay, my dear; and I dare say Charles was thinking of him too when he went away."

"Poor Charles," said Ellen, "I really felt for him."

And so she did, she pitied him; but she soon found that this pity was of a degrading nature; it was a pity that lowered the object of it,—it was a sort of pity which a man could not with any safety excite in the woman who loved him. Certain it is that Ellen's musical taste had never been so highly gratified as it was that evening; and she went to bed wondering how she could ever have so much admired Charles Mandeville's singing.

"Now, Ellen," said Mrs. Ainslie to her on the Tuesday morning, "you shall see that rare, but to me always pleasing object, a true gentleman, and a real man of fashion. Colonel Delborough is to dine with us, and accompany us to the opera; but though he is a single man, and has a foible for pretty girls, I insist on your not preferring him to Sir Henry; for here is another basket of fruit and flowers arrived, and some carp to boot. Tell me, Ellen, has Sir Henry ever seen you eat ravenously, that he thus feeds you?"

"Oh, no; I dare say he sends them, because he knows that I shall have pleasure in presenting them to you."

"Well, I am glad to see that you do his motives justice,—that is a good sign."

The Hon. Hugh Delborough was a man who at forty retained a considerable share of the beauty of early life, and all its pretensions; but his vanity, however great, never wounded the vanity of others; he was generally courteous, so much so that he was reckoned a complete pattern of a fine gentleman, and a high-bred man. He was sometimes, indeed, cold and proud, and severe in his manner to those whom he thought coxcombs and pretenders to the rank and consequence which they had not; therefore, as his acquaintance was known to be never granted but to those who were worthy to associate with a man like him, the privilege of being known to Colonel Delborough was eagerly courted, and deemed a sort of passport into the best and most select circles in the fashionable world. Colonel Delborough, with many virtues, had some weaknesses, one of the chief of which was a tendency to fall in love with every young and pretty face that appeared in the world in which he moved, attended with a full persuasion, that he himself was irresistible. But his preferences never amounted to passions; never urged him to take the desperate step of marrying. Love was to him little better than the gentle intoxication produced by champaign; exhilarating, not disordering; and he changed his favourites nearly as often as he did his gloves, always taking care to do so before his assiduities were become so dangerous as to induce the lady's father or brother to ask him what his intentions were. He was, therefore, a very harmless flirt; and while even the youngest girl of fashion was proud and desirous of his attentions, the eldest and most experienced woman of the world was never alarmed, lest these passionless and bounded attentions should injure the peace of her child or *protégée*; consequently he was welcome everywhere; and as he united rank to fashion, being an Earl's younger son, he was more courted and more invited than any man in London society. Mrs. Ainslie was desirous of obtaining him as her beau to the opera, not only because he knew every one personally who was worth knowing, but because she wished, by showing Ellen, in him, what a real man of fashion was, to give her a model with which to compare Charles Mandeville. She was, therefore, much disappointed when Mandeville said he could not dine with her that day, but she expected he would come to her box during the evening, and this expectation was rendered certainty by the receipt of a note from Charles to Ellen, in which he told her that he would make a point of coming to their box as early as he possibly could; that, as he knew almost every person of rank and fashion at the opera, he might point out to her all the persons worth seeing.

" Yes," said the pleased Ellen, " Charles knows every one, I dare say."

" I have no doubt," replied Mrs Ainslie, " but that Colonel Delborough knows them better, especially as he himself is one of the very set to whom Mr. Mandeville alludes."

Colonel Delborough was captivated with Ellen as soon as he beheld her; and, as usual, on hearing that she was of a good family, he said to himself, " Now, if I were inclined to marry, here is an opportunity." As Colonel Delborough was a man of real fashion, he was not afraid of being thought unfashionable, by going to the opera to hear the overture, and, as he loved music, he had no objection to the early hour at which Mrs. Ainslie ordered the carriage. He and his fair companions, therefore, had the satisfaction of hearing a fine overture of Mozart performed in a manner worthy of it. I shall not attempt to describe Ellen's raptures at the singing and scenery, but she was not so well pleased with the dancing, for she was not always sure that she ought to look at it, and she was not sorry when the first ballet was ended.

By this time, Ellen was almost fascinated with the grace, the attentions, and the conversation of the Colonel. He could not fail to know every person of rank and distinction in the house, and had many pleasant anecdotes to relate of them whom he pointed out. Mrs. Ainslie had given the fourth ticket to her husband, in case his professional engagements allowed him to use it, therefore the Colonel had no rival, and was enjoying the privilege of being sole beau to a very fine woman, and a beautiful girl, when an acquaintance of Mandeville's entered the box to pay his compliments to the ladies, and Colonel Delborough heard him say something concerning Mandeville, whom he only knew by sight, and who was particularly disagreeable to him. When the young man was gone, he turned round and exclaimed,

" Mandeville ! Do you know Mr. Mandeville, that consummate coxcomb, that would-be somebody? My dear Mrs. Ainslie, how came you to know that man? He is so entirely out of your way."

" I agree with you," she said, " but my acquaintance with him was unavoidable." Here she looked at Ellen, who sat in ill-suppressed agitation to hear her cousin, and once most dear Charles, so spoken of ; but Mrs. Ainslie motioned to her not to betray their relationship, and the Colonel went on.

" The boy expected to get into the Alfred, but I am happy to say he has been disappointed."

" Is he not elected, sir ?" said Ellen eagerly.

" Oh ! no, he is not the sort of person for us. I have reason to know all about him. The name is a high name, but I find his father was only what is called a wholesale dealer at Bristol, a man who kept a general warehouse, and died very rich. I inquired, because the young man thought proper to pay marked attention to one of my nieces, Lady Julia L——, and the silly girl encouraged him; but I soon put a stop to her folly, by inquiring into the youth's pretensions, and pride conquered love."

Scarcely had he ended his philippic against Mandeville, when he himself made his appearance, and just as poor Ellen, seeing how much the Colonel disliked him, was wishing that he might not come. Mrs. Ainslie could not present him to her friend after what had passed, and, on his first entrance, Charles was too full of his disappointment at the Alfred to attend to aught besides, and he talked of nothing else, though he saw that the conversation did not interest Mrs. Ainslie. At length, however, he remembered that he came to do the honours of the opera to Ellen, and he pointed out this Countess, that Duchess, such a beauty, and such a distinguished character; and so far he was right, but Ellen had been told all this before.

"And *there*," said Mandeville, "that is the Dowager Duchess of ———."

"Are you sure of that, sir!" said the Colonel, coldly. "Do you know the lady."

"I have met her in company, sir."

"Indeed! but still you are mistaken, at least I hope so, for she died two days ago,"

Mandeville could only say she was very like her.

"Not at all, sir; that lady is fair as alabaster, and the Duchess was dark as ebony."

Nothing daunted, Mandeville then pointed out other persons of rank.

"Is he right now?" said Mrs. Ainslie.

"Perhaps so, but they are lords and ladies, of whom I know nothing," he proudly replied.

Mandeville felt piqued, and observed, "that they were well worth knowing for all that."

"Humph!" said the Colonel, shrugging up his shoulders and looking on the stage.

Mandeville now named lords and ladies to the right and left out of bravado, and then the Colonel coldly said, sometimes,

"It is not she, or it is not he."

Mandeville, little suspecting who this contradicting gentleman was, disputed the point and insisted on it that he was right. At last, he pointed out a lady just come into the opposite box as Lady Harriet H. The Colonel said it was not. Mandeville persisted, and declared he knew her perfectly.

"Do you mean that you are acquainted with her, sir?"

"No, sir; but I have seen her; I met her a few evenings ago coming into Lady D.'s as I went out."

"You must therefore know her well, no doubt, sir?"

"I do know her well, sir."

"But not quite so well as I do, sir; for Lady Harriet H. is my own niece, sir."

Mandeville was excessively confused, and stammered out an apology, while Mrs. Ainslie could not help laughing, exchanging as she did so certain meaning looks with the Colonel, while Ellen pitied Charles with a sense of the ridiculous connected with him, which it was painful, but salutary to her to feel. Mrs. Ainslie now, lest Charles should expose himself again, whispered to him;

"Do you not know this gentleman is the Hon. Colonel Delborough?"

Again Charles was confounded; he had long been ambitious to have the honour of that gentleman's acquaintance; and, now that he had the opportunity as it seemed, for he was in the same box with him, he had not only not been presented to him, but he saw that there was no intention of presenting him, and also that the Colonel beheld him with proud contempt. Ellen, too, he found was cold and absent in her replies, and Mrs. Ainslie not disposed to talk. He therefore rose and took his leave, telling Ellen that he hoped to see her again before she quitted London.

"To be sure," said Mrs. Ainslie, "this is only Tuesday, and Ellen does not go till Friday. You know," she added in a whisper, "as I cannot see her to the mail myself, and Ainslie dines out that day, *you must*."

"Must! oh dear! no, really, I am very sorry; but I dine out on Friday, and really—indeed, I—it is most probable I *dine* when the mail sets out; and if Ellen will go by such vulgar conveyances, she must take the consequences, I really *cannot* go with her."

"Ellen does not go by the mail," said Mrs. Ainslie, "and I said what I did *only* to try you, and your regard for your cousin."

This put the finishing stroke to Mandeville's discomfiture, and he quitted the box, shutting it after him with great violence.

"I never saw such ill-breeding and impertinence," said the Colonel, colouring violently; "and to call you Ellen too, that young man deserves to—"

"He is my first-cousin, sir," said Ellen, calmly, but firmly.

The Colonel was shocked, confounded, and silenced.

"Miss Mortimer," said he, at length, "there is no apology too humble, which I am not willing to make to you for what I have uttered; had I known, as indeed I ought to have been informed, that Mr. Mandeville was your relation, I would not only have been silent when I could not commend, but I would even have endeavoured to like him for your sake. Why did you not tell me who he was?"

"It was my place to do that, Colonel," said Mrs. Ainslie: "but I had my reasons for not doing it; and I am sure my young friend will forgive you your unintentional offence."

"Yes, certainly, sir;" cried Ellen; "but what you said of poor Charles gave me great pain. I own that he was positive and contradicting, but then one ought to make allowances for him. He was full of irritation from his disappointment concerning the Alfred, and when one is uneasy and mortified, one is so apt to be disagreeable and tenacious, and—and—"

"And what, Ellen?"

"Why, there was something very provoking both in Colonel Delborough's manner and yours too, my dear friend."

"Granted, granted; and I like you for your candid and spirited defence of your relation: so does the Colonel, I dare say."

"Oh! I adore her for it; and, indeed, charming Miss Mortimer, I should not care how often I was so attacked, if I could be sure to be so defended. Now tell me how I can expiate my offence? To appease and please you, I will call to-morrow, and leave my card for Mr. Mandeville; will that do?"

"Generously and delicately felt, and like you, Colonel; but I trust Ellen will not exact such an *amende* from you."

"By no means; I am too proud for poor Charles, to do it. Let him be thought deserving the honour of being known to Colonel Delborough, before he has it; but I will not impose my cousin, as an acquaintance, on any man."

"Proudly and honourably felt, Miss Mortimer; and I sincerely hope, that before long, I shall not only know, but like Mr. Mandeville; at least, no endeavour on my part shall be wanting to enable me to do so; and I must own that I saw him and heard him this evening with prejudiced eyes."

"See Ellen," said Mrs. Ainslie, soon after; "Mandeville did not go home to take poison, however mortified he might be; for there he is yonder, the life of the set in one of the pit boxes, and laughing with all his power."

It was so; and Ellen, being assured that Charles did not remember or feel as much for his late painful embarrassment as she did, forgot it also, and enjoyed as much of the last ballet as she dared to look at, and enjoyed also the buzz of admiration which her new and beautiful face excited in the crush-room, while the gallant Colonel enjoyed it still more, and was in raptures, when every now and then, some man of ton or rank whispered in his ear, "Oh, Delborough, you are always a happy fellow."

When Mrs. Ainslie thought over all that had passed, she was startled, on recollection, as she had been at the time, with the manner in which Ellen had defended Charles; but at length she reflected that it was her relation whom she defended; she considered that if she had seemed less hurt, her tranquillity must have been *assumed*, which would have been a very suspicious circumstance; and that had she been *violently agitated* by still struggling, conscious love, she would have been unable to speak at all, or only in broken, faltering tones; whereas, on the contrary, she was voluble and judicious in Charles's defence; evidently proving, therefore, that she defended him from a sense of justice, and a feeling of relationship alone. It is well, thought Mrs. Ainslie, and I see that this faithless boy's reign is over.

He certainly thought so himself; he therefore wished to dismiss, rather than wait to be dismissed; he chose to assure Ellen that he loved her no longer, rather than receive from her a previous assurance that her attachment to him was at end, and he wrote to her as follows:

"DEAR ELLEN,—I meant to see you once more; but, as I find that I am no favourite with Mrs. Ainslie, and indeed she was not far from being downright rude when I last saw her, even though she was in the box which I procured for her, I do not mean to call at the house again; therefore take this method of wishing you health and happiness. I am going abroad, and it will be many years probably before we meet again; both of us by that time will probably have changed our situations, but I shall always be,
"My dear Ellen's
"Affectionate friend and cousin,
"CHARLES MANDEVILLE."

When Ellen received this letter, she could not help weeping bitterly over it; not that she was sorry, or even mortified that Mandeville's attachment to her was at an end, but she wept for the loss of those pleasing illusions which had so long given interest to her existence. She wept for the loss of the love, not the lover; and she felt a blank in her heart which seemed to remain there a sad and dreary void, till the day before her departure arrived; then the idea of home, and the welcome which awaited her there, from many an affectionate heart, diffused a glow of cheering and impatient tenderness to her own.

To part with Mrs. Ainslie, was now the only thing that clouded over her brow, for that lady had twined herself round her affections, by entering with tender sympathy, and almost with intuitive penetration, into all her fears, her sorrows, her triumphs, and her escapes.

But, that pang over, she was cheerful, and willing to try and make her companions so; when she found herself seated in a travelling chariot, by the side of a lady and gentleman, friends of Mrs. Ainslie, who were going through the village of R——, in their way to a more distant country.

The travellers slept on the road, and at so short a distance from London that it was nearly evening the next day, before Ellen saw each well-remembered object, and beheld the lodge at Sir Henry Claremont's park-gate. Perhaps, thought she, he will be there, waiting for my arrival. But he was not there, and Ellen felt disappointed; perhaps he was at her uncle's: he was not there either; and in the midst of the affectionate greetings of her family Ellen felt sad, because she was not welcomed by one friend more: and he had professed so much, and had been so markedly attentive in sending her presents to London; was he, too, inconstant? Was she doomed to find all men false? If not, where was Sir Henry Claremont; she dared not inquire, because, as she said to herself, she did not like to show she was mortified; but perhaps it was because she did not feel it easy to name him. But when she had been home near an hour, her uncle said,

"Ungrateful girl! Why, Ellen, you have never yet inquired for Sir Henry Claremont!"

"Oh, dear, no;—I hope he is well."

"No, certainly not, or you would have seen him long ere this. He has been so ill that he has kept his bed."

"Indeed! but I earnestly hope he is better?"

"Yes."

"Then I am satisfied;" and Ellen was really ashamed to feel that she was glad to find necessity, not choice, kept him away, even though that necessity was caused by indisposition.

But a few minutes after, pale, thin, and wrapt up as in the depth of winter, Sir Henry Claremont himself appeared.

"I would have come," said he, "Miss Mortimer, when I heard you were arrived, in spite of nurses and physicians, for I was sure the sight of you would do me more good than all of them; but I am very weak, and I need not tell you I am very ill-looking."

Ellen was affected, nay, overpowered; for she could not help contrasting this welcome, this eagerness to see her, with that of Charles Mandeville; and, while overwhelming sensations of affectionate gratitude and painful recollections throbbed tumultuously in her soul, she hurried out of the room, having almost returned Sir Henry's pressure of her hand as she passed him. But she soon came back, and eagerly, anxiously entreated Sir Henry not to risk a life so precious, by staying out any longer in the night air.

"If you say my life is precious, I will go directly," said he; "and if you will add, pray come again soon."

"I will say anything rather than detain you now, you look so pale; and yet very like your picture."

"My picture! have you seen my picture?"

"Yes, frequently; for Mrs. Ainslie fell in love with it."

"Mrs. Ainslie fell in love with it; O kind Mrs. Ainslie! but could not she make her love catching? But you are impatient for my departure, so good-night. Oh! I am so happy to see you again returned, I feel well already."

I have little more to relate; in six months after Ellen's return, she was the happy wife of Sir Henry Claremont: and, as Mrs. Ainslie wrote to her in her letter of congratulation, she felt that she had indeed cause to bless her Journey to London, as it had taught her to distinguish the FALSE from the TRUE.

END OF FALSE OR TRUE; OR, THE JOURNEY TO LONDON.

THE CONFESSIONS OF AN ODD-TEMPERED MAN.

WRITTEN BY HIMSELF.

How strange it is that I, whose life has been rendered miserable by the consequences of the reserve and closeness of my disposition, should now be going to unveil my secret thoughts and feelings to the world! But such are the changes incident to human character, when operated upon by the vicissitudes of human life;—and where is the change, however extraordinary, that may not one day be effected by the influence of misery and the impulses of self-reproach?

I was born to the possession of a comfortable fortune; and unhappily lost my parents before my temper could be regulated, and my character formed, by parental judgment or parental authority.

My disposition was naturally, as it is called, reserved, and my pride great. The voice of admonition had rarely reached me except from masters whom I cared not for, and it always excited in me resentment rather than amendment of any sort;—for who, thought I, has any right to reprove or control me? My natural reprovers and directors are in their grave, and I spurn the officious interference of these my would-be friends. Still, I had affections, I had sensibility; but as circumstances had early in life shown me the danger sometimes incurred by a display of affection and of feeling, and that they exposed their possessor to be often cruelly enslaved and trampled upon, I resolved to conceal my susceptibility within my own bosom, and entrench myself behind a rampart of apparently impenetrable coldness, from the dangers attendant on any assaults on my affections.

Time insensibly elapsed. I had gone through school without disgrace, if without honour; and I had taken rather a high degree at the university, when at the age of one-and-twenty I left college, entered myself at Lincoln's Inn, and took possession of my paternal inheritance. My estate lay near a large city, and it will be readily believed that I immediately became an object for matrimonial speculations.

But though my manner was generally polite, it was so cold where I saw it was most desired that it should be the contrary, that neither mothers nor daughters had any reason to flatter themselves their wishes would succeed.

I was, besides, a great speculator on character, and was fond of sitting in observant silence, when I was expected to join the dance, or make the fourth at a card-table.

During this time I regularly kept my terms in London; and when I returned to my house, I continued to appear so insensible to the many flattering advances which I received, that at length parties were formed without considering whether I was in the country or not; and the general opinion I believe was—that to be sure I could be very agreeable when I chose, but that really I took so much courting before I would say a word, that it was not worth while for any one to take much trouble about me. But I had one advocate and one admirer, and a disinterested one too—one whose good opinion I never attempted to gain by flattery or attention of any kind, but who, from the natural benevolence of a pure and generous heart, always loved to protect the absent from severe animadversions.

And what a creature had I thus unconsciously enlisted on my side! But I will not anticipate. As I am going to confess my faults, I hope I may also be allowed to mention my good qualities. I was rich, and I loved to impart some of my wealth to others; but this in me was no merit; I was not a man of expensive habits, therefore I had few personal wants, and I gave, not so much from principle as from impulse; for my charities were not the result of any self-denial, any surrender of my own gratifications.

It so happened that some kind action, which I thought unknown, reached the ear of my amiable defender and eulogist in the town of C——, and laid the foundation of an attachment which—But, as I said before, I will *not* anticipate.

Still she ought not to have loved me; I was never worthy of her. My ruggedness of nature never deserved her gentleness, her tenderness, her forbearance, her pardoning spirit—Pshaw! I am digressing.

She was beautiful, if countenance rather than regularity of features can entitle any one to that epithet, and her smile spoke the unaffected cheerfulness of a heart at peace with itself and with all the world beside. Benevolence beamed in her soft blue eye, spoke in the soothing accents of her voice, and it seemed as if happiness must reign wherever she deigned to take up her abode—Oh! busy memory, peace! and let me proceed with my story.

Though always on my guard against the fascinations of women, I could not but desire the acquaintance of a being like this.

She danced well—I liked to be her partner.
She sung delightfully—I was the most attentive of her hearers.

She talked eloquently, yet unaffectedly—and I used to love to converse with her.

With her I often wholly forgot my reserve; and the coldness of my manner, at times, vanished before the kindness and ingenuousness of hers.

This was indeed a homage, and a proof of power most dear to the heart of woman. To make that man unreserved, cordial in manner, and agreeable in conversation, who was usually guarded, cold, and taciturn, was a triumph that even her modest nature could not but delight in; and I was told that she would allow no one to deny in her presence that I was the most conversable, warm-hearted, and agreeable of men. She always added that she had the best grounds for being assured I was the most benevolent too. She used even to insist on it that I was *handsome;* though the utmost of my personal pretensions were to the praise of being a well-made manly-looking man, with a sensible countenance.

But that countenance was, I know, very austere and unprepossessing. She, however, used to dwell on the effect of my *smile*, and to declare that the radiance of my expression, when animated into smiles of benevolence and complacence, was such as she had never seen before in any human being. Sweet enthusiast! Alas! alas!

It is not to be supposed that this strange prepossession in my favour could fail at length of influencing me in hers; cautious though I was of forming any tender attachment, and resolved also never to let any woman know the extent of her power over me.

But, spite of myself, I looked—I listened—and I loved; and I soon was enabled to pay my kind advocate a marked compliment; which, though it did not betray the extent of my feeling towards her, was sufficient to strengthen the regard which she loved to cherish towards me.

Some circumstances, not worth relating, involved me in severe but wholly unmerited obloquy; and those who have lived in a country town must know that the greatest delight of its inhabitants, in general, is to detract from the merit of any one distinguished in the slightest degree above the rest, and that to destroy a reputation is the climax of enjoyment.

The calumny against me was related often with minute and even with increasing details before my lovely friend; and every time—not merely from her particular respect for me, but from her knowledge of human nature in general, which taught her that persons are usually consistent with themselves, and that certain virtues are incompatible with certain vices, and *vice versâ*—she always undertook my defence; declared her perfect conviction that the whole story was false, or that, if rightly told, it would redound to my honour, and not to my disgrace; and was always sure, by her benevolent and candid eloquence, to silence those whom she was unable to convince.

As soon as I heard what she had done, my resolution was taken.

Pride of heart, which I could not subdue, but which at the same time I never presumed to justify, led me to preserve an indignant silence on the subject of the charge against me to my accusers, though the proofs of my innocence had always been in my possession.

But to her who had generously undertaken my defence, without any ground to go upon but the noble confidence of her nature, her wise distrust of calumny and reports, and her consistent respect for me and my character—to her I owed every respect, every feeling of gratitude; and it was my duty to show her that I valued *her* good opinion, though I despised that of others.

Accordingly I waited on her; laid the whole details of the affair before her; forced her to listen to my exculpation, though she assured me it was wholly unnecessary; and then left her with a heart and mind in which her image reigned triumphant.

From that hour my attentions became so constant, and the language of my looks so tender, that the object of them could not be blind to the conquest which she had made, though the most feminine delicacy and restraint guided her looks and actions; and though she could not but expect to engross my attention when we met, she never seemed to think she had any decided claim on it. This surrender of a right which most women would have imperiously asserted, and have looked displeased if their claim was not acknowledged, riveted me in her chains for ever; for I was consciously the slave of a petty pride, which made me resist all claims on my attentions, and *particularly* resist the claims of women.

So far all was well; but unluckily the gossips of C—— thought proper to interfere; and I was engaged to Caroline, and on the point of marriage with her, according to report, before I had breathed one word of love to her.

This very natural report, after the attentions I had paid her, awakened my jealousy of independence, and the suspicion incident to my character.

I fancied the people of C—— believed I had advanced too far to retreat; and also that Caroline's friends had perhaps spread the report, in order to hasten my proposals.

A generous man would not have imagined this; but I was not a generous man; and I not only thought it, but I *acted* upon it, and became suddenly cold in my manner towards the gentle being whose affections I believed were awakened in my favour, merely because I could not bear any interference with my actions, and was resolved not to be talked or compelled into a marriage even with the woman whom I adored.

Accordingly, at the next ball, instead of soliciting the hand of Caroline, I kept at a distance from her after my first salutation, and had resolution to withstand the wandering, but not reproachful, glance of her soft and speaking eye; and I saw, with mean satisfaction, how listlessly and joylessly the usually active and gay Caroline went down every dance that evening.

I was as cold and as distant at two succeeding parties, when a rival, and a formidable one too, now entered on the field.

It was well known that Caroline had refused several offers; but then they were not eligible ones; but the gentleman who now came forward as a pretender to her hand, was, in every respect, worthy even of *her*. I must do him justice, and I have often wondered that *she* did not. Nay, I felt that she ought to have loved him; and that nothing but a blind infatuation for an undeserving object—namely, myself—could have led her to reject a being so perfect. Indeed, I carried my self-judgment so far, that I thought it a *fault* in Caroline to love me and refuse him. He was handsome, learned, highly-gifted in point of talents; and he was good, fine-tempered, benevolent, and pious. In rank, he was her superior—for he was the younger son of a nobleman; in income, being a beneficed clergyman, he was her *equal; yet still* he was rejected, because *I* was preferred! What is that passion called love, that thus sets the judgment at defiance, and rejects a true, to worship a false divinity!

I was not sure, however, that my formidable rival would *not* succeed; and I began to relax in my assumed coldness, when I saw his marked attentions, and their aim; especially when the sarcastic eye of a shrewd married friend of Caroline's, who disliked me and adored him, was fixed on me with a look which seemed to say—"You have lost her now for ever."

Accordingly, I requested Caroline's hand for the two first dances at the next ball—she was engaged to my rival, but she accepted me for the two next; and I found a perceptible difference in her expression when dancing with me and when dancing with him. While she was his partner, her eye wandered about, or carelessly turned on him as he led her down the dance. While she was mine, her conscious looks were fixed upon the ground, and her cheek was flushed with a degree of pleasurable emotion, which her apprehensive, and rather wounded pride, made her ashamed to feel.

Some women would have retorted on me my own coldness, and, with some propriety, perhaps, assumed indifference, though they felt it not; but the heart of Caroline was a stranger to disguise; she was above the common artifices of her sex; and though I have sometimes, in a splenetic humour, accused her of being ingenuous almost to indelicacy, I now do her justice, and am convinced, that were all women like her, the fate of lovers and of husbands would be much happier than it is. But then I must also own, that men must be refined, in order to deserve such women as she was—Digressing again—but I will try to improve.

After this effort of my self-love—and as it had convinced me my rival, charming as he was, had not yet undermined my influence—I became less assiduous than I had been at the ball; and as it was certain I was not yet an actual *pretender* to the hand of Caroline, my rival ventured to offer himself to her acceptance; and the lady whom I mentioned before strongly urged her to marry him—but urged in vain; and with well-principled, though I must call it rash decision, she at once declined the honour which he offered her; and the rejected lover left C——.

It was now confidently expected that I should come forward, as no one doubted but he had been refused on my account; but because I knew such a step was expected from me, I would not take it; and I persevered in my resolution though I own that it was often nearly overset whenever I met Caroline, and was exposed to the fascinations of her countenance, her voice, and her manner, which all acquired added charms in my eyes from the evident pensiveness of the former, the increased softness of the second, and the timid consciousness which, spite of her self-command, was visible in the third.

To be as cold and distant as I had been when I first heard of the report concerning us, was, however, impossible; and I had, in the insolence of conscious power, the assurance of assuming towards her, familiarity and easiness of manner.

Instead of approaching her with my usual respectful softness, I put out my hand to take hers, with a sort of abrupt " How do you? how do you?" I nodded my head when I met her, instead of touching or taking off my hat like a gentleman; and I soon found that the indignation which Caroline's friend expressed towards me both by her countenance and manner, was beginning to be felt by the gentle girl herself.

And why was I thus acting? I can only say that I was obeying one of the many obliquities of temper, and that I earnestly exhort my female readers never to put their happiness in the power of a man who has ever exhibited such marks of caprice and humour as I now did.

After thus trifling with the feelings of a heart too ingenuous to hide itself at all times from my interested observation, I went to London to keep my terms; but it was known that I meant to eat my Christmas dinner in the country, and I returned two or three days before the 25th of December.

On my return I called on Caroline, and found her friend with her; and I was sensibly struck with the change in Caroline's manner towards me; it was calm and almost cold; and it was not long before she told me that she was going the next day to Sir Charles D.'s to spend the Christmas week. I had some difficulty in concealing the pain this intelligence gave me, as I knew that Sir Charles's house would be the resort of many agreeable persons of both sexes, and that Caroline would be the object of much attention amongst men who would have great opportunities of ingratiating themselves with her, and might succeed in driving me from her mind.

But seeing her friend's eyes fixed on me, I recovered myself immediately, and said I was glad she was likely to pass her Christmas week so pleasantly; but I strongly urged her to stay through the next week, which no doubt would, from the hospitable nature of the master, be as gay as the first.

" Are you going thither?" asked Caroline's friend eagerly, while Caroline betrayed, I thought, some pleasurable emotion—" Are you going? I know you were asked."

" I was," replied I, " but I am not going; therefore, my advice to your fair friend was wholly disinterested and truly benevolent, as I urged her prolonged absence to my own discomfiture—as what is C—— but a desert without her?" I glanced my eye over Caroline as I said this, and saw her cheek redden with a mixed feeling, I believe, of disappointment and resentment, while her friend in a very sarcastic tone complimented me on the *disinterested benevolence* on which I seemed to value myself. She might well ridicule my assumption of a feeling which I certainly had given no proofs of in my conduct to her friend; and seeing Caroline apparently sinking into no agreeable reverie, I called forth all my powers of entertaining, and soon succeeded in drawing her into conversation.

Insensibly, too, her manner resumed its unaffected unreserve, and her countenance its animation, and we both appeared to derive as much pleasure from each other's converse as we had ever expressed and experienced before; while in proportion to our increasing gaiety and evident delight in each other, the brow of Mrs. Belson became clouded, and her manner harsh and petulant.

Contrary, I dare say, to her wish, which was to be a spy on her friend and me, she was called out of the room, and I was alone with Caroline. In an instant our animation and our volubility were suspended, and Caroline's eye avoided mine, though mine involuntarily sought hers. At length, thrown off my guard by the situation, I approached her; and as I leaned on the mantel-piece close to which she was seated, I said, in a voice of great tenderness, "So then, you are going away for a fortnight; for a month perhaps!"

"Very likely; and you advise it you know," she replied, playing with the handle of the bell-rope.

"I advise!" exclaimed I, and was going to utter some of the feelings of my heart, when Mrs. Belson returned; and finding I had no chance of being again left alone with Caroline, I took my leave, but not till I had obtained her permission to call again the next morning before she and her friend set off, to bring her a book which she had asked me to lend her.

I could have wished certainly, to have left a friend, not an enemy, in possession of my mistress's ear, as I well knew that I laid myself open by the capriciousness of my conduct to severe and just animadversion. However, I knew I had an advocate in the heart of Caroline, and I returned to her house the next day, more full of hope than of fear; but I had no reason to be pleased with my reception from either lady. Mrs. Belson was, as usual, repellant and abrupt in her manner; and Caroline, who had, with justice no doubt, considered the tenderness of my manner almost at the moment of her departure, as only one instance more of coquetry evident in my conduct, received me with a degree of reserved dignity which I had never seen in her before, and which, though it wounded my feelings, was approved by my judgment. It was in vain that I started the most interesting subjects—Caroline was not disposed to converse; in vain I endeavoured to meet her eyes, and express by mine the affection and the regret which I experienced. Without either effort or emotion she seemed to avoid looking at me; and I began to fear I had deceived myself in thinking that she entertained for me any strong and decided feeling of regard. The idea was nearly insupportable, and finding how little pleasure my presence seemed to impart, I should have taken my leave very soon, had I not found it absolutely impossible to rise; so strong was my feeling of awkwardness and embarrassment, and so difficult did it seem to me to bid Caroline farewell without betraying the state of my heart—and of *that* my pride could not endure the idea.

I therefore lingered on, sometimes speaking, sometimes turning over a music-book which lay near me, and sometimes looking at a picture opposite through my glass.

The carriage at length drove up, and the ladies retired to put on their shawls. I could not do less than wait to hand them into the carriage; accordingly, when they returned, I offered my arm to Mrs. Belson, and was going to take Caroline's hand to assist her, when she defeated my purpose by springing in without my assistance. This action piqued my self-love, and enabled me to utter my parting compliments in a firm and steady tone of voice.

Nay, more, coxcomb as I was, I gave Caroline, as she bowed her last adieu when the carriage drove off, one of my *smiles*, of which I was told she had expressed herself so much enamoured, as I was desirous that her last remembrance of me should be a pleasant one. I then returned home, displeased with Caroline, angry with myself, almost muttering curses on Mrs. Belson; but, above all, triumphant was the painful idea, that I should not see Caroline again for many, many days, and that she was going where she would be surrounded by candidates for her favour, whose pretensions to it were as great, if not greater than my own. Sometimes I resolved that I would follow her in a day or two; but as I had refused the invitation when it was sent me, pride forbade me to take this step, however tempting, because I was sure my change of resolution would be attributed to the *true cause*—Caroline's power to attract me.

Now, for the first time, did I feel the force of the well-known phrase of time's hanging heavy on the hands. I had refused to join the Christmas party at Sir Charles's, because I wished to study some law-books which I had lately purchased; but alas, in vain did I sit down to my learned labours—the blue eyes of Caroline gazed on me from every page, and I found that studies of a lighter nature were more suited to my present deplorable condition. Accordingly, I had recourse to the belles-lettres and to history; but whenever I came to a beautiful passage in the classics, my first idea was, that I would repeat it to Caroline; and if I remarked and noted down any event in the pages of history, it was with a view to mention it to her at her return. Nor did my chains sit easily upon me; on the contrary, I spurned at the fetters I could not break, and lamented that a man of my pride and independence of soul should thus have sacrificed his freedom to a woman, although that woman was one of the most distinguished of her sex. Thus passed the first week of Caroline's absence. The second was begun and ended, and still her return was not at all expected. At this period, a gentleman left Sir Charles's, and returned to C——, and immediately on his arrival he called to impart to me the pleasure which he had experienced, and to describe the scenes in which he had been a delighted actor.

It was with difficulty that I could endure the narration. Caroline the life of every thing! her playing, her dancing, her singing, the theme of every praise! and the young, the rich, the noble, hanging enamoured on her looks and graces! Scarcely could I forbear to affront the chattering and happy being, who smiled complacently while he plunged a dagger in my heart. But the worst was yet to come; " The honourable Mr. Douglas arrived," he added at last, "two days before I came away; and if I have any penetration, Caroline Orville and he will make a match of it at last."

Luckily for me he took his leave after he had given me this last blow, which, however, was softened by his saying, as he closed the door, "In short, the party at L—— is so delightful, that it grieved me to be forced to leave it; and Sir Charles says, if *you* had been there, he should not have had a social wish ungratified." " Then, as Sir Charles says so," thought I to myself, " it gives me an excuse for joining the party, in spite of my refusal, and there I will soon be."

But there was an influenza in the town of C——; and whether I had caught it before I saw my communicative acquaintance, or whether the agitation of my mind affected my body, I cannot say; but certain it is, that I became very ill as soon as he left me, so ill as to be forced to send for advice, and I was confined to my bed for three days successively.

On the fifth day, however, I was quite recovered, and on the sixth I resolved to set off for L——.

But when I looked in the glass and saw how pale and thin my illness had made me, and when I recollected that I was going to put myself in comparison with my handsome and blooming rivals, my courage failed me, and I resolved to stay at home. But then I recollected that Caroline could never have admired me for my personal graces, and that if she knew my increased plainness of person proceeded from love for her, she would love me the better for the change. But how was she to know that the change proceeded from such a cause, unless I told her? And could my proud spirit and close temper ever allow me to make such a confession? "No, never!" I exclaimed, "never shall any woman know to what a state of degradation and dependence her power can bring me!"

Then again, I said to myself, "If this account be true, and she is engaged to Douglas, why should I go to witness his triumph?" But the next minute something whispered me that all hope for me was *not* at an end, and to L—— I went.

I arrived there about two hours before dinner, and when the company, having returned from their morning walks, rides, or drives, were lounging in the apartments till the time for dressing arrived; or amusing themselves with the different games or books of prints with which the tables were abundantly supplied.

As the doors of the first room of the suite were open, my entrance made no noise; and as I felt very nervous, I desired the servant not to announce me; for I know nothing more painful to a nervous man, than to follow his own name into a room, especially if he believes that room to contain many persons, and amongst them one whom his heart flutters at the idea of meeting.

As I entered, I saw myself whole-length in a pier-glass, and I thought I had never looked so pale and ugly before. And while I thought so, I beheld an absolute contrast to myself in the form of Douglas, leaning enamoured over Caroline Orville, who was playing chess with a man I had never seen, and who, at the very moment of my entrance, was looking up in Douglas's face with delighted eagerness, because she was just going, as she thought, to check-mate her adversary. I did not stop one minute in that room, nor did I look a second time towards them; but I saw her start when she beheld me; and immediately after I heard Douglas say that she had not made the right move. I now entered the third room in the suite, and saw my host, of whom I was in search. My welcome from *him* was all that I could wish; but Mrs. Belson, who was with him, changed colour, I thought, at seeing me, and looked for a moment as repellant as usual. She came forward to meet me, however; but exclaimed, and not in a tone of pity, "Dear me, how ill you look! Why, I declare I could not have believed anything could change a man so much for the worse in a few days!"

"That is not the way to make any one look better," observed the good-natured Sir Charles.

"Pardon me! see! it has improved him already. It has given him colour, and he does not look quite so ghastly as he did."

"If you had been as ill as *I* have been, *you* might perhaps look ghastly too," replied I.

"Ill! ill!" cried she; "Well, I thought you never ailed anything, but were as strong as a horse. Really, one would think you were in love—poor soul! If so, indeed I *pity* you," she added significantly and sarcastically; then humming an opera tune, and almost dancing into the other room, as if impelled by some very pleasant thoughts, she left me with a dagger in my breast; for her words and her manner convinced me that she had no longer any fear that my amiable rival would not succeed.

Sir Charles saw my emotion, and my increasing paleness; and, having given me a chair and some wine, for I was really quite overcome with the fatigue of my journey, and Mrs. Belson's attack, he kindly inquired into the nature and duration of my illness; and having heard my reply, he said laughing, "Well, well, this was enough to make you ill, without love's having anything to do in the matter."

He then expatiated on the excellence of the society which he had been able to collect around him, and begged leave to present me to those ladies and gentlemen to whom I was not personally known. I therefore, not without great emotion, followed him into the first room. Caroline had finished her game, and was just rising. As soon as she saw me, she came forward, and met me with an extended hand—a proof of ease and unembarrassment which I would readily have excused; and in proportion as she was at her ease, I was confused and awkward. I saw that Douglas obamined us both with very observant eyes; and my spirits were not raised by the conviction which I felt, that his countenance brightened the longer he regarded Caroline.

Caroline even rallied me on my changeableness of nature, but wondered that if I meant to come at all I did not come before.

"I should have come before," I replied, "if I had not been prevented by illness."

"Illness!" echoed Caroline in a tone of kind alarm; but she was prevented adding more by her friend, who rather pettishly led her away by the arm, saying that if she did not go to her room directly she would not have time to finish her letter before dinner. Caroline went with her; and the little hope which Mrs. Belson's evident wish to get her away from me gave me, was completely crushed by Douglas's offering her his arm across the hall, and by her accepting it. That day I thought my toilet would never have been finished; I could not tie my neckcloth in my opinion at all to my mind; my hair would not obey the brush, and form itself becomingly as usual; and as I looked at my pale and thin face, I could not but repeat to myself Mrs. Belson's expression of *ghastly*, and I mournfully added, "Ghastly indeed!"

The bell rang, and I went down to dinner. As I expected, Douglas led Caroline; though, being the first man in rank present, he ought to have led a married lady. This little circumstance gave me exquisite pain; and the lady whom I conducted, and, consequently, sat next, found me any thing, I am sure, rather than an *entertaining* companion; while to complete my misery, Mrs. Belson sat opposite to me, and showed me by her looks of triumph how much to her satisfaction matters were going on at the head of the table on my side, towards which I really dared not look.

At length, however, some of my silent sufferings ceased; for on the dinner being over, the dessert on the table, and the servants withdrawn, subjects of general conversation were started; and as I felt quite at home on some of them, I was able, when particularly addressed by my host, to talk with volubility; and I had soon the satisfaction of seeing Caroline's head bending forward, as if in the act of listening very attentively; nor could I be unobservant of the pettish and angry manner in which Mrs. Belson at that moment drew on her glove, and then drummed on the table. Nor was it long before she gave the lady on Sir Charles's right hand the signal for retiring, being resolved my little triumph should be as short as possible. I contrived, however, to open the door for the ladies; and as they passed, and Caroline civilly raised her eyes to mine, I gave her a look too full of meaning to be misunderstood, and sighed as I did so. A faint flush instantly overspread her cheek, and I thought she gently sighed in return. At what straws do persons in love catch in order to save themselves from sinking into despair! I returned to the table quite another man; and when we joined the ladies, my cheeks were flushed, and my eyes were no longer dim.

But my spirits were as quickly and as easily depressed again, as they had been easily and quickly elevated; for the pleased attention with which Caroline listened to Douglas, having first made room for him on the sofa by her, made me even worse than I had been before; and I did not let Sir Charles rest, till by summoning Caroline to the piano forte he removed her from a situation so agonizing to my feelings. But Douglas handed her to the instrument, and retained his post by her side, while I stationed myself in front of her, and had soon the satisfaction of seeing that my earnest gaze confused her, and that her voice was not as steady as usual. I do not know how I contrived it, but I got the start of Douglas, and handed her back to her seat; nor did I relinquish it without such a pressure as I had never before hazarded, and a sigh which spoke a heart too deeply touched to be able any longer to conceal its feelings. It was not to the sofa which she had *quitted* that I led her, but to a single chair, which was soon surrounded by flattering men, in whose compliments I could not prevail on myself to bear a part.

Caroline, too, did not smile on her flatterers with her usual sweetness, but seemed disposed to fall into reverie; but on Douglas's approaching her, her usual animation seemed to return; and while she carefully avoided my eyes, she looked up in his with a degree of complacency which I was tempted to think indelicate. It was more than returned by the expression of Douglas's; and I was rejoiced when another lady began a concerto on the piano forte, which would, I knew, prevent any conversation and any language of looks for a long time to come.

During this performance I watched Caroline very narrowly, and I saw her evidently lost in thought, though her head was turned towards the performer. Still there was nothing promising to me in her thoughtfulness, and there was a vexation rather than an emotion in her manner.

I cannot describe the succession of hopes and fears which agitated me that evening, and which, contrary to my usual caution, I did not attempt to conceal from the observation of others; and scarcely could I believe the change in myself which the dread of losing Caroline had effected in me. My reserve, my pride, my dread of ridicule, my sense of independence, were all annihilated; and love, with all its train of doubts, fretfulness, and fears, reigned triumphant over my heart.

The next day, the day after that, and the succeeding day, were nearly duplicates of each other; except that every day Mrs. Belson contrived some new method of tormenting me, and letting me know that Caroline would certainly at last accept Mr. Douglas. My own fears confirmed the truth of this assurance;—"for how," thought I, "can a sincere, generous, and correct woman, give encouragement to a man whom she has once rejected, unless she intends to recompense him by ultimately accepting his offers?"

On the evening of the fourth day after my arrival, as I was going to light a candle that stood on a table near the door against which Douglas and Caroline were standing in earnest conversation, I heard him say, "Well then, you will meet me to-morrow morning at eight, in the garden?"

"I will—indeed I will," she replied; on which he took her hand and pressed it to his lips.

This action and these words, appeared to me the destruction of all my hopes; and whether I had been weakened not only by illness, but also by continued uneasiness of mind ever since I arrived at L———, I cannot say; but certain it is, that a sudden sort of faintness came over me, and letting go the candle, I staggered to the side of the wall, and with some difficulty got out of the room. At this moment, (as I have been told since,) Douglas turned away from Caroline to speak to some one else, and neither saw my seizure, nor the alarm which observing it occasioned her; while Caroline, alive only to that alarm, hastily left the room in search of me, as she heard a noise in the hall, as she imagined, as if some one had fallen down. Her heart and her ear did not deceive her. I had only just reached the door of a small parlour which stood open, when my senses failed me for one moment, and I fell; but I had raised and seated myself before Caroline discovered me—I am now going to describe one of the happiest and proudest moments of my life;—but the recollection overcomes me.

The paroxysm of unavailing agony is past, and I resume my narration.

Judge of what my feelings must have been, when on opening my eyes, I beheld Caroline standing near me with a face colourless from alarm, and asking in a voice inarticulate from emotion, how I did, and whether she should ring for assistance.

It was not a moment for further reserve or further hesitation—we were alone, and the door had closed itself upon us—but in an agony of passion I demanded of her why she expressed such interest in the wretch whom she alone had made; or pity for that illness which she alone had occasioned.

"I—I make you ill!" she faintly exclaimed.

"Can you doubt it? But go—why do you stay here? Go back to the happy Douglas—go and renew your promise to meet him to-morrow morning, and leave me here to perish!"

"Leave you here to perish!" replied Caroline, bursting into tears;—"ungrateful man!"

I awaited in trembling impatience till this burst of feeling, so precious to my soul, had a little subsided; then taking her trembling hand, I said, "Then do you not love Mr. Douglas, Caroline?"

"Love him! Oh no!"

"And need I not despair? And will you bid me live, and hope, Caroline?"

She did not—could not speak. Such a proof of ardent attachment as she was now receiving from a man whose conduct towards her had been marked—she thought and others had told her—by nothing but cold and heartless coquetry, and one too whom she had vainly endeavoured to banish from her affections, was too much for her sensitive nature, and for a few minutes she leaned her head against my shoulder in agitated silence; but that silence was eloquent—and I was happy. Nor did we leave the room we had so unexpectedly entered, till she had assured me that Mr. Douglas's attentions should no longer disturb my peace; but that, though she should certainly keep her appointment next day, it was one of business only, and in which Mrs. Belson was always to have accompanied her; and she would take advantage of the opportunity to let him know the true state of her affections, and that her hand was now promised to the possessor of her heart.

Oh! with what different feelings did I return to the drawing-room, to those with which I left it! But Caroline was too full of agitation to join the company again that night; nor did I long remain below, for I wished to retire to the solitude of my own chamber, in order to enjoy the new and delightful prospects which that blessed evening had so unexpectedly opened upon me.

My night, if not passed in sleep, was passed in reflections even more cheering still, and I gazed on returning morn with sensations as new as they were delightful.

Let me, however, do myself the justice to say, that there was one drawback to my pleasure; namely, the misery which Caroline was, by her ingenuous declaration, to inflict on my amiable rival that very morning; and it was not without a feeling of true compassion that I saw her from my window, accompanied by Mrs. Belson, join Douglas on the lawn, according to their appointment, and set off on their projected walk; which was, as I afterwards found, to the cottage of a poor widow, in whose welfare he wished to interest her.

After they were out of sight, I came down and walked round and round the shrubbery that shaded the lawn, awaiting their return; and it seemed a long time indeed to me before they came in sight. When they did so, I found that Mrs. Belson preceded Caroline and Mr. Douglas by at least a hundred yards, and that the two latter appeared engaged in an earnest conversation.

On seeing me, Mrs. Belson came forward to meet me, with an air of smiling triumph.

"You see," said she, when I joined her, "what is going forward yonder; I don't like to be in the way on such occasions, therefore I walked off."

This convinced me that she was wholly ignorant of the nature of their conference; and I must own that I rather enjoyed the prospect of her mortification, especially as, while she spoke, she fixed her eyes earnestly on my face, in order, evidently, to enjoy my embarrassment and distress; but she looked for them in vain; and with great calmness, not unmixed with sarcasm, I replied, that I could not but admire her consideration for the feelings of others.

"What self-command some people have!" she exclaimed, conscious of, but not *amended* by the sarcasm. "I suppose, now, you expect to make me believe that you do not envy Douglas at this moment?"

By this time they had nearly reached us. "No, on my *honour*," replied I, "I do not envy him. Look at him, madam, and tell me whether he appears to you an object of envy?"

She did look at him; while I, seeing the pale cheek of Caroline, evidently rendered so by painful emotion, flush with conscious pleasure at sight of me, while she welcomed me with a smile, could not resist eagerly hastening to meet her; and I was just going to draw her arm under mine, when I recollected myself and desisted, lest I should unnecessarily wound the agitated bosom of my rival. He saw and felt my forbearance, and with a generous effort worthy of him he grasped my hand—tried to join it with Caroline's—then, bursting into tears, relinquished his hold, and hastened down the path that led to the stables; while Mrs. Belson, with a countenance far more "ghastly," to use her own word, than mine had ever been, exclaimed, "For mercy's sake! tell me what all this means! Mr. Douglas—Mr. Douglas! pray, pray let me hear an explanation from you!" So saying, she ran after him, but she did not stay with him long. The explanation was soon given; and we saw her return with her handkerchief at her eyes. Caroline stepped forward to speak to her; but angrily waving her from her she rushed into the house, and ran up into her own apartment.

Affected, but not surprised, Caroline returned to me; and taking her under my arm, I led her into an unfrequented walk, where I drew from her an account of what had passed; and learned that on her requesting a conference alone with Mr. Douglas, her friend had gladly left them together, little suspecting what the result of the conference would be.

I was now almost at the summit of my wishes;—my rival was dismissed, and I accepted; nor could the intelligence which was brought Sir Charles at the breakfast-table, that Mr. Douglas was gone, give me one added feeling of security and triumph.

But, in compliance with Caroline's wishes, *one* engagement was to be kept secret a little while longer, as our courtship might be reckoned, she was aware, too short for such a decisive proceeding; and after breakfast, at which Mrs. Belson did not choose to appear, she went to that lady's chamber, to beg her to keep the secret, and also to endeavour to appease her resentment at the failure of her darling expectations.

She found Mrs. Belson really ill from disappointment, and very averse to receive me as the betrothed lover of her friend; but Caroline's gentle and soothing persuasions succeeded at length, and I was admitted into her dressing-room.

But the storm had not subsided, and I was obliged to hear what my heart whispered were unwelcome truths. For she justified her preference of Mr. Douglas, on the ground of his being, she believed, a more amiable man than myself, and possessed of a finer temper; not to mention his superiority in rank, and in all those accomplishments, both mental and personal, which usually command the admiration both of men and women. Contrary to her expectations, I agreed to all she advanced; and I even owned that I wondered, as much as she herself could do, at Caroline's blindness in preferring me to Douglas.

Spite of her prepossession against me, she was pleased with what she called my generous candour; and putting out her hand to me, she said she really believed I should make her like me in time.

I replied, that I had no doubt of it; because in one respect, and that an *essential* one, I was fully Mr. Douglas's equal, and that was in the strength of my attachment to her amiable friend, whose happiness would, I assured her, be the study of my life.

She shook her head, and exclaimed, "We shall see, we shall see;" and even at the moment her words struck on my heart as full of a painful foreboding of unhappiness to come. Ill-fated! but affectionate woman!

I could not resent, however I might be hurt by her dislike to my union with Caroline, as it proceeded from a strong and I may call it quick-sighted interest which she took in her friend's happiness; and she had convinced herself that mine was a temper calculated, in all probability, to destroy her peace. Let me mention here one anecdote of myself, in order to gain me a little approbation from my readers, to set against the censure which they may load me with as I proceed.

Mrs. Belson's father was the steward of Caroline's father, and he had left her a very large fortune, which a most unworthy husband entirely dissipated, not many years ago; and at this very moment this much-injured woman is supported entirely on an income which *I* allow her, without her being at all conscious who her unknown friend is. But to return to my subject.

Caroline had now been more than a month at Sir Charles D.'s, and I had been there a fortnight. I ventured to suggest a wish to Sir Charles, who had been Caroline's guardian and the intimate friend of her father, that he would try to prevail on her to shorten my term of probation, and consent to give me her hand before we left L——.

My request was perfectly consonant with the inclinations of the good old man, as he was very desirous that the child of his dearest friend, and the daughter of his own adoption, should be married from his own house; and in spite of the earnest dissuasions of Mrs. Belson, who said we had as yet been lovers too short a time, Caroline consented to be mine, at the end of two months from that period.

To Sir Charles I left the necessary arrangements for drawing up a draft of the marriage settlements, &c., and I gave him a *carte blanche* to settle on Caroline whatever he thought fit; insisting at the same time that the whole of her own fortune should be settled on her and her children; with the income of it, even during my life, wholly at her disposal, to save or to spend, according to her own will, without my having any power over it whatever.

To this Sir Charles strongly objected, and so did Caroline herself; Sir Charles because he did not approve a wife's total independence in money matters, of her husband ; and Caroline, because her tenderness of nature made her desire to be dependent for every thing on the being whom she loved best. But I was resolute; and Sir Charles (respecting what he called my liberality, though he reprobated my sentiments as pernicious) was obliged to obey me; and he congratulated the gratified Caroline, with much feeling, on the generous nature of her future husband. Generous! Oh, how easy is that sort of generosity!—at least to me it was easy. But to another sort of generosity, and one more necessary to the happiness of domestic life, I was, alas! entirely a stranger.

However, this imaginary virtue of mine softened even Mrs. Belson's heart in my favour; at least it led her to tell me, with her usual frankness, that I was a strange and most provoking man ; for I would neither let her love me entirely, nor dislike me entirely. And I must own that I soon gave her apprehensive friendship only too much reason to believe the feeling of dislike towards me was a more just feeling than that of affection. For, I must confess that the natural obliquity and pride of my nature returned, and my jealousy of influence, as soon as I had nearly gained all I wished for, and found that Caroline would certainly be mine beyond all visible means of separating us.

"What have I done?" said I, mentally; "I have acted contrary to all the rules I have ever laid down for myself; I have allowed a woman, the woman too whom I am to marry, to *see* the whole extent of her power over me, and to convince herself, that even my *health* depended on her acceptance of me! Yes; I, who, till now, piqued myself on my pride of spirit and manly independence of character; I have been laid prostrate by my affections—been rendered ill by the emotions of my heart; and the fair cause of it has seen, and no doubt has triumphed over the irresistible influence of her charms! But she shall not triumph long," I added, as I finished my toilet, and went down to breakfast, which had been ordered that morning an hour earlier than usual.

I was unusually grave in my morning salutations ; and I scarcely smiled in return, when Caroline greeted me with a smile full of affection and benevolence, and put out her hand to welcome me. I saw her countenance change instantly ; and I observed, I must own, with gratified vanity, the anxious attention with which she followed my averted eye, and watched for one of those expressive glances which, however transient, is sufficient for lovers, even when they are separated by intervening crowds, to impress on each other the sweet consciousness of ever-enduring affection.

Caroline had been accustomed to receive such looks from me; but now my eyes were silent. What could the change mean? What, indeed! and at length, being ashamed of my conscious unkindness, I addressed some unimportant questions to her, but which obliged me, in common politeness, to look her in the face; and having done so, and met the kind glance of her mild blue eyes, I could not, even if I had wished it, retain my unamiable and repelling coldness ; and the meal, which began in a degree of dullness and gloom, for which no one could account, and which no one could venture to observe, ended in cheerfulness and pleasant conversation, apparently as unaccountable as the silence had been.

Our party was now dwinded to our host, Mrs. Belson, Caroline, and myself. And when breakfast was over, I saw Sir Charles's landau drive up to the door.

"What does this mean?" said I, "and who is going out?"

"Did you not know we were going to pay a visit to a new-married couple, nine miles off?" replied Caroline.

"No; if you ever told me of it I had forgotten it.—You will have a cold drive; pray, when am I to expect you back?"

"What!" exclaimed Mrs. Belson, "will you not go with us?"

"No; I am not prepared—I knew nothing of it—and I have letters to write."

"And was it then necessary, sir," angrily replied Mrs. Belson, "to prepare a lover to accompany his mistress? Is it not your first duty, under existing circumstances, to attend on *her?*"

"There," said Sir Charles, "there, Harry; you see what dependent creatures these women expect us to be. So, then, you see you are no longer an independent being, but you are considered merely as a necessary appendage to that young creature."

I felt my anger equally rise against Mrs. Belson's angry reproof, and Sir Charles's good-natured pleasantry, for both aggravated my already wounded self-love; and I was preparing an angry reply, when, casting my eyes on Caroline, I saw her cheek was pale, and her bosom heaving with emotion, and I had just humanity enough to forbear; and with some effort I said, "What man would not willingly, Sir Charles, resign his independence for the sake of being with such a company as the present? But, indeed, I have letters to write, and it is unfortunate; but I must beg to be excused—you can go without me, you know."

"Certainly, certainly," said Mrs. Belson, hastening to the door; "I am sure *I* don't want you to go. Come, Sir Charles."

"Patience, patience," he replied, slowly buttoning his coat, while Caroline as slowly closed her pelisse, and tied her bonnet under her chin.

"Pray, clothe yourself well," said I to Caroline, as I put her fur tippet on her shoulders; "and I hope you will not stay out till it is dark."

She did not answer—her heart was full—and had she spoken she would have burst into tears.

"Come, Harry, come with us," cried Sir Charles, "and write your letters another day." As he said this, he left the room, and I felt like a culprit, now that I was alone with Caroline. Would she had had some of her friend's spirit! that is, I think, if she had, I should have behaved better to her; for I was too sure of her affection to prove myself deserving of it—But I wander from the point.

Well, I was alone with her; and I knew that sorrowful emotion had deprived her of utterance, for sullenness was a stranger to her nature.

"This is very, very provoking," said I, in a hoarse voice, as I closed her tippet, and insisted on putting another shawl round her.

"What is provoking?" she asked in a faint tone.

"That I should have these letters to write."

"Provoking indeed;" and she moved towards the door.

"Stop!" cried I, a little mortified that she would not *urge* me to go; "I think I will defer writing till to-morrow, and lay the fault on you; will you allow me to plead you as my excuse?"

She did not reply, but she turned round and gave me such a smile! But she smiled through her tears; and as I pressed her to my heart, I almost vowed that I would never so distress her gentle and generous nature again.

"So! you are coming after all, are you?" observed Mrs. Belson; "I am sure if I had been Miss Orville *I* would not have asked you to come."

"Nor did Miss Orville ask me," replied I, coolly, "but I go because I should have been uneasy to have stayed at home."

Sir Charles now got in, good-naturedly observing that he was glad to find that I had made my business yield to my inclinations.

But neither Mrs. Belson nor Caroline could shake off the uncomfortable feelings which this display of my disposition had excited in both of them, and while one was silent from resentment, the other was so from sorrow. I therefore exerted myself to the utmost to draw them from their silence and their reserve; while I endeavoured, by every attention in my power, to soothe the feelings of Caroline, and heal the wound which I had so wantonly inflicted.

And in her bosom resentment never could tarry long. She was the most placable of human beings;—too much so for the man to whom she had intrusted her happiness; for the consciousness of her aptitude to forgive made me careless of giving her offence, and her virtue became her enemy. We had not gone far before she was able to talk and look on me as usual; and as even Mrs. Belson was at length unable to resist the influence of her enlivening good-humour, our drive turned out a very pleasant expedition.

I behaved very well for the next week; but with my odd temper and my system it was impossible for me not to err soon again. I fancied that I was too fond and too amiable, and if I did not take care, I thought I should become a thorough woman's slave. The idea was insupportable, and I took the first opportunity of rebelling again against that rule laid down by Mrs. Belson—that a lover is always to consider himself as the appendage of his mistress, and is to follow her whithersoever she goes, whether he likes it or not.

An opportunity soon occurred. Sir Charles had accepted a dinner engagement in the neighbourhood without consulting me; and it was at the house of persons whom I did not like, or rather, whose conduct I deemed reprehensible. My resolution therefore was taken, but I concealed it till the carriage was ordered to come round. I then told Sir Charles, that on mature deliberation I had resolved not to accompany him in the projected visit; for that, as I did not approve the character of the parties, and did not mean, when I married, to receive them on my visiting list; going to their houses would, I thought, be insuring a call from them—a civility which I wished to avoid; besides, I thought the visit would be a very dull one, and I should be more amused at home.

At this unexpected communication, Caroline changed colour, but looked more indignant than distressed. Mrs. Belson, after uttering an angry ejaculation, had wisdom enough to leave the room; and Sir Charles, drawing up his head, with evident displeasure in his look, replied as follows:

"I have only to say, Mr. Aubrey, that I do not wish any gentleman in my house to do what he does not like. No, not even an act of civility, or an act of *justice*; but I beg leave to observe, that when an engagement to a dinner-visit is accepted, it appears to me only an act of justice to keep it, as a place at table has been reserved, which might have been otherwise filled up. And if you and Caroline—for no doubt she has promised to stay at home with you—stay away—"

"Not I, indeed, sir!" exclaimed Caroline eagerly; "I never allow myself on *any* pretence to break an engagement."

"No!" replied Sir Charles, "then my surprise is increased. But setting aside any idea of propriety on the subject of keeping engagements, I must observe, Mr. Aubrey, that as my friend and his wife, I must allow, have made themselves only too much talked of, your not accompanying us would certainly appear like a marked disrespect; and as I loved and venerated their parents, it would grieve me that they should receive from any guest of mine a personal slight; therefore I *request* you to go with us, however dull and disagreeable the visit may be to *you*. But I must say, that in urging a lover to bear with the society of his mistress during a few hours, though it be in the company of *others*, I cannot think—if I may venture to judge of what young men are now by what I was myself—that I urge you to do any thing so *very trying*, and so very painful to endure."

I felt ashamed, confounded, yet angry. I saw that without affronting Sir Charles I could not refuse to go; but if I went I was resolved that Caroline, whose words and manner had wounded my self-love, should not suppose that the wish to appease her had influenced my change of plan. I therefore told Sir Charles that his request was sufficient; and that, as I would on no account do any thing likely to hurt the feelings of a friend of his, I would get my great-coat and follow them.

I then left the room without looking at Caroline; and while I was putting on my coat, Sir Charles handed her into the carriage, a ceremony which, in the irritated state of my temper, I wished to avoid.

It is not to be expected that our drive was a very comfortable one. Even Sir Charles's fine temper had been a little ruffled; and Mrs. Belson sat swelling with indignation in one corner of the coach, while Caroline could with difficulty suppress the tears of wounded pride and tenderness; and I, the guilty cause of all this vexation, was too painfully self-reproved to be able to break the perturbed and discomforting silence. Fortunately, however, the roads were very bad, and the jolting of the coach was intolerable, for the physical inconvenience which we suffered, diverted our attention in a slight degree from our moral disturbance, and involuntary exclamations of "Dear me! Well, I thought we were overset," broke the above mentioned silence ever and anon, whether we would or no, and gradually paved the way for a renewal of conversation. Nothing, however, seemed to steal one thought of Caroline's from the gloom that overhung her mind; no exclamation opened her fast-closed lips; and she seemed wholly unconscious of what was passing in the external world, though her eyes were fixed on the window next me. I would have given half my possessions to have held her motionless hand in mine; but I dared not even touch her; and though we sat on the same seat, we had each retired to the corner, and I felt convinced that it was with the greatest effort alone the heart which I had so wantonly wounded could prevent its misery from venting itself in sighs and tears.

At length a jolt of the coach, from one of the wheels being suddenly plunged in a very deep rut in the road, at the great risk of our being completely overturned, threw Caroline, who was off her guard, against the window near her, and the glass cut her forehead till the blood streamed down her face. This gave a welcome excuse for the long-smothered agony to burst forth; and she gave way to a sort of hysterical seizure, which Sir Charles attributed to the sudden alarm; but I knew better; and amidst the sobs of the hysteric I distinguished only too well the tones of heartfelt distress. The wound was slight, and an immediate application of gold-beater's skin stopped the bleeding, but the agitation did not subside so soon. And, alas! it was not against my shoulder that Caroline leaned, for she seemed to reject my offered service; but she suffered Sir Charles's arm to sustain her trembling frame, and her hand grasped that of Mrs. Belson. This was a trial to me; but I had deserved it. Having thus unburthened her heart of its heavy load, Caroline became quite composed and gave a decided negative to their proposals to return home; saying that the wound in her forehead would excuse her discoloured cheeks and disordered head-dress, and she was very sure she had quite recovered.

It was more than I was; her sobs still rung in my ears, and I still read in her averted looks, that I had, in a measure, chilled the ardour of her attachment towards me. And why had I done so? I could not answer the question satisfactorily; and overcome with a variety of feelings, I complained of being made unwell by the motion of the carriage, and desired the coachman to stop that I might get on the box.

"Why, you will be frozen to death, Harry," said Sir Charles.

"No matter," replied I; "I shall be frozen to death if I remain here, and be ill also. I must—indeed I must get out."

These words, uttered in a tone of deep and painful emotion, found their way to the placable bosom of Caroline, and she looked at me; but I avoided her eyes; and, having opened the door, jumped out, in spite of Sir Charles's remonstrances, and ascended the box; but I had not gone far when the check-string was again pulled; and Sir Charles looking out, with a very meaning countenance assured me Miss Orville was so unhappy lest I should catch a bad cold, (as I had been so recently ill,) that he earnestly wished I would re-enter the coach, especially as we were within two miles of our journey's end.

For one instant the angry obstinacy of my nature still held out, but *only* for an instant, and in another minute I was re-seated by the side of Caroline; whose soft eyes swelling with tears, met mine as I entered. Immediately, without uttering one word, we both felt that we were reconciled to each other; and every one looked relieved but Mrs. Belson, who every now and then, by a sudden jerk of her chin, and a shake of her head, proclaimed that tranquillity was by no means restored to her mind or temper.

At last, overjoyed, we reached the end of our journey, and I got out first to assist the ladies.

Mrs. Belson would not take my offered hand or arm; and I almost feared that Caroline might evade accepting them. But I did not do her justice; as her heart had forgiven me, she was too sincere to let her actions tell a different story; and when I pressed her hand to my heart, as I carefully assisted her down the frozen step, and when I whispered in her ear, "Dearest Caroline, forgive me!" her hand returned the pressure of mine, and we entered the house with buoyant tread and with renewed spirits. Nay, so strong was the rebound of mine, from great depression to unusual hilarity, that I was even more amiable in my manner to the master and mistress of the house than my kind host could have desired; and conscious as I was that my behaviour during the visit had gratified both Caroline and Sir Charles, and that my agreeableness, while it pleased the woman who loved me, had provoked the woman who hated me—the drive home, during which Caroline's hand was locked in mine, still lives in my memory as replete with some of the most delightful moments of my life.

After some refreshment, when we reached home, Sir Charles and Caroline (who complained that her wound was painful) retired to their rooms, and I thought Mrs. Belson was following them; but she suddenly shut the door, and I found she was going to address me.

"This is now the second time, Mr. Aubrey," said she, "that your strange temper has shown itself, sir; and I think it but fair to tell you, that if I can help it, Miss Orville shall *never be your wife*, though your wedding day is fixed. If such is the lover, sir, what will not the husband be? and my friend is too meek, too placable, too yielding, to marry such a man as you are, without the *certain* risk of utter destruction to her happiness. Sir, what passed to-day—"

"Well, madam," said I, "and what passed to-day to justify what you are now saying?"

"I own, sir," she replied, "that in detail it would appear a trifle; but it is on trifles that the happiness of wedded life depends. Well has that woman said, who is an ornament to her sex, that

"'Since trifles make the sum of human things,
And half our misery from our foibles springs;
Since life's best gifts consist in peace and ease,
And few can save,or serve,but all may please;—
O! let the ungentle spirit learn from hence,
A small unkindness is a great offence.'"

I felt to the bottom of my soul the truth of what she said; and as I could not confute, I would not answer what she advanced; but I replied, in a tone expressive of anything but good-humour—

"Are you aware, madam, that in a case like this, your interference cannot do good, and may do harm?"

"Not if I can convince my friend that she had better not marry you."

"If you can convince her—Good night, madam—*C'est là où je vous attends.*"

So saying, I left her. But I was not as secure of my prize as my words seemed to imply; and though my pride whispered that I would not put any restraint on myself, and that Caroline should take me with my faults, and love me with my faults, or that we should break our engagement by mutual consent; still, love got the better of pride, and I resolved to disarm Mrs. Belson of all power to hurt me, by every possible affectionate attention, and lover-like obsequiousness, in my power to display.

I kept my resolution, though not without exhibiting some tendencies to err again. I gave way occasionally to sudden coldnesses and reserve of manner, which I saw tried the unvaryingly affectionate feelings of Caroline, and made her fancy I felt a remission of attachment. But as soon as I saw that ingenuous and happy countenance overclouded by a pensiveness unnatural to it, I subdued my systematic aversion to admit the necessity of a lover's being always attentive and ardent in his manner towards his mistress; and in a moment Caroline's sweet and placable nature made her forget my recent coldness, and all was happiness again.

At length our wedding-day arrived, and we were married at the parish church at L——; and from the church-door we set off by ourselves to a small house of mine in Worcestershire, at the foot of Malvern Hills. O, the happiness of that journey! Never, never, till consciousness is lost in dissolution, can I forget our six weeks' residence in that sequestered spot! And she was happy, quite happy, then! for I was contented that she saw the real feelings of my heart towards her; and as there was no witness of the thraldom, in which love had bound me, I believe, that during that short time, there was no cloud visible on the brow of either.

At length, business called me to London, and we took a ready-furnished house there for four months. One of our first visiters was Mrs. Belson, who, I saw plainly, by her manner, expected to be received by me as one with whose visits, in future, I should gladly dispense.

But she was agreeably disappointed; for I met her with a smile of welcome, and told her before we parted, that, as I respected her highly for the strong attachment which she had ever displayed towards Caroline, I should always be truly happy to see her as our guest; and tears of real feeling started in the eyes of this affectionate woman while I spoke, which affected me, as well as my beloved wife, who thanked me by a look which, though I noticed it not, I valued beyond expression.

But, alas! now that I was to enter the world in a new character—that of a husband—and that the novelty of my change of situation was worn off, my usual habits of temper and manner returned; and while every day convinced me, how much the wife was dearer than the bride, still I could not bear to let her know the extent of the influence which she had over my heart; and when I found that the coldness of my manner, at times, alarmed her with the idea that I was becoming indifferent to her, I felt an ungenerous triumph in witnessing the depression which I had caused. My pride, too, enjoyed the consciousness that this lovely and admired being watched every turn of my countenance, in order to judge by it how my heart was at the moment affected towards her; and when, which I could not sometimes help, my looks expressed some of the admiration and tenderness which she had excited in my bosom, there was an expression of gratified and grateful affection in her eyes, which was so beautiful that I wonder the pleasure of beholding it did not make me eager to call it forth. Certain it is, however, that the more I felt myself dependent on her for happiness, the more I made a parade of independence. If she hoped I should accompany her to a party, declaring that unless I was with her the evening would have no charms for her, I used to reply, though I meant to go the whole time, "Perhaps I may go with you, but do not depend on me,—you had better get some friend to accompany you;" and then I have purposely come very late, in order to have the gratification of seeing her sitting by the door, and evidently watching for my entrance. And how did I, at such moments, requite this tender solicitude?—By meeting with equal kindness her warmest look of love and welcome? No; feigning the coldness which I did not feel, I sometimes stood and talked to her with eyes that wandered towards every one but her; or, contenting myself with giving her a passing nod, I walked to the other end of the room or rooms, always contriving, however, to stand where I could see the only object which I really loved to look upon, and where I could observe that her glances followed me wherever I went;—and when I returned to her, (O cutting, yet gratifying recollection!) she used to receive me with such a smile!

Well, the London season over, and all my terms kept, we returned to C——; and the frequent recurrence of little slights and coldnesses on my part certainly produced the pernicious conviction on hers, that I did not love her in any degree as well as I once loved her; and that though every faculty of her loving nature was devoted to me, my feelings towards her were fast approaching to indifference.

And yet never did the prodigality of nature form a being in every respect more worthy of being beloved! But humility always attends on real passion; and this creature, formed to be adored, could believe, from the timidity attendant on affection, that her husband did not adequately return her love! But what is more incredible still, I, who loved her deeply and ardently—I, who knew that she entertained this painful conviction, and suffered, daily suffered from it; for sometimes she would gently hint her fears on the subject—I, from some obliquity of temper and feeling, which, while I reprobate, I cannot describe or account for—I allowed her to remain under this distressing impression; and though a few kind words and tender assurances would have banished her doubts and restored her tranquillity, I made no answer either by word of mouth, or by letter whenever we were in correspondence, to her implied affectionate fears, but preserved on the subject a chilling, and to her boding heart, an ominous and convincing silence.

To return. We left London for my seat near C——; and having been visited on our arrival by all the principal persons in that city, and returned their calls, we resolved to visit only those families who gave and paid dinner visits. By this means we were sure to avoid the busy and unproductive idleness of constant engagements, and enable ourselves to enjoy the comfort of evenings at home, spent in rational and instructive pursuits; for while Caroline worked or drew, I read aloud; and certainly time flew on rapid wings to us both. Yet still, though contented to pass all my evenings at home, and desiring evidently no other company than hers, this too susceptible, this too apprehensive being would allow my occasional oddity to disturb her peace, and set *trifles* against such substantial proofs of affection. But what does this prove? The importance of attention to *trifles* in wedded life, and the truth of those lines of wisdom which Mrs. Belson repeated to me. And alas! of what use was my consciously rich store of affection for this beloved object? It was as if I had willed to her an income of a thousand a year at my death, and during my life refused to honour her draft for a guinea to save her from inanition!

In a few months after we returned to C——, Caroline had the prospect of becoming a mother; and though my affection could not admit of increase, my anxiety became stronger in proportion as the period of her danger advanced; and it was with a degree of unhappiness which I would not gratify her by showing, that I saw myself forced to leave her when she was within a month of her confinement.

But, spite of myself, my feelings of regret were very visible when I parted with her; and I am sure that the joy of seeing she was dear to me overcame the grief which parting with me occasioned her. Still, ever consistent, I could not bring myself to promise to write to her as soon as I reached Worcester, whither I was going on very urgent business; but, ridiculing her anxiety, I left it uncertain whether I should write or not.

I went by one of the Worcester mails; but I got out within a few miles of Worcester, at the house of a friend whom I wanted to see on the business which carried me away from home. I had time enough to write to Caroline, and I thought of doing it; but a strange wish to avoid indulging her fond uneasiness, and to conceal from her, how precious her wishes were to me, made me resolve, as I had not promised her that I would write, to defer writing to the next day, and not seem, by writing when she desired it, to acknowledge her claims on my time and attention. But retributive justice awaited the unworthy, the ungenerous feeling.

It so happened that, unknown to me, the mail was overturned after I left it; and the *only* inside passenger (a gentleman) was, in attempting to jump out, killed on the spot.

The news was immediately sent to the paper; and as no name was mentioned, and there was only one mail, my unhappy wife read the paragraph; and concluding, as I had not written, that I was the unfortunate gentleman, she fell into strong convulsions, during which she gave birth to a dead child, and in a few hours her life was thought in danger.

Perhaps the punishment may seem too strong for my offence, as I could not foresee the terrible consequences. True; I well knew that by not writing I should undoubtedly wound the feelings, and disappoint the expectations of that being who had made me the depository of her happiness; and I also knew, that by writing I should give pleasure to the heart that doted on me.

Oh! what an important power is that we are vested with, of inflicting pain and conferring pleasure at our will! Oh! what an awful thing it is to be the depository of another's happiness!—Let no one presume ever to enter the marriage state, or even to put on the ties of mutual affection in any way, who is not deeply sensible of this awful responsibility.

Forgive my digressions, reader;—but there are parts of my story yet to tell which I like to defer as long as I possibly can.

An express was sent by Mrs. Belson, who happened to be at our house, with orders to find me wherever I was; for the name of the *real* victim was mentioned in another paper, and my fortunate escape by stopping on the road. The express reached me just as I had written to Caroline, and told her of the accident from which I had so providentially been preserved.

The news I received overwhelmed me with agony amounting to frenzy; and I cursed, bitterly cursed, my own cruel conduct, to which I justly attributed the misery which I underwent. The mail was just setting off, and I entered it, with feelings which I will not pretend to describe. That agony was renewed in all its force when I reached home, and when I beheld those windows closed whence Caroline used to be watching my return, even after a two days' absence. I rushed into the house like a distracted man; but Mrs. Belson, before I could speak, relieved me by exclaiming, "She is better; and when she sees you I doubt not she will be quite easy, and will do well."

I burst into tears; and she considerately left me, to go and break my arrival to the dear sufferer. She was allowed to see me, provided she did not speak; and with trembling steps, though in the agony of the moment I forgot my delinquency, I approached the door of her chamber. She had promised to be silent; but when she saw me—saw him alive whom she had bewailed as dead, her feelings burst through the restraints imposed on them, and she wildly exclaimed, "It is true then, you have not deceived me; he lives! he lives!—My God, my gracious God, I thank thee!" and then sunk back fainting on her pillow.

The fit was long and alarming, but she recovered; and as a deep refreshing sleep succeeded it, her mind was now at ease; she grew better from that moment, and was declared out of danger.

"We have lost our child," said she mournfully, as I hung over her pillow.

"But you are saved," I replied, "and that is happiness enough." Yes, for once I gave way to the full feelings of my heart; and I blushed to think with what tears of unutterable tenderness and gratitude I, undeserving as I was, was instantly repaid.

Caroline left her sick room at the end of the month; but so changed, so weak, that I was desired to take her instantly to the sea-side; and I chose the most retired place possible. Caroline objected to this for my sake; because she said I should find it so very dull.

I was, for the time, enough amended by what I had undergone, not to grudge her the soothing assurance, that the restoration of her health was my only object in going; and that all others were indifferent to me. She thanked me as if I had conferred the greatest favour on her—O Caroline!

When we set off she was so feeble that I was forced to lift her into the carriage, and she was so faint from the exertion that I could scarcely conceal my misery and remorse; the latter of which I had not been able to hide from Mrs. Belson, and it was so great as to make my peace even with her.

But to Caroline I could not prevail on myself to express it; nor would she have listened to me on such a subject if I had attempted it. The sight of Caroline's weakness, however, and the consciousness of my having contributed to cause it, had softened my heart so much, that when with her usual want of confidence in herself, she said, " I *wish* you would have let me gone without you to the coast; I am sure you would rather have gone back to Worcester; it will be such a burthen to you to stay with me, without your books, or any society—"

I could not help replying "Foolish woman! I want nothing but you! and to see you well again!" And as I did so, I laid my cheek on hers, which reclined on my shoulder.

How happy was her countenance during that journey! how calm was her sleep upon my bosom! and when she awoke and found me fondly watching her, she said, " I would always rather be unwell than well to be so nursed." And as she felt during that journey that she was beloved, even her strength seemed recovered before we reached the end of it. Nay, I am convinced that my attentions did more for her than change of air; and I had the satisfaction of bringing her home again, as well, apparently, as she had ever been.

Well—month succeeded to month, and witnessed the same inequality in my conduct, and the same susceptibility of it in Caroline, when we were invited to stay at the house of a friend some distance off, and we accepted the invitation. But some law business at home, which I could not get rid of, (for since I had been called to the bar I had accepted business, from the dislike I felt to be a man without a pursuit,) forced me to give up the projected journey. Caroline immediately entreated to be allowed to give it up also.

But I insisted that she should go; and did it in such a manner, that her countenance and even her words evinced she believed that I wished for her absence; and she prepared to depart with that terrible *serrement de cœur*, the bitterness of which no one but those who have experienced it can even conceive.

"You will write to me?" said Caroline as I put her into the carriage.

"That depends on the length of your stay."

"I will come home whenever you choose; next week, if you like."

"Next week! Oh, no; it is not worth while going so many miles for a week."

"But as you do not accompany me, all my expected pleasure is at an end."

"Poh!" replied I, "you will be very well entertained when you get there; and I do not expect to see you again till the month is over."

"Perhaps you do not wish it?" she timidly observed.

I only replied by a smile; and bidding the postilion drive on, I kissed my hand to her in silence; for the tears which filled her eyes, while she wrung my hand at parting, filled me with self-reproach, and I wished to stop the carriage, and tell her I should not be happy till she returned; but I let her go with the terrible fear on her mind that I wished to get rid of her for a while, and I returned into the house self-reproved. I consoled myself, however, with the idea that I could recall her whenever I chose, and that I would write most kindly to her.

She reached the place of her destination in safety, as I learned from a short but most affectionate letter which she wrote to me the next day.

Perhaps if it had been less tender, I could have answered it better; but men cannot express their feelings as women can; nor do they, I believe, ever feel those little niceties of affection which women so well understand, and which it wounds them often so deeply not to find in the objects of their attachment. Indeed, there were two rocks on which the happiness of Caroline unavoidably made shipwreck; the one was her not being able to conceive that I loved her, because my affection was not an active principle as hers was, and she thought no one could really love, that did not testify affection as she did; and the other was, her distrust of herself, and her own capability of inspiring affection equal to what she felt. I will give an extract which appears to me to describe a similar failing, (if I may use such a term,) to this of Caroline:

Madame de la Fayette says, speaking of Madame de Sevigné, "In your *distrustfulness* consists your only fault;" and that admirable woman was known to distrust the strength of her daughter's attachment *to her*, just as Caroline doubted that of mine. But I digress again.

Well then, I wrote to Caroline; but consciously with a cold and restrained pen. I could not write like her; and feeling that my expressions would be ice to hers, I did not attempt to write a letter of sentiment at all, nor did I try to combat, by assurances of the contrary, her delicately hinted conviction that I wished her to be absent from me. This, I well knew, was the only part of her letter to which she desired an answer; but this I would not notice at all — and thus I always behaved to her on such occasions. Thus wantonly and cruelly did I sport with the humble fondness and the apprehensive tenderness of that creature, who hung on me for happiness with all the contented dependence of virtuous woman's love. Alas! power, conscious power, corrupts every one, from the despot on his throne to the tyrant in domestic life. I, spoiled by her contented and willing slavery, tyrannized, because I could do it with impunity, over the heart that only lived and breathed and beat for me! Still let me say that she ought to have had more confidence both in me and in herself. And if anxious affection had not blinded her usually acute penetration into character, she would have seen that I loved her as much as I was capable of loving; and that she was the only passion of my heart. Madame de Sevigné says of her son:

"He shows me a great deal of tenderness *in his way;* I think his regard worth having, provided one understands it to be all *that he knows* on the subject. Can any one require *more* from him?"

But Caroline, alas! did not understand my regard to be all I was capable of feeling, and she tormented herself with fears that had really no foundation. Yet that does not exonerate me, who knew the disease of her mind, from unkindness, in not endeavouring to administer a cure to it. I knew that she required merely kind words and looks, and assurances of affection; but a something of temper that I could not conquer, made me still refuse to make her happy her own way, and happy in mine she could not be.

A week elapsed, and Caroline wrote to request a summons home. I refused it, and urged her staying longer. Another week elapsed, and I could not yet prevail on myself to send the desired recall.

"I do not flatter myself that you miss me," she then wrote; "nay, I am sure you do not, or you would have obliged me by sending for me; but I will not importune you any longer. I will stay here as long as I think right, and then, if you again wish me to leave you, I will go somewhere else."

I wrote, and suffered her to remain convinced that her absence was a pleasure to me! Such is the obliquity of some tempers, and of mine.

In the meanwhile, I certainly regretted, though I did not mourn over Caroline's protracted stay; for she stayed five weeks, and then sent me word she should be home such a day.

How long the day on which I expected her appeared to me! though I had been tranquil during her absence, especially as I had found, thrown carelessly in her drawer, the following songs:

SONG.

They told me I was born to love,
   When first in youth's soft bloom I shone,
They told me I was form'd to prove
   The bliss that waits on love alone.

I gave the tale but little heed,
   For mine was yet life's laughing morn;
Till Henry came, and then indeed
   I found that I to love was born.

But while I with my fondness strove,
   This mournful truth too soon I knew;
The tender heart that's form'd to love,
   Is form'd, alas! to sorrow, too.

I could not read this true picture of her own feelings, without considerable self-reproach, and a resolution to try to prevent her from ever "sorrowing" again.

The next lines were these:

Hast thou e'er loved, and know'st thou not
   Love's chain is form'd of bitter tears—
Of joys in one short hour forgot,
   Of griefs remember'd still for years?

Of gladness lighting lovers' eyes,
   With beams that mock the painter's art;
And also form'd of secret sighs,
   That dim the eye, and break the heart?

Love! contradiction's darling child,
   Thou prize, thou scourge to mortals given;
By turns thou'rt blest, by turns reviled,
   Art now a hell, and now a heaven.

Alas! I had only too much reason to fear, that with her, it was much oftener the former than the latter.

On the day fixed for her return, I did nothing but wander up and down the house and garden; and during the last two hours before she came in sight, I was watching at the window incessantly for the carriage.

She met me with tears, with a languid smile, and an expression of resigned suffering in her countenance, which cut me to the soul, and which called forth all the signs of tenderness which I could at that moment display. For an instant her countenance brightened; but on my asking her if she had not much enjoyed her visit, she burst into a flood of tears, which I only too well understood; and getting up she retired to her chamber.

When we met again, she was quite composed; but her eyes and discoloured cheeks showed that she had been weeping bitterly.

Time went on. We were again disappointed of our hopes of a family, and Caroline's pale cheeks appeared to grow still paler. But she said she was well; and it was my way always to turn from every thing that it distressed me to dwell upon — the usual resources of the selfish.

I was now unexpectedly, and most unwelcomely, forced to go into Worcestershire, on business that might detain me some weeks, or might be finished in a few days; therefore, though at first I thought of taking Caroline with me, I gave up the design, and contented myself with urging her to invite Mrs. Belson to stay with her during my absence. But this she declined; for she knew, though I did not, that Mrs. Belson had been offended with the coldness of her manner, and kept up little or no intercourse with her.

Mrs. Belson, no doubt, laid all the fault on me; but I was wholly innocent of it. The truth was, that Caroline, fearful that her quick-sighted friend should see that she was unhappy, and discover that I made her so, purposely separated herself gradually from her affectionate friend, and sacrificed friendship to her ideas of wedded duty.

The day for my departure arrived; and Caroline looked even so unusually ill, that I could scarcely prevail on myself to leave her; and if she had only expressed the slightest wish to accompany me, I should have gladly acceded to it. But her mind was so impressed with the idea that I preferred leaving her behind me, she did not think of preferring such a request; and I went — but not till I had given her repeated charges to write constantly.

Are there such things as forebodings? or were the altered looks of Caroline sufficient to account for my agony when I lost sight of my house, and of her faded form, which lingered at the door to catch the last glimpse of me as I looked back at her from the open window? I know not. But certain it is, that I once resolved to return and take her with me; but the hope of coming back in a few days again prevented me, and on I went.

At first the necessary cares of business diverted my mind from the gloomy thoughts which oppressed it, and as I received a letter from Caroline, which, though evidently written under great depression of spirits, assured me she was not worse, if not better, I became tolerably cheerful; but I was much distressed to find that my stay must considerably exceed the length of time which I had hoped to appropriate to it.

Accordingly, week succeeded to week, and still my stay was prolonged contrary to my expectations, and still more so to my wishes; and so completely busied and engrossed was I by the disagreeable business which detained me, that my letters, which never at any time did justice to my feelings, partook of the uncomfortable dryness of my state of mind; and though I wished to write tenderly, I know that I wrote coldly and reservedly. And soon, to my great alarm, Caroline's letters grew shorter and shorter, and she ceased to express any desire whatever for my speedy return. She seemed to have borrowed my pen, and it appeared as if her glowing expressions were chilled by some unusual feelings before they reached the paper. Her hand-writing also became slovenly and illegible; and so great a terror of I know not what took possession of me, that I hastened the business I was engaged on by every possible means; resolving on no account to delay my return three days longer.

By the next post after I had formed this resolution, I received a letter from an old and confidential servant, in which he informed me, that he was sure his lady was very ill, very ill indeed, though she would not own it; that at last she had sent for advice; and that, though she had positively forbidden the doctor to write, he was sure he thought ill of her; but as she had not forbidden him to write, he had thought it his duty to do it. Caroline wrote by the same post, telling me she had been ill, and was ill, but she was likely to be *better soon. Oh! much better!* and desiring me not to hasten home on her account.

I knew not what to think when I received these letters; but alarm was my predominant feeling. Shocking as the account contained in my servant's letter was, there were words in Caroline's more terrible still; for what did she mean by her being "*likely to be better soon. Oh! much better?*"

These letters made me wholly unfit to go on with what I was engaged in; and having arranged matters so that I could be allowed to go home for a few days, I prepared to set off as soon as the post should come in the next day.

It came, and brought me a letter from the physician, begging me to set off directly, as he feared that my beloved wife was indeed on her death-bed.

My servant also wrote, saying—"Oh! sir, come directly, if you wish to see my poor mistress alive."

And Caroline wrote herself—such a letter! It was as follows:

"They deceive you, my beloved husband, if they tell you you can arrive time enough to see me before I have breathed my last; for when this reaches you, I feel that the last struggle will be over! Let me then, with a shaking hand, but a firm heart, bid thee thus my last farewell; and conjure thee to forgive those errors of feeling in me, which militated against your comforts, and alienated your affections from me, and have ultimately destroyed both my own peace and my own health. But the chastisement is just, and I humbly kiss the rod.

"I have been, I own it, an exacting wife;— true, mine have not been the exactions of temper, but of too tender love; still, though different in their nature, their effect has been the same; and whether a wife injures her husband's happiness by ill-humour or by too much softness of disposition, she equally violates the duty of ministering to a husband's comfort.

"Oh! why was I not contented to be loved according to your capability of loving, and your ideas of the dues of affection? Why did I weakly expect you to make affection, as I did, the business and the passion of my life? Why did I not, till it was too late, remember, that even a virtuous passion, if carried to excess, becomes a vice? When on my bended knee I have responded to that awful injunction—'Thou shalt make to thyself no graven image,'— how often has my heart reproached me with idolatrous worship of you, my beloved husband! and the tear of conscious disobedience has fallen while I listened; but the warning remorse has been soon disregarded, and your image has again swallowed up every other.

"Yes, in apprehensions of your coldness, in plans to recover what I fancied your alienated love, or in mournful reverie, have often passed those hours which I once devoted to the cultivation of my talents and the purposes of benevolence.

"But a heart as susceptible, a conscience as timorous, and a frame as weak as mine, could not long sustain this terrible mental conflict; and my weakness has been made at once my chastisement and my relief.

"But must I indeed die without seeing you once more? Yet, perhaps, it is better as it is. If I fancied you beheld me expiring, with less sorrow than my too ardent love deserves, even my last thoughts would be riveted by mental agony on you, and stolen from my God; and if your grief was violent, and your pangs evidently severe, even in death, I should mourn for the misery of which I was the cause.

"No: it is wisely ordained that you will not see me again, till I am lying in the calm stillness of death, and you can have the satisfaction of knowing that this troubled heart has at last beat itself to rest.

"May you live long and happy! May you be united to some happier woman, who will love you *well enough* for *your* happiness, and not *too well* for *her own!* Oh! I have been very weak and very faulty; therefore, blame not yourself; and remember that this is my *last dying charge*. My eyes grow dim— I must leave off.

"Receive my last blessing.
"CAROLINE."

Desperation gave me energy—gave me, as it were, perception. I spoke to no one; but going to the first livery stable, I hired the swiftest horse in it, and set off at full speed for that home to which I was so painfully recalled. Nor did I stop till my horse could positively go on no longer. Another was instantly procured, and I proceeded.

I must pause—yet wherefore? The task which I have set myself must be gone through, and my whole tale be told.

The second horse brought me to my journey's end; and seeing a man whom I knew, I dismounted at the park gate and gave my horse to him. I ran with all the speed I could across the park; but found my course impeded by groups of men, women, and children, talking over the danger and the virtues of their benefactress, and watching there to catch every new account that could be given them of her situation; for she was their guide, their instructress, their comforter, and often their preserver.

At sight of me, they formed a sort of line, to let me pass; but no one spoke, till one woman said, "God comfort you, sir!" and another said, "Amen." It was too much—I increased my speed, nor stopped till I reached the door. My faithful William met me in the hall.

"Oh! sir, I fear—" was all he could articulate. I rushed up stairs, and to the door of our chamber. Two of the women servants, who were sobbing violently, begged me not to go in; but I proceeded; and by the countenance of the nurse and the physician I concluded that all was over.

Oh! the agony of that moment, when I threw myself beside that pale and motionless being! when I called her by every endearing name which tongue can utter; when I conjured her to speak to me once more; and declared that I could not and would not survive her! The physician would fain have led me away; but I resisted, and continued to kiss her cold lips and press her to my bursting bosom; while again and again I called upon her name in the fondest accents of love, and conjured her to speak and look on me once more.

That voice—those accents—recalled her fleeting spirit, and roused departing consciousness. She moved—she opened her eyes—she gazed on me, and she knew me; while I repeated again every term of agonizing and despairing tenderness, soothed a little by a faint glimmering hope.

"Do I hear aright?" she said, with a choked, impeded and sepulchral tone; "and you *do* love me! *do* love me dearly! Oh, happier in death than in life!—I—"

She could utter no more; but she smiled on me so fondly, yet so piteously! As I bent over her I felt her cold arms gently clasp themselves round my neck, and her cold lip press mine. The arms unclosed, and all was over in one short moment!!

* * * * * *

Months of existence succeeded, of which I knew nothing. And when I first recovered my senses, it was to lothe that consciousness which only taught me the extent of my misery.

But better and more thankful thoughts ensued, though the image of her whom I had lost was for ever present to my view, attended with bitter feelings of self-blame and agonizing regret.

I had been removed from my own house, but thither I now insisted on returning; and it was not long before I set off, accompanied by Sir Charles D—— and my faithful William, for that once welcome home which I had rendered a desert.

It was some days before I could prevail on Sir Charles to leave me to myself; and when I did so, I was aware that he gave orders to William never to lose sight of me. But such precautions would have been useless, as they always are, if I had had any intention of committing suicide; and as I had not, they were annoying. However, I at last convinced William that I was to be trusted alone, as my religion taught me to feel it a sort of gratification as well as a duty, to live on, and patiently endure that load of suffering which I had helped to bring on myself.

At length I had resolution to enter Caroline's own dressing-room, which had been locked up on her decease, by Sir Charles's orders, and not a single thing removed. On her writing-table was the portfolio that contained her paper and her MSS. and near it lay the last pen she had ever touched.

I do not think that I had shed one tear before since the sad event; but now they flowed abundantly. A few faded flowers lay by the pen—the last nosegay she culled no doubt—*I have them still.*

It now became the first and only desire of my heart, to obey in every thing the slightest wish that Caroline had ever expressed, and to do all things that she had ever recommended, except not blaming myself and my cruel indulgence of my own obliquity of temper. That she was wrong in loving so strongly and so pertinaciously a being so faulty as I was, I could not but admit; but I knew that I was culpable in persisting in that silence and concealment of the real strength of my attachment, which would have made her affectionate soul completely happy.

But regret was vain; my sufferings were deserved; and she, I trusted, was in a state of being more worthy of her pure and tender nature.

And what employment had she left me here? To take care of those whom she cherished; to love and serve those whom she loved and served; to remember all she had ever thought it right to do; and to act on her recommendation.

I now recollected that she had once said she thought it would be beneficial to ourselves, and might be made so to others, if we were to write down, not only our actions, and the events of our lives, but the feelings and the sentiments which had given rise to them. I therefore resolved to write the preceding narrative; believing that in so doing I should do what she approved, and also inflict on my close and fatally reserved disposition, a proper punishment, in forcing myself to unveil my heart and my sorrows to uninterested and indifferent strangers.

The narrative is ended; and if it should teach any one to whom the happiness of another is confided, to consider the sacredness of the deposit, and to watch carefully over those selfish indulgences of temper, which may lead to its utter destruction, my purpose and my wishes will be fulfilled;—and should departed souls be allowed to witness what is passing on earth, the gentle spirit of Caroline will be soothed by the consciousness that *I* have not *suffered*, and that *she* has not *died*, in vain.

END OF THE CONFESSIONS OF AN ODD-TEMPERED MAN.

ILLUSTRATIONS OF LYING,

IN ALL ITS BRANCHES.

TO DR. ALDERSON, OF NORWICH.

To thee, my beloved father, I dedicated my first, and to thee I also dedicate my present work;—with the pleasing conviction that thou art disposed to form a favourable judgment of any production, however humble, which has a tendency to promote the moral and religious welfare of mankind.

AMELIA OPIE.

PREFACE.

I AM aware that a preface must be short, if its author aspires to have it read. I shall therefore content myself with making a very few preliminary observations, which I wish to be considered as apologies.

My first apology is, for having throughout my book, made use of the words lying and lies, instead of some gentler term, or some easy paraphrase, by which I might have avoided the risk of offending the delicacy of any of my readers.

Our great satirist speaks of a Dean who was a favourite at the church where he officiated, because

"He never mentioned hell to ears polite,—"

and I fear that to "ears polite," my coarseness, in uniformly calling lying and lie by their real names, may sometimes be offensive.

But, when writing a book against lying, I was obliged to express my meaning in the manner most consonant to the *strict truth;* nor could I employ any words with such propriety as those hallowed and sanctioned for use, on such an occasion, by the practice of inspired and holy men of old.

Moreover, I believe that those who accustom themselves to call lying and lie by a softening appellation, are in danger of weakening their aversion to the fault itself.

My second apology is, for presuming to come forward, with such apparent boldness, as a didactic writer, and a teacher of truths, which I ought to believe that every one knows already, and better than I do.

But I beg permission to deprecate the charge of presumption and self-conceit, by declaring that I pretend not to lay before my readers any new knowledge; my only aim, is to bring to their recollection, knowledge which they already possess, but do not constantly recall and act upon.

I am to them, and to my subject, what the picture-cleaner is to the picture; the restorer to observation of what is valuable, and not the artist who created it.

In the next place, I wish to remind them that a weak hand is as able as a powerful one to hold a mirror, in which we may see any defects in our dress or person.

In the last place, I venture to assert that there is not in my whole book a more common-place truth, than that kings are but men, and that monarchs, as well as their subjects, must surely die.

Notwithstanding, Philip of Macedon was so conscious of his liability to forget this awful truth, that he employed a monitor to follow him every day, repeating in his ear, "Remember, thou art but a man." And he who gave this salutary admonition neither *possessed* superiority of wisdom, nor *pretended* to possess it.

All, therefore, that I require of my readers is to do me justice to believe that, in the following work, my pretensions have been as humble and as confined as those of the REMEMBRANCER of PHILIP OF MACEDON.

CHAPTER I.

INTRODUCTION.

WHAT constitutes lying?

I answer, the *intention to deceive.*

If this be a correct definition, there must be *passive* as well as *active* lying; and those who withhold the truth, or do not tell the whole truth, with an intention to deceive, are guilty of lying, as well as those who tell a direct or positive falsehood.

Lies are many, and various in their nature and in their tendency, and may be arranged under their different names, thus:—

Lies of Vanity;
Lies of Flattery;
Lies of Convenience;
Lies of Interest;
Lies of Fear;
Lies of first-rate Malignity;
Lies of second-rate Malignity;

ON LIES OF VANITY.

Lies, falsely called Lies of Benevolence;
Lies of real Benevolence;
Lies of mere Wantonness, proceeding from a depraved love of lying, or contempt for truth.

There are others probably; but I believe that this list contains all those which are of the most importance; unless, indeed, we may add to it—

Practical Lies; that is, Lies acted, not spoken.

I shall give an anecdote, or tale, in order to illustrate each sort of lie in its turn, or nearly so, lies for the sake of lying *excepted*; for I should find it very difficult so to illustrate this, the most despicable species of falsehood.

CHAPTER II.

ON THE ACTIVE AND PASSIVE LIES OF VANITY.

I SHALL begin my observations, by defining what I mean by the Lie of Vanity, both in its active and passive nature; these lies being undoubtedly the most common, because vanity is one of the most powerful springs of human action, and is usually the besetting sin of every one. Suppose, that, in order to give myself consequence, I were to assert that I was actually acquainted with certain great and distinguished personages, whom I had merely met in fashionable society. Suppose also, I were to say that I was at such a place, and such an assembly, on such a night, without adding, that I was there, not as an invited guest, but only because a benefit concert was held at these places, for which I had tickets. These would both be lies of vanity; but the one would be an active, the other a passive lie.

In the first, I should assert a direct falsehood; in the other, I should withhold part of the truth; but both would be lies, because, in both, my intention was to deceive.*

But though we are frequently tempted to be guilty of the active lies of vanity, our temptations to its passive lies are more frequent still; nor can the sincere lovers of truth be too much on their guard against this constantly-recurring danger. The following instances will explain what I mean by this observation.

If I assert that my motive for a particular action was virtuous, when I know that it was worldly and selfish, I am guilty of an *active*, or *direct* lie. But I am equally guilty of falsehood, if, while I hear my actions or forbearances praised, and imputed to decidedly worthy motives, when I am conscious that they sprung from unworthy or unimportant ones, I listen with silent complacency, and do not positively disclaim my right to commendation; only, in the one case I lie *directly*, in the other, *indirectly;* the lie is *active* in the one, and *passive* in the other. And are we not all of us conscious of having sometimes accepted incense to our vanity, which we knew that we did not deserve?

Men have been known to boast of attention, and even of avowals of serious love from women, and women from men, which, in point of fact, they never received, and therein have been guilty of positive falsehood; but they who, without any contradiction on their own part, allow their friends and flatterers to insinuate that they have been, or are, objects of love and admiration to those who never professed either, are as much guilty of deception as the utterers of the above-mentioned assertion. Still, it is certain, that many who would shrink with moral disgust from committing the latter species of falsehood, are apt to remain silent, when their vanity is gratified, without any overt act of deceit on their part, and are contented to let the flattering belief remain uncontradicted. Yet the turpitude is, in my opinion, at least, nearly equal, if my definition of lying be correct: namely, *the intention to deceive.*

This disingenuous passiveness, this deceitful silence, belongs to that extensive and common species of falsehood, *withholding the truth.*

But this *tolerated* sin, denominated *white lying*, is a sin which I believe that some persons commit, not only without being conscious that it is a sin, but frequently, with a belief that, to do it readily, and without confusion, is often a merit, and always a proof of *ability*. Still more frequently, they do it unconsciously, perhaps, from the force of habit; and, like Monsieur Jourdain, "the Bourgeois gentilhomme," who found out that he had talked prose all his life without knowing it, these persons utter lie upon lie, without knowing that what they utter deserves to be considered as falsehood.

I am myself convinced, that a passive lie is equally as irreconcilable to moral principles as an active one; but I am well aware that most persons are of a different opinion. Yet, I would say to those who thus differ from me, if you allow yourselves to violate truth—that is, to *deceive*, for any purpose whatever—who can say where this sort of self-indulgence will submit to be bounded? Can you be sure that you will not, when strongly tempted, utter what is equally false, in order to benefit yourself at the expense of a fellow-creature?

All mortals are, at times, accessible to temptation; but, when we are not exposed to it, we dwell with complacency on our means of resisting it, on our principles, and our tried

---

* This passive lie is a very frequent one in certain circles in London; as many ladies and gentlemen there purchase tickets for benefit concerts, held at great houses, in order that they may be able to say, "I was at Lady such-a-one's on such a night."

and experienced self-denial; but, as the life-boat and the safety-gun, which succeeded in all that they were made to do while the sea was calm and the winds still, have been known to fail when the vessel was tost on a tempestuous ocean; so those who may successfully oppose principle to temptation when the tempest of the passions is not awakened within their bosoms, may sometimes be overwhelmed by its power when it meets them in all its awful energy and unexpected violence.

But in every warfare against human corruption, habitual resistance to little temptations is, next to prayer, the most efficacious aid. He who is to be trained for public exhibitions of feats of strength, is made to carry small weights at first, which are daily increased in heaviness, till at last he is almost unconsciously able to bear, with ease, the greatest weight possible to be borne by man. In like manner, those who resist the daily temptation to tell what are apparently trivial and innocent lies, will be better able to withstand allurements to serious and important deviations from truth, and be more fortified in the hour of more severe temptation against every species of dereliction from integrity.

The active lies of vanity are so numerous, but at the same time, are so like each other, that it were useless, as well as endless, to attempt to enumerate them. I shall therefore mention one of them only, before I proceed to my tale on the ACTIVE LIE OF VANITY, and that is the most common of all; namely, the violation of truth which persons indulge in relative to their age; an error so generally committed, especially by the unmarried of both sexes, that few persons can expect to be believed when declaring their age at an advanced period of life. So common, and therefore so little disreputable, is this species of lie considered to be, that a sensible friend of mine said to me the other day, when I asked him the age of the lady whom he was going to marry, "She *tells* me she is five-and-twenty; I therefore *conclude* that she is five-and-thirty." This was undoubtedly spoken in joke; still it was an evidence of the toleration generally granted on this point.

But though it is *possible* that my friend believed the lady to be a year or two older than she owned herself to be, and thought a deviation from truth on this subject was of no consequence, I am very sure that he would not have ventured to marry a woman whom he suspected of lying on any other occasion. This however is a lie which does not expose the utterer to severe animadversion, and for this reason probably, that all mankind are so averse to be thought old, that the wish to be considered younger than the truth warrants meets with complacent sympathy and indulgence, even when years are notoriously annihilated at the impulse of vanity.

I give the following story in illustration of the ACTIVE LIE OF VANITY.

THE STAGE COACH.

AMONGST those whom great success in trade had raised to considerable opulence in their native city, was a family by the name of Burford; and the eldest brother, when he was the only surviving partner of that name in the firm, was not only able to indulge himself in the luxuries of a carriage, country-house, garden, hot-houses, and all the privileges which wealth bestows, but could also lay by money enough to provide amply for his children.

His only daughter had been adopted, when very young, by her paternal grandmother, whose fortune was employed in her son's trade, and who could well afford to take on herself all the expenses of Annabel's education. But it was with painful reluctance that Annabel's excellent mother consented to resign her child to another's care; nor could she be prevailed upon to do so, till Burford, who believed that his widowed parent would sink under the loss of her husband, unless Annabel was permitted to reside with her, commanded her to yield her maternal rights in pity to this beloved sufferer. She could therefore presume to refuse no longer;—but she yielded with a mental conflict only too prophetic of the mischief to which she exposed her child's mind and character, by this enforced surrender of a mother's duties.

The grandmother was a thoughtless woman of this world—the mother, a pious, reflecting being, continually preparing herself for the world to come. With the latter, Annabel would have acquired principles — with the former, she could only learn accomplishments; and that weakly judging person encouraged her in habits of mind and character which would have filled both her father and mother with pain and apprehension.

Vanity was her ruling passion; and this her grandmother fostered by every means in her power. She gave her elegant dresses, and had her taught showy accomplishments. She delighted to hear her speak of herself, and boast of the compliments paid her on her beauty and her talents. She was even weak enough to admire the skilful falsehood with which she embellished every thing which she narrated; but this vicious propensity the old lady considered only as a proof of a lively fancy; and she congratulated herself on the consciousness how much more agreeable her fluent and inventive Annabel was, than the *matter of fact* girls with whom she associated. But while Annabel and her grandmother were on a visit at Burford's country-house, and while the parents were beholding with sorrow the conceit and flippancy of their only daughter, they were plunged at once into comparative poverty, by the ruin of some of Burford's correspondents abroad, and by the fraudulent conduct of a friend in whom he had trusted. In a few short weeks, therefore, the ruined grandmother and her adopted child, together with the parents and their boys, were forced to seek an asylum in the heart of Wales, and live on the slender marriage settlement of Burford's amiable wife. For her every one felt, as it was thought she had always discouraged that expensive style of living which had exposed her husband to envy, and its concomitant detractions, amongst those whose increase in wealth had not kept pace with his own. He had also carried his ambition so far, that he had even aspired to represent his native city in parliament; and, as he was a violent politician, some of the opposite party not only rejoiced in his downfall, but were ready to believe and to propagate that he had made a fraudulent bankruptcy in concert with his friend who had absconded, and that he had secured or conveyed away from his creditors money to a considerable amount. But the tale of calumny, which has no foundation in truth, cannot long retain its power to injure; and, in process of time, the feelings of the creditors in general were so completely changed towards Burford, that some of them who had been most decided against signing his certificate, were at length brought to confess that it was a matter for *reconsideration*. Therefore, when a distinguished friend of his father's, who had been strongly prejudiced against him at first, repented of his unjust credulity, and, in order to make him amends, offered him a share in his own business, all the creditors, except two of the principal ones, became willing to sign the certificate. Perhaps there is nothing so difficult to remove from some minds as suspicions of a derogatory nature; and the creditors in question were envious, worldly men, who piqued themselves on their shrewdness, could not brook the idea of being overreached, and were perhaps not sorry that he whose prosperity had excited their jealousy, should now be humbled before them as a dependant and a suppliant. However, even they began to be tired at length of holding out against the opinion of so many; and Burford had the comfort of being informed, after he had been some months in Wales, that matters were in train to enable him to get into business again, with restored credit and renewed prospects.

"Then, who knows, Anna," said he to his wife, "but that in a few years I shall be able, by industry and economy, to pay all that I owe, both principal and interest? for, till I have done so, I shall not be really happy; and then poverty will be robbed of its sting."

"Not only so," she replied,—"we could never have given our children a better inheritance than this proof of their father's strict integrity; and, surely, my dear husband, a blessing will attend thy labours and intentions."

"I humbly trust that it will."

"Yes," she continued; "our change of fortune has humbled our pride of heart, and the cry of our contrition and humility has not ascended in vain."

"*Our* pride of heart!" replied Burford, tenderly embracing her; "it was *I*, I alone, who deserved chastisement, and I cannot bear to hear thee blame thyself; but it is like thee, Anna,—thou art ever kind, ever generous; however, as I like to be obliged to thee, I am contented that thou shouldst talk of *our* pride and *our* chastisement."

While these hopes were uppermost in the minds of this amiable couple, and were cheering the weak mind of Burford's mother, which, as it had been foolishly elated by prosperity, was now as improperly depressed by adversity, Annabel had been passing several months at the house of a school-fellow some miles from her father's dwelling. The vain girl had felt the deepest mortification at this blight to her worldly prospects, and bitterly lamented being no longer able to talk of her grandmother's villa and carriages, and her father's hot-houses and grounds; nor could she help repining at the loss of indulgences to which she had been accustomed. She was therefore delighted to leave home on a visit, and very sorry when unexpected circumstances in her friend's family obliged her to return sooner than she intended. She was compelled also to return by herself in a public coach,—a great mortification to her still existing pride; but she had now no pretensions to travel otherwise, and found it necessary to submit to circumstances. In the coach were one young man and two elderly ones; and her companions seemed so willing to pay her attention, and make her journey pleasant to her, that Annabel, who always believed herself an object of admiration, was soon convinced that she had made a conquest of the youth, and that the others thought her a very sweet creature. She therefore, gave way to all her loquacious vivacity; she hummed tunes in order to show that she could sing; she took out her pencil and sketched wherever they stopped to change horses, and talked of her own *boudoir*, her own maid, and all the past glories of her state, as if they still existed. In short, she tried to impress her companions with a high idea of her consequence, and as if unusual and unexpected circumstances had led her to travel *incog.*, while she put in force all her attractions against their poor condemned hearts. What an odious thing is a coquette of sixteen! and such was Annabel Burford. Certain it is, that she became an object of great attention to the gentlemen with her, but of admiration, probably, to the young man alone, who, in her youthful beauty, might possibly overlook her obvious defects. During the journey, one of the elderly gentlemen opened a basket which stood near him, containing some fine hothouse grapes and flowers.

"There, young lady," he said to her, "did you ever see such fruit as this before?"

"Oh dear yes, in my papa's grapery."

"Indeed! but did you ever see such fine flowers?"

"Oh dear, yes, in papa's succession-houses. There is nothing, I assure you, of that sort," she added, drawing up her head with a look of ineffable conceit, "that I am not accustomed to;"—condescending, however, at the same time, to eat some of the grapes, and accept some of the flowers.

It was natural that her companions should now be very desirous of finding out what princess in disguise was deigning to travel in a manner so unworthy of her; and when they stopped within a few miles of her home, one of the gentlemen, having discovered that she was known to a passenger on the top of the coach, who was about to leave it, got out and privately asked him who she was.

"Burford! Burford!" cried he, when he heard the answer; "what! the daughter of Burford the bankrupt?"

"Yes, the same."

With a frowning brow he re-entered the coach, and, when seated, whispered the old gentleman next him; and both of them having exchanged glances of sarcastic and indignant meaning, looked at Annabel with great significance. Nor was it long before she observed a marked change in their manner towards her. They answered her with abruptness, and even with reluctance; till, at length, the one who interrogated her acquaintance on the coach said, in a sarcastic tone,

"I conclude that you were speaking just now, young lady of the fine things which were *once* yours. You have no graperies and succession-houses *now*, I take it."

"Dear me! why not, sir?" replied the conscious girl, in a trembling voice.

"Why not? Why, excuse my freedom, but are you not the daughter of Mr. Burford the bankrupt?"

Never was child more tempted to deny her parentage than Annabel was; but though with great reluctance, she faltered out,

"Yes; and to be sure, my father was once unfortunate; but—"

Here she looked at her young and opposite neighbour; and, seeing that his look of admiring respect was exchanged for one of ill-suppressed laughter, she felt irresistibly urged to add,

"But we are very well off now, I assure you; and our present residence is so pretty! Such a sweet garden! and such a charming hot-house!"

"Indeed!" returned the old man, with a significant nod to his friend; "well, then, let your papa take care he does not make his house too hot to hold him, and that *another* house be not added to his list of residences." Here he laughed heartily at his own wit, and was echoed by his companion. "But pray, how long has he been thus again favoured by fortune?"

"Oh dear! I cannot say, but for some time, and I assure you our style of living is very complete."

"I do not doubt it; for children and fools speak truth, says the proverb; and sometimes," added he in a low voice, "the child and the fool are the same person. So, so," he muttered aside to the other traveller; "gardens! hot-house! carriage! swindling, specious rascal!"

But Annabel heard only the first part of the sentence; and being quite satisfied that she had recovered all her consequence in the eyes of her young beau by two or three *white lies*, as she termed them, (flights of fancy in which she was apt to indulge,) she resumed her attack on his heart, and continued to converse, in her most seducing manner, till the coach stopped, according to her desire, at a cottage by the road-side, where, as she said, her father's groom was to meet her and take her portmanteau. The truth was, that she did not choose to be set down at her own humble home, which was at the further end of the village, because it would not only tell the tale of her fallen fortunes, but would prove the falsehood of what she had been asserting. When the coach stopped, she exclaimed with well-acted surprise, "Dear me! how strange that the servant is not waiting for me! But it does not signify; I can stop here till he comes." She then left the coach scarcely greeted by her elderly companions, but followed, as she fancied, by looks of love from the youth, who handed her out, and expressed his great regret at parting with her.

The parents, meanwhile, were eagerly expecting her return; for though the obvious defects in her character gave them excessive pain, and they were resolved to leave no measures untried in order to eradicate them, they had missed her amusing vivacity; and even their low and confined dwelling was rendered cheerful, when, with her sweet and brilliant tones, she went carolling about the house. Besides, she was coming, for the first time, alone and unattended; and as the coach was later than usual, the anxious tenderness of the paternal heart was worked up to a high pitch of feeling, and they were even beginning to share the fantastic fears of the impatient grandmother, when they saw the coach stop at a distant turn of the road, and soon after beheld Annabel coming towards them; who was fondly clasped to those affectionate bosoms, for which her unprincipled falsehoods, born of the most contemptible vanity, had prepared fresh trials and fresh injuries; for her elderly companions were her father's principal and relentless creditors, who had been down to Wynstaye on business, and were returning thence to London; intending when they arrived there to assure Sir James Alberry,—that friend of Burford's father, who resided in London, and wished to take him into partnership,—that they were no longer averse to sign his certificate; being at length convinced he was a calumniated man. But now all their suspicions were renewed and confirmed; since it was easier for them to believe that Burford was still the villain which they always thought him, than that so young a girl should have told so many falsehoods at the mere impulse of vanity. They therefore became more inveterate against her poor father than ever; and though their first visit to the metropolis was to the gentleman in question, it was now impelled by a wish to injure, not to serve him. How differently would they have felt, had the vain and false Annabel allowed the coach to set her down at her father's lowly door! and had they beheld the interior arrangement of his house and family! Had they seen neatness and order giving attraction to cheap and ordinary furniture; had they beheld the simple meal spread out to welcome the wanderer home, and the Bible and Prayer-book ready for the evening service, which was deferred till it could be shared again with her whose return would add fervour to the devotion of that worshipping family, and would call forth additional expressions of thanksgiving!

The dwelling of Burford was that of a man improved by trials past; of one who looked forward with thankfulness and hope to the renewed possession of a competence, in the belief that he should now be able to make a wiser and holier use of it than he had done before. His wife had needed no such lesson; though, in the humility of her heart, she thought otherwise; and she had helped her husband to impress on the yielding minds of her boys, who (happier than their sister) had never left her, that a season of worldly humiliation is more safe and blessed than one of worldly prosperity —while their Welch cottage and wild mountain garden had been converted, by her resources and her example, into a scene of such rural industry and innocent amusement, that they could no longer regret the splendid house and grounds which they had been obliged to resign. The grandmother, indeed, had never ceased to mourn and to murmur; and, to her, the hope of seeing a return of brighter days, by means of a new partnership, was beyond measure delightful. But she was doomed to be disappointed, through those errors in the child of her adoption which she had at least encouraged, if she had not occasioned.

It was, with even clamorous delight, that Annabel, after this absence of a few months, was welcomed by her brothers; the parents' welcome was of a quieter, deeper nature; while the grandmother's first solicitude was to ascertain how she looked; and having convinced herself that she was returned handsomer than ever, her joy was as loud as that of the boys.

"Do come hither, Bell," said one of her brothers, "we have so much to show you! The old cat has such nice kittens!"

"Yes; and my rabbits have all young ones!" cried another.

"And I and mamma," cried the third boy, "have put large stones into the bed of the mountain rill; so now it makes such a nice noise as it flows over them! Do come, Bell; do, pray, come with us!"

But the evening duties were first to be performed; and performed they were, with more than usual solemnity; but after them, Annabel had to eat her supper; and she was so engrossed in relating her adventures in the coach, and with describing the attentions of her companions, that her poor brothers were not attended to. In vain did her mother say, "Do, Annabel, go with your brothers!" and added, "Go now; for it is near their bed-time!" She was too fond of hearing herself talk, and of her grandmother's flatteries, to be willing to leave the room; and though her mother was disappointed at her selfishness, she could not bear to chide her on the first night of her return.

When Annabel was alone with her grandmother, she ventured to communicate to her what a fearful consciousness of not having done right had led her to conceal from her parents; and, after relating all that had passed relative to the fruit and flowers, she repeated the cruel question of the old man, "Are you not the daughter of Mr. Burford the bankrupt?" and owned what her reply was; on which her grandmother exclaimed, with great emotion,

"Unthinking girl! you know not what injury you have done your father!" She then asked for a particular description of the persons of the old men, saying, "Well, well, it cannot be helped now—I may be mistaken; but be sure not to tell your mother what you have told me."

For some days after Annabel's return, all went on well; and their domestic felicity would have been so complete, that Burford and his wife would have much disliked any idea of change, had their income been sufficient to give their boys good education; but, as it was only just sufficient for their maintenance, they looked forward with anxious expectation to the arrival of a summons to London, and to their expected residence there. Still, the idea of leaving their present abode was really painful to all, save Annabel and her grandmother. They thought the rest of the family devoid of proper spirit, and declared that living in Wales was not living at all.

But a stop was now put to eager anticipations on the one hand, or tender regrets on the other; for, while Burford was expecting daily to receive remittances from Sir James Alberry, to enable him to transport himself and his family to the metropolis, that gentleman wrote to him as follows:—

"Sir,—All connexion between us is for ever at an end; and I have given the share in my business, which was intended for you, to the *worthy* man who has so long solicited it. I thought that I had done you injustice, sir; I wished therefore to make you amends. But I find you are, what you are represented to be, a fraudulent bankrupt; and your certificate *now will never be signed*. Should you wonder what has occasioned this change in my feelings and proceedings, I am at liberty to inform you, that your daughter travelled in a stage-coach, a few days ago, with your two principal creditors; and I am desired to add, *that children and fools speak truth*.
"JAMES ALBERRY."

When Burford had finished reading this letter, it fell from his grasp, and clasping his hands convulsively together, he exclaimed, "Ruined and disgraced for ever!" then rushed into his own chamber. His terrified wife followed him with the unread letter in her hand, looking the inquiries which she could not utter.

"Read that," he replied, "and see that Sir James Alberry deems me a villain!" She did read, and with a shaking frame; but it was not the false accusation of her husband, nor the loss of the expected partnership, that thus agitated her firm nerves, and firmer mind; it was the painful conviction, that Annabel, by some means unknown to her, had been the cause of this mischief to her father;—a conviction which considerably increased Burford's agony, when she pointed out the passage in Sir James's letter alluding to Annabel, who was immediately summoned, and desired to explain Sir James's mysterious meaning.

"Dear me! papa," cried she, changing colour, "I am sure, if I had thought,—I am sure, I could not think,—nasty, ill-natured old man! I am sure I only said—"

"But what *did* you say?" cried her agitated father.

"I can explain all," said his mother, who had entered uncalled for, and read the letter. She then repeated what Annabel had told, but softening it as much as she could;—however, she told enough to show the agonizing parents that their child was not only the cause of disappointment and disgrace to them, but a mean, vain-glorious, and despicable liar!

"The only amends which you can now make us," said Burford, "is to tell the whole truth, unhappy child! and then we must see what can be done; for my reputation must be cleared, even at the painful expense of exposing you."

Nor was it long before the mortified Annabel, with a heart awakened to contrition by her mother's gentle reproofs, and the tender teachings of a mother's love, made an ample confession of all that had passed in the stage-coach; on hearing which, Burford instantly resolved to set off for London. But how was he to get thither? He had no money; as he had recently been obliged to pay some debts of his still thoughtless and extravagant mother; nor could he bear to borrow of his neighbour what he was afraid he might be for some time unable to return.

"Cruel, unprincipled girl!" cried he, as he paced their little room in agony; "see to what misery thou hast reduced thy father! However, I must go to London immediately, though it be on foot."

"Well, really, I don't see any very great harm in what the poor child did," cried his mother, distressed at seeing Annabel's tears. "It was very trying to her to be reproached with her father's bankruptcy and her fallen fortunes; and it was very natural for her to say what she did."

"Natural!" exclaimed the indignant mother; "natural for my child to utter falsehood on falsehood, and at the instigation of a mean vanity! Natural for my child to shrink from the avowal of poverty, which was unattended with disgrace! Oh! make us not more wretched than we were before, by trying to lessen Annabel's faults in her own eyes! Our only comfort, is the hope that she is ashamed of herself."

"But neither her shame nor penitence," cried Burford, "will give me the quickest means of repairing the effects of her error. However, as I cannot ride, I must walk to London;" while his wife, alarmed at observing the dew of weakness which stood upon his brow, and the faint flush which overspread his cheek, exclaimed,

"But will not writing to Sir James be sufficient?"

"No. My appearance will corroborate my assurances too well. The only writing necessary will be a detail from Annabel of all that passed in the coach, and a confession of her fault."

"What! exact from your child such a disgraceful avowal, William!" cried the angry grandmother.

"Yes; for it is a punishment due to her transgression;—and she may think herself happy if its consequences end here."

"Here's a fuss, indeed, about a little harmless puffing and white lying!"

"Harmless!" replied Burford, in a tone of indignation; while his wife exclaimed, in the agony of a wounded spirit,

"Oh! mother, mother! do not make us deplore, more than we already do, that fatal hour when we consented to surrender our dearest duties at the call of compassion for your sorrows, and entrusted the care of our child's precious soul to your erroneous tenderness! But, I trust that Annabel deeply feels her sinfulness, and that the effects of a mistaken education may have been counteracted in time."

The next day, having procured the necessary document from Annabel, Burford set off on his journey, intending to travel occasionally on the tops of coaches, being well aware that he was not in a state of health to walk the whole way.

In the meanwhile, Sir James Alberry, the London merchant, to whom poor Burford was then pursuing his long and difficult journey, was beginning to suspect that he had acted hastily, and, perhaps, unjustly. He had written his distressing letter in the moments of his first indignation, on hearing the statement of the two creditors; and he had moreover written it under their dictation; and, as the person who had long wished to be admitted into partnership with him, happened to call at the same time, and had taken advantage of Burford's supposed delinquency, he had, without further hesitation, granted his request. But as Sir James, though a *rash* was a *kind-hearted* man, when his angry feelings had subsided, the rebound of them was in favour of the poor accused; and he reproached himself for having condemned and punished a supposed culprit, before he was even heard in his defence. Therefore, having invited Burford's accusers to return to dinner, he dismissed them as soon as he could, and went in search of his wife, wishing, but not expecting, his hasty proceeding to receive the approbation of her candid spirit and discriminating judgment.

"What is all this?" cried Lady Alberry, when he had done speaking. "Is it possible that, on the evidence of these two men, who have shown themselves inveterate enemies of the poor bankrupt, you have broken your promise to him, and pledged it to another?"

"Yes; and my letter to Burford is gone. I wish I had shown it to you before it went; but surely Burford's child could not have told them falsehoods."

"That depends on her education."

"True, Jane; and she was brought up, you know, by that paragon, her mother, who cannot do wrong."

"No; she was brought up by that weak woman, her grandmother, who is not likely, I fear, ever to do right. Had her pious mother educated her, I should have been sure that Annabel Burford could not have told a lie. However, I shall see, and interrogate the accusers. In the meanwhile, I must regret your excessive precipitancy."

As Lady Alberry was a woman who scrupulously performed all her religious and moral duties, she was, consequently, always observant of that holy command, "not to take up a reproach against her neighbour." She was, therefore, very unwilling to believe the truth of this charge against Burford; and thought that it was more likely an ill-educated girl should tell a falsehood, which had also, perhaps, been magnified by involuntary exaggeration, than that the husband of such a woman as Anna Burford should be the delinquent which his old creditors described him to be. For she had in former days been thrown into society with Burford's wife, and had felt attracted towards her by the strongest of all sympathies, that of entire unity on those subjects most connected with our welfare here, and hereafter; those sympathies which can convert strangers into friends, and draw them together in the enduring ties of pure, christian love. "No, no," said she to herself; "the beloved husband of such a woman cannot be a villain;" and she awaited, with benevolent impatience, the arrival of her expected guests.

They came, accompanied by Charles Danvers, Annabel's young fellow-traveller, who was nephew to one of them; and Lady Alberry lost no time in drawing from them an exact detail of all that had passed.

"And this girl, you say, was a forward, conceited, set-up being, full of herself and her accomplishments; in short, the creature of vanity."

"Yes," replied one of the old men, "it was quite a comedy to look at her, and hear her!"

"But what says my young friend?"

"The same. She is very pretty; but a model of affectation, boasting, and vanity. Now she was hanging her head on one side—then looking languishingly with her eyes; and when my uncle, *coarsely*, as I thought, talked of her father as a bankrupt, her expression of angry mortification was so ludicrous that I could scarcely help laughing. Nay, I do assure you," he continued, "that had we been left alone a few minutes, I should have been made the confidant of her love affairs; for she sighed deeply once, and asked me with an affected lisp, if I did not think it a dangerous thing to have a too susceptible heart!"

As he said this, after the manner of Annabel, both the old men exclaimed, "Admirable! that is she to the life! I think that I see her and hear her!"

"But, I dare say," said Lady Alberry gravely, "that you paid her compliments, and pretended to admire her, notwithstanding."

"I own it; for how could I refuse the incense which every look and gesture demanded?"

"A principle of truth, young man! would have enabled you to do it. What a fine lesson it would be, for poor flattered women, if we could know how meanly men think of us, even when they flatter us the most."

"But, dear Lady Alberry, this girl seemed to me a mere child; a coquette of the nursery; still, had she been older, her evident vanity would have secured me against her beauty."

"You are mistaken, Charles; this child is

almost seventeen. But now, gentlemen, as *just men*, I appeal to you all, whether it is not more likely that this vain-glorious girl told lies, than that her father, the husband of one of the best of women, should be guilty of the grossest dishonesty?"

"I must confess, Jane, that you have convinced me," said Sir James; but the two creditors only frowned, and spoke not.

"But consider," said this amiable advocate; "if the girl's habitation was so beautiful, was it not inconsistent with her boasting propensities that she should not choose to be set down at it? And if her father still had carriages and servants, would they not have been sent to meet her? And if he were really rich, would she have been allowed to travel alone in a stage-coach? Impossible: and I conjure you to suspend your severe judgment of an unfortunate man, till you have sent some one to see how he really lives."

"I am forced to return to Wynstaye to-morrow," growled out Charles's uncle; "therefore, suppose I go myself."

"We had fixed to go into Wales ourselves, next week," replied Lady Alberry, "on a visit to a dear friend who lives not far from Wynstaye. Therefore, what say you, Sir James? Had we not better go with our friend? For if you have done poor Burford injustice, the sooner you make him reparation, and *in person*, the better."

To this proposal Sir James gladly assented; and they set off for Wales the next day, accompanied by the uncle and the nephew.

As Lady Alberry was going to her chamber, on the second night of their journey, she was startled by the sound of deep groans, and a sort of delirious raving, from a half-open door.

"Surely," said she to the landlady, who was conducting her, "there is some one very ill in that room."

"Oh, dear! yes, my lady; a poor man who was picked up on the road yesterday. He had walked all the way from the heart of Wales, till he was so tired he got on a coach; and he supposes that, from weakness, he fell off in the night; and not being missed, he lay till he was found and brought hither."

"Has any medical man seen him?"

"Not yet; for our surgeon lives a good way off; and, as he had his senses when he first came, we hoped he was not much hurt. He was able to tell us that he only wanted a garret, as he was very poor; and yet, my lady, he looks and speaks so like a gentleman!"

"Poor creature! he must be attended to, and a medical man sent for directly, as he is certainly not sensible *now*."

"Hark! he is raving again, and all about his wife, and I cannot tell what."

"I should like to see him," said Lady Alberry, whose heart always yearned towards the afflicted; "and I think that I am myself no bad doctor."

Accordingly, she entered the room just as the sick man exclaimed, in his delirium, "Cruel Sir James! I a fraudulent . . . . . Oh! my dearest Anna!" . . . . and Lady Alberry recognised, in the poor raving being before her, the calumniated Burford!

"I know him!" she cried, bursting into tears: "We will be answerable for all expenses."

She then went in search of Sir James; and having prepared him as tenderly as she could for the painful scene which awaited him, she led him to the bedside of the unconscious invalid;—then, while Sir James was shocked and distressed beyond measure, interrogated the landlady, Lady Alberry examined the nearly threadbare coat of the *supposed rich man*, which lay on the bed, and searched for the slenderly-filled purse, of which he had himself spoken. She found there Sir James's letter, which had, she doubted not, occasioned his journey and his illness; and which, therefore, in an agony of repentant feeling, her husband tore *into atoms*. In the same pocket he found Annabel's confession; and when they left the chamber, having vainly waited, in hopes of being recognised by the poor invalid, they returned to their fellow-travellers, carrying with them the evidences of Burford's scanty means, in corroboration of the tale of suffering and fatigue which they had to relate.

"See!" said Lady Alberry, holding up the coat, and emptying the purse on the table, "are these signs of opulence? and is travelling on foot, in a hot June day, a proof of splendid living?" while the harsh creditor, as he listened to the tale of delirium, and read the confession of Annabel, regretted the hasty credence which he had given to her falsehoods.

But what was best to be done? To send for Burford's wife;—and, till she arrived to nurse him, Sir James and Lady Alberry declared that they would not leave the inn. It was therefore agreed that the nephew should go to Burford's house, in the barouche, and escort his wife back. He did so; and while Annabel, lost in painful thought, was walking on the road, she saw the barouche driving up, with her young fellow-traveller in it. As it requires great suffering to subdue such overweening vanity as Annabel's, her first thought, on seeing him, was, that her youthful beau was a young heir, who had travelled in disguise, and was now come in state, to make her an offer! She, therefore, blushed with pleasure, as she approached, and received his bow with a countenance of joy. But his face expressed no answering pleasure; and, coldly passing her, he said his business was with her mother, who, alarmed, she scarcely knew why, stood trembling at the door; nor was she less alarmed, when the feeling youth told his errand, in broken and faltering accents, and delivered Lady Alberry's letter.

"Annabel must go with me!" said her mother, in a deep and solemn tone. Then lowering her voice, because unwilling to reprove her before a stranger, she added, "Yes, my child! thou must go, to see the effects of thy errors, and take sad, but salutary warning, for the rest of thy life. We shall not detain you long, sir," she continued, turning to Charles Danvers; "our *slender wardrobe* can be soon prepared."

In a short time, the calm, but deeply-suffering wife, and the weeping, humbled daughter, were on their road to the inn. The mother scarcely spoke during the whole of the journey; but she seemed to pray a great deal; and the young man was so affected, with the subdued anguish of the one, and the passionate grief of the other, that, he declared to Lady Alberry, he had never been awakened to such serious thought before, and hoped to be the better for the journey, through the whole of his existence; while, in her penitent sorrow, he felt inclined to forget Annabel's fault, coquetry, and affectation.

When they reached the inn, the calmness of the wife was entirely overcome at the sight of Lady Alberry, who opened her arms to receive her with the kindness of an attached friend; whispering, as she did so, " He has been sensible; and he knew Sir James; knew him as an affectionate friend and nurse!"

"Gracious Heaven, I thank thee!" she replied, hastening to his apartment, leading the reluctant Annabel along. But he did not know them; and his wife was at first speechless with sorrow; at length, recovering her calmness, she said, "See, dear unhappy girl! to what thy sinfulness has reduced thy fond father! Humble thyself, my child, before the Great Being whom thou hast offended; and own his mercy in the awful warning!"

"I am humbled, I am warned, I trust," cried Annabel, falling on her knee; "but, if he die, what will become of me?"

"What will become of us *all*?" replied the mother, shuddering at the bare idea of losing him, but preparing with forced composure, for her important duties. Trying ones indeed they were, through many days and nights, that the wife and daughter had to watch beside the bed of the unconscious Burford. The one heard herself kindly invoked, and tenderly desired, and her *absence wondered at*; while the other never heard her name mentioned, during the ravings of fever, without heart-rending upbraidings, and just reproofs. But Burford's life was granted to the prayers of agonizing affection; and when recollection returned, he had the joy of knowing that his reputation was cleared, that his angry creditors were become his kind friends, and that Sir James Alberry lamented, with bitter regret, that he could no longer prove his confidence in him by making him his partner. But, notwithstanding this blight to his prospects, Burford piously blessed the event which had had so salutary an influence on his offending child; and had taught her a lesson which she was not likely to forget. Lady Alberry, however, thought that the lesson was not yet sufficiently complete; for, though Annabel might be cured of lying by the consequences of her falsehoods, the vanity which prompted them might still remain uncorrected. Therefore, as Annabel had owned that it was the wish not to lose consequence in the eyes of her supposed admirer, which had led her to her last fatal falsehood, Lady Alberry, with the mother's approbation, contrived a plan for laying the axe, if possible, to the root of her vanity; and she took the earliest opportunity of asking Charles Danvers in her presence, and that of her mother, some particulars concerning what passed in the coach, and his opinion on the subject. As she expected, he gave a softened and favourable representation; and would not allow that he did not form a favourable opinion of his fair companion.

"What! Charles," said she, "do you pretend to deny that you mimicked her voice and manner?"

She then repeated all that he had said, and his declaration that her evident vanity and coquetry steeled his heart against her, copying at the same time, his accurate mimicry of Annabel's manner; nor did she rest till she had drawn from him a full avowal that what he had asserted was true; for, Lady Alberry was not a woman to be resisted; while the mortified, humbled, but corrected Annabel, could only hide her face in her mother's bosom; who, while she felt for the salutary pangs inflicted on her, mingled caresses with her tears, and whispered in her ear, that the mortification which she endured, was but for a moment; and the benefit would be, she trusted, of eternal duration. The lesson was now complete indeed. Annabel found that she had not only, by her lies of vanity, deprived her father of a lucrative business, but that she had exposed herself to the ridicule and contempt of that very being who had been the cause of her error; and, in the depth of her humbled and contrite heart, she resolved from that moment to struggle with her besetting sins and subdue them. Nor was the resolve of that trying moment ever broken. But when her father, whose original destination had been the church, was led by his own wishes to take orders, and was in process of time inducted into a considerable living, in the gift of Sir James Alberry, Annabel rivalled her mother in performing the duties of her new station; and, when she became a wife and mother herself, she had a mournful satisfaction in relating the above story to her children; bidding them beware of all lying, but more especially of that common lie, the lie of vanity, whether it be active or passive.

"Not," said she, "that retributive justice in this world, like that which attended mine, may always follow your falsehoods, or those of others; but because all lying is contrary to the moral law of God; and that the liar, as scripture tells us, is not only liable to punishment and disgrace here, but will be the object of certain and more awful punishment in the world to come."

The following tale illustrates the PASSIVE LIE OF VANITY.

UNEXPECTED DISCOVERIES.

THERE are two sayings — the one derived from divine, the other from human authority — the truth of which is continually forced upon us by experience. They are these ; — "A prophet is not without honour, except in his own country;" and " No man is a hero to his valet de chambre."—" Familiarity breeds contempt," is also a proverb to the same effect; and they all three bear upon the tendency in our natures to undervalue the talents, and the claims to distinction, of those with whom we are closely connected and associated; and on our incapability to believe that they, whom we have always considered as our equals only, or perhaps as our inferiors, can be to the rest of the world objects of admiration and respect.

No one was more convinced of the truth of these sayings than Darcy Pennington, the only child of a pious and virtuous couple, who thought him the best of sons, and one of the first of geniuses; but, as they were not able to persuade the rest of the family of this latter truth, when they died, Darcy's uncle and guardian insisted on his going into a merchant's counting-house, in London, instead of being educated for one of the learned professions. Darcy had a mind too well disciplined, to rebel against his guardian's authority. He therefore submitted to his allotment in silence; resolving that his love of letters and the muses should not interfere with his duties to his employer, but he devoted all his leisure hours to literary pursuits; and, as he had real talents, he was at length raised from the unpaid contributor to the poetical columns in the newspaper, to the *paid* writer in a popular magazine; while his poems, signed *Alfred*, became objects of eager expectation. But Darcy's own family and friends could not have been more surprised at his growing celebrity than he himself was; for he was a sincere, humble christian; and, having been accustomed to bow to the opinion of those whom he considered as his superiors in intellect and knowledge, he could scarcely believe in his own eminence. But it was precious to his heart, rather than to his vanity; as it enabled him to indulge those benevolent feelings, which his small income had hitherto restrained. At length he published a duodecimo volume of poems and hymns, still under the name of Alfred, which was highly praised in reviews and journals, and a strong desire was expressed to know who the modest, promising, and pious writer was.

Notwithstanding, Darcy could not prevail upon himself to disclose his name. He visited his native town every year, and in the circle of his family and friends, was still considered only as a good sort of lad, who had been greatly overrated by his parents — was just suited for the situation in which he had been placed — and was very fortunate to have been received into partnership with the merchant to whom he had been clerk. In vain did Darcy sometimes endeavour to hint that he was an author; he remembered the contempt with which his uncle and relations had read one of the earliest fruits of his muse, when exhibited by his fond father, and the advice given to burn such stuff, and not turn the head of a dull boy, by making him fancy himself a genius. Therefore, recollecting the wise saying quoted above, he feared that the news of his literary celebrity would not be received with pleasure, and that the affection with which he was now welcomed might suffer diminution. " Besides," thought he, — and then his heart rose in his throat, with a choking, painful feeling,— " those tender parents, who would have enjoyed my little fame, are cold, and unconscious now ; and the ears, to which my praises would have been sweet music, cannot hear; therefore, methinks, I have a mournful pleasure in keeping on that veil, the removal of which cannot confer pleasure on them."

Consequently he remained contented to be warmly welcomed at D—— for talents of an humble sort, such as his power for mending toys, making kites, and rabbits on the wall; which talents endeared him to all the children of his family and friends; and, through them, to their parents. Yet it may be asked, was it possible that a young man so gifted, could conceal his abilities from observation ?

Oh, yes. Darcy, to borrow Addison's metaphor concerning himself, though he could draw a bill for 1000*l*., had never any small change in his pocket. Like him, he could write, but he could not talk ; he was discouraged in a moment; and the slightest rebuff made him hesitate to a painful degree. He had, however, some flattering moments, even amidst his relations and friends; for he heard them repeating his verses, and singing his songs. He had also far greater joy in hearing his hymns in places of public worship ; and then, too much choked with grateful emotion to join in the devotional chorus himself, he used to feel his own soul raised to heaven upon those wings which he had furnished for the souls of others. At such moments, he longed to discover himself as the author ; but was withheld by the fear that his songs would cease to be admired, and his hymns would lose their usefulness, if it were known that he had written them. However, he resolved to

UNEXPECTED DISCOVERIES.

feel his way; and once, on hearing a song of his commended, he ventured to observe,

"I think I can write as good a one."

"You!" cried his uncle; "what a conceited boy! I remember that you used to scribble verses when a child; but I thought you had been laughed out of that nonsense."

"My dear fellow, nature never meant thee for a poet, believe me," said one of his cousins conceitedly,—a young collegian. "No, no; like the girl in the drama, thou wouldst make 'love' and 'joy' rhyme, and know no better."

"But I have written, and I can rhyme," replied Darcy colouring a little.

"Indeed!" replied his formal aunt; "Well, Mr. Darcy Pennington, it really would be very amusing to see your erudite productions; perhaps you will indulge us some day."

"I will; and then you may probably alter your opinion."

Soon after, Darcy wrote an anonymous prose tale, in one volume, interspersed with poetry, which had even a greater run than his other writings; and it was attributed first to one person, and then to another, while his publisher was excessively pressed to declare the name of the author; but he did not himself know it, as he only knew Darcy, *avowedly*, under a feigned name. But, at length, Darcy resolved to disclose his secret, at least to his relatives and friends at D——; and, just as the second edition of his tale was nearly completed, he set off for his native place, taking with him the manuscript, full of the printer's marks, to prove that he was the author of it.

He had one *irresistible* motive for thus walking out from his *incognito*, like Homer's deities from their cloud. He had fallen in love with his second-cousin, Julia Vane, an heiress, and his uncle's ward; and had become jealous of himself, as he had, for some months, wooed her in anonymous poetry, which she, he found, attributed to a gentleman in the neighbourhood, whose name he knew not; and she had often declared that, such was her passion for poetry, he who could woo her in beautiful verse, was alone likely to win her heart.

On the very day of his arrival, he said in the family-circle, that he had brought down a little manuscript of his own, which he wished to read to them. Oh! the comical grimaces! the suppressed laughter, growing and swelling, however, till it could be restrained no longer, which was the result of this request! And oh! the looks of consternation when Darcy produced the manuscript from his pocket!

"Why, Darcy," said his uncle, "this is really a word and a blow; but you cannot read it to-night; we are engaged."

"Certainly, Mr. Darcy Pennington," said his aunt, "if you wish to read your astonishing productions, we are bound in civility to hear them; but we are all going to Sir Hugh Belson's, and shall venture to take you with us, though it is a great favour and privilege to be permitted to go on such an occasion; for a gentleman is staying there who has written such a sweet book! It is only just out, yet it cannot be had; because the first edition is sold, and the second not finished. So Sir Hugh, for whom your uncle is exerting himself against the next election, has been so kind as to invite us to hear the author read his own work. This gentleman does not, indeed, *own* that he wrote it; still he does not *deny* it; and it is clear, by his *manner*, that he did write it, and that he would be very sorry not to be considered as the writer."

"Very well, then; the pleasure of hearing another author read his own work shall be delayed," replied Darcy, smiling.

"Perhaps, when you have heard this gentleman's, you will not be so eager to read yours, Darcy," said Julia Vane; "for you *used* to be a modest man."

Darcy sighed, looked significantly, but remained silent.

In the evening they went to Sir Hugh Belson's, where, in the Captain Eustace, who was to delight the company, Darcy recognised the gentleman who had been pointed out to him as the author of several meagre performances handed about in manuscript in certain circles; which owed their celebrity to the birth and fashion of the writer, and to the bribery which is always administered to the self-love of those who are the *select few* chosen to see and judge on such occasions.

Captain Eustace now prepared to read; but when he named the title of the book which he held in his hand, Darcy started from his seat in surprise; for it was the title of his own work! But there might be two works with the same title; and he sat down again; but when the reader continued, and he could doubt no longer, he again started up, and with stuttering eagerness said,

"Wh—wh—who, sir, did you say, wrote this book?"

"I have named no names, sir," replied Eustace conceitedly; "the author is unknown, and wishes to remain so."

"Mr. Darcy Pennington," cried his aunt, "sit down and be quiet;" and he obeyed.

"Mr. Pennington," said Sir Hugh, affectedly, "the violet must be sought, and is *discovered* with difficulty, you know; for it shrinks from observation, and loves the shade."

Darcy bowed assent; but fixed his eyes on the discovered violet before him with such an equivocal expression, that Eustace was disconcerted; and the more so, when Darcy, who could not but feel the ludicrous situation in which he was placed, hid his face in his handkerchief, and was evidently shaking with laughter.

"Mr. Darcy Pennington, I am really ashamed of you," whispered his aunt; and Darcy recovered his composure.

He had now two hours of great enjoyment. He heard that book admirably read which he had intended to read the next day, and knew that he should read ill. He heard that work applauded to the skies as the work of another, which would, he feared, have been faintly commended, if known to be his; and he saw the fine eyes of the woman he loved drowned in tears, by the power of his own simple pathos. The poetry in the book was highly admired also; and, when Eustace paused to take breath, Julia whispered in his ear, "Captain Eustace is the gentleman who, I have every reason to believe, wrote some anonymous poetry sent me by the post; for Captain Eustace pays me, as you see, marked attention; and as he denies that he wrote the verses, exactly as he denies that he wrote the book which he is now reading, it is very evident that he wrote both."

"I dare say," replied Darcy, colouring with resentment, "that he as much wrote the *one* as he wrote the *other*."

"What do you mean, Darcy! There can be no doubt of the fact; and I own that I cannot be insensible to such talent; for poetry and poets are my passion, you know; and in his authorship I forget his plainness. Do you not think a woman would be justified in loving a man who writes so morally, so piously, and so delightfully?"

"Certainly," replied Darcy, eagerly grasping her hand, "provided his conduct be in unison with his writings; and I advise you to give the writer in question *your whole heart*."

After the reading was over, the delighted audience crowded round the reader, whose manner of receiving their thanks was such as to make every one but Darcy believe the work was his own; and never was the PASSIVE LIE OF VANITY more completely exhibited; while Darcy, intoxicated, as it were, by the feelings of gratified authorship, and the hopes excited by Julia's words, thanked him again and again for the admirable manner in which he had read the book; declaring, with great earnestness, that he could not have done it such justice himself; adding, that this evening was the happiest of his life.

"Mr. Darcy Pennington, what ails you?" cried his aunt; "you really are not like yourself!"

"Hold your tongue, Darcy," said his uncle, drawing him on one side; "do not be such a forward puppy; who ever questioned or cared whether you could have done it justice or not? But here is the carriage; and I am glad you have no longer an opportunity of thus exposing yourself by your literary and critical raptures, which sit as ill upon you as the caressings of the ass in the fable did on him, when he pretended to compete with the lapdog in fondling his master."

During the drive home, Darcy did not speak a word; not only because he was afraid of his severe uncle and aunt, but because he was meditating how he should make that discovery, on the success of which hung his dearest hopes. He was also communing with his own heart, in order to bring it back to that safe humility out of which it had been led by the flattering and unexpected events of the evening.

"Well," said he, while they drew round the fire, "as it is not late, suppose I read *my* work to you *now*. I assure you that it is quite as good as that which you have heard."

"Mr. Darcy Pennington, you really quite alarm me," cried his aunt.

"Why so?"

"Because I fear that you are a little *delirious!*" on which Darcy nearly laughed himself into convulsions.

"Let me feel your pulse, Darcy," said his uncle very gravely,—"too quick. I shall send for advice, if you are not better to-morrow; you look so flushed, and your eyes are so bright!"

"My dear uncle," replied Darcy, "I shall be quite well, if you will but hear my manuscript before you go to bed."

They now all looked at each other with increased alarm; and Julia, in order to please him, (for she really loved him) said, "Well, Darcy, if you insist upon it;" but, interrupting her, he suddenly started up, and exclaimed, "No; on second thoughts, I will not read it till Captain Eustace and Sir Hugh and his family can be present; and they will be here the day after to-morrow."

"What! read your nonsense to them!" cried his uncle, "poor fellow! poor fellow!"

But Darcy was gone! he had caught Julia's hand to his lips, and quitted the room, leaving his relations to wonder, to fear, and to pity. But as Darcy was quite composed the next day, they all agreed that he must have drunk more wine than he or they had been aware of the preceding evening. But though Darcy was willing to wait the ensuing evening, before he discovered his secret to the rest of the family, he could not be easy till he had disclosed it to Julia; for he was mortified to find that the pious, judicious Julia Vane had, for one moment, believed that a mere man of the world, like Captain Eustace, could have written such verses as he had anonymously addressed to her; verses breathing the very quintessence of pure love; and full of anxious interest not only for her temporal, but her eternal welfare. "No, no," said he; "she shall not remain in such a degrading error one moment longer;" and having requested a private interview with her, he disclosed the truth.

"What! are *you*—can *you* be—did you write all!" she exclaimed in broken accents; while Darcy gently reproached her for having believed that a mere worldly admirer could so have written; however, she justified herself by declaring how impossible it was to suspect that a man of honour, as Eustace seemed, could be so base as to assume a merit which was not his own. Here she paused, turning away from Darcy's penetrating look, covered with conscious blushes, ashamed that he should see how pleased she was. But she readily acknowledged her sorrow at having been betrayed, by the unworthy artifice of Eustace, into encouraging his attentions, and was eager to concert with Darcy the best plan for revealing the surprising secret.

The evening, so eagerly anticipated by Darcy and Julia, now arrived; and great was the consternation of all the rest of the family, when Darcy took a manuscript out of his pocket, and began to open it.

"The fellow is certainly possessed," thought his uncle.

"Mr. Darcy Pennington," whispered his aunt, "I shall faint if you persist in exposing yourself!"

"Darcy, I will shut you up if you proceed," whispered his uncle; "for you must positively be mad."

"Let him go on, dear uncle," said Julia; "I am *sure* you will be delighted, or *ought* to be so;" and, spite of his uncle's threats and whispers, he addressed Captain Eustace thus:

"Allow me, sir, to thank you again for the more than justice which you did my humble performance the other evening. Till I heard you read it, I was unconscious that it had so much merit; and I again thank you for the highest gratification which, as an author, I ever received."

New terror seized every one of his family who heard him, except Julia; while wonder filled Sir Hugh and the rest of his party— Eustace excepted; he knew that he was not the author of the work; therefore he could not dispute the fact that the real author now stood before him; and blushes of detected falsehood covered his cheek; but ere he could falter out a reply, Darcy's uncle and sons seized him by the arm, and insisted on speaking with him in another room. Darcy, laughing violently, endeavoured to shake them off, but in vain.

"Let him alone," said Julia, smiling, and coming forward. "Darcy's 'eye may be in a fine frenzy rolling,' as you have all of you owned him to be a poet; but other frenzy than that of a poet he has *not*, I assure you—so pray set him at liberty; *I* will be answerable for his sanity."

"What does all this mean?" said his uncle, as he and his sons unwillingly obeyed.

"It means," said Darcy, "that I hope not to quit this room till I have had the delight of hearing these yet unpublished poems of mine read by Captain Eustace. Look, sir," continued he, "here is a signature well known, no doubt, to you; that of *Alfred*."

"Are you indeed Alfred, the celebrated Alfred?" faltered out Eustace.

"I believe so," he replied with a smile; "though on some occasions, you know, it is difficult to prove one's *personal identity*."

"True," answered Eustace, turning over the manuscript to hide his confusion.

"And I, Captain Eustace," said Julia, "have had the great satisfaction of discovering that my unknown poetical correspondent is my long-cherished friend and cousin, Darcy Pennington. Think how satisfactory this discovery has been to *me!*"

"Certainly, madam," he replied, turning pale with emotion; for he not only saw his *Passive Lies of Vanity* detected, though Darcy had too much christian forbearance even to insinuate that he intended to appropriate to himself the fame of another, but he also saw, in spite of the kindness with which she addressed him, that he had lost Julia, and that Darcy had probably gained her.

"What is all this?" cried Sir Hugh at last, who with the uncle and aunt had listened in silent wonder. "Why, Eustace, I thought you owned that?"

"That I deny; I *owned nothing*;" he eagerly replied. "You *insisted* on it, nay, everybody insisted, that I was the *author* of the beautiful work which I read, and of other things; and if Mr. Pennington asserts that he is the author, I give him joy of his genius and his fame."

"What do I hear!" cried the aunt; "Mr. Darcy Pennington a genius, and famous, and I not suspect it!"

"Impossible!" cried his uncle, pettishly; "that dull fellow turn out a wit! It cannot be. What! are you Alfred, boy? I cannot credit it; for if so, I have been dull indeed;" while his sons seemed to feel as much mortification as surprise.

"My dear uncle," said Darcy, "I am now a professed author. I wrote the work which you heard last night. Here it is in the manuscript, as returned by the printer; and here is the last proof of the second edition, which I received at the post-office just now, directed to A. B.; which is, I think, *proof positive* that I may be Alfred also, who by your certainly *impartial* praises, is for *this* evening, at least, in his own eyes, elevated into ALFRED THE GREAT."

CHAPTER III.

ON THE LIES OF FLATTERY.

THE Lies of Flattery are next on my list. These lies are, generally speaking, not only unprincipled, but offensive; and though they are usually told to conciliate good will, the flatterer often fails in his attempt; for his intended dupe frequently sees through his art, and he excites indignation where he meant to obtain regard. Those who know aught of human nature, as it really is, and do not throw the radiance of their own Christian benevolence over it, must be well aware that *few* persons hear with complacency the praises of others, even where there is no competition between the parties praised and themselves. Therefore, the objects of excessive flattery are painfully conscious that the praises bestowed on them, in the hearing of their acquaintances, will not only provoke those auditors to under-value their pretensions, but to accuse them of believing in and enjoying the gross flattery offered to them. There are no persons, in my opinion, with whom it is so difficult to keep up "the relations of peace and amity," as flatterers by system and habit. Those persons, I mean, who deal out their flatteries on the same principle as boys throw a handful of burs. However unskilfully the burs are thrown, the chances are that some will stick; and flatterers expect that some of their compliments will dwell with, and impose on their intended dupe. Perhaps their calculation is not, generally considered, an erroneous one; but if there be any of their fellow-creatures with whom the sensitive and the discerning may be permitted to loathe association, it is with those who presume to address them in the language of compliment, too violent and unappropriate to deceive even for a moment; while they discover on their lips the flickering sneer of contempt contending with its treacherous smile, and mark their wily eye looking round in search of some responsive one, to which it can communicate their sense of the uttered falsehood, and their mean exultation over their imagined dupe. The lies of benevolence, even when they can be resolved into lies of flattery, may be denominated amiable lies; but the lie of flattery is usually uttered by the bad-hearted and censorious; therefore, to the term LIE OF FLATTERY, might be added an alias;—*alias*, the LIE OF MALEVOLENCE.

Coarse and indiscriminating flatterers lay it down as a rule, that they are to flatter all persons on the qualities which they have not. Hence, they flatter the plain, on their beauty; the weak, on their intellect; the dull, on their wit; believing, in the sarcastic narrowness of their conceptions, that no one possesses any self-knowledge; but that every one implicitly believes the truth of the eulogy bestowed. This erroneous view, taken by the *flatterer* of the penetration of the *flattered*, is common only in those who have more cunning than intellect; more shrewdness than penetration; and whose knowledge of the weakness of our nature has been gathered, not from deep study of the human heart, but from the depravity of their own, or from the pages of ancient and modern satirists;—those who have a mean, malignant pleasure, in believing in the absence of all moral truth amongst their usual associates; and are glad to be able to comfort themselves for their own conscious dereliction from a high moral standard, by the conviction that they are, at least, as *good as their neighbours.* Yes; my experience tells me that the above-mentioned rule of flattery is acted upon only by the half-enlightened, who take for superiority of intellect that *base* low cunning,

...... which, in fools, supplies,
And amply too, the place of being wise.

But the deep observer of human nature knows that where there is real intellect, there are discernment and self-knowledge also; and that the really intelligent are aware to how much praise and admiration they are entitled, be it encomium on their personal or mental qualifications.

I beg to give one illustration of the Lie of Flattery, in the following tale, of which the offending heroine is a *female*; though, as men are the *licensed* flatterers of women, I needed not to have feared the imputation of want of candour, had I taken my example from one of the wiser sex.

THE TURBAN; OR THE LIE OF FLATTERY.

Some persons are such determined flatterers both by nature and habit, that they flatter unconsciously, and almost involuntarily. Such a flatterer was Jemima Aldred; but, as the narrowness of her fortune made her unable to purchase the luxuries of life in which she most delighted, she was also a *conscious* and *voluntary* flatterer whenever she was with those who had it in their power to indulge her favourite inclinations.

There was one distinguished woman in the circle of her acquaintance, whose favour she was particularly desirous of gaining, and who was therefore the constant object of her flatteries. This lady, who was rendered, by her situation, her talents, and her virtues, an object of earthly worship to many of her associates, had a good-natured indolence about her, which made her receive the incense offered, as if she believed in its sincerity. But the flattery of young Jemima was so gross, and so indiscrimate, that it sometimes converted the usual gentleness of Lady Delaval's nature into gall; and she felt indignant at being supposed capable of relishing adulation so excessive, and devotion so servile. But, as she was full of christian benevolence, and, consequently, her first desire was to do good, she allowed pity for the poor girl's ignorance to conquer resentment, and laid a plan, in order to correct and amend her, if *possible*, by salutary mortification.

Accordingly, she invited Jemima, and some other young ladies, to spend a whole day with her at her house in the country. But, as the truly benevolent are always reluctant to afflict any one, even though it be to *improve*, Lady Delaval would have shrunk from the task which she had imposed on herself, had not Jemima excited her into perseverance, by falling repeatedly and grossly into her besetting sin during the course of the day. For instance; Lady Delaval, who usually left the choice of her ribbons to her milliner, as she was not studious of her personal appearance, wore colours at breakfast that morning which she thought ill-suited both to her years and complexion; and having asked her guests how they liked her scarf and ribbons, they pronounced them to be beautiful.

"But, surely, they do not become my olive, ill-looking skin!"

"They are certainly not becoming," was the ingenuous reply of all but Jemima Aldred, who persisted in asserting that the colour was as becoming as it was brilliant; adding,

"I do not know what dear Lady Delaval means by undervaluing her own clear complexion."

"The less that is said about that the better, I believe," she drily replied, not trying to conceal the sarcastic smile which played upon her lip, and feeling strengthened, by this new instance of Jemima's duplicity, to go on with her design; but Jemima thought she had endeared herself to her by flattering her personal vanity; and, while her companions frowned reproach for *her insincerity*, she wished for an opportunity of reproving *their rudeness*. After tea, Lady Delaval desired her maid to bring her down the foundation for a turban, which she was going to pin up, and some other finery prepared for the same purpose; and in a short time, the most splendid materials for millinery shone upon the table. When she began her task, her other guests, Jemima excepted, worked also, but she was sufficiently employed, she said, in watching the creative and tasteful fingers of her friend. At first, Lady Delaval made the turban of silver tissue; and Jemima was in ecstasies; but the next moment she declared that covering to be too simple; and Jemima thought so too;—while she was in equal ecstasies at the effect of a gaudy many-coloured gauze, which replaced its modest costliness. But still her young companions openly preferred the silver covering, declaring that the gay one could only be tolerated if nothing else of showy ornament were superadded. They gave, however, their opinion in vain. Coloured stones, a gold band, and a green, spun-glass feather, were all in their turn heaped upon this showy head-dress, while Jemima exulted over every fresh addition, and admired it as a new proof of Lady Delaval's taste.

"Now, then, it is completed," cried Lady Delaval; "but no; suppose I add a scarlet feather to the green one; oh! that would be superb;" and having given this desirable finish to her performance, Jemima declared it to be perfect; but the rest of the company were too honest to commend it. Lady Delaval then put it on her head; and it was as unbecoming as it was ugly; but Jemima exclaimed that her dear friend had never worn anything before in which she looked so well, adding,

"But then *she* looks well in *everything*. However, that lovely turban would become any one."

"Try how it would fit you!" said Lady Delaval, putting it on her head. Jemima looked in a glass, and saw that to her short, small person, little face, and little turned-up nose, such an enormous mass of finery was the destruction of all comeliness; but, while the by-standers laughed immoderately at her appearance, Jemima was loud in her admiration, and volunteered a wish to wear it at some public place—

"For I think I *do* look so well in it!" cried Jemima.

"If so," said her hostess, "*you*, young ladies, on this occasion, have neither taste nor eye;" while Jemima danced about the room, exulting in her heavy head-dress, in the triumph of her falsehood, and in the supposed superior ascendency it had gained her over her hostess, above that of her more sincere companions. Nor, when Lady Delaval expressed her fear that the weight might be painful, would she allow it to be removed; but she declared that she liked her burden. At parting, Lady Delaval, in a tone of great significance, told her that she should *hear from her the next day*. The next morning Jemima often dwelt on these marked words, impatient for an explanation of them; and between twelve and one o'clock, a servant of Lady Delaval's brought a letter and a bandbox.

The letter was first opened; and was as follows:

"Dear Jemima,—As I know that you have long wished to visit my niece, Lady Ormsby, and also to attend the astronomical lecture on the grand transparent orrery, which is to be given at the public rooms this evening, for the benefit of the Infirmary; though your praiseworthy prudence prevented you from subscribing to it, I have great pleasure in enclosing you a ticket for the lecture, and in informing you that I will call and take you to dinner at Lady Ormsby's at four o'clock, whence you and I, and the rest of the party, (which will be a splendid one,) shall adjourn to the lecture.".... "How kind, how very kind!" exclaimed Jemima; but, in her heart, imputing these favours to her recent flatteries; and reading no farther, she ran to her mother's apartment to declare the joyful news. "Oh, mamma!" exclaimed she, "how fortunate it was that I made up my dyed gauze when I did! and I can wear natural flowers in my hair; and they are so becoming, as well as cheap." She then returned to her own room, to finish the letter, and explore the contents of the box. But what was her consternation on reading the following words:..... "But I shall take you to the dinner, and I give you the ticket for the lecture, only on this express condition,—that you wear the accompanying turban, which was decorated according to *your* taste and judgment, and in which you were conscious of looking so well!— Every *additional* ornament was bestowed to please you; and as I know that your wish will be not to deprive me of a head-dress in which your *partial* eyes thought I looked so *charmingly*, I positively assure you, that no consideration shall ever induce you to wear it; and that I expect you to meet my summons, arrayed in your youthful loveliness, and my turban."

Jemima sat in a sort of stupor after perusing this epistle; and when she started from it, it was to carry the letter and the turban to her mother.

"Read that! and look at that!" she exclaimed, pointing to the turban.

"Why, to be sure, Jemima, Lady Delaval must be making game of you," she replied.

"What could produce such an absurd requisition?"

When called upon to answer this question, Jemima blushed; and, for the first time, feeling some compunctious visitings of conscience, she almost hesitated to own, that the annoying conditions were the consequence of her flatteries. Still, to comply with them was impossible; and to go to the dinner and lecture without them, and thereby perhaps affront Lady Delaval, was impossible also.

"What! expect me to hide my pretty hair under that preposterous mountain! Never, never!" Vainly, now, did she try to admire it; and she felt its weight insupportable.

"To be sure," said she to herself, "Captain Leslie and George Vaux will dine at Lady Ormsby's and go to the lecture; but then they will not bear to look at me in this frightful head-dress, and will so quiz me; and I am sure they will think me too great a *quiz* to sit by! No, no; much as I wish to go, and I do so very, very much wish it, I cannot go on these cruel conditions."

"But what excuse can you make to Lady Delaval?"

"I must tell her that I have a bad tooth-ache, and cannot go; and I will write her a note to say so; and at the same time return the ugly turban."

She did so;—but when she saw Lady Delaval pass to the fine dinner, and heard the carriages at night going to the crowded lecture, she shed tears of bitterness and regret, and lamented that she had not dared to go without the conditional and detestable turban. The next day she saw Lady Delaval's carriage drive up to the door, and also saw the servant take a band-box out.

"Oh dear, mamma," cried Jemima, "I protest that ridiculous old woman has brought her ugly turban back again!" and it was with a forced smile of welcome that she greeted Lady Delaval.—That lady entered the room with a graver and more dignified mien than usual; for she came to reprove, and, she hoped, amend an offender against those principles of truth which she honoured, and to which she uniformly acted up. Just before Lady Delaval appeared, Jemima recollected that she was to have the tooth-ache; therefore she tied up her face, adding a PRACTICAL LIE to the many already told;—for one lie is sure to make many.

"I was sorry to find that you were not able to accompany me to the dinner and lecture," said she, "and were kept at home by the tooth-ache. Was that your only reason for staying at home?"

"Certainly, madam; can you doubt it?"

"Yes; for I have strong suspicion that the tooth-ache is a pretence, not a reality."

"This from you, Lady Delaval! my once kind friend."

"Jemima, I am come to prove myself a far kinder friend than ever I did before. I am glad to find you alone; because I should not like to reprove a child before her mother."

Lady Delaval then reproached her astonished auditor with the mean habit of flattery, in which she was so apt to indulge; assuring her that she had never been for one moment her dupe, and had insisted on her wearing the turban, in order to punish her despicable duplicity.

"Had you not acted thus," continued Lady Delaval, "I meant to have taken you to the dinner and lecture, without conditions; but I wished to inflict on you a salutary punishment, in hopes of convincing you that there are no qualities so safe, or so pleasing as truth and ingenuousness.—I saw you cast an alarmed look at the hat-box," she added, in a gayer tone; "but fear not; the turban is no more! and, in its stead, I have taken the liberty of bringing you a Leghorn bonnet; and should you, while you wear it, feel any desire to flatter, in your usual degrading manner, may it remind you of this conversation, and its *cause*, —and make your present mortification the means of your future good."

At this moment Jemima's mother entered the room, exclaiming; "Oh! Lady Delaval! I am glad you are come! my poor child's toothache is so bad! and how unfortunate that" .... Lady Delaval cast on the mistaken mother a look of severe reproof, and on the daughter one of pity and unavailing regret; for she felt that, for the child who is hourly exposed to the contagion of an unprincipled parent's example, there can be little chance of amendment; and she hastened to the carriage, convinced that for the poor Jemima Aldred her labours of christian duty had been exerted in *vain*. She would have soon found how just her conviction was, had she heard the dialogue between the mother and daughter, as soon as she drove off. Jemima dried up her hypocritical tears, and exclaimed, "A cross, methodistical creature! I am glad she is gone!"

"What do you mean, child? and what is all this about?" Jemima having told her, she exclaimed, "Why the woman is mad! What! object to a little harmless flattery! and call that lying, indeed! Nonsense! it is all a pretence. She hate *flattery!* no, indeed; if you were to tell her the truth, she would hate you like poison."

"Very likely; but see, mamma, what she has given me. What a beautiful bonnet! But she owed it to me, for the trick she played me, and for her preaching."

"Well, child," answered her mother, "let her preach to you every day and welcome, if she comes as to-day, full-handed."

Such was the effect of Lady Delaval's kind efforts on a mother so teaching, and a daughter so taught; for indelible indeed are those habits of falsehood and disingenuousness which children acquire, whose parents do not make a *strict adherence* to truth, the *basis* of their children's education; and punish all deviation from it with salutary rigour. But, whatever be the *excellencies* or the *errors* of parents or preceptors, there is one necessary thing for them to remember, or their excellences will be useless, and their faults irremediable; namely, that they are not to form their children for the present world alone;—they are to educate them not merely as the *children of time*, but as the *heirs of eternity.*

CHAPTER IV.

LIES OF FEAR.

I ONCE believed that the lie of fear was confined to the low and uneducated of both sexes, and to children; but further reflection and observation have convinced me that this is by no means the case; but that, as this lie springs from the want of *moral courage*, and as this defect is by no means confined to any class or age, the result of it, that fear of man which prompts to the lie of fear, must be universal also; though the nature of the dread may be various, and of different degrees of strength. For instance; a child or servant (of course I speak of ill-educated children) breaks a toy or glass, and denies having done so. Acquaintances forget to execute commissions entrusted to them; and either say that they are executed, when they are not, or make some false excuses for an omission which was the result of forgetfulness only. No persons are guilty of so many of this sort of lies, in the year, as negligent correspondents; since excuses for not writing sooner are usually *lies of fear*—fear of having forfeited favour by too long a silence.

As the lie of fear always proceeds, as I have before observed, from a want of *moral courage*, it is often the result of want of resolution to say "no," when "yes" is more agreeable to the feelings of the questioner. "Is not my new gown pretty?" "Is not my new hat becoming?" "Is not my coat of a good colour?" There are few persons who have courage to say "no," even to these trivial questions; though the negative would be *truth*, and the affirmative, *falsehood*. And still less are they able to be honest in their replies to questions of a more delicate nature. "Is not my last work the best?" "Is not my wife beautiful?" "Is not my daughter agreeable?" "Is not my son a fine youth?"—those ensnaring questions, which contented and confiding egotism is only too apt to ask.

Fear of wounding the feelings of the interrogator prompts an affirmative answer. But, perhaps, a lie on these occasions is one of the least displeasing, because it may possibly proceed from a kind aversion to give pain, and occasion disappointment; and has a *degree* of relationship, a distant family resemblance, to the LIE OF BENEVOLENCE; though, when accurately analyzed, even this good-natured falsehood may be resolved into *selfish dread* of losing favour by speaking the truth. Of these *pseudo-lies* of benevolence I shall treat in their turn; but I shall now proceed to relate a story, to illustrate THE LIE OF FEAR, and its important results, under apparently unimportant circumstances.

THE BANK-NOTE.

"ARE you returning immediately to Worcester?" said Lady Leslie, a widow residing near that city, to a young officer who was paying her a morning visit.

"I am; can I do any thing for you there?"

"Yes; you can do me a great kindness. My confidential servant, Baynes, is gone out for the day and night; and I do not like to trust my new footman, of whom I know nothing, to put this letter in the post-office, as it contains a fifty-pound note."

"Indeed! that is a large sum to trust to the post."

"Yes; but I am told it is the safest conveyance. It is, however, quite necessary that a person whom I can trust, should put the letter in the box."

"Certainly," replied Captain Freeland. Then, with an air that showed he considered *himself* as a person to be trusted, he deposited the letter in safety in his pocket-book, and took leave; promising he would return to dinner the next day, which was *Saturday*.

On his road, Freeland met some of his brother officers, who were going to pass the day and night at Great Malvern; and as they earnestly pressed him to accompany them, he wholly forgot the letter entrusted to his care; and, having despatched his servant to Worcester, for his *sac-de-nuit** and other things, he turned back with his companions, and passed the rest of the day in that sauntering but amusing idleness, that *dolce far niente,*† which may be reckoned *comparatively* virtuous, if it leads to the forgetfulness of little duties only, and is not attended by the positive infringement of greater ones. But, in not putting this important letter into the post, as he had engaged to do, Freeland violated a real duty; and he might have put it in at Malvern, had not the rencontre with his brother-officers banished the commission given him entirely from his thoughts. Nor did he remember it till, as they rode through the village the next morning, on their way to Worcester, they met Lady Leslie walking in the road.

At sight of her, Freeland recollected with shame and confusion that he had not fulfilled the charge committed to him, and fain would he have passed her unobserved; for, as she was a woman of high fashion, great talents, and some severity, he was afraid that his negligence, if avowed, would not only cause him to forfeit her favour, but expose him to her powerful sarcasm.

To avoid being recognised was, however, impossible; and as soon as Lady Leslie saw him, she exclaimed, "Oh! Captain Freeland, I am so glad to see you! I have been quite uneasy concerning my letter since I gave it to your care; for it was of such consequence! Did you put it in the post yesterday?"

"Certainly," replied Freeland, hastily, and in the hurry of the moment, "certainly. How could you, dear madam, doubt my obedience to your commands?"

"Thank you! thank you!" cried she, "how you have relieved my mind!"

He had so; but he had painfully burthened his own. To be sure it was only a white lie, —the LIE OF FEAR. Still he was not used to utter falsehood; and he felt the *meanness* and degradation of *this.* He had yet to learn that it was mischievous also; and that none can presume to say where the consequences of the most apparently trivial lie will end. As soon as Freeland parted with Lady Leslie, he bade his friends farewell, and, putting spur to his horse, scarcely slackened his pace till he had reached a general post-office, and deposited the letter in safety. "Now, then," thought he, "I hope I shall be able to return and dine with Lady Leslie, without shrinking from her penetrating eye."

He found her, when he arrived, very pensive and absent; so much so, that she felt it necessary to apologize to her guests, informing them that Mary Benson, an old servant of hers, who was very dear to her, was seriously ill, and painfully circumstanced; and that she feared she had not done her duty by her. "To tell you the truth, Captain Freeland," said she, speaking to him in a low voice, "I blame myself for not having sent for my confidential servant, who was not very far off, and despatched him with the money, instead of trusting it to the post."

"It would have been better to have done so, *certainly!*" replied Freeland, deeply blushing.

"Yes; for the poor woman, to whom I sent it, is not only herself on the point of being confined, but she has a sick husband, unable to be moved; and as (but owing to no fault of his) he is on the point of bankruptcy, his cruel landlord has declared that, if they do not pay their rent by to-morrow, he will turn them out into the street, and seize the very bed they lie on! However, as you put the letter into the post *yesterday,* they must get the fifty-pound note to-day, else they could not; for there is no delivery of letters in London on a *Sunday,* you know."

"True, very true," replied Freeland, in a tone which he vainly tried to render steady.

"Therefore," continued Lady Leslie, "if you had told me, when we met, that the letter was not gone, I should have recalled Baynes, and sent him off by the mail to London; and then he would have reached Somerstown, where the Bensons live, in good time; but now, though I own it would be a comfort to me to send him, for fear of accident, I could not get him back again soon enough; therefore, I must let things take their chance; and, as letters seldom miscarry, the only danger is, that the note may be taken out."

She might have talked an hour without answer or interruption; for Freeland was too much shocked, too much conscience-stricken, to reply; as he found that he had not only told a falsehood, but that, if he had had moral courage enough to tell the truth, the mischievous negligence, of which he had been guilty, could have been repaired; but now, as Lady Leslie said, "it was too late!"

But, while Lady Leslie became talkative, and able to perform her duties to her friends, after she had thus unburthened her mind to Freeland, he grew every minute more absent, and more taciturn; and, though he could not eat with appetite, he *threw down,* rather than *drank,* repeated glasses of hock and champagne, to enable him to rally his spirits; but in vain. A naturally ingenuous and generous nature cannot shake off the first compunctious visitings of conscience for having committed an unworthy action, and having also been the means of injury to another. All on a sudden, however, his countenance brightened; and as soon as the ladies left the table, he started up, left his compliments and excuses with Lady Leslie's nephew, who presided at dinner; said he had a pressing call to Worcester; and

---
* Night bag.   † Sweet doing nothing.

when there, as the London mail was gone, he threw himself into a post-chaise, and set off for Somerstown, which Lady Leslie had named as the residence of Mary Benson.

"At least," said Freeland to himself with a lightened heart, "I shall now have the satisfaction of doing all I can to repair my fault."

But owing to the delay occasioned by want of horses, and by finding the ostlers at the inns in bed, he did not reach London and the place of his destination till the wretched family had been dislodged; while the unhappy wife was weeping, not only over the disgrace of being so removed, and for her own and her husband's increased illness in consequence of it, but from the agonizing suspicion that the mistress and friend, whom she had so long loved, and relied upon, had disregarded the tale of her sorrows, and had refused to relieve her necessities! Freeland soon found a conductor to the mean lodging in which the Bensons had obtained shelter; for they were well known; and their hard fate was generally pitied; but it was some time before he could speak, as he stood by their bed-side—he was choked with painful emotion at first; with pleasing emotions afterwards; for his conscience smote him for the pain which he had occasioned, and applauded him for the pleasure which he came to bestow.

"I come," said he, at length, (while the sufferers waited in almost angry wonder, to hear his reason for thus intruding on them) "I come to tell you, from your kind friend, Lady Leslie—"

"Then she has *not* forgotten me!" screamed out the poor woman, almost gasping for breath.

"No, to be sure not; she could not forget you; she was incapable . . . . ." here his voice wholly failed him.

"Thank heaven!" cried she, tears trickling down her pale cheek. "I can bear any thing now; for that was the bitterest part of all!"

"My good woman," said Freeland, "it was owing to a mistake; pshaw! no, it was owing to *my fault*, that you did not receive a 50*l.* note by the post yesterday."

"Fifty pounds!" cried the poor man, wringing his hands, "why that would have more than paid all we owed; and I could have gone on with my business, and our lives would not have been risked, nor I disgraced!"

Freeland now turned away, unable to say a word more; but recovering himself, he again drew near them; and, throwing his purse to the agitated speaker, said, "there! get well! *only get well!* and whatever you want shall be yours! or I shall never lose this horrible choking again while I live!"

Freeland took a walk after this scene, and with hasty, rapid strides; the painful choking being his companion very often during the course of it—for he was haunted by the image of those whom he had disgraced; and he could not help remembering that, however blameable his negligence might be, it was nothing, either in sinfulness or mischief, to the lie told to conceal it; and that, but for that LIE OF FEAR, the effects of his negligence might have been *repaired* in time.

But he was resolved that he would not leave Somerstown till he had seen these poor people settled in a good lodging. He therefore hired a conveyance for them, and superintended their removal that evening to apartments full of every necessary comfort.

"My good friends," said he, "I cannot recall the mortification and disgrace which you have endured through my fault; but I trust that you will have gained, in the end, by leaving a cruel landlord, who had no pity for your unmerited poverty. Lady Leslie's note will, I trust, reach you to-morrow;—but if not, I will make up the loss; therefore be easy! and when I go away may I have the comfort of knowing that your removal has done you no harm!"

He then, but not till then, had courage to write to Lady Leslie, and tell her the whole truth; concluding his letter thus:

"If your interesting *protégés* have not suffered in their health, I shall not regret what has happened; because I trust that it will be a lesson to me through life, and teach me never to tell even the most apparently *trivial* white lie again. How unimportant this violation of truth appeared to me at the moment! and how sufficiently motived! as it was to avoid falling in your estimation; but it was, you see, overruled for evil;—and agony of mind, disgrace, and perhaps risk of life, were the consequences of it to innocent individuals; —not to mention my own pangs;—the pangs of an upbraiding conscience. But forgive me, my dear Lady Leslie. However, I trust that this evil, so deeply repented of, will be blessed to us all; but it will be long before I forgive myself."

Lady Leslie was delighted with this candid letter, though grieved by its painful details, while she viewed with approbation the amends which her young friend had made, and his modest disregard of his own exertions.

The note arrived in safety; and Freeland left the afflicted couple better in health, and quite happy in mind;—as his bounty and that of Lady Leslie had left them nothing to desire in a pecuniary point of view.

When Lady Leslie and he met, she praised his virtue, while she blamed his fault; and they fortified each other in the wise and moral resolution, never to violate truth again, even on the slightest occasion; as a lie, when told, however unimportant it may at the time appear, is like an arrow shot over a house, whose course is unseen, and may be unintentionally the cause, to some one, of agony or death.

CHAPTER V.

LIES FALSELY CALLED LIES OF BENEVOLENCE.

THESE are lies which are occasioned by a selfish dread of losing favour, and provoking displeasure by speaking the truth, rather than by real benevolence. Persons, calling themselves benevolent, withhold disagreeable truths, and utter agreeable falsehoods, from a wish to give pleasure, or to avoid giving pain. If you say that you are looking ill, they tell you that you are looking well. If you express a fear that you are growing corpulent, they say you are only just as fat as you ought to be. If you are hoarse in singing, and painfully conscious of it, they declare that they did not perceive it. And this not from the desire of flattering you, or from the malignant one of wishing to render you ridiculous by imposing on your credulity, but from the desire of making you pleased with yourself. In short, they lay it down as a rule, that you must never scruple to sacrifice the truth, when the alternative is giving the slightest pain or mortification to any one.

I shall leave my readers to decide whether the lies of fear or of benevolence preponderate, in the following trifling, but characteristic anecdote.

A TALE OF POTTED SPRATS.

MOST mistresses of families have a family receipt-book, and are apt to believe that no receipts are so good as their own.

With one of these notable ladies a young house-keeper went to pass a few days both at her town and country house. The hostess was skilled, not only in culinary lore, but in economy; and was in the habit of setting on her table, even when not alone, whatever her taste or carefulness had led her to pot, pickle, or preserve, for occasional use.

Before a meagre family-dinner was quite over, a dish of POTTED SPRATS was set before the lady of the house, who, expatiating on their excellence, derived from a family-receipt of a century old, pressed her still unsatisfied guest to partake of them.

The dish was as good as much salt and little spice could make it; but it had one peculiarity;—it had a strong flavour of garlic, and to garlic the poor guest had a great dislike.

But she was a timid woman; and good-breeding, and what she called benevolence, said, "persevere a swallow," though her palate said, "no."

"Is it not excellent," said the hostess.

"Very;" faltered out the half-suffocated guest;—and this was lie the first.

"Did you ever eat any thing like it before?"

"Never," replied the other more firmly; for *then* she knew that she spoke the truth, and *longing* to add, "and I hope I never shall eat any thing like it again."

"I will give you the receipt," said the lady kindly; "it will be of use to you as a young housekeeper; for it is economical as well as good, and serves to make out when we have a scrap dinner. My servants often dine on it." "I wonder you can get any servants to live with you," thought the guest; "but I dare say you do not get any one to stay long!"

"You do not, however, *eat as* if you liked it."

"Oh, yes, *indeed,* I do, very much," (lie the second) she replied; "but you forget that I have already eaten a *good dinner;*" (lie the third. Alas! what had benevolence, *so called*, to answer for on this occasion!)

'"Well, I am delighted to find that you like my sprats," said the flattered hostess, while the cloth was removing; adding, "John! do not let those sprats be eaten in the kitchen!" an order which the guest heard with indescribable alarm.

The next day they were to set off for the country-house or cottage. When they were seated in the carriage, a large box was put in, and the guest fancied she smelt *garlic;* but

"... Where ignorance is bliss,
'Tis folly to be wise."

She therefore asked no questions; but tried to enjoy the present, regardless of the future. At a certain distance they stopped to bait the horses. There the guest expected that they should get out, and take some refreshment; but her economical companion with a shrewd wink of the eye, observed, "I always sit in the carriage on these occasions. If one gets out, the people at the inn expect one to order a luncheon. I therefore take mine with me." So saying, John was summoned to drag the carriage out of sight of the inn windows. He then unpacked the box, took out of it knives and forks, plates, &c. and also a *jar*, which impregnating the air with its effluvia, even before it was opened, disclosed to the alarmed guest that its contents were the dreaded sprats!

"Alas!" thought she, "Pandora's box was nothing to this! for in that Hope remained behind; but, at the bottom of this, is Despair!" In vain did the unhappy lady declare (lie the fourth) that "she had no appetite, and (lie the fifth) that she never ate in the morning." Her hostess would take no denial. However, she contrived to get a piece of sprat down, enveloped in bread; and the rest she threw out of the window when her companion was looking another way—who on turning round, exclaimed, "so you have soon despatched the fish! let me give you another; do not refuse, because you think they are nearly finished; I assure you there are several left; and (delightful information!) we shall have a fresh supply to-morrow!" However, this time she was allowed to know when she had eaten enough;

LIES OF BENEVOLENCE.

and the travellers proceeded to their journey's end.

This day, the sprats did not appear at dinner;—but there being only a few left, they were kept for a *bonne bouche*, and reserved for supper! a meal, of which, this evening, on account of indisposition, the hostess did not partake, and was therefore at liberty to attend entirely to the wants of her guest, who would fain have declined eating also, but it was impossible; she had just declared that she was quite well, and had often owned that she enjoyed a piece of supper after an *early dinner*. There was therefore no retreat from the maze in which her insincerity had involved her; and eat she must, but when she again smelt on her plate the nauseous composition, which being near the bottom of the pot, was more disagreeable than ever, human patience and human infirmity could bear no more; the scarcely tasted morsel fell from her lips, and she rushed precipitately into the open air, almost disposed to execrate, in her heart, potted sprats, the good breeding of her officious hostess, and even Benevolence itself.

Some may observe, on reading this story, "What a foolish creature the guest must have been! and how improbable it is that any one should scruple to say the dish is disagreeable, and I hate garlic!" But it is my conviction that the guest on this occasion, exhibited only a slightly-exaggerated specimen of the usual conduct of those who have been taught to conduct themselves wholly by the artificial rules of civilized society, of which, generally speaking, falsehood is the basis.

Benevolence is certainly one of the first of virtues; and its result is an amiable aversion to wound the feelings of others, even in trifles; therefore benevolence and politeness may be considered as the same thing; but WORLDLY POLITENESS is only a *copy* of benevolence. Benevolence is gold; this politeness a paper currency, contrived as its *substitute;* as society being aware that benevolence is as rare as it is precious, and that few are able to distinguish in any thing, the false from the true, resolved, in lieu of benevolence, to receive WORLDLY POLITENESS, with all her train of deceitful welcomes, heartless regrets, false approbations, and treacherous smiles; those alluring seemings, which shine around her brow, and enable her to pass for BENEVOLENCE herself.

But how must the religious and the moral dislike the one, though they venerate the other! The kindness of the worldly Polite only lives its little hour in one's presence; but that of the Benevolent retains its life and sweetness in one's absence. The worldly polite will often make the objects of their greatest flatteries and attentions, when present, the butt of their ridicule as soon as they see them no more; while the benevolent hold the characters and qualities of their associates in a sort of *holy keeping* at all times, and are as *indulgent* to the *absent* as they were *attentive* to the *present*. The kindness of the worldly polite is the gay and pleasing flower worn in the bosom, as the ornament of a few hours; then suffered to fade, and thrown by, when it is wanted no longer;—but that of the really benevolent, is like the fresh-springing evergreen, which blooms on through all times, and all seasons, unfading in beauty, and undiminishing in sweetness. But, it may be asked, whether I do not admit that the principle of never wounding the self-love or feelings of any one is a benevolent principle; and whether it be not commendable to act on it continually. Certainly; if sincerity goes hand-in-hand with benevolence. But where is your benevolence, if you praise those to their faces whom you abuse as soon as they have left you?—where your benevolence, if you welcome those, with smiling urbanity, whom you see drive off with a "Well; I am glad they are gone!" and how common is it to hear persons, who think themselves very moral, and very kind, begin, as soon as their guests are departed, and even when they are scarcely out of hearing, to criticise their dress, their manners, and their characters; while the poor unconscious visiters, the dupes of their deceitful courtesy, are going home delighted with their visit, and saying "what a charming evening they have passed, and what agreeable and kind-hearted persons the master and mistress of the house, and their family, are!" Surely, then, I am not refining too much when I assert that the cordial seemings with which these deluded guests were received, treated, and parted with, were any thing rather than the LIES OF BENEVOLENCE. I also believe that those who scruple not, even from well-intentioned kindness, to utter spontaneous falsehoods, are not gifted with much judgment and real feeling, nor are they given to think deeply; for the virtues are nearly related, and live in the greatest harmony with each other;—consequently, sincerity and benevolence must always agree, and not, as is often supposed, be at variance with each other. The truly benevolent feel, and cultivate such candid and kind views of those who associate with them, that *they* need not *fear* to be sincere in *their* answers; and if obliged to speak an unwelcome truth, or an unwelcome opinion, their well-principled kindness teaches them some way of making what they utter palatable; and benevolence is gratified without injury to sincerity.

It is a common assertion, that society is so constituted, that it is impossible to tell the truth *always*;—but, if those who possess good sense would use it as zealously to remove obstacles in the way of spontaneous truth as they do to justify themselves in the practice of falsehood, the difficulty would vanish. Besides, truth is so uncommon an ingredient in society, that few are acquainted with it sufficiently to know whether it be admissible or not. A pious and highly gifted man said in my presence, to a friend whom I esteem and admire, and who had asserted that truth cannot always be told in society, "Has any one tried it!—We have all of us, in the course of our lives, seen dead birds of Paradise so often, that we should scarcely take the trouble of going to see one now. But the Marquis of Hastings has brought over a *living* bird of Paradise; and every one is eagerly endeavouring to procure a sight of *that*. I therefore prognosticate that, were spontaneous truth to be told in society, where it now is, rarely, if ever, heard, *real, living truth* would be as much sought after and admired, as the living bird of Paradise."*

The following anecdote exhibits that Lie which some may call the lie of Benevolence, and others, the lie of *fear*;—that is, the dread of losing favour, by wounding a person's self-love. I myself denominate it the latter.

AN AUTHORESS AND HER AUDITORS.

A YOUNG lady, who valued herself on her benevolence and good-breeding, and had as much respect for truth as those who live in the world usually have, was invited by an authoress, whose favour she coveted, and by whose attention she was flattered, to come and hear her read a manuscript tragi-comedy. The other auditor was an old lady, who, to considerable personal ugliness, united strange grimaces, and convulsive twitchings of the face, chiefly the result of physical causes.

The authoress read in so affected and dramatic a manner, that the young lady's boasted benevolence had no power to curb her propensity to laughter; which being perceived by the reader, she stopped in angry consternation, and desired to know whether she laughed at her, or her composition. At first she was too much fluttered to make any reply;—but as she dared not own the truth, and had no scruple against being guilty of deception, she cleverly resolved to excuse herself by a practical lie. She therefore trod on her friend's foot, elbowed her, and, by winks and signs, tried to make her believe that it was the grimaces of her opposite neighbour, who was quietly knitting and twitching as usual, which had had such an effect on her risible faculties; and the deceived authoress, smiling herself, when her young guest directed her eye to her unconscious *vis-à-vis*, resumed her reading with a lightened brow and increased energy.

This added to the young lady's amusement; as she could now indulge her risibility occasionally at the authoress's expense without exciting her suspicions; especially as the manuscript was sometimes intended to excite smiles, if not laughter; and the self-love of the writer led her to suppose that her hearer's mirth was the result of her comic powers. But the treacherous gratification of the auditor was soon at an end. The manuscript was meant to move tears, as well as smiles; but as the matter became more pathetic, the manner became more ludicrous; and the youthful hearer could no more force a tear than she could restrain a laugh; till the mortified authoress, irritated into forgetfulness of all feeling and propriety, exclaimed, "Indeed, Mrs. ——, I must desire you to move your seat, and sit where Miss —— does not see you; for you make such queer grimaces, that you draw her attention, and cause her to laugh, when she should be listening to me." The erring, but humane girl was overwhelmed with dismay at the unexpected exposure; and when the poor, infirm old lady replied, in a faltering tone, "Is she indeed laughing at me?" she could scarcely refrain from telling the truth, and assuring her that she was incapable of such cruelty.

"Yes;" rejoined the authoress, in a paroxysm of wounded self-love, "she owned to me soon after she began, that you occasioned her ill-timed mirth; and when I looked at you, I could hardly help smiling myself; but I am sure you could help making such faces, if you would."

"Child!" cried the old lady, while tears of wounded sensibility trickled down her pale cheeks, "and you, my unjust friend, I hope and trust that I forgive you both; but, if ever you should be paralytic yourselves, may you remember this evening, and learn to repent of having been provoked to laugh by the physical weakness of a palsied old woman!"

The indignant authoress was now penitent, subdued, and ashamed,—and earnestly asked pardon for her unkindness; but the young offender, whose acted lie had exposed her to seem guilty of a fault which she had not committed, was in an agony to which expression was inadequate. But to exculpate herself was impossible; and she could only give her wounded victim tear for tear.

To attend to a farther perusal of the manuscript was impossible. The old lady desired that her carriage should come round directly; the authoress locked up her composition that had been so ill-received; and the young lady, who had been proud of the acquaintance of each, became an object of suspicion and dislike both to the one and the other; since the former considered her to be of a cruel and un-

---

* I fear that I have given the words weakly and imperfectly; but I know I am correct, as to the sentiment and the illustration. The speaker was EDWARD IRVING.

feeling nature, and the latter could not conceal from herself the mortifying truth, that her play must be wholly devoid of interest, as it had utterly failed either to rivet or to attract her young auditor's attention.

But, though this girl lost two valued acquaintances by acting a lie (a harmless white lie, as it is called,) I fear she was not taught or amended by the circumstance; but deplored her want of luck, rather than her want of integrity; and had her deception met with the success which she expected, she would probably have boasted of her ingenious artifice to her acquaintance;—nor can I help believing that she goes on in the same way whenever she is tempted to do so, and values herself on the lies of SELFISH FEAR, which she dignifies by the name of LIES OF BENEVOLENCE.

It is curious to observe that the kindness which prompts to really erroneous conduct, cannot continue to bear even a remote connexion with real benevolence. The mistaken girl, in the anecdote related above, begins with what she calls a virtuous deception. She could not wound the feelings of the authoress by owning that she laughed at her mode of reading; she therefore accused herself of a much worse fault: that of laughing at the personal infirmities of a fellow-creature; and then, finding that her artifice enabled her to indulge her sense of the ridiculous with impunity, she at length laughs treacherously and systematically, because she dares do so, and not *involuntarily*, as she did at first, at her unsuspecting friend. Thus, such hollow, unprincipled benevolence as hers soon degenerated into absolute *malevolence*. But, had this girl been a girl of principle and of *real benevolence*, she might have healed her friend's vanity at the same time that she wounded it, by saying, after she had owned that her mode of reading made her laugh, that she was now convinced of the truth of what she had often heard; namely, that authors rarely do justice to their own works, when they read them aloud themselves, however well they may read the works of others; because they are naturally so nervous on the occasion, that they are laughably violent, because painfully agitated.

This reply could not have offended her friend greatly, if at all; and it might have led her to moderate her *outré* manner of reading. She would in consequence have appeared to more advantage; and the interests of real benevolence, namely, the doing good to a fellow-creature, would have been served, and she would not, by a vain attempt to save a friend's vanity from being hurt, have been the means of wounding the feelings of an afflicted *woman*; have incurred the charge of inhumanity, which she by no means deserved; and have vainly, as well as grossly, sacrificed the interests of Truth.

37*

CHAPTER VI.

LIES OF CONVENIENCE.

I HAVE now before me a very copious subject; and shall begin by that most common *lie of convenience;* the order to servants, to say "Not at home;" a custom which even some moralists defend, because they say that it is not lying; as it deceives no one. But this I deny;—as I know it is often *meant* to deceive. I know that if the person, angry at being refused admittance, says, at the next meeting with the denied person, "I am sure you *were* at home such a day, when I called, but did not *choose to see me*," the answer is, "Oh dear, no;—how can you say so? I am *sure* I was not at home;—for I am never *denied* to *you;*" though the speaker is conscious all the while that "not at home" was intended to *deceive*, as well as to deny. But, if it be true that "not at home" is not intended to deceive, and is a form used merely to exclude visiters with as little trouble as possible, I would ask whether it were not just as easy to say, "my master, or my mistress, is engaged; and can see no one this morning." Why have recourse even to the appearance of falsehood, when truth would answer every purpose just as well?

But if "not at home" be understood amongst *equals*, merely as a legitimate excuse, it still is highly objectionable; because it must have a most pernicious effect on the minds of *servants*, who cannot be supposed parties to this implied compact amongst their superiors, and must therefore understand the order *literally;* which is, "go, and lie for my convenience!" How then, I ask in the name of justice and common sense, can I, after giving such an order, resent any lie which servants may choose to tell me for their own convenience, pleasure, or interest?

Thoughtless and injudicious, (I do not like to add,) *unprincipled* persons, sometimes say to servants, when they have denied their mistress, "Oh fy! how can you tell me such a fib without blushing! I am ashamed of you! You know your lady *is* at home;—well;—I am really *shocked* at your having so much effrontery as to tell such a lie with so grave a face! But give my compliments to your mistress, and tell her, I hope that she will see me the next time I call;" and all this uttered in a laughing manner, as if this moral degradation of the poor servant were an *excellent joke!* But on these occasions, what can the effect of such joking be on the conscious liars? It must either lead them to think as lightly of truth as their reprovers themselves, (since they seem more amused than shocked at the detected violation of it,) or they will turn away distressed in conscience, degraded in their own eyes, for having obeyed their employer, and

ILLUSTRATIONS OF LYING.

feeling a degree of virtuous indignation against those persons who have, by their immoral command, been the means of their painful degradation;—nay, their master and mistress will be for ever lowered in their servants' esteem; they will feel that the *teacher* of a lie is brought down on a level with the utterer of it; and the chances are that, during the rest of their service, they will without scruple use *against their employers* the dexterity which they have taught them to use *against others.**

But amongst the most frequent lies of convenience are those which are told relative to engagements, which they who make them are averse to keep. "Headaches, bad colds, unexpected visiters from the country," all these, in their turn, are used as lies of convenience, and gratify indolence, or caprice, at the expense of integrity.

How often have I pitied the wives and daughters of professional men, for the number of lies which they are obliged to tell, in the course of the year! "Dr. —— is very sorry; but he was sent for to a patient just as he was

---

* As I feel a great desire to lay before my readers the strongest arguments possible, to prove the vicious tendency of even the most tolerated lie of convenience; namely, the order to servants to say "Not at home;" and as I wholly distrust my own powers of arguing with *effect* on this, or any other subject, I give the following extracts from Dr. Chalmers's "Discourses on the Application of Christianity to the Commercial and Ordinary Affairs of Life;"—discourses which abundantly and eloquently prove the sinfulness of deceit in general, and the fearful responsibility incurred by all who depart, even in the most common occurrences, from that undeviating practice of truth which is everywhere enjoined on Christians in the pages of Holy Writ. But I shall, though reluctantly, confine myself, in these extracts, to what bears immediately on the subject before us. I must, however, state, in justice to myself, that my remarks *on the same* points were not only written, but printed and published, in a periodical work, before I knew that Dr. Chalmers had written the book in question.

"You put a lie into the mouth of a dependant, and that for the purpose of protecting your time from such an encroachment as you would not feel to be convenient or agreeable. Look to the little account that is made of a brother's and sister's eternity. Behold the guilty task that is thus unmercifully laid upon one who is shortly to appear before the judgment-seat of Christ. Think of the entanglement that is thus made to beset the path of a creature who is unperishable. That, at the shrine of Mammon, such a bloody sacrifice should be rendered, by some of his unrelenting votaries, is not to be wondered at; but, that the shrine of elegance and fashion should be bathed in blood;—that *soft and sentimental ladyship* should put forth her hand to such an enormity;—that she, who can sigh so gently, and shed her graceful tear over the sufferings of others, should thus be accessary to the second and more awful death of her own domestics;—that one, who looks the mildest and loveliest of human beings, should exact obedience to a mandate which carries wrath, and tribulation, and anguish in its train. Oh! how it should confirm every Christian in his defiance of the authority of fashion, and lead him to spurn at all its folly, and all its worthlessness. And it is quite in vain to say that the servant, whom you thus employ as the deputy of your falsehood, can possibly execute the commission without the conscience being at all tainted or defiled by it; that a simple cottage maid can so sophisticate the matter, as, without any violence to her original principles, to utter the language of what she assuredly knows to be a downright lie;—that she, humble and untutored soul! can sustain no injury, when thus made to tamper with the plain English of these realms;—that she can at all satisfy herself how, by the prescribed utterance of "not at home," she is not pronouncing such words as are substantially untrue, but merely using them in another and perfectly understood meaning;—and which, according to their modern translation, denote that the person, of whom she is thus speaking, is securely lurking in one of the most secure and intimate of its receptacles.

"You may try to darken this piece of casuistry as you will, and work up your minds into the peaceable conviction, that it is all right, and as it should be. But, be very certain that, where the moral sense of your domestic is not already overthrown, there is, at least, one bosom, within which you have raised a war of doubts and difficulties, and where, if the victory be on your side, it will be on the side of him who is the great enemy of righteousness.

"There is, at least, one person, along the line of this conveyance of deceit, who condemneth herself in that which she alloweth; who, in the language of Paul, esteeming the practice to be unclean, to her will it be unclean; who will perform her task with the offence of her own conscience, and to whom, therefore, it will indeed be evil; who cannot render obedience in this matter to her earthly superior, but, by an act, in which she does not stand clear and unconscious of guilt before God; and with whom, therefore, the sad consequences of what we can call nothing else than a barbarous combination against the principles and prospects of the lower orders, is—that, as she has not cleaved fully unto the Lord, and has not kept by the service of the one Master, and has not forsaken all but His bidding, she cannot be the disciple of Christ.

"And let us just ask a master, or a mistress, who can thus make free with the moral principle of their servants in one instance, how they can look for pure or correct principle from them in other instances? What right have they to complain of unfaithfulness against themselves, who have deliberately seduced another into a habit of unfaithfulness against God? Are they so utterly unskilled in the mysteries of our nature, as not to perceive, that the servant whom you have taught to lie, has gotten such rudiments of education at your hand, as that, without any further help, he can now teach himself to purloin?—and yet nothing more frequent than loud and angry complainings against the treachery of servants; as if, in the general wreck of their other principles, a principle of consideration for the good and interest of their employer, and who has at the same time been their seducer, was to survive in all its power and sensibility. It is just such a retribution as was to be looked for. It is a recoil, upon their own heads, of the mischief which they themselves have originated. It is the temporal part of the punishment which they have to bear for the sin of our text; but not the whole of it; far better for them both, that both person and property were cast into the sea, than that they should stand the reckoning of that day, when called to give an account of

PROJECTS DEFEATED.

coming with me to your house."—" Papa's compliments, and he is very sorry; but he was forced to attend a commission of bankruptcy ; he will certainly come, if he can, by-and-by," when the chances are, that the physician is enjoying himself over his book and his fire, and the lawyer also, congratulating themselves on having escaped that terrible bore, a party, at the expense of teaching their wife, or daughter, or son, to tell what they call a white lie! But, I would ask those fathers and those mothers who make their children the bearers of similar excuses, whether after giving them such commissions, they could conscientiously resent any breach of veracity, or breach of confidence, or deception, committed by their children in matters of more importance. " *Ce n'est que le premier pas qui coute*," says the proverb; and I believe that habitual, permitted, and encouraged lying, in little and seemingly unimportant things, leads to want of truth and principle in great and serious matters; for when the barrier, or restrictive principle, is once thrown down, no one can say where a stop will be put to the inroads and the destruction.

I forgot, in the first edition of my work, to notice one falsehood which is only too often uttered by young women in a ball-room; but I shall now mention it with due reprehension, though I scarcely know under what head to class it. I think, however, that it may be named without impropriety, one of the LIES OF CONVENIENCE.

But, I cannot do better than give an extract on this subject, from a letter addressed to me by a friend, on reading this book, in which she has had the kindness to praise, and the still greater kindness to admonish me.[*] She says, as follows; " One falsehood that is very often uttered by the lips of youth, I trust not without a blush, you have passed unnoticed; and, as I always considered it no venial one, I will take the present opportunity of pointing out its impropriety. A young lady, when asked by a gentleman to dance, whom she does not approve, will, without hesitation, say, though unprovided with any other partner, " If I dance, I am engaged;" this positive untruth is calculated to wound the feelings of the person to whom it is addressed, for it generally happens that such person discovers he has been deceived, as well as rejected. It is very seldom that young men, to whom it would really be improper that a lady should give her hand for the short time occupied in one or two dances, are admitted into our public places : but, in such a case, could not a reference be made by her, to any friends who are present; pride and vanity too often prompt the refusal, and, because the offered partner has not sufficiently sacrificed to the graces, is little versed " in the poetry of motion," or derives no consequence from the possession of rank, or riches, he is treated with what he must feel to be contempt. True politeness, which has its seat in the heart, would scorn thus to wound another, and the real votaries of sincerity would never so violate its rules to escape a temporary mortification."

I shall only add that I have entire *unity of sentiment* with the foregoing extract.

Here I beg leave to insert a short tale, illustrative of *Lies of Convenience*.

PROJECTS DEFEATED.

THERE are a great many match-makers in the world; beings who dare to take on themselves the *fearful responsibility* of bringing two persons together into that solemn union which only death or guilt can dissolve; and thus make themselves answerable for the possible misery of two of their fellow creatures.

One of these busy match-makers, a gentleman named Byrome, was very desirous that Henry Sanford, a relation of his, should become a married man; and he called one morning to inform him that he had at length met with a young lady who would, he flattered himself, suit him in all respects as a wife. Henry Sanford was not a man of many words; nor had he a high opinion of Byrome's judgment. He therefore only said, in reply, that he was willing to accompany his relation to the lady's house, where, on Byrome's invitation, he found that he was expected to drink tea.

The young lady in question, whom I shall call Lydia L——, lived with her widowed aunt, who had brought her and her sisters up, and supplied to them the place of parents, lost in their infancy. She had bestowed on them an expensive and showy education; had, both by precept and example, given every worldly polish to their manners; and had taught them to set off their beauty by tasteful and fashionable dress; that is, she had done for them all that she thought was necessary to be done; and she, as well as Byrome, believed that they possessed every requisite to make the marriage state happy.

But Henry Sanford was not so easy to please. He valued personal beauty and external accomplishments far below christian graces

---

the souls that they have murdered, and the blood of so mighty a destruction is required at their hands."

These remarks at first made part of a chapter on the Lie of Convenience, but thinking them not suited to that *period* of my work, I took them out again, and not being able to introduce them in any subsequent chapter, because they treat of one particular lie, and not of lying in general, I have been obliged to content myself with putting them in a note.

[*] Vide a (printed) letter addressed " to Mrs. Opie, with observations on her recent publication, ' Illustrations of Lying in all its branches.'" The Authoress is Susan Reeve, wife of Dr. Reeve, M.D., and daughter of E. Bonhote of Bungay, authoress of many interesting publications.

and moral virtues; and was resolved never to unite himself to a woman whose conduct was not entirely under the guidance of a strict religious principle.

Lydia L—— was not in the room when Sanford arrived, but he very soon had cause to doubt the moral integrity of her aunt and sisters; for, on Byrome's saying, "I hope you are not to have any company but ourselves to-day," the aunt replied, "Oh, no; we put off some company that we expected, because we thought you would like to be alone;" and one of the sisters added, "Yes; I wrote to the disagreeable D——s, informing them that my aunt was too unwell, with one of her bad headaches, to see company;" "and I," said the other, "called on the G——s, and said that we wished them to come another day, because the beaux whom they liked best to meet were engaged."

"Admirable!" cried Byrome, "let women alone for excuses!" while Sanford looked grave, and wondered how any one could think admirable what to *him* appeared so reprehensible. "However," thought he, "*Lydia* had no share in this treachery and white lying, but may dislike them as I do." Soon after, she made her appearance, attired for conquest; and so radiant did she seem in her youthful loveliness and grace, that Sanford earnestly hoped she had better principles than her sisters.

Time fled on rapid wings; and Byrome and the two elder sisters frequently congratulated each other that "the disagreeable D——s, and tiresome G——s," had not been allowed to come and destroy, as they would have done, the pleasure of the afternoon. But Lydia did not join in this conversation; and Sanford was glad of it. The hours passed in alternate music and conversation, and also in looking over some beautiful drawings of Lydia's; but the evening was to conclude with a French game, a *jeu-de-société* which Sanford was unacquainted with, and which would give Lydia an opportunity of telling a story gracefully.

The L——s lived in a pleasant village near the town where Sanford and Byrome resided; and a long avenue of fine trees led to their door; when, just as the aunt was pointing out their beauty to Sanford, she exclaimed, "Oh, dear! girls, what shall we do? there is Mrs. Carthew now entering the avenue! Not at home, John! not at home!" she eagerly vociferated.

"My dear aunt, that will not do for her," cried the eldest sister; "for she will ask for us all in turn, and inquire where we are, that she may go after us."

"True," said the other, "and if we admit her, she is so severe and methodistical, that she will spoil all our enjoyment."

"However, in she must come," observed the aunt, "for, as she is an old friend, I should not like to affront her."

Sanford was just going to say, "If she be an old friend, admit her by all means;" when on looking at Lydia, who had been silent all this time, and was, he flattered himself, of his way of thinking, he saw her put her finger archly to her nose, and heard her exclaim, "I have it! there, there; go all of you into the next room, and close the door!" she then bounded gracefully down the avenue, while Sanford, with a degree of pain which he could have scarcely thought possible, heard one of the sisters say to Byrome, "Ah! Lydia is to be trusted; she tells a white lie with such an innocent look, that no one can suspect her."

"What a valuable accomplishment," thought Sanford, "in a woman! what a recommendation in a wife!" and he really dreaded the fair deceiver's return.

She came back, "nothing doubting," and, smiling with great self-complacency, said, "It was very fortunate that it was I who met her; for I have more presence of mind than you, my dear sisters. The good soul had seen the D——s; and hearing my aunt was ill, came to inquire concerning her. She was even coming on to the house, as she saw no reason why she should not; and I, for a moment, was at a loss how to keep her away, when I luckily recollected her great dread of infection, and told her that, as the typhus fever was in the village, I feared it was only too possible that my poor aunt had caught it!"

"Capital!" cried the aunt and Byrome.

"Really, Lydia, that was even out-doing yourself," cried her eldest sister.

"Poor Carthew! I should not wonder, if she came at all near the house, that she went home, and took to her bed from alarm!"

Even Byrome was shocked at this unfeeling speech; and could not help observing, that it would be hard indeed if such was the result, to a good old friend, of an affectionate inquiry.

"True," replied Lydia, "and I hope and trust she will not really suffer; but, though very good, she is very troublesome; and could we but keep up the hum for a day or two, it would be such a comfort to us! as she comes very often, and now cannot endure cards, nor any music but hymn-singing."

"Then I am glad she was not admitted;" said Byrome, who saw with pain, by Sanford's folded arms and grave countenance, that a change in his feelings towards Lydia had taken place. Nor was he deceived; Sanford was indeed gazing intently, but not as before, with almost overpowering admiration, on the consciously blushing object of it. No; he was likening her as he gazed, to the beautiful apples that are said to grow on the shores of the Dead Sea, which tempt the traveller to pluck and eat, but are filled only with dust and bitter ashes.

"But we are losing time," said Lydia; "let us begin our French game!" Sanford coldly bowed assent: but he knew not what she said; he was so inattentive, that he had to forfeit continually; he spoke not; he smiled not; except with a sort of sarcastic expression; and Lydia felt conscious that she had *lost him*, though she knew not why; for her moral sense was too dull for her to conceive the effect which her falsehood and want of feeling, towards an old and pious friend, had produced on him. This consciousness was a painful one, as Sanford was handsome, sensible, and rich; therefore, he was what match-seeking girls (odious vulgarity!) call a *good catch*. Besides, Byrome had told her that she might depend on making a conquest of his relation, Henry Sanford. The evening, therefore, which began so brightly, ended in pain and mortification, both to Sanford and Lydia. The former was impatient to depart as soon as supper was over, and the latter, piqued, disappointed, and almost dejected, did not join her sisters in soliciting him to stay.

"Well," said Byrome, as soon as they left the house, "how do you like the beautiful and accomplished Lydia?"

"She is beautiful and accomplished; but that is all."

"Nay, I am sure you seemed to admire her exceedingly, till just now, and paid her more animated attention than I ever saw you pay any woman before."

"True; but I soon found that she was as hollow-hearted as she is fair."

"Oh! I suppose you mean the deception which she practised on the old lady. Well; where was the great harm of that? she only told a white lie; and nobody, that is not a puritan, scruples to do that, you know."

"I am no puritan, as you term it; yet I scruple it; but, if I were to be betrayed into such meanness, (and no one perhaps can be always on his guard,) I should blush to have it known; but this girl seemed to glory in her shame, and to be proud of the disgraceful readiness with which she uttered her falsehood."

"I must own that I was surprised she did not express some regret at being forced to do what she did, in order to prevent our pleasure from being spoiled."

"Why should she? Like yourself, she saw no harm in a *white lie*; but mark me, Byrome, the woman whom I marry shall not think there is such a thing as a *white* lie;—she shall think all lies *black*; because the intention of *all* lies is to *deceive*; and, from the highest authority we are forbidden to deceive one another. I assure you, that if I were married to Lydia, I should distrust her expressions of love towards me;—I should suspect that she married my fortune, not me; and that whenever strong temptation offered, she would deceive me as readily as, for a very slight one indeed, she deceived that kind friend who came on an errand of love, and was sent away alarmed, and anxious, by this young hypocrite's unblushing falsehood! Trust me, Byrome, that my wife shall be a strict moralist."

"What! a moral philosopher?"

"No; a far better thing. She shall be an *humble relying christian*;—thence she will be capable of speaking the truth, even to her own condemnation;—and on all occasions her fear of man will be wholly subservient to her fear of her Creator."

"And, pray, how can you ever be able to assure yourself that any girl is this paragon?"

"Surely, if what we call chance could so easily exhibit to me Lydia L—— in all the ugliness of her falsehood, it may equally, one day or other, disclose to me some other girl in all the beauty of her truth. Till then, I hope, I shall have resolution enough to remain a bachelor."

"Then," replied Byrome, shaking his head, "I must bid you good night, an old bachelor in prospect and perpetnity!"

And as he returned his farewell, Sanford sighed to think that his prophecy was only too likely to be fulfilled; since his observation had convinced him that a strict adherence to truth, on little as well as on great occasions, is, though one of the most IMPORTANT, the RAREST of all virtues!

CHAPTER VII.

ON LIES OF INTEREST.

THESE lies are very various, and are more excusable and less offensive, than many others.

The pale, ragged beggar, who, to add to the effect of his or her ill looks, tells of the large family which does not exist, has a strong motive to deceive in the penury which does;—and one cannot consider as a very *abandoned* liar, the tradesman, who tells you he cannot afford to come down to the price which you offer, because he gave almost as much for the goods himself. It is not from persons like these that we meet with the most disgusting marks of interested falsehood. It is when habitual and petty lying profanes the lips of those whom independence preserves from any strong temptation to violate truth, and whom religion and education might have taught to value it.

The following story will illustrate the LIES OF INTEREST.

THE SCREEN, OR "NOT AT HOME."

THE widow of Governor Atherling returned from the East Indies, old, rich, and childless; and as she had none but very distant relations, her affections naturally turned towards the earliest friends of her youth; one of whom she found still living, and residing in a large country-town.

She therefore hired a house and grounds adjacent, in a village very near to that lady's abode, and became not only her frequent but welcome guest. This old friend was a widow in narrow circumstances, with four daughters slenderly provided for; and she justly concluded that, if she and her family could endear themselves to their opulent guest, they should in all probability inherit some of her property. In the meanwhile as she never visited them without bringing with her, in great abundance, whatever was wanted for the table, and might therefore be said to contribute to their maintenance, without seeming to intend to do so, they took incessant pains to conciliate her more and more every day, by flatteries which she did not see through, and attentions which she deeply felt. Still, the Livingstones were not in spirit united to their amiable guest. The sorrows of her heart had led her by slow degrees, to seek refuge in a religious course of life; and, spite of her proneness to self-deception, she could not conceal from herself that, on this most important subject the Livingstones had never thought seriously, and were, as yet, entirely women of the world. But still her heart longed to be attached to something; and as her starved affections craved some daily food, she suffered herself to love this plausible, amusing, agreeable, and seemingly affectionate family; and she every day lived in hope, that, by her precepts and example, she should ultimately tear them from that "world they loved too well." Sweet and precious to their own souls, are the illusions of the good; and the deceived East Indian was happy, because she did not understand the true nature of the Livingstones.

On the contrary, so fascinated was she by what she fancied they were, or might become, that she took very little notice of a shame-faced, awkward, retiring, silent girl, the only child of the dearest friend that her childhood and her youth had known,—and who had been purposely introduced to her *only as Fanny Barnwell.* For the Livingstones were too selfish, and too prudent, to let their rich friend know that this poor girl was the orphan of *Fanny Beaumont. Withholding,* therefore, the most *important part of the truth,* they only informed her that Fanny Barnwell was an orphan, who was glad to live amongst her friends, that she might make her small income sufficient for her wants; taking care not to add that she was mistaken in supposing that Fanny Beaumont, whose long silence and subsequent death she had bitterly deplored, had died childless; for that she had married a second husband, by whom she had the poor orphan in question, and had lived many years in sorrow and obscurity, the result of this imprudent marriage; resolving, however, in order to avoid accidents, that Fanny's visit should not be of long duration. In the meanwhile, they confided in the security afforded them by what may be called their PASSIVE LIE OF INTEREST. But, in order to make "assurance doubly sure," they had also recourse to the ACTIVE LIE OF INTEREST; and, in order to frighten Fanny from ever daring to inform their visiter that she was the child of Fanny Beaumont, they assured her that that lady was so enraged against her poor mother, for having married her unworthy father, that no one dared to mention her name to her; because it never failed to draw from her the most violent abuse of her once dearest friend.

"And you know Fanny," they took care to add, "that you could not bear to hear your poor mother abused."

"No; that I could not, indeed," was the weeping girl's answer.

The Livingstones therefore felt safe and satisfied. However, it still might not be amiss to make the old lady dislike Fanny, if they could; and they contrived to render the poor girl's virtue the means of doing her injury.

Fanny's mother could not bequeath much money to her child; but she had endeavoured to enrich her with principles and piety. Above all, she had impressed her with the strictest regard for truth;—and the Livingstones artfully contrived to make her integrity the means of displeasing their East Indian friend.

This good old lady's chief failing was believing implicitly whatever was said in her commendation; not that she loved flattery, but that she liked to believe she had conciliated *good will;* and being sincere *herself,* she never thought of distrusting the sincerity of *others.*

Nor was she at all vain of her once fine person, and finer face, or improperly fond of dress. Still, from an almost pitiable degree of *bonhommie,* she allowed the Livingstones to dress her as they liked; and as they chose to make her wear fashionable and young-looking attire, in which they declared that she looked "so handsome! and so well!" she believed they were the best judges of what was proper for her, and always replied, "well, dear friends, it is entirely a matter of indifference to me; so dress me as you please;" while the Livingstones, not *believing* that it was a *matter of indifference,* used to laugh as soon as she was gone, at her obvious credulity.

But this ungenerous and treacherous conduct excited such strong indignation in the usually gentle Fanny, that she could not help expressing her sentiments concerning it; and by that means made them the more eager to betray her into offending their unsuspicious friend. They therefore asked Fanny, in her presence, one day, whether their dear guest did not dress most *becomingly?*

The poor girl made sundry sheepish and awkward contortions, now looking down, and then looking up; unable to lie, yet afraid to tell the truth.

"Why do you not reply, Fanny?" said the artful questioner. "Is she not well-dressed?"

"Not in my opinion," faltered out the distressed girl.

"And pray, Miss Barnwell," said the old lady, "what part of my dress do you disapprove?"

After a pause, Fanny took courage to reply, "All of it, madam."

"Why, do you think it too young for me?"

"I do."

"A plain-spoken young person that!" she observed in a tone of pique;—while the Livingstones exclaimed, "impertinent! ridiculous!"—and Fanny was glad to leave the room, feeling excessive pain at having been forced to wound the feelings of one whom she wished to be permitted to love, because she had once been her mother's dearest friend. After this scene, the Livingstones, partly from the love of mischief, and partly from the love of fun, used to put similar questions to Fanny, in the old lady's presence, till at last, displeased and indignant at her bluntness and ill-breeding, she scarcely noticed or spoke to her. In the meanwhile, Cecilia Livingstone became an object of increasing interest to her; for she had a lover to whom she was greatly attached; but who would not be in a situation to marry for many years.

This young man was frequently at the house, and was as polite and attentive to the old lady, when she was present, as the rest of the family; but, like them, he was ever ready to indulge in a laugh at her credulous simplicity, and especially at her continually expressing her belief, as well as her hopes, that they were all beginning to think less of the present world and more of the next; and as Alfred Lawrie, (Cecilia's lover,) as well as the Livingstones, possessed no inconsiderable power of mimickry, they exercised them with great effect on the manner and tones of her whom they called the *over-dressed* saint, unrestrained, alas! by the consciousness that she was their present, and would, as they expected, be their *future*, benefactress.

That confiding and unsuspecting being was, meanwhile, considering that though her health was injured by a long residence in a warm climate, she might still live many years; and that, as Cecilia might not therefore possess the fortune which she had bequeathed to her till "youth and genial years were flown," it would be better to give it to her during her lifetime. "I will do so," she said to herself, (tears rushing into her eyes as she thought of the happiness which she was going to impart,) "and then the young people can marry directly!"

She took this resolution one day when the Livingstones believed that she had left her home on a visit. Consequently, having no expectation of seeing her for some time, they had taken advantage of her long vainly expected absence, to make some engagements which they knew she would have excessively disapproved. But though, as yet, they knew it not, the old lady had been forced to put off her visit; a circumstance which she did not at all regret; as it enabled her to go sooner on her benevolent errand.

The engagement of the Livingstones for that day was a rehearsal of a private play at their house, which they were afterwards, and during their saintly friend's absence, to perform at the house of a friend; and a large room, called the library, in which there was a wide, commodious screen, was selected as the scene of action.

Fanny Barnwell, who disliked private and other theatricals as much as their old friend herself, was to have no part in the performance; but, as they were disappointed of their prompter that evening, she was, though with great difficulty, persuaded to perform the office, for *that night only*.

It was to be a dress rehearsal; and the parties were in the midst of adorning themselves, when, to their great consternation, they saw their supposed distant friend coming up the street, and evidently intending them a visit. What was to be done? To admit her was impossible. They therefore called up a new servant, who only came to them the day before, and who did not know the worldly consequence of their unwelcome guest; and Cecilia said to her, "you see that old lady yonder; when she knocks, be sure to say that *we are not at home*; and you had better add, that we shall not be at home *till bed-time*;" thus adding the *lie of* CONVENIENCE to other deceptions. Accordingly, when she knocked at the door, the girl spoke as she was desired to do, or rather she improved upon it; for she said that "her ladies had been out all day, and would not return till two o'clock in the morning."

"Indeed! that is unfortunate;" said their disappointed visiter, stopping to deliberate whether she should not leave a note of agreeable surprise for Cecilia; but the girl, who held the door in her hand, seemed so impatient to get rid of her, that she resolved not to write, and then turned away.

The girl was really in haste to return to the kitchen; for she was gossiping with an old fellow-servant. She therefore neglected to go back to her anxious employers; but Cecilia ran down the back stairs to interrogate her, exclaiming, "Well, what did she say? I hope she did not suspect that we were at home."

"No, to be sure not, Miss;—how should she?—for I said even more than you told me to say," repeating her additions; being eager to prove her claim to the confidence of her new mistress.

"But are you sure that she is really gone from the door?"

"To be sure, Miss."

"Still, I wish you would go and see; because we have not seen her pass the window, though we heard the door shut."

"Dear me, Miss, how should you? for I looked out after her, and I saw her go down the street under the windows, and turn.... yes,—I am sure that I saw her turn into a shop. However, I will go and look, if you desire it." She did so; and certainly saw nothing of the dreaded guest. Therefore, her young ladies finished their preparations devoid of fear. But the truth was, that the girl, little aware of the importance of this unwelcomed lady, and concluding she could not be a *friend*, but merely some *troublesome nobody*, showed her contempt and her anger at being detained so long, by throwing to the street-door with such violence, that it did not really close; and the old lady, who had ordered her carriage to come for her at a certain hour, and was determined on second thoughts to sit down and wait for it, was able, unheard, to push open the door, and to enter the library unperceived; —for the girl lied to those who bade her lie, when she said she saw her walk away.

In that room Mrs. Atherling found a sofa; and though she wondered at seeing a large screen opened before it, she seated herself upon it, and, being fatigued with her walk, soon fell asleep. But her slumber was broken very unpleasantly; for she heard as she awoke the following dialogue, on the entrance of Cecilia and her lover, accompanied by Fanny.

"Well—I am so glad we got rid of Mrs. Atherling so easily!" cried Cecilia. "That new girl seems apt. Some servants deny one so as to show one is at home."

"I should like them the better for it," said Fanny. "I hate to see any one ready at telling a falsehood."

"Poor little conscientious dear!" said the lover, mimicking her, "one would think the dressed-up saint had made you as methodistical as herself."

"What, I suppose, Miss Fanny, you would have had us let the old quiz in?"

"To be sure I would; and I wonder you could be denied to so kind a friend.—Poor, dear Mrs. Atherling! how hurt she would be if she knew you were at home!"

"*Poor dear*, indeed! Do not be so affected, Fanny. How should you care for Mrs. Atherling, when you know that she dislikes you!"

"*Dislikes* me! Oh, yes; I fear she does!"

"I am *sure* she does," replied Cecilia; "for you are downright rude to her. Did you not say, only the day before yesterday, when she said, 'There, Miss Barnwell, I hope I have *at last* gotten a cap which you like,'— 'No; I am sorry to say you have not!'"

"To be sure I did; I could not tell a falsehood, even to please Mrs. Atherling, though she was my own dear mother's dearest friend."

"Your mother's friend, Fanny? I never heard *that* before;" said the lover.

"Did you not know that, Alfred?" said Cecilia, eagerly adding, "but *Mrs. Atherling* does not know it;" giving him a meaning look, as if to say, "and do not you *tell* her."

"Would she *did* know it!" said Fanny, mournfully, "for, though I dare not tell her so, lest she should abuse my poor mother, as you say she would, Cecilia, because she was so angry at her marriage with my misguided father, still, I think she would look kindly on her once dear friend's orphan child, and like me in spite of my honesty."

"No, no, silly girl; honesty is usually its own reward. Alfred, what do you think? Our old friend, who is not very penetrating, said one day to her, 'I suppose you think my caps too young for me;' and that true young person replied, 'Yes, madam, I do.'"

"And would do so again, Cecilia;—and it was far more friendly and kind to say so than flatter her on her dress, as you do, and then laugh at it when her back is turned. I hate to hear any one mimicked and laughed at; and more especially my mamma's old friend."

"There, there, child! your sentimentality makes me sick. But come, let us begin."

"Yes," cried Alfred, "let us rehearse a little before the rest of the party come. I should like to hear Mrs. Atherling's exclamations, if she knew what we were doing. She would say thus;".... Here he gave a most accurate representation of the poor old lady's voice and manner, and her fancied abuse of private theatricals, while Cecilia cried "bravo! bravo!" and Fanny, "shame, shame!" till the other Livingstones, and the rest of the company, who now entered, drowned her cry in their loud applauses and louder laughter.

The old lady, whom surprise, anger, and wounded sensibility, had hitherto kept *silent* and *still* in her involuntary hiding-place, now rose up, and, mounting on the sofa, looked over the top of the screen, full of reproachful meaning, on the conscious offenders!

What a moment to them of overwhelming surprise and consternation! The cheeks, flushed with malicious triumph and satirical pleasure, became covered with the deeper blush of detected treachery, or pale with fear of its consequences; and the eyes so lately beaming with ungenerous, injurious satisfaction, were now cast with painful shame upon the ground, unable to meet the justly indignant glance of her whose kindness they had repaid with such palpable and base ingratitude!

"An admirable likeness, indeed, Alfred Lawrie," said their undeceived dupe, breaking her perturbed silence, and coming down from her elevation; "but it will cost you more than you are at present aware of.—But who art thou?" she added, addressing Fanny (who, though it might have been a moment of triumph to her, felt and looked as if she had been a sharer in the guilt,) "Who art *thou*, my honourable, kind girl! And who was your mother!"

"Your Fanny Beaumont," replied the quick-feeling orphan, bursting into tears.

"Fanny Beaumont's child! and it was concealed from me!" said she, folding the weeping girl to her heart. "But it was all of a piece;—all treachery and insincerity, from the beginning to the end. However, I am undeceived before it was too late." She then disclosed to the detected family her generous motive for the unexpected visit; and declared her thankfulness for what had taken place, as far as she was herself concerned; though she could not but deplore, as a christian, the discovered turpitude of those whom she had fondly loved.

"I have now," she continued, "to make amends to one whom I have hitherto not treated kindly; but I have at length been enabled to discover an undeserved friend, amidst undeserved foes.... My dear child," added she, parting Fanny's dark ringlets, and gazing fearfully in her face, "I must have been *blind* as well as blinded, not to see your likeness to your dear mother.—Will you live with me, Fanny, and be unto me as a DAUGHTER!"

"Oh, most gladly!" was the eager and agitated reply.

"You artful creature!" exclaimed Cecilia, pale with rage and mortification, "you knew very well that she was behind the screen."

"I know that she could *not* know it," replied the old lady; "and you, Miss Livingstone, assert what you do not yourself believe. But come, Fanny, let us go and meet my carriage; for, no doubt, your presence here is now as unwelcome as mine."

But Fanny lingered, as if reluctant to depart. She could not bear to leave the Livingstones in anger. They had been kind to her; and she would fain have parted with them affectionately; but they all preserved a sullen, indignant silence, and scornfully repelled her advances.

"You see that you must not tarry here, my good girl," observed the old lady, smiling; "so let us depart." They did so, leaving the Livingstones and the lover, not deploring their fault, but lamenting their detection;—lamenting also the hour when they added the lies of CONVENIENCE to their other deceptions, and had thereby enabled their unsuspecting dupe to detect those falsehoods, the result of their avaricious fears, which may be justly entitled the LIES OF INTEREST.

CHAPTER VIII.

LIES OF FIRST-RATE MALIGNITY.

LIES OF FIRST-RATE MALIGNITY come next to be considered; and I think that I am right in asserting that such lies,—lies intended *wilfully* to destroy the reputation of men and women, to injure their characters in public or private estimation, and for ever cloud over their prospects in life,—are less frequent than falsehoods of any other description.

Not that malignity is an unfrequent feeling; —not that dislike, or envy, or jealousy, would not gladly vent itself in many a malignant falsehood, or other efforts of the same kind, against the peace and fame of its often innocent and unconscious objects;—but that the arm of the law, *in some measure* at least, defends reputations; and if it should not have been able to deter the slanderer from his purpose, it can at least avenge the slandered.

Still, such is the prevailing tendency, in society, to prey on the reputations of others (especially of those who are at all *distinguished,* either in public or private life;) such the propensity to impute BAD MOTIVES to GOOD ACTIONS: so common the fiend-like pleasure of finding or imagining blemishes in beings on whom even a *motive-judging world* in general gazes with respectful admiration and bestows the sacred tribute of well-earned praise; that I am convinced there are many persons, worn both in mind and body by the consciousness of being the objects of calumnies and suspicions which they have it not in their power to combat, who steal broken-hearted to their graves, thankful for the summons of death, and hoping to find refuge from the injustice of their fellow-creatures in the bosom of their God and Saviour.

With the following *illustration* of the LIE OF FIRST-RATE MALIGNITY I shall conclude my observations on this subject.

THE ORPHAN.

THERE are persons in the world whom circumstances have so entirely preserved from intercourse with the base and the malignant, and whose dispositions are so free from bitterness, that they can scarcely believe in the existence of baseness and malignity. Such persons, when they hear of injuries committed, and wrongs done, at the instigation of the most trivial and apparently worthless motives, are apt to exclaim, "You have been imposed upon. No one could be so wicked as to act thus upon such slight grounds; and you are not relating as a sober observer of human nature and human action, but with the exaggerated view of a dealer in fiction and romance!" Happy, and privileged beyond the ordinary charter of human beings, are those who can thus exclaim;—but the inhabitants of the tropics might, with equal justice, refuse to believe in the existence of that thing called snow, as these unbelievers in the moral turpitude in question refuse their credence to anecdotes which disclose it. All they can with propriety assert is, that such instances have not come under their cognizance. Yet, even to these favoured few, I would put the following questions:—Have you never experienced feelings of selfishness, anger, jealousy, or envy, which, though habits of religious and moral restraint taught you easily to subdue them, had yet troubled you long enough to make you fully sensible of their existence and their power? If so, is it not easy to believe that such feelings, when excited in the minds of those not under religious and moral guidance, may grow to such an unrestrained excess as to lead to actions and lies of terrible malignity?

I cannot but think that even the purest and best of my friends must answer in the affirmative. Still, they have reason to return thanks to their Creator, that their lot has been cast amongst such "pleasant places;" and that it is theirs to breathe an atmosphere impregnated only with airs from heaven.

My lot, from a peculiar train of circumstances, has been somewhat differently cast; and when I give the following story, to illustrate a lie of FIRST-RATE MALIGNITY, I do so with the certain knowledge that its foundation is truth.

CONSTANTIA GORDON was the only child of a professional man of great eminence, in a provincial town. Her mother was taken from her before she had attained the age of womanhood, but not before the wise and pious precepts which she gave her had taken deep root, and had therefore counteracted the otherwise pernicious effects of a showy and elaborate education. Constantia's talents were considerable; and as her application was equal to them, she was, at an early age, distinguished in her native place for her learning and accomplishments.

Among the most intimate associates of her father, was a gentleman of the name of Overton; a man of some talent, and some acquirement; but, as his pretensions to eminence were not as universally allowed as he thought that they ought to have been, he was extremely tenacious of his own consequence, excessively envious of the slightest successes of others, while any dissent from his dogmas was an offence which his mean soul was incapable of forgiving.

It was only too natural that Constantia, as she was the petted, though not spoiled child of a fond father, and the little sun of the circle in which she moved, was, perhaps, only too forward in giving her opinion on literature, and on some other subjects, which are not usually discussed by women at all, and still less by girls at her time of life; and she had sometimes ventured to disagree in opinion with Oracle Overton—the nickname by which this man was known. But he commonly took refuge in sarcastic observations on the ignorance and presumption of women in general, and of blue-stocking girls in particular, while on his face a grin of conscious superiority contended with the frown of pedantic indignation.

Hitherto this collision of wits had taken place in Constantia's domestic circle only; but, one day, Overton and the former met at the house of a nobleman in the neighbourhood, and in company with many persons of considerable talent. While they were at table, the master of the house said that it was his birth-day; and some one immediately proposed that all the guests, who could write verses, should produce one couplet at least in honour of the day.

But as Overton and Constantia were the only persons present who were known to be so gifted, they alone were assailed with earnest entreaties to employ their talents on the occasion. The latter, however, was prevented by timidity from compliance; and she persevered in her refusal, though Overton loudly conjured her to indulge the company with a display of her *wonderful genius*; accompanying his words with a sarcastic smile, which she well understood. Overton's muse, therefore, since Constantia would not let hers enter into the competition, walked over the course; having been highly applauded for a *médiocre* stanza of eight doggerel lines. But, as Constantia's timidity vanished when she found herself alone with the ladies in the drawing-room, who were most of them friends of hers, she at length produced some verses, which not only delighted her affectionate companions, but, when shown to the gentlemen, drew from them more and warmer encomiums than had been bestowed on the frothy tribute of her competitor; while the writhing and mortified Overton forced himself to say they were very well, very well indeed, for a scribbling Miss of sixteen; insinuating at the same time that the pretended extempore was one written by her father at home, and gotten by heart by herself. But the giver of the feast declared that he had forgotten it was his birth-day, till he sat down to table; therefore, as every one said, although the verses were written by a girl of sixteen only, they would have done honour to a riper age, Overton gained nothing, but added mortification from his mean attempt to blight Constantia's well-earned laurels, especially as his ungenerous conduct drew on him severe animadversions from some of the other guests. His fair rival also unwittingly deepened his resentment against herself, by venturing, in a playful manner, being emboldened by success, to dispute some of his paradoxes;—and once she did it so successfully, that she got the laugh against Overton, in a manner so offensive to his self-love, that he suddenly left the company, vowing revenge in his heart, against the being who had thus shone at his expense. However, he continued to visit at her father's house; and was still considered as their most intimate friend.

Constantia, meanwhile, increased not only both in beauty and accomplishments, but in qualities of a more precious nature; namely, in a knowledge of her christian duties. But her charities were performed in secret, and so fearful was she of being deemed righteous overmuch, and considered as an enthusiast, even by her father himself, that the soundness of her religious character was known only to the sceptical Overton, and two or three more of her associates, while it was a notorious fact, that the usual companions of her father and herself were free-thinkers and latitudinarians, both in politics and religion. But, if Constantia did not lay open her religious faith to those by whom she was surrounded, she fed its lamp in her own bosom, with never-ceasing watchfulness; and, like the solitary light in a cottage on the dark and lonely moors, it beamed on her hours of solitude and retirement, cheering and warming her amidst surrounding darkness.

It was to do yet more for her. It was to support her, not only under the sudden death of a father whom she tenderly loved, but under the unexpected loss of income which his death occasioned. On examining his affairs, it was discovered that, when his debts were all paid, there would be a bare maintenance only remaining for the afflicted orphan. Constantia's sorrow, though deep, was quiet and gentle as her nature; and she felt, with unspeakable thankfulness, that she owed the tranquillity and resignation of her mind, to her religious convictions alone.

The interesting orphan had only just returned into the society of her friends, when a Sir Edward Vandeleur, a young baronet of large fortune, came on a visit in the neighbourhood.

Sir Edward was the darling and pride of a highly-gifted mother, and several amiable sisters; and Lady Vandeleur, who was in declining health, had often urged her son to let her have the satisfaction of seeing him married before she was taken away from him.

But, it was no easy thing for a man like Sir Edward Vandeleur to find a wife suited to him. His feelings were too much under a strong religious restraint, to admit of his falling violently in love, as the phrase is; and beauty and accomplishments had no chance of captivating his heart, unless they were accompanied by qualities which fully satisfied his principles and his judgment.

It was at this period of his life that Sir Edward Vandeleur was introduced to Constantia Gordon, at a small conversation party, at the house of a mutual acquaintance.

Her beauty, her graceful manners, over which sorrow had cast a new and sobered charm, and her great conversational powers, made her presently an object of interest to Sir Edward; and when he heard her story, that interest was considerably increased by pity for her orphan state and altered circumstances.

Therefore, though Sir Edward saw Constantia rarely, and never except at one house, he felt her at every interview growing more on his esteem and admiration; and he often thought of the recluse in her simple mourning attire, and wished himself by her side, when he was the courted, flattered, attendant on a reigning belle.

Not that he was in love;—that is, not that he had imbibed an attachment which his reason could not at once enable him to conquer, if it should ever disapprove its continuance; but his judgment, as well as his taste, told him that Constantia was the sort of woman to pass life with. "Seek for a companion in a wife!" had always been his mother's advice. "Seek for a woman who has understanding enough to know her duties, and piety and principle enough to enable her to fulfil them; one who can teach her children to follow in her steps, and form them for virtue here, and happiness hereafter!" "Surely," thought Sir Edward, as he recalled this natural advice, "I have found the woman so described in Constantia Gordon!" But he was still too prudent to pay her any marked attention; especially as Lady Vandeleur had recommended caution.

At this moment his mother wrote thus:

"I do not see any apparent objection to the lady in question. Still, be cautious! Is there no one at —— who has known her from her childhood, and can give you an account of her and her moral and religious principles, which can be relied upon? Death, that great discoverer of secrets, proved that her father was not a very worthy man: still, bad parents have good children, and *vice versâ*; but, inquire and be wary."

The day after Sir Edward received this letter, he was introduced to Overton at the house of a gentleman in the neighbourhood; and at the most unfortunate period possible for Constantia Gordon. Overton had always pretended to have a sincere regard for the poor orphan, and no one was more loud in regrets for her reduced fortune; but, as he was fond of giving her pain, he used to mingle with his pity, so many severe remarks on her father's thoughtless conduct, that had he not been her father's most familiar friend, she would have forbidden him her presence.

One day having found her alone at her lodgings, he accompanied his expressions of affected condolence with a proposal to give her a bank-note now and then, to buy her a new gown; as he was (he said) afraid that she would not have money sufficient to set off her charms to advantage. To real kindness, however vulgarly worded, Constantia's heart was ever open; but she immediately saw that this offer, prefaced as it was by abuse of her father, was merely the result of malignity and coarseness combined; and her spirit, though habitually gentle, was roused to indignant resentment.

But who, that has ever experienced the bitterness of feeling excited by the cold, spiteful efforts of a malignant temper to irritate a gentle and generous nature, can withhold their sympathy and pardon from Constantia on this occasion? At last, gratified at having made his victim awhile forego her nature, and at being now enabled to represent her as a vixen; he took his leave with hypocritical kindness, calling her his "*naughty scolding Con*," leaving her to humble herself before that Being whom she feared to have offended by her violence, and to weep over the recollection of an interview which had added, to her other miseries, that of self-reproach.

Overton, meanwhile, did not retire unhurt from the combat. The orphan had uttered, in her agony, some truths which he could not forget. She had held up to him a mirror of himself, from which he found it difficult to turn away, while in proportion to his sense of suffering was his resentment against its fair cause; and his desire of revenge was in proportion to both.

It was on this very day that he dined in company with Sir Edward Vandeleur, who was soon informed by the master of the house, that Overton had been from her childhood, the friend and intimate of Constantia Gordon; and the same gentleman informed Overton in private, that Sir Edward was supposed to entertain thoughts of paying his addresses to Constantia.

Inexpressible was Overton's consternation at hearing that this girl, whose poverty he had insulted, whom he disliked because she had been a thorn to his self-love, and under whose just severity he was still smarting, was likely, not only to be removed from his power to torment her, but to be raised above him by a fortunate marriage.

Great was his triumph, therefore, when Sir Edward, before they parted, requested an interview with him the following morning, at his lodgings in the town of ——, adding, that he wished to ask him some questions concerning their mutual friend, Constantia Gordon.

Accordingly they met; and the following conversation took place. Sir Edward began by candidly confessing the high opinion which he had conceived of Constantia, and his earnest wish to have its justice confirmed by the testimony of her oldest and most intimate friend.

"Sir Edward," replied the exulting hypocrite, with well-acted reluctance, "you put an honourable and a kind-hearted man, like myself, into a complete *embarras*—"

"Sir, what do I hear?" cried Sir Edward starting from his seat. "Can you feel any embarrassment, when called upon to bear testimony in favour of Constantia Gordon?"

"I dare say *you* cannot think such a thing possible," he replied with a sneer; "for men in love are usually blind."

"But I am not in love yet," eagerly replied Sir Edward; "and it very much depends on this conversation whether I ever am so with the lady in question."

"Well then, Sir Edward, however unpalatable, I must speak the truth. I need not tell you that Constantia is beautiful, accomplished, and *talented*, is, I think, the *new* word."

"No, sir; I already know she is all these; and she appears to me to be as gentle, virtuous, and pious, as she is beautiful."

"I dare say she does; but, as to her *gentleness*, however, I might provoke her improperly;—but, I assure you, she flew into such a passion with me yesterday, that I thought she would have struck me!"

"Is it possible? I really feel a difficulty in believing you!"

"No doubt; so let us talk of something else."

"No, no,—Mr. Overton; I came hither to be informed on a subject deeply interesting to me, and, at whatever risk of disappointment, I will await all you have to say."

"I have nothing to say, Sir Edward, you know Con is beautiful and charming; and is not that enough?"

"No! it is *not* enough. Outward graces are not sufficient to captivate and fix me, unless they are accompanied by charms that fade not with time, but blossom to eternity."

"Whew!" exclaimed Overton, with well-acted surprise, "I see that you are a methodist, Sir Edward; and if so, my friend Con will not suit you."

"Does it follow that I am a methodist, because I require that my wife should be a woman of pious and moral habits?"

"Oh! for *morals*, in these, indeed, my friend Con would suit you well enough. Let her morals pass; but as to her *piety*, religion will never turn her head."

"What do you mean, Mr. Overton?"

"Why, sir, our lovely friend has learned from the company which she has kept, to think freely on such subjects, very freely;—for women, you know, always go to extremes. Men keep within the rational bounds of *deism*; but the female sceptic, weaker in intellect, and incapable of reasoning, never rests, till she loses herself in the mazes and absurdities of atheism."

Had Sir Edward Vandeleur seen the fair smooth skin of Constantia suddenly covered with leprosy, he would not have been more shocked than he was at being informed of this utter blight to her mental beauty in his rightly judging eyes: and starting from his seat, he exclaimed, "Do you really mean to assert that your fair friend is an atheist?"

"Sir Edward, I am Constantia's friend; and I was her father's friend; and I am sorry these things have been forced upon me, but I could not deceive an honourable man, who placed confidence also in my honour; though as Constantia is the child of an old friend, and poor, it would be, perhaps, a saving to my pocket if she were well-married."

"Then, it is true!" said Sir Edward, clasping his hands in agony; "and this lovely girl is what I hate to name! Yet, she looks so right-minded! and I have thought the expression of her dark-blue eye was that of pious resignation!"

"Yes, yes; I know that look; and she knows that is her *prettiest* look. That eye, half turned up, shows her fine long dark eyelashes to great advantage!"

"Alas!" replied Sir Edward deeply sighing, "if this be so—oh! what are looks? Good morning. You have distressed, but you have *saved* me."

When Overton soon after saw Sir Edward drive past in his splendid curricle, he exulted that he had prevented Constantia from ever sitting there by his side.

Yet he was, as I have said before, one of the few who knew how deeply and sincerely Constantia was a believer; for he had himself in vain attempted to shake her belief, and thence he had probably a double pleasure in representing her as he did.

Sir Edward was engaged that evening to meet Constantia at the accustomed house; and as his attentions to her had been rather marked, and her friends, with the usual dangerous officiousness on such occasions, had endeavoured to convince her that she had made a *conquest*, as the phrase is, of the young baronet, the expectation of meeting him was become a circumstance of no small interest to her; though she was far too humble to be convinced that they were right in their conjectures.

But the mind of Constantia was too much under the guidance of religious principle, to allow her to love any man, however amiable, unless she was sure of being beloved by him. She was too delicate, and had too much self-respect, to be capable of such a weakness; she therefore escaped that danger, of which I have seen the peace of some young women become the victims; namely, that of being talked and flattered into a hopeless passion by the idle wishes and representations of gossiping acquaintances. And well was it for her peace that she had been thus *holily* on her guard; for, when Sir Edward Vandeleur, instead of keeping his engagement, sent a note to inform her friend that he was not able to wait on her, as he thought of going to London the next day, Constantia felt that the idea of his attachment was as unfounded as it had been pleasing, and she rejoiced that the illusion had not been long enough to endanger her tranquillity. Still, she could not but own, in the secret of her heart, that the prospect of passing life with a being apparently so suited to herself, was one on which her thoughts had dwelt with involuntary pleasure; and a tear started to her eyes, at the idea that she might see him no more. But she considered it as the tear of weakness, and though her sleep that night was short, it was tranquil, and she rose the next morning to resume the duties of the day with her accustomed alacrity. In her walks she met Sir Edward, but happily for her, as he was leaning on Overton's arm, whom she had not seen since she had parted with him in anger, a turn was given to her feelings, by the approach of the latter, which enabled her to conquer at once her emotion at the unexpected sight of the former. Still the sight of Overton occasioned in her disagreeable and painful recollections, which gave an unpleasing and equivocal expression to her beautiful features, and enabled Overton to observe, "You see, Sir Edward, how her conscience flies in her face at seeing me! How are you? How are you?" said Overton, catching her hand as she passed. "Have you forgiven me yet? Oh! you vixen, how you scolded me the other day!"

Constantia, too much mortified and agitated to speak, and repel the charge, replied by a look of indignation; and snatching her hand away, she bowed to Sir Edward, and hastened out of sight.

"You see," cried Overton, "that she resents still! and how like a fury she looked! You must be convinced that I told you the truth. Now, could you believe, Sir Edward, that pretty Con could have looked in that manner?"

"Certainly not; and appearances are indeed deceitful."

Still, Sir Edward wished Constantia had given him an opportunity of bidding her farewell; however, he left his good wishes and respects for her with their mutual friend, and set off that evening to join his mother at Hastings.

"But are you sure, Edward," said Lady Vandeleur, when he had related to her all that had passed, "that this Overton is a man to be depended upon?"

"Oh, yes! and he could have no *motive* for calumniating her, but the contrary, as it would have been a relief to his mind and pocket to get his old friend's daughter well married."

"But, does she appear to her other friends neglectful of her religious duties, as if she had really no religion at all?"

"So far from it, that she has always been punctual in the *outward* performance of them; therefore, no one but Overton, the confidential friend and intimate of the family, could suspect or *know* her real opinions; thus she adds, I fear, *hypocrisy* to scepticism. Overton also accuses her of being violent in her temper; and I was unexpectedly enabled to see the truth of this accusation, in a measure, confirmed. Therefore, indeed, dear mother, all I have to do is to forget her, and resume my intention of accompanying you and my sisters to the continent." Accordingly they set off very soon on a foreign tour.

Constantia, after she left Overton and Sir Edward so hastily and suddenly, returned home in no enviable state of mind; because she felt sure that her manner had been such as to convince the latter that she was the violent creature which Overton had represented her to be; and though she had calmly resigned all idea of being beloved by Sir Edward Vandeleur, she was not entirely indifferent to his good opinion. Besides, she feared that her quitting him without one word of kind farewell, might appear to him a proof of pique and disappointment; nor could she be quite sure that somewhat of that feeling did not impel her to hasten abruptly away; and it was some time before she could conquer her self-blame and her regret. But at length she reflected that there was a want of proper self-government in dwelling at all on recollections of Sir Edward Vandeleur; and she forced herself into society and absorbing occupations.

Hitherto Constantia had been contented to remain in idleness; but, as her income was, she found, barely equal to her maintenance, and she was therefore obliged to relinquish nearly all her charities, she resolved to turn her talents to account; and was just about to decide between two plans, which she had thought desirable, when an uncle in India died, and the question was decided in a very welcome and unexpected manner. Till this gentleman married, her father had such large expectations from him, that he had fancied them a sufficient excuse for his profuse expenditure; but, when his brother, by having children, destroyed his hopes of wealth from that quarter, he had not strength of mind enough to break the expensive habits which he had acquired. To the deserving child, however, was destined the wealth withheld from the undeserving parent. Constantia's uncle's wife and children died before he did, and she became sole heiress to his large fortune. This event communicated a sensation of gladness to the whole town in which the amiable orphan resided.

Constantia had borne her faculties so meekly, had been so actively benevolent, and was thence so generally beloved, that she was now daily overpowered with thankful and pleasing emotion, at beholding countenances which, at sight of her, were lighted up with affectionate sympathy and joy.

Overton was one of the first persons whom she desired to see, on this accession of fortune. Her truly christian spirit had long made her wish to hold out to him her hand in token of forgiveness; but she wished to do so more especially now, because he could not suspect her of being influenced by any mercenary views. Overton, however, meant to call on her, whether she invited him or not; as, such was his love and respect for *wealth*, that though the *poor* Constantia was full of faults in his eye, the *rich* Constantia was very likely to appear in time, impeccable. He was at this period Mayor of the place in which he lived; and having been knighted for carrying up an address, he became desirous of using the privilege, which, according to Shakspeare's Falconbridge, knighthood gives a man, of making "any Joan a lady." Nor was it long before he entertained serious thoughts of marrying; and why not? as he was only fifty; was very young-looking for his age; was excessively handsome still; and had now a title, in addition to a good fortune. The only difficulty was to make a choice; for he was very sure that *he* must be the choice of any one to whom he offered himself.

But where could he find in one woman all the qualities which he required in a wife! She must have youth, and beauty, or he could not love her; good principles, or he could not trust her; and, though he was not religious himself, he had a certain consciousness that the best safeguard for a woman's principles was to be found in piety; *therefore*, he resolved that his wife should be a *religious* woman. Temper, patience, and forbearance, were also requisites in the woman he married; and, as the last and best recommendation, she must have a large fortune. Reasonable man! youth, beauty, temper, virtue, piety, and riches! but what woman of his acquaintance possessed all these? No one, he believed, but that forgiving being whom he had represented as an atheist; "that vixen Con!" and while this conviction came over his mind, a blush of shame passed over even his brassy brow. However, it was soon succeeded by one of pleasure, when he thought that, as Constantia was evidently uneasy till she had *made it up with him*, as the phrase is, it was not unlikely that she had a secret liking to him; and as to her scribbling verses, and pretending to be literary, he would take care that she should not write when she was his wife; and he really thought he had better propose to her at once, especially as it was a duty in him to make her a lady himself, since he had prevented another man's doing so. There was, perhaps, another inducement to marry Constantia. It would give him an opportunity of tormenting her now and then, and making her smart for former impertinences. Perhaps this motive was nearly as strong as the rest. Be that as it may, Overton had, at length, the presumption to make proposals of marriage to the young and *lovely* heiress, who, though ignorant of his base conduct to her, and the LIE OF FIRST-RATE MALIGNITY with which he had injured her fame, and blighted her prospects, had still a dislike to his manners and character, which it was impossible for any thing to overcome. He was therefore refused,—and in a manner so decided, and, spite of herself, so haughty, that Overton's heart renewed all its malignity towards her; and his manner became so rude and offensive, that she was constrained to refuse him admittance, and go on a visit to a friend at some distance, intending not to return till the house which she had purchased in a village near to —— was ready for her. But she had not been absent many months when she received a letter one evening, to inform her that her dearest friend at —— was supposed to be in the greatest danger, and she was requested to set off directly. To disobey this summons was impossible; and, as the mail passed the house where she was, and she was certain of getting on faster that way than any other, she resolved, accompanied by her servant, to go by the mail, if possible; and, happily, there were two places vacant. It was night when Constantia and her maid entered the coach, in which two gentlemen were already seated; and, to the consternation of Constantia, she soon saw, as they passed near a lamp, that her *vis-à-vis* was Overton! He recognised her at the same moment; and instantly began, in the French language, to express his joy at meeting her and to profess the faithfulness of his fervent affection. In vain did she try to force conversation with the other passenger, who seemed willing to talk, and who, though evidently not a gentleman, was much preferable, in her opinion, to the new Sir Richard. He would not allow her to attend to any conversation but his own; and, as it was with difficulty that she could keep her hand from his rude grasp, she tried to change seats with her maid; but Overton forcibly withheld her; and she thought it was better to endure the evil patiently, than violently resist it. When the mail stopped, that the passengers might sup, Constantia hoped *Overton* would, at least, leave her for a time; but, though the other passenger got out, he kept his seat, and was so persevering, and was so much more disagreeable when the restraint imposed on him by the presence of others was removed, that she was glad when the coach was again full, and the mail drove off.

Overton, however, became so increasingly offensive to her, that at length, she assured him, in language the most solemn and decided, that *nothing* should ever induce her to be his wife; and that, were she penniless, *service* would be more desirable to her, than union with him.

This roused his anger even to frenzy; and, still speaking French, a language which he was sure the illiterate man in the corner could not understand, he told her that she refused him only because she loved Sir Edward Vandeleur; "but," said he, "you have no chance of obtaining him. I have taken care to prevent *that*. I gave him such a character of you, as frightened him away from you, and—"

"Base-minded man!" cried Constantia; "what did you, what could you say against my character?"

"Oh! I said nothing against your morals. I only told him that you were an atheist, and a vixen, that is all; and, you know, you are the latter, though not the former; but are more like a methodist than an atheist!"

"And you told him these horrible falsehoods! And if you had not, would he have—did he then!—but I know not what I say; and I am miserable! Cruel, wicked man! how could you thus dare to injure and misrepresent an unprotected orphan? and the child of your friend! and to calumniate me to *him* too! to Sir Edward Vandeleur! Oh, it was cruel indeed!"

"What! then you wished to please him, did you? answer me!" he vociferated, seizing both her hands in his; "Are you attached to Sir Edward Vandeleur?" But, before Constantia could answer no, and while screaming with apprehension and pain, she vainly tried to free herself from Overton's nervous grasp, a powerful hand rescued her from the ruffian gripe. Then, while the dawn shone brightly upon his face, Constantia and Overton at the same moment recognised, in her rescuer, Sir Edward Vandeleur himself!

He was just returned from France; and was on his way to the neighbourhood of ——, being now, as he believed, able to see Constantia with entire indifference, when, as one of his horses became ill, he resolved to take that place in the mail which the other passenger had quitted for the box; and had thus the pleasure of hearing all suspicions, all imputations, against the character of Constantia cleared off, and removed, at once, and for ever! Constantia's joy was little inferior to his own; but it was soon lost in terror at the probable result of the angry emotions of Sir Edward and Overton. Her fear, however, vanished, when the former assured the latter, that the man who could injure an innocent woman, by a lie of FIRST-RATE MALIGNITY, was beneath even the resentment of an honourable man.

I shall only add, that Overton left the mail at the next stage, baffled, disgraced, and miserable; that Constantia found her friend recovering; and that the next time she travelled along that road, it was as the bride of Sir Edward Vandeleur.

CHAPTER IX.

LIES OF SECOND-RATE MALIGNITY.

I HAVE observed, in the foregoing chapter, that LIES OF FIRST-RATE MALIGNITY are not frequent, because the arm of the law defends reputations;—but, against lies of second-rate malignity, the law holds out no protection; nor is there a tribunal of sufficient power either to deter any one from uttering them, or to punish the utterer. The lies in question spring from the spirit of detraction; a spirit more widely diffused in society than any other; and it gives birth to satire, ridicule, mimicry, quizzing, and lies of second-rate malignity, as certainly as a wet season brings snails.

I shall now explain what I consider as lies of SECOND-RATE MALIGNITY;—namely, tempting persons, by dint of flattery, to do what they are incapable of doing well, from the mean, malicious wish of leading them to expose themselves, in order that their tempter may enjoy a hearty laugh at their expense. Persuading a man to drink more than his head can bear, by assurances that *the wine is not strong*, and that he has not drunk as much as he thinks he has, in order to make him intoxicated, and that his persuaders may enjoy the cruel delight of witnessing his drunken silliness, his vain-glorious boastings, and those physical contortions, or mental weaknesses, which intoxication is always sure to produce. Complimenting either man or woman on qualities which they do not possess, in hopes of imposing on their credulity; praising a lady's work, or dress, to her face; and then, as soon as she is no longer present, not only abusing both her work and her dress, but laughing at her weakness, in believing the praise sincere. Lavishing encomiums on a man's abilities and learning in his presence; and then, as soon as he is out of hearing, expressing contempt for his credulous belief in the sincerity of the praises bestowed; and wonder that he should be so blind and conceited as not to know that he was in learning only a smatterer, and in understanding, just not a fool. All these are lies of *second-rate malignity*, which cannot be exceeded in *base and petty treachery*.

The following story will, I trust, explain fully what, in the common intercourse of society, I consider as LIES OF SECOND-RATE MALIGNITY.

THE OLD GENTLEMAN AND THE YOUNG ONE.

NOTHING shows the force of habit more than the tenaciousness with which those adhere to economical usages who, by their own industry and unexpected good fortune, are become rich in the decline of life.

A gentleman, whom I shall call Dr. Albany, had, early in life, taken his degree at Cambridge, as a doctor of physic, and had settled in London as a physician; but had worn away the best part of his existence in vain expectation of practice, when an old bachelor, a college friend, whom he had greatly served, died, and left him the whole of his large fortune.

Dr. Albany had indeed *deserved* this bequest; for he had rendered his friend the greatest of all services. He had rescued him, by his friendly advice and enlightened arguments, from scepticism, apparently the most hopeless; and, both by precept and example, had allured him along the way that leads to salvation.

But, as wealth came to Dr. Albany too late in life for him to think of marrying, and as he had no relations who needed all his fortune, he resolved to leave the greatest part of it to those friends who wanted it the most.

Hitherto, he had scarcely ever left London; as he had thought it right to wait at home to receive business, even though business never came; but now he was resolved to renew the neglected acquaintances of his youth; and, knowing that some of his early friends lived near Cheltenham, Leamington, and Malvern, he resolved to visit those watering-places, in hopes of meeting there some of these well-remembered faces.

Most men, under his circumstances, would have ordered a handsome carriage, and entered Cheltenham in style; but, as I before observed, habits of economy adhere so closely to persons thus situated, that Dr. Albany could not prevail on himself to travel in a manner more in apparent accordance with the acquisition of such a fortune. He therefore went by a cheap day coach; nor did he take a servant with him. But, though still denying indulgences to himself, the first wish of his heart was to be generous to others; and, surely, that economy which is unaccompanied by avarice may, even in the midst of wealth, be denominated a virtue.

While dinner was serving up, when they stopped on the road, Albany walked up a hill near the inn, and was joined there by a passenger from another coach. During their walk he observed a very pretty house on a rising ground in the distance, and he asked his companion, who lived there. The latter replied that it was the residence of a clergyman, of the name of Musgrave.

"Musgrave!" he eagerly replied, "what Musgrave! Is his name Augustus?"

"Yes."

"Is he married?"

"Yes."

"Has he a family?"

"Oh yes; a large one; six daughters, and one son; and he has found it a hard task to bring them up, as he wished to make them accomplished. The son is now going to college."

"Are they an amiable family?"

"Very; the girls sing and play well, and draw well."

"And what is the son to be?"

"A clergyman."

"Has he any chance of a living?"

"Not that I know of; but he must be something; and a legacy which the father has just had, of a few hundred pounds, will enable him to pay college expenses, till his son gets ordained, and can take curacies."

"Is Musgrave," said Albany after a pause, "a likely man to give a cordial welcome to an old friend, whom he has not seen for many years?"

"Oh yes; he is very hospitable; and there he is, now going into his own gate."

"Then I will not go on," said Albany, hastening to the stables. "There, coachman," cried he, "take your money; and give me my little portmanteau."

Augustus Musgrave had been a favourite college friend of Dr. Albany, and he had many associations with his name and image, which were dear to his heart.

The objects of them were gone for ever; but, thus recalled, they came over his mind like strains of long-forgotten music, which he had loved and carolled in youth; throwing so strong a feeling of tenderness over the recollection of Musgrave, that he felt an irresistible desire to see him again, and greet his wife and children in the language of glowing good will.

But, when he was introduced into his friend's presence, he had the mortification of finding that he was not recognised; and was obliged to tell his name.

The name, however, seemed to electrify Musgrave with affectionate gladness. He shook his old friend heartily by the hand, presented him to his wife and daughters, and for some minutes moved and spoke with the brightness and alacrity of early youth.

But the animation was momentary. The cares of a family, and the difficulty of keeping up the appearance of a gentleman with an income not sufficient for his means, had preyed on Musgrave's spirits; especially as he knew himself to be involved in debt. He had also other cares. The weakness of his nature, which he dignified by the name of tenderness of heart, had made him allow his wife and children to tyrannize over him; and his son, who was a universal quizzer, did not permit even his father to escape from his impertinent ridicule. But then Musgrave was assured, by his own family, that his son Marmaduke was a wit; and that, when he was once in orders, his talents would introduce him into the first circles, and lead to ultimate promotion in his profession.

I have before said that Dr. Albany did not travel like a gentleman; nor were his every-day clothes at all indicative of a well-filled purse. Therefore, though he was a physician, and a man of pleasing manners, Musgrave's fine lady wife, and her *tonnish* daughters, could have readily excused him, if he had not persuaded their unexpected guest to stay a week with them; and, with a frowning brow, they saw the portmanteau, which the *strange person* had brought himself, carried into the best chamber.

But oh! the astonishment and the comical grimaces with which Marmaduke Musgrave, on his coming in from fishing, beheld the new guest! Welcome smiled on one side of his face, but scorn sneered on the other; and when Albany retired to dress, he declared that the only thing which consoled him for finding such a person forced on them, was the consciousness that he could extract great fun out of the old quiz, and serve him up for the entertainment of himself and friends.

To this amiable exhibition, the mother and daughters looked forward with great satisfaction; while his father, having vainly talked of the dues of hospitality, gave in, knowing that it was in vain to contend; comforting himself with the hope that, while Marmaduke was quizzing his guest, he must necessarily leave him alone.

In the meanwhile, how different were the cogitations and the plans of the benevolent Albany! He had a long *tête-à-tête* walk with Musgrave, which had convinced him that his old friend was not happy, owing, he suspected, to his narrow income and expensive family.

Then his son was going to college; a dangerous and ruinous place; and, while the good old man was dressing for dinner, he had laid plans of action which made him feel more deeply thankful than ever for the wealth so unexpectedly bestowed on him. Of this wealth, he had as yet said nothing to Musgrave. He was not purse-proud; and when he heard his friend complain of his poverty, he shrunk from saying how rich he himself was. He had therefore simply said that he was enabled to retire from business; and when Musgrave saw his friend's independent, economical habits, as evinced by his mode of travelling, he concluded that he had only gained a small independence, sufficient for his slender wants.

To those to whom amusement is every thing, and who can enjoy fun, even when it is procured by the sacrifice of every benevolent feeling, that evening at the rectory, when the family party was increased by the arrival of some of the neighbours, would have been an *exquisite treat ;* for Marmaduke played off the unsuspicious old man to admiration; mimicked him even to his face, unperceived by him; and having found out that Albany had not only a passion for music, but unfortunately fancied he could sing himself, he urged his guest, by his flatteries, lies of SECOND-RATE MALIGNITY, to sing song after song, in order to make him expose himself for the entertainment of the company, and give him an opportunity of perfecting his mimickry.

Blind, infatuated, contemptible boy! short-sighted trifler on the path of the world! Marmaduke Musgrave saw not that the very persons who seemed to idolize his pernicious talent must, unless they were lost to all sense of moral feeling, despise and distrust the youth who could play on the weakness of an unoffending, artless old man, and violate the rights of hospitality to his father's friend.

But Marmaduke had no heart, and but little mind; for mimickry is the lowest of the talents; and to be even a successful quizzer requires no talent at all. But his father had once a heart, though cares and pecuniary embarrassments had choked it up, and substituted selfishness for sensibility; the sight of his early companion had called some of the latter quality into action; and he seriously expostulated with his son on his daring to turn so respectable a man into ridicule. But Marmaduke answered him by insolent disregard; and when he also said, "if your friend be so silly as to sing, that is, do what he *cannot* do, am I not justified in laughing at him?" Musgrave assented to the proposition. He might, however, have replied, "but you are not justified in lying, in order to urge him on, nor in saying to him ' you can sing,' when you know he *cannot*. If he be *weak*, it is not necessary that you should be *treacherous*." But Musgrave always came off halting from a combat with his undutiful son; he therefore sighed, ceased, and turned away. On one point Marmaduke was right; when vanity prompts us to do what we cannot do well, while conceit leads us to fancy that our efforts are successful, we are perhaps fit objects for ridicule. A consideration which holds up to us this important lesson; namely, that our *own weakness* alone can, for any length of time, make us victims of the satire and malignity of others.

When Albany's visit to Musgrave was drawing near to its conclusion, he was very desirous of being asked to prolong it, as he had become attached to his friend's children, from living with them, and witnessing their various accomplishments, and was completely the dupe of Marmaduke's treacherous compliments. He was therefore glad when he, as well as the Musgraves, was invited to dine at a house in the neighbourhood, on the very day intended for his departure. This circumstance led them all, with one accord, to say that he must remain at least a day longer, while Marmaduke exclaimed, "Go you shall not! Our friends would be so disappointed, if they and their company did not hear you sing and act that sweet song about Chloe! and all the pleasure of the evening would be destroyed to me, dear sir, if you were not there!"

This was more than enough to make Albany put off his departure; and he accompanied the Musgrave's to the dinner party. They dined at an early hour; so early, that it was yet daylight, when, tea being over, the intended amusements of the afternoon began, of which the most prominent was to be the vocal powers of the mistaken Albany, who, without much pressing, after sundry flatteries from Marmaduke, cleared his throat, and began to sing and act the song of " Chloe." At first, he was hoarse, and stopped to apologize for want of voice; "Nonsense!" cried Marmaduke, "you were never in better voice in your life! Pray go on; you are only nervous!" while the side of his face *not* next to Albany was distorted with laughter and ridicule, Albany, believing him, continued his song; and Marmaduke, sitting a little behind him, took off the distorted expression of his countenance, and mimicked his odd action. But, at this moment, the broadest splendour of the setting sun threw its beams into a large pier glass opposite, with such brightness, that Albany's eyes were suddenly attracted to it, and thence to his treacherous neighbour, whom he detected in the act of mimicking him in mouth, attitude, and expression—while behind him he saw some of the company laughing with a degree of violence which was all but audible!

Albany paused, in speechless consternation —and when Marmaduke asked why " he did not go on, as every one was delighted," the susceptible old man hid his face in his hands, shocked, mortified, and miserable, but taught and enlightened. Marmaduke however, nothing doubting, presumed to clap him on the back, again urging him to proceed; but the indignant Albany, turning suddenly round, and throwing off his arm with angry vehemence, exclaimed, in the touching tone of wounded feeling, "Oh! thou serpent, that I would have cherished in my bosom, was it for thee to sting me thus? But I was an old fool; and the lesson, though a painful one, will, I trust, be salutary."

"What is all this? what do you mean?" faltered out Marmaduke; but the rest of the party had not courage enough to speak; and many of them rejoiced in the detection of baseness which, though it amused their depraved taste, was very offensive to their moral sense.

"What does it mean?" cried Albany, "I appeal to all present, whether they do not understand my meaning, and whether my resentment be not just!"

"I hope, my dear friend, that you acquit *me*," said the distressed father.

"Of all," he replied, "except of the fault of not having taught your son better morals and manners. Young man!" he continued, "the next time you exhibit any one as your butt, take care that you do not sit opposite a pier-glass. And now, sir," addressing himself to the master of the house, "let me request to have a post-chaise sent for to the nearest town directly."

"Surely, you will not leave us, and in anger," cried all the Musgraves, Marmaduke excepted.

"I hope I do not go in anger, but I cannot stay," cried he, "because I have lost my confidence in you."

The gentleman of the house, who thought

Albany right in going, and wished to make him all the amends he could, for having allowed Marmaduke to turn him into ridicule, interrupted him, to say that his own carriage waited his orders, and would convey him whithersoever he wished.

"I thank you, sir, and accept your offer," he replied, "since the sooner I quit this company, in which I have so lamentably exposed myself, the better it will be for you, and for us all."

Having said this, he took the agitated Musgrave by the hand, bowed to his wife and daughters, who hid their confusion under distant and haughty airs; *then*, stepping opposite to Marmaduke, who felt it difficult to meet the expression of that eye, on which just anger and a sense of injury had bestowed a power hitherto unknown to it, he addressed him thus; "Before we part, I must tell you, young man, that I intended, urged, I humbly trust, by virtuous considerations, to expend on your maintenance at college a part of that large income which I cannot spend on myself. I had also given orders to my agent to purchase for me the advowson of a living now on sale, intending to give it to you; here is the letter, to prove that I speak the truth; but I need not tell you that I cannot make the fortune, which was left me by a pious friend, assist a youth to take on himself the sacred profession of a christian minister, who can utter falsehoods, in order to betray a fellow-creature into folly, utterly regardless of that christian precept, 'Do unto others as ye would that others should do unto you.'"

He then took leave of the rest of the company, and drove off, leaving the Musgraves chagrined and ashamed, and bitterly mortified at the loss of the intended patronage to Marmaduke, especially when a gentleman present exclaimed, "No doubt, this is the Dr. Albany, to whom Clewes of Trinity left his large fortune!"

Albany, taught by his misadventure in this worldly and treacherous family, went, soon after, to the abode of another of his college friends, residing near Cheltenham. He expected to find this gentleman and family in unclouded prosperity; but they were labouring under unexpected adversity, brought on them by the villany of others; he found them, however, bowed in lowly resignation before the inscrutable decree. On the pious son of these reduced, but contented parents, he, in due time, bestowed the living intended for the treacherous Marmaduke. Under their roof he experienced gratitude which he felt to be sincere, and affection in which he dared to confide; and, ultimately, he took up his abode with them, in a residence suited to their early prospects and his riches; for even the artless and unsuspecting can, without danger, associate and sojourn with those whose thoughts and actions are under the guidance of religious principle, and who live in this world as if they every hour expected to be summoned away to the judgment of a world to come.

CHAPTER X.

LIES OF BENEVOLENCE.

In a former chapter I commented on those lies which are, at best, of a mixed nature, and are made up of worldly motives, of which fear and selfishness compose the principal part, although the utterer of them considers them as LIES OF BENEVOLENCE.

Lies of real benevolence are, like most other falsehoods, various in their species and degrees; but, as they are, however, in fact objectionable, the most amiable and respectable of all lies, and seem so like virtue that they may easily be taken for her children; and as the illustrations of them, which I have been enabled to give, are so much more connected with our tenderest and most solemn feelings, than those afforded by other lies; I thought it right that, like the principal figures in a procession, they should bring up the rear.

The lies which relations and friends generally think it their duty to tell an unconsciously dying person, are prompted by real benevolence, as are those which medical men deem themselves justified in uttering to a dying patient; though, if the person dying, or the surrounding friends, be strictly religious characters, they must be, on principle, desirous that the whole truth should be told.*

---

* Richard Pearson, the distinguished author of the Life of William Hey of Leeds, says, in that interesting book, p. 261, "Mr. Hey's sacred respect for truth, and his regard for the welfare of his fellow-creatures, never permitted him intentionally to deceive his patients by flattering representations of their state of health, by assurances of the existence of no danger, when he conceived their situation to be hopeless, or even greatly hazardous. "The duty of a medical attendant," continues he. "in such delicate situations, has been a subject of considerable embarrassment to men of integrity and conscience, who view the uttering of a falsehood as a crime, and the practice of deceit as repugnant to the spirit of christianity. That a sacrifice of truth may sometimes contribute to the comfort of a patient, and be medically beneficial, is not denied; but that a wilful and deliberate falsehood can, in any case, be justifiable before God, is a maxim not to be lightly admitted. The question may be stated thus; Is it justifiable for a man deliberately to violate a moral precept of the law of God, *from a motive of prudence and humanity?* If this be *affirmed*, it must be admitted that it would be no less justifiable to infringe the laws of his country from similar motives; and, consequently, it would be an act of injustice to punish him for such a transgression. But, will it be contended, that the divine, or even the human legislator, must be subjected to the control of this sort of casuistry? If falsehood, under these circumstances, be no crime,

Methinks I hear some of my readers exclaim, can any one suppose it a duty to run the risk of killing friends or relations, by telling the whole truth; that is, informing them that they are dying! But if the patient be not really dying, or in danger, no risk is incurred; and if they be near death, which is it of most importance to consider,—their momentary quiet here, or their interests hereafter? Besides, many of those persons who would think that for spiritual reasons merely, a disclosure of the truth was improper, and who declare that, on *such occasions*, falsehood is *virtue*, and concealment, humanity, would hold a different language, and act differently, were the unconsciously dying person one who was known not *to have made a will*, and who had *considerable property to dispose of*. Then, consideration for their own temporal interests, or for those of others, would probably make them advise

---

then, as no detriment can result from uttering it, very little merit can be attached to so light a sacrifice; whereas, if it were presumed that some guilt were incurred, and that the physician voluntarily exposed himself to the danger of future suffering, for the sake of procuring temporary benefit to his patient, he would have a high claim upon the gratitude of those who derived the advantage. But, is it quite clear that pure benevolence commonly suggests the deviation from truth, and that neither the low consideration of conciliating favour, nor the view of escaping censure, and promoting his own interest, have any share in prompting him to adopt the measure he defends? To assist in this inquiry, let a man ask himself whether he carries this caution and shows this kindness, indiscriminately on all occasions; being as fearful of giving pain, by exciting apprehension in the mind of the poor, as of the rich; of the meanest as of the most elevated rank. Suppose it can be shown that these humane falsehoods are distributed promiscuously, it may be inquired further, whether, if such a proceeding were a manifest breach of a municipal law, exposing the delinquent to suffer a very inconvenient and serious punishment, a medical adviser would feel himself obliged to expose his person or his estate to penal consequences, whenever the circumstances of his patient should seem to require the intervention of a falsehood. It may be presumed without any breach of charity, that a demur would frequently, perhaps generally, be interposed on the occasion of such a requisition. But, surely, the laws of the Moral Governor of the universe are not to be esteemed less sacred, and a transgression of them less important in its consequences, than the violation of a civil statute; nor ought the fear of God to be less powerful in deterring men from the committing of a crime, than the fear of a magistrate. Those who contend for the necessity of violating truth, that they may benefit their patients, place themselves between two conflicting rules of morality; their obligation to obey the command of God, and their presumed duty to their neighbour; or in other words, they are supposed to be brought by the Divine Providence into this distressing alternative of necessarily sinning against God or their fellow-creatures. When a moral and a positive duty stand opposed to each other, the Holy Scriptures have determined that obedience to the former is to be preserved, before compliance with the latter."

---

or adopt a contrary proceeding. Yet, who that seriously reflects can, for a moment, put worldly interests in any comparison with those of a spiritual nature? But perhaps, an undue preference of worldly over spiritual interests might not be the leading motive to tell truth in the one case, and withhold it in the other. The persons in question would probably be influenced by the conviction satisfactory to them, but awful and erroneous in my apprehension, that a death-bed repentance, and a death-bed supplication, must be wholly unavailing for the soul of the departing; that, as the sufferer's work for himself is wholly done, and his fate fixed for time, and for eternity, it were needless cruelty to let him know his end was approaching; but that, as his work for *others* is not done, if he has not made a testamentary disposal of his property, it is a duty to urge him to make a will, even at all risk to himself.

My own opinion, which I give with great humility, is, that the truth is never to be violated or withheld, in order to deceive; but I know myself to be in such a painful minority on this subject, that I almost doubt the correctness of my own judgment.

I am inclined to think that lies of Benevolence are more frequently passive, than active —are more frequently instanced in withholding and concealing the truth, than in direct spontaneous lying. There is one instance of withholding and concealing the truth from motives of mistaken benevolence, which is so common, and so pernicious, that I feel it particularly necessary to hold it up to severe reprehension. It is withholding or speaking only half the truth in giving the character of a servant.

Many persons, from reluctance to injure the interests even of very unworthy servants, never give the whole character unless it be required of them, and then, rather than tell a positive lie, they disclose the whole truth. But are they not lying, that is, are they not meaning to *deceive*, when they *withhold* the truth?

When I speak to ladies and gentlemen respecting the character of a servant, I of course conclude that I am speaking to honourable persons. I therefore expect that they should give me a correct character of the domestic in question; and should I omit to ask whether he, or she, be honest, or sober, I require that information on those points should be given me unreservedly. They must leave me to judge whether I will run the risk of hiring a drunkard, a thief, or a servant otherwise ill-disposed; but they would be dishonourable if they betrayed me into receiving into my family, to the risk of my domestic peace, or my property, those who are addicted to dishonest practices, or otherwise of immoral habits. Besides, what an erroneous and bounded benevolence this conduct exhibits! If it be bene-

MISTAKEN KINDNESS.

volence towards the servant whom I hire, it is *malevolent* towards *me*, and unjust also. True christian kindness is just and impartial in its dealings, and never serves even a friend at the expense of a third person. But, the masters and mistresses, who thus do what they call a benevolent action at the sacrifice of truth and integrity, often, no doubt, find their sin visited on their own heads; for they are not likely to have trustworthy servants. If servants know that, owing to the sinful kindness and lax morality of their employers, their faults will not receive their proper punishment —that of disclosure—when they are turned away, one of the most powerful motives to behave well is removed; for those are not likely to abstain from sin, who are sure that they shall sin with impunity. Thus then, the master or mistress who, in mistaken kindness, conceals the fault of a single servant, leads the rest of the household into the temptation of sinning also; and what is fancied to be benevolent to one, becomes, in its consequences, injurious to many. But, let us now see what is the probable effect on the servants so screened and befriended? They are instantly exposed, by this withholding of the truth, to the peril of temptation. Nothing, perhaps, can be more beneficial to culprits, of all descriptions, than to be allowed to take the *immediate* consequences of their offences, provided those consequences stop short of death, that most awful of punishments, because it cuts the offender off from all means of amendment; therefore it were better for the interest of servants, in every point of view, to let them abide by the certainty of not getting a new place, because they cannot have a character from their last; by this means the humane wish to punish, in order to *save*, would be gratified, and consequently, if the truth was always told on occasions of this nature, the feelings of REAL BENEVOLENCE would, in the end, be gratified. But, if good characters are given to servants, or incomplete characters, that is, if their good qualities are mentioned, and their bad withheld, the consequences to the beings so mistakenly befriended may be of the most fatal nature; for, if *ignorant* of their besetting sin, the heads of the family cannot guard against it, but, unconsciously, may every hour put temptations in their way; while, on the contrary, had they been made acquainted with that besetting sin, they would have taken care never to have risked its being called into action.

But who, it may be asked, would hire servants, knowing that they had any "besetting sins?"

I trust there are many who would do this from the pious and benevolent motive of saving them from further destruction, especially if penitence had been satisfactorily manifested.

I will now endeavour to illustrate some of my positions by the following story.

MISTAKEN KINDNESS.

ANN BELSON had lived in a respectable merchant's family, of the name of Melbourne, for many years, and had acquitted herself to the satisfaction of her employers in successive capacities of nurse, house-maid, and lady's maid. But it was at length discovered that she had long been addicted to petty pilfering; and, being emboldened by past impunity, she purloined some valuable lace, and was detected; but her kind master and mistress could not prevail on themselves to give up the tender nurse of their children to the just rigour of the law, and as their children themselves could not bear to have "poor Ann sent to gaol," they resolved to punish her in no other manner, than by turning her away *without a character*, as the common phrase is. But without a character she could not procure another service, and might be thus consigned to misery and ruin. This idea was insupportable! However she might deserve punishment, they shrunk from inflicting it! and they resolved to keep Ann Belson themselves, as they could not recommend her conscientiously to any one else. This was a truly benevolent action; because, if she continued to sin, they alone were exposed to suffer from her fault. But they virtuously resolved to put no further temptation in her way, and to guard her against herself by unremitting vigilance.

During the four succeeding years, Ann Belson's honesty was so entirely without a stain, that her benevolent friends were convinced that her penitence was sincere, and congratulated themselves that they had treated her with such lenity.

At this period the pressure of the times, and losses in trade, produced a change in the circumstances of the Melbournes; and retrenchment became necessary. They therefore felt it right to discharge some of their servants, and particularly the lady's maid.

The grateful Ann would not hear of this dismissal, she insisted on remaining on any terms, and in any situation; nay, she declared her willingness to live with her indulgent friends for nothing; but, as they were too generous to accept her services at so great a disadvantage to herself, especially as she had poor relations to maintain, they resolved to procure her a situation; and having heard of a very advantageous one, for which she was admirably calculated, they insisted on her trying to procure it.

"But what shall we do, my dear," said the wife to her husband, "concerning Ann's character? Must we tell the whole truth? As she has been uniformly honest during the last four years, should we not be justified in concealing her fault?"

"Yes; I think, at least I hope so," replied he. "Still, as she was dishonest more years

VOL. III.——39   3 H

than she has now been honest, I really . . . . I . . . . it is a very puzzling question, Charlotte; and I am but a weak casuist."

A strong christian might not have felt the point so difficult. But the Melbournes had not studied serious things deeply; and the result of the consultation was, that Ann Belson's past faults should be concealed, if possible.

And possible it was. Lady Baryton, the young and noble bride who wished to hire her, was a thoughtless, careless, woman of fashion; and as she learned that Ann could make dresses, and dress hair to admiration, she made few other inquiries; and Ann was installed in her new place.

It was, alas! the most improper of places, even for a sincere penitent, like Ann Belson; for it was a place of the most dangerous trust. Jewels, laces, ornaments of all kinds, were not only continually exposed to her eyes, but placed under her especial care. Not those alone. When her lady returned home from a run of good luck at loo, a reticule, containing bank-notes and sovereigns, was emptied into an unlocked drawer; and Ann was told how fortunate her lady had been. The first time that this heedless woman acted thus, the poor Ann begged she would lock up her money. "Not I; it is too much trouble; and why should I?"

"Because, my lady, it is not right to leave money about; it may be stolen."

"Nonsense! who should steal it? I know you must be honest; the Melbournes gave you such a high character."

Here Ann turned away in agony and confusion.

"But, my lady, the other servants," she resumed in a faint voice.

"Pray, what business have the other servants at my drawers? However, do you lock up the drawer, and keep the key."

"No; keep it *yourself*, my lady."

"What, I go about with keys, like a housekeeper? Take it, I say!"

Then flinging the key down, she went singing out of the room, little thinking to what peril, temporal and spiritual, she was exposing a hapless fellow-creature.

For some minutes after this *new danger* had opened upon her, Ann sat leaning on her hands, absorbed in painful meditation, and communing seriously with her own heart; nay, she even prayed for a few moments to be delivered from evil; but the next minute she was ashamed of her own self-distrust, and tried to resume her business with her usual alacrity.

A few evenings afterwards, her lady brought her reticule home, and gave it to Ann, filled as before.

"I conclude, my lady, you know how much money is in this purse."

"I did know; but I have forgotten."

"Then let me tell it."

"No, no; nonsense!" she replied as she left the room; "lock it up, and then it will be safe, you know, as I can trust you."

Ann sighed deeply, but repeated within herself, "Yes, yes; I am certainly now to be trusted;" but, as she said this, she saw two sovereigns on the carpet, which she had dropped out of the reticule in emptying it, and had locked the drawer without perceiving. Ann felt fluttered when she discovered them; but, taking them up, resolutely felt for the key to add them to the others;—but the image of her recently widowed sister, and her large destitute family, rose before her, and she thought she would *not return* them, but ask her lady to give them to the poor widow. But then, her lady had already been very bountiful to her, and she would not ask her; however, she would consider the matter, and it seemed as if it was *intended* she should have the sovereigns; for they were separated from the rest, *as if for her*. Alas! it would have been safer for her to believe that they were left there as a *snare* to try her penitence, and her faith; but she took a different view of it; she picked up the gold, then laid it down; and long and severe was the conflict in her heart between good and evil.

We weep over the woes of romance; we shed well-moved tears over the sorrows of real life; but where is the fiction, however highly wrought, and where the sorrows, however acute, that can deserve our pity and our sympathy so strongly, as the *agony* and conflicts of a *penitent*, yet *tempted* soul! Of a soul that has turned to virtue, but is as forcibly pulled back again to vice,—that knows its own danger, without power to hurry from it; till, fascinated by the glittering bait, as the bird by the rattlesnake, it yields to its fatal allurements, regardless of consequences! It was not without many a heartache, many a struggle, that Ann Belson gave way to the temptation, and put the gold in her pocket; and when she had done so, she was told her sister was ill, and had sent to beg she would come to her, late as it was. Accordingly, when her lady was in bed, she obtained leave to go to her, and while she relieved her sister's wants with the two purloined sovereigns, the poor thing almost fancied she had done a good action! Oh! never is sin so dangerous as when it has allured us in the shape of a deed of benevolence. It had so allured the Melbournes when they concealed Ann's faults from Lady Baryton; and its bitter fruits were only too fast preparing.

"*Ce n'est que le premier pas qui coute;*" says the proverb, or "the first step is the only difficult one." The next time her lady brought her winnings to her, Ann pursued a new plan; she insisted on telling the money over; but took care to make it less than it was, by two or three pounds. Not long after, she told Lady Baryton that she must have a new lock put on the drawer that held the money, as she had certainly dropped the key *somewhere;* and that, before she missed it, some one, she was sure, had been trying at the lock; for it was evidently hampered the last time she unlocked it.

"Well, then, get a new lock," replied her careless mistress; "however, let the drawer be forced now; and then we had better tell over the money."

The drawer was forced; they told the money; and even Lady Baryton was conscious that some of it was missing. But, the *missing key*, and *hampered lock*, exonerated Ann from suspicion; especially as Ann owned that she had *discovered* the loss before; and declared that, had not her lady insisted on telling over the money, she had intended to replace it gradually; because she felt herself responsible; while Lady Baryton, satisfied and deceived, recommended her to be on the watch for the thief, and soon forgot the whole circumstance.

Lady Baryton thought herself, and perhaps she was, a woman of feeling. She never read the Old-Bailey convictions without mourning over the prisoners condemned to death; and never read an account of an execution without shuddering. Still, from want of reflection, and a high-principled sense of what we owe to others, especially to those who are the members of our own household, she never for one moment troubled herself to remember that she was daily throwing temptations in the way of a servant to commit the very faults which led those convicts, whom she pitied, to the fate which she deplored. Alas! what have those persons to answer for, in every situation of life, who consider their dependants and servants merely as such, without remembering that they are, like themselves, heirs of the invisible world to come; and that, if they take no pains to enlighten their minds, in order to *save* their immortal souls, they should, at least, be careful never to *endanger* them.

In a few weeks after the dialogue given above, Lady Baryton bought some strings of pearls at an India sale; and having, on her way thence, shown them to her jeweller, that he might count them, and see if there were enough to make a pair of bracelets, she brought them home, because she could not yet afford proper clasps to fasten them; and these were committed to Ann's care. But, as Lord Baryton, the next week, gave his lady a pair of diamond clasps, she sent the pearls to be made up immediately. In the evening, however, the jeweller came to tell her that there were two strings less than when she brought them before.

"Then they must have been stolen!" she exclaimed; "and now I remember that Belson told me she was sure there was a thief in the house."

"Are you sure," said Lord Baryton, "that Belson is not the thief herself?"

"Impossible! I had such a character of her! and I have trusted her implicitly!"

"It is not right to tempt even the most honest," replied Lord Baryton; "but we must have strict search made; and all the servants must be examined."

They were so; but, as Ann Belson was not a hardened offender, she soon betrayed herself by her evident misery and terror; and was committed to prison on her own *full confession;* but she could not help exclaiming, in the agony of her heart, "Oh, my lady! remember that I conjured you not to trust me!" and Lady Baryton's heart reproached her, at least for *some hours.* There were other hearts also that experienced self-reproach, and of a far longer duration; for the Melbournes, when they heard what had happened, saw that the seeming benevolence of their concealment had been a real injury, and had ruined her whom they meant to save. They saw, that had they told Lady Baryton the truth, that lady would either not have hired her, in spite of her skill, or she would have taken care not to put her in situations calculated to tempt her cupidity. But, neither Lady Baryton's regrets, nor self-reproach, nor the greater agonies of the *Melbournes*, could alter or avert the course of justice;—and Ann Belson was condemned to death. She was, however, strongly recommended to mercy, both by the jury and the noble prosecutor; and her conduct in prison was so exemplary, so indicative of the deep contrition of a trembling, humble Christian, that, at length, the intercession was not in vain; and the Melbournes had the comfort of carrying to her, what was to them at least, joyful news; namely, that her sentence was commuted for transportation.

Yet, even this mercy was a severe trial to the self-judged Melbournes; since they had the misery of seeing the affectionate nurse of their children, the being endeared to them by many years of active services, torn from all the tender ties of existence, and exiled for life as a felon to a distant land! exiled too, for a crime which, had they performed their SOCIAL DUTY, she might never have committed. But the pain of mind which they endured on this lamentable occasion was not thrown away on them; as it awakened them to serious reflection; they learned to remember, and to teach their children to remember, the holy command, "that we are not to do evil, that good may come;" and that no deviation from truth and ingenuousness can be justified, even if it claims for itself the plausible title of the active or *passive* LIE OF BENEVOLENCE.

There is another species of withholding the truth, which springs from so amiable a source, and is so often practised even by pious Christians, that, while I venture to say it is at variance with reliance on the wisdom and mercy of the Creator, I do so with reluctant awe. I mean a *concealment* of the whole extent of a calamity from the person afflicted, lest the blow should fall too heavily upon them.

I would ask, whether such conduct be not inconsistent with the belief that trials are *mercies* in disguise? that the Almighty "loveth those whom he chasteneth, and scourgeth every son that he receiveth?"

If this assurance be true, we set our own judgment against that of the Deity, by concealing from the sufferer the extent of the trial inflicted; and seem to believe ourselves more capable than he is to determine the quantity of suffering that is good for the person so visited; and we set up our *finite* against *infinite* wisdom.

There are other reasons, besides religious ones, why this sort of deceit should no more be practised than any other.

The motive for withholding the whole truth, on these occasions, is *to do good;* but will the desired good be effected by this opposition to the Creator's revealed will towards the sufferer? Is it certain that good will be performed at all, or that concealment is necessary?

What is the reason given for concealing half the truth? Fear lest the whole would be more than the sufferer could bear; which implies that it is already mighty, to an awful degree. Then, surely, a degree more of suffering, at such a moment, cannot possess much added power to destroy; and if the trial be allowed to come in its full force, the mind of the victim will make exactly the same efforts as minds always do when oppressed by misery. A state of heavy affliction is so repulsive to the feelings, that even in the first paroxysms of it we all make efforts to get away from under its weight; and, in proof of this assertion, I ask, whether we do not always find the afflicted less cast down than we expected? The religious pray as well as weep; the merely moral look around for consolation here, and, as a dog, when cast into the sea, as soon as he rises and regains his breath, strikes out his feet, in order to float securely upon the waves; so, be their sorrows great or small, all persons instantly strive to find support somewhere; and they do find it, while, in proportion to the depth of the affliction, is often the subsequent rebound.

I could point out instances (but I shall leave my readers to imagine them) in which, by concealing from bereaved sufferers the most affecting part of the truth, we stand between them and the balm derived from that very incident which was mercifully intended to heal their wounds.

I also object to such concealment; because it entails upon those who are guilty of it, a series of falsehoods; falsehoods too, which are often fruitlessly uttered; since the object of them is apt to suspect deceit, and endure that restless, agonizing suspicion, which those who have ever experienced it could never inflict on the objects of their love. Besides, religion and reason enable us, in time, to bear the calamity of which we *know* the extent; but we are always on the watch to find out that which we only *suspect*, and the mind's strength, frittered away in vain and varied conjectures, runs the risk of sinking beneath the force of its own indistinct fears.

Confidence, too, in those dear friends whom we trusted before, is liable to be entirely destroyed; and in *all* its bearings, this well-*intentioned* departure from the truth is pregnant with mischief.

Lastly, I object to such concealment, from a conviction that its continuance is IMPOSSIBLE; for, some time or other, the whole truth is revealed at a moment when the sufferers are not so well able to bear it, as they were in the first paroxysms of grief.

In this, my next and last tale, I give another illustration of those amiable, but pernicious lies, the LIES OF REAL BENEVOLENCE.

THE FATHER AND SON.

"WELL, then, thou art willing that Edgar should go to a public school?" said the vicar of a small parish in Westmoreland to his weeping wife.

"Quite willing."

"And yet thou art in tears, Susan?"

"I weep for his faults; and not because he is to quit us. I grieve to think he is so disobedient and unruly, that we can manage him at home no longer. And yet I loved him so dearly! so much more than—" Here her sobs redoubled; and, as Vernon rested her aching head on his bosom, he said, in a low voice,

"Ay; and so did I love him, even better than our other children; and therefore, probably, our injustice is thus visited. But, he is so clever! He learned more Latin in one week than his brothers in a month!"

"And he is so *beautiful!*" observed his mother.

"And so generous!" rejoined his father; "but cheer up, my beloved; under stricter discipline than ours, he may yet do well, and turn out all we could wish."

"I hope, however," replied the fond mother, "that his master will not be very severe; and I will try to look forward." As she said this, she left her husband with something like comfort; for a tender mother's hopes for a darling child are easily revived, and she went, with recovered calmness, to get her son's wardrobe ready against the day of his departure. The equally affectionate father, meanwhile, called his son into the study, to prepare his mind for that parting which his undutiful conduct had made unavoidable.

But Vernon found that Edgar's mind required no preparation; that the idea of change was delightful to his volatile nature; and that he panted to distinguish himself on a wider field of action, than a small retired village afforded to his daring, restless spirit; while his father saw with agony, which he could but ill conceal, that this desire of entering into a new situation, had power to annihilate all regret at leaving the tenderest of parents, and the companions of his childhood.

However, his feelings were a little soothed when the parting hour arrived; for then the heart of Edgar was so melted within him at the sight of his mother's tears, and his father's agony, that he uttered words of tender contrition, such as they had never heard from him before; the recollection of which spoke comfort to their minds when they beheld him no longer.

But short were the hopes which that parting hour had excited. In a few months the master of the school wrote to complain of the insubordination of his new pupil. In his next letter he declared that he should be under the necessity of expelling him; and Edgar had not been at school six months, before he prevented the threatened expulsion, only by running away, no one knew whither! Nor was he heard of by his family for four years; during which time not even the dutiful affection of their other sons, nor their success in life, had power to heal the breaking heart of the mother, nor cheer the depressed spirits of the father. At length the prodigal returned, ill, meagre, penniless, and penitent; and was received, and forgiven.

"But where hast thou been, my child, this long, long time?" said his mother, tenderly weeping, as she gazed on his pale sunk cheek.

"Ask me no questions! I am here; that is enough;" Edgar Vernon replied, shuddering as he spake.

"It *is* enough!" cried his mother, throwing herself on his neck! "For this my son was dead, and is alive again; was lost, and found!"

But the father felt and thought differently; he knew that it was his duty to interrogate his son; and he resolved to insist on knowing where and how those long four years had been passed. He, however, delayed his questions till Edgar's health was re-established, but when that time arrived, he told him that he expected to know all that had befallen him since he ran away from school.

"Spare me till to-morrow," said Edgar Vernon, "and then you shall know all."

His father acquiesced; but the next morning Edgar had disappeared, leaving the following letter behind him:—

"I cannot, dare not, tell you what a wretch I have been! though I own your right to demand such a confession from me. Therefore, I must become a wanderer again! Pray for me, dearest and tenderest of mothers! Pray for me, best of fathers and of men! I dare not pray for myself, for I am a vile and wretched sinner, though your grateful and affectionate son, E. V."

Though this letter nearly drove the mother to distraction, it contained for the father a degree of soothing comfort. She dwelt only on the conviction which it held out to her, that she should probably never behold her son again; but *he* dwelt with pious thankfulness on the sense of his guilt expressed by the unhappy writer; trusting that the sinner who knows and owns himself to be "vile" may, when it is least expected of him, repent and amend.

How had those four years been passed by Edgar Vernon? That important period of a boy's life, the years from fourteen to eighteen? Suffice it that, under a feigned name, in order that he might not be traced, he had entered on board a merchant-ship; that he had left after he had made one voyage; that he was taken into the service of what is called a *sporting character*, whom he had met on board ship, who saw that Edgar had talents and spirit which he might render serviceable to his own pursuits. This man, finding he was the son of a gentleman, treated him as such, and initiated him gradually into the various arts of gambling, and the vices of the metropolis; but one night they were both surprised by the officers of justice at a noted gaming-house; and, after a desperate scuffle, Edgar escaped wounded, and nearly killed, to a house in the suburbs. There he remained till he was safe from pursuit, and then, believing himself in danger of dying, he longed for the comfort of his paternal roof; he also longed for paternal forgiveness; and the prodigal returned to his forgiving parents.

But, as this was a tale which Edgar might well shrink from relating to a pure and pious father, flight was far easier than such a confession. Still, "so deceitful is the human heart, and desperately wicked," that I believe Edward was beginning to feel the monotony of his life at home, and therefore was glad of an excuse to justify to himself his desire to escape into scenes more congenial to his habits and, now, perverted nature. His father, however, continued to hope for his reformation, and was therefore little prepared for the next intelligence of his son, which reached him through a private channel. A friend wrote to inform him that Edgar was taken up for having passed forged notes, knowing them to be forgeries; that he would soon be fully committed to prison for trial; and would be tried with his accomplices at the ensuing assizes for Middlesex.

At first, even the firmness of Vernon yielded to the stroke, and he was bowed low unto the earth. But the confiding christian struggled against the sorrows of the suffering father, and overcame them; till, at last, he was able to exclaim, "I will go to him! I will be near him at his trial! I will be near him even at his death, if death be his portion! And no doubt, I shall be permitted to awaken him to a sense of his guilt. Yes, I may be permitted to see him expire contrite before God and man, and calling on his name who is able to save to the uttermost!"

But, just as he was setting off for Middlesex, his wife, who had long been declining, was, to all appearance, so much worse, that he could not leave her. She having had suspicions that all was not right with Edgar, contrived to discover the TRUTH, which had been *kindly*, but erroneously concealed from her, and had sunk under the sudden *unmitigated* blow; and the welcome intelligence, that the *prosecutor had withdrawn the charge*, came at a moment when the sorrows of the bereaved husband had closed the father's heart against the voice of gladness.

"This news came too late to save the poor victim!" he exclaimed, as he knelt beside the corpse of her whom he had loved so long and so tenderly; "and I feel that I cannot, cannot *yet* rejoice in it as I ought." But he soon repented of this ungrateful return to the mercy of Heaven; and, even before the body was consigned to the grave, he thankfully acknowledged that the liberation of his son was a ray amidst the gloom that surrounded him.

Meanwhile, Edgar Vernon, when unexpectedly liberated from what he knew to be certain danger to his life, resolved, on the ground of having been falsely taken up, and as an innocent injured man, to visit his parents; for he had heard of his mother's illness, and his heart yearned to behold her once more. But it was only in the dark hour that he dared venture to approach his home; and it was his intention to discover himself at first to his mother only.

Accordingly, the grey parsonage was scarcely visible in the shadows of twilight, when he reached the gate that led to the back door; at which he gently knocked, but in vain. No one answered his knock; all was still within and around. What could this mean? He then walked round the house, and looked in at the window; all there was dark and quiet as the grave; but the church-bell was tolling, while alarmed, awed, and overpowered, he leaned against the gate. At this moment he saw two men rapidly pass along the road, saying, " I fear we shall be too late for the funeral! I wonder how the poor old man will bear it! for he loved his wife dearly!"

"Ay; and so he did that wicked boy who has been the death of her;" replied the other.

These words shot like an arrow through the not yet callous heart of Edgar Vernon, and throwing himself on the ground, he groaned aloud in his agony; but the next minute, with the speed of desperation, he ran towards the church, and reached it just as the service was over, the mourners departing, and as his father was borne away, nearly insensible, on the arms of his *virtuous* sons.

At such a moment Edgar was able to enter the church unheeded; for all eyes were on his afflicted parent, and the self-convicted culprit dared not force himself, at a time like that, on the notice of the father whom he had so grievously injured. But his poor bursting heart felt that it must vent his agony, or break; and, ere the coffin was lowered into the vault, he rushed forward, and throwing himself across it, called upon his mother's name, in an accent so piteous and appalling, that the assistants, though they did not recognise him at first, were unable to drive him away; so awed, so affected, were they by the agony which they witnessed.

At length he rose up and endeavoured to speak, but in vain; then, holding his clenched fists to his forehead, he screamed out, " Heaven preserve my senses!" and rushed from the church with all the speed of desperation. But whither should he turn those desperate steps! He longed, earnestly longed, to go and humble himself before his father, and implore that pardon for which his agonized soul pined. But, alas! earthly pride forbade him to indulge the salutary feeling; for he knew his worthy, unoffending brothers were in the house, and he could not endure the mortification of encountering those whose virtues must be put in comparison with his vices. He therefore cast one long lingering look at the abode of his childhood, and fled for ever from the house of mourning, humiliation, and safety.

In a few days, however, he wrote to his father, detailing his reasons for visiting home, and all the agonies which he had experienced during his short stay. Full of consolation was this letter to that bereaved and mourning heart! for to him it seemed the language of contrition; and he lamented that his beloved wife was not alive, to share in the hope which it gave him. " Would that he had come, or would *now* come to me!" he exclaimed; but the letter had no date; and he knew not whither to send an invitation. But *where* was he, and *what* was he, at that period? In gambling-houses, at cock-fights, sparring-matches, fairs; and in every scene where profligacy prevailed the most; while at all these places he had a pre-eminence in skill which endeared these pursuits to him, and made his occasional contrition powerless to influence him to amendment of life. He therefore continued to disregard the warning voice within him; till at length it was no longer heeded.

One night, when on his way to Y——, where races were to succeed the assizes, which had just commenced, he stopped at an inn, to refresh his horse; and, being hot with riding, and depressed by some recent losses at play, he drank very freely of the spirits which he had ordered. At this moment he saw a schoolfellow of his in the bar, who, like himself, was on his way to Y——. This young man was of a coarse, unfeeling nature; and, having had a fortune left him, was full of the consequence of newly-acquired wealth.

Therefore, when Edgar Vernon impulsively approached him, and, putting his hand out, asked how he did, Dunham haughtily drew back, put his hands behind him, and, in the hearing of several persons, replied, "I do not know you, sir!"

"Not *know* me, Dunham?" cried Edgar Vernon, turning very pale.

"That is to say, I do not *choose* to know you."

"And why not?" cried Edgar, seizing his arm, and with a look of menace.

"Because ..... because ..... I do not choose to know a man who murdered his mother."

"Murdered his mother!" cried the by-standers, holding up their hands, and regarding Edgar Vernon with a look of horror.

"Wretch!" cried he, seizing Dunham in his powerful grasp, "explain yourself this moment, or . . . ."

"Then take your fingers from my throat!" Edgar did so; and Dunham said, "I meant only that you broke your mother's heart by your ill conduct; and pray, was not that murdering her?"

While he was saying this, Edgar Vernon stood with folded arms, rolling his eyes wildly from one of the by-standers to the other; and seeing, as he believed, disgust towards him in the countenances of them all. When Dunham had finished speaking, Edgar Vernon wrung his hands in agony,—"True, most true, I am a murderer! I am a parricide!" Then, suddenly drinking off a large glass of brandy near him, he quitted the room, and, mounting his horse, rode off at full speed. Aim and object in view, he had *none*; he was only trying to ride from himself; trying to escape from those looks of horror and aversion which the remarks of Dunham had provoked. But what right had Dunham so to provoke him?

After he had put this question to himself, the image of Dunham, scornfully rejecting his offered hand, alone took possession of his remembrance, till he thirsted for revenge; and the irritation of the moment urged him to seek it immediately.

The opportunity, as he rightly suspected, was in his power; Dunham would soon be coming that way, on his road to Y——; and he would meet him. He did so; and, riding up to him, seized the bridle of his horse, exclaiming,

"You have called me a murderer, Dunham; and you were right; for, though I loved my mother dearly, and would have died for her, I killed her by my wicked course of life!"

"Well, well; I know *that*," replied Dunham, "so let me go! for I tell you, I do not like to be seen with such as you. Let me go, I say!"

He *did* let him go; but it was as the tiger lets go its prey, to spring on it again. A blow from Edgar's nervous arm knocked the rash insulter from his horse. In another minute, Dunham lay on the road a bleeding corpse; and the next morning officers were out in pursuit of the murderer. That wretched man was soon found, and soon secured. Indeed, he had not desired to *avoid* pursuit; but, when the irritation of drunkenness and revenge had subsided, the agony of remorse took possession of his soul; and he confessed his crime with tears of bitterest penitence. To be brief; Edgar Vernon was carried into that city as a manacled criminal, which he had expected to leave as a successful gambler; and, before the end of the assizes, he was condemned to death.

He made a full confession of his guilt before the judge pronounced condemnation; gave a brief statement of the provocation which he received from the deceased; blaming himself at the same time for his criminal revenge, in so heart-rending a manner, and lamenting so pathetically the disgrace and misery in which he had involved his father and family, that every heart was melted to compassion; and the judge wept, while he passed on him the awful sentence of the law.

His conduct in prison was so exemplary, that it proved he had not forgotten his father's precepts, though he had not acted upon them; and his brothers, for whom he sent, found him in a state of mind which afforded them the only and best consolation. This contrite, lowly state of mind accompanied him to the awful end of his existence; and it might be justly said of him, that "nothing in his life became him like the losing it."

Painful, indeed, was the anxiety of Edgar and his brothers, lest their father should learn this horrible circumstance; but as the culprit was arraigned under a feigned name, and as the crime, trial, and execution had taken, and would take up, so short a period of time, they flattered themselves that he would never learn how and where Edgar died; but would implicitly believe what was told him. They therefore wrote him word that Edgar had been taken ill at an inn, near London, on his road *home;* that he had sent for them; and they had hopes of his recovery. They followed this letter of BENEVOLENT LIES as soon as they could, to inform him that all was over.

This plan was wholly disapproved by a friend of the family, who, on principle, thought all concealment wrong; and, probably, useless too.

When the brothers drove to his house, on their way home, he said to them, "I found your father in a state of deep submission to the divine will, though grieved at the loss of a child, whom not even his errors could drive from his affections. I also found him consoled by those expressions of filial love and reliance on the merits of his Redeemer, which you transmitted to him from Edgar himself. Now, as the poor youth died penitent, and as his crime was palliated by great provocation, I conceive that it would not add much to your father's distress, were he to be informed of the truth. You know that, from a principle of obedience to the implied designs of Providence, I object to any concealment on such occasions, but on this, disclosure would certainly be a *safer*, as well as more *proper*, mode of proceeding; for, though he does not read newspapers, he may, one day, learn the fact as it is, and then the consequence may be fatal to life or reason. Remember how ill concealment answered in your poor mother's case." But he argued in vain. However, he obtained leave to go with them to their father, that he might judge of the possibility of making the disclosure which he advised.

They found the poor old man leaning his head upon an open Bible, as though he had been praying over it. The sight of his sons in mourning told the tale which he dreaded to hear; and, wringing their hands in silence, he left the room, but soon returned; and with surprising composure said, "Well; now I can bear to hear particulars." When they had told him all they chose to relate, he exclaimed, melting into tears, "Enough!—Oh, my dear sons and dear friend, it is a sad and grievous thing for a father to own; but I feel this sorrow to be a blessing! I had always feared that he would die a violent death, either by his own hand, or that of the executioner; (here the sons looked triumphantly at each other;) therefore his dying a penitent, and with humble christian reliance, is *such a relief to my mind!* Yes; I feared he might commit forgery, or even murder; and that would have been dreadful!"

"Dreadful, indeed!" faltered out both the brothers, bursting into tears; while Osborne, choked, and almost convinced, turned to the window. "Yet," added he, "even in that case, if he had died penitent, I trust that I could have borne the blow, and been able to believe the soul of my unhappy boy would find mercy!" Here Osborne eagerly turned round, and would have ventured to tell the truth; but was withheld by the frowns of his companions, and the truth *was not told*.

Edgar had not been dead above seven months, before a visible change took place in his father's spirits, and expression of countenance; for the constant dread of his child's coming to a terrible end had hitherto preyed on his mind, and rendered his appearance haggard; but now he looked, and *was* cheerful; therefore, his sons rejoiced, whenever they visited him, that they had not taken Osborne's advice.

"You are wrong," said he, "he would have been just as well, if he had known the manner of Edgar's death. It is not his *ignorance*, but the cessation of anxious suspense, that has thus renovated him. However, he may go in his ignorance to his grave; and I earnestly hope he will do so."

"Amen;" said one of his sons; "for his life is most precious to our children as well as to us. Our little boys are improving so fast under his tuition!"

The consciousness of recovering health, as a painful affection of the breast and heart had greatly subsided since the death of Edgar, made the good old man wish to visit, during the summer months, an old college friend who lived in Yorkshire; and he communicated his intentions to his sons. But they highly disapproved them, because, though Edgar's dreadful death was not likely to be revealed to him in the little village of R——, it might be disclosed to him by some one or other during a long journey.

However, as he was bent on going, they could not find a sufficient excuse for preventing it; but they took every precaution possible. They wrote to their father's intended host, desiring him to keep all papers and magazines for the last seven months out of his way; and when the day of his departure arrived, Osborne himself went to take a place for him; and took care it should be in that coach which did not stop at, or go through York, in order to obviate all possible chance of his hearing the murder discussed. But it so happened that a family, going from the town whence the coach started, wanted the whole of it; and, without leave, Vernon's place was transferred to the other coach, which went the very road Osborne disapproved.

"Well, well; it is the same thing to me;" said the good old man, when he was informed of the change; and he set off, full of pious thankfulness for the affectionate conduct and regrets of his parishioners at the moment of his departure, as they lined the road along which the coach was to pass, and expressed even clamorously their wishes for his return. The coach stopped at an inn outside the city of York; and as Vernon was not disposed to eat any dinner, he strolled along the road till he came to a small church, pleasantly situated, and entered the church-yard to read, as was his custom, the inscriptions on the tombstones. While thus engaged, he saw a man filling up a new-made grave, and entered into conversation with him. He found it was the sexton himself; and he drew from him several anecdotes of the persons interred around them.

During this conversation they had walked over the whole of the ground, when, just as they were going to leave the spot, the sexton stopped to pluck some weeds from a grave near the corner of it, and Vernon stopped also; taking hold, as he did so, of a small willow sapling, planted near the corner itself.

As the man rose from his occupation, and saw where Vernon stood, he smiled significantly and said,

"I planted that willow; and it is on a grave, though the grave is not marked out."

"Indeed!"

"Yes; it is the grave of a murderer."

"Of a murderer!" echoed Vernon, instinctively shuddering and moving away from it.

"Yes," resumed he, "of a murderer who was hanged at York. Poor lad! it was very right that he should be hanged; but he was not a hardened villain! and he died so penitent! and, as I knew him when he used to visit where I was groom, I could not help planting this tree for old acquaintance sake."

Here he drew his hand across his eyes.

"Then he was not a low-born man."

"Oh no; his father was a clergyman, I think."

"Indeed! poor man; was he living at the time?" said Vernon, deeply sighing.

"Oh yes; for his poor son did so fret, lest his father should ever know what he had done; for he said he was an angel upon earth; and he could not bear to think how he would grieve; for, poor lad, he loved his father and mother too, though he did so badly."

"Is his mother living?"

"No; if she had, he would have been alive; but his evil courses broke her heart; and it was because the man he killed reproached him for having murdered his mother, that he was provoked to murder him."

"Poor, rash, mistaken youth! then he had provocation."

"Oh yes; the greatest; but he was very sorry for what he had done; and it would have broken your heart to hear him talk of his poor father."

"I am glad I did not hear him," said Vernon hastily, and in a faltering voice, (for he thought of Edgar.)

"And yet, sir, it would have done your heart good too."

"Then he had virtuous feelings, and loved his father amidst all his errors?"

"Ay."

"And I dare say his father loved him in spite of his faults."

"I dare say he did," replied the man; "for one's children are our own flesh and blood, you know, sir, after all that is said and done; and may be this young fellow was spoiled in the bringing up."

"Perhaps so," said Vernon, sighing deeply.

"However, this poor lad made a very good end."

"I am glad of that! and he lies here," continued Vernon, gazing on the spot with deepening interest, and moving nearer to it as he spoke. "Peace be to his soul! but was he not dissected?"

"Yes; but his brothers got leave to have the body after dissection. They came to me; and we buried it privately at night."

"His brothers came! and who were his brothers?"

"Merchants in London; and it was a sad cut on them; but they took care that their father should not know it."

"No!" cried Vernon, turning sick at heart.

"Oh no; they wrote *him* word that his son was ill; then went to Westmoreland, and—"

"Tell me," interrupted Vernon, gasping for breath, and laying his hand on his arm, "tell me the name of this poor youth?"

"Why, he was tried under a false name, for the sake of his family; but his real name was Edgar Vernon!"

The agonized parent drew back, shuddered violently and repeatedly, casting his eyes to heaven at the same time, with a look of mingled appeal and resignation. He then rushed to the obscure spot which covered the bones of his son, threw himself upon it, and stretched his arms over it, as if embracing the unconscious deposit beneath, while his head rested on the grass, and he neither spoke nor moved. But he uttered one groan! then all was stillness!

His terrified and astonished companion remained motionless for a few moments,—then stooped to raise him; but the FIAT OF MERCY had gone forth, and the paternal heart, broken by the sudden shock, had suffered, and breathed its last.

CHAPTER XI.

LIES OF WANTONNESS.

I COME now to LIES OF WANTONNESS; that is, lies told from no other motive but a love of lying, and to show the utterer's total contempt of truth, and for those scrupulous persons of their acquaintance who look on it with reverence, and endeavour to act up to their principles; lies, having their origin merely in a depraved fondness for speaking and inventing falsehood. Not that persons of this description confine their falsehoods to this sort of lying; on the contrary, they lie after this fashion, because they have exhausted the strongly motived and more natural sorts of lying. In such as these, there is no more hope of amendment than there is for the man of intemperate habits, who has exhausted life of its pleasures, and his constitution of its energy. Such persons must go despised and (terrible state of human degradation!) untrusted, unbelieved, into their graves.

PRACTICAL LIES come last on my list; lies not UTTERED BUT ACTED; and dress will furnish me with most of my illustrations.

ILLUSTRATIONS OF LYING.

It has been said that the great art of dress is to CONCEAL DEFECTS and HEIGHTEN BEAUTIES; therefore, as concealment is deception, this great art of dress is founded on falsehood; but, certainly, in some instances, on falsehood, *comparatively*, of an innocent kind.

If the false-hair be so worn, that no one can fancy it natural; if the bloom on the cheek is such, that it cannot be mistaken for nature; or, if the person who "conceals defects, and heightens beauties," openly avows the practice, then is the deception annihilated. But, if the cheek be so artfully tinted, that its hue is mistaken for natural colour; if the false-hair be so skilfully woven, that it passes for natural hair; if the crooked person, or meagre form, be so cunningly assisted by dress, that the uneven shoulder disappears, and becoming fulness succeeds to unbecoming thinness, while the man or woman thus assisted by art expects their charms will be imputed to *nature* alone; then these aids of dress partake of the nature of other lying, and become equally vicious in the eyes of the religious and the moral.

I have said, the *man* or woman so assisted by art; and I believe that, by including the *stronger* sex in the above observation, I have only been *strictly just*.

While men hide baldness by gluing a piece of false-hair on their heads, *meaning* that it should pass for their own, and while a false calf gives muscular beauty to a shapeless leg, can the observer on human life do otherwise than include the wiser sex in the list of those who indulge in the permitted artifices and mysteries of the toilet? Nay; bolder still are the advances of some men into its sacred mysteries. I have seen the eyebrows, even of the young, darkened by the hand of art, and their cheeks reddened by its touch; and who has not seen, in Bond street, or *the* Drive, during the last twenty or thirty years, certain notorious men of fashion glowing in immortal bloom, and rivalling the dashing belle beside them?

As the foregoing observations on the practical lies of dress, have been mistaken by many, and have exposed me to severe, (and I think I may add) unjust animadversions, I take the opportunity afforded me by a second edition, to say a few words in explanation of them.

I do not wish to censure any one for having recourse to art to hide the defects of nature; and, I have *expressly said*, that such practices are comparatively innocent; but, it seems to me, that they cease to be innocent, and become passive and practical lies also, if, when men and women hear the fineness of their complexion, hair, or teeth, commended in their presence, they do not own that the beauty so commended is entirely artificial, provided such be really the case. But,

I am far from advising any one to be guilty of the unnecessary *egotism* of *volunteering* such an assurance; all I contend for is, that when we are praised for qualities, whether of mind or person, which we do not possess, we are guilty of *passive* if not *practical* lying, if we do not disclaim our right to the encomium bestowed.

The following also are PRACTICAL LIES of every day's experience.

Wearing paste for diamonds, intending that the false should be taken for the true; and purchasing brooches, pins, and rings of mock jewels, intending that they should pass for real ones; passing off gooseberry wine at dinner for real Champaigne, and English *liqueurs* for foreign ones. But, on these occasions, the motive is not always the mean and contemptible wish of imposing on the credulity of others; but it has sometimes its source in a dangerous as well as deceptive ambition, *that of making an appearance beyond what the circumstances of the person so deceiving really warrant; the wish to be supposed to be more opulent than they really are; that most common of all the practical lies; as ruin and bankruptcy follow in its train*. The lady who purchases and wears paste which she hopes will pass for diamonds, is usually one who has no right to wear jewels at all; and the gentleman who passes off gooseberry wine for Champaigne is, in all probability, aiming at a style of living beyond his situation in society.

On some occasions, however, when ladies substitute paste for diamonds, the substitution tells a tale of greater error still. I mean when ladies wear mock for real jewels, because their extravagance has obliged them to raise money on the latter; and they are therefore constrained to keep up the appearance of their necessary and accustomed splendour by a PRACTICAL LIE.

The following is another of the PRACTICAL LIES in common use.

The medical man, who desires his servant to call him out of church, or from a party, in order to give him the appearance of the great business which he has *not*, is guilty not of uttering, but of *acting* a falsehood; and the author also, who makes his publisher put second and third editions before a work of which, perhaps, not even the first edition is sold.

But, the most fatal to the interests of others, though perhaps the most pitiable of practical lies, are those acted by men who, though they know themselves to be in the gulf of bankruptcy, either from wishing to put off the evil day, or from the visionary hope that something will occur unexpectedly to save them, launch out into increased splendour of living, in order to obtain further credit, and induce their acquaintances to entrust their money to them.

There is, however, one PRACTICAL LIE more fatal still, in my opinion; because it is the practice of schools, and consequently the sin of early life;—a period of existence in which it is desirable, both for general and individual

PRACTICAL LIES.

good, that habits of truth and integrity should be acquired, and strictly adhered to. I mean the pernicious custom which prevails amongst boys, and probably girls, of getting their schoolfellows to do their exercises for them, or consenting to do the same office for others.

Some will say, "but it would be so ill-natured to refuse to write one's school-fellows' exercises, especially when one is convinced that they cannot write them for themselves." But, leaving the question of truth and falsehood *unargued* awhile, let us examine coolly that of the probable good or evil done to the parties obliged.

What are children sent to school for?—to learn. And when there, what are the motives which are to make them learn? dread of punishment, and hope of distinction and reward. There are few children so stupid, as not to be led on to industry by one or both of these motives, however indolent they may be; but, if these motives be not allowed their proper scope of action, the stupid boy will never take the trouble to learn, if he finds that he can avoid punishment, and gain reward, by prevailing on some more diligent boy to do his exercises for him. Those, therefore, who indulge their school-fellows, do it at the expense of their future welfare, and are in reality *foes* where they fancied themselves *friends*. But, generally speaking, they have not even *this* excuse for their pernicious compliance, since it springs from want of sufficient firmness to say no,— and deny an earnest request at the command of principle. But, to such I would put this question. "Which is the real friend to a child, the person who gives it the sweetmeats which it asks for, at the risk of making it ill, merely because it were *so hard* to refuse the dear little thing; or the person who, considering only the interest and health of the child, resists its importunities, though grieved to deny its request?" No doubt that they would give the palm of *real* kindness, *real* good-nature to the *latter*; and in like manner, the boy who *refuses* to do his school-fellow's task is more truly kind, more truly good-natured to him, than he who, by indulging his indolence, runs the risk of making him a dunce for life.

But some may reply, "It would make one *odious* in the school, were one to refuse this common compliance with the wants and wishes of one's companions."— Not if the refusal were declared to be the result of principle, and every aid not contrary to it were offered and afforded; and there are many ways in which schoolfellows may assist each other, without any violation of truth, and without sharing with them in the PRACTICAL LIE, by imposing on their masters, as theirs, lessons which they never wrote.

This common practice in schools is a PRACTICAL LIE of considerable importance, from its frequency; and because, as I before observed, the result of it is, that the first step which a child sets in a school is into the midst of deceit—tolerated, cherished deceit. For, if children are quick at learning, they are called upon immediately to enable others to deceive; and, if dull, they are enabled to appear in borrowed plumes themselves.

How often have I heard men in mature life say, "Oh! I knew such a one at school; he was a very good fellow, but so dull! I have often done his exercises for him." Or, I have heard the contrary asserted. "Such a one was a very clever boy at school indeed; he has done many an exercise for me; for he was *very good-natured*." And in neither case was the speaker conscious that he had been guilty of the meanness of deception himself, or been accessary to it in another.

Parents also correct their children's exercises, and thereby enable them to put a deceit on the master; not only by this means convincing their offspring of their own total disregard of truth; a conviction doubtless most pernicious in its effects on their young minds; but as full of folly as it is of laxity of principle; since the deceit cannot fail of being detected, whenever the parents are not at hand to afford their assistance.

But, is it *necessary* that this school delinquency should exist? Is it not advisable that children should learn the rudiments of truth, rather than falsehood, with those of their mother tongue and the classics? Surely masters and mistresses should watch over the morals, while improving the *minds* of youth. Surely parents ought to be tremblingly solicitous that their children should always speak truth, and be corrected by their preceptors for uttering falsehood. Yet, of what use could it be to correct a child for telling a spontaneous lie, on the impulse of strong temptation, if that child be in the daily habit of deceiving his master on system, and of assisting others to do so? While the present practice with regard to exercise-making exists; while boys and girls go up to their preceptors with lies in their hands, whence, sometimes, no doubt, they are transferred to their lips; every hope that truth will be taught in schools, as a necessary moral duty, must be totally, and for ever, annihilated.

CHAPTER XII.

OUR OWN EXPERIENCE OF THE PAINFUL RESULTS OF LYING.

I CANNOT point out the mischievous nature and impolicy of lying better, than by referring my readers to their own experience. Which of them does not know some few persons, at least, from whose habitual disregard of truth they have often suffered; and with whom they find intimacy unpleasant, as well as unsafe; because confidence, that charm and cement of intimacy, is wholly wanting in the intercourse? Which of my readers is not sometimes obliged to say, "I ought to add, that my authority for what I have just related, is only Mr. and Mrs. such-a-one, or a certain young lady, or a certain young gentleman; therefore, you know what credit is to be given to it."

It has been asserted, that every town and village has its idiot; and, with equal truth, probably, it may be advanced, that every one's circle of acquaintance contains one or more persons known to be habitual liars, and always mentioned as such. I may be asked, "If this be so, of what consequence is it? And how is it mischievous? If such persons are known and chronicled as liars, they can deceive no one, and, therefore, can do no harm." But this is not true; we are not always on our guard, either against our own weakness, or against that of others; and if the most notorious liar tells us something that we wish to believe, our wise resolution, never to credit or repeat what he has told us, fades before our desire to confide in him on this occasion. Thus, even in spite of caution, we become the agents of his falsehood; and, though lovers of truth, are the assistants of lying.

Nor are there many of my readers, I venture to pronounce, who have not, at some time or other of their lives, had cause to lament some violation of truth, of which they themselves were guilty, and which, at the time, they considered as wise, or positively unavoidable.

But the greatest proof of the impolicy even of occasional lying is, that it exposes one to the danger of never being believed in future. It is difficult to give implicit credence to those who have once deceived us; when they did so deceive, they were governed by a motive sufficiently powerful to overcome their regard for truth; and how can one ever be sure, that equal temptation is not always present, and always overcoming them?

Admitting, that perpetual distrust attends on those who are known to be frequent violators of truth, it seems to me that the liar is, as if he was *not*. He is, as it were, annihilated for all the important purposes of life. That man or woman is no better than a nonentity, whose simple assertion is not credited immediately. Those whose words no one dares to repeat, without naming the *authority*, lest the information conveyed by them should be too implicitly credited, such persons, I repeat it, exist, as if they existed *not*. They resemble that diseased eye, which, though perfect in colour and appearance, is wholly useless, because it cannot perform the function for which it was created, that of *seeing;* for, of what use to others, and of what benefit to themselves, can those be whose tongues are always suspected of uttering falsehood, and whose words, instead of inspiring confidence, that soul and cement of society, and of mutual regard, are received with offensive distrust, and never repeated without caution and apology?

I shall now endeavour to show, that speaking the truth does not imply a necessity to wound the feelings of any one; but that, even if the unrestricted practice of truth in society did at first give pain to self-love, it would, in the end, further the best views of benevolence; namely, moral improvement.

There cannot be any reason why *offensive* or *home* truths should be *volunteered*, because one lays it down as a principle that truth must be spoken when *called for*. If I put a question to another which may, if truly answered, wound either my sensibility or my self-love, I should be rightly served if replied to by a *home truth;* but, taking conversation according to its general tenor — that is, under the usual restraints of decorum and propriety — truth and benevolence will, I believe, be found to go hand-in-hand; and not, as is commonly imagined, be opposed to each other. For instance, if a person in company be old, plain, affected, vulgar in manners, or dressed in a manner unbecoming their years, my utmost love of truth would never lead me to say, "how old you look! or how plain you are! or how improperly dressed! or how vulgar! and how affected!" But, if this person were to say to me, "do I not look old? am I not plain? am I not improperly dressed? am I vulgar in manners?" and so on, I own that, according to my principles, I must, in my reply, adhere to the strict truth, after having vainly tried to avoid answering, by a serious expostulation on the folly, impropriety, and indelicacy of putting such a question to any one. And what would the consequence be? The person so answered would, probably, never like me again. Still, by my reply, I might have been of the greatest service to the indiscreet questioner. If ugly, the inquirer being convinced that not on outward charms could he or she build their pretensions to please, might study to improve in the more permanent graces of mind and manner. If growing old, the inquirer might be led by my reply to reflect seriously on the brevity of life, and try to grow in grace while advancing in years. If ill-dressed, or in a manner unbecoming a certain time of life, the inquirer might be led to improve in this particular, and be no longer exposed to the sneer of detraction. If vulgar, the inquirer might be induced to keep a watch in future over the admitted vulgarity; and if affected, might endeavour at greater simplicity, and less pretension in appearance.

Thus, the temporary wound to the self-love of the inquirer might be attended with lasting benefit; and benevolence in reality be not

PAINFUL RESULTS OF LYING.

wounded, but gratified. Besides, as I have before observed, the truly benevolent can always find a balm for the wounds which duty obliges them to inflict.

Few persons are so entirely devoid of external and internal charms, as not to be subjects for some kind of commendation; therefore, I believe, that means may always be found to smooth down the plumes of that self-love which principle has obliged us to ruffle. But, if it were to become a general principle of action in society to utter spontaneous truth, the difficult situation in which I have painted the utterers of truth to be placed, would, in time, be impossible; for, if certain that the truth would be spoken, and their suspicions concerning their defects confirmed, none would dare to put such questions as I have enumerated. Those questions sprung from the hope of being contradicted and flattered, and were that hope annihilated, no one would ever so question again.

I shall observe here, that those who make mortifying observations on the personal defects of their friends, or on any infirmity, either of body or mind, are not actuated by the love of truth, or by any good motive whatever; but that such unpleasant sincerity is merely the result of coarseness of mind, and a mean desire to inflict pain and mortification; therefore, if the utterer of them be noble, or even royal, I should still bring a charge against them, terrible to "ears polite," that of ill-breeding and positive *vulgarity*.

All human beings are convinced in the closet of the importance of truth to the interests of society, and of the mischief which they experience from lying, though few, comparatively, think the practice of the one, and avoidance of the other, binding either on the christian or the moralist, when they are acting in the busy scenes of the world. Nor can I wonder at this inconsistency, when boys and girls, as I have before remarked, however they may be taught to speak the truth at home, are so often tempted into the tolerated commission of falsehood as soon as they set their foot into a public school.

But we must wonder still less at the little shame which attaches to what is called WHITE LYING, when we see it sanctioned in the highest assemblies in this kingdom.

It is with fear and humility that I venture to blame a custom prevalent in our legislative meetings; which, as christianity is declared to be "part and parcel of the law of the land," ought to be christian as well as wise; and where every member, feeling it binding on him individually to act according to the legal oath, should speak the truth, and nothing *but* the truth. Yet what is the real state of things there on some occasions?

In the heat, (the pardonable heat, perhaps,) of political debates, and from the excitement produced by collision of wits, a noble lord, or an honourable commoner, is betrayed into severe personal comment on his antagonist. The *unavoidable* consequence, as it is *thought*, is apology, or duel.

But as these assemblies are called christian, even the warriors present deem apology a more proper proceeding than duel. Yet how is apology to be made consistent with the dignity and dictates of worldly honour? And how can the necessity of duel, that savage, heathenish disgrace to a civilized and christian land, be at once obviated? Oh! the method is easy enough. "It is as easy as lying," and lying is the remedy. A noble lord, or an honourable member gets up, and says, that undoubtedly his noble or honourable friend used such and such words; but, no doubt, that by those words he did not mean what those words usually mean; but he meant so and so. Some one on the other side immediately rises on behalf of the *offended*, and says, that if the *offender* will say that by so and so, he did not mean so and so, the *offended* will be perfectly satisfied. On which the offender rises, declares that by *black* he did not mean *black*, but *white;* in short, that black is white, and white black; the offended says, Enough; I am satisfied! the honourable house is satisfied also that life is put out of peril; and what is called honour is satisfied by the sacrifice ONLY of truth.

I must beg leave to state, that no one can rejoice more fervently than myself when these disputes terminate without duels; but must there be a victim? and must that victim be Truth? As there is no intention to deceive on these occasions, nor wish, nor expectation to do so, the soul, the essence of lying, is not in the transaction on the side of the *offender*. But the *offended* is forced to say that *he* is satisfied, when he certainly can *not* be so. He knows that the *offender* meant, at the moment, what he said; therefore he is *not* satisfied when he is told, in order to return his half-drawn sword to the scabbard, or his pistol to the holster, that black means white, and white means black.

However, he has his resource; he may ultimately tell the truth, declare himself, when out of the house, unsatisfied; and may (horrible alternative!) *peril his* life, or that of his opponent. But is there no other course which can be pursued by him who gave the offence? Must apology to *satisfy* be made in the language of falsehood? Could it not be made in the touching and impressive language of truth? Might not the perhaps already penitent offender, say "no; I will not be guilty of the meanness of subterfuge. By the words which I uttered, I meant at the moment what those words conveyed, and nothing else. But I then saw through the medium of passion; I spoke in the heat of resentment; and I now scruple not to say that I am sorry for what I said, and entreat the pardon of him whom I offended. If he be not satisfied, I know the consequences, and must take the responsibility."

Surely an apology like this would satisfy any one, however offended; and if the adversary were not contented, the noble or honourable house would undoubtedly deem his resentment brutal, and he would be constrained to pardon the offender in order to avoid disgrace.

But I am not contented with the conclusion of the apology which I have put into the mouth of the offending party; for I have made him willing, if necessary, to comply with the requirings of *worldly honour*. Instead of ending his apology in that unholy manner, I should have wished to end it thus:—" But if this heart-felt apology be not sufficient to appease the anger of him whom I have *offended*, and he expects me, in order to expiate my fault, to meet him in the lawless warfare of single combat, I solemnly declare that I will not so meet him; that not even the dread of being accused of cowardice, and being frowned on by those whose respect I value, shall induce me to put in peril either his life or my own."

If he and his opponent be married men, and, above all, if he be *indeed* a christian, he might add, " I will not, for any *personal* considerations, run the risk of making his wife and mine a widow, and his children and my own fatherless. I will not run the risk of disappointing that confiding tenderness which looks up to us for happiness and protection, by any rash and selfish action of mine. But I am not actuated to this refusal by this consideration alone; I am withheld by one more binding and more powerful still. For I remember the precepts taught in the Bible, and confirmed in the New Testament; and I cannot, will not, *dare* not, enter into single and deadly combat, in opposition to that awful command, ' thou shalt not kill!' "

Would any one, however narrow and worldly in his conceptions, venture to condemn as a coward, meanly shrinking from the responsibility he had incurred, the man that could dare to put forth sentiments like these, regardless of that fearful thing, " the world's dread laugh ?"

There might be some among his hearers by whom this truly noble daring could not possibly be appreciated. But though in both houses of parliament, there might be heroes present, whose heads are even bowed down by the weight of their laurels; men, whose courage has often paled the cheeks of their enemies in battle, and brought the loftiest low; still, (I must venture to assert) he who can dare, for the sake of conscience, to speak and act counter to the prejudices and passions of the world, at the risk of losing his standing in society, such a man is a hero in the best sense of the word, his is courage of the most difficult kind; that moral courage, founded indeed on *fear*, but a fear that tramples firmly on every fear of man; for it is that holy fear, the FEAR OF GOD.

CHAPTER XIII.

LYING THE MOST COMMON OF ALL VICES.

I HAVE observed in the preceding chapter, and elsewhere, that all persons, in *theory*, consider lying as a most odious, mean, and pernicious practice. It is also one which is more than almost any other reproved, if not punished, both in servants and children;—for parents, those excepted whose moral sense has been rendered utterly callous, or who never possessed any, mourn over the slightest deviation from truth in their offspring, and visit it with instant punishment. Who has not frequently heard masters and mistresses of families declaring that some of their servants were such liars that they could keep them no longer! Yet trying and painful as *intercourse* with liars is universally allowed to be, since confidence, that necessary guardian of domestic peace, cannot exist where they are; lying is *undoubtedly*, THE MOST COMMON OF ALL VICES. A friend of mine was once told by a confessor, that it was the one most *frequently confessed* to him; and I am sure that if we enter society with eyes open to detect this propensity, we shall soon be convinced, that there are few, if any, of our acquaintance, however distinguished for virtue, who are not, on some occasions, led by good and sufficient motive, in their own opinion at least, either to violate or withhold the truth with intent to deceive. Nor do their most conscious or even detected deviations from veracity fill the generality of the world with shame or compunction. If they commit any other sins, they shrink from avowing them; but I have often heard persons confess, that they had, on certain occasions, uttered a direct falsehood, with an air which proved them to be proud of the deceptive skill with which it was uttered, adding, " but it was only a white lie, you know," with a degree of self-complacency which showed that, in their eyes, a white lie was no lie at all. And what is more common than to hear even the professedly pious, as well as the moral, assert that a deviation from truth, or at least, withholding the truth, so as to deceive, is sometimes absolutely necessary? Yet, I would seriously ask of those who thus argue, whether, when they repeat the commandment, " thou shalt not steal," they feel willing to admit, either in themselves or others, a mental reservation, allowing them to *pilfer* in any degree, or even in the slightest particular make free with the property of another? Would they think that pilfering tea or sugar was a venial fault in a servant, and excusable under strong temptations? They would answer "no;" and be ready to say in the words of the apostle, "whosoever in this respect shall offend in one point, he is guilty of all." Yet, I venture to assert, that *little lying*, alias white lying, is as much an infringement of the moral law against "speaking leasing" as little pilfering is of the commandment not to steal; and I defy any consistent moralist to escape from the obligation of the principle which I here lay down.

The economical rule, "take care of the pence, and the pounds will take care of themselves," may, with great benefit, be applied to morals. Few persons, comparatively, are exposed to the danger of committing *great crimes*, but all are daily and hourly tempted to commit *little sins*. Beware, therefore, of slight deviations from purity and rectitude, and great ones *will take care of themselves*; and the habit of resistance to trivial sins will make you able to resist temptation to errors of a more culpable nature; and as those persons will not be likely to exceed improperly in pounds, who are laudably saving in pence, and as little lies are to *great ones*, what pence are to pounds, if we acquire a habit of telling truth on trivial occasions, we shall never be induced to violate it on serious and important ones.

I shall now borrow the aid of others to strengthen what I have already said on this important subject, or have still to say; as I am painfully conscious of my own inability to do justice to it; and if the good which I desire be but effected, I am willing to resign to others the merit of the success.

CHAPTER XIV.

EXTRACTS FROM LORD BACON, AND OTHERS.

In a gallery of moral philosophers, the rank of Bacon, in my opinion, resembles that of Titian in a gallery of pictures; and some of his successors not only look up to him as authority for certain excellences, but, making him, in a measure, their study, they endeavour to diffuse over their own productions the beauty of his conceptions, and the depth and breadth of his manner. I am, therefore, sorry that those passages in his Essay on Truth which bear upon the subject before me, are so unsatisfactorily brief;—however, as even a sketch from the hand of a master is valuable, I give the following extracts from the essay in question.

"But to pass from theological and philosophical truth — to truth, or rather veracity, in civil business, it will be acknowledged, even by those that practise it not, that clear and sound dealing is the honour of man's nature, and that mixture of falsehood is like alloy in coin of gold and silver, which may make the metal work the better, but it embaseth it. For these winding and crooked courses are the goings of the serpent, which goeth basely upon the belly, and not upon the feet. There is no vice that does so overwhelm a man with shame, as to be found false or perfidious; and therefore Montaigne saith very acutely, when he inquired the reason, why the giving the lie should be such a disgraceful and odious charge, 'If it be well weighed,' said he, 'to say that a man lies, is as much as to say, he is a bravado towards God and a coward towards man. For the liar insults God and crouches to man.'" *Essay on Truth*.

I hoped to have derived considerable assistance from Addison; as he ranks so very high in the list of moral writers, that Dr. Watts said of his greatest work, "There is so much virtue in the eight volumes of the Spectator, such a reverence of things sacred, so many valuable remarks for our conduct in life, that they are not improper to lie in parlours, or summerhouses, to entertain one's thoughts in any moments of leisure." But, in spite of his fame as a moralist, and of this high eulogium from one of the best authorities, Addison appears to have done very little as an advocate for spontaneous truth, and an assailant of spontaneous lying; and has been much less zealous and effective than either Hawkesworth or Johnson. However, what he has said, is well said; and I have pleasure in giving it.

"The great violation of the point of honour from man to man is, giving the lie. One may tell another that he drinks and blasphemes, and it may pass unnoticed; but to say he lies, though but in jest, is an affront that nothing but blood can expiate. The reasons perhaps may be, because no other vice implies a want of courage so much as the making of a lie; and, therefore, telling a man he lies, is touching him in the most sensible part of honour, and, indirectly, calling him a coward. I cannot omit, under this head, what Herodotus tells us of the ancient Persians; that, from the age of five years to twenty, they instruct their sons only in three things; — to manage the horse, to make use of the bow, and to *speak the truth*." SPECTATOR, Letter 99.

I know not whence Addison took the extract, from which I give the following quotation, but I refer my readers to No. 352 of the Spectator.

"Truth is always consistent with itself, and needs nothing to help it out; it is always near at hand, and sits upon our lips, and is ready to drop out, before we are aware; whereas, a LIE is troublesome, and sets a man's invention upon the rack; and one break wants a great many more to make it good. It is like building on a false foundation, which continually stands in need of props to keep it up, and proves at last more chargeable than to have raised a substantial building at first upon a true and solid foundation; for sincerity is firm and substantial, and there is nothing hollow and unsound in it; and, because it is plain and open, fears no discovery, of which the crafty man is always in danger. All his pretences are so transparent, that he that runs may read them; he is the last man that finds himself to be found out; and while he takes it for granted that he makes fools of others, he renders himself ridiculous. Add to all this, that sincerity is the most compendious wisdom, and an excellent instrument for the speedy despatch of business. It creates confidence in those we have to deal with, saves the labour of many inquiries, and brings things to an issue in a few words. It is like travelling in a plain-beaten road, which commonly brings a man sooner to his journey's end than by-ways, in which men often lose themselves. In a word, whatsoever convenience may be thought to be in falsehood and dissimulation, it is soon over; but the inconvenience of it is perpetual, because it brings a man under an everlasting jealousy and suspicion, so that he is not believed when he speaks truth, nor trusted perhaps when he means honestly. When a man has once forfeited the reputation of his integrity, he is set fast, and nothing will serve his turn; neither truth nor falsehood."

Dr. Hawkesworth, in the "Adventurer," makes lying the subject of a whole number; and begins thus:—"When Aristotle was once asked what a man could gain by uttering falsehoods," he replied, "not to be credited when he shall speak the truth." "The character of a liar is at once so hateful and contemptible, that even of those who have lost their virtue it might be expected that, from the violation of truth, they should be restrained by their pride;" and again, "almost every other vice that disgraces human nature may be kept in countenance by applause and association..... The liar, and only the liar, is invariably and universally despised, abandoned, and disowned. It is natural to expect that a crime thus generally detested should be generally avoided, &c. Yet, so it is, that in defiance of censure and contempt, truth is frequently violated; and scarcely the most vigilant and unremitted circumspection will secure him that mixes with mankind from being hourly deceived by men of whom it can scarcely be imagined that they mean any injury to him, or profit to themselves." He then enters into a copious discussion of the lie of vanity, which he calls the most common of lies, and not the least mischievous; but I shall content myself with only one extract from the conclusion of this paper. "There is, I think, an ancient law in Scotland, by which LEASING MAKING was capitally punished. I am, indeed, far from designing to increase in this country the number of executions; yet, I cannot but think that they who destroy the confidence of society, weaken the credit of intelligence, and interrupt the security of life, might very properly be awakened to a sense of their crimes by denunciations of a whipping-post or pillory; since many are so insensible of right and wrong, that they have no standard of action *but the law*, nor feel *guilt* but as they dread *punishment*."

In No. 54 of the same work, Dr. Hawkesworth says, "that these men, who consider the imputation of some vices as a compliment, would resent that of a lie as an insult, for which *life* only could atone. Lying, however," he adds, "does not incur more infamy than it deserves, though other vices incur less. But," continues he, "there is equal *turpitude* and yet greater *meanness*, in those forms of speech which deceive without direct falsehood. The crime is committed with greater deliberation, as it requires more contrivance; and by the offenders the use of language is totally perverted. They conceal a meaning opposite to that which they express; their speech is a kind of riddle propounded for an evil purpose.

"Indirect lies, more effectually than others, destroy that mutual confidence which is said to be the band of society. They are more frequently repeated, because they are not prevented by the dread of detection. Is it not astonishing that a practice so universally infamous should not be more generally avoided! To think, is to renounce it; and, that I may fix the attention of my readers a little longer upon the subject, I shall relate a story which, perhaps, by those who have much sensibility, will not soon be forgotten."

He then proceeds to relate a story which is, I think, more full of moral teaching than any one I ever read on the subject; and so superior to the preceding ones written by myself that I am glad there is no necessity for me to bring them in immediate competition with it; —and that all I need do, is to give the moral of that story. Dr. Hawkesworth calls the tale "the Fatal Effects of False Apologies and Pretences;" but "the fatal effects of *white lying*," would have been a juster title; and perhaps, my readers will be of the same opinion, when I have given an extract from it. I shall preface the extract by saying that, by a series of white lies, well-intentioned, but, like all lies, mischievous in their result, either to the purity of the moral feeling, or to the interests of those who utter them, jealousy was aroused in the husband of one of the heroines, and duel and death were the consequences. The following letter, written by the too successful combatant to his wife, will sufficiently explain all that is necessary for my purpose.

"My dear Charlotte, I am the most wretched of all men; but I do not upbraid you as the cause. Would that I were not more guilty than you! We are the martyrs of dissimulation. But your dissimulation and falsehood were the effects of mine. By the success of *a lie put into the mouth of a chairman*, I was prevented reading a letter which would at last have undeceived me; and, by persisting in dissimulation, the Captain has made his friend a fugitive, and his wife a widow. Thus does insincerity terminate in misery and confusion, whether in its immediate purpose it succeeds, or is disappointed. If we ever meet again (to meet again in peace is impossible, but if we ever meet again,) let us resolve to be sincere; to be *sincere* is to be *wise, innocent*, and *safe*. We venture to commit faults, which shame or fear would prevent, if we did not hope to conceal them by a lie. But in the labyrinth of falsehood men meet those evils which they seek to avoid; and, as in the straight path of truth alone they can see before them, in the straight path of truth alone they can pursue felicity with success. Adieu! I am ...... dreadful! ...... I can subscribe nothing that does not reproach and torment me."

Within a few weeks after the receipt of this letter, the unhappy lady heard that her husband had been cast away on his passage to France.

I shall next bring forward a greater champion of truth than the author of the Adventurer; and put her cause into the hands of the mighty author of the Rambler. Boswell, in his Life of Dr. Johnson, says thus:—

"He would not allow his servant to say he was not at home when he really was. 'A servant's strict regard for truth,' said he, 'must be weakened by the practice. A *philosopher* may know that it is merely a *form of denial*; but few servants are such *nice distinguishers*. If I accustom a servant to tell a lie for *me*, have I not reason to apprehend that he will tell many lies for *himself?*'"*

* Boswell adds, in his own person, "I am however satisfied that every servant, of any degree of intelligence, understands saying, his master is not at home, not at all as the affirmation of a fact, but as customary words, intimating that his master wishes not to be seen; so that there can be no bad effect from it." So says the *man of the world;* and so say almost *all* the men of the world, and women too. But, even they will admit that the opinion of Johnson is of more weight, on a question of morals, than that of *Boswell;* and I beg leave to add that of another powerfully-minded and pious man. Scott, the editor of the Bible, says, in a note to the fourth chapter of Judges, " A very criminal deviation from simplicity and godliness is become customary amongst professed Christians. I mean the instructing and requiring servants to *prevaricate* (to word it no more harshly), in order that their masters may be preserved from the inconvenience of unwelcome visitants. And it should be considered whether they who require their servants to disregard the truth for their pleasure, will not teach them an evil lesson, and habituate them to use falsehood for their own pleasure also." When I first wrote on this subject, I was not aware that writers of such eminence as those from whom I *now* quote had written concerning this *Lie of Convenience;* but it is most gratifying to me to find

"The importance of strict and scrupulous veracity," says Boswell, vol. ii., pp. 454–55, "cannot be too often inculcated. Johnson was known to be so rigidly attentive to it, that, even in his common conversation, the slightest circumstance was mentioned with exact precision. The knowledge of his having such a principle and habit made his friends have a perfect reliance on the truth of EVERY THING THAT HE TOLD, however it might have been DOUBTED, if told by OTHERS.

"What a bribe and a reward does this anecdote hold out to us to be accurate in relation! for, of all *privileges,* that of being considered as a person on whose veracity and accuracy every one can implicitly rely, is perhaps the most valuable to a social being."—Vol. iii., p. 450.

"Next morning, while we were at breakfast," observes the amusing biographer, "Johnson gave a very earnest recommendation of what he himself practised with the utmost conscientiousness; I mean, a strict regard to truth, even in the most minute particulars. 'Accustom your children,' said he, 'constantly to this. If a thing happened at one window, and they, when relating it, say that it happened at another, do not let it pass; but instantly check them; *you don't know where deviation from truth will end.*' Our lively hostess, whose fancy was impatient of the rein, fidgeted at this, and ventured to say, 'this is too much. If Mr. Johnson should forbid me to drink tea, I would comply; as I should feel the restraint only twice a day; but little variations in narrative must happen a thousand times a day, if one is not perpetually watching.'—JOHNSON. 'Well, madam, and you *ought to be perpetually watching.* It is more from *carelessness about truth,* than from *intentional lying,* that there is so much falsehood in the world.'"

"Johnson inculcated upon all his friends the importance of perpetual vigilance against the slightest degree of falsehood; the effect of which, as Sir Joshua Reynolds observed to me, has been that all who were of his *school* are distinguished for a love of truth and accuracy, which they would not have possessed in the same degree, if they had not been acquainted with Johnson."†

"We talked of the casuistical question," says Boswell, vol. iv. 334, "whether it was allowable at any time to depart from truth."—JOHNSON. 'The general rule is, that truth

the truth of my humble opinion confirmed by such men as Johnson, Scott, and Chalmers.

I know not who wrote a very amusing and humorous book, called " Thinks I to myself;" but this subject is admirably treated there, and with effective ridicule, as, indeed, is worldly insincerity in general.

† However Boswell's self-flattery might blind him, what he says relative to the harmlessness of servants denying their masters, makes him an exception to this general rule.

should never be violated; because it is of the utmost importance to the comfort of life that we should have a full security by mutual faith; and occasional inconveniences should be willingly suffered, that we may preserve it. I deny,' he observed further on, 'the lawfulness of telling a lie to a sick man, for fear of alarming him. *You have no business with consequences; you are to tell the truth.'*"

Leaving what the great moralist himself added on this subject, because it is not necessary for my purpose, I shall do Boswell the justice to insert the following testimony, which he himself bears to the importance of truth.

"I cannot help thinking that there is much weight in the opinion of those who have held that truth, as an eternal, an immutable principle, is never to be violated for supposed, previous, or superior obligations, of which, every man being led to judge for himself, there is great danger that we too often, from partial motives, persuade ourselves that they exist; and, probably, whatever extraordinary instances may sometimes occur, where some evil may be prevented by violating this noble principle, it would be found that human happiness would, *upon the whole*, be more perfect, were truth universally preserved."

But, however just are the above observations, they are inferior in pithiness, and practical power, to the following few words, extracted from another of Johnson's sentences. "All truth is not of equal importance; but, if *little violations be allowed, every violation will, in time, be thought little.*"

The following quotation is from the 96th number of the Rambler. It is the introduction to an Allegory, called Truth, Falsehood, and Fiction; but, as I think his didactic is here superior to his narrative, I shall content myself with giving the first.

"It is reported of the Persians, by an ancient writer, that the sum of their education consisted in teaching youth to ride, to shoot with the bow, and to speak truth. The bow and the horse were easily mastered; but it would have been happy if we had been informed by what arts veracity was cultivated, and by what preservations a Persian mind was secured against the temptations of falsehood.

"There are, indeed, in the present corruptions of mankind, many incitements to forsake truth; the need of palliating our own faults, and the convenience of imposing on the ignorance or credulity of others, so frequently occur; so many immediate evils are to be avoided, and so many present gratifications obtained by craft and delusion; that very few of those who are much entangled in life, have spirit and constancy sufficient to support them in the steady practice of open veracity. In order that all men may be taught to speak truth, it is necessary that all likewise should learn to hear it; for no species of falsehood is more frequent than flattery, to which the coward is betrayed by fear, the dependant by interest, and the friend by tenderness. Those who are neither servile nor timorous, are yet desirous to bestow pleasure; and, while unjust demands of praise continue to be made, there will always be some whom hope, fear, or kindness, will dispose to pay them."

There cannot be a stronger picture given of the difficulties attendant on speaking the strict truth; and I own I feel it to be a difficulty which requires the highest of motives to enable us to overcome. Still as the old proverb says, "where there is a will, there is a way;" and if that will be derived from the only right source, the only effective motive, I am well convinced, that all obstacles to the utterance of spontaneous truth would at length vanish, and that falsehood would become as rare as it is contemptible and pernicious.

The contemporary of Johnson and Hawkesworth, Lord Kames, comes next on my list of moral writers, who have treated on the subject of truth; but I am not able to give more than a short extract from his Sketches of the History of Man; a work which had no small reputation in its day, and was in every one's hand, till eclipsed by the depth and brilliancy of modern Scotch philosophers.

He says, p. 169, in his 7th section, with respect to veracity in particular, "man is so constituted that he must be indebted to information for the knowledge of most things that benefit or hurt him; and if he could not depend on information, society would be very little benefited. Further, it is wisely ordered, that we should be bound by the moral sense to speak truth, even where we perceive no harm in transgressing that duty, *because it is sufficient that harm may come, though not foreseen; at the same time, falsehood always does mischief.* It may happen not to injure us externally in our reputation, or goods; but it never fails to injure us internally; the sweetest and most refined pleasure of society is a candid intercourse of sentiments, of opinion, of desires, and wishes; and it would be poisonous to indulge any falsehood in such an intercourse."

My next extracts are from two celebrated divines of the Church of England, Bishop Beveridge, and Archdeacon Paley. The Bishop, in his "Private Thoughts," thus heads one of his sections (which he denominates resolutions ;—)

"RESOLUTION III.—*I am resolved, by the grace of God, always to make my tongue and heart go together, so as never to speak with the one, what I do not think with the other.*

"As my happiness consisteth in nearness and vicinity, so doth my holiness in likeness and conformity, to the chiefest good. I am so much the better, as I am the liker the best; and so much the holier, as I am more conformable to the holiest, or rather to him who is holiness itself. Now, one great title which the Most High is pleased to give himself, and

EXTRACTS FROM LORD BACON, AND OTHERS. 475

by which he is pleased to reveal himself to us, is the God of truth; so that I shall be so much the liker to the God of Truth, by how much I am the more constant to the truth of God. And, the farther I deviate from this, the nearer I approach to the nature of the devil, who is the father of lies, and liars too; John viii. 44. And therefore to avoid the scandal and reproach, as well as the dangerous malignity, of this damnable sin, I am resolved, by the blessing of God, always to tune my tongue in unison to my heart, so as never to speak any thing, but what I think really to be true. So that, if ever I speak what is not true it shall not be the error of my will, but of my understanding.

"I know, lies are commonly distinguished into officious, pernicious, and jocose; and some may fancy some of them *more tolerable than others*. But, for my own part, I think they are *all* pernicious; and therefore, not to be jested withal, nor indulged, *upon any pretence or colour whatsoever*. Not as if it was a sin, not to speak exactly as a thing is in itself, or as it seems to me in its literal meaning, without some liberty granted to rhetorical tropes and figures; [for so, the Scripture itself would be chargeable with lies; many things being contained in it which are not true in a literal sense.] But, I must so use *rhetorical*, as not to abuse my *Christian* liberty; and therefore, never to make use of hyperboles, ironies, or other tropes and figures, to deceive or impose upon my auditors, but only for the better adorning, illustrating, or confirming the matter.

"I am resolved never to promise any thing with my mouth, but what I intend to perform in my heart; and never to intend to perform any thing, but what I am sure I can perform. For, though I may intend to do as I say now, yet there are a thousand weighty things that intervene, which may turn the balance of my intentions, or otherwise hinder the performance of my promise."

I come now to an extract from Dr. Paley, the justly-celebrated author of the work entitled "Moral Philosophy."

"A lie is a breach of promise; for whosoever seriously addresses his discourse to another, tacitly promises to speak the truth, because he knows that the truth is expected. Or the obligation of veracity may be made out from the direct ill-consequences of lying to social happiness; which consequences consist, either in some specific injury to particular individuals, or in the destruction of that confidence which is essential to the intercourse of human life; for which latter reason a lie may be pernicious in its general tendency; and therefore, criminal, though it produce no particular or visible mischief to any one. There are falsehoods which are not lies; that is, which are not criminal, as where no one is deceived; which is the case in parables, fables, jests, tales to create mirth, ludicrous embellishments of a story, where the declared design of the speaker is not to inform but to divert; *compliments in the subscription of a letter; a servant's denying his master; a prisoner's pleading not guilty; an advocate asserting the justice, or his belief in the justice, of his client's cause. In such instances no confidence is destroyed, because none was reposed; no promise to speak the truth is violated, because none was given or understood to be given.*

"In the first place, it is almost impossible to pronounce beforehand with certainty, concerning any lie, that it is inoffensive, *volat irrevocabile*, and collects oft-times reactions in its flight, which entirely changes its nature. It may owe, possibly, its mischief to the officiousness or misrepresentation of those who circulate it; but the mischief is, nevertheless, in some degree chargeable upon the original editor. In the next place, this liberty in conversation defeats its own end. Much of the pleasure, and all the benefit of conversation, depend upon our opinion of the speaker's veracity, for which this rule leaves no foundation. The faith, indeed, of a hearer must be extremely perplexed, who considers the speaker, or believes that the speaker considers himself, as under no obligation to *adhere to truth*, but according to the *particular importance of what he relates*. But, beside and above both these reasons, *white lies* always introduce others of a darker complexion. I have seldom known any one who deserted *truth in trifles*, that could be trusted *in matters of importance*.*

"Nice distinctions are out of the question upon occasions which, like those of speech, return every hour. The habit, therefore, when once formed, is easily extended to serve the designs of malice or interest; like all habits, it spreads indeed of itself.

"As there may be falsehoods which are not lies, so there are many lies without literal or direct falsehood. An opening is always left for this species of prevarication, when the literal and grammatical signification of a sentence is different from the popular and customary meaning. It is the wilful deceit that makes the lie; and we wilfully deceive when our expressions are not true in the sense in which we believe the hearer apprehends them. Besides, it is absurd to contend for any sense of words, in opposition to usage, and upon nothing else;—or a man may *act* a lie, as by pointing his finger in a wrong direction, when a traveller inquires of him his road;—or when a tradesman shuts up his windows, to induce his creditors to believe that he is abroad; for, to all moral purpose, and therefore as to veracity, speech and action are the same;—speech

---

* How contrary is the spirit of this wise observation, and the following ones, to that which Paley manifests in his toleration of servants being taught to deny their masters!

being only a mode of action. Or, lastly, there may be lies of omission. A writer on English history, who, in his account of the reign of Charles the 1st, should wilfully suppress any evidence of that Prince's despotic measures and designs, might be said to lie; for, by entitling his book a History of England, he engages to relate the whole truth of the history, or, at least, all he knows of it."

I feel entire unity of sentiment with Paley on all that he has advanced in these extracts, except in those passages which are printed in italic; but Chalmers and Scott have given a complete refutation to his opinion on the innocence of a servant's denying his master, in the extracts given in a *preceding* chapter; and it will be ably refuted in some succeeding extracts. But, eloquent and convincing as Paley generally is, it is not from his Moral Philosophy that he derives his purest reputation. He has long been considered as lax, negligent, and inconclusive, on many points, as a moral philosopher.

It was when he came forward as a Christian warrior against infidelity, that he brought his best powers into the field; and his name will live for ever as the author of Evidences of Christianity, and the Horæ Paulinæ.[*] I shall now avail myself of the assistance of a powerful and eloquent writer of more modern date, William Godwin, with whom I have entire correspondence of opinion on the subject of spontaneous truth, though, on some other subjects, I decidedly differ from him. "It was further proposed," says he, "to consider the value of truth in a practical view, as it relates to the incidents and commerce of ordinary life, under which form it is known by the denominations of sincerity.

"The powerful recommendations attendant on sincerity are obvious. It is intimately connected with the general dissemination of *innocence*, energy, intellectual improvement, and philanthropy. Did every man impose this law upon himself; did he regard himself as not authorized to conceal any part of his character and conduct; this circumstance alone would prevent millions of actions from being perpetrated, in which we are now induced to engage, by the prospect of success and impunity." "There is a further benefit that would result to me from the habit of telling every man the truth, regardless of the dictates of worldly prudence and custom; I should acquire a clear, ingenuous, and unembarrassed air. According to the established modes of society, whenever I have a circumstance to state which would require some effort of mind and discrimination, to enable me to do it justice, and state it with proper effect, I fly from the task, and take refuge in silence and equivocation."

"But the principle which forbade me concealment would keep my mind for ever awake, and for ever warm. I should always be obliged to exert my attention, lest, in pretending to tell the truth, I should tell it in so imperfect and mangled a way, as to produce the effect of falsehood. If I spoke to a man of my own faults, or those of his neighbour, I should be anxious not to suffer them to come distorted or exaggerated to his mind, or permit what at first was fact, to degenerate into *satire*. If I spoke to him of the errors he had himself committed, I should carefully avoid those inconsiderate expressions, which might convert what was in itself beneficent, into offence, and my thoughts would be full of that kindness and generous concern for his welfare, which such a task necessarily brings with it. The effects of sincerity upon others would be similar to its effects on him that practised it. Plain dealing, truth spoken with kindness, but spoken with sincerity, is the most wholesome of all disciplines." .... "The only species of sincerity which can, in any degree, prove satisfactory to the enlightened moralist and politician, is that where frankness is perfect, and every degree of reserve is discarded."

"Nor is there any danger that such a character should degenerate into ruggedness and brutality.

"Sincerity, upon the principles on which it is here recommended, is practised from a consciousness of *its utility*, and from sentiments of philanthropy.

"It will communicate frankness to the voice, fervour to the gesture, and kindness to the heart.

"The duty of sincerity is one of those general principles which reflection and experience have enjoined upon us as conducive to the happiness of mankind.

"Sincerity and plain dealing are eminently conducive to the interests of mankind at large, because they afford that ground of confidence and reasonable expectation which are essential to wisdom and virtue."

I feel it difficult to forbear giving further extracts from this very interesting and well-argued part of the work from which I quote; but the limits necessary for my own book forbid me to indulge myself in copious quotations from this. I must, however, give two further extracts from the conclusion of this chapter. "No man can be eminently either respectable, or amiable, or useful, who is not distinguished for the frankness and candour of his manners ..... He that is not conspicuously sincere, either very little partakes of the passion of doing good, or is pliably ignorant of the means by which the objects of true benevolence are to be effected." The writer proceeds to discuss the mode of *excluding visiters*, and

---

[*] I heard the venerable bishop of —— say, that when he gave Dr. Paley some very valuable preferment, he addressed him thus: "I give you this, Dr. Paley, not for your Moral Philosophy, nor for your Natural Theology, but for your Evidences of Christianity, and your Horæ Paulinæ."

it is done in so powerful a manner, that I must avail myself of the aid which it affords me.

"Let us then, according to the well-known axiom of MORALITY, put ourselves in the place of that man upon whom is imposed this ungracious task. Is there any of us that would be contented to perform it in person, and to say that our father and brother was not at home, when they were really in the house? Should we not feel ourselves contaminated by the PLEBEIAN LIE? Can we thus be justified in requiring that from another which we should shrink from as an act of dishonour in ourselves?" I must here beg leave to state that, generally speaking, masters and mistresses only command their servants to tell a lie which they would be very willing *to tell themselves*. I have heard wives deny their husbands, husbands their wives, children their parents, parents their children, with as much unblushing effrontery as if there were no such thing as truth, or its obligations; but I respect his question on this subject, envy him his ignorance, and admire his epithet PLEBEIAN LIE.

But then, I think that *all* lies are plebeian. Was it not a king of France, a captive in his kingdom, who said, (with an honourable consciousness, that a sovereign is entitled to set a high example to his people,) "if honour be driven from every other spot, it should always inhabit the breast of kings!" and if truth be banished from every other description of persons, it ought more especially to be found on the lips of those whom rank and fortune have placed above the reach of strong temptation to falsehood.

But, while I think that, however exalted be the rank of the person who utters a lie, that person suffers by his deceit a worse than plebeian degradation, I also assert, that the humblest plebeian, who is known to be incapable of falsehood, and to utter, on all occasions, spontaneous truth, is raised far above the mendacious patrician in the scale of real respectability; and in comparison, the plebeian becomes patrician, and the patrician plebeian.

I shall conclude my references, with extracts from two modern Scotch philosophers of considerable and deserved reputation, Dr. Reid, and Dr. Thomas Browne.*

"Without fidelity and trust, there can be no human society. There never was a society even of savages, nay, even of robbers and pirates, in which there was not a great degree of veracity and fidelity amongst themselves. Every man thinks himself injured and ill-used when he is imposed upon. Every man takes it as a reproach when falsehood is imputed to him. There are the clearest evidences that all men disapprove of falsehood, when their judgment is not biassed." *Reid's Essays on the Power of the Human Mind*, chap vi. "On the nature of a Contract."

"The next duty of which we have to treat, is that of veracity, which relates to the knowledge or belief of others, as capable of being affected by the meanings, true or false, which our words or our conduct may convey; and consists in the faithful conformity of our language, or of our conduct, when it is intended tacitly to supply the place of language to the truth which we profess to deliver; or, at least, to that which is at the time believed by us to be true. So much of the happiness of social life is derived from the use of language, and so profitless would the mere power of language be, but for the truth which dictates it, that the abuse of the confidence which is placed in our declarations may not merely be in the highest degree injurious to the individual deceived, but would tend, if general, to throw back the whole race of mankind into that barbarism from which they have emerged, and ascended through still purer air, and still brighter sunshine, to that noble height which they have reached. It is not wonderful, therefore, that veracity, so important to the happiness of all, and yet subject to so many temptations of personal interest in the violation of it, should in all nations, have had a high place assigned to it among the virtues." *Dr. Thomas Browne's Lectures on the Philosophy of the Human Mind*, vol. iv. p. 225.

It may be asked, why I have taken the trouble to quote from so many authors, in order to prove what no one ever doubted; namely, the importance and necessity of speaking the truth, and the meanness and mischief of uttering falsehood. But I have added authority to authority, in order renewedly to force on the attention of my *readers* that not one of the writers mentions any allowed *exception* to the general rule, that truth is always to be spoken; no *mental reservation* is pointed out as permitted on *special occasions*; no individual is authorized to be the judge of right or wrong in his own case, and to set his own opinion of the propriety and necessity of lying, in particular instances, against the positive precept to abstain from lying; an injunction which is so commonly enforced in the page of the moralist, that it becomes a sort of imperative command. Still, in spite of the universally acknowledged conviction of mankind, that truth is virtue, and falsehood vice, I scarcely know an individual who does not occasionally shrink from acting up to his conviction on this point, and is not, at times, irresistibly impelled to qualify that conviction, by saying, that on "ALMOST all occasions the truth is to be spoken, and never withheld." Or they may, perhaps, quote the well-known proverb, that "truth is not to be spoken at all times." But the *real* meaning of that proverb

* This latter gentleman, with whom I had the pleasure of being personally acquainted, has, by his early death, left a chasm in the world of literature, and in the domestic circle in which he moved, which cannot easily be filled up.

appears to me to be simply this; that we are never *officiously* or *gratuitously* to utter offensive truth; not that truth, when required, is ever to be *withheld*. The principle of truth is an immutable principle, or it is of no use as a guard, nor safe as the foundation of morals. A moral law on which it is dangerous to act to the uttermost, , however admirable, no better than Harlequin's horse, which was the very best and finest of all horses, and worthy of the admiration of the whole world; but, unfortunately, the horse was DEAD; and if the law to tell the truth inviolably, is not to be strictly adhered to, without any regard to consequences, it is, however admirable, as useless as the merits of Harlequin's dead horse. King Theodoric, when advised by his courtiers to debase the coin, declared, "that nothing which bore his image should ever lie." Happy would it be for the interests of society, if, having as much proper self-respect as this good monarch had, we could resolve never to allow our looks or words to bear any impress, but that of the *strict truth;* and were as reluctant to give a false impression of ourselves, in any way, as to circulate light sovereigns and forged bank-notes. Oh! that the day may come, when it shall be thought as dishonourable to commit the slightest breach of veracity, as to pass counterfeit shillings; and when both shall be deemed equally detrimental to the safety and prosperity of the community.

I intend, in a future work, to make some observations on several *collateral descendants* from the large family of lies: such as INACCURACY IN RELATION;—PROMISE-BREAKING;—ENGAGEMENT-BREAKING,—and WANT OF PUNCTUALITY. Perhaps PROCRASTINATION comes in a degree under the head of lying; at least, procrastinators lie to themselves; they say, "I will do so and so to-morrow," and as they believe their own assertions, they are guilty of self deception, the most dangerous of all deceptions. But those who are enabled, by constant watchfulness, never to deceive others, will at last learn never to deceive *themselves;* for truth being their constant aim in all their dealings, they will not shrink from that most effective of all means to acquire it, SELF-EXAMINATION.

CHAPTER XV.

OBSERVATIONS ON THE EXTRACTS FROM HAWKESWORTH AND OTHERS.

IN the preceding chapter, I have given various extracts from authors who have written on the subject of truth, and borne their testimony to the necessity of a strict adherence to it on all occasions, if individuals wish not only to be safe and respectable themselves, but to establish the interests of society on a sure foundation; but, before I proceed to other comments on this important subject, I shall make observations on some of the above-mentioned extracts.

Dr. Hawkesworth says, "that the liar, and only the liar, is universally despised, abandoned, and disowned." But is this the fact? Inconvenient, dangerous, and disagreeable, though it be, to associate with those on whose veracity we cannot depend; yet which of us has ever known himself, or others, refuse intercourse with persons who habitually violate the truth? We dismiss the servant indeed, whose habit of lying offends us, and we cease to employ the menial or the tradesman; but when did we ever hesitate to associate with the liar of rank and opulence? When was our moral sense so delicate as to make us refuse to eat of the costly food, and reject the favour or services of any one, because the lips of the obliger were stained with falsehood, and the conversation with guile? *Surely*, this writer overrates the delicacy of moral feeling in society, or we, of these latter days, have fearfully degenerated from our ancestors.

He also says, "that the imputation of a lie is an insult for which life only can atone." And amongst men of worldly honour, duel is undoubtedly the result of the lie given and received. Consequently, the interests of truth are placed under the secure guardianship of fear on great occasions. But, it is not so on daily, and more common ones, and the man who would thus fatally resent the imputation of falsehood, does not even reprove the lie of convenience in his wife or children, nor refrain from being guilty of it himself; he will often, perhaps, be the bearer of a lie to excuse them from keeping a disagreeable engagement; and will not scruple to make lying apologies for some negligence of his own. But, is Dr. Hawkesworth right in saying that offenders like *these* are shunned and despised? Certainly not; nor are they even *self-reprobated*, nor would they be censured by others, if their falsehood were detected. Yet, are they not liars? and is the lie imputed to them (in resentment of which imputation they were willing to risk their life, and the life of another,) a greater breach of the *moral law*, than the little lies which they are so willing to tell? and who, that is known to tell lies on trivial occasions, has a right to resent the imputation of lying on great ones? Whatever flattering unction we may lay to our souls, there is only one wrong and one right; and I repeat, that as those servants who pilfer grocery only are with justice called thieves, because they have thereby shown that the principle of honesty is not in them,—so may the utterers of little lies be with justice called liars, because they equally show that they are strangers to the restraining and immutable principles of truth.

OBSERVATIONS ON THE EXTRACTS.

Hawkesworth says, "that indirect lies more effectually destroy mutual confidence, that band of society, than any others;" and I fully agree with him in his idea of the "great turpitude, and greater meanness of those forms of speech, which deceive without direct falsehood;" but I cannot agree with him, that these deviations from truth are "*universally infamous;*" on the contrary, they are even scarcely reckoned a fault at all; their very frequency prevents them from being censured, and they are often considered both necessary and justifiable.

In that touching and useful tale by which Hawkesworth illustrates the pernicious effect of *indirect*, as well as direct lies, "a lie put into the mouth of a chairman, and another lie, accompanied by WITHHOLDING OF THE WHOLE TRUTH, are the occasion of duel and of death."

And what were these lies, direct and indirect, active and passive? Simply these. The bearer of a note is desired to *say* that he comes from a *milliner*, when, in reality, he comes from a lady in the neighbourhood; and one of the principal actors in the story leaves word that he is gone to a coffee-house, when, in point of fact, he is gone to a friend's house. That friend, on being questioned by him, *withholds*, or conceals part of the truth, meaning to *deceive*; the wife of the questioner *does the same*, and thus, though both are innocent even in thought, of any thing offensive to the strictest propriety, they become involved in the fatal consequences of imputed guilt, from which a disclosure of the whole truth would at once have preserved them.

Now, I would ask if there be any thing *more common* in the daily affairs of life, than those *very lies* and dissimulations which I have selected?

Who has not given, or heard given, this order, "do not say where you come from;" and often accompanied by "if you are asked, say you do not know, or you come from *such* a place." Who does not frequently conceal where they have been; and while they own to the questioner that they have been to such a place, and seen such a person, *keep back* the information that they *have been* to *another* place, and seen *another person*, though they are very conscious that the two latter were the *real* objects of the *inquiry* made?

Some may reply, "yes; I do these things every day perhaps, and so does every one; and where is the harm of it? You cannot be so absurd as to believe that such innocent lies, and a concealment such as I have a *right* to indulge in, will certainly be visited by consequences like those imagined by a writer of fiction?"

I answer, no; but though I cannot be *sure* that *fatal* consequences will be the result of that IMPOSSIBLE thing, an INNOCENT LIE, some consequences attend on *all* deviations from truth, which it were better to avoid. In the first place, the lying order given to a servant, or *inferior*, not only lowers the standard of truth in the mind of the person so commanded, but it *lowers* the person who GIVES it; it weakens that *salutary respect* with which the lower orders regard the higher; servants and inferiors are shrewd observers; and those domestics who detect a laxity of morals in their employers, and find that they do not hold truth sacred, but are ready to teach others to lie for their service, deprive themselves of their best claim to respect and obedience from them, that of a deep conviction of their MORAL SUPERIORITY. And they who discover in their intimate friends and associates a systematic habit, an assumed and exercised right of telling only as *much of the truth as suits their inclinations and purposes*, must feel their confidence in them most painfully destroyed; and listen, in future, to their disclosures and communications with unavoidable suspicion, and degrading distrust.

The account given by Boswell of the regard paid by Dr. Johnson to truth on all occasions, furnishes us with a still better shield against deviations from it, than can be afforded even by the best and most *moral fiction*. For, as Longinus was said, "to be himself the great sublime he draws," so Johnson was himself the great example of the benefit of those precepts which he lays down for the edification of others; and what is still more useful and valuable to us, he proves that however difficult it may be to speak the truth, and to be accurate on all occasions, it is certainly *possible;* for, as Johnson could do it, why cannot others? It requires not his force of intellect to enable us to follow his example; all that is necessary is a knowledge of right and wrong, a reverence for truth, and an abhorrence of deceit.

Such was Johnson's *known* habit of telling the truth, than even improbable things were believed, if *he* narrated them! Such was the respect for truth which his practice of it excited, and such the beneficial influence of his example, that all his intimate companions "were distinguished for a love of truth and an accuracy" *derived* from association with him.

I can never read this account of our great moralist, without feeling my heart glow with EMULATION and TRIUMPH! With emulation, because I know that it must be my own fault, if I become not as habitually the votary of truth as he himself was; and with triumph, because it is a complete refutation of the commonplace arguments against enforcing the necessity of spontaneous truth, that it is *absolutely impossible;* and that, *if possible*, what would be gained by it?

What would be gained by it? Society at large would, in the end, gain a degree of safety and purity far beyond what it has hitherto known; and, in the meanwhile, the individuals who speak truth would obtain a prize worthy the highest aspirings of earthly ambition,—the constant and involuntary confidence and reverence of their fellow-creatures.

The consciousness of truth and ingenuousness gives a radiance to the countenance, a freedom to the play of the lips, a persuasion to the voice, and a graceful dignity to the person, which no other quality of mind can equally bestow. And who is not able to recollect the direct contrast to this picture exhibited by the conscious utterer of falsehood and disingenuousness? Who has not observed the downcast eye, the snapping restless eyelid, the changing colour, and the hoarse, impeded voice, which sometimes contradict what the hesitating lip utters, and stamp, on the positive assertion, the undoubted evidence of deceit and insincerity?

Those who make up the usual mass of society are, when tempted to its common dissimulations, like little boats on the ocean, which are continually forced to shift their sail, and row away from danger; or, if obliged to await it, are necessitated, from want of power, to get on one side of the billow, instead of directly meeting it. While the firm votaries of truth, when exposed to the temptations of falsehood, proceed undaunted along the direct course, like the majestic vessel, coming boldly and directly on, breasting the waves in conscious security, and inspiring confidence in all whose well-being is entrusted to them. Is it not delightful to know, when we lie down at night, that however darkness may envelope us, the sun will undoubtedly rise again, and chase away the gloom? True, he may rise in clouds, and his usual splendour may not shine out upon us during the whole diurnal revolution; still we know that though there be not sunshine, there will be light, and we betake ourselves to our couch, confiding in the assurances of past experience, that day will succeed to night, and light to darkness. But, is it not equally delightful to feel this cheering confidence in the moral system of the circle in which we move? And can any thing inspire it so much as the constant habit of truth in those with whom we live? To know that we have friends on whom we can always rely for honest counsel, ingenuous reproof, and sincere sympathy, — to whom we can look with never-doubting confidence in the night of our soul's despondency, knowing that they will rise on us like the cheering, never-failing light of day, speaking unwelcome truths perhaps, but speaking them with tenderness and discretion,—is, surely, one of the dearest comforts which this world can give. It is the most precious of the earthly staffs, permitted to support us as we go, trembling, short-sighted, and weary pilgrims, along the chequered path of human existence.

And is it not an ambition worthy of thinking and responsible beings, to endeavour to qualify ourselves, and those whom we love, to *be* such friends as these? And if habits of unblemished truth will bestow this qualification, were it not wise to labour hard in order to attain them, undaunted by difficulty, undeterred by the sneers of worldlings, who cannot believe in the possibility of that moral excellence which they feel themselves unable to obtain?

To you, O ye parents and preceptors! I particularly address myself. Guard your own lips from "speaking leasing," that the quickly-discerning child or servant, may not, in self-defence, set the force of your example against that of your precepts. If each individual family would seriously resolve to avoid every species of falsehood themselves, whether authorized by custom or not, and would visit every deviation from truth, in those accused, with punishment and disgrace, the example would unceasingly spread; for, even now, wherever the beauty of truth is seen, its influence is immediately felt, and its value acknowledged. Individual efforts, however humble, if firm and repeated, must be ultimately successful, as the feeble mouse in the fable was, at last, enabled, by its perseverance, to gnaw the cords asunder which held the mighty lion. Difficult, I own, would such general purification be; but what is impossible to zeal and enterprise?

Hercules, as fabulous but instructive story tells us, when he was required to perform the apparently impossible task of cleansing the Augean stables, exerted all his strength, and turned the course of a river through them to effect his purpose, proving by his success, that nothing is impossible to perseverance and exertion; and, however long the duration, and wide-spreading the pollutions of falsehood and dissimulation in the world, there *is* a river, which, if suffered to flow over their impurities, is powerful enough to wash away every stain, since it flows from the "FOUNTAIN OF EVER-LIVING WATERS."

CHAPTER XVI.

RELIGION THE ONLY BASIS OF TRUTH.

ALL the moralists from whom I have quoted, and those on whom I have commented in the preceding chapters, have treated the subject of truth, as moralists only. They do not lay it down as an indisputable fact, that truth, as a principle of action, is obligatory on us all, in enjoined obedience to the clear dictates of revealed religion. Therefore, they have kept out of sight the strongest motive to abhor lying, and cleave unto truth, OBEDIENCE TO THE DIVINE WILL; yet, as necessary as were the shield and buckler to the ancient warriors, is the "breastplate of faith" to the cause of spontaneous truth. It has been asserted, that morality might exist in all its power and purity, were there no such thing as religion, since it is conducive to the earthly interests and happiness of man. But, are moral motives sufficient to protect us in times of particular temptations? There appears to me the same difference between morality, unprotected by religious motives, and morality derived from them, as between the palace of ice, famous in Russian story, and a castle built of ever-during stone; perfect to the eye, and, as if formed to last for ever, was the building of frost-work, ornamented and lighted up for the pleasure of the sovereign; but, it melted away before the power of natural and artificial warmth, and was quickly resolved to the element from which it sprung.— But the castle formed of stones, joined together by a strong and enduring cement, is proof against all assailment; and, even though it may be occasionally shattered by the enemy, it still towers in its grandeur, indestructible, though impaired. In like manner, unassailable and perfect, in appearance, may be the virtue of the mere moralist; but, when assailed by the warmth of the passions on one side, and by different enemies on the other, his virtue, like the palace of ice, is likely to melt away, and be as though it had not been. But, the virtue of the truly religious man, even though it may, on occasion, be slightly shaken, is yet proof against any important injury; and remains, spite of temptation and danger, in its original purity and power. The moral man *may*, therefore, utter spontaneous truth, but the *religious* man *must*; for he remembers the following precepts, which amongst others he has learned from the Scriptures; and knows, that to speak lies, is displeasing to the GOD OF TRUTH.

In the 6th chapter of Leviticus, the Lord threatens the man " Who lies to his neighbour, and who deceives his neighbour." Again he says, "Ye shall not deal falsely, neither lie to one another." We read in the Psalms that "The Lord will destroy those who speak leasing." He is said to be angry with the wicked every day, who have conceived mischief, and brought forth falsehood. "He that worketh deceit," says the Psalmist, "shall not dwell within my house — he that telleth lies shall not tarry in my sight." The Saviour, in the 8th chapter of John, calls the devil "A liar, and the father of lies." Paul, in the 3d chapter of Colossians, says, "Lie not one to another!" Prov. vi. 19, "The Lord hates a false-witness that speaketh lies." Prov. ix. "And he that speaketh lies shall perish." Prov. xix. 22, "A poor man is better than a liar." James iii. 14, "Lie not against the truth." Isaiah xvii. "The Lord shall sweep away the refuge of lies." Prov. xviii. "Let the lying lips be put to silence." Psalm cxix. 29, "Remove from me the way of lying." Psalm lxiii. 11, "The mouth that speaketh lies shall be stopped." The fate of Gehazi, in the 5th chapter of the second book of Kings, who lied to the prophet Elisha, and went out of his presence "a leper whiter than snow;" and the judgment on Ananias and Sapphira, in the 5th chapter of Acts, on the former for WITHHOLDING THE TRUTH, INTENDING TO DECEIVE, and on the latter for telling a DIRECT LIE, are awful proofs how hateful falsehood is in the sight of the Almighty; and, that though the seasons of his immediate judgments may be past, his vengeance against every species of falsehood is tremendously certain.

But though, as I have stated more than once, all persons, even those who are most negligent of truth, exclaim continually against lying; and liars cannot forgive the slightest imputation against their veracity, still, few are willing to admit that telling lies of courtesy, or convenience, is lying; or that the occasional violator of truth, for what are called innocent purposes, ought to be considered as a liar; and *thence* the universal falsehood which prevails. And surely, that moral precept which every one claims a right to violate, according to his wants and wishes, loses its restraining power, and is, as I have before observed, for all its original purposes, wholly annihilated.

But, as that person has no right to resent being called a sloven, who goes about in a stained garment, though that stain be a single one; so that being who allows himself to indulge in any one species of lie, cannot declare with justice that he deserves not the name of a liar. The general voice and tenor of Scripture say, "lie not at all."

This may appear a command very difficult to obey, but he who gave it, has given us a still more appalling one; "Be ye perfect, as your Father in heaven is perfect." Yet, surely, he would never have given a command impossible for us to fulfil. However, be that as it may, we are to try to fulfil it. The drawing-master who would form a pupil to excellence, does not set incorrect copies before him, but the most perfect models of immortal art; and that tyro who is awed into doing nothing by the perfection of his model, is not more weak than those who persevere in the practice of lying by the seeming *impossibility* of constantly telling the truth. The pupil may never be able to copy the model set before him, because his aids are only human and earthly ones. But,

He who has said that "As our day our strength shall be;" He whose ear is open to the softest cry; He whom the royal Psalmist called upon to deliver him from those "Whose mouth speaketh vanity, and whose right hand is a right hand of falsehood;"—This pure, this powerful, this perfect Being, still lives to listen to the supplications of all who trust *in him*; and will, in the hour of temptation to utter falsehood and deceit, strengthen them out of Zion.

In all other times of danger the believer supplicates the Lord to grant him force to resist temptation; but, who ever thinks of supplicating him to be enabled to resist daily temptation to what is called little, or *white lying?* Yet, has the Lord revealed to us what species of lying he tolerates, and what he reproves? Does he tell us that we may tell the lie of courtesy and convenience, but avoid all others? The lying of Ananias was only the passive lie of concealing that he had kept back part of *his own property*, yet he was punished with instant death! The only safety is in believing, or remembering, that all lying and insincerity whatever, is rebellion against the revealed will of the great God of Truth; and they who so believe or remember, are prepared for the strongest attacks of the soul's adversary, "that devil, who is the father of lies;" for their weapons are derived from the armory of heaven; their steps are guided by light from the sanctuary, and the cleansing river by which they are enabled to drive away all the pollutions of falsehood and deceit, is that pure river of "the water of life, flowing from the throne of God, and of the Lamb."

I trust, that I have not in any of the preceding pages underrated the difficulty of always speaking the truth;—I have only *denied* that it was *impossible* to do so, and I have pointed out the only means by which the possibility of resisting the temptation to utter falsehood might be secured to us on all occasions; namely, religious motives derived from obedience to the will of God.

Still, in order to prove how well aware I am of the difficulty in question, I shall venture to bring forward some distinguished instances on record of holy men, who were led by the fear of death and other motives to lie against their consciences; thereby exhibiting, beyond a doubt, the difficulty of a constant adherence to the practice of sincerity. But they also prove that the real christian must be miserable under a consciousness of having violated the truth, and that to escape from the most poignant of all pangs, the pangs of self-reproach, the delinquents in question sought for refuge from their remorse, by courting that very death which they had endeavoured to escape from, by being guilty of falsehood. They at the same time furnish convincing proofs that it is in the power of the sincere penitent to retrace his steps, and be reinstated in the height of virtue whence he has fallen, if he will humble himself before the great Being whom he has offended, and call upon Him who can alone "save to the uttermost."

My first three examples are taken from the martyred reformers, who were guilty of the most awful species of lying, in signing recantations of their opinions, even when their belief in them remained unchanged; but who, as I have before observed, were compelled by the power of that word of God written on the depth of the secret heart, to repent with agonizing bitterness of their apostasy from truth, and to make a public reparation for their short-lived error, by a death of patient suffering, and even of rejoicing.

JEROME OF PRAGUE comes first upon the list. He was born at the close of the thirteenth century; and in the year 1415, after having spent his youth in the pursuit of knowledge at the greatest Universities in Europe,—namely, those of Prague, Paris, Heidelberg, and Cologne,—we find him visiting Oxford, at which place he became acquainted with the works of Wickliffe; and at his return to Prague he not only professed himself an open favourer of the doctrines of that celebrated reformer; but, finding that John Huss was at the head of Wickliffe's party in Bohemia, he attached himself immediately to that powerful leader. It were unnecessary for me to follow him through the whole of his polemical career, as it is the close of it only which is fitted for my purpose; suffice, that having been brought before the Council of Constance, in the year 1415, to answer for what they deemed his heresies, a thousand voices called out, even after his first examination, "away with him! burn him! burn him! burn him!" On which, little doubting that his power and virtuous resistance could ever fail him in time of need, Jerome replied, looking round on the assembly with dignity and confidence, "Since nothing can satisfy you but my blood, God's will be done!"

Severities of a most uncommon nature were now inflicted on him, in order to constrain him to recant, a point of which the council were excessively desirous. So rigorous was his confinement, that at length it brought upon him a dangerous illness, in the course of which he entreated to have a confessor sent to him; but he was given to understand, that only on certain terms would this indulgence be granted; notwithstanding, he remained immoveable. The next attempt on his faithfulness was after the martyrdom of Huss; when all its affecting and appalling details were made known to him, he listened, however, without emotion, and answered in language so resolute and determined, that they had certainly no hope of his *sudden* conversion. But, whether, too confident in his own strength, he neglected to seek, as he had hitherto done, that only strength "which cometh from above," it is certain that his constancy at length gave way. "He withstood," says Gilpin, in his Lives of the Reformers, "the simple fear of death, but imprisonment, chains, hunger, sickness, and torture, through a succession of months, was more than human nature could bear; and though he still made a noble stand for the truth, when brought three times before the infuriated council, he began at last to waver, and to talk obscurely of his having misunderstood the tendency of some of the writings of Huss. Promises and threats were now redoubled upon him, till, at last, he read aloud an ample recantation of all the opinions that he had recently entertained, and declared himself in every article a firm believer with the church of Rome.

But with a heavy heart he retired from the council; chains were removed from his body, but his mind was corroded by chains of his conscience, and his soul was burthened with a load, till then unknown to it. Hitherto, the light of an approving conscience had cheered the gloom of his dungeon, but now all was dark to him both without and within.

But in this night of his moral despair, the day-spring from on high was again permitted to visit him, and the penitent was once more enabled to seek assistance from his God. Jerome had long been apprized that he was to be brought to a second trial, upon some new evidence which had appeared; and this was his only consolation in the midst of his painful penitence. At length the moment so ardently desired by him arrived; and, rejoicing at an opportunity of publicly retracting his errors, and deploring his unworthy falsehood, he eagerly obeyed the summons to appear before the council in the year 1416. There, after delivering an oration, which was, it is said, a model of pathetic eloquence, he ended by declaring before the whole assembly, "that, though the fear of death, and the prevalence of human infirmity, had induced him to retract those opinions with his lips which had drawn on him the anger and vengeance of the council, yet they were *then* and *still* the opinions near and dear to his heart, and that he solemnly declared they were opinions in which he alone believed, and for which he was ready, and even glad to die." "It was expected," says Poggé the Florentine who was present at his examination, "that he would have retracted his errors; or, at least, have apologized for them; but he plainly declared that he had nothing to retract." After launching forth into the most eloquent encomiums on Huss, declaring him to be a wise and holy man, and lamenting his unjust and cruel death, he avowed that he had armed himself with a firm resolution to follow the steps of that blessed martyr, and suffer with constancy whatever the malice of his enemies should inflict; and he was mercifully enabled to keep his resolution.

When brought to the stake, and when the wood was beginning to blaze, he sang a hymn, which he continued with great fervency, till the fury of the fire scorching him, he was heard to cry out, "Oh Lord God! have mercy on me!" and a little afterwards, "thou knowest," he cried, "how I have loved thy truth;" and he continued to exhibit a spectacle of intense suffering, made bearable by as intense devotion, till the vital spark was in mercy permitted to expire; and the contrite, but then triumphant spirit was allowed to return unto the God who gave it.

THOMAS BILNEY, the next on my list, "was brought up from a child, (says Fox, in his Acts and Monuments) in the University of Cambridge, profiting in all kind of liberal sciences, even unto the profession of both laws. But, at last, having gotten a better schoolmaster, even the Holy Spirit of Christ enduing his heart by privie inspiration with the knowledge of better and more wholesome things, he came unto this point, that forsaking the knowledge of man's lawes, he converted his studie to those things which tended more unto godlinesse, than gainfulnesse. At the last, Bilney forsaking the university, went into many places teaching and preaching, being associate with Thomas Arthur, which accompanied him from the universitie. The authority of Thomas Wolsey, Cardinall of York, at that time was greate in England, but his temper and pride much greater, which did evidently declare unto all wise men the manifest vanitie, not only of his life, but also of all the Bishops and clergie; whereupon, Bilney with other good men, marvelling at the incredible insolence of the clergie, which they could no longer suffer or abide, began to shake and reprove this excessive pompe, and also to pluck at the authority of the Bishop of Rome."

It therefore became necessary that the cardinal should rouse himself and look about him. A chapter being held at Westminster for the occasion, Thomas Bilney, with his friends, Thomas Arthur and Hugh Latimer, were brought before them. Gilpin says, "that, as Bilney was considered as the Heresiarch, the rigour of the court was chiefly levelled against him. The principal persons at this time concerned in Ecclesiastical affairs besides Cardinal Wolsey, were Warham, Archbishop of Canterbury, and Tunstall, Bishop of London." The latter was of all the prelates of these times the most deservedly esteemed, "as he was not influenced by the spirit of popery, and had just notions of the mild genius of Christianity;" but every deposition against Bilney was enlarged upon with such unrelenting bitterness, that Tunstall, though the president of the court, despaired of being able to soften by his influence the enraged proceedings of his colleagues. And, when the process came to an end, "Bilney, declaring himself what they called an obstinate heretic, was found guilty." Tunstall now proved the kindness of his heart. He could not come forward in Bilney's favour by a judicial interference, but he laboured to save him by all means in his power. "He first set his friends upon him to persuade him to recant, and when that would not do, he joined his entreaties to theirs; had patience with him day after day, and begged he would not oblige him, contrary to his inclinations, to treat him with severity."

The man whom fear was not able to move was not proof against the language of affectionate persuasion. " Bilney could not withstand the winning rhetoric of Tunstall, though he withstood the menaces of Warham. He therefore recanted, bore a fagot on his shoulders, in the Cathedral church of Paul, bareheaded, according to the custom of the times, and was dismissed with Latimer and the others who had met with milder treatment and easier terms."

The liberated heretics, as they were called, returned directly to Cambridge, where they were received with open arms by their friends; but in the midst of this joy, Bilney kept aloof, bearing on his countenance the marks of internal suffering and incessant gloom. " He received the congratulations of his officious friends with confusion and blushes;" he had sinned against his God, therefore he could neither be gratified nor cheered by the affection of any earthly being. In short, his mind at length preying on itself, nearly disturbed his reason, and his friends dared not allow him to be left alone, either by night or day. They tried to comfort him; but they tried in vain; and when they endeavoured to soothe him by certain texts in Scripture, " It was as though a man would run himself through with a sword." In the agonies of his despair he uttered pathetic and eager accusations of his friends, of Tunstall, and above all, of himself. At length, his violence having had its course, it subsided, by degrees, into a state of profound melancholy. In this state he continued from the year 1629 to 1631, " reading much, avoiding company; and, in all respects, preserving the severity of an ascetic."

It is interesting to observe in how many different ways our soul's adversary deals with us, in order to allure us to perdition; and he is never so successful as when he can make the proffered sin assume the appearance of what is amiable. This seems to have been the case with the self-judged Bilney. To the fear of death, and the menaces of Warham, we are told that he opposed a resolution and an integrity which could not be overcome; but the gentle entreaties of affection, and the tender, persuasive eloquence of Tunstall, had power to conquer his love of truth, and make the pleadings of conscience vain; while he probably looked upon his yielding as a proof of affectionate gratitude, and that, not to consider the feelings of those who loved him, would have been offensive, and ungrateful hardness of heart.

But, whatever were his motives to sin, that sin was indeed visited with remorse as unquestionable as it was efficacious; and it is pleasant to turn from the contemplation of Bilney's frailty, to that of its exemplary and courted expiation.

The consequence of this salutary period of sorrow and seclusion was, that after having, for some time, thrown out hints that he was meditating an extraordinary design; after saying that he was almost prepared, that he would shortly go up to Jerusalem, and that God must be glorified in him; and keeping his friends in painful suspense by this mysterious language, he told them at last that he was fully determined to expiate his late shameful abjuration, that *wicked lie* against his conscience, by death.

There can be no doubt but that his friends again interposed to shake his resolution; but that Being who had lent a gracious ear to the cry of his penitence and his agony, " girded up his loins for the fight," and enabled him to sacrifice every human affection at the foot of the cross, and strengthened him to take up that cross, and bear it, unfainting, to the end. He therefore broke from all his Cambridge ties, and set out for Norfolk, the place of his nativity, and which, for that reason, he chose to make the place of his death.

When he arrived there, he preached openly in the fields, confessing his fault, and preaching publicly that doctrine which he had before abjured, to be the VERY TRUTH, and willed all men to beware by him, and never to trust to their *fleshly friends in causes of religion;* and so setting forward in his journey towards the celestial Jerusalem, he departed from thence to the Anchresse in Norwich, (whom he had converted to Christ,) and there gave her a New Testament of Tindall's translation, and " the obedience of a Christian man;" whereupon he was apprehended, and carried to prison.

Nixe, (the blind Bishop Nixe, as Fox calls him) the then Bishop of Norwich, was a man of a fierce, inquisitorial spirit, and he lost no time in sending up for a writ to burn him.

In the meanwhile, great pains were taken by divers religious persons to re-convert him to what his assailants believed to be the truth; but he having " planted himselfe upon the firm rocke of God's word, was at a point, and so continued to the end."

While Bilney lay in the county gaol, waiting the arrival of the writ for his execution, he entirely recovered from that melancholy which had so long oppressed him; and " like an honest man who had long lived under a difficult debt, he began to resume his spirits when he thought himself in a situation to discharge it."—*Gilpin's Lives of the Reformers*, p. 358.

" Some of his friends found him taking a hearty supper the night before his execution, and expressing their surprise, he told them he was but doing what they had daily examples of in common life; he was only keeping his cottage in repair while he continued to inhabit it." The same composure ran through his whole behaviour, and his conversation was more agreeable that evening than they had ever remembered it to be.

Some of his friends put him in mind, " that though the fire which he should suffer the next day should be of great heat unto his body, yet the comfort of God's Spirit should coole it to his everlasting refreshing." At this word, the said Thomas Bilney putting his hand toward the flame of the candle burning before them, (as he also did divers times besides,) and feeling the heat thereof, "Oh!" said he, "I feel by experience, and have knowne it long by philosophie, that fire, by God's ordinance, is naturally hot, but yet I am persuaded by God's holy word, and by the experience of some spoken of in the same, that in the flame they felt no heate, and in the fire they felt no consumption; and I constantly believe that, howsoever the stubble of this my bodie shall be wasted by it, yet my soule and spirit shall be purged thereby; a paine for the time, whereon, notwithstanding, followeth joy unspeakable." He then dwelt much upon a passage in Isaiah. "Fear not, for I have redeemed thee, and called thee by thy name.— Thou art my own; when thou passest through the waters, I will be with thee; when thou walkest in the fire, it shall not burn thee, and the flame shall not kindle upon thee; for I am the Lord thy God, the Holy One of Israel."

"He was led to the place of execution* without the citie gate, called Bishop's gate, in a low valley, commonly called the Lollard's pit, under Saint Leonard's hill. At the coming forth of the said Thomas Bilney out of the prison doore, one of his friends came to him, and prayed him, in God's behalf, to be constant, and take his death as patiently as he could. Whereunto the said Bilney answered with a quiet and mild countenance, "Ye see when the mariner is entered his ship to saile on the troublous sea, how he is for a while tossed in the billows of the same, but yet in hope that he shall come to the quiet haven, he beareth in better comfort the perils which he feeleth; so am I now toward this sayling; and whatsoever stormes I shall feele, yet shortly after shall my ship be in the haven, as I doubt not thereof, by the grace of God, desiring you to helpe me with your prayers to the same effect."

While he kneeled upon a little ledge coming out of the stake, upon which he was afterwards to stand, that he might be better seen, he made his private prayers with such earnest elevation of his eyes and hands to heaven, "and in so good quiet behaviour, that he seemed not much to consider the terror of his death," ending his prayer with the 43d Psalm, in which he repeated this verse thrice, "Enter not into judgment with thy servant, O Lord! for in thy sight shall no man living be justified;" and so finishing the Psalm, he concluded. "Nor did that God in whom he trusted forsake him in the hour of his need; while the flames raged around him, he held up his hands, and knocked upon his breast, crying 'Jesus,' and sometimes 'Credo,' till he gave up the ghost, and his body being withered, bowed downward upon the chaine, 'while triumphing over death, (to use the words of the poet laureate) 'he ren-

---

* "In the Lollard's pit, I find that many persons of a sect, known by the name of Lollards, in the city of Norwich, were thrown, after being burnt, in the year 1424, and for many years afterwards; and thence it was called the *Lollard's pit;* and the following account of the meaning of the term Lollard may not be unacceptable. Soon after the commencement of the 14th century, the famous sect of the Cellite brethren and sisters arose at Antwerp; they were also styled the Alexian brethren and sisters, because St. Alexius was their patron; and they were named Cellites, from the cells in which they were accustomed to live. As the clergy of this age took but little care of the sick and the dying, and deserted such as were infected with those pestilential disorders which were then very frequent, some compassionate and pious persons at Antwerp formed themselves into a society for the performance of these religious offices which the sacerdotal orders so shamefully neglected. In the prosecution of this agreement, they visited and comforted the sick, assisted the dying with their prayers and exhortations, took care of the interment of those who were cut off by the plague, and on that account forsaken by the terrified clergy, and committed them to the grave with *a solemn funeral dirge.* It was with reference to this last office that the common people gave them the name of *Lollards.* The term Lollhard, or Lullhard, or as the ancient Germans wrote it, Lollert, Lullert, is compounded of the old German word lullen, lollan, lallen, and the well-known termination of hard, with which many of the old High Dutch words end. Lollen, or Lullen, signifies to sing with a low voice. It is yet used in the same sense among the English, who say *lulla sleep,* which signifies to sing any one into a slumber with a sweet indistinct voice.

"Lollhard, therefore, is a singer, or one who frequently sings. For, as the word beggen, which universally signifies to request any thing fervently, is applied to devotional requests, or prayers, so the word lollen, or lallen, is transferred from a common to a sacred song, and signifies, in its most limited sense, to sing a hymn. Lollhard, therefore, in the vulgar tongue of the ancient Germans, denotes a person who is continually praising God with a song, or singing hymns to his honour.

"And as prayers and hymns are regarded as an external sign of piety towards God, those who were more frequently employed in singing hymns of praise to God than others, were, in the common popular language, called Lollhards.

"But the priests and monks, being inveterately exasperated against these good men, endeavoured to persuade the people, that innocent and beneficent as the Lollhards appeared to be, they were tainted with the most pernicious sentiments of a religious kind, and secretly addicted to all sorts of vices; hence the name of Lollard at length became infamous. Thus, by degrees it came to pass, that any person who covered heresies, or crimes, under the appearance of piety, was called a Lollard, so that this was not a name to denote any one particular sect, but was formerly common to all persons, and all sects, who were supposed to be guilty of impiety towards God and the church, under an external profession of extraordinary piety."—*Maclane's Eccles. History*, p. 355–356.

dered up his soul in the fulness of faith, and entered into his reward.'"

"So exemplary," says Bloomfield, in his History of Norwich, " was Bilney's life and conversation, that when Nixe, his persecutor, was constantly told how holy and upright he was, he said he feared that he had burnt *Abel.*"

I have recently visited the Lollard's pit; that spot where my interesting martyred countryman met his dreadful death. The top of the hill retains, probably, much the same appearance as it had when he perished at its foot; and, without any great exertion of fancy, it would have been easy for me to figure to myself the rest of the scene, could I have derived sufficient comfort from the remembrance of the fortitude with which he bore his sufferings, to reconcile me to the contemplation of them. Still it is, I believe, salutary to visit the places hallowed in the memory, as marked by any exhibition of virtuous acts and sufferings endured for the sake of conscience. To the scaffold, and to the stake, on account of their religious opinions, it is humbly to be hoped that Christians will never again be brought. But all persecution, on the score of religion, is, in a degree, an infliction of martyrdom on the mind and on the heart. It matters not that we forbear to kill the body of the Christian, if we afflict the soul by aught of a persecuting spirit.

Yet does not our daily experience testify, that, there is nothing which calls forth petty persecutions, and the mean warfare of a detracting spirit, so much as any marked religious profession?

And while such a profession is assailed, by ridicule on the one hand, by distrust of its motives on the other; while it exposes the serious Christian, converted from the errors of former days, to the stigma of wild enthusiasm, or of religious hypocrisy; who shall say that the persecuting spirit of the Lauds, and the Bonners, is not still the spirit of the world? Who shall say to the tried and shrinking souls of those who, on account of their having made a religious profession, are thus calumniated, and thus judged, the time of martyrdom is over, and we live in mild, and liberal, and truly Christian days?

Such were the thoughts uppermost in my mind, while I stood perhaps on the very spot where Bilney suffered, and where Bilney died; and though I rejoiced to see that the harmless employment of the lime-burner had succeeded to the frightful burning of the human form, I could not but sigh as I turned away, while I remembered that so much of an intolerant, uncandid spirit still prevailed amongst professed Christians, and that the practice of persecution still existed, though applied in a very different manner. I could not but think, that many of the present generation might do well to visit scenes thus fraught with the recollection of martyrdom. If it be true that "our love of freedom would burn brighter on the plains of Marathon," and that our devotion "must glow more warmly amidst the ruins of Iona," sure am I that the places where the martyrs for conscience' sake have passed through the portals of fire and agony to their God, must assist in bestowing on us power to endure with fortitude the mental martyrdom which may, unexpectedly, become our portion in life; and by recalling the sufferings of others, we may, meekly bowing to the hand that afflicts us for good, be in time enabled to bear, and even to love, our own.

The last, and third, on my list, is THOMAS CRANMER, Archbishop of Canterbury, who was promoted to that see by the favour of Henry the Eighth, and degraded from it in consequence of his heretical opinions, by virtue of an order from the sovereign pontiff, in the reign of Queen Mary. "The ceremony of his degradation," says Gilpin, which took place at Oxford, " was performed by Thirlby, Bishop of Ely, a man recently converted, it should seem, to catholicism; who, in Cranmer's better days, had been honoured with his particular friendship, and owed him many obligations.

As this man, therefore, had long been so much attached to the Archbishop, it was thought proper by his new friends, that he should give an extraordinary test of his zeal; for this reason the ceremony of his degradation was committed to him. He had undertaken, however, too hard a task. The mild benevolence of the primate, which shone forth with great dignity, though he stood in mock grandeur of canvass robes, struck the old apostate to the heart. All the past came throbbing to his breast, and a few repentant tears began to trickle down the furrows of his aged cheek. The Archbishop gently exhorted him not to suffer his private to overpower his public affections. At length, one by one, the canvass trappings were taken off, amidst the taunts and exultations of Bonner, bishop of London, who was present at the ceremony.

Thus degraded, he was attired in a plain frieze gown, the common habit of a yeoman at that period, and had what was then called a townsman's cap put upon his head. In this garb he was carried back to prison, Bonner crying after him, " He is now no longer my Lord! he is now no longer my Lord!"—*Gilpin's Lives of the Reformers.*

I know not what were Cranmer's feelings at these expressions of mean exultation from the contemptible Bonner; but, I trust that he treated them, and the ceremony of degradation at the time, with the indifference which they merited. Perhaps, too, he might utter within himself, this serious and important truth, that none of us can ever be truly *degraded*, but by *ourselves alone;* and this moment of his external humiliation was, in the eyes of all whose esteem was worth having, one of triumph and honour to the bereaved ecclesiastic. But what, alas! were those which succeeded to it? That period, and that alone, was the period of his real degradation, when overcome by the flatteries and the kindness of his real and seeming friends, and subdued by the entertainments given him, the amusements offered him, and, allowed to indulge in the "lust of the eye, and the pride of life," he was induced to lend a willing ear to the proposal of being reinstated in his former dignity, on condition that he would conform to the present change of religion, and "gratify the queen by being wholly a catholic!"

The adversary of man lured Cranmer, as well as Bilney, by the unsuspected influence of mild and amiable feelings, rather than the instigations of fear; and he who was armed to resist, to the utmost, the rage and malice of his enemies, was drawn aside from truth and duty by the suggestions of false friends.

After the confinement of a full year in the gloomy walls of a prison, his sudden return into social intercourse dissipated his firm resolves. That love of life returned, which he had hitherto conquered; and when a paper was offered to him importing his assent to the tenets of popery, his better resolutions gave way, and in an evil hour, he signed the fatal scroll!

Cranmer's recantation was received by the popish party with joy beyond expression; but, as all they wanted was to blast the reputation of a man whose talents, learning, and virtue, were of such great importance to the cause which he espoused, they had no sooner gained what they desired, than their thirst for his blood returned, and though he was kept in ignorance of the fate which awaited him, a warrant was ordered for his execution with all possible expedition.

But long before the certainty of his approaching fate was made known to him, the self-convicted culprit sighed for the joy and the serenity which usually attend the last days of a martyr for the truth which he loves.

Vainly did his friends throw over his faults the balm afforded by those healing words, "the spirit was willing, but the flesh was weak." In his own clear judgment he was fully convicted, while his days were passed in horror and remorse, and his nights in sleepless anguish.

To persevere in his recantation was an insupportable thought; but to retract it was scarcely within the verge of possibility; but he was allowed an opportunity of doing so which he did not expect, and, though death was the means of it, he felt thankful that it was afforded him, and deemed his life a sacrifice not to be regarded for the attainment of such an object.

When Dr. Cole, one of the heads of the popish party, came to him on the twentieth of March, the evening preceding his intended execution, and insinuated to him his approaching fate, he spent the remaining part of the evening in drawing up a full confession of his apostasy, and of his bitter repentance, wishing to take the best opportunity to speak or publish it, which he supposed would be afforded him when he was carried to the stake; but, beyond his expectation, a better was provided for him. It was intended that he should be conveyed immediately from his prison to the place of his execution, where a sermon was to be preached; but, as the morning of the appointed day was wet and stormy, the ceremony was performed under cover.

About nine o'clock, the Lord Williams of Thame, attended by the magistrates of Oxford, received him at the prison-gate, and conveyed him to St. Mary's church, where he found a crowded audience awaiting him, and was conducted to an elevated place, in public view, opposite to the pulpit. If ever there was a broken and a contrite heart before God and man; if ever there was a person humbled in the very depths of his soul, from the consciousness of having committed sin, and of having deserved the extreme of earthly shame and earthly suffering; that man was Cranmer!

He is represented as standing against a pillar, pale as the stone against which he leaned. "It is doleful," says a popish, but impartial spectator, "to describe his behaviour during the sermon, part of which was addressed to him; his sorrowful countenance; his heavy cheer, his face bedewed with tears; sometimes lifting up his eyes to heaven in hope; sometimes casting them down to the earth for shame. To be brief, he was an image of sorrow. The dolour of his heart burst out continually from his eyes in gushes of tears; yet he retained ever a quiet and grave behaviour, which increased pity in men's hearts, who unfeignedly loved him, *hoping that it had been his repentance for his transgressions.*" And so it was; though not for what many considered his transgressions; but it was the deep contrition of a converted heart, and of a subdued and penitent soul, prepared by the depth of human degradation and humility, to rise on the wings of angels, and meet in another world its beloved and blessed Redeemer.

The preacher having concluded his sermon, turned round to the audience, and desired all who were present to join with him in silent prayers for the unhappy man before them. A solemn stillness ensued; every eye and heart were instantly lifted up to heaven. Some minutes having been passed in this affecting manner, the degraded primate, who had also fallen on his knees, arose in all the dignity of sorrow, accompanied by conscious penitence and Christian reliance, and thus addressed his audience.

"I had myself intended to desire your prayers. My desires have been anticipated, and I return you all that a dying man can give, my sincerest thanks. To your prayers for me let me add my own! Good Christian people!" continued he, "my dearly beloved brethren and sisters in Christ, I beseech you most heartily, to pray for me to Almighty God, that he will forgive me all my sins and offences, which are many, without number, and great beyond measure. But one thing grieveth my conscience more than all the rest; whereof, God willing, I mean to speak hereafter. But, how great and how many soever my sinnes be, I beseech you to pray God, of his mercy, to pardon and forgive them all." He then knelt down and offered up a prayer as full of pathos as of eloquence; then he took a paper from his bosom, and read it aloud, which was to the following effect.

"It is now, my brethren, no time to dissemble—I stand upon the verge of life—a vast eternity before me—what my fears are, or what my hopes, it matters not here to unfold. For one action of my life, at least, I am accountable to the world. My *late shameful subscription to opinions, which are wholly opposite to my real sentiments.* Before this congregation I solemnly declare, that the fear of death alone induced me to this ignominious action—that it hath cost me many bitter tears — that, in my heart, I totally reject the Pope, and doctrines of the church of Rome, and that——"

As he was continuing his speech, the whole assembly was in an uproar. "Stop the audacious heretic," cried Lord Williams of Thame. On which several priests and friars, rushing from different parts of the church, seized, or pulled him from his seat, dragged him into the street, and, with indecent precipitation, hurried him to the stake, which was already prepared.

As he stood with all the horrid apparatus of death around him, amidst taunts, revilings, and execrations, he alone maintained a dispassionate behaviour. Having discharged his conscience, he seemed to feel, even in his awful circumstances, an inward satisfaction, to which he had long been a stranger. His countenance was not fixed, as before, in sorrow on the ground; but he looked round him with eyes full of sweetness and benignity, as if at peace with all the world.

Who can contemplate the conduct of Cranmer, in the affecting scene that followed, without feeling a deep conviction of the intensity of his penitence for the degrading lie, of which he had been guilty! and who can fail to think that Cranmer, in his proudest days, when the favourite, the friend, the counsellor of the king, and bearing the highest ecclesiastical rank in the country, was far inferior in real dignity and real consequence to Cranmer, when, prostrate in soul before his offended, yet pardoning God, but erect and fearless before his vindictive enemies, he thrust the hand, with which he had signed the lying scroll of recantations, into the fast-rising flames, crying out, as he did so, "this hand hath offended! this hand hath offended!"

It is soothing to reflect, that his sufferings were quickly over; for, as the fire rose fiercely round him, he was involved in a thick smoke, and it was supposed that he died very soon.

"Surely," says the writer before quoted, "his death grieved every one; his friends sorrowed for love; his enemies for pity; and strangers through humanity."

To us of these latter days, his crime and his penitence afford an awful warning, and an instructive example.

The former proves how vain are talents, learning, and even exalted virtues, to preserve us in the path of rectitude, unless we are watchful unto prayer, and unless, wisely distrustful of our own strength, we wholly and confidently lean upon "that rock, which is higher than we are." And the manner in which he was enabled to declare his penitence and contrition for his falsehood and apostasy, and to bear the tortures which attended on his dying hours, is a soothing and comforting evidence, that sinners, who prostrate themselves with contrite hearts before the throne of their God, and their Redeemer, "he will in no wise cast out," but will know his Almighty arm to be round about them, "till death is swallowed up in victory."

It is with a degree of fearfulness and awe, that I take my fourth example from one who, relying too much on his own human strength, in his hour of human trial, was permitted to fall into the commission of human frailty, and to utter the most decided and ungrateful of falsehoods; since he that thus erred was no less a person than the apostle Peter himself, who, by a thrice-told lie, denied his Lord and Master; but who, by his bitter tearful repentance, and by his subsequent faithfulness unto death, redeemed, in the eyes of his Saviour and of men, his short-lived frailty, and proved himself worthy of that marked confidence in his active zeal which was manifested by our great Redeemer, in his parting words.

The character of Peter affords us a warning, as well as an example; while the affectionate reproofs of the Saviour, together with the tender encouragement, and generous praise, which he bestowed upon him, prove to us, in a manner the most cheering and indisputable, how merciful are the dealings of the Almighty with his sinful creatures; how ready he is to overlook our offences, and to dwell with complacency on our virtues; and that he willeth not the death of a sinner, but had rather that he should turn from his wickedness and live."

Self-confidence, and self-righteousness, proceeding perhaps from his belief in the superior depth and strength of his faith in Christ, seem to have been the besetting sins of Peter; and that his faith was lively and sincere, is sufficiently evidenced by his unhesitating reply to the questions of his Lord; "Thou art the Christ, the Son of the living God!" A reply so satisfactory to the great being whom he addressed, that he answered him saying, "Blessed art thou, Simon Barjona; for flesh and blood have not revealed it unto thee, but my Father which is in Heaven; and I say unto thee, that thou art Peter; and upon this rock will I build my church, and the gates of hell shall not prevail against it."

It seems as if Peter became, from this assurance, so confident in his own strength, that he neglected to follow his master's injunction, "Watch and pray, lest ye enter into temptation;" and therefore became an easy victim to the first temptation which beset him; for soon after, with surprising confidence in his own wisdom, we find him rebuking his Lord, and asserting, that the things which he prophesied concerning himself should not happen unto him. On which occasion, the Saviour says, addressing the adversary of Peter's soul, then powerful within him, "Get thee behind me, Satan! thou art an offence to me!" His want of implicit faith on this occasion was the more remarkable, because he had *just before* uttered that strong avowal of his confidence in Christ, to which I have already alluded.

In an early part of the history of the Gospel we read that Peter beholding the miraculous draught of fishes, fell on his knees, and exclaimed, in the fullness of surprise and admiration, and in the depth of conscious sinfulness and humility, "Depart from me, for I am a sinful man, O Lord!"

On a subsequent occasion, ever eager as he was to give assurances of what he believed to be his undoubting faith, we find him saying to the Saviour, when he had removed the terror of his disciples at seeing him walking on the sea, by those cheering words, "'It is I, be not afraid!'—'Lord! if it be thou, bid me come to thee on the water!'—And he walked on the water to come to Jesus; but when he saw the wind boisterous he *was again afraid*, and beginning to sink, he cried, saying, 'Lord, save me!' Immediately, Jesus stretched forth his hand and caught him, saying unto him, 'O thou of *little faith*, wherefore didst thou doubt?'" The first of these facts show the great sensibility of his nature, and his exemplary aptitude to acknowledge and admire every proof of the power and goodness of his Redeemer; and the second is a further corroborating instance of his eager confidence in his own courage and belief, followed by its accustomed falling off in the hour of trial.

His unsubmitted and self-confident spirit shows itself again in his declarations, that Christ should not wash his feet; as if he still set human wisdom against that of the Redeemer, till, subdued by the Saviour's reply, he exclaims, "not my feet only, but also my hands and my head."

The next instance of the mixed character of Peter, and of the solicitude which it excited in our Saviour, is exhibited by the following address to him, "'And the Lord said, Simon, Simon, behold! Satan hath desired to have thee, that he may sift thee as wheat; but I have prayed for thee, (added the gracious Jesus,) that thy faith fail not; and when thou art converted, strengthen thy brethren.' Peter replied, in the fulness of self-confidence, 'Lord, I am ready to go with thee into prison, and unto death!' And he said, 'I tell thee, Peter, that before the cock crows, thou shalt deny me thrice.'" It does not appear what visible effect this humiliating prophecy had on him to whom it was addressed, though Matthew says that he replied, "though I should die with thee, still I will not deny thee;" but it is probable that, by drawing his sword openly in his defence, when they came out "with swords and with staves to take him," he hoped to convince his Lord of his fidelity. But this action was little better than one of mere physical courage, the result of sudden excitement at the time; and was consistent with that want of moral courage, that most difficult courage of *all*, which led him, when the feelings of the moment had subsided, to deny his master, and to utter the degrading *lie of fear*. After he had thus sinned, the Lord turned and looked upon Peter; and Peter remembered the words of the Lord, how he had said unto him, "Before the cock crow, thou shalt deny me thrice. And Peter went out, and wept bitterly."

It seems as if that self-confidence, that blind trusting in one's own strength, that tendency which we all have to believe, like Hazael, that we can never fall into certain sins, and yield to certain temptations, was conquered, for a while, in the humbled, self-judged, and penitent apostle. Perhaps the look of mild reproach which the Saviour gave him was long present to his view, and that in moments of subsequent danger to this truth, those eyes seemed again to admonish him, and those holy lips to utter the salutary and saving precept, "watch and pray, lest ye enter into temptation."

Nevertheless, rendered too confident, probably, in his own unassisted strength, we find him shining once more in the same way; namely, from *fear of man;* for, being convinced that the Mosaic law was no longer binding on the conscience, he ate and drank freely at Antioch with the Gentiles; but, when certain Jewish converts were sent to him from the apostle James, he separated from the Gentiles, lest he should incur the censure of the Jews; being thus guilty of a sort of *practical lie*, and setting those Jews, as it proved, a most pernicious example of dissimulation; for

3 M

which disingenuous conduct, the apostle Paul publicly and justly reproved him before the whole Church. But as there is no record of any reply given by Peter, it is probable that he bore the rebuke meekly; humbled, no doubt, in spirit, before the great Being whom he had again offended; and not only does it seem likely that he met this public humiliation with silent and Christian forbearance, but, in his last Epistle, he speaks of Paul, "as his beloved brother," generously bearing his powerful testimony to the wisdom contained in his Epistles, and warning the hearers of Paul against rejecting aught in them which from want of learning, they may not understand, and "therefore wrest them, as the unlearned and unstable do also the other Scriptures, to their own destruction."

The closing scene of this most interesting apostle's life, we have had no means of contemplating, though the Saviour's last affecting and pathetic address to him, in which he prophesies that he will die a martyr in his cause, makes one particularly desirous to procure details of it.

"So when they had dined, Jesus saith to Simon Peter, 'Simon, son of Jonas, lovest thou me more than these?' He saith unto him, 'Yea, Lord, thou knowest that I love thee.' He saith unto him, 'Feed my lambs!' He saith unto him again the second time, 'Simon, son of Jonas, lovest thou me?' He saith unto him, 'Yea, Lord! thou knowest that I love thee.' He saith unto him, 'Feed my sheep!' He saith unto him the third time, 'Simon, son of Jonas, lovest thou me?' Peter was grieved because he said unto him the third time, Lovest thou me? and he said unto him, 'Lord, thou knowest that I love thee.' Jesus saith unto him, 'Feed my sheep. Verily, verily, I say unto thee, when thou wast young, thou girdedst thyself, and walkedst whither thou wouldst; but when thou shalt be old, thou shalt stretch forth thy hands, and another shall gird thee, and carry thee whither thou wouldst not.' This spake he, signifying by what death he should glorify God; and when he had spoken this he saith unto him, Follow me!"

"The case of Peter," says the pious and learned Scott, in his Notes to the Gospel of John, "required a more particular address than that of the other apostles, in order that both he and others might derive the greater benefit from his fall and his recovery. Our Lord, therefore, asked him by his original name, as if he had forfeited that of PETER by his instability, whether he loved him more than these. The latter clause might be interpreted of his employment and gains as a fisherman, and be considered as a demand whether he loved Jesus above his secular interests; but Peter's answer determines us to another interpretation. He had before his fall, in effect, said that he loved his Lord more than the other disciples did; for he had boasted that, though all men should forsake him, yet would not he. Jesus now asked him whether he would stand to this, and aver that he loved him more than the others did. To this he answered modestly by saying, 'thou knowest that I love thee,' without professing to love him more than the others. Our Lord therefore renewed his appointment to the ministerial and apostolical office; at the same time commanding him to feed his lambs, or his *little lambs*, even the least of them, for the word is diminutive; this intimated to him that his late experience of his own weakness ought to render him peculiarly condescending, complaisant, tender, and attentive to the meanest and feeblest believers. As Peter had *thrice* denied Christ, so he was pleased to repeat the same question a third time; this grieved Peter, as it reminded him that he had given sufficient cause for being thus repeatedly questioned concerning the sincerity of his love to his Lord. Conscious, however, of his integrity, he more solemnly appealed to Christ, as knowing all things, even the secrets of his heart, that he knew he loved him with cordial affection, notwithstanding the inconsistency of his late behaviour. Our Lord thus tacitly allowed the truth of his profession, and renewed his charge to him to feed his sheep.

"Peter," continues the commentator, "had earnestly professed his readiness to die with Christ, yet had shamefully failed when put to the trial; but our Lord next assured him that he would at length be called on to perform that engagement, and signified the death by which he would, as a martyr for his truth, glorify God." No doubt that this information, however awful, was gratefully received by the devoted, ardent, though, at times, the unstable follower of his beloved master; as it proved the Saviour's confidence in him notwithstanding all his errors.

There was, indeed, an energy of character in Peter, which fitted him to be an apostle and a martyr. He was the questioning, the observing, the conversing disciple. The others were probably withheld by timidity from talking with their Lord, and putting frequent questions to him; but Peter was the willing spokesman on all occasions; and to him we owe that impressive lesson afforded us by the Saviour's reply, when asked by him how often he was to forgive an offending brother, "I say not unto thee until seven times, but unto seventy times seven."

But, whether we contemplate Peter as an example, or as a warning, in the early part of his religious career, it is cheering and instructive, indeed, to acquaint ourselves with him in his writings, when he approached the painful and awful close of it. When, having been enabled to fight a good fight, in fulfilment of his blessed Lord's prayer, that "his faith might not fail;" and having been "converted himself, and having strengthened his brethren, he addressed his last awfully impressive Epistle to his Christian brethren, before he himself was summoned to that awful trial, after which he was to receive the end of "his faith," even "the salvation of his soul!" Who can read, without trembling awe, his eloquent description of the day of judgment; "that day," which, as he says, "will come like a thief in the night, in which the heavens shall pass away with a great noise, and the elements shall melt with fervent heat; and the works that are therein shall be burned up," while he adds this impressive lesson, " seeing then that all things shall be dissolved, what manner of persons ought ye to be in all holy conversation and godliness?" And who can contemplate, without affectionate admiration, the *undoubting* but *unfearing* certainty with which he speaks of his approaching death, as foretold by our Lord; "knowing," said he, "that shortly I must put off this my tabernacle, even as our Lord Jesus Christ has showed us!"

Soon after he had thus written, it is probable that he repaired to the expected scene of his suffering, and met his doom—met it, undoubtedly, as became one taught by experience to his own recurring weakness, admonished often by the remembrance of that eye, which had once beamed in mild reproof upon him; but which, I doubt not, he beheld in the hour of his last trial and dying agonies, fixed upon him with tender encouragement and approving love; while, in his closing ear, seemed once again to sound the welcome promise to the devoted follower of the cross, "Well done, good and faithful servant, enter thou into the joy of thy Lord."

We, of these latter days, can see the founder of our religion only in the record of his word, and hear him only in his ever-enduring precepts; but, though we hear him not externally with our ears, he still speaks in the hearts of us all, if we will but listen to his purifying voice; and, though the look of his reproachful eye can be beheld by us only with our mental vision, still, that eye is continually over us and when, like the apostle, we are tempted to feel too great security in our own strength, and to neglect to implore the assistance which cometh from above, let us recall the look which Jesus gave the offending Peter, and remember that the same eye, although unseen, is watching and regarding us still.

Oh! could we ever lie, even upon what are called trifling occasions, if we once believed the certain, however disregarded *truth*, that the Lord takes cognizance of every species of falsehood, and that the eye, which looked the apostle into shame and agonizing contrition, beholds our lying lips with the same indignation with which it reproved him, reminding us that "all liars shall have their part in the lake that burneth with fire and brimstone," and that *without* the city of life is " whosoever loveth and maketh a lie."

CHAPTER XVII.

THE SAME SUBJECT CONTINUED.

I SHALL not give many individual instances of those whom even the fear of death has not been able to terrify into falsehood, because they were supported in their integrity by the fear of God; but such facts are on record. The history of the primitive Christians contains many examples, both of men and women, whom neither threats nor bribes could induce for a moment to withhold or falsify the truth, or to conceal their newly-embraced opinions, though certain that torture and death would be the consequence; *fearless* and *determined* beings, who, though their rulers, averse to punish them, would gladly have allowed their change to pass unnoticed, persisted, like the prophet Daniel, openly to display the faith that was in them, exclaiming at every interrogatory, and in the midst of tortures and of death, "We are Christians; we are Christians!" Some martyrs of more modern days, Catholics as well as Protestants, have borne the same unshaken testimony to what they believed to be religious truth; but Latimer, more especially, was so famous among the latter, not only for the pureness of his life, but for the *sincerity* and goodness of his *evangelical doctrine;* (which, since the beginning of his preaching, had, in all points, been conformable to the teaching of Christ and of his apostles), that the very adversaries of God's truth, with all their menacing words and cruel imprisonment, could not withdraw him from it. But, "whatsoever he had *once preached, he valiantly defended* the same before the world, *without fear of any mortal creature,* although of ever so great power and high authority; wishing and minding rather to suffer not only loss of worldly possessions, but of life, than that the glory of God and the truth of Christ's Gospel should in any point be obscured or defaced through him."

Thus, this eminent person exhibited a striking contrast to that fear of man, which is the root of all lying, and all *dissimulation;* that mean, grovelling, and pernicious fear, which every day is leading us either to disguise or withhold our real opinion; if not to be absolutely guilty of uttering falsehood, and which induces us but too often, to remain silent and ineffective, even when the oppressed and the insulted require us to speak in their defence, and when the cause of truth and of righteousness is injured by our silence. The early FRIENDS were exemplary instances of the power of faith to lift the Christian above all fear of man; and not only George Fox himself, but many of his humblest followers, were known to be persons "*who would rather have died than spoken a lie.*"

There was one female Friend amongst others,

of the name of Mary Dyar, who, after undergoing some persecution for the sake of her religious tenets at Boston, in America, was led to the gallows between two young men, condemned, like herself, to suffer for conscience' sake; but, having seen them executed, she was reprieved, carried back to prison, and then, being discharged, was permitted to go to another part of the country; but, apprehending it to be her duty to return to "the bloody town of Boston," she was summoned before the general court. On her appearance there, the governor, John Endicott, said, "Are you the same Mary Dyar that was here before?" And it seems *he was preparing an evasion for her;* there having been another of that name returned from Old England. But she was so far from disguising the truth, that she answered undauntedly, "I am the *same Mary Dyar that was here the last general court.*" The consequence was immediate imprisonment, and soon after, death.

But the following narrative, which, like the preceding one, is recorded in Sewell's History of the people called Quakers, bears so directly on the point in question, that I am tempted to give it to my readers in all its details.

"About the fore part of this year, if I mistake not, there happened a case at Edmond's Bury, which I cannot well pass by in silence; viz. a certain young woman was committed to prison for child murder. Whilst she was in jail, it is said, William Bennet, a prisoner for conscience' sake, came to her, and in discourse asked her whether, during the course of her life, she had not many times transgressed against her conscience? and whether she had not often thereupon felt secret checks and inward reproofs, and been troubled in her mind because of the evil committed; and this he did in such a convincing way, that she not only assented to what he laid before her, but his discourse so reached her heart, that she came clearly to see, that if she had not been so stubborn and disobedient to those inward reproofs, in all probability she would not have come to such a miserable fall as she now had; for man, not desiring the knowledge of God's ways, and departing from him, is left helpless, and cannot keep himself from evil, though it may be such as formerly he would have abhorred in the highest degree, and have said with Hazael, 'what! is thy servant a dog, that he should do this great thing?'

"W. Bennet thus opening matters to her, did, by his wholesome admonition, so work upon her mind, that she, who never had conversed with the Quakers, and was altogether ignorant of their doctrine, now came to apprehend that it was the grace of God that brings salvation, which she so often had withstood, and that this grace had not yet quite forsaken her, but now made her sensible of the greatness of her transgression. This consideration wrought so powerfully, that, from a most grievous sinner, she became a true penitent; and with hearty sorrow she cried unto the Lord, 'that it might please him not to hide his countenance.' And continuing in this state of humiliation and sincere repentance, and persevering in supplication, she felt, in time, ease; and giving heed to the exhortations of the said Bennet, she obtained, at length, to a sure hope of forgiveness by the precious blood of the immaculate Lamb, who died for the sins of the world. Of this, she gave manifest proofs at her trial before Judge Matthew Hale, who, having heard how penitent she was, would fain have spared her; she being asked, according to the form, '*guilty or not guilty?*' readily answered, 'guilty.' This astonished the judge, and therefore he told her that she seemed not duly to consider what she said, since it could not well be believed that such a one as she, who, it may be, inconsiderately, and roughly handled her child, should have killed it 'wilfully and designedly.' Here the judge opened a back-door for her to avoid the punishment of death. But now the fear of God had got so much room in her heart, that no tampering would do; no fig-leaves could serve her for a cover; for she now knew that this would have been adding sin to sin, and to cover herself with a covering, but not of God's spirit; and therefore she plainly signified to the court, that indeed she had committed the mischievous act intendedly, thereby to hide her shame; and that having sinned thus grievously, and being affected now with true repentance, she could by no means excuse herself, but was willing to undergo the punishment the law required; and, therefore, she could but acknowledge herself guilty, since, otherwise, how could she expect forgiveness from the Lord? This undisguised and free confession being spoken with a serious countenance, did so affect the judge that, tears trickling down his cheeks, he sorrowfully said, 'Woman! such a case as this, I never met with before. Perhaps you, who are but young, and speak so piously, as being struck to the heart with repentance, might yet do much good in the world; but now you force me so that *ex officio*, I must pronounce sentence of death against you, since you will admit of no excuse.' Standing to what she had said, the judge pronounced the sentence of death; and when, afterward, she came to the place of execution, she made a pathetical speech to the people, exhorting the spectators, especially those of the young, 'to have the fear of God before their eyes; to give heed to his secret reproofs for evil, and so not to grieve and resist the good of the Lord, which she herself not having timely minded, it had made her run on in evil, and thus proceeding from wickedness to wickedness, it had brought her to this dismal exit. But, since she firmly trusted to God's infinite mercy, nay, surely believed her sins, though of a bloody dye, to be washed off by the pure blood of Christ, she could contentedly depart this life.' Thus she preached at the gallows the doctrine of the Quakers, and gave heart-melting proofs that her immortal soul was to enter into Paradise, as well as anciently that of the thief on the cross."

The preceding chapter contains three instances of martyrdom, undergone for the sake of religious truth, and attended with that animating publicity which is usual on such occasions, particularly when the sufferers are persons of a certain rank and eminence in society.

But, she who died, as narrated in the story given above, for the cause of *spontaneous* truth, and *willingly* resigned her life, rather than be guilty of a *lie* to save it, though that lie was considered by the law of the country, and by the world at large, to be no lie at all; this bright example of what a true and lively faith can do for us in an hour of strong temptation, was not only an humble, guilty woman, but a *nameless* one also. She was an obscure, friendless individual, whose name on earth seems to be nowhere recorded; and, probably, no strong interest was felt for her disastrous death, except by the preacher who converted her, and by the judge who condemned her. This afflicted person was also well aware that the courage with which she met her fate, and died rather than utter a falsehood, would not be cheered and honoured by an anxious populace, or by the tearful farewells of mourning, but admiring friends; she also knew that her honest avowal would brand her with the odious guilt of murdering her child, and yet she persevered in her adherence to the truth. Therefore, I humbly trust that, however inferior she may appear, in the eyes of her fellow-mortals, to martyrs of a loftier and more important description, this willing victim of what she thought her duty, offered as acceptable a sacrifice as theirs, in the eyes of her Judge and her Redeemer.

No doubt, as I before observed, the history of both public and private life may afford many more examples of equal reverence for truth, derived from religious motives; but, as the foregoing instance was more immediately before me, I was induced to give it as an apt illustration of the precept which I wish to enforce.

The few, and not the many, are called upon to earn the honours of public martyrdom, and to shine like stars in the firmament of distant days; and, in like manner, few of us are exposed to the danger of *telling* great and *wicked* falsehoods. But, as it is more difficult, perhaps, to bear with fortitude the little *daily* trials of life, than great calamities, because we summon up all our spiritual and moral strength to resist the latter, but often do not feel it to be a necessary duty to bear the former with meekness and resignation; so is it more difficult to overcome and resist temptations to every-day lying and deceit, than to falsehoods of a worse description; since, while these little lies often steal on us unawares, and take us unprepared, we know them to be so trivial, that they escape notice, and to be so *tolerated*, that even if detected, they will not incur reproof. Still, I must again and again repeat the burden of my song, the *moral result*, which, however weakly I may have performed my task, I have laboured incessantly, through the whole of my work, to draw, and to illustrate; namely, that this little tolerated lying, as well as great and reprobated falsehood, is wholly inconsistent with the character of a serious Christian, and sinful in the eyes of the God of Truth; that, in the daily recurring temptation to deceive, our only security is to lift up our soul, in secret supplication, to be preserved faithful in the hour of danger, and always to remember, without any *qualification* of the monitory words, that "lying lips are an abomination to the Lord."

CONCLUSION.

I SHALL now give a summary of the didactic part of these observations on lying, and the principles which, with much fearlessness and humility, I have ventured to lay down.

I have stated, that if there be no other true definition of lying than an intention to deceive, withholding the truth, with such an intention, partakes as much of the nature of falsehood as direct lies; and that, therefore, lies are of two natures, active and passive; or, in other words, direct and indirect.

That a PASSIVE LIE is equally as irreconcilable to moral principles as an active one.

That the LIES OF VANITY are of an active and passive nature; and that, though we are tempted to be guilty of the former, our temptations to the latter are stronger still.

That many, who would shrink with moral disgust from committing the latter species of falsehood, are apt to remain silent when their vanity is gratified, without any overt act of deceit on their part; and are contented to let the flattering representation remain uncontradicted.

That this disingenuous passiveness belongs to that common species of falsehood, *withholding the truth.*

That lying is a common vice, and the habit of it so insensibly acquired, that many persons violate the truth, without being conscious that it is a sin to do so, and even look on dexterity in *white lying*, as it is called, as a thing to be proud of; but, that it were well to consider whether, if we allow ourselves liberty to lie on trivial occasions, we do not weaken our power to resist temptation to utter falsehoods which may be dangerous, in their results, to our own well-being, and that of others.

That, if we allow ourselves to violate the truth, that is, deceive for any purpose whatever, who can say where this self-indulgence will submit to be bounded?

That those who learn to resist the daily temptation to tell what are deemed trivial and innocent lies, will be better able to withstand allurements to serious and important deviations from truth.

That the LIES OF FLATTERY are, generally speaking, not only unprincipled, but offensive.

That there are few persons with whom it is so difficult to keep up the relations of peace and amity as flatterers by system and habit.

That the view taken by the flatterer of the penetration of the flattered is often erroneous. That the really intelligent are usually aware to how much praise and admiration they are entitled, be it encomium on their personal or mental qualifications.

That the LIE OF FEAR springs from the want of moral courage; and that, as this defect is by no means confined to any class or age, the result of it, that fear of man, which prompts to the lie of fear, must be universal.

That some lies, which are thought to be LIES OF BENEVOLENCE, are not so in reality, but may be resolved into lies of fear, being occasioned by a dread of losing favour by speaking the truth, and not by real kindness of heart.

That the daily lying and deceit tolerated in society, and which are generally declared necessary to preserve good will, and avoid offence to the self-love of others, are the result of false, not real benevolence, — for that those who practise it the most to their acquaintances when present, are only too apt to make detracting observations on them when they are out of sight.

That true benevolence would insure, not destroy, the existence of sincerity, as those who cultivate the benevolent affections always see the good qualities of their acquaintance in the strongest light, and throw their defects into shade; that, consequently, they need not shrink from speaking truth on all occasions. That the kindness which prompts to erroneous conduct cannot long continue to bear even a remote connexion with real benevolence; that *unprincipled benevolence* soon degenerates into *malevolence*.

That if those who possess good sense would use it as zealously to remove obstacles in the way of spontaneous truth, as they do to justify themselves in the practice of falsehood, the difficulty of always speaking the truth would in time vanish.

That the LIE OF CONVENIENCE—namely, the order to servants to say, " not at home," that is, teaching them to lie for our convenience, is at the same time teaching them to lie for their own, whenever the temptation offers.

That those masters and mistresses who show their domestics that they do not themselves value truth, and thus render the consciences of the latter callous to its requirings, forfeit their right, and lose their chance, of having servants worthy of confidence, degrade their own characters also in their opinions, and incur an awful guilt by endangering their servants' well-being here and hereafter.

That husbands who employ their wives, and wives their husbands, and that parents who employ their children to utter for them the lies of convenience, have no right to be angry, or surprised if their wedded or parental confidence be afterwards painfully abused, since they have taught their families the habit of deceit, by encouraging them in the practice of what they call *innocent white lying*.

That LIES OF INTEREST are sometimes more excusable, and less offensive than others, but are disgusting when told by those whom conscious *independence* preserves from any strong temptation to violate truth.

That LIES OF FIRST RATE MALIGNITY, namely, lies intended wilfully to destroy the reputation of men and women, are less frequent than falsehoods of any other description, because the arm of the law defends reputations.

That, notwithstanding, there are many persons, worn both in body and mind by the consciousness of being the object of calumnies and suspicions which they have not the power to combat, who steal broken-hearted into their graves, thankful for the summons of death, and hoping to find refuge from the injustice of their fellow-creatures in the bosom of their Saviour.

That against LIES OF SECOND RATE MALIGNITY the law holds out no protection.

That they spring from the spirit of detraction, and cannot be exceeded in base and petty treachery.

That LIES OF REAL BENEVOLENCE, though the most amiable and respectable of all lies, are, notwithstanding, objectionable, and ought not to be told.

That, to deceive the sick and the dying, is a dereliction of principle which not even benevolence can excuse; since, who shall venture to assert that a deliberate and wilful falsehood is justifiable?

That, withholding the truth with regard to the character of a servant, *alias*, the passive lie of benevolence, is a pernicious and reprehensible custom; that, if benevolent to the hired, it is malevolent to the hiring, and may be fatal to the person so favoured.

That the masters and mistresses who thus perform what they call a benevolent action, at the expense of sincerity, often, no doubt, find their sin visited on their own heads; because, if servants know that owing to the lax morality of their employers, their faults will not receive their proper punishment, that is, disclosure, when they are turned away,—one of the most powerful motives to behave well is removed,

CONCLUSION.

since those are not likely to abstain from sin, who are sure that they shall sin with impunity.

That it would be REAL BENEVOLENCE to tell, and not to withhold, the whole truth on such occasions; because those who hire servants so erroneously befriended, may, from ignorance of their besetting sins, put temptations in their way to repeat their fault; and may thereby expose them to incur, some day or other, the severest penalty of the law.

That it is wrong, however benevolently meant, to conceal the whole extent of a calamity from an afflicted person, not only because it shows a distrust of the wisdom of the Deity, and implies that he is not a fit judge of the proper degree of trial to be inflicted on his creatures, but because it is a *withholding of the truth with an intention to deceive*, and that such a practice is not only wrong, but *inexpedient*; as we may thereby stand between the sufferer and the consolation which might have been afforded in some cases by the very nature and intensity of the blow inflicted; and lastly, because such concealment is seldom ultimately successful, since the truth comes out usually in the end, when the sufferer is not so well able to bear it.

That LIES OF WANTONNESS, are lies which are often told for no other motive than to show the utterer's total contempt for truth; and that there is no hope for the amendment of such persons, since they thus sin from a depraved fondness for speaking and inventing falsehood.

That dress affords good illustrations of PRACTICAL LIES.

That if false hair, false bloom, false eyebrows, and other artificial aids to the appearance, are so well contrived, that they seem palpably intended to pass for natural beauties, then do these aids of dress partake of the vicious nature of other lying.

That the medical man who desires his servant to call him out of church, or from a party, when he is not wanted, in order to give him the appearance of the great business which he has *not*; and the author who makes his publisher put second and third edition before a work of which, perhaps even the *first* is not wholly sold, are also guilty of PRACTICAL LIES.

That the practical lies most fatal to others, are those acted by men who, when in the gulf of bankruptcy, launch out into increased splendour of living, in order to obtain further credit, by inducing an opinion that they are rich.

That another pernicious *practical* lie is acted by boys and girls at school, who employ their school-fellows to do exercises for them; or who themselves do them for others; that, by this means, children become acquainted with the practice of deceit as soon as they enter a public school; and thus is counteracted the effect of those principles of spontaneous truth which they may have learnt at home.

That lying is mischievous and impolitic, because it destroys confidence, that best charm and only cement of society; and that it is almost impossible to believe our acquaintances, or expect to be believed ourselves, when we or they have once been detected in falsehood.

That speaking the truth does not imply a necessity to wound the feelings of any one. That offensive, or home truths, should never be *volunteered*, though one lays it down as a principle, that truth must be spoken *when called for*.

That often the temporary wound given by us, on principle, to the self-love of others, may be attended with lasting benefit to them, and benevolence in reality be not wounded, but gratified; since the truly benevolent can always find a balm for the wounds which duty obliges them to inflict.

That, were the utterance of spontaneous truth to become a general principle of action in society, no one would dare to put such questions concerning their defects as I have enumerated; therefore the difficulty of always speaking truth would be almost annihilated.

That those who, in the presence of their acquaintance, make mortifying observations on their personal defects, or wound their self-love in any other way, are not actuated by the love of truth, but that their sincerity is the result of *coarseness of mind*, and of the *mean wish to inflict pain*.

That all human beings are, in their closets, convinced of the importance of truth to the interests of society, though few, comparatively, think the practice binding on them, when acting in the busy scene of the world.

That we must wonder still less at the little shame attached to white lying, when we see it sanctioned in the highest assemblies in the kingdom.

That, in the heat of political debate, in either house of parliament, offence is given and received, and the unavoidable consequence is thought to be apology, or duel; that the necessity of either is obviated only by LYING, the offender being at length induced to declare that by black he did not mean black, but white, and the offended says, "enough—I am satisfied."

That the supposed necessity of thus making apologies, in the language of falsehood, is much to be deplored; and that the language of truth might be used with equal effect.

That, if the offender and offended were married men, the former might declare, that he would not, for any worldly consideration, run the risk of making his own wife a widow, and his own children fatherless, nor those of any other man; and that he was also withheld by obedience to the divine command, "Thou shalt not kill."

That, though there might be many heroes present on such an occasion, whose heads were bowed down with the weight of their laurels, the man who could thus speak and act against the bloody custom of the world would be a greater hero, in the best sense of the word, as he would be made superior to the fear of man, by *fear of God*.

That some persons say, that they have lied so as to deceive, with an air of complacency, as if vain of their deceptive art, adding, "but it was only a white lie, you know;" as if, therefore, it was no lie at all.

That it is common to hear even the pious and the moral assert that deviation from truth, or a withholding of the truth, is *sometimes* absolutely necessary.

That persons who thus reason, if asked whether, while repeating the commandment, "thou shalt not steal," they may, nevertheless, pilfer in some small degree, would undoubtedly answer in the negative; yet, that white-lying is as much an infringement of the moral law as little pilfering is of the commandment not to steal.

That I have thought it right to give extracts from many powerful writers, in corroboration of my own opinion on the subjects of lying.

That, if asked why I have taken so much trouble to prove what no one ever doubted, I reply, that I have done so in order to force on the attention of my readers that not one of these writers mentions any allowed exception to the general rule of truth; and it seems to be their opinion that no *mental reservation* is to be permitted on *special occasions*.

That the principle of truth is an *immutable principle*, or it is of no use as a guard to morals.

That it is earnestly to be hoped and desired, that the day may come, when it shall be as dishonourable to commit the slightest breach of veracity as to pass counterfeit shillings.

That Dr. Hawkesworth is wrong in saying that the liar is universally abandoned and despised; for, although we dismiss the servant whose habit of lying offends us, we never refuse to associate with the liar of rank and opulence.

That, though, as he says, the imputation of a lie is an insult for which life only can atone, the man who would thus fatally resent it does not even reprove the *lie of convenience* in his wife or child, and is often guilty of it himself.

That the lying order given to a servant entails consequences of a mischievous nature; that it lowers the standard of truth in the person who receives it, lowers the persons who give it, and deprives the latter of their best claim to their servants' respect; namely, a conviction of their MORAL SUPERIORITY.

That the account given, by Boswell, of Johnson's regard to truth, furnishes us with a better argument for it than is afforded by the best moral fictions.

That, if Johnson could always speak the truth, others can do the same; as it does not require his force of intellect to enable us to be sincere.

That, if it be asked what would be gained by always speaking the truth; I answer, that the individuals so speaking would acquire the involuntary confidence and reverence of their fellow-creatures.

That the consciousness of truth and ingenuousness gives a radiance to the countenance, and a charm to the manner, which no other quality of mind can equally bestow.

That the contrast of this picture must be familiar to the memory of every one.

That it is a delightful sensation to feel and inspire confidence.

That it is delightful to know that we have friends on whom we can always rely for honest counsel and ingenuous reproof.

That it is an ambition worthy of thinking beings, to endeavour to qualify ourselves, and those whom we love, to be such friends as these.

That if each individual family would resolve to avoid every species of falsehood, whether authorized by custom or not, the example would soon spread.

That nothing is impossible to zeal and enterprise.

That there is a river which, if suffered to flow over the impurities of falsehood and dissimulation in the world, is powerful enough to wash them all away; since it flows from the FOUNTAIN OF EVER-LIVING WATERS.

That the powerful writers, from whom I have given extracts, have treated the subject of truth as *moralists only*; and have, therefore, kept out of sight the only *sure* motive to resist the temptation to lie; namely, OBEDIENCE TO THE DIVINE WILL.

That the moral man *may* utter spontaneous truth on all occasions; but, the religious man, if he acts consistently, *must* do so.

That both the Old and New Testament abound in facts and texts to prove how odious the sin of lying is in the sight of the Almighty: as I have shown in several quotations from Scripture, to that effect.

That, as no person has a right to resent being called a sloven who goes about in a stained garment, though that stain be a single one; so that person who indulges in any one species of lie, cannot declare, with justice, that he deserves not the name of liar.

That the all-powerful Being who has said, "as is our day, our strength shall be," still lives to hear the prayer of all who call on Him, and in the hour of temptation will " strengthen them out of Zion."

That, though in all other times of danger, the believer supplicates for help, but few persons think of praying to be preserved from *little lying*, though the Lord has not revealed to us what species of lying he *tolerates*, and what he *reproves*.

That, though I am sure it is not impossible to speak the truth always, when persons are powerfully influenced by religious motives, I admit the extreme difficulty of it, and have given the conduct of some distinguished religious characters as illustrations of the difficulty.

That other instances have been stated, in order to exemplify the power of religious motives on some minds to induce undaunted utterance of the truth, even when death was the sure consequence.

That temptations to little lying are far more common than temptations to *great* and *important* lies; that they are far more difficult to resist, because they come upon us daily and unawares, and because we know that we may utter white lies without fear of detection; and, if detected, without any risk of being disgraced by them in the eyes of others.

That, notwithstanding, they are equally, with great lies, contrary to the will of God, and that it is necessary to be "watchful unto prayer," when we are tempted to commit them.

I conclude this summary, by again conjuring my readers to reflect that there is no moral difficulty, however great, which COURAGE, ZEAL, and PERSEVERANCE will not enable them to overcome; — and, never, probably, was there a period, in the history of man, when those qualities seemed more successfully called into action, than at the present moment.

Never was there a better opportunity of establishing general society on the principles of truth, than that now afforded by the enlightened plan of educating the INFANT POPULATION of these United Kingdoms.

There is one common ground on which the most sceptical philosopher and the most serious Christian meet, and cordially agree; namely, on the doctrines of the *omnipotence of motives*. They differ only on the *nature* of the motives to be applied to human actions; the one approving of moral motives alone, the other advocating the propriety of giving religious ones.

But, these motives only can be made to act upon the *infant* mind, which it is able to understand; and they are, chiefly, the hope of reward for obedience, and the dread of punishment for disobedience. But, these motives are all-sufficient; therefore, even at the earliest period of life, a love of truth, and an abhorrence of lying, may be inculcated with the greatest success. Moreover, HABIT, that best of friends, or worst of foes, according to the direction given to its power, may form an impregnable barrier to defend the pupils thus trained, against the allurements of falsehood.

Children taught to tell the truth from the motive of fear and of hope, and from the force of habit, will be so well prepared to admit and profit by the highest motives to do so, as soon as they can be unfolded to their minds, that, when they are removed to other schools, as they advance in life, they will be found to abhor every description of lying and deceit; and thus the cause of *spontaneous truth* and general education will go forward, progressing and prospering together.

Nor can the mere moralist, or the man of the world, be blind to the benefit which would accrue to them, were society to be built on the foundation of truth and of sincerity. If our servants, a race of persons on whom much of our daily comfort depends, are trained up in habits of truth, domestic confidence and security will be the happy result; and we shall no longer hear the common complaint of their lies and dishonesty; and, the parents who feel the value of truth in their domestics, will doubtless take care to teach their children those habits which have had power to raise even their inferiors in the scale of utility and of moral excellence. Where are the worldlings who, in such a state of society, would venture to persevere in what they now deem *necessary white lying*, when the lady may be shamed into truth by the refusal of her *waiting-maid* to utter the lie required; and the gentleman may learn to feel the meanness of falsehood, alias, of the LIE OF CONVENIENCE, by the respectful, but firm, resistance to utter it of his *valet-de-chambre?* But, if the minds of the poor and the laborious, who must always form the most extensive part of the community, are formed in infancy to the practice of moral virtue, the happiness, safety, and improvement, of the higher classes will, I doubt not, be thereby secured. As the lofty heads of the pyramids of Egypt were rendered able to resist the power of the storm and the whirlwind, through successive ages, by the extent of their basis, and by the soundness and strength of the materials of which they were constructed, so, the continued security, and the very existence, perhaps, of the higher orders in society, may depend on the extended moral teaching and sound principles of the lowest orders; for treachery and conspiracy, with their results, rebellion and assassination, are not likely to be the crimes of those who have been taught to practise *truth* and *openness* in all their dealings, on the ground of MORAL ORDER, and of obedience to the WILL OF GOD.

But it is the bounden duty of the rich and of the great, to maintain their superiority of mind and morals, as well as that of wealth and situation. I beseech them to remember, that it will always be their place to give, and not to *take* example; and they must be careful, in the race of morality, to be neither outstripped, nor overtaken by their inferiors. They must also believe, in order to render their efforts successful, that, although morality without religion is comparatively weak, yet when these are combined, they are strong enough to overcome all obstacles.

Lying is a sin which tempts us on every side, but is more to be dreaded when it allures us in the shape of white lies; for against

ILLUSTRATIONS OF LYING.

these, as I have before observed, we are not on our guard; and, instead of looking on them as enemies, we consider them as friends.

BLACK LIES, if I may so call them, are beasts and birds of prey, which we rarely see; and which, when seen, we know that we must instantly avoid; but white lies approach us in the pleasing shape of *necessary courtesies and innocent self-defence.*

Finally, I would urge them to remember, that if they believe in the records of holy writ, they can thence derive sufficient motives to enable them to tell spontaneous truth, in defiance of the sneers of the world, and of "evil and good report."

That faith in a life to come, connected with a close dependence on divine grace, will give them power in this, as well as in other respects, to emancipate themselves from their own bondage of corruption, as well as to promote the purification of others. For Christians possess what Archimedes wanted; they have *another* sphere on which to fix their hold; and, by that means, can be enabled to move, to influence, and to benefit, this present world of transitory enjoyments; a world which is in reality safe and precious to those alone who "use it without abusing it," and who are ever looking beyond it " to a building of God, a home not made with hands, eternal in the heavens."

THE END.

THE
WORKS OF
MRS OPIE
VOL. 3.

236663

Lightning Source UK Ltd.
Milton Keynes UK
UKHW022133010519
341961UK00007B/176/P